COMPUTER GRAPHICS

PROCEEDINGS

Annual Conference Series   1997

SIGGRAPH 97
Conference Proceedings
August 3–8, 1997
Papers Chair: Turner Whitted
Panels Chair: Barbara Mones-Hattal

A Publication of ACM SIGGRAPH

Sponsored by the ACM's Special
Interest Group on Computer
Graphics

The Association for Computing Machinery, Inc.
1515 Broadway
New York, NY 10036

Sample Citation Information:
...Proceedings of SIGGRAPH 97 (Los Angeles, California, August 3–8, 1997). In *Computer Graphics* Proceedings, Annual Conference Series, 1997, ACM SIGGRAPH, pp. xx – yy.

Orders from nonmembers of ACM:

U.S.A. and Canada:
ACM Order Department
P.O. Box 12114
Church Street Station
New York, NY 10257
    Telephone: +1-800-342-6626
    Telephone: +1-212-626-0500
    Fax: +1-212-944-1318
    E-mail: `orders@acm.org`
    URL: `http://www.acm.org/`

All other countries:
ACM European Service Center
108 Cowley Road
Oxford OX4 1JF
United Kingdom
    Telephone: +44-1-865-382338
    Fax: +44-1-865-381338
    E-mail: `acm_europe@acm.org`

ACM Order Number: 428970
ACM ISBN: 0-89791-896-7
ACM ISSN: 1069-529X

Orders from nonmembers of ACM:

Addison-Wesley will pay postage and handling on orders accompanied by check. Credit card orders may be placed by mail or by calling the Addison-Wesley Order Department at the number above. Followup inquiries should be directed at the same number. Please include the Addison-Wesley ISBN with your order:
    A-W Softcover Proceedings and
    CD-ROM Package ISBN:
    0-201-32230-7

United States:
Addison-Wesley Publishing Company
Order Department
Jacob Way
Reading, MA 01867
    Telephone: +1-800-447-2226

Europe/Middle East:
Addison-Wesley Publishing Group
Concertgebouwplein 25
1071 LM Amsterdam
The Netherlands
    Telephone: +31-20-6717296
    Fax: +31-20-6645334

Germany/Austria/Switzerland:
Addison-Wesley Verlag Deutschland GmbH
Hildachstraße 15d
Wachsbleiche 7-12
53111 Bonn
Germany
    Telephone: +49-228-98-515-0
    Fax: +49-228-98-515-99

United Kingdom/Africa:
Addison-Wesley Publishers Ltd.
Finchampstead Road
Wokingham, Berkshire RG11 2NZ
United Kingdom
    Telephone: +44-734-794000
    Fax: +44-734-794035

Asia:
Addison-Wesley Singapore Pte. Ltd.
15 Beach Road
#05-02/09/10 Beach Centre
Singapore 0718
    Telephone: +65-339-7503
    Fax: +65-339-9709

Japan:
Addison-Wesley Publishers Japan Ltd.
Nichibo Building
1-2-2 Sarugakucho
Chiyoda-ku, Tokyo 101
Japan
    Telephone: +81-33-2914581
    Fax: +81-33-2914592

Australia/New Zealand:
Addison-Wesley Publishers Pty. Ltd.
6 Byfield Street
North Ryde, N.S.W. 2113
Australia
    Telephone: +61-2-878-5411
    Fax: +61-2-878-5830

Latin America:
Addison-Wesley Iberoamericana S.A.
Boulevard de las Cataratas #3
Colonia Jardines del Pedregal
Delegacion Alvaro Obregon
01900 Mexico D.F.
    Telephone: +52-5-660-2695
    Fax: +52-5-660-4930

Canada:
Addison-Wesley Publishing (Canada) Ltd.
26 Prince Andrew Place
Don Mills, Ontario M3C 2T8 Canada
    Telephone: +1-416-447-5101
    Fax: +1-416-443-0948

Contents

Papers Sessions, Wednesday, 6 August

Papers Sessions, Thursday, 7 August

Papers Sessions, Friday, 8 August

Panels Sessions, Wednesday, 6 August

Panels Sessions, Thursday, 7 August

Panels Sessions, Friday, 8 August

Special Session, Thursday, 7 August

Special Session, Friday, 8 August

Papers Preface

Whether this issue of the SIGGRAPH Conference Proceedings serves as your introduction to computer graphics or as another half inch along your already full bookshelf, you can be assured that it contains the best examples of research from our discipline. It is worth reminding each of you who attend the conference's Technical Program that the quality of this result comes not only from the effort and ingenuity of the authors and the experience and diligence of the reviewers, but also from the enthusiasm of the attendees. To the authors presenting papers at SIGGRAPH 97, your acceptance of their work is powerful motivation and a rich reward.

Submitting six copies of each of 265 papers along with their associated videotapes is not only a chore for those who create them, but a logistical challenge to those on the receiving end. This year, the Computer Science Department of the University of North Carolina at Chapel Hill generously set aside an office purely for the purpose of receiving and sorting papers. My administrative assistant, Nereida Segura-Rico along with Cathy and Chris Whitted spent days unpacking and sorting papers. In the meantime, Michael Cohen, SIGGRAPH 98 Papers Chair, traveled to Chapel Hill so that he and I could assign papers to senior reviewers. Illness did not slow Michael down, and he completed the job in two days.

Papers review has evolved into a streamlined and extremely fair process. Each submission is forwarded to two senior reviewers (members of the Papers Committee), one of whom solicits reviews from at least three other reviewers. Each senior reviewer coordinates the review of 10-12 papers, as well as reviewing 10-12 papers he or she is asked to review. Finally, each senior reviewer collects the reviews from the outside reviewers, summarizes the reviews, and consults with the other senior reviewer to whom each paper is assigned.

The 24 members of the Papers Committee met in Atlanta during the weekend of March 7, to confer, occasionally argue, and to ultimately select 48 outstanding papers from the 265 submissions. It is impossible to adequately praise these men and women for their dedication and hard work.

Accepted papers were forwarded to Stephen Spencer, SIGGRAPH Director for Publications. Similarly, videotapes accompanying papers were forwarded to Jim Rose. Both have done an outstanding job of assembling the printed and video versions of the Conference Proceedings and deserve sincere thanks.

In a recent survey attendees were asked to name their most memorable SIGGRAPH conference. The most common answer was "my first." If this is your first SIGGRAPH conference, welcome, and I hope that you find it memorable. If this is your 20th time, we all hope that you find the Technical Program as exciting and valuable as your first.

Turner Whitted
SIGGRAPH 97 Papers Chair

Panels Preface

The SIGGRAPH 97 Panel Committee vision was to support the broadly based and growing SIGGRAPH community, with outstanding, stimulating,and provocative panel topics and presentations. Concurrently, we made it part of our mission to invite the many new communities that have emerged as a result of evolving technical developments to participate in the dialog. The definition of our vision led to the design of three new methodologies in order to encourage the full participation of these diverse, international and intercultural audiences.

We will extend the reach of the panels this year by introducing the use of simultaneous translation for our Japanese speaking participants in order to provide for them a more comfortable environment for information exchange. In order to expand the horizons of our geographical connections, and improve the quality and quantity of the interactive experience, we have offered, for the first time, four pre-conference Online Panels that commenced in early May. They were the following:

- Putting a Human Face on Cyberspace: Designing Avatars and the Virtual Worlds They Live In
- Sounding Off on Audio: The Future of Internet Sound
- Motion Capture and CG Character Animation
- Medical Illustration & Visualization: Why Do We Use CG and Does It Really Make a Difference in Creating Meaningful Images?

Those panels will culminate in onsite panel presentations during the conference. Fortunately Janet McAndless, the SIGGRAPH 97 Online Chair, worked tirelessly to "make this happen" for us.

In addition, several panels will present complementary technology displays and interactive experiences before, during, or after their panels in the Creative Applications Laboratory, thus providing an innovation in the overall conference experience. The opportunity to enhance the information presented, with a "hands on" experience, or simply to take a closer look at the material presented during the panel, will encourage the integration and extension of the whole technical program experience.

The expanded desciptions of the SIGGRAPH 97 Panels are documented here in the Conference Proceedings. And this year, panel participants had the unique opportunity to include color images with their individual panel descriptions. We proudly present to you the fruit of their efforts. Credit for the excellent text and images captured here goes to the Panels Committee, panel organizers and speakers, and the SIGGRAPH Director for Publications, Stephen Spencer.

Just a few words about the process used to design the Panels Program. Our panels, by intent, highlight emerging technologies, provide a forum for the debate of technical and creative controversies, allow for the potential of diverse opinions and present the effects of these technologies on the graphics and animation communities.

Our Committee continued the practice of reviewing early proposals in order to provide constructive and useful feedback for the final proposal process. In December, we received and reviewed twenty early proposals. In January we received thirty-seven final proposals, many of which were revised versions of reviewed early proposals.

In early March, the Committee met to evaluate the final proposals and recommend final selections. The Panels Committee worked carefully, with enthusiasm, and expertise to review the final proposals and mentor the sixteen panels and one special session that were selected for the conference. The goal in selecting these panels was to select a combination of panels that would cover important and developing topics, represent new insights, and illuminate different viewpoints. It was especially important to present controversial approaches and opinions. After the selection process, our Committee members provided extensive ongoing help to the selected panels by acting as individual mentors to the Panel Organizers. The mentors and Panel Organizers enhanced communication among and between the individual panel members and the rest of the conference community.

This year, the technical program chairs defined several content tracks to make it easier for attendees to investigate and pursue their interests that pass through more than one part of the technical program. Those participating in courses, papers, panels and educators program may find it useful for scheduling their time spent in the technical sessions.

High praise goes to the members of the Panels Committee who defined and nurtured this program to its completion at the conference: Leo Hourvitz, Alyce Kaprow, Mike Mcgrath, Celia Pearce, Theresa Marie Rhyne, Carl Rosendahl, Alan Turransky, and Mary Whitton.

Our Panels Administrator Dawn Truelsen provided great assistance, support, and focus.

We also worked closely with the other technical chairs to ensure the highest quality content for all of the venues. We trust that this will result in a well organized and coordinated experience for the conference participants.

I would like to personally thank all of the SIGGRAPH 97 technical chairs, and especially Turner Whitted, the Papers Chair, whose wealth of experience, knowledge of the graphics community and collaborative spirit was an invaluable resource to me and to the whole Panels Committee. In addition, I thank Scott Owen, this year's Conference Chair, for his support in helping us reach for the vision. We hope that you will enjoy the results of our labor and find the Panels Program a worthwhile learning experience!

Barbara Mones-Hattal
SIGGRAPH 97 Panels Chair

1997 ACM SIGGRAPH Awards

Steven A. Coons Award for Outstanding Creative Contributions to Computer Graphics

James Foley

The 1997 Steven A. Coons Award for Outstanding Creative Contributions is presented to Dr. James Foley for his strong and sustained leadership in computer graphics education and research, and for his dedication to the profession through books and his work with ACM/SIGGRAPH and ACM publications.

Foley received the BS in electrical engineering from Lehigh University in 1964 and completed graduate studies at the University of Michigan in 1969. His interest in computer graphics began when he took an early course from Bert Herzog: he was instantly "hooked" and, recalling a lecture from the course, chose distributed graphics computing as his Ph.D. topic. He began his professional career at the University of North Carolina. After a stint at the Bureau of the Census he joined the faculty at the George Washington University (GWU) in 1977. In 1991 he moved to Georgia Tech and in 1996 became Executive Vice President, Mitsubishi Electric Information Technology Center, MERL.

Dr. Foley is the lead author of *Fundamentals of Computer Graphics* and of *Computer Graphics: Principles and Practice*. He is recognized as the organizer and motivator whose vision made possible these complex multi author texts and their subsequent updated editions. More than 300,000 copies have introduced an entire generation of graphics students to computer graphics not only in English but, via translations, in Chinese, German, Japanese, French, Polish, Russian and Spanish.

Foley has been a driving force in the graphics community by recognizing that the power of computer graphics can be achieved only through a carefully crafted user interface. At the University of North Carolina he co-authored the important 1974 paper "The Art of Natural Graphic Man-Machine Conversation." This inspired a career-long emphasis on research and teaching dedicated to the integration of computer technology with human-centered concerns. He launched an on going series of research projects focused on user interface management systems and development environments. In the late 1970's, at the George Washington University, he introduced one of the first courses on user interface design, a short form of which many of us took at SIGGRAPH, SIGCHI, or NCGA conferences.

Having recognized the importance of user interface studies within computer graphics, Foley combined his research talent with his people skills to build and nurture growing organizations. His group at GWU and, more recently, the world-class Graphics, Visualization and Usability Center (GVU) he established and led at Georgia Tech demonstrate this outstanding leadership. At Georgia Tech he set an interdisciplinary standard for graphics and user interface research. He successfully integrated computer science, human factors, cognitive science, graphics and multimedia design, and engineering disciplines. In a remarkably short period, Foley created an environment in which over thirty faculty and a hundred graduate students worked together. Foley not only built the GVU Center but also taught students and led research projects. He won the College of Computing Graduate Student Award, "Most likely to make students want to grow up to be professors," and the Sigma XI sustained research award.

He has devoted time and talent to fostering today's flourishing SIGGRAPH organization and conferences. He and Paul Oliver organized the first short courses at the 1974 conference in Boulder, precursor of the SIGGRAPH conferences. As Vice Chair of SIGGRAPH (1974-76), he established the annual SIGGRAPH conferences beginning with Bowling Green in 1975 and Philadelphia in 1976. His GWU colleague John Sibert and he proposed that SIGGRAPH support student and faculty attendance through volunteer positions and scholarships. He was an early influence on computer graphics standards. With Ira Cotton, he organized the 1974 NBS (now NIST) workshop on graphics standards. He later co-chaired, with Dan Bergeron, the team that specified the 1977 SIGGRAPH Core Graphics Standard. He was section editor of the *Communications of the ACM* for graphics and image processing from 1975 to 1982, and editor-in-chief of *ACM Transactions on Graphics* from 1991 to 1995.

Through his books, courses, papers, organizational, and professional contributions, Foley has made a broad and lasting impact on our field. He was an early and vigorous champion of the science, technology, and art of computer graphics, and remains a leader in his efforts to support and strength the computer graphics community. In recognition of these accomplishments and contributions to Computer Graphics, SIGGRAPH is pleased to present Dr. James Foley the Steven Anson Coons Award.

Selected References: Books

J. Foley and A. van Dam, Fundamentals of Interactive Computer Graphics, Addison- Wesley (IBM Systems Programming Series), Reading, MA, 664 pp., 1982. Translated into Chinese, Japanese, and Russian.

J. Foley, A. van Dam, S. Feiner, J. Hughes, Interactive Computer Graphics: Principles and Practice, Addison-Wesley, Reading, MA, 1174 pp., 1990, C Edition,1995.

J. Foley, A. van Dam, S. Feiner, J. Hughes, and R. Phillips, Introduction to Computer Graphics, Addison-Wesley, Reading, MA, 559 pp., 1993. Translated into German, French, and Spanish.

Selected References: Papers

Sukaviriya, P., J. Foley and T. Griffith, A Second Generation User Interface Design Environment: The Model And The Runtime Architecture, CHI '93, ACM, New York, pp. 375-382.

Foley, J., W. Kim, S. Kovacevic and K. Murray, The User Interface Design Environment - A Computer Aided Software Engineering Tool for the User-Computer Interface, IEEE Software, Special Issue on User Interface Software, 6(1), January 1989, pp. 25-32.

Foley, J., Interfaces for Advanced Computing, Scientific American, Special Issue on Advanced Computing, 257(4), October 1987, pp. 126-135.

Foley, J., V.L. Wallace and P. Chan, The Human Factors of Computer Graphics Interaction Techniques, IEEE Computer Graphics and Applications, 4(11), Nov. 1984, pp. 13-48.

Garrett, M. and J. Foley, Graphics Programming Using a Database System with Dependency Declarations, ACM Transactions on Graphics, 1(2), April 1982, pp.109-128.

Foley, J. and V. Wallace, The Art of Natural Graphic Man-Machine Conversation (Invited Paper), Proceedings of the IEEE , 62(4) (Special Issue on Computer Graphics), April 1974, pp. 462-470.

Previous Award Recipients

1995	Jose Luis Encarnação
1993	Edwin E. Catmull
1991	Andries van Dam
1989	David C. Evans
1987	Donald P. Greenberg
1985	Pierre Bézier
1983	Ivan E. Sutherland

1997 ACM SIGGRAPH Awards

Computer Graphics Achievement Award

Przemyslaw Prusinkiewicz

The 1997 SIGGRAPH Achievement Award is presented to Przemyslaw Prusinkiewicz for his work pertaining to modeling and visualizing of biological structures.

Dr. Prusinkiewicz's interest in computer graphics began in the late 1970s. By 1986 he originated a method for visualizing the structure and growth of plants based on L-systems, a mathematical theory of development of multicellular organisms introduced by the late Professor Aristid Lindenmayer. Professor Prusinkiewicz, his students, and collaborators transformed L-systems into a powerful programming language for expressing plant models, and extended the range of phenomena that can be simulated. Specifically, parametric L-systems facilitate the construction of models by assigning attributes to their components. Differential L-systems make it possible to simulate plant growth in continuous time, which is essential to the animation of developmental processes. Environmentally-sensitive and open L-systems provide a framework for simulating the interactions between plants and their environment. The power of these concepts is demonstrated by the wide range of biological structures already modeled, from algae to wild flowers to gardens and stands of trees competing for light.

In addition to the important extensions of L-systems, Professor Prusinkiewicz's research also includes studies of fundamental problems of morphogenesis - emergence of patterns and three dimensional forms in nature. This includes the modeling of spiral phyllotactic patterns in plants, and developmental patterns and forms of seashells.

Professor Prusinkiewicz received his M.S. (1974) and Ph.D. (1978) degrees in Computer Science from the Technical University of Warsaw. His initial research interests were in digital design, fault-tolerant computing, computer arithmetic and computer music. He held Assistant Professorships at the Technical University of Warsaw (1974-1979) and at the University of Science and Technology of Algiers (1979-1982). He joined the University of Regina in 1982 and was appointed to his current position as Professor of Computer Science at the University of Calgary in 1991. He has also held Visiting Professorships at Yale University and l'Ecole Polytechnique Federale de Lausanne, and was a visiting researcher at the University of Bremen and the Center for Tropical Pest Management in Brisbane.

As a result of his research, plants can be modeled with unprecedented visual and behavioral fidelity to nature. The book, "The Algorithmic Beauty of Plants," his contributed chapters to other books, and many papers demonstrate that plant models can be combined artistically into stunning and inspiring images. Growth of realistic and artificial life forms now can be included in computer graphics animation. His modeling methods have been incorporated into commercial products and reproduced in public-domain programs.

Dr. Prusinkiewicz's work stands out for its scholarly approach and for his collaboration with biologists, agronomists, horticulturists, theoretical computer scientists, and mathematicians. Biologists, inspired by these thoroughly researched models, have initiated international research programs including a study of the impact of microclimates on the growth of crop plants, the modeling of interactions between plants and insects for crop pest control, and a study of the relationships between plant genetics and the development of plant architecture.

These achievements produced a large impact by making complex natural environments a visible part of computer graphics. The impact can only increase as these environments become richer and even more realistic. In recognition of these contributions SIGGRAPH is pleased to present the SIGGRAPH Computer Graphics Achievement Award to Przemyslaw Prusinkiewicz.

Selected References

Prusinkiewicz, P., Lindenmayer, A., Hanan, J. S., Fracchia, F. D., Fowler, D. R., de Boer, M. J. M., and Mercer, L.. The Algorithmic Beauty of Plants, 1990 and 1996.

Mech, R. and Prusinkiewicz, P.. Visual Models of Plants Interacting with Their Environment, in Holly Rushmeier, editor, *SIGGRAPH 96 Conference Proceedings,* Annual Conference Series. ACM SIGGRAPH, Addison Wesley, August 1996.

Prusinkiewicz, P., James, M., and Mech, R.. Synthetic Topiary, *SIGGRAPH 94 Conference Proceedings,* Annual Conference Series. ACM SIGGRAPH, Addison Wesley, August 1994.

Prusinkiewicz, P., Hammel, M., and Mjolsness, E.. Animation of Plant Development, in *SIGGRAPH 93 Conference Proceedings,* Annual Conference Series. ACM SIGGRAPH, Addison Wesley, August 1993.

Fowler, D., Meinhardt, H., and Prusinkiewicz, P.. Modeling Seashells. In *Computer Graphics (SIGGRAPH 92 Conference Proceedings),* volume 26. Addison Wesley, July 1992.

Fowler, D. and Prusinkiewicz, P.. A Collision-based Model of Spiral Phyllotaxis. In *Computer Graphics (SIGGRAPH 92 Conference Proceedings),* volume 26. Addison Wesley, July 1992.

Prusinkiewicz, P., Lindenmeyer, A., and Hanan, J.. Developmental Models Of Herbaceous Plants For Computer Imagery Purposes. In *Computer Graphics (SIGGRAPH 88 Conference Proceedings),* volume 22. Addison Wesley, August 1988.

Prusinkiewicz, P.. Graphical Applications of L-systems. In Graphics Interface 1986 Conference Proceedings.

Previous Award Recipients

1996	Marc Levoy
1995	Kurt Akeley
1994	Kenneth E. Torrance
1993	Pat Hanrahan
1992	Henry Fuchs
1991	James T. Kajiya
1990	Richard Shoup and Alvy Ray Smith
1989	John Warnock
1988	Alan H. Barr
1987	Robert Cook
1986	Turner Whitted
1985	Loren Carpenter
1984	James H. Clark
1983	James F. Blinn

Quantifying Immersion in Virtual Reality

Randy Pausch[1], Dennis Proffitt, George Williams[2]

University of Virginia

pausch@cmu.edu, drp@virginia.edu, gcw@best.com

ABSTRACT

Virtual Reality (VR) has generated much excitement but little formal proof that it is useful. Because VR interfaces are difficult and expensive to build, the computer graphics community needs to be able to predict which applications will benefit from VR. In this paper, we show that users with a VR interface complete a search task faster than users with a stationary monitor and a hand-based input device. We placed users in the center of the virtual room shown in Figure 1 and told them to look for camouflaged targets. VR users did not do significantly better than desktop users. However, when asked to search the room and conclude *if* a target existed, VR users were substantially better at determining when they had searched the entire room. Desktop users took 41% more time, re-examining areas they had already searched. We also found a positive transfer of training from VR to stationary displays and a negative transfer of training from stationary displays to VR.

INTRODUCTION

In 1968, Ivan Sutherland implemented the first virtual reality system. Using wire-frame graphics and a head-mounted display (HMD), it allowed users to occupy the same space as virtual objects [Sutherland]. In the 1980's, VR captured the imagination of the popular press and government funding agencies [Blanchard, Fisher]. Potential VR applications include architectural walkthrough [Brooks], simulation [Bryson], training [Loftin], and entertainment [Pausch 1996]. For the purpose of this paper, we define "virtual reality" to mean any system that allows the user to look in all directions and updates the user's viewpoint by passively tracking head motion. Existing VR technologies include HMDs and CAVEs[tm] [Cruz-Neira].

[1]Currently at Carnegie Mellon University.

[2]Currently at Fakespace, Inc. 241 Polaris Ave. Mountain View, CA 94043

Figure 1: *Users Stood in the Center of This Room and Looked For Target Letters.*

The National Academy of Sciences report on VR [NAS] recommends an agenda to determine when VR systems are better than desktop displays, and states that without scientific grounding many millions of dollars could be wasted. Ultimately, we would like a predictive model of what tasks and applications merit the expense and difficulty of VR interfaces. In this paper, we take a step towards quantifying immersion, or the sense of "being there." We asked users, half using an HMD and half using a stationary monitor, to search for a target in heavily camouflaged scenes. In any given search, there was a 50/50 chance that the target was somewhere in the scene. The user's job was to either find the target or claim no target was present. Our major results are:

1) VR users *did not* find targets in camouflaged scenes faster than traditional users.

2) VR users were substantially faster when no target was present. Traditional users needed to re-search portions of the scene to be confident there was no target.

From these two findings, we infer that the VR users built a better mental frame-of-reference for the space. Our second two conclusions are based on search tasks where the users needed to determine that no target existed in the scene:

3) Users who practiced first in VR *positively transferred* that experience and improved their performance when using the traditional display.

4) Users who practiced first with the traditional display *negatively transferred* that experience and performed *worse* when using VR. This negative transfer may be relevant in applications that use desktop 3D graphics to train users for real-world tasks.

In a practical sense, the only way to demonstrate that VR is worthwhile is to build real applications that have VR interfaces, and show that users do better on real application tasks. That can be expensive, and new technologies take time to mature. But the computer graphics community has not even achieved a lower standard: showing, *even for a simple task*, that VR can improve performance. We show improvement in a search task and discuss *why* a VR interface improved user performance.

RELATED WORK

Several researchers have attempted to qualitatively define immersion with taxonomies [Robinett, Zeltzer] or subjective ratings by users [Heeter]. Others have measured "fish tank VR" head-tracked performance [Authur, McKenna, Ware 1993, Ware 1996], or compared variables such as resolution and frame rate in virtual environments [Smets]. We know of no work that formally measures that VR is better than a desktop interface for any search task; the closest is Chung, who compared VR against hand-based manipulation of an object, rather than the viewpoint [Chung].

COMPARING VR AND DESKTOP INTERFACES

To see if VR is useful, one could pick a representative task, such as finding an object in a scene, and compare performance with the best possible VR and desktop interfaces. That introduces many variables, as shown in Table 1. We do not wish to ask if *current* VR interfaces are useful, but rather if VR will *ever* be useful. Simply put, do users perform measurably better when controlling the viewpoint with their head instead of with their hand?

	Desktop	HMD
resolution	1280x1024	240x120
horizontal FOV	40 degrees	93 degrees
vertical FOV	30 degrees	61 degrees
input device	mouse or joystick	6 DOF tracker

Table 1: *Typical Values for Displays*

To hold the variables constant we used the same HMD as both the head-tracked display and the stationary monitor. In both cases, the scenes were rendered in stereo (The use of stereo was probably not significant, as all objects in the scene were at least two meters from the user). Figure 2 shows the stationary condition, where we bolted

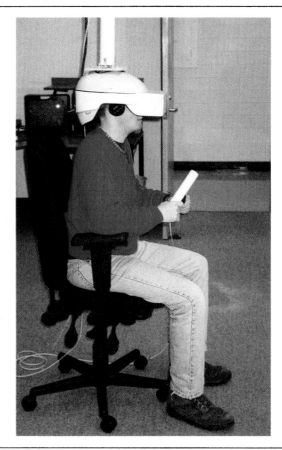

Figure 2: *Using the HMD as a Stationary Monitor.*

the HMD onto a ceiling-mounted post, thus turning the HMD into a stationary monitor. This provided the same resolution, field of view, and image quality in both VR and desktop interfaces. Table 1 gives the values for this particular HMD, the Virtual Research Flight Helmet[tm] [HMD]. We chose a task where the display resolution was unimportant because the targets were large and easily visible. Using a mouse or joystick as the desktop input device would have introduced variables in lag and sampling rate. Therefore, we used the same magnetic 6DOF electromagnetic tracker [Tracker] from the HMD as our hand input device. All we did to create the desktop interface was to seat the user in a chair and take the 6DOF tracker off the user's head and place it in a comfortable device held in user's hands. By holding all other variables constant, we can claim our results are dependent on head-input versus hand-input. For the remainder of this paper, we refer to these groups as "the VR users" and "the desktop users." While we acknowledge that our desktop users are hardly using a conventional configuration, we claim their setup contains the essential components: a stationary monitor and a hand-input device.

We attempted a pilot experiment [Pausch 1993] where 28 users searched for easy-to-find, uncamouflaged, targets at random locations in a virtual room. VR users found the targets 42% faster than desktop users. We feared we had measured how fast users could move the camera, rather than how immersed they were. For example, finding the red 'Y' in Figure 3 is a *pre-attentive* task, where the human visual system can find the target without having to consider the camouflage. In a room surrounding the user, the time to find a red Y might be limited only by how fast one could move the camera. But the time to find an object like the black 'Y' in Figure 3 is limited by one's ability to serially examine the items. Searching for a black 'K' in Figure 3 is another mentally limited task; there is no 'K', and the only way to be certain of that is to systematically search the entire scene. We claim that VR users are much better at systematic searches because they can better remember where they have already looked in the scene that surrounds them.

We placed users in the center of a simple virtual room, 4 meters on each side. The room contained a door and two windows which served as orientation cues. During each search task, the room contained 170 letters arranged on the walls, ceiling and floor. Figure 1 shows a third-person view of the scene, with one wall removed. Letters measured 0.6 meters in length and were easily visible through the display. Users needed to apply some degree of concentration and focused attention to locate the target letter among the similar looking "camouflage" letters. In any given task, we chose target and camouflage letters from either the set "AKMN-VWXYZ" (whose primarily visual features are slanted lines), or "EFHILT" (whose primary features are horizontal and vertical lines). We began each search by displaying the target letter in a fixed location over the door, and waiting for the user to say the target letter in order to begin the search. On the user's cue, we rendered the 170 camouflage letters, placing the target letter at a random location. When they found the target letter, users said "there it is," which we confirmed by watching an external monitor which displayed what the users were seeing.

48 users participated in the experiment, 24 using VR and 24 using the desktop configuration created by bolting the HMD into a fixed position. Desktop users controlled their viewpoint with the handheld "camera" controller shown in Figure 4, which contained the same 6DOF tracker used to track the VR users' heads. We did a large number of informal experiments to design a reasonable handheld camera controller. Based on that experience, we also removed the roll component of tracking for the hand input device. The end-to-end system latency in all cases was roughly 100 milliseconds, measured by the technique described by Liang [Liang], and we rendered a constant 60 frames per second on an SGI Onyx Reality Engine2.

```
AVMNVWXZWXZWXZAVMNVWXZWXZAVMNVVWXZWXZAVMNV
AMNVNYVAVMNVWXZMNVAVMNVWXZWXZAVMNVAVMNVWX
ZWXZANVWAVMNVWAVMNVWXZXZXVMAVMNVMWXZNVZAV
MNVWMNZAVMNVAVMNVWXZWXZWXZWXZAVMNVWMAVYNV
AMNVNVAVMNVWXZWXZAVMNVAVMNVWXZAVMNVWXZMXZ
```

Figure 3: *Find the red Y, the Black Y, and the Black K.*

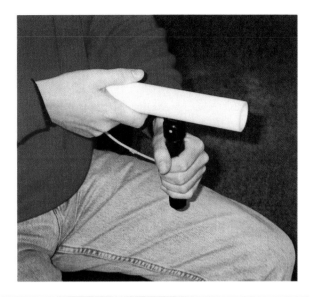

Figure 4: *The Hand Input Device, Containing the 6DOF Tracker.*

RESULTS

Graph 1 shows the average time users needed to locate a target.

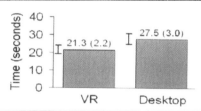

Graph 1: *VR versus Desktop Performance. The difference is not statistically significant.*

Each user performed five searches which we averaged together to form a single data point for that user. The bars in Graph 1 are the average of the 24 VR users and the 24 desktop users. The error bars show the standard error for each data set. The VR and desktop times are very similar, and their difference is not statistically significant. We constructed a cognition-limited task, so it is reasonable that the VR and desktop times are similar. We informally observed that users never physically turned the camera as fast as they could have. The cognitive portion of the search task slowed the users down.

Practice did not appear to be a factor. We asked users to do practice searches until they were comfortable; we required two practice, searches, and some users did three. We did not count practice searches in the results. Users took roughly 15 minutes to perform the searches, and none appeared fatigued. To measure practice and fatigue, we ran separate control groups with eight users each, who ran double the number of trials on both the VR and desktop interfaces. These users showed no statistically significant differences between their earlier and later trials. Users made essentially no errors. All users were between 18 and 25 years old, mostly undergraduates with no VR experience. Both groups were evenly balanced by gender. All users said they could easily see the targets. In addition to the 48 users we report, 3 other users began but did not complete this study. All 3 felt slightly nauseous, and they all reported that they were generally prone to motion sickness.

We now consider searching for a target which is *not* in the scene. Of course, if the user *knows* the target is not there, then the task is pointless. Therefore, we had users perform a sequence of searches, each of which had a 50% likelihood of containing a target. Users were instructed to either locate the target, or claim no target existed. In this way, we measured the time users needed to *confidently* search the entire scene.

If the targets are dense, and the users are efficient in their searching, we can predict how long this will take. Working backwards, consider an efficient user who takes 40 seconds to completely search a scene, with no wasted effort. On average, when a target *is* present, that user should find it in 20 seconds. Random placement may make the letter appear earlier or later in the search process, but on average the user will find the target halfway through the search. We know how long it takes users to find targets when they are present. If the users searched perfectly, it should take twice that long to search the entire room and confidently conclude the target is not there. Any time over that would imply that the users were re-examining portions of the room that they had already searched. This prediction is shown in Graph 2.

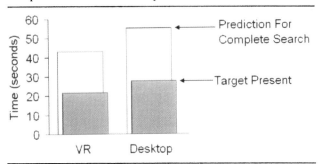

Graph 2: *Predicted Times for A Complete Search.*

Graph 1 showed the results of users who each performed five searches for targets that were in the room. In fact, these users each performed a sequence of ten searches, where on any given search, the target might or might not have existed. For each of the ten searches, the user was told to either find the target, or announce that it was not there. Users did not know beforehand whether a target would be present in any given search. Graph 3 shows the average time users required to locate a target that was in the room (Graph 1 results), the predicted time to search the entire room (Graph 2 results), and the observed time to search the entire room and conclude that no target existed.

The VR user data is only 1.4% above the prediction for efficient search. This concurs with our personal observations of VR users, who appeared to search the entire room without rescanning. However, desktop users typically examined portions of the room a second time. As shown in Graph 3, the desktop users spent 41% above the time that a perfect search would take.

IMPLICATIONS

The VR community claims that a head-tracked, egocentric camera control provides a stronger sense of immersion, or "being there," than does a desktop display. Our results indicate that VR can help users remember where they have and have not looked. The ratio shown in the "desktop" performance in Graph 3 implies that back-

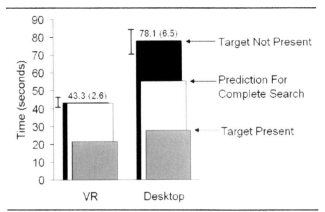

Graph 3: *Observed Times To Search the Entire Room and Determine that No Letter is Present.*

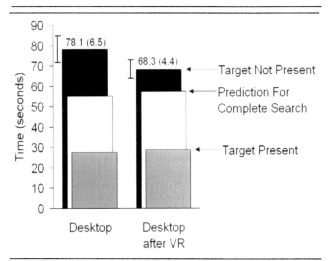

Graph 4: *Positive Transfer: Users Who Practice in VR Improve Their Performance on the Desktop*

tracking is occurring [Braddick]. If the desktop users were slower for some biomechanical reason, such as our choice of input device, we assume it would have also slowed them when the target was present.

TRANSFER EFFECTS

We wondered how users would perform the desktop search tasks if they first practiced in VR. If VR allows the user to develop a good frame-of-reference for a space, perhaps that memory would carry over to a desktop interface. We had each of the VR users perform their ten searches, rest for five to ten minutes, and then perform ten more searches using the desktop interface. In this way, we could see if the experience with VR affected later use of the desktop interface. The ten desktop searches, just like the first ten VR searches, contained five with a present target and five without. Graph 4 shows a *positive transfer effect*, where practicing in VR improves performance of the same task when using a desktop interface. This result is statistically significant (p < 0.0096). We also performed the reverse experiment — we had the desktop users rest and then perform ten more searches using the VR interface. Graph 5 presents the results, which show a *negative transfer of training*. Practicing on the desktop decreases performance of the same task when using a VR interface. This result is statistically significant (p < 0.0493). The implications here are powerful. If we assume that VR and the real world are similar, Graph 5 indicates that training with desktop 3d graphics could potentially degrade real-world performance.

FUTURE WORK

Our claims, particularly about negative transfer of training, rely on VR search performance being similar to real-world search performance. Therefore, we should perform the study using real objects in a real scene. While the absolute times may improve due to improved vision and reduced lag, we expect that "no target exists" searches will take twice as long as searches where the target exists. In a similar vein, we expect that we would see similar results in a CAVE or a BOOM, and we are curious what the results would be for a PUSH device [PUSH]. In general, we believe the computer graphics community should actively pursue this kind of evaluation, which was a primary recommendation of a recent National Academy of Science study on VR [NAS]. Especially given our finding on the potential negative transfer of training, we feel the computer graphics community can benefit from performing this kind of measurement.

CONCLUSIONS

Proponents of virtual reality claim that it can improve user performance via *immersion*, or giving an enhanced sense of "being there." We compared the performance of users searching for targets in heavily camouflaged scenes. Half of the users used VR and the other half used a stationary display with view controlled by a hand input device. In 50% of the searches, we randomly placed a target in the scene. For each search, we asked the user to either find the target, or conclude that no target was in the scene.

1) When targets were present, VR did not improve performance. We believe this is because the task was cognitively limited, and the ability to move the camera quickly and/or naturally was not the bottleneck.

2) When there was no target present, VR users concluded this substantially faster than traditional users. We believe that VR users built a better mental frame-of-reference for the space, and avoided redundant searching.

3) Users of traditional displays improved by practicing first with VR. This underscores that something occurred in the user's mental state and could be transferred to using a different interface.

4) VR users who practiced first with traditional displays hurt their performance in VR. This may imply problems with using desktop 3D graphics to train users for real world search tasks.

We believe this is the first formal demonstration that VR can improve search task performance versus a traditional interface. More importantly, the results give us insight into *why* VR is beneficial. This is a step towards our long term goal of being able to predict which real-world tasks will benefit from having a VR interface.

REFERENCES

Arthur, K.W. Booth, Kellogg S., Ware, Colin. 1993. Evaluating 3D Task Performance for Fish Tank Virtual Worlds, ACM Transactions on Information Systems, vol.11, no.3, 239-265.

Blanchard, C., Burgess, S., Harvill, Y., Lanier, J., Lasko, A, Reality Built for Two: A Virtual Reality Tool, ACM SIGGRAPH 1990 Symposium on Interactive 3D Graphics, March 1990.

Braddick, O.J., & Holliday, I.E. (1991). Serial search for targets defined by divergence or deformation of optic flow. Perception, 20_, 345-354.

Brooks, Frederick P, Walkthrough - A Dynamic Graphics System for Simulating Virtual Buildings. In Proceedings of the 1986 ACM Workshop on 3D Graphics, Chapel Hill, NC, October 23-24, 1986, pages 9-21.

Bryson, S., Levit, C., The Virtual Wind Tunnel, IEEE Computer Grahpics and Applications, July 1992, pages 25-34.

Chung, J., A Comparison of Head-tracked and Non-head-tracked SteeringModes in the Targeting of Radiotherapy Treatment Beams, In Proceedings of the 1992 ACM Symposium on Interactive 3D Graphics., pages 193-196.

Cruz-Neira, C., Sandin, T.A., DeFanti R.V. 1993. Surround screen projection-based virtual reality: the design and implementation of the cave. Proceedings of SIGGRAPH 1993. 135-142.

Fisher, S., McGreevy, A, Humphries, J., Robinett, W., Virtual ENvironment Diplay System, Proceedings on the 1986 Workshop on Interactive 3D Graphics, October 23-24, 1986, pages 77-87.

Heeter, Carrie. 1992. Being There: The Subjective Experience of Presence. Presence, vol.1, no.2, 262-271.

HMD: Virtual Research Flight Helmet[tm]. Company information available via www.virtualresearch.com.

Liang, J., Shaw, C., and Green, M., On Temporal-Spatial Realism in the VIrutal Reality Environment, In Proceedings of the ACM SIGGRAPH Symposium on User Interface Software and Technology, 1991, pages 19-25.

Loftin, R., Kenny, Patrick. 1995. Training the Hubble Space Telescope Flight Team. IEEE Computer Graphics and Applications, 31-37.

McKenna, Michael. 1992. Interactive viewpoint control and three-dimensional operations. In Proceedings of the 1992 ACM Symposium on Interactive 3D Graphics., pages 53-56.

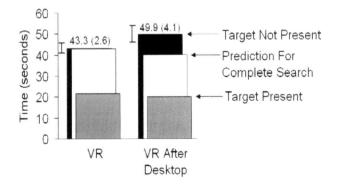

Graph 5: *Negative Transfer: Users Who Practice with the Desktop Interface Degrade Later Performance with the VR Interface.*

NAS: Virtual Reality: Scientific and Technological Challenges, Committe on VIrtual Reality Research and Development, National Research Council, Nathaniel Durlach and Anne Mavor, editors, National Academy of Science Press, 1995, ISBN 0-309-05135-5.

PUSH: Information for the PUSH device can be found at http:// www.fakespace.com

Pausch Randy, Shackelford M. Aanne., Proffitt, Dennis., A User Study Comparing Head-Mounted and Stationary Displays, IEEE 1993 Symposium on Research Frontiers in Virtual Reality, October, 1993, pages 41-45.

Pausch, Randy, Snoddy, Jon., Taylor, Robert., Watson, Scott., Haseltine, Eric, Disney's Aladdin: First Steps Toward Storytelling in Virtual Reality, Proceedings of SIGGRAPH, 1996, pages 193-203.

Robinett, Warren. 1992. Synthetic Experience: A Proposed Taxonomy. Presence, vol. 1, no. 2, 229- 247.

Smets, G., and Overbeeke, K., Trade-Off Between Resolution and Interactivity in Spatial Task Performance.

Sutherland, I. 1968. A head-mounted three-dimensional display. In Proceeding of the Fall Joint Computer Conference. AFIPS Conference Proceedings, vol. 33. AFIPS, Arlington, VA., 757- 764.

Tracker: Polhemus FASTRACK[tm]. Company information available via www.polhemus.com.

Ware, C. and Franck, G. (1996) Evaluating and stereo and motion cues for visualizing information nets in 3D. ACM TOG 15(2). 121-139.

Ware, Arthur and Booth. (1993) "FishTank Virtual Reality" ACM CHI'93 Proceedings, 37-42. is also somewhat relevant in that it looks at the phenomenological perception of space. Motion parallax is found to be more important that stereo information.

Zeltzer, D. 1992. Autonomy, interaction, and presence. Presence vol. 1, no. 1, 127-132.

Moving Objects In Space: Exploiting Proprioception In Virtual-Environment Interaction

Mark R. Mine, Frederick P. Brooks Jr.[1]

University of North Carolina at Chapel Hill

Carlo H. Sequin[2]

University of California at Berkeley

Abstract

Manipulation in immersive virtual environments is difficult partly because users must do without the haptic contact with real objects they rely on in the real world to orient themselves and their manipulanda. To compensate for this lack, we propose exploiting the one real object every user has in a virtual environment, his body. We present a unified framework for virtual-environment interaction based on *proprioception*, a person's sense of the position and orientation of his body and limbs. We describe three forms of body-relative interaction:

- Direct manipulation—ways to use body sense to help control manipulation
- Physical mnemonics—ways to store/recall information relative to the body
- Gestural actions—ways to use body-relative actions to issue commands

Automatic scaling is a way to bring objects instantly within reach so that users can manipulate them using proprioceptive cues. Several novel virtual interaction techniques based upon automatic scaling and our proposed framework of proprioception allow a user to interact with a virtual world intuitively, efficiently, precisely, and lazily. We report the results of both informal user trials and formal user studies of the usability of the body-relative interaction techniques presented.

CR Categories and Subject Descriptors: I.3.6 [Computer Graphics]: Methodology and Techniques - Interaction Techniques; I.3.7 [Computer Graphics]: Three-Dimensional Graphics and Realism - Virtual Reality.
Additional Keywords: virtual worlds, virtual environments, navigation, selection, manipulation.

----

[1]CB #3175 Sitterson Hall, Chapel Hill, NC 27599-3175. Tel: +1-919-962-1700. Email: {mine, brooks}@cs.unc.edu. URL: http://www.cs.unc.edu/~mine

[2]Computer Science Division, Department of Electrical Engineering and Computer Science, University of California, Berkeley, CA 94720. Tel: +1-510-642-5103. Email: sequin@cs.berkeley.edu

1 MANIPULATION IN A VIRTUAL WORLD: WHY IS IT HARD?

1.1 The Problem

The promise of immersive virtual environments is one of a three-dimensional environment in which a user can directly perceive and interact with three-dimensional virtual objects. The underlying belief motivating most virtual reality (VR) research is that this will lead to more natural and effective human-computer interfaces. Promising results in several key application domains have been demonstrated:

Domain	Example Applications
"Being There", experience for the sake of experience	Phobia therapy: [Rothbaum 1995] Aesthetics: [Davies 1996] Entertainment: [Pausch 1996]
Training and practice of different skills	Surgery: [Hunter 1993] Military : [Macedonia 1994] Maintenance: [Wilson 1995] Wayfinding: [Witmer 1995]
Visualization of unrealized or unseeable objects	Architecture: [Brooks 1986] Fluid Flow: [Bryson 1992] Nano-surfaces: [Taylor 1993]
Design	3D models: [Butterworth 1992] Cityscapes: [Mapes 1995]

Table 1: Successful Virtual-World Application Domains

The number of successful virtual-environment applications, however, still remains small, with even fewer applications having gone beyond the research laboratory. Why?

Many of these successes fall within the realm of spatial visualization. The applications exploit the intuitive view specification (via head tracking) offered by VR systems but make little use of direct virtual-object manipulation. Why is it difficult to do much more than look around in a virtual world?

Besides the well known technological limitations such as system latency and display resolution, several less obvious factors have hampered development of "real-world" virtual-environment applications.

1) *The precise manipulation of virtual objects is hard.* Although immersion, head-tracked view specification, and six degree-of-freedom (DoF) hand tracking facilitate the coarse manipulation of virtual objects, the precise manipulation of virtual objects is complicated by:

- *Lack of haptic feedback*: Humans depend on haptic feedback and physical constraints for precise interaction in the real world; the lack of physical work-surfaces to align against and rest on limits precision and exacerbates fatigue. Though there is considerable ongoing research in the area of active haptic feedback [Durlach 1995], general-purpose haptic feedback devices that do not restrict the mobility of the user are not yet practical or available.

- *Limited input information*: Most virtual-environment systems accept position and orientation (pose) data on the user's head and (if lucky) two hands. One also typically has a button or glove to provide signal/event information. This suffices for specifying simple 6 DoF motion and placement. In the real world, we do this and much more:

  a) Object modification, usually with tools.
  b) Directing the cooperation of helping hands, by spoken commands ("Put that there").
  c) Measuring.
  d) Annotating objects with text.

  Today in most VR systems:

  a) Tool selection is difficult.
  b) Voice command technology is marginal.
  c) Measuring tools are rarely available.
  d) Alphanumeric input is difficult.

- *Limited precision*: The lack of haptic and acoustic feedback, inaccurate tracking systems, and whole-hand input typical of current VR systems restricts users to the coarse manipulation of virtual objects. Fine-grained manipulations are extremely difficult using this "boxing glove" style interface. Shumin Zhai of the University of Toronto, for example, has demonstrated that users' task completion times were slower in a 3D docking task when using a 3D input device which excluded the use of the fingers (vs. a similar device that utilized the fingers) [Zhai 1996].

2) *Virtual environments lack a unifying framework for interaction,* such as the desktop metaphor used in conventional through-the-window computer applications. Without haptics, neither real-world nor desktop computer interaction metaphors are adequate in a virtual environment. Knowledge on how to manipulate objects or controls can no longer be "stored in the world" [Norman 1988], with the physical constraints of the devices giving the user clues as to their use (e.g. a dial can only be rotated about its axis).

The desktop metaphor further breaks down when the user is inside the user interface. Interface controls and displays must move with the user as he moves through the environment and be made easy to locate. The differences between working in a conventional computer environment and working immersed are analogous to the differences between a craftsman at a workbench and one moving about a worksite wearing a toolbelt. His toolbelt had better be large and filled with powerful tools.

1.2 A Solution: Use What You Have

Without touch, a user can no longer feel his surroundings to tell where he is nor use the felt collision of a manipulandum with stationary objects to refine spatial perception. It is imperative, therefore, to take advantage of the one thing a user can still feel in the virtual world, his body.

A person's sense of the position and orientation of his body and its several parts is called *proprioception* [Boff 1986]. We propose that proprioception can be used to develop a unified set of interaction techniques that allow a user to interact with a virtual world intuitively, efficiently, precisely, and lazily.

We describe several novel body-relative interaction techniques based on the framework of proprioception. These techniques provide better control, precision, and dynamic range during manipulation and take advantage of additional input information such as data from the user's head or second hand.

We present automatic scaling as a means of instantly bringing objects in reach so that users can manipulate them using proprioceptive cues.

Finally, we present the results of formal users studies designed to evaluate several core aspects of body-relative interaction. In addition, throughout the paper, we provide anecdotal data from the tens of demonstrations that were given to students, faculty and visitors at the University of North Carolina during development of the interaction techniques presented in this paper.

2 PROPRIOCEPTION AND BODY-RELATIVE INTERACTION

In a series of user observations, we have found that body-relative interaction techniques (exploiting proprioceptive feedback) are more effective than techniques relying solely on visual information. Such body-relative interaction techniques provide:

- a physical real-world frame of reference in which to work
- a more direct and precise sense of control
- "eyes off" interaction (the user doesn't have to constantly watch what he's doing)

A user can take advantage of proprioception during body-relative interaction in at least three ways:

- *Direct manipulation*: If a virtual object is located directly at the user's hand position, the user has a good sense of the position of the object (even with eyes closed) due to proprioception, and thus a greater sense of control. It is easier to place an object precisely by hand than when it is attached to the end of a fishing rod.

- *Physical mnemonics*: Users can store virtual objects, in particular menus and widgets [Conner 1992], relative to his body. Since a user can no longer feel the world around him, it can be difficult to find, select, and use virtual controls in world space, especially if the user is free to walk about the environment. If, however, controls are fixed relative to the user's body, he can use proprioception to find the controls, as one finds his pen in his pocket, or his pliers in his tool belt. If controls are attached to the user's body, they move with him as he moves through the environment and are always within reach. Finally, controls can be stored out of view (behind the user's back for example), reducing visual clutter, yet remaining easily accessible (like an arrow from a quiver).

- *Gestural actions*: Just as a user's body sense can be used to facilitate the recall of objects, it can be used to facilitate the recall of actions, such as gestures used to invoke commands or to communicate information.

3 WORKING WITHIN ARM'S REACH

Interacting within a user's natural working volume (i.e. within arm's reach) has these advantages:

- takes advantage of proprioceptive information
- provides a more direct mapping between hand motion and object motion
- yields stronger stereopsis and head-motion parallax cues
- provides finer angular precision of motion

Often the target of manipulation lies outside of the user's reach. Though he can move to reach it, constantly switching between object interaction and movement control breaks the natural rhythm of the operation and adds significant cognitive over-

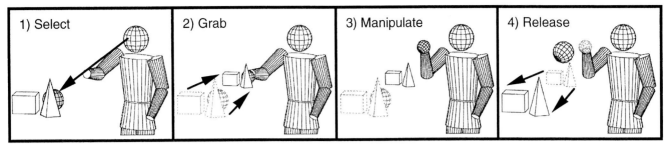

Figure 1: Automatic scaling of the world when the user grabs and releases an object.

head. We developed a convenient automatic scaling mechanism as a way to allow the user to interact instantly with objects lying at any distance as though they were within arm's reach.

Selected objects that fall outside of the reach of the user are brought instantly into reach by automatically scaling down the world about the user. For example, if the user's arm is extended 0.5 meters, the application brings a selected object that is 5 meters away to the user's hand by scaling down the world by a factor of 10 (see Figure 1)[1]. Scaling takes place at the start of each manipulation and is reset when the user is done (when the user grabs and then releases an object, for example).

The scaling factor used to scale down the world (or conversely, scale up the user) is equal to the ratio of the distance of the object being manipulated to the distance of the user's hand:

$$\frac{\|head\_object\|}{\|projection\ of\ head\_hand\ onto\ head\_object\|}$$

where head_object is the vector from the user's head (defined to be the midpoint between the user's eyes) to the object, and head_hand is the vector from the user's head to his hand.

If the center of the scaling operation is chosen to be the point midway between the user's eyes, he will be unaware, usually, that scaling has taken place, due to the ambiguity of perspective projections. This is particularly true if the inter-pupilary distance used to compute stereo images is also adjusted by the same scaling factor. This saves the user's having to reconverge the eyes. The most noticeable change is an apparent change in the size of the user's hand (which was not scaled). This can be offset by using non-realistic hand representations such as 3D crosshairs whose size is harder for the user to estimate visually.

A more implicit effect of the scaled-down world is the more dramatic effects of head movements; a small movement left-to-right may enable the user to see a big object such as a house from different sides, as though it were a dollhouse. While, in general, this is desirable, in some cases head motion can result in distracting movement of small, nearby objects.

---

[1] More precisely the object will move to a point on the surface of a sphere whose radius is equal to the user's current arm extension. The object will move to the user's hand only if his hand lies along the vector from the scaling center (the point midway between the user's eyes) to the object. This is the case when the user's hand visually occludes the object.

4 SAMPLE INTERACTION TECHNIQUES

4.1 Direct Manipulation

4.1.1 Scaled-world grab for manipulation

An example of the power of automatic scaling is *scaled-world grab*. In scaled-world grab, the world is automatically scaled down about the user's head every time he grabs an object and scaled back up when he releases it. With the object at the user's hand he can exploit proprioception, stereopsis, and head-motion parallax as he grabs an object and moves it.

Scaled-world grab is a powerful technique with an important property: it minimizes user work for a given result. With scaled-world grab the user can bring the most remote object in the scene to his side in a single operation; he doesn't have to fly (or worse, walk) to reach it or repeatedly grab, drop, and re-grab the object to reel it in. Furthermore, since the scale factor is automatically set, the user can manipulate near and far objects with equal ease. Scaled-world grab makes excellent use of a user's proprioceptive information for radial object movement, too: if the user halves his arm extension, the distance to the object will be halved. Movement of an object is easy for the user to control, predict and understand. Scaled-world grab is a surprising yet intuitive technique. In our informal user trials we have observed that users are often surprised to learn that scaling has taken place, and that they have no problem using the technique.

Related Work

The principles on which scaled-world grab is based have their foundations in the lessons we learned while exploring other forms of remote object manipulation.

Originally, for example, we tried the remote manipulation of objects via laser beams [Mine 1996, Mine 1997] (and later spotlights, following [Liang 1994]). We found, however, that even though these beams extend a user's reach, they are effective only for translations perpendicular to the beam direction and rotations about the beam axis. While it is easy to move an object about in an arc, translations in the beam direction and arbitrary rotations are much more difficult, requiring the user to repeatedly grab, move, drop, and re-grab the object.

A very effective way to specify arbitrary rotations is to use an *object centered interaction* paradigm [Wloka 1995, Mine 1997] in which changes in pose of the user's hand are mapped onto the center of a remote object. One technique we developed that grows out of this paradigm we call *extender grab*. Changes in orientation of the user's hand are applied 1:1 to the object's orientation. Translations are scaled by a factor which depends upon the distance of the object from the user at the start of the grab. The further away the object, the larger the scale factor.

By automatically setting the scale factor based on object distance, extender grab enables a large dynamic range of manipulation. No matter how far away an object lies, it can be brought to the user's side in a single operation. A key distinction between scaled-world grab and extender grab is that in the latter, manipulanda are not necessarily co-located with a user's hand as they are in scaled-world grab. This makes it harder for the user to exploit proprioception to determine object position and orientation. Similar techniques have been presented in [Bowman 1997] and [Pierce 1997]. In Pierce's techniques, the user interacts with the two-dimensional projections of 3D objects on the image plane.

A closely related technique for extending a user's reach called *go-go interaction* has been developed by Poupyrev et al. at the University of Washington [Poupyrev 1996]. In go-go interaction a user's virtual arm extension is a function of his physical arm extension, with a 1:1 mapping applied close to the user's body and a nonlinear function used further out. The maximum distance a user can reach depends upon the length of the user's arm and the scaling function used. Go-go interaction may require different scaling functions in scenes with different distributions of objects (i.e. mostly nearby or faraway).

Scaled-world grab has some common features with the Worlds-in-Miniature (WIM) paradigm (see [Pausch 1995, Stoakley 1995, Mine 1996, Mine 1997] and related earlier work in [Teller 1991]), in which objects are brought into reach in the form of a miniature copy of the environment floating in front of the user. WIMs have shown excellent promise in areas such as remote object manipulation and wayfinding. With a WIM, users can perform large scale manipulations of remote objects (moving a chair from one room in the house to another, for example) simply by manipulating the corresponding miniature copy in the WIM.

One drawback we have found with WIMs is that they force one to split limited display real estate between the miniature copy and the original environment. In addition, we have found that fine-grained manipulations can be difficult, particularly if the user is forced to hold a copy of the entire environment in his hand (as was the case in our system). If the entire environment has been scaled down to WIM size, individual scene elements may be quite small, and thus difficult to see, select, and manipulate. Note that manipulations at arbitrary resolutions would be easier if the user could interactively select a subset of the environment to view in the WIM (choosing to look at a single room instead of the whole house, for example). In that case the WIM could be thought of as a more general three-dimensional windowing system.

4.1.2 Scaled-world grab for locomotion

Automatic world-scaling also yields a useful locomotion mode, in which the user transports himself by grabbing an object in the desired travel direction and pulling himself towards it. With scaled-world grab the user can reach any visible destination in a single grab operation.

Since the point of interest is attached to the user's hand he can quickly view it from all sides by simply torquing his wrist. Alternately, if the virtual world stays oriented with the laboratory (which aids wayfinding), the user can swing himself about the point of interest, in a fashion similar to orbital mode (discussed later), by holding it in front of his face while he turns around (the world pivoting about his hand).

A similar movement metaphor called *virtual walking* is used in MultiGen's SmartScene™ application [MultiGen 1997]. With virtual walking users can pull themselves through the environment hand-over-hand, like climbing a rope. Virtual walking, however, is more suitable for the exploration of nearby objects since the extent of the pulling operation is limited to the reach of the user. To go much further the user must either invoke a separate scaling operation, to scale down the world until the desired destination is within reach, or switch to an alternate movement mode such as two-handed flying.

4.2 Physical Mnemonics

We call the storing of virtual objects and controls relative to the user's body *physical mnemonics.*

4.2.1 Pull-down menus

A thorny problem is the management and placement of virtual menus. If menus are left floating in space they are difficult to find. If they are locked in screen space they occlude parts of the scene. One solution is to keep the menu hidden and use a virtual button (like a menu bar) or a physical button to invoke the menu. However, small virtual buttons that minimally occlude are difficult to hit, and the cost of dedicating a physical button just for menu activation is high, since the number of buttons available on an input device is inherently limited.

As an alternative, we propose that one can hide virtual menus in locations fixed relative to the user's body, just above his current field of view for example. To access a menu the user simply reaches up, grabs it, and pulls it into view. The user can then interact with the menu using his other hand (if two hands are available) or through some form of gaze-directed interaction. Once the user is done with the menu he lets go, and it returns to its hiding place. This obviates a dedicated menu button, avoids occlusion by the menu, uses an existing operation for menu invocation, and keeps menus easy to find and access. In informal trials we have found that the user can easily select among three menus from above his field of view; one up and to the left, one just above, and one up and to the right.

The user's body can similarly be used to locate other tools or mode switches. Widgets for changing the viewing properties can be stored by the user's head; widgets for manipulating objects can be stored by the user's hands. The user 's own body parts act as physical mnemonics which help in the recall and acquisition of frequently used controls. Furthermore, since the user is interacting relative to his own body, controls can remain invisible until acquired and can snap back to their hiding place when no longer needed. This minimizes occlusion of the scene by the virtual controls.

4.2.2 Hand-held widgets

In [Conner 1992], widgets (such as handles to stretch an object) were attached directly to the objects they control. To use such object-bound widgets in an immersive environment requires either the ability to reach the widget or some form of at-a-distance interaction. As an alternative we developed *hand-held widgets:* 3D objects with geometry and behavior that appear in the user's virtual hand(s). Hand-held widgets can be used to control objects from afar like using a TV remote control (see Figure 2).

We prefer hand-held widgets to object-bound ones for several reasons. First, we have observed in both formal user studies (Section 5) and informal user trials that users can select and work with hand-held widgets (assisted by proprioceptive in-

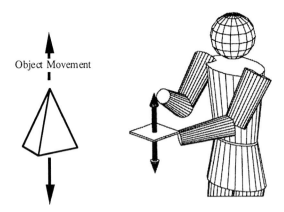

Figure 2: Using a hand-held widget.

formation) more easily than they can with object-bound widgets (whose position can be deduced only visually). Second, hand-held widgets enable a user to interact with selected objects from afar; he doesn't have to reach an object to use its widgets. Third, hand-held widgets reduce visual clutter, since each object doesn't have to have its own set of widgets, only a single copy of each kind of widget is needed. Finally, hand-held widgets eliminate obscuration of an object by its widgets. As a result of these factors, we find that it is preferable to work with widgets held in the hand, even though at-a-distance interaction with object-bound widgets could be accomplished using image-plane interaction techniques or automatic scaling.

4.2.3 FoV-Relative mode switching

One knows when one's hand or foot is in one's field of view (FoV), and one knows intuitively how to bring it into view. We have found that this can be effectively used for mode switching. Applications can, for example, switch between different forms of object selection. Occlusion selection, the selection of objects that visually lie behind a hand-attached cursor [Pierce 1997], requires the user's hand to be visible. The selection of objects pointed at by a laser beam or spotlight attached to the user's hand, does not. A logical and intuitive form of body-relative mode switching is to automatically change between occlusion selection to ray casting whenever the user's hand moves out of/into his current field of view.

4.3. Gestural Actions

We demonstrate how intuitive gestures can be augmented in powerful ways.

4.3.1 Head-butt zoom

Promising results have been reported on the potential of head pose as an auxiliary channel into the system. In orbital mode, for example, the user's head orientation is tracked and mapped so as to move the viewpoint of the user about the surface of a virtual sphere surrounding an object [Chung 1994]. Orbital mode is an excellent example of a technique not possible in the real world that gives the user power in the virtual environment. Chung found radiologists preferred it over six other methods of view-direction control such as mouse, joystick, and walka-round, and hypothesized that that was because it minimized work.

We developed head-butt zoom as another way for head motion to be used in controlling interaction. We have observed that users routinely and frequently switch between close-up local (and detailed) views and pulled-back global (and simplified) views when using interactive design systems, whether architectural CAD, molecular map tracing, or technical illustration preparation. Head-butt zoom enables a user to switch quickly between these two types of views as simply as leaning forward for a closer look.

Setting up head-butt zoom is similar to using a zoom tool in a conventional through-the-window application. The user frames the chosen detailed subset of his current view using a screen-aligned rectangle in front of his face. He sizes the rectangle like a movie director framing a shot; the position of his hands setting the corners of the rectangle (Figure 3). The size of this rectangle determines the zoom factor; its placement in world space determines the transition point. To remind the user that he is in head-butt zoom mode, a semi-transparent rectangle is left floating in space.

Figure 3: Setting up head-butt zoom

The user switches between the two views simply by leaning forward and backward. Lean forward (across the plane of the rectangle) to get a close-up and detailed view; lean back to return to the normal view.[2] If the user wishes to remain in the close-up view, he simply steps forward, at which point he will translate to the point of view of the zoomed-in view. Stepping back, he will return to the original view.

Instead of having the user explicitly frame a region of interest, the current zoom factor can be based upon the currently selected object (chosen so that when he leans forward the object fills his field of view). This mode makes it easier to integrate head-butt zoom with other forms of interaction, since the user does not have to interrupt his current operation in order to switch modes and specify a zoom rectangle.

Head-butt zoom makes good use of an additional input channel, i.e., head position. Users can change zoom levels without having to interrupt the current operation they are performing with their hands. Head-butt zoom also makes good use of limited display space, since one no longer needs to share screen space between versions of the same scene at different scales, as in World-In-Miniature.

---

[2] Note that head-butt zoom can also be used to switch between other kinds of viewing modes. E.g., the user could lean forward to get a wireframe view, lean back to get a full shaded representation.

4.3.2 Look-at Menus

Head orientation can be used instead of the traditional hand position to control the cursor used to select an item from a menu. To select one turns the head instead of moving the hand. The pick ray is fixed relative to the head (thus tracking head motion, see Figure 4). This gives an intuitive way to select an item simply by looking at it. To confirm selection, the user presses a physical button or, with pull-down menus, releases the menu.

Figure 4: Look-at menu.

4.3.3 Two-handed flying

Numerous results describe the benefits of two-handed input in interactive applications ([Buxton 1986, Bier 1993, Shaw 1994, Goble 1995, Mapes 1995, Cutler 1997, Zeleznik 1997] and [Guiard 1987] for more theoretical foundations). We have found two-handed flying an effective technique for controlled locomotion. The direction of flight is specified by the vector between the user's two hands, and the speed is proportional to the user's hand separation (see Figure 5)[3]. A dead zone (some minimum hand separation, e.g. 0.1 meters) enables users to stop their current motion quickly by bringing their hands together (a quick and easy gesture). Two-handed flying exploits proprioception for judging flying direction and speed.

Two-handed flying is easier ergonomically than conventional one-handed flying in which the user's hand orientation specifies direction and arm extension specifies speed. Flying backwards using one-handed flying, for example, requires the user to regrab the input device or to turn his hand around awkwardly. With two-handed flying the user simply swaps his hands. Moreover, speed control based on hand separation is less tiring than speed control based on arm extension, the user doesn't have to hold his hands out in front of his body.

4.3.4 Over-the-shoulder deletion

A common operation is deletion; users need an easy way to get rid of virtual objects. Over-the-shoulder deletion is an intuitive gesture that exploits body sense. To delete an object the user simply throws it over his shoulder. It is easy to do, easy to remember, and it does not use up any buttons or menu space. It is

---
[3] A similar flying technique has been implemented by Mapes and colleagues in MultiGen's SmartScene[TM] [MultiGen 1997].

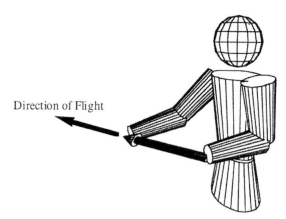

Direction of Flight

Figure 5: Two-handed flying.

unlikely to be accidentally invoked, since users do not typically manipulate objects in that region.

The space behind a user's head can be treated as a virtual clipboard. A user can later retrieve the last object deleted by simply reaching over his shoulder and grabbing it.

5 USER STUDIES

To evaluate some of the core aspects of body-relative interaction we performed two formal user studies, a virtual-object docking task, and a widget interaction task.

5.1 Virtual-Object Docking

The goal of this experiment was to explore the differences between manipulating virtual objects that are co-located with one's hand and manipulating objects at a distance. The experiment was a repeated measures design with three primary experimental conditions: the manipulation of objects held in one's hand, objects held at a fixed offset, and objects held at an offset which varied with the subject's arm extension. These three conditions were abstractions of three forms of remote object manipulation: scaled-world grab, laser beam interaction, and extender grab. Our hypothesis was that the manipulation of objects co-located with one's hand is more efficient than the manipulation of objects held at an offset.

5.1.1 The Experiment

Subjects

Eighteen unpaid subjects (7 female, 11 male) were recruited from staff and students at the University of North Carolina-CH.

The Task

The virtual environment consisted of target shapes and handheld docking shapes. Target shapes were semi-transparent red cubes floating in space in front of the subject. Hand-held docking shapes were fully opaque blue cubes attached to the subject's hand. Docking shapes were either co-located with the subject's dominant hand or at some random initial offset ranging from 0.1 - 0.6 meters.

The task given to the subjects was to align the hand-held docking cube with the target cube floating in space as quickly as possible. Target cubes were presented to the subject one at a time. Each time the subject successfully aligned the docking cube with the target cube, both the target cube and docking cube would disappear from their current locations and then reappear in their new locations.

The subject controlled the virtual docking cube using a small styrofoam cube held in his dominant hand.

5.1.2 The Results

Table 2 presents the overall means obtained in each experimental condition.

Condition	Mean (sec)	Std. Dev. (sec)
In hand	3.87	2.05
Fixed offset	5.10	3.83
Variable offset	4.96	4.48

Table 2: Mean trial completion time.

Results were analyzed using a one-way multivariate analysis of variances (MANOVA), repeated measures design. This analysis revealed significant differences among the mean trial completion times for the three manipulation techniques $F(2,16) = 7.86$; $p < 0.005$. Contrasts of trial completion times showed that the manipulation of objects co-located with one's hand was significantly faster than the manipulation of objects at a fixed offset ($F(1,17) = 16.70$; $p < 0.001$), and the manipulation of objects at a variable offset ($F(1,17) = 8.37$; $p = 0.01$). No significant difference was found between the manipulation of an object at a fixed offset and one at a variable offset ($F(1,17) = 0.25$; $p = 0.62$).

Analysis of a post-test questionnaire also revealed a preference for the manipulation of an object co-located with one's hand, subjects rated it significantly higher than the manipulation of an object with an offset.

5.2 Virtual-Widget Interaction

This experiment explored the differences between interacting with a widget held in one's hand and interacting with a widget floating in space. Our goal was to see if subjects could take advantage of proprioception when interacting with widgets held in their hand. Our hypothesis was that it would be easier for subjects to interact with hand-held widgets than it would be for them to interact with widgets floating in space.

5.2.1 The Experiment

Subjects

The same eighteen subjects used in the object-docking experiment were used in this experiment.

Task

The virtual environment consisted of a three-dimensional cursor, a virtual widget, a current-color indicator, and target objects. The three-dimensional cursor was a small sphere attached to the subject's dominant hand. The virtual widget consisted of three orthogonal rods with colored spheres at each end (for a total of six spheres). The widget was either attached to the subject's non-dominant hand or was fixed floating in space. The current-color indicator was an additional colored sphere that was fixed in the upper right hand corner of the subject's display. Finally, the target objects were red semi-transparent cubes which appeared at random positions and orientations about the subject.

Each trial was broken down into three phases. First, the subject moved the 3D cursor to the indicated point on a virtual widget (one of the six colored spheres). Next, he performed an

unrelated abstract task (moving his hand from the widget to a target cube and clicking on the input button). This made the target cube and widget disappear. Finally, he returned his hand as closely as possible to the original point of interaction on the virtual widget, without visual feedback. The dependent variable measured was the positional accuracy with which the user could return his hand to a point in space.

5.2.2 The Results

Table 3 presents the overall means obtained in each experimental condition.

Condition	Mean (cm)	Std. Dev. (cm)
Hand held	5.1	4.0
In space	10.4	6.1

Table 3: Mean positional offsets

Results were analyzed using a one-way analysis of variances (ANOVA), repeated measures design. This analysis revealed a significant difference in positional accuracy between widgets held in one's hand and widgets fixed in space $F(1,17) = 115.52$; $p < 0.001$. Contrasts of positional accuracy showed that subjects were able to return to a position relative to their own hand more accurately than a position fixed in virtual space.

Analysis of a post-test questionnaire also revealed a preference for interaction with widgets held in one's hand, subjects rated it as being easier, more precise and better overall.

6 FUTURE WORK

We continue to explore additional means for compensating for the lack of haptic feedback in immersive virtual worlds. Though proprioception greatly enhances virtual-environment interaction, precise manipulation is still harder in virtual spaces than in real space. Several factors complicate fine-grained manipulation.

First, the lack of physical work surfaces and haptic feedback makes the controlled manipulation of virtual objects much more difficult. Users typically manipulate virtual objects by holding their arms out without support. In the real world, a person generally grounds the arm at the forearm, or elbow, or heel of hand to steady hand motions and to reduce fatigue when performing precise manipulation.

Second, humans depend upon naturally occurring physical constraints to help determine the motion of objects they are manipulating (sliding a chair along a floor, for example). Whereas it is possible to implement virtual equivalents of physical constraints [Bukowski 1995], it is more difficult for the user to take advantage of these constraints without haptic feedback. He can only see that the chair is on the floor, he can't feel the contact, hear it, or sense the vibration as the chair slides.

Third, users in a virtual world must typically do without the fingertip control they rely on for the fine-grained manipulation of objects in the real world. Instrumented gloves have shown some promise for the fine-grained manipulation of objects, but they have proven difficult to use in practice [Kijima 1996].

One approach we are exploring to give users a real surface on which they can work using haptic constraints is to provide a hand-held tablet (following the lead of [Sachs 1991] and [Stoakley 1995]). The tablet can be used as a two-dimensional drawing surface (to define detailed two-dimensional shapes) or it can be used as the input space for a two-dimensional menu (allowing users to interact precisely with widgets and controls).

If the user interacts with the tablet using a hand-held stylus, he can take advantage of the user's fingertip control precision. In addition the friction between tablet and stylus and the grounding of the stylus against the tablet give the user better control.

To provide a larger work surface the tablet can be docked in a larger fixed physical surface such as a lectern or a drafting table which can also provide grounding and support during object manipulations (see related work in [Mapes 1995]).

7 ACKNOWLEDGMENTS

Special thanks to Robert Zeleznik of Brown University for his invaluable contributions to this paper. Thanks to Hans Weber of UNC; Andrew Forsberg, Seung Hong, Loring Holden of Brown University; and Jeff Pierce, and Dennis Cosgrove of the University of Virginia for numerous discussions about virtual-environment interaction and their many helpful comments and suggestions. Thanks to Todd Gaul of UNC for his assistance in the production of the associated video tape. As always, thanks to Sandra, Dylan, and Baby X.

This funding for this work was provided by DARPA Contract DABT63-93-C-0048, and Lockheed Missile and Space Co., Inc. (indirect DARPA).

REFERENCES

[Bier 1993] Bier, E.A., M.C. Stone, K. Pier, W. Buxton and T.D. DeRose. "Tooolglass and magic lenses: the see-through interface." *Proceedings of SIGGRAPH 93*, Anaheim, CA, ACM: 73-80.

[Boff 1986] Boff, K.R., L. Kaufman and J.P. Thomas, Eds.. *Handbook of Perception and Human Performance*. New York, John Wiley and Sons.

[Bowman 1997] Bowman, D. and L.F. Hodges. "An Evaluation of Techniques for Grabbing and Manipulating Remote Objects in Immersive Virtual Environments." *Proceedings of the 1997 Symposium on Interactive 3D Graphics*, Providence, RI, ACM: 35-38.

[Brooks 1986] Brooks, F.P., Jr. "Walkthrough-a dynamic graphics system for simulating virtual buildings." *Computer Graphics. 1986 Workshop on Interactive 3D Graphics* 21(1): 3.

[Bryson 1992] Bryson, S. and C. Levit. "The Virtual Wind Tunnel." *IEEE Computer Graphics & Applications* : 25-34.

[Bukowski 1995] Bukowski, R.W. and C.H. Sequin. "Object Associations: A Simple and Practical Approach to Virtual 3D Manipulation." *Proceedings of the 1995 Symposium on Interactive 3D Graphics*, Monterey, CA, ACM: 131-138.

[Butterworth 1992] Butterworth, J., A. Davidson, S. Hench and T.M. Olano. "3DM: A Three Dimensional Modeler Using a Head-Mounted Display." *Computer Graphics. Proceedings 1992 Symposium on Interactive 3D Graphics* 25(2): 135-138.

[Buxton 1986] Buxton, W. and B.A. Myers. "A Study in Two-Handed Input." *Human Factors in Computing Systems (ACM SIGCHI 86 Conference Proceedings)*, Boston, MA, ACM, New York: 321-326.

[Chung 1994] Chung, J. *Intuitive Navigation in the Targeting of Radiation Therapy Treatment Beams*. University of North Carolina, Ph.D. Thesis

[Conner 1992] Conner, D.B., S.S. Snibbe, K.P. Herndon, D.C. Robbins, R.C. Zeleznik and A. vanDam. "Three-dimensional widgets." *Computer Graphics (1992 Symposium on Interactive 3D Graphics)* 25(2): 183-188.

[Cutler 1997] Cutler, L.D., B. Fröhlich and P. Hanrahan. "Two-Handed Direct Manipulation on the Responsive Workbench." *Proceedings of the 1997 Symposium on Interactive 3D Graphics*, Providence, RI, ACM: 107-114.

[Davies 1996] Davies, C. and J. Harrison. "Osmose: Towards Broadening the Aesthetics of Virtual Reality." *Computer Graphics* 30(4):

[Durlach 1995] Durlach, N.I. and A.S. Mavor, Eds.. *Virtual Reality: Scientific and Technological Challenges*. Washington, D.C., National Academy Press.

[Goble 1995] Goble, J.C., K. Hinckley, R. Pausch, J. W. Snell and N.F. Kassell. "Two-handed spatial interface tools for neurosurgical planning." *Computer* 28,(7): p. 20-6.

[Guiard 1987] Guiard, Y. "Asymmetric Division of Labor in Human Skilled Bimanual Action: The Kinematic Chain as a Model." *The Journal of Motor Behavior* 19(4): 486-517.

[Hunter 1993] Hunter, I.W., D.D. Tilemachos, S.R. Lafontaine, P.G. Charette, L.A. Jones, M.A. Sagar, G.D. Mallinson and P.J. Hunter. "A Teleoperated Microsurgical Robot and Associated Virtual Environment for Eye Surgery." *Presence* 2(4): 265-280.

[Kijima 1996] Kijima, R. and M. Hirose. "Representative Spherical Plane Method and Composition of Object Manipulation Methods." *1996 Virtual Reality Annual International Symposium*, Santa Clara, CA, IEEE: 196-202.

[Liang 1994] Liang, J. and M. Green. "JDCAD: a highly interactive 3D modeling system." *Computers & Graphics* 18(4): 499-506.

[Macedonia 1994] Macedonia, M.R., M.J. Zyda, D.R. Pratt, P.T. Barham and S. Zeswitz. "NPSNET: A Network Software Architecture for Large Scale Virtual Environments." *Presence* 3(4): 265-287.

[Mapes 1995] Mapes, D.P. and J.M. Moshell. "A Two-Handed Interface for Object Manipulation in Virtual Environments." *Presence* 4(4): 403-416.

[Mine 1997] Mine, M.R. "ISAAC: A Meta-CAD System for Virtual Environments." *Computer-Aided Design* : to appear.

[Mine 1996] Mine, M.R. "Working in a Virtual World: Interaction Techniques Used in the Chapel Hill Immersive Modeling Program." *University of North Carolina*, Technical Report TR96-029

[MultiGen 1997] MultiGen Inc. "SmartScene^TM" *for more information see:* http://www.multigen.com/smart.htm

[Norman 1988] Norman, D.A. *The psychology of everyday things*. New York, Basic Books.

[Pausch 1995] Pausch, R., T. Burnette, D. Brockway and M.E. Weiblen. "Navigation and locomotion in virtual worlds via flight into hand-held miniatures." *Proceedings of SIGGRAPH 95*, Los Angeles, CA, ACM: 399-400.

[Pausch 1996] Pausch, R., J. Snoddy, R. Taylor, S. Watson and E. Haseltine. "Disney's Aladdin: First Steps Toward Storytelling in Virtual Reality." *Proceedings of SIGGRAPH 96*, New Orleans, LA, ACM: 193-202.

[Pierce 1997] Pierce, J.S., A. Forsberg, M.J. Conway, S. Hong, R. Zeleznik and M.R. Mine. "Image Plane Interaction Techniques in 3D Immersive Environments." *Proceedings of the 1997 Symposium on Interactive 3D Graphics*, Providence, RI, ACM: 39-44.

[Poupyrev 1996] Poupyrev, I., M. Billinghurst, S. Weghorst and T. Ichikawa. "The Go-Go Interaction Technique: Non-Linear Mapping for Direct Manipulation in VR." *Proceedings of UIST 96*, Seattle, WA, ACM:

[Rothbaum 1995] Rothbaum, B., L. Hodges, R. Kooper, D. Opdyke, J. Williford and M. North. "Effectiveness of computer-generated (virtual reality) graded exposure in the treatment of acrophobia." *American Journal of Psychiatry* 152(4): 626-628.

[Sachs 1991] Sachs, E., A. Roberts and D. Stoops. "3-Draw: a tool for designing 3D shapes." *IEEE Computer Graphics and Applications* 11(6): 18- 26.

[Shaw 1994] Shaw, C. and M. Green. "Two-handed polygonal surface design." *Proceedings of UIST 94*, Marina del Rey, CA, p. 226, 205-12.

[Stoakley 1995] Stoakley, R., M.J. Conway and R. Pausch. "Virtual Reality on a WIM: Interactive Worlds in Miniature." *Proceedings of CHI 95*, Denver, CO, ACM: 265-272.

[Taylor 1993] Taylor, R.M., W. Robinett, V.L. Chi, F.P. Brooks Jr., W.V. Wright, S. Williams and E.J. Snyder. "The Nanomanipulator: A Virtual-Reality Interface for a Scanning Tunnel Microscope." *Proceedings of SIGGRAPH 93*, Anaheim, CA, ACM:

[Teller 1991] Teller, S.J. and C.H. Sequin. "Visibility Preprocessing for Interactive Walkthroughs." *Computer Graphics (Proceedings of SIGGRAPH 91)* 25(4): 61-69.

[Wilson 1995] Wilson, J.R., D.J. Brown, S.V. Cobb, M.M. D'Cruz and R.M. Eastgate. "Manufacturing Operations in Virtual Environments (MOVE)." *Presence* 4(3): 306-317.

[Witmer 1995] Witmer, B.G., J.H. Bailey and B. Knerr, W. "Training Dismounted Soldiers in Virtual Environments: Route Learning and Transfer." *United States Army Research Institute for the Behavioral and Social Sciences*, Technical Report 1022

[Wloka 1995] Wloka, M.M. and E. Greenfield. "The Virtual Tricorder: A Uniform Interface for Virtual Reality." *Proceedings UIST 95*, Pittsburgh, PA, ACM: 39-40.

[Zeleznik 1997] Zeleznik, R.C., A.S. Forsberg and P.S. Strauss. "Two pointer input for 3D interaction." *Proceedings of the 1997 Symposium on Interactive 3D Graphics*, Providence, RI, ACM: 115-120.

[Zhai 1996] Zhai, S., P. Milgram and W. Buxton. "The Influence of Muscle Groups on Performance of Multiple Degree-of-Freedom Input." *Proceedings of CHI 96*, Vancouver, BC, Canada, ACM: 308-315.

Virtual Voyage: Interactive Navigation in the Human Colon

Lichan Hong*   Shigeru Muraki†   Arie Kaufman*   Dirk Bartz‡   Taosong He§

Center for Visual Computing
State University of New York at Stony Brook

Abstract

Virtual colonoscopy is a non-invasive computerized medical procedure for examining the entire colon to detect polyps. We present an interactive virtual colonoscopy method, which uses a physically-based camera control model and a hardware-assisted visibility algorithm. By employing a potential field and rigid body dynamics, our camera control supplies a convenient and intuitive mechanism for examining the colonic surface while avoiding collisions. Our Z-buffer-assisted visibility algorithm culls invisible regions based on their visibility through a chain of portals, thus providing interactive rendering speed. We demonstrate our method with experimental results on a plastic pipe phantom, the Visible Human, and several patients.

CR Categories: I.3.3 [Picture/Image Generation]: Display Algorithms; I.3.5 [Computational Geometry and Object Modeling]: Physically Based Modeling; I.3.6 [Methodologies and Techniques]: Interaction Techniques; I.3.7 [Three-Dimensional Graphics and Realism]: Hidden Line/Surface Removal; I.3.8 [Applications];

Keywords: Virtual Colonoscopy, Endoscopy, Camera Control, Visibility, Physically-Based Navigation, Potential Field, Interactive Rendering, Virtual Environment

1   Introduction

Cancer of the colon and rectum is the second leading cause of cancer deaths in the USA. Approximately 150,000 new cases of colorectal cancer are diagnosed every year. Consequently, it is imperative that an effective diagnostic procedure be found to detect colonic polyps or tumors at an early stage. Currently, optical colonoscopy and barium enema are the only two procedures available for examining the entire colon to detect polyps larger than *5mm* in diameter,

*Department of Computer Science, State University of New York at Stony Brook, Stony Brook, NY 11794-4400, USA. Email: {lichan|ari}@cs.sunysb.edu

†Machine Understanding Division, Electrotechnical Laboratory, 1-1-4 Umezono, Tsukuba, 305 Japan. Email: muraki@etl.go.jp

‡University of Tübingen, WSI/GRIS, Auf der Morgenstelle 10/C9, D72076 Tübingen, Germany. Email: bartz@gris.uni-tuebingen.de

§Software Production Research Department, Bell Laboratories, Lucent Technologies, Naperville, IL 60566, USA. Email: taosong@research.bell-labs.com

which are clinically considered to have a high probability of being malignant. In optical colonoscopy, a fiber optical probe is introduced into the colon through the rectum. By manipulating the tiny camera attached to the tip of the probe, the physician examines the inner surface of the colon to identify abnormalities. This invasive procedure requires intravenous sedation, takes about one hour, and is expensive. Barium enema requires a great deal of physical cooperation from the patient when the X-ray radiographs of the colon are taken at different views. Additionally, its sensitivity can be as low as 78% in detecting polyps in the range of *5mm* to *20mm* [13].

In the past few years, at Stony Brook we have been independently developing an innovative technique called *virtual colonoscopy* [7], which was proposed as an alternative procedure for examining the entire colon [7, 11, 14, 20]. In general, this procedure consists of three steps. First, the patient's colon is cleansed and inflated with air in a way similar to that of optical colonoscopy. Second, while the patient is holding his or her breath, a helical CT scan of the patient's abdomen is taken, capturing a sequence of 2D slices which covers the entire range of the colon. This scan takes 30 – 45 seconds and produces several hundred transaxial slices of 512×512 pixels, which are subsequently reconstructed into a 3D volume of 100 – 250 MBytes. Finally, the colonic surface is extracted, and the physician virtually navigates inside the colon to examine the surface for possible polyps. This non-invasive procedure can potentially improve the diagnostic sensitivity and specificity with fewer complications, lower expense, shorter examination time, and reduced patient discomfort [20].

Previous work [7, 11, 14] has focused primarily on generating a fly-through animation (i.e., planned navigation) inside the colon, by moving a virtual camera from one end of the colon to the other. Specifically, after the camera parameters at the keyframes have been either manually specified [14] or automatically calculated [7, 11], intermediate frames are rendered *off-line* in several hours. Although this planned navigation provides a general overview of the colonic surface, helping to quickly exclude many benign cases, it is rather limited because no user interaction is possible. A detailed study requires close interactions such as observing the shape of an abnormality from different angles, measuring its size, and even examining the tissues beneath the abnormality.

2   Interactive Virtual Colonoscopy

In this paper, we describe a technique called *interactive virtual colonoscopy*. In addition to providing an overview of the colonic surface as in planned navigation, our technique allows the physician to interactively manipulate the virtual camera to explore detailed structures as desired. The resulting virtual voyage inside the colon may remind one of *Fantastic Voyage* (20th Century Fox, 1966), an Academy-Award winning science fiction movie, in which a team of doctors aboard a miniaturized submarine cruised inside a patient's arteries to perform brain surgery. Fig. 1 shows the process of interactive virtual colonoscopy comprised of two primary components: camera control and interactive rendering. These two technical challenges are the main focus of this paper.

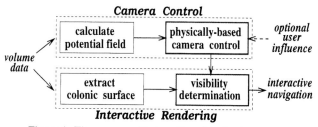

Figure 1: The process of interactive virtual colonoscopy.

Camera control essentially defines how the physician navigates inside the colon. A desirable camera control should enable the physician to examine the surface easily and intuitively, and prevent the camera from penetrating through the surface (an inescapable concern while navigating inside the colon). In this work, we have developed a physically-based camera control model. To balance between guiding the physician through the colonic interior and the physician's freedom to manipulate the camera, our model employs a potential field and rigid body dynamics. Section 3 describes the general concept of our camera control model, how we calculate the potential field for the colonic interior from two volumetric distance fields, and move the camera using kinematic rules.

Interactive rendering speed is indispensable for virtual colonoscopy to be accepted by the medical community. For an effective navigation, at least 10 frames/second is required. From the acquired CT data, in a preprocess, we reconstruct the colonic surface using the Marching Cubes algorithm [10]. During navigation, based on the camera parameters supplied by the camera control model, we render the isosurface triangles on-the-fly to generate an image. Unfortunately, the number of triangles is enormous and can not be processed at interactive speed. Section 4 describes how we achieve high frame rates by reducing the number of triangles delivered to the graphics engine, without compromising image quality. Specifically, we present a hardware-assisted visibility algorithm which exploits the twisted nature of the colon. In Section 5, we briefly describe our user interface and present our experimental results on a pipe phantom, the Visible Human data, and patient studies.

3 Camera Control

3.1 Design Concepts

The following properties are desirable for our camera control:

(1) Given a user-specified source point (e.g., the rectum) and a user-specified target point (e.g., the appendix), the camera automatically moves from the source point towards the target point, or vice versa.

(2) When necessary, the physician can intuitively and easily change the camera position and direction.

(3) To obtain a wide view of the colonic surface, the camera stays away from the surface.

(4) Since in virtual colonoscopy the concern is the inner surface of the colon, the camera should never penetrate through the surface, even when incorrectly handled by the physician.

There has been a great deal of research on camera control for navigating within a 3D virtual environment. Roughly speaking, there are three groups of camera control techniques: planned navigation, manual navigation, and guided navigation. Planned navigation (e.g., [7, 11, 14]) does not satisfy properties 2 and 4. Manual navigation (e.g., [4, 19, 21]), which requires the user to control the camera parameters at every step, does not satisfy properties 1, 3 and 4. Guided navigation [3], which provides some guidance for

the camera and allows the user to control it when desired, does not satisfy property 4 but satisfies properties 1 – 3 quite well. Nevertheless, Galyean's technique [3], which uses a pre-computed path as a guide and employs a spring-based model for the user control, lacks implementation details. It is unclear how the camera parameters (particularly the orientation) are interactively influenced by the user.

In this section, we present our guided-navigation camera control model which satisfies all four properties. Our camera is mounted on a *submarine*, which is immersed within a potential field [9] and moved according to a set of kinematic equations (see Fig. 2). With

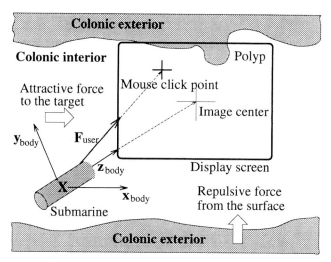

Figure 2: Our physically-based submarine model.

this physically-based model, the colonic interior mimics a "water tunnel", with the water running downstream. The submarine is moved by the water flow as well as by any external influence imposed by the physician, but never collides with the tunnel walls. As the end user, the physician watches the display screen on which the view from the submarine is projected. When desired, the physician repeatedly clicks the mouse at a spot on the screen to maneuver the submarine closer to that spot.

3.2 Potential Field

As shown in Fig. 2, we approximate the submarine with a small cylinder, whose mass is 1. The center of mass is $\mathbf{X}$, where the camera is attached. $\mathbf{x}_{body}$, $\mathbf{y}_{body}$, and $\mathbf{z}_{body}$ define the body-space coordinate system of the submarine. The major axis of the cylinder, $\mathbf{z}_{body}$, corresponds to the camera direction, and $\mathbf{y}_{body}$ corresponds to the up-vector of the camera. The submarine is under the influence of the potential field $V(\mathbf{X})$, which is a volume data set of the same resolution as the CT data. Assuming that the submarine is sufficiently small, the following equation of motion is satisfied for the submarine, which is pushed toward the steepest descending direction of $V(\mathbf{X})$:

$$\dot{\mathbf{P}}(t) = -\nabla V(\mathbf{X}) - k_l \mathbf{P}(t) \qquad (1)$$

$\dot{\mathbf{P}}(t)$ is the time derivative of the submarine linear momentum $\mathbf{P}(t)$ at time t; $\nabla V(\mathbf{X})$ is the gradient of $V(\mathbf{X})$ at point $\mathbf{X}$; and $k_l \mathbf{P}(t)$ is a dissipative force to prevent the submarine from moving too fast, where k_l is the friction coefficient.

To make the submarine motion satisfy properties 1, 3 and 4, we define $V(\mathbf{X})$ by using two distance fields: distance from the colonic surface $D_s(\mathbf{X})$ and distance from the target point $D_t(\mathbf{X})$. $D_s(\mathbf{X})$ and $D_t(\mathbf{X})$ are calculated using 3D image processing techniques. Since the colon is inflated with air, the voxels inside the colon are easily extracted with a region growing method (for simplicity, we explain the process with 2D examples; see Fig. 3a). Then, for these inside voxels, we compute $D_t(\mathbf{X})$ using the single-source shortest path algorithm [2]. Fig. 3b shows the resulting $D_t(\mathbf{X})$ with the appendix as the target point. Similarly, $D_s(\mathbf{X})$ is calculated as an Euclidean distance map [15] (see Fig. 3c).

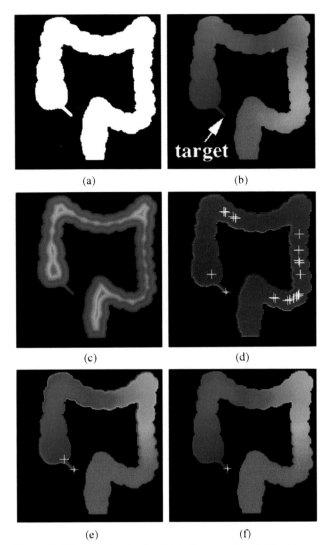

(a)   (b)

(c)   (d)

(e)   (f)

Figure 3: 2D example of potential field generation: (a) Inside voxels (white). (b) Distance from the target point (*min*: blue, *max*: red). (c) Distance from the surface (*min*: blue, *max*: red). (d) $V(\mathbf{X})$: $C_t = 1, C_s = 5, \rho = 30$ (the white cross markers show the local minima). (e) $V(\mathbf{X})$: $C_t = 30, C_s = 5, \rho = 30$. (f) $V(\mathbf{X})$: $C_t = 30, C_s = 5, \rho = 15$.

Based on $D_t(\mathbf{X})$ and $D_s(\mathbf{X})$, we generate an attractive force to the target point and a repulsive force from the surface, respectively. Specifically, $V(\mathbf{X})$ is defined as:

$$V(\mathbf{X}) = \begin{cases} C_t D_t(\mathbf{X}) + C_s(\rho/D_s(\mathbf{X}) - 1)^2, & 0 < D_s < \rho \\ C_t D_t(\mathbf{X}), & \text{otherwise} \end{cases} \quad (2)$$

where C_t and C_s are coefficients controlling the strength of the attractive and repulsive forces, respectively, and ρ is a parameter changing the distance-of-influence of the repulsive force. The repulsive potential term in Eq. 2 is a variant of the function used in robot path planning [9], which keeps the submarine away from the surface. As a result, when the submarine approaches the sur-

face, the value of $V(\mathbf{X})$ drastically increases and the submarine is bounced back as if there was a solid wall.

During preprocessing, $D_t(\mathbf{X})$ and $D_s(\mathbf{X})$ are computed as two volumes of the same resolution as the CT data. In order to save memory space, we only store $D_t(\mathbf{X})$ and $D_s(\mathbf{X})$ for the inside voxels along with their coordinate indices and sort them by the indices, since the submarine is inside the colon and only the distance values for the inside voxels are needed in the evaluation of $V(\mathbf{X})$. Subsequently, to calculate $V(\mathbf{X})$ during navigation, we access the distance values of an arbitrary voxel by performing a binary search on the voxel index. For a location not coinciding with any voxel vertex, trilinear interpolation is used to reconstruct the distance values from those of its eight neighboring voxels. Additionally, central differences are employed to estimate $\nabla V(\mathbf{X})$ for Eq. 1.

Like any other potential field method, the submarine may get stuck at a local minimum of $V(\mathbf{X})$. Eliminating local minima by modifying a particular $V(\mathbf{X})$ is possible [9]. However, our goal is not only to reach the target point, but also to provide a flexible submarine model. For example, if the physician increases the value of C_t, the submarine accelerates towards the target point. On the other hand, if the physician wants to examine an abnormality on the surface from close proximity, he or she can stop the influence of the attractive force by setting $C_t = 0$ and weaken the repulsive force by reducing the values of C_s and/or ρ. Thus, instead of using a static $V(\mathbf{X})$, we allow the physician to interactively adjust the values of C_t, C_s, and ρ during navigation. Figs. 3d, 3e, and 3f show how local minima depend on these values. From our experience, a small ρ and a large C_t usually reduce the number of local minima. Another way to propel the submarine out of local minima is to apply an external force, as described next.

3.3 Submarine Dynamics

To allow the physician to control the submarine, Eq. 1 is extended to:

$$\dot{\mathbf{P}}(t) = -\nabla V(\mathbf{X}) - k_l \mathbf{P}(t) + \mathbf{F}_{user}(t), \quad (3)$$

where $\mathbf{F}_{user}(t)$ is the external force applied to the submarine by mouse-clicking (see Fig. 2). Based on the geometry of the viewing frustum of the camera, the 3D location of the screen pixel clicked on by the mouse is computed. The direction of $\mathbf{F}_{user}(t)$ is then assigned as a unit vector pointing from the camera at $\mathbf{X}$ to the screen pixel. The magnitude of $\mathbf{F}_{user}(t)$ is a parameter which can be interactively modified by the physician. $\mathbf{F}_{user}(t)$ changes not only the submarine location, but also its orientation. As a result, when the physician wants to examine an abnormality on the surface from close proximity, he or she can simply point the mouse on that region and click.

In our model, a small cylinder with six degrees of freedom is used to approximate the submarine. To represent the submarine orientation, instead of Euler's angles which tend to cause gimbal lock problem [17], we employ the quaternion $\mathbf{q}(t)$ [17] as follows:

$$\mathbf{q}(t) = [s(t), \mathbf{v}(t)] = [s, (v_x, v_y, v_z)^T]$$

The quaternion is subsequently converted into the orientation matrix $R(t)$:

$$\begin{pmatrix} 1 - 2v_y^2 - 2v_z^2 & 2v_x v_y - 2s v_z & 2v_x v_z + 2s v_y \\ 2v_x v_y + 2s v_z & 1 - 2v_x^2 - 2v_z^2 & 2v_y v_z - 2s v_x \\ 2v_x v_z - 2s v_y & 2v_y v_z + 2s v_x & 1 - 2v_x^2 - 2v_y^2 \end{pmatrix},$$

where the three column vectors correspond to $\mathbf{x}_{body}$, $\mathbf{y}_{body}$, and $\mathbf{z}_{body}$, respectively. Additionally, to handle the submarine as a rigid object [1], we need to define its inertia tensor I_{body}. We approximate I_{body} with the inertia tensor of a cylinder as follows:

$$\begin{pmatrix} \frac{3r^2+h^2}{12} & 0 & 0 \\ 0 & \frac{3r^2+h^2}{12} & 0 \\ 0 & 0 & \frac{r^2}{2} \end{pmatrix},$$

where r and h are the radius and the length of the submarine, respectively. Note that the values of r and h are used only for the orientation calculation. In other words, the submarine can actually navigate through any constriction that is less than its size.

In addition to the translation depicted by Eq. 3, the rotation of the submarine is described as:

$$\dot{\mathbf{L}}(t) = \mathbf{z}_{body} \times \mathbf{F}_{user} - k_a\omega(t) + \tau_{option}(t). \tag{4}$$

$\dot{\mathbf{L}}(t)$ is the time derivative of the angular momentum $\mathbf{L}(t)$; $\mathbf{z}_{body} \times \mathbf{F}_{user}$ is the torque caused by $\mathbf{F}_{user}$; $k_a\omega(t)$ is a dissipative torque to stop the rotation of the submarine, where $\omega(t)$ is the angular velocity and k_a is the friction coefficient; and $\tau_{option}(t)$ is an optional torque which can be applied by the physician.

The differential equations, Eqs. 3 and 4, are integrated from certain initial values with the Euler method:

$$\begin{align} \mathbf{P}(t+\Delta t) &= \mathbf{P}(t) + \dot{\mathbf{P}}(t)\Delta t, \tag{5} \\ \mathbf{X}(t+\Delta t) &= \mathbf{X}(t) + \mathbf{P}(t+\Delta t)\Delta t, \tag{6} \\ \mathbf{L}(t+\Delta t) &= \mathbf{L}(t) + \dot{\mathbf{L}}(t)\Delta t, \tag{7} \\ \omega(t+\Delta t) &= R(t)I_{body}^{-1}R(t)^T\mathbf{L}(t+\Delta t), \tag{8} \\ \mathbf{q}(t+\Delta t) &= \Delta\mathbf{q}(t+\Delta t)\cdot\mathbf{q}(t). \tag{9} \end{align}$$

Accordingly, we obtain the location and orientation of the submarine at every time step Δt. Eq. 9 computes the quaternion product [17] of $\Delta\mathbf{q}(t+\Delta t)$ and $\mathbf{q}(t)$, where

$$\Delta\mathbf{q}(t) = [\frac{\cos|\omega(t)|\Delta t}{2}, \frac{\sin|\omega(t)|\Delta t}{2}\frac{\omega(t)}{|\omega(t)|}]$$

is the quaternion representation of the submarine rotation during time step Δt. To prevent the submarine from moving erratically, we regularly check the change of $\mathbf{X}$ in Eq. 6 and subdivide Δt when necessary.

There are a few optional controls, which are also provided by our submarine model:

(1) **Compass mode**: When using the torque

$$\tau_{compass}(t) = -\mathbf{z}_{body} \times \nabla V(\mathbf{X}),$$

as part of $\tau_{option}(t)$, the submarine rotates its $\mathbf{z}_{body}$ to match the descending direction of $V(\mathbf{X})$. This mode is useful for keeping the submarine orientation along the traveling direction of the submarine.

(2) **Leveling mode**: If we define a certain gravity direction $\mathbf{G}$ and apply the torque

$$\tau_{leveling}(t) = -\mathbf{y}_{body} \times \mathbf{G},$$

the submarine rotates its $\mathbf{y}_{body}$ towards the opposite direction of the gravity. This mode is useful for maintaining the camera up-vector pointing upward during navigation.

(3) **Still mode**: If we do not execute Eqs. 5 and 6 at every time step, we essentially fix the submarine location while enabling other functionalities. This mode is useful for panning the camera around, yet keeping its location fixed.

4 Interactive Rendering

4.1 Reducing the Number of Triangles

Given the camera positions and orientations generated by the submarine model, we need to rapidly render images of the colonic surface. To reduce the number of triangles submitted to the graphics pipeline, one may suggest using surface simplification (e.g., [8, 16]). However, we strongly believe that in virtual colonoscopy, image fidelity should always be considered a top priority, not to be compromised. Essentially, this requires that the simplified surface should not lose any detail contained in the original highly curved surface. Otherwise, during navigation, since the camera might be very close to the colonic wall, the appearance of the surface could be degraded. More seriously, a small polyp on the surface may be faded out into the surrounding area and no longer recognizable. Such an image fidelity requirement means a very low, if any, simplification rate. Hence, no simplification has been employed in this work.

Fortunately, the twisted nature of the colon can be exploited to reduce the triangle count. As shown in Fig. 4, at any particular instant, what the camera sees is usually a small fraction of the entire surface. Therefore, to generate that snapshot, we do not need to ren-

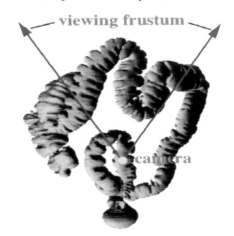

Figure 4: At any given camera position, only a small fraction of the colonic surface is visible to the camera.

der all the triangles, since most of them are invisible to the camera anyway. This essentially becomes an issue of visibility determination (e.g., [5, 6, 12, 18]). Commonly, in a visibility algorithm, the virtual environment is subdivided into a set of cells. Then, by conservatively estimating the *potentially visible set (PVS)* of cells from the camera, the number of polygons submitted to the graphics pipeline is substantially reduced. Prior work on visibility can be roughly classified into two approaches. One (e.g., [18]) determines the PVS for viewpoints inside a cell in a preprocess. The other approach (e.g., [5, 6, 12]) computes the PVS for the camera on-the-fly during rendering. In this work we have adopted the latter approach because of concerns with large memory space and long preprocessing time required by the first approach.

To determine the PVS, Greene et al. [5, 6] employed a hierarchical Z-buffer algorithm. Potentially, this algorithm can solve the visibility problem quite efficiently. Unfortunately, it relies on a Z-buffer query which is not supported in most of the currently-available graphics hardware and thus has to be implemented in software. In Luebke and Georges [12], the problem of determining which cell is potentially visible is reduced to the problem of checking whether the intersection area of the projections from the portal sequence is empty. This algorithm is particularly suitable for an architectural model [18], where cells are convex. Yet, as below, our cells are likely to be *concave*. All the triangles in a concave cell can potentially occlude the "see through" of a portal sequence and thus be exploited to improve rendering performance.

4.2 Subdividing into Cells

Our objective is to use graphics hardware to scan-convert the triangles and consider cell concavity to substantially reduce the size of PVS. Due to the twisted nature of the colon, instead of a BSP tree or a k-D tree [6, 18], we employ a simple subdivision method which is based on the *center-line* (or *skeleton*) of the colon. To determine the center-line, we use the distance field from the colonic surface $D_s(\mathbf{X})$, described in Section 3.2. We denote the maximal value of $D_s(\mathbf{X})$ as D_{max}. For each inside voxel, we assign a cost value of $D_{max} - D_s(\mathbf{X})$. As a result, voxels close to the surface have high cost values, while the cost values of voxels near the center of the colon are relatively low. Based on this cost assignment, we subsequently employ the single-source shortest path algorithm [2] to efficiently compute a minimum cost path from the user-specified source point to the target point. This is exactly the colonic center-line that we want to compute.

In the colon subdivision step, we start from the source point, and march along the center-line towards the target point, while continuously trying to partition the colon with the cross-section through the current position and perpendicular to the center-line (see Fig. 5). As a "cut" is desired (for example, when we have traversed enough

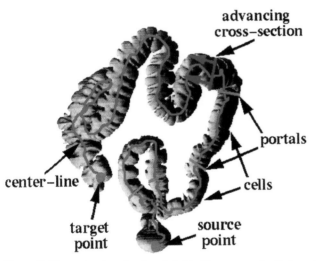

Figure 5: The patient's colon is subdivided into a set of cells based on the colonic center-line.

distance along the center-line or the accumulated number of surface polygons has reached a certain threshold), we generate a cell which has two cross-sections as portals. Consequently, each inside voxel belongs uniquely to one cell and a list of isosurface triangles is associated with each cell. Note that the boundary of the concave cells, particularly the haustra which appears frequently (see Fig. 6), can be used to reduce the size of PVS, as described below.

4.3 Hardware-Assisted Visibility

During navigation, given a certain camera location, we identify the cell that contains the camera using a binary search on the location index, similar to that in Section 3.2. Then, starting from that cell, we traverse two portal sequences (towards the source and target points, respectively), in a near-to-far order. Specifically, for each portal sequence, we set up an *aggregate cull rectangle (ACR)*, which is initialized as the whole screen. As we traverse a portal

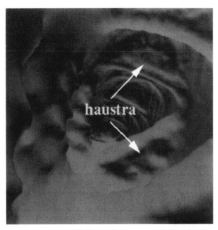

Figure 6: The concave cell boundary, especially the haustra which protrudes from the surface, potentially blocks the view of distant cells.

sequence, we render the triangles of the cells and shrink the ACR in an *alternating* pattern.

In other words, as we encounter a new cell, we first deliver all the triangles in the cell to the graphics engine. Note that at the farther end of this cell, we also have a new portal, which controls what can be seen beyond this cell. The ACR size is reduced in two steps (see Figs. 7a and 7b). At the first step, we project the vertices of the new

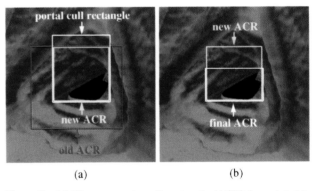

(a)   (b)

Figure 7: (a) The aggregate cull rectangle (ACR) is updated by intersecting it with the cull rectangle of the portal. (b) The size of the ACR is further reduced by checking the Z-buffer content.

portal onto the screen and compute the 2D axis-aligned bounding rectangle of the projected vertices. This bounding rectangle, called *cull rectangle*, represents a conservative bound of the portal. We update the ACR by intersecting it with the cull rectangle of the portal, as illustrated in Fig. 7a. At the second step, if the ACR has not fully degenerated, the ACR size is further reduced by checking the Z-buffer. Otherwise, no triangle is visible beyond the current portal, so we simply terminate the portal sequence.

As shown in Fig. 7b, if the first or last several scanlines of the ACR have been covered (i.e., the Z values of the pixels have been changed due to the projection of previous cells), the ACR size can be reduced. When we check the Z-buffer, instead of loading in the whole content of the Z-buffer (which takes milliseconds according to our experiments and [5]), we only read from the Z-buffer to the memory those pixels inside the ACR. Since an initialization cost is imposed in communicating with the Z-buffer, it is more efficient to read a block of pixels than reading them one-by-one. Therefore, at each step, we read in n consecutive scanlines of the ACR (top-down or bottom-up), where n is inversely proportional to the ACR width

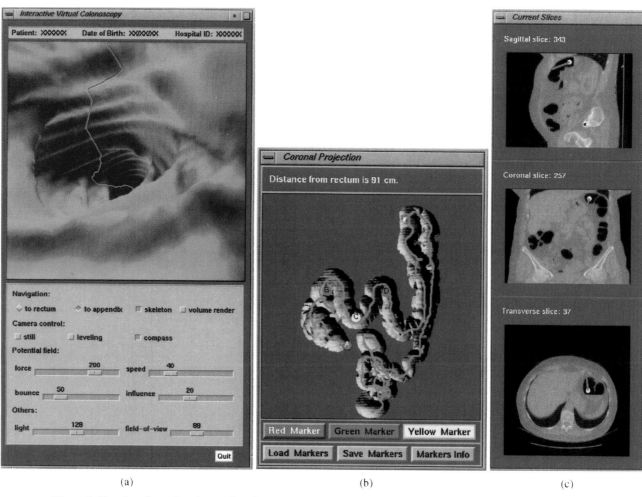

(a) (b) (c)

Figure 8: User interface of our interactive virtual colonoscopy: (a) endoscopy panel; (b) scout panel; (c) slice panel.

w. In the extreme case, we need to read $p + h/n$ times from the Z-buffer to generate an image, where h is the height of the ACR and p is the number of visible cells.

During navigation, since the camera parameters change only slightly and smoothly, most of the cells visible in the previous frame are probably still visible in the current frame. In other words, to generate the new frame, we encounter most of the same portals of the previous frame as we traverse the portal sequences. We have exploited this temporal coherence by reusing the visibility information of the previous image to render the new image. Specifically, without updating the ACRs, we first render 80% of the cells along the portal sequences of the previous frame. Then, we start to render the farther cells and compute the ACRs alternately, as described above.

5 Experimental Studies

Based on feedback from the two physicians involved in developing the navigation system, we have designed a user interface mimicking the visual effects of optical colonoscopy. As shown in Fig. 8, our interface consists of three components: endoscopy panel, scout panel, and slice panel. The endoscopy panel provides the patient's medical record, endoscopic view, and navigation controls. The physician can choose to navigate from the rectum to the appendix, or vice versa. The colonic center-line (shown in green in Fig. 8a) can be turned on to help the physician to better monitor the movement of

the submarine. The "volume render" option, turned on if desired, allows the physician to visualize the tissues beneath the surface to differentiate residual stool from polyps (see Fig. 9). The scout panel shows the actual shape of the patient's entire colon, with markers placed to identify points of interest. The current position and orientation of the submarine is also depicted on the scout panel. The slice panel displays the sagittal, coronal, and transverse slices through the current submarine position.

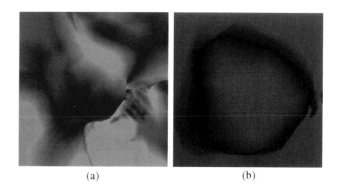

(a) (b)

Figure 9: (a) An abnormality on the surface. (b) With close-up volume rendering, the abnormality of (a) was confirmed to be a polyp.

Our initial experiments with virtual colonoscopy used a pipe phantom and the Visible Male data. In the pipe simulation, we looped a plastic respirator pipe of *20mm* radius inside a water tank. To simulate colonic polyps, we attached three small rubber objects of sizes *7mm*, *5mm*, and *3mm* to the inner surface of the pipe. The CT scan of the pipe produced a volume of $512 \times 512 \times 107$. The image in Fig. 10a, which was captured during a navigation inside the pipe, clearly depicts the three simulated polyps. In the Visible Male data set, we primarily focused on the physical cross-sections (24-bit color slices) of the abdomen, from slice *1595* to slice *1848*. For the navigation, the 24-bit color slices were downsampled, converted into 8-bit grayscale, segmented, and subsequently assembled into a volume of $683 \times 406 \times 254$. Fig. 10b shows an abnormality on the colonic surface of the Visible Male.

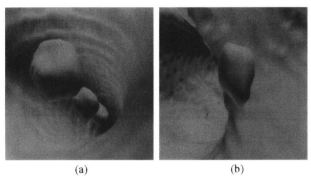

(a)　　　　　　　　　　(b)

Figure 10: (a) An image from the pipe phantom clearly depicts the three simulated polyps. (b) An image from the Visible Male colon shows an abnormality on the surface.

Due to the encouraging results obtained from the previous two experiments, we acquired about a dozen patient data sets (see Figs. 4-9, 11). Polyps discovered by our collaborating physicians using our interactive virtual colonoscopy technique have been documented. They were subsequently evaluated and compared with the results of optical colonoscopy, performed by gastroenterologists and recorded on video immediately following the CT scan. In Fig. 11 we compare two diagnostic results of virtual colonoscopy with those of optical colonoscopy.

Table 1 shows the results that we obtained on three patient data sets. Column *MC* is the number of isosurface triangles generated by the Marching Cubes algorithm [10]; column *LG* shows the number of triangles per frame rendered with Luebke's and Georges' algorithm [12]; and column *Our* is the average triangles per frame using our visibility algorithm. Note that the number of visible triangles is determined mainly by the twisted degree of the colon as well as the amount of air inflated into the colon in the preparation routine.

Table 1: Triangles/frame rendered with the Marching Cubes algorithm (*MC*), Luebke's and Georges' method (*LG*), and our visibility scheme (*Our*).

Data Set	MC	LG	Our
P1 ($512 \times 512 \times 361$)	1,339*K*	212*K*	146*K*
P2 ($512 \times 512 \times 370$)	1,117*K*	132*K*	72*K*
P3 ($512 \times 512 \times 358$)	1,249*K*	96*K*	53*K*

We have achieved adequate interactive speeds for image size 512×512 on a single SGI R10000 processor with InfiniteReality. Average frames/second for patient data sets P1 – P3 were 14.8, 18.7, and 22.7, respectively. Rendering performances on an SGI RealityEngine2 were 5.6, 7.9, and 10.0 frames/second, respectively. The timings include not only the rendering expense but also the cost involved in solving the submarine motion equations.

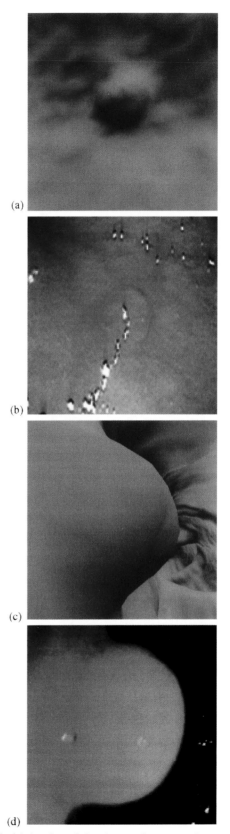

(a)

(b)

(c)

(d)

Figure 11: (a) A polyp of size *4mm* at the center of the image discovered in virtual colonoscopy. (b) The corresponding polyp of (a) confirmed by optical colonoscopy. (c) Close-up of another polyp of size *8mm* from virtual colonoscopy. (d) The corresponding polyp of (c) confirmed by optical colonoscopy.

6 Conclusions

In this work our primary contributions have been an intuitive and physically-based submarine model with collision avoidance using a potential field and kinematic rules, and an efficient Z-buffer-assisted visibility method which both employs a center-line-based subdivision and exploits cell concavity. We have harnessed these interactive computer graphics advances for the benefit of the important application of interactive virtual colonoscopy.

As a cost-effective, non-invasive, and patient-comfort procedure, interactive virtual colonoscopy provides a potential alternative for mass screening of patients for possible colon cancer. Unlike optical colonoscopy, our technique allows the physician to examine the tissues underneath abnormalities and measure polyp size, without physical biopsy and surgery. Our physically-based submarine model provides an intuitive mechanism to navigate inside the colon for examining the surface, as testified by our collaborating physicians. From their experience, usually after one hour of training, a computer-illiterate physician is able to master the system quite well, while two years of training is commonly required for optical colonoscopy. In addition, due to the accelerated rendering speed achieved by our technique, diagnostic time has been greatly reduced. Usually only several minutes are required to navigate through the entire colon for locating abnormalities, in contrast to one hour for optical colonoscopy.

In general, the preprocessing stage takes a few hours on our SGI workstations. It includes computing the two distance fields $D_s(\mathbf{X})$ and $D_t(\mathbf{X})$, extracting the center-line of the colon, subdividing the colon into cells, and generating isosurface triangles from the CT data. We are currently working on a variety of techniques to speed up the preprocess. Additionally, we plan to improve the speed of the volume rendering option by exploiting the depth information produced by our visibility algorithm. Together with our collaborating physicians, we are evaluating our technique on clinical cases. We are also working on "subtracting" residual stool and liquid from the colonic interior, and highlighting abnormalities with color mapping to attract the physician's attention. Furthermore, our technique is being extended to virtual endoscopy for examining other human organs where traditional medical procedures are invasive or difficult to perform.

Acknowledgments

This work has been supported by the Center for Biotechnology of New York State and E-Z-EM Inc. The Visible Human data set is courtesy of the National Library of Medicine and the Visible Human Project. The pipe and patient data were provided by our collaborating physicians at the Stony Brook University Hospital. We thank Ajay Viswambharan, Mark Wax, Jerome Liang, Yong Zhou, and Suya You for their contributions to this project. Special thanks to Amitabh Varshney, Claudio Silva, Lan Yu, Edmond Prakash, Ming Wan, Nilo Stolte, and Kathleen McConnell for their helpful comments on drafts of this paper.

References

[1] D. Baraff. Rigid Body Simulation. *SIGGRAPH 95 Course Note 34*. ACM SIGGRAPH, August 1995.

[2] E. Dijkstra. A Note on Two Problems in Connection with Graphs. *Numerische Mathematik*, vol. 1, 1959, pp. 269-270.

[3] T. Galyean. Guided Navigation of Virtual Environments. *ACM Symposium on Interactive 3D Graphics*, pp. 103-104. ACM, April 1995.

[4] M. Gleicher and A. Witkin. Through-the-Lens Camera Control. *Computer Graphics (SIGGRAPH 92 Conference Proceedings)*, vol. 26, pp. 331-340. ACM SIGGRAPH, July 1992.

[5] N. Greene, M. Kass, and G. Miller. Hierarchical Z-Buffer Visibility. *SIGGRAPH 93 Conference Proceedings*, Annual Conference Series, pp. 231-236. ACM SIGGRAPH, August 1993.

[6] N. Greene. Hierarchical Polygon Tiling with Coverage Masks. *SIGGRAPH 96 Conference Proceedings*, Annual Conference Series, pp. 65-74. ACM SIGGRAPH, August 1996.

[7] L. Hong, A. Kaufman, Y. Wei, A. Viswambharan, M. Wax, and Z. Liang. 3D Virtual Colonoscopy. *IEEE Symposium on Biomedical Visualization*, pp. 26-32. IEEE, October 1995.

[8] H. Hoppe, T. DeRose, T. Duchamp, J. McDonald, and W. Stuetzle. Mesh Simplification. *SIGGRAPH 93 Conference Proceedings*, Annual Conference Series, pp. 19-26. ACM SIGGRAPH, August 1993.

[9] J. Latombe. Robot Motion Planning. *Kluwer Academic Publishers*, 1991.

[10] W. Lorensen and H. Cline. Marching Cubes: A High Resolution 3D Surface Construction Algorithm. *Computer Graphics (SIGGRAPH 87 Conference Proceedings)*, vol. 21, pp. 163-169. ACM SIGGRAPH, July 1987.

[11] W. Lorensen, F. Jolesz, and R. Kikinis. The Exploration of Cross-Sectional Data with a Virtual Endoscope. In R. Satava and K. Morgan (eds.), *Interactive Technology and New Medical Paradigm for Health Care*, IOS Press, 1995, pp. 221-230.

[12] D. Luebke and C. Georges. Portals and Mirrors: Simple, Fast Evaluation of Potential Visible Sets. *ACM Symposium on Interactive 3D Graphics*, pp. 105-106. ACM, April 1995.

[13] C. Morosi, G. Ballardini, and P. Pisani. Diagnostic Accuracy of the Double-Contrast Enema for Colonic Polyps in Patients with or without Diverticular Disease. *Gastrointest Radiology*, vol. 16, 1991, pp. 346-347.

[14] G. Rubin, C. Beaulieu, V. Argiro, H. Ringl, A. Norbash, J. Feller, M. Dake, R. Jeffey, and S. Napel. Perspective Volume Rendering of CT and MR Images: Applications for Endoscopic Imaging. *Radiology*, vol. 199, May 1996, pp. 321-330.

[15] T. Saito and J. Toriwaki. New Algorithms for Euclidean Distance Transformation of an N-Dimensional Digitized Picture with Applications. *Pattern Recognition*, vol. 27, no. 11, 1994, pp. 1551-1565.

[16] W. Schroeder, J. Zarge, and W. Lorensen. Decimation of Triangle Meshes. *Computer Graphics (SIGGRAPH 92 Conference Proceedings)*, vol. 26, pp. 65-70. ACM SIGGRAPH, July 1992.

[17] K. Shoemake. Animation Rotation with Quaternion Curves. *Computer Graphics (SIGGRAPH 85 Conference Proceedings)*, vol. 19, pp. 245-254. ACM SIGGRAPH, July 1985.

[18] S. Teller and C. Sequin. Visibility Preprocessing For Interactive Walkthroughs. *Computer Graphics (SIGGRAPH 91 Conference Proceedings)*, vol. 25, pp. 61-69. ACM SIGGRAPH, July 1991.

[19] R. Turner, F. Balaguer, E. Gobbetti, and D. Thalmann. Physically-Based Interactive Camera Motion Control Using 3D Input Devices. *Computer Graphics International '91*, pp. 135-145. Springer-Verlag, June 1991.

[20] D. Vining, D. Gelfand, R. Bechtold, E. Scharling, E. Grishaw, and R. Shifrin. Technical Feasibility of Colon Imaging with Helical CT and Virtual Reality. *Annual Meeting of American Roentgen Ray Society*, 1994, pp. 104.

[21] C. Ware and S. Osborne. Exploration and Virtual Camera Control in Virtual Three Dimensional Environments. *ACM Symposium on Interactive 3D Graphics*, pp. 175-183. ACM, March 1990.

Interactive Simulation of Fire in Virtual Building Environments

Richard Bukowski*   Carlo Séquin†

Computer Science Department ‡
University of California, Berkeley

Abstract

This paper describes the integration of the Berkeley Architectural Walkthrough Program with the National Institute of Standards and Technology's CFAST fire simulator. The integrated system creates a simulation based design environment for building fire safety systems; it also allows fire safety engineers to evaluate the performance of building designs, and helps make performance-based fire codes possible. We demonstrate that the visibility preprocessing and spatial decomposition used in the Walkthru also allow optimization of the data transfer between the simulator and visualizer. This optimization improves the ability to use available communication bandwidth to get needed simulation data to the Walkthru in the best order to visualize results in real time; an appropriate communication model and data structures are presented. General issues arising in the integration of environmental simulations and virtual worlds are discussed, as well as the specifics of the Walkthru-CFAST system, including relevant aspects of the user interface and of the visualization and simulation programming interfaces. A recommendation is made to structure future simulators in such a way that they can selectively direct their computational efforts toward specified spacetime regions of interest and thereby support real-time, interactive virtual environment visualization more effectively.

CR Categories: I.3.2 [Computer Graphics]: Graphics Systems—Distributed/Network Graphics; I.3.6 [Computer Graphics]: Methodology and Techniques—Graphics Data Structures and Data Types; I.3.6 [Computer Graphics]: Methodology and Techniques—Interaction Techniques; I.3.7 [Computer Graphics]: Three-Dimensional Graphics and Realism—Virtual Reality; I.6.7 [Simulation and Modeling]: Simulation Support Systems—Environments; J.6 [Computer-Aided Engineering]: Computer-Aided Design.

Keywords: Virtual/Interactive Environments, Scientific Visualization, Simulation, Virtual Reality, Interactive Techniques, Information Visualization

*bukowski@cs.berkeley.edu
†sequin@cs.berkeley.edu
‡Soda Hall, Berkeley, CA 94720

1 INTRODUCTION

Virtual environments are of major interest to computer graphics researchers; this is due, in part, to their ability to immerse the user in a computer-generated alternate reality in which we can easily recreate scenarios which are too dangerous, difficult, or expensive to play out in real life. One application domain with a particularly high expected payoff is building design evaluation, where scientists, engineers, architects, and other professionals can enter a virtual space and evaluate its physical structure without actually building or affecting a real instance of that structure. With such a system, users could preview architectural designs, evaluate their performance with various metrics, and do simulations and potentially destructive "what-if" experiments (such as fire safety studies; see figure 1) cheaply and with no risk. To obtain useful answers to such experiments, we need to integrate good physical simulations with virtual environment interfaces. Integration of powerful simulation technology with virtual reality visualization systems affords the possibility of intuitive interpretation and visualization of the results of complex and powerful simulations via 3D computer graphics.

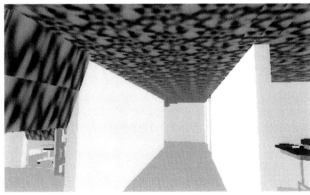

Figure 1: *Above, a pool fire, three-quarters of a meter in diameter, rages in a student office in Soda Hall; 100 seconds after ignition, smoke nearly fills the room. Below, smoke has spread into the hallways.*

We are attempting to realize some of these advantages for the benefit of fire safety in architectural environments. We are in the process of integrating the National Institute of Standards and Technology's (NIST) Consolidated Model of Fire and Smoke Transport (CFAST) [15] into the Berkeley Architectural Walkthrough (Walkthru) system [17, 10]. CFAST currently provides the world's most accurate simulation of the impact of fire and its byproducts on a building environment. Integrated into the Walkthru, it provides real-time, intuitive, realistic and scientific visualization of building conditions in a fire hazard situation from the perspective of a person walking through a burning building. The viewer can observe the natural visual effects of flame and smoke in fire hazard conditions; alternatively, scientific visualization techniques allow the user to "observe" the concentrations of toxic compounds such as carbon monoxide and hydrogen cyanide in the air, as well as the temperatures of the atmosphere, walls, and floor. Warning and suppression systems such as smoke detectors and sprinkler heads can be observed in action to help determine their effectiveness. This technology can be used to improve fire safety by helping engineers and architects evaluate a building's potential safety and survivability through performance-based standards (i.e. how well the building protects its occupants from the fire). With more development, it could also be used to help train personnel in firefighting techniques and rescue operations by presenting them with practice situations that are too risky to be simulated in the real world.

While the combination of virtual reality and environmental simulation constitutes a framework for very powerful tools, it also raises many implementation challenges. Among these challenges are interaction with the virtual world, setting up and dynamically changing simulation conditions from within the virtual world to a simulator, designing "visualization-oriented" simulators, transporting simulation results to the visualizer, integrating the simulator's results with the virtual environment, and visualizing those results in a way that is useful to the user; either descriptively, in the case of scientific visualization applications, or realistically, in the case of training or entertainment applications. These problems are compounded by an additional desire to distribute both the virtual environment and the simulation over multiple computers – potentially connected by relatively high-latency, low-bandwidth networks such as the Internet – when attempting to simulate and visualize large buildings with hundreds of rooms.

In this paper, we present an approach to the problem of distributed simulation-visualization data management that is optimized for densely occluded polyhedral environments (i.e. buildings) based on the Walkthru and CFAST programs. Walkthru has already addressed some of the problems of distributed visualization and of the interaction between the user and the virtual world [16, 11, 4]. We show that the basic virtual environment structure used in the Walkthru, a spatial subdivision of the world into densely occluded cells with connecting portals, can be put to good use for simulation data management. In addition to optimizing the visualization task, it is also useful for optimizing bandwidth requirements between a visualizer and simulator, both for communicating scenario information to the simulator and for communicating simulated states back to the visualizer. Using this structure, we can minimize bandwidth requirements for arbitrarily large visualizations and simulations, and relieve the visualization and simulation designers of the complexity of the data management problem. The solution is extensible to multiple distributed visualizers and simulators operating on one virtual world. It also suggests an important attribute of future simulation design for simulation developers who wish to make "virtual reality-oriented" real-time simulators: the ability to partition a simulation effort so as to concentrate computation on parts of the environment of immediate interest to the observer (i.e. those parts that affect the areas which are currently being viewed). This issue is also being studied by other groups at Berkeley [5].

In section 2, we discuss the simulation/visualization data management problem in the context of other related work in virtual environment simulation. In section 3, we present an overview of the two components of the system, Walkthru and CFAST, the issues involved in combining these two programs, and more generally, issues in combining visualization software with simulation software in a densely occluded building environment. In section 4, we present the most important abstract representations for the exchange of simulation data and the corresponding communication system. Section 5 explains the APIs and functionality provided to the visualization front end, the user, and the simulator. Finally, in section 6, we discuss some of the details of the internal workings of the simulation data management system.

2 RELATED WORK

The most frequent application of virtual reality technology so far has been visualization of static spatial environments. The majority of current virtual worlds are nearly static environments with a few movable objects and avatars inside. The most common applications of these systems are either peer-to-peer simulation of the user's interaction with other users or simulated entities, or systems that use physics to make the world seem more "real" to an immersed user. Some more famous examples of the former include the Iowa driving simulator [7], where the user's vehicle interacts with other independently-simulated road vehicles, and the department of defense's NPSNET [13, 19], where "units" of military vehicles engage in simulated combat on static terrain. Each simulated unit (or vehicle) communicates its status to each other unit, but since the environment (i.e. the terrain) is fixed, the communication requirements are bounded by the number of simulation entities, not the size of the environment. Though these systems may be doing some actual physical simulations, because only a few "detail objects" in the world are actually changing, the amount of data being transferred is relatively small. Other systems are typically concerned with the physics of everyday object interaction, such as impenetrability and collisions [9, 6, 14]; they have been used to evaluate the ergonomics of environments like kitchens, automobiles, or work spaces. In these systems, simulations are typically limited to objects being directly manipulated, and the computations are simplified so that they can be done directly in the visualization environment without seriously loading down the computer.

On the other hand, many virtual-reality visualization systems have been built to allow the user to perform and interact with complex physical simulations, but they tend not to involve what we would consider "interactive simulation;" that is, the user is simply exploring precomputed data, without being able to interactively change the conditions under which that data was derived, and observe the results of their tampering. NASA's virtual windtunnel [2], in which airflow around a particular object is calculated, is a well documented example of this approach. An observer can enter a "black void" in which the object is suspended, insert "ink" sources to produce streamers along flow lines, and view the airflow computations from within the air space around the object. This system visualizes a precomputed computational fluid dynamics solution, and only allows the user to explore the space of the computed solution, without the ability to interactively modify the object or wind conditions for which the solution was generated.

The architectural community is very interested in full-scale interactive environmental simulation of planned environments from the point of view of an immersed human observer. Parameters of interest include lighting, temperature, and airflow throughout an entire building, and the computations can become very complex. Some architectural firms have constructed non-interactive, predefined video-tape visualizations comprising many moving people [18]. Realistic world simulation, where the environment itself is changing based on a reasonable subset of physical and chemical laws, and under the possible influence of user-initiated changes to the scenario set-up, is a much more difficult task. Combining such simulations with immersive visualization by one or more active observers adds particular challenges with respect to synchronization and data management.

For systems that do offer interactive, real-time scientific visualization of complex simulations, the data transmission problem is well documented [3, 8, 10]. As the simulated system grows more complex, the amount of data needed to describe the full simulation state of the system in each time step can easily exceed the available bandwidth between simulator and visualizer. Efficient encodings, even lossy compression, have been employed to alleviate this communications bottleneck [8]. Another approach is to run the visualizer on the same (super)computer that performs the simulation, thereby hopefully gaining access to any needed data for visualization on demand in less than a frame time. However, this requires that the observer be physically close to the simulation engine, or that there exist a fast video link between the visualizer and the display screen used by the observer [9]. The video link approach also requires an extremely low-latency command line from the observer to the simulator to make the user's normal movements and interactions with the environment reasonably responsive. In such a set-up it might be more difficult to realize a collaborative environment in which individual observers can sign on at will from anywhere in the country at any time.

Densely occluded interior environments such as buildings, boats, planes, or caves offer certain advantages for immersive environmental simulation. They can take advantage of the same kind of preprocessing that has already been demonstrated in the context of visualization of static models [17]. Only those simulation results that affect the currently visible set of spaces need to be transmitted to the visualizer. A cell-based decomposition of the densely occluded world allows an effective estimation of a tight yet still conservative superset of the data which is absolutely necessary for visualization at any moment in time. As long as the number and complexity of the cells visible at any time remains bounded, the size of the whole world model can be, in principle, arbitrarily large – as long as there is sufficient (super)computer power to keep the ongoing simulation up-to-date.

3 PROBLEM FORMULATION

The first problem we faced was to combine two existing large and relatively well-developed programs into an integrated system that leaves room for growth and experimentation. We will now briefly introduce the two preexisting systems and define the key integration issues.

3.1 Walkthru and CFAST

The Berkeley Walkthru program was designed to support real-time interactive visualization of large (several million polygons), densely occluded building models at interactive frame rates (greater than 10 frames per second). To accomplish this goal, the Walkthru subdivides the "world" into rectilinear *cells*, connected by *portals*. In a preprocessing step, the system associates with each cell the set of all other cells that can be seen by an observer from any point within that cell. From this information, plus constraints on how quickly the observer can move through the database, the Walkthru can compute a set of cells for each frame that tightly, but conservatively, bound the set of cells visible in the next few frames. There are only two types of object in the Walkthru: "major occluders," which are two-dimensional wall, ceiling, or floor polygons, whose planes define cell boundaries; and "detail objects," which are 3D models of building contents (such as furniture and light fixtures), and which are as-

sociated with the cells that intersect the object's bounding box. During each frame, the detail objects and major occluders incident to any visible cell are drawn, and visibility is reevaluated from the new position. If the user wishes to voluntarily disallow changes in major occluders by the database editor and any in-use simulators during a visualization run, many visibility relationships can be precomputed for the database. Otherwise, the update rate of the visibility computations is easily quick enough to support relatively small-scale changes in the visibility structure of the world (i.e. punching some new holes in walls, or opening a new shaft in the floor or ceiling). In the last few years, Walkthru has provided a testbed for several applications including database construction [4], large scale radiosity computation [16], and scalable distributed walkthroughs with up to thousands of simultaneous users [11]. This technology can now be leveraged into support for distributed virtual environment simulation.

NIST's CFAST is the world's premier "zone model" fire chemistry and physics simulator. Similar to the Walkthru, it assumes an environment composed of rectilinear 3D regions (called "volumes") which are interconnected by portals (called "vents"). Within each volume, physical quantities such as gas species concentrations, raw fuel density, combustion byproducts, atmospheric pressure and temperature, and wall, ceiling, and floor temperature are tracked. A system of differential equations monitors the flow and exchange of these quantities through vents into adjoining volumes. Although CFAST's building partition concept is analogous to the Walkthru's cell structure, CFAST does not require similarly precise geometry. Volumes have a floor and ceiling height as well as length and width, but only the area of the volume (length times width) is relevant. Volumes are also not positioned in 3D space; only their size and height matters, and their connectivity through vents. Similarly, the exact X and Y location of the vents is irrelevant to the physics and is not represented; only orientation (horizontal or vertical) and cross-sectional area of the vent are needed, as well as the height at which it connects to the two prismatic volumes. As in the Walkthru, walls and floors are differentiated from "detail objects" such as furniture. Wall specifications include material and thickness information. The furniture database contains no geometry, but does include mass, materials, chemistry, and ignition and combustion detail curves for each type of object. Objects will ignite at predefined temperatures and burn as separate fires, producing appropriate physical and chemical effects on the environment. Other fire-related objects, such as sprinklers and HVAC ducts, affect the physics of the situation in realistic ways, but their only geometric component is positional information. Thus, the geometry of the CFAST situation can be derived from a Walkthru model, but the Walkthru model contains much more geometric information than CFAST represents; likewise, the unadorned Walkthru database contains none of the chemical, material, or "building systems" information (i.e. in-wall ductwork, piping, and wiring) needed by CFAST.

CFAST's main engine is a differential equation solver, computing flows of physical quantities and chemical species over time in the upper and lower parts of each volume. The formulation of the problem as a set of differential equations makes it feasible to create a parallelized version of CFAST, but this has not been done yet. CFAST provides large quantities of physical and chemical information, including concentrations of each of 10 chemical species, combustion products, temperatures of atmosphere, walls, floors, and ceilings, ignition times of objects, toxicology results, and many other physical and chemical quantities for each volume per time point.

While our system was designed specifically to integrate the Walkthru with CFAST, we attempted to make the combining framework sufficiently general to be useful for any environmental simulation one might want to do in a densely occluded world. Throughout this paper, we will refer to a generic "visualizer" and a generic "simulator;" for this project, the reader may infer "Walkthru" for visualizer

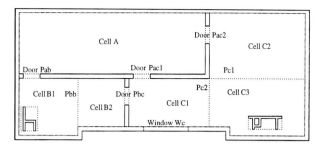

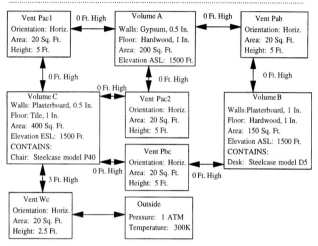

Figure 2: *How Walkthru (top) and CFAST (bottom) would "see" the same model. The Walkthru model contains detailed geometric information, but little else; the CFAST model is geometrically much simpler, but contains chemical and materials information that Walkthru lacks.*

and "CFAST" for simulator, but should keep in mind that the described framework is designed to be useful for other visualization and simulation engines.

3.2 Integration of Visualization and Simulation

Given CFAST and Walkthru, and with consideration to future visualization/simulation integration efforts, we are assuming the following model for our system:

We have a simulator and a visualizer, each of which operates on a cell-and-portal style environmental database. This database may be arbitrarily large, i.e., we could be operating on a building that will not fit into memory, and each of the two component systems can deal with the paging problem in its own way. However, due to occlusion, the visible "working set" of volumes will be tractable for any observer position. There is a mapping between the volumes of the visualization database and the simulation database, but the two are not be expected to be the same (i.e. a simulator "cell" might cover multiple visualizer "cells", or vice versa). Presently, we do not support arbitrarily complex geometric mappings between the two databases; we assume that one or more visualizer cells correspond to one simulator cell. We assume that the visualizer will transmit any setup information needed to begin simulation before issuing the start command. Furthermore, the visualizer may provide a front end by which the scenario being simulated may be changed on-the-fly. For example, the user may start a wastebasket fire in some room and then explore how the spread of the fire is influenced by opening or closing various doors or windows in the visualizer, thus repeatedly changing the situation being simulated. In such a case, the visualizer must

transmit an update to the simulator in real time, and the simulator should recalculate previously computed simulation results that are affected by the change, as well as alter the course of the simulation in progress. CFAST explicitly supports opening and closing of vents at certain times in the model; however, we can make other interactive modifications by "restarting" CFAST in the middle of a run. We store the internal state of the solver at each time point, and, if necessary, "roll back" the simulator to the time of the modification by resetting the appropriate internal state if a change is made to the simulation conditions at a previously-computed simulation time. The solution is rather brute-force, as it requires complete recomputation of all conditions from that point forward. Hopefully in the future CFAST will directly support interactive modification without requiring discarding all simulation results past the time of the change.

Either one or both of the two component systems may be distributed, and may be operating on computers connected by anything from a LAN to a potentially high-latency, low-bandwidth network such as the Internet. We would also like to be able to attach and detach visualizers to a simulation in progress, to allow multiple observers to independently observe different portions of the data from the ongoing simulation. Each component system maintains its own world database during operation. The simulator generates data about subsequent world states observing relevant dependencies. CFAST operates with a fixed time step and produces its results in time slices that span all volumes in the database; these contain the current values of all the variables that are being tracked, and some derived quantities such as aggregate toxicity. Only a subset of that information will be of relevance to the visualizer at any particular time. We refer to a discrete piece of simulated information that is associated with one time slice and one spatial cell, a simulation "chunk." These chunks might be generated in different order depending on the demands of the visualizer.

The bottleneck in getting simulation data to the visualizer for rendering in real time may be in one of two places: either the simulator is too slow to generate data in real time, or the communication process between the simulator and visualizer has insufficient bandwidth to transmit the necessary chunks in a timely fashion. The simulation speed bottleneck is likely to hold for single-CPU simulations of reasonably sized databases; CFAST on a single 150MHz R4400 can only simulate about 16 cells (depending on degree of interconnection and density of furniture) in real time. Our goal in this situation is to increase the simulator's potential effectiveness by letting it know what areas of the world are of current interest to the visualizer. Specifically, the visualizer will inform the simulator of the currently visible cells and of the cells that may become visible in the very near future. The simulator can then concentrate on calculating and shipping the corresponding chunks with priority. In the near future, we expect simulator technology to improve; simulators will become faster, and their designs will evolve to provide better support for interactive visualization. Recent work has shown that this can be a promising approach for modeling the dynamics of physical structures [5]. In the specific case of CFAST, NIST is working on a version that will be able to concentrate its computational efforts on critical areas of the simulation, improving the speed and potential size of the simulation. We are also considering parallelizing the CFAST core for the Berkeley Network of Workstations (NOW) [1].

For the case where communication bandwidth is the bottleneck, the framework provides mechanisms that are easy to use and that optimally exploit the available bandwidth, while hiding communications concerns from the simulation designer. Of course, it is not possible to guarantee that all needed simulation chunks will be at the visualizer in time: the user might jump to a different part of the building or suddenly advance the time slider far into the future. To minimize the visible discontinuities associated with such a switch, we use a "just-in-time" chunk transmission scheme. Our scheme keeps the communication channel in a state of near-starvation, allowing unanticipated "emergency" chunks to be sent through a nearly-empty transmission queue. This approach minimizes latency in the emergency case while still transmitting chunks at the highest possible rate for the channel.

4 KEY ABSTRACTIONS

The key primitives that define the interactions between simulator and visualizer are the *Simulation Data Set* and the *Real-Time Channel* over which this information gets exchanged. In this section we define these two abstractions.

4.1 The Simulation Data Set

In order to provide efficient data exchange between simulator and visualizer, we need a general structure for simulation data that can be easily managed and which is flexible enough to accommodate any information that a particular simulator may want to convey to the visualizer. This structure, called the *simulation data set*, which holds all simulation results, is organized in a three-level hierarchy as a set of sets. At the top level, it is indexed by simulation time. At the second level (i.e. within a particular timeslice) it is indexed by an identifier corresponding to one of the volumes into which the two databases are partitioned. At the third level, each spacetime volume contains a set of one or more integer-indexed subvolumes which together provide an arbitrarily sized data subspace for each volume. The leaf nodes of this hierarchy are the aforementioned "simulation chunks;" they are fixed-size data structures that represent part of the simulation output for a particular volume at a particular simulation time. The structure of a chunk is user-definable, so it can be easily modified to accommodate different simulator models. Because the system has a known mapping between simulator volume IDs and Walkthru cells, the visualizer can transmit desired simulation time and cell visibility information to the simulator, allowing the latter to determine exactly which chunks still need to be transmitted.

We do not currently manage distributed simulations, since the latest version of the CFAST code is unable to operate in parallel. However, assuming that any multicomputer simulator subsystem would be able to distribute the problem appropriately, the chunks generated by the separate simulators are easily recombined via simple set unions. Furthermore, since the subsystem controller knows how the problem is distributed, it should also be able to appropriately distribute the visibility lookahead data provided by the simulation manager.

4.2 The Basic Communication Mechanism

A simple and robust communications model is critical to both the performance and ease of use of a system that will be used to integrate a visualizer and a simulator for real time operation. Our communication model is based on a primitive we call a *real-time channel* (RTC). This is a 2-way, buffered, asynchronous mechanism that can operate in either a nonblocking polling or an interrupt-driven mode. Each channel has two separate 2-way byte streams: a data stream for most communication, and a command stream, intended to be used relatively infrequently, for user commands and simulator status packets that need to arrive quickly. The interface to a channel is independent of the specific low-level mechanism used (currently either Internet- or Unix-domain sockets), and provides the ability to send either single-integer "commands" or arbitrary-length "packets" across either of the two streams. A server mechanism is provided that allows a simulator to open a server port on a machine and wait for connections, which will launch an instance of a simulator

connected to an instance of a channel. Channels can be opened locally or over a network; the appropriate low-level protocol is automatically selected by the system when it connects.

5 PROGRAMMING, INTEGRATION, AND USER INTERFACES

With the data format and the basic communication mechanism defined, we now look at the system's interface and functionality from the point of view of both visualization designer and simulation designer.

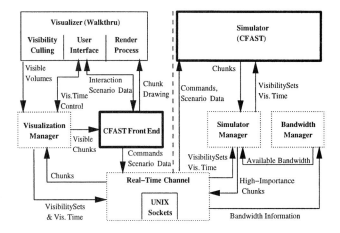

Figure 3: *A diagram of how the system components connect simulator to visualizer. Components in bold outline are created by the simulator designer; components in dotted outline are provided by the integration framework.*

5.1 Visualizer User Interface Constructs

The visualizer's user interface needs to allow the user to connect and disconnect the simulator, as well as to control the progress of "visualization time." The selection of which volumes are being visualized is determined simply by "walking" to the appropriate area. We provide a standardized simulator controller consisting of a panel with simulator connection and status controls, a time slider bar that covers the timespan of the currently running simulation, and a set of VCR-style controls (play, reverse play, fast forward, reverse, and pause) that allows the user to control the rate at which time passes. The slider bar may be directly manipulated to change the current viewing time to any desired value; the VCR controls alter the "time velocity" of the user in simulation time (Play is velocity 1, Fast Forward and Rewind are 10 and -10 respectively, Pause is velocity 0, etc.). The portion of the slider corresponding to data that has been computed by the running simulation is colored green; the portion corresponding to the as yet unsimulated timespan is colored red. This provides immediate feedback to the user about how far the simulation has progressed. The slider is prevented from entering the red region.

The controller also includes a tool intended to mitigate the inherent "burstiness" of most simulations, including CFAST. This tool, called the *autopause* mechanism, will automatically "pause" the visualization time in two cases. At the beginning of the simulation run, it allows the simulator to get a certain distance ahead of the current visualization time, in order to provide a buffer of data that allows the visualization to proceed smoothly if the simulation output becomes bursty. Second, at any time, if the visualization time "catches up" to the simulator, the pause is engaged in the same fashion. In either case, when the simulation provides enough of a buffer, the pause will automatically be removed and visualization time will once again move forward.

5.2 Establishing a Connection

There are two mechanisms for establishing a connection between a simulator and visualizer. A local connection can be established by the visualizer forking a simulator process, which is connected via a local channel. Alternatively, the simulator can establish a server on either a local or remote machine, and the visualizer can connect to it. Once a connection is established, negotiation and setup are handled by the simulator-specific visualization front-end and the simulator being run. In the case of CFAST, the CFAST visualization front-end within the Walkthru transmits the simulation scenario across the channel in the form of a native CFAST data file, which it can create and/or interpret from the Walkthru model geometry, registration information, and chemistry data provided by the user. Negotiation is specific to the particulars of the simulation being run, so the only mechanism provided is the communication channel. When both sides are ready to begin, they each establish their respective "manager" (either a visualization manager or a simulation manager). With the managers attached to the channel, the simulator may begin generating data and submitting it to the simulation manager, and the visualizer can begin visualizing simulation data provided by the visualization manager, each side trusting the managers to handle the communication process. Attaching the managers does not restrict use of the channel; "out-of-band" information such as condition changes and commands from the visualizer can pass through the managers and across the channel, where the simulator can account for these changes by adjusting or re-simulating all or part of the current run.

5.3 Visualization Manager and API

The visualizer's access to simulation data is controlled by the visualization manager and the simulator's visualization "front-end;" the former is a standard component of our architecture, while the latter must be provided by the simulation designer for each simulator to be integrated into the system. When launched, the visualization manager establishes a connection to a simulation manager on the other end of a channel, as well as registering a callback with the visibility lookahead system of the Walkthru. The simulator's visualization front-end launches both the simulator and the visualization manager, and must provide the visualization manager with a starting visualization time and time velocity; these values are typically derived from the simulation scenario. The visualization manager keeps the simulation manager apprised of both the currently visible set of volumes (from the renderer's visibility system) and the current visualization time and velocity; this is done via corrections which are transmitted across the command stream of the channel whenever the time, time velocity, or lookahead set changes.

The simulator visualization front-end provides the user with both direct and indirect control of the simulator and visual interpretation of the simulation results. It may include arbitrary user interface controls for the simulation scenario, and it is required to include a rendering function for simulation chunks. The rendering function accepts a Walkthru database cell and a set of chunks describing the current conditions in the cell, and renders the chunks' contents into the GL window. During each frame, it is called with all visible cells in the frame that have simulation chunks associated with them at the current visualization time. It is never called for a cell or simulation chunk that is not visible in the current frame; this provides efficient, rapid rendering of simulation conditions. The front-end is also provided with hooks into the visualizer's event processing system and

is required to interpret any user interactions that might affect the ongoing simulation scenario. If such an interaction happens, the necessary changes to the scenario are transmitted to the simulator, and, by default, all simulation chunks from that simulation time forward are invalidated. The simulator then has the option to either re-validate (i.e. tag valid without regenerating) or regenerate any portion of that data.

CFAST simulation chunks come in two types. The first type contains temperature, energy output, location, and fuel conversion rate of one particular fire; there can be many of these in one spacetime volume, corresponding to active fires from individual fuel sources such as pieces of furniture. The second type, of which there is only one per spacetime volume, contains the chemical concentrations of nine different gases, fuel concentration, atmospheric pressure and toxicity level, and smoke interface height for the volume as a whole. The user can select a "natural" viewing mode or one of several "scientific visualization" modes. In the natural mode, the drawing function renders the smoke interface with texture-mapped smoke flowing in the appropriate direction. If there are active fires in the volume, a texture-mapped, animated flame is drawn at each flame location with a physically accurate height and base area. If the user is actually inside the smoke, hardware-enhanced fogging of the viewing volume is used to simulate visibility attenuation. A side panel indicates the chemical composition of the atmosphere; an alarm sounds when the user experiences toxic chemical levels. These panels and signals help the user determine what sort of conditions would be experienced by someone inside the burning building. Alternatively, one of the scientific visualization modes can be used. For example, if the user is interested in temperature, "infravision" can be activated; the observer can look at the walls, floor, or smoke, and the surfaces are pseudo-colored according to their temperature. Thermal distributions on the walls can be directly viewed, and the spread of heat can be observed. Selection of appropriate visualization modes is an ongoing research topic of this project. Good combinations of visualization and realistic rendering are being explored to provide maximum information transfer to the user.

5.4 Simulation Manager and API

The simulation manager allows the simulator to generate simulation data as rapidly as possible without worrying about how that data is being transmitted to the visualizer. Once the manager is engaged, the simulator simply generates data, and "submits" the data in the form of simulation sets to the simulation manager. Submissions may be made for any timeslice or volume ID; if a simulation chunk is submitted for the same time, volume ID, and subvolume ID as a previously submitted chunk, it supersedes the older chunk. In this way, a simulator may "retract" any subportion of the previously generated data that is incorrect or that was generated as a quick approximation to be improved later. This will generally happen when the user makes a change in the environment at a particular simulation time, rendering many or all of the chunks after that time invalid.

If the simulator has the necessary capabilities, it may request the current set of visible volumes and the current visualization time from the simulation manager, and selectively generate or improve the corresponding simulation data to ensure that the visualization can proceed without pausing. We believe that this will be an important feature of future simulators that intend to provide visualization data in real-time while operating on very large databases.

6 SIMULATION DATA MANAGEMENT

We have stated that the visualizer and simulator can rely on the visualization manager and simulation manager to get the simulation data to the visualizer in time to be viewed. In this section, we explain how this is implemented via "just-in-time" data management.

6.1 "Just-In-Time" Simulation Data Management

In order for the visualization manager to ensure that the appropriate simulation chunks are either already present or en route from the simulation manager, it has to provide the simulation manager with enough information to determine which chunks are most critically needed. To do this, we define an "importance function" over spacetime, in which the chunks associated with spacetime cells of higher importance will be transmitted to the visualizer earlier. Clearly, the spacetime cells that are visible to the user at the current visualization time are the most important ones, and are needed immediately by the visualizer. Given the user's location, maximum velocities in space and time, the current visualization time, the current visualization time velocity, and the preprocessed volume visibility information from the Walkthru's cull process, we can compute for each spacetime cell the earliest real time in the future in which the user might be able to see that cell. This defines the desired function; smaller "earliest-possible-time-to-visibility" values correspond to higher importance. The information needed to compute this function is available to the visualization manager, which is directly linked to the visualizer; one of the visualization manager's tasks is to transmit this information to the simulation manager, which evaluates the importance function over the set of chunks generated by the simulator, and thereby determines which unsent chunks are most important at any given time.

Our current system does not support the full computation of this function. We implement a heuristic approximation by maintaining a *visibility set* and an up-to-date visualization time at the simulation manager. The visibility set contains the set of Walkthru cells that are either currently visible to the observer, or may be visible in the next several frames. This information is normally computed as part of a Walkthru frame. The visualization manager monitors the visibility set and transmits an update to the simulation manager if the set changes from one frame to the next. Similarly, the visualization time and time velocity are updated if the user alters the time velocity or moves the time slider. Note that, though the visualization time changes as real time passes, the simulation manager can keep accurate track of the current visualization time without continuous updates from the visualization manager; updates are only necessary if the user manipulates a control setting.

The simulation manager then assigns highest importance to the transmission of chunks that are in the visible set and whose time is closest to the current visualization time in the direction of the current time velocity. The next highest importance is assigned to chunks in the visibility set in the *opposite* direction of the current time velocity, since the user often wants to review preceding time slices in the current location to find out how the situation has evolved. All other chunks are of tertiary importance. This corresponds to an approximation of the "ideal" importance function discussed above for very high values of time velocity; it can be computed quickly and does not require the full visibility information of the Walkthru's visibility processing. The simulation manager uses the communications channel to transmit those chunks that have not already been sent and are of highest importance as denoted by the heuristic function.

A sudden change in the time, time velocity, or visibility set can result in a need to get a new set of chunks to the visualizer as quickly as possible. If the user has been visualizing simulation time $t_s = 10$, for example, and the time slider is moved to $t_s = 200$, the simulation manager may have this data, but it is unlikely that the data has been transmitted already. In this case, the simulation manager *immediately* evaluates the most critical chunks to be sent to the visualizer, and transmits those chunks as soon as possible.

It is interesting to note that limiting the user's maximum "time acceleration" (i.e. disallowing direct manipulation of the time slider, allowing the user to move in time only with the VCR buttons) has the effect of allowing us to compute a "time lookahead" to go along with the visibility lookahead. This means that we can establish a

tight superset of the number of spacetime chunks that might be visible in the next few seconds of real time. Without such a bound, the potentially visible set from one frame to the next includes the set of potentially visible cells for *all* timeslices of simulation data available, because the user can drag the time slider from any point to any point within one frame time. With such a bound, and a bound on the number of chunks that will be submitted per spacetime volume (which is easy to derive for most simulators, including CFAST), we can compute a minimum required bandwidth so that we can *guarantee* that all of the needed chunks will be available if there has been at least enough time since the chunk's submission to overcome the latency of the communication channel.

If memory is limited on the visualization machine, it is possible for our system to run the visualization manager as a *cache*, rather than as an *accumulator* of the entire simulation data set. In this case, the visualization manager is allowed to "throw out" old or not recently used chunks. The visualization manager reports to the simulation manager which chunks have been discarded, so that they may be retransmitted if they need to be viewed again,. In the case of very large precomputed data sets, the simulation manager can also be run on a local machine, managing access to a huge disk file instead of an active simulation, while the visualization manager manages the set of simulation data being cached in memory.

6.2 Bandwidth Management

Given only the importance function on the set of simulation chunks that have been submitted, there is no indication of *how much* data should be sent by the simulation manager per unit time. Because the channel is buffered, if no bandwidth usage constraint is enforced, then every time some conditions are submitted by the simulator, all of that data could be queued for transmission through a channel which will not be able to actually finish transmitting that data for quite some time. In a priority situation, when the importance function has changed due to user input, and a different set of chunks are needed *immediately*, queued "old" chunks would delay the transmission of urgent data until those older chunks had drained through the pipe. This "clogging" reduces or eliminates the system's ability to respond to sudden changes in visibility or time. Unfortunately, with most physical simulators, this situation would occur fairly often; physical simulators, including CFAST, tend to exhibit "bursty" output corresponding to sets of solutions for conditions across a slice of time for the entire model. If we use our importance function to determine which chunks are to be sent, the situation becomes even worse; sudden changes of the user's time or position generate even larger spikes, as new, potentially huge sets of chunks become highly important when the user walks into a new region of the database.

An early solution we tried for this problem is to include a priority bypass which provides the ability to interrupt the channel's normal input queue with a second queue of chunks which are to be transmitted first. In an interactive system, this priority bypass often proves ineffective, due to the fact that *two* of the aforementioned sudden changes in the importance function could cause the system to send priority data down an already busy priority channel, and the more recent priority packets, which are now more critical, are delayed in the same fashion that the one-channel strategy delays the first set of priority packets. The situation is made worse in larger databases; in the unmanaged condition the size of these spikes grows with the size of the database. Adding bypasses on top of bypasses quickly becomes unwieldy and inefficient; once all of the data is sitting in multiply-bypassed queues, control of transmission order becomes impossible, the amount of storage needed for redundant queues quickly becomes prohibitive, and the work needed to override a chunk which has been regenerated by the simulator grows without bound.

The core of the problem is the inherent buffering of data in the communication channel. This buffering is unavoidable due to its ubiquity in the low-level communication structures provided by the operating system and the network itself, which use buffering to optimize throughput. Unfortunately, the more buffering there is in the channel, the larger the potential latency for a high-priority packet to be transmitted through the channel; since guaranteed-receipt network protocols guarantee arrival in order of transmission, every bit of buffered data in the channel must clear the channel before our high-priority packet can get through. Thus, we would like to operate the channel in a near-starvation mode, which simultaneously minimizes buffering while using all or nearly all of the bandwidth to transmit useful chunks as quickly as possible. This job is handled by our *bandwidth manager*, which closely controls the speed at which the simulation manager is allowed to transmit chunks to the visualization manager. Available bandwidth is currently specified to the bandwidth manager in total kilobytes (kb) per second. The bandwidth number should be selected to closely approximate real bandwidth (i.e. on two machines on an Ethernet, bandwidth might be on the order of 1,000 kb per second, whereas two machines connected by 28.8 kilobaud [kbps] modem would only be able to manage about 3 kb per second). Several times a second, the bandwidth manager "wakes up" and gives the simulation manager permission to transmit another x kb worth of simulation chunks on the data stream, where x is the given bandwidth divided by the manager's wakeup frequency. When this happens, the simulation manager selects x kb worth of chunks from the unsent chunk pool in order of importance, and gives those chunks to the channel for immediate transmission. By the time the manager wakes up again, all of the submitted chunks should have cleared or nearly cleared the channel; thus, if an emergency situation happens while the manager is asleep, when the manager next wakes up, the most important chunks will be transmitted on a nearly empty channel, which minimizes the transmission latency for those chunks. At the same time, if no emergency occurs, the channel is still being utilized at nearly its maximum capacity, with the next most important set of chunks being sent "just-in-time" for the channel to have completed transmitting the last set; clogging cannot occur if the bandwidth estimate is accurate or conservative.

In our current system, the bandwidth manager's settings are provided by the user. In the future, we intend to have the bandwidth manager dynamically determine via feedback how much bandwidth is available in the pipe, and scale its notion of available bandwidth appropriately [12].

6.3 Performance

Figures 4 through 6 show a typical example and comparison of the performance of three strategies for data management. The most basic is the naive, *oldest-data-first* strategy (figure 4A) which simply queues timeslice data into the communication channel as it becomes available. The second is the *visibility-guided* strategy (figure 4B), in which simulation data is transmitted only for visible or almost-visible volumes (i.e. in order of the basic heuristic importance function), but with no bandwidth management, so that it queues *all* unsent available data for the visible volume set after a change in visualization time or the visible set. The third strategy is our full *bandwidth-managed-importance* strategy (figure 4C), which incorporates all of the subsystems mentioned in this paper. The data was gathered from our instrumented RTC package during identical prerecorded runs of both the visualizer and simulator, in which all simulation data generation, user motion, and manipulation of the time slider and VCR controls were recorded and reproduced in exactly the same way for each run. The communication bandwidth was artificially reduced to 3 kb/s for these runs in order to demonstrate the difference between the strategies; at present, our largest test case is insufficient to stress the switched Ethernet in our office. The reader may wish to note that this bandwidth was selected to correspond to that available from a 28.8 kbps modem link.

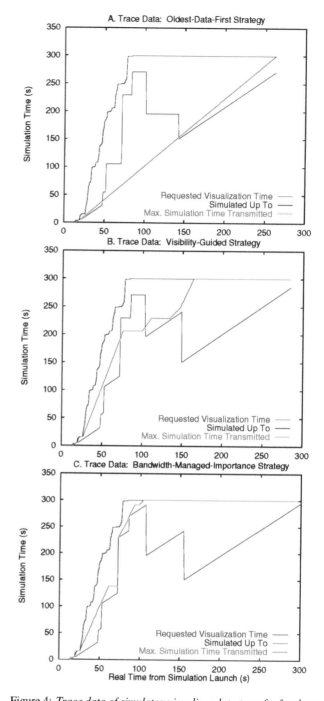

Figure 4: *Trace data of simulator-visualizer data transfer for three strategies: the oldest-data-first strategy (top), the visibility-guided strategy (middle), and the bandwidth-managed-importance strategy (bottom). The horizontal axis is real time; the vertical axis is simulation (i.e. virtual) time. Three functions are plotted for each strategy: the amount of simulation time completed by the simulator, the viewer's current visualization time, and the timestamp of the latest chunk that has been transmitted from simulator to visualizer. Note the vertical lines in the requested visualization time, which denote user-created time discontinuities, and the horizontal lines in the requested visualization time, which show regimes for which data is available from the simulator, but for which that data had not been transmitted in time to be viewed. The "maximum simulation time transmitted" curves give an indication of how responsive each strategy is to user movement in space and time.*

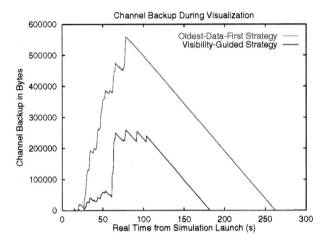

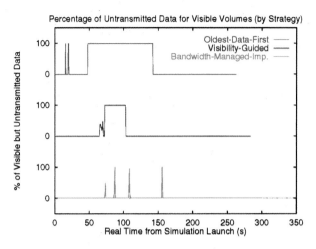

Figure 5: *Trace data of communication pipe backup (i.e. clogging) for the oldest-data-first and visibility-guided strategies. The former is much worse than the latter, although it is in the latter that it actually makes a difference. Pipe blockage in the bandwidth-managed-importance case is negligible (less than 1.5 KPS on this graph, where the others peak at about 550 KPS and 250 KPS respectively), and can in fact be reduced to an arbitrarily small amount on a fast computer by increasing the manager's callback frequency.*

Figure 6: *Trace data of the percentage of spacetime volumes visible to the user which have simulation data available, but for which that data has not yet been transmitted to the visualizer. The oldest-data-first strategy exhibits massive gaps in viewable data; the visibility-guided strategy fares better, but there is still a 40-second period where the user should be seeing smoke and flame, but instead sees nothing. The bandwidth-managed-importance case shows only brief, 1- to 2-second gaps at time discontinuities (i.e. where the user unpredictably drags the time slider far into the untransmitted data).*

The three graphs in figure 4 compare three functions of real time for each strategy: how far the simulator has progressed through the simulation, labeled *Simulated Up To*; the latest simulation time for which simulation data has actually been sent to the visualizer (i.e. the maximum possible viewable simulation time at the visualizer), labeled *Max. Simulation Time Transmitted*, and the simulation time currently being requested by the user within the Walk-thru, labeled *Requested Visualization Time*. If bandwidth were infinite, the user should be able to "see" simulation results whenever the requested visualization time is less than the simulated-up-to time, and the maximum simulation time transmitted would be identical to the simulated-up-to time (which is the most recent simulation time available from the simulator). Under bandwidth limitations, however, it may be that the requested visualization time is less than the simulated-up-to time, but the data is not yet available (i.e. the maximum simulation time transmitted is *less* than the requested visualization time) due to failure of the communication channel to transport the needed data. The most visible evidence of this in the graphs is where the requested visualization time becomes a horizontal line, indicating that the autopause mechanism has engaged due to the visualizer not having the needed data (resulting in a zero time velocity and unchanging visualization time). Many such flats are seen in the case of the *oldest-data-first* strategy; the channel is far too narrow at 3 kb/s to transmit the data in time. The *visibility-guided* strategy does better toward the beginning of the run, where the fact that few volumes are visible allows it to get more timesteps to the visualizer, since those steps contain fewer volumes. However, when the user walks out into the hallway at time 70, the new set of visible volumes results in a deluge of newly important data being queued into the channel. When the user proceeds to move the time slider at time 83, the channel is clogged with the (as yet unsent, but already obsolete) "priority" data from the hallway transition, and the system is unable to respond, resulting in a period of no data being visible. A graph of the communication channel blockage per unit real time (figure 5) shows that a large "clog" occurs at time 70 in the visibility guided case; this clog is what prevents the adaptation to the time discontinuity at time 83. The *oldest-data-first* strategy shows much more extensive clogging. Ironically, since the naive strategy has no ability

to adapt to changing conditions anyway, the clogging is somewhat moot.

In the *bandwidth-managed-importance* case, the system adds the data to the pipeline a little at a time, never adding enough to clog it for more than a fraction of a second; when the user enters the hallway, the system immediately switches to transmitting the needed data for the hallway, and when the time slider is moved, a similar switch is performed that sends the data for the new time. Since the pipe is never clogged, the needed data can be transmitted quickly in subsequent emergency situations.

Figure 6 shows the crucial data of concern; that is, the percentage of volumes per unit real time that are visible to the user and for which simulation data has been generated, but for which that simulation data has not been transmitted yet. The top curve shows that the *oldest-data-first* strategy spends almost half of the simulation run in this state; the viewer is looking at blank volumes when they should be seeing smoke. The center curve shows that the *visibility-guided* strategy does well until the second discontinuity at $t = 83$, at which point it breaks down as well; however, it recovers just after $t = 100$, whereas the *oldest-data-first* strategy doesn't recover for another 20 seconds. Finally, the *bandwidth-managed-importance* strategy is shown at the bottom. The spikes are 1 to 2 seconds long, and are only present at gross visualization time discontinuities (compare the locations with the vertical jumps in visualization time in figure 4). This corresponds closely with the minimum response latency for an emergency; it takes about 1 second just to transmit the data for a timestep at 3 kb/s, and the bandwidth manager makes new bandwidth available once every 0.5 seconds in our system, so the total response latency in our test case has a lower bound of 1 second, and an expected time of 1.25 seconds if the channel had absolutely no latency (which is the ideal case). Thus, our bandwidth manager approaches ideal performance under these conditions. If we bound the user's time velocity, we can further reduce the frequency of these spikes; with a bandwidth of about 30 kb/s, we could eliminate them entirely for any user manipulation of the VCR controls (i.e. any time velocity under 10 virtual seconds per real second). This claim cannot be made for the other two strategies.

7 CONCLUSION

We have developed an example of a simulation based environment for the study of fire hazards and their environmental effects in buildings. An existing simulator, NIST's CFAST, and an existing visualizer, the Berkeley Building Walkthru program have been integrated via a new general framework.

To achieve the most effective simulation for real-time visualization, we have exploited the "cell-and-portal" data structures of both systems. The resulting spatial subdivision and localization of the overall world allows the visualizer to concentrate the expensive rendering task on only those cells that are possibly visible to the observer. With a suitably structured simulator, preference could also be given to simulating the environment in the neighborhood of the observer; but even with an unstructured simulator that produces data in a strictly time-ordered fashion, the cell-based subdivision permits an efficient grouping and prioritizing of the simulation data for its transmission to the visualizer over a potentially bandwidth-limited, high-latency network.

The integration of CFAST into the Walkthru visualizer makes the results of this powerful fire simulator much more understandable at several levels and allows the user to interfere with and redirect the ongoing simulation. Previously, CFAST operated in a batch mode, and provided limited, one- and two-dimensional graphs and data dumps that had to be pieced together with substantial cognitive effort. The use of 3D computer graphic techniques employing suitable symbolic visualizations permits scientists to perceive several variable values such as temperature, smoke levels, or air toxicity in a parallel and quantitative manner. On the other hand, using more natural rendering techniques showing flickering flames and drifting smoke clouds, gives even lay-persons an intuitive understanding of the environmental phenomena being simulated. Such realistic-looking virtual worlds offer the promise of practicing fire-fighting and rescue strategies without any physical danger to the trainee.

The abstractions, integration mechanisms, and high-level data structures that define the interface between the CFAST fire simulator and the Walkthru visualization program are also applicable to other virtual environments combining one or more simulators with first-person interactive visualizers in densely occluded worlds. The demonstrated programming interfaces will also allow rapid prototyping and integration of other environmental simulations into the Walkthru.

Acknowledgments

The authors would like to thank Walter Jones of the Building Fire Research Laboratory for intellectual guidance and technical support for CFAST, and Professor Patrick Pagni of Berkeley, for encouraging us to undertake this project. This work was primarily supported by NIST under contract number 60NANB5D0082, and received further financial assistance from Lockheed-Martin Missles and Space, NEC, and ONR MURI grant N00014-96-1-1200.

References

[1] Anderson, T.E., Culler, D.E., and Patterson, D. A Case for Networks of Workstations: NOW. *IEEE Micro* 15:1, Feb. 1995, pp. 54-64.

[2] Bryson, S. The Virtual Windtunnel: A High-Performance Virtual Reality Application. *IEEE Virtual Reality Annual International Symposium* (Seattle, WA, Sept. 1993), pp. 20-26.

[3] Bryson, S. Virtual Reality in Scientific Visualization. *Communications of the ACM* 38:5, May 1996, pp. 62-71.

[4] Bukowski, R.W. and Séquin, C.H. Object Associations: A Simple and Practical Approach to Virtual 3D Manipulation. *Proc. of the 1995 Symposium on Interactive 3D Graphics* (Monterey, CA, April 1995), pp. 131-138.

[5] Chenney, S., and Forsyth, D. View-Dependent Culling of Dynamic Systems in Virtual Environments. *Proc. of the 1997 Symposium on Interactive 3D Graphics* (Providence, RI, April 1997), pp. 55-58.

[6] Cohen, J., Lin, M., Manocha, D., and Ponamgi, M. I-COLLIDE: An Interactive and Exact Collision Detection System for Large-Scale Environments. *Proc. of the 1995 Symposium on Interactive 3D Graphics* (Monterey, CA, April 1995), pp. 189-196.

[7] Cremer, J., Kearney, J. and Ko, H. Simulation and Scenario Support for Virtual Environments. *Computers and Graphics* 20:2, March/April 1996, pp. 199-200.

[8] DeFanti, T.A., Sandin, D.J., Lindahl, G. et. al. High Bandwidth and High Resolution Immersive Interactivity. *Very High Resolution and Quality Imaging* (San Jose, CA, 1996), pp. 198-204.

[9] Doi, S., Takei, T., Akiba, Y., et. al. Real-Time Visualization System for Computational Fluid Dynamics. *NEC Research and Development* 37:1, Jan 1996, pp. 114-123.

[10] Funkhouser, T.A., Séquin, C.H. , and Teller, S.J. Management of Large Amounts of Data in Interactive Building Walkthroughs. *ACM SIGGRAPH Special Issue: 1992 Symposium on Interactive 3D Graphics*, March, 1992, pp. 11-20.

[11] Funkhouser, T. A. RING: A Client-Server System for Multi-User Virtual Environments. *Proc. of the 1995 Symp. on Interactive 3D Graphics* (Monterey, CA, April 1995), pp. 85-92.

[12] Gong, K. and Rowe, L.A. Parallel MPEG-1 Video Encoding. *Proc. 1994 Picture Coding Symposium* (Sacramento, CA, September 1994).

[13] Macedonia, M.R., Brutzman, D.P., Zyda, M.J. et. al. NPSNET: A Multi-Player 3D Virtual Environment over the Internet. *Proc. of the 1995 Symposium on Interactive 3D Graphics* (Monterey, CA, April 1995), pp. 93-94.

[14] Mirtich, B., and Canny, J. Impulse-Based Simulation of Rigid Bodies. *Proc. of the 1995 Symposium on Interactive 3D Graphics* (Monterey, CA, April 1995), pp. 181-188.

[15] Peacock, R.D., Forney, G.P., Reneke, P. et al. CFAST, the Consolidated Model of Fire Growth and Smoke Transport. NIST technical note 1299, U.S. Department of Commerce, Feb. 1993.

[16] Teller, S., Fowler, C., Funkhouser, T. and Hanrahan, P. Partitioning and Ordering Large Radiosity Computations. *Proc. of SIGGRAPH 94* (Orlando, FL, July 1994), pp. 443-450.

[17] Teller, S.J., and Séquin, C.H. Visibility Preprocessing for Interactive Walkthroughs. *Proc. of SIGGRAPH 91* (Las Vegas, Nevada, Jul. 28-Aug. 2, 1991). In *Computer Graphics*, 25, 4 (Jul. 1991), pp. 61-69.

[18] Taisei corporation. "Yebisu Garden Palace." Video, 1994.

[19] Zyda, M.J., Pratt, D.R., Monahan, J.G. and Wilson, K.P. NPSNET: Constructing a 3D virtual world. *ACM SIGGRAPH Special Issue: 1992 Symposium on Interactive 3D Graphics*, March, 1992.

Fitting Virtual Lights For Non-Diffuse Walkthroughs

Bruce Walter   Gün Alppay   Eric Lafortune   Sebastian Fernandez   Donald P. Greenberg

Cornell Program of Computer Graphics *

Abstract

This paper describes a technique for using a simple shading method, such as the Phong lighting model, to approximate the appearance calculated by a more accurate method. The results are then suitable for rapid display using existing graphics hardware and portable via standard graphics API's. Interactive walkthroughs of view-independent non-diffuse global illumination solutions are explored as the motivating application.

CR Categories: I.3.7 [Computer Graphics]: Three Dimensional Graphics and Realism—Shading

Keywords: interactive walkthroughs, non-diffuse appearance, global illumination, Phong shading

1 INTRODUCTION

This paper describes a method to take a view-independent non-diffuse global illumination solution and approximate it in a form that is suitable for rapid display and interactive walkthroughs. The method fits "virtual lights" to each object that, when displayed using a simple Phong lighting model, will closely reproduce its correct appearance.

One goal of realistic computer graphics is to let a viewer experience a virtual space as if they were physically present in a real space. There are many possible aspects to this mimicry, but here we will emphasize two facets. We want the viewer to be able to move about and explore the space in a natural and unrestricted way, and we want to match the appearance of the real space as closely as possible.

Real lighting is complex and subtle. Global illumination calculations are necessary if we hope to duplicate its appearance. These calculations are expensive, but if we are willing to restrict ourselves to a static environment, this part of the simulation can done as a pre-process. However, we still need to display the results rapidly if we want interactive walkthroughs. To accomplish this, we would like to leverage the existing 3D graphics hardware/software infrastructure.

Unfortunately, there is no standard format for storing non-diffuse lighting information; previously this has meant displaying a diffuse-only approximation to the actual appearance. While the results can be impressive, the absence of

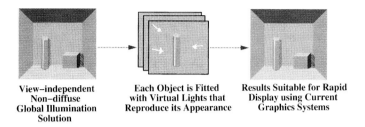

| View–independent Non–diffuse Global Illumination Solution | Each Object is Fitted with Virtual Lights that Reproduce its Appearance | Results Suitable for Rapid Display using Current Graphics Systems |

Figure 1: Approximation process.

directionally dependent lighting effects, such as glossy highlights, means that important perceptual cues are missing.

The continuing popularity of the Phong [10] lighting model[1] is a testament to the importance of including such highlights. Most current graphics API's include a Phong-style lighting model for fast shading. These lighting models are much too simplistic to accurately compute global illumination, but we can still make use of them. Instead of viewing Phong as a lighting model, we can think of it as a set of "appearance basis functions" which can be used to approximately reproduce the results of a more accurate method.

The basic process is outlined in Figure 1. We start from a view-independent non-diffuse global illumination solution. For each non-diffuse object, we fit a set of "virtual lights" that, under the Phong lighting model, will reproduce its computed appearance as closely as possible. By utilizing directionally varying parts of the Phong model, the results will contain non-diffuse aspects of the original solution, although there will also be some loss of directional information due to the limitations of the Phong "basis functions". The results can then be displayed using a standard Phong lighting model.

The translated model can easily be displayed using standard graphics API's (e.g. OpenGL, VRML, or Direct3D) and can even be embedded in display lists. This makes the model portable and suitable for the existing highly optimized 3D graphics display systems. The results are also much more compact than the original global illumination solutions. Most importantly, we apply the lesson of the popular but physically impossible Phong lighting model: even fairly approximate highlights are better than none.

1.1 Related Work

Several researchers have proposed methods for generating and displaying view-independent non-diffuse global illumination solutions (e.g. [6, 11]). Practical application of such methods has so far been hampered by their high computational cost, large storage requirements, and slow display

---

[1]In this paper we use the term Phong somewhat loosely to mean the Phong model, the Blinn-Phong model [3] or any similar simple direct lighting model.

speeds. We hope the methods presented here may help push them toward greater use.

Image-based techniques represent a very different route to non-diffuse walkthroughs. They store the illumination in a set of images instead of on surfaces. Image rendering algorithms such as [4, 7, 8] are then used to quickly interpolate new viewpoints from the precomputed images for a walkthrough. These methods offer some potential advantages, but it is not yet known how well they will scale to walkthroughs of larger environments. We consider them to be promising, but take a different approach here.

Environment or reflection maps [1, 5, 12] have long been used for the rapid display of directionally dependent effects. Their main difference from our work lies in their application. They are usually used as a small extension to a simplistic direct lighting model, whereas we are fitting our directional effects in order to reproduce the appearance computed by a physically-based method. In the future, environment maps may be used in a manner similar to our virtual lights.

Multi-pass rendering techniques are another way to perform walkthroughs with non-diffuse effects. They can implement a variety of extensions to the standard Phong lighting model such as shadows, mirror reflections, refraction, and translucency [2]. The results can be striking and they can handle dynamic environments, which is a major advantage. The problem is that the number of passes required per image increases rapidly with the number of lights and the number of lighting effects simulated. To keep the frame rate interactive, one is forced to limit the environment and choose a somewhat *ad hoc* lighting model.

2 OVERVIEW

Before our technique is used, we assume that a view-independent non-diffuse global illumination solution has been computed for the environment of interest. For each object, this solution will specify its appearance as the amount of light leaving (by emission and/or reflection) every point on the object and in each direction. For simplicity we will assume that this information is specified at a number of selected points which we will refer to as vertices.

An example of a directional light pattern leaving a vertex is shown in 2D at the left in Figure 2. Our goal is to reproduce this pattern using parts of the Phong lighting model. The Phong model allows us two kinds of basis functions: a diffuse or directionally invariant type and the "Phong lobes", or directionally dependent parts, which are caused by specific lights. The diffuse basis is commonly used to encode diffuse global illumination solutions. The new idea of this paper is to also use the "Phong lobes" to approximate non-diffuse appearance as illustrated in Figure 2.

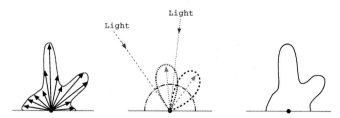

Figure 2: Directional light pattern leaving a vertex. Left: exact or computed pattern, Middle: diffuse basis and two "Phong lobe" basis functions, Right: approximated pattern using the basis functions.

We need to be aware of the many limitations in the Phong model. Some of these make perfect sense (e.g. limit on the number of active lights). Others are somewhat arbitrary and due to the fact that the designers were thinking of Phong as a lighting model rather than as "appearance basis functions". For instance, there is a specular exponent parameter which controls the width of the Phong lobes. We would like to use different exponents for different lights, and thus fit using lobes of several different sizes. We cannot because in the usual Phong lighting model, the exponent is a property of the surface and not a property of the lights.

Given these various restrictions, we must decide which parts and parameters will be the most useful. For each object, we have chosen to use a single set of directional light sources and a single specular exponent. Additionally, at each vertex we set a diffuse coefficient and a specular coefficient. Together, the exponent, light positions, and light intensities determine the shape of the specular basis function at each vertex as shown in Figure 3. The vertex coefficients then specify the mixture of the diffuse and specular basis functions which will serve as our approximation.

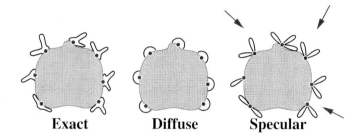

Exact **Diffuse** **Specular**

Figure 3: Directional light patterns at selected vertices on an object. Left: exact or computed patterns, Middle: diffuse basis function, Right: specular basis functions induced by three directional lights shown as arrows. Previous methods approximated the exact pattern using only the diffuse basis, while we use both the diffuse and specular.

Setting these parameters is a non-linear optimization problem. At first we tried using a general purpose non-linear optimization procedure, but found that this took a long time and often did not converge. Instead, we have developed a simple set of heuristics for choosing reasonable values. Further optimization could then be done using these values as the initial guess, although we do not currently do this. We iteratively perform a simple three stage fitting process, where a subset of the parameters are set in each stage.

For each object we start by assuming some value for the specular exponent which fixes the shape of the specular lobes, and iteratively fitting a set of lights. We find the brightest value among all vertices and directions on the object, and select the light direction that will create a Phong lobe centered in that direction for that vertex and the light intensity that will reproduce this maximum value (assuming the specular coefficient is 1.0 for now). The effect of this new light is subtracted from each vertex and the process is repeated until some maximum number of lights have been fit.

Once the exponent and lights are chosen, the shape of the specular basis functions is determined. The problem is now a linear optimization, and we set the two coefficients for each vertex using simple least squares fitting. Finally, we repeat this process with different values of the exponent and choose the exponent which gives the best fit in the least squares step.

Figure 4: An environment containing a teapot shown using virtual lights.

We cannot expect to achieve an exact fit, but this procedure guarantees there will be highlights in the places where the object has its brightest highlights. Note that each object gets its own set of "virtual lights" which do not affect other objects. These lights do not cast shadows and need not correspond to real lights in the environment. For example, several lights may be used to better simulate a highlight whose shape is different than that of a Phong lobe, or lights may correspond to an indirect light source such as the ceiling above a halogen light.

3 IMPLEMENTATION

For our implementation we have worked with OpenGL's version of the Phong shading model [9].

3.1 OpenGL's Lighting Model

OpenGL uses a simple lighting model to approximate the direct illumination of surfaces by light sources. This lighting model consists of four components: emitted, ambient, diffuse, and specular. These are intended to simulate, respectively: light emitted by a surface (glow), multiply reflected indirect lighting, diffusely reflected direct lighting, and specularly reflected glossy highlights from lights. Lights can be ambient, directional, positional, or spotlights and have ambient, diffuse and specular coefficients. OpenGL guarantees that at least eight lights are available. Surfaces have emitted, ambient, diffuse, and specular coefficients, and a shininess parameter that controls the size of the highlights.

In our implementation, we only use the emitted and specular components, along with directional light sources. The emitted, ambient, and diffuse components all produce directionally invariant lighting at a vertex and are thus redundant for our purposes. We use the emitted component to encode the diffuse part of our solution. The specular component is directionally varying and depends on the shininess of the material, the light direction relative to the surface, the surface normal, and the viewing direction relative to the surface.

Using only the emitted and specular components, the OpenGL lighting equation for determining vertex colors becomes:

$$\text{emitted} + \sum_{\text{lights}} \max(\mathbf{s} \cdot \mathbf{n}, 0)^{\text{shininess}} * \text{specular}_{\text{light}} * \text{specular}_{\text{vertex}}$$

where $\mathbf{n}$ is the vertex normal, and $\mathbf{s}$ is the vector obtained by adding the light direction and the view direction and normalizing.

Figure 5: Comparison of original data for the teapot (left) and our approximation using 8 lights (right) shown from three viewpoints.

3.2 The Fitting Process

We compute the initial data by computing a radiosity solution via density estimation [13] and then performing a gather at each vertex and storing the results for a discrete set of outgoing directions. The details are not important and many other methods are possible. For each object, we then need to find the emitted and specular values for each vertex, the directions and intensity values for its lights, and its shininess value. Our algorithm for a single object is:

Repeat
  Choose a shininess value
  Repeat
    Subtract effects of existing lights from input light data
    Find the maximum difference
    Add directional light to cause a highlight at this maximum
    Set light intensities to match input data at their maxima
  until all lights have been fit
  For each vertex
    Set emitted and specular values by least squares fitting
until shininess search is done

We search for the shininess (i.e. exponent) which minimizes the least squares error. We currently use a golden section search method which eliminates a portion of the search interval on each iteration.

4 RESULTS

We computed a global illumination solution for the environment shown in Figure 4 displayed using eight "virtual lights" per specular object. This scene contains the familiar Utah teapot which we use as a an example object to demonstrate our results. A comparison between the computed teapot and our fitted approximation with eight "virtual lights" is shown in Figure 5. The results are perceptually convincing overall although small differences can easily be seen. We also compare results when using fewer fitted lights in Figure 6.

The real test of our techniques is in walkthroughs of non-diffuse environments. We can only show images here, but

Figure 6: Comparison of original data for the teapot (left) and our approximation using 2 (middle) and 8 (right) virtual lights.

Figure 7: Our environment shown with virtual lights and diffuse only (virtual lights turned off).

we have included a live walkthrough of our environment in the video proceedings. Figure 7 shows images of this environment both with and without the virtual lights to demonstrate how much they contribute perceptually.

4.1 Limitations and Open Issues

While our results match the computed solutions surprisingly well, there are many limitations to how well we can currently mimic real appearance. Some of these are fundamental to the technique (e.g. mirrors simply require too much directional information), but others could be alleviated with changes in both our implementation and in the graphics display interfaces.

Some improvements, such as using positional instead of directional lights or finding a perceptually better fitting process, are possible now. But many others would require extensions or additions to the current graphics API's. Some potentially useful extensions would be the ability to vary the specular exponent per light and having a separate specular coefficient for each light at each vertex.

Gouraud interpolation is a major source of artifacts and requires that the curved surfaces be finely tessellated. True Phong shading would reduce these problems, but is rarely available because it is more computationally demanding.

While we use standard graphics API's, we use them in a hitherto unusual way. Many systems are not properly optimized for the sequence of operations we use. For instance on many OpenGL systems there is a very large ($> 4\times$) performance penalty for varying more than one property per vertex (in our case emitted and specular coefficients). We have achieved good performance using a two pass technique, one pass for the diffuse component and a second for the specular. Another possibility is to leave the specular coefficient fixed at the cost of some additional loss of quality. But this problem should largely disappear if our method gains acceptance and is considered during system optimization.

5 CONCLUSIONS

We have presented a technique for using a simple shading model, such as Phong, to approximate the non-diffuse appearance calculated by some more accurate method. This technique can translate view-independent non-diffuse global illumination solutions into a form that is more compact, portable, and suitable for fast display. This allows for non-diffuse walkthroughs which are perceptually better than traditional diffuse-only walkthroughs.

Moreover, by targeting our results toward standard graphics API's such as OpenGL, we can utilize the existing 3D graphics display infrastructure and allow designers to easily optimize their systems for our type of solutions. Finally, we have suggested a few ways in which future graphics API's could be enhanced to better enable the reproduction of non-diffuse appearance.

Acknowledgments

Our thanks to Ben Trumbore, the modelers, and our anonymous reviewers. This work was supported by the NSF Science and Technology Center for Computer Graphics and Scientific Visualization (ASC-8920219) and by NSF ASC-9523483 and performed with workstations generously donated by the Hewlett-Packard Corporation.

References

[1] J. Blinn and M. Newell. Texture and reflection in computer generated images. *Communications of the ACM*, 19(10):542–547, October 1976.

[2] P. J. Diefenbach. *Pipeline Rendering: Interaction and Realism through Hardware-base Multi-pass Rendering*. PhD thesis, University of Pennsylvania, 1996.

[3] A. S. Glassner. *Principles of Digital Image Synthesis*. Morgan-Kaufman, San Francisco, 1995.

[4] S. J. Gortler, R. Grzeszczuk, R. Szeliski, and M. Cohen. The lumigraph. *Computer Graphics*, pages 43–54, August 1996. ACM Siggraph '96 Conference Proceedings.

[5] N. Greene. Environment mapping and other applications of world projections. *IEEE Computer Graphics and Applications*, 6(11):21–29, Nov. 1986.

[6] D. S. Immel, M. F. Cohen, and D. P. Greenberg. A radiosity method for non-diffuse environments. *Computer Graphics*, 20(4):133–142, August 1986. ACM Siggraph '86 Conference Proceedings.

[7] M. Levoy and P. Hanrahan. Light field rendering. *Computer Graphics*, pages 31–42, August 1996. ACM Siggraph '96 Conference Proceedings.

[8] L. McMillan and G. Bishop. Plenoptic modeling: An image-based rendering system. *Computer Graphics*, pages 39–46, August 1995. ACM Siggraph '95 Conference Proceedings.

[9] J. Neider, T. Davis, and M. Woo. *OpenGL Programming Guide*. Addison-Wesley, New York, 1993.

[10] B.-T. Phong. Illumination for computer generated images. *Communications of the ACM*, 18(6):311–317, June 1975.

[11] F. X. Sillion, J. Arvo, S. Westin, and D. Greenberg. A global illumination algorithm for general reflection distributions. *Computer Graphics*, 25(4):187–196, July 1991. ACM Siggraph '91 Conference Proceedings.

[12] D. Voorhies and J. Foran. Reflection vector shading hardware. *Computer Graphics*, 28(3):163–166, July 1994. ACM Siggraph '94 Conference Proceedings.

[13] B. Walter, P. M. Hubbard, P. Shirley, and D. P. Greenberg. Global illumination using local linear density estimation. *ACM Transactions on Graphics*, October 1997.

Instant Radiosity

Alexander Keller*

Universität Kaiserslautern

Abstract

We present a fundamental procedure for instant rendering from the radiance equation. Operating directly on the textured scene description, the very efficient and simple algorithm produces photorealistic images without any finite element kernel or solution discretization of the underlying integral equation. Rendering rates of a few seconds are obtained by exploiting graphics hardware, the deterministic technique of the quasi-random walk for the solution of the global illumination problem, and the new method of jittered low discrepancy sampling.

CR Categories: I.3.3 [Computer Graphics]: Picture/ Image Generation—Antialiasing| Bitmap and framebuffer operations| Display algorithms| Viewing algorithms; I.3.7 [Computer Graphics]: Three-Dimensional Graphics and Realism—Animation| Color, shading, shadowing, and texture| Radiosity

Keywords: Radiance equation, radiosity, shading, Monte Carlo integration, quasi-Monte Carlo integration, quasi-random walk, jittered low discrepancy sampling, hardware, accumulation buffer, realtime rendering algorithms, photorealism.

1 Introduction

Provided a realistic scene description, rendering from the radiance integral equation [Kaj86] yields realistic images. Under the assumption of diffuse reflection, the most popular approaches to approximate the solution of the Fredholm integral equation are radiosity algorithms. In the classical algorithms [CW93], the kernel of the radiance integral equation is projected onto some finite base, yielding the form factor matrix which is of quadratic order in the number of scene elements. For its sparse representation, hierarchical methods with hierarchical base functions have been introduced. Nevertheless, these Galerkin algorithms need to store the kernel and solution discretization of the integral equation. In addition to the high complexity of accurate mesh generation for shadow representation [LTG92], such projections introduce a discretization error.

From the domain of Monte Carlo simulation, algorithms without kernel discretization are available, using the random integration scheme for only projecting the solution onto a finite base. Similar to the random approaches, a deterministic particle simulation scheme based on low discrepancy sampling has been introduced in [Kel96b].

*Fachbereich Informatik, AG Numerische Algorithmen, keller@informatik.uni-kl.de, http://www.uni-kl.de/ AG-Heinrich/Alex.html

This deterministic scheme converges smoother at a slightly superior rate and exposes no variance as compared to stochastic algorithms. In bidirectional path tracing [LW93, VG94], even the discretization of the solution of the radiance equation has been avoided, but the rendering time is far from realtime.

On the other hand, graphics hardware is capable of illuminating and shadowing textured scenes by extended light sources [HA90, Hei91, SKvW+92] in realtime.

In our new approach we combine the advantages of deterministic particle simulation of light, i.e. the quasi-random walk principle, with the available hardware capabilities to consistently render from the radiance equation, neither using a kernel nor an intermediate solution projection of the integral equation, resulting in a very fast, robust and straightforward to implement procedure.

Following this introduction, in the second section of this paper we briefly resume the mathematical model of the global illumination problem. The third section explains the new rendering procedure and its underlying techniques of quasi-Monte Carlo integration and the quasi-random walk principle. After pointing out some extensions of the basic algorithm for including antialiasing by jittered low discrepancy sampling, specular effects, and modifications for realtime application in section four, the algorithm is discussed in the fifth section. The final section draws the conclusion and points out directions of future research.

2 Global Illumination

Our eyes perceive radiance, which is power per unit area per unit solid angle. In vacuum the radiance L fulfills the *radiance equation* [Kaj86]

$$L(y, \vec{\omega}_r) = L_e(y, \vec{\omega}_r)$$
$$+ \int_{\Omega} f_r(\vec{\omega}_i, y, \vec{\omega}_r) L(h(y, \vec{\omega}_i), -\vec{\omega}_i) \cos\theta_i d\omega_i,$$

where Ω is the set of all directions $\vec{\omega} = (\theta, \phi)$ of the unit hemisphere aligned normal to the surface in point y. S is the surface of the scene modeled as boundary representation. The function h returns the first point hit when shooting a ray from y into direction $\vec{\omega}_i$. The term $\cos\theta_i$ projects the incoming radiance normal to the surface, where θ_i is the azimuth angle between the surface normal in y and the direction of incidence $\vec{\omega}_i$. The radiance L in a point $y \in S$ into direction $\vec{\omega}_r \in \Omega$ so is the sum of the source radiance L_e and the reflected radiance. Using operator notation we have the shorthand

$$L = L_e + T_{f_r} L.$$

The bidirectional reflectance distribution function f_r accounts for the surface properties like color and gloss. In the general setting this function depends on the incident direction $\vec{\omega}_i$ and reflection direction $\vec{\omega}_r$ of radiance and the location y. In the *radiosity setting* $f_r = f_d(y) := \frac{\rho_d(y)}{\pi}$ is restricted to only diffuse reflection. Then the radiance becomes isotropic, too:

$$L(y) = L_e(y) + \frac{\rho_d(y)}{\pi} \int_{\Omega} L(h(y, \vec{\omega}_i)) \cos\theta_i d\omega_i,$$

where $\rho_d(y)$ is the reflectivity of the diffuse surface texture.

Given the quadruple (S, f_r, L_e, Ψ), the *global illumination problem* consists in calculating functionals of the form

$$\langle L, \Psi \rangle := \int_S \int_\Omega L(y, \vec{\omega}) \Psi(y, \vec{\omega}) \cos \theta d\omega dy$$

either in the radiosity setting or for the full radiance equation. There are various choices for the detector functional Ψ, e.g. the sum of orthonormal base vectors of a finite vector space, as used in classical or hierarchical radiosity approaches [CW93]. Instead of discretizing the solution of the integral equation and then having to render it in a separate pass, we directly select

$$\Psi_{mn}(y, \vec{\omega}) := \frac{\delta(\vec{\omega} - \vec{\omega}_{y_f})}{\cos \theta} \frac{1}{|P_{nm}|} \chi_{P_{mn}}(h(y, \vec{\omega}))$$

detecting the average radiance passing through the pixel P_{mn} of the image matrix as seen by a pinhole camera[1] from the focal point y_f. $\vec{\omega}_{y_f} := P - y_f$ is the direction of a point P in the support of P_{mn} through y_f. $\chi_{P_{mn}}$ is the characteristic function of the pixel's support and δ the Kronecker delta function.

3 The new Algorithm

Our new algorithm generates a particle approximation of the diffuse radiance in the scene using the quasi-random walk [Kel96b] based on the method of quasi-Monte Carlo integration. Then the graphics hardware renders an image with shadows for each particle used as point light source. Global illumination finally is obtained by summing up the single images in an accumulation buffer [HA90] and displaying the result. The algorithm calculates the average radiance

$$\begin{aligned}\overline{L}_{mn} := \langle L, \Psi_{mn} \rangle &= \langle L_e, \Psi_{mn} \rangle + \langle T_{f_r} L, \Psi_{mn} \rangle \\ &= \langle L_e, \Psi_{mn} \rangle + T_{mn} L \qquad (1)\end{aligned}$$

passing through a pixel P_{mn}, where the shorthand $T_{mn}L$ defines the rendering operator, which determines the at least once reflected radiance through P_{mn}. If the radiance L in the radiosity setting can be approximated by a discrete density of M point light sources

$$L(y) \approx \sum_{i=0}^{M-1} L_i \delta(y - P_i), \qquad (2)$$

where L_i is the radiance and P_i is the position of the i-th light source, the application of T_{nm} to the particle approximation yields the very fast rendering algorithm

$$\overline{L}_{mn} \approx \langle L_e, \Psi_{mn} \rangle + \sum_{i=0}^{M-1} T_{mn} L_i \delta(y - P_i).$$

T_{mn} applied to a point light source simultaneously can be evaluated for all pixels of the image matrix by calling a standard graphics hardware illumination routine in the manner of [Hei91, SKvW$^+$92], producing the shaded image of the textured scene including shadows. The directly visible light sources in $\langle L_e, \Psi_{mn} \rangle$ are rendered on the fly by assigning emission to the corresponding surface elements (see the light source in figure 7). The algorithm thus directly operates on the textured scene description in image space and does not apply any kernel or solution discretization to the integral equation. In consequence, no mesh artifacts will occur and also no topological data structure like e.g. a winged-edge representation

---
[1] For more elaborate camera models we refer to [KMH95].

 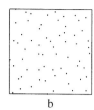 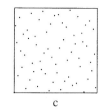

a   b   c

Figure 1: Two-dimensional uniform sampling patterns: a) random, b) jittered, and c) Halton for $N = 64$ samples.

is required for interpolation or overlapping coefficients evaluation. A small number M (usually $50 \ldots 300$) of point light sources will be sufficient, since from multipass rendering with expensive local pass calculations [CSSD94, Kel95, Kel96a], it is known that a very coarse radiosity solution suffices to produce realistic images. So the speed of the algorithm mainly depends on the frame generation rate of the graphics hardware, promising interactive rates of photorealistic image generation.

3.1 Quasi-Monte Carlo Integration

Similar to [Kel96b], we use the method of quasi-Monte Carlo integration for the evaluation of the integrals. For the approximation

$$\int_{[0,1)^s} f(x) dx \approx \frac{1}{N} \sum_{i=0}^{N-1} f(x_i)$$

we generate the N sample points $x_0, \ldots, x_{N-1} \in [0, 1)^s$ using the Halton sequence. Based on the radical inverse function

$$\Phi_b(i) := \sum_{j=0}^{\infty} a_j(i) b^{-j-1} \in [0, 1) \Leftrightarrow i = \sum_{j=0}^{\infty} a_j(i) b^j,$$

the s-dimensional Halton low discrepancy sequence (see comparison in figure 1) is

$$x_i = (\Phi_{b_1}(i), \ldots, \Phi_{b_s}(i)), i \in \mathbb{N}_0,$$

where b_j is the j-th prime number. Note that each segment $P_{N'}$ of a larger segment P_N, $N' < N$, of successive points of the Halton sequence is a quadrature rule, too, which is not the case for variance reduced sampling methods like jittered or N-rooks sampling. In addition, the Halton points are available for any choice of N independent of dimension s. Compared to N-rooks sampling, where for each dimension a random permutation of size $\mathcal{O}(N)$ and unknown quality has to be stored, the Halton points can be generated for arbitrary i (see figure 2) or successively (see figure 3) by the algorithm of [HW64] at a speed comparable to usual pseudo-random generators without additional storage.

The integrands in computer graphics are discontinuous, allowing only very pessimistic upper error bounds (for details see [Nie92]) for the integral approximation. Nevertheless, the numerical evidence in [Kel95, Kel96a, Kel96b] shows that the calculation of functionals of the solution of the radiance equation by means of low discrepancy sequences results in a much smoother convergence at a slightly superior rate as compared to random sampling. In [PTVF92] a plausibility argument gives the rate of $\mathcal{O}(N^{-\frac{s+1}{2s}})$ as upper bound for the quasi-Monte Carlo method applied to discontinuous functions. For high dimension, this rate converges to the random rate of $\mathcal{O}(N^{-\frac{1}{2}})$, but since $s \ll \infty$, the rate of sampling with Halton points is superior to random sampling. The above arguments also apply to jittered sampling [Mit96], but the low discrepancy pattern is deterministic and therefore works without variance!

```
void Φ(int b, int i)
{
    double x = 0.0, f = 1/b;

    while(i)
    {
        x += f * (double) (i % b);
        i /= b;
        f *= 1/b;
    }

    return x;
}
```

Figure 2: Direct calculation of the radical inverse function.

```
void Φ(int b, double x)
{
    double h, hh, r = 1.0 - x - 1e - 10;

    if(1/b < r)
        x += 1/b;
    else
    {
        h = 1/b;

        do
        {
            hh = h;
            h *= 1/b;
        }
        while(h >= r);

        x += hh + h - 1.0;
    }

    return x;
}
```

Figure 3: Incremental calculation of the radical inverse function.

3.2 The Quasi-Random Walk

In realistic applications the transport operator norm $\|T_{f_r}\| < 1$, meaning that less than 100% of the incident radiance is reflected. So the Neumann series

$$L = (I - T_{f_r})^{-1} L_e = \sum_{j=0}^{\infty} T_{f_r}^j L_e$$

converges and can be used to solve the integral equation. Inserted in (1), after some transformations, for the radiosity setting we get

$$T_{mn} L = \frac{1}{|P_{mn}|} \sum_{j=0}^{\infty} \int_{P_{mn}} \int_{\Omega^j} \int_{S_e} p_j(y_0, \vec{\omega}_0, \ldots, \vec{\omega}_j)$$

$$V(y_j, y') f_d(y') \frac{\cos \theta_j \cos \theta'}{|y_j - y'|^2} dy_0 d\omega_0 \cdots d\omega_j dP. \quad (3)$$

Here $S_e := \mathrm{supp}\, L_e \subseteq S$ is the support of the light sources, and $y' = h(y_f, P - y_f) \in S$ is the first point hit when shooting a ray from the eye at y_f through the point $P \in P_{mn}$ into the scene. $V(y_j, y')$ checks the mutual visibility of the points y_j and y', yielding 1 in case of visibility and 0 else. The radiance density

$$p_j(y_0, \vec{\omega}_0, \ldots, \vec{\omega}_j) := L_e(y_0) \prod_{l=1}^{j} (\cos \theta_{l-1} f_d(y_l))$$

represents the source radiance after j reflections. Here $y_0 \in S_e$ is a point on a light source, and the subsequent points $y_{l+1} := h(y_l, \vec{\omega}_l) \in S, 0 \leq l < j$, of a path are determined by ray shooting. Taking the diffuse part of the scene, the operator norm can be estimated by the mean reflectivity

$$\bar{\rho} := \frac{\sum_{k=1}^{K} \rho_{d,k} |A_k|}{\sum_{k=1}^{K} |A_k|} \approx \|T_{f_d}\|,$$

where the scene $S := \cup_{k=1}^{K} A_k$ is composed of K surface elements A_k with average diffuse reflectivity of $\rho_{d,k}$.

As in [Kel96b], the radiance density is simulated by its particle nature using the technique of the quasi-random walk. Since in realistic scene models the actual diffuse reflectivity has only small deviation from $\bar{\rho}$, we can use fractional absorption and avoid Russian Roulette absorption [AK90]. So from N particles started at the light sources, $\bar{\rho} N$ particles are supposed not to be absorbed by the first reflection, $\bar{\rho}^2 N$ survive the second reflection and so on. Then the number M of radiance points generated is bounded by

$$M < \sum_{j=0}^{\infty} \bar{\rho}^j N = \frac{1}{1 - \bar{\rho}} N =: \bar{l} N$$

and thus is linear in N depending on the average scene reflectivity $\bar{\rho}$, where $\bar{l}$ is the mean path length. The quasi-random walk scheme now evaluates $T_{mn} L_e$ using N point lights, $T_{mn} T_{f_d} L_e$ by using $\lfloor \bar{\rho} N \rfloor$ point lights, and so on, where the particles are generated using the Halton sequence. As a consequence, the particles are concentrated in the lower powers of the reflection operator, which due to the operator norm contribute the most important parts of the image, thus fully exploiting the advantages of low discrepancy sampling.

3.3 Implementation

The pseudocode of the instant radiosity algorithm is given in figure 4. To generate the discrete density approximation of p_j by low discrepancy points, we first fix the number N of particles to start off the light source. By an isometry y_0 (e.g. see the collection in [Shi92]) the first two components of the Halton sequence are mapped from the unitsquare onto the surface of the light source, yielding the starting point $y = y_0(\Phi_2, \Phi_3)$ with power $L = L_e(y)$ supp L_e. In the case of multiple light sources, first a light source is selected by the composition method identical to [Kel96b], then the isometry is applied. Exploiting the property of the Halton sequence that segments of the sequence have small discrepancy, too, the $\lfloor \bar{\rho} N \rfloor$ first points are used to shoot a ray into direction $\vec{\omega}$ using

$$\vec{\omega} = \vec{\omega}_d(\Phi_{b_{2j+2}}, \Phi_{b_{2j+3}}) = (\arcsin \sqrt{\Phi_{b_{2j+2}}}, 2\pi \Phi_{b_{2j+3}}),$$

where the direction already is distributed with respect to the cosine-term in the density p_j. In the next hitpoint $y = h(y, \vec{\omega})$ the particle's radiance is attenuated by $f_d(y)$. From these particles the first $\lfloor \bar{\rho}^2 N \rfloor$ continue their paths, repeating the diffuse scattering procedure until no particles remain. The starting points and the subsequent hitpoints of the above quasi-random walk then form the discrete density approximation (2) which is used for the hardware lighting call glRenderShadowedScene, i.e. the scene is rendered with shadows and the point light source located in y with the power $\frac{N}{\lfloor w \rfloor} L$. The term $w = \bar{\rho}^j N$ is used to compensate the attenuation by $\prod_{l=1}^{j} f_d(y_l)$, making the contribution of each image equally important. Finally the quasi-Monte Carlo integration is performed by accumulating all images with the weight $\frac{1}{N}$.

```
void InstantRadiosity(int N, double ρ̄)
{
    double w, Start; int End, Reflections = 0;
    Color L; Point y; Vector ω⃗;

    Start = End = N;

    while(End > 0)
    {
        Start *= ρ̄;

        for(int i = (int) Start; i < End; i++)
        {
            // Select starting point on light source
            y = y₀(Φ₂(i),Φ₃(i));
            L = Lₑ(y) * supp Lₑ;
            w = N;

            // trace reflections
            for(int j = 0; j <= Reflections; j++)
            {
                glRenderShadowedScene(N/⌊w⌋ L, y);
                glAccum(GL_ACCUM, 1/N);
                // diffuse scattering
                ω⃗ = ω⃗_d(Φ_{b_{2j+2}}(i),Φ_{b_{2j+3}}(i));
                //trace ray from y into direction ω⃗
                y = h(y,ω⃗);
                // Attenuate and compensate
                L *= f_d(y);
                w *= ρ̄;
            }
        }

        Reflections++;
        End = (int) Start;
    }

    glAccum(GL_RETURN, 1.0);
}
```

Figure 4: Instant radiosity pseudocode (see section 3.3).

4 Extensions

The fast, deterministic radiosity algorithm introduced in the previous section consistently renders diffuse global illumination for still images. By the new concept of jittered low discrepancy sampling, we treat issues of antialiasing in order to improve image quality at low sampling rates by random elements. Then specular effects are added to the algorithm. Finally modifications for realtime walkthroughs are indicated.

4.1 Jittered Low Discrepancy Sampling

Taking a look at the two-dimensional Hammersley sequence $\left(\frac{i}{N}, \Phi_2(i)\right)_{i=0}^{N-1}$ in figure 5, it becomes obvious that the low discrepancy points based on radical inversion are aligned to a grid. This grid structure guarantees a minimum distance property, and thus an implicit stratification, but is prone to aliasing. The new concept of jittered low discrepancy sampling joins the two worlds of Monte Carlo and quasi-Monte Carlo integration by using low discrepancy point sets as stratification. Approximating the grid resolution by $\frac{1}{N}$, this is done by randomizing each low discrepancy point in its raster cell, i.e. replacing the radical inverse Φ_b by $\Phi_b + \frac{\xi}{N}$, where ξ is a random variable, assuring that the sample remains in the unit interval. From the images in figure 5 it also becomes obvious that the jittered Hammersley sequence in two dimensions is a special case of N-rooks sampling. The Hammersley points, however, can

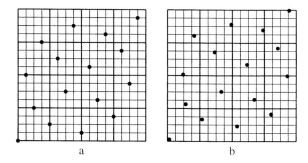

Figure 5: Grid structure of the a) Hammersley and b) jittered Hammersley sampling patterns for $N = 16$.

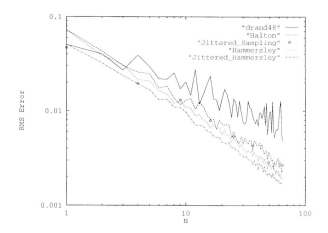

Figure 6: Convergence of different sampling patterns.

be generated without storing a random permutation; they implicitly are a permutation with low discrepancy.

Applied to pixel supersampling for antialiasing as in [HA90], the two dimensional jittered Hammersley sequence exposes an even faster convergence than standard variance reduced sampling. This can be seen in figure 6, where the RMS-error is plotted versus the sampling rate N for an experiment where images of the textured scene in figure 8 at a sampling rate of $N = 1 \ldots 64$ were compared to a master calculation at 640 samples per pixel.

In our new algorithm then, according to the path number i, the corresponding x_i of the Hammersley sequence is jittered for each image produced by the particles of the path. Using this sampling pattern in the manner of [HA90], hardware antialiasing, as available on some graphics accelerators, becomes redundant. Concerning the quasi-random walk, the components of the Halton vector have to be jittered by different ranges. Starting on the light sources we have N particles, where the coordinates (Φ_2, Φ_3) will be jittered by $\frac{\xi}{N}$, in the next step only $\lfloor \bar{\rho}N \rfloor$ particles are traced, so the jitter range is $\frac{1}{\lfloor \bar{\rho}N \rfloor}$, and so on. By this procedure aliasing is reduced, even improving the convergence rate.

4.2 Specular Effects

To add specular effects, we first let T_{mn} use the full BRDF f_r in the hardware lighting pass, enabling specular highlights as can be seen in figure 8. In the particle generation phase, by a random decision each surface is tested to be specular or diffuse according to its BRDF [CRMT91, War92]. In case of specular reflection a virtual light source is generated, i.e. the origin of the ray is mirrored by the specular surface under consideration. The virtual light source now illuminates the part of the scene inside the pyramid spanned by itself and the contour of the reflecting element using techniques of [DB94, Die96]. Note that virtual light sources can only be applied at planar polygon level. Afterwards the incoming particle is randomly scattered according to the specular part of the BRDF. Particles hitting specular surfaces so produce a virtual light source raising M and cause a lengthening of the low discrepancy path by a random piece. If the graphics hardware supports spot lights and the particles $(L_i, P_i, \vec{\omega}_i)$ are equipped with their direction of incidence, even more general light source emission, i.e. with a $\cos^d$-distribution, and caustics can be simulated. Finally the visible specular objects have to be treated separately by ray tracing or advanced hardware techniques as illustrated in [DB94, Die96].

4.3 Realtime Walkthroughs

The algorithm designed so far produces still images. In an animated environment, the quasi-random walk is substituted by tracing fixed length paths generated by the Halton sequence as introduced in [Kel95, Kel96a]. All images produced by one path are accumulated and the resulting image is stored with its time of generation. Keeping the last N images of the last N paths, each time a new path is completed, the oldest image is replaced by the new one. The current N images then are accumulated and displayed, thus implicitly performing temporal antialiasing. As path length we choose the maximal length of the paths obtained in the quasi-random walk procedure

$$l_{max} := \left\lfloor -\frac{\log N}{\log \overline{\rho}} \right\rfloor .$$

Then the maximal frame rate of the graphics accelerator is reduced by the factor $\frac{1}{l_{max}}$ for one time step, allowing for realtime rendering rates (e.g. $\overline{\rho} = 0.5774$ of the scene in figure 7 with $N = 64$ yields $l_{max} = 7$), and since the algorithm directly operates on the scene graph, dynamic environments can be treated without further effort!

Using texture mapping hardware for displaying illumination maps, generalizing the method of [HH96] yields another approach to realtime walkthroughs for static environments. Instead of using jittered sampling and $\overline{\rho} = 0$, i.e. only direct illumination, we replace the light samples of [HH96] by our discrete density approximation of radiance (see section 3.3). By this simple enhancement the algorithm of [HH96] renders the global diffuse illumination into textures, which then interactively can be displayed. Besides considerable memory consumption, the solution of the radiance equation now is discretized in textures, which may result in visible artifacts if the texture resolution has been chosen too small.

5 Discussion of the Algorithm

The algorithm displayed in figure 4 is illustrated by figure 7. For a path number of $N = 10$ the single images created by the point light sources (red balls) are shown. In addition, the results of accumulating $N \in \{10, 32, 64\}$ paths (i.e. $M = 20, 42,$ or 147 images in PAL-resolution 720x576 pixels) are displayed. The images of the scene of 402 quadrangles have been produced on a Silicon Graphics Onyx with Reality Engine[2] graphics and a 75MHz R8000 processor in 24 seconds by the shadow algorithm of [Hei91], i.e. by evaluating the shadow volume of each primitive drawn over the depth buffer image of the scene for stenciling out the shadows. Using the shadow techniques of [SKvW+92] would result in an at least twice as fast algorithm. This emphasizes the fact that the performance of our approach mainly depends on the hardware rendering speed, since the particle approximation can be generated instantly. Note that the smooth shadows and the indirect illumination are obtained without any meshing which would have raised the number of polygons to a multiple.

Two problems of the algorithm become apparent at very low sampling rates N. The first problem is the weak singularity of the operator T_{mn}, when the distance $|y_j - y'|^2$ of point light source y_j and point y' to be lit comes close to zero (see figure 7). Then the value to be entered into the frame buffer is overmodulated and will be clipped to the maximal representable value. The second problem is that each light point colored by a texture has a large influence on the overall color of the scene. Since all images are weighted by $\frac{1}{N}$ in the accumulated image, however, the impact of one of the above cases is at most of order $\frac{1}{N}$, which in most cases is hardly perceivable.

Our access to graphics hardware was restricted to the above example, so we exploited shadow caching and eye ray coherence, to simulate the hardware evaluation of T_{mn} for the point lights by ray tracing. For the conference room consisting of 39584 scene primitives, N was chosen independent of the number of extended light sources, as demonstrated in figure 9, where only $N = 128$ paths are used for a scene with 248 light sources.

Since the algorithm directly operates on the scene graph without additional storage for discretizations animated environments, cyclic graphs as used for plant modeling, or level-of-detail modeling easily can be rendered in a photorealistic way. The only additional data structure required is a space order like e.g. a BSP-tree for accelerating the ray shooting $h(y, \vec{\omega})$. On the one hand it is possible to generate the discrete density approximation $(L_i, P_i)_{i=0}^{M-1}$ of the radiance and to affix these point light sources to the scene description, e.g. MGF or VRML. Then the final rendering process, i.e. loading the scene graph and illuminating it by the point light sources, does not need the space order for ray shooting. On the other hand the BSP can be used for rendering with impostors similar to [SLS+96] and hierarchical clipping, speeding up the frames-per-second rate. These techniques have not yet been included in the implementation used for the time measurements, but reduce the constant of the time complexity $\mathcal{O}(NK)$ of our algorithm, where the number N of paths can be freely chosen with respect to the frame and accumulation buffer accuracy, and K is the number of elements in the scene.

6 Conclusion and Future Work

A new method for rendering from the radiance equation has been introduced. Based on the quasi-random walk, point light sources are generated for fast hardware illumination. The single images are superimposed, yielding one of the fastest physically correct rendering procedures. Working in image space, the algorithm does not need any storage for kernel or solution discretization or topological information. The efficient algorithm itself is very compact and can be easily implemented using a standard graphics API, requiring only a ray intersection routine and an isometry from the unit square onto the surface of each light source. The deterministic algorithm has been extended by the new concept of jittered low discrepancy sampling.

Since our method already includes importance sampling, stratification of low discrepancy, and jittering for antialiasing, future work will be spent on the investigation of the adjoint transport operator for efficiently sampling the light sources with high impact on the final image (especially in large and/or indirectly illuminated environments), reducing the number M of point lights, and decreasing the influence of the weak singularity of the transport operator. Provided that the rendering hardware supplies fog attenuation, even an extension to participating media is possible, since the direct simulation is easily extended for volume scattering.

7 Acknowledgements

The author would like to thank Stefan Heinrich and Hans-Christian Rodrian for the discussions. Special thanks go to Marc Stamminger for providing access to the Reality Engine[2].

The models of this paper (except for figure 8, which has been modeled by Christian Keller) are taken from the *Material and Geometry Format* (MGF)-package of Greg Ward (available via `http://radsite.lbl.gov/mgf/HOME.html`). The greyscale scene has been provided by Peter Shirley. The conference room has been modeled by Anat Grynberg and Greg Ward. A photograph of the original room can be found in [FvDFH96].

References

[AK90] J. Arvo and D. Kirk. Particle Transport and Image Synthesis. In *Computer Graphics (SIGGRAPH 90 Conference Proceedings)*, pages 63 – 66, 1990.

[CRMT91] S. Chen, H. Rushmeier, G. Miller, and D. Turner. A progressive Multi-Pass Method for Global Illumination. In *Computer Graphics (SIGGRAPH 91 Conference Proceedings)*, pages 165 – 174, 1991.

[CSSD94] P. Christensen, E. Stollnitz, D. Salesin, and T. DeRose. Wavelet Radiance. In *Proc. 5th Eurographics Workshop on Rendering*, pages 287–302, 1994.

[CW93] M. Cohen and J. Wallace. *Radiosity and Realistic Image Synthesis*. Academic Press Professional, Cambridge, 1993.

[DB94] P. Diefenbach and N. Badler. Pipeline Rendering: Interactive Refractions, Reflections, and Shadows. *Displays: Special Issue on Interactive Computer Graphics*, 15(3):173–180, 1994.

[Die96] Paul J. Diefenbach. *Pipeline Rendering: Interaction and Realism through Hardware-Based Multi-Pass Rendering*. Ph.D. thesis, University of Pennsylvania, 1996.

[FvDFH96] J. Foley, A. van Dam, S. Feiner, and J. Hughes. *Computer Graphics, Principles and Practice, 2nd Edition in C*. Addison-Wesley, 1996.

[HA90] P. Haeberli and K. Akeley. The Accumulation Buffer: Hardware Support for High-Quality Rendering. In *Computer Graphics (SIGGRAPH 90 Conference Proceedings)*, pages 309–318, 1990.

[Hei91] T. Heidmann. Real Shadows - Real Time. *Iris Universe*, (18):28–31, 1991.

[HH96] M. Herf and P. Heckbert. Fast Soft Shadows. In *Technical Sketches (SIGGRAPH 96 Visual Proceedings)*, page 145, 1996.

[HW64] J. Halton and G. Weller. Algorithm 247: Radical-inverse quasi-random point sequence. *Comm. ACM*, 7(12):701–702, 1964.

[Kaj86] J. Kajiya. The Rendering Equation. In *Computer Graphics (SIGGRAPH 86 Conference Proceedings)*, pages 143–150, 1986.

[Kel95] A. Keller. A Quasi-Monte Carlo Algorithm for the Global Illumination Problem in the Radiosity Setting. In H. Niederreiter and P. Shiue, editors, *Monte Carlo and Quasi-Monte Carlo Methods in Scientific Computing*, volume 106, pages 239–251. Springer, 1995.

[Kel96a] A. Keller. Quasi-Monte Carlo Methods in Computer Graphics: The Global Illumination Problem. *Lectures in App. Math.*, 32:455–469, 1996.

[Kel96b] A. Keller. Quasi-Monte Carlo Radiosity. In X. Pueyo and P. Schröder, editors, *Rendering Techniques '96 (Proc. 7th Eurographics Workshop on Rendering)*, pages 101–110. Springer, 1996.

[KMH95] C. Kolb, D. Mitchell, and P. Hanrahan. A Realistic Camera Model for Computer Graphics. In *SIGGRAPH 95 Conference Proceedings*, Annual Conference Series, pages 317–324, 1995.

[LTG92] D. Lischinski, F. Tampieri, and D. Greenberg. Discontinuity Meshing for Accurate Radiosity. *IEEE Computer Graphics & Applications*, 12(6):25–39, 1992.

[LW93] E. Lafortune and Y. Willems. Bidirectional Path Tracing. In *Proc. 3rd International Conference on Computational Graphics and Visualization Techniques (Compugraphics)*, pages 145–153, 1993.

[Mit96] D. Mitchell. Consequences of Stratified Sampling in Graphics. In *SIGGRAPH 96 Conference Proceedings*, Annual Conference Series, pages 277–280, 1996.

[Nie92] H. Niederreiter. *Random Number Generation and Quasi-Monte Carlo Methods*. SIAM, Pennsylvania, 1992.

[PTVF92] H. Press, S. Teukolsky, T. Vetterling, and B. Flannery. *Numerical Recipes in C*. Cambridge University Press, 1992.

[Shi92] P. Shirley. Nonuniform Random Point Sets via Warping. In D. Kirk, editor, *Graphics Gems III*, pages 80–83. Academic Press Professional, 1992.

[SKvW+92] M. Segal, C. Korobkin, R. van Widenfelt, J. Foran, and P. Haeberli. Fast Shadows and Lighting Effects using Texture Mapping. In *Computer Graphics (SIGGRAPH 92 Conference Proceedings)*, pages 249–252, 1992.

[SLS+96] J. Shade, D. Lischinski, D. Salesin, T. DeRose, and J. Snyder. Hierarchical Image Caching for Accelerated Walkthroughs of Complex Environments. In *SIGGRAPH 96 Conference Proceedings*, Annual Conference Series, pages 75–82, 1996.

[VG94] E. Veach and L. Guibas. Bidirectional Estimators for Light Transport. In *Proc. 5th Eurographics Worshop on Rendering*, pages 147 – 161, Darmstadt, Germany, June 1994.

[War92] G. Ward. Measuring and Modeling Anisotropic Reflection. In *Computer Graphics (SIGGRAPH 92 Conference Proceedings)*, pages 265 – 272, 1992.

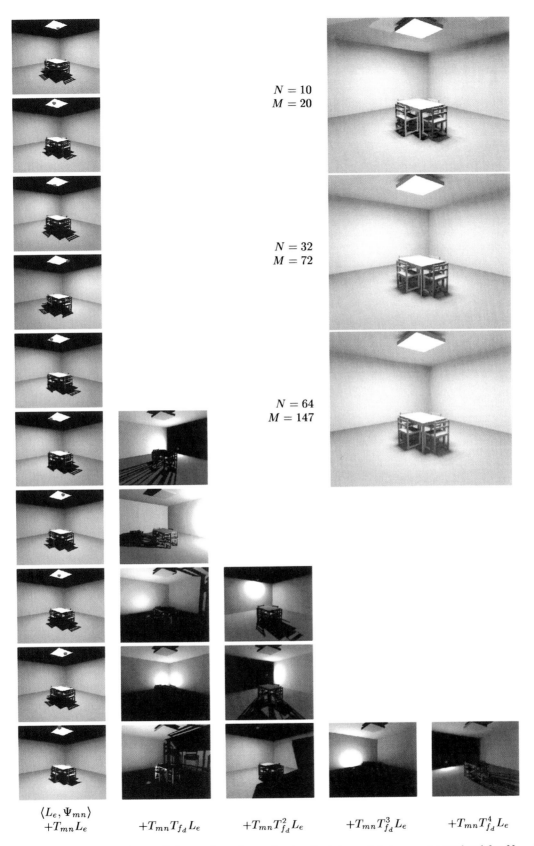

$$N = 10$$
$$M = 20$$

$$N = 32$$
$$M = 72$$

$$N = 64$$
$$M = 147$$

| $\langle L_e, \Psi_{mn}\rangle$ $+T_{mn}L_e$ | $+T_{mn}T_{f_d}L_e$ | $+T_{mn}T_{f_d}^2 L_e$ | $+T_{mn}T_{f_d}^3 L_e$ | $+T_{mn}T_{f_d}^4 L_e$ |

Figure 7: Illustration of the quasi-random walk integration scheme showing the intermediate images accumulated for $N = 10$ paths with $\overline{\rho} = 0.5774$ and the resulting images for $N \in \{10, 32, 64\}$.

Figure 8: Specular effects of the standlight on the floor by using the full BRDF f_r in T_{mn} for $N = 128$.

Figure 9: Conference room image for $N = 128$.

Interactive Update Of Global Illumination
Using A Line-Space Hierarchy

George Drettakis and François X. Sillion

iMAGIS[†]- GRAVIR/IMAG - INRIA

Abstract

Interactively manipulating the geometry of complex, globally illuminated scenes has to date proven an elusive goal. Previous attempts have failed to provide interactive updates of global illumination and have not been able to offer well-adapted algorithms controlling the frame rate. The need for such interactive updates of global illumination is becoming increasingly important as the field of application of radiosity algorithms widens. To address this need, we present a novel algorithm which provides interactive update rates of global illumination for complex scenes with moving objects. In the context of clustering for hierarchical radiosity, we introduce the idea of an implicit *line-space hierarchy*. This hierarchy is realized by augmenting the links between hierarchical elements (clusters or surfaces) with *shafts*, representing the set of lines passing through the two linked elements. We show how line-space traversal allows rapid identification of modified links, and simultaneous cleanup of subdivision no longer required after a geometry move. The traversal of line-space also limits the amount of work required to update and solve the new hierarchical system after a move, by identifying the modified paths in the scene hierarchy. The implementation of our new algorithm allows interactive updates of illumination after object motion for scenes containing several thousand polygons, including global illumination effects. Finally, the line-space hierarchy traversal provides a natural control mechanism allowing the regulation of the tradeoff between image quality and frame rate.

Keywords: Global illumination, Dynamic environments, Hierarchical radiosity, Form-factors, Interactivity, Frame-rate control.

1   Introduction

The use of realistic global illumination is becoming more and more widespread. As a consequence, users demand more flexibility, and better interaction with lighting systems. Ideally, a user would like to be able to interact with a scene and interactively perceive at least some degree of global illumination effects. A major limitation of current systems is the inability to move or change geometry in a scene, with simultaneous update of global illumination effects. Applications such as virtual studios, tele-conferencing in virtual environments, driving simulators etc., all require interactive manipulation of the scene geometry, without loss of important illumination information.

Although significant advances have been made towards accelerating radiosity calculations for changing geometry [7, 4, 11], all previous approaches fail to provide interactive global illumination updates even for moderately complex scenes, and do not provide a way to control the quality/speed tradeoff for interactive display. The new solution we present uses the subdivision of line-space implied by the link structure of hierarchical radiosity to achieve efficient interactive radiosity updates for scenes of moderate complexity.

The goal of our approach is to provide a unified framework which will allow a user of a hierarchical radiosity system to move objects in a lighting simulation, and interactively perceive global illumination changes. We also provide a mechanism permitting the user to sacrifice quality for speed, but still maintain at least some of the important visual cues due to global illumination.

In any hierarchical radiosity system, and in particular a clustering-based approach, the elements of the scenes are linked together following the potential interactions of light between such pairs. These links induce a subdivision of the line-space of the scene, or more accurately the space of line-segments, following the flow of light between scene elements. We augment links with an explicit representation of all lines passing between two elements via a *shaft* [9]. In particular, when an object moves, we can efficiently identify the parts of the system which are modified, by hierarchically descending in this line-space. This traversal permits efficient cleanup of the mesh where subdivision is no longer needed because of geometry changes, and allows us to mark the paths in the hierarchy which are modified. As a consequence, fast resolution of the modified part of the system of equations is achieved. Finally, the line-space hierarchy provides a natural way to control the expense incurred at every frame. This is achieved by limiting the descent into line-space by the time available at each frame.

We present an implementation of these ideas which shows that, using the line-space hierarchy we can achieve interactive updates of illumination (2-3 frames per second) for scenes of moderate complexity (up to about 14,500 input polygons). This includes the treatment of scenes almost exclusively lit by secondary illumination.

2   Context and Previous Work

The fact that the movement of an object often causes limited changes to a global illumination solution became evident early on in graphics research, in particular for "radiosity" algorithms. Several algorithms have been proposed which deal specifically with changes to geometry, and their evolution follows closely the progress of radiosity solutions. In what follows we present a brief overview of these methods.

2.1   Progressive radiosity solutions

The initial "full-matrix" radiosity solution [8], led to the development of an algorithm which took advantage of coherence properties of the hemi-cube, used to calculate form-factors [3]. This solution suffered from all the limitations of full-matrix radiosity (including

[†]iMAGIS is a joint research project of CNRS/INRIA/UJF/INPG. Address: iMAGIS/GRAVIR, BP 53, F-38041 Grenoble Cedex 09 France. Email: {George.Drettakis|Francois.Sillion}@imag.fr

quadratic storage and lack of adaptive subdivision), and most notably was limited to predetermined trajectories. Despite these drawbacks, this algorithm is noteworthy in the insight that form-factor changes can be limited spatially, by means of a swept volume restricting the part of space affected by the move.

The advent of progressive refinement solutions led to the development of two similar approaches which took advantage of the "shooting" process of radiosity propagation [4, 7]. By treating all object movements as deletions and re-insertions in the scene, shadows were removed by re-shooting energy, and new shadows were correctly inserted where appropriate by shooting "negative energy". This approach achieved impressive update times for direct illumination, even though global updates remained very expensive. An improvement to these methods was developed by Müller et al. [11], who added an intelligent data structure maintaining shadow-lists accelerating potentially modified interactions between surfaces. The main drawback of all these approaches is due to the fact that they are based on progressive refinement, for which the global energy balance is hard to control. In addition these methods cannot achieve interactive update rates (several frames per second) for scenes of moderate size or larger.

2.2   Hierarchical radiosity solutions

Some of the limitations of progressive refinement solutions can be addressed in the context of hierarchical radiosity. An overall "snapshot" of the global energy balance is maintained in the link structure, and the corresponding hierarchy. When an object moves, a limited number of links, and thus a limited part of the hierarchy, are modified. This can be seens by examining the block form-factor matrices resulting from hierarchical subdivision. In Fig. 1(a) the chair has just moved to the right. The block form-factor matrix (collapsed up to a certain hierarchical level for display) is shown in Fig. 1(b), "warmer" colors representing larger values of form-factors. The matrix in Fig. 1(c) represents the difference in the matrices produced by the move. As we can see, few regions of the matrix change.

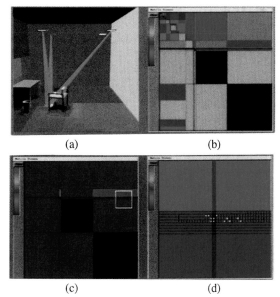

(a)   (b)

(c)   (d)

Figure 1: The chair in (a) has moved to the right. The block form-factor matrix is shown in (b), color coded (see text), before motion. In (c) we show the difference (dark blue = no change); (d) zoom of the modified matrix area, yellow blocks are the links shown in (a).

By zooming into a modified region (Fig. 1(d)), we realize that the changes are due to the moving shadow of the chair. In particular the region of the matrix selected in Fig. 1(d) corresponds to the element

shown in red in Fig. 1(a), and the yellow blocks are a collapsed representation of the links arriving at this element.

Two first solutions have been developed exploiting hierarchical radiosity for dynamic environments. Forsyth et al. [6] present the idea of "promoting" and "demoting" links based on a refinement criterion which moves links up and down in the hierarchy, depending on the position of the objects at each frame. This is similar to the idea of "ghost" links presented by Shaw [12]. A first approach to the problems incurred by changes in visibility was presented in Shaw's work, by introducing special "shadow" links connected to the source and containing blocker information. A final optimisation was presented by which a "motion volume" is built with the bounding planes of the two positions of the dynamic object; All links are then tested against this volume to determine if they may have changed or not.

2.3   Shortcomings of previous methods

The algorithms for hierarchical radiosity in dynamic environments described above achieve significant improvement over the progressive refinement approaches developed earlier. Nonetheless, interactive updates rates are not achievable using these methods, especially for complex scenes, and since they were developed using traditional hierarchical radiosity, the quadratic cost of initial linking presents an important obstacle to their practical use.

More importantly, all previous approaches lack a unified mechanism which can rapidly identify the part of the system modified and at the same time control the simulation quality/time tradeoff in a coherent manner. In what follows we show that the *line-space hierarchy*, exploited by accessing the links attached to the scene hierarchy, provides this functionality. We will show how the hierarchical traversal of line-space allows rapid identification of the parts of the system which change, provides an efficient mechanism to update the hierarchy, and finally allows fine control of the quality/speed tradeoff for dynamic environments.

2.4   Objectives: user interaction with the scene

We assume that any object in the scene can be chosen to be dynamic. The only restriction is that each potential dynamic object must be included in a cluster of its own. When the user selects a dynamic object, the corresponding cluster is attached to the root of the hierarchy.

Changing the dynamic object during the simulation is not too complicated, since we can identify the links which were affected by the previous and the new dynamic object. This can be performed efficiently by traversing line space as described later, updating the links and the corresponding visibility information. Since the dynamic object clusters are attached to the root, a change in the object chosen can be accompanied by a re-insertion into the cluster hierarchy.

Once the object is chosen, the user can freely interact with the object to change its position (for example by translation or rotation). At each frame, all that is required is the previous and current position of the dynamic object bounding box. What is required next is to identify the links of the system whose shaft cuts either of these bounding boxes.

3   Hierarchical Line-Space Traversal

To rapidly identify the necessary modifications of the global illumination system of equations, we need a data structure which will isolate the parts of space which are affected by the motion of an object. The *line-space hierarchy* we introduce is such a representation encoded using the traditional link structure of hierarchical radiosity.

3.1 Introduction to the Line-Space Hierarchy

In the original hierarchical radiosity algorithm [10], the scene, as well as subsequent subdivision, is represented as a hierarchy. In addition, when the clustering algorithm is used, the polygons of the scene are grouped together to form a complete hierarchical representation of the environment. We will refer to such an element as an H-element h_e (*Hierarchical* element [13]), be it a cluster or a surface element. This scene hierarchy is augmented by *link* information, which is used to represent radiant exchanges between two H-elements of this hierarchy. A typical hierarchical solution process proceeds by *refining* the links: when the link is considered to insufficiently or incorrectly represent the light transfer, the element is subdivided and sub-links are created [10, 15]. The decision to subdivide is based on a "subdivision criterion" which may be based on error-estimation or magnitude of energy transfer across a link. We will refer to a "refiner", which is the module responsible for the refinement operation.

We represent the set of light paths in a hierarchical manner by augmenting the link structure. The shaft shown for example in Fig. 2(a) represents the entire set of lines which pass between the two elements. More precisely, this is the set of *line segments* rather than infinite lines. For simplicity however, we will use the term *line-space hierarchy* throughout this paper. In this respect, we build a coarse approximation to structures which encode visibility information of maximal free segments such as the visibility complex [5].

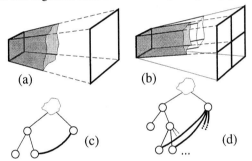

Figure 2: We show here a line space hierarchy: (a) the original link l^p (shown as a shaft) is subdivided, resulting in four sub-links (b), which are the line-space children of l^p. P-links (c) and the subsequent children links (d) are embedded in the H-element hierarchy.

When a link is subdivided, the four resulting links can be considered as children of the original link, Fig. 2(b). To store this hierarchy, subdivided links are not discarded, and are stored as *passive links* or *p-links* with the H-elements. Thus our new link hierarchy is actually *embedded* in the H-element hierarchy itself. For example, the thick black line in Fig. 2(c) corresponds to a (subdivided) p-link, and the four thick lines in Fig. 2(d) to the four resulting links. These ideas are related to the approach developed by Teller and Hanrahan [17], where a similar link hierarchy was used to incrementally maintain blocker lists, as well as the "ghost-link" idea [12] or link "demotion/promotion" approach [6].

3.2 Data structures

To explicitly work in line-space, we need a representation of the set of lines between surfaces. One possibility would be the approach using Plücker coordinates as was presented by Teller [16], or the intercepts of lines on two parallel planes [1]. Another approach would be that of ray-classification [2].

We have preferred to use the *shaft* structure [9] for its simplicity, and because it is well defined and easy to manipulate for the case when one endpoint of a link is a bounding box. In addition the shaft structure permits efficient intersection tests with bounding

boxes, which is an operation central to the algorithms presented below. Since our algorithm operates in the context of clustering radiosity, this allows the use of the same structure for links between any combination of cluster and surface element. Another interesting aspect of the shaft representation is that shafts are truncated, and thus operate on line *segments*, as opposed to infinite lines.

The line-space hierarchy is built during the traditional refinement process of clustering hierarchical radiosity. The list of links arriving at a H-element is stored on the element itself, as well as all the p-links (see Figs. 2 and 3) Both active links and p-links are augmented with the shaft corresponding to the part of line-space they respectively cover.

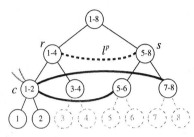

Figure 3: Numbering of the H-element hierarchy into index ranges.

One final component is required to allow efficient traversal the line-space hierarchy. Consider a given passive link $l^p_{s \to r}$, stored at H-element r and emanating from H-element s. Since this p-link has been subdivided, it is possible that the element s has been subdivided also. In addition, what originally was the p-link $s \to r$ is now a set of links at possibly different levels of the hierarchy, emanating from children of s, also at different levels. Links originating from other sources may also co-exist on the element r and its children. To be able to quickly identify the links which are children of $l^p_{s \to r}$, we need to be able to tell if a given link originates from an H-element which is a child of s. To avoid repeated traversals of the hierarchy which become overwhelmingly expensive, we apply a numbering scheme of all hierarchical elements. In particular, we traverse the entire hierarchy once at the beginning of the lighting simulation process, and assign an interval to each node, corresponding to the largest possible number of children which can be created. This number can be calculated based on the value of the *area threshold* A_ϵ [10], which limits the size of the smallest surface. To see this, consider the partially subdivided hierarchy shown in Fig. 3, where subdivided nodes are represented with solid lines. The index ranges assigned to each node correspond to the maximum subdivision which can possibly be incurred, shown as the complete tree, where currently unsubdivided nodes are shown with dashed lines.

3.3 Traversing Line-Space

Consider that we are situated on a given H-element h_e of the hierarchy and we wish to traverse the part of line space related to a p-link arriving at h_e. To effect the line-space descent, we need to visit exclusively the children links of the passive link considered. Each passive link l^p is connected to a source node s, which has a corresponding index range following the numbering scheme elaborated above. To visit the line-space children of l^p, we descend to each H-element child c of the current node h_e, and examine only those passive links originating from s or s's children, arriving at c. These are the links attached to a node with an index within the interval of the index of s.

For example, in Fig. 3, we are at receiver node r. P-link l^p is the thick dashed line. When descending to its line-space children, we visit for example H-element c. The only links we consider however are those emanating from H-element in the range $[5 - 8]$, i.e., children of the original H-element s, linked by l^p. This procedure is summarized in Fig. 4.

```
traverseLineSpace(H-element he, IndexRange ind)
{
    for each p-link l^p of he
        // find the "source" node q
        H-element q = l^p →LinkedNode()
        if( ind contains q→IndexRange() )
            for each child c of he
                // limit traversal to the index of q
                traverseLineSpace( c, q→Index )
}
```

Figure 4: Hierarchical Line Space Traversal

3.4 Efficient illumination update

To perform an update we first need to find the links affected by object motion. We consider as potentially changed the links whose *shafts* are touched by the bounding box of the *dynamic object* (i.e., the object which moves) before or after the move. After motion, the subdivision of parts of the hierarchy (for example due to shadow motion) may no longer be needed. We need to identify these parts of the hierarchy and perform the cleanup.

For the links which have been thus identified, new form-factor values need to be computed, since visibility may have changed with respect to the dynamic object. We call this operation *link update*.

To perform form-factor update efficiently, we maintain two-part occlusion information with each link: occlusion with respect to the dynamic object, and occlusion with respect to the rest of the scene. Thus at each frame, visibility is checked only with respect to the dynamic object. This information must of course be updated when we change dynamic objects; a line traversal to find the sub-spaces affected by the old and new object suffices to achieve this. Also, when a new link is created, its visibility with the rest of the scene is computed (but not for reinstated p-links).

After link update, it may be the case that certain links have to be refined, in particular when a visibility change occurs. The new values of the radiosity need to be computed and gathered on the links. The hierarchical system must then be updated to reflect the new position of the moving object. Finally the new system must be solved. The line-space hierarchy provides the necessary mechanism to efficiently perform all of the above steps. We thus summarize our new approach as follows:

1. Find the links potentially changed by traversing line-space and remove subdivision unnecessary due to geometry change;

2. Update the modified links and refine where necessary;

3. Solve the hierarchical system efficiently.

Step (1) occurs during the line-space traversal, resulting in the information necessary to perform steps (2) and (3).

4 Rapid Identification of Modified Links and Subdivision Cleanup

We next show how line-space traversal can be used to rapidly identify the links which have potentially changed. This traversal allows simultaneous removal of subdivision which is no longer required due to the new position of the moving object.

4.1 Finding the modified links efficiently

To find the modified links, the line-space traversal can be thought of as "zooming-in" to the region of space which has changed. The traversal algorithm starts at the root of the hierarchical elements (a cluster whose extent is the bounding volume of the scene), and descends recursively. At a given hierarchical node h_e, we visit all its

passive links. For each such p-link l^p, we determine whether its corresponding line-space (represented by the shaft), was affected by the object motion. This is performed by testing the link shaft against the previous and current positions of the dynamic object. If the link was affected, we will potentially descend into its corresponding line-space. Given the new position of the dynamic object, we first test whether passive link l^p would no longer satisfy the subdivision criteria; this could occur for example if the p-link was partially occluded by the previous position of the dynamic object, but is completely unoccluded in the new position. If this is the case, the link can be reinstated as active, and the descent into the line-space hierarchy is stopped. If, on the other hand, the passive link l^p is maintained, the line-space children of l^p are visited, and the same process is applied recursively.

Finally, when the traversal of the passive links of h_e is complete, we examine all of the active links corresponding to the current part of line space (links originating from s or s's children) to determine if they are affected by the object motion. If this is the case, i.e., the active link shaft cuts the dynamic object before or after the move, it is added to a list of candidates for update and potential refinement. An example of a candidate list is shown in Fig. 5(b); notice that few of the numerous links describing energy exchanges in the left room or with the left wall of the right-hand office appear in this list.

4.2 Cleanup of unnecessary subdivision

The traversal described above also provides the benefit of cleaning up unneeded refinement in the same step as the determination of the links which need to be updated. In particular when we have decided that a p-link l^p (linked to H-element s) on H-element h_e does not merit refinement due to the new position of the dynamic object, we can remove the entire set of links and p-links which are (line-space) children of l^p. This is performed by descending to the children of H-element h_e and removing all passive and active links linked to s and its children. After this removal, if there are no links remaining on any of the children of h_e (or its intermediate nodes), the subdivision is cleaned up. A similar approach to subdivision cleanup presented in [12] required a special pass, and multiple hierarchy passes to mark attached sources and their children.

The line space traversal is summarized in Fig. 6. In this algorithm, notice that when a potential change is found (either for a p-link re-installation or the required update of an link), the corresponding H-element is marked changed. For example, the H-elements marked "changed" are shown in red in Fig. 5(c). This will be used in what follows to limit the system solution at each frame. In addition, this approach is particularly efficient in the context of a clustering algorithm, since the number of links is limited.

5 Fast System Solution By Hierarchy Pruning

The line-space traversal algorithm described above results in fast identification of the links which need to be refined and at the same time allows the un-refinement of unnecessary subdivision. Once this step has been performed, we need to update the links which are changed, and potentially refine certain links. This additional refinement will be required for example around new shadow boundaries. Once these steps are complete, we have a complete hierarchical system which is ready to be resolved. In hierarchical radiosity [10, 15], system resolution is performed by performing complete sweeps of the hierarchy: *Gather* and *Push-Pull*. In the context of clustering [13], irradiance is gathered through the links onto the H-elements; this irradiance is subsequently pushed down the hierarchy. Finally, the radiosity values are computed at the leaves, and pulled up the hierarchy to provide the new solution.

Such an approach was used for a dynamic solution in [12] for example. For large scenes containing thousands of input polygons,

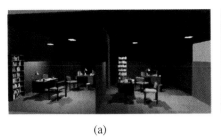  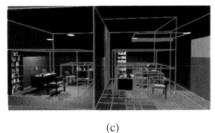

(a) (b) (c)

Figure 5: This example contains 14,572 input polygons. The chair in the right-hand room moves to the right (a) - (b). The average update time is approximately .3 s. In (b) we show the links modified and in (c) the parts of the hierarchy affected by the move and marked "changed" by the line-space traversal. Note how the several thousand surfaces of the left-hand room are unaffected.

```
findModifiedLinks(H-element he, IndexRange ind)
{
    for each p-link pl of he {
        H-element q = pl→LinkedNode()   // "source" node
        if( ind contains q→IndexRange()
            and affectedByMotion(pl→Shaft()) {
            if( wouldBeRefined( pl ) ) {
                for each child c of he
                    // limit traversal to the index of q
                    findModifiedLinks( c, q→IndexRange() )
                    if a child changed
                        he→setChanged()
            }
            else
                reInstateLink( pl )
                he→setChanged()
        }
    }
    // if any links of he are modified they are added
    // to the list of links to refine, and he is marked changed
    checkAddLinks( he )
}
```

Figure 6: Efficient Modified Link Identification

these multiple sweeps of the hierarchy result in an unacceptable overhead in an interactive context. Furthermore, such complete hierarchy traversal is unnecessary: only a small number of elements has actually been changed.

In what follows, we show that we can perform a *Gather* exclusively for links which have been affected by object motion, during link update. The line-traversal algorithm returns a list of links potentially changed. The form-factors for these links are recomputed to reflect the new position of the dynamic object. This update operation may result in the need for certain links to be refined.

Once the refinement is complete, the global solution can be efficiently performed. In particular the marking of the changed paths performed during line-space traversal allows us to limit the *Push-Pull* to the subsections of the hierarchy which have been modified, for one bounce of illumination. Subsequent bounces may potentially be required but can also be treated efficiently.

There is one essential assumption for the following discussion: we assume that before any motion is performed, the system has run to convergence. We define a solution as converged when no more links can be refined for the given error threshold, and the energy balance has been computed using all links.

5.1 Link update and in-place *Gather*

Once a link has been identified by the line-space traversal algorithm as potentially changed, we need to update its form-factor value. There are two possibilities: either the link has changed little and as a consequence it will not be refined or the link has changed in a way which requires further subdivision.

In the first case we need to modify the irradiance of the receiving patch by the difference of the previous irradiance and the current irradiance. For source s and receiver r, B_s the radiosity of H-element s, F^k the form-factor before the move and F^{k+1} the form-factor after the move, this difference is simply:

$$I_{diff} = B_s \left(F^{k+1} - F^k \right) \tag{1}$$

For clusters, we also need to distribute the irradiance down to the cluster contents.

When refinement occurs, we need to remove the irradiance which arrived at the receiving node from the previous transfer on the link. After subdivision, the new irradiance will be transferred when the sub-links are established. For element r, the irradiance I_r becomes:

$$I_r^{k+1} = I_r^k - F^k B_s \tag{2}$$

After subdivision, the new links will be established at a different level in the hierarchy, and we then simply add in the new irradiance. We thus avoid the *Gather* sweep of the hierarchy.

5.2 Non-recursive refinement for modified links

At each frame, certain links will be identified as requiring refinement. This typically occurs when the dynamic object touches a link shaft for the first time. Previous hierarchical radiosity (e.g., [10]) performed recursive refinement of links. In such an approach, when a link is refined, we immediately attempt to refine its children and so on recursively until subdivision is no longer possible given current subdivision criteria.

For the requirements of controlling the solution, we need to achieve two goals: (a) refine the most important links first and (b) potentially truncate the refinement process if we wish to limit the amount of time spent for a frame. The latter point becomes essential for the time/quality control algorithm presented in Section 6.1.

To achieve this, when refining a link, the resulting refined sub-links are added to a heap. The refiner then extracts the link with the highest potential power transfer for refinement, thus achieving goal (a). The refiner keeps track of the number of links it still needs to refine n_l, and the number n_r of links already refined. When the sum of n_l and n_r exceed the limit fixed by the subdivision process, the refinement is terminated. The n_l form-factors of the remaining links are then updated to correspond to the new position of the dynamic object, and established at the given level without being refined.

5.3 Global solution

Once the line-space traversal and the refinement are complete, we have a new hierarchy for which the irradiance at each node corresponds to the new position of the object. In addition, we have marked as "changed" all the elements in the hierarchy which have been modified, as well as all the paths in the hierarchy leading to these elements. The only remaining step is the *Push-Pull* process of the hierarchical solution which will result in the correct hierarchical representation of radiosity at every level of the hierarchy.

As mentioned earlier, we exploit the information of the paths and elements marked "changed", to accelerate the *Push-Pull* since it will only be performed on a small part of the hierarchy.

5.3.1   Single Bounce

We modify the *Push-Pull* procedure to visit only the parts of the hierarchy which are modified. At a given node, we check if it is marked "changed": if it is we proceed as normal, descending to the children, and if not we use the radiosity already calculated at this level instead of continuing the hierarchy descent. This procedure is summarized in the pseudo-code of Fig. 7.

```
Spectrum partialPushPull(Helement* he, Spectrum IrradDown)
{
    Spectrum RadUp
    if he→changed() { // normal PushPull
        if ( he→isLeaf() )
            RadUp = ComputeLeafRad
        else foreach child c of he
            RadUp += partialPushPull(c, IrradDown + he→Irrad())
    }
    else // use previous values
        RadUp = he→Radiosity()
    he→Radiosity = RadUp
    return RadUp
}
```

Figure 7: Partial Push-Pull

This update algorithm will result in a system which is updated to reflect the new position of the dynamic object. This new state includes changes to all links, for direct *and* indirect illumination. In most cases, this is largely sufficient, since it represents a system which in many cases has converged. This solution always provides updated shadows due to primary illumination, as well as for some shadows due to indirect illumination.

5.3.2   Subsequent bounces of illumination

It may be the case however that the system has changed sufficiently so that subsequent iterations are needed to achieve convergence. Consider the example of a dark room with a door (initially closed) opening to a bright corridor (see Fig. 10). When opening the door, some direct light will flow into the room due to links which will be refined. If the previous algorithm were to be used as described above, certain light transfers would not occur (e.g., from the floor to the ceiling), since the radiosity values in the hierarchy would not be modified until after the call to *partialPushPull*.

To determine the modified links, we perform a partial traversal of the hierarchy, visiting only the elements marked "changed" by the line-space traversal. At each H-element h_e, the H-elements it is linked to are stored, that is the H-elements for which h_e acts as a "source." In addition, we store the old value of radiosity, corresponding to the previous dynamic object position. Thus at every H-element changed by the first bounce, we can calculate the difference in irradiance, and perform an in-place gather to the receiving node as described above. Some links may need to be refined, and as such are inserted into the heap. Subsequent refinement is then performed, followed by a new partial push pull. Care must be taken to re-initialize the "changed" markings of every node, as well as the old value of radiosity after each iteration. In particular, H-elements updated by the difference in irradiance are marked as "changed" as well as their parents and children. The difference in global effects is generally limited, and thus the extents of these updates is not very large, even for cases where global illumination effects are very important (e.g., Fig. 10).

6   Controlling Simulation Time and Rendering Quality

The solution presented above allows rapid updates for scene of moderate complexity. Nonetheless, the update rate can be too slow for certain applications where 1 or 2 frames per second is simply not acceptable. In addition, for very complex scenes, we need to be able to provide the user with the choice of "give me N frames per second, with the best possible quality."

The limitation of the algorithm presented above is that there is no control on the number of links that need to be updated. Thus, if the dynamic object moves into a part of space which contains a large number of links, the line-space traversal will create a large candidate list. A large amount of time will thus be required to update the form-factors of these links, and to potentially refine some of them.

To avoid this problem we present an algorithm that updates as much of the modified link hierarchy as possible, in the sense of a user-defined time limit, and unrefines the rest. This can be performed naturally with the aid of the line-space hierarchy, and is very much in the spirit of the original hierarchical radiosity approach.

6.1   Controlled update algorithm

To achieve a controlled update time the user first selects a target frame rate. The system then calculates the number of link updates that it can perform in a given frame. Thus we consider as our "time" or cost unit, the time required for a link update.

To achieve the control of the number of link updates, and adapt the hierarchy to the desired frame rate, we first calculate the number of child links and p-links for each p-link in the hierarchy. This is performed while traversing line-space to find modified links, as presented above in Fig. 4, and "pulling" the number of links resulting from the subdivision of each p-link.

To perform the link update, we traverse line-space for a second time. During this sweep, we only traverse the parts of the hierarchy actually modified.

The update control algorithm is very similar to the line space traversal. The important difference is that we always update the links of the current node *first*. We are thus assured that the state of the hierarchy above the current node h_e is correctly up to date. This is an essential requirement, since we can not otherwise truncate the update without incurring inconsistencies. The time spent updating links of this node is subtracted from the remaining time.

We then compute the minimum amount of work required if we are to descend in line-space. This is equal to the total of all line-space children active and passive links arriving at the children of h_e. If this number is larger than the remaining "time", we cannot guarantee that we will be able to update the remaining sub-links in the allotted time. In this case, we reinstate the appropriate p-links of h_e and cleanup underlying links (and remove subdivision if necessary). We then stop the descent.

If we can still descend, we continue the traversal of line-space. We assign to each child the fraction of time calculated as follows. We sum the total number n_{cl} of children links stored with each p-link of h_e, in the current index range. The fraction assigned to each child c of h_e is the number of active sub links of p_l arriving at c plus the number of active sub links below c, also stored during the push-pull of line-space. This can be seen as a local and adaptive form of progressive multi-gridding [14].

A very important feature of this controlled update strategy is that no matter how much time is allocated for the update, a consistent solution is computed. This is due to the fact that the set of links always completely covers the entire line space. The availability of a *complete* hierarchy is a benefit of using hierarchical clusters. In other words, the algorithm ensures that all possible energy transfers are accounted for, although they may be included in links very high

```
controlledUpdate(Helement he, IndexRange ind, int remainingCost )
{
    updateLinks(he)
    remainingCost = remainingCost− links updated
    plinkCost = number of children p-links and links in ind range
    if pLinkCost ≤ remainingCost {
        for each p-link lᵖ of he
            H-element q = lᵖ →LinkedNode()  // "source" node
            if ind contains q →IndexRange()
                for each child c of he with c →changed()
                    cost = fraction of child links of lᵖ in c
                    controlledUpdate( c, q →IndexRange(), cost )
    }
    else
        update and reinstate all p-links of he in ind range
}
```

Figure 8: Controlled Update Algorithm

up the hierarchy (probably as a significant approximation, inducing some error). This consistency comes in contrast to all previous approaches to incremental updates of radiosity solutions, and is an important asset for many practical applications.

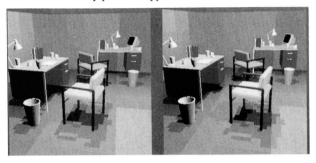

(a)   (b)

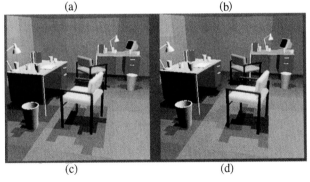

(c)   (d)

Figure 9: The chair is the dynamic object, moving to the right, with no additional bounces. Update rates (a)-(b) average .5s. In (c) and (d) the same motion is shown with time/quality tradeoff, limited to 330 link updates per frame. The average update takes .3s.

6.2 Maintaining consistent quality

The controlled line-space descent presented above performs well for many configurations. Nonetheless, due to the quadtree nature of the subdivision on surfaces, it is often the case that new refinement does not occur as desired. In particular we may notice that subdivision is not propagated across quadtree edges.

To counter this problem, we influence link refinement. Consider a p-link inserted into the heap for refinement because the dynamic object cuts its shaft, and that there was no interaction in the position at the previous frame. In this case, we increase the key used to sort elements in the heap, making refinement of this link more probable.

7 Implementation and Results

We have implemented the new algorithms on a clustering hierarchical radiosity algorithm following [13]. The modules for line-space traversal and all modified refinement routines required around 5000 additional lines of C++. All test results are reported on an Indigo 2 Impact, with an R4400 processor at 200MHz.

7.1 Basic algorithm

The first example is a single scene containing 5,405 polygons shown in Fig. 9, with four light sources. For this scene, we show one chair moving to the right, which is an object containing 870 polygons. The update rates are close to 0.5 seconds per frame, which can be satisfactory in many cases. The breakdown of the computation time for the first move for example is: 0.08 s. for line-space traversal, 0.40 s. for link update/refinement and 0.05 s. for partial push-pull.

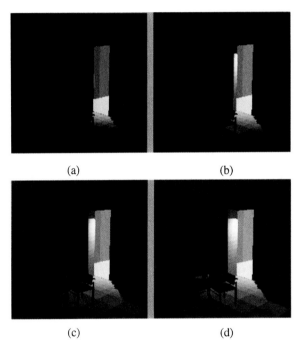

(a)   (b)

(c)   (d)

Figure 10: In this example, a door opens onto a dark room (5,295 polygons). Additional bounces are performed, and global illumination is updated. Updates takes (a)-(b): 3.20 s.; (b)-(c): 3.47 s.; (c)-(d): 2.52 s.

The second example is shown in Fig. 10, where the additional iterations are required. Initially the room is completely black. While the door is gradually opened, global illumination is rapidly updated. We see that a reasonable representation of global illumination is provided with update rates of around 3 seconds per frame. For the second update for example, the single bounce took a total of 2.15 seconds and the subsequent two bounces 0.55 and 0.5 seconds each.

The third example shows that we can handle complex geometry without significant degradation in speed. In Fig. 5, we have a scene with 14,572 input polygons, with the chair in the right-hand room moving to the right. The update takes around 0.6s. per frame, but sometimes improves to 0.2s per frame (5 fps) when the chair traverses "sparse" regions of line-space (i.e. with few links).

7.2 Time/quality tradeoff

The controlled update algorithm was tested on the scene used previously to demonstrate the basic approach. In Fig. 9(c) and (d) we present the output of the algorithm for a selected value of 330 link updates per frame, which results in an average update rate of approximately .3 seconds/frame. The shadows are of lower quality compared to the image shown in Fig. 9, but are still definitely usable.

7.3 Higher quality movement

Our approach is also well adapted if the user requires higher quality, and is prepared to wait longer (several seconds). An example is shown in Fig. 11, where an update takes about 4 s., but we see that the quality of shadows is improved compared to Fig. 9. To achieve this, we simply decrease the ϵ threshold for BF refinement [10].

8 Conclusions and Future Work

We have presented a new framework for the efficient calculation of incremental changes of global illumination using hierarchical radiosity. This set of algorithms allows interactive updates of the lighting solutions in scenes with moving geometry. The heart of our approach is the introduction of a *line-space* hierarchy associated with the links between scene elements. This hierarchy is distinct from, but related to, the hierarchy of surfaces and clusters in the scene, and can be traversed efficiently using the implicit correspondence between the two hierarchies. In terms of data structures, the main addition with respect to hierarchical radiosity is the introduction of shaft structures representing a portion of line segment space associated to each link.

The line-space traversal algorithm is beneficial in many respects. First, it allows the fast identification of the links that should be modified in response to object motion. These links are collected to accelerate later processing. In addition, it permits simultaneous cleanup of object subdivision that has become unnecessary due to visibility changes induced by object motion. The line-space traversal marks the modified parts of the hierarchy, resulting in an accelerated solution of the modified system.

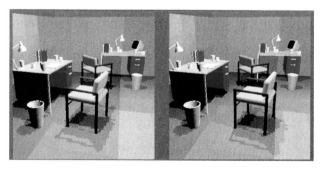

Figure 11: Higher-quality solution, 4 s. per frame on average.

The set of links marked during line-space traversal embodies all of the form factor changes in the scene, although at a hierarchical level which may not be sufficiently detailed for the desired accuracy. Hierarchical refinement of these links is carried out in a non-recursive manner, using a set of refinement criteria to resolve fine radiosity variations and shadow details. The marking mechanism results in a very fast solution of the updated system of equations.

Finally, the line-space hierarchy also provides a natural mechanism to control the time/quality tradeoff for incremental updates, by constantly monitoring the expected cost of refinement operations and ensuring that the refinement budget is not exceeded. The nature of the refinement algorithm ensures that the solution is always consistent in that it takes into account all possible energy transfers in the scene, although possibly at high hierarchical levels.

Future work includes the design of improved quality control mechanisms. The very notion of solution quality is difficult to define. For instance, it is well accepted that the presence of shadows for moving objects is an important visual cue for understanding object location and motion, but these shadows need not necessarily be very precise. Recent work on accelerated approximate shadow calculations using the hierarchy of clusters and feature-based error metrics may be applicable to dynamic updates [14].

Finally, more involved visibility structures, which provide detailed line-space information, such as the Visibility Complex [5], will probably be very useful for dynamic updates of illumination.

Acknowledgements

Thanks to Frédo Durand, Mathieu Desbrun and Rachel Orti for crucial help.

References

[1] N. Amenta. Finding a line transversal of axial objects in three dimensions. In *Proc. 3rd ACM-SIAM Sympos. Discrete Algorithms*, pages 66–71, 1992.

[2] James Arvo and David Kirk. Fast ray tracing by classification. *Computer Graphics*, 21(4):55–64, July 1987. Proceedings SIGGRAPH '87 in Anaheim.

[3] Daniel R. Baum, John R. Wallace, Michael F. Cohen, and Donald P. Greenberg. The back-buffer algorithm : an extension of the radiosity method to dynamic environments. *The Visual Computer*, 2:298–306, 1986.

[4] Shenchang Eric Chen. Incremental radiosity: An extension of progressive radiosity to an interactive image synthesis system. *Computer Graphics*, 24(4):135–144, August 1990. Proceedings SIGGRAPH '90 in Dallas.

[5] Frédo Durand, George Drettakis, and Claude Puech. The 3d visibility complex, a new approach to the problems of accurate visibility. In X. Pueyo and P. Shroeder, editors, *Rendering Techniques '96*, pages 245–257. Springer Verlag, June 1996. Proc. 7th EG Workshop on Rendering in Porto.

[6] David Forsyth, Chien Yang, and Kim Teo. Efficient radiosity in dynamic environments. In Sakas et al., editor, *Photorealistic Rendering Techniques*, Darmstadt, D, June 1994. Springer Verlag. Proc. 5th EG Workshop on Rendering.

[7] David W. George, François Sillion, and Donald P. Greenberg. Radiosity redistribution for dynamic environments. *IEEE Computer Graphics and Applications*, 10(4), July 1990.

[8] Cindy M. Goral, Kenneth E. Torrance, Donald P. Greenberg, and Bennett Battaile. Modeling the interaction of light between diffuse surfaces. *Computer Graphics*, 18(3):213–222, July 1984. Proc. SIGGRAPH '84 in Minneapolis.

[9] Eric A. Haines. Shaft culling for efficient ray-traced radiosity. In Brunet and Jansen, editors, *Photorealistic Rendering in Comp. Graphics*, pages 122–138. Springer Verlag, 1993. Proc. 2nd EG Workshop on Rendering (Barcelona, 1991).

[10] Pat Hanrahan, David Saltzman, and Larry Aupperle. A rapid hierarchical radiosity algorithm. *Computer Graphics*, 25(4):197–206, August 1991. SIGGRAPH '91 Las Vegas.

[11] Stefan Müller and Frank Schöffel. Fast radiosity repropagation for interactive virtual environments using a shadow-form-factor-list. In Sakas et al., editor, *Photorealistic Rendering Techniques*, Darmstadt, D, June 1994. Springer Verlag. Proc. 5th EG Workshop on Rendering.

[12] Erin Shaw. Hierarchical radiosity for dynamic environments. Master's thesis, Cornell University, Ithaca, NY, August 1994.

[13] François Sillion. A unified hierarchical algorithm for global illumination with scattering volumes and object clusters. *IEEE Trans. on Vis. and Comp. Graphics*, 1(3), September 1995.

[14] François Sillion and George Drettakis. Feature-Based Control of Visibility Error: A Multiresolution Clustering Algorithm for Global Illumination. In Robert Cook, editor, *SIGGRAPH 95 Conference Proceedings*, Annual Conference Series, pages 145–152. ACM SIGGRAPH, August 1995.

[15] Brian E. Smits, James R. Arvo, and David H. Salesin. An importance-driven radiosity algorithm. *Computer Graphics*, 26(4):273–282, July 1992. Proc. SIGGRAPH '92 in Chicago.

[16] Seth J. Teller. Computing the antipenumbra of an area light source. *Computer Graphics*, 26(4):139–148, July 1992. Proc. SIGGRAPH '92 in Chicago.

[17] Seth J. Teller and Patrick M. Hanrahan. Global visibility algorithms for illumination computations. In J. Kajiya, editor, *SIGGRAPH 93 Conf. Proc. (Anaheim)*, Annual Conf. Series, pages 239–246. ACM SIGGRAPH, August 1993.

Metropolis Light Transport

Eric Veach   *Leonidas J. Guibas*

Computer Science Department
Stanford University

Abstract

We present a new Monte Carlo method for solving the light transport problem, inspired by the Metropolis sampling method in computational physics. To render an image, we generate a sequence of light transport paths by randomly mutating a single current path (e.g. adding a new vertex to the path). Each mutation is accepted or rejected with a carefully chosen probability, to ensure that paths are sampled according to the contribution they make to the ideal image. We then estimate this image by sampling many paths, and recording their locations on the image plane.

Our algorithm is unbiased, handles general geometric and scattering models, uses little storage, and can be orders of magnitude more efficient than previous unbiased approaches. It performs especially well on problems that are usually considered difficult, e.g. those involving bright indirect light, small geometric holes, or glossy surfaces. Furthermore, it is competitive with previous unbiased algorithms even for relatively simple scenes.

The key advantage of the Metropolis approach is that the path space is explored locally, by favoring mutations that make small changes to the current path. This has several consequences. First, the average cost per sample is small (typically only one or two rays). Second, once an important path is found, the nearby paths are explored as well, thus amortizing the expense of finding such paths over many samples. Third, the mutation set is easily extended. By constructing mutations that preserve certain properties of the path (e.g. which light source is used) while changing others, we can exploit various kinds of coherence in the scene. It is often possible to handle difficult lighting problems efficiently by designing a specialized mutation in this way.

CR Categories: I.3.7 [Computer Graphics]: Three-Dimensional Graphics and Realism; I.3.3 [Computer Graphics]: Picture/Image Generation; G.1.9 [Numerical Analysis]: Integral Equations—Fredholm equations.

Keywords: global illumination, lighting simulation, radiative heat transfer, physically-based rendering, Monte Carlo integration, variance reduction, Metropolis-Hastings algorithm, Markov Chain Monte Carlo (MCMC) methods

E-mail: ericv@cs.stanford.edu, guibas@cs.stanford.edu

1   Introduction

There has been a great deal of work in graphics on solving the light transport problem efficiently. However, current methods are optimized for a fairly narrow class of input scenes. For example, many algorithms require a huge increase in computer resources when there is bright indirect lighting, or when most surfaces are non-diffuse reflectors. For light transport algorithms to be widely used, it is important to find techniques that are less fragile. Rendering algorithms must run within acceptable time bounds on real models, yielding images that are physically plausible and visually pleasing. They must support complex geometry, materials, and illumination — these are all essential components of real-life environments.

Monte Carlo methods are an attractive starting point in the search for such algorithms, because of their generality and simplicity. Especially appealing are unbiased algorithms, i.e. those that compute the correct answer on the average. For these algorithms, any error in the solution is guaranteed to show up as random variations among the samples (e.g., as image noise). This error can be estimated by simply computing the sample variance.

On the other hand, many methods used in graphics are biased. To make any claims about the correctness of the results of these algorithms, we must bound the amount of bias. In general this is very difficult to do; it cannot be estimated by simply drawing a few more samples. Biased algorithms may produce results that are not noisy, but are nevertheless incorrect. This error is often noticeable visually, in the form of discontinuities, excessive blurring, or objectionable surface shading.

In graphics, the first unbiased Monte Carlo light transport algorithm was proposed by Kajiya [10], building on earlier work by Cook et al. [4] and Whitted [26]. Since then many refinements have been suggested (e.g. see [1]). Often these improvements have been adapted from the neutron transport and radiative heat transfer literatures, which have a long history of solving similar problems [22].

However, it is surprisingly difficult to design light transport algorithms that are general, efficient, and artifact-free.[1] From a Monte Carlo viewpoint, such an algorithm must efficiently sample the transport paths from the light sources to the lens. The problem is that for some environments, most paths do not contribute significantly to the image, e.g. because they strike surfaces with low reflectivity, or go through solid objects. For example, imagine a brightly lit room next to a dark room containing the camera, with a door slightly ajar between them. Naive path tracing will be very inefficient, because it will have difficulty generating paths that

---

[1] In this regard, certain ray-tracing problems have been shown to be *undecidable*, i.e. they cannot be solved on a Turing machine [19]. We can expect that any light transport algorithm will perform very badly as the geometry and materials of the input scene approach a provably difficult configuration.

go through the doorway. Similar problems occur when there are glossy surfaces, caustics, strong indirect lighting, etc.

Several techniques have been proposed to sample these difficult paths more efficiently. One is *bidirectional path tracing*, developed independently by Lafortune and Willems [12, 13], and Veach and Guibas [24, 25]. These methods generate one subpath starting at a light source and another starting at the lens, then they consider all the paths obtained by joining every prefix of one subpath to every suffix of the other. This leads to a family of different importance sampling techniques for paths, which are then combined to minimize variance [25]. This can be an effective solution for certain kinds of indirect lighting problems.

Another idea is to build an approximate representation of the radiance in a scene, which is then used to modify the directional sampling of the basic path tracing algorithm. This can be done with a particle tracing prepass [9], or by adaptively recording the radiance information in a spatial subdivision [14]. Moderate variance reductions have been reported (50% to 70%), but there are several problems, including inadequate directional resolution to handle concentrated indirect lighting, and substantial space requirements. Similar ideas have been applied to particle tracing [17, 5].

We propose a new algorithm for importance sampling the space of paths, which we call *Metropolis light transport* (MLT). The algorithm samples paths according to the contribution they make to the ideal image, by means of a random walk through path space. In Section 2, we give a high-level overview of MLT, then we describe its components in detail. Section 3 summarizes the classical Metropolis sampling algorithm, as developed in computational physics. Section 4 describes the path integral formulation of light transport, upon which our methods are based. Section 5 shows how to combine these two ideas to yield an effective light transport algorithm. Results are presented in Section 6, followed by conclusions and suggested extensions in Section 7. To our knowledge, this is the first application of the Metropolis method to transport problems of any kind.

2 Overview of the MLT algorithm

To make an image, we sample the paths from the light sources to the lens. Each path $\bar{x}$ is a sequence $\mathbf{x}_0 \mathbf{x}_1 \ldots \mathbf{x}_k$ of points on the scene surfaces, where $k \geq 1$ is the length of the path (the number of edges). The numbering of the vertices along the path follows the direction of light flow.

We will show how to define a function f on paths, together with a measure μ, such that $\int_D f(\bar{x}) \, d\mu(\bar{x})$ represents the power (flux) that flows from the light sources to the image plane along a set of paths D. We call f the *image contribution function*, since $f(\bar{x})$ is proportional to the contribution made to the image by light flowing along $\bar{x}$.

Our overall strategy is to sample paths with probability proportional to f, and record the distribution of paths over the image plane. To do this, we generate a sequence of paths $\bar{X}_0, \bar{X}_1, \ldots, \bar{X}_N$, where each $\bar{X}_i$ is obtained by a random mutation to the path $\bar{X}_{i-1}$. The mutations can have almost any desired form, and typically involve adding, deleting, or replacing a small number of vertices on the current path.

However, each mutation has a chance of being rejected, depending on the relative contributions of the old and new paths. For example, if the new path passes through a wall, the mutation will be rejected (by setting $\bar{X}_i = \bar{X}_{i-1}$). The Metropolis framework gives a recipe for determining the acceptance probability for each mutation, such that in the limit

the sampled paths $\bar{X}_i$ are distributed according to f (this is the *stationary distribution* of the random walk).

As each path is sampled, we update the current image (which is stored in memory as a two-dimensional array of pixel values). To do this, we find the image location (u, v) corresponding to each path sample $\bar{X}_i$, and update the values of those pixels whose filter support contains (u, v). All samples are weighted equally; the light and dark regions of the final image are caused by differences in the number of samples recorded there.

The MLT algorithm is summarized below. In the following sections, we will describe it in more detail.

$$\bar{x} \leftarrow \text{INITIALPATH}()$$
$$image \leftarrow \{ \text{ array of zeros } \}$$
$$\textbf{for } i \leftarrow 1 \textbf{ to } N$$
$$\quad \bar{y} \leftarrow \text{MUTATE}(\bar{x})$$
$$\quad a \leftarrow \text{ACCEPTPROB}(\bar{y}|\bar{x})$$
$$\quad \textbf{if } \text{RANDOM}() < a$$
$$\quad\quad \textbf{then } \bar{x} \leftarrow \bar{y}$$
$$\quad \text{RECORDSAMPLE}(image, \bar{x})$$
$$\textbf{return } image$$

3 The Metropolis sampling algorithm

In 1953, Metropolis, Rosenbluth, Rosenbluth, Teller, and Teller introduced an algorithm for handling difficult sampling problems in computational physics [15]. It was originally used to predict the material properties of liquids, but has since been applied to many areas of physics and chemistry.

The method works as follows (our discussion is based on [11]). We are given a state space Ω, and a non-negative function $f : \Omega \to \mathbb{R}^+$. We are also given some initial state $\bar{X}_0 \in \Omega$. The goal is to generate a random walk $\bar{X}_0, \bar{X}_1, \ldots$ such that $\bar{X}_i$ is eventually distributed proportionally to f, no matter which state $\bar{X}_0$ we start with. Unlike most sampling methods, the Metropolis algorithm does not require that f integrate to one.

Each sample $\bar{X}_i$ is obtained by making a random change to $\bar{X}_{i-1}$ (in our case, these are the path mutations). This type of random walk, where $\bar{X}_i$ depends only on $\bar{X}_{i-1}$, is called a *Markov chain*. We let $K(\bar{y} \mid \bar{x})$ denote the probability density of going to state $\bar{y}$, given that we are currently in state $\bar{x}$. This is called the *transition function*, and satisfies the condition $\int_\Omega K(\bar{y} \mid \bar{x}) \, d\mu(\bar{y}) = 1$ for all $\bar{x} \in \Omega$.

The stationary distribution. Each $\bar{X}_i$ is a random variable with some distribution p_i, which is determined from p_{i-1} by

$$p_i(\bar{x}) = \int_\Omega K(\bar{x} \mid \bar{y}) \, p_{i-1}(\bar{y}) \, d\mu(\bar{y}) \,. \tag{1}$$

With mild conditions on K (discussed further in Section 5.2), the p_i will converge to a unique distribution p, called the *stationary distribution*. Note that p does not depend on the initial state $\bar{X}_0$.

To give a simple example of this idea, consider a state space consisting of n^2 vertices arranged in an $n \times n$ grid. Each vertex is connected to its four neighbours by edges, where the edges "wrap" from left to right and top to bottom as necessary (i.e. with the topology of a torus). A transition consists of randomly moving from the current vertex $\bar{x}$ to one of the neighboring vertices $\bar{y}$ with a probability of $1/5$ each, and otherwise staying at vertex $\bar{x}$.

Suppose that we start at an arbitrary vertex $\bar{X}_0 = \bar{x}^*$, so that $p_0(\bar{x}) = 1$ for $\bar{x} = \bar{x}^*$, and $p_0(\bar{x}) = 0$ otherwise. After one transition, $\bar{X}_1$ is distributed with equal probability among $\bar{x}^*$ and its four neighbors. Similarly, $\bar{X}_2$ is randomly distributed among 13 vertices (although not with equal probability). If this process is continued, eventually p_i converges to a fixed probability distribution p, which necessarily satisfies

$$p(\bar{x}) = \sum_{\bar{y}} K(\bar{x} \mid \bar{y}) \, p(\bar{y}) \, .$$

For this example, p is the uniform distribution $p(\bar{x}) = 1/n^2$.

Detailed balance. In a typical physical system, the transition function K is determined by the physical laws governing the system. Given some arbitrary initial state, the system then evolves towards equilibrium through transitions governed by K.

The Metropolis algorithm works in the opposite direction. The idea is to invent or construct a transition function K whose resulting stationary distribution will be proportional to the given f, and which will converge to f as quickly as possible. The technique is simple, and has an intuitive physical interpretation called *detailed balance*.

Given $\bar{X}_{i-1}$, we obtain $\bar{X}_i$ as follows. First, we choose a tentative sample $\bar{X}_i'$, which can be done in almost any way desired. This is represented by the *tentative transition function* T, where $T(\bar{y} \mid \bar{x})$ gives the probability density that $\bar{X}_i' = \bar{y}$ given that $\bar{X}_{i-1} = \bar{x}$.

The tentative sample is then either accepted or rejected, according to an acceptance probability $a(\bar{y} \mid \bar{x})$ which will be defined below. That is, we let

$$\bar{X}_i = \begin{cases} \bar{X}_i' & \text{with probability } a(\bar{X}_i' \mid \bar{X}_{i-1}) \, , \\ \bar{X}_{i-1} & \text{otherwise} \, . \end{cases} \tag{2}$$

To see how to set $a(\bar{y} \mid \bar{x})$, suppose that we have already reached equilibrium, i.e. p_{i-1} is proportional to f. We must define $K(\bar{y} \mid \bar{x})$ such that the equilibrium is maintained. To do this, consider the density of transitions between any two states $\bar{x}$ and $\bar{y}$. From $\bar{x}$ to $\bar{y}$, the transition density is proportional to $f(\bar{x}) \, T(\bar{y} \mid \bar{x}) \, a(\bar{y} \mid \bar{x})$, and a similar statement holds for the transition density from $\bar{y}$ to $\bar{x}$. To maintain equilibrium, it is sufficient that these densities be equal:

$$f(\bar{x}) \, T(\bar{y} \mid \bar{x}) \, a(\bar{y} \mid \bar{x}) = f(\bar{y}) \, T(\bar{x} \mid \bar{y}) \, a(\bar{x} \mid \bar{y}) \, , \tag{3}$$

a condition known as *detailed balance*. We can verify that if $p_{i-1} \propto f$ and condition (3) holds, then equilibrium is preserved:

$$\begin{aligned} p_i(\bar{x}) &= \left[1 - \int_\Omega a(\bar{y} \mid \bar{x}) \, T(\bar{y} \mid \bar{x}) \, d\mu(\bar{y}) \right] p_{i-1}(\bar{x}) \quad (4) \\ &\quad + \int_\Omega a(\bar{x} \mid \bar{y}) \, T(\bar{x} \mid \bar{y}) \, p_{i-1}(\bar{y}) \, d\mu(\bar{y}) \\ &= p_{i-1}(\bar{x}) \, . \end{aligned}$$

The acceptance probability. Recall that f is given, and T was chosen arbitrarily. Thus, equation (3) is a condition on the ratio $a(\bar{y} \mid \bar{x}) / a(\bar{x} \mid \bar{y})$. In order to reach equilibrium as quickly as possible, the best strategy is to make $a(\bar{y} \mid \bar{x})$ and $a(\bar{x} \mid \bar{y})$ as large as possible [18], which is achieved by letting

$$a(\bar{y} \mid \bar{x}) = \min \left\{ 1, \frac{f(\bar{y}) \, T(\bar{x} \mid \bar{y})}{f(\bar{x}) \, T(\bar{y} \mid \bar{x})} \right\} \, . \tag{5}$$

According to this rule, transitions in one direction are always accepted, while in the other direction they are sometimes rejected, such that the expected number of moves each way is the same.

Comparison with genetic algorithms. The Metropolis method differs from genetic algorithms [6] in several ways. First, they have different purposes: genetic algorithms solve optimization problems, while the Metropolis method solves sampling problems (there is no search for an optimum value). Genetic algorithms work with a population of individuals, while Metropolis stores only a single current state. Finally, genetic algorithms have much more freedom in choosing the allowable mutations, since they do not need to compute the conditional probability of their actions.

Beyer and Lange [2] have applied genetic algorithms to the problem of integrating radiance over a hemisphere. They start with a population of rays (actually directional samples), which are evolved to improve their distribution with respect to the incident radiance at a particular surface point. However, their methods do not seem to lead to a feasible light transport algorithm.

4 The path integral formulation of light transport

Often the light transport problem is written as an integral equation, where we must solve for the equilibrium radiance function L. However, it can also be written as a pure integration problem, over the domain of all transport paths. The MLT algorithm is based on this formulation.[2] We start by reviewing the light transport and measurement equations, and then show how to transform them into an integral over paths.

The light transport equation. We assume a geometric optics model where light is emitted, scattered, and absorbed only at surfaces, travels in straight lines between surfaces, and is perfectly incoherent. Under these conditions, the *light transport equation* is given by[3]

$$L(\mathbf{x}' \to \mathbf{x}'') = L_e(\mathbf{x}' \to \mathbf{x}'') \tag{6}$$
$$+ \int_{\mathcal{M}} L(\mathbf{x} \to \mathbf{x}') \, f_s(\mathbf{x} \to \mathbf{x}' \to \mathbf{x}'') \, G(\mathbf{x} \leftrightarrow \mathbf{x}') \, dA(\mathbf{x}).$$

Here $\mathcal{M}$ is the union of all scene surfaces, A is the area measure on $\mathcal{M}$, $L_e(\mathbf{x}' \to \mathbf{x}'')$ is the emitted radiance leaving $\mathbf{x}'$ in the direction of $\mathbf{x}''$, L is the equilibrium radiance function, and f_s is the bidirectional scattering distribution function (BSDF). The notation $\mathbf{x} \to \mathbf{x}'$ symbolizes the direction of light flow between two points of $\mathcal{M}$, while $\mathbf{x} \leftrightarrow \mathbf{x}'$ denotes symmetry in the argument pair.[4] The function G represents the throughput of a differential beam between $dA(\mathbf{x})$ and $dA(\mathbf{x}')$, and is given by

$$G(\mathbf{x} \leftrightarrow \mathbf{x}') = V(\mathbf{x} \leftrightarrow \mathbf{x}') \, \frac{|\cos(\theta_o) \, \cos(\theta_i')|}{\|\mathbf{x} - \mathbf{x}'\|^2} \, ,$$

where θ_o and θ_i' represent the angles between the segment $\mathbf{x} \leftrightarrow \mathbf{x}'$ and the surface normals at $\mathbf{x}$ and $\mathbf{x}'$ respectively, while $V(\mathbf{x} \leftrightarrow \mathbf{x}') = 1$ if $\mathbf{x}$ and $\mathbf{x}'$ are mutually visible and is zero otherwise.

---

[2] Note that two different formulations of bidirectional path tracing have been proposed: one based on a measure over paths [24, 25], and the other based on the *global reflectance distribution function* (GRDF) [13]. However, only the path measure approach defines the notion of probabilities on paths, as required for combining multiple estimators [25] and the present work.

[3] Technically, the equations of this section deal with *spectral radiance*, and apply at each wavelength seperately.

[4] There is redundancy in this representation; e.g. $L(\mathbf{x} \to \mathbf{x}') = L(\mathbf{x} \to \mathbf{x}'')$ whenever $\mathbf{x}'$ and $\mathbf{x}''$ lie in the same direction from $\mathbf{x}$.

The measurement equation. Light transport algorithms estimate a finite number of measurements of the equilibrium radiance L. We consider only algorithms that compute an image directly, so that the measurements consist of many pixel values $m_1, \ldots, m_M$, where M is the number of pixels in the image. Each measurement has the form

$$m_j = \int_{\mathcal{M} \times \mathcal{M}} W_e^{(j)}(\mathbf{x} \to \mathbf{x}') \, L(\mathbf{x} \to \mathbf{x}') \, G(\mathbf{x} \leftrightarrow \mathbf{x}') \, dA(\mathbf{x}) \, dA(\mathbf{x}'),$$

$$(7)$$

where $W_e^{(j)}(\mathbf{x} \to \mathbf{x}')$ is a weight that indicates how much the light arriving at $\mathbf{x}'$ from the direction of $\mathbf{x}$ contributes to the value of the measurement.[5] For real sensors, $W_e^{(j)}$ is called the *flux responsivity* (with units of $[\mathrm{W}^{-1}]$), but in graphics it is more often called an *importance function*.[6]

The path integral formulation. By recursively expanding the transport equation (6), we can write measurements in the form

$$m_j = \int_{\mathcal{M}^2} L_e(\mathbf{x}_0 \to \mathbf{x}_1) \, G(\mathbf{x}_0 \leftrightarrow \mathbf{x}_1) \, W_e^{(j)}(\mathbf{x}_0 \to \mathbf{x}_1) \, dA(\mathbf{x}_0) \, dA(\mathbf{x}_1)$$
$$+ \int_{\mathcal{M}^3} L_e(\mathbf{x}_0 \to \mathbf{x}_1) \, G(\mathbf{x}_0 \leftrightarrow \mathbf{x}_1) \, f_s(\mathbf{x}_0 \leftrightarrow \mathbf{x}_1 \leftrightarrow \mathbf{x}_2)$$
$$G(\mathbf{x}_1 \leftrightarrow \mathbf{x}_2) \, W_e^{(j)}(\mathbf{x}_1 \to \mathbf{x}_2) \, dA(\mathbf{x}_0) \, dA(\mathbf{x}_1) \, dA(\mathbf{x}_2)$$
$$+ \cdots. \qquad (8)$$

The goal is to write this expression in the form

$$m_j = \int_\Omega f_j(\bar{x}) \, d\mu(\bar{x}), \qquad (9)$$

so that we can handle it as a pure integration problem.

To do this, let Ω_k be the set of all paths of the form $\bar{x} = \mathbf{x}_0 \mathbf{x}_1 \ldots \mathbf{x}_k$, where $k \geq 1$ and $\mathbf{x}_i \in \mathcal{M}$ for each i. We define a measure μ_k on the paths of each length k according to

$$d\mu_k(\mathbf{x}_0 \ldots \mathbf{x}_k) = dA(\mathbf{x}_0) \cdots dA(\mathbf{x}_k),$$

i.e. μ_k is a product measure. Next, we let Ω be the union of all the Ω_k, and define a measure μ on Ω by[7]

$$\mu(D) = \sum_{k=1}^{\infty} \mu_k(D \cap \Omega_k). \qquad (10)$$

The integrand f_j is defined by extracting the appropriate term from the expansion (8) — see Figure 1. For example,

$$f_j(\mathbf{x}_0 \mathbf{x}_1) = L_e(\mathbf{x}_0 \to \mathbf{x}_1) \, G(\mathbf{x}_0 \leftrightarrow \mathbf{x}_1) \, W_e^{(j)}(\mathbf{x}_0 \to \mathbf{x}_1).$$

We call f_j the *measurement contribution function*.

There is nothing tricky about this; we have just expanded and rearranged the transport equations. The most significant aspect is that we have removed the sum over different path lengths, and replaced it with a single integral over an abstract measure space of paths.

---

[5]The function $W_e^{(j)}$ is zero almost everywhere. It is non-zero only if $\mathbf{x}'$ lies on the virtual camera lens, and the ray $\mathbf{x} \to \mathbf{x}'$ is mapped by the lens to the small region of the image plane corresponding to the filter support of pixel j.

[6]Further references and discussion may be found in [23].

[7]This measure on paths is similar to that of Spanier and Gelbard [22, p. 85]. However, in our case infinite-length paths are excluded. This makes it easy to verify that (10) is in fact a measure, directly from the axioms [7].

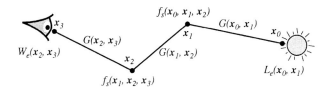

Figure 1: The measurement contribution function f_j is a product of many factors (shown for a path of length 3).

5 Metropolis light transport

To complete the MLT algorithm outlined in Section 2, there are several tasks. First, we must formulate the light transport problem so that it fits the Metropolis framework. Second, we must show how to avoid *start-up bias*, a problem which affects many Metropolis applications. Most importantly, we must design a suitable set of mutations on paths, such that the Metropolis method will work efficiently.

5.1 Reduction to the Metropolis framework

We show how the Metropolis method can be adapted to estimate all of the pixel values m_j simultaneously and without bias.

Observe that each integrand f_j has the form

$$f_j(\bar{x}) = w_j(\bar{x}) \, f(\bar{x}), \qquad (11)$$

where w_j represents the filter function for pixel j, and f represents all the other factors of f_j (which are the same for all pixels). In physical terms, $\int_D f(\bar{x}) \, d\mu(\bar{x})$ represents the radiant power received by the image area of the image plane along a set D of paths.[8] Note that w_j depends only on the last edge $\mathbf{x}_{k-1} \mathbf{x}_k$ of the path, which we call the *lens edge*.

An image can now be computed by sampling N paths $\bar{X}_i$ according to some distribution p, and using the identity

$$m_j = E\left[\frac{1}{N} \sum_{i=1}^{N} \frac{w_j(\bar{X}_i) f(\bar{X}_i)}{p(\bar{X}_i)} \right].$$

If we could let $p = (1/b) \, f$ (where b is the normalization constant $\int_\Omega f(\bar{x}) \, d\mu(\bar{x})$), the estimate for each pixel would be

$$m_j = E\left[\frac{1}{N} \sum_{i=1}^{N} b \, w_j(\bar{X}_i) \right].$$

This equation can be evaluated efficiently for all pixels at once, since each path contributes to only a few pixel values.

This idea requires the evaluation of b, and the ability to sample from a distribution proportional to f. Both of these are hard problems. For the second part, the Metropolis algorithm will help; however, the samples $\bar{X}_i$ will have the desired distribution only in the limit as $i \to \infty$. In typical Metropolis applications, this is handled by starting in some fixed initial state $\bar{X}_0$, and discarding the first k samples until the random walk has approximately converged to the equilibrium distribution. However, it is often difficult to know how large k should be. If it is too small, then the samples will be strongly influenced by the choice of $\bar{X}_0$, which will bias the results (this is called *start-up bias*).

---

[8]We assume that $f(\bar{x}) = 0$ for paths that do not contribute to any pixel value (so that we do not waste any samples there).

Eliminating start-up bias. We show how the MLT algorithm can be initialized to avoid start-up bias. The idea is to start the walk in a random initial state $\bar{X}_0$, which is sampled from some convenient path distribution p_0 (we use bidirectional path tracing for this purpose). To compensate for the fact that p_0 is not the desired distribution $(1/b) f$, the sample $\bar{X}_0$ is assigned a weight: $W_0 = f(\bar{X}_0)/p_0(\bar{X}_0)$. Thus after one sample, the estimate for pixel j is $W_0 \, w_j(\bar{X}_0)$. All of these quantities are computable since $\bar{X}_0$ is known.

Additional samples $\bar{X}_1$, $\bar{X}_2$, ..., $\bar{X}_N$ are generated by mutating $\bar{X}_0$ according to the Metropolis algorithm (using f as the target density). Each of the $\bar{X}_i$ has a different distribution p_i, which only approaches $(1/b) f$ as $i \to \infty$. To avoid bias, however, it is sufficient to assign these samples the same weight $W_i = W_0$ as the original sample, where the following estimate is used for pixel j:

$$m_j = E\left[\frac{1}{N} \sum_{i=1}^{N} W_i \, w_j(\bar{X}_i) \right] . \qquad (12)$$

To show that this is unbiased, recall that the initial state was chosen randomly, and so we must average over all choices of $\bar{X}_0$ when computing expected values. Consider a group of starting paths obtained by sampling p_0 many times. If we had $p_0 = (1/b) f$ and $W_0 = b$, then obviously this starting group would be in equilibrium. For general p_0, the choice $W_0 = f/p_0$ leads to exactly the same distribution of weight among the starting paths, and so we should expect that these initial conditions are unbiased as well. (See Appendix A for a proof.)

This technique for removing start-up bias is not specific to light transport. However, it requires the existence of an alternative sampling method p_0, which for many Metropolis applications is not easy to obtain.

Initialization. In practice, initializing the MLT algorithm with a single sample does not work well. If we generate only one path $\bar{X}_0$ (e.g. using bidirectional path tracing), it is quite likely that $W_0 = 0$ (e.g. the path goes through a wall). Since all subsequent samples use the same weight $W_i = W_0$, this would lead to a completely black final image. Conversely, the initial weight W_0 on other runs may be much larger than expected. Although the algorithm is unbiased, this statement is only useful when applied to the average result over many runs. The obvious solution is to run n copies of the algorithm in parallel, and accumulate all the samples into one image.

The strategy we have implemented is to sample a moderately large number of paths $\bar{X}_0^{(1)}$, ..., $\bar{X}_0^{(n)}$, with corresponding weights $W_0^{(1)}$, ..., $W_0^{(n)}$. We then resample the $\bar{X}_0^{(i)}$ to obtain a much smaller number n' of equally-weighted paths (chosen with equal spacing in the cumulative weight distribution of the $\bar{X}_0^{(i)}$). These are used as independent seeds for the Metropolis phase of the algorithm.

The value of n is determined indirectly, by generating a fixed number of eye and light subpaths (e.g. 10 000 pairs), and considering all the ways to link the vertices of each pair. Note that it is not necessary to save all of these paths for the resampling step; they can be regenerated by restarting the random number generator with the same seed.

It is often reasonable to choose $n' = 1$ (a single Metropolis seed). In this case, the purpose of the first phase is to estimate the mean value of W_0, which determines the absolute image brightness.[9] If the image is desired only up

to a constant scale factor, then n can be chosen to be very small. The main reasons for retaining more than one seed (i.e. $n' > 1$) are to implement convergence tests (see below) or lens subpath mutations (Section 5.3.3).

Effectively, we have separated the image computation into two subproblems. The initialization phase estimates the overall image brightness, while the Metropolis phase determines the relative pixel intensities across the image. The effort spent on each phase can be decided independently. In practice, however, the initialization phase is a negligible part of the total computation time (e.g., even 100 000 bidirectional samples typically constitute less than one sample per pixel).

Convergence tests. Another reason to run several copies of the algorithm in parallel is that it facilitates convergence testing. (We cannot apply the usual variance tests to samples generated by a single run of the Metropolis algorithm, since consecutive samples are highly correlated.)

To test for convergence, the Metropolis phase runs with n' independent seed paths, whose contributions to the image are recorded separately (in the form of n' separate images). This is done only for a small representative fraction of the pixels, since it would be too expensive to maintain many copies of a large image. The sample variance of these test pixels is then computed periodically, until the results are within prespecified bounds.[10]

Spectral sampling. Our discussion so far has been limited to monochrome images, but the modifications for color are straightforward.

We represent BSDF's and light sources as point-sampled spectra (although it would be easy to use some other representation). Given a path, we compute the energy delivered to the lens at each of the sampled wavelengths. The resulting spectrum is then converted to a tristimulus color value (we use RGB) before it is accumulated in the current image.

The image contribution function f is redefined to compute the luminance of the corresponding path spectrum. This implies that path samples will be distributed according to the luminance of the ideal image, and that the luminance of every filtered image sample will be the same (irrespective of its color). Effectively, each color component h is sampled with an estimator of the form h/p, where p is proportional to the luminance.

Since the human eye is substantially more sensitive to luminance differences than other color variations, this choice helps to minimize the apparent noise.[11]

5.2 Designing a mutation strategy

The main disadvantage of the Metropolis method is that consecutive samples are correlated, which leads to higher variance than we would get with independent samples. This can happen either because the proposed mutations to the path are very small, or because too many mutations are rejected.

This problem can be minimized by choosing a suitable set of path mutations. We consider some of the properties that these mutations should have, to minimize the error in the final image.

---

[9] More precisely, $E[W_0] = \int f = b$, which represents the total power falling on the image region of the film plane.

[10] Note that in all of our tests, the number of mutations for each image was specified manually, so that we would have explicit control over the computation time.

[11] Another way to handle color is to have a separate run for each wavelength. However, this is inefficient (we get less information from each path) and leads to unnecessary color noise.

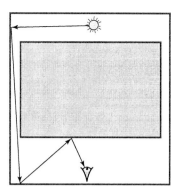

Figure 2: If only additions and deletions of a single vertex are allowed, then paths cannot mutate from one side of the barrier to the other.

High acceptance probability. If the acceptance probability $a(\bar{y} \mid \bar{x})$ is very small on the average, there will be long path sequences of the form $\bar{x}, \bar{x}, \ldots, \bar{x}$ due to rejections. This leads to many samples at the same point on the image plane, and appears as noise.

Large changes to the path. Even if the acceptance probability for most mutations is high, samples will still be highly correlated if the proposed path mutations are too small. It is important to propose mutations that make substantial changes to the current path, such as increasing the path length, or replacing a specular bounce with a diffuse one.

Ergodicity. If the allowable mutations are too restricted, it is possible for the random walk to get "stuck" in some subregion of the path space (i.e. one where the integral of f is less than b). To see how this can happen, consider Figure 2, and suppose that we only allow mutations that add or delete a single vertex. In this case, there is no way for the path to mutate to the other side of the barrier, and we will miss part of the path space.

Technically, we want to ensure that the random walk converges to an *ergodic* state. This means that no matter how $\bar{X}_0$ is chosen, it converges to the same stationary distribution p. To do this, it is sufficient to ensure that $T(\bar{y} \mid \bar{x}) > 0$ for every pair of states $\bar{x}, \bar{y}$ with $f(\bar{x}) > 0$ and $f(\bar{y}) > 0$. In our implementation, this is always true (see Section 5.3.1).

Changes to the image location. To minimize correlation between the sample locations on the image plane, it is desirable for mutations to change the lens edge $\mathbf{x}_{k-1}\mathbf{x}_k$. Mutations to other portions of the path do not provide information about the path distribution over the image plane, which is what we are most interested in.

Stratification. Another potential weakness of the Metropolis approach is the random distribution of samples across the image plane. This is commonly known as the "balls in bins" effect: if we randomly throw n balls into n bins, we cannot expect one ball per bin. (Many bins may be empty, while the fullest bin is likely to contain $\Theta(\log n)$ balls.) In an image, this unevenness in the distribution produces noise.

For some kinds of mutations, this effect is difficult to avoid. However, it is worthwhile to consider mutations for which some form of stratification is possible.

Low cost. It is also desirable that mutations be inexpensive. Generally, this is measured by the number of rays cast, since the other costs are relatively small.

5.3 Good mutation strategies

We now consider three specific mutation strategies, namely *bidirectional mutations*, *perturbations*, and *lens subpath mutations*. These strategies are designed to satisfy different subsets of the goals mentioned above; our implementation uses a mixture of all three (as we discuss in Section 5.3.4).

Note that the Metropolis framework allows us greater freedom than standard Monte Carlo algorithms in designing sampling strategies. This is because we only need to compute the *conditional* probability $T(\bar{y} \mid \bar{x})$ of each mutation: in other words, the mutation strategy is allowed to depend on the current path.

5.3.1 Bidirectional mutations

Bidirectional mutations are the foundation of the MLT algorithm. They are responsible for making large changes to the path, such as modifying its length. The basic idea is simple: we choose a subpath of the current path $\bar{x}$, and replace it with a different subpath. We divide this into several steps.

First, the subpath to delete is chosen. Given the current path $\bar{x} = \mathbf{x}_0 \ldots \mathbf{x}_k$, we assign a probability $p_\mathrm{d}[s,t]$ to the deletion of each subpath $\mathbf{x}_s \ldots \mathbf{x}_t$. The subpath endpoints are not included, i.e. $\mathbf{x}_s \ldots \mathbf{x}_t$ consists of $t - s$ edges and $t - s - 1$ vertices, with indices satisfying $-1 \leq s < t \leq k+1$.

In our implementation, $p_\mathrm{d}[s,t]$ is a product two factors. The first factor $p_{\mathrm{d},1}$ depends only on the subpath length; its purpose is to favor the deletion of short subpaths. (These are less expensive to replace, and yield mutations that are more likely to be accepted, since they make a smaller change to the current path). The purpose of the second factor $p_{\mathrm{d},2}$ is to avoid mutations with low acceptance probabilities; it will be described in Section 5.4.

To determine the deleted subpath, the distribution $p_\mathrm{d}[s,t]$ is normalized and sampled. At this point, $\bar{x}$ has been split into two (possibly empty) pieces $\mathbf{x}_0 \ldots \mathbf{x}_s$ and $\mathbf{x}_t \ldots \mathbf{x}_k$.

To complete the mutation, we first choose the number of vertices s' and t' to be added to each side. We do this in two steps: first, we choose the new subpath length, $l_\mathrm{a} = s' + t' + 1$. It is desirable that the old and new subpath lengths be similar, since this will tend to increase the acceptance probability (i.e. it represents a smaller change to the path). Thus, we choose l_a according to a discrete distribution $p_{\mathrm{a},1}$ which assigns a high probability to keeping the total path length the same. Then, we choose specific values for s' and t' (subject to $s' + t' + 1 = l_\mathrm{a}$), according to another discrete distribution $p_{\mathrm{a},2}$ that assigns equal probability to each candidate value of s'. For convenience, we let $p_\mathrm{a}[s',t']$ denote the product of $p_{\mathrm{a},1}$ and $p_{\mathrm{a},2}$.

To sample the new vertices, we add them one at a time to the appropriate subpath. This involves first sampling a direction according to the BSDF at the current subpath endpoint (or a convenient approximation, if sampling from the exact BSDF is difficult), followed by casting a ray to find the first surface intersected. An initially empty subpath is handled by choosing a random point on a light source or the lens as appropriate.

Finally, we join the new subpaths together, by testing the visibility between their endpoints. If the path is obstructed, the mutation is immediately rejected. This also happens if any of the ray casting operations failed to intersect a surface.

Notice that there is a non-zero probability of throwing away the entire path, and generating a new one from scratch. This automatically ensures the ergodicity condition (Section 5.2), so that the algorithm can never get "stuck" in a small subregion of the path space.

Parameter values. The following values have provided reasonable results on our test cases. For the probability $p_{d,1}[l_d]$ of deleting a subpath of length $l_d = t - s$, we use $p_{d,1}[1] = 0.25$, $p_{d,1}[2] = 0.5$, and $p_{d,1}[l_d] = 2^{-l}$ for $l_d \geq 3$. For the probability $p_{a,1}[l_a]$ of adding a subpath of length l_a, we use $p_{a,1}[l_d] = 0.5$, $p_{a,1}[l_d - 1] = 0.15$, and $p_{a,1}[l_d + 1] = 0.15$, with the remaining probability assigned to the other allowable subpath lengths.

Evaluation of the acceptance probability. Observe that $a(\bar{y} \,|\, \bar{x})$ can be written as the ratio

$$a(\bar{y} \,|\, \bar{x}) = \frac{R(\bar{y} \,|\, \bar{x})}{R(\bar{x} \,|\, \bar{y})} \,, \qquad \text{where} \quad R(\bar{y} \,|\, \bar{x}) = \frac{f(\bar{y})}{T(\bar{y} \,|\, \bar{x})} \,. \quad (13)$$

The form of $R(\bar{y} \,|\, \bar{x})$ is very similar to the sample value $f(\bar{y})/p(\bar{y})$ that is computed by standard Monte Carlo algorithms; we have simply replaced an absolute probability $p(\bar{y})$ by a conditional probability $T(\bar{y} \,|\, \bar{x})$.

Specifically, $T(\bar{y} \,|\, \bar{x})$ is the product of the discrete probability $p_d[s, t]$ for deleting the subpath $\mathbf{x}_s \ldots \mathbf{x}_t$, and the probability density for generating the $s' + t'$ new vertices of $\bar{y}$. To calculate the latter, we must take into account all $s' + t' + 1$ ways that the new vertices can be split between subpaths generated from $\mathbf{x}_s$ and $\mathbf{x}_t$. (Although these vertices were generated by a particular choice of s', the probability $T(\bar{y} \,|\, \bar{x})$ must take into account all ways of going from state $\bar{x}$ to $\bar{y}$.)

Note that the unchanged portions of $\bar{x}$ do not contribute to the calculation of $T(\bar{y} \,|\, \bar{x})$. It is also convenient to ignore the factors of $f(\bar{x})$ and $f(\bar{y})$ that are shared between the paths, since this does not change the result.

An example. Let $\bar{x}$ be a path $\mathbf{x}_0 \mathbf{x}_1 \mathbf{x}_2 \mathbf{x}_3$, and suppose that the random mutation step has deleted the edge $\mathbf{x}_1 \mathbf{x}_2$. It is replaced by new vertex $\mathbf{z}_0$ by casting a ray from $\mathbf{x}_1$, so that the new path is $\bar{y} = \mathbf{x}_0 \mathbf{x}_1 \mathbf{z}_0 \mathbf{x}_2 \mathbf{x}_3$. (This corresponds to the random choices $s = 1$, $t = 2$, $s' = 1$, $t' = 0$.)

Let $p_s(\mathbf{x}_0 \to \mathbf{x}_1 \to \mathbf{z}_0)$ be the probability density of sampling the direction from $\mathbf{x}_1$ to $\mathbf{z}_0$, measured with respect to projected solid angle.[12] Then the probability density of sampling $\mathbf{z}_0$ (measured with respect to surface area) is given by $p_s(\mathbf{x}_0 \to \mathbf{x}_1 \to \mathbf{z}_0)\, G(\mathbf{x}_1 \leftrightarrow \mathbf{z}_0)$.

We now have all of the information necessary to compute $R(\bar{y} \,|\, \bar{x})$. From (8), the numerator $f(\bar{y})$ is

$$f_s(\mathbf{x}_0, \mathbf{x}_1, \mathbf{z}_0)\, G(\mathbf{x}_1, \mathbf{z}_0)\, f_s(\mathbf{x}_1, \mathbf{z}_0, \mathbf{x}_2)\, G(\mathbf{z}_0, \mathbf{x}_2)\, f_s(\mathbf{z}_0, \mathbf{x}_2, \mathbf{x}_3) \,,$$

where the factors shared between $R(\bar{y} \,|\, \bar{x})$ and $R(\bar{x} \,|\, \bar{y})$ have been omitted (and we have dropped the arrow notation for brevity). The denominator $T(\bar{y} \,|\, \bar{x})$ is

$$p_d[1, 2] \left[\begin{array}{l} p_a[1, 0]\, p_s(\mathbf{x}_0, \mathbf{x}_1, \mathbf{z}_0)\, G(\mathbf{x}_1, \mathbf{z}_0) \\ + \, p_a[0, 1]\, p_s(\mathbf{x}_3, \mathbf{x}_2, \mathbf{z}_0)\, G(\mathbf{x}_2, \mathbf{z}_0) \end{array} \right] \,.$$

In a similar way, we find that $R(\bar{x} \,|\, \bar{y})$ is given by

$$\{ f_s(\mathbf{x}_0, \mathbf{x}_1, \mathbf{x}_2)\, G(\mathbf{x}_1, \mathbf{x}_2)\, f_s(\mathbf{x}_1, \mathbf{x}_2, \mathbf{x}_3) \} \,/\, \{ p_d[1, 3]\, p_a[0, 0] \} \,,$$

where p_d and p_a now refer to $\bar{y}$. To implement this calculation in general, it is convenient to define functions

$$C(\mathbf{x}_0, \mathbf{x}_1, \mathbf{x}_2, \mathbf{x}_3) = f_s(\mathbf{x}_0, \mathbf{x}_1, \mathbf{x}_2)\, G(\mathbf{x}_1, \mathbf{x}_2)\, f_s(\mathbf{x}_1, \mathbf{x}_2, \mathbf{x}_3)$$

$$S(\mathbf{x}_0, \mathbf{x}_1, \mathbf{x}_2) = f_s(\mathbf{x}_0, \mathbf{x}_1, \mathbf{x}_2)/p_s(\mathbf{x}_0, \mathbf{x}_1, \mathbf{x}_2) \,, \quad (14)$$

and then express $1/R(\bar{y} \,|\, \bar{x})$ in terms of these functions. This formulation extends easily to subpaths of arbitrary length, and can be evaluated efficiently by precomputing C and S for each edge. In this form, it is also easy to handle specular BSDF's, since the ratio S is always well-defined.

---

[12]If $p'_s(\mathbf{x}_0 \to \mathbf{x}_1 \to \mathbf{z}_0)$ is the density with respect to ordinary solid angle, then $p_s = p'_s/|\cos(\theta_o)|$, where θ_o is the angle between $\mathbf{x}_1 \to \mathbf{z}_0$ and the surface normal at $\mathbf{x}_1$.

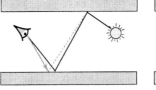 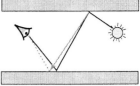

Lens perturbation   Caustic perturbation

Figure 3: The lens edge can be perturbed by regenerating it from either side: we call these *lens perturbations* and *caustic perturbations*.

5.3.2 Perturbations

There are some lighting situations where bidirectional mutations will almost always be rejected. This happens when there are small regions of the path space in which paths contribute much more than average. This can be caused by caustics, difficult visibility (e.g. a small hole), or by concave corners where two surfaces meet (a form of singularity in the integrand). The problem is that bidirectional mutations are relatively large, and so they usually attempt to mutate the path outside the high-contribution region.

One way to increase the acceptance probability is to use smaller mutations. The principle is that nearby paths will make similar contributions to the image, and so the acceptance probability will be high. Thus, rather than having many rejections on the same path, we can explore the other nearby paths of the high-contribution region.

Our solution is to choose a subpath of the current path, and move the vertices slightly. We call this type of mutation a *perturbation*. While the idea can be applied to arbitrary subpaths, our main interest is in perturbations that include the lens edge $\mathbf{x}_{k-1}\mathbf{x}_k$ (since other changes do not help to prevent long sample sequences at the same image point). We have implemented two specific kinds of perturbations that change the lens edge, termed *lens perturbations* and *caustic perturbations* (see Figure 3). These are described below.

Lens perturbations. We delete a subpath $\mathbf{x}_t \ldots \mathbf{x}_k$ of the form $(L|D)DS^*E$ (where we have used Heckbert's regular expression notation [8]; S, D, E, and L stand for specular, non-specular, lens, and light vertices respectively). This is called the *lens subpath*, and consists of $k-t$ edges and $k-t-1$ vertices. (Note that if $\mathbf{x}_t$ were specular, then any perturbation of $\mathbf{x}_{t-1}$ would result in a path $\bar{y}$ for which $f(\bar{y}) = 0$.)

To replace the lens subpath, we perturb the old image location by moving it a random distance R in a random direction ϕ. The angle ϕ is chosen uniformly, while R is exponentially distributed between two values $r_1 < r_2$:

$$R = r_2 \exp(-\ln(r_2/r_1)\, U) \,, \quad (15)$$

where U is uniformly distributed on $[0, 1]$.

We then cast a ray at the new image location, and extend the subpath through additional specular bounces to be the same length as the original. The mode of scattering at each specular bounce is preserved (i.e. specular reflection or transmission), rather than making new random choices.[13] This allows us to efficiently sample rare combinations of events, e.g. specular reflection from a surface where 99% of the light is transmitted.

The calculation of $a(\bar{y} \,|\, \bar{x})$ is similar to the bidirectional case. The main difference is the method used for directional sampling (i.e. distribution (15) instead of the BSDF).

---

[13]If the perturbation moves a vertex from a specular to a non-specular material, then the mutation is immediately rejected.

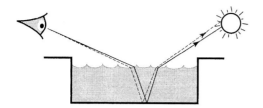

Figure 4: Using a two-chain perturbation to sample caustics in a pool of water. First, the lens edge is perturbed to generate a point $\mathbf{x}'$ on the pool bottom. Then, the direction from original point $\mathbf{x}$ toward the light source is perturbed, and a ray is cast from $\mathbf{x}'$ in this direction.

Caustic perturbations. Lens perturbations are not possible in some situations; the most notable example occurs when computing caustics. These paths have the form LS^+DE, which is unacceptable for lens perturbations.

However, there is another way to perturb paths with a suffix $\mathbf{x}_t \ldots \mathbf{x}_k$ of the form $(D|L)S^*DE$. To do this, we generate a new subpath starting from $\mathbf{x}_t$. The direction of the segment $\mathbf{x}_t \to \mathbf{x}_{t+1}$ is perturbed by an amount (θ, ϕ), where θ is exponentially distributed and ϕ is uniform. The technique is otherwise similar to lens perturbations.

Multi-chain perturbations. Neither of the above can handle paths with a suffix of the form $(D|L)DS^*DS^*DE$, i.e. caustics seen through a specular surface (see Figure 4). This can be handled by perturbing the path through more than one specular chain. At each non-specular vertex, we choose a new direction by perturbing the corresponding direction of the original subpath.

Parameter values. For lens perturbations, the image resolution is a guide to the useful range of values. We use $r_1 = 0.1$ pixels, while r_2 is chosen such that the perturbation region is 5% of the image area. For caustic and multi-chain perturbations, we use $\theta_1 = 0.0001$ radians and $\theta_2 = 0.1$ radians. The algorithm is not particularly sensitive to these values.

5.3.3 Lens subpath mutations

We now describe *lens subpath mutations*, whose goal is to stratify the samples over the image plane, and also to reduce the cost of sampling by re-using subpaths. Each mutation consists of deleting the lens subpath of the current path, and replacing it with a new one. (As before, the lens subpath has the form $(L|D)S^*E$.) The lens subpaths are stratified across the image plane, such that every pixel receives the same number of proposed lens subpath mutations.

We briefly describe how to do this. We initialize the algorithm with n' independent seed paths (Section 5.1), which are mutated in a rotating sequence. At all times, we also store a current lens subpath $\bar{x}_e$. An eye subpath mutation consists of deleting the lens subpath of the current path $\bar{x}$, and replacing it with $\bar{x}_e$.

The current subpath $\bar{x}_e$ is re-used a fixed number of times n_e, and then a new one is generated. We chose $n' \gg n_e$, to prevent the same lens subpath from being used multiple times on the same path.

To generate $\bar{x}_e$, we cast a ray through a point on the image plane, and follow zero or more specular bounces until we obtain a non-specular vertex.[14] To stratify the samples

---

[14] At a material with specular and non-specular components, we randomly choose between them.

on the image plane, we maintain a tally of the number of lens subpaths that have been generated at each pixel. When generating a new subpath, we choose a random pixel and, if it already has its quota of lens subpaths, we choose another one. We use a rover to make the search for a non-full pixel efficient. We also control the distribution of samples within each pixel, by computing a Poisson minimum-disc pattern and tiling it over the image plane.

The probability $a(\bar{y} \mid \bar{x})$ is similar to the bidirectional case, except that there is only one way of generating the new subpath. (Subpath re-use does not influence the calculation.)

5.3.4 Selecting between mutation types

At each step, we assign a probability to each of the three mutation types. This discrete distribution is sampled to determine which kind of mutation is applied to the current path.

We have found that it is important to make the probabilities relatively balanced. This is because the mutation types are designed to satisfy different goals, and it is difficult to predict in advance which types will be the most successful. The overall goal is to make mutations that are as large as possible, while still having a reasonable chance of acceptance. This can be achieved by randomly choosing between mutations of different sizes, so that there is a good chance of trying an appropriate mutation for any given path.

These observation are similar to those of *multiple importance sampling* (an alternative name for the technique in [25]). We would like a set of mutations that cover all the possibilities, even though we may not (and need not) know the optimum way to choose among them for a given path. It is perfectly fine to include mutations that are designed for special situations, and that result in rejections most of the time. This increases the cost of sampling by only a small amount, and yet it can increase robustness considerably.

5.4 Refinements

We describe several ideas that improve the efficiency of MLT.

Direct lighting. We use standard techniques for direct lighting (e.g. see [21]), rather than the Metropolis algorithm. In most cases, these standard methods give better results at lower cost, due to the fact that the Metropolis samples are not as well-stratified across the image plane (Section 5.2). By excluding direct lighting paths from the Metropolis calculation, we can apply more effort to the indirect lighting.

Using the expected sample value. For each proposed mutation, there is a probability $a(\bar{y} \mid \bar{x})$ of accumulating an image sample at $\bar{y}$, and a probability $1 - a(\bar{y} \mid \bar{x})$ of accumulating a sample at $\bar{x}$. We can make this more efficient by always accumulating a sample at both locations, weighted by the corresponding probability. Effectively, we have replaced a random variable by its expected value (a common variance reduction technique [11]). This is especially useful for sampling the dim regions of the image, which would otherwise receive very few samples.

Importance sampling for mutation probabilities. We describe a technique that can increase the efficiency of MLT substantially, by increasing the average acceptance probability. The idea is to implement a form of importance sampling which with respect to $a(\bar{y} \mid \bar{x})$, when deciding which mutation to attempt. This is done by weighting each possible mutation according to the probability with which the

(a) Bidirectional path tracing with 40 samples per pixel.

(b) Metropolis light transport with an average of 250 mutations per pixel [the same computation time as (a)].

Figure 5: All of the light in the visible portion of this scene comes through a door that is slightly ajar, such that about 0.1% of the light in the adjacent room comes through the doorway. The light source is a diffuse ceiling panel at the far end of a large adjacent room, so that virtually all of the light coming through the doorway has bounced several times. The MLT algorithm efficiently generates paths that go through the small opening between the rooms, by always preserving a path segment that goes through the doorway. The images are 900 by 500 pixels, and include the effects of all paths up to length 10.

deleted subpath can be regenerated. (This is the factor $p_{d,2}$ mentioned in Section 5.3.1.)

Let $\bar{x}$ be the current path, and consider a mutation that deletes the subpath $\mathbf{x}_s \ldots \mathbf{x}_t$. The insight is that given only the deleted subpath, it is already possible to compute some of the factors in the acceptance probability $a(\bar{y} \,|\, \bar{x})$. In particular, from (13) we see that $a(\bar{y} \mid \bar{x})$ is proportional to $1 \,/\, R(\bar{x} \,|\, \bar{y})$, and that it is possible to compute all the com-

ponents of $R(\bar{x} \mid \bar{y})$ except for the discrete probabilities p_d and p_a (these apply to $\bar{y}$, which has not been generated yet). The computable factors of $1 \,/\, R(\bar{x} \,|\, \bar{y})$ are denoted $p_{d,2}$. In the example of Section 5.3.1, for instance, we have

$$p_{d,2}[1,2] = 1/C(\mathbf{x}_0, \mathbf{x}_1, \mathbf{x}_2, \mathbf{x}_3) \,.$$

The discrete probabilities for each mutation type are weighted by this factor, before a mutation is selected.

6   Results

We have rendered test images that compare Metropolis light transport with classical and bidirectional path tracing. Our path tracing implementations support efficient direct lighting calculations, importance-sampled BSDF's, Russian roulette on shadow rays, and several other optimizations.

Figure 5 shows a test scene with difficult indirect lighting. For equal computation times, Metropolis light transport gives far better results than bidirectional path tracing. Notice the details that would be difficult to obtain with many light transport algorithms: contact shadows, caustics under the glass teapot, light reflected by the white tiles under the door, and the brighter strip along the back of the floor (due to the narrow gap between the table and the wall). This scene contains diffuse, glossy, and specular surfaces, and the wall is untextured to clearly reveal the noise levels.

For this scene, MLT gains efficiency from its ability to change only part of the current path. The portion of the path through the doorway can be preserved and re-used for many mutations, until it is successfully mutated into a different path through the doorway. Note that perturbations are not essential to make this process efficient, since the path through the doorway needs to change only infrequently.

Figure 6 compares MLT against bidirectional path tracing for a scene with strong indirect illumination and caustics. Both methods give similar results in the top row of images (where indirect lighting from the floor lamp dominates). However, MLT performs much better as we zoom into the caustic, due to its ability to generate new paths by perturbing existing paths. The image quality degrades with magnification (for the same computation time), but only slowly. Notice the streaky appearance of the noise at the highest magnification. This is due to caustic perturbations: each ray from the spotlight is perturbed within a narrow cone; however, the lens maps this cone of directions into an elongated shape. The streaks are due to long strings of caustic mutations that were not broken by successful mutations of some other kind.

Even in the top row of images, there are slight differences between the two methods. The MLT algorithm leads to lower noise in the bright regions of the image, while the bidirectional algorithm gives lower noise in the dim regions. This is what we would expect, since the number of Metropolis samples varies according to the pixel brightness, while the number of bidirectional samples per pixel is constant.

Figure 7 shows another difficult lighting situation: caustics on the bottom of a small pool, seen indirectly through the ripples on the water surface. Path tracing does not work well, because when a path strikes the bottom of the pool, a reflected direction is sampled according to the BRDF. In this case, only a very small number of those paths will contribute, because the light source occupies about 1% of the visible hemisphere above the pool. (Bidirectional path tracing does not help for these paths, because they can be generated only starting from the eye.) As with Figure 6, perturbations are the key to sampling these caustics efficiently (recall Figure 4). One interesting feature of MLT is that it obtains these results without special handling of the light sources or specular surfaces — see [16] or [3] for good examples of what can be achieved if this restriction is lifted.

We have measured the performance of MLT relative to path tracing (PT) and bidirectional path tracing (BPT), for the same computation time. To do this, we computed the relative error $e_j = (\tilde{m}_j - m_j)/m_j$ at each pixel, where $\tilde{m}_j$ is the value computed by MLT, PT, or BPT, and m_j is the

(a)   (b)

Figure 6: These images show caustics formed by a spotlight shining on a glass egg. Column (a) was computed with bidirectional path tracing using 25 samples per pixel, while (b) uses Metropolis light transport with the same number of ray queries (varying between 120 and 200 mutations per pixel). The solutions include all paths of up to length 7, and the images are 200 by 200 pixels.

value from a reference image (computed using BPT with a large number of samples). Next, we computed the l_1, l_2, and l_∞ norms of the resulting error image (i.e. the array of e_j). Finally, we normalized the results, by dividing the error norms for PT and BPT by the corresponding error norm for MLT. This gave the following table:

Test Case	PT vs. MLT			BPT vs. MLT		
	l_1	l_2	l_∞	l_1	l_2	l_∞
Fig. 5	7.7	11.7	40.0	5.2	4.9	13.2
Fig. 6 (top)	2.4	4.8	21.4	0.9	2.1	13.7
Fig. 7	3.2	4.7	5.0	4.2	6.5	6.1

Note that the efficiency gain of MLT over the other methods is proportional to the *square* of the table entries, since the

(a) Path tracing with 210 samples per pixel.

(b) Metropolis light transport with an average of 100 mutations per pixel [the same computation time as (a)].

Figure 7: Caustics in a pool of water, viewed indirectly through the ripples on the surface. It is difficult for unbiased Monte Carlo algorithms to find the important transport paths, since they must be generated starting from the lens, and the light source only occupies about 1% of the hemisphere as seen from the pool bottom (which is curved). The MLT algorithm is able to sample these paths efficiently by means of perturbations. The images are 800 by 500 pixels.

error for PT and BPT decreases according to the square root of the number of samples. For example, the RMS relative error in Figure 5(a) is 4.9 times higher than in Figure 5(b), and so approximately 25 times more BPT samples would be required to achieve the same error levels. Even in the topmost images of Figure 6 (for which BPT is well-suited), notice that MLT and BPT are competitive.

The computation times were approximately 15 minutes for each image in Figure 6, 2.5 hours for the images in Figure 7, and 4 hours for the images in Figure 5 (all times measured on a 190 MHz MIPS R10000 processor). The memory requirements are modest: we only store the scene model, the current image, and a single path (or a small number of paths, if the mutation technique in Section 5.3.3 is used). For high-resolution images, the memory requirements could be reduced further by collecting the samples in batches, sorting them in scanline order, and applying them to an image on disk.

7 Conclusions

We have presented a novel approach to global illumination problems, by showing how to adapt the Metropolis sampling method to light transport. Our algorithm starts from a few seed light transport paths and applies a sequence of random mutations to them. In the steady state, the resulting Markov chain visits each path with a probability proportional to that path's contribution to the image. The MLT algorithm is notable for its generality and simplicity. A single control structure can be used with different mutation strategies to handle a variety of difficult lighting situations. In addition, the MLT algorithm has low memory requirements and always computes an unbiased result.

Many refinements of this basic idea are possible. For example, with modest changes we could use MLT to compute view-independent radiance solutions, by letting the m_j be the basis function coefficients, and defining $f(\bar{x}) = \sum_j f_j(\bar{x})$. We could also use MLT to render a sequences of images (as in animation), by sampling the the entire space-time of paths at once (thus, a mutation might try to perturb a path forward or backward in time). Another interesting problem is to determine the optimal settings for the various parameters used by the algorithm. The values we use have not been extensively tuned, so that further efficiency improvements may be possible. We hope to address some of these refinements and extensions in the future.

8 Acknowledgements

We would especially like to thank the anonymous reviewers for their detailed comments. In particular, review #4 led to significant improvements in the formulation and exposition of the paper. Thanks also to Matt Pharr for his comments and artwork.

This research was supported by NSF contract number CCR-9623851, and MURI contract DAAH04-96-1-0007.

References

[1] ARVO, J., AND KIRK, D. Particle transport and image synthesis. *Computer Graphics (SIGGRAPH 90 Proceedings) 24*, 4 (Aug. 1990), 63–66.

[2] BEYER, M., AND LANGE, B. Rayvolution: An evolutionary ray tracing algorithm. In *Eurographics Rendering Workshop 1994 Proceedings* (June 1994), pp. 137–146. Also in *Photorealistic Rendering Techniques*, Springer-Verlag, New York, 1995.

[3] COLLINS, S. Reconstruction of indirect illumination from area luminaires. In *Rendering Techniques '95* (1995), pp. 274–283. Also in *Eurographics Rendering Workshop 1996 Proceedings* (June 1996).

[4] COOK, R. L., PORTER, T., AND CARPENTER, L. Distributed ray tracing. *Computer Graphics (SIGGRAPH 84 Proceedings) 18*, 3 (July 1984), 137–145.

[5] DUTRE, P., AND WILLEMS, Y. D. Potential-driven Monte Carlo particle tracing for diffuse environments with adaptive probability density functions. In *Rendering Techniques '95* (1995), pp. 306–315. Also in *Eurographics Rendering Workshop 1996 Proceedings* (June 1996).

[6] GOLDBERG, D. E. *Genetic Algorithms in Search, Optimization, and Machine Learning.* Addison-Wesley, Reading, Massachusetts, 1989.

[7] HALMOS, P. R. *Measure Theory.* Van Nostrand, New York, 1950.

[8] HECKBERT, P. S. Adaptive radiosity textures for bidirectional ray tracing. In *Computer Graphics (SIGGRAPH 90 Proceedings)* (Aug. 1990), vol. 24, pp. 145–154.

[9] JENSEN, H. W. Importance driven path tracing using the photon map. In *Eurographics Rendering Workshop 1995* (June 1995), Eurographics.

[10] KAJIYA, J. T. The rendering equation. In *Computer Graphics (SIGGRAPH 86 Proceedings)* (Aug. 1986), vol. 20, pp. 143–150.

[11] KALOS, M. H., AND WHITLOCK, P. A. *Monte Carlo Methods, Volume I: Basics.* John Wiley & Sons, New York, 1986.

[12] LAFORTUNE, E. P., AND WILLEMS, Y. D. Bi-directional path tracing. In *CompuGraphics Proceedings* (Alvor, Portugal, Dec. 1993), pp. 145–153.

[13] LAFORTUNE, E. P., AND WILLEMS, Y. D. A theoretical framework for physically based rendering. *Computer Graphics Forum 13*, 2 (June 1994), 97–107.

[14] LAFORTUNE, E. P., AND WILLEMS, Y. D. A 5D tree to reduce the variance of Monte Carlo ray tracing. In *Rendering Techniques '95* (1995), pp. 11–20. Also in *Eurographics Rendering Workshop 1996 Proceedings* (June 1996).

[15] METROPOLIS, N., ROSENBLUTH, A. W., ROSENBLUTH, M. N., TELLER, A. H., AND TELLER, E. Equations of state calculations by fast computing machines. *Journal of Chemical Physics 21* (1953), 1087–1091.

[16] MITCHELL, D. P., AND HANRAHAN, P. Illumination from curved reflectors. In *Computer Graphics (SIGGRAPH 92 Proceedings)* (July 1992), vol. 26, pp. 283–291.

[17] PATTANAIK, S. N., AND MUDUR, S. P. Adjoint equations and random walks for illumination computation. *ACM Transactions on Graphics 14* (Jan. 1995), 77–102.

[18] PESKUN, P. H. Optimum monte-carlo sampling using markov chains. *Biometrika 60*, 3 (1973), 607–612.

[19] REIF, J. H., TYGAR, J. D., AND YOSHIDA, A. Computability and complexity of ray tracing. *Discrete and Computational Geometry 11* (1994), 265–287.

[20] SHIRLEY, P., WADE, B., HUBBARD, P. M., ZARESKI, D., WALTER, B., AND GREENBERG, D. P. Global illumination via density-estimation. In *Eurographics Rendering Workshop 1995 Proceedings* (June 1995), pp. 219–230. Also in *Rendering Techniques '95*, Springer-Verlag, New York, 1995.

[21] SHIRLEY, P., WANG, C., AND ZIMMERMAN, K. Monte Carlo methods for direct lighting calculations. *ACM Transactions on Graphics 15*, 1 (Jan. 1996), 1–36.

[22] SPANIER, J., AND GELBARD, E. M. *Monte Carlo Principles and Neutron Transport Problems.* Addison-Wesley, Reading, Massachusetts, 1969.

[23] VEACH, E. Non-symmetric scattering in light transport algorithms. In *Eurographics Rendering Workshop 1996 Proceedings* (June 1996) Also in *Rendering Techniques '96*, Springer-Verlag, New York, 1996.

[24] VEACH, E., AND GUIBAS, L. Bidirectional estimators for light transport. In *Eurographics Rendering Workshop 1994 Proceedings* (June 1994), pp. 147–162. Also in *Photorealistic Rendering Techniques*, Springer-Verlag, New York, 1995.

[25] VEACH, E., AND GUIBAS, L. J. Optimally combining sampling techniques for Monte Carlo rendering. In *SIGGRAPH 95 Proceedings* (Aug. 1995), Addison-Wesley, pp. 419–428.

[26] WHITTED, T. An improved illumination model for shaded display. *Communications of the ACM 32*, 6 (June 1980), 343–349.

Appendix A

To prove that (12) is unbiased, we show that the following identity is satisfied at each step of the random walk:

$$\int_{\mathbf{R}} w \, q_i(w, \bar{x}) \, dw = f(\bar{x}) \,, \qquad (16)$$

where q_i is the joint probability distribution of the i-th weighted sample $(W_i, \bar{X}_i)$. Clearly this condition is satisfied by q_0, noting that $q_0(w, \bar{x}) = \delta(w - f(\bar{x})/p_0(\bar{x})) \, p_0(\bar{x})$ (where δ denotes the Dirac delta distribution).

Next, observe that (4) is still true with p_j replaced by $q_j(w, \bar{x})$ (since the mutations set $W_i = W_{i-1}$). Multiplying both sides of (4) by w and integrating, we obtain

$$\int_{\mathbf{R}} w \, q_i(w, \bar{x}) \, dw = \int_{\mathbf{R}} w \, q_{i-1}(w, \bar{x}) \,,$$

so that (16) is preserved by each mutation step.

Now given (16), the desired estimate (12) is unbiased since

$$E[W_i \, w_j(\bar{X}_i)] = \int_{\Omega} \int_{\mathbf{R}} w \, w_j(\bar{x}) \, p_i(w, \bar{x}) \, dw \, d\mu(\bar{x})$$

$$= \int_{\Omega} w_j(\bar{x}) \, f(\bar{x}) \, d\mu(\bar{x}) \; = \; m_j \,.$$

Visibility Culling using Hierarchical Occlusion Maps

Hansong Zhang   Dinesh Manocha   Tom Hudson   Kenneth E. Hoff III

Department of Computer Science
University of North Carolina
Chapel Hill, NC 27599-3175
{zhangh,dm,hudson,hoff}@cs.unc.edu
http://www.cs.unc.edu/~{zhangh,dm,hudson,hoff}

Abstract: We present hierarchical occlusion maps (HOM) for visibility culling on complex models with high depth complexity. The culling algorithm uses an object space bounding volume hierarchy and a hierarchy of image space occlusion maps. Occlusion maps represent the aggregate of projections of the occluders onto the image plane. For each frame, the algorithm selects a small set of objects from the model as occluders and renders them to form an initial occlusion map, from which a hierarchy of occlusion maps is built. The occlusion maps are used to cull away a portion of the model not visible from the current viewpoint. The algorithm is applicable to all models and makes no assumptions about the size, shape, or type of occluders. It supports approximate culling in which small holes in or among occluders can be ignored. The algorithm has been implemented on current graphics systems and has been applied to large models composed of hundreds of thousands of polygons. In practice, it achieves significant speedup in interactive walkthroughs of models with high depth complexity.
CR Categories and Subject Descriptors: I.3.5 [**Computer Graphics**]: Computational Geometry and Object Modeling
Key Words and Phrases: visibility culling, interactive display, image pyramid, occlusion culling, hierarchical data structures

1 Introduction

Interactive display and walkthrough of large geometric models currently pushes the limits of graphics technology. Environments composed of millions of primitives (e.g. polygons) are not uncommon in applications such as simulation-based design of large mechanical systems, architectural visualization, or walkthrough of outdoor scenes. Although throughput of graphics systems has increased considerably over the years, the size and complexity of these environments have been growing even faster. In order to display such models at interactive rates, the rendering algorithms need to use techniques based on visibility culling, levels-of-detail, texturing, etc. to limit the number of primitives rendered in each frame. In this paper, we focus on visibility culling algorithms, whose goal is to cull away large portions of the environment not visible from the current viewpoint.

Our criteria for an effective visibility culling algorithm are *generality*, *interactive performance*, and *significant culling*. Additionally, in order for it to be *practical*, it should be implementable on current graphics systems and work well on large real-world models.

Main Contribution: In this paper, we present a new algorithm for visibility culling in complex environments with high depth

Figure 1: *Demonstration of our algorithm on the CAD model of a submarine's auxiliary machine room. The model has 632,252 polygons. The green lines outline the viewing frustum. Blue indicates objects selected as occluders, gray the objects not culled by our algorithm and transparent red the objects culled away. For this particular view, 82.7% of the model is culled.*

complexity. At each frame, the algorithm carefully selects a small subset of the model as occluders and renders the occluders to build *hierarchical occlusion maps* (HOM). The hierarchy is an image pyramid and each map in the hierarchy is composed of pixels corresponding to rectangular blocks in the screen space. The pixel value records the *opacity* of the block. The algorithm decomposes the visibility test for an object into a two-dimensional overlap test, performed against the occlusion map hierarchy, and a conservative Z test to compare the depth. The overall approach combines an *object space* bounding volume hierarchy (also useful for view frustum culling) with the *image space* occlusion map hierarchy to cull away a portion of the model not visible from the current viewpoint. Some of the main features of the algorithm are:

1. **Generality:** The algorithm requires no special structures in the model and places *no restriction* on the types of occluders. The occluders may be polygonal objects, curved surfaces, or even not be geometrically defined (e.g. a billboard).

2. **Occluder Fusion:** A key characteristic of the algorithm is the ability to *combine* a "forest" of small or disjoint occluders, rather than using only large occluders. In most cases,

the union of a set of occluders can occlude much more than what each of them can occlude taken separately. This is very useful for large mechanical CAD and outdoor models.

3. **Significant Culling:** On high depth complexity models, the algorithm is able to cull away a significant fraction (up to 95%) of the model from most viewpoints.

4. **Portability:** The algorithm can be implemented on most current graphics systems. Its main requirement is the ability to read back the frame-buffer. The construction of hierarchical occlusion maps can be accelerated by texture mapping hardware. It is not susceptible to degeneracies in the input and can be parallelized on multiprocessor systems.

5. **Efficiency:** The construction of occlusion maps takes a few milliseconds per frame on current medium- to high-end graphics systems. The culling algorithm achieves significant speedup in interactive walkthroughs of models with high depth complexity. The algorithm involves no significant preprocessing and is applicable to dynamic environments.

6. **Approximate Visibility Culling:** Our approach can also use the hierarchy of maps to perform *approximate* culling. By varying an *opacity threshold* parameter the algorithm is able to fill small transparent holes in the occlusion maps and to cull away portions of the model which are visible through small gaps in the occluders.

The resulting algorithm has been implemented on different platforms (SGI Max Impact and Infinite Reality) and applied to city models, CAD models, and dynamic environments. It obtains considerable speedup in overall frame rate. In Figure 1 we demonstrate its performance on a submarine's Auxiliary Machine Room.

Organization: The rest of the paper is organized as follows: . We briefly survey related work in Section 2 and give an overview of our approach in Section 3. Section 4 describes occlusion maps and techniques for fast implementation on current graphics systems. In Section 5 we describe the entire culling algorithm. We describe its implementation and performance in Section 6. Section 7 analyses our algorithm and compares it with other approaches. Finally, in Section 8, we briefly describe some future directions.

2 Related Work

Visibility computation and hidden surface removal are classic problems in computer graphics [FDHF90]. Some of the commonly used visibility algorithms are based on Z-buffer [Cat74] and view-frustum culling [Cla76, GBW90]. Others include Painter's Algorithm [FDHF90] and area-subdivision algorithms [War69, FDHF90].

There is significant literature on visible surface computation in computational geometry. Many asymptotically efficient algorithms have been proposed for hidden surface removal [Mul89, McK87] (see [Dor94] for a recent survey). However, the practical utility of these algorithms is unclear at the moment.

Efficient algorithms for calculating the visibility relationship among a static group of 3D polygons from arbitrary viewpoints have been proposed based on the binary space-partitioning (BSP) tree [FKN80]. The tree construction may involve considerable pre-processing in terms of time and space requirements for large models. In [Nay92], Naylor has given an output-sensitive visibility algorithm using BSPs. It uses a 2D BSP tree to represent images and presents an algorithm to project a 3D BSP tree, representing the model in object space, into a 2D BSP tree representing its image.

Many algorithms structure the model database into *cells* or regions, and use a combination of off-line and on-line algorithms for cell-to-cell visibility and the conservative computation of the potentially visible set (PVS) of primitives [ARB90, TS91, LG95]. Such approaches have been successfully used to visualize architectural models, where the division of a building into discrete rooms lends itself to a natural division of the database into cells. It is not apparent that cell-based approaches can be generalized to an arbitrary model.

Other algorithms for densely-occluded but somewhat less-structured models have been proposed by Yagel and Ray [YR96]. They used regular spatial subdivision to partition the model into cells and describe a 2D implementation. However, the resulting algorithm is very memory-intensive and does not scale well to large models.

Object space algorithms for occlusion culling in general polygonal models have been presented by Coorg and Teller [CT96b, CT96a] and Hudson et al. [Hud96]. These algorithms dynamically compute a subset of the objects as occluders and use them to cull away portions of the model. In particular, [CT96b, CT96a] compute an arrangement corresponding to a linearized portion of an aspect graph and track the viewpoint within it to check for occlusion. [Hud96] use shadow frusta and fast interference tests for occlusion culling. All of them are object-space algorithms and the choice of occluder is restricted to convex objects or simple combination of convex objects (e.g. two convex polytope sharing an edge). These algorithms are unable to combine a "forest" of small non-convex or disjoint occluders to cull away large portions of the model.

A hierarchical Z-buffer algorithm combining spatial and temporal coherence has been presented in [GKM93, GK94, Gre95]. It uses two hierarchical data structures: an octree and a Z-pyramid. The algorithm exploits coherence by performing visibility queries on the Z-pyramid and is very effective in culling large portions of high-depth complexity models. However, most current graphics systems do not support the Z-pyramid capability in hardware, and simulating it in software can be relatively expensive. In [GK94], Greene and Kass used a quadtree data structure to test visibility throughout image-space regions for anti-aliased rendering. [Geo95] describes an implementation of the Z-query operation on a parallel graphics architecture (PixelPlanes 5) for obscuration culling.

More recently, Greene [Gre96] has presented a hierarchical tiling algorithm using coverage masks. It uses an image hierarchy named a "coverage pyramid" for visibility culling. Traversing polygons from front to back, it can process densely occluded scenes efficiently and is well suited to anti-aliasing by oversampling and filtering.

For dynamic environments, Sudarsky and Gotsman [SG96] have presented an output-sensitive algorithm which minimizes the time required to update the hierarchical data structure for a dynamic object and minimize the number of dynamic objects for which the structure has to be updated.

A number of techniques for interactive walkthrough of large geometric databases have been proposed. Refer to [RB96] for a recent survey. A number of commercial systems like *Performer* [RH94], used for high performance graphics, and *Brush* [SBM+94], used for visualizing architectural and CAD models, are available. They use techniques based on view-frustum culling, levels-of-detail, etc., but have little support for occlusion culling on arbitrary models.

There is substantial literature on the visibility problem from the flight simulator community. An overview of flight simulator architectures is given in [Mue95]. Most notably, the Singer Company's Modular Digital Image Generator [Lat94] renders front to back using a hierarchy of mask buffers to skip over already cov-

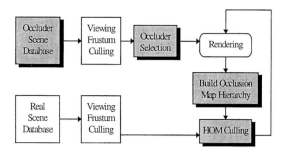

Figure 2: *Modified graphics pipeline showing our algorithm. The shaded blocks indicate components unique to culling with hierarchical occlusion map.*

ered spans, segments or rows in the image. General Electric's COMPU-SCENE PT2000 [Bun89] uses a similar algorithm but does not require the input polygons to be in front-to-back order and the mask buffer is not hierarchical. The Loral GT200 [LORA] first renders near objects and fills in a mask buffer, which is used to cull away far objects. Sogitec's APOGEE system uses the Meta-Z-buffer, which is similar to hierarchical Z buffer [Chu94].

The structure of hierarchical occlusion maps is similar to some of the hierarchies that have been proposed for images, such as image pyramids [TP75], MIP maps [Wil83], Z-pyramids [GKM93], coverage pyramids [Gre96], and two-dimensional wavelet transforms like the non-standard decomposition [GBR91].

3 Overview

In this paper we present a novel solution to the visibility problem. The heart of the algorithm is a hierarchy of occlusion maps, which records the aggregate projection of occluders onto the image plane at different resolutions. In other words, the maps capture the cumulative occluding effects of the occluders. We use occlusion maps because they can be built quickly and have several unique properties (described later in the paper). The use of occlusion maps reflects a decomposition of the visibility problem into two sub-problems: a two-dimensional overlap test and a depth test. The former decides whether the screen space projection of the potential occludee lies completely within the screen space projection of the union of all occluders. The latter determines whether or not the potential occludee is behind the occluders. We use occlusion maps for the overlap tests, and a *depth estimation buffer* for the conservative depth test. In the conventional Z-buffer algorithm (as well as in the hierarchical Z-buffer algorithm), the overlap test is implicitly performed as a side effect of the depth comparison by initializing the Z-buffer with large numbers.

The algorithm renders the occluders at each frame and builds a hierarchy (pyramid) of occlusion maps. In addition to the model database, the algorithm maintains a separate *occluder database*, which is derived from the model database as a preprocessing step. Both databases are represented as bounding volume hierarchies. The rendering pipeline with our algorithm incorporated is illustrated in Figure 2. The shaded blocks indicate new stages introduced due to our algorithm. For each frame, the pipeline executes in two major phases:

1. Construction of the Occlusion Map Hierarchy: The occluders are selected from the occluder database and rendered to build the occlusion map hierarchy. This involves:

- **View-frustum culling:** The algorithm traverses the bounding volume hierarchy of the occluder database to find occluders lying in the viewing frustum.

- **Occluder selection:** The algorithm selects a subset of the occluders lying in the viewing frustum. It utilizes temporal coherence between successive frames.

- **Occluder rendering and depth estimation:** The selected occluders are rendered to form an image in the framebuffer which is the highest resolution occlusion map. Objects are rendered in pure white with no lighting or texturing. The resulting image has only black and white pixels except for antialiased edges. A depth estimation buffer is built to record the depth of the occluders.

- **Building the Hierarchical Occlusion Maps:** After occluders are rendered, the algorithm recursively filters the rendered image down by averaging blocks of pixels. This process can be accelerated by texture mapping hardware on many current graphics systems.

2. Visibility Culling with Hierarchical Occlusion Maps: Given an occlusion map hierarchy, the algorithm traverses the bounding volume hierarchy of the model database to perform visibility culling. The main components of this stage are:

- **View-frustum Culling:** The algorithm applies standard view-frustum culling to the model database.

- **Depth Comparison:** For each potential occludee, the algorithm conservatively checks whether it is behind the occluders.

- **Overlap test with Occlusion Maps:** The algorithm traverses the occlusion map hierarchy to conservatively decide if each potential occludee's screen space projection falls completely within the opaque areas of the maps.

Only objects that fail one of the latter two tests (depth or overlap) are rendered.

4 Occlusion Maps

In this section, we present occlusion maps, algorithms using texture mapping hardware for fast construction of the hierarchy of occlusion maps, and state a number of properties of occlusion maps which are used by the visibility culling algorithm.

When an opaque object is projected to the screen, the area of its projection is made opaque. The *opacity* of a block on the screen is defined as the ratio of the sum of the opaque areas in the block to the total area of the block. An *occlusion map* is a two-dimensional array in which each pixel records the opacity of a rectangular block of screen space. Any rendered image can have an accompanying occlusion map which has the same resolution and stores the opacity for each pixel. In such a case, the occlusion map is essentially the α channel [FDHF90] of the rendered image (assuming α values for objects are set properly during rendering), though generally speaking a pixel in the occlusion map can correspond to a block of pixels in screen space.

4.1 Image Pyramid

Given the lowest level occlusion map, the algorithm constructs from it a hierarchy of occlusion maps (HOM) by recursively applying the average operator to rectangular blocks of pixels. This operation forms an *image pyramid* as shown in Figure 3. The resulting hierarchy represents the occlusion map at multiple resolutions. It greatly accelerates the overlap test and is used for approximate culling. In the rest of the paper, we follow the convention that the *highest* resolution occlusion map of a hierarchy is at *level* 0.

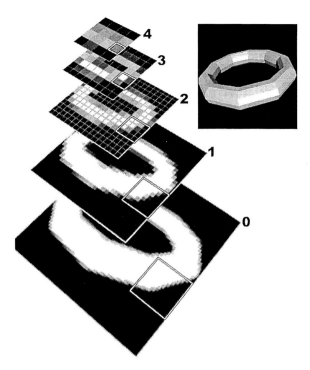

Figure 3: *The hierarchy of occlusion maps. This particular hierarchy is created by recursively averaging over 2 blocks of pixels. The outlined square marks the correspondence of one top-level pixel to pixels in the other levels. The image also shows the rendering of the torus to which the hierarchy corresponds.*

The algorithm first renders the occluders into an image, which forms the lowest-level and highest resolution occlusion map. This image represents an *image-space fusion* of all occluders in the object space. The occlusion map hierarchy is built by recursively filtering from the highest-resolution map down to some minimal resolution (e.g. 4×4). The highest resolution need not match that of the image of the model database. Using a lower image resolution for rendering occluders may lead to inaccuracy for occlusion culling near the edges of the objects, but it speeds up the time for constructing the hierarchy. Furthermore, if hardware multi-sampled anti-aliasing is available, the lowest-level occlusion map has more accuracy. This is due to the fact that the anti-aliased image in itself is already a filtered down version of a larger super-sampled image on which the occluders were rendered.

4.2 Fast Construction of the Hierarchy

When filtering is performed on 2×2 blocks of pixels, hierarchy construction can be accelerated by graphics hardware that supports bilinear interpolation of texture maps. The averaging operator for 2×2 blocks is actually a special case of *bilinear interpolation*. More precisely, the bilinear interpolation of four scalars or vectors $\mathbf{v}_0, \mathbf{v}_1, \mathbf{v}_2, \mathbf{v}_3$ is:

$$(1 - \alpha)(1 - \beta)\mathbf{v}_0 + \alpha(1 - \beta)\mathbf{v}_1 + \alpha\beta\mathbf{v}_2 + (1 - \alpha)\beta\mathbf{v}_3,$$

where $0 \leq \alpha \leq 1, 0 \leq \beta \leq 1$ are the weights. In our case, we use $\alpha = \beta = 0.5$ and this formula produces the average of the four values. By carefully setting the texture coordinates, we can filter a $2N \times 2N$ occlusion map to $N \times N$ by drawing a two dimensional rectangle of size $N \times N$, texturing it with the $2N \times 2N$ occlusion map, and reading back the rendered image as the $N \times N$ occlusion map. Figure 4 illustrates this process.

The graphics hardware typically needs some setup time for the required operations. When the size of the map to be filtered is relatively small, setup time may dominate the computation. In such cases, the use of texture mapping hardware may slow down the computation of occlusion maps rather than accelerate it, and hierarchy building is faster on the host CPU. The break-even point between hardware and software hierarchy construction varies with different graphics systems.

[BM96] presents a technique for generating mipmaps by using a hardware accumulation buffer. We did not use this method because the accumulation buffer is less commonly supported in current graphics systems than texture mapping.

4.3 Properties of Occlusion Maps

The hierarchical occlusion maps for an occluder set have several desirable properties for accelerating visibility culling. The visibility culling algorithm presented in Section 5 utilizes these properties.

1. Occluder fusion: Occlusion maps represent the fusion of small and possibly disjoint occluders. No assumptions are made on the shape, size, or geometry of the occluders. Any object that is renderable can serve as an occluder.

2. Hierarchical overlap test: The hierarchy allows us to perform a fast overlap test in screen space for visibility culling. This test is described in more detail in Section 5.1.

3. High-level opacity estimation: The opacity values in a low-resolution occlusion map give an estimate of the opacity values in higher-resolution maps. For instance, if a pixel in a higher level map has a very low intensity value, it implies that almost all of its descendant pixels have low opacities, i.e. there is a low possibility of occlusion. This is due to the fact that occlusion maps are based on the average operator rather than the minimum or maximum operators. This property allows for a *conservative early termination* of the overlap test.

The opacity hierarchy also provides a natural method for *aggressive early termination*, or approximate occlusion culling. It may be used to cull away portions of the model visible only through small gaps in or among occluders. A high opacity value of a pixel in a low resolution map implies that most of its descendant pixels are opaque. The algorithm uses the *opacity threshold* parameter to control the degree of approximation. More details are given in Section 5.4.

5 Visibility Culling with Hierarchical Occlusion Maps

An overview of the visibility culling algorithm has been presented in Section 3. In this section, we present detailed algorithms for overlap tests with occlusion maps, depth comparison, and approximate culling.

5.1 Overlap Test with Occlusion Maps

The two-dimensional overlap test of a potential occludee against the union of occluders is performed by checking the opacity of the pixels it overlaps in the occlusion maps. An exact overlap test would require a scan-conversion of the potential occludee to find out which pixels it touches, which is relatively expensive to do in software. Rather, we present a simple, efficient, and *conservative* solution for the overlap test.

For each object in the viewing frustum, the algorithm conservatively approximates its projection with a screen-space bounding rectangle of its bounding box. This rectangle covers a superset of the pixels covered by the actual object. The extremal values of the bounding rectangle are computed by projecting the corners

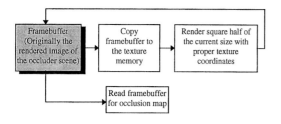

Figure 4: *Use of texture-mapping hardware to build occlusion maps*

of the bounding box. The main advantage of using the bounding rectangle is the reduced cost of finding the pixels covered by a rectangle compared to scan-converting general polygons.

The algorithm uses the occlusion map hierarchy to accelerate the overlap test. It begins the test at the level of the hierarchy where the size of a pixel in the occlusion map is approximately the same size as the bounding rectangle. The algorithm examines each pixel in this map that overlaps the bounding rectangle. If any of the overlapping pixels is not completely opaque [1], the algorithm recursively descends from that pixel to the next level of the hierarchy and checks all of its sub-pixels that are covered by the bounding rectangle. If all the pixels checked are completely opaque, the algorithm concludes that the occludee's projection is completely inside that of the occluders. If not, the algorithm conservatively concludes that the occludee may not be completely obscured by the occluders, and it is rendered.

The algorithm supports *conservative early termination* in overlap tests. If the opacity of a pixel in a low-resolution map is too low, there is small probability that we can find high opacity values even if we descend into the sub-pixels. So the overlap test stops and concludes that the object is not occluded. The *transparency thresholds* are used to define these lower bounds on opacity below which traversal of the hierarchy is terminated.

5.2 Depth Comparison

Occlusion maps do not contain depth information. They provide a necessary condition for occlusion in terms of overlap tests in the image plane, but do not detect whether an object is in front of or behind the occluders. The algorithm manages depth information separately to complete the visibility test. In this section, we propose two algorithms for depth comparison.

5.2.1 A Single Z Plane

One of the simplest ways to manage depth is to use a single Z plane. The Z plane is a plane parallel to and beyond the near plane. This plane separates the occluders from the potential occludees so that any object lying beyond the plane is farther away than any occluder. As a result, an object which is contained within the projection of the occluders and lies beyond the Z plane is completely occluded. This is an extremely simple and conservative method which gives a rather coarse bound for the depth values of all occluders.

5.2.2 Depth Estimation Buffer

The depth estimation buffer is a software buffer that provides a more general solution for conservatively estimating the depth of occluders. Rather than using a single plane to capture the depth

of the entire set of occluders, the algorithm partitions the screen-space and uses a separate plane for each region of the partition. By using a separate depth for each region of the partition, the algorithm obtains a finer measure of the distances to the occluders. The depth estimation buffer is essentially a general-purpose software Z buffer that records the farthest distances instead of the nearest.

An alternative to using the depth estimation buffer might be to read the accurate depth values back from a hardware Z buffer after rendering the occluders. This approach was not taken mainly because it involves further assumptions of hardware features (i.e. there is a hardware Z-buffer, and we are able to read Z-values reasonably fast in a easily-usable format).

Construction of the depth estimation buffer: The depth estimation buffer is built at every frame, which requires determining the pixels to which the occluders project on the image plane. Scan-converting the occluders to do this would be unacceptably expensive. As we did in constructing occlusion maps, we conservatively estimate the projection and depth of an occluder by its screen-space bounding rectangle and the Z value of its bounding volume's farthest vertex. The algorithm checks each buffer entry covered by the rectangle for possible updates. If the rectangle's Z value is greater than the old entry, the entry is updated. This process is repeated for all occluders.

Conservative Depth Test: To perform the conservative depth test on a potential occludee, it is approximated by the screen space bounding rectangle of its bounding box (in the same manner as in overlap tests), which is assigned a depth value the same as that of the nearest vertex on the bounding box. Each entry of the depth estimation buffer covered by the rectangle is checked to see if any entry is greater than the rectangle's Z value. If this is the case then the object is conservatively regarded as being partly in front of the union of all occluders and thus must be rendered.

The cost of the conservative Z-buffer test and update, though far cheaper than accurate operations, can still be expensive as the resolution of the depth estimation buffer increases. Furthermore, since we are performing a conservative estimation of the objects' screen space extents, there is a point where increasing the resolution of the depth estimation buffer does not help increase the accuracy of depth information. Normally the algorithm uses only a coarse resolution (e.g. 64×64).

5.3 Occluder Selection

At each frame, the algorithm selects an occluder set. The *optimal* set of occluders is exactly the visible portion of the model. Finding this optimal set is the visible surface computation problem itself. Another possibility is to pre-compute global visibility information for computing the useful occluders at every viewpoint. The fastest known algorithm for computing the effects on global visibility due to a single polyhedron with m vertices can take $O(m^6 \log m)$ time in the worst case [GCS91].

We present algorithms to estimate a set of occluders that are used to cull a significant fraction of the model. We perform preprocessing to derive an occluder database from the model. At runtime the algorithm dynamically selects a set of occluders from that database.

5.3.1 Building the Occluder Database

The goal of the pre-processing step is to discard objects which do not serve as good occluders from most viewpoints. We use the following criteria to select good occluders from the model database:

- **Size:** Small objects will not serve as good occluders unless the viewer is very close to them.

---

[1] By definition, a pixel is completely opaque if its value is above or equal to the *opacity threshold*, which is defined in Section 5.4.

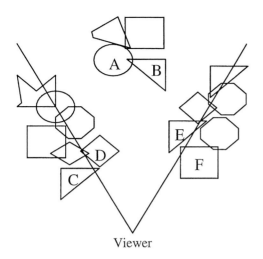

Viewer

Figure 5: *Distance criterion for dynamic selection*

- **Redundancy:** Some objects, e.g. a clock on the wall, provide redundant occlusion and should be removed from the database.

- **Rendering Complexity:** Objects with a high polygon count or rendering complexity are not preferred, as scan-converting them may take considerable time and affect the overall frame rate.

5.3.2 Dynamic Selection

At runtime, the algorithm selects a set of objects from the occluder database. The algorithm uses a distance criterion, size, and temporal coherence to select occluders.

The single Z-plane method for depth comparison, presented in Section 5.2.1, is also an occluder selection method. All objects not completely beyond the Z-plane are occluders.

When the algorithm uses the depth estimation buffer, it dynamically selects occluders based on a distance criterion and a limit ($\mathcal{L}$) on the number of occluder polygons. These two variables may vary between frames as a function of the overall frame rate and percentage of model culled. Given $\mathcal{L}$, the algorithm tries to find a set of good occluders whose total polygon count is less than $\mathcal{L}$.

The algorithm considers each object in the occluder database lying in the viewing frustum. The distance between the viewer and the center of an object's bounding volume is used as an estimate of the distance from the viewer to the object. The algorithm sorts these distances, and selects the nearest objects as occluder until their combined polygon count exceeds $\mathcal{L}$. This works well for most situations, except when a good occluder is relatively far away. One such situation has been shown in Figure 5. The distance criterion will select C, D, E, F, etc. as occluders, but $\mathcal{L}$ will probably be exceeded *before* A and B are selected. Thus, we lose occlusion that would have been contributed by A and B. In other words, there is a hole in the occlusion map which decreases the culling rate.

Dynamic occluder selection can be assisted by visibility preprocessing of the occluder scene. The model space is subdivided by a uniform grid. Visibility is sampled at each grid point by surrounding the grid point with a cube and using an item buffer algorithm similar to the hemi-cube algorithm used in radiosity. Each grid point gets a lists of visible objects. At run-time, occluders can be chosen from visible object lists of grid points nearest to the viewing point.

5.4   Approximate Visibility Culling

A unique feature of our algorithm is to perform approximate visibility culling, which ignores objects only visible through small holes in or among the occluders. This ability is based on an inherent property of HOM: it naturally represents the combined occluder projections at different levels of detail.

In the process of filtering maps to build the hierarchy, a pixel in a low resolution map can obtain a high opacity value even if a small number of its descendant pixels have low opacity. Intuitively, a small group of low-opacity pixels (a "hole") in a high-resolution map can dissolve as the average operation (which involves high opacity values from neighboring pixels) is recursively applied to build lower-resolution maps.

The opacity value above which the pixel is considered completely opaque is called the *opacity threshold*, which is by default 1.0. The visibility culling algorithm varies the degree of approximation by changing the opacity threshold. As the threshold is lowered, the culling algorithm becomes more approximate. This effect of the opacity threshold is based on the fact that if a pixel is considered completely opaque, the culling algorithm does not go into the descendant pixels for further opacity checking. If the opacity of a pixel in a low-resolution map is not 1.0 (because some of the pixel's descendents have low opacities), but is still higher than the opacity threshold assigned to that map, the culling algorithm does not descend to the sub-pixels to find the low opacities. In effect, some small holes in higher-resolution maps are ignored. The opacity threshold specifies the size of the holes that can be ignored; the higher the threshold, the smaller the ignorable holes.

The opacity thresholds for each level of the hierarchy are computed by first deciding the maximum allowable size of a hole. For example, if the final image is 1024×1024 and a map is 64×64, then a pixel in the map corresponds to 16×16 pixels in the final image. If we consider 25 black pixels among 16×16 total pixels an ignorable hole, then the opacity threshold for the map is $1 - 25/(16 * 16) = 0.90$. Note that we are considering the worst case where the black pixels gather together to form the biggest hole, which is roughly a 5×5 black block. One level up the map hierarchy, where resolution is 32×32 and where a map pixel corresponds to 32×32 screen pixels, the threshold becomes $1 - 25/(32 * 32) = 0.98$.

Consider the k-th level of the hierarchy. Let n black pixels among m total pixels form an ignorable hole, then the opacity threshold is $O_k = 1 - \frac{n}{m}$. Since at the $k + 1$-th level[2] each map pixel corresponds to four times as many pixels in the final image, the opacity threshold is

$$O_{k+1} = 1 - \frac{n}{4m} = 1 - \frac{1 - O_k}{4} = \frac{3 + O_k}{4}.$$

Let the opacity threshold in the highest resolution map be O_{min}. If a pixel in a lower resolution map has opacity lower than O_{min}, then it is not possible for all its descendant pixels have opacities greater than O_{min}. This means that if a high-level pixel is completely covered by a bounding rectangle and its opacity is lower than O_{min}, we can immediately conclude that the corresponding object is potentially visible. For pixels not completely covered by the rectangle (i.e. pixels intersecting the rectangle's edges), the algorithm always descends into sub-pixels.

To summarize the cases in the overlap test, a piece of pseudo-code is provided in 5.4.

Approximate visibility is useful because in many cases we don't expect to see many meaningful parts of the model through small holes in or among the occluders. Culling such portions of the model usually does not create noticeable visual artifacts.

---

[2]Remember that highest resolution map is level 0. See Figure 3.

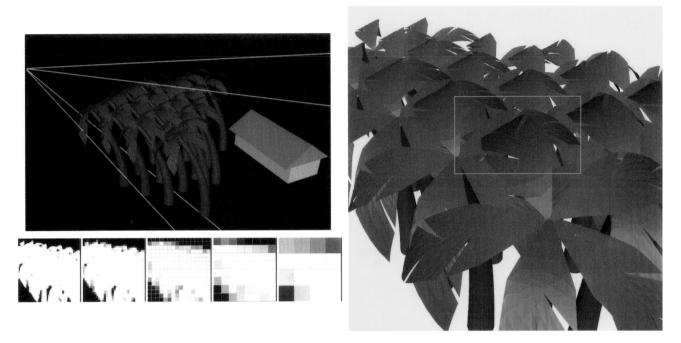

Figure 6: *These images show a view of an environment composed of trees and a house, with the trees as oclcuders. The green line in the left image indicates the view-frustum. The right image highlights the holes among the leaves with a yellow background. The screen space bounding rectangle of the house is shown in cyan. The occlusion map hierarchy is shown on the left.*

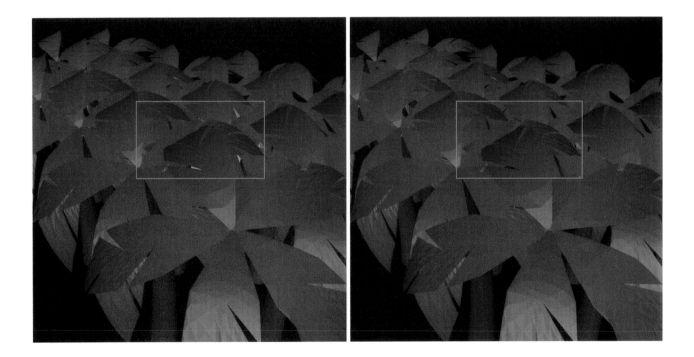

Figure 7: *Two images from the same view as in Figure 6. The left image is produced with no approximate culling. The right image uses opacity threshold values from 0.7 for the highest resolution map up to 1.0 for the lowest resolution map.*

```
CheckPixel(HOM, Level, Pixel, BoundingRect)
{
    Op = HOM[Level](Pixel.x, Pixel.y);
    Omin = HOM[0].OpacityThreshold;

    if (Op > HOM[Level].OpacityThreshold)
        return TRUE;
    else if (Level = 0)
        return FALSE;
    else if (Op < Omin AND
            Pixel.CompletelyInRect = TRUE)
        return FALSE;
    else
    {
        Result = TRUE;
        for each sub-pixel, Sp, that
                overlaps BoundingRect
        {
            Result = Result AND CheckPixel(HOM,
                Level-1, Sp, BoundingRect);
            if Result = FALSE
            return FALSE;
        }
    }
    return TRUE;
}


OverlapTest(HOM, Level, BoundingRect)
{
    for each pixel, P, in HOM[HOM.HighestLevel]
            that intersects BoundingRect
    {
        if (CheckPixel(HOM, HOM.HighestLevel, P)
                = FALSE)
            return FALSE;
    }
    return TRUE
}
```

Figure 8: *Pseudo-code for the overlap test between the occlusion map hierarchy and a bounding rectangle. This code assumes that necessary information is available as fields in the HOM and Pixel structures. The meaning of the fields are easily inferred from their names. The* CheckPixel *function check the opacity of a pixel, descending into sub-pixels as necessary. The* OverlapTest *function does the whole overlap test, which returns* TRUE *if bounding rectangle falls within completely opaque areas and* FALSE *otherwise.*

Omitting such holes can significantly increase the culling rate if many objects are potentially visible only through small holes. In Figure 6 and Figure 7, we illustrate approximate culling on an environment with trees as occluders.

It should be noted that in some situations approximate culling may result in noticeable artifacts, even if the opacity threshold is high. For example, if objects visible only through small holes are very bright (e.g. the sun beaming through holes among leaves of a tree), then strong popping can be observed as the viewer zooms closer. In such cases approximate culling should not be applied. Furthermore, approximate culling decreases accuracy of culling around the edges of occluders, which can also result in visual artifacts.

5.5 Dynamic Environments

The algorithm easily extends to dynamic environments. As no static bounding volume hierarchy may be available, the algorithm uses oriented bounding boxes around each object. The occluder selection algorithm involves no pre-processing, so the occluder database is exactly the model database. The oriented bounding boxes are used to construct the depth estimation buffer as well as to perform the overlap test with the occlusion map hierarchy.

6 Implementation and Performance

We have implemented the algorithm as part of a walkthrough system, which is based on OpenGL and currently runs on SGI platforms. Significant speed-ups in frame rates have been observed on different models. In this section, we discuss several implementation issues and discuss the system's performance on SGI Max Impacts and Infinite Reality platforms.

6.1 Implementation

As the first step in creating the occlusion map hierarchy, occluders are rendered in a 256×256 viewport in the back framebuffer, in full white color, with lighting and texture mapping turned off. Any one of the three color channels of the resulting image can serve as the highest-resolution occlusion map on which the hierarchy is based. An alternate method could be to render the occluders with the original color and shading parameters and use the α channel of the rendered image to construct the initial map. However, for constructing occlusion maps we do not need a "realistic" rendering of the occluders, which may be more expensive. In most cases the resolution of 256×256 is smaller than that of the final rendering of the model. As a result, it is possible to have artifacts in occlusion. In practice, if the final image is rendered at a resolution of 1024×1024, rendering occluders at 256×256 is a good trade-off between accuracy and time required to filter down the image in building the hierarchy.

To construct the occlusion map hierarchy, we recursively average 2×2 blocks of pixels using the texture mapping hardware as well as the host CPU. The resolution of the lowest-resolution map is typically 4×4. The break-even point between hardware and software hierarchy construction (as described in Section 4.2) varies with different graphics systems. For SGI Maximum Impacts, we observed the shortest construction time when the algorithm filters from 256×256 to 128×128 using texture-mapping hardware, and from 128×128 to 64×64 and finally down to 4×4 on the host CPU. For SGI InfiniteReality, which has faster pixel transfer rates, the best performance is obtained by filtering from 256×256 to 64×64 using the hardware and using the host CPU thereafter. Hierarchy construction time is about 9 milliseconds for the Max Impacts and 4 milliseconds for the Infinite Reality, with a small variance (around 0.5 milliseconds) between frames.

The implementation of the depth estimation buffer is optimized for block-oriented query and updates. The hierarchical overlap test is straight-forward to implement; It is relatively harder to optimize, as it is recursive in nature.

6.2 Performance

We demonstrate the performance of the algorithm on three models. These are:

- **City Model:** this is composed of models of London and has $312,524$ polygons. A bird's eye view of the model has been shown in Figure 11.

- **Dynamic Environment:** It is composed of dinosaurs and teapots, each undergoing independent random motion. The total polygon count is $986,800$. It is shown in Figure 12.

- **Submarine Auxiliary Machine Room (AMR):** It is a real-world CAD model obtained from industrial sources. The

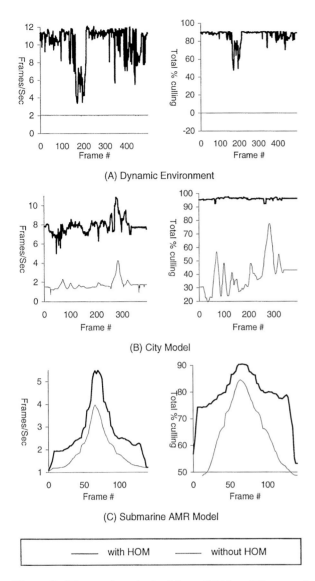

(A) Dynamic Environment

(B) City Model

(C) Submarine AMR Model

——— with HOM   ——— without HOM

Figure 9: *The speed-up obtained due to HOM on different models. The left graphs show the improvement in frame rate and the right graphs show the percentage of model culled. The statistics were gathered over a path for each model.*

model has 632, 252 polygons. Different views of the model are shown in Figure 1 and Figure 13.

As mentioned earlier, our algorithm uses a bounding volume hierarchy (i.e. a scene graph) for both the original model database as well as the occluder database. Each model we used is originally a collection of polygons with no structure information. We construct an axis-aligned bounding box hierarchy for each database.

For the dynamic environment and the city model, we use the model database itself as the occluder database, without any preprocessing for static occluder selection. For the AMR model, the pre-processing yields an occluder database of 217, 636 polygons. The algorithm removes many objects that have little potential of being a good occluder (like the bolts on the diesel engine, thin pipes etc.) from the original model. Further, most of these parts are densely tessellated, making them to expensive to be directly used as occluders. We use the simplified version of the parts which are produced by algorithms in [Cohen96]. Although many

simplification algorithms give good error bounds on the simplified model, they do not guarantee that the projection of the simplified object lies within that of the original. Therefore, visibility artifacts may be introduced by the simplified occluders. We use very tight error bounds so that artifacts are rarely noticeable.

The performance of the algorithms has been highlighted in Figure 9. The graphs on the left show the frame rate improvement, while the graphs on the right highlight the percentage of the model culled at every frame. The performance of the city model was generated on a SGI Maximum Impact while the other two were rendered on an SGI Infinite Reality. The actual performance varies due to two reasons:

1. Different models have varying depth complexities. Furthermore, the percentage of occlusion varies with the viewpoint.

2. The ability of the occluder selection algorithm to select the "right" subset of occluders. The performance of the greedy algorithm, e.g. distance based criterion, varies with the model distribution and the viewpoint.

The occluder polygon count budget ($\mathcal{L}$) per frame is important for the performance of the overall algorithm. If too few occluders are rendered, most of the pixels in the occlusion map have low opacities and the algorithm is not able to cull much. On the other hand, if too many occluder polygons are rendered, they may take a significant percentage of the total frame time and slow down the rendering algorithm. The algorithm starts with an initial guess on the polygon count and adaptively modifies it based on the percentage of the model culled and frame rate. If the percentage of the model culled is low, it increases the count. If the percentage is high and the frame rate is low, it decreases the count.

Average time spent in the different stages of the algorithm (occluder selection and rendering, hierarchy generation, occlusion culling and final rendering) has been shown in Figure 10. The average time to render the model without occlusion culling is normalized to 100%. In these cases, the average time in occluder rendering varies between $10 - 25\%$.

7 Analysis and Comparison

In this section we analyze some of the main features of our algorithm and compare it with other approaches.

Our algorithm is generally applicable to all models and obtains significant culling when there is high depth complexity. This is mainly due to its use of occlusion maps to combine occluders in image space. The extensive use of screen space bounding rectangles as an approximation of the object's screen space projection makes the overlap tests and depth tests fast and cheap.

In terms of hardware assumptions, the algorithm requires only the ability to read back the framebuffer. Texture mapping with bilinear interpolation, when available, can be directly used to accelerate the construction of the occlusion map hierarchy.

In general, if the algorithm is spending a certain percentage of the total frame time in occluder rendering, HOM generation and culling (depth test and overlap test), it should at least cull away a similar percentage of the model so as to justify the overhead of occlusion culling. If a model under some the viewing conditions does *not* have sufficient occlusion, the overall frame rate may decrease due to the overhead, in which case occlusion culling should be turned off.

7.1 Comparison to Object Space Algorithms

Work on cells and portals[ARB90, TS91, LG95] addresses a special class of densely occluded environments where there are plenty

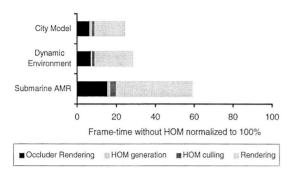

Figure 10: *Average speed-up obtained due to HOM culling on different models. The total time to render each model without HOM culling is normalized to 100%. Each bar shows the percentage of time spent in different stages of our algorithm.*

of cell and portal structures, as in an indoor architectural model. [ARB90, TS91] pre-processes the model to identify potentially visible set of primitives for each cell. [LG95] developed a dynamic version which eliminates the visibility pre-processing. These methods work very well for this particular type of environment, but are not applicable to models without cell/portal structures.

Our algorithm works without modification for environments with cells and portals, but occluder selection can be optimized for these environments. The cell boundaries can be used to form the occluder database. As an alternative, we can fill a viewport with white pixels and then render the portals in black to form the occlusion map. In general, however, we do not expect to outperform the specialized algorithms in cell/portal environments.

Two different object space solutions for more general models have been proposed by [CT96a, CT96b] and [Hud96]. They dynamically choose polygons and convex objects (or simple convex combination of polygons) as occluders and use them to cull away invisible portions of the model. However, many models do not have single big convex occluders. In such cases, merging small, irregular occluders is critical for significant culling, which is a difficult task in object space. Our algorithm lies between object space and image space and the occluder merging problem is solved in image space.

7.2   Comparison with Hierarchical Z-buffer Algorithm

In many ways, we present an alternative approach to hierarchical Z-buffer visibility [GKM93]. The main algorithm presented in [GKM93] performs updates of the Z-buffer hierarchy as geometry is rendered. It assumes special-purpose hardware for fast depth updating and querying to obtain interactive performance. It is potentially a very powerful and effective algorithm for visibility culling. However, we are not aware of any hardware implementation.

There is a possible variation of hierarchical Z-buffer algorithm which selects occluders, renders them, reads back the depth buffer once per frame, builds the Z-pyramid, and use the screen-space bounding rectangles for fast culling. The algorithm proposed in [GKM93] uses the exact projection of octree nodes, which requires software scan-conversion. In this case, the HOM approach and the hierarchical Z-buffer are comparable, each with some advantages over the other.

The HOM approach has the following advantages:

1. There is no need for a Z-buffer. Many low-end systems do

not support a Z-buffer and some image generators for flight simulators do not have one. Tile-based architectures like PixelFlow[MEP92] and Talisman[TK96] do not have a full-screen Z-buffer, but instead have volatile Z-buffers the size of a single tile. This makes getting Z values for the entire screen rather difficult.

2. The construction of HOM has readily-available hardware support (in the form of texture mapping with bilinear interpolation) on many graphics systems. Further, if filtering is performed in software, the cost of the average operator is smaller than the minimum/maximum operator (due to the absence of branch instructions).

3. HOM supports conservative early termination in the hierarchical test by using a transparency threshold (Section 5.1) and approximate occlusion culling by using an opacity threshold (Section 5.4). These features result from using an average operator.

On the other hand, the Hierarchical Z-buffer has depth values, which the HOM algorithm has to manage separately in the depth estimation buffer. This results in the following advantages of Hierarchical Z-buffer:

1. Culling is less conservative.

2. It is easier to use temporal coherence for occluder selection because nearest Z values for objects are available in the Z-buffer. Updating the active occluder list is more difficult in our algorithm since we only have estimated farthest Z values.

7.3   Comparison with Hierarchical Tiling with Coverage Masks

Hierarchical polygon tiling [Gre96] tiles polygons in front-to-back order and uses a "coverage" pyramid for visibility culling. The coverage pyramid and hierarchical occlusion maps serve the same purpose in that they both record the aggregate projections of objects. (In this sense, our method has more resemblance to hierarchical tiling than to the hierarchical Z-buffer.) However, a pixel in a mask in the coverage pyramid has only three values (covered, vacant or active), while a pixel in an occlusion map has a continuous opacity value. This has lead to desirable features, as discussed above. Like HOM, the coverage masks do not contain depth information and the algorithm in [Gre96] uses a BSP-tree for depth-ordering of polygons. Our algorithm is not restricted to rendering the polygons front to back. Rather, it only needs a conservatively estimated boundary between the occluders and potential occludees, which is represented by the depth estimation buffer. Hierarchical tiling is tightly coupled with polygon scan-conversion and has to be significantly modified to deal with non-polygonal objects, such as curved surfaces or textured billboards. Our algorithm does not directly deal with low-level rendering but utilizes existing graphics systems. Thus it is readily applicable to different types of objects so long as the graphics system can render them. Hierarchical tiling requires special-purpose hardware for real-time performance.

8   Future Work and Conclusion

In this paper we have presented a visibility culling algorithm for general models that achieves significant speedups for interactive walkthroughs on current graphics systems. It is based on hierarchical occlusion maps, which represent an image space fusion of all the occluders. The overall algorithm is relatively simple, robust and easy to implement. We have demonstrated its performance on a number of large models.

There are still several areas to be explored in this research. We believe the most important of these to be occlusion preserving simplification algorithms, integration with levels-of-detail modeling, and parallelization.

Occlusion Preserving Simplification: Many models are densely tessellated. For fast generation of occlusion maps, we do not want to spend considerable time in rendering the occluders. As a result, we are interested in simplifying objects under the constraint of occlusion preservation. This implies that the screen space projection of the simplified object should be a subset of that of the original object. Current polygon simplification algorithms can reduce the polygon count while giving tight error bounds, but none of them guarantees an occlusion preserving simplification.

Integration with Level-of-Detail Modeling: To display large models at interactive frame rates, our visibility culling algorithm needs to be integrated with level-of-detail modeling. The latter involves polygon simplification, texture-based simplification and dynamic tessellation of higher order primitives.

Parallelization: Our algorithm can be easily parallelized on multi-processor machines. Different processors can be used for view frustum culling, overlap tests and depth tests.

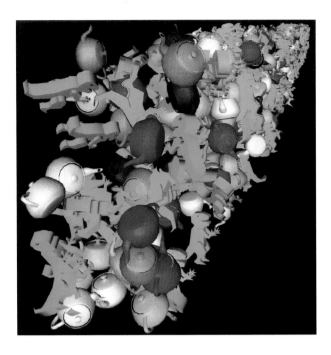

Figure 12: *Dynamic environment composed of dinosaurs and teapots. The total polygon count is 986,800. The HOM algorithm achieves about five times speed-up.*

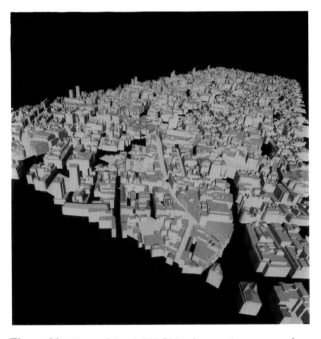

Figure 11: *City model with 312,524 polygons. Average speed-up obtained by our visibility culling algorithm is about five times.*

9   Acknowledgements

We are grateful to the reviewers for their comments and to Fred Brooks, Gary Bishop, Jon Cohen, Nick England, Ned Greene, Anselmo Lastra, Ming Lin, Turner Whitted, and members of UNC Walkthrough project for productive discussions. The Auxiliary Machine Room model was provided to us by Greg Angelini, Jim Boudreaux and Ken Fast at Electric Boat, a subsidiary of General Dynamics. Thanks to Sarah Hoff for proofreading the paper.

This work was supported in part by an Alfred P. Sloan Foundation Fellowship, ARO Contract DAAH04-96-1-0257, DARPA Contract DABT63-93-C-0048, Intel Corp., NIH/National Center for Research Resources Award 2 P41RR02170-13 on Interactive Graphics for Molecular Studies and Microscopy, NSF grant CCR-9319957 and Career Award, an ONR Young Investigator Award, the NSF/ARPA Center for Computer Graphics and Scientific Visualization, and a UNC Board of Governors Fellowship.

References

[ARB90]   J. Airey, J. Rohlf, and F. Brooks. Towards image realism with interactive update rates in complex virtual building environments. In *Symposium on Interactive 3D Graphics*, pages 41–50, 1990.

[BM96]   D. Blythe and T. McReynolds. Programming with Opengl: Advanced course. *Siggraph'96 Course Notes*, 1996.

[Bun89]   M. Bunker and R. Economy. Evolution of GE CIG Systems, SCSD document, General Electric Company, Daytona Beach, FL, 1989

[Car84]   L. Carpenter. The A-buffer, an antialiased hidden surface method. *Proc. of ACM Siggraph*, pages 103–108, 1984.

[Cat74]   E. Catmull. *A subdivision algorithm for computer display of curved surfaces*. PhD thesis, University of Utah, 1974.

[Chu94]   J. C. Chauvin (Sogitec). An advanced Z-buffer technology. IMAGE VII, pages 76–85, 1994.

[Cla76]   J.H. Clark. Hierarchical geometric models for visible surface algorithms. *Communications of the ACM*, 19(10):547–554, 1976.

[CT96a]   S. Coorg and S. Teller. A spatially and temporally coherent object space visibility algorithm. Technical Report TM 546, Laboratory for Computer Science, Massachusetts Institute of Technology, 1996.

[CT96b]   S. Coorg and S. Teller. Temporally coherent conservative visibility. In *Proc. of 12th ACM Symposium on Computational Geometry*, 1996.

[Dor94]   S. E. Dorward. A survey of object-space hidden surface removal. *Internat. J. Comput. Geom. Appl.*, 4:325–362, 1994.

[FDHF90]   J. Foley, A. Van Dam, J. Hughes, and S. Feiner. *Computer Graphics: Principles and Practice*. Addison Wesley, Reading, Mass., 1990.

[FKN80]   H. Fuchs, Z. Kedem, and B. Naylor. On visible surface generation by a priori tree structures. *Proc. of ACM Siggraph*, 14(3):124–133, 1980.

[GBR91]   R. Coifman G. Beylkin and V. Rokhlin. Fast wavelet transforms and numerical algorithms: I. *Communications of Pure and Applied Mathematics*, 44(2):141–183, 1991.

Figure 13: *A top view of the auxiliary machine room of a submarine composed of 632,252 polygons. Average speed-up is about two due to occlusion culling.*

[GBW90] B. Garlick, D. Baum, and J. Winget. Interactive viewing of large geometric databases using multiprocessor graphics workstations. *Siggraph'90 course notes: Parallel Algorithms and Architectures for 3D Image Generation*, 1990.

[GCS91] Z. Gigus, J. Canny, and R. Seidel. Efficiently computing and representing aspect graphs of polyhedral objects. *IEEE Transactions on Pattern Analysis and Machine Intelligence*, 13(6):542–551, 1991.

[GK94] N. Greene and M. Kass. Error-bounded antialiased rendering of complex environments. In *Proc. of ACM Siggraph*, pages 59–66, 1994.

[GKM93] N. Greene, M. Kass, and G. Miller. Hierarchical Z-buffer visibility. In *Proc. of ACM Siggraph*, pages 231–238, 1993.

[Geo95] C. Georges. Obscuration culling on parallel graphics architectures. Technical Report TR95-017, Department of Computer Science, University of North Carolina, Chapel Hill, 1995.

[Gre95] N. Greene. *Hierarchical rendering of complex environments*. PhD thesis, University of California at Santa Cruz, 1995.

[Gre96] N. Greene. Hierarchical polygon tiling with coverage masks. In *Proc. of ACM Siggraph*, pages 65–74, 1996.

[Hud96] T. Hudson, D. Manocha, J. Cohen, M. Lin, K. Hoff and H. Zhang. Accelerated occlusion culling using shadow frusta. Technical Report TR96-052, Department of Computer Science, University of North Carolina, 1996. To appear in Proc. of ACM Symposium on Computational Geometry, 1997.

[Lat94] R. Latham (CGSD). Advanced image generator architectures. Course reference material, 1994.

[LG95] D. Luebke and C. Georges. Portals and mirrors: Simple, fast evaluation of potentially visible sets. In *ACM Interactive 3D Graphics Conference*, Monterey, CA, 1995.

[LORA] Loral ADS. GT200T Level II image generator product overview, Bellevue, WA.

[McK87] M. McKenna. Worst-case optimal hidden-surface removal. *ACM Trans. Graph.*, 6:19–28, 1987.

[MEP92] S. Molnar, J. Eyles and J. Poulton. PixelFlow: High speed rendering using image composition. *Proc. of ACM Siggraph*, pp. 231-248, 1992.

[Mue95] C. Mueller. Architectures of image generators for flight simulators. Technical Report TR95-015, Department of Computer Science, University of North Carolina, Chapel Hill, 1995.

[Mul89] K. Mulmuley. An efficient algorithm for hidden surface removal. *Computer Graphics*, 23(3):379–388, 1989.

[Nay92] B. Naylor. Partitioning tree image representation and generation from 3d geometric models. In *Proc. of Graphics Interface*, pages 201–12, 1992.

[RB96] R. Brechner et al. Interactive walkthrough of large geometric databases. *Siggraph'96 course notes*, 1996.

[RH94] J. Rohlf and J. Helman. Iris performer: A high performance multiprocessor toolkit for realtime 3d graphics. In *Proc. of ACM Siggraph*, pages 381–394, 1994.

[SBM$^+$94] B. Schneider, P. Borrel, J. Menon, J. Mittleman, and J. Rossignac. Brush as a walkthrough system for architectural models. In *Fifth Eurographics Workshop on Rendering*, pages 389–399, July 1994.

[SG96] O. Sudarsky and C. Gotsman. Output sensitive visibility algorithms for dynamic scenes with applications to virtual reality. *Computer Graphics Forum*, 15(3):249–58, 1996. Proc. of Eurographics'96.

[TK96] J. Torborg and J. Kajiya. Talisman: Commodity Realtime 3D Graphics for the PC. *Proc. of ACM Siggraph*, pp. 353-363, 1996.

[TP75] S. Tanimoto and T. Pavlidis. A hierarchical data structure for picture processing. *Computer Graphics and Image Processing*, 4(2):104–119, 1975.

[TS91] S. Teller and C.H. Sequin. Visibility preprocessing for interactive walkthroughs. In *Proc. of ACM Siggraph*, pages 61–69, 1991.

[War69] J. Warnock. A hidden-surface algorithm for computer generated half-tone pictures. Technical Report TR 4-15, NTIS AD-753 671, Department of Computer Science, University of Utah, 1969.

[Wil83] L. Williams. Pyramidal parametrics. *ACM Computer Graphics*, pages 1–11, 1983.

[YR96] R. Yagel and W. Ray. Visibility computations for efficient walkthrough of complex environments. *Presence*, 5(1):1–16, 1996.

The Visibility Skeleton:
A Powerful And Efficient Multi-Purpose Global Visibility Tool

Frédo Durand, George Drettakis and Claude Puech

iMAGIS[†]- GRAVIR/IMAG - INRIA

Abstract

Many problems in computer graphics and computer vision require accurate *global* visibility information. Previous approaches have typically been complicated to implement and numerically unstable, and often too expensive in storage or computation. The Visibility Skeleton is a new powerful utility which can efficiently and accurately answer visibility queries for the entire scene. The Visibility Skeleton is a *multi-purpose* tool, which can solve numerous different problems. A simple construction algorithm is presented which only requires the use of well known computer graphics algorithmic components such as ray-casting and line/plane intersections. We provide an exhaustive catalogue of visual events which completely encode all possible visibility changes of a polygonal scene into a graph structure. The nodes of the graph are extremal stabbing lines, and the arcs are critical line swaths. Our implementation demonstrates the construction of the Visibility Skeleton for scenes of over a thousand polygons. We also show its use to compute exact visible boundaries of a vertex with respect to any polygon in the scene, the computation of global or on-the-fly discontinuity meshes by considering any scene polygon as a source, as well as the extraction of the exact blocker list between any polygon pair. The algorithm is shown to be manageable for the scenes tested, both in storage and in computation time. To address the potential complexity problems for large scenes, on-demand or lazy contruction is presented, its implementation showing encouraging first results.

Keywords: Visibility, Global Visibility, Extremal Stabbing Lines, Aspect Graph, Global Illumination, Form Factor Calculation, Discontinuity Meshing, View Calculation.

1 INTRODUCTION

Ever since the early days of computer graphics, the problems of determining visibility have been central to most computations required to generate synthetic images. Initially the problems addressed concerned the determination of visibility of a scene with respect to a given point of view. With the advent of interactive walkthrough systems and lighting calculations, the need for *global* visibility queries has become much more common. Many examples of such requirements exist, and are not limited to the domain of computer graph-

ics. When walking through a complex building, real-time visualization algorithms require the information of which objects are visible to limit the number of primitives rendered, and thus achieve better frame rates. In global illumination computations, the dominant part of any calculation concerns the determination of the proportion of light leaving surface s and arriving at surface r. This determination depends heavily on the relative occlusion of the two objects, requiring the calculation of which parts of s are visible from r. All such applications need detailed data structures which completely encode global visibility information; previous approaches have fallen short of this goal.

1.1 Motivation

The goal of the research presented here is to show that it is possible to construct a data structure encompassing all global visibility information and to show that our new structure is useful for a number of different applications. We expect the structure we present to be of capital importance for any application which requires detailed visibility information: the calculation and maintenance of the view around a point in a scene, the calculation of exact form-factors between vertices and surfaces, the computation of discontinuity meshes between any two pairs of objects in a scene as well as applications in other domains such as aspect graph calculations for computer vision etc.

Previous algorithms have been unable to provide efficient and robust data structures which can answer global visibility queries for typical graphics scenes. In what follows we present a new data structure which can provide *exact* global visibility information. Our structure, called the *Visibility Skeleton*, is easy to build, since its construction is based exclusively on standard computer graphics algorithms, i.e., ray casting and line-plane intersections. It is a *multi-purpose* tool, since it can be used to solve numerous different problems which require global visibility information; and finally it is well-adapted to *on-demand* or *lazy* construction, due to the locality of the construction algorithm and the data structure itself. This is particularly important in the case of complex geometries.

The central component of the Visibility Skeleton are *critical lines* and *extremal stabbing lines*, which, as will be explained in detail in what follows, are the foci of all visibility changes in a scene. All modifications of visibility in a polygonal scene can be described by these critical lines, and a set of *line swaths* which are necessarily adjacent to these lines. In this paper we present the construction of the Skeleton, and the implementations of several applications. As an example, consider Fig. 1(a), which is a scene of 1500 polygons. After the construction of the skeleton, many different queries can be answered efficiently. We show the view from the green selected point to the left wall which only required 1.4 ms to compute; in Fig. 1(b), the complete discontinuity mesh on the right wall is generated by considering the screen of the computer as an emitter which required 8.1 ms.

After a brief overview of previous work (Section 1.2), we will provide a complete description of all possible nodes, and all the adjacent line swaths in Section 2. In Section 3 the construction algorithm and the actual data structure are described in detail. The results of our implementation are then presented in Section 4, giving the complete construction of the Visibility Skeleton for a suite of test

[†]iMAGIS is a joint research project of CNRS/INRIA/UJF/INPG. iMAGIS/GRAVIR, BP 53, F-38041 Grenoble Cedex 09 France. E-mail: {Frederic.Durand|George.Drettakis|Claude.Puech}@imag.fr http://www-imagis.imag.fr/

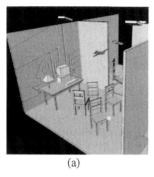 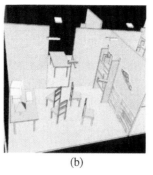

(a)   (b)

Figure 1: (a) Exact computation of the part of the left wall as seen by the green vertex. (b) Complete discontinuity mesh on the right wall when considering the computer screen as source.

scenes. We show how the Skeleton is then used to provide exact point-to-surface visibility information for any vertex in the scene, to calculate the complete discontinuity mesh between any two surfaces in the scene, extract exact blocker lists between two objects, and compute all visibility interactions of one object with all other objects in a scene, which could be used for dynamic illumination updates in scenes with moving objects. Section 5 addresses the issues arising when treating more complex scenes, and in particular we present a first attempt at on-demand construction. The results of the implementation show that this allows significant speedup compared to the complete algorithm. In Section 6 we sketch how the structure can be extended to environments in which objects move, as well as other potential extensions, and we conclude.

1.2 Previous Work

Many researchers in computer graphics, computational geometry and computer vision have addressed the issue of calculating global visibility. We present here a quick overview of closely related previous work, which is of course far from exhaustive.

Interest in visibility structures in computer graphics was expressed by Teller [26], when presenting an algorithm for the calculation of anti-penumbra. This work was in part inspired by the wealth of research in computer vision related to the *aspect graph* (e.g., [21, 10, 9]). The work of Teller is closely related to the development of discontinuity meshing algorithms (pioneered by [14, 17]). These algorithms lead to structures closely resembling the aspect graph which contain visibility information (*backprojections*) with respect to a light source [5, 24]. Discontinuity meshes have been used in computer graphics to calculate visibility and improve meshing for global illumination calculations [18, 6]. Nonetheless, these structures have always been severely limited by their inability to treat visibility between objects other than the primary light sources. This is caused by the fact that the calculation of the discontinuity mesh with respect to a source is expensive and prone to numerical robustness problems.

An alternative approach to calculating visibility between two patches for global illumination has been proposed by Teller and Hanrahan [27]. In this work a conservative algorithm is presented which answers queries concerning visibility between any two patches in the scene but does not provide exact visibility information. In addition, this approach provides tight blocker lists of potential occluders between a patch pair. Information on the potential occluders between a patch pair is central in the design of any refinement strategy for hierarchical radiosity [12]. The ability to determine analytic visibility information between two arbitrary patches would render practical the error bound refinement strategy of [16], which requires this information.

In computational geometry, the problem of visibility has been extensively studied in two dimensions. The visibility complex [22] provides all the information necessary to compute global visibility. This was successfully used in a 2D study of the problem applied to radiosity [19]. A similar structure in 3D, called the *asp*, has been presented in computer vision by Plantinga and Dyer [21], to allow the computation of aspect graphs. This structure provides the information necessary to compute exact visibility information. A related, but more efficient structure called the 3D visibility complex [7] has been proposed. Both structures have remained at the theoretical level for the full 3D perspective case which is the only case of interest for 3D computer graphics, despite partial implementations of orthographic and other limited cases for the *asp* [21]. Other related work in a computational geometry framework can be found in [15, 20].

Moreover, most of the work done on static visibility does not easily extend to dynamic environments. Most of the time, motion volumes enclosing all the positions of the moving objects are built [3, 8, 23].

2 THE VISIBILITY SKELETON

The new structure we will present addresses many of the shortcomings of previous work in global visibility. As mentioned earlier, the emphasis is on the development of a multi-purpose tool which can be easily used to resolve many different visibility problems, a structure which is easy and stable to build and which lends itself to on-demand construction and dynamic updates.

In what follows, we will consider only the case of polygonal scenes.

2.1 Visual Events

In previous global visibility algorithms, in particular those relating to aspect graph computations (e.g., [21, 10, 9]), and to antipenumbra [26] or discontinuity meshing [5, 24], visibility changes have been characterized by *critical lines sets* or *line swaths* and by *extremal stabbing lines*.

Following [20] and [26], we define an extremal stabbing line to be incident on four polygon edges. There are several types of extremal stabbing lines, including vertex-vertex (or VV) lines, vertex-edge-edge (or VEE) lines, and quadruple edge (or $E4$) lines. As explained in Section 2.3.1, we will also consider here extremal lines associated to faces of polyhedral objects.

A *swath* is the surface swept by extremal stabbing lines when they are moved after relaxing exactly one of the four edge constraints defining the line. The swath can either be planar (if the line remains tight on a vertex) or a regulus, whose three generator lines embed three polygon edges.

We call *generator elements* the vertices and edges participating in the definition of an extremal stabbing line.

We start with an example: after traversing an EV line swath from left to right as shown in Figure 2(a), the vertex as seen from the observer will lie upon the polygon adjacent to the edge and no longer upon the floor. This is a visibility change (often called visibility event). The topology of the view is modified whenever the vertex and the edge are aligned, that is, when there is a line from the eye going through both e and v.

This EV line swath is a one dimensional ($1D$) set of lines, passing through the vertex v and the edge e_1, thus it has one degree of freedom (varying for example over the edge e). When two such EV surfaces meet as in Figure 2(b) a unique line is defined by the intersection of the two planes defined by the EV surfaces. This line is an extremal stabbing line; it has zero degrees of freedom.

In what follows we will develop the concepts necessary to avoid any direct treatment of the line swaths themselves since sets of lines

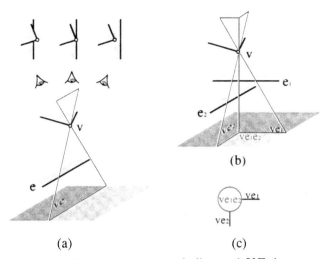

(a)　　　　　　　　(b)

(c)

Figure 2: (a) While the eye traverses the line swath VE, the vertex v passes over the edge e. (b) Two line swaths meet at an extremal stabbing line (c) and induce a graph structure

or the surfaces described by these sets are difficult to handle, in part because they can be ruled quadrics. All computations will be performed by line – or ray – casting in the scene.

We will be using the extremal stabbing lines to encode all visibility information, by storing a list of all line swaths adjacent to each extremal stabbing line. In our first example of Figure 2(b), the VEE line ve_1e_2 is adjacent to the two $1D$ elements ve_1 and ve_2 described above; i.e., the swaths ve_1 and ve_2. Additional adjacencies for the VEE line ve_1e_2 are implied by the interaction of ve_2 and e_1 (Fig 3(a)).

To complete the adjacencies of a VEE line, we need to consider the EEE line swaths related to the edges e_4 and e_2, and the two edges e_4 and e_3 which are adjacent to the vertex v (Fig. 3(b) and (c)).

The simple construction shown above introduces the fundamental idea of the Visibility Skeleton: by determining all the appropriate extremal stabbing lines in the scene, and by attaching all adjacent line swaths, we can completely describe all possible visibility relationships in a 3D scene. They will be encoded in a graph structure as shown on Fig.3, to be explained in Section 2.3.2. Consider the example shown in Fig.3(a): The node associated to extremal stabbing line ve_1e_2 is adjacent in the graph structure to the arcs associated with line swaths ve_1, $ve_1\prime$ and ve_2.

2.2 The 3D Visibility Complex, the Asp and the Visibility Skeleton

The *Visibility Complex* [7], is a structure which also contains all relevant visibility information for a 3 dimensional scene. It is also based on the adjacencies between visibility events and considers sets of maximal free segments of the scene (these are lines limited by intersections with objects).

The zero and one-dimensional components of the visibility complex are in effect the same as those introduced above, which we will be using for the construction of the Visibility Skeleton. Similar constructions were presented (but not implemented to our knowledge for the complete perspective case) for the *asp* structure [21] for aspect graph construction.

In both cases, higher dimensional line sets are built. For the visibility complex in particular, faces of 2, 3 and 4 dimensions are considered. For example, the set of lines tangent to two objects has 2 degrees of freedom, those tangent to one object 3 degrees of free-

dom, etc. (see [7] for details).

These sets and their adjacencies could theoretically be useful for some specific queries such as view computation or dynamic updates, for example in some specific worst cases such as scenes composed of grids aligned and slightly rotated. In such cases, almost all objects occlude each other and the high number of line swaths and extremal stabbing lines makes the grouping of lines into higher dimensional sets worthwhile.

The *Visibility Complex* and *asp* are intricate data-structures with complicated construction algorithms since they require the construction of a $4D$ subdivision. In addition they are difficult to traverse due to the multiple levels of adjacencies. Our approach is different: we have developed a data structure which is easy to implement and easy to use.

These facts also explain the name *Visibility Skeleton*, since our new structure can be thought of as the skeleton of the complete Visibility Complex.

2.3 Catalogue of Visual Events and their Adjacencies

The Visibility Skeleton is a graph structure. The nodes of the graph are the extremal stabbing lines and the arcs correspond to line swaths. In this section (and in Appendix 7.1) we present an exhaustive list of all possible types of arcs and nodes of the Visibility Skeleton.

2.3.1 1D Elements: Arcs of the Visibility Skeleton

In Figure 4, we see the four possible types of $1D$ elements: an EV line swath (shown in blue), an EEE line swath (shown in purple) and two line swaths relating a polygonal face (F) to one of its vertices (Fv) or an edge of another polygon(FE) (both are shown in blue). In the upper part of the figure we show the view (with changes in visibility), as seen from a viewpoint located above the scene and, from left to right in front of, on, or behind the line swath.

Note that the interaction of an edge e and a vertex v can correspond to many ve arcs of the skeleton. These arcs are separated by nodes. Consider, for example, arcs ve_1 and $ve_1\prime$ adjacent to node ve_1e_2 in Fig. 3(a).

2.3.2 0D Elements: Nodes of the Visibility Skeleton

As explained in Section 2.1, two line swaths which meet define an extremal stabbing line, which in the Visibility Skeleton is the node at which the arcs meet. This section presents a list of the configurations creating nodes and their corresponding adjacencies. A figure is given in each case.

The simplest node corresponds to the interaction of two vertices shown in Figure 5(a).

The interaction of a vertex v and two edges e_1 and e_2 can result in two configurations, depending on the relative position of the vertex with respect to the edges. The first node was presented previously in Figure 3 and the second is shown in Figure 5(b).

The interaction of four edges is presented in Figure 6, together with the six corresponding adjacent EEE arcs. Face related nodes are given in detail in the appendix: EFE, FEE, FF, E and Fvv (see Fig. 18 to 19).

3 DATA STRUCTURE AND CONSTRUCTION ALGORITHM

Given the catalogues of nodes and arcs presented in the previous section, we can present the details of a suitable data structure to rep-

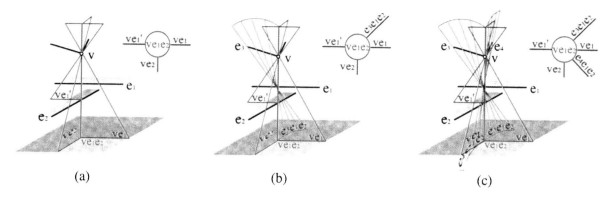

Figure 3: (a) An additional EV line swath is adjacent to the extremal stabbing line, (b) (c) and two EEE line swaths

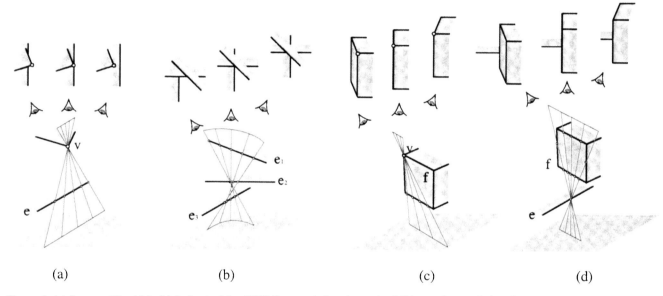

Figure 4: (a) Same as Fig. 1(a). (b) In front of the EEE line swath the edge e_2 is visible, on the swath the edges meet at a point and behind e_2 is hidden. (c) In front of the FV we see the front side of F, on the swath we see a line and behind we see the other side of F. (d) The FE swath is similar to the FV case.

resent the Visibility Skeleton graph structure, as well as the algorithm to construct it.

Preliminaries: Our scene model provides the adjacencies between vertices, edges and faces. Before processing the scene, we traverse all vertices, edges and faces, and assign a unique number to each. This allows us to index these elements easily. In addition, we consider all edges to be uniquely oriented. This operation is arbitrary (i.e., the orientation does not depend on the normal of one of the two faces attached to the edge), and facilitates consistency in the calculations we will be performing.

3.1 Data Structure

The simplest element of the structure is the node. The $Node$ structure contains a list of arcs, and pointers to the polygonal faces F_{up} and F_{down} (possibly void) which block the corresponding extremal stabbing line at its endpoints P_{up} and P_{down}.

The structure for an Arc is visualized in the Fig.7(a). The arc represented here (swath shown in blue) is an EV line set. There are two adjacent nodes N_{start}, N_{end}, represented as red lines. All the adjacency information is stored with the arc. Details of the structures $Node$ and Arc are given in Fig. 7(b).

To access the arc and node information, we maintain arrays of

balanced binary search trees corresponding to the different type of swaths considered. For example, we maintain an array ev of trees of EV arcs (see Fig.7(b)). These arrays are indexed by the unique identifiers of the endpoints of the arcs. These can be faces, vertices or edges (if the swath is interior, that is if the lines traverse the polyhedron).

This array structure allows us to efficiently query the arc information when inserting new nodes and when performing visibility queries. The balanced binary search tree used to implement the query structure is ordered by the identifiers of the generators and by the value of t_{start}.

3.2 Finding Nodes

Before presenting the actual construction of each type of node, we briefly discuss the issue of "local visibility". As has been presented in other work (e.g., [10]), for any edge adjacent to two faces of a polyhedron, the negative half-space of a polygonal face is locally invisible. Thus when considering interactions of an edge e, we do not need to process any other edge e' which is "behind" the faces adjacent to e. This results in the culling of a large number of potential events.

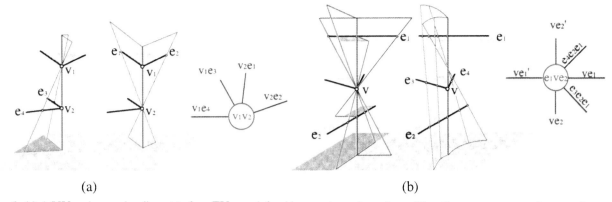

(a) (b)

Figure 5: (a) A VV node v_1v_2 is adjacent to four EV arcs defined by a vertex and an edges of the other vertex: v_1e_3 and v_1e_4 and e_1v_2 and e_2v_2. (b) An EVE node e_1ve_2: each edge defines two EV arcs with v depending on the polygon at the extremity, and to two EEE defined by e_1, e_2 and the two edges adjacent to v.

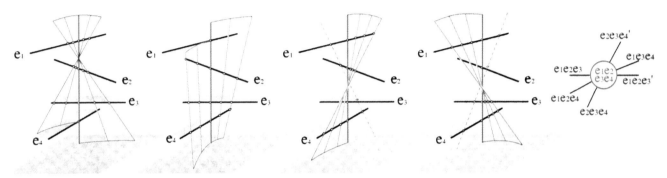

Figure 6: An $E4$ node is adjacent to six EEE arcs.

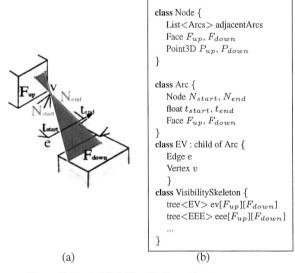

```
class Node {
    List<Arcs> adjacentArcs
    Face F_up, F_down
    Point3D P_up, P_down
}

class Arc {
    Node N_start, N_end
    float t_start, t_end
    Face F_up, F_down
}
class EV : child of Arc {
    Edge e
    Vertex v
}
class VisibilitySkeleton {
    tree<EV> ev[F_up][F_down]
    tree<EEE> eee[F_up][F_down]
    ...
}
```

(a) (b)

Figure 7: Basic Visibility Skeleton Structure.

3.2.1 Trivial Nodes

The simplest nodes are the VV, Fvv and Fe nodes. For these, we simply loop over the appropriate scene elements (vertices, edges and faces). The appropriate lines are then intersected with the scene using a traditional ray-caster to determine if there is an occluding object between the related scene elements, in which case no extremal stabbing line is reported. Otherwise it gives the elements and points

at the extremities of the lines, and thus the appropriate location in the overall arc tree array.

3.2.2 VEE and EEEE Nodes

We consider two edges of the scene e_i and e_j. All the lines going through two segments are within an extended tetrahedron (or double wedge) shown in Fig. 8, defined by four planes. Each one of these planes is defined by one of the edges and an endpoint of the other.

To determine the vertices of the scene which can potentially generate a VEE or EVE stabbing line, we need only consider vertices within the wedge. If a vertex of the scene is inside the double wedge, there is a potential VEE or EVE event.

We next consider a third edge e_k of the scene. If e_k cuts a plane of the wedge, a VEE or EVE node is created. If edge e_k of the scene intersects the plane of the double wedge defined by edge e_i and vertex v of e_j, there is a ve_ie_k or e_ive_k event (Fig. 8(a)).

We next proceed to the definition of the $E4$ nodes. The intersections of e_k and the planes of the double wedge *restrict* the third edge e_k. To compute a line going through e_i, e_j, e_k we need only consider the restriction of e_k to the double wedge defined by e_i and e_j. This process is re-applied to restrict a fourth edge e_l by the wedge of e_i and e_j, by that of e_i and e_k and by that of e_j and e_k. This multiple restriction process eliminates a large number of candidates.

Once the restriction is completed, we have two EEE line sets, those passing through e_l, e_i and e_j and those passing through e_l, e_i and e_k. A simple binary search is applied to find the point on e_l (if it exists) which defines the $E4$ node. We perform this search for a point P of e_l by searching for the root of the angle formed by the two lines defined by the intersection of the plane (P, e_i) with e_j and with e_k. This is shown on Fig.8(c).

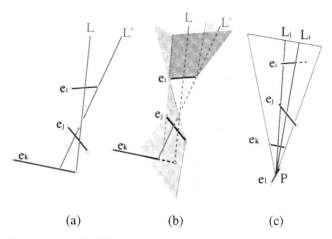

(a)   (b)   (c)

Figure 8: (a) (b) VEE enumeration and EEE restriction. (c) $E4$ computation: find the root of the angle of the lines going through $e_j e_k e_l$ and that through $e_l e_k e_i$.

A more robust algorithm such as the one given in [28] could be used, but the simpler algorithm presented here seems to perform well in practice. This is true mainly because we are not searching for infinite stabbing lines, but for restricted edge line segments. The potential VEE and $E4$ enumeration algorithm is given in Fig. 9.

We have developed an acceleration scheme to avoid the enumeration of all the triples of edges. For each pair of edges, we reject very quickly most of the third potential edges using a regular grid. Instead of checking if each cell of the grid intersects the extended tetrahedron, we use the projection on the three axis-aligned planes. For each such plane, we project the extended tetrahedron (which gives us an hourglass shape), and we perform the actual edge-tetrahedron intersection only for the edges contained in the cells whose three projections intersect the three pixelized hourglasses.

3.2.3 Non-Trivial Face Nodes

To calculate the non-trivial face-related nodes, we start by intersecting the plane of each face f_1 with every edge of the scene. For edges intersecting the face we attempt to create an FvE node (Fig.18).

For each pair of intersections, we search for a FEE node. To do this we determine if the line joining the two intersections intersects the face f_1. The last operation required is the verification of the existence of an FF node. This case occurs if the faces adjacent to the edge of the intersection cause an FF. The construction for the FEE and FF nodes is described in Fig. 10 (a).

3.3 Creating the Arcs

The creation of the arcs of the Visibility Skeleton is performed simultaneously with the detection of the nodes. When inserting a new node, we create all the adjacent arcs from the corresponding catalogue presented in Section 2.3.2. For each of these arcs a we calculate the arc parameter t corresponding to the node to be inserted, and proceed as explained in Fig.12. We then access the list of arcs in the Skeleton with the same extremities (thus in the same list of the array) and which have the same generator elements (*vertices and edges*) as the arc a. If the value of t indicates that the node is contained in the arc, we determine whether this node is the start of the end node of the arc. This is explained in more detail in the following paragraph. If this position is already occupied we split the arc, else we assign the node the corresponding extremity of the arc. This process is summarized in Fig. 11.

We have seen above that each time an arc adjacent to a node is considered, we have to know if it is its *start node* or its *end node*. In some cases this operation is trivial, for example for a $v_1 v_2$ node and one if its adjacent $v_1 e$ arcs, we simply determine if v_2 is the starting vertex of e. In other cases, this can be more involved, especially for the $E4$ case. This case and the necessary criteria for the other cases are summarized in Table 2 in the Appendix.

In Fig. 12, we illustrate the construction algorithm. Initially a trivial vv_e node is created. The second node identified is vfe, which is adjacent the arc ve. Thus the arc ve is adjacent to both vv_e and vfe. The third node to be created is vee_3. When this node is inserted, we realize that the start node for ve already exists, and we thus split the ve arc. This splitting operation will leave the end of the ve arc connected to vv_e undefined. The final insertion shown is $ve_2 e$ which will fill an undefined node previously generated.

4 IMPLEMENTATION AND FIRST APPLICATIONS

We have completed a first implementation of the data structure described. We have run the system on a set of test scenes, with varying visibility properties. In its current form, we have successfully computed the Visibility Skeleton for scenes up to 1500 polygons.

In what follows we first present Visibility Skeleton construction statistics for the different test scenes used. We then proceed to demonstrate the flexible nature of our construction, by presenting the use of our data structure to efficiently answer several different global visibility queries.

4.1 Implementation and Construction Statistics

Our current implementation requires convex polyhedra as input. However, this is not a limitation of the approach since we use polyhedral adjacencies simply for convenience when performing local visibility tests.

We treat touching objects by detecting this occurrence and slightly modifying the ray-casting operation. We also reject coplanar edge triples. Other degeneracies such as intersecting edges are not yet treated by the current implementation.

We present statistics on the size of our structure and construction time in Table 1. Evidently, these tests can only be taken as an indication of the asymptotic behavior of our algorithm. As such, we see that our test suite indicates quadratic growth of the memory requirements and super-quadratic growth of the running time. In particular, for the test suite used, the running time increases with $n^{2.4}$ on average, where n is the number of polygons.

The VEE nodes are the most numerous. There are approximately a hundred times fewer $E4$ nodes, even though theoretically there should be an order of magnitude more.

We believe that the memory requirements could be greatly decreased by an improved implementation of the arrays of trees. Currently, a large percentage of the memory required is used by these arrays (e.g. for scene (d) of Table 1., the arrays need 53.7Mb out of a total 135Mb). Since these arrays are very sparse (e.g. 99.3% empty for scene (d)), it is clear that storage requirements can be greatly reduced.

In the case of densely occluded scenes, the memory requirements grow at a slower rate, on average much closer to linear than quadratic with respect to the number of polygons. As an example, we replicated scene (a) 2, 4 and 8 times, thus resulting in isolated rooms containing a single chair each. The memory requirements (excluding the quadratic cost of the arrays) are 1.2Mb, 2.8Mb, 8.6Mb and 17.3Mb, for respectively 78, 150, 300 and 600 polygons.

The theoretical upper bounds are very pessimistic, $O(n^4)$ in size because every edge quadruple can have two lines going through it

```
potential VEE and EEEE enumeration
{
foreach edge eᵢ from 1 to n
    foreach edge eⱼ from i + 1 to n locally visible
        foreach edge eₖ from j + 1 to n locally visible
            compute the EEE restrictions eᵢeⱼeₖ
        foreach edge eₖ from j + 1 to n locally visible
            foreach segment of its restrictions
                foreach edge eₗ from k + 1 to n locally visible
                    foreach segment of its restrictions
                        search for E4
}
```
(a)

```
EEE restriction
{
foreach of the 4 planes
    compute the intersection inter with the line of the edge
        if it inter on the edge
            propose a VEE
            restrict the edge
foreach of the edge endpoints sₑₚ
    if sₑₚ is inside the double wedge
        propose a VEE
        restrict the edge
}
```
(b)

Figure 9: Enumeration of Potential VEE and E4 Nodes.

```
Find Face Nodes {
foreach face f₁ of the scene
    foreach edge e of the scene
        compute the intersection of the edge e with the plane of f₁
        foreach intersection Pᵢ
            create a FvE
            foreach intersection Pⱼ
                if (PᵢPⱼ) intersects f₁
                    create FEE
            foreach of the 2 faces f₂ adjacent to the edge of Pi
                find Pⱼ the intersection of a second edge of f₂ with f₁
                if (PᵢPⱼ) intersects f₁
                    create FF
}
```
(a)

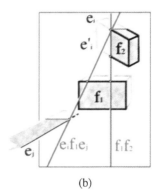

(b)

Figure 10: Finding Face Nodes.

[28], and $O(n^5)$ in time because such potential extremal stabbing lines have to be ray-cast with the whole scene. But such bounds occur only in uncommon worst case scenes such as grids aligned and rotated or infinite lines. It is clear that our construction algorithm would be very inefficient for such cases. More efficient construction algorithms are possible, but these approaches suffer from all the problems described previously in Section 2.2.

In what concerns the robustness of the computation, previous aspect graph and discontinuity meshing algorithms depend heavily on the construction of the arrangement (of the mesh or aspect graph "cells"), as the algorithm progresses. In the construction presented here, this is not the case since all operations are completely local. Since we perform ray-casting and line-plane intersections, the number of potential numerical problems is limited. Degeneracies can occasionally cause some problems, but due to the locality, this does not effect the construction of the Skeleton elsewhere. More efficient sweep-based algorithms are particularly sensitive to such instabilities, since an error in one position in space can render the rest of the construction completely incorrect and inconsistent.

4.2 Point-to-Area Form-Factor for Vertices

The calculation of point-to-area form factors has become central in many radiosity calculations. In most radiosity systems, point-to-area calculations are used to approximate area-to-area calculations [4, 2], and in others the actually point-to-area value is computed at the vertices [29].

In both theoretical [16] and experimental [6] studies, previous research has shown that error of the visibility calculation is a predominant source of inaccuracies. This is typically the case when ray casting is used. Lischinski et al. [16] have developed a very promising approach to bounding the error committed during light transfer for

hierarchical radiosity. For it to be useful for general environments, access is required to the exact visibility information between a point on one element with respect to the polygon face it is linked to. This information is inherently global, since a pair of linked elements can contain *any* two surface elements of the scene.

The Visibility Skeleton in its initial form can answer this query exactly and efficiently for the original vertices of the input scene.

To calculate the view of a polygonal face from a vertex v, with respect to a face f, we first access all the EV arcs of the skeleton related to the face f. This is simply the traversal of the line of our global two-dimensional array of arcs, indexed by f. For each entry of this list (many of which are empty), we search for the EV arcs related to v. These EV arcs are exactly the visible boundary of f seen from v.

An example is shown in Fig. 13(a) and (b) For scene (b), containing 312 and 1488 polygons, the extraction of the point-to-area boundary takes respectively 1.2 ms and 1.5 ms (all query time are given without displaying the result).

4.3 Global and On-The-Fly Discontinuity Meshing

In radiosity calculations, it is often very beneficial to subdivide the mesh of a surface by following some [14, 18], or all [6] of the discontinuity surfaces between two surfaces which exchange energy. The partial [14, 17] or complete [5, 24] construction of such meshes has in the past been restricted to the discontinuity mesh between a source (which is typically a small polygon) and the receivers (which are the larger polygons of the scene). For all other interactions between surfaces of scenes, the algorithmic complexity and the inherent robustness problems related to the construction of these structures has not permitted their use [25].

For many secondary transfers in an environment, the construc-

```
Creation of a Visibility Skeleton Node
{
    foreach adjacent arc n
        compute t
        foreach arc a with same extremities and same generators
            if a → t_start < t < a → t_end
            AddNodeToArc(n, a)
        if no arc found
            create new Arc
}
```

```
AddNodeToArc(Node n, Arc a)
{
    pos = decideStartOrEnd(n, a)
    if pos in a undefined
        set pos to n
    else
        split a into two parts
}
```

Figure 11: Node Creation

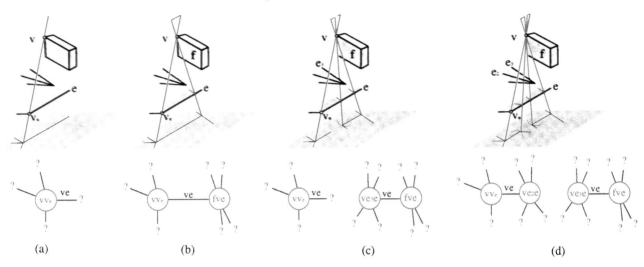

(a)　　　　　　　(b)　　　　　　　(c)　　　　　　　(d)

Figure 12: Example of node insertions: (a) Insertion node vv_e. (b) Insertion of node f_ve. Arc ve has now two ending nodes. (c) Insertion of node ve_3e. Arc ve is split. (c) Insertion of node ve_4e, the two arcs ve have their actual adjacent nodes.

tion of a global discontinuity mesh (i.e., from any surface (emitting/reflecting) to any other receiving surface in a scene), can aid in the accuracy of the global visibility computation. This was shown in the discontinuity driven subdivision used by Hardt and Teller [13]. In their case, the discontinuity surfaces are simply intersected with the scene polygons, and thus visibility on the line swath is not computed. With the Visibility Skeleton, the complete global discontinuity mesh between two surfaces can be efficiently computed.

To efficiently perform this query, we add an additional two-dimensional array $DM(i, j)$, storing all the arcs from face f_i to f_j. Insertion into this array of lists and well as subsequent access is performed in constant time. To extract the discontinuity mesh between to surfaces f_i and f_j we simply access the entry $DM(i, j)$, and traverse the corresponding list. In Fig. 14(a), the complete discontinuity mesh between the source and the floor is extracted in 28.6 ms. The mesh caused by the small lamp on the table in Fig 14(b) was extracted in 1.3 ms (note that the arrangement is not built).

The resulting information is a set of arcs. These arcs can be used as in Hardt and Teller to guide subdivision, or to construct the arrangement of the discontinuity mesh on-the-fly, to be used as in [6] for the construction of a subdivision which follows the discontinuities. The adjacency information available in the Skeleton arcs and nodes should permit a robust construction of the mesh arrangement.

4.4 Exact Blocker Lists, Occlusion Detection and Efficient Initial Linking

When considering the interaction between two surfaces, it is often the case that we wish to have access to the exact list of blocker surfaces hiding one surface from the other. This is useful in the context of blocker list maintenance approaches such as that presented by Teller and Hanrahan [27].

The Visibility Skeleton can again answer this query exactly and efficiently. In particular, we use the global array $DM(i, j)$, and we traverse the related arcs. All the polygons related to the intervening arcs are blockers. It is important to note that this solution results in the *exact* blocker list, in contrast with all previous methods. Consider the example shown in Fig. 13(c) where we compute the occluders between the left ceiling lamp and the floor in 4 ms.

The *shaft* structure [11] would report all objects on the table though they are hidden by the table. In this case the Visibility Skeleton reports the exact set of blockers.

When constructing the Visibility Skeleton, we compute all the mutually visible objects of the scene: if two object see each other, there will be at least one extremal stabbing line which touches them or their edges and vertices. This is fundamental for hierarchical radiosity algorithms since it avoids the consideration of the interaction of mutually visible objects in the initial linking stage.

Similarly, the Skeleton allows for the detection of the occlusions caused by an object. This can be very useful for the case of a moving object m allowing the detection of the form factors to be recomputed. To detect if the form factor F_{ij} has to be recomputed we perform a query similar to the discontinuity mesh between two polygons: we traverse $DM(i, j)$ and search for an arc caused by an element (vertex, edge or face) of m. This gives us the limits of occlusions of m between f_i and f_j. Moreover, by considering all the arcs of the skeleton, we report all the form factors to be recomputed, and not a superset. Fig 14(c) shows the occlusions caused by the body of

Scene	a	b	c	d	e	f	g
Polygons	84	168	312	432	756	1056	1488
Nodes ($*10^3$)	7	37	69	199	445	753	1266
Arcs ($*10^3$)	16	91	165	476	1074	1836	3087
Construction	1 s 71 s	12 s 74	37 s 07	1 min 39 s	5 min 36 s	14 min 36 s	31 min 59
Memory (Mb)	1.8	9	21	55	135	242	416

Table 1: Construction statistics (all times on a 195Mhz R10000 SGI Onyx 2). Storage is scene dependent and can be greatly reduced.

(a)

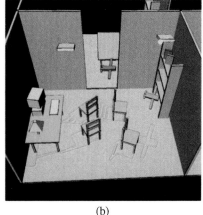

(b)

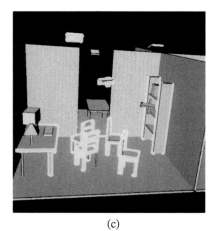

(c)

Figure 13: (a) Part of the scene visible from a vertex of the airplane. (b) Part of the floor seen by a vertex of the right-hand light source. (c) List of occluding blockers between the left light source and the floor. Note that the objects on the table that are invisible from the floor are not reported as blockers.

the plane between the screen and the right wall. This computation required 1.3 ms.

5 DEALING WITH SPATIAL COMPLEXITY: ON-DEMAND CONSTRUCTION

We propose here an on-demand or *lazy* scheme to compute visibility information only where and when needed. For example, if we want the discontinuity mesh between two surfaces, we just need to compute the arcs of the complex related to these two faces, and for this we only need to detect the nodes between these two faces.

The key for this approach is the locality of the Visibility Skeleton construction algorithm. We only compute the nodes of the complex where needed. The fact that some arcs might have missing nodes causes no problem since no queries will be made on them. Later on, other queries can appropriately link the missing nodes with those arcs.

Two problems must be solved: determination of what is to be computed, and determination of what has already been computed.

We propose two approaches: a source driven computation, and an adaptive subdivision of ray-space in the spirit of [1].

In the context of global illumination, the information related to "sources" (emitters or reflectors) is crucial. Thus the part of the visibility skeleton we compute in an on-demand construction is related to lines cutting the sources. The event detection has to be modified: every time a double wedge or a face does not cut the source, the pair of edges or the face is discarded, and if a potential node is detected, the ray-casting is performed only if the corresponding critical line cuts the source.

We use our grid-acceleration scheme here too: for each first edge, an edge pair is formed only for the edges that lie inside the hourglass defined by the source and the first edge.

When considering many sources one after the other, we also have to detect nodes already computed. If the sources are small, it is not worth rejecting double wedges, and only the final ray-casting and node insertion can be avoided (in our implementation they account for a third of the running time). We can perform a "final computation" if we want all the nodes that have not yet been computed: we just test before ray-casting if the critical line cuts one of the sources.

For scene (g) of Table 1, the part of the Visibility Skeleton with respect to one of the sources is computed in 4 min. 15 s. instead of 31 min. 59 s. for the entire scene.

When the number of sources becomes large, most of the time would be spent in checking if lines intersect the sources or if they have already been subdivided. If we need visibility information only between two objects, not between an object and the whole scene, we propose the use of ray classification of [1] together with the notions of dual space of [7] to build the visibility skeleton only where and when needed. The idea (which is not currently implemented) is to parameterize the lines of the 3D space (which is a set in 4D space), for example by their direction and projection on a plane or by their intersections with two parallel planes. We then perform a subdivision of the space of lines with a simple scheme (e.g., grid, hierarchical subdivision) and compute the nodes of the complex located inside a given cell of this subdivision.

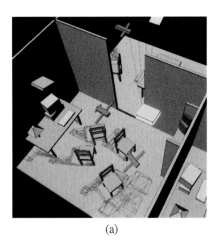 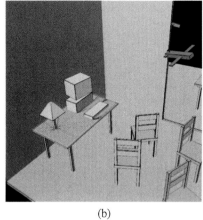 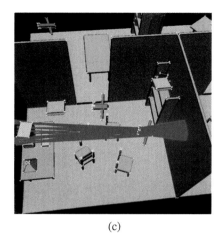

(a) (b) (c)

Figure 14: (a)The complete discontinuity mesh with respect to the right source. (b) Discontinuity mesh between the lamp and the table. (c) Limits of the occlusions caused by a part of the plane between the computer screen and the right wall.

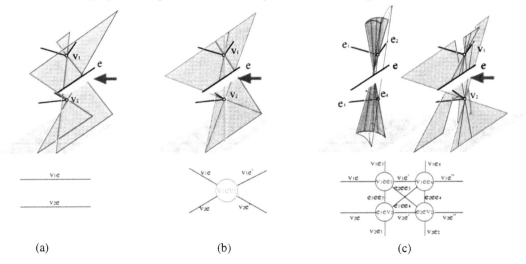

(a) (b) (c)

Figure 15: The edge moving from right to left causes a VEV temporal visibility event which is the meeting of two EV with the the two same extremities and with a common element (here the edge e). Four nodes are created, the EV arcs are split into three parts and eight arcs are created. These events and the topological visibility changes are local in the visibility skeleton.

6 CONCLUSIONS AND FUTURE WORK

We have presented a new data structure, called the *Visibility Skeleton*, which encodes all global visibility information for polygonal scenes. The data structure is a graph, whose nodes are the extremal stabbing lines generated by the interaction of edges and vertices in the scene. These lines can be found using standard computer graphics algorithms, notably ray-casting and line-plane intersections. The arcs of the graph are critical line sets or swaths which are adjacent to nodes. The key idea for simplicity was to treat the nodes and deduce the arcs using the full catalogues of all possible nodes and adjacent arcs we have presented for polygonal scenes. A full construction algorithm was then given, detailing insertion of nodes and arcs into the Skeleton.

We presented an implementation of the construction algorithm and several applications. In particular, we have used the Skeleton to calculate the visible boundary of a polygonal face with respect to a scene vertex, the discontinuity mesh between any two polygons of the scene, the exact list of blockers between any two polygons, as well as the complete list of all interactions of a polygon with all other polygons of the scene.

The implementation shows that despite unfavorable asymptotic complexity bounds, the algorithm is manageable for the test suite used, both in storage and in computation time. In addition, we have developed and implemented a first approach to on-demand or lazy construction which opens the way to hierarchical and progressive construction techniques for the Skeleton.

The use of our implemented system shows the great wealth of information provided by the Visibility Skeleton. Only a few of the many potential applications were presented here, and we believe that there are many computer graphics (and potentially computer vision) domains which can exploit the capacities of the Skeleton.

In future work many issues remain to be investigated. From a theoretical point of view, the most challenging problems are the development of a hierarchical approach so that the Visibility Skeleton can be used for very complex scenes as well as the resolution of all theoretical issues for the treatment of dynamic scenes. Some of the problems for the dynamic solution are sketched in Fig 15. Adapting the algorithm to curved objects requires the enumeration of all relevant events and definitely has many applications.

Finally the field of applications must be extended: exact point to area form-factor from any point on a face, aspect graph construction, and incorporation into a global illumination algorithm.

Acknowledgements

We would like to thank Jean-Dominique Gascuel for his AVL-tree code and Seth Teller for the very fruitful discussions we had and for all the suggestions he gave on conservative, lazy and practical approaches.

7 Appendix

7.1 Complete Catalogue of FACE Adjacencies

Face related events are adjacent to FE elements Fv elements as well as EEE arcs when two non-coplanar edges are involved.

The interaction of a face with two edges is shown in Fig. 16, the interaction of a face a vertex and an edge is shown in Fig. 18 and finally the interaction of two faces is shown in Fig. 17.

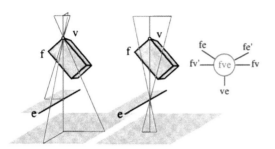

Figure 18: A FvE node.

7.2 Details of the Construction to find the Orientation of Arcs

Finding the correct extremity of an arc when inserting a node is crucial for the construction algorithm to function correctly. We present here the most complex case, which is the insertion of an $E4$ node.

Consider the node $e_1 e_2 e_3 e_4$ shown in Fig. 19, and the adjacent arc $e_1 e_2 e_3$. The question that needs to be answered is whether the node $e_1 e_2 e_3 e_4$ is the start or the end node of this arc. To answer this query, we examine the movement of the line l going through e_1, e_2 and e_3, when moving on e_1. The side of e_4 to which we move will determine whether we are a start or an end node.

Consider the infinitesimal motion $d\vec{e_1}$ on e_1. The corresponding point of e_3 on the EEE will lie on the intersection of the plane defined by e_2 and the defining point on e_1. The motion of $d\vec{e_1}$ on e_1 corresponds to a rotation of $\alpha = \frac{\vec{e_1}.\vec{n}}{d_1}$ of the plane around e_2. Symmetrically, this rotation corresponds to the motion $d\vec{e_3}$ on e_3 and we have $\alpha = \frac{d\vec{e_3}.\vec{n}}{d_3}$, by angle equality. Thus, $d\vec{e_3} = e_3 \frac{d_3 d\vec{e_1}.\vec{n}}{d_1 \vec{e_3}.\vec{n}}$.

Now we want to obtain $d\vec{e_4}$, the infinitesimal motion of the line going through the three edges around e_4. We consider the line as being defined by its origin on e_1 and by its unnormalized direction vector $\vec{dir}$ from e_1 to e_3. For the motion $d\vec{e_1}$ of the origin, the direction vector of moves by $d\vec{e_3} - d\vec{e_1}$, and thus $d\vec{e_4} = d\vec{e_1} + \frac{d_4}{d_3 - d_1}(d\vec{e_3} - \vec{e_1})$.

The sign of $(\vec{e_4} \times \vec{e_4}').node$ determines on which side of e_4 the line l will move.

The adjacencies also depend on the face related to the edges which are visible from the other edges. The other cases are simpler and summarized in Table 2.

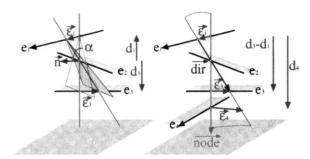

Figure 19: Determining the direction of an E4 node insertion.

Node	Adjacent arc	Start or End Criterion
$v_1 v_2$	$v_1 e_3$	$v_1 == startV(e)$
$v e_1 e_2$	$v e_2$	$(\vec{e_2} \times \vec{e_1}).\vec{node} > 0$
	$e_3 e_1 e_2$	$v == startV(e_3)$
	$e_2 e_1 e_3$	$\vec{n} = normal(v, \vec{e_2})$
		$\vec{e_3}.\vec{n} * \vec{e_1}.\vec{n} > 0$
$e_1 v e_2$	$v e_2$	$(\vec{e_1} \times \vec{e_2}).\vec{node} > 0$
	$e_2 e_1 e_3$	$\vec{n} = normal(v, \vec{e_2})$
		$\vec{e_3}.\vec{n} * \vec{e_2}.\vec{n} > 0$
$e_1 e_2 e_3 e_4$	$e_1 e_2 e_3$	$\vec{n} = normal(\vec{e_2}, \vec{node});$
		$\vec{e_3} = e_3 \frac{d_3 \vec{e_1}.\vec{n}}{d_1 \vec{e_3}.\vec{n}}$
		$\vec{e_4} = \vec{e_1} + \frac{d_4}{d_3 - d_1}(\vec{e_3} - \vec{e_1})$
		$(\vec{e_4} \times \vec{e_4}').\vec{node} > 0$
$e_1 f e_2$	$f e_1$	$\vec{e_2}.\vec{normal(f)} > 0$
	$e_1 e_{f1} e_2$	$\vec{e_1}.\vec{normal(f)} > 0$
$f e_1 e_2$	$f e_2$	$\vec{e_1}.\vec{normal(f)} > 0$
	$e_2 e_1 e_{f1}$	$\vec{n} = normal(\vec{node}, \vec{e_1})$
		$\vec{n}.\vec{e_2} * \vec{n}.\vec{e_{f1}} > 0$
$f v e$	$f v$	$\vec{e}.\vec{normal(f)} > 0$
	$v e$	$\vec{e}.\vec{normal(f)} > 0$

Table 2: for each arc adjacent to a created node, there is a criterion that tells if it is a start node or an ending node.

References

[1] James Arvo and David B. Kirk. Fast ray tracing by ray classification. In Maureen C. Stone, editor, *Computer Graphics (SIGGRAPH '87 Proceedings)*, volume 21, pages 55–64, July 1987.

[2] Daniel R. Baum, Holly E. Rushmeier, and James M. Winget. Improving radiosity solutions through the use of analytically determined form-factors. *Computer Graphics*, 23(3):325–334, July 1989. Proceedings SIGGRAPH '89 in Boston, USA.

[3] Daniel R. Baum, John R. Wallace, Michael F. Cohen, and Donald P. Greenberg. The back-buffer algorithm : an extension of the radiosity method to dynamic environments. *The Visual Computer*, 2:298–306, 1986.

[4] Michael F. Cohen and Donald P. Greenberg. The hemi-cube : A radiosity solution for complex environments. *Computer Graphics*, 19(3):31–40, July 1985. Proceedings SIGGRAPH '85 in San Francisco (USA).

[5] George Drettakis and Eugene Fiume. A fast shadow algorithm for area light sources using back projection. In Andrew Glassner, editor, *SIGGRAPH 94 Conference Proceedings (Orlando, FL)*, Annual Conference Series, pages 223–230. ACM SIGGRAPH, July 1994.

[6] George Drettakis and Francois Sillion. Accurate visibility and meshing calculations for hierarchical radiosity. In X. Pueyo and P. Shröder, editors, *Rendering Techniques '96*, pages 269–279. Springer Verlag, June 1996. Proc. 7th EG Workshop on Rendering in Porto.

[7] Frédo Durand, George Drettakis, and Claude Puech. The 3d visibility complex, a new approach to the problems of accurate visibility. In X. Pueyo and P. Shröder, editors, *Rendering Techniques '96*, pages 245–257. Springer Verlag, June 1996.

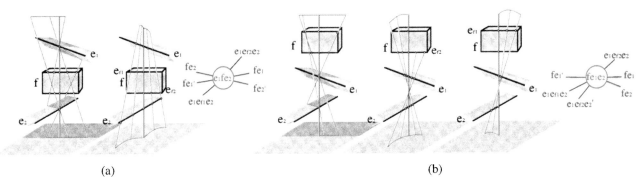

Figure 16: An EFE node.

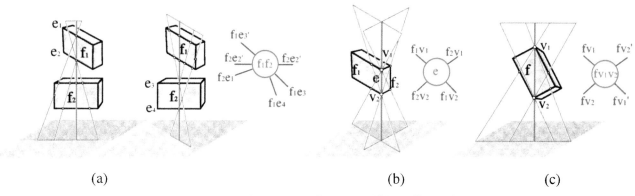

Figure 17: (a) A FF node, (b) an Fe node and (c) and Fvv node.

Proc. 7th EG Workshop on Rendering in Porto.

[8] David W. George, François Sillion, and Donald P. Greenberg. Radiosity redistribution for dynamic environments. *IEEE Computer Graphics and Applications*, 10(4), July 1990.

[9] Ziv Gigus, John Canny, and Raimund Seidel. Efficiently computing and representing aspect graphs of polyhedral objects. *IEEE Trans. on Pat. Matching & Mach. Intelligence*, 13(6), June 1991.

[10] Ziv Gigus and Jitendra Malik. Computing the aspect graph for the line drawings of polyhedral objects. *IEEE Trans. on Pat. Matching & Mach. Intelligence*, 12(2), February 1990.

[11] Eric A. Haines. Shaft culling for efficient ray-traced radiosity. In Brunet and Jansen, editors, *Photorealistic Rendering in Comp. Graphics*, pages 122–138. Springer Verlag, 1993. Proc. 2nd EG Workshop on Rendering (Barcelona, 1991).

[12] Pat Hanrahan, David Saltzman, and Larry Aupperle. A rapid hierarchical radiosity algorithm. *Computer Graphics*, 25(4):197–206, August 1991. SIGGRAPH '91 Las Vegas.

[13] Stephen Hardt and Seth Teller. High-fidelity radiosity rendering at interactive rates. In X. Pueyo and P. Shröder, editors, *Rendering Techniques '96*. Springer Verlag, June 1996. Proc. 7th EG Workshop on Rendering in Porto.

[14] Paul Heckbert. Discontinuity meshing for radiosity. *Third Eurographics Workshop on Rendering*, pages 203–226, May 1992.

[15] Michael Mc Kenna and Joseph O'Rourke. Arrangements of lines in space: A data structure with applications. In *Proc. 4th Annu. ACM Sympos. Comput. Geom.*, pages 371–380, 1988.

[16] Dani Lischinski, Brian Smits, and Donald P. Greenberg. Bounds and error estimates for radiosity. In Andrew S. Glassner, editor, *SIGGRAPH 94 Conference Proceedings (Orlando, FL)*, Annual Conference Series, pages 67–74. ACM SIGGRAPH, July 1994.

[17] Dani Lischinski, Filippo Tampieri, and Donald P. Greenberg. Discontinuity meshing for accurate radiosity. *IEEE Computer Graphics and Applications*, 12(6):25–39, November 1992.

[18] Dani Lischinski, Filippo Tampieri, and Donald P. Greenberg. Combining hierarchical radiosity and discontinuity meshing. In Jim Kajiya, editor, *SIGGRAPH 93 Conference Proceedings (Anaheim, CA)*, Annual Conference Series, pages 199–208. ACM SIGGRAPH, August 1993.

[19] Rachel Orti, Stéphane Rivière, Frédo Durand, and Claude Puech. Radiosity for dynamic scenes in flatland with the visibility complex. In Jarek Rossignac and François Sillion, editors, *Computer Graphics Forum (Proc. of Eurographics '96)*, volume 16, pages 237–249, Poitiers, France, September 1996.

[20] M. Pellegrini. Stabbing and ray shooting in 3-dimensional space. In *Proc. 6th Annu. ACM Sympos. Comput. Geom.*, pages 177–186, 1990.

[21] H. Plantinga and C. R. Dyer. Visibility, occlusion, and the aspect graph. *Internat. J. Comput. Vision*, 5(2):137–160, 1990.

[22] M. Pocchiola and G. Vegter. The visibility complex. 1996. special issue devoted to ACM-SoCG'93.

[23] Erin Shaw. Hierarchical radiosity for dynamic environments. Master's thesis, Cornell University, Ithaca, NY, August 1994.

[24] A. James Stewart and Sherif Ghali. Fast computation of shadow boundaries using spatial coherence and backprojections. In Andrew Glassner, editor, *SIGGRAPH 94 Conference Proceedings (Orlando, FL)*, Annual Conference Series, pages 231–238. ACM SIGGRAPH, July 1994.

[25] Filippo Tampieri. *Discontinuity Meshing for Radiosity Image Synthesis*. PhD thesis, Department of Computer Science, Cornell University, Ithaca, New York, 1993. PhD Thesis.

[26] Seth J. Teller. Computing the antipenumbra of an area light source. *Computer Graphics*, 26(4):139–148, July 1992. Proc. SIGGRAPH '92 in Chicago.

[27] Seth J. Teller and Patrick M. Hanrahan. Global visibility algorithms for illumination computations. In J. Kajiya, editor, *SIGGRAPH 93 Conf. Proc. (Anaheim)*, Annual Conf. Series, pages 239–246. ACM SIGGRAPH, August 1993.

[28] Seth J. Teller and Michael E. Hohmeyer. Computing the lines piercing four lines. Technical report, CS Dpt. UC Berkeley, 1991.

[29] John R. Wallace, Kells A. Elmquist, and Eric A. Haines. A ray tracing algorithm for progressive radiosity. *Computer Graphics*, 23(3):315–324, July 1989. Proceedings SIGGRAPH '89 in Boston.

Rendering Complex Scenes with Memory-Coherent Ray Tracing

Matt Pharr　　　　Craig Kolb　　　　Reid Gershbein　　　　Pat Hanrahan

Computer Science Department, Stanford University

Abstract

Simulating realistic lighting and rendering complex scenes are usually considered separate problems with incompatible solutions. Accurate lighting calculations are typically performed using ray tracing algorithms, which require that the entire scene database reside in memory to perform well. Conversely, most systems capable of rendering complex scenes use scan-conversion algorithms that access memory coherently, but are unable to incorporate sophisticated illumination. We have developed algorithms that use caching and lazy creation of texture and geometry to manage scene complexity. To improve cache performance, we increase locality of reference by dynamically reordering the rendering computation based on the contents of the cache. We have used these algorithms to compute images of scenes containing millions of primitives, while storing ten percent of the scene description in memory. Thus, a machine of a given memory capacity can render realistic scenes that are an order of magnitude more complex than was previously possible.

CR Categories: I.3.3 [Computer Graphics]: Picture/Image Generation; I.3.7 [Computer Graphics]: Three-Dimensional Graphics and Realism—Raytracing

Keywords: scene data management, caching, computation reordering, coherence

1 Introduction

Rendering systems are challenged by three types of complexity: geometric, surface, and illumination. Geometric complexity is necessary to model detailed environments; many more primitives than can fit into memory may be necessary to model a scene accurately. Surface complexity is a result of programmable shading and many texture maps. Illumination complexity arises from realistic lighting models and the interreflection of light. Previous rendering algorithms have not been able to handle all of these types of complexity simultaneously. Generally, they either perform illumination computations assuming that the entire scene fits in main memory, or only store part of the scene in memory and simplify the lighting computation. In order to be able to use algorithms that compute accurate illumination with such complex scenes, the coherence of scene data reference patterns must be greatly improved.

Exploiting coherence to increase efficiency is a classic technique in computer graphics[19]. Increasing the coherence of a computation can reduce the amount of memory used, the time it requires, or both. For example, Z-buffer rendering algorithms operate on a single primitive at a time, which makes it possible to build rendering hardware that does not need access to the entire scene. More recently, the Talisman architecture was designed to exploit frame-to-frame coherence as a means of accelerating rendering and reducing memory bandwidth requirements[21].

Kajiya has written a whitepaper that proposes an architecture for Monte Carlo ray tracing systems that is designed to improve coherence across all levels of the memory hierarchy, from processor caches to disk storage[13]. The rendering computation is decomposed into parts—ray-object intersections, shading calculations, and calculating spawned rays—that are performed independently. The coherence of memory references is increased through careful management of the interaction of the computation and the memory that it references, reducing overall running time and facilitating parallelism and vectorization. However, no system based on this architecture has been implemented.

We have independently developed similar algorithms, based on two main ideas: caching and reordering. We cache a subset of large geometric and texture databases in main memory for fast access by the rendering system. Data is added to these caches on demand when needed for rendering computation. We ensure coherent access to the cache by statically reordering scene data, dynamically placing it in memory, and dynamically reordering ray intersection calculations. This reordering is critical for good performance with small caches. These algorithms have made it possible to efficiently compute images using global illumination algorithms with scenes containing roughly ten times as many primitives as can fit into memory. This marks a large increase in the complexity of scenes that can be rendered effectively using Monte Carlo methods.

In this paper, we describe the algorithms we have developed and the system we have built that uses them. We first discuss how previous rendering systems have managed complexity. We then introduce and describe our algorithms in detail and discuss their implementation. Finally, we present results from applying our algorithms to a variety of realistic complex scenes and discuss the performance of the algorithms.

2 Background

Previously developed techniques that address the problems of rendering complex scenes include culling algorithms, lazy evaluation and caching, and reordering independent parts of a computation to improve its memory coherence. In this section, we briefly describe some of this previous work and how our work draws from and builds upon it.

While most ray tracing systems do not explicity address scene memory management, several researchers have investigated this issue, particularly in the context of managing scene distribution on multiprocessors. Jansen and Chalmers have written a survey of past work in parallel rendering that investigated these issues[11], and in particular, Green used geometry caching techniques to manage scene distribution on a multiprocessor[7]. Pharr and Hanrahan later used geometry caching to manage large amounts of displacement-mapped geometry in a serial ray tracer[17]. Global illumination calculations were not performed in these geometry caching systems, so the rays that were traced passed through coherent regions of space and the caches performed well. In general, however, Monte Carlo ray tracing systems that evaluate the trees of rays in depth-first order access scene data too incoherently for caching algorithms to be effective.

A number of techniques have been presented to increase the coherence of rays traveling through a scene. Fröhlich traversed ray trees iteratively in order to be able to gather rays into coherent bundles. The bundles were stored in the intersection acceleration data structure and voxels of rays and geometry were processed in order based on how many rays were contained within. Rays in voxels were processed as a group so that candidate objects for intersection tests could be found and so that the overhead of octree traversal could be reduced. In a manner similar to shaft culling[9], Reinhard and Jansen gathered rays with common origins into frustums that were traced together so that a set of the objects inside the frustum could be found to accelerate ray-object intersection tests[18]. Pharr and Hanrahan reordered eye rays using space-filling curves over the image plane to improve the coherence of spawned rays in a depth-first ray tracer, which in turn improved geometry cache performance[17].

Scanline-based rendering algorithms are able to render images of scenes that are too complex to fit into memory; the REYES architecture[4] is representative of these approaches. Sorting, culling, and lazy evaluation techniques further increase the efficiency of REYES. At startup time, geometric primitives are sorted into the screen-space buckets that they overlap. When a bucket is rendered, the primitives overlapping it are subdivided into grids of pixel-sized micropolygons that are shaded all at once and discarded as soon as they have been sampled in the image plane. As rendering progresses, most hidden geometry is culled before being shaded by an algorithm similar to the hierarchical Z-buffer[8, 1]. This sorting and culling process allows REYES to store in memory only a small fraction of the total number of potential micropolygons.

Two major features of REYES are programmable shading[3, 10] and support for large amounts of texture data. A texture caching scheme, described by Peachey[16], makes it possible to render scenes with much more texture than can fit into memory. Textures are pre-filtered into a set of multiresolution images (used for anti-aliasing) that are stored on disk in tiles of approximately 32 by 32 texels. A fixed number of texture tiles are cached in memory, and when the cache fills up, the least recently used tile is discarded. Since texture is only read into memory when needed, startup time is low and textures that do not contribute to the image do not affect performance. Furthermore, since texture is resampled from the pre-filtered images, each shading calculation makes a small number of accesses to a local part of the texture, which further improves locality of reference and, thus, performance. The texture cache in REYES performs extremely well: Peachey found that less than 1% of the texture in a scene can typically be kept in memory without any degradation in performance. Our system uses texture caching in a similar manner, and extends these ideas to support efficient geometry caching.

Algorithms that explicitly take advantage of the dense occlusion present in large architectural models have been used to compute radiosity solutions in scenes that would otherwise be intractable[20, 6]. These algorithms break the computation into nearly independent sub-problems, based on sets of mutually-interacting objects. Computation is reordered so that only a spatially local part of the data is processed at a time, and computation is scheduled based on which parts of the scene are already in memory to minimize the time spent reading additional data from disk. These algorithms make it possible to compute radiosity solutions for models that would require enormous resources using traditional techniques. Our computation reordering techniques build on the reordering frameworks of these systems.

3 Overview

In the next two sections, we describe the techniques we have investigated for managing scene data and for finding and exploiting coherence in ray tracing based rendering algorithms. Figure 1 illustrates how the various parts of our system interact. Disk storage is used to manage texture, geometry, queued rays and image samples. First, the camera generates eye rays to form the image, and these are partitioned into coherent groups. The scheduler selects groups of rays to trace, based on information about which parts of the scene are already in memory and the degree to which processing the rays will advance the computation. Intersection tests are performed with the chosen rays, which causes geometry to be added to the cache as needed. As intersections are found, shading calculations are performed, and the texture maps used for shading are managed by the texture cache. Any new rays that are spawned during shading are returned to the scheduler to be added to the queues of waiting rays. Once all of the rays have terminated, the image samples are filtered and the image is reconstructed.

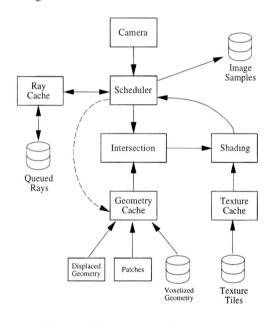

Figure 1: Block diagram of our system.

4 Caching Scene Data

Our system uses texture caching and geometry caching to manage scene complexity. Our texture cache is much like Peachey's[16], and texture access is driven by procedural shaders written in a language similar to the RenderMan shading language. Our geometry caching scheme draws upon ideas from the texture cache: a limited amount of geometry is stored in memory, and lazy loading limits the amount of data added to the cache to that which is needed for ray intersection tests. The only information needed by the geometry cache at startup time is the spatial bounds of each model in the scene. Both caches use a least recently used replacement policy.

4.1 Geometry Sources

A distinguishing feature of our ray tracer is that we cache a single type of geometric primitive: triangles. This has a number of advantages. Ray intersection tests can be optimized for a single case, and memory management for the geometry cache is easier, since there is less variation in the amount of space needed to store different types of primitives. It is also possible to optimize

Figure 2: Trees by a lake

many other parts of the renderer when only one type of primitive is supported. The REYES algorithm similarly uses a single internal primitive—micropolygons—to make shading and sampling more efficient[4]. Unlike REYES, we optimize the system for handling large databases of triangles; this allows our system to efficiently handle a wide variety of common sources of geometry, including scanned data, scientific data, and tessellated patches. A potential drawback of this single representation is that other types of primitives, such as spheres, require more space to store after they are tessellated. We have found that the advantages of a single representation outweigh this disadvantage.

A number of different sources can supply the geometry cache with triangles:

- *Secondary storage.* We store triangle meshes on disk pre-sorted into voxels. All of the geometry in each voxel is stored contiguously, so that it may be quickly read from disk. The model's bounding box is stored in the file header for efficient access at startup time. Because geometry may be read from disk many times during rendering, it is stored in a compact format in order to minimize time spent parsing the file. As with tiled texture maps, the time to create these files is negligible: a mesh of slightly more than 1 million primitives stored in a traditional format can be read, parsed, sorted, and written out in the new format in well under a minute.

- *Tessellated patches and subdivision surfaces.* In our system, patches are tessellated into triangles for the geometry cache. The only information that must be stored in memory until these triangles are generated is the bounding box of the patch or group of patches and, possibly, the control points.

- *Displacement mapping.* Our system supports displacement mapping. We subdivide input geometry into small triangles, the vertices of which are perturbed by a displacement shader. This can result in enormous amounts of geometry to be stored, since the triangles created must be the size of a pixel if they are not to be individually visible.

- *Procedurally generated geometry.* Relatively simple programs can be used to describe complex objects; the geometry needed to represent these objects can be stored in the geometry cache. The program need only be run again to regenerate the geometry if it is discarded and later needed again.

4.2 Geometry Cache Properties

Our geometry cache is organized around regular voxel grids termed *geometry grids.* Each collection of geometric objects is stored in its own grid, which tightly encloses it. The volume of the grid's voxels (and hence the amount of geometry in each voxel) determines the granularity of the cache, since the cache fills and discards all of the geometry in a voxel as a block. We have found that a few thousand triangles per voxel is a good level of granularity for caching. However, this is too coarse a granularity for ray intersection acceleration, so we insert another voxel grid, the *acceleration grid,* inside geometry grid voxels that hold more than a few hundred triangles. This two-level intersection acceleration scheme is similar to a method described by Jevans and Wyvill[12].

By construction, all geometry in a voxel occupies a contiguous block of memory independent of geometry in other voxels. In particular, triangles that span multiple voxels are stored independently in each of them. Thus, spatial locality in the three-dimensional space of the scene is tied to spatial locality in memory. If these two types of spatial locality were not coupled in this way, the cache would almost always perform poorly, since coherent access in three dimensional space would not generate coherent access in memory.

Memory management in the geometry cache is more complicated than it is in the texture cache. Whereas all texture tiles are the same size, each geometry voxel may require a different amount of space. These differences lead to repeated allocation and freeing of different-sized blocks of memory, which causes heap fragmentation. Before memory management was addressed in our system, fragmentation would often cause our renderer's size to double or triple after a few hours of execution. After replacing the system library's allocation routines with our own (based on segregated storage with bitmapped usage tables and no coalescing[23]), heap fragmentation was negligible. More recently, preliminary experiments suggest that Lea's allocator[15] also eliminates growth due to fragmentation.

The geometry cache could be implemented with virtual memory, with some loss of direct control of and information about the contents of the cache. Furthermore, the data being cached must still be organized to ensure coupled spatial locality as described above, and computation must still be reordered if the cache is to perform well.

5 Reordering Rendering Computation

These geometry and texture caching algorithms provide a framework for rendering large scenes. However, since cache misses are orders of magnitude more expensive then cache hits, we must find a way to minimize misses if overall system performance is to be acceptable. In order to ensure coherent access of the caches, we dynamically reorder ray-object intersection tests. Rather than evaluating ray trees in a fixed order, such as depth-first or breadth-first, all rays are placed on ray queues. The system chooses rays from the queues, simultaneously trying to minimize cache misses and advance computation toward completion. The degree to which we can minimize the number of times geometry must be added to the cache determines how efficiently we make use of the cache, and how well the system performs in the face of extreme complexity.

In order to perform this reordering, we would like each queued ray not to depend on the results or state of other queued rays. This independence implies that we must store with each ray all of the information needed to compute its contribution to the image; furthermore, the space occupied by this information must be minimized given the potentially large number of queued rays. Both of these goals can be achieved by decomposing the computation of outgoing radiance into a simple sum of weighted incoming radiances. To our knowledge, this decomposition was first used by Cleary et al.[2] to reduce storage and communication demands in a parallel ray tracing system.

5.1 Computation Decomposition

We can take advantage of the structure of the rendering equation[14] to decompose the rendering computation into parts that can be scheduled independently. When we sample the rendering equation to computing outgoing radiance at a point x in the direction ω_r, the result is:

$$L_o(x, \omega_r) = L_e(x, \omega_r) + \frac{1}{N} \sum_N f_r(x, \omega_i, \omega_r) L_i(x, \omega_i) \cos \theta_i, \tag{1}$$

where L_o is the outgoing radiance, L_e is the emitted radiance, f_r is the bidirectional reflectance distribution function (BRDF) at x, L_i is the radiance incoming from direction ω_i, and θ_i is the angle between ω_i and the surface normal at x. We can make use of the separability of (1) to decompose the computation in such a way as to make each queued ray independent from the others, and to minimize the amount of state stored with each queued ray. Given a ray r to be traced in direction ω_i, the weight of its contribution to the outgoing radiance at x is given by

$$w(x, \omega_i) = \frac{1}{N} f_r(x, \omega_i, \omega_r) \cos \theta_i. \tag{2}$$

If r, in turn, intersects a reflective surface at a point x', additional rays will be spawned from this point to determine the total radiance traveling along r. The contribution that one of these spawned rays r' will make to the outgoing radiance at x is simply the product of $w(x, \omega_i)$ and $w(x', \omega_i')$.

When an initial camera ray r_0 is spawned, we record a unit weight and its corresponding image plane location. When the intersection of r_0 is found and a secondary ray is spawned, we compute the total weight for the new ray as above, store this weight and the same image plane location, and repeat the process. The weight associated with a ray r thus represents the product of the weighted BRDF values of all the surfaces on the path from a point on r to the image-plane location. Once a ray intersects an emissive object, the emitted differential irradiance that it carries is multiplied by the ray's weight, and the result can be immediately added to the radiance stored at the ray's associated image-plane location.

This decomposition does introduce limitations. For example, because all of the information about the point being shaded is discarded once secondary rays are generated, adaptive sampling (of area light sources, for example) is not possible. Although more state could be stored with each ray, including information about the surface from which it originated, this would increase memory requirements. Furthermore, the scheduling algorithm's interest in deferring rays that will cause cache misses means that this state information might have to be stored for a great many points (until all of their spawned rays have been traced.)

For high resolution images with many samples per pixel, the storage needed to hold intermediate results for all of the image samples can be hundreds of megabytes. The result for each image sample is found in parts, and results are generated in an unknown order, so we write results to disk as they are computed rather than storing them in main memory. When rendering finishes, we make a number of passes through this file, accumulating sample values and filtering them into pixel values.

5.2 Ray Grouping

Given this decomposition of the illumination computation into pieces that can be easily reordered, we must find effective reordering techniques. A perfect scheduling system would cause each primitive to be added to the geometry cache only once. However, this is not generally possible for ray tracing algorithms, since there is a strict order relationship in ray trees: it is not possible to spawn secondary rays until we find the intersection positions of the rays that cause them to be spawned.

One early reordering approach we tried organizes rays with nearby origins into clusters. When a cluster of rays is traced, its rays are sorted by direction to increase their coherence, and each ray is then traced through the scene until an intersection is found. This technique is good at exploiting coherence in scenes where the majority of rays are spawned from a few locations, such as the eye and the light sources. However, it has two drawbacks. First, because each ray is traced to completion before starting another ray, this method fails to exploit coherence between rays in a beam as they move through the scene together. Secondly, this technique fails to exploit coherence that exists between rays that pass through the same region of space, but whose origins are not close together.

The approach we currently use is designed to account for the spatial coherence between all rays, including those whose origins are not close to each other. We divide the scene into another set of voxels, the *scheduling grid*. Associated with each scheduling voxel is a queue of the rays that are currently inside it and information about which of the geometry voxels overlap its extent. When a scheduling voxel is processed, each queued ray in it is tested for intersection with the geometry inside each overlapping geometry voxel. If an intersection is found, we perform shading calculations and calculate spawned rays, which are added to the ray queue. Otherwise, the ray is advanced to the next non-empty voxel it enters and is placed on that voxel's ray queue. Figure 4 summarizes the rendering process.

If the subset of the scene geometry that overlaps each scheduling voxel can fit into the geometry cache, the cache will not thrash while the rays in an individual voxel are being traced. Conversely, if a scheduling voxel contains too much geometry to fit into memory at once, the geometry cache will thrash (this is the analogue of trying to render a scene that cannot fit into memory without computation reordering). To account for variations in geometric complexity in different regions of the scene, the regular scheduling grid we use could be replaced with an adaptive spatial data structure, such as an octree.

To amortize the expense of cache misses over as much ray intersection work as possible, we attempt to defer tracing rays in voxels where there will be misses. We preferentially process scheduling voxels that have all of their corresponding geometry cached in

Figure 3: Indoor scene, with dense occlusion, and Cathedral scene.

```
Generate eye rays and place them in queues
While there are queued rays
        Choose a voxel to process
        For each ray in voxel
                Intersect the ray with the voxel's geometry
                If there is an intersection
                        Run the surface shader and compute the BRDF
                        Insert spawned rays into the voxel's queue
                        If the surface is emissive
                                Store radiance contribution to the image
                        Terminate the ray
                Else
                        Advance the ray to the next voxel queue
```

Figure 4: Basic reordering algorithm.

memory, and accumulate rays in the queues of voxels that will incur geometry cache misses. This can lead to prohibitively many rays to store in memory, so we use a simple mechanism to manage the untraced rays. We store a limited number of rays in memory in a *ray cache*; excess rays are written to disk until needed for intersection calculations. When we trace the rays in a given voxel, those in the ray cache are traced first, and then those on disk are read and processed.

5.3 Voxel Scheduling

Given a set of scheduling voxels with rays in their queues, the scheduler must choose an order in which to process the voxels. It could simply loop through all of the voxels, processing the rays that are waiting in each of them until all rays have terminated. However, we can reduce cache misses and improve efficiency by more carefully choosing when to process each voxel.

We associate a cost value and a benefit value with each voxel. The cost is computed using a function that estimates how expensive it will be to process the rays in the voxel (for example, the cost should be high if the voxel encompasses a large amount of geometry, none of which is currently in memory). The benefit function estimates how much progress toward the completion of the computation will be made as a result of processing the voxel. For example, voxels with many rays in their queues have a higher benefit. Furthermore, voxels full of rays with large weights have a greater ben-

efit than voxels full of rays with low weights, since the rays with large weights are likely to spawn a larger number new rays. The scheduler uses these values to choose voxels to work on by selecting the voxel with the highest ratio of benefit to cost.

Both of these functions are only approximations to the true cost and benefit of processing the voxel. It is difficult to estimate *a priori* how many cache misses will be caused by a group of rays in a voxel since the geometry caching algorithms add geometry to the cache lazily. If the rays in a voxel don't access some geometry, that geometry is never added to the cache. It is also difficult to estimate how many new rays will be spawned by a group of rays before they are actually traced, since the number and weights of the spawned rays depend on the reflectances and orientations of the surfaces the rays hit.

In our implementation, the cost of processing a voxel is based on an estimate of how much of the geometry in a voxel that will be accessed is already present in memory. If some but not all of the geometry in a voxel is in memory, we reduce its expected cost by 90% if we have already traced rays inside the voxel and no geometry that overlaps the voxel has been removed from the geometry cache in the meantime. This reduction keeps voxels with geometry that cannot be accessed by the rays currently passing through them from seeming to be more expensive than they actually are. The benefit is the product of the the number of rays in the voxel and the sum of their weighted contributions to the final image. Other possible cost and benefit functions could account for a user interested in seeing results for one part of an image as soon as possible, or for minimizing the number of queued rays.

6 Results

We have implemented our caching and reordering algorithms as part of a ray tracing based rendering system. Like most ray tracers, our renderer supports several mechanisms for accurately simulating light transport. However, because it was specifically designed to manage scene complexity, our system also supports features usually only found in scanline-based systems, including displacement mapping, the ability to render large geometric databases and NURBS, and programmable shaders that use large numbers of texture maps.

We conducted a number of experiments to determine how our algorithms performed on complex scenes that would be difficult to renderer using traditional approaches. Our experiments were performed on a lightly loaded 190 MHz MIPS R10000 processor with 1GB of memory. So that our results would be indicative of performance on machines with less memory (where there wouldn't be excess memory that the operating system could use to buffer I/O), we disabled I/O buffering for our tests. In practice, performance would be improved if buffering was permitted. Running time was measured in wall clock time, which ensured that time spent waiting for I/O was included. Heap fragmentation caused by the large amount of memory allocation and freeing necessary to manage the geometry cache was accounted for by basing memory use statistics on the total size of the process. Although our algorithms make use of disk I/O in a number of ways, all of our tests were performed using a single disk; using more disks, a RAID system, or asynchronous prefetching of data would further improve performance.

Each of our test scenes would be considered complex by current standards, requiring between 431MB and 1.9GB of memory to store in their entirety. The scenes cover a variety of common situations, including an indoor scene that is densely occluded and an outdoor scene with little occlusion. We use no instantiation of geometry in these scenes; all objects are distinct and managed individually.

- The first test scene is a Cathedral model that was used to demonstrate algorithms simulating the effects of weathering due to water flowing over surfaces[5] (Figure 3). The base Cathedral model itself consists of only 11,000 triangles, but displacement mapping is used to add a great deal more geometric detail. There is also a statue modeled using 36,000 polygons and three gargoyle models comprised of roughly 20,000 polygons each. The surface shaders access four or five different texture maps at each point being shaded, and the displacement shader accesses one texture map. After displacement mapping, total geometric complexity is 5.1 million primitives when the image is rendered at a resolution of 576 by 864 pixels. All tests were performed at this resolution, using four samples per pixel[1]. A total of 1,495 texture maps that use 116MB of disk space are used to store the displacement maps and the results of the flow simulations over the surface (wetness, the thickness of dirt deposited on it, and so on). The illumination in this scene is simple, consisting of one shadow-casting light source and one fill light.

- Next, we modeled a room in a small office building (Figure 3). The building has two floors, each with four offices; the floors are connected by a staircase. The floors and ceilings are modeled using procedural displacement shaders, and each of the rooms is filled with complex models, including dense meshes from Cyberware scans and plant models from an organic modeling program. Total geometric complexity is 46.4 million primitives, which would require approximately 1.9GB of memory to store in memory at once. Most of the light in the main room is due to to sunlight shining through a window, modeled as a large area light source. The hallway and nearby offices are further illuminated by light sources in the ceiling. The reflective column in the hallway causes light from rooms not directly visible to the camera to strike the image, and forces additional scene geometry to be be brought into memory. We rendered this scene at a resolution of 672 by 384 pixels.

- Lastly, we constructed an outdoor test scene consisting of group of trees by a lake (Figure 2). There are four tree models comprised of 400,000 to 3.3 million triangles. Even the individual leaves of the trees are modeled explicitly; nothing is instantiated. The terrain and lake were created using displacement mapping, resulting in a total scene complexity

---

[1]The test scenes were rendered at higher resolution with more samples per pixel for the color plates. Our scheduling and reordering techniques performed as well when rendering the plates as when used for the test cases.

of over 9.6 million primitives, which would require approximately 440MB to store in memory in their entirety. Almost all of the geometry in this scene is visible from the eye. The only direct lighting in the scene comes from the sun, which is back-lighting the trees. Most of the illumination is due to indirect lighting from the sky and indirect reflections from other surfaces in the scene. For our tests, we rendered the scene at 677 by 288 pixels.

6.1 Caching and Lazy Evaluation

We first tested the impact of lazy loading of scene data on both running time and memory use. We started with the Cathedral, a scene where most of the modeled geometry and texture was visible. The scene was rendered twice: once with caches of unlimited size that were filled lazily, and once with all texture and geometric data read into memory at startup time (Figure 5). As shown in the table, both running time and memory use decreased when scene data is brought into memory lazily. Memory use was reduced by 22% using lazy loading, indicating that approximately 22% of the scene data was never accessed. Given that this test scene was chosen as a case where we would expect little improvement, this was a particularly encouraging result. To investigate further, we rendered the office scene to see how well lazy loading of data worked in a scene exhibiting dense occlusion. For this test, we computed only direct illumination from the light sources. We were unable to read the entire database for this scene into memory at startup time, due to its large size. However, when we lazily read the data into memory only 18% of the memory that would have been necessary to store the entire scene was used.

	Cathedral	Cathedral Lazy	Indoor Lazy
Running Time	163.4 min	156.9 min	35.3 min
Memory Use	431MB	337MB	316MB
% Texture Accessed	100%	49.6%	100%
% Geometry Accessed	100%	81.6%	17.8%

Figure 5: The overhead introduced by lazy loading of data is very small, and doing so improves performance even for scenes with little occlusion. For the scene with dense occlusion, lazy evaluation makes it possible to render a scene that could not fit into memory otherwise.

Using the Cathedral scene, we investigated how well the geometry cache performs if standard depth-first ray tracing is used in a scene that spawns a limited number of illumination rays (Figure 6). We rendered the scene using different geometry cache sizes, and recorded running time and geometry cache hit rates. We found that when geometry caching was used we could efficiently render the scene using only 90MB of memory, which is 21% of the space needed to store the scene in its entirety, or 27% of the space needed to store all of the data that was ever accessed.

Next, we investigated the performance of the texture cache using the Cathedral scene. We rendered the scene a number of times, each with a different cache size, in order to determine how hit rate and running time were affected. To increase the number of texture accesses for displacement map lookups, we used a moderately sized geometry cache for this test, ensuring that some of the displacement mapped geometry would be discarded from the cache and later recreated. We found that the texture cache performed extremely well. Even with only 32 tiles in memory, the cache hit rate was was 99.90%, and running time was 179 minutes, compared to 177 minutes when using a cache of unlimited size. A cache of 32 tiles uses 128kB of memory, which is 0.1% of all of the texture data in the scene.

Maximum Memory Use	Running Time	% of time with unlimited cache
90MB	184.3 min	117%
100MB	177.7 min	113%
300MB	156.9 min	100%

Figure 6: Time to render the Cathedral scene with varying limits on memory use. Although performance degraded slowly as maximum memory use was reduced from 300MB to 90MB, performance degrades catastrophically when it is smaller than 90MB. The working set for this scene is between 80 and 90MB–we were unable to complete any runs with maximum memory use of 80MB or below.

6.2 Scheduling and Reordering

We used the lake scene to test the performance of the reordering algorithms. The scene was rendered with Monte Carlo path tracing and no limit to the length of each path; instead, rays with low contributions were terminated probabilistically with Russian Roulette. A ray cache of 100,000 rays was used, representing 6% of the total number of rays traced. As shown in Figure 7, rendering the lake scene with global illumination algorithms and a small geometry cache was feasible only if computation reordering was performed. If reordering was not used, storing any less than 80% of the scene in memory caused running time to increase rapidly, as rendering was dominated by cache misses. Using reordering, we were able to render the lake scene using a cache of only 10% of the total size of the scene.

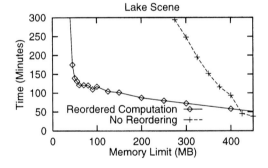

Figure 7: Running time for rendering the lake scene as the maximum amount of memory used is varied. When the cache is large enough to hold the entire scene database, the difference in time between the reordered and depth-first computation represents the overhead introduced by reordering. As can be seen, this overhead is not excessive. When maximum memory use is reduced to a small percentage of scene complexity, the reordered algorithm's performance allows us to efficiently render the scene using far less memory.

I/O performance had a greater impact on running time as we decreased cache sizes, but only significantly affected running time when the cache was thrashing. When the lake scene was rendered with all of the geometry stored in memory, the renderer performed 120MB of I/O to read models from disk. CPU utilization was 96%, indicating that little time was spent waiting for I/O. When we limited the total rendering memory to 50MB, the renderer performed 938MB of I/O managing models on disk, though CPU utilization was still 93%. For both of these tests, less than 70MB of I/O for the ray queues was done. Without computation reordering, much more I/O is performed: when we rendered the lake scene without reordering using a 325MB geometry cache, 2.1GB of data was read from disk to satisfy misses in the thrashing geometry cache.

Finally, we gathered statistics to gain insight into the interplay between our scheduling algorithm and the geometry cache. Figure

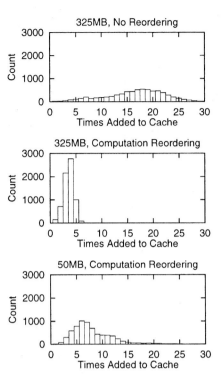

Figure 8: Histogram of the number of times each voxel of geometry was added to the geometry cache for the lake scene. When the scene is rendered without computation reordering with a cache of 325MB (left), geometry is added to the cache many more times than when computation is reordered with a cache of the same size (middle). When the cache size is limited to just 50MB and computation is reordered (right), cache performance is significantly better than the 325MB cache without reordering.

8 is a histogram of how many times each voxel of geometry was added to the geometry cache when the lake scene was rendered. Depth-first ray tracing led to poor performance with a medium-sized cache, as illustrated by the fact that most voxels were added to the cache between fifteen and twenty times. However, if computation reordering was used, the number of times each voxel was added to the cache was greatly reduced. With a very small cache of 50MB and computation reordering, voxels were inserted into the cache an average of approximately eight times. This compares well to the three complete passes through the database that systems such as REYES would make in rendering the shadow map, water reflection map, and final image for this scene. Of course, REYES would be unable to accurately reproduce the reflections in the water, or other effects due to indirect illumination.

7 Summary and Conclusion

We have presented a set of algorithms that improve locality of data storage and locality of data reference for rendering algorithms that use ray tracing. We have implemented these algorithms as part of a rendering system that supports programmable shading, large amounts of texture, displacement mapping and global illumination. These algorithms have enabled us to render scenes with far greater geometric, surface, and illumination complexity than previously possible on a machine of given capacity.

Our algorithms decompose the rendering computation into separate parts that can be worked on in any order, while minimizing the amount of state that needs to be stored for the rays waiting to be traced. Our decomposition of rendering computation is based on forward ray tracing; determining how to incorporate algorithms such as bidirectional path tracing[23, 15] is an interesting future challenge. Other questions to examine include how performance would be affected by other scheduling algorithms, and whether it is possible to greatly reduce the number of queued rays without causing performance to degrade.

Another area of future work is applying these techniques to parallel and hardware accelerated ray tracing. Management of shared texture and geometry caches on distributed shared memory architectures offers challenges of coordination of cache access and modification, scheduling rays over groups of processors, and effective management of the increased I/O demands that multiple processors would generate. Furthermore, by presenting a framework for ray tracing without holding the entire scene in memory (as Z-buffering does for scan-conversion), this works suggests a new approach to the long-elusive goal of effective hardware accelerated ray tracing.

Improving performance by gathering related data together with related computation is a powerful technique, as evidenced by its central position in computer architecture today; we believe that it will lead to further benefits in other areas of computer graphics.

8 Acknowledgments

Special thanks to Jim Kajiya for sharing a copy of his whitepaper, and to Radomír Měch and Przemyslaw Prusinkiewicz for sharing their wonderfully complex Chestnut tree model which was used in Figure 2. John Gerth was a source of valuable discussions and suggestions. Tony Apodaca, Tom Duff, Larry Gritz, and Mark VandeWettering in the RenderMan group at Pixar explained the intricacies of REYES. Julie Dorsey and Hans Pedersen kindly shared the Cathedral model used in Figure 3. James Davis wrote the code to tessellate NURBS for the geometry cache, and Chase Garfinkle provided much-needed editing help at the last minute. This research was supported by Silicon Graphics, Inc., NSF contract number CCR-9508579-001, and DARPA contracts DABT63-96-C-0084-P00002 and DABT63-95-C-0085-P00006.

References

[1] Tony Apodaca. Personal communication. 1996.

[2] J. G. Cleary, B. M. Wyvill, G. M. Birtwistle, and R. Vatti. Multiprocessor ray tracing. *Computer Graphics Forum*, 5(1):3–12, March 1986.

[3] Robert L. Cook. Shade trees. In Hank Christiansen, editor, *Computer Graphics (SIGGRAPH '84 Proceedings)*, volume 18, pages 223–231, July 1984.

[4] Robert L. Cook, Loren Carpenter, and Edwin Catmull. The Reyes image rendering architecture. In Maureen C. Stone, editor, *Computer Graphics (SIGGRAPH '87 Proceedings)*, pages 95–102, July 1987.

[5] Julie Dorsey, Hans Køhling Pedersen, and Pat Hanrahan. Flow and changes in appearance. In Holly Rushmeier, editor, *SIGGRAPH 96 Conference Proceedings*, pages 411–420. Addison Wesley, August 1996.

[6] Thomas A. Funkhouser. Coarse-grained parallelism for hierarchical radiosity using group iterative methods. In Holly Rushmeier, editor, *SIGGRAPH 96 Conference Proceedings*, pages 343–352. Addison Wesley, August 1996.

[7] Stuart Green. *Parallel Processing for Computer Graphics*. Research Monographics in Parallel and Distributed Computing. The MIT Press, 1991.

[8] Ned Greene and Michael Kass. Hierarchical Z-buffer visibility. In *Computer Graphics (SIGGRAPH '93 Proceedings)*, pages 231–240, August 1993.

[9] Eric Haines and John Wallace. Shaft culling for efficient ray-traced radiosity. In *Eurographics Workshop on Rendering*, 1991.

[10] Pat Hanrahan and Jim Lawson. A language for shading and lighting calculations. In Forest Baskett, editor, *Computer Graphics (SIGGRAPH '90 Proceedings)*, volume 24, pages 289–298, August 1990.

[11] Frederik W. Jansen and Alan Chalmers. Realism in real time? In Michael F. Cohen, Claude Puech, and Francois Sillion, editors, *Fourth Eurographics Workshop on Rendering*, pages 27–46. Eurographics, June 1993.

[12] David Jevans and Brian Wyvill. Adaptive voxel subdivision for ray tracing. In *Proceedings of Graphics Interface '89*, pages 164–72, Toronto, Ontario, June 1989. Canadian Information Processing Society.

[13] James Kajiya. A ray tracing architecture. unpublished manuscript, 1991.

[14] James T. Kajiya. The rendering equation. In David C. Evans and Russell J. Athay, editors, *Computer Graphics (SIGGRAPH '86 Proceedings)*, volume 20, pages 143–150, August 1986.

[15] Eric P. Lafortune and Yves D. Willems. A theoretical framework for physically based rendering. *Computer Graphics Forum*, 13(2):97–107, June 1994.

[16] Doug Lea. A memory allocator. Available on the web at http://g.oswego.edu/dl/html/malloc.html, 1996.

[17] Darwyn R. Peachey. Texture on demand. unpublished manuscript, 1990.

[18] Matt Pharr and Pat Hanrahan. Geometry caching for ray tracing displacement maps. In Xavier Pueyo and Peter Schröder, editors, *Eurographics Workshop on Rendering*, pages 31–40, 1996.

[19] E. Reinhard and F. W. Jansen. Rendering large scenes using parallel ray tracing. In A. G. Chalmers and F. W. Jansen, editors, *First Eurographics Workshop of Parallel Graphics and Visualization*, pages 67–80, September 1996.

[20] Ivan E. Sutherland, Robert F. Sproull, and R. A. Schumacker. A characterization of ten hidden-surface algorithms. *Computing Surveys*, 6(1):1–55, March 1974.

[21] Seth Teller, Celeste Fowler, Thomas Funkhouser, and Pat Hanrahan. Partitioning and ordering large radiosity computations. In Andrew Glassner, editor, *Proceedings of SIGGRAPH '94*, pages 443–450, July 1994.

[22] Jay Torborg and Jim Kajiya. Talisman: Commodity Realtime 3D graphics for the PC. In Holly Rushmeier, editor, *SIGGRAPH 96 Conference Proceedings*, pages 353–364. Addison Wesley, August 1996.

[23] Eric Veach and Leonidas Guibas. Bidirectional estimators for light transport. In *Fifth Eurographics Workshop on Rendering*, pages 147–162, Darmstadt, Germany, June 1994.

[24] Paul R. Wilson, Mark S. Johnstone, Michael Neely, and David Boles. Dynamic storage allocation: A survey and critical review. In *International Workshop on Memory Management*, September 1995. held in Kinross, Scotland, UK.

Illustrating Surface Shape in Volume Data
via Principal Direction-Driven 3D Line Integral Convolution

Victoria Interrante
Institute for Computer Applications in Science and Engineering (ICASE)

ABSTRACT

This paper describes how the set of principal directions and principal curvatures can be understood to define a natural "flow" over the surface of an object and, as such, can be used to guide the placement of the lines of a stroke texture that seeks to represent 3D shape in a perceptually intuitive way.

The driving application for this work is the visualization of layered isovalue surfaces in volume data, where the particular identity of an individual surface is not generally known *a priori* and observers will typically wish to view a variety of different level surfaces from the same distribution, superimposed over underlying opaque structures.

This paper describes how, by advecting an evenly distributed set of tiny opaque particles, and the empty space between them, via 3D line integral convolution through the vector field defined by the principal directions and principal curvatures of the level surfaces passing through each gridpoint of a 3D volume, it is possible to generate a single scan-converted solid stroke texture that can be used to illustrate the essential shape information of any level surface in the data.

By redefining the length of the filter kernel according to the magnitude of the maximum principal curvature of the level surface at each point around which the convolution is applied, one can generate longer strokes over more the highly curved areas, where the directional information is both most stable and most relevant, and at the same time downplay the visual impact of the directional information indicated by the stroke texture in the flatter regions.

In a voxel-based approach such as this one, stroke narrowness will be constrained by the resolution of the volume within which the texture is represented. However, by adaptively indexing into multiple pre-computed texture volumes, obtained by advecting particles of increasing sizes, one may selectively widen the strokes at any point by a variable amount, determined at the time of rendering, to reflect shading information or any other function defined over the volume data.

Keywords: visualization, transparent surfaces, shape representation, principal directions, stroke textures, line integral convolution, solid texture, isosurfaces, volume rendering.

MS 403, NASA Langley Research Center, Hampton, VA 26801
interran@icase.edu; http://www.icase.edu/~interran/lic

1 INTRODUCTION

The texturing method described in this paper is intended as a partial solution to the problem of effectively visualizing the complex spatial relationships between two or more overlapping surfaces. Applications requiring the simultaneous appreciation of multiple layers of information arise in a number of fields in scientific visualization, and particularly in situations where surfaces of interest are defined by a level set of intensities in a volume distribution. The specific application that motivated this research is radiation therapy treatment planning, in which physicians need to evaluate the extent to which a particular three-dimensional distribution of radiation dose might satisfy the twin objectives of maximizing the probability of tumor control and minimizing the probability of complications due to the excess irradiation of normal tissues.

Although transparent surface rendering offers the best possibility for enabling an integrated appreciation of the 3D spatial relationship between two superimposed structures, it can often be difficult, under ordinary conditions, to adequately perceive the full three-dimensional shape of a layered transparent surface or to accurately judge its depth distance from an underlying opaque object. To compensate for the lack of naturally-occurring shape and depth cues, one may artificially enhance the transparent surface with a small, stable set of appropriately defined, sparsely distributed, opaque markings.

It is universally recognized that shape and depth judgements can improve markedly when surfaces are covered with an appropriately-defined texture rather than left plain or inappropriately textured, and that shape and depth may be understood more accurately and more readily from some texture patterns rather than others [6, 31, 32, 35, 37, 5, 14]. These results have been shown for actual objects viewed directly [9], as well as for photographs of actual objects [10] and for computer-generated images of objects viewed either monocularly [3] or in stereo [5, 14], and have been deftly exploited by op artists such as Victor Vasarely [40].

What are the characteristics of texture that are most important for showing shape, and how can we define a texture pattern that conveys shape information both accurately and intuitively? Although research toward a definitive explanation of the role of texture in shape perception remains ongoing, some key observations help motivate the underlying philosophy behind the work described in the remainder of this paper.

Gradients of element compression, or the relative orientations of naturally elongated elements, appear to play a central role in the perception of surface curvature [6, 35, 37]. The perception of shape from texture may be inhibited when the texture pattern is non-homotropic [33] or when texture anisotropies mimic the effects of foreshortening [44]. Although we can estimate local surface orientation remarkably well from the projective deformation of a circle to an ellipse [30], recent research suggests that we do not understand shape as a collection of mutually independent local estimates of the surface normal directions at scattered points but rather as an *organization of space* based on local depth order relationships [17, 36].

There are a number of advantages, for dynamic 3D applications, in choosing a texture definition that will be essentially viewpoint independent. Densely spaced planar contours have historically been a popular device for applications such as this one; however recent work [14] inspired by empirical observations of the use of line by pen-and-ink illustrators suggests that lines carefully defined to "follow the form" may convey surface shape in a more effective and intuitive manner.

This paper advances the state of the art in surface shape representation by proposing that the set of principal directions and principal curvatures [16] can be understood to define the intrinsic geometrical and perceptual "flow" of the surface of an object, and can be used as such to automatically define a continuous stroke texture that "follows the shape" in a perceptually intuitive and geometrically meaningful way. Specifically, this paper describes how, by advecting an evenly distributed set of tiny opaque particles, and the empty space between them, via 3D line integral convolution through the vector field defined by the principal directions and principal curvatures of the level surfaces implicitly defined by the values at each gridpoint of a 3D volume, it is possible to automatically generate a single solid texture [24, 25] of scan-converted strokes that can be simply and efficiently applied during rendering to more effectively convey the essential shape features of every level surface in the volume distribution.

2 PREVIOUS AND RELATED WORK

Dooley and Cohen [7] suggested using screen-space opacity-masking texture patterns to help disambiguate the depth order of overlapping transparent surfaces; such patterns, however, may give a false impression of flatness when applied to curved surfaces. To more clearly represent the shapes of transparent surfaces in volume data, Levoy et al. [20] proposed using a solid grid texture, comprised of planes of voxels evenly spaced along the two orthogonal axes of the volume most nearly aligned with the image plane, to increase the opacity of selected planar cross-sections. Interrante et al. [13] suggested selectively opacifying valley and sharp ridge regions on transparent skin surfaces to emphasize their distinctive shape features in the style of a viewpoint-independent "3D sketch". Rheingans [26] described how surface retriangulation could be used in combination with a procedurally-defined 2D opacity-masking texture of small circles to accurately portray fine-grained information about the orientation of a smoothly curving layered transparent surface, and Interrante et al. [14] proposed a method for covering a transparent surface with individually-defined short opaque strokes locally aligned with the direction of maximum surface curvature. Although the results presented in [14] are encouraging, the stroke definition proposed there is cumbersome, the lines do not bend to follow the principal directions along the length of their extent, and the texture definition is inherently tied to a specific surface definition and would have to be completely reiterated in order to be applied to multiple level surfaces from the same 3D distribution.

In terms of more general inspiration, Saito and Takahashi [27] showed how the comprehensibility of 3D shaded surface renderings could be improved via highlighting the first- and second-order depth discontinuities in an image, and they suggested defining a hatching pattern, based on the latitude and longitude lines of a sphere, or on the parametric representation of a surface, that could be applied according to the values in an illumination map to evoke the impression of a pen-and-ink illustration. Winkenbach and Salesin defined intricately detailed resolution-independent fine stroke textures [42] and showed how they could be applied in accordance with the directions of the surface parameterization to represent a class of curved surfaces in the style of a pen-and-ink drawing [43]. Other textures that "follow the surface" in some sense include the reaction-diffusion textures proposed by Turk [38] and Witkin and Kass [45]. Most recently, Turk and Banks [39] described a method for evenly distributing streamlines over a 2D vector field, to represent the flow in a visually pleasing manner akin to a hand-drawn illustration.

Slightly farther afield, researchers in computer-aided design [2, 12, 23] have developed suites of methods for illustrating various geometrical properties on analytically-defined surfaces, for purposes such as facilitating NC milling and evaluating surface "fairness".

The direction taken in this paper was most fundamentally inspired by the elegant vector field visualization work that began with van Wijk's introduction of spot noise [41] and Cabral and Leedom's line integral convolution method [4], and was advanced by Stalling and Hege [29] and others [8, 18, 1, 15, 28]. Line integral convolution is particularly attractive as a device for generating strokes through a volume because by advecting the empty space in a point distribution along with the full it is possible, by and large, to finesse the problem of appropriate streamline placement, at least as far as the æsthetic requirements of this particular application are concerned.

3 DEFINING THE TEXTURE

In many of the applications that call for the visualization of superimposed surfaces, it is necessary to view not just one but *multiple* level surfaces through a volume distribution. Sophisticated methods for improving the comprehensibility of a transparent surface via texture are of greatest practical utility in these cases when the texture used to convey surface shape is applicable throughout the volume and does not have to be derived separately for each level surface examined.

3.1 Distributing the particles

The first step in the process of defining a volume texture of principal direction strokes is the task of defining the evenly-distributed set of points that will be advected to form them. I try to approximate a minimum distance Poisson disk sampling distribution by applying a random jitter of 0-1 times the inter-element spacing of points on a uniform grid and throwing away and recomputing any sample that falls within a specified minimum distance of a previously computed neighbor. Because the points are processed in a predetermined order, there are only 13 possible predecessors, out of all of the points already derived, that could conceivably be too close to any new candidate, so only 13 comparisons are needed to decide whether to accept or reject a particular random amount of jitter for each new point. As long as the minimum allowable distance between points is reasonably less than the inter-element spacing before jittering, this procedure turns out to be very efficient and it has the advantage of producing a point distribution in which the number of samples contained within any arbitrary plane of neighboring voxels is more or less equivalent and at the same time avoids letting samples bunch up too closely in any one spot.

The final set of points chosen defines the voxels of the input to LIC that will be turned "on" (set to 255). The remainder of the voxels are left "off" (set to zero). I have found that introducing varying levels of grey into the input texture, unless for the purpose of representing larger particles, only seems to complicates matters unnecessarily. The resolution of the volume data will usually be coarse enough, relative to the resolution of the final image, that unit-width input points will produce strokes of ample thickness. However, wider strokes may sometimes be desirable, for representing shading or some other variable, as will be discussed in section 6.3.

3.2 Defining the principal directions

In addition to defining a suitable set of particles to advect, it is necessary to define the vector field of principal directions along which the particles will be made to flow. Principal directions and principal curvatures are classical geometric measures that can be used to describe the local shape of a surface around any given point. Although they are amply described in almost any text on differential geometry, and various algorithms for defining them have been explained in great detail elsewhere in the literature [16, 22, 12], for the sake of completeness and to help make these concepts perhaps somewhat more easily accessible I will briefly restate the basic process and definitions given by Koenderink [16] and used in [12].

At any point on a smoothly curving surface, there will in general be one single direction in which the curvature of the surface is greatest. This direction is the *first principal direction*, and the curvature of the surface in this direction is the *first principal curvature*. The *second principal direction* is mutually orthogonal to both the first principal direction and to the surface normal, and represents the direction in which the surface curvature is most nearly flat. Starting from an orthogonal frame $(\vec{e}_1, \vec{e}_2, \vec{e}_3)$ at a point $P_{x,y,z}$, where $\vec{e}_1$ and $\vec{e}_2$ are arbitrary orthogonal vectors lying in the tangent plane to the surface and $\vec{e}_3$ points in the surface normal direction, it is possible to determine the principal directions by diagonalizing the *Second Fundamental Form*, a matrix of partial derivatives

$$A = \begin{bmatrix} \tilde{\omega}_1^{13} & \tilde{\omega}_1^{23} \\ \tilde{\omega}_2^{13} & \tilde{\omega}_2^{23} \end{bmatrix},$$

in which the elements $\tilde{\omega}_j^{i3}$ can be computed as the dot product of $\vec{e}_i$ and the first derivative of the gradient in the $\vec{e}_j$ direction.

Specifically, diagonalizing A means computing the matrices

$$D = \begin{bmatrix} \kappa_1 & 0 \\ 0 & \kappa_2 \end{bmatrix} \text{ and } P = \begin{bmatrix} v_{1u} & v_{2u} \\ v_{1v} & v_{2v} \end{bmatrix},$$

where $A = P D P^{-1}$ and $|\kappa_1| > |\kappa_2|$. The principal curvatures are the eigenvalues κ_1 and κ_2, and the principal directions are the corresponding eigenvectors, expressed in 3D object space coordinates as $\vec{e}_i' = v_{iu} \vec{e}_1 + v_{iv} \vec{e}_2$.

To ensure the best possible results it is useful to represent the gradients at full floating point precision, and use a Gaussian-weighted derivative operator over a 3x3x3 neighborhood rather than central differences when computing the values of $\tilde{\omega}_j^{i3}$. As an extra precaution, I enforce the expected equality of $\tilde{\omega}_2^{13}$ and $\tilde{\omega}_1^{23}$ by replacing each of these twist terms by the average of the two of them before performing the diagonalization.

Where the surface is locally spherical (at points called *umbilics*) or locally planar, the principal directions will be undefined. These "non-generic" points arise relatively infrequently in nature, but of course are found everywhere over manmade surfaces. A texturing technique based on principal directions could potentially run into a lot of trouble if it were applied to an object made up of spheres and rectangular slabs. For this application, however, a few zeros are no problem, and the LIC program has to check for such points in any case.

In this implementation, I use unit length principal direction vectors for streamline tracing, and save the principal curvature values in a companion volume so that they may be accessed independently.

3.3 Advecting the particles via 3D LIC

The implementation of LIC that I use to obtain the scan-converted strokes is basically a straightforward 3D extension of the "fast-LIC" method described by Stalling and Hege [29]. Voxels are processed in block-sequential order, and streamlines are traced in both directions through each voxel using a 4th-order Runge Kutta method with maximum-limited adaptive step size control, and are resampled at equally spaced points ($h_t = 0.5$) via a cubic spline interpolation that preserves C^1 continuity.

Because the orientation indicated by the first principal direction is actually an axis that can point either way, there is no way to guarantee the consistency of any particular chosen direction *a priori*; recognition of this must be built into the LIC program and taken into consideration during streamline tracing. I use a reference vector to keep track of the direction of the most recently obtained sample from the vector field of principal directions, and use comparisons with this vector to determine which of the two possible orientations of the first principal direction to select at each gridpoint before performing the trilinear interpolation to retrieve the next sample. When using a constant-length box filter kernel, I take advantage of the method suggested in [29] for incrementally computing the convolution integral, but go back to computing the convolution separately for each point when the filter length is allowed to vary.

Since most of the space in the input texture is empty, the average intensity at each voxel after LIC will be quite low. To avoid loss of precision and maintain a reasonable dynamic range in the grey levels of the output texture (which is necessary to avoid aliasing artifacts), one may either estimate an appropriate scaling factor, based on the length of the filter used for the convolution, to apply during the normalization step of the LIC (where final voxel intensity is set to the accumulated intensity divided by the number of streamlines contributing to this accumulation), or, alternatively, output the results as a floating point volume and use standard image processing utilities to window and rescale the results into an appropriate range.

4 APPLYING THE TEXTURE

Once a 3D scan-converted stroke texture is obtained, it can be used during rendering to selectively increase the opacity of the corresponding points on the transparent surface being displayed.

If the isosurface is defined by a marching cubes [21] triangulation, one may determine the amount of additional opacity to be added at any surface point by trilinearly interpolating from the values in the texture volume. If the isosurface is defined by a volume region of finite thickness, as described in [19], one must be careful to add the additional opacity indicated by the texture only to those voxels occupied or partially occupied by the isovalue contour surface.

One advantage of the polygonal representation produced by marching cubes is that it facilitates discounting all but the first occurrence of the transparent surface in depth along the viewing direction. I usually take advantage of this option during rendering to help simplify the images and avoid a "gauze curtain" look where the transparent surface overlaps itself multiple times in the projection. This technique was used to produce the images in figure 1. The "strokes" on each of the level surfaces shown in this figure are obtained from a single solid texture, defined in a 241x199x181 volume, equal in resolution to the dose data.

It is of course possible to define the resolution of the stroke texture to be several times finer than the resolution of the volume data defining the isosurface to which it is applied. When this is done, somewhat better-looking results may be achieved by using Levoy's [19] volume definition for the isosurface and displaying

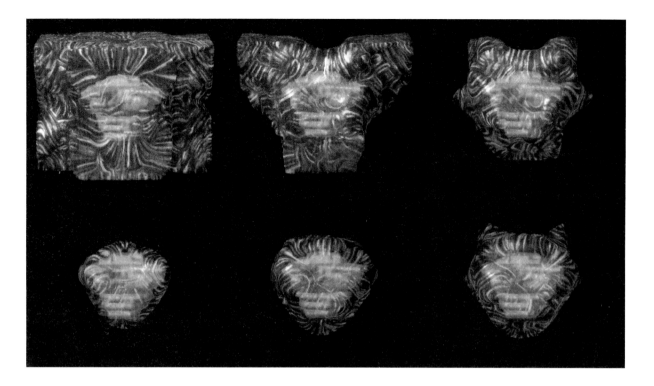

Figure 1: A single solid texture is applied to the volume data shown in each of these pictures. Nevertheless, the image of the texture on each isolevel surface conveys shape information specific to that surface. These images depict a series of level surfaces of radiation dose enclosing an opaque treatment region. This data, defined in a 241x199x181 voxel volume, represents a five-beam treatment plan for cancer of the prostate. Clockwise from the upper left, dose concentrations, relative to the prescribed level, are: 4%, 28%, 36%, 47%, 55%, and 82%.

all strokes that fall within the isosurface region. This approach is illustrated by the image in figure 2. The opaque treatment region has been left out of this particular image so that it may be easier to appreciate the detail of the strokes. The 3D nature of the irregularities in the positions of the tiny strokes in this kind of representation may also more aptly evoke a "hand-drawn" look, when that is the aim.

5 SOME EMPIRICAL COMPARISONS

The potential effectiveness of the proposed principal direction stroke texturing method may perhaps be best appreciated through comparison with alternatively rendered images. Figure 3 shows three different representations of the same pair of overlapping surfaces. On the left, the external transparent surface is left plain. Cues to its shape are given by the subtle intensity variations in the diffuse surface shading and by the shapes and locations of the reflected specular highlights. However there are no cues to the depth distance between the overlapping surfaces in this image; even the introduction of stereo and/or motion can do little in this case to improve the perceptibility of the depth information [14].

In the image on the right, a "solid grid" texture has been applied which increases the opacity of the external transparent surface along selected planar cross-sections. When this image is viewed in motion or in stereo, the relative depth distances between the opacified points on the external surface and points on the inner object become immediately apparent. However, it is not easy to obtain an intuitive understanding of the overall surface shape from this representation; the grid lines demand our attention, and the directions they indicate are only indirectly related to features of the surface shape.

Figure 2: Narrower strokes may be represented via higher resolution textures. The resolution of the texture volume in this image is 482x398x362, twice as great as the resolution of the texture used to compute the images in figure 1.

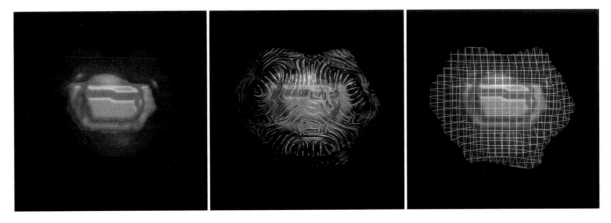

Figure 3: A comparison of methods for displaying overlapping surfaces, illustrated on a 433x357x325 voxel dataset representing a radiation treatment plan for cancer of the nasopharynx. Left: a plain transparent isointensity surface of radiation dose surrounds the opaque treatment region. Center: the same dataset, with principal direction-driven 3D LIC texture added to the outer surface. Right: the same dataset, with a solid grid texture used to highlight selected contour curves.

The image in the center shows a principal direction-driven 3D LIC stroke texture. At every point, the lines are oriented in the direction of maximum surface curvature. Important shape information is readily available even in this static image, and with the addition of stereo and motion cues, the shapes and depths of the two surfaces may be yet more easily and accurately perceived.

6 REFINING THE TEXTURE DEFINITION

The quality of the shape description provided by the principal direction texturing approach described in this paper may be improved somewhat when curvature magnitude information is incorporated into the texture definition process, and other interesting effects may be achieved when stroke color and/or width are allowed to vary in accordance with the values of a second function over the volume data.

6.1 Stroke length

Stroke length is controlled by the length of the filter kernel used for convolving the intensities at successive points along each streamline. Figure 4, after figure 5 in [4], illustrates the effect on the stroke texture of using different constant values for this parameter.

Because the visual prominence of the indication of a specific direction should ideally reflect the significance of that particular direction, it can be advantageous to adaptively modify the length of the filter kernel applied at each point in correspondence with the magnitude of the first principal curvature there. The principal directions and principal curvatures have already been precomputed and stored for every gridpoint, and it is straightforward to define a mapping from relative curvature (κ_1/κ_{max}) to filter kernel length that can be locally applied during the LIC. The effect of adaptively controlling stroke length in this fashion can be seen in figure 5.

6.2 Stroke width

Because the strokes are scan-converted, the resolution of the stroke texture volume fundamentally limits the narrowness with which any stroke may be represented. For example, if the texture volume is only 100 voxels wide, the thinnest stroke will occupy 1% of the total width of the image. To apply a finer stroke texture to surfaces obtained from more coarsely sampled data, it is necessary to compute a texture volume that has higher resolution than the data. To achieve a stroke texture of wider strokes, one may run the LIC on an input texture containing larger spots.

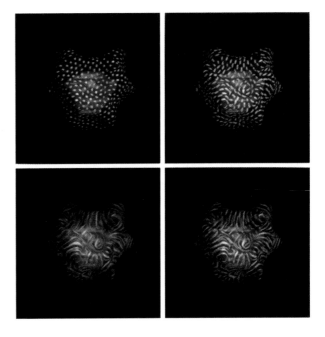

Figure 4: An illustration of the effect of filter kernel length on the lengths of the strokes in the texture. Clockwise from the upper left, these images were computed using filter kernel lengths of 2, 6, 20 and 40. The initial spots were defined by a point-spread function approximately four voxels in diameter, applied at evenly-distributed surface points in the 241x199x181 voxel volume.

Figure 5: Stroke lengths and widths in this image have each been adaptively defined according to the magnitude of the curvature in the stroke direction.

Stroke thickness in the scan-converted texture is directly related to the size of the spots advected by LIC. Supersampling during traditional LIC to get a higher resolution output won't result in thinner strokes unless the values interpolated from the input texture are windowed or ramped before being used. The best way to obtain a texture of very thin strokes is to either supersample the directional data and index into a higher resolution input texture, which is the approach I have taken, or, as Battke *et al.* [1] suggest, to define the input texture procedurally, in which case resolution is not a limiting factor.

There are several different ways in which stroke width can be used to convey additional information about the volume data. One possibility is to vary stroke width according to a static variable such as the magnitude of the principal curvature at a point, as has been done in figure 5. Such an approach can be used to emphasize the stroke texture in the specific areas where the directional information it indicates is most perceptually relevant and play down the visual impact of the texture in flatter regions, where it is less helpful for shape understanding. By using stroke width rather than stroke opacity to modulate the texture prominence, one may more easily maintain the impression of a continuous and coherent surface and avoid imparting an ephemeral or "moth-eaten" look to the outer object.

It may alternatively be desirable to allow the stroke width to be locally determined by the value of a dynamically changing variable such as surface shading. While adaptive stroke width might be approximated in the former case by defining a single input texture containing spots of different sizes, as in the "multi-frequency" LIC texturing approach suggested by Kiu and Banks [15], to efficiently reflect the value of a dynamically changing function it is far preferable to precompute a short series of LIC texture volumes from inputs containing a succession of spot sizes at identical points, and then adaptively index into any particular one of these during rendering, depending on the value of the dynamically-defined function. The right-hand image in figure 6 was computed from a combination of five different LIC textures, and the particular texture applied at each point was determined by the value of the local illumination, illustrated in the picture to its left. An advantage of this approach is that it allows quick and easy experimentation with different function value to stroke width mappings; computing the 3D LIC can sometimes be a fairly slow process, but recombining the precomputed texture volumes is fast.

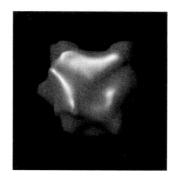

Figure 6: The width of a stroke at any point along its extent may be adaptively determined, at the time of rendering, by selecting texture values from any of a series of multiple predefined volumes, indexed by the value of a second function computed over the data. In this case the shading at each point is used to determine the volume from which the local texture sample is retrieved. The texture shown here was defined in a 409x338x307 voxel volume.

6.3 Stroke color

The most effective use of color (hue) in this application is as a *label*. Color can be used to help differentiate the inner surface from the outer, or to convey information about a third scalar distribution. One particularly effective use of color, shown in fig. 7, is as an indicator of the depth distance between the outer and inner surfaces. To make it easier to intuitively appreciate the relationship between the successive colors and the amount of distance represented, I've found it useful to vary luminance along with hue, in an approximation of a heated-object colorscale.

6.4 Limiting texture computations to a region of interest in the volume

One of the principal advantages of the texturing technique described in this paper is its applicability in situations where one needs to view arbitrary level surfaces in a 3D volume dataset. However, it may also be used with some efficiency in situations when more limited regions of interest (ROI) are defined. In such cases one may evenly distribute input points among the voxels within the ROI, and trace streamlines around the voxels in the ROI only. The images in figures 6 and 7 were computed using such an approach.

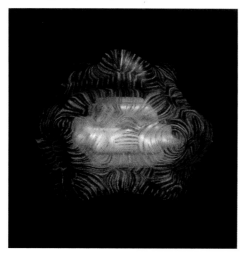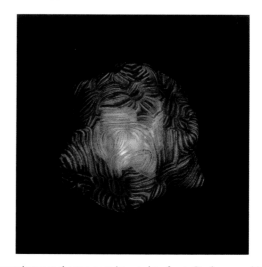

Figure 7: Color is used here to convey the relative magnitude of the depth distance between the two superimposed surfaces. Strokes are whitest where the surfaces are relatively widely separated, and become progressively redder as the proximity of the outer surface to the to the inner increases. Stroke length varies slightly according to the magnitude of the principal curvature, as in figure 3, but stroke width is held constant. The resolution of this data is 433x357x325.

7 CONCLUSIONS

Line direction is an essential element in surface shape description. An appropriate use of line can reveal the curvature of a 3D form in a single static image; inappropriate uses of line can make smoothly curving surfaces appear flattened or distorted, even when binocular disparity cues provide veridical depth information. Artists and illustrators have historically emphasized the importance of stroke direction in line drawing, advising that "as a general rule, a subject offers some hint as to a natural arrangement of lines" [11] and warning that

> ... all a fastidious spectator's pleasure in a drawing may
> be destroyed by a wrong use of direction... no matter
> how fine the lines composing it may be, or how pretty
> the general effect [34].

This paper has described how the set of principal directions and principal curvatures, classical shape descriptors from differential geometry, can be used to define a natural flow of lines over the surface of an object, and used to guide the placement of a stroke texture that seeks to reveal shape in a perceptually intuitive way.

The method described here is fully automatic, easy to implement, and requires very little fine-tuning. The strokes are defined as static entities in 3D space, and when applied to the surface they create a texture pattern that is stable under changes in viewpoint or object orientation. The problem of defining an even stroke distribution, and avoiding the unæsthetic merging and colliding of elements, is finessed by the tracing, via LIC, of the empty space along with the full space in a volume of approximately Poisson-disk distributed point samples. A few, simple parameters can be adjusted to globally or locally control seed point spacing, stroke length and stroke width, and the resulting scan-converted texture will be applicable to all level surfaces in a smooth volume distribution, facilitating data exploration. When investigations are known *a priori* to be limited to a specific region of interest within the volume, this ROI information can be easily incorporated into the texture definition process so that excess calculations may be avoided.

8 FUTURE WORK

There are several directions for future work. Of particular interest is the problem of portraying multiple superimposed transparent layers. A key issue is the difficulty of facilitating the perceptual segregation of multiple overlapping texture patterns. Preliminary investigations suggest that color differences alone will not be sufficient to enable the effortless, exclusive perceptual grouping of the texture elements comprising any individual surface.

In another direction, it is possible that principal direction-driven LIC texturing methods might potentially be useful for generating non-photorealistic "line drawing" style images of objects with complex geometries. Several important issues would need to be addressed before such an application could be recommended, however. Of foremost concern is the issue of algorithmic efficiency, or the need for a more cost effective approach for generating what would basically be a 2D texture. Other challenges include improving the artistic quality of the line definition, maintaining the overall continuity of a lower-scale indication of direction across broad surface areas that contain irrelevant higher frequency details, and defining a technique for more gracefully merging opposing lines of force. Figure 8 shows the results of applying the texturing method described in this paper to the bone/soft tissue boundary surface in a 343x195x241 voxel CT volume.

Figure 8: A principal-direction-driven LIC texture applied to the bone/soft tissue boundary surface in a CT volume dataset.

ACKNOWLEDGMENTS

This research was supported by ICASE under NASA contract NAS1-19480, and grew out of work supported by NIH grant # PO1 CA47982. The radiation therapy datasets were provided by Dr. Julian Rosenman, UNC Hospitals. I am grateful to Marc Levoy for allowing me to build on top of his original volume rendering platform, to Jim Chung for providing the implementation of the marching cubes isosurface extraction routine, and to Kwan-Liu Ma, Hans-Christian Hege, David Banks, and the anonymous reviewers for offering insightful comments and suggestions that aided this work.

REFERENCES

[1] H. Battke, D. Stalling, H.-C. Hege. "Fast Line Integral Convolution for Arbitrary Surfaces in 3D", Visualization and Mathematics, H.-C. Hege and K. Polthier, eds., Springer-Verlag, 1997.

[2] James M. Beck, Rida T. Farouki and John K. Hinds. "Surface Analysis Methods", *IEEE Computer Graphics and Applications*, **6**(12): 18-36, December 1986.

[3] Myron L. Braunstein and John W. Payne. "Perspective and Form Ratio as Determinants of Relative Slant Judgments", *Journal of Experimental Psychology*, **81**(3): 584-590, 1969.

[4] Brian Cabral and Casey Leedom. "Imaging Vector Fields Using Line Integral Convolution", *SIGGRAPH 93 Conference Proceedings*, Annual Conference Series, pp. 263-270.

[5] Bruce G. Cumming, Elizabeth B. Johnston and Andrew J. Parker. "Effects of Different Texture Cues on Curved Surfaces Viewed Stereoscopically", *Vision Research*, **33**(5/6): 827-838, 1993.

[6] James E. Cutting and Robert T. Millard. "Three Gradients and the Perception of Flat and Curved Surfaces", *Journal of Experimental Psychology: General*, **113**(2): 198-216, 1984.

[7] Debra Dooley and Michael F. Cohen. "Automatic Illustration of 3D Geometric Models: Surfaces", *IEEE. Visualization '90*, pp. 307-313.

[8] Lisa K. Forsell. "Visualizing Flow Over Curvilinear Grid Surfaces Using Line Integral Convolution", *IEEE Visualization '94*, pp. 240-247.

[9] Howard R. Flock and Anthony Moscatelli. "Variables of Surface Texture and Accuracy of Space Perceptions", *Perceptual and Motor Skills*, **19**: 327-334, 1964.

[10] James J. Gibson. "The Perception of Visual Surfaces", *American Journal of Psychology*, **63**: 367-384, 1950.

[11] Arthur Guptill. Rendering in Pen and Ink, Watson-Guptill Publications, 1976.

[12] Hans Hagen, Stefanie Hahmann, Thomas Schreibner, Yasuo Nakajima, Bukard Wördenweber and Petra Hollemann-Grundestedt. "Surface Interrogation Algorithms", *IEEE Computer Graphics and Applications*, **12**(5): 53-60, September 1992.

[13] Victoria Interrante, Henry Fuchs and Stephen Pizer. "Enhancing Transparent Skin Surfaces with Ridge and Valley Lines", *IEEE Visualization '95*, pp. 52-59.

[14] Victoria Interrante, Henry Fuchs and Stephen Pizer. "Conveying the 3D Shape of Smoothly Curving Transparent Surfaces via Texture", *IEEE Transactions on Visualization and Computer Graphics*, **3**(2): 211-218.

[15] Ming-Hoe Kiu and David C. Banks. "Multi-Frequency Noise for LIC", *IEEE Visualization '96*, pp. 121-126.

[16] Jan Koenderink. Solid Shape, MIT Press, 1990.

[17] Jan J. Koenderink and Andrea J. van Doorn. "Relief: pictorial and otherwise", *Image and Vision Computing*, **13**(5): 321-334, June 1995.

[18] Willem C. de Leeuw and Jarke J. van Wijk. "Enhanced Spot Noise for Vector Field Visualization", *IEEE Visualization '95*, pp. 233-239.

[19] Marc Levoy. "Display of Surfaces from Volume Data", *IEEE Computer Graphics and Applications*, **8**(3): 29-37, May 1988.

[20] Marc Levoy, Henry Fuchs, Stephen Pizer, Julian Rosenman, Edward L. Chaney, George W. Sherouse, Victoria Interrante and Jeffrey Kiel. "Volume Rendering in Radiation Treatment Planning", *First Conference on Visualization in Biomedical Computing*, 1990, pp. 4-10.

[21] William Lorensen and Harvey Cline. "Marching Cubes: A High Resolution 3D Surface Reconstruction Algorithm", *Computer Graphics* (SIGGRAPH 87 Conference Proceedings), **21**(4): 163-169, July 1987.

[22] Olivier Monga, Serge Benayoun and Olivier D. Faugeras. "From Partial Derivatives of 3D Density Images to Ridge Lines", *proc. of the IEEE Computer Society Conference on Computer Vision and Pattern Recognition*, 1992, pp. 354-359.

[23] Henry P. Moreton. "Simplified Curve and Surface Interrogation via Mathematical Packages and Graphics Libraries and Hardware", *Computer-Aided Design*, **27**(7): 523-543, 1995.

[24] Darwyn Peachey. "Solid Texturing of Complex Surfaces", *Computer Graphics* (SIGGRAPH 85 Conference Proceedings), **19**(3): 279-286, July 1985.

[25] Ken Perlin. "An Image Synthesizer", *Computer Graphics* (SIGGRAPH 85 Conference Proceedings), **19**(3): 287-296, July 1985.

[26] Penny Rheingans. "Opacity-modulating Triangular Textures for Irregular Surfaces", *IEEE Visualization '96*, pp. 219-225.

[27] Takafumi Saito and Tokiichiro Takahashi. "Comprehensible Rendering of 3-D Shapes", *Computer Graphics* (SIGGRAPH 90 Conference Proceedings), **24**(4): 197-206, August 1990.

[28] Han-Wei Shen, Christopher R. Johnson and Kwan-Liu Ma. "Visualizing Vector Fields Using Line Integral Convolution and Dye Advection", *proc. 1996 Symposium on Volume Visualization*, pp. 63-70.

[29] Detlev Stalling and Hans-Christian Hege. "Fast and Resolution Independent Line Integral Convolution", *SIGGRAPH 95 Conference Proceedings*, Annual Conference Series, pp. 249-256.

[30] Kent A. Stevens and Allen Brookes. "Probing Depth in Monocular Images", *Biological Cybernetics*, **56**: 355-366, 1987.

[31] Kent A. Stevens. "The Information Content of Texture Gradients", *Biological Cybernetics*, **42**: 95-105, 1981.

[32] Kent A. Stevens. "The Visual Interpretation of Surface Contours", *Artificial Intelligence*, **17**: 47-73, 1981.

[33] James V. Stone. "Shape From Local and Global Analysis of Texture", *Philosophical Transactions of the Royal Society of London, B*, **339**: 53-65, 1993.

[34] Edmund J. Sullivan. Line; an art study, Chapman & Hall, 1922.

[35] James. T. Todd and Robin Akerstrom. "Perception of Three-Dimensional Form from Patterns of Optical Texture", *Journal of Experimental Psychology: Human Perception and Performance*, **13**(2): 242-255, 1987.

[36] James T. Todd and Francene D. Reichel. "Ordinal Structure in the Visual Perception and Cognition of Smoothly Curved Surfaces", *Psychological Review*, **96**(4): 643-657, 1989.

[37] James T. Todd and Francene D. Reichel. "Visual Perception of Smoothly Curved Surfaces from Double-Projected Contour Patterns", *Journal of Experimental Psychology: Human Perception and Performance*, **16**(3): 665-674, 1990.

[38] Greg Turk. "Generating Textures for Arbitrary Surfaces Using Reaction-Diffusion", *Computer Graphics* (SIGGRAPH 91 Conference Proceedings), **25**(4): 289-298, July 1991.

[39] Greg Turk and David Banks. "Image-Guided Streamline Placement", *SIGGRAPH 96 Conference Proceedings*, Annual Conference Series, pp. 453-460.

[40] Victor Vasarely. Vasarely III, Éditions du Griffon Neuchâtel, 1974.

[41] Jarke J. van Wijk. "Spot Noise-Texture Synthesis for Data Visualization", *Computer Graphics* (SIGGRAPH 91 Conference Proceedings), **25**(4): 309-318, July 1991.

[42] Georges Winkenbach and David H. Salesin. "Computer-Generated Pen-and-Ink Illustrations", *SIGGRAPH 94 Conf. Proceedings*, Annual Conference Series, pp. 91-100.

[43] Georges Winkenbach and David H. Salesin. "Rendering Parametric Surfaces in Pen and Ink", *SIGGRAPH 96 Conf. Proceedings*, Annual Conference Series, pp. 469-476.

[44] Andrew P. Witkin. "Recovering Surface Shape and Orientation from Texture", *Artificial Intelligence*, **17**:17-45, 1981.

[45] Andrew Witkin and Michael Kass. "Reaction-Diffusion Textures", *Computer Graphics* (SIGGRAPH 91 Conference Proceedings), **25**(4): 299-308, July 1991.

Non-Linear Approximation of Reflectance Functions

Eric P. F. Lafortune   Sing-Choong Foo*   Kenneth E. Torrance   Donald P. Greenberg

Program of Computer Graphics
Cornell University †

Abstract

We introduce a new class of primitive functions with non-linear parameters for representing light reflectance functions. The functions are reciprocal, energy-conserving and expressive. They can capture important phenomena such as off-specular reflection, increasing reflectance and retro-reflection. We demonstrate this by fitting sums of primitive functions to a physically-based model and to actual measurements. The resulting representation is simple, compact and uniform. It can be applied efficiently in analytical and Monte Carlo computations.

CR Categories: I.3.7 [Computer Graphics]: Three-Dimensional Graphics and Realism; I.3.3 [Computer Graphics]: Picture/Image Generation

Keywords: Reflectance function, BRDF representation

1   INTRODUCTION

The bidirectional reflectance distribution function (BRDF) of a material describes how light is scattered at its surface. It determines the appearance of objects in a scene, through direct illumination and global interreflection effects. Local reflectance *models* therefore play an essential role in local and global illumination simulations.

The diagram of Figure 1 illustrates the importance of a proper representation of reflectance data. The data originate from physical measurements, from scattering simulations on surfaces, from physically-based reflectance models, or from a set of empirical parameters input by the user. The representation should capture the necessary information in a way that allows it to be used in global illumination algorithms. Several factors contribute to the quality and usefulness of a representation: *accuracy*, *physical correctness* and *computational efficiency*.

First of all, the original data should be represented accurately enough to obtain physically faithful results. However, in practice, precise measurements are often not available. As a very precise representation cannot improve imprecise data, a simpler model that naturally interpolates the data may be preferable. It can also be

---
*Currently at Blue Sky Studios, Harrison, NY.

†580 Rhodes Hall, Ithaca, NY 14853, USA.

WWW: http://www.graphics.cornell.edu/

E-mail: eric@graphics.cornell.edu

useful to have a model with a limited set of parameters that are intuitive to use. Such parameters provide an easy way to control or to monitor the behavior of the model.

Secondly, the representation should be physically plausible. Reflectance functions are positive, reciprocal and energy-conserving [12]. Preferably, their representations should satisfy these constraints as well, because global illumination algorithms may rely on it.

Thirdly, for actual application in global illumination computations, the ideal model should be computationally efficient. It is usually an element in the larger context of an illumination simulation algorithm. One thus looks for a proper balance between accuracy, memory use and computation times of the various components. In the context of physically-based rendering, it makes little sense to use an overly precise and computationally expensive or memory-hungry model, when small subtleties are overwhelmed by global illumination effects, or when the simulation is relatively inaccurate.

At present, many reflectance models are not physically plausible. More precise physical models are often computationally expensive and geared toward specific types of surfaces. The most expressive models, such as spherical harmonics or wavelet representations, may require significant memory to obtain acceptable representations of even the simplest BRDFs. Yet we want to efficiently represent the relatively complex reflectance of common surfaces such as the wooden table shown in Figure 2. The pictures illustrate the varying specular and diffuse reflectance for different viewing angles.

In this paper we introduce a representation based on a new class of functions with non-linear parameters. While the representation does not offer the arbitrary accuracy that linear basis functions can achieve, it is expressive enough to fit complex reflectance behavior. Importantly, a single function can capture a complete BRDF over its entire domain of incident and exitant directions. It is therefore uniform and compact, as well as computationally efficient.

The next section gives a brief overview of previous work. Section 3 discusses the concept of non-linear approximation. We then present our specific primitive functions for modeling reflectance in Section 4. The qualitative properties of functions are discussed in Section 5, while quantitative fits to complex reflectance functions are presented in Section 6. Section 7 shows more results.

2   PREVIOUS WORK

Previous research focuses on various aspects of reflectance functions: their derivation, their measurement, and their representation. Torrance and Sparrow [22], and Cook and Torrance [3, 4] derived physical models based on geometrical optics, assuming specular V-grooves, and incorporating masking and self-shadowing effects. Their models correctly predict the off-specular reflection that they had previously measured [21]. Extending this work, He *et al.* [9] derived a model based on physical optics. The final representation of the model consists of an ideal diffuse component, a directional-diffuse component and a specular mirror component, which are all expressed by a set of analytic expressions. These can be evaluated numerically, albeit at a fair computational expense. Poulin

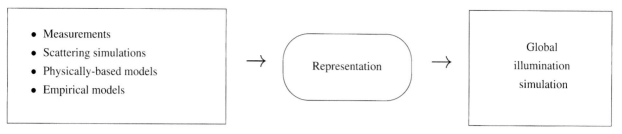

Figure 1: The representation of reflectance data constitutes the essential link between the origin of the raw data and their application in global illumination algorithms.

Figure 2: These pictures show a table exhibiting typical increasing specular reflection for increasingly grazing angles. At the same time the diffuse component, which results from subsurface scattering, fades out; the wood-grain texture and color disappear.

and Fournier [16] constructed a model assuming a surface consisting of microscopic cylinders. Oren and Nayar [14] derived a non-Lambertian diffuse model on the basis of diffuse micro-facets.

An alternative approach for deriving theoretical models is to perform a deterministic or Monte Carlo simulation on a surface model at a micro-scale. Kajiya [10] computed anisotropic reflectance functions based on the Kirchoff laws. He proposed storing the results in a table from which the values are linearly interpolated. Cabral [2] also stored reflectance simulation results in a table, but then represented them using spherical harmonics for a rendering step. Westin *et al.* [24] directly estimated the coefficients of the spherical harmonics. Hanrahan and Krueger [8] simulated subsurface scattering and stored the results in a uniform subdivision of the hemisphere. Gondek *et al.* [7] stored results in an adaptive subdivision of the geodesic sphere.

Empirical models, on the other hand, are not constructed from physical first principles. Instead, they capture reflectance effects using basis functions or other generic functions. The functions usually do not have any inherent physical meaning. Their physical validity stems from the theoretical or measured data to which they are fitted. For this purpose the functions should be expressive, while still being compact and efficient to use. Lambert's approximation, which assumes that the reflectance function of a diffuse surface is simply a constant, is widespread and sufficiently accurate for many applications. Phong [15] introduced one of the first more general shading models into computer graphics. Although it was not presented in the context of physically-based rendering, Lewis [12] showed how a physically plausible reflectance function can be derived from it. Ward [23] presented a model based on a Gaussian lobe, stressing its physical plausibility and ease of use. He successfully fitted the model to measurements of various surfaces and presented an equation to sample directions for it, which is important for Monte Carlo applications such as stochastic ray tracing. Schlick [17, 18] presented a model in which the important factors of previous physically-based models are approximated numerically, making it more convenient for use in Monte Carlo algorithms. Fournier [6] experimented with sums of separable functions for representing reflectance models, for application in radios-

ity algorithms. Schröder and Sweldens [19] represented reflectance functions using spherical wavelets. Koenderink *et al.* [11] recently introduced a compact representation based on Zernike polynomials.

Our work falls within the latter category of representations. We take a novel approach, using non-linear approximation with a sum of one or more appropriate functions. In the next section, we explain the general principle of non-linear approximation.

3 NON-LINEAR APPROXIMATION

Approximating functions with linear basis functions is well studied. Some common basis functions are Fourier bases, Chebychev polynomials and piece-wise linear functions. When approximating a function, the coefficients of the basis functions are determined by a set of linear equations. Non-linear approximation, for instance with rational functions or with Gaussians, is somewhat less known. In this approach, the parameters of the approximating functions are not necessarily linear with respect to the original function. They therefore generally have to be determined using non-linear optimization. Figure 3 shows an example of a peaked one-dimensional function that is approximated using the first four terms of a Fourier series and using two Gaussian functions. The Fourier terms vary in amplitude and in phase. Due to the relatively sharp peaks in the original function, their sum is only a rough approximation, which becomes negative at some point. The Gaussians are parametrized by a position, a standard deviation and a size. Their sum approximates the original function much better and remains positive over the interval. Obviously, this is not true in general, for all possible functions. However, the non-linear functions can be chosen such that they span a region of the function space that suits a specific application. Functions can then be approximated using a more compact representation. Furthermore, the parameters can be more intuitive when interpreting or controlling the model.

In the context of modeling BRDFs, more general representations are usually linear, e.g. spherical harmonics [2, 24], sums of separable bicubic polynomials [6] or wavelets [19]. Especially the former representations may require many coefficients, for instance

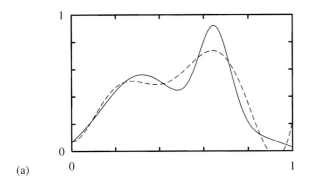
(a)

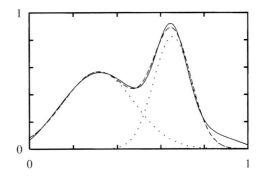
(b)

Figure 3: (a) A one-dimensional function (solid line) and its approximation by the first four terms of the Fourier series (dashed line). (b) The same function (solid line) and its approximation by the sum of two unconstrained Gaussians (dashed line). The Gaussians (dotted lines) correspond directly to the main features of the function.

for specular surfaces, which have reflectance functions with high frequencies. On the other hand, many popular models are simple non-linear approximations. The cosine lobe model [12] and the Gaussian model by Ward [23] are probably the most widely used examples, being simple and efficient. Instead of fitting a function in one dimension as in Figure 3, these approximations are defined in the four directional dimensions of the reflectance function.

In this work we take the idea of non-linear approximation a step further, paying close attention to physical plausibility and ensuring computational efficiency.

4 THE GENERALIZED COSINE MODEL

Our representation is a generalization of the cosine lobe model that is based on the Phong shading model. As such, it is intended to approximate the directional-diffuse component and possibly a non-Lambertian diffuse component of a reflectance function. We first discuss the cosine lobe model and then our generalization.

4.1 The Classical Cosine Lobe Model

The original cosine lobe model is attractively simple, but it has a few major shortcomings for representing directional-diffuse reflection. Figure 5 shows the appearance of the model for different viewing angles. The behavior contrasts sharply with the reflectance behavior of most real surfaces, which appear more specular at grazing angles, because the apparent roughness decreases (Figure 2). So why do the reflections in the images of Figure 5 disappear? There are two related reasons. Figure 4a shows how the shape and size of the reflectance lobe remain the same for all incident directions. For grazing angles, up to half the lobe disappears under the surface. Furthermore, the remaining part has to be multiplied by the cosine of the angle with the normal when computing the reflected power. As illustrated in Figure 4b, this results in the albedo (the directional-hemispherical reflectance) decreasing rapidly towards grazing angles. Visually, this means that the directional-diffuse reflection will disappear rather than increase.

In spite of these flaws, the original cosine lobe model is still widely used for illumination simulations. The model is physically plausible: it is reciprocal and conservation of energy can be ensured easily. It is simple and computationally inexpensive to evaluate. It is attractive for Monte Carlo algorithms as one can easily sample directions according to the function. In the context of deterministic algorithms, Arvo [1] showed how irradiance tensors can be applied to analytically compute cosine lobe reflections on surfaces illuminated by diffuse luminaires.

We briefly recall that the original cosine lobe model for a given position and wavelength can be written formally as follows:

$$f_r(\mathbf{u}, \mathbf{v}) \quad = \quad \rho_s C_s \cos^n \alpha, \qquad (1)$$

where α is the angle between the exitant direction $\mathbf{v}$ and the mirror direction of the incident direction $\mathbf{u}$, which we will denote by $\mathbf{u}_m$. In order not to burden our notation we will define the power of negative values as 0; the lobe is clamped to 0 for negative cosine values. If we choose C_s to be the normalization factor $(n+2)/(2\pi)$, then ρ_s is a value between 0 and 1, expressing the maximum albedo of the lobe. This maximum is reached for perpendicularly incoming light. The maximum albedo ρ_s and the specular exponent n are the parameters that determine the size and shape of the reflectance function. The cosine can be written as a dot product, and as mentioned in [1], the mirroring around the normal $\mathbf{n}$ can be written using a Householder matrix:

$$\begin{aligned} f_r(\mathbf{u}, \mathbf{v}) \quad &= \quad \rho_s C_s \left[\mathbf{u}_m \cdot \mathbf{v}\right]^n \\ &= \quad \rho_s C_s \left[\mathbf{u}^T (2\mathbf{n}\mathbf{n}^T - \mathbf{I})\mathbf{v}\right]^n. \qquad (2) \end{aligned}$$

4.2 The Generalized Cosine Lobe Model

Our model can be regarded as a generalization of the original cosine lobe model. Most known generalizations simply scale the reflectance lobes in some way, violating reciprocity in the process. Changing the model while still satisfying the reciprocity constraint is hard. Physical plausibility, and reciprocity in particular, are therefore important merits of the generalization presented. Yet the representation is conceptually simple and it retains the original advantages for Monte Carlo sampling and analytical evaluation. As a result, it can easily be integrated into existing code.

The essential observation is that Equation 2 can be generalized by replacing the Householder transform together with the normalization factor by a general 3×3 matrix $\mathbf{M}$:

$$f_r(\mathbf{u}, \mathbf{v}) \quad = \quad \rho_s \left[\mathbf{u}^T \mathbf{M} \mathbf{v}\right]^n, \qquad (3)$$

where we assume that the direction vectors are defined with respect to a fixed local coordinate system at the surface. This representation provides us with 9 coefficients and an exponent to shape the reflectance function. Of course, certain physical restrictions apply to these parameters. In order for this reflectance function to be reciprocal, the matrix has to be symmetrical: $\mathbf{M} = \mathbf{M}^T$.

We can now apply a singular value decomposition of $\mathbf{M}$ into $\mathbf{Q}^T \mathbf{D} \mathbf{Q}$. This yields the transformation $\mathbf{Q}$ for going to a new local coordinate system, in which the matrix simplifies to the diagonal matrix $\mathbf{D}$. Except for unusual types of anisotropy, the axes

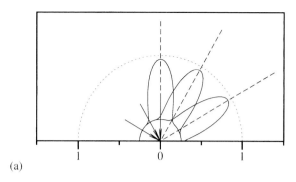
(a)

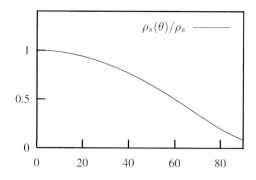
(b)

Figure 4: (a) Polar plots of the classical cosine lobe reflectance model ($\rho_s = 0.2$, $n = 20$) with a Lambertian term ($\rho_d = 0.8$) in the incidence plane, for incidence angles $0°$, $30°$ and $60°$. (b) The relative decrease of the albedo of the directional-diffuse term as a function of incidence angle.

Figure 5: Rendered pictures of a scene with the classical cosine lobe model, for various viewing angles. The glossy reflection on the table disappears at grazing angles, which is exactly the opposite of real surface behavior.

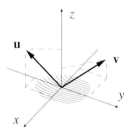

Figure 6: The incident direction **u** and exitant direction **v** are defined in a local coordinate system at the surface. The coordinate system is aligned to the normal and to the principal directions of anisotropy, if any.

are now aligned to the normal and to the principal directions of anisotropy, as illustrated in Figure 6. The diagonal matrix can be seen as weighting the terms of the dot product $\mathbf{u} \cdot \mathbf{v}$:

$$f_r(\mathbf{u}, \mathbf{v}) = \rho_s \left[C_x u_x v_x + C_y u_y v_y + C_z u_z v_z \right]^n. \quad (4)$$

This formulation of the model is the most convenient to use. In the case of isotropic reflection, $C_x = C_y$. The original cosine lobe model is obtained by choosing $-C_x = -C_y = C_z = \sqrt[n]{C_s}$. However, much more expressive functions than the cosine lobe model can be obtained by varying the different parameters, as we will show in more detail in Section 5. Note that the function is defined for all incident and exitant directions. It is thus fully four-dimensional and we apply and fit it as such.

4.3 The Generalized Function as a Cosine Lobe

The generalized function has an elegant and very practical property: for each given incident direction **u** the function can be rewritten as a scaled version of an ordinary cosine lobe. Simply rewriting Equation 3:

$$
\begin{aligned}
f_r(\mathbf{u}, \mathbf{v}) &= \rho_s \, \|\mathbf{u}^T\mathbf{M}\|^n \, \left[\frac{\mathbf{u}^T\mathbf{M}}{\|\mathbf{u}^T\mathbf{M}\|} \mathbf{v} \right]^n \\
&= \rho_s C_s(\mathbf{u}) \, [\mathbf{u}' \cdot \mathbf{v}]^n \\
&= \rho_s C_s(\mathbf{u}) \, \cos^n \alpha'. \quad (5)
\end{aligned}
$$

The direction $\mathbf{u}' = (\mathbf{u}^T\mathbf{M}/\|\mathbf{u}^T\mathbf{M}\|)^T$ is a transformed and normalized version of the incident direction **u**, and the angle α' is its angle with **v**. The scaling factor $C_s(\mathbf{u}) = \|\mathbf{u}^T\mathbf{M}\|^n$ is a power of the normalization factor and therefore varies with the incident direction. For the specific case of Equation 4, the direction $\mathbf{u}' = (C_x u_x, C_y u_y, C_z u_z)^T / \sqrt{C_x^2 u_x^2 + C_y^2 u_y^2 + C_z^2 u_z^2}$ and the scaling factor $C_s(\mathbf{u}) = \sqrt{C_x^2 u_x^2 + C_y^2 u_y^2 + C_z^2 u_z^2}^n$. This observation shows how the original cosine lobe function is now generalized in its orientation and its scaling. The changes in orientation and scale are specific results of Equation 3 – if they were just arbitrary, reciprocity would generally not be preserved.

Practically, the equation makes it straightforward to continue using the same Monte Carlo sampling strategies and deterministic evaluation techniques as for the original cosine lobe model. One only needs to substitute the mirror direction $\mathbf{u}_m$ by $\mathbf{u}'$ (or the angle α by α') and scale the results as required. For instance, the albedo $\rho_s(\mathbf{u})$ for each incident direction **u** can be computed analytically, using the procedures presented by Arvo [1]. This is specifically useful to ensure energy conservation.

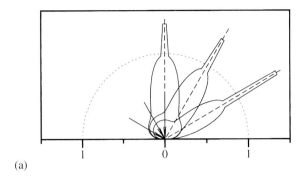

(a)

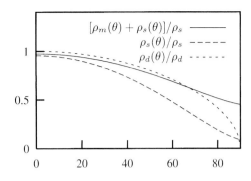

(b)

Figure 7: (a) Polar plots of the classical cosine lobe model ($\rho_s = 0.2$, $n = 20$) with a generalized diffuse term ($\rho_d = 0.8$, $n = 0.5$) and an additional mirror term ($R_m = 0.4$). (b) The albedos of the diffuse and directional-diffuse terms, $\rho_d(\theta)$ and $\rho_s(\theta)$ respectively, decrease towards grazing angles; the mirror term $\rho_m(\theta)$ gradually takes over.

Figure 8: Rendered pictures of a scene with the classical cosine lobe model, now including the mirror term and a generalized diffuse term. The mirror term gradually takes over from the directional-diffuse term, and the diffuse term fades out. Even with these minor changes the table surface already shows a more realistic reflective behavior.

5 QUALITATIVE PROPERTIES

In this section, we illustrate the qualitative properties of our generalized model. We construct a few simple reflectance functions with diffuse, directional-diffuse and specular components, to demonstrate how the model can simulate important aspects of real-life reflectance behavior. Section 6 will then demonstrate the quantitative properties of the model, by fitting sums of primitive functions to a complex physically-based model and to actual measurements.

5.1 Non-Lambertian Diffuse Reflection

An effect apparent in the pictures of Figure 2 is the fading out of the diffuse component for grazing angles. As more light is reflected off the coating of the surface, the subsurface scattering responsible for the diffuse reflection diminishes. The surface looks less saturated and the wood texture disappears. While our generalized cosine lobe model encompasses the Lambertian model (by setting $n = 0$), a more general *rotationally symmetric* diffuse component can be derived from Equation 4, by setting $C_x = C_y = 0$:

$$f_r(\mathbf{u}, \mathbf{v}) \quad = \quad \rho_d C_d \left[u_z v_z \right]^n, \qquad (6)$$

where the normalization factor $C_d = (n + 2)/(2\pi)$, and ρ_d is the parameter between 0 and 1 specifying the maximum albedo. For grazing incident or exitant directions the reflectance decreases proportionally to a power of the cosine of the angle with the normal. This instance actually corresponds to the model presented by Minnaert [13], in the context of modeling the reflectance of the lunar surface. The non-Lambertian diffuse component is plotted in Figure 7a (appearing as the small circular component near the origin), along with directional-diffuse and mirror components that will be

discussed in the next section. Figure 7b shows the behavior of the albedo $\rho_d(\mathbf{u})$ as a function of incidence angle θ, normalized by the parameter ρ_d. Figure 8 illustrates the effect visually: the diffuse component of the table surface fades out for grazing angles.

5.2 Specularity at Grazing Angles

The other important visual effect shown in the pictures of Figure 2 is the increasing specularity of the polished table surface at grazing angles. This behavior can be accounted for by extending the model of a diffuse lobe and a directional-diffuse lobe with a specular mirror term. The directional-diffuse lobe can in the simplest case be an ordinary cosine lobe. The mirror term can be made to reflect a fraction of the power that is not reflected by the directional-diffuse lobe. A simple instance of these two components thus becomes:

$$\begin{aligned} f_r(\mathbf{u}, \mathbf{v}) \quad = \quad & \rho_s C_s \left[\mathbf{u}_m \cdot \mathbf{v} \right]^n \qquad (7) \\ & + (\rho_s - \rho_s(\mathbf{u})) \, R_m \, \delta(\mathbf{u}_m - \mathbf{v}), \end{aligned}$$

where $\delta(\mathbf{u}_m - \mathbf{v})$ is the Dirac delta function with respect to the canonical measure on the sphere. In this case it is convenient to choose $C_s = (n + 1)/(2\pi)$. The factor $\rho_s - \rho_s(\mathbf{u})$ is the difference between the directional-diffuse scaling factor and the actual albedo for direction $\mathbf{u}$. The parameter R_m expresses the fraction of the power lost in the directional-diffuse lobe that is reflected in the mirror term. In Monte Carlo simulations this can be taken quite literally. One can sample a direction according to the cosine lobe. Any sample is then tested against the cosine of the angle with the normal, with rejection sampling. The fraction R_m of rejected samples is sent into the mirror direction. In analytical computations each of the terms, including the mirror term, can be computed.

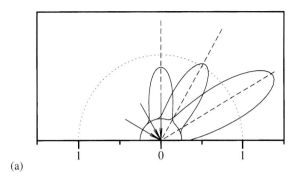
(a)

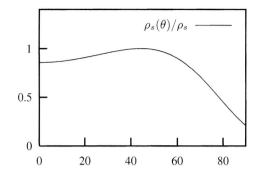
(b)

Figure 9: (a) Polar plots of the generalized cosine lobe model ($\rho_s = 0.2$, $n = 20$, $C_z/C_x = 0.95$) with a Lambertian term ($\rho_d = 0.8$). The lobes are slightly off-specular and increase in size towards grazing angles. (b) The albedo of the directional-diffuse term only decreases for larger incidence angles as a result.

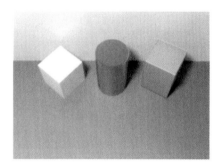  

Figure 10: Rendered pictures of a scene with the generalized cosine lobe model. The off-specular directional-diffuse reflectance of the table surface gradually increases for grazing angles.

Figure 7 presents an example function, including the non-Lambertian diffuse reflection that was discussed in the previous section. Note that the mirror term is actually a Dirac delta function; it is broadened here to visualize its behavior. Figure 7b displays the albedos $\rho_s(\theta)$ and $\rho_m(\theta)$ for the directional diffuse and the mirror terms, respectively. Figure 8 then shows the example scene rendered with the extended model.

The results look reasonably realistic because the mirror term is a rough approximation of an actual Fresnel term multiplied by masking-shadowing and roughness factors (e.g. [9]). If it is known, a more accurate approximation can be used by attenuating the mirror term, so that R_m becomes a function of incidence angle.

5.3 Off-Specular Reflection

Application of the model becomes more interesting by varying the individual parameters of Equation 4. Torrance and Sparrow [21] already observed that the directional-diffuse lobe for a given incident direction generally does not reach its maximum for the mirror direction, but rather for a more grazing direction. At the same time the size of the reflectance lobe increases. The original cosine lobe model obviously does not account for these effects. This shortcoming is sometimes overcome by dividing by the cosine of the exitance angle, which breaks reciprocity. In the generalized model, parameters C_z that are smaller than $-C_x = -C_y$ yield a range of off-specular reflection effects, without compromising the physical plausibility. Figure 9 gives an example with moderately increasing reflectance, and Figure 10 shows a set of rendered images. The table surface exhibits off-specular reflection. It looks mostly diffuse from above, while the directional-diffuse component increases for grazing angles.

5.4 Retro-Reflection

Many surfaces not only scatter light in the forward direction, but also backwards, in the direction of the illuminant. This phenomenon is called retro-reflection. The moon surface is an extreme example, where a large fraction of light from the sun is reflected in the incident direction. In the generalized model, a retro-reflective lobe can be represented in the same uniform framework by using a set of parameters C_x, C_y and C_z that are all positive. The reflectance measurements of paint in section 6.2 will illustrate this effect.

5.5 Anisotropy

Anisotropic reflection can be modeled with a single primitive function, by assigning different values to the parameters C_x and C_y. As with the parameter C_z that controls the off-specular reflection, this will pull the reflectance lobes for all incident directions in a preferential direction and scale them. More general anisotropy, e.g. with a splitting lobe, can be obtained by constructing a matrix $\mathbf{M}$ for Equation 3 that is not necessarily symmetrical. Adding a reflectance term with its transpose $\mathbf{M}^T$ then yields a new reciprocal model.

6 QUANTITATIVE PROPERTIES

In this section, we show how the model is also suitable for representing complex real-life reflectance functions. The representation is a sum of several primitive functions of the form of Equation 4. Absorbing the albedo ρ_s in the other parameters, each primitive function i is defined by the parameters $C_{x,i}(= C_{y,i})$, $C_{z,i}$ and n_i.

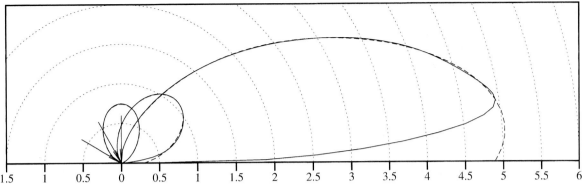

Figure 11: Polar plots of the fitted reflectance model (dashed lines) against the original physically-based model of a roughened aluminum surface (solid lines) in the plane of incidence, for $\theta = 0°, 30°, 60°$, at $500nm$. The reflectance function becomes more off-specular and strongly increases in size towards grazing angles. The sum of generalized cosine functions captures these effects.

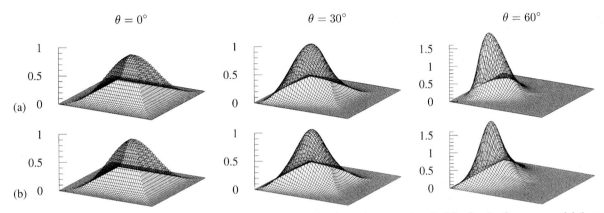

Figure 12: Plots of the original physically-based model of roughened aluminum (top row, a) and of the fitted reflectance model (bottom row, b), now multiplied by the cosines of the incidence and exitance angles with the normals, fitted and shown over the entire hemisphere, for various incidence angles.

The model can thus be written as:

$$f_r(\mathbf{u}, \mathbf{v}) = \sum_i [C_{x,i} u_x v_x + C_{y,i} u_y v_y + C_{z,i} u_z v_z]^{n_i}. \quad (8)$$

The model is fitted to the BRDF of aluminum, based on the physically-based reflectance model of He *et al.*, and to the measured BRDF of blue paint. We minimize the mean-square error of the reflectance functions multiplied by the cosines of the incidence and exitance angles with the normal. As the primitive functions are non-linear, a non-linear optimization technique is required to determine the parameters. The Levenberg-Marquardt optimization algorithm has proven to be efficient for this application; computing each approximation requires only a few minutes in a standard numerical package. This is not a serious penalty, as it only has to be done once for each measured material.

In both case studies, we first look at the BRDFs in the incidence plane, and then in the entire function space. In the incidence plane the function space is two-dimensional, depending on the incident polar angle and the exitant polar angle. The entire function space of isotropic BRDFs is three-dimensional, additionally depending on the exitant azimuthal angle.

6.1   Fit to a Physically-Based Model

The reflectance model derived by He *et al.* [9] is generally acknowledged as the most sophisticated model in use in computer graphics.

It consists of a Lambertian term, a directional-diffuse term and a mirror term. Here we concentrate on approximating the directional-diffuse term. In our example, the Lambertian term and the mirror term are mostly negligible, but in any case representing and using these terms is straightforward. We present the results for roughened aluminum, as in their original paper for wavelength $\lambda = 500nm$, roughness $\sigma_0 = 0.28\mu m$ and autocorrelation length $\tau = 1.77\mu m$.

Figure 11 shows the results of a fit in the incidence plane, using the sum of three primitive functions. It is important to note that the function has not been fitted for each of the individual lobes, which would be a lot easier, but to the reflectance function as a whole. The fit is visually perfect, except for more grazing angles. In this regime of angles, most of the difference is due to the masking term, which is not present in the representation. These values are less important, however, as they are multiplied in illumination computations by the cosine of the angle between the direction and the surface normal. Additionally, the mirror reflection becomes more important than the directional-diffuse reflection for grazing angles.

Figure 12 shows the results of fitting the approximation to the reflectance function in the entire three-dimensional space of directions. The functions are plotted for three different incidence angles, in a uniform parametrization of the hemisphere [20]. The creases along the diagonals of the square are a result of the parametrization and are not related to the functions. The functions are multiplied by the cosine of the exitance angle with the normal, so that the volumes below the surfaces are proportional to the albedos. Both the shapes of the functions and the albedos match very well.

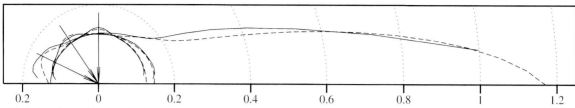

Figure 13: Polar plots of the fitted reflectance model (dashed lines) against the original measured BRDF data of blue paint (solid lines) in the plane of incidence, for $\theta = 0°, 35°, 65°$, at $550nm$. The model successfully reproduces both the increasing retro-reflection and off-specular reflection.

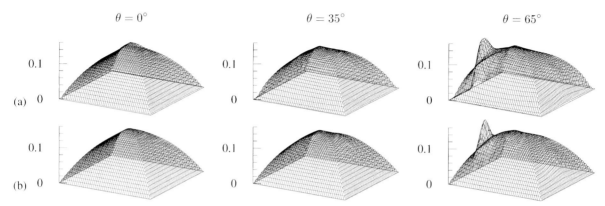

Figure 14: Plots of the original measured model of blue paint (top row, a) and of the fitted reflectance model (bottom row, b), now fitted and shown over the entire hemisphere, for various incidence angles.

6.2 Fit to Reflectance Measurements

The second comparison is with the measured reflectance data of a blue paint sample (spray-painted latex blue paint, Pratt & Lambert, Vapex Interior Wall Base 1, Color #1243, Cal. III) [5]. Figure 13 shows the data and the approximation in the incidence plane at $550nm$, for three incidence angles.

Compared to the strong forward-scattering behavior of the roughened aluminum, the paint is largely diffuse. Due to measurement noise, the data are more irregular. Still, there are important other phenomena. The forward scattering lobe increases rapidly for grazing angles and is very off-specular. The measurements did not include highly grazing angles, for which theory predicts a drop-off. The measurements did show increasing retro-reflection. The approximation, which uses a sum of three directional-diffuse functions and a Lambertian term, captures this effect.

Figure 14 shows the data and the approximation fitted over the three-dimensional space of incident and exitant directions. Table I lists the coefficients for this approximation, illustrating how simple and compact the model is. The positive value of C_x for lobe I indicates that it is a retro-reflective lobe, while lobes II and III account for the forward scattering. The ratios of the parameters C_x and C_z give an idea of how off-specular the lobes are and how fast they increase in size for grazing angles. Note that the exponents are not necessarily integers. For Monte Carlo simulations using the model, this is generally not a problem. For analytical computations the exponents would have to be constrained to integer values.

Lobe	$C_x = C_y$	C_z	n
I	0.86	0.77	18.6
II	−0.41	0.018	2.58
III	−1.03	0.70	63.8
Diffuse	0.13		

Table 1: The coefficients of the representation for the three-dimensional fit of Figure 14.

7 RESULTS

We have approximated the measured reflectance data of the blue paint presented in Section 6.2 and of a standardized steel sample (Matte finished steel, Q-Panel Laboratory Products, Q-panel R-46) at 6 discrete wavelengths. The resulting models were then used for global illumination rendering, using a Monte Carlo path tracing program. The implementation required only a few additional lines of code. The reflectance functions are evaluated using Equation 8. For sampling an exitant direction for a given incident direction we construct a probability density function that is a linear combination of the primitive cosine reflectance lobes.

Figure 15 shows a rendering of a simple scene with two spheres, a Q-panel, and two colored light sources, positioned symmetrically with respect to the viewer. A larger white light source above the viewer illuminates the whole scene. The sphere on the left is rendered with a Lambertian diffuse approximation of the measured blue paint, while the sphere on the right is rendered with the generalized reflectance model. The latter sphere has both red and green highlights due to strong forward scattering. These are lacking on the Lambertian sphere. With a light source near the viewer, the right sphere has a slightly flatter appearance due to retro-reflection. The Q-panel has a completely different appearance, displaying a blurry metallic reflection of the colored lights and of the objects. The representation successfully captures these very different reflectance characteristics.

8 CONCLUSIONS

We have introduced an efficient representation for a wide range of bidirectional reflectance distribution functions. It is an interesting alternative for previous models of directional-diffuse reflectance, which required either simplified single-term representations, complex analytical expressions for specific classes of functions, or general but large representations with linear basis functions.

Figure 15: Rendered picture of a scene with two spheres and a Q-panel, illuminated by two colored light sources and one larger white light source. The sphere on the left has a Lambertian approximation of the measured paint reflectance; the sphere on the right is rendered with the non-linear approximation. The Q-panel has the non-linear approximation of the measured steel reflectance.

- The representation is compact. Each primitive function is determined by two or three coefficients and an exponent. Because the representation is memory-efficient, any complex wavelength dependency can be modeled by constructing independent approximations at discrete wavelengths.

- The functions are expressive. They can represent complex reflectance behavior, such as off-specular reflection, increasing directional-diffuse reflectance for grazing angles, retro-reflection and non-Lambertian diffuse reflection in a uniform way.

- The functions handle noise in the raw reflectance data gracefully. They can capture sharp reflectance lobes without suffering from small spurious errors in the data. If the data are sparse, the model interpolates them naturally.

- The functions themselves are physically plausible, irrespective of how they were constructed. They are inherently reciprocal. Energy-conservation can be verified analytically for each incident direction.

- On the algorithmic side, the representation is efficient and easy to use in both local and global illumination algorithms. Its simplicity and uniformity make it practical for implementation in hardware. In Monte Carlo algorithms, reflection directions for a given incident direction can be sampled according to the transformed cosine lobe. In deterministic algorithms, illumination from diffuse emitters can be computed analytically, using a straightforward extension of the calculations for ordinary cosine lobes.

- While the representation cannot approximate all possible reflectance functions to any desired accuracy, it adequately represents a range of measured BRDF data, which usually only have a very limited accuracy. In our tests, we have obtained satisfactory results with as few as three primitive functions to represent directional-diffuse reflections from roughened metals and paints. Broad, glossy reflectance lobes are relatively easy to approximate. Sharp directional-diffuse peaks, such as for smooth metal surfaces, may be harder to represent, due to a strong dependency on the Fresnel factor, which is not explicitly included in the representation.

As future work, we will look into the details of representing anisotropic reflectance measurements with one or more terms of the current model, e.g. to model the effect of splitting reflectance lobes at anisotropic surfaces.

Acknowledgements

Thanks to Pete Shirley for many helpful discussions on BRDF representations. Jon Blocksom provided the implementation of the He model. Also thanks to Ben Trumbore and Dan Kartch for critically reading the paper. Measurement equipment was provided by NSF CTS-9213183 and by the Imaging Science Division of the Eastman Kodak Company. Q-Panel Lab Products kindly provided the Q-panels. This work was supported by the NSF Science and Technology Center for Computer Graphics and Scientific Visualization (ASC-8920219) and by NSF ASC-9523483, and performed on workstations generously donated by the Hewlett-Packard Corporation.

References

[1] J. Arvo. Applications of irradiance tensors to the simulation of non-Lambertian phenomena. In *SIGGRAPH 95 Conference Proceedings*, pages 335–342, Los Angeles, California, August 1995.

[2] B. Cabral, N. Max, and R. Springmeyer. Bidirectional reflection functions from surface bump maps. *Computer Graphics*, 21(4):273–281, July 1987.

[3] R.L. Cook and K.E. Torrance. A reflectance model for computer graphics. *Computer Graphics*, 15(4):187–196, July 1981.

[4] R.L. Cook and K.E. Torrance. A reflectance model for computer graphics. *ACM Transactions on Graphics*, 1(1):7–24, January 1982.

[5] S.C. Foo. A gonioreflectometer for measuring the bidirectional reflectance of materials for use in illumination computations. Master's thesis, Cornell University, Ithaca, New York, July 1997.

[6] A. Fournier. Separating reflection functions for linear radiosity. In *Proceedings of the Sixth Eurographics Workshop on Rendering*, pages 383–392, Dublin, Ireland, June 1995.

[7] J.S. Gondek, G.W. Meyer, and J.G. Newman. Wavelength dependent reflectance functions. In *SIGGRAPH 94 Conference Proceedings*, pages 213–220, Orlando, Florida, July 1994.

[8] P. Hanrahan and W. Krueger. Reflection from layered surfaces due to subsurface scattering. In *SIGGRAPH 93 Conference Proceedings*, pages 165–174, Anaheim, California, August 1993.

[9] X.D. He, K.E. Torrance, F.X. Sillion, and D.P. Greenberg. A comprehensive physical model for light reflection. *Computer Graphics*, 25(4):175–186, July 1991.

[10] J. Kajiya. Anisotropic reflectance models. *Computer Graphics*, 19(4):15–21, July 1985.

[11] J.J. Koenderink, A.J. van Doorn, and M. Stavridi. Bidirectional reflection distribution function expressed in terms of surface scattering modes. In *European Conference on Computer Vision*, pages 28–39, 1996.

[12] R.R. Lewis. Making shaders more physically plausible. In *Proceedings of the Fourth Eurographics Workshop on Rendering*, pages 47–62, Paris, France, June 1993.

[13] M. Minnaert. The reciprocity principle in lunar photometry. *Astrophysical Journal*, 93:403–410, 1941.

[14] M. Oren and S.K. Nayar. Generalization of Lambert's reflectance model. In *SIGGRAPH 94 Conference Proceedings*, pages 239–246, Orlando, Florida, July 1994.

[15] B.T. Phong. Illumination for computer generated pictures. *Communications of the ACM*, 18(6):311–317, 1975.

[16] P. Poulin and A. Fournier. A model for anisotropic reflection. *Computer Graphics*, 24(4):273–282, August 1990.

[17] Ch. Schlick. A customizable reflectance model for everyday rendering. In *Proceedings of the Fourth Eurographics Workshop on Rendering*, pages 73–83, Paris, France, June 1993.

[18] Ch. Schlick. A survey of shading and reflectance models. *Computer Graphics Forum*, 13(2):121–131, June 1994.

[19] P. Schröder and W. Sweldens. Spherical wavelets: Efficiently representing functions on the sphere. In *SIGGRAPH 95 Conference Proceedings*, pages 161–172, Los Angeles, California, August 1995.

[20] P. Shirley and K. Chiu. Notes on adaptive quadrature on the hemisphere. Technical Report 411, Department of Computer Science, Indiana University, Bloomington, Indiana, 1994.

[21] K.E. Torrance and E.M. Sparrow. Off-specular peaks in the directional distribution of reflected thermal radiation. In *Transactions of the ASME*, pages 1–8, Chicago, Ill., November 1965.

[22] K.E. Torrance and E.M. Sparrow. Theory for off-specular reflection from roughened surfaces. *Journal of the Optical Society of America*, 57(9):1105–1114, September 1967.

[23] G.J. Ward. Measuring and modeling anisotropic reflection. *Computer Graphics*, 26(2):265–272, July 1992.

[24] S.H. Westin, J.R. Arvo, and K.E. Torrance. Predicting reflectance functions from complex surfaces. *Computer Graphics*, 26(2):255–264, July 1992.

Fake Fur Rendering

Dan B Goldman*

Industrial Light and Magic

Abstract

A probabilistic lighting model is presented for thin coats of fur over skin. Previous methods for rendering furry objects and creatures have addressed the case where individual strands or tufts of hair may be resolvable at the pixel level. These methods are often computationally intensive. However, a large class of real-world cases where individual hairs are much smaller than the size of a pixel can be addressed using a probabilistic model for the expected value of reflected light within a small surface area. Under the assumption that hair parameters are slowly varying across the skin, lighting calculations are performed on a reference hair with prefiltered parameters. The reflected light from individual hairs and from the skin below is blended using the expectation of a ray striking a hair in that area as the opacity of the fur coating. Approximations for hair-to-hair shadowing and hair-to-skin shadowing can be made using the same hit-expectation model. Our system can be implemented in existing commercial surface-rendering software at a much lower computational cost than typical resolvable-hair methods.

CR Categories and Subject Descriptors: I.3.7 [Computer Graphics]: Three-Dimensional Graphics and Realism - Color, shading, shadowing and texture.

Additional Keywords: natural phenomena, animals, fur, anisotropic shading

1. INTRODUCTION

At first glance, fur appears to be one natural phenomenon which doesn't "cheat" easily. The appearance of a furry object is so distinctive that many approaches have utilized hair-by-hair methods to achieve an acceptable level of realism. Indeed, some of the most striking images of creatures with fur have been rendered using techniques in which individual strands of hair are visible [11][19]. But since many real-world creatures have millions of

*P.O. Box 2459, San Rafael, CA 94912.
email: dgoldman@cs.stanford.edu

hairs, object-based rendering techniques typically have running times which do not decrease as the image size decreases. Volumetric rendering algorithms render smaller images faster, but tend to be memory and computation-intensive.

Our solution does not attempt to address the 'closeup' situations which are well-handled by the existing models. Instead we address the common case where hair geometry is not visible at the final image resolution, but the visual characteristics of fur, such as glossy sheen and soft illumination, are still observed. Our model falls into a class of secondary approximations, in which hairs are not rendered directly, but are used as the underlying model for the furry surface's lighting properties.

2. RELATED WORK

Most attempts to render fur have used brute force methods, representing hairs with large numbers of polygons or particles [7],[15],[20],[13],[2]. The primary drawbacks of these types of methods are severe aliasing and/or computational costs which, in some algorithms, actually increase as the subject decreases in screen size.

Kajiya [12] has addressed the illumination and rendering of hairs using a volume technique, by precomputing a volume 'texel' which is tiled across a furry surface. Hair geometry is rasterized into this texel, and final rendering is accomplished using volume rendering. This technique lends itself well to uniformly furry surfaces which can be tiled using a small number of such texels. Others eschew texels in favor of procedural hair generation [18]. Unfortunately, these are some of the more computationally intensive methods available.

Many lighting models for complex surfaces take a probabilistic approach to microstructure [4],[21]. Recent work [22] has extended this paradigm to more complex surfaces by describing a general method for estimating the bidirectional reflectance distribution function (BRDF) via Monte Carlo sampling and parametrizing it using spherical harmonics. This method is well suited to complex but uniformly patterned surfaces.

A number of proprietary fur renderers have been developed, but published details are rare [8][17]. The true ancestors of this work are the proprietary renderers used at our facility for high-detail fur rendering [19] ([11]). These renderers were useful not only for creating reference images for quality comparisons, but also as working models forming a basis for comparisons of tradeoffs and limitations of alternative rendering methods.

3. FAKE FUR RENDERING

We call our probabilistic fur rendering algorithm method the 'fakefur' algorithm, to distinguish it from our proprietary high-detail method not covered here, which by comparison became known as the 'realfur' algorithm. Despite the nomenclature, both methods are approximations of varying degrees to the appearance of real mammalian fur.

It should be noted that the goal of this method is to render creatures to be composited into live-action feature films Although the model can be used for other purposes, this goal has motivated its parametrization and allowed us to ignore certain lighting behaviours uncommon in such a setting:

The fakefur rendering method hinges on a probabilistic method for computing fur visibility, which we call the fakefur opacity function.

3.1. Outline

A sketch of the fakefur illumination process for a given area is as follows:

  I. Compute the mean hair geometry within the sample region. This is the 'reference hair'.

  II. For each light:

    1. Using the fakefur opacity function, compute the hair-over-hair shadow attenuation.

    2. Compute the reflected luminance of the average hair in the sample region.

    3. Using the fakefur opacity function, compute the hair-over-skin shadow factor.

    4. Compute the reflected luminance of the underlying skin.

    5. Using the fakefur opacity function, compute the hair/skin visibility ratio.

    6. Blend the reflected luminance of the skin and hair using the visibility ratio to obtain the final reflected luminance of the sample region.

  III. Sum the reflected luminances for each light to obtain the total reflected luminance for the sample region.

3.2. Parametrization

We parameterize hair geometry on a surface by hair length, hair radius, density of hairs, and hair tangents at the root and tip. The reflectivity of individual hairs is parameterized by diffuse reflectivity, specular reflectivity, specular exponent, and several directionality factors for reflectivity/transmissivity control and Lambertian macro-behaviour. Of the aforementioned parameters, only the diffuse reflectivity is wavelength dependent.

The parameters for the hairs in a particular region may vary over the surface, either in a procedural manner or defined via texture maps.

3.3. The Fakefur Illumination Function

To describe the reflected luminance of a single hair, we use a modified version of the hair reflectance model described in [12]. The equations from [12] (with some notation modified for consistency) are:

$$\Psi_{\text{diffuse}} = K_d \sin(\overline{T}, \overline{L}) \tag{1}$$

$$\Psi_{\text{specular}} = K_s [(\overline{T} \cdot \overline{L})(\overline{T} \cdot \overline{E}) + \sin(\overline{T}, \overline{L})\sin(\overline{T}, \overline{E})]^p \tag{2}$$

$$\Psi_{\text{hair}} = \Psi_{\text{diffuse}} + \Psi_{\text{specular}} \tag{3}$$

The vectors $\overline{T}$, $\overline{L}$, and $\overline{E}$ represent the normalized hair tangent vector, the normalized light direction vector, and the normalized eye direction vector, respectively. Ψ and its subscripts are the reflectivity components.

One limitation of this model is its lack of directionality: hairs are fully lit even if $\overline{L}$ is opposite $\overline{V}$. We are interested in both reflection and transmission. To increase directionality, we utilize two new attenuation factors, introduced by [24], which may be used to tune the relative transmissivity and reflectivity of a hair.

We first characterize the relative directionality of a given incident light ray, eye ray, and hair tangent using the cosine of the dihedral angle between the planes containing each pair.

$$\kappa = \cos(\overline{T} \times \overline{L}, \overline{T} \times \overline{E}) = \frac{(\overline{T} \times \overline{L}) \cdot (\overline{T} \times \overline{E})}{|\overline{T} \times \overline{L}||\overline{T} \times \overline{E}|} \tag{4}$$

Note that when $\overline{L}$ and $\overline{E}$ strike the same side of the hair (frontlighting), $\kappa > 0$, and when $\overline{L}$ and $\overline{E}$ lie on opposite sides of the hair (backlighting), $\kappa < 0$.

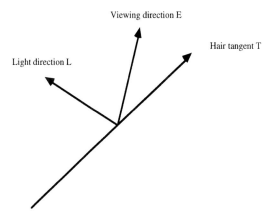

Figure 1. Frontlighting

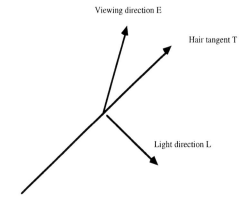

Figure 2. Backlighting

We represent the amounts of forward and backward scattering of the hair by the parameters ρ_{transmit} and ρ_{reflect}, which vary in the range $[0,1]$. Then our directional attenuation factor f_{dir} is computed as follows:

$$f_{\text{dir}} = \frac{1+\kappa}{2}\rho_{\text{reflect}} + \frac{1-\kappa}{2}\rho_{\text{transmit}} \tag{5}$$

White or gray hairs are well-represented by nearly equal reflectance and transmission coefficients. Hairs with more pigment will have much higher reflectance than transmission. When both ρ_{reflect} and ρ_{transmit} are 1, no attenuation occurs.

We also include a surface normal factor as a quick and dirty way to adjust shadowing. Since the layer of fur is approximated geometrically by a flat surface, if we were to use only shadow mapping or shadow tracing to determine the shadowed areas, a hard termination line would result. Instead we specify a smooth gradation from full illumination to full shadow:

$$f_{\text{surface}} = 1 + \rho_{\text{surface}}(\text{smoothstep}(\overline{N} \cdot \overline{L}, \omega_{\min}, \omega_{\max}) - 1) \qquad (6)$$

where $\overline{N}$ is the normalized surface normal, and smoothstep is the smooth Hermite interpolation between $\omega_{\min}$ and $\omega_{\max}$:

$$\text{smoothstep}(x, a, b) = \begin{cases} 0, \forall x < a \\ 1, \forall x > b \\ -2\left(\dfrac{x-a}{b-a}\right)^3 + 3\left(\dfrac{x-a}{b-a}\right)^2, \forall a < x < b \end{cases} \qquad (7)$$

When ρ_{surface} is 0, no attenuation occurs. $\omega_{\min}$ and $\omega_{\max}$ are the cosines of the starting and ending shadow termination angles, and can be easily adjusted to match reference images.

In our model, both f_{dir} and f_{surface} are multiplied into the r.h.s. of equation [III.3] above:

$$\Psi_{\text{hair}} = f_{\text{dir}} f_{\text{surface}}(\Psi_{\text{diffuse}} + \Psi_{\text{specular}}) \qquad (8)$$

If hairs are bent along their trajectory, or if the hair parameters are otherwise varying from root to tip, multiple samples along the reference hair can be computed for Ψ_{hair} and averaged. In practice, we found using a very small number of samples (3 or 4) is sufficient.

Because the hairs in question are relatively short and slowly varying, we disregard the possibility of hairs with widely disparate parameters reflecting light in the same sample region.

Like [12], this model is a first-order approximation, which is most accurate when the hair albedo is low. No secondary scattering of light off of hairs onto other hairs or onto skin is considered.

3.4. The Fakefur Opacity Function

The fur opacity function, denoted α_f, computes the mean opacity of a patch of fur as viewed from a given angle. α_f is a function of the hair geometry, the distribution of hairs, and the viewing angle. In general, both the hair geometry and the distribution of hairs can be quite complex, and we must make some simplifying assumptions in order to generate an easily computible form for α_f.

We make the following assumptions concerning hair geometry:

• Hairs are truncated cones of radius r_b at their base, r_t at their tip and length l.

$$\bullet \ l >> r_b \qquad (9)$$

$$\bullet \ r_b \geq r_t \qquad (10)$$

In general, the projection of a truncated cone into a viewing plane is the union of two ellipses (the projection of the base and

top) and a trapezoid (the projection of the sides). The area of the projection of the base and top are proportional to r^2, while the area of the projection of the sides is proportional to $l(r_b + r_t)$. So the constraint $l >> r_b, r_t$ implies that r^2 is vanishingly small for most viewing directions. Therefore, we will consider only the projection of the sides onto the viewing plane.

Under these assumptions, we compute the area of the projection of a hair onto the viewing plane as the projection of its trapezoidal profile,

$$A_h = l(r_b + r_t)/2 \qquad (11)$$

$$A_h' = A_h \sin(\overline{E}, \overline{T}) \qquad (12)$$

We make the following assumptions concerning distribution of hairs:

• All hairs in the sampled region share identical geometry and orientation.

• The distribution of hairs in a small region has Poisson characteristics: Within a zone of uniform density, a sample of half the size will contain half the hairs and hairs are placed independently of each other .

It may be noted that the distribution of hairs on mammal fur seems to follow a Poisson-disk pattern, not the Poisson pattern described by our model [12].[1] Nevertheless, the assumption of a Poisson pattern vastly simplifies the computation of the fur opacity function, and as we will see in the following section, does not significantly alter the results.

Under the above assumptions, we compute the average area on the skin covered by n_i hairs:

$$A_s = \frac{n_i}{D} \qquad (13)$$

where n_i is a constant denoting the number of hairs in a sample region and D is the local density of hairs. The projection of that area is

$$A_s' = A_s(\overline{E} \cdot \overline{N}) \qquad (14)$$

Thus, the coverage of a single hair in this area, and the probability of a random ray striking the single hair from direction $\overline{E}$ is

$$\alpha_h = \frac{A_h'}{A_s'} = \frac{A_h}{A_s} \frac{\sin(\overline{E}, \overline{T})}{\overline{E} \cdot \overline{N}} = \frac{A_h}{A_s} g(\overline{E}, \overline{T}, \overline{N}) \qquad (15)$$

We isolate the projection-dependent part of α_h above as the fakefur projection function

$$g(\overline{E}, \overline{T}, \overline{N}) = \frac{\sin(\overline{E}, \overline{T})}{\overline{E} \cdot \overline{N}}. \qquad (16)$$

The coverage of the entire distribution of hairs, assuming their independence, is computed as:

$$\alpha_f = 1 - (1 - \alpha_h)^{n_i} = 1 - \left(1 - \frac{DA_h g(\overline{E}, \overline{T}, \overline{N})}{n_i}\right)^{n_i} \qquad (17)$$

As the number of hairs in the sample region increases, this

[1]There is some ambiguity in the literature concerning the difference between a Poisson pattern and a Poisson-disk pattern. In this paper, a Poisson pattern refers to independently distributed samples, while a Poisson-disk pattern is defined, as in [9], as one in which "no two samples are closer together than some distance r_p' defining a non-overlapping radius surrounding each sample. [9] notes that "we also usually want the samples to be as close together as the disks allow."

simplifies to:

$$\lim_{n_i \to \infty} \alpha_f = 1 - \frac{1}{e^{DA_h g(\overline{E}, \overline{T}, \overline{N})}} \qquad (18)$$

This is the fakefur opacity function.

3.5. Using the Fakefur Opacity Function

In the illumination process, the fakefur opacity function is used for three separate computations: hair-over-skin shadows, hair-over-hair shadows, and hair-over-skin visibility.

Hair-over-skin shadows are handled by computing the opacity of the fur as seen from the light direction, and attenuating the light intensity by this opacity before illuminating the skin:

$$\lambda_{\text{skin}} = I[1 - \alpha_f(\overline{L})]\Psi_{\text{skin}} \qquad (19)$$

where I is the illuminance, and λ and its subscripts are the reflected luminance and its summed skin and hair components, respectively.

Hair-over-hair shadows are simulated by using some fraction of the hair-over-skin shadows to similarly attenuate the hair illuminance:

$$\lambda_{\text{hair}} = I[1 - s\alpha_f(\overline{L})]\Psi_{\text{hair}} \qquad (20)$$

A physical model should include an integral summing the shadowed regions along a hair. The tips of the hairs will be unshadowed by other hairs, while the roots of the hairs will be completely shadowed by other hairs. We approximate this integral with the constant s. This constant can be adjusted to increase or decrease the density of the hair-over-hair shadows, but a value of $s = 0.5$ seems to work well for essentially straight cylindrical hairs. This corresponds to a coat of fur in which, on average, half of each hair is in shadow and half is not in shadow.

The hair-over-skin visibility computation is the simplest. The opacity of the fur as seen from the camera viewing direction is computed, and this value used to blend the skin luminance with the hair luminance:

$$\lambda = \alpha_f(\overline{E})\lambda_{\text{hair}} + [1 - \alpha_f(\overline{E})]\lambda_{\text{skin}} \qquad (21)$$

3.6 Large-scale geometry

Certain other steps involving large-scale geometry are not included in the above outline. The three most notable omissions are shadows cast by skin onto hairs (skin-on-hair shadows), shadows cast by skin onto other skin surfaces (skin-on-skin shadows), and the skin illumination model. These are not central to the algorithm, and are well-handled by existing methods, so they will be covered fairly briefly:

An implementation emphasizing physical accuracy might opt for ray-traced shadows [5] and a skin substructure illumination model such as [10]. However, in keeping with the high priority of efficiency, our implementation applies the most expedient methods available: For the scales at which we wish to render furry things, shadow maps [23] are adequate mechanisms for skin-on-hair and skin-on-skin shadows. And since the underlying skin is visible only in a few areas where fur is thin or sparse, we use a variant of the Torrance-Sparrow illumination model [21] for computing the reflected luminance of the skin.

4. DISCUSSION

4.1. Validating the Opacity Approximation

Since the fakefur opacity function is so essential to the illumination equation, it's important to establish that it's a valid approximation.

How well does α_f approximate the density of real fur? The distribution of hairs on mammal fur has been observed to be distributed in a poisson-disk pattern [12]. Our model, on the other hand, assumes that within a local region hairs are distributed independently. We might expect that our model underestimates opacity, because hairs in a poisson-disk distribution will overlap less frequently than in a poisson distribution.

However, the approximation can be justified as follows: Very short hairs can only overlap other hairs whose roots lie immediately adjacent. In a poisson-disk distribution, there is high correlation between adjacent hairs, while in an independent scatter, there is no correlation. Therefore, for short hairs, the fur opacity function is indeed a poor approximation of a poisson-disk distribution's opacity. However, as hairs grow longer relative to the distance between their roots, they may overlap hairs whose roots lie far from their own. In a poisson-disk distribution such that the disk radius is much larger than the hair radius, there are no direct placement constraints on hairs which lie further away, so the odds of overlapping hairs are well approximated by the poisson distribution. (This is not true if the disk radius is not much larger than the hair radius, but in this case the density is probably very close to 1, by the assumption of equation 9, so the error is very small.)

Figure 3. Poisson-disk pattern of triangles scan-converted into a 512x512 grid. r = .1, l = 1.5

We have verified empirically that the poisson distribution

density model approximates a poisson-disk distribution's density quite closely when hairs are long relative to the distance between them. Figure 3 shows a poisson-disk distribution of identically oriented hairs with $l = 1.5$, $r_b = .2$, and $r_t = 0$ scan-converted into a 512x512 buffer of size 3.5. Poisson scatters of varying densities were similarly scan-converted and the resulting coverage α_f plotted against D. The results are shown in figure 4. The fur opacity function approaches 1 slightly more slowly than the empirical data, as expected, but the discrepancy is small, and narrows even further for longer hairs.

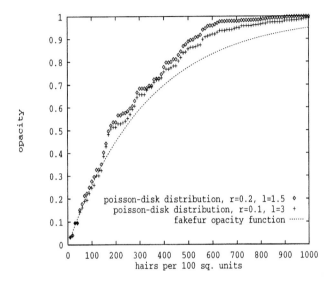

Figure 4. Fakefur opacity function compared to poisson-disk distribution densities.

4.2. Special Cases

There are two special cases which the above model does not consider.

The first special case is the 'hot_spot': the viewing vector $\overline{E}$ is close to the illumination vector $\overline{L}$. Because the shadows of hairs are almost entirely occluded from view by the hairs themselves, the overall brightness is greater than predicted by this model. This effect can be observed by looking at one's own shadow in a patch of grass on a sunny day. The area immediately surrounding the shadow, where the viewing and illumination vectors are very close, appears brighter than the rest of the grass.

The second special case is the 'halo': the viewing and illumination vectors are nearly opposite. In this case, the approximation of the fur layer as a flat surface and the use of shadow maps underestimates the strong transmission of light through the fur around the silhouette edges of the creature.

Although these are easily observed in the real world, such illumination environments are generally avoided by cinematographers: When frontlighting, it is common to offset the frontmost lights by several degrees from the camera axis, and when backlighting, lights are often placed above and out of frame to separate foreground and background without appearing unnatural. Therefore, we have not found these limitations to be of great practical concern for our usage.

5. RESULTS

The fakefur algorithm was used with resounding success to simulate the appearance of dog fur in live-action feature films [1][14]. The algorithm was implemented using the RenderMan shading language and PhotoRealistic RenderMan rendering software.

The color images below illustrates the degree of realism attainable with this technique. In figures 5 and 6., only the two adult dogs were filmed on location. All of the puppies in these two images are computer-generated models illuminated using only the fakefur method.[2]

The fakefur model was eventually used to render most of the computer-generated dalmatians featured in this film. Where additional detail and nonlocal effects were required in closeups, the 'realfur' hair renderer was employed. Figures 7 and 8 illustrate the close match that was achieved between the 'realfur' model and the probabilistic 'fakefur' model. Images were generated at a variety of scales to verify the similarity of appearance. Note in particular the specular sheen on the ears, the effect of high opacity along the silhouette edges, and the pinkness of the underlying skin showing through the thin coat of fur, which is itself colored a neutral off-white.

Although actual rendering times are highly dependent on hardware and software, the 'fakefur' images in figures 7 and 8 rendered about 6 times faster than the 'realfur' images on the same machines.

As shown in this plate, the two rendering techniques generate almost indistinguishable images at a sufficiently small scale. This allowed us to utilize both techniques in the same shots. In some cases, individual dalmatians were rendered using the fakefur method when distant from the camera, and using the realfur method as they approached (or vice versa). The dissolve between the two is essentially invisible.

6. FUTURE WORK

Some of the limitations of this work are fundamental, such as the lack of high-frequency detail. However, others are merely simplifications and could be improved with some additional work.

The constraint that hairs must be short is imposed in order to enforce locality of texture influence and to avoid geometry displacement away from the underlying surface. This constraint could be relaxed by convolving the hair parameters with a variable length and direction linear kernel [3] before applying them, and by including a displacement computation for the underlying surface.

The current hair-to-hair shadow formula could be made more accurate by extending the fur opacity function into three-dimensions, taking into account the change of hair radius and the bend of the hairs along their length.

The model has an unwieldy number of parameters. Although some may be determined by direct measurement, many must be assigned by trial and error. This allows considerable freedom for aesthetic considerations, but makes achieving a specific appearance somewhat cumbersome. In the future we hope to find ways of reducing the number of free parameters.

Although this model itself is applied here to a single breed of

[2]Color plates have been color-corrected to match photographic film response.

dog, it can be applied to any animal with reasonably short fur. The concepts underlying the fakefur model also show promise in creating effective lighting models for certain classes of fabrics.

7. ACKNOWLEDGEMENTS

The Dalmatian model shown here was created by Geoff Campbell, Kyle Odermatt, and Wayne Kennedy. Textures and hairstyles by Carol Hayden. The shots pictured in Color Plate I were animated by Mike Eames, John Campanaro, and Daniel Jeannette. Color Plate I.a. was lit and composited by Samir Hoon.

Thanks to Barry Armour, Gail Currey, Christian Rouet, Doug Smythe, Chrissie England, Jeff Yost, and Florian Kainz. Thanks also to the SIGGRAPH paper reviewers, whose insightful comments helped me close a number of holes.

Very special thanks to Jocelyn Lamm and Ellen Pasternack at ILM, and Mary Lippold at Disney Rights Administration, and to Disney for allowing some of the above images to appear in this paper.

8. REFERENCES

[1] *101 Dalmatians*, Walt Disney Studios 1996.

[2] Anjyo, Ken-Ichi, Yoshiaki Usami, and Tsuneya Kurihara, "A Simple Method for Extracting the Natural Beauty of Hair." In Edwin C. Catmull, editor, *Computer Graphics (SIGGRAPH 92 Conference Proceedings)*, volume 26, pages 111-120. Addison Wesley, July 1992. ISBN 0-89791-479-1.

[3] Cabral, Brian, and Leith Leedom, "Imaging Vector Fields Using Line Integral Convolution." In James T. Kajiya, editor, *SIGGRAPH 93 Conference Proceedings*, Annual Conference Series, pages 263-270. ACM SIGGRAPH, Addison Wesley, 1993. ISBN 0-89791-601-8.

[4] Cook, Robert L. and Kenneth Torrance, "A Reflectance Model for Computer Graphics," In *Computer Graphics (SIGGRAPH 81 Conference Proceedings)*, volume 15(3), pages 307-316. ACM SIGGRAPH, Addison Wesley, August 1981.

[5] Cook, Robert L., "Shade Trees." In *Computer Graphics (SIGGRAPH 84 Conference Proceedings)*, volume 18(3), pages 223-231. ACM SIGGRAPH, Addison Wesley, July 1984.

[6] Cook, Robert L., Tom Porter, and Loren Carpenter, "Distributed Ray Tracing." In *Computer Graphics (SIGGRAPH 84 Conference Proceedings)*, volume 18(3), pages 137-145. ACM SIGGRAPH, Addison Wesley, July 1984.

[7] Csuri, C., et al., "Towards an interactive high visual complexity animation system." In *Computer Graphics (SIGGRAPH 79 Conference Proceedings)*, volume 13(2), pages 289-299. ACM SIGGRAPH, Addison Wesley, August 1979.

[8] Duncan, Jodi. "The Island of Dr. Moreau: Moreau's Menagerie," *Cinefex* 68, pages 59-65, 123-124, and 142, December 1996.

[9] Glassner, Andrew S. *Principles of Digital Image Synthesis*, Morgan Kaufmann Publishers, 1995. ISBN 1-55860-276-3

[10] Hanrahan, Pat, and Wolfgang Krueger. "Reflection from Layered Surfaces due to Subsurface Scattering." In James T. Kajiya, editor, *SIGGRAPH 93 Conference Proceedings*, Annual Conference Series, pages 165-174. ACM SIGGRAPH, Addison Wesley, August 1993. ISBN 0-89791-601-8.

[11] *Jumanji*, Tri-Star Pictures, 1996.

[12] Kajiya, James T., and Timothy L.. Kay, "Rendering Fur with Three Dimensional Textures." In *Computer Graphics (SIGGRAPH 89 Conference Proceedings)*, volume 23(3), pages 271-277. ACM SIGGRAPH, Addison Wesley, July 1989. ISBN 0-89791-312-4.

[13] LeBlanc, André M., Russell Turner, and Daniel Thalmann, "Rendering Hair using Pixel Blending and Shadow Buffers," In *The Journal of Visualization and Computer Animation*, Vol 2, pages 92-96, 1991. ISSN 1049-8907

[14] *Mars Attacks*, Warner Brothers, 1996.

[15] Miller, Gavin S.P., "From Wire-Frames to Furry Animals.", In *Graphics Interface '88 Proceedings*, pages 138-145, 1988.

[16] Neyret, Fabrice. "A General And Multiscale Method For Volumetric Textures." In *Graphics Interface '95 Proceedings*, pages 83-91, May 1995.

[17] Peishel, Bob, "Feline Fabrication." *Cinefex* 56, November 1993, 17-18.

[18] Perlin, Ken, and Eric M. Hoffert, "Hypertexture." In *Computer Graphics (SIGGRAPH 89 Conference Proceedings)*. volume 23(3), pages 253-262. Addison Wesley, July 1989.

[19] Pourroy, Janine, "The Game Board Jungle." *Cinefex* 64, pages 54-71, December 1995.

[20] Rosenblum, Robert E., Wayne E. Carlson, and Edwin Tripp III, "Simulating the Structure and Dynamics of Human Hair: Modeling, Rendering, and Animation." In *The Journal of Visualization and Computer Animation*, volume 2, pages 141-148, 1991. ISSN 1049-8907

[21] Torrance, Kenneth, and E.M. Sparrow, "Theory for Off-Specular Reflection from Roughened Surfaces." In *Journal of the Optical Society of America*, volume 57(9), pages 1105-1114, September 1967.

[22] Westin, Stephen .H., James R. Arvo, and Kenneth E. Torrance, "Predicting Reflectance Functions from Complex Surfaces" In Edwin C. Catmull, editor, *Computer Graphics (SIGGRAPH 92 Conference Proceedings)*, volume 26(2), pages 255-264. Addison Wesley, July 1992.

[23] Williams, Lance, "Casting Curved Shadows on Curved Surfaces." In *Computer Graphics (SIGGRAPH 78 Conference Proceedings)*, volume 12(3), pages 270-274. Addison Wesley, August 1978.

[24] Yost, Jeffrey, "Fur Lighting Parameters", ILM internal memo, 1995.

Figure 5. A frame from the film *101 Dalmatians*. © Disney 1996, All Rights Reserved.

Figure 6. A frame from the film *101 Dalmatians*. © Disney 1996, All Rights Reserved.

Figure 7. Comparison of 'realfur' and 'fakefur' methods at different scales.

Figure 8. Comparison of 'realfur' and 'fakefur' methods at different scales.

A Model for Simulating the Photographic Development Process on Digital Images

Joe Geigel [*]
The George Washington University

F. Kenton Musgrave[+]
Digital Domain

ABSTRACT [*] [+]

In this paper we present a model for the simulation of the photographic development process for use on computer generated and other digital images. The model provides us with a tone reproduction operator based on photographic principles that mimics the creation process of black and white photographic prints. We focus on four characteristics of photographic materials: density response, spectral sensitivity, resolution and granularity. These characteristics are described quantitatively using empirical data thus making the simulation of the response of actual photographic materials a straight forward application of the model. The result of the simulation is a device independent image of floating point values between 0 and 1 which represent shades of gray on a linear scale. This image can be quantized for display on a given output device.

CR Categories and Subject Descriptions: I.3.3 [Computer Graphics]: Picture / Image Generation; I.3.7 [Computer Graphics]: Three-dimensional Graphics and Realism; I.4.9 [Image Processing] : Applications

Additional Keywords and Phrases: Photography, Tone Reproduction, Digital Effects, Post-processing, Simulation.

1 INTRODUCTION

Since its inception, one of the major goals of computer graphics has been the quest for photorealism in the synthesis of computer generated imagery. The field has utilized a photographic metaphor to achieve this goal where renderings are produced by following the path of visible radiation from a virtual scene, through a camera and onto a film plane. This process can be viewed as a large simulation problem, where the tracing of the light in the scene can be divided into the three stages: a simulation of the distribution and reflection of light within a scene, the capture and focus of this light by a camera model, and the translation of captured radiance values to quantized pixel values for producing a displayable image.

Over the past decade, a great deal of research in image synthesis has focused on the first stage. This research has resulted in a wealth of shading techniques, reflection models and illumination algorithms. Advances in the second stage have resulted in realistic camera models, far more sophisticated than original pinhole models, that are based on an accurate treatment of lens optics[1,2].

The rendering process is not complete, however, until the third stage is considered. The results produced by the first two stages provide us with representative illuminance values at each pixel, but give no indication of how these values should be interpreted or translated to produce an appropriate image. Taking an ad-hoc approach in this stage can lead to extremely misleading results especially in rendering scenes with different levels of contrast[3].

This third phase, known as the *tone reproduction problem*, involves the definition of a response function that converts representative illuminance values to appropriate tones for final display. Recent research efforts in this area have concentrated on simulating the response of the human visual system [3,4,5,6] (usually in conjunction with a given output device) thus faithfully reproducing how the eye would perceive a given virtual scene.

There are instances, however, where visual accuracy may not be the desired goal. Looking again to photography, the famed photographer Ansel Adams viewed photography as an expression not of what one sees, but instead, how one interprets what one sees. His philosophy of "artistic visualization" has the photographer mentally visualizing the final print based on what is seen and using the controls of photography to realize his or her vision.[7]

In this paper, we approach the tone reproduction problem by modeling the response of photographic materials. Such a model can provide the computer graphic artists with the means to interact with images using the same controls that photographers have learned to use so effectively. With the increased use of computer generated elements in images and film, this model also becomes essential in the seamless composition of computer graphic elements with real scenes recorded on film.

[*] current address: Eastman Kodak Company, Networked Image Technology Center, 1447 St. Paul Street, Rochester, NY 14626.
Email: **geigel@kodak.com**
[+] 300 Rose Avenue, Venice, CA 90274 Email: **musgrave@d2.com**

Although the mechanism of photographic image formation operates independently of the human visual system, photographic engineers have spent over a century designing photographic materials that have optimal response for human viewing, even under a variety of circumstances and viewing conditions (e.g. slide film is designed to take into effect the fact that the resultant image will be viewed in dark surroundings [8]). With a generalized photographic model, one will be able to take advantage of the knowledge derived from years of photographic film design and apply it to computer generated imagery.

Our model is designed to mimic the process by which actual photographs are created. As such, we rely heavily on the existing photographic process and on photographic data commonly available for existing photographic materials.   In order to clearly illustrate this process, we focus on the generation process of black and white positive prints. Although all photography is based on the same fundamental concepts, the discussions below are specific to black and white print photography. Issues regarding the extension of the model to color photography are discussed in Section 7.

Our paper proceeds with a summary of the process by which photographic prints are created. The photographic data used by the model is described in Section 3, followed by a full description of our model in Section 4. In Section 5, we provide some implementation details. We conclude by showing some results of the application of the model on computer generated images and by a giving a discussion of future work.

2 PHOTOGRAPHIC IMAGE FORMATION

Photographic images are the result of the chemical interaction of silver halide with radiant energy to produce metallic silver [9].

Photographic materials consist of microscopic silver halide grains embedded in a gelatin (*photographic emulsion*). When exposed to radiation, these grains undergo an invisible chemical change to form a *latent image*. This latent image becomes realized during the chemical development process, where fractions of grains adequately exposed to the radiation transform to metallic silver thus creating a visible density. The conversion from silver halide to metallic silver is a binary one (i.e. a grain is either silver halide or metallic sliver) with the threshold for the change being dependent upon the chemical developer used and the time of processing.

Both photographic film and photographic paper comprise an emulsion. In film, the emulsion is mounted in a transparent support, whereas, with paper, the emulsion is spread on a paper base.

2.1 Photographic Print Formation

In print photography (Figure 1), the illumination from a scene is captured by a camera and focused onto the plane of photographic film. Once processed, this film produces a negative image where dark areas represent regions of high illuminance. This negative is then placed into a printer/enlarger, where light is shown through

it onto photographic paper. The printing process acts as a second reversal procedure and re-establishes the relationship of light and dark that exists in the original scene. Once developed, the processed paper results in the final print.

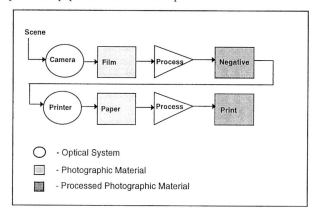

Figure 1 - Block diagram of the print photography process

2.2 Exposure and Density

In describing the response of photographic materials, a given emulsion is said to produce a *density* as a response to a given *exposure*.

Exposure is defined as the product of the irradiance incident upon the photosensitive surface (I) and the time during which the surface is exposed (t).

$$E = It \qquad (1)$$

Photographic exposure data is generally given in photometric rather than radiometric units. Photometric units take into account the response of human visual system by weighting the power at each wavelength by its corresponding value in the luminosity function[10].   In Equation 1 above, I is usually given as an illuminance value (in lumens/m^2 or lux) and exposure is given in lux-sec.

In cases where the incoming flux is a continuous spectral distribution, which is usually the case, the exposure is given by the integral:

$$E = \int E_\lambda d\lambda = \int I_\lambda t d\lambda \qquad (2)$$

where E_λ is the exposure at wavelength λ, I_λ is the illuminance at wavelength λ and t is the time of exposure.

The definition of exposure is concerned only with the product of illuminance by time, and does not discriminate between the contributions of the individual components. Because of the chemical nature of the process, this definition breaks down at very low values of I or t. This breakdown is known as the *reciprocity law failure* and must be considered when trying to capture low luminance scenes (as in the case of astronomical photography).

The measured response of a photographic material is given in density. Density is a unit less, logarithmic measure that indicates the opacity of an emulsion that results from processing.

Density comes in two flavors. Transmission density is used in describing the response of photographic film. It is defined as:

$$D_T = \log_{10} 1 / T \qquad (3)$$

where T is a transmission value, between 0 and 1, that gives the ratio of light transmitted through an emulsion to the quantity of light incident to it.

Reflective density, used for describing the response of photographic papers, indicates the quantity of light that is transmitted through the emulsion and reflected off the paper base. It is defined as:

$$D_R = \log_{10} 1 / R \qquad (4)$$

where R is the ratio of the light reflected off the paper base to the light incident to it.

3 SENSITOMETRY

The quality of an image is directly related to the quality of the emulsions that comprise the film and the photographic paper used in creating the image.   For over a century, photographic scientists have been concerned with the measurement and study of the response of photographic emulsions to radiant energy. This science, called *sensitometry*, provides us with empirical measures that can be used to quantify the characteristics of an emulsion [11]. In our analysis, we consider four characteristics of the emulsion: density response, spectral sensitivity, resolution, and granularity.

3.1 Density Response

On a macroscopic level, emulsions have a non-linear response to radiant energy. This relationship is customarily illustrated by an emulsion's *characteristic curve* (Figure 2), a plot that relates input exposure to output density.[1]

The gradient of the characteristic curve in its straight line section is an important characteristic of an emulsion as it defines the change in density due to a given change in log exposure. This measure, termed *gamma*, is analogous to gain measures in other display systems and acts as a gauge for the contrast range of an emulsion. It is important to note that although gamma measures the slope of the curve in its linear portion, it really describes the non-linearity of an emulsion's response as the characteristic curve is plotted on a log-log scale.[8] Recall that density is already a logarithmic measure.

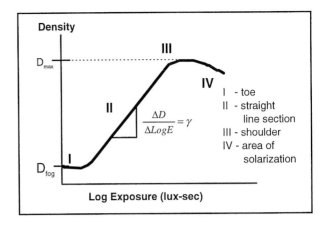

Figure 2 - A Typical Characteristic Curve

Sensitivity of an emulsion is indicated by its speed. A higher speed emulsion is more sensitive to light than a lower speed emulsion. Speed is defined as

$$SP = K / E_m \qquad (5)$$

where K is a constant and E_m represents the exposure necessary to produce a density of m units above the fog density. Current standards for the speed of photographic materials define $K = 0.8$ and $m = 0.1$ for photographic films [12], and $K = 1000$ and $m = 0.6$ and for photographic papers[13].

The density response of a processed emulsion depends not only on the nature of the emulsion, but on also development conditions (i.e. developer solution, temperature, time of development). Consequently, the shape and positioning of a characteristic curve, and thus its gamma, speed, and density scale , will also vary based on these conditions.

Note that for photographic papers, the density reported in the characteristic curve represents transmission density whereas with photographic papers, reflection density is recorded.

3.2 Spectral Sensitivity

Untreated, silver halide grains are only sensitive to the blue and ultraviolet wavelengths of the spectrum. Specially formulated dyes that extend the responses of the grains to longer wavelengths are injected into emulsions in order to the increase the spectral sensitivity to include the rest of the visible spectrum.

The spectral sensitivity of an emulsion is very often expressed by means of a *spectral response curve* which provides a measure of relative sensitivity of the emulsion to each wavelength in the spectrum.   Figure 3 shows the spectral response curves for three film types with different spectral sensitivities: panchromatic (sensitive to entire visible spectrum), orthochromatic (sensitive to green and blue light), and blue-sensitive (untreated).

---

[1] The characteristic curve is also known as the D-Log E curve or the H & D Curve (after Hurter and Driffield who introduced its use in 1890).

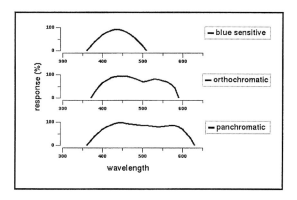

Figure 3 - Spectral response curves for three types of film with different spectral sensitivities (after [7])

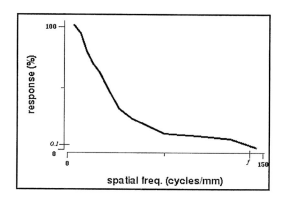

Figure 4 - Modulation Transfer Function (MTF) of a typical emulsion (after [15]).

3.3 Resolution

The resolution of an emulsion defines its ability to clearly reproduce the spatial detail of the scene being recorded on it. Internal scattering of light between the grains within an emulsion, causes a degradation of the recorded image. A point source ray of light incident to a film's surface, rather than producing a single transmitted ray, will instead produce a distribution of light. This distribution, termed the *point spread function (PSF)*, is instrumental in determining the resolution of an emulsion. Assuming the film to be isotropic, the point spread function is rotationally invariant.

The *line spread function, A(x)*, which is defined by:

$$A(x) = \int_{-\infty}^{\infty} PSF(x, y)\, dy \qquad (6)$$

gives the scattering response to an infinitesimal line of light. This function can be determined by measuring the response to a knife-edge exposure. Since most films can be considered isotropic, this function serves as a primary means for obtaining the PSF of an emulsion.

Although the macroscopic response of an emulsion is non-linear (as is evident by the characteristic curve), the internal scattering of light due to the microscopic grains can be modeled as a linear system and the response due to scattering determined by performing a convolution of the input image with the point spread function[14]. In the frequency domain, the effect of the scattering is given by the *modulation transfer function (MTF(ω))* which is the Fourier transform of the line spread function (Figure 4). The MTF can be determined directly from the line spread function, measured using the response of a sinusoidal exposure input, or calculated mathematically using Monte Carlo methods. [16]

A numerical measure for an emulsion's resolution is its resolving power. This measure, expressed in cycles/mm, is an estimate of the finest detail that can visibly be observed on the photographic material[17]. Its value can be roughly inferred from the MTF by determining the frequency at which the modulation transfer function falls to 0.1 (*f* in Figure 4).

3.4 Graininess and Granularity

Graininess is the visual perception of the non-uniformity in a uniformly exposed emulsion due to the random placements of the grains within it. Since grains in an emulsion are microscopic in nature, graininess for most emulsions is observable only upon magnification. The graininess becomes more apparent as the magnification of an exposed emulsion is increased.

The objective measure of graininess is called *granularity* and can be determined by examining the micro structure of an emulsion. Using the traces obtained a microdensitometer, fluctuations in density of a uniformly exposed emulsion can be measured and recorded. These measurements can be used to statistically model the grains within an emulsion and provide a measure for the granularity.

The *root mean square (rms)* deviation provides an indication of the uniformity of a sample and is obtained by computing the differences in density from a mean over an entire photographic sample. Assuming N independent sample points in a trace, the rms is calculated as:

$$\sigma^2 = \frac{1}{N} \sum_{i=1}^{N} (\Delta D_i)^2 \qquad (7)$$

where ΔD_i is the deviation from the density mean of the ith sample point.

Although the rms is a natural choice for a measure of granularity, it is ineffective as an absolute measure as its value depends upon the area of the aperture used in making the measurement. Selwyn developed a classic measure based on his observation that for large aperture areas (with respect to grain size), the product of the square root of the rms by the area of the aperture is constant. The *Selwyn granularity*, is given by:

$$G = \sqrt{(2A)}\,\sigma \qquad (8)$$

where A is the area of the scanning aperture and σ the square root of the rms density fluctuation.

Analysis of microdensitometer traces of many films has indicated that the density fluctuations of processed emulsions tend to follow a Gaussian distribution[15], although the above definitions hold for any probability distribution assumed.

Granularity, and as a result graininess, is also dependent on the density level of a sample. Experiments have shown granularity to be approximately proportional to the cube root of the density[11].

4 SIMULATION MODEL

In this section, we present our model for the photographic processing of photographic materials. The model is based on emulsion characteristics expressed using the sensitometric measures mentioned above.

Like the process described in Section 2.1, our full model is a two-step process whereby film development is simulated first, followed by a simulation of the printing process. In the summary below, we describe the simulation of the processing of a single photographic material, i.e. a single step of our full model. An image will have to run through the described process twice with the first run resulting in a virtual negative. This simulated negative is then used during the second simulation run which results in a simulated print.

In an attempt to base our model solely on reported photographic data, we assume ideal processing conditions and ignore adjacency effects[11] that may occur during processing. The H & D curves used by the simulation should be carefully chosen to reflect appropriate sets of processing conditions and materials.

The model is an extension of a computation model developed by Kelly[18] and is presented as a pipeline of image processing modules (Figure 5). Each module performs a given image processing operation and passes the result to the next module in the pipeline. The pipeline takes as input a color image where each pixel represents the illuminance values at given sample wavelengths as detected on the film plane. The pipeline can be separated into three stages.

During the first stage, the wavelength based illuminance values are converted to exposure values. This stage consists of three modules. The **expose** module converts the illuminance values to exposure by multiplying each pixel by a time value. This time parameter represents the amount of time the photographic material is exposed. After passing through this module, the image is still a color image with each color channel giving the exposure at a given sample wavelength. These color channels are merged in the **spectral sensitivity** module where the image is filtered by a spectral response curve and exposure integrated over the wavelengths to produce a single channel of exposure data per pixel. Resolution is modeled by the **internal scattering** module which makes use of an emulsion's MTF to spatially filter the image and approximate the effects of scattering due to grains within an emulsion.

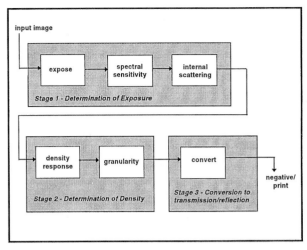

Figure 5 - Simulation pipeline for a single processing step

During the next stage of the pipeline, density values are determined. The **density response** module uses a characteristic curve to determine density from the exposure values calculated in the first stage. To simulate film grain, these density values are stochastically modulated using Gaussian noise in the **granularity** module. The deviation at each pixel is based upon a Selwyn Granularity value, the size and magnification of the image, and the density value at the pixel.

During the third and final stage, density values are converted to transmission values (for film) or reflection values (for papers) by the **convert** module. The conversion is done by directly applying the definitions of density as presented in Section 2.2.

After passing through the pipeline, the resulting image consists of floating point values between 0 and 1 that represent transmission or reflectance values. This is a convenient final format as it provides us with a device independent solution which can then be quantized for a given output device. The only caveat is that the output device will have to be adjusted to display these values on a photometric linear gray scale[8].

A table summarizing the various modules of the pipeline is given in Table 1.

5 IMPLEMENTATION

We have implemented our model into a system called the Virtual Darkroom (VDR). VDR takes a rendered image as input and allows for user specification of the parameters required by the simulation pipeline modules. Sensitometric curves are specified to the system as sampled functions with curve values between sample points determined by linear interpolation. These curves can be intuitively created using graphical input tools provided by VDR.

MODULE	PARAMS	OUTPUT UNITS	OUTPUT RANGE	RGB?
Input Image	--	lux/λ	10^{-3} - 10^4	Yes
Expose	time (sec)	lux-sec/λ	10^{-3} - 10^4	Yes
Spectral Sensitivity	spectral response curve	lux-sec	10^{-3} - 10^4	No
Internal Scattering	MTF	lux-sec	10^{-3} - 10^4	No
Density Response	H & D Curve	density	0 - 3	No
Granularity	Selwyn Granularity magn, size	density	0 - 3	No
Convert	--	trans or reflect	0 - 1	No

Table 1- Summary of Simulation Pipeline Modules

Implementing the model itself can be most easily performed using an image processing library that supports a rendering chain paradigm. Our initial implementation was written using the ImageVision library[19] and we are currently in the process of re-implementing the system using Java.

Physically based illuminance values are expected as input to the simulation pipeline. Certain renderers (such as RADIANCE[20]) will output these values. However, for images produced by renderers that do not, a conversion from the pixel values to illuminance values needs to be made. VDR performs a simple linear scaling from 0 to a user supplied maximum to make this conversion. (More sophisticated, non-linear mappings may be required if the image had been optimized for display on a particular output device such as a CRT[8]).

Similarly, the illuminance that falls on the surface of photographic paper during the printing process must also be estimated. Much like a camera, a printer/enlarger is a complex optical system whose properties highly affect the quality of the final print. VDR simplifies this estimation by using a simulated negative as a transparency map ignoring any optical effects that may occur during the printing process. The intensity and spectral distribution of the light source used in printing is supplied by the user.

Most renderers provide only three channels of color data per pixel (usually in RGB color space). VDR performs spectral filtering (as is required by the spectral sensitivity module) in XYZ color space, converting the spectral response curves to XYZ triplets and then using these XYZ components as scale factors for the corresponding spectrally dependent exposure values. Note that pixel values must also be converted to XYZ space. (See [10] for details on these conversion). The integration over the range of wavelengths is approximated by summing the results of the scaling operation.

6. RESULTS

In our examples, we focus on the effects due to the characteristics of the film. Representative data from data sheets of actual films are used. In all the examples, the paper being simulated uses data from a medium grade paper with gamma of 1.67 and speed of 250.

In figure 6, the effects of film speed on the contrast of the final image is illustrated. The original image is processed using data from films with speeds of 100, 200, and 400 with exposure time for each of the images remaining constant.

(a) Original image

(b) Simulated 100 speed film

(c) Simulated 200 speed film

(d) Simulated 400 speed film

Figure 6 - Effects of film speed

Figure 7 illustrates the effects of a film's spectral sensitivity on the final image. In this example, an artistic challenge is to properly expose the image as to maintain the brightness of the scene yet at the same time, emphasize the detail in the rocks. Attempts using a panchromatic, orthochromatic and untreated film are shown with exposure time chosen so that the mountain is properly exposed. Because of the extended spectral sensitivity in the panchromatic and orthochromatic films, it is difficult to capture the bright blue sky in its full brilliance without running the risk of overexposure of the mountain area. With the untreated, blue-sensitive film, this is not a problem since the majority of the film's sensitivity lies in the blue range of the spectrum. Increasing the exposure as to capture the detail in the rocks, an area to which the film is not very sensitive, will only result in the overexposure of the sky. When processed, the sky appears white in the final print, thus given a feeling of brilliance. This kind of image is indicative of many old time landscape photographs taken before the introduction of sensitizing dyes that extend the spectral sensitivity of an emulsion.

The effects of granularity are illustrated in Figure 8. The figure shows three magnifications of an image, all processed using the same granularity value. As the magnification of the image increases, the graininess in the image becomes more apparent.

(a) original scene   (b) Using panchromatic film

(c) Using orthochromatic film   (d) Using blue sensitive film

Figure 7 - Effects of spectral sensitivity

Using the MTF to model the resolution can be useful when degradation of an image is required (e.g. when compositing computer generated elements with existing photographic images.) The combination of MTF filtering and the addition of grain produces a more striking degradation which results in a more photographic look to computer generated imagery. Figure 9 shows a magnified portion of the image presented in Figure 8 processed with and without MTF filtering. The MTF used is exaggerated to illustrate the effect. Grain is added in Figure 9c to complete the simulated photographic look.

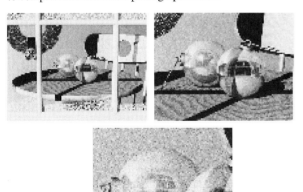

Figure 8 - Simulation of grain

7 CONCLUSION

We have presented a practical model for the simulation of photographic processing for use on digital images. The model makes use of empirical sensitometric data commonly reported

in film and paper data sheets, thus making the simulation of the response of actual photographic materials a straightforward exercise.

7.1 Discussion

The simulation model essentially describes a tone reproduction operator for digital images. It is not, however, meant as a replacement for other tone reproduction operators that are based on the response of the human visual system. The eye's response to light generally differs from that of photographic materials thus leading to different goals of the operators that mimic the response of each. In fact, taking Adams' idea of artistic visualization to an extreme, the tone reproduction operators that mimic the response of the eye should be used *in conjunction with* that which models photographic response. In this scenario, tone reproduction operators that mimic the response of the visual system can be used to generate a rendering of what a photographer *sees* when viewing a virtual scene, whereas the photographic model presented can be used to realize the photographer's artistic vision in the final print.

7.2 Future Directions

The natural next direction for this work would be to extend the model to color photography. Color photography, although based on the same fundamental principles, does provide an additional set of challenges. Photographic materials for color photography consists of three emulsion layers, each layer sensitive to different portions of the visible spectrum. During development, the silver is converted to dyes that acts as color filters that absorb red, blue, and green light.[21] As a result, the number of parameters needed to simulate the color development process will triple as each emulsion layer of the material will have its own unique set of sensitometric data associated with it. (Note that this is true not only for the spectral response and characteristic curves, as would be expected, but also for the resolution and granularity parameters)[9]. The simulation for producing color prints also provides an additional challenge as the inter-reflections of light between emulsion layers of color paper should be considered [21].

Although our model produces predictable results, we have no quantitative measure of its effectiveness in reproducing the photographic qualities of an image. The next step in our investigation will involve the validation of our model by both visually and computationally comparing a simulated print of a virtual scene with carefully created photographs of an equivalent real-world scene.

Our model and system assumes a priori knowledge of the photographic materials to be simulated. In practical situations where computer generated elements are composed with existing photographic images, the details of the film stock used is very often unknown. An interesting extension to this work would be a reversal of the model as to obtain the model parameter values from scanned negatives and prints. This is especially true with grain modeling as the accuracy of grain matching during compositing is critical in the creation of computer generated special effects for motion pictures. Our model considers each emulsion characteristic independently. However, when analyzing and modeling emulsions at the grain level, the interdependencies between the characteristics should be considered (see [14] for a complete treatment). Additional research in this area would prove to be a valuable addition to the model.

ACKNOWLEDGEMENTS

We would like to thank Price Pethel at Digital Domain for his insight into simulating grain, David Florek from the George Washington University for the generous use of his Christmas image, and the reviewers for their valuable comments. Joe would like offer a special thanks to Dr. David Deerfield II from the Pittsbugh Supercomputing Center for his support and encouragement during the early stages of this project, and the folks at Eastman Kodak's NITC for their help and support in the later stages.

REFERENCES

[1] C. Kolb, D. Mitchell, and P. Hanrahan, "A Realistic Camera Model for Computer Graphics", *Computer Graphics (SIGGRAPH '95 Proceedings),* pp 317-324, 1995.

[2] M.Potmesil and I. Chakravarty, "Synthetic Image Generation with a Lens and Aperture Camera Model", *ACM Transaction on Graphics*, 1(2), pp 85-108, April 1982.

[3] J. Tublin and H. Rushmeier, "Tone Reproduction for Realistic Images", *IEEE Computer Graphics and Applications*, 13(6), pp 42-48, November 1993.

[4] G. Ward, "A contrast-based scalefactor for luminance display" in P.S. Heckbert, ed, *Graphics Gems IV*, Academic Press Professional, 1994.

[5] J.A. Ferwerda, S.N. Pattanaik, P. Shirley, D.P. Greenberg, "A Model of Visual Adaptation for Realistic Image Synthesis*", Computer Graphics (SIGGRAPH '96 Proceedings)*, pp.249-258, 1996.

[6] G. Spencer, P. Shirley, K. Zimmerman, D.P. Greenberg, "Physically-based Glare Effects for Digital Images", *Computer Graphics (SIGGRAPH '95 Proceedings)*, pp 325-334, 1995

[7] A. Adams, *The Negative*, New York Graphic Society, 1981.

[8] C.A. Poynton, *A Technical Introduction to Digital Video*, John Wiley and Sons, 1996.

[9] T.H. James, ed*., The Theory of the Photographic Process, 4th Edition*, Macmillian, 1977

[10] G. Wyszecki and W.S. Styles, *Color Science - Concepts and Methods, Quantitative Data and Formulas* , John Wiley & Sons, 1967

[11] H.N. Todd and R.D. Zakia, *Photographic Sensitometry: The Study of Tone Reproduction, 2nd Ed.*, Morgan and Morgan, 1974.

[12] American National Standards Institute, "Method for Determining Speed of Photographic Negative Materials (Monochrome, Continuous-Tone)", ANSI Standard PH2.5-1979.

[13] American National Standards Institute, "Black and White Continuous Tone Papers - Determination of ISO Speed and ISO Range", ANSI Standard ANSI/NAPM IT2.2-1993.

[14] J.C. Dainty and R. Shaw, *Image Science: principles, analysis, and evaluation of photographic-type imaging processes*, Academic Press, 1974.

[15] J.H. Altman, "The Sensitometry of Black and White Materials", in T.H. James, ed*., The Theory of the Photographic Process, 4th Edition*, Macmillian, 1977

[16] J.J. DePalma and J. Gasper, "Determining the optical properties of photographic emulsions by the Monte Carlo method", *Photographic Science and Engineering*, 16(3), May/June, 1972.

[17] American National Standards Institute, "Determination of ISO Resolving Power", ANSI Standard PH2.33-1993.

[18] D.H. Kelly, "System Analysis of the Photographic Process. I. A Three-Stage Model", *Journal of the Optical Society of America*, 50(3), March,1960.

[19] Silicon Graphics, Inc, *ImageVision Library*, Silicon Graphics, Inc, Mountain View, CA,

[20] G. Ward, "The RADIANCE Lighting Simulation and Rendering System", *Computer Graphics (SIGGRAPH '94 Proceedings)*, pp 459-472.

[21] R.W.G. Hunt, *The Reproduction of Colour in Photography, Printing, and Television, 5th Ed.*, Fountain Press, 1995.

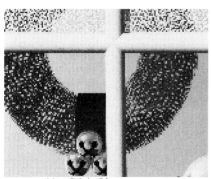

(a)   Original image

(b) Degraded using MTF filtering

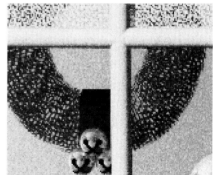
(c) Degraded using MTF filtering with grain

Figure 9 - Using the simulation model to degrade an image

A Model of Visual Masking for Computer Graphics

James A. Ferwerda, Cornell University *
Peter Shirley, University of Utah

Sumanta N. Pattanaik, Cornell University
Donald P. Greenberg, Cornell University

Abstract

In this paper we develop a computational model of visual masking based on psychophysical data. The model predicts how the presence of one visual pattern affects the detectability of another. The model allows us to choose texture patterns for computer graphics images that hide the effects of faceting, banding, aliasing, noise and other visual artifacts produced by sources of error in graphics algorithms. We demonstrate the utility of the model by choosing a texture pattern to mask faceting artifacts caused by polygonal tesselation of a flat-shaded curved surface. The model predicts how changes in the contrast, spatial frequency, and orientation of the texture pattern, or changes in the tesselation of the surface will alter the masking effect. The model is general and has uses in geometric modeling, realistic image synthesis, scientific visualization, image compression, and image-based rendering.

CR Categories: I.3.0 [Computer Graphics]: General;

Keywords: visual perception, masking, image quality, error metrics

1 Introduction

In "A Framework for the Analysis of Error in Global Illumination Algorithms", Arvo et. al. [1994] introduce a taxonomy for classifying sources of error in realistic image synthesis. They define three categories of error: errors in the input data caused by limitations in measurement or modeling; discretization errors introduced when analytical functions are replaced by finite-dimensional linear systems that can be computed; and computational errors that occur because the numerical precision of calculations is limited.

These errors can produce visual artifacts in synthetic images. *Faceting* due to tesselation of curved surfaces, *banding* caused by quantization, *aliasing* due to insufficient sampling, and *noise* introduced by stochastic methods are all well known visual consequences of error in computer graphics algorithms. For many years graphics practitioners have observed that visual texture can mask these image artifacts.

---

*Program of Computer Graphics, 580 Rhodes Hall, Cornell University, Ithaca, NY 14853, USA. http://www.graphics.cornell.edu.

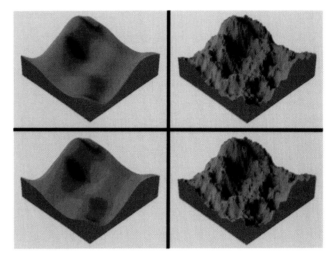

Figure 1: Masking in computer graphics: The upper pair of images are quantized to 8 bits. The lower pair are quantized to 4 bits. Banding is visible in the smooth surface on the lower left but not in the rough surface on the lower right due to masking effects from the visual texture created by the rough surface. From [Bolin95].

A recent example is shown in Figure 1 where banding due to quantization is much more apparent in the smooth surface on the left than in the rough surface on the right. Here the visual texture produced by the rough surface masks the banding artifact. With few exceptions [Bolin95, Mitchell87], the effects of masking have been applied in an ad hoc manner with unpredictable results.

Masking is a robust perceptual phenomenon that has been studied for more than 30 years by physiologists and psychologists. Masking was first observed in auditory perception [Fletcher52] but analogues in the visual domain were soon discovered [Campbell66, Pantle69]. Figure 2 from a classic study by Harmon and Julesz [1973] illustrates the characteristics of visual masking.

A continuous tone photograph of Abraham Lincoln was low-pass filtered to 10 cycles/picture height and then coarsely sampled and quantized to produce the image shown in Figure 2a. Notice how this processing seriously disturbs our ability to recognize the subject. If this blocky image is once again low pass filtered as in Figure 2b, recognition is restored. Thus it first appears that the image discontinuities introduced by high spatial frequencies in the block edges interfere with recognition. However Harmon and Julesz showed that it is not simply high frequencies that disturb recognition, but frequencies adjacent to the picture spectrum. They termed this *critical band masking*. Thus in Figure 2c where spatial frequencies above 40 cycles have been removed, the block edges are softened but recognition is still difficult. However in Figure 2d where frequencies between 12 and 40 cycles have been removed, the block edges are still apparent, but the subject is identifiable. This shows that masking is caused by interactions within a limited spatial frequency band because removal of a critical band of frequencies directly adjacent to the picture's 10 cycle spectrum limit eliminates the masking effect but removal of higher frequencies does not.

In this paper we develop a computational model of visual masking derived from psychophysical experiments. The model predicts how the presence of one visual pattern affects the detectability of another. The model is general and has uses in geometric modeling, realistic image synthesis, scientific visualization, image compression, and image-based rendering. We demonstrate the utility of the model by predicting when a texture pattern will mask visual artifacts caused by tesselation of a flat-shaded curved surface. The model takes into account how changes in the contrast, spatial frequency, and orientation of the texture pattern, or changes in the tesselation of the curved surface will alter the masking effect.

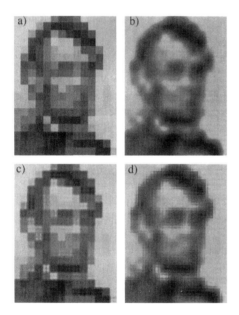

Figure 2: Demonstration of critical band masking. From [Harmon73].

2 Spatial Vision

Spatial vision is the field of psychology that studies of how patterns of light on the retina are interpreted by the visual system. The goal of the research in spatial vision is to understand the visual mechanisms that transform the patterns of light in the retinal image into the colors, sizes, shapes, locations, and motions of the three-dimensional objects we perceive in the world around us. The field has a long tradition which draws on both *physiological* studies of the electrical responses of cells in the visual pathways of primates and lower animals, as well as on *psychophysical* studies of the responses of human observers to simple visual stimuli.

2.1 Physiological foundations of spatial vision

One of the most fundamental physiological findings in the field of spatial vision is that the rod and cone photoreceptors which transduce light into electrical impulses in our nerve

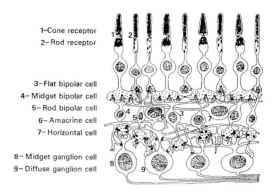

Figure 3: Neural networks in the primate retina: The rod and cone photoreceptors synapse on a variety of cells in the plexiform layers of the retina. These cells form networks which comprise the receptive fields of the retinal ganglion cells whose axons make up the optic nerve. From [Dowling66].

fibers are not independent of one another but interact in various ways. Figure 3 shows a diagram of a cross section through the retina. Amacrine, bipolar, and horizontal cells form neural networks in the plexiform layers of the retina that synapse on ganglion cells whose axons make up the optic nerve.

2.1.1 Receptive fields

To understand the properties of these neural networks, Kuffler [1953] made electrophysiological measurements of the responses of retinal ganglion cells in the cat. He found that each ganglion cell took its input from a spatially localized region of the retina called its *receptive field*.

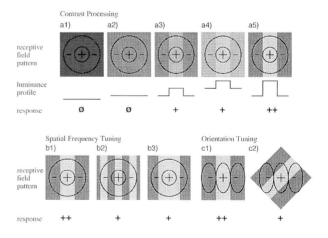

Figure 4: Properties of visual system receptive fields: (a) contrast processing; (b) spatial frequency tuning; (c) orientation tuning.

Kuffler found that these receptive fields had a characteristic center/surround organization with antagonism between the center and surround. Center/surround antagonism in receptive fields results in ganglion cells that respond primarily to contrast rather than to simple light intensity. This is illustrated in Figure 4a which shows the response of an idealized ganglion cell to various types of stimuli. In the dark, (Figure 4a1) the ganglion cell fires spontaneously at its base rate.

If the intensity of light falling on the ganglion cell's receptive field is raised uniformly, (Figure 4a2) the excitatory and inhibitory regions of the field cancel and the cell continues to fire at its base rate. If however, a bar pattern is introduced with contrast between the bar and the background (Figure 4a3), the excitation produced by the center will exceed the inhibition produced by the surround and the cell will increase its firing rate. Figures 4a4 and 4a5 show that the cell's response depends upon the contrast of the pattern rather than it's absolute intensity. In Figure 4a4 the luminance of the bar and background have both increased, but the cell continues to give the same response. However when the contrast between the bar and background is increased, (Figure 4a5) the response goes up as well.

Researchers have also found that different ganglion cells have receptive fields of different sizes and that these receptive fields overlap in the retina so that at any retinal location receptive fields of many sizes can be found.

2.1.2 Spatial tuning in receptive fields

Enroth-Cugell and Robson [1966] measured the response properties of retinal ganglion cells in the cat to sinusoidal grating patterns of different spatial frequencies. They found that the cells responded to limited ranges of spatial frequencies related to the sizes of their receptive fields. This spatial frequency selectivity of ganglion cell receptive fields is illustrated in Figure 4b.

The receptive field of the idealized ganglion cell has an excitatory center and inhibitory surround. If the receptive field is illuminated with the grating pattern shown in Figure 4b1 where the spatial frequency of the grating is such that the bars match the widths of the center and surround, there will be significant excitation from the center and not much inhibition from the surround so the cell will respond near its maximum rate. If however, we raise or lower the grating's spatial frequency as shown in Figures 4b2 and 4b3 there will be both less excitation from the center, and more inhibition from the surround so the cell will respond at a lower rate. The *spatial frequency tuning* of a cell depends upon the size of its receptive field. Cells with small receptive fields will respond to high ranges of spatial frequencies. Cells with larger fields will respond to lower ranges.

Although early studies focused on the response properties of cells in the retina, as more sophisticated electrophysiological techniques became available researchers began to investigate higher levels in the visual system including the visual cortex. These studies found that the receptive field organization first seen in the retina is in evidence throughout the visual system.

2.1.3 Orientation tuning in receptive fields

Hubel and Wiesel [1962,1968] did electrophysiological studies of cells in the visual cortex of the cat and monkey, mapping the properties of cortical receptive fields. They found that many cells responded maximally to patterns at a particular orientation and that response declined rapidly as the pattern was tilted away in either direction. Figure 4c1 shows an idealized receptive field for a cortical cell. The receptive field still has an antagonistic center surround organization, but the field is elongated in a particular direction. This elongation of the field accounts for the cell's orientation selectivity. If a grating pattern of the right spatial frequency and orientation stimulates the cell's receptive field then there will be significant excitation and little inhibition and the cell will respond maximally. However, if the orientation of the

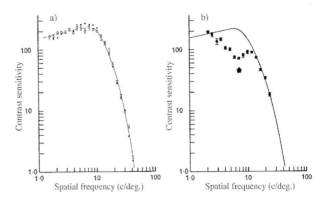

Figure 5: (a) The contrast sensitivity function of subject F.W.C.: Patterns were sine-wave gratings. Mean luminance of the gratings was 100 cd/m^2. Contrast sensitivity is plotted on a logarithmic scale against spatial frequency. Filled and open symbols show two independent measurements on the same subject. (b) Contrast sensitivity function for F.W.C. after adaptation to a sine-wave grating of 7.1 cpd. Note the depression in sensitivity in the spatial frequency band near the adapting frequency. Adapted from [Blakemore69].

grating is changed as in Figure 4c2 then there will be a mix of excitation and inhibition and the response will be reduced. Thus the cell exhibits *orientation tuning*.

2.2 Psychophysics of Spatial Vision

Given the physiological evidence for visual mechanisms in animals selective for contrast, spatial frequency, and orientation, psychophysicists began to test for the existence of similar mechanisms in human vision.

2.2.1 Contrast processing

The psychophysical evidence for contrast processing mechanisms in human vision has a long history going back at least as far as Mach [Ratliff65] who suggested that *lateral inhibition* could account for the bright and dark bands seen at discontinuities in luminance profiles, and Hering who proposed in his *opponent process theory* that antagonism between visual mechanisms was a fundamental principle of color and lightness perception and could explain such visual phenomena as simultaneous contrast and color constancy (see [Hurvich81] for a review). Modern psychophysical evidence for these mechanisms comes from the work of Campbell and Robson [1968] who measured the *contrast sensitivity function* of human vision for sine wave gratings of different spatial frequencies.

Campell and Robson tested contrast thresholds for sine wave gratings over a range of spatial frequencies and plotted the contrast sensitivity function shown in Figure 5a. In the fovea, at the luminance level tested, contrast sensitivity peaks for a pattern of 4-5 cycles/degree where a contrast of 0.5% can be detected. The graph shows that threshold contrast sensitivity declines for both higher and lower spatial frequencies.

2.2.2 Spatial frequency tuning

As was shown in the previous section, the receptive field organization of visual processing in cats and primates leads to

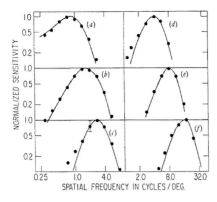

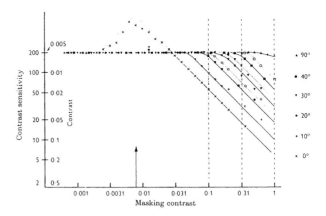

Figure 6: Model of spatial frequency tuned mechanisms in the human visual system: Points show mean data from three subjects on the spatial frequency tuning of six visual mechanisms. The curves show difference-of-Gaussian (DOG) function fits to the data for each mechanism. Mechanisms a-f are arranged in order of increasing peak spatial frequency. Each curve is plotted on a normalized sensitivity scale. Note that the spatial frequency scales in the right and left halves of the figure are different. From [Wilson84].

Figure 7: Orientation tuned mechanisms in the human visual system: Curves show contrast sensitivity for a vertical sine-wave test grating as a function of the contrast of a masking grating. Individual curves show how the orientation of the masking grating modulates the masking effect. Note that the magnitude of masking diminishes with the angular difference between the masking and test gratings. The anomalous data seen at low contrasts of the 0° masker is a *facilitation* effect that will be described in a later section. From [Campbell66].

visual mechanisms that are tuned to different ranges of spatial frequencies. Blakemore and Campbell [1969] conducted a series of psychophysical experiments to see if frequency tuned mechanisms exist in human vision.

They used an *adaptation* paradigm in their experiments. Prior to the experiment they measured the subject's contrast sensitivity function. They then had the subject inspect a grating pattern of a particular spatial frequency for one minute, instructing the subject to move their eyes constantly to avoid afterimages. They then re-measured the subject's contrast sensitivity function. Their results are shown in Figure 5b.

Contrast sensitivity is depressed for spatial frequencies close to the adapting frequency. The loss of sensitivity is greatest at the adapting frequency, but sensitivity is also depressed for spatial frequencies within a 2 octave band around the adapting frequency. Frequencies outside of this range are unaffected.

Wilson and Gelb [1984] performed a set of related experiments on spatial frequency discrimination to estimate the spatial frequency tuning of visual mechanisms in the fovea. Their *multiple mechanism* model illustrated in Figure 6 has six spatial frequency tuned mechanisms with different peak frequencies and spatial bandwidths. While there is ongoing debate about the number, peak frequencies, and bandwidths of spatially tuned mechanisms in human vision (see [Wilson91] for a review), the number of mechanisms in this model and their tuning parameters were derived by fitting experimental data and therefore provide a good account of actual visual performance.

2.2.3 Orientation tuning

A similar pattern of results can be found from psychophysical experiments testing the orientation tuning of human visual mechanisms. Campbell and Kulikowski [1969] used a *masking* paradigm to measure contrast sensitivity for a test grating in a vertical orientation, superimposed on a background grating which varied in orientation. Their results are shown in Figure 7.

When the test and background gratings have the same orientation (indicated by the x's in the 0° curve) sensitivity for the test grating drops in direct proportion to the suprathreshold contrast of the background grating. The apparent enhancement in sensitivity at low background contrasts is a *facilitation* effect that will be described in the following section on visual masking.

When the test and background gratings have different orientations, the drop in contrast sensitivity is a function of the angle between the gratings. The greater the angle between the gratings the less effect the background grating has on sensitivity for the test grating. This is indicated by the parallel curves in Figure 7 which show that as the angle between the gratings is increased, higher and higher background contrasts are needed to produce the same reduction in contrast sensitivity.

Phillips and Wilson [1984] performed a related set of experiments to determine the orientation tuning of human visual mechanisms at different spatial frequencies. The test pattern was a spatially localized grating patch superimposed upon a background grating that varied in orientation. Figure 8 shows the orientation tuning half-bandwidths of the visual mechanisms at different spatial frequencies. The results show that the visual system is more tightly tuned to orientation at high spatial frequencies than at low spatial frequencies. At a spatial frequency of 0.5 cycles/degree the orientation bandwidth of the visual system is approximately 60° (half-bandwidth × 2) and at 11 cycles/degree it has narrowed to approximately 30°.

2.3 Visual masking

The visual mechanisms described above are selective for bands of spatial frequencies and orientations. Interactions between image components within these bands result in masking effects like the ones illustrated in Figures 1 and 2 where the visual response to one component depends upon the presence of other components. The parameters of these masking effects were investigated by Legge and Foley [1980].

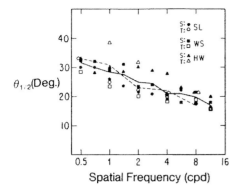

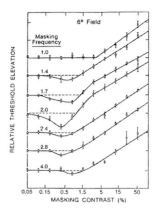

Figure 8: Bandwidth estimates of orientation-tuned mechanisms in the human visual system. The data shows the 50% amplitude, half-bandwidths of orientation-tuned visual mechanisms at different spatial frequencies. Different symbols are used for each of the three subjects. The filled symbols are for sustained presentations. The open symbols are for transient presentations. The solid line runs through the average half-bandwidth value at each spatial frequency. The dashed line compares these results to physiological data from primates [DeValois82]. Note that the orientation bandwidths of the mechanisms become progressively narrower with increasing spatial frequency. From [Phillips84].

Figure 9: Facilitation and threshold elevation due to masking: Curves show contrast thresholds for a 2.0 cycle/degree sine-wave grating as a function of the masking grating contrast. The individual curves show the results for different spatial frequency masks. Each curve is plotted on its own arbitrary scale. The dotted line through each curve indicates the unmasked threshold for the 2.0 cycle/degree test grating. Note that the curves show a pattern of facilitation or increased sensitivity at low mask contrasts and threshold elevation at higher mask contrasts. From [Legge80].

They performed a series of experiments to determine how the presence of one grating affects the detectability of another. The first grating is called the *mask* and the other is the *test*. Their test grating was a sine-wave grating of 2.0 cycles/degree. The masks were phase-coherent sine-wave gratings that ranged in frequency from 1.0 to 4.0 cycles/degree. They measured the threshold contrast necessary to detect the test grating while varying the contrast and spatial frequency of the mask. Their results are shown in Figure 9.

The individual curves show the results for each mask frequency. Each curve is plotted on its own vertical scale showing in arbitrary units, the relative threshold elevation produced by the mask at different mask contrasts. The general form of the results is that very low mask contrasts have no significant effect on the detectability of the test grating, but as the mask contrast is increased, at first the threshold drops showing increased sensitivity or *facilitation* and then rises again showing a loss in sensitivity or *threshold elevation* for high contrast masks. The shape of the threshold elevation curve is evidence of a contrast nonlinearity in the visual system caused by masking. This contrast nonlinearity is an accelerating function at low mask contrasts and a compressive function at higher mask contrasts.

The curves in Figure 9 also shows the spatial frequency tuning of visual masking. Threshold elevation is greatest when the mask and test gratings have the same spatial frequency. As the spatial frequencies of the mask and test become different greater and greater mask contrasts are necessary to produce the same threshold elevation. The effects of orientation tuning on masking can be understood in a similar way.

2.4 Extensions to color

There is now substantial physiological and psychophysical evidence for *spectrally-tuned opponent mechanisms* in color vision [Hurvich81]. The evidence supports a description of color vision in terms of the responses of an *achromatic chan-*

nel and two *chromatic channels*, one tuned to a red/green dimension and the other to a yellow/blue dimension. If we want to predict masking effects in complex color images we need to correctly model masking in both the chromatic and achromatic visual channels.

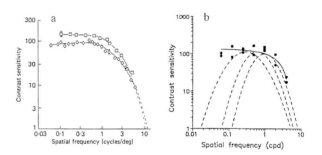

Figure 10: (a) Chromatic contrast sensitivity functions: The curves show contrast sensitivity as a function of spatial frequency for red/green (□ 602, 526nm) and yellow/blue (◇ 470, 577nm) isoluminant sine-wave gratings. From [Mullen85]. (b) Bandpass chromatic mechanisms underlying the chromatic CSF. The solid line shows the average contrast sensitivity data from three subjects for a red/green grating. The dashed curves show Gaussian fits to the average spatial frequency tuning functions measured in the experiments. Peak frequencies are 0.25, 0.5 and 1 cpd. The sensitivities of the mechanisms have been adjusted to fit the shape of the CSF. From [Losada94].

Mullen [1985] measured the contrast sensitivity function of the chromatic channels. The results are shown in Figure 10a. The separate curves show the results for red/green and yellow/blue gratings. Several differences between these *chromatic* CSF's and the *achromatic* CSF shown in Figure 5a should be noted. First, the chromatic CSF's have a low-pass frequency characteristic unlike the bandpass nature of the achromatic CSF. Second, the high frequency cutoff is approximately 11 cycles/degree rather than more than 30 for the comparable achromatic CSF. This means that the chromatic channels have much lower spatial resolution than the achromatic channel. Finally, the absolute sensitivity of the chromatic channels is lower than that of the achromatic channel except at very low spatial frequencies.

Losada and Mullen [1994] measured the spatial frequency tuning of the red/green chromatic channel. The results are shown in Figure 10b. The three bandpass mechanisms shown provide a good fit to the psychophysically measured chromatic CSF.

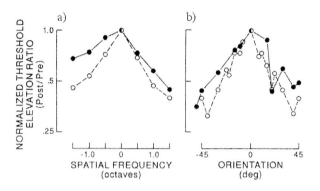

Figure 11: Normalized tuning functions for the achromatic and chromatic channels: (a) Spatial frequency tuning. Tuning is measured in octaves (doubling of spatial frequency). Open circles are for the achromatic channel, filled circles are for the red/green chromatic channel. (b) Orientation tuning. Tuning is measured in degrees. In both cases note the similarity between the tuning characteristics of the achromatic and chromatic channels. From [Bradley88].

Bradley [1988] has shown that the absolute spatial frequency and orientation tuning of the chromatic channels is broader than the achromatic channel, however when this data is normalized for contrast sensitivity differences between the channels, the relative spatial frequency and orientation tuning of the channels is very similar. This is shown in Figure 11. This allows us to use same spatial frequency and orientation tuned mechanisms for both the chromatic and achromatic channels in our masking model. Of course the scaling factors will be different to fit their respective CSF's.

Finally to predict masking effects in color images we must consider interactions between the chromatic and achromatic channels. Switkes [1988] found an asymmetric relationship between luminance masking and chromatic masking for sinewave grating patterns. While luminance masks can facilitate detection of chromatic test gratings, high contrast chromatic masks raise thresholds for luminance test gratings. However, Gegenfurther [1992] failed to find significant cross-channel effects for sine-wave gratings presented in chromatic and achromatic noise. Given the lack of consistent data on cross-channel effects we have decided to model only in-channel masking effects which should provide good results except for pathological cases.

3 Computational Model of Visual Masking

We will now draw on the physiological and psychophysical evidence outlined in the previous sections to develop a computational model of visual masking. Our goal is to create an algorithm that can predict when a texture will mask visual artifacts in a synthetic image.

Figure 12 illustrates our approach. To determine the visibility of image artifacts we take a *reference* image and a *test* image containing artifacts. The images are processed through the masking model. The model contains four stages. In the first stage the spectral radiances in the images are transformed into responses in an opponent color space to produce a *color representation*. In the next stage this color representation is decomposed into a *pattern representation* that accounts for the sensitivities of the spatial frequency and orientation tuned mechanisms in the visual system. In the third stage an appropriate *masking function* is applied to each visual mechanism to account for masking effects between the image components contained within a mechanism's sensitive band. Finally the responses of the mechanisms are compared in the *detection model* to determine when the artifacts will be visible and when they will be masked.

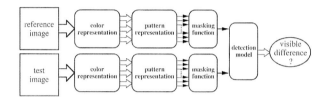

Figure 12: Components of the masking model.

3.1 Color representation

Figure 13 illustrates how the color representation is formed. At the first stage, the spectral irradiance at each point in the retinal image is encoded into the responses of three different classes of cone photoreceptors sensitive to long (L), middle (M) and short (S) wavelength ranges of visible light. The response (R) of each cone is calculated as a nonlinear function (Γ) of the effective light absorption by the cone, where the effective light absorption is given by the light spectrum $I(\lambda)$, times the cone's spectral sensitivity, $S(\lambda)$, and integrated over the wavelength range. Thus we have,

$$R_j = \Gamma \left(\int_{380nm}^{780nm} I(\lambda)S_j(\lambda)d\lambda \right),$$

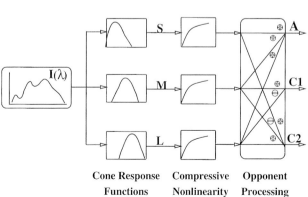

Cone Response Functions **Compressive Nonlinearity** **Opponent Processing**

Figure 13: Color representation.

where j = S, M, or L. The function Γ is normally chosen to be a compressive nonlinearity, e.g., a square root, or a logarithm (which yields Weber's law behaviour [Wilson91]).

At the next stage, the cone responses are transformed by opponent mechanisms. This opponency results in a color representation that can be described in terms of the signals in an achromatic channel and two chromatic channels. This model is based on work by Bolin [1995] and Meyer [1988].

3.2 Pattern representation

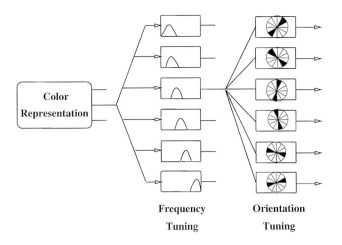

Figure 14: Pattern representation.

As was discussed in detail in earlier sections, the visual system processes spatial patterns with mechanisms tuned to various ranges of frequencies and orientations. The achromatic and chromatic representations of the image undergo transformation by each of these mechanisms and give rise to the pattern representation. Figure 14 illustrates this process.

To implement a model of these mechanisms, we need to choose a particular set of mechanism response functions. A number of mathematical functions such as Gabor functions [Marcelja80], Cortex transforms [Watson87], and differences-of-Gaussians (DOGs) [Marr82] have been proposed to emulate these mechanisms. While all of these functions have been used to model visual processing, and some like the Cortex transform offer greater computational efficiency, we have chosen to use the DOG functions defined by [Wilson84] because they provide an accurate quantitative fit to both physiological and psychophysical data.

Figure 6 shows the normalised response curves for these functions. The expression for the corresponding visual filter functions is:

$$\mathcal{RF}_i = A_i \left[e^{-x^2/\sigma_{x1i}^2} - B_i e^{-x^2/\sigma_{x2i}^2} + C_i e^{-x^2/\sigma_{x3i}^2} \right] e^{-y^2/\sigma_{yi}^2} \tag{1}$$

where x, y are spatial positions in foveal degrees. Different scalings of the gaussians provide filters tuned to different spatial frequencies.

The parameter, A_i, in the equation determines the gain of each mechanism which varies with adaptation and chromatic conditions. Since the psychophysically measured CSF is the envelope of these mechanism gains, by determining the chromatic and achromatic CSF's for our display conditions we can compute the appropriate A_i's. CSF data were generated from the equations given in [Martin92]. We computed the A_i's by least-squares fits to this data.

To account for the orientation tuning of the mechanisms, the filters are used with rotated coordinates. The data given in Figure 8 was used to determine the orientation bandwidths of the mechanisms which range from approximately 60° (for low frequencies) to 30° (for high frequencies). These differences in orientation tuning mean that the number of orientation channels in the pattern representation is different for each mechanism.

Given a visual mechanism $\mathcal{RF}$ with spatial frequency tuning i and orientation tuning θ, the sensitivity of this mechanism to a pattern $I(x', y')$ is given by the expression:

$$S_{i,\theta} = \int_{-\infty}^{+\infty} \int_{-\infty}^{+\infty} \mathcal{RF}_{i,\theta}(x - x', y - y') I(x', y') dx' dy'. \tag{2}$$

3.3 Masking function

If the visual system behaved in a linear fashion then it would be possible to predict the appearance of an image directly from the mechanism sensitivities $S_{i,\theta}$ given in equation 2. However, the response (R) of each mechanism is nonlinear due to masking interactions among the spatial frequency components within the mechanism's sensitive band. Wilson [1984] developed the following expression to take these nonlinearities into account in determining the responses of each mechanism in the pattern representation.

$$R_{i,\theta} = R(S_{i,\theta}) = \frac{S_{i,\theta}^2 + K_i S_{i,\theta}^{3-\epsilon_i}}{K_i + S_{i,\theta}^2} \tag{3}$$

In this expression $R_{i,\theta}$ is the response of the (i, θ)-th mechanism to an input pattern. $S_{i,\theta}$ is the mechanism's sensitivity given by equation 2. K_i is given by

$$K_i = 1/H_i(1 - \epsilon_i) \tag{4}$$

and H_i and ϵ_i are empirically derived constants specific to each mechanism that Wilson [1984] determined by fitting the expression to the results of masking experiments performed by [Nachmias74].

3.4 Detection model

Given the mechanism responses we can determine how detectable artifacts in the test image will be. If we neglect response variability for the moment then the responses to two identical images should be the same. Artifacts in one of the images should result in differences in the responses. For each mechanism this difference can be described by:

$$\Delta R_{i,\theta} = | R_{i,\theta}(\text{Image}_1) - R_{i,\theta}(\text{Image}_2) | \tag{5}$$

where $R_{i,\theta}(\text{Image}_1)$ and $R_{i,\theta}(\text{Image}_2)$ are the responses of the (i, θ)-th mechanism to each of the images.

These differences can be used to determine how visible the artifacts will be by the following formula:

$$\Delta R = \left[\sum_i \sum_\theta \Delta R_{i,\theta}^Q \right]^{\frac{1}{Q}} \tag{6}$$

In this formulation each image is represented as a point in a multidimensional response space and the visibility of artifacts in the test image is related to the distance between the reference and test images in this space. This model is essentially similar to the classic line-element model for color discrimination developed by Stiles [1978]. However in this case the metric is based on differences in the responses of the spatial frequency and orientation tuned mechanisms in the pattern representation. Choosing a value of 2.0 for Q gives the response space a Euclidean distance metric which has been shown to provide a good fit to experimental data on pattern discrimination [Wilson84].

Finally, there is variability in visual response due to noise within the visual mechanisms as well as uncertainty in the observer's decision making processes. These effects can be modeled by the *psychometric function* [Graham89], which in this case relates the distance between the reference and test images in the response space, to the likelihood that the images will be discriminable. The psychometric function is given by:

$$P(\Delta R) = 1 - 2^{-(1+k\Delta R)^3} \qquad (7)$$

The constant k has been given a value of 0.2599, to scale the function so that a ΔR value of 1.0 corresponds to $P = 0.75$, the standard threshold value for discrimination in a two-alternative forced choice (2AFC) task [Wilson91].

3.5 Applying the masking model

To demonstrate the utility of the masking model we applied the model in an algorithm to predict how masking provided by a texture map affects the visibility of shading artifacts caused by polygonal tesselation of a curved surface. The results are shown in Figure 15.

(a1) shows the flat-shaded approximation to the cylinder used in the first three rows of the figure. We examined how three aspects of the texture: its contrast, spatial frequency spectrum, and orientation, affected masking and the visibility of the artifacts. We generated synthetic textures for our study using Perlin's [1989] texture synthesis algorithm.

Row (a) shows how masking is affected by the contrast of the texture map. The texture contrast increases from left to right. Faceting is visible at the lower contrasts shown in (a2) and (a3) but not at the higher contrasts shown in (a4) and (a5).

Row (b) shows how masking is affected by the relationship between the spatial frequency components of the cylinder's luminance profile and the texture map. Since masking only occurs within limited frequency bands, high frequencies will not mask low frequencies and vice-versa. Thus we expect masking to occur only when the texture frequencies and facet frequencies are similar, and this can be observed in the figure. At each end of the row where the spatial frequencies of the texture and the spatial frequencies due to the faceting are very different, the faceting is visible. As we move toward the center of the row where the frequencies become more similar masking increases.

Row (c) shows how masking and the visibility of faceting is affected by the relative orientation of the facets and the texture map. In (c1) where the facets and the dominant orientation of the texture are orthogonal, little masking occurs and the facets can be seen. As the texture is rotated toward the vertical in (c2)-(c5) the masking effect increases. In (c4) some faceting is still detectable, but only with careful scrutiny. In (c5) the faceting has become invisible.

Finally in row (d) we show that the masking effect can be used to find tesselations for curved surface so that faceting artifacts won't be seen. Given a particular texture we want to find low tesselations where the faceting will still be masked by the texture. The tesselation increases from left to right.

At the lower levels of detail the given texture fails to mask the facet artifacts, but in (d3) the faceting is just barely detectable and when it is increased in (d4) it is no longer visible. Thus the minimum visually acceptable tesselation for this texture falls between these two levels.

All these effects are predicted by the masking model. The numbers listed at the top of each image give the ΔR values computed by the model for the visibility of faceting in each image. Values smaller than 1.0 indicate that the image is not visibly different from the reference image in a standard forced-choice discrimination task.

4   Conclusions and future work

In this paper we have developed a computational model of visual masking for computer graphics. The model analyzes how the presence of one visual pattern affects the detectability of another. The model allows us to choose texture patterns for synthetic images that hide visual artifacts caused by errors in graphics algorithms. We have demonstrated how the model can be used to determine when a texture will mask the faceting artifacts caused by polygonal tesselation of a curved surface, but the model can be applied to in the same manner to predict masking of other artifacts such as banding, aliasing, and noise. Since the model takes into account how masking is affected by the relationships between the contrast, spatial frequency spectrum, and orientation of the texture and the artifacts it can be used to choose the texture features required to mask artifacts with given characteristics. Conversely if the texture properties are given, the model can predict the precision required in modeling and rendering processes to bring the artifacts to a level that can be masked by the texture. Because the model is based on data from psychophysical experiments on human vision, it is *predictive* and allows us to determine a priori whether a texture pattern will mask a given visual artifact.

There is still much work to be done on this model: structured patterns and unstructured noise masks exhibit different patterns of masking due to learning effects [Watson97]; Chromatic and achromatic cross-channel masking effects are still being investigated in the psychophysics literature [Switkes88, Gegenfurther92]; Foley [1994] has shown that better fits to psychophysical masking experiments may require a model with a divisive inhibitory term that pools activity across mechanisms; and finally, dynamic effects and changes in visual function across the visual field must certainly play a role in masking. All these dimensions should be incorporated into future models and the models should be tested and validated in a wider variety of applications.

In his "Visible Difference Predictor" Daly [1992] incorporated a model of visual masking that is similar in many ways to our own. Daly uses data on threshold elevation from masking studies to predict when an original image and image with artifacts will be visibly different. His method determines visibility differences by calculating the differences in contrast between "images" that represent the activity within spatial frequency and orientation tuned visual mechanisms. We originally tried to apply his approach to our texture masking problem but encountered difficulty in developing a meaningful formulation of the effects of the texture mask in terms of the differences in contrast between our reference and test images. Therefore we based our masking model on Wilson's formulation which has been shown to predict actual psychophysical results, and which offers a more natural interpretation of visible differences in terms of differences in the *responses* of visual mechanisms and the distance between

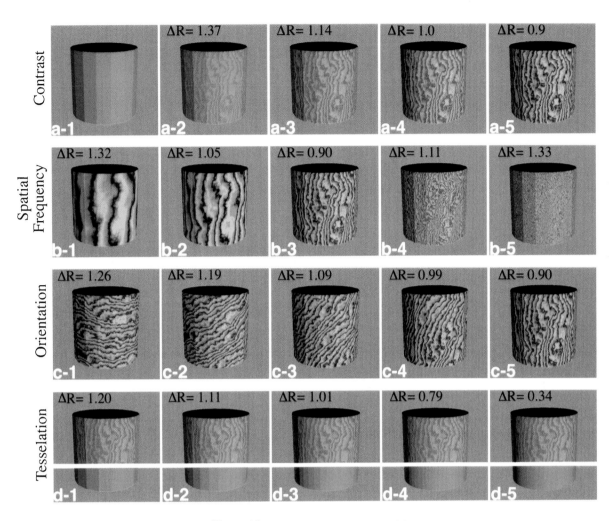

Figure 15: Applying the masking model.

images in a multidimensional response space. Although we have ended up with a somewhat different model than Daly's there is much to commend his approach especially in terms of accounting for learning effects in masking, and in producing visualizations of visible difference maps. We hope that further work will be able to unify the two models.

While we have demonstrated the utility of our masking model in a specific computer graphics application, the model is general and has uses in geometric modeling, realistic image synthesis, scientific visualization, image compression, and image-based rendering. In geometric modeling the masking model should allow us to determine the minimum level-of-detail necessary so a textured object will not exhibit visible shading artifacts. In realistic rendering, Monte Carlo methods often produce noisy images. Here, the model should allow us to determine the thresholds for visible noise in textured scenes to improve the quality and efficiency of these algorithms. In scientific visualization, abstract data is often coded as color or texture patterns superimposed on the surface of a shaded three-dimensional object. At times these patterns can obscure the shape of the underlying geometry leading to misinterpretations of the data. By using the model to predict when masking *won't* occur, we should be able to choose scales for abstract data that don't obscure the object's shape. In compression, methods such as JPEG and MPEG follow the same general visual model we've used, but do not consider the effects of masking. Applying the masking model should allow more aggressive quantization of the DCT coefficients and thereby achieve higher compression factors without losses in visual fidelity (see also [Watson93]). Finally, the model may have applicability in newly developed image-based rendering schemes [Torborg96] where objects are rendered and then their images are warped to efficiently simulate perspective changes. We may be able to use the masking model to determine how much perspective distortion is acceptable for a given relationship between the surface texture and the underlying geometry. This could provide a perceptual basis for the distortion criterion which may allow higher levels of distortion and thereby improve performance.

Acknowledgements

Special thanks to Linda Stephenson for securing permissions for the figures used in this paper.

This work was supported by the NSF/ARPA Science and Technology Center for Computer Graphics and Scientific Visualization (ASC-8920219) and by NSF CCR-9401961 and NSF ASC-9523483 and performed on workstations generously provided by the Hewlett-Packard Corporation.

References

[Arvo94] Arvo, J., Torrance, T., and Smits, B. (1994). A framework for the analysis of error in global illumination algorithms. Proceedings SIGGRAPH 94, 75-84.

[Blakemore69] Blakemore, C. and Campbell, F.W. (1969). On the existence of neurones in the human visual system selectively sensitive to the orientation and size of retinal images. J. Physiol., 203, 237-260.

[Bolin95] Bolin, M.R. and Meyer, G.M. (1995). A frequency based ray tracer. Proceedings SIGGRAPH 95, 409-418.

[Bradley88] Bradley, A., Switkes, E., and DeValois, K.K. (1988). Orientation and spatial frequency selectivity of adaptation to color and luminance patterns. Vision Res., 28, 841-856.

[Campbell66] Campbell, F.W. and Kulikowski, J.J. (1966). Orientation selectivity of the human visual system. J. Physiol., 187, 437-445.

[Campbell68] Campbell, F.W. and Robson, J.G. (1968). Application of Fourier analysis to the visibility of gratings. J. Physiol., 197, 551-566.

[Daly92] Daly, S. (1992). The visible difference predictor: an algorithm for the assessment of image fidelity. Human Vision, Visual Processing and Digital Display, SPIE Vol. 1666, 2-15.

[DeValois82] DeValois, R.L., Yund, E.W., and Hepler, N. (1982). The orientation and direction selectivity of cells in macaque visual cortex. Vision Res., 22, 531-544.

[Dowling66] Dowling, J.E. and Boycott, B.B. (1966). Organization of the primate retina: electron microscopy. Proc. Royal Soc. Lond. Ser. B., 166, 80-111.

[Enroth-Cugell66] Enroth-Cugell, C. and Robson, J.G. (1966). The contrast sensitivity of retinal ganglion cells of the cat. J. Physiol., 187, 517-552.

[Fletcher52] Fletcher, H. (1952). *Speech and hearing* (revised ed.). New York: van Nostrand.

[Foley94] Foley, J.M. (1994). Human luminance pattern-vision mechanisms: masking experiments require a new model. J. Opt. Soc. Am. A, 11(6), 1710-1719.

[Gegenfurther92] Gegenfurther, K.R. and Kiper, D.C. (1992). Contrast detection in luminance and chromatic noise. J. Opt. Soc. Am. A, 9(11). 1880-1888.

[Graham89] Graham, N.V. (1989). *Visual Pattern Analyzers*. New York: Oxford University Press.

[Harmon73] Harmon, L.D. and Julesz, B. (1973). Masking in visual recognition: effects of two-dimensional filtered noise. Science, 180, 1194-1197.

[Hubel62] Hubel, D.H. and Wiesel, T.N. (1962). Receptive fields, binocular interaction, and functional architecture in the cat's visual cortex. J. Physiol., 160, 106-154.

[Hubel68] Hubel, D.H. and Wiesel, T.N. (1968). Receptive fields and functional architecture of monkey striate cortex. J. Physiol., 195, 215-243.

[Hurvich81] Hurvich, L. (1981). *Color Vision*. Sunderland, MA: Sinauer Assoc.

[Kuffler53] Kuffler, S.W. (1953). Discharge patterns and functional organization of the mammalian retina. J. Neurophysiol., 16, 37-68.

[Legge80] Legge, G.E. and Foley, J.M. (1980). Contrast masking in human vision. J. Opt. Soc. Am., 70, 1458-1470.

[Losada94] Losada, M.A. and Mullen, K.T. (1994). The spatial tuning of chromatic mechanisms identified by simultaneous masking. Vision Res., 34(3), 331-341.

[Marcelja80] Marcelja, S. (1980). Mathematical description of the responses of simple cortical cells. J. Opt. Soc. Am., 70, 1297-1300.

[Marr82] Marr, D. *Vision*. San Francisco: W.H. Freeman.

[Martin92] Martin, R.A., Ahumada, A.J. and Larimer J.A. (1992). Color matrix display simulation based upon luminance and chromatic contrast sensitivity of early vision. Human Vision, Visual Processing and Digital Display, SPIE Vol. 1666, 336-342.

[Meyer88] Meyer, G.M. (1988). Wavelength selection for synthetic image generation. Computer Vision, Graphics, and Image Processing, 41, 57-79.

[Mitchell87] Mitchell, D.P. (1987). Generating antialiased images at low sampling densities. Proceedings SIGGRAPH 87, 65-72.

[Mullen85] Mullen, K.T. (1985). The contrast sensitivity of human color vision to red-green and blue-yellow chromatic gratings. J. Physiol., 359, 381-400.

[Nachmias74] Nachmias, J. and Sansbury, R.V. (1974). Grating contrast: discrimination may be better than detection. Vision Res., 14, 1039-1042.

[Pantle69] Pantle, A. and Sekuler, R.W. (1969). Contrast response of human visual mechanisms sensitive to orientation and direction of motion. Vision Res., 9, 397-406.

[Perlin89] Perlin, K. (1989). Hypertexture. Proceedings SIGGRAPH 89, 253-262.

[Phillips84] Phillips, G.C. and Wilson H.R. (1984). Orientation bandwidths of spatial mechanisms measured by masking. J. Opt. Soc. Am. A, 1, 226-232.

[Ratliff65] Ratliff, F. (1965). *Mach Bands: Quantitative Studies on Neural Networks in the Retina*. San Francisco: Holden-Day.

[Stiles78] Stiles, W.S. (1978). *Mechanisms of Color Vision*. London: Academic Press.

[Switkes88] Switkes, E., Bradley, A. and DeValois, K.K. (1988). Contrast dependence and mechanisms of masking interactions among chromatic and luminance gratings. J. Opt. Soc. Am. A, 5, 1149-1162.

[Torborg96] Torborg, J. and Kajiya, J.T. (1996). Talisman: commodity realtime 3d graphics for the PC. Proceedings SIGGRAPH 96, 353-363.

[Watson87] Watson, A.B. (1987). Efficiency of a model human image code. J. Opt. Soc. Am. A, 4, 2401-2417.

[Watson93] Watson, A.B. (1993) DCT quantization matrices visually optimized for individual images. Human Vision, Visual Processing and Digital Display, SPIE

[Watson97] Watson, A.B., Borthwick, R. and Taylor, M. (1997). Image quality and entropy masking. To appear in: Proceedings SPIE, Vol. 3016.

[Wilson84] Wilson H.R. and Gelb, D.J. (1984). Modified line-element theory for spatial-frequency and width discrimination. J. Opt. Soc. Am. A, 1, 124-131.

[Wilson91] Wilson, H.R. (1991). Psychophysical models of spatial vision and hyperacuity. in D. Regan (Ed.) *Spatial Vision*, Vol. 10, Vision and Visual Dysfunction. Boca Raton, FL, CRC Press.

Adapting Simulated Behaviors For New Characters

Jessica K. Hodgins and Nancy S. Pollard

College of Computing and Graphics, Visualization and Usability Center*

Abstract

This paper describes an algorithm for automatically adapting existing simulated behaviors to new characters. Animating a new character is difficult because a control system tuned for one character will not, in general, work on a character with different limb lengths, masses, or moments of inertia. The algorithm presented here adapts the control system to a new character in two stages. First, the control system parameters are scaled based on the sizes, masses, and moments of inertia of the new and the original characters. Then a subset of the parameters is fine-tuned using a search process based on simulated annealing. To demonstrate the effectiveness of this approach, we animate the running motion of a woman, child, and imaginary character by modifying the control system for a man. We also animate the bicycling motion of a second imaginary character by modifying the control system for a man. We evaluate the results of this approach by comparing the motion of the simulated human runners with video of an actual child and with data for men, women, and children in the literature. In addition to adapting a control system for a new model, this approach can also be used to adapt the control system in an on-line fashion to produce a physically realistic metamorphosis from the original to the new model while the morphing character is performing the behavior. We demonstrate this on-line adaptation with a morph from a man to a woman over a period of twenty seconds.

CR Categories: I.3.7 [Computer Graphics]: Three Dimensional Graphics and Realism: Animation—; G.1.6 [Numerical Analysis]: Optimization—; I.3.5 [Computer Graphics]: Computational Geometry and Object Modeling—Physically-Based Modeling

Keywords: Human Motion, Motion Control, Dynamic Simulation, Simulated Annealing

1 Introduction

If simulated, humanlike characters are to be useful in animations and virtual environments, we must be able to create new, appealing characters easily. Appealing human motion has several components: the kinematics and dynamics of the figure must be physically correct and the control algorithms must make the figure perform in ways that appear natural and are stylistically appropriate for the setting and character. In this paper, we describe an algorithm for adapting existing control systems to new dynamic models

*Georgia Institute of Technology, Atlanta, GA 30332-0280, [jkh|nsp]@cc.gatech.edu

Figure 1: Image of running child, woman, and man.

to facilitate the rapid creation of new characters. We demonstrate this approach for running and cycling behaviors. A running behavior designed for a male figure is adapted to control the running motion for a woman, child, and imaginary character, and a cycling behavior designed for a male figure is adapted to control a second imaginary character. The running motion of three different figures with markedly different dynamic properties is shown in figure 1. A simple, or geometric, scaling is not adequate to transform one model or control system into another. For example, the man and the child differ not only in height but also in proportion because the child has a proportionally heavier torso and shorter arms and legs.

An algorithm such as the one described in this paper should allow an animator to develop a new character by using a commercial modeling package to define the shape of the body parts and then to automatically adapt an existing behavior to animate the new model. The animation process proceeds in two stages. First, the volume and mass distribution of each body part are computed from a polygonal representation of the new model, and an approximation to the new control system is obtained by scaling based on the sizes, masses, and moments of inertia of the new and the old models. Second, a search process is used to tune the new control system. When the old and new models differ substantially, the transformation may require adapting the control system to one or more intermediate models rather than moving directly from the original to the new model.

This algorithm can be used not only to adapt a control system to a new model but also to perform a physically realistic metamorphosis between two models. In the transformation, the graphical model, the dynamic system, and the control system are interpolated on-line while the character performs the behavior. The trajectories of the control system parameters for the transformation are found using a two-stage process of scaling and tuning that is similar to the procedure used for the off-line adaptation. Figure 2 shows the metamorphosis of a man into a woman while running.

Figure 2: Images of the metamorphosis of a man into a woman while running. The metamorphosis occurred over 20 seconds and the images are spaced by 3 seconds.

2 Background

Generating appealing motion is the central problem in animation. Dynamic simulation and other procedural approaches are one potential solution to this problem. Simulation guarantees physical realism (or at least adherence to a set of consistent "pseudo-physical" laws), but the design of control systems for characters with interesting complexity has proved difficult. Control systems or procedural algorithms can be hand-designed[11, 25, 6, 5, 14, 32], but this approach is labor intensive and requires that the animator or programmer have extensive knowledge about the details of the behavior.

A more appealing approach is automatic or semi-automatic design. One such approach treats the problem of generating motion as a trajectory optimization problem. Witkin and Kass[38] used this approach to control a jumping Luxo lamp. Cohen and Liu[8, 19] divided the optimization problem into smaller spacetime windows thereby providing more control for the animator and reducing the time required for the optimization. They used this approach to control a two-link acrobot and a planar diving figure. Liu, Gortler, and Cohen[20] implemented a hierarchical wavelet-based version of spacetime constraints to allow finer detail where necessary without increasing the computation cost uniformly. Zhao and his colleagues at the University of Pennsylvania[40] represented the trajectory of the control variables as a spline and then optimized the locations of the control points for the spline. They used this approach to control a planar human figure performing a vertical jump.

A second approach to automatically generating motion uses techniques from optimal control to find a control algorithm instead of a desired trajectory. Once found, control algorithms have the advantage that different but similar motions can be generated to respond to a disturbance or interaction without further optimization. As optimization techniques for complex systems approach realtime, however, this distinction becomes less significant because trajectories can be computed for new situations as they arise. In the most general case, an optimal controller must contain information on how to get from every state of the system to every other state. This problem is of higher dimension than the problem of finding a trajectory that reaches a particular goal state from a particular start state. As a result, optimal control approaches have focused on simple systems, on problem domains where the space is dense with solutions, or on techniques that allow the space to be represented without a fine discretization.

The first paper to introduce optimal control to the graphics community was Brotman and Netravali[4]. They used a linear quadratic regulator to control the motion of a single body on the plane. Huang and van de Panne[15] used a best-first search to discover a sequence of set points that, when combined with a proportional-derivative servo, allowed a two link acrobot to hop and flip. Closed loop controllers were synthesized by van de Panne and his colleagues[35, 36] for the jumping Luxo lamp and

other simple systems using dynamic programming. A generate-and-test strategy was used by van de Panne and Fiume[34] to produce neural network-based control systems for a wide variety of planar creatures with 3-6 links. Ngo and Marks and their colleagues[23, 1] relied on a similar generate and test approach to find stimulus/response systems that animate a variety of behaviors for planar and three-dimensional figures. Sims[30, 29] used genetic algorithms to construct linked creatures and competitive behaviors for the task of capturing a block. Grzeszczuk and Terzopoulos[13] used simulated annealing to learn low-level controllers and higher-level behaviors for locomotion of fish and snakes.

Automatic techniques that begin the optimization or search process without significant knowledge of the behavior have not yet been successfully used for complex models such as three-dimensional humanlike figures. For a human figure with a realistic number of degrees of freedom, the search space is substantial and the density of acceptable solutions is low; however, knowledge about the behavior can be used to focus the search. Knowledge can be incorporated in the form of external guiding forces, via an existing but imperfect control system, or through motion capture data. External forces were used by Lamouret and van de Panne[37] to maintain the attitude of the body of a walking human figure, thereby guiding the optimization process towards the desired solution. The external force was eliminated in later stages of the optimization. Laszlo et al.[17] used limit cycle control to stabilize open-loop trajectories for walking of a human model with 19 degrees of freedom. Ringrose[26] adapted the control system of a planar quadruped to carry additional weight or to have longer leg lengths or heavier feet. In this paper, we take a similar approach by automatically adapting an existing control system for a new dynamic model. Because our control system is more complex and has more parameters, we include more extensive knowledge about the behavior in the form of a priori scaling and parameter selection. We believe that incorporating this knowledge improves the resulting control system and allows us to use fewer intermediate models for transitioning between more complex systems.

Other researchers have realized that if generating motion directly proves too difficult, perhaps we can obtain desired motion by adapting or smoothly blending between existing motion sequences derived from procedural approaches, simulation, or motion capture[39, 7, 33, 27, 12]. Techniques for adapting existing trajectories via optimization share with our work the idea that optimization procedures can be used to adapt to new situations. The two approaches differ in the level of the parameters used by the optimization. Motion trajectories contain little explicit knowledge of the task to be performed, but a well-parameterized control system contains extensive knowledge about the task.

We also draw from research in biomechanics for data and inspiration in this work. McMahon's elegant work on scaling between species inspired the idea that the control parameters could be approximately scaled based on knowledge about the dynamics of the system[21]. The biomechanics literature also contains data about the running motions of men, women, and children, and we use this information as a point of comparison for the simulated running motion in the last section of the paper. Finally, the biomechanics literature provides data on the anthropomorphic parameters of men, women, and children of various ages that we used in developing our models. In the computer graphics area, these data have been used extensively in the Jack system developed at the University of Pennsylvania[2] to allow the construction of models of various anthropomorphic dimensions for ergonomic analysis and human factors engineering as well as distributed interactive simulation.

In the remainder of the paper, we describe the algorithm for adapting control systems for steady-state running, bicycling, and physically realistic morphing. We briefly describe the dynamic models and the control systems. The algorithm for adapting the control system through scaling and tuning is described next, followed by an analysis of the performance of the algorithm.

3 Dynamic Simulation

The animated motions described in this paper are computed using dynamic simulation. Each simulation contains the equations of motion for a rigid-body model of a human or humanlike character, constraint equations for the interaction with the ground, parameterized control algorithms for running or bicycling, a graphical image for viewing the motion, and a user interface for changing the parameters of the simulation. During each simulation time step, the control algorithm computes desired positions and velocities for each joint based on the state of the system and the requirements of the task as specified by the user. Proportional-derivative servos compute joint torques based on the desired and actual value of each joint. The equations of motion of the system are integrated forward in time, taking into account the internal joint torques and the external forces and torques from interactions with the ground plane or other objects. A description of the graphical and dynamic models and an overview of the control algorithms are given below (for details see [14]).

3.1 Graphical and Dynamic Models

The models we used to animate the running and bicycling motions were constructed from rigid links connected by rotary joints with one, two, or three degrees of freedom. The human graphical models were created by modifying models purchased from Viewpoint Datalabs, and the imaginary characters were modeled in Alias. Intermediate models for the morph scene were created by first shrinking a cube or cylinder onto the polygonal model for each body part. Models created in this fashion have the same number of vertices, and corresponding vertices can be linearly interpolated from one character to the other to perform a morph or create intermediate models. This simple algorithm for three-dimensional morphing is not as elegant as algorithms published in the literature (for example, [16]), but it provides acceptable results for our application because the polygonal models for the body parts are generally convex and because a close correspondence exists between the physical characteristics of the models.

The dynamic models were derived from graphical models by computing the mass and moment of inertia of each body part using algorithms for computing the moment of inertia of a polygonal object of uniform density[18] and density data measured from cadavers[9]. The mass parameters of the four models used to test the scaling and tuning algorithms are given in figure 3.

The controlled degrees of freedom of the models are shown in figure 4. Each internal joint has a torque source that allows the con-

	Woman	Child	Running Character	Cycling Character
Mass (kg)				
head	4.22 (0.90)	5.63 (0.99)	5.98 (1.01)	7.19 (1.07)
torso	17.62 (0.87)	8.47 (0.68)	12.55 (0.78)	28.95 (1.03)
pelvis	11.08 (0.94)	3.71 (0.65)	9.51 (0.89)	7.89 (0.84)
leg	8.32 (0.92)	2.98 (0.65)	6.84 (0.86)	5.03 (0.78)
arm	2.51 (0.87)	1.20 (0.68)	2.38 (0.85)	2.70 (0.89)
wheel				1.93 (1.20)
frame				1.52 (0.76)
Length (m)				
height	1.63 (0.91)	1.08 (0.60)	1.64 (0.92)	1.74 (0.97)
leg length	0.68 (0.91)	0.39 (0.52)	0.72 (0.96)	0.70 (0.93)
arm length	0.50 (1.01)	0.29 (0.59)	0.55 (1.12)	0.54 (1.11)
hip spacing	0.15 (0.77)	0.13 (0.67)	0.17 (0.84)	0.22 (1.10)
wheel radius				0.58 (0.87)
Moment of Inertia ($kg\,m^2$)				
leg/hip	1.17 (0.89)	0.13 (0.58)	1.58 (0.95)	0.48 (0.84)
body/ankle	45.40 (0.90)	10.10 (0.67)	36.55 (0.86)	74.80 (0.99)
body/hip	6.50 (0.90)	2.26 (0.73)	5.16 (0.86)	17.67 (1.10)

Figure 3: Measurements of the mass and size of body and bicycle parts for the woman, child, and two imaginary characters. Moment of inertia parameters express moment of inertia of several body parts about a particular joint. Numbers in parentheses show the geometric scaling factor from the man to the other characters based on that parameter alone. Variation in these numbers is an indication that geometric scaling alone will not adequately describe the transformation from the man to the new character.

trol algorithms to apply a torque between the two links that form the joint. The equations of motion for each system were generated using a commercially available package[28, 31]. The points of contact with the ground are modeled using constraints with Baumgarte stabilization[3].

3.2 Running Control Algorithms

Running is a cyclic behavior in which the legs swing fore and aft and provide support for the body in alternation. Because the legs perform different functions during the phases of the locomotion cycle, the muscles are used for different control actions at various times in the cycle. For example, when the foot of the simulated runner is on the ground, the ankle, knee, and hip provide support and balance. During the flight phase, a leg is swung forward in preparation for the next touchdown. These distinct phases and corresponding changes in control actions make a state machine a natural tool for selecting the control actions that should be active at a particular time. The states correspond to the points of contact with the ground: flight, heel contact, heel and metatarsus contact, and metatarsus contact.

To generate steady-state running, the control system must maintain three parameters: forward speed, flight duration, and balance. Each state includes control laws that compute desired values for each joint with the goal of controlling those three parameters of the running cycle. Because they control the high-level attributes of the running motion, parameters of these control laws will be adjusted in the search step described in Section 4.3.

During flight, one leg is swung forward in anticipation of touchdown. The foot is positioned at touchdown to correct for errors in forward speed and to maintain balance. The disturbances caused by the impact of touchdown can be reduced by decreasing the relative speed between the foot and the ground at touchdown. This technique is commonly called *ground speed matching*. In our control system, ground speed matching is accomplished by swinging the leg further forward in the direction of travel during flight and moving it back just before touchdown.

Flight duration is controlled by extending the ankle and knee

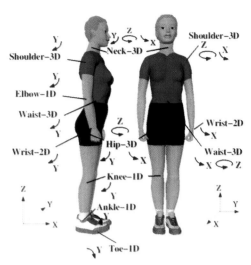

Figure 4: The controlled degrees of freedom for the dynamic model of the runner. The runner models have 17 body segments and 30 controlled degrees of freedom. The bicyclist models are similar, but have only a single degree of freedom at the neck and hips and no degree of freedom at the toes. The direction of the arrows indicates the positive direction of rotation for each degree of freedom.

joints during stance, causing the heel to lift off the ground and adding energy to the system for the next flight phase. Thrust is initiated when the metatarsus is in contact with the ground and the hip has moved a certain distance in front of the foot.

Throughout stance, proportional-derivative servos are used to compute torques for the hip joint of the stance leg that will cause the attitude of the body (roll, pitch, and yaw) to move toward the desired values. The desired angle for pitch is inclined slightly forward and the desired angles for roll and yaw are zero.

The control laws for forward speed, flight duration, and balance result in desired values for each joint. Proportional-derivative servos are used to control the position of all joints. For each internal joint the control equation is

$$\tau = k(\theta_d - \theta) + k_v(\dot{\theta}_d - \dot{\theta}) \tag{1}$$

where θ is the angle of the joint, θ_d is the desired angle, $\dot{\theta}$ is the velocity of the joint, $\dot{\theta}_d$ is the desired velocity, and k and k_v are the proportional and derivative gains.

3.3 Bicycling Control Algorithms

The underlying principles of the control system for the bicyclist are similar to those of the runner. High level control laws are used to compute desired values for each joint with the goal of controlling balance, speed, and facing direction. The rider navigates by applying forces to the handlebars and controls speed by applying forces to the pedals. Proportional-derivative servos are used to control the positions of all joints.

4 Scaling and Tuning

For motions as complex as running and bicycling, the parameters of a control system must be carefully tuned to match the physical attributes of each character. A control system that has been tuned for one dynamic model will not, in general, work on a different dynamic model. Figure 5 shows the result of using the controller designed for the male model to control the running motion for a model whose characteristics fall halfway between those of the male

and female models. The model fails to run because the control system gains and the desired forward speed that are appropriate for the male model are too high for the smaller, lighter intermediate model. This section describes how the control system of one character can be adapted to produce similar motion in a different character through a two step process involving scaling and search.

4.1 Geometric Scaling

Control systems for geometrically similar characters can be scaled based on size alone[25]. Two characters are geometrically similar if the model for one can be obtained by scaling the model of the other by a constant factor. For example, a model of the female runner can be geometrically scaled to be the same height as the child by scaling the position of each model vertex by the ratio of the characters' heights. A control system can then be generated for the scaled model based on the scaling rules in figure 6. These rules are derived assuming that scaling is uniform in all dimensions and that densities and acceleration due to gravity are the same for the two characters. For example, a geometric scaling factor L and the assumption that acceleration due to gravity (in units of $\frac{L}{T^2}$) is constant means that time must scale as $L^{1/2}$. This relationship in turn implies that desired velocity for the scaled character should scale as $\frac{L}{T} = \frac{L}{L^{1/2}} = L^{1/2}$.

The scaling rules in figure 6 allow us to adapt each parameter of the control system to account for the physical differences between two geometrically similar characters. We apply geometric scaling to the following parameters:

- The state of the system (joint angles, position and orientation of the torso, and their derivatives)

- Gains for all proportional-derivative joint servos

- Values used to control the motion such as desired forward speed and desired time of flight

- Constants referenced by the control system such as the desired clearance of the foot during flight

- The integration time step for the dynamic simulation

Once the designer of the behavior has identified the control parameters and their units, this process is automatic, and requires only that the animator supply the geometric model for the new character.

In general, two characters will not be geometrically similar, as figure 7 demonstrates. Figure 3 further illustrates this point by giving the scaling factors based on various parameters of the dynamic models. Although these scaling factors vary substantially, geometric scaling can serve as a good first approximation, capturing some of the physical differences between two characters. Figure 8 illustrates the effects of geometric scaling on stable running time for characters with physical characteristics ranging from the male model to the female model. For example, the 50% model illustrated in figure 5 runs for less than 4 seconds when the control system has not been scaled, but geometric scaling is sufficient to give it a stable running gait (i.e. the model runs for at least 100 seconds without falling).

Because geometric scaling is approximate for the models that we would like to animate, we must pick an appropriate scaling factor. For the runner, we tried scaling factors based on the height and the leg length of the characters. Leg length was found to be a more reliable scaling factor, perhaps because the control and appearance of the running motion depend much more on the lower body than on the upper body. For the bicyclist, the ratio of wheel radii was found to be a more reliable measure than either height or leg length.

Figure 5: Images showing the result of using the control system designed for the man to control the running motion for a model that is halfway between the man and the woman. The images show successive touchdowns (1.8, 2.17, 2.53, 2.8, 3, 3.53 seconds).

Quantity	Units	Geom. Scaling	Mass Scaling
Basic variables			
length	L	L	—
time	T	$L^{1/2}$	—
force	F	L^3	M
torque	FL	L^4	IL^{-1}
Motion variables			
displacement	L	L	—
velocity	LT^{-1}	$L^{1/2}$	—
acceleration	LT^{-2}	1	—
angular displacement	—	1	—
angular velocity	T^{-1}	$L^{-1/2}$	—
angular acceleration	T^{-2}	L^{-1}	—
Mechanical parameters			
mass	$FL^{-1}T^2$	L^3	M
stiffness	FL^{-1}	L^2	ML^{-1}
damping	$FL^{-1}T$	$L^{5/2}$	$ML^{-1/2}$
moment of inertia	FLT^2	L^5	I
torsional stiffness	FL	L^4	IL^{-1}
torsional damping	FLT	$L^{9/2}$	$IL^{-1/2}$

Figure 6: Scaling rules that capture differences in size, mass, and moment of inertia. The geometric scaling factor is derived assuming uniform scaling by factor L in all dimensions (geometric similarity), and assuming that the acceleration of gravity and the density of the material are invariant to scale. The mass scaling factor assumes also that mass scales by factor M and moment of inertia scales by factor I. A "−" in the mass scaling column indicates that there is no change in the scaling rule.

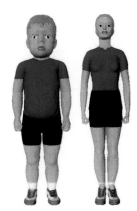

Figure 7: Woman scaled to the height of a 3-year-old child.

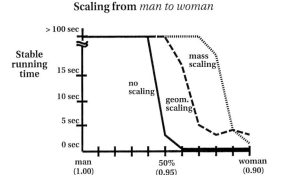

Figure 8: Effects of scaling on stable running time for characters with physical characteristics ranging from the man to the woman. The control system for each character was derived in three ways: (1) directly from that of the man, (2) by geometric scaling, and (3) by mass scaling. The scaled control systems were not tuned. Scaling factors for the characters are shown in parentheses.

4.2 Mass Scaling

An additional scaling step is needed to adapt the control system to physical differences not captured through geometric scaling. Differences in proportion between the man and woman, for example, are sufficient to prevent a geometrically scaled control system for the man from producing steady-state running in the woman (figure 8). Many of these differences can be accounted for through mass scaling rules, which correct for differences in masses and relative moments of inertia.

As an example, we first derive the mass scaling rule for torsional stiffness. For a system with one rigid body and one angular joint, torque τ at the joint produces angular acceleration $\ddot{\theta}$:

$$\tau = I\ddot{\theta} \qquad (2)$$

where I is the moment of inertia of the body about the axis of rotation. This joint is controlled with gains k and k_v as in equation 1.

Based on equations 1 and 2, a second system with moment of inertia I' and the same link lengths as the first system could be controlled to have the same angular positions, velocities, and accelerations over time by adjusting the gains as follows:

$$k' = k\left(\frac{I'}{I}\right) \quad \text{and} \quad k_v' = k_v\left(\frac{I'}{I}\right) \qquad (3)$$

Given appropriate ratios for the moment of inertia terms, equation 3 expresses the scaling relationships for torsional stiffness and damping that are required to account for differences in moments of inertia between two characters that have the same link lengths but very different inertia properties.

If link lengths also differ, equation 3 can be combined with the rules for geometric scaling. For torsional stiffness:

$$k' = kL^4 \left(\frac{I'}{IL^5} \right) = k \left(\frac{I'}{I} \right) L^{-1} \qquad (4)$$

Torsional stiffness k has been scaled by geometric scaling factor L^4, and moment of inertia I has been scaled by geometric scaling factor L^5.

The complete set of rules for scaling based on mass and moment of inertia properties is given in the rightmost column of figure 6. All of the mass scaling rules in figure 6 can be derived from the single design decision to eliminate the observable effects of differing mass distributions. Gains are scaled to keep angular and positional terms the same over time for two systems of the same scale. The derivation of all mass scaling rules is similar to that for torsional stiffness, although terms related to linear motion rather than angular motion will scale based on mass ratios rather than moment of inertia ratios. For example, the hands of the cyclist are attached to the handlebars with linear springs, and the stiffness of those springs will scale based on the ratio of relevant masses of two characters.

Applying the mass scaling rules requires selecting the relevant body segments for each gain so that mass ratio M or moment of inertia ratio I can be computed. The relevant body segments are determined for each state based on knowledge of the behavior. For example, during the flight phase of the running motion, torque applied at the hip is primarily responsible for swinging the entire leg forward, and so the flight gains for the hip should depend on the moment of inertia of the entire leg about the hip.

For each gain in the control systems for the running and cycling behaviors, the appropriate mass or moment of inertia was determined by identifying the body parts whose motion is significantly affected by that gain and summing their masses or their moments of inertia about the joint. Identification of the body segments most closely associated with each gain is something that must be done once by the designer of the behavior. Mass scaling rules can then be automatically applied to create a new control system based only on the geometric model of a new character.

Figure 8 illustrates the effect of mass scaling on characters ranging from the male model to the female model. Application of mass scaling rules can result in a substantial improvement over geometric scaling alone. For example, a character generated by transforming the physical attributes of the male model 70% of the distance toward the female model does not run a single step when the control system of the man is used without scaling or tuning, runs for 5 seconds with geometric scaling based on the ratio of leg lengths of the man and the new model, and runs with a stable gait for at least 100 seconds when mass scaling rules are applied. This plot is typical of the results we observed when scaling between any two characters, although when the physical characteristics were very different (e.g. when scaling the control system from the woman to the child) the curves would be shifted to the left on the x-axis of the plot.

Although the mass scaling rules result in a far better control system than geometric scaling alone, these rules are still approximate because they depend on the choice of a single ratio for each gain. One source of error is introduced by scaling each gain based only on a subset of the body parts, although torque applied at a joint actually affects all parts of the body. A second source of error is that the moment of inertia of a set of body parts about a joint changes as the joint angles change. For example, the moment of inertia of the leg about the hip is smaller when the leg is bent than when it is

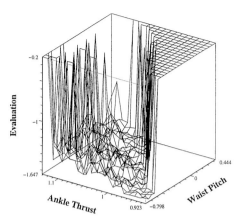

Figure 9: The evaluation function used to tune the runner control system has many local minima. This plot shows a sampling of the evaluation function as two of the tuning parameters responsible for body attitude and thrust are varied. The front corner of the figure shows a near optimal solution for this part of the search space. Values of -0.2 for the evaluation function indicate that the runner did not run for the desired running time.

straight. To obtain a single scaling factor for each gain, we calculated the moments of inertia with the body standing upright in the position shown in figure 4. This approximation is similar to the assumption underlying the use of a proportional-derivative servo with constant gains despite changes in joint angles.

4.3 Tuning the Motion

Development of a control system for steady-state performance of a behavior requires a final search step to compensate for the approximations inherent in the mass scaling rules. Because the mass scaling rules provide us with a good initial guess at a control system, a search over a small number of high-level parameters is sufficient to produce a control system for stable, repeatable motion.

4.3.1 Running

To constrain the search process for the running behavior, we restricted the search to five high-level control parameters covering forward speed, body attitude, and flight duration. One parameter, ground speed matching, controlled foot velocity relative to the ground at landing and affected the running speed. The second parameter controlled the desired pitch angle of the body during stance. Three parameters affected the duration of the flight phase: the timing of thrust and the extension of the ankle and knee during stance.

The direction of the search was determined by an evaluation function designed to capture the quality and appearance of the running motion. Values assigned to the search parameters defined a control system. The runner was commanded to run for a fixed duration (15 seconds in our experiments), and the resulting motion was evaluated. The evaluation function contained penalties for falling, for errors in velocity, for head acceleration, and for deviations in roll, pitch, and yaw from one stride to the next. Penalty coefficients could be adjusted to alter the style of the motion. For example, the evaluation function was adjusted to convert a stride where the feet of the runner were barely skimming over the ground to a stride that was more bouncy, to pull a runner out of a crouched running stride, and to eliminate a limp from a running character.

The search space for this problem contains a large number of local minima. For example, figure 9 shows the evaluation function as two of the search parameters controlling body attitude and thrust are varied. The local minima in this plot result from the fact that the optimization function combines a variety of criteria that together provide a high-level evaluation of a complex motion. In an informal evaluation of search techniques, simulated annealing[24] appeared to provide better results on this search space than Powell's method, a line-search technique. Simulated annealing was used to tune the control system for the characters described in this paper. A typical search required approximately 1500 evaluations and 15 hours of processing time on an SGI R8000 computer.

The tuning process required several stages, because scaling the control system of one character directly to reflect the parameters of a second character did not, in general, result in a stable running motion for the second character. To tune the control systems, we used intermediate characters that created smaller jumps in the physical parameters. The intermediate characters were then tuned in sequence. For example, in creating a control system for the woman, we scaled and tuned control systems for intermediate characters at 50%, 70%, and then 90% of the distance from the man to the woman. Similarly, two intermediate characters were used in tuning the control system of the child from that of the woman, and three intermediate characters were used in tuning the control system of the imaginary character from that of the man. We obtained good performance from the tuning process when a scaled, but untuned, control system would allow a character to run for approximately 10 seconds without falling. Such a heuristic could be used to determine automatically which intermediate characters should be created.

The results of scaling and tuning a control system for the man to control a woman, child, and imaginary character are shown in figure 10 along with a sequence of video frames showing a four-year-old child. Each of the animated characters had a stable running motion, measured by verifying that they would run with a stable gait for at least 100 seconds.

4.3.2 Bicycling

The search process for the bicycling behavior was similar to that for running. To constrain the search process, we grouped search parameters into high level categories for control of roll and yaw of the bicycle, control of the handlebars and pedals, and stiffness of the arms and shoulders. The bicyclist was commanded to ride a challenging course involving straight riding, turning, and speed changes, and the evaluation function included penalties for falling, excessive yaw velocity, head acceleration, and poor tracking of the desired course.

We used scaling and search to obtain a bicycling control system for an imaginary character from a working control system for a man (figure 11). The scaling and tuning process worked very well for this problem, requiring no intermediate characters, although we found that the bicycle design had to be well adapted to the character. If the bicycle was too heavy or too light, or if the handlebars could not be reached in a "comfortable" position, the resulting motion was poor. For an integrated system such as this, the constraints of physical realism may require the animator to experiment with different bicycle designs.

4.4 Metamorphosis

The algorithm described here can be used not only for adapting control systems to achieve steady-state running but also to perform an on-line metamorphosis from one model to another. To perform the metamorphosis, the graphical models, the physical models, and the control system are interpolated to create a dynamic simulation where one model is transformed to another over a period of time. Figure 2 shows the transition from a running man to a running woman over a period of 20 seconds.

The physical metamorphosis from the man to the woman was performed by creating nine equally spaced dynamic models between the man and the woman and linearly interpolating the limb lengths, masses, and moments of inertia to create a new dynamic model for each simulation step. The initial control system was created in a similar fashion by interpolating between the scaled parameters for each of the nine intermediate models. This initial control system was not stable, and the morphing runner fell over before it had completed the transition to the woman model. As in the adaptation of the steady-state control system, five parameters of the running motion were tuned to achieve stable running for the 20-second morph and steady-state running using the female model for a subsequent 7 seconds. The initial values for the five parameters were those that were found by tuning the running motion of the male model. The tuning process then determined a rate of change for each parameter, creating a linear ramp for each parameter as the dynamic system made the transition from the man to the woman.

The metamorphosis shown in figure 2 was performed over a 20-second period. A faster morph would be preferable, but physically realistic metamorphosis is difficult for several reasons. The primary difficulty is that the dynamic system, while physically realistic at each moment in time, is changing in a way that violates physical laws. For example, the body is changing in mass during the flight phase so angular momentum is not conserved. Similarly, while the foot is on the ground, the ground contact forces are applied to a constantly changing model. Physically realistic morphing of the control system is also difficult because the running is not steady-state. The control system has step-to-step goals of maintaining forward speed, flight duration, and balance and immediate goals of moving the joints to the right angles. When the dynamic model is continuously changing, these two sets of goals and the choice of corresponding gains are no longer synchronized. For example, forward speed is controlled by the position of the foot at touchdown with the new desired speed achieved by liftoff. When the dynamic model is morphing, the system in effect at the time the desired foot position angle was selected is no longer active when the new speed is achieved, resulting in errors in the control of forward speed.

5 Discussion

One goal of this research is to demonstrate that simulations of human motion can be automatically adapted to new dynamic models while maintaining the important properties of the running motion. Figure 10 compares video footage of a human child with images of a simulated child, and figure 12 compares biomechanical data from the literature[22, 10] with measurements of the simulated runners. We found that our simulation results were very similar to the quantitative data from the human runners. These results also captured some of the male/female and adult/child differences found in the literature. A comparison of the video footage for the child, however, showed that the human child had more variability in his motion.

We have presented algorithms that allow an animator to generate running or bicycling motion for several different dynamic systems in an automatic fashion. By dividing the algorithm into two stages, scaling and tuning, we chose a hybrid approach based on explicit knowledge about the system and on automatic search. We made this decision because of our intuition that a fully automatic approach that attempted to tune approximately 100 control gains would not be successful. We also felt that an exclusively knowledge-based approach would fail because our understanding of human running and bicycling, as represented by the control laws, is far from complete. The tuning process allows for some imprecision in the exact form of the control laws by adjusting several important parameters for an individual model.

To be widely applicable, this approach to adapting control systems must be independent of the particular behavior that we chose

Figure 10: Images of a running man, woman, child, and imaginary character, and a video of a four-year-old human child. The human child weighs 20 kilograms and is 1.07 meters tall. In each case, the spacing of the images is 0.066 seconds.

Figure 11: Images of a bicycling man and imaginary character following a slalom course. The spacing of the images is 1 second.

Quantity	Man	Woman	Child
Speed (*m/s*)			
human	4.83	4.83	2.13
simulated	4.41	4.45	2.52
Step Frequency (*steps/s*)			
human	2.92	3.05	3.8
simulated	3.18	3.33	4.3
Step Length (*m*)			
human	1.66	1.60	0.56
simulated	1.39	1.33	0.58
Stance Time / Step Time (%)			
human	57.9	55.2	68.5
simulated	59.6	54.3	63.3

Figure 12: A comparison of data from the biomechanical literature with data recorded from our simulated runners. The match between the human child and the simulated child is within the variability between subjects. Simulated data from the male and female runners captures the male/female differences found in the literature.

for our experiments. Would the same approach work for adapting control systems for diving and vaulting to new models? Both the scaling laws and the selection of parameters for tuning are based on information about the control system and behavior. This information, however, is readily available to the designer of the behavior. For example, geometric scaling requires that we know the units of each gain in the control system, but that information can be easily determined by examining the units of each control equation. Scaling based on mass and moment of inertia requires that we identify the bodies that are most affected by a particular joint gain. We assumed that the lighter of two bodies (or chains of bodies) would be most affected by joint motion except when that body was in contact with the ground. Only the selection of parameters for tuning is specific to the behavior. We chose higher-level parameters that we thought best represented the important properties of each motion: forward speed, flight duration, and balance for the runner and balance, support, and control of handlebars and pedals for the bicyclist. In principle, it should be possible to pick a similar set of parameters for other behaviors.

To be widely applicable, the scaling and tuning process must

also be very easy for animators and researchers to use. Once the designer of the behavior has incorporated the scaling laws into the behavior and selected a set of search parameters, the scaling and tuning process can be completely automatic, requiring only that a geometric model for the new character be supplied. In practice, we found that creating appealing motion may require experimenting with the evaluation function, but this could easily be done without knowledge of the control system for that behavior. Although the search process is time consuming, it makes scaling accessible to users with no knowledge of the control system.

To be useful as part of a modeling and animation package, an algorithm for automatically adapting control systems must be robust for a wide variation in models. The child is markedly different from the woman or man, but there are certainly parameter changes that are too extreme to be accounted for by the combination of scaling laws and tuning presented here. For example, creatures whose physique demands a fundamentally different style of bipedal running could not be controlled using this approach. Birds and bipedal dinosaurs, for example, are "toe-strike" runners rather than "heel-strike" runners. The control laws for toe running probably differ not only in parameter values but also in structure from the control laws for heel-strike running.

The scaling rules presented in this paper were applied to control systems developed for simulation, but they apply equally well to data obtained through motion capture. Motion capture data describing, for example, the position of the torso and the joint angles of a human actor over time can be scaled according to the rules in figure 6. Only torso positions and the length of time between data points are affected. Because joint angle positions are dimensionless, they do not scale.

Scaling is not sufficient for adapting motion capture data to fit new characters, however. Kinematic constraints for characters with different relative link lengths still need to be resolved. For example, the feet of the runners must make contact with the ground, and the feet of the bicyclist must touch the pedals. A more subtle issue is the expected variation of motion with changes in physical characteristics such as mass. This variation is not captured by the scaling rules, which attempt to generate identical motions over time for characters with the same geometric scaling parameters but different masses or mass distributions. Perhaps simulation results demonstrating physical responses to changes in physical properties will provide some insight into more sophisticated scaling rules to capture effects such as these.

The animations described in this paper can be seen on the WWW at: `http://www.cc.gatech.edu/gvu/animation/`.

Acknowledgments

The authors would like to thank Elizabeth de Goursac for her help in developing the early versions of the tools used in this paper, James O'Brien for the use of his rendering and modeling software, Joe Marks for the loan of his child, Christopher, and Sherry Strickland and Victor Zordan for use of their Alias models. We would also like to thank the anonymous reviewers for their detailed comments. This project was supported in part by NSF NYI Grant No. IRI-9457621, by Mitsubishi Electric Research Laboratory, and by a Packard Fellowship.

References

[1] J. Auslander, A. Fukunaga, H. Partovi, J. Christensen, L. Hsu, P. Reiss, A. Shuman, J. Marks, and J.T. Ngo. Further experience with controller-based automatic motion synthesis for articulated figures. *ACM Transactions on Graphics*, 14(4):311–336, October 1995.

[2] N. I. Badler, C. B. Phillips, and B. L. Webber. *Simulating Humans: Computer Graphics Animation and Control.* Oxford University Press, New York, 1993.

[3] J. Baumgarte. Stabilization of constraints and integrals of motion in dynamical systems. *Computer Methods in Applied Mechanics and Engineering*, 1:1–16, 1972.

[4] L. S. Brotman and A. N. Netravali. Motion interpolation by optimal control. In J. Dill, editor, *Computer Graphics (SIGGRAPH 88 Proceedings)*, volume 22, pages 309–315, August 1988.

[5] A. Bruderlin and T. Calvert. Interactive animation of personalized human locomotion. In *Proceedings of Graphics Interface '93*, pages 17–23, Toronto, Ontario, Canada, May 1993. Canadian Information Processing Society.

[6] A. Bruderlin and T. W. Calvert. Goal-directed, dynamic animation of human walking. In *Computer Graphics (SIGGRAPH 89 Proceedings)*, volume 23, pages 233–242, July 1989.

[7] A. Bruderlin and L. Williams. Motion signal processing. In *SIGGRAPH 95 Proceedings*, Annual Conference Series, pages 97–104. ACM SIGGRAPH, Addison Wesley, August 1995.

[8] M. F. Cohen. Interactive spacetime control for animation. In E. E. Catmull, editor, *Computer Graphics (SIGGRAPH 92 Proceedings)*, volume 26, pages 293–302, July 1992.

[9] W. T. Dempster and G. R. L. Gaughran. Properties of body segments based on size and weight. *American Journal of Anatomy*, 120:33–54, 1965.

[10] V. L. Fortney. The kinematics and kinetics of the running pattern of two-, four-, and six-year-old children. *Research Quarterly for Exercise and Sport*, 54(2):126–135, 1983.

[11] M. Girard and A. A. Maciejewski. Computational modeling for the computer animation of legged figures. In B. A. Barsky, editor, *Computer Graphics (SIGGRAPH 85 Proceedings)*, volume 19, pages 263–270, July 1985.

[12] M. Gleicher. Motion editing with spacetime constraints. In *Proceedings of the 1997 Symposium on Interactive 3D Graphics*, pages 139–148, Providence, RI, April 1997.

[13] R. Grzeszczuk and D. Terzopoulos. Automated learning of muscle-actuated locomotion through control abstraction. In *SIGGRAPH 95 Proceedings*, Annual Conference Series, pages 63–70. ACM SIGGRAPH, Addison Wesley, August 1995.

[14] J. K. Hodgins, W. L. Wooten, D. C. Brogan, and J. F. O'Brien. Animating human athletics. In *SIGGRAPH 95 Proceedings*, Annual Conference Series, pages 71–78. ACM SIGGRAPH, Addison Wesley, August 1995.

[15] P. S. Huang and M. van de Panne. A planning algorithm for dynamic motions. In *7th Eurographics Workshop on Animation and Simulation*, pages 169–182, 1996.

[16] J. R. Kent, W. E. Carlson, and R. E. Parent. Shape transformation for polyhedral objects. In E. E. Catmull, editor, *Computer Graphics (SIGGRAPH 92 Proceedings)*, volume 26, pages 47–54, July 1992.

[17] J. Laszlo, M. van de Panne, and E. Fiume. Limit cycle control and its application to the animation of balancing and walking. In *SIGGRAPH 96 Proceedings*, Annual Conference Series, pages 155–162. ACM SIGGRAPH, ACM Press, August 1996.

[18] S. Lien and J. T. Kajiya. A symbolic method for calculating the integral properties of arbitrary nonconvex polyhedra. *IEEE Computer Graphics and Applications*, 4(10):35–41, 1984.

[19] Z. Liu and M. Cohen. Decomposition of linked figure motion: Diving. In *5th Eurographics Workshop on Animation and Simulation*, 1994.

[20] Z. Liu, S. J. Gortler, and M. F. Cohen. Hierarchical spacetime control. In *SIGGRAPH 94 Proceedings*, Annual Conference Series, pages 35–42. ACM SIGGRAPH, ACM Press, July 1994.

[21] T. A. McMahon. *Muscles, Reflexes, and Locomotion.* Princeton University Press, Princeton, 1984.

[22] R. Nelson, C. Brooks, and N. Pike. Biomechanical comparison of male and female distance runners. *Annals of the NY Academy of Sciences*, 301:793–807, 1977.

[23] J. T. Ngo and J. Marks. Spacetime constraints revisited. In J. T. Kajiya, editor, *Computer Graphics (SIGGRAPH 93 Proceedings)*, volume 27, pages 343–350, August 1993.

[24] W. H. Press, S. A. Teukolsky, W. T. Vetterling, and B. P. Flannery. *Numerical Recipes in C.* Cambridge University Press, New York, 1992.

[25] M. H. Raibert and J. K. Hodgins. Animation of dynamic legged locomotion. In T. W. Sederberg, editor, *Computer Graphics (SIGGRAPH 91 Proceedings)*, volume 25, pages 349–358, July 1991.

[26] R. Ringrose. Simulated creatures: Adapting control for variations in model or desired behavior. M.S. Thesis, Massachusetts Institute of Technology, 1992.

[27] C. F. Rose, B. Guenter, B. Bodenheimer, and M. F. Cohen. Efficient generation of motion transitions using spacetime constraints. In *SIGGRAPH 96 Proceedings*, Annual Conference Series, pages 155–162. ACM SIGGRAPH, Addison Wesley, August 1996.

[28] D. E. Rosenthal and M. A. Sherman. High performance multibody simulations via symbolic equation manipulation and Kane's method. *Journal of Astronautical Sciences*, 34(3):223–239, 1986.

[29] K. Sims. Evolving 3d morphology and behavior by competition. In *Artificial Life IV*, pages 28–39, 1994.

[30] K. Sims. Evolving virtual creatures. In *SIGGRAPH 94 Proceedings*, Annual Conference Series, pages 15–22. ACM SIGGRAPH, ACM Press, July 1994.

[31] Symbolic Dynamics Inc. *SD/Fast User's Manual.* 1990.

[32] X. Tu and D. Terzopoulos. Artificial fishes: Physics, locomotion, perception, behavior. In *SIGGRAPH 94 Proceedings*, Annual Conference Series, pages 43–50. ACM SIGGRAPH, ACM Press, July 1994.

[33] M. Unuma, K. Anjyo, and R. Takeuchi. Fourier principles for emotion-based human figure animation. In *SIGGRAPH 95 Proceedings*, Annual Conference Series, pages 91–96. ACM SIGGRAPH, Addison Wesley, August 1995.

[34] M. van de Panne and E. Fiume. Sensor-actuator networks. In J. T. Kajiya, editor, *Computer Graphics (SIGGRAPH 93 Proceedings)*, volume 27, pages 335–342, August 1993.

[35] M. van de Panne, E. Fiume, and Z. Vranesic. Reusable motion synthesis using state-space controllers. In F. Baskett, editor, *Computer Graphics (SIGGRAPH 90 Proceedings)*, volume 24, pages 225–234, August 1990.

[36] M. van de Panne, E. Fiume, and Z. G. Vranesic. Optimal controller synthesis using approximating-graph dynamic programming. In *Proceedings of the American Control Conference*, pages 2668–2673, 1993.

[37] M. van de Panne and A. Lamouret. Guided optimization for balanced locomotion. In *Eurographics Workshop on Computer Animation and Simulation '95*, pages 165–177, 1995.

[38] A. Witkin and M. Kass. Spacetime constraints. In J. Dill, editor, *Computer Graphics (SIGGRAPH 88 Proceedings)*, volume 22, pages 159–168, August 1988.

[39] A. Witkin and Z. Popović. Motion warping. In *SIGGRAPH 95 Proceedings*, Annual Conference Series, pages 105–108. ACM SIGGRAPH, Addison Wesley, August 1995.

[40] X. Zhao, D. Tolani, B. Ting, and N. I. Badler. Simulating human movements using optimal control. In *Eurographics Workshop on Computer Animation and Simulation '96*, pages 109–120, 1996.

Anatomy-Based Modeling of the Human Musculature

Ferdi Scheepers*   Richard E. Parent†   Wayne E. Carlson‡   Stephen F. May‡

* *Satellite Applications Centre*
CSIR
South Africa

† *Department of Computer and*
Information Science
The Ohio State University

‡ *Advanced Computing Center for*
the Arts and Design
The Ohio State University

"Anatomy increases the sensitivity of the artist's eye and makes the skin transparent; it allows the artist to grasp the true form of the surface contours of the body because he knows the parts that lie hidden beneath a veil of flesh."
Gerdy

Abstract

Artists study anatomy to understand the relationship between exterior form and the structures responsible for creating it. In this paper we follow a similar approach in developing anatomy-based models of muscles. We consider the influence of the musculature on surface form and develop muscle models which react automatically to changes in the posture of an underlying articulated skeleton. The models are implemented in a procedural language that provides convenient facilities for defining and manipulating articulated models. To illustrate their operation, the models are applied to the torso and arm of a human figure. However, they are sufficiently general to be applied in other contexts where articulated skeletons provide the basis of modeling.

CR Categories and Subject Descriptors: I.3.5 [Computer Graphics]: Computational Geometry and Object Modeling *Surfaces and Object Representations*; I.3.7 [Computer Graphics]: Three-Dimensional Graphics and Realism.

Additional Keywords: Articulated Models, Procedural Modeling, Deformations, Muscles, Tendons, Bones, Human Figure Animation

1   INTRODUCTION

Human figure modeling and animation has been one of the primary areas of research in computer graphics since the early 1970's. The complexity of simulating the human body and its behavior is directly proportional to the complexity of the human body itself, and is compounded by the vast number of movements it is capable of. Although articulated structures containing rigid segments is a reasonable approximation of the human skeleton, most researchers use articulated structures that are too simple to be deemed anatomically appropriate. The shoulder, spine, forearm, and hand are typical examples where accuracy is sacrificed for simplicity. The more difficult problem of fleshing-out a skeleton is currently an active area of research [6][9][23][28][29]. In several of these cases, oversim-

---

*Ferdi.Scheepers@csir.co.za
†parent@cis.ohio-state.edu
‡[waynec | smay]@cgrg.ohio-state.edu

plification causes undesirable or distracting results. Using flexible surfaces at or near joints is a poor approximation because many deformations (like bulging muscles) occur far away from joints. Also, producing intricate joint-dependent changes in the shape of the skin without considering the motivators for those shape changes seems implausible.

In this paper we present an approach to human figure modeling similar to the one taken in artistic anatomy—by analyzing the relationship between exterior form and the underlying structures responsible for creating it, surface form and shape change may be understood and represented best. We focus on the musculature by developing anatomy-based models of skeletal muscles, but many of the principles apply equally well to the modeling of other anatomical structures that create surface form, such as bones and fatty tissue.

1.1   Related Work

Because of demands for rapid feedback and the limitations of present-day technology, human figures are often represented with stick figures, curves, or simple geometric primitives. This approach sacrifices realism of representation for display efficiency. Recently, a layered approach to the representation of human figures has been adopted [2][20][23][28] in which skeletons support one or more layers, typically muscle, fatty tissue, skin, and clothing layers. The additional layers serve to flesh-out the skeleton and to enhance the realism of the representation.

Anatomy-based skeletal models

Most human figure models use a simplified articulated skeleton consisting of relatively few jointed segments. Magnenat-Thalmann and Thalmann [11] challenged researchers to develop more accurate articulated models for the skeletal support of human figures. They observe that complex motion control algorithms which have been developed for primitive articulated models better suit robot-like characters than they do human figures. To address this issue, researchers have revisited the skeletal layer of human figure models to solve some specific problems. In Jack [1], the shoulder is modeled accurately as a clavicle and shoulder pair. The spatial relationship between the clavicle and shoulder is adjusted based on the position and orientation of the upper arm. In another treatment of the shoulder-arm complex, the Thalmanns [11] use a moving joint based on lengthening the clavicle which produces good results. Monheit and Badler [14] developed a kinematic model of the human spine that improves on the realism with which the torso can be bent or twisted. Scheepers *et al.* [21] developed a skeleton model which supports anatomically accurate pronation and supination of the two forearm bones. Gourret *et al.* [9] use realistic bones in their hand skeleton to assist in producing appropriate deformations of the fingers in a grasping task.

Modeling deformable tissues

Ignoring the effects that gravity and other external forces may have on tissue, some researchers have concentrated on the deformations that occur in the vicinity of joints. One simplifying assumption considers the human body as consisting of rigid body parts connected with flexible surfaces at joints. Chadwick *et al.* [2] use free-form deformations [22] (FFDs) to deform skin surfaces that surround the underlying skeleton. By using abstract muscle operators, a relationship between skeletal parameters (such as joint angles) and the control points of the FFDs is established. For example, tendon muscle operators are used to control deformations near joints. The Thalmanns[12] use joint-dependent local deformation operators to control the changes that surfaces undergo near flexing joints. Singh [23] models the skin surfaces near joints with polyhedral objects embedded in implicit functions. As the joints move, the implicit functions deform the polyhedral definition, and therefore the skin surface in the vicinity of the joint.

Surfaces may also be deformed in areas other than near joints. Chadwick *et al.* [2] use flexor muscle operators based on FFDs to simulate the visible result of muscle contraction, while Nahas *et al.* [15] manipulate the control points of a B-spline model to mimic deformations. Henne [10] and Singh [23] both use implicit function primitives to model muscles and pseudo-physical models to cause these muscles to bulge. None of these methods model individual muscles in an anatomically appropriate way, nor do any of them attempt to account for all muscles that create or influence the visible surfaces surrounding the underlying skeleton.

Early physically-based techniques for modeling facial expressions consider the face to be sufficiently representable by its skin, applying abstract muscle actions to the skin to produce facial expressions [17]. The work of Waters [26] in this regard is particularly noteworthy. More recent physically-based techniques are anatomically more appropriate [25]. Pieper [16] developed a model of soft tissue which accounts for the 3D structure and mechanical properties of human facial tissue, allowing accurate simulation of the interaction between soft tissue, muscles, and bony structures in the face. Waters [27] extended his earlier work by using a physical model of the epidermis, subcutaneous fatty tissues, and bone to model facial expressions more realistically.

Chen and Zeltzer [3] developed a finite element model of muscle to simulate muscle forces and to visualize the deformations that muscles undergo during contraction. They used polygonal data derived from MRI scans or data digitized from anatomically accurate plastic models to represent muscles. Their model accounts for shape changes due to external forces, such as gravity, or due to internal muscle forces which produce movement.

In her approach to modeling and animating animals, Wilhelms [28] uses ellipsoids to model bones, muscles, and fatty tissue. She uses an iso-surface extraction program to generate polygonal skin surfaces around the ellipsoids in some rest posture of the body, and anchors the skin to the underlying body components, allowing the skin to be adjusted automatically when the body moves. Her research concentrates on the generation of models that may be developed at least semi-automatically.

1.2 Overview

The remainder of this paper is organized as follows. In Section 2 we identify the anatomical structures that influence surface form and discuss the musculature and its influence in some detail. In Section 3 we briefly describe a procedural model for skeletons. Section 4 presents anatomy-based muscle models for simulating the deformable nature of skeletal muscles. We illustrate the operation of each muscle model and show how the muscle models may be used in conjunction with the skeleton model presented in Section 3.

Concluding remarks are given in Section 5 where we discuss possibilities for future research.

2 ARTISTIC ANATOMY

Anatomy is a biological science concerned with the form, position, function, and relationship of structures in the human body. *Artistic anatomy* [8][19][30] is a specialized discipline concerned only with those structures that create and influence surface form. Whereas medical anatomies consider the human body in an erect and motionless stance, artistic anatomy is also concerned with changes that occur when the body moves into different stances.

Three general anatomical structures create surface form:

1. *The skeleton*, consisting of bones and joints organized into an articulated structure;

2. *The musculature*, consisting of contractile muscles and nonelastic tendons; and

3. *The panniculus adiposus* (or fat layer), consisting of fatty tissue located beneath the skin.

Before discussing the musculature and its effect on surface form, we briefly mention the influence of the skeleton. Interested readers should consult reference [20] for more detail.

2.1 The skeleton

The *skeleton* is the basis of all surface form [30]. It determines the general shape of the body and each of its constituent parts. The skeleton also affects surface form more directly: bones create surface form where skin abuts to bones, such as at the elbows and knees. Bones are attached at *joints* which allow the bones to move relative to one another. Parts of bones that appear not to create surface form in some postures do so in others. For example, the heads of the metacarpal bones cannot be seen unless the hand is clenched into a fist.

2.2 The musculature

Of the anatomical systems that determine surface form, the musculature is the most complex. Muscles are arranged side by side and in layers on top of bones and other muscles [8]. They often span multiple joints. Muscles typically consist of different kinds of tissue, allowing some portions to be contractile and others not. Depending on their state of contraction, muscles have different shapes and they influence surface form in different ways.

Muscles

Skeletal muscles are voluntary muscles which contract in order to move the bones they connect. Located throughout the body, these muscles form a layer between the bones of the skeleton and subcutaneous fatty tissue.

Structurally, skeletal muscles consist of a contractile *belly* and two extremities, often tendinous, called the *origin* and the *insertion*. The origin is usually the more stationary end of a contracting muscle, and the insertion the more movable. Skeletal muscles consist of elongated muscle fibers and fibrous connective tissue which anchors the muscles to the underlying skeleton. The composition of muscle fibers in a muscle determines the potential strength of muscle contraction and the possible range of motion due to contraction. The shapes of muscles often reveal their function.

Anatomists distinguish between two types of muscle contraction. In *isotonic contraction*, the length of a muscle changes and the muscle produces movement, while in *isometric contraction*, the muscle contracts or tenses without producing movement or undergoing a change in length.

Skeletal muscles act across one or more movable joints, working together in groups to produce movement or to modify the actions of other muscles. Depending on the types of joints involved and the points of attachment of the muscle [4], a standard name can be given to any movement so produced, for example flexion/extension or protraction/retraction [7].

Tendons

Skeletal muscles attach to other structures directly or by means of tendons. A *tendon* is a dense band of white connective tissue that connects the belly of a muscle to its attachment on the skeleton. Tendons are nonelastic, flexible, and extremely strong. They concentrate the force produced by the contractile muscle belly, transmitting it to the structure to be moved. Tendons decrease the bulk of tissue around certain joints, obviating the need for long fibers in the belly portion of the muscle. For example, in the forearm and lower leg, long tendons shift the weight away from the hand and foot, making the ends of the arm and leg lighter.

Influence on surface form

Skeletal muscles can be thought of as independent convex forms [8] placed in layers on top of the underlying skeleton. Although the forms of adjacent muscles tend to blend with each other, furrows or grooves are present between some muscles and muscle groups, especially between those that have different or opposing actions. This arrangement of muscles is visible on the surface as a series of convexities [8], especially when the muscles are put into action. In their relaxed state, however, muscles are soft and appear less defined, even hanging loosely because of the pull of gravity [19]. Upon contraction, the belly of muscles become shorter and thicker. In superficial muscles, this change in shape can be observed on the surface where the muscle's relief becomes increasingly defined.

When muscles with narrow tendons contract, the tendons often stand out prominently on the surface of the skin. For example, some of the tendons of the forearm muscles can be seen on the wrist when the fingers are clenched into a fist. In superficial muscles, the area of attachment of a tendon and its muscle belly is often apparent on the surface.

3 SKELETAL SUPPORT

In this section we give a brief overview of a procedural model for skeletal support [21]. The model is implemented in AL [13], a procedural modeling and animation language with facilities for defining and manipulating articulated models. We introduce articulation variables (or *avars* [18]) to the model and use them to provide animation and interaction controls. The model is applied to the arm skeleton to illustrate its operation. This example will be extended in the next section when the modeling of muscles is considered.

3.1 Bones and joints

Since bones are hard relative to other anatomical structures in the human body, a rigid model for individual bones is appropriate. We model bones with functions that select one representation out of a number of alternatives based on a complexity parameter. Two of these alternatives, constructed in piecewise fashion from predefined *geometric primitives* (*g-prims*), are shown in Figure 1. If necessary, arbitrarily complex boundary representations could be included as alternatives, but for our purposes the *g-prims* representations suffice.

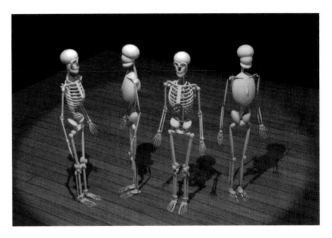

Figure 1: *Stage-fright*—stylized representations of a human skeleton assembled from spheres, cylinders, tori, hyperboloids, and bilinear patches.

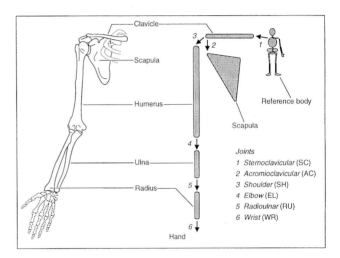

Figure 2: Conceptual model of the arm skeleton.

The different types of movable joints in the human skeleton can also be modeled with functions. Conceptually, each function applies the required transformations to locate and orient the joint. Joint motions may be restricted to predetermined excursion ranges, one for each of the degrees of freedom of the joint. We use an object-oriented style of programming in AL to encapsulate the implementation details into a joints class. This abstraction allows the instantiation of joint types to be stated succinctly, which, in turn, simplifies the arrangement of bones and joints into hierarchies.

3.2 The arm skeleton

The upper limb of the human body is supported by a complex and intricate skeleton which provides an excellent testbed for developing articulated models. To simplify interaction, we introduce 'anatomically appropriate' simplifications to the arm skeleton. For example, since the acromioclavicular joint is capable of very little motion in itself [24], we separate the scapula from the arm skeleton (see Figure 2) and define its motion functionally in terms of *avars*.

Figure 3 shows a hierarchical definition of the arm skeleton. We place the rooted reference skeleton first, and use nested blocking constructs to specify the kinematic chain from the sternoclavicular joint and the clavicle bone down to the wrist joint and the hand

```
(define (the-arm-skeleton)
 (lambda
  (reference-skeleton)

  (model "clavicle" (ElevateDepress ProtractRetract)
   (SC-joint (ElevateDepress) (ProtractRetract))
   (clavicle)

   (separator
    (AC-joint (ElevateDepress) (ProtractRetract))
    (scapula))

   (model "humerus" (AbductAdduct FlexExtend Rotate)
    (SH-joint (AbductAdduct) (FlexExtend) (Rotate))
    (humerus)

    (model "ulna" (ElbowFlexExtend)
     (EL-joint (ElbowFlexExtend))
     (ulna)

     (model "radius" (PronateSupinate)
      (RU-joint (PronateSupinate))
      (radius)

      (model "hand" (FlexDorsiflex RabductUabduct)
       (WR-joint (FlexDorsiflex) (RabductUabduct))
       (hand)
 )))))))
```

Figure 3: AL function defining the arm skeleton (*avars* associated with each model appear in *italics* and are named for joint movements).

skeleton. Low-level motion control is provided by binding *avars* to joint angles. High-level motion control is also possible. For example, by relating a normalized *avar clench* to the flexion angles of interphalangeal joints, the fingers of the hand can be clenched into a fist simply by setting *clench* equal to one.

4 THE MUSCULATURE

In this section we present three anatomy-based muscle models for simulating the behavior of skeletal muscles. Before doing so, however, we discuss the representation of muscle bellies.

4.1 Muscle bellies

We use ellipsoids to represent muscle bellies. As Wilhelms argues [28], the ellipsoid is a natural and convenient primitive for representing muscle bellies because it can be scaled along its three major axes to simulate bulging. We automatically adjust the dimensions of the muscle belly when its extremities are moved further apart or when they are brought closer together. These adjustments not only preserve the ratio of the belly's height to its width, but also the volume of the muscle belly—an approach justified by considering the anatomical structure of muscles and their behavior during isotonic contraction.

Let E be an ellipsoid whose principal axes have lengths $2a$, $2b$, and $2c$, respectively, and let $l = 2c$ denote the length of a muscle belly to be represented. Given the required volume $v = \frac{4\pi abc}{3}$ and the ratio of the width and height $r = \frac{a}{b}$ of the muscle belly, isotonic muscle contraction can be simulated by adjusting a and b when the length of the muscle belly changes. Since $a = br$,

$$v = \frac{4\pi r b^2 c}{3} \implies b^2 = \frac{3v}{4\pi rc}.$$

Letting l' denote the new length of the muscle belly, we have

$$c' = \frac{l'}{2} \tag{1}$$

$$b' = \sqrt{\frac{3v}{4\pi rc'}} \tag{2}$$

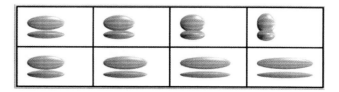

Figure 4: Volume preserving contraction (top) and stretching (bottom) of a muscle belly. Front and side views of the same muscle belly are shown in each frame.

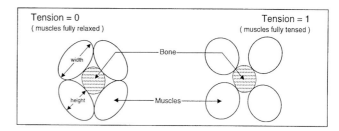

Figure 5: Simulating isometric muscle contraction.

$$a' = b'r. \tag{3}$$

Figure 4 shows how the muscle belly bulges when contracting, and how it thins out when stretching.

To simulate isometric muscle contraction, we introduce a *tension* parameter t to adjust the ratio r (see Figure 5). Assuming that $r_n = \frac{a_n}{b_n}$ is given for a muscle in a fully relaxed state, we define

$$r = (1 - t)r_n + ktr_n = (1 - t + kt)r_n, \tag{4}$$

where k is a tension control parameter[1] that regulates the amount of muscle bulging (increased height, reduced width) due to isometric contraction.

4.2 Fusiform muscles

Many skeletal muscles are fusiform and act in straight lines between their points of attachment. For these muscles we use a simple model with relatively few parameters, called the *fusiform muscle model*. This model provides a convenient mechanism for locating muscle bellies relative to underlying skeletal bones. Specifically, since muscles attach to different bones, the origin may be given in the local coordinate system of the bone where the muscle originates. Similarly, the insertion may be given in the local coordinate system of the bone where the muscle inserts. Muscles with tendons may be defined by giving two additional points, as illustrated in Figure 6. The model takes care of transforming all the points to a common coordinate system.

Like the joint types in Section 3.1, the fusiform muscle model is implemented in a class. We use two *class* parameters to define the volume v and ratio r of the muscle in its natural state, and a number of *instance* parameters to specify the location and orientation of the muscle.

Figure 7 shows a few frames of an animation sequence to illustrate the operation of the fusiform muscle model. Two fusiform muscles of the same volume are modeled, but only one has tendons. Notice the effect of the tendons on the perceived bulging of the muscle belly on the right. Notice also that the tendons retain their lengths, an important attribute of tendons which is not incorporated in Wilhelms' modeling of animal muscles [28].

---

[1]Empirical evidence shows a value of $k = 2.56$ provides reasonable bulging for acceptable visual representation.

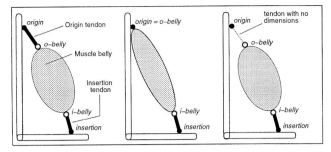

Figure 6: Parameters of the fusiform muscle model.

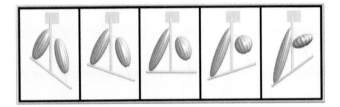

Figure 7: Operation of the fusiform muscle model with and without tendons.

4.3 Multi-belly muscles

Wide muscles with complex shapes cannot be modeled with the same ease as straight fusiform muscles. Although one could use multiple instances of fusiform muscles to approximate the shape of a complex muscle, a better alternative would be to use a generative approach in which any number of muscle bellies may be positioned automatically. The *multi-belly muscle model* accomplishes this task.

In order to locate and orient a number of muscle bellies automatically, we need to define the origin and insertion of the muscle to be represented. Spline curves [5] provide a convenient alternative to merely enumerating the individual origin and insertion points. Relatively few control points are needed to define these curves, and by using a parametric formulation of the spline curve, points along the curve can be sampled simply and efficiently. Thus, instead of origin and insertion *points*, the multi-belly muscle model requires that origin and insertion *curves* be specified.

Figure 8 illustrates the procedure for locating and orienting n muscle bellies between pairs of spline curves. Locating each muscle involves finding two points of attachment on each curve for every muscle belly, a task easily accomplished by sampling the curves and pairing-off corresponding sample points. Orientation of individual muscle bellies requires finding a reference vector to indicate the 'up-direction' of a muscle belly. As illustrated in Figure 8, the reference vector for each pair of points $(\mathbf{o}_j, \mathbf{i}_j)$ is the normal vector of the plane through three sample points, specifically:

$$\mathbf{o}_j, \mathbf{o}_{j+1}, \mathbf{i}_j \quad \text{if} \quad j = 1;$$
$$\mathbf{o}_{j-1}, \mathbf{o}_{j+1}, \mathbf{i}_j \quad \text{if} \quad 1 < j < n; \quad \text{and}$$
$$\mathbf{o}_{j-1}, \mathbf{o}_j, \mathbf{i}_j \quad \text{if} \quad j = n.$$

The implementation of the multi-belly muscle model resembles that of the fusiform muscle model. The origin of each multi-belly muscle is represented by a list of control points defining the origin curve. Another list defines the insertion curve in a similar way. As before, the origin and insertion curves may be defined in whichever local coordinate system necessary; the class transforms the control points (and hence, the curves) into world coordinates prior to storing them. By default, ten muscle bellies are created between the origin and insertion curves. This default behavior can be changed

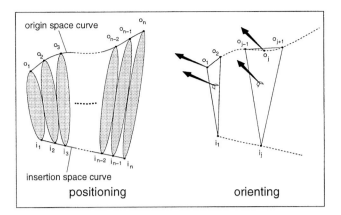

Figure 8: Locating and orienting muscle bellies in the multi-belly muscle model.

by specifying a different belly count before instantiating the muscle.

4.4 Muscles that bend

The *general muscle model* allows muscles with complex shapes to be modeled. It is useful for representing muscles that bend around underlying anatomical structures.

Motivation

The fusiform and multi-belly muscle models can be used to represent most skeletal muscles in the human body. Exceptions are muscles for which the simplifying assumptions of these models are unreasonable. Specifically, some muscles bend around underlying anatomical structures, others cannot be represented accurately by one or more straight muscle bellies, and yet others attach via wide, flat tendons to the underlying skeletal bones. Also, using many independent muscle bellies to approximate a single muscle with a complex shape is not always anatomically appropriate—the real muscle may not even have muscle bellies that can be individually differentiated.

Representation and parameters

To model muscles with complex shapes, we use tubularly-shaped bicubic patch meshes capped with elliptic hemispheres at either end. Figure 9 illustrates the construction of such a patch mesh. It is defined by sweeping an ellipse along the path defined by the control points $\mathbf{o}_c$, $\mathbf{o}_v$, $\mathbf{i}_v$, and $\mathbf{i}_c$. During the sweep, the lengths of the major axes of the ellipse are adjusted to create fusiform-like profiles in directions orthogonal to the path. In Figure 9, this fusiform profile is easily observed in the rendered side view of the muscle[2].

Parameters that control the shape of general muscles are given in Table 1. As before, *class* parameters are used to define the shape of the muscle in its natural state, while the location, direction, and orientation of the muscle are specified before the muscle is instantiated.

Two points $\mathbf{o}_1$ and $\mathbf{o}_2$ specify the origin of the muscle. The midpoint $\mathbf{o}_c$ of $\mathbf{o}_1$ and $\mathbf{o}_2$ is where the path originates. Together with another parameter, $\mathbf{o}_v$, point $\mathbf{o}_c$ determines the general direction of the muscle near its origin. The points $\mathbf{o}_1$, $\mathbf{o}_2$, and $\mathbf{o}_v$ are all given

---

[2]A similar (but less conspicuous) profile is present in the rendered front view; however, the bend in the muscle and the eccentricity of the ellipse tend to disguise the profile.

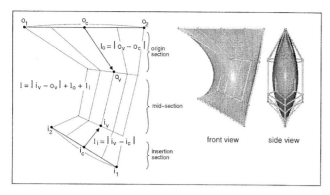

Figure 9: The general muscle model: contruction of a bicubic patch mesh by sweeping a varying ellipse along a cubic Bezier curve. For simplicity of illustration, the Bezier curve is defined in the plane of the page.

Parameters	Comment
Class parameters	*defines natural state of muscle*
V	muscle volume
r	height-to-width ratio of muscle's bulge
Other parameters	*locates, directs, and orients muscle*
$\mathbf{o}_1, \mathbf{o}_2$	defines origin of muscle
$\mathbf{o}_v$	directs origin section of muscle
$\mathbf{i}_1, \mathbf{i}_2$	defines insertion of muscle
$\mathbf{i}_v$	directs insertion section of muscle
h_o, h_i	height of muscle at origin and insertion
c	'depth' of capping elliptic hemisphere

Table 1: Parameters of the general muscle model.

in the local coordinate system of the bone where the muscle originates. Similarly, the points $\mathbf{i}_1$ and $\mathbf{i}_2$ specify the insertion of the muscle, and $\mathbf{i}_c$ and $\mathbf{i}_v$ determine the general direction of the muscle near its insertion. These points are given in the local coordinate system of the bone where the muscle inserts. The points $\mathbf{o}_c$, $\mathbf{o}_v$, $\mathbf{i}_v$, and $\mathbf{i}_c$ determine three lengths which are used in calculating the muscle's volume:

- the length of the origin section, $l_o = |\mathbf{o}_v - \mathbf{o}_c|$,

- the length of the insertion section, $l_i = |\mathbf{i}_v - \mathbf{i}_c|$, and

- the overall length of the muscle, $l = |\mathbf{o}_v - \mathbf{i}_v| + l_o + l_i$.

The parameters h_o and h_i determine the height of the muscle at each of its extremities, and c gives the undetermined radius of the capping hemispheres. The remaining parameters specify the volume of the muscle in its natural state, and the height-to-width ratio of the bulge of the muscle's mid-section.

Construction

The path along which the varying ellipse is swept is a cubic Bezier curve[3] defined by the control points $\mathbf{o}_c$, $\mathbf{o}_v$, $\mathbf{i}_v$, and $\mathbf{i}_c$. At $\mathbf{o}_c$ the ellipse has major axes with lengths $a_o = |\mathbf{o}_c - \mathbf{o}_1|$ and $b_o = \frac{h_o}{2}$, respectively. The major axes themselves are easily determined: the first is defined by the vector $\overrightarrow{\mathbf{o}_1 \mathbf{o}_c}$, and the second by the vector $\overrightarrow{\mathbf{o}_{up}} = \overrightarrow{\mathbf{o}_c \mathbf{o}_v} \times \overrightarrow{\mathbf{o}_1 \mathbf{o}_c}$. Similarly, the ellipse at $\mathbf{i}_c$ has major axes

---

[3]A cubic Bezier curve is used for the natural way in which it allows the direction of the path, and therefore the way the muscle bends, to be controlled.

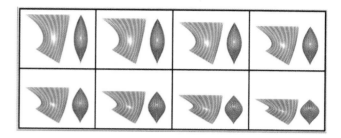

Figure 10: Operation of the general muscle model.

defined by $\overrightarrow{\mathbf{i}_1 \mathbf{i}_c}$ and $\overrightarrow{\mathbf{i}_{up}} = \overrightarrow{\mathbf{i}_c \mathbf{i}_v} \times \overrightarrow{\mathbf{i}_1 \mathbf{i}_c}$, with lengths $a_i = |\mathbf{i}_c - \mathbf{i}_1|$ and $b_i = \frac{h_i}{2}$, respectively.

To determine the lengths a and b of the major axes of the ellipses at $\mathbf{o}_v$ and $\mathbf{i}_v$, we use the volume of the muscle and the height-to-width ratio of the muscle's bulge at $\mathbf{o}_v$ and $\mathbf{i}_v$. First, consider the muscle's volume, V. Since the area of an ellipse with major axes x and y is $\pi x y$, the volume of the muscle may be approximated[4] by

$$
\begin{aligned}
V &= l_o \pi \left(\frac{a_o b_o + ab}{2} \right) + \\
&\quad (l - l_o - l_i)\pi \left(\frac{ab + ab}{2} \right) + l_i \pi \left(\frac{ab + a_i b_i}{2} \right) \\
&= \frac{\pi}{2} (l_o a_o b_o + (2l - l_o - l_i)ab + l_i a_i b_i) \\
&= \frac{\pi}{2} (C + Lab),
\end{aligned} \tag{5}
$$

where

$$
C = l_o a_o b_o + l_i a_i b_i \quad \text{and} \quad L = 2l - l_o - l_i > 0.
$$

Next, let the height-to-width ratio of the muscle's bulge at $\mathbf{o}_v$ and $\mathbf{i}_v$ be $r = \frac{a}{b}$, then Equation 5 becomes

$$
V = \frac{\pi}{2} \left(C + Lb^2 r \right).
$$

Equations expressing the lengths a and b of the major axes of the ellipses at $\mathbf{o}_v$ and $\mathbf{i}_v$ may now be stated:

$$
\begin{aligned}
b &= \sqrt{\frac{2V - C\pi}{\pi L r}} \tag{6} \\
a &= br. \tag{7}
\end{aligned}
$$

Implementation

As before, we implement the general muscle model in a class with two class parameters corresponding to V and r in Table 1. Before instantiating a muscle of this class, the origin and insertion should be specified. Two lists of the form $(\mathbf{o}_1, \ \mathbf{o}_2, \ \mathbf{o}_v)$ and $(\mathbf{i}_1, \ \mathbf{i}_2, \ \mathbf{i}_v)$ should be used. The class transforms these points to world coordinates before storing them. Figure 10 shows the general muscle model in action. The figure illustrates how a general muscle deforms when the relative locations of its extremities are changed. Notice how the curvature of the muscle is maintained, and how the muscle deforms automatically when its extremities are moved closer together.

---

[4]The volumes of the capping hemispheres, which are small relative to the volume enclosed by the patch mesh, are ignored; also, the volume enclosed by the patch mesh is approximated by summing the volumes of three truncated elliptic cones, one for each section of the patch mesh, as annotated in Figure 9.

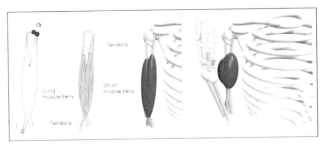

Figure 11: Front view of the biceps brachii and its behavior when the forearm is flexed at the elbow joint.

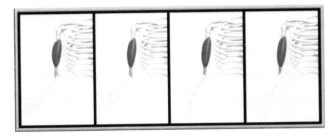

Figure 12: Behavior of the biceps brachii when the forearm is pronated while the elbow joint is flexed to 90.°

4.5 Muscles of the arm and torso

To illustrate the application of the muscle models, we consider three typical muscles of the arm and torso:

1. *The biceps brachii*, the familiar muscle on the upper arm that flexes and supinates the forearm;

2. *The pectoralis major*, a large, fan-shaped muscle on the upper front part of the chest; and

3. *The brachioradialis*, a muscle that twists around the elbow joint and assists in flexing the forearm.

Two instances of the fusiform muscle model are used to represent the biceps brachii (see Figure 11). We define two functions for specifying the muscle's attachments and one for instantiating the muscle. Notice that the biceps brachii is a multi-joint muscle. It originates from the scapula, spans over the shoulder, elbow, and radioulnar joints, and inserts into the radius bone. Therefore, when specifying the attachments of the muscle in the hierarchy, the origin function must be called just after creating the scapula, and the insertion function must be called just after creating the radius. This ensures that the origin and insertion points will be transformed together with their underlying parts; the scapula in case of the origin, and the radius in case of the insertion. Another action performed by the biceps brachii is supination of the forearm, an action that is most powerful when the elbow joint is flexed to 90.° In this position, if the forearm is pronated and supinated in alternation, the biceps brachii can be seen to elongate and shorten correspondingly. Even though this motion is less dramatic in its effect on the biceps brachii, it nevertheless is important to simulate. Figure 12 shows the behavior of the biceps brachii when the forearm in pronated with the elbow joint in a state of flexion. Figure 13 repeats the hierarchical definition of the arm skeleton presented earlier, but now it includes calls to the origin, insertion, and instantiation functions of the biceps brachii. These function calls appear in *italics* in the figure.

The pectoralis major originates from the clavicle and the sternum (see Figure 14) and inserts into the humerus. Because of this natural

```
(define (the-arm-skeleton)
 (lambda
  (reference-skeleton)

  (model "clavicle" (ElevateDepress ProtractRetract)
   (SC-joint (ElevateDepress) (ProtractRetract))
   (clavicle)

   (separator
    (AC-joint (ElevateDepress) (ProtractRetract))
    (scapula)
    (biceps-brachii-origin))

   (model "humerus" (AbductAdduct FlexExtend Rotate)
    (SH-joint (AbductAdduct) (FlexExtend) (Rotate))
    (humerus)

    (model "ulna" (ElbowFlexExtend)
     (EL-joint (ElbowFlexExtend))
     (ulna)

     (model "radius" (PronateSupinate)
      (RU-joint (PronateSupinate))
      (radius)
      (biceps-brachii-insertion)

      (model "hand" (FlexDorsiflex RabductUabduct)
       (WR-joint (FlexDorsiflex) (RabductUabduct))
       (hand))))))

   (biceps-brachii)
  ))
```

Figure 13: AL function defining the arm skeleton and the multi-joint biceps brachii muscle.

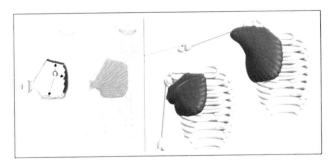

Figure 14: Front view of the pectoralis major and its behavior when the forearm is abducted at the shoulder joint.

division into two sections, we use two instances of the multi-belly class to represent the muscle. The figure shows the behavior of the pectoralis major when the arm is abducted at the shoulder joint. The model represents the general shape of the muscle quite well, and it even creates the armpit where the muscle bellies overlap near the insertion into the humerus.

We use the general muscle model and a simple tendon model [20] to represent the fleshy and tendinous portions of the brachioradialis (Figure 15), respectively. Figure 16 shows the behavior of this muscle when the forearm is flexed at the elbow joint. Notice how the muscle folds quite naturally as the elbow joint approaches full flexion. This behavior is made possible by allowing the two points defining the mid-section of the muscle ($\mathbf{o}_v$ and $\mathbf{i}_v$ in Table 1) to approach each other. Recall that these points are the second and third control points of the cubic curve defining the muscle's axis. As the angle between the origin and insertion section of the axis becomes more acute, the second and third control points move closer together and the bend in the muscle's mid-section becomes more pronounced. Of course, if the fold is not desired, the positions of the second and third control points can be adjusted as needed.

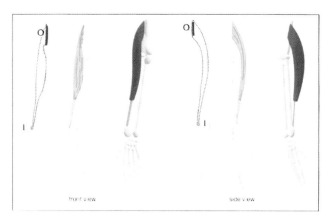

Figure 15: Front and side views of the brachioradialis.

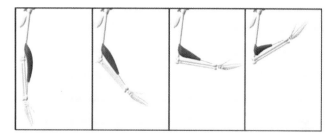

Figure 16: Behavior of the brachioradialis with flexion at the elbow joint.

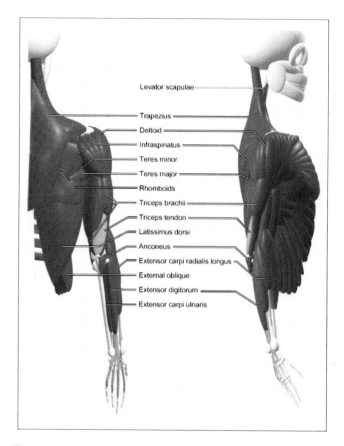

Figure 17: Muscles and tendons of the neck, trunk, shoulder, and upper limb.

4.6   Results and evaluation

We tested the muscle models on a variety of superficial and middle-layer muscles [8] that are responsible for joint movement in the upper limb. Figure 17 presents back and side views of some of these muscles. Notice how the general muscle model is used very successfully to model large muscles such as the trapezius and the latissimus dorsi. We also tested the deformation characteristics of the muscle models by creating an animation sequence to show how the biceps brachii muscle bulges when the forearm is flexed at the elbow joint. Selected frames of the animation sequence are shown in Figure 18.

Figures 17 and 18 show that the muscle models are capable of representing complex shapes with a high degree of realism, and that natural muscle shape deformation occurs when the underlying skeleton is moved. By implementing the muscle models in classes with well-defined interfaces, the instantiation of individual muscles is greatly simplified. Also, integrating the muscle layer into the hierarchical definition of the skeleton is straightforward. Origin, insertion, and instantiation functions for each muscle may be invoked at appropriate points in the hierarchy, allowing muscles that span over one or more joints to be defined with the same ease as the underlying bones in the skeleton.

5   CONCLUSION

This paper has presented a number of anatomy-based muscle models appropriate for simulating the behavior of skeletal muscles in humans. Each muscle model allows the extremities of muscles to be specified relative to different underlying bones, whether adjacent or not, and automatically adjusts the dimensions of the muscle when the extremities are moved closer together or further apart. The models are implemented in classes with consistent interfaces, thereby creating reusable components which may be used in con-

texts other than in human figure modeling, such as in 3D character animation and the animation of other animals with endoskeletons.

The muscle models manage the deformation of muscles due to isotonic contraction. These deformations are inherent in the models, completely automatic, and functionally dependent on the configuration (or pose) of the underlying articulated skeleton. To allow for isometric muscle contraction, we introduced a tension parameter to control the ratio of a muscle's height to its width, independent of the current pose. The muscle models take the muscle's tension as an instance parameter and deform the muscle accordingly. By binding the tension of individual muscles to articulation variables, users have complete control over the deformations of individual muscles.

We used a procedural modeling language to describe all our anatomy-based models. A language-based definition of complex hierarchical models is elegant and intuitive, and affords the creation of functional dependencies between different components. Interactive control is supported through the use of articulation variables, which may be used either directly, or in expressions, to modify components of the hierarchical model. Cooperating tools can be made available to give nontechnical users interactive control over the complex models.

We adopted an approach to modeling which parallels the one taken in the discipline of artistic anatomy. By analyzing the relationship between exterior form and the structures responsible for creating it, surface form and shape change may be understood best. We identified three general anatomical structures responsible for creating surface form and described one of these, the musculature, in some detail. Application of knowledge of the human anatomy to the development of human figure models is necessary if we hope to achieve a high degree of realism.

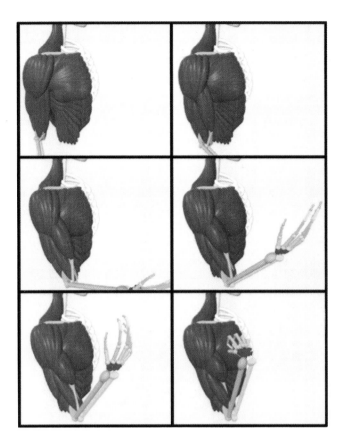

Figure 18: Behavior of the various muscle models with flexion at the elbow joint—isotonic and isometric contraction of the biceps muscle is simulated.

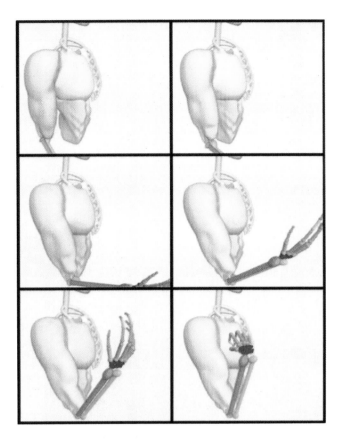

Figure 19: Application of a skin and fatty tissue model to muscles of the upper arm and torso.

We are currently investigating anatomy-based models for generating skin surfaces based on the influence of underlying deformable structures. The capability of implicit functions to blend individual primitives together is exploited in the generation of surfaces to represent the skin. Initial results look promising (see Figure 19). Implicit versions of the simple geometric modeling primitives are used to adjust the control points of bicubic patch meshes representing the skin. This technique also allows us to model fatty tissue between the muscles and the skin—adjusting the radius of influence of the implicit functions allows different thicknesses of fatty tissue deposits to be modeled.

Future research could analyze the structure and function of muscles further to enable a more automated approach to their creation than the one used here. If the origin, insertion, volume, and general shape of a muscle could be determined heuristically, perhaps based on the type of joint(s) being acted upon, or the desired action of the muscle, the creation of human figure models may be greatly simplified. Used in conjunction with a method for generating articulated skeletons automatically, this approach has great potential in creating new or fictional articulated figures for 3D animation applications.

References

[1] BADLER, N. I. Graphical behaviors and animated agents. In *Advanced Techniques in Human Modeling, Animation, and Rendering*. ACM SIGGRAPH, July 1992. (SIGGRAPH '92 Course Notes #17).

[2] CHADWICK, J. E., HAUMANN, D. R., AND PARENT, R. E. Layered construction for deformable animated characters. *Computer Graphics (SIGGRAPH 89 Conference Proceedings) 23*, 3 (July 1989), 243–252.

[3] CHEN, D. T., AND ZELTZER, D. Pump it up: Computer animation of a biomechanically based model of muscle using the finite element method. *Computer Graphics (SIGGRAPH 92 Conference Proceedings) 26*, 2 (July 1992), 89–98.

[4] DAWSON, H. L. *Basic Human Anatomy*, 2nd ed. Appleton-Century-Crofts, New York, 1974.

[5] DUFF, T. Splines in animation and modeling. In *SIGGRAPH 1986 Course Notes*. ACM SIGGRAPH, Aug. 1986.

[6] GASCUEL, M.-P. Welding and pinching spline surfaces: New methods for interactive creation of complex objects and automatic fleshing of skeletons. In *Graphics Interface '89 Proceedings* (June 1989), pp. 20–27.

[7] GAUDIN, A. J., AND JONES, K. C. *Human Anatomy and Physiology*. Harcourt Brace Jovanovich, San Diego, 1989.

[8] GOLDFINGER, E. *Human Anatomy for Artists: The Elements of Form*. Oxford University Press, New York, 1991.

[9] GOURRET, J.-P., THALMANN, N. M., AND THALMANN, D. Simulation of object and human skin deformations in a grasping task. *Computer Graphics (SIGGRAPH 89 Conference Proceedings) 23* (July 1989), 21–30.

[10] HENNE, M. A constraint-based skin model for human figure animation. Master's thesis, University of California, Santa Cruz, Santa Cruz, CA 95064, June 1990.

[11] MAGNENAT-THALMANN, N., AND THALMANN, D. Complex models for animating synthetic actors. *IEEE Computer Graphics and Applications 11*, 5 (Sept. 1991), 32–44.

[12] MAGNENAT-THALMANN, N., AND THALMANN, D. Environment-independent deformations and JLD operators. In *Advanced Techniques in Human Modeling, Animation, and Rendering*. ACM SIGGRAPH, July 1992. (SIGGRAPH '92 Course Notes #17).

[13] MAY, S. F., CARLSON, W., PHILLIPS, F., AND SCHEEPERS, F. AL: A language for procedural modeling and animation. Tech. Rep. OSU-ACCAD-12/96-TR5, ACCAD, The Ohio State University, Dec. 1996.

[14] MONHEIT, G., AND BADLER, N. I. A kinematic model of the human spine and torso. *IEEE Computer Graphics and Applications 11*, 2 (Mar. 1991), 29–38.

[15] NAHAS, M., HUITRIC, H., AND SAINTOURENS, M. Animation of a B-spline figure. *The Visual Computer 3*, 5 (1988), 272–276.

[16] PIEPER, S. Physically-based animation of facial tissue. In *State of the Art in Facial Animation*. ACM SIGGRAPH, 1989, pp. 71–124. (SIGGRAPH '89 Course Notes #22).

[17] PLATT, S. M., AND BADLER, N. Animating facial expressions. *Computer Graphics (SIGGRAPH 81 Conference Proceedings) 15*, 3 (Aug. 1981), 245–252.

[18] REEVES, W. T., OSTBY, E. F., AND LEFFLER, S. J. The Menv modelling and animation environment. *Journal of Visualization and Computer Animation 1*, 1 (Aug. 1990), 33–40.

[19] RICHER, P. *Artistic Anatomy*. Watson-Guptill Publications, New York, 1981. Translated by Robert Beverly Hale.

[20] SCHEEPERS, C. F. *Anatomy-based Surface Generation for Articulated Models of Human Figures*. PhD thesis, The Ohio State University, 1996. Adviser: Richard E. Parent.

[21] SCHEEPERS, F., PARENT, R. E., MAY, S. F., AND CARLSON, W. E. A procedural approach to modeling and animating the skeletal support of the upper limb. Tech. Rep. OSU-ACCAD-1/96-TR1, ACCAD, The Ohio State University, Jan. 1996.

[22] SEDERBERG, T. W., AND PARRY, S. R. Free-form deformation of solid geometric models. *Computer Graphics (SIGGRAPH 86 Conference Proceedings) 20*, 4 (Aug. 1986), 151–160.

[23] SINGH, K. *Realistic Human Figure Synthesis and Animation for VR Applications*. PhD thesis, The Ohio State University, 1995. Adviser: Richard E. Parent.

[24] STEINDLER, A. *Kinesiology of the Human Body*, 5th ed. Charles C. Thomas, Springfield, IL, 1977.

[25] TERZOPOULOS, D., AND WATERS, K. Physically-based facial modeling, analysis, and animation. *Journal of Visualization and Computer Animation 1*, 2 (Dec. 1990), 73–80.

[26] WATERS, K. A muscle model for animating three-dimensional facial expression. *Computer Graphics (SIGGRAPH 87 Conference Proceedings) 21*, 4 (July 1987), 17–24.

[27] WATERS, K. Modeling 3D facial expressions: Tutorial notes. In *State of the Art in Facial Animation*. ACM SIGGRAPH, 1989, pp. 127–160. (SIGGRAPH '89 Course Notes #22).

[28] WILHELMS, J. Modeling animals with bones, muscles, and skin. Tech. Rep. UCSC-CRL-95-01, University of California, Santa Cruz, Jan. 1995.

[29] WILHELMS, J., AND VAN GELDER, A. Anatomically based modeling. In *SIGGRAPH 97 Conference Proceedings* (Aug. 1997), T. Whitted, Ed., Annual Conference Series, ACM SIGGRAPH, Addison Wesley.

[30] WOLFF, E. *Anatomy for Artists*, 4th ed. H. K. Lewis & Co., London, 1968. Illustrated by George Charlton.

Anatomically Based Modeling

Jane Wilhelms and Allen Van Gelder*

University of California, Santa Cruz

Abstract

We describe an improved, anatomically based approach to modeling and animating animals. Underlying muscles, bones, and generalized tissue are modeled as triangle meshes or ellipsoids. Muscles are deformable discretized cylinders lying between fixed origins and insertions on specific bones. Default rest muscle shapes can be used, or the rest muscle shape can be designed by the user with a small set of parameters. Muscles automatically change shape as the joints move. Skin is generated by voxelizing the underlying components, filtering, and extracting a polygonal isosurface. Isosurface skin vertices are associated with underlying components and move with them during joint motion. Skin motion is consistent with an elastic membrane model. All components are parameterized and can be reused on similar bodies with non-uniformly scaled parts. This parameterization allows a non-uniformly sampled skin to be extracted, maintaining more details at the head and extremities.

CR Categories and Subject Descriptors: I.3 [Computer Graphics]; I.3.5 [Computational Geometry and Object Modeling]; I.3.7 [Three-Dimensional Graphics and Realism] Animation, Virtual Reality.

Additional Keywords: Human and Animal Modeling, Anatomically-Based Modeling.

1 INTRODUCTION

Humans, and other animals, are among the most important and interesting objects simulated using computer graphics, but they are also the most difficult to realistically model and animate. In general, computer graphics has achieved greater realism by developing methods that *simulate* the real world, rather than using ad hoc methods. As a step in this direction, we present a modeling and animation approach that is more closely based on anatomical principles than previously described methods. This model consists of individual muscles, bones, and generalized tissues covered by an elastic skin. The components mimic actual components of the animal body. In real animals, muscles stretch across joints to cause motion, and skin movements caused by underlying muscles can occur across a wide area. For simulated animals (and humans) to appear realistic, these widespread skin effects must be seen, and what better way to simulate these effects than to actually model individual muscles?

*Computer Science Dept, Univ. of California, Santa Cruz, CA 95064, USA. E-mail: {wilhelms,avg}@cs.ucsc.edu

Our modeling approach involves the following steps: (1) specify a body hierarchy and rest position; (2) design individual muscles, bones, and generalized tissues; (3) voxelize components into a 3D grid; filter; extract triangle-mesh skin; (4) map skin vertices parametrically from world space into the coordinate system of the nearest underlying component.

Animation involves repetition of the following steps: (1) specify motion at joints; (2) reposition and deform underlying components according to new positions; (3) map skin vertices back to world space; (4) apply iterative relaxation algorithm, adjusting skin vertices to achieve equilibrium of the elastic membrane forces. Table 2 shows performance times for these steps.

A longer version of this paper is available as a technical report [20]. Examples from our work on anatomically based modeling can be found on our web site www.cse.ucsc.edu/~wilhelms/fauna.

2 BACKGROUND AND RELATED WORK

Blinn's seminal work on implicit surface modeling included a "blobby man" made by extracting a surface from around an articulated skeleton [1]. Magnenat-Thalmann and Thalmann developed joint-local deformations (JDL's) where procedures are associated with each joint to simulate natural changes [10].

Chadwick *et al.* presented a method for layered construction of flexible animated characters [2] using *free-form deformations* [12]. The free-form deformation approach was also used by Komatsu [8] for skin. Mark Henne used a layered approach [6], in which *implicit fields* simulated body tissue. Singh *et al.* also used implicit functions to simulate skin behavior [13]. Turner *et al.* used an elastic skin model for character animation [14]. Skin wrinkling has been explored by Wu *et al.* [21]. Gourret *et al.* [5] used a finite element method to model the hand during grasping. None of these methods attempted to model individual three-dimensional muscles.

Chen and Zeltzer presented a biomechanically based muscle model using a finite element method to realistically simulate a few individual muscles without an overlying skin [3]. Another example from biomechanics is the work of Delp and Loan [4].

Recent work by Scheepers *et al.* is most closely related to ours [11]. Their emphasis is on modeling musculature, using a variety of geometric primitives.

The most anatomically detailed simulations have been done for the human face. Skin is generally modeled as a surface mesh whose points must move as expression changes. Physical simulation has been integrated into facial modeling by Lee *et al.* [9]. Koch *et al.* described a system for simulating facial surgery using finite element models [7]. None of these models used individual muscles with a physical presence to deform overlying tissue, though some do mimic individual muscle actions.

3 THE BASIC MODEL

Our body model uses a standard hierarchy of rigid segments connected by joints and emanating from a single root. The body consists of four types of materials. Individual *bones* are rigidly embedded in segments. Individual *muscles* are attached to bones.

Figure 1: Anatomical components in rest posture: skeleton (white), muscles (red), generalized tissue (purple), and skin (lower right).

Generalized tissue gives shape to regions where detailed bones and muscles aren't used, and for features such as eyes and nails. An elastic overlying triangle-mesh *skin* is attached to underlying tissues with anchors, but adjusts in response to forces from neighboring skin vertices. The model is appropriate for any vertebrate; we illustrate it here with a monkey body model. Figure 1 shows the underlying components and the skin in the rest position of the body.

The monkey model has 85 segments, including all segments connected by major moving joints in a vertebrate body: skull, jaw, 44 vertebrae, pelvis, arms, legs, wrists, ankles, fingers, and toes. All joints are capable of three revolute degrees of freedom, but their range can be limited by a maximum and minimum angle. Also, one can designate "synergies", so that a requested rotation is distributed over a *series* of joints. Synergies help to control many degrees of freedom easily, particularly in the spine and hands. E.g., a 12 degree rotation of the thoracic region is interpreted as a one degree rotation at each thoracic vertebra. Each segment has a *basic segment size* based on the long diagonal of the segment bounding box in the rest position, which is used in parameterizing components.

The skeleton and generalized tissues are modeled as triangle meshes or ellipsoids. These components do not change shape during motion, but can change position relative to each other. Each has its own local coordinate system. When stored, the sizes and locations of bones and generalized tissues are parameterized by the basic segment size, so that the same components can be used in an individual where segments are different sizes.

The monkey skeleton consists of 88 individual triangle-mesh bones based on a human skeleton model from *Viewpoint DataLabs* and altered using the *SGI Alias/Wavefront* software to be more monkey-like. There are 68 ellipsoidal bones for the tail, hands, and feet. Generalized tissue is represented by 54 ellipsoids. Eyes and nails are also ellipsoids. (See Figure 1.)

4 MUSCLES

A typical skeletal muscle is an elastic, contractile material. In anatomical terminology it *originates* via tendons at fixed *origin* locations on one or more bones, passes across one or more joints, and *inserts* via tendons on fixed *insertion* locations on one or more other bones more distal to the body center. When the muscle contracts, and shortens, the bones to which the muscles are attached are pulled toward each other. The diameter and shape of the muscle changes depending on the relative positions of origins and insertions. In a

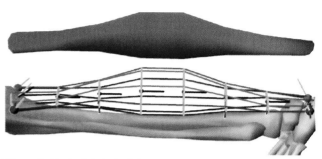

Figure 2: Typical default *deformed-cylinder* muscle, also illustrating anatomical terminology. The *proximal* direction is left, *distal* is right. The muscle is defined by two *origins* (red and green spheres at left) and two *insertions* (same at right). In the wireframe view below, eight yellow cross-sectional slices are connected by red edges to form a polygon mesh. The short blue and green lines are slice coordinate frame $Z-$ and $Y-$axes. The shaded polygon mesh is shown above.

Figure 3: A (user-adjusted) deformed-cylinder muscle, seen from side and front at three different levels of contraction.

real animal, muscle contraction causes joint motion. In our virtual animal, muscles change shape because of joint motion, to cause realistic skin deformations during animation. Initial work [19] used ellipsoids for muscles, which is adequate for those with a simple fusiform shape and a single origin and insertion. This model is insufficiently general for many muscles; e.g., only the lower arm muscles of the monkey model are ellipsoidal.

4.1 Deformed Cylinder Model for Muscles

Many muscles originate from or insert on more than one location. The various origins may be in different segments, and the same is true for insertions. To model such muscles, we have developed a muscle model based on a *deformed cylinder*. Our interests lie in producing relatively realistic animals that can be animated quickly and designed in a reasonable time frame. We have found this model to provide a good compromise between realism and speed.

The system generates, on request, a default deformed-cylinder muscle that is completely defined by two *origins* and two *insertions* (Figure 2). Origin and insertion points are described as three-dimensional locations on specific bones, parameterized by the size of the bounding box of the bone. In this way, the same muscle model can be used in different individuals. Origins must be proximal relative to insertions in the body hierarchy.

Each muscle is a discretized, deformed cylinder whose axis is a curve that proceeds from the midpoint of the origins to the midpoint of the insertions. Generally, the cylinder is discretized into 7 longitudinal *muscle sections* demarcated by 8 elliptical cross-sectional *slices*, as shown in Figure 2 (see also Figure 6).

The first elliptical slice lies between the two origins, and the last elliptical slice lies between the two insertions. The six intervening elliptical slices lie between and define the shape and longitudinal axis of the muscle. (There are no explicit tendons.) Each cross-sectional slice is then discretized into regularly spaced radial points, defining a planar polygon. Connecting the radial points between neighboring muscle cross-sections produces a polygon mesh, as shown in Figure 2.

There are approximately 80 major muscles that affect the shape of the arms, legs, and trunk (ignoring fingers and toes), most of which occur symmetrically on the right and left sides of the body [18]. The monkey model used here groups some of these muscles, divides a few, and ignores others. 40 deformed-cylinder muscles are used altogether.

The basic muscle definitions are provided to the program by an ascii file giving the muscle name, its origin and insertion bones, and the parameterized two origin and two insertion locations for each muscle. Origins and insertions can be interactively adjusted as needed for best effect, and the results saved.

4.2 Setting the Default Muscle Shape

The default muscle shape is automatically created based on the origins and insertions and can be altered interactively by the user. A *slice* coordinate frame is associated with each of the sliced segments of the muscle. The origins of these coordinate frames define the piecewise linear longitudinal axis of the muscle, and lie at the center of each slice ellipse. The X, Y, and Z axes of these slice frames are shown as red, green, and blue lines (respectively) in Figure 2. The XY planes of these slice coordinate frames define cross-sections of the muscle, and their Z-axis points along the longitudinal axis of the muscle, from muscle origins to muscle insertions. (We somewhat verbosely describe the (fixed) origin points of the muscle on bone as *muscle origins* and the origins of the slice coordinate frames as *coordinate frame origins* to prevent confusion in the different use of the word *origin*.)

The polyhedral vertices of the muscle's surface lie in the XY plane of each slice, arranged symmetrically around the slice coordinate frame origin, discretizing the ellipse. The number of vertices in each slice is under user control; the default number is 8. Figure 2 connects the muscle vertices within each slice with yellow lines, and muscle vertices between slices by reddish lines.

The locations of these frames and vertices are found as follows: First, all muscle origin and insertion locations are converted into the frame of the first muscle origin location's segment (i.e. the segment that contains the bone that the first muscle origin is attached to). The first muscle origin is just the one listed first in the muscle description file. This must be done anew each time any joint between origins and insertions changes.

Next, two end-slice coordinate frames are created. The midpoint of the two muscle origins becomes the origin of one end-slice frame, and the midpoint of the two insertions becomes the origin of the other. The lines between origins, and between insertions, define X-axes of end frames. The Z-axis of the origin slice coordinate frame is perpendicular to the X-axis and points outward from the origin bone. The Z-axis of the insertion slice frame is similarly perpendicular to the insertion frame X-axis, but points into the insertion bone. These Z-axes are found by averaging the outward normal vectors to the bones at the origin locations, and the inward normal vectors to the bones at the insertion locations. The Y-axes for these coordinate frames complete right-handed systems.

Now, the planes of the intermediate slices are calculated. Initially, they are arranged along a straight line between the origins of the two end coordinate frames described above, and equidistant from each other along this line. The intermediate slice frames have their Z-axes aligned along the line between end coordinate frame origins, and their X-axes are interpolated between the X-axes of the end frames. Once the thickness of the muscle slices is found, the origins of the intermediate frames are slightly displaced in the negative Y direction (outward from the underlying bone), to compensate for the greater thickness of the muscle near its center,

Figure 4: A. (at left) The right pectoralis major muscle shown shaded and the left in outline, illustrating a non-default muscle shape set interactively by the user. B. (at right) The quadriceps femoris muscles illustrating the use of a pivot. The right lower leg is in the rest position, and the left lower leg is flexed showing the muscle bending around its pivot.

creating a curved path from origin to insertions.

Finally, the vertices around each slice frame, which define the actual polygon mesh muscle surface, are calculated. These points are radially located around the coordinate frame origin of the slice in its XY-plane. The two end coordinate frames are constrained so that the width of the muscle (in X) is the distance between muscle origin points, and muscle insertion points, respectively. The vertex locations for the intermediate slices are scaled in X and Y to produce a fusiform shape, larger in the middle slices than in the end slices, and larger across (in X) than in thickness (in Y).

4.3 Non-Default Muscle Shapes

The user can interactively alter the size of a muscle, and the orientation and location of slice coordinate frames, and the locations of origins and insertions. Figure 4 shows two non-default muscle shapes, which illustrate the topics of this section.

First, the interface provides a facility to change the scale factors defining the X-width and Y-thickness of a muscle or any individual muscle slice. The cross-section of the muscle is always elliptical. Muscles such as the gastrocnemius in the leg, the biceps in the arm, and the sterno-cleido-mastoid in the neck are well represented by slightly scaling the default muscle shape (Figure 3).

Other muscle modification parameters alter location and orientation of the muscle slice coordinate frames. Any intermediate slice can be interactively translated from the default position. The orientation of the slice frames can also be rotated, in X, Y, or Z for intermediate frames, or in X alone for end frames. Figure 4.A. shows the pectoralis major muscles in the chest. Note that the shape of the muscle is more triangular than fusiform, the muscle is quite flat, and the slice coordinate frames are in an arc around the ribs, not in a straight line from origin to insertion.

Another modification method is to designate a *pivot* coordinate frame. In this case, the path of the muscle is not from muscle origins to insertions, but from origins to pivot, then from pivot to insertions. Pivots are helpful in modeling muscles such as the quadriceps femoris, which runs across the front of the thigh and bends over the knee (Figure 4.B). The origins of pivot coordinate frames are shown as blue spheres in outline figures. Generally, pivots can reduce the problem of interpenetration of the muscle with the material beneath it. (See Section 7 for further discussion of this problem.)

The pivot frame is defined relative to a specific segment, usually that of the segment containing the bone to which the first muscle origin is attached. Its location and orientation are under user control. A specific slice uses the pivot frame as its slice frame, and other frames arrange themselves on the line to the pivot frame, or from the pivot frame, depending on their position relative to the

> 2 origin locations parameterized on bones (x,y,z)
> 2 insertion locations parameterized on bones (x,y,z)
> x,y scale of each muscle shape slice
> x,y,z translate of slice coordinate frame from default
> x,y,z rotation of slice coordinate frame from default
> whether pivot is on, off, or variable
> which muscle shape slice acts as the pivot
> location of the origin of the pivot coordinate frame
> orientation of the pivot coordinate frame

Table 1: Muscle parameters controllable by the user.

pivot slice. The pivot frame can be permanently in effect (always used), or it can be used intermittently depending on whether the joint angles make it natural to use it. In Figure 4.B, the pivot frame is the seventh frame, as the bend occurs near the very end of the muscle. The right leg is in its rest position, and the left lower leg is flexed, showing the muscle bending around its pivot.

Table 1 summarizes the user-controllable parameters for muscle design. Nearly all the muscles in the monkey model shown in Figure 1 used some non-default parameters.

4.4 Muscle Animation

Muscle animation involves the automatic recalculation of the muscle shape whenever a joint lying between muscle origins and insertions moves. The muscle origins and insertions are converted to the frame of the first origin, given the new joint positions. A default shape is found, and automatically adjusted using the user-specified non-default muscle parameters described in the previous section.

Finally, the muscle width and thickness are scaled to maintain approximately constant muscle volume during joint changes. The *rest length* of the muscle is the distance from the midpoint of the muscle origins, through the pivot, if present, to the midpoint of the insertions, while the muscle is in the resting position, as designed. A *present length* is similarly calculated for when the muscle is repositioned due to joint changes. The width and thickness of the internal slices of the muscle (not the end slices) are scaled by $\sqrt{rest\ length\ /\ present\ length}$. This increases the cross-sectional area if the muscle shortens, and decreases it if it lengthens. Volume is preserved exactly in regions between parallel slices, and is changed as a second order effect in regions between two nonparallel scaled slices. However, end slices do not change shape, so regions involving an end slice will normally vary in volume. In any case, exact volume preservation of muscles is not biologically justified. Isometric deformations provide a case in point. Future work should address a more flexible and more biologically sophisticated method for adjusting muscle volume.

The new muscle shape is stored and reused for display and skin adjustment purposes until another joint change necessitating recalculation occurs. Figure 3 shows a muscle from the front and side at three levels of contraction.

5 SKIN

The skin is an elastic triangle-mesh surface that is attached to underlying components but can move relative to them; i.e., a separate, controllably loose layer over underlying components. The initial creation of the surface is based on fairly standard implicit surface techniques, and is summarized below. The novel contribution of this paper is the methodology for skin deformation in response to deformation of the underlying tissue, described in subsequent subsections.

The region around the animal in the rest position is voxelized to create a three-dimensional discrete grid of points. Values at

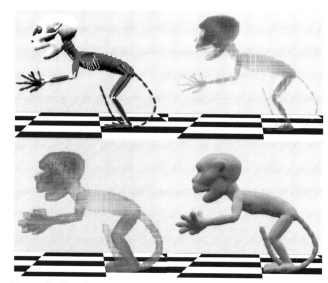

Figure 5: Voxelization and skin extraction illustrated: underlying parts with extremities enlarged (upper left); initial "density" function (upper right); after filtering (lower left); extracted skin (lower right).

points define an artificial *density function* that is positive if the point is inside any body part and zero otherwise. (In addition, certain artificial components may have a *negative* density to create a repulsion effect, discussed below.) Then the initial density function is filtered with a Gaussian kernel, whose width is under user control. The user chooses a threshold, and an isosurface of the filtered density is extracted as a triangulated surface mesh.

Figure 5 shows these steps. Upper left shows the underlying components; the head and extremities are enlarged for better skin detail in those areas, as described in Section 5.3. Upper right is a voxel grid whose maximum resolution is 200, showing interior grid points in magenta. Grid points outside the body are not shown. The purple spheres near the eyes contribute negative values to the field, making deep orbits for the eyes. Lower left is the voxel grid after filtering, showing the grid points with positive field values in cyan. The Gaussian filter kernel had a standard deviation of about 3 voxel separations. Lower right is the extracted skin.

5.1 Anchoring Skin

After surface extraction, in a second stage called *anchoring*, each vertex in the triangle-mesh skin is associated with the closest underlying body component (muscle, bone, or generalized tissue).

The *anchor* of a particular skin vertex is the nearest point on its underlying component. More important for animation is the *virtual anchor*, which is the initial position of a skin vertex relative to its underlying component. This is the position of the vertex when the skin was extracted in the animal's rest position. The anchors and virtual anchors are stored parameterized in the local space of the component. If shape changes occur in the underlying component, they are transmitted through the anchors and virtual anchors, to affect the skin vertices correspondingly. Each skin vertex is considered to be connected to its virtual anchor by a spring of rest length zero, and a specified spring stiffness. (See Section 5.2.)

Anchoring refers to the process of finding the nearest underlying component of each skin vertex, converting that skin vertex to a parameterized local location relative to the component, and storing this local position of the skin vertex as its virtual anchor. Anchoring skin to ellipsoids was previously described [19]. To anchor skin to triangle-mesh bones, skin vertices are converted into the coordinate

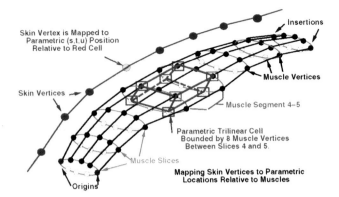

Figure 6: Illustration of mapping skin vertices to parametric trilinear functions over muscle segments. The lightest skin vertex lies between muscle slices 4 and 5, and is mapped into an (s, t, u) coordinate system defined by the eight muscle vertices shown in red.

Figure 7: This figure illustrates the concepts of anchors, virtual anchors, and elastic relaxations, on a shoulder and raised left arm. It corresponds to the center third of Figure 8. Skin vertices are connected by brown edges to form a triangle mesh. In the left image, skin vertices coincide with their virtual anchors, as no elastic relaxation has been done. In the right image, after elastic relaxation, the virtual anchor positions are unchanged, while the skin vertices have been redistributed more uniformly. In both images yellow lines connect skin vertices to their muscle anchors. In the right image red lines connect the skin vertices to their virtual anchors, showing the displacement necessary to equalize spring forces.

system of the bone and scaled by the size of its bounding box in each dimension. Anchoring points to deformed-cylinder muscles is a more interesting problem, described next.

The skin vertex is associated with a section of the muscle that lies between two muscle slices. In Figure 6, the lighter skin vertex lies nearest to the muscle segment between slices 4 and 5, and will be mapped to a parametric location in this region. One cannot simply map the skin vertices into the frame of single slice, because bumps appear in the skin when the muscles change shape, due to the abrupt changes in mapping from one slice frame to the next.

Rather, we define a *parametric trilinear transformation* (more precisely named "tri-affine") over the space between the planes of the two slices in rest position, and assign parameters to the virtual anchor in accordance with the inverse of this transformation. A parametric trilinear transformation is a three-vector of independent trilinear functions, each of which maps parameter-space (s, t, u) into physical-space (x, y, z). The parametric trilinear transformation maps a unit cube into a warped cell such that edges in the original cell remain as straight lines. Parametric trilinear transformations are defined on adjacent cubes so that they map each shared corner of their cubes to the same point. This ensures that they combine to make a $C0$ continuous transformation. Related ideas are found in free-form deformations of computer modeling [12].

The parametric trilinear transformation for a muscle segment is found by taking four corresponding muscle vertices from each of the slice planes that bound the segment. The four from the "proximal" slice will be the image of a parametric unit cube's $u = 0$ face, while the four from the "distal" slice will be the image of the same unit cube's $u = 1$ face. Joining corresponding vertices of the two slices makes the warped image of the unit cube. In Figure 6 such a warped cell is shown in red. These eight vertices provide the 24 unknowns necessary to specify the coefficients of the parametric trilinear transformation. Each skin vertex associated with a particular muscle segment is then mapped inversely to a parametric position (s, t, u) within the domain of the parametric trilinear transformation defining that segment. The inverse mapping has no closed form, and requires 3D Newton-Raphson iteration [15]. The (s, t, u) parameterized position is the virtual anchor for that skin vertex. This expensive operation needs to be done only once per vertex, during anchoring.

When the body is moved, new world space positions are calculated for the slices (see Section 4.4). Then for each adjacent pair of slices a *new* parametric trilinear transformation is defined. (This process is not expensive, compared to calculating general inverse mappings.) Virtual anchor points associated with this segment are

mapped from (s, t, u) to world space, using the new parametric trilinear transformation, in the *forward* direction. Each virtual anchor provides an initial skin position for its corresponding skin vertex, for this body configuration.

Figure 7 illustrates these concepts on the left shoulder and arm of the monkey. The arm is raised away from the rest position, with consequent deformation of nearby muscles. Virtual anchor points have been remapped from parameter space to world space, taking into account both the rigid motion and deformation of their respective muscles.

5.2 The Elastic Model

To simulate an elastic membrane each edge of the skin triangle mesh is considered to be a spring with a certain rest length and stiffness. Together with other forces and constraints in the system, these springs are brought into equilibrium by means of a series of relaxation operations. The initial skin positions, from which relaxation commences, are provided by the positions of the virtual anchor, as described in Section 5.1. Relaxation operations continue iteratively until a user-defined convergence tolerance is reached, or a user-defined maximum number of iterations has occurred.

The spring stiffness coefficient (stiffness, for short), for edges between skin vertices is denoted as k_e. This value is automatically calculated as

$$k_e(v, v_j) \quad = \quad \frac{a_1 + a_2}{len^2} \tag{1}$$

where *len* is the length of the edge between skin vertices v and v_j, and a_1 and a_2 are the areas of the two triangles sharing the edge, all calculated once in the rest position. This formula provides a more accurate model of uniformly elastic skin than would uniform stiffness for all springs [17]. The formula used is simplified from the general case by assuming the Poisson coefficient for skin is 0. (A more complicated formula with the more realistic Poisson coefficient of 0.25 did not produce observable differences.)

The spring stiffness for the edge between the skin vertex and its virtual anchor is denoted as k_a. This "edge" has zero rest length. For each skin triangle, the force resulting from pulling the skin away from the underlying material is assumed to be proportional to the area of the triangle (as is standard for "body forces" in elasticity), and this area is distributed equally to the three skin

177

vertices incident upon the triangle. Consequently,

$$k_a(v) \quad = \quad C_a \sum_i \frac{a_i}{3} \tag{2}$$

where a_i denotes the area of the i-th triangle incident upon the skin vertex v, and the sum is over all such triangles. The coefficient C_a is a proportionality constant to control the relative strengths of skin-skin springs (k_e's) and skin-virtual-anchor springs (k_a's). For the monkey model, the anchor spring stiffness is generally scaled by $C_a = 0.10$, which allows the skin to slide readily over the underlying parts.

If constant spring stiffness coefficients are used instead of the geometrically determined values in Eqs. 1–2), then we observed that the equilibrium position of the skin appears irregularly stretched.

To find the change in position to be applied to a vertex due to the influence of a connected edge, the elastic force vector is calculated. First, the vector $w_j = v_j - v$ is defined, where v is the vertex being analyzed, and v_j is the vertex at the far end of the edge. The length of w_j is the present length of the edge. The rest length of the edge is subtracted from the present length, giving the *length excess*, which may be negative. Now the spring stiffness, $k_e(v, v_j)$ may be modified, based on the *length excess*, providing a form of nonlinear spring (see below). The *length excess* is multiplied by the (possibly modified) spring stiffness for the edge to give the scalar value of elastic force due to this edge. The direction of the elastic force is just the direction of w_j. Thus the elastic force is toward v_j if the *length excess* is positive, and away from v_j if it is negative.

For each vertex v, the sum of the elastic forces due to each of its edges to other skin vertices v_j, and due to the edge to its virtual anchor, defines the *net elastic force* acting on this vertex. This net force is divided by the sum of the spring stiffness coefficients that contributed to the net force, giving the *elastic relaxation vector* for v. (This denominator is conservatively large, as various forces tend to cancel each other; however it stabilizes the relaxation.) All skin vertex positions are translated by their relaxation vectors in one round of relaxation. The relaxations are iterated until the maximum relaxation vector is below the user-specified threshold, or the user-specified maximum number of iterations occurs.

Figures 7 and 8 show the effect of elastic relaxation on the skin. The smooth redistribution seen in the right images is important to achieve a natural appearance for fur [16] or skin with markings.

A few other parameters can be applied to the skin. First, we want the skin to *pull* from a stretched position toward its rest state more strongly than it *pushes* back when it is compressed. Therefore, a user-controlled scale factor can be applied to scale down the spring force if the present length is less than the rest length. Typically this scale factor is 0.1.

Second, the skin can appear more smooth if we adjust the model so that the skin is slightly stretched in its extracted configuration. I.e., the *rest length* of the edge is taken to be some percentage of the measured *default length* of the edge when extracted. Suppose the user has chosen 90% for this parameter, and 0.1 for the above "pushing back" parameter. Then k_e, the spring stiffness will be modified by the following continuous function of *length excess*, discussed above. If *length excess* is positive, k_e is used as is (100%). If *length excess* is more negative than $-0.1 \times$(rest length), then $0.1k_e$ is used (10%). If *length excess* is between these bounds, the multiplier for k_e is interpolated between 10% and 100%.

Finally, a collision influence can be applied to prevent the skin from sinking into underlying components. Each skin vertex is prohibited from penetrating a sphere whose center is somewhat below the anchor point in the underlying component. The surface of this sphere is tangent to the tangent plane of the skin at the virtual anchor point. I.e., if the calculated new position of the skin vertex penetrates such a sphere, a repelling force is activated to displace the skin vertex outward toward the sphere surface.

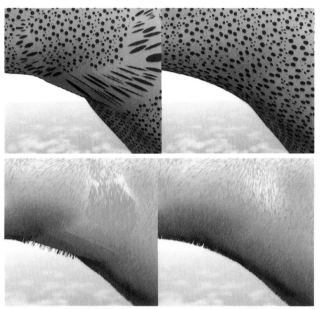

Figure 8: This figure illustrates the effect on skin of elastic relaxation. At left, no elastic relaxation has occurred, and skin vertices coincide with their virtual anchors. At right, 30 relaxations have occurred, the skin has largely stabilized, and skin vertices are more uniformly distributed (see wireframe detail view in Figure 7). Red dots appearing in the top images are produced by texture maps on the triangles of the skin surface, which vary in size and shape, even in the rest position. Dots are proportional in area to their triangles, and are circular in the rest position. Before relaxation (left) unequal distortions of the red dots are apparent, while after relaxation (right) they exhibit smoothly varying deformations. Bottom images show the effect on fur, which is attached to skin triangles. Before relaxation, the unequal skin stretching produces gaps and irregularities; after relaxation, fur and skin appear normal.

This approach only handles collisions between the skin and its nearby underlining tissues. A second collision type occurs when a joint is bent so that skin on either side of the joint meet. In this case interpenetration can occur, but it is hidden within the folds of the skin. A third collision type occurs when skin from one part of the body presses on another. This would require modeling the influence of external collision forces on the skin, which we do not do.

5.3 Non-Uniform Scaling and Re-usability

Because all components are parameterized, they can be re-used to a large extent in different individuals. The basic reference for all components is ultimately the basic segment size (see Section 3). If a model with larger or smaller segments is used, components compensate automatically for the change in size. It is also possible to scale the basic size by applying an extra scale factor to each segment when the body is read in. In this way, we created the model shown in Figure 5, with extra large extremities. By voxelizing such a model, more detail is preserved in the hands and feet. The skin is then saved, and can be re-used on a model with more normal-sized segments. All the monkeys shown in this paper used such scaling. Because of the similarity between vertebrates, many of the components of one model can be used for other species as well. It is also possible to scale the thickness of the skin, by moving the virtual anchors further from their underlying components.

Figure 9 shows the effects of scaling. These three monkeys were made from the identical underlying components and skin as all the other monkeys in the paper but in the left image the arms are

Figure 9: Three monkeys were made from the identical underlying components and skin, but with long arms (left), thick skin (middle), and long legs (right).

lengthened, in the right image the legs are lengthened, and in the center the skin thickness is increased to create a plump monkey.

6 RESULTS AND DISCUSSION

The monkey model contains 85 body segments, 156 bones, 52 muscles, and 54 generalized components. The skin was voxelized over a grid whose maximum dimension was 225. Internal points were assigned 200 as density, outside points were 0. It was filtered by a Gaussian kernel with standard deviation 3.2. The isosurface threshold was 35. There are about 75,000 skin vertices and about 150,000 skin triangles. Table 2 gives times for various steps.

Figure 10 shows a selection of monkey images in various positions. The "mohawk" fur [16] is a whimsical addition to make the monkey seem less bald without obscuring the skin deformations that we wish to emphasize.

The parameterized muscle shape model is fast and easy to change, and provides a good approximation to the shape of most muscles (but see below). The monkey model could be improved by making more muscles. There can be problems in certain extreme positions. However, as the images and animations show, the body looks good over a wide range of motions.

The most time-consuming part of creating the model was to model individual muscles. Although each change is easy, a tedious trial-and-error process was needed to customize difficult muscles. Knowledge of anatomy is helpful, although students with no background in anatomy were able to perform many modeling tasks with light supervision of a trained biologist, and appropriate texts on anatomy (e.g., [18]).

An alternative to adjusting a permanent skin in response to underlying tissue deformations would be to re-extract skin over new positions. However, this would raise questions about consistency from one position to the next. For example, how would a texture be associated with the skin that appears to shift realistically?

The current skin model produces a smooth surface that is visu-

Figure 10: A selection of monkey images. Notice the effect of individual muscles, and the ability of the model to simulate both stretching and folds.

ally close to equilibrium after about 30 iterations; after this, changes from one iteration to the next are barely noticeable. Even after 5 or 10 iterations, acceptable convergence is found in many cases.

7 FUTURE WORK

This remains a very approximate model when compared to actual animal anatomy. It is a reasonable compromise between detailed realism and acceptable modeling and animation speed, and is a considerable step forward from ellipsoidal models.

The major next step we envision is underlying components that interact with each other, and do not interpenetrate. This will allow more detailed, space-filling components to be created, which reposition themselves based on influences from neighboring components. Generalized tissue should also be extended to accommodate shape changes, as muscles do now. While these additions will be more expensive, the minimal computational cost of adjusting the present underlying components suggest it will still be feasible in a fairly interactive system.

It would be a relatively simple matter to have muscles pull on their bones and implement a real physically based simulation of joint motion. This could be useful for educational purposes or for research in biomechanics. However, the control problems of physically simulating general realistic motion using contraction of individual muscles is really beyond present capabilities.

It would be desirable to have more detail in the face than provided by the non-uniform scaling. Because the skin is initially a

Steps Done Once to Create Skin	
Voxelization (Max. Dim. 225)	185
Filtering (3.2 std.dev. kernel)	160
Isosurface Extraction	16
Anchoring	645
Steps Required if Joints Moved	
Redraw of Underlying Components	Less than 1
Skin Repositioning - 0 relaxations	3
Skin Repositioning - 10 relaxations	9
Skin Repositioning - 30 relaxations	25

Table 2: Elapsed times in seconds for various steps, on an SGI with four 150-MHz R4400 processors, using shared-memory multiprocessing.

separate polygonal layer that is then connected to the underlying components, it would be possible to connect a triangle-mesh skin from elsewhere to underlying components. For example, a digitized head model or a model extracted from CT scans could be connected to the underlying parts. This would require appropriate positioning and scaling.

The skin and underlying components should also react to outside forces, such as gravity, and detect and respond to all collision types.

8 CONCLUSIONS

This paper describes a new and improved modeling and animation approach for animals and humans that is based on actual three-dimensional representations of individual body components such as bones, muscles, and miscellaneous tissue, covered by a skin. We believe this is the most natural approach to use for creating realistic animals and humans. The scheme is a good compromise between realism and complexity, and can be displayed and animated interactively. We believe the approach can be extended to produce much greater realism at an acceptable computational cost.

Acknowledgments

List processing software by Yumi Tsuji was used in this software package. Marlon Veal helped with programming. Research supported by a gift from Research and Development Laboratories, and by NSF Grant CDA-9115268.

References

[1] James F. Blinn. A Generalization of Algebraic Surface Drawing. *ACM Transactions on Graphics*, 1(3):235–256, July 1982.

[2] John E. Chadwick, David R. Haumann, and Richard E. Parent. Layered Construction for Deformable Animated Characters. In *Computer Graphics (SIGGRAPH 89 Conference Proceedings)*, volume 23 of *Annual Conference Series*, pages 242–252. Addison Wesley, August 1989.

[3] David T. Chen and David Zeltzer. Pump It Up: Computer Animation Based Model of Muscle Using the Finite Element Method. In *Computer Graphics (SIGGRAPH 92 Conference Proceedings)*, volume 26, pages 89–98. Addison Wesley, July 1992.

[4] Scott L. Delp and J. Peter Loan. A Graphics-based Software System to Develop and Analyze Models of Musculoskeletal Structures. *Computers in Biology and Medicine*, 25(1):21–34, 1995.

[5] Jean-Paul Gourret, Nadia Magnenat-Thalmann, and Daniel Thalmann. Simulation of Object and Human Skin Deformations in a Grasping Task. In *Computer Graphics (SIGGRAPH 89 Conference Proceedings)*, volume 23, pages 21–30. Addison Wesley, July 1989.

[6] Mark Henne. A Constraint-Based Skin Model for Human Figure Animation. Master's thesis, University of California, Santa Cruz, Santa Cruz, CA 95064, June 1990.

[7] R. M. Koch, M. H. Gross, F. R. Carls, D. F. von Buerin, G. Fankhauser, and Y. I. H. Parish. Simulating Facial Surgery Using Finite Element Models. In *SIGGRAPH 96 Conference Proceedings*, Annual Conference Series, pages 421–428. ACM SIGGRAPH, Addison Wesley, August 1996.

[8] K. Komatsu. Human Skin Model Capable of Natural Shape Variation. *The Visual Computer*, 4(3):265–271, 1988.

[9] Yuencheng Lee, Demetri Terzopoulos, and Keith Waters. Realistic modeling for facial animation. In *SIGGRAPH 95 Conference Proceedings*, Annual Conference Series, pages 55–62. ACM SIGGRAPH, Addison Wesley, 1995.

[10] Nadia Magnenat-Thalmann and Daniel Thalmann. Human Body Deformations Using Joint-Dependent Local Operators and Finite Element Theory. In N. Badler, B. Barsky, and D. Zeltzer, editors, *Making Them Move*. Morgan Kaufmann Publishers, Inc., San Mateo, CA, 1991.

[11] Ferdi Scheepers, Richard E. Parent, Wayne E. Carlson, and Stephen F. May. Anatomy-based modeling of the human musculature. In *SIGGRAPH 97 Conference Proceedings*, Annual Conference Series. ACM SIGGRAPH, Addison Wesley, August 1997.

[12] Thomas W. Sederberg and Scott R. Parry. Free-form deformations of solid geometric objects. In *Computer Graphics (SIGGRAPH 92 Conference Proceedings)*, volume 20, pages 151–160. Addison Wesley, August 1986.

[13] Karansher Singh, Jun Ohya, and Richard Parent. Human figure synthesis and animation for virtual space teleconferencing. In *Proceedings of the Virtual Reality Annual International Symposium '95*, pages 118–126, Research Triangle Park, N.C., March 1995. IEEE Computer Society Press.

[14] R. Turner and D. Thalmann. The Elastic Surface Layer Model for Animated Character Construction. In N. M. Thalmann and D. Thalmann, editors, *Proceedings of Computer Graphics International '93*, pages 399–412, Lausanne, Switzerland, June 1993. Springer-Verlag.

[15] Allen Van Gelder and Jane Wilhelms. Interactive Animated Visualization of Flow Fields. In *1992 Workshop on Volume Visualization*, pages 47–54, Boston, Mass., October 1992. ACM.

[16] Allen Van Gelder and Jane Wilhelms. An Interactive Fur Modeling Technique. In *Proceedings of Graphics Interface*, May 1997.

[17] Allen Van Gelder and Jane Wilhelms. Simulation of Elastic Membranes and Soft Tissue with Triangulated Spring Meshes. Technical Report UCSC-CRL-97-12, CS Dept., University of California, 225 A.S., Santa Cruz, CA 95064, January 1997.

[18] Marvalee H. Wake, editor. *Hyman's Comparative Vertebrate Anatomy*. University of Chicago Press, Chicago, Illinois, third edition edition, 1979.

[19] Jane Wilhelms. Animals with Anatomy. *IEEE Computer Graphics and Applications*, 17(3):22–30, May 1997.

[20] Jane Wilhelms and Allen Van Gelder. Anatomically Based Modeling. Technical Report UCSC-CRL-97-10, CS Dept., University of California, 225 A.S., Santa Cruz, CA 95064, April 1997.

[21] Yin Wu, P. Kalra, and N. M. Thalmann. Simulation of Static and Dynamic Wrinkles of Skin. In *Proceedings of Computer Animation '96*, pages 90–97, Geneva, Switzerland, June 3–4 1996. IEEE Computer Society Press.

Modeling the Motion of a Hot, Turbulent Gas

Nick Foster and Dimitris Metaxas

Center for Human Modeling and Simulation
University of Pennsylvania, Philadelphia
{fostern | dnm}@graphics.cis.upenn.edu

Abstract

This paper describes a new animation technique for modeling the turbulent rotational motion that occurs when a hot gas interacts with solid objects and the surrounding medium. The method is especially useful for scenes involving swirling steam, rolling or billowing smoke, and gusting wind. It can also model gas motion due to fans and heat convection. The method combines specialized forms of the equations of motion of a hot gas with an efficient method for solving volumetric differential equations at low resolutions. Particular emphasis is given to issues of computational efficiency and ease-of-use of the method by an animator. We present the details of our model, together with examples illustrating its use.

Keywords: Animation, Convection, Gaseous Phenomena, Gas Simulations, Physics-Based Modeling, Steam, Smoke, Turbulent Flow.

1. Introduction

The turbulent motion of smoke and steam has always inspired interest amongst graphics researchers. The problem of modeling the complex inter-rotational behavior that arises as gases of different temperatures mix and interact with solid objects is still an open one. This behavior forms the part of so many everyday scenes (*e.g.*, steam rising from street gratings) that it remains an important topic in computer graphics.

There have been several previous approaches to modeling gas motion for computer graphics. Wejchert and Haumann [18] and Sims [13] modeled gases using the manual superposition of deterministic wind fields. This gives an animator control over the flow in an animation by placing vortices and flow field components by hand. More random motion, due to turbulence and diffusion, has proved amenable to spectral analysis. Shinya and Fournier [15], Stam and Fiume [16], and Sakas [12] define stochastic models of turbulent motion in Fourier space, and then transform them to give periodic, chaotic looking vector fields that can be used to convect gas particles or interact with simple objects.

These and similar approaches to modeling turbulent gases require that the animator has micro-control over the behavior of the gas. They characterize the visual behavior of gases without accurately modeling the physics-based components of gas flow. This leaves the animator with the sometimes difficult task of defining wind field parameters and small scale stochastic turbulence parameters wherever the visual characteristics of the flow vary significantly. For simple scenes and homogeneous effects this leads to good results which can be

easily controlled. However, for scenes involving complex motion or a lot of interaction between a gas and other objects, it is almost impossible to manually create and control a natural looking animation. This is because the appearance of this kind of phenomena is very sensitive to the behavior of the gas as a volume. Rising steam, for example, is directed by the interaction and mixing between it and the surrounding air, as well as the convective flow field around static or moving objects. It would be prohibitively difficult to model these effects by hand even using existing methods for defining stochastic turbulence and laminar wind fields. The best way to achieve realism would be to model these effects in a physically accurate way, but the methods available to do so are inefficient, and tailored to computational fluid mechanics rather than computer graphics.

Another popular method has been to treat gases as collections of particles. Ebert, Carlson, and Parent [3], Reeves and Blau [11], and Stam and Fiume [17] reduced the complexity of the gas volume modeling problem in this way by using discrete particles to represent gaseous motion. Particle systems are generally efficient, but have two inherent drawbacks. First, a real gas is a continuous medium; selecting particular regions, and then estimating the interaction between them, can lead to unpredictable results for the animator. It is also unclear how interaction between volumes of gas is modeled using forces between particles. Often, the rotational component of such interaction still needs to be added manually. Second, the most visually interesting gaseous behavior is due to the fact that the gas being modeled is mixing with its surrounding medium. This medium has not been modeled in the particle system methods and so its effects can only be estimated. This may lead to visual simulations that have an unrealistic feel to them. Yaeger, Upson, and Myers [10] generated an excellent animation of the surface of the planet Jupiter by building a vorticity field from a particle-based motion system. The results were very realistic, but the method does not generalize to three dimensions and cannot account for flow around obstacles. In addition, a Cray X-MP was required to achieve reasonable computation times. A similar combination of vortex field and particle motion was used by Chiba *et. al.* [1] for their 2D simulations of flames and smoke. This technique does generalize to three dimensions and handles laminar gas flow around objects very nicely, but it isn't strictly physics-based. Again, this puts responsibility on the animator to achieve realism. These methods do show however, that the combination of visual simulation and physics-based simulation can lead to satisfying results for computer graphics.

In this paper we develop a new physics-based model specifically designed to realistically animate the complex rotational component of gaseous motion, effects due to regions of different temperature within a gas, and the interaction between gases and other objects. This work directly addresses the problem that no graphics models exist for the precise calculation of the turbulent, buoyant, or rotational motion that develops as a gas interacts with itself and solid objects. In the past, definition of this component of gas motion has been done via ad hoc methods or left to the skill of the animator. The paper's main contribution is a method for the efficient animation of both the turbulent and swirling behavior of a three-dimensional volume of hot gas in an arbitrary environment. The model we have developed accounts for convection, turbulence, vorticity and thermal buoyancy, and can also accurately model gas flowing around complex objects. This gives rise to a number of realistic effects that could not be modeled previously, such as hot steam being vented into a boiler room or the rolling smoke cloud from an explosion. We show that not only is the proposed method accurate, it is also fast, straightforward, and can be used as a general graphics tool. Fast, because we use a simplified set of equations (compared to those used in the computational fluid dynamics literature) which are adequate for modeling the desired effects. Straightforward, because boundary conditions are set automatically and can be used to model different types of objects (rough or smooth for example). The model is mathematically nontrivial, but we will show that its solution proceeds in relatively simple computational steps.

2. Developing a gas model for computer graphics

Before trying to model a hot gas for computer graphics purposes, it is important to have some intuition for those factors that influence its motion. Consider as an example, an old fashioned steam engine venting a jet of hot gas from its boiler. A governing factor in the motion of the gas is the velocity it has when rushing into the surrounding air. As it mixes with the slower moving air, the steam experiences drag (shearing forces), and starts to rotate in some places. This rotation causes more mixing with the air, and results in the characteristic turbulent swirling that we see when gases mix. A second important factor that governs gas motion is temperature. As the steam is vented, it tends to rise. Hotter parts of the gas rise more quickly than regions which have mixed with the cooler air. As the gas rises, it causes internal drag, and more turbulent rotation is produced. This effect is known as thermal buoyancy. Turbulent motion is further exaggerated if the gas flows around solid objects. At first the gas flows smoothly along the surface, but it eventually becomes chaotic as it mixes with the still air behind the object. Finally, even when conditions are calm, diffusion due to molecular motion keeps the gas in constant motion.

In the next sections we derive a "customized" numerical model for animating visually accurate gaseous behavior based on the motion components described above. We call the model customized, because it incorporates only the physical elements of gaseous flow that correspond to interesting visual effects, not those elements necessary for more scientific accuracy. The model is built around a physics-based framework, and achieves speed without sacrificing realism as follows.

A volume of gas is represented as a combination of a scalar temperature field, a scalar pressure field, and a vector velocity field. The motion of the gas is then broken down into two components: 1) convection due to Newton's laws of motion, and 2), rotation and swirling due to drag and thermal buoyancy. The rotational, buoyant, and convective components of gaseous motion are modeled by coupling a reduced form of the Navier-Stokes equations with an equation for turbulent mixing due to temperature differences in a gas. This coupling provides realistic rotational and chaotic motion for a hot gaseous volume.

In general, solving a nonlinear system throughout a 3D volume is much too time consuming for animation because any algorithm that does so accurately has a complexity of $O(n^3)$ [4]. However, the authors have recently shown that for computer graphics, realistic looking results can be obtained in a reasonable amount of time if such a system is suitably approximated and solved at very low resolutions [5]. For a gas this is done in two stages. First, we solve equations corresponding to the two motion components in a voxel environment containing rectangular approximations to arbitrary static objects. This significantly reduces scene complexity, makes the application of boundary conditions trivial, and yet keeps the basic structure of the objects intact allowing for interaction between them and the gas. Second, the solution proceeds using a finite difference approximation scheme which preserves

the turbulent and rotational component of gaseous motion even at very low resolution, making the scheme efficient and suitable for use as a general graphics tool. So even though the method is still $O(n^3)$, we have reduced n significantly (40–60 in the examples given).

The result is a scheme that calculates the movement and mixing of a gas within interesting environments in a visually and physically accurate way. The output from the system is a pre-sampled, regular grid of time varying velocity or temperature values, which, when combined with massless particles, can be rendered in a number of ways using popular volume density rendering methods.

For the following discussion of the method, we take a Newtonian approach and treat finite regions in space as individual gaseous elements. An element can vary in temperature and pressure and allows gas to flow through it with arbitrary velocity, but its position remains fixed. We now present the model used to calculate the components of gaseous motion mentioned above.

2.1. Convection and Drag

The velocity of gas in an element is affected by a number of factors. First, it is pushed along, or convected, by its neighbors. Second, the gas is drawn into adjacent regions of greater velocity (or lower pressure). This is called vorticity, or drag. Third, the element is affected by forces such as gravity. In some extreme gaseous phenomena there may also be motion caused by shock and pressure waves that arise because gas can be locally compressed. If, however, the class of effects that we want to model is restricted to day-to-day sub-sonic effects such as smoke from fires, steam from steam engines, and so on, then the terms due to the compressibility of the gas will have only a minor effect on the overall motion. Therefore, we make a simplifying assumption that locally, the gas is incompressible. Furthermore, we assume that motion due to molecular diffusion is negligible relative to other effects. When these assumptions are applied to the Navier-Stokes equations, which fully describe the forces acting within a gas, a reduced form can be derived. For brevity the full equations are not reproduced here, but the reduced form, without compressive effects, or gravity forces is

$$\frac{\partial \mathbf{u}}{\partial t} = \nu \nabla \cdot (\nabla \mathbf{u}) - (\mathbf{u} \cdot \nabla)\mathbf{u} - \nabla p, \qquad (1)$$

where ∇ is the gradient operator, $\mathbf{u}$ is the velocity of the gas, $\cdot$ is the inner product operator, and p is the pressure of the gas. This equation models how the velocity of a gas changes over time depending on convection ($(\mathbf{u} \cdot \nabla)\mathbf{u}$), its pressure gradient (∇p), and drag ($\nu \nabla \cdot (\nabla \mathbf{u})$). It is generally combined with the continuity equation which models mass conservation and which is discussed later in this paper. The ν coefficient is the kinematic viscosity. Intuitively, small ν models a less viscous gas in which rotational motion is more easily induced. Equation (1) models the convective and rotational velocity in our customized gas.

2.2. Thermal Buoyancy

Forces due to thermal buoyancy also induce motion in a gas. If a hot gaseous element is surrounded by cooler elements, the gas will rise (or move against gravity in cases of interest to us). We model this effect by defining a buoyant force on a gaseous element, as

$$\mathbf{F}_{bv} = -\beta \mathbf{g}_v (T_0 - T_k), \qquad (2)$$

where $\mathbf{g}_v$ is gravity in the vertical direction, β is the coefficient of thermal expansion, T_0 is an initial reference temperature (a balmy $28^\circ C$ for the examples in this paper), and T_k is the average temperature on the boundary between a gaseous cell and the one above it. Although simple, this equation seems to work very well.

In order to use (2) to calculate buoyant forces, the evolution of temperature within the gas must also be modeled. Adjacent elements exchange energy by straight convection (hot gas flowing from one element to another) and also by small scale turbulent mixing through molecular collisions with adjacent elements. Thus, the change in temperature of a gas over time can be characterized as a combination of the convection and diffusion of heat from adjacent regions. The differential equation that governs this process is [14]

$$\frac{\partial T}{\partial t} = \lambda \nabla \cdot (\nabla T) - \nabla \cdot T\mathbf{u}, \qquad (3)$$

where $\mathbf{u}$ is the velocity of the gas, T is its temperature, and λ can be chosen to represent both turbulent and molecular diffusion processes. The structural similarity between (1) and (3) should be apparent. The second term on the right describes how temperature at a point changes due to convection, whereas the first term on the right takes into account changes in temperature due to diffusion and turbulent mixing. By solving (3) for a volume of hot gas, it is possible to calculate the force on a gaseous element due to thermal buoyancy using (2). This force affects velocity and so can be added as a new term to (1) giving

$$\frac{\partial \mathbf{u}}{\partial t} = \nu \nabla \cdot (\nabla \mathbf{u}) - (\mathbf{u} \cdot \nabla)\mathbf{u} - \nabla p + \mathbf{F}_{bv}. \qquad (4)$$

Equations (3) and (4) together provide us with a model for the rotational and turbulent motion that makes the mixing of hot and cold regions of a gas so interesting to watch.

3. Building a Useful Animation Tool from the Model

To obtain realistic motion from a volume of gas, the governing equations must be solved over time in three dimensions. The authors recently showed that for liquids, such volume calculations can be made with computational times and accuracy acceptable for a computer animation application if the environment and equations are suitably approximated [5]. A similar method is used here to solve the gas motion equations. A voxel-based scene approximation is combined with a numerical scheme known as finite differences. For (3) and (4), this leads to a straightforward algorithm that solves for the motion of a hot gas and takes into account arbitrary (approximated) objects as well as animator-controlled special effects. In addition, the method can be solved over a coarse grid without losing any of the behavioral characteristics of the gas, making it relatively efficient for even complex scenes.

3.1. Modeling the Simulation Environment

In order to solve the gas motion equations so that they represent the behavior of a gas in an animation environment, we need to represent the scene in a meaningful way with respect to the equations. We first approximate the scene as a series of cubic cells to reduce its complexity, and to form a grid upon which we can define temperature, pressure, and velocity.

A collection of solid 3D objects can be approximated as a series of regular voxels that are axially aligned to a coordinate system x,y,z (see Fig. 1a). If a portion of the medium (gas) surrounding the objects is likewise voxelized using the same coordinate system, then the boundaries of the objects can be made to coincide with the faces of gas voxels (Fig. 1b). The resulting grid can be used to solve physics-based differential equations in an efficient and straightforward way [5].

Consider a single cell in this grid (Fig. 2). It can be identified by its position relative to the origin in the x, y, z, directions, as i, j, k, respectively. At the center of the cell, we define variables $T_{i,j,k}$ and $p_{i,j,k}$ to represent the average temperature and average pressure within the cell. Likewise, in the center of each face of the cell we define a variable to

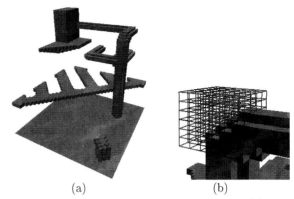

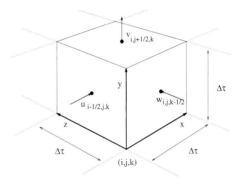

Figure 1: *Using regular voxels to approximate (a) a scene containing solid objects and (b) the medium around those objects.*

Figure 2: *Numbering convention for a single cell in the voxel grid. $\Delta\tau$ is the side length for each face of the cell.*

represent the gas velocity perpendicular to that face. This leads to the velocities u,v,w shown in Fig. 2. Intuitively, cells at i,j,k and $i+1,j,k$ will share the face velocity $u_{i+1/2,j,k}$. Once the environment over which we wish to calculate gas motion is discretized in this way, it is possible to calculate, using (3) and (4), how the temperature, pressure, and velocity throughout the grid vary over time. By using linear interpolation, the temperature (or velocity and pressure) at any point in the volume can be found. As an example, the u velocity of the gas at the center of the cell can be found from $(u_{i-1/2,j,k} + u_{i+1/2,j,k})/2$.

3.2. Applying the Equations to the Grid

To solve (3) and (4) we recast them to a form that is applicable to the regular voxel grid, using a numerical method called finite differences. A differential term such as

$$\frac{\partial T}{\partial y}$$

is approximated using a Taylor series to give a new expression for the derivative,

$$\frac{\partial T}{\partial y} = \frac{1}{2h}(T(y+h) - T(y-h)) + O(h^2), \qquad (5)$$

where h is the finite distance over which the derivative is being taken, and $O(h^2)$ denotes that terms of order 2 or higher exist. Likewise, a second order derivative,

$$\frac{\partial^2 T}{\partial y^2},$$

is written as

$$\frac{\partial^2 T}{\partial y^2} = \frac{1}{h^2}(T(y+h) - 2T(y) + T(y-h)) + O(h^2), \qquad (6)$$

where h is as before. If h is taken to be $\Delta\tau$, the grid width, then for a single voxel, we approximate (6) such that

$$\frac{\partial^2 T}{\partial y^2} = \frac{1}{\Delta\tau^2}(T_{i,j+1,k} - 2T_{i,j,k} + T_{i,j-1,k})$$

using terms that correspond directly to variables on the voxelized grid, and ignoring terms of order 2 or higher (in h). Using this basic technique, (3) is first expanded as a series of first and second order differential terms,

$$\frac{\partial T}{\partial t} = \lambda\left(\frac{\partial^2 T}{\partial x^2} + \frac{\partial^2 T}{\partial y^2} + \frac{\partial^2 T}{\partial z^2}\right) - \frac{\partial Tu}{\partial x} - \frac{\partial Tv}{\partial y} - \frac{\partial Tw}{\partial z}, \qquad (7)$$

and then completely rewritten in terms of the free variables on the finite grid,

$$
\begin{aligned}
T_{i,j,k}^{n+1} =\ & T_{i,j,k}^n + \Delta t\{(1/\Delta\tau)[(Tu)_{i-1/2,j,k}^n - (Tu)_{i+1/2,j,k}^n \\
& + (Tv)_{i,j-1/2,k}^n - (Tv)_{i,j+1/2,k}^n + (Tw)_{i,j,k-1/2}^n \\
& - (Tw)_{i,j,k+1/2}^n] + \frac{\lambda}{\Delta\tau^2}[(T_{i+1,j,k}^n - 2T_{i,j,k}^n + T_{i-1,j,k}^n) \\
& + (T_{i,j+1,k}^n - 2T_{i,j,k}^n + T_{i,j-1,k}^n) \\
& + (T_{i,j,k+1}^n - 2T_{i,j,k}^n + T_{i,j,k-1}^n)]\},
\end{aligned}
\qquad (8)
$$

where a term such as $(Tu)_{i+1/2,j,k}^n$ represents the temperature flow between cells (i,j,k) and $(i+1,j,k)$, and is calculated as

$$(Tu)_{i+1/2,j,k}^n = \frac{u_{i+1/2,j,k}^n}{2}(T_{i,j,k}^n + T_{i+1,j,k}^n).$$

Using (8), the temperature at the center of cell i,j,k at time $t + \Delta t$ can be found in terms of the temperatures at time t in adjacent cells. T^{n+1} denotes the value of T at time $t + \Delta t$, while T^n, denotes the value at time t. It is simply a matter of plugging in the old values of T in order to find the new value. In a similar way, (4) is also expanded as first and second order differentials, written in terms of cell face velocities and cell pressures, and then solved to find $\mathbf{u}_{i,j,k}^{n+1}$ in terms of $\mathbf{u}_{i,j,k}^n$ (see Appendix A). Thus, to find how the velocity and temperature change over a time interval Δt, (8) and (17) are applied simultaneously to each cell in the grid. Because $\Delta\tau$ is a constant, this calculation involves only floating point multiplication and addition, making it reasonably efficient. The change in pressure for a cell is calculated separately and is a fortunate side effect of mass conservation which is described in the next section.

3.3. Ensuring Accuracy

The approximation of the animation environment as regular voxels is the main source of efficiency for our algorithm. The drawback, however, is that low resolution variable sampling can introduce error into the calculation. Because the free variables $\mathbf{u}$ and T are sampled at fixed positions in space $\Delta\tau$ apart, an error of order $O(\Delta\tau^2)$ is introduced into T and $\mathbf{u}$ when the finite difference approximation is applied to the voxels (the $O(h^2)$ terms from (5) and (6)). For temperature this is not significant, but for $\mathbf{u}$ it represents mass that has been created (or destroyed) as a side effect of the algorithm. This means that each cell in the scene acts as a small gas source or sink, slightly altering the total mass of gas in a scene. To correct for this change in mass, we need to ensure that at any point in the scene (unless we specifically want a source or sink), the mass of gas flowing in, is the same as the mass flowing out. This can be characterized by a constraint equation that is actually part of the Navier-Stokes equations,

$$\nabla \cdot \mathbf{u} = 0. \qquad (9)$$

For a single grid cell, the left hand side of (9) is approximated using the Taylor series method, and rewritten in terms of the grid variables, giving

$$
\begin{aligned}
(\nabla \cdot \mathbf{u})_{i,j,k} =\ & \frac{1}{\Delta\tau}[u_{i+1/2,j,k} - u_{i-1/2,j,k} + v_{i,j+1/2,k} \\
& - v_{i,j-1/2,k} + w_{i,j,k+1/2} - w_{i,j,k-1/2}],
\end{aligned}
\qquad (10)
$$

where $(\nabla \cdot \mathbf{u})_{i,j,k}$ is the mass divergence at the center of the cell. For mass to be conserved, this scalar field must be zero in every cell. This requires a solution to the classic three dimensional Poisson equation. The computational method described by Harlow and Welch [8] was one of the earliest in print, and although that approach is two-dimensional in scope, it can be modified so that it is suitable for our gas model.

We define a potential field, ψ, which is sampled at the center of each grid cell and is initially zero everywhere. Then, for every frame of animation, we iterate over the grid, updating ψ according to

$$
\begin{aligned}
\psi_{i,j,k}^{h+1} =\ & \frac{2}{8/\Delta\tau^2}\{-(\nabla \cdot \mathbf{u})_{i,j,k} + \frac{1}{\Delta\tau^2}[\psi_{i+1,j,k}^h + \psi_{i-1,j,k}^h + \psi_{i,j+1,k}^h \\
& + \psi_{i,j-1,k}^h + \psi_{i,j,k+1}^h + \psi_{i,j,k-1}^h]\} - \psi_{i,j,k}^h,
\end{aligned}
\qquad (11)
$$

where $(\nabla \cdot \mathbf{u})_{i,j,k}$ is given by (10). This field is considered to have converged, i.e., the iteration stops, when, for every cell in the grid,

$$\left| \frac{|\psi_{i,j,k}^{h+1}| - |\psi_{i,j,k}^h|}{|\psi_{i,j,k}^{h+1}| + |\psi_{i,j,k}^h|} \right| < \epsilon. \qquad (12)$$

For the examples given later in this paper, ϵ is taken to be on the order of 10^{-4}, and convergence is achieved in about 8-20 iterations per frame.

After convergence, the ψ field represents the relative discrepancy in mass between adjacent cells. By adjusting $\mathbf{u}$ according to the gradient in ψ, $\mathbf{u}$ can be made to satisfy (9) directly [8]. The velocity components on the grid cell faces are adjusted to correct for the divergence field by

$$
\begin{aligned}
u_{i+1/2,j,k}^{n+1} &= u_{i+1/2,j,k}^{n+1} - \frac{\psi_{i+1,j,k} - \psi_{i,j,k}}{\Delta\tau}, \\
v_{i,j+1/2,k}^{n+1} &= v_{i,j+1/2,k}^{n+1} - \frac{\psi_{i,j+1,k} - \psi_{i,j,k}}{\Delta\tau}, \\
w_{i,j,k+1/2}^{n+1} &= w_{i,j,k+1/2}^{n+1} - \frac{\psi_{i,j,k+1} - \psi_{i,j,k}}{\Delta\tau}.
\end{aligned}
\qquad (13)
$$

The temperature, $T_{i,j,k}^{n+1}$, need not be changed. This final step makes the necessary small adjustments in the velocity field to preserve mass and ensure that the calculation remains physically accurate. In addition, it can be shown that the gradient in the pressure field, $p_{i,j,k}$, is equal to the gradient in $\psi_{i,j,k}$ [8]. Because (4) depends only on the gradient in p, we can use the ψ field directly when calculating gas motion, instead of calculating the pressure.

3.3.1. Stability

An important issue with respect to accuracy is the numerical stability of the algorithm. Instability can occur when small oscillations in the variables resonate and dominate the solution. With the model we have described this can happen when the velocity of any part of the gas allows it to move further than $\Delta\tau$ in a single timestep. To ensure stability for an animation with a maximum gas velocity of $|\mathbf{u}|$, the timestep, Δt, must be set according to,

$$\Delta t \, |\mathbf{u}| < \Delta\tau. \qquad (14)$$

For all the examples given in this paper Δt was set to $\frac{1}{30}Sec$, to achieve the standard animation framerate. This is an order of magnitude lower than the maximum stable timestep for even the most violent of the examples shown. A further

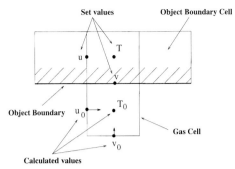

Figure 3: *Setting temperature and velocity conditions at the boundary between a gas and an object.*

Object Type	u	v	T	Result
Rough and rocky	$-u_0$	0	T_0	Lots of turbulence close to the object
Concrete	0	0	T_0	Some turbulence, object slows flow
Smooth Plastic	u_0	0	T_0	No turbulence, flow unaffected
Open Window	0	v_x	T_x	Gas can flow in or out depending on T_x and v_x
Hot Fan	0	v_x	T_x	Hot gas is forced into the scene
Steaming soup	0	0	T_x	Gas cells next to boundary are heated

Table 1: *Examples of different object boundary conditions. A subscript x represents a value chosen by the animator. A subscript 0 means that the value is taken directly from the adjacent gas cell (see Fig. 3).*

condition for numerical stability is a necessary feature of the finite-difference method and it forces a lower bound on the kinematic viscosity, ν. Linear analysis has shown that for the Navier-Stokes equations, ν must satisfy [4]

$$\nu > (\Delta t/2) max[u^2, v^2, w^2] \qquad (15)$$

for the system to remain stable.

3.4. Boundary Conditions for Special Effects

The regular voxel grid makes application of the gaseous motion equations efficient and straightforward. It also makes it easy to specify temperature, pressure, and velocity along the edges of solid objects so that interaction between objects and gas can be modeled accurately. Such "boundary conditions" can also be used to specify special effects involving gas flowing into or out of the environment. Referring to Fig. 3, the application of the finite difference forms of (3) and (4) to the gas cell may require grid values from an adjacent object cell. These values are set automatically depending on the type of material or object that the cell represents.

For example, a hot radiator cannot allow gas to pass through it, so the velocity, $\mathbf{u}$, (v in the 2D figure) is set to zero for cell faces that represent the radiator boundary. Tangentially however, we want gas to flow freely along the surface. Therefore u, is set equal to the external tangential velocity u_0. Temperature flows freely from the radiator to the air, so the temperature, T, within the boundary cell is set to the desired temperature of the radiator. If a heating fan were being modeled instead of a radiator, then $\mathbf{u}$ on the object cell faces would be set to model air flowing into the environment. For a standard obstacle, such as a wall or table, $\mathbf{u}$ is set to zero and T is set to the ambient temperature. The pressure is more difficult to set with a desired effect in mind. Therefore the object pressure is simply set equal to the external gas pressure so that it has no local effect on the flow. There are no restrictions on how boundary conditions can be set. Some examples of $\mathbf{u}$ and T for interesting effects are given in Table 1.

3.5. The Turbulent Gas Algorithm

The complete algorithm for animating turbulent gas has two stages. The first involves decisions that need to be made by an animator in order to create a particular effect. The steps the animator must take are:

1. Subdivide the environment into regular voxels with side length $\Delta\tau$. The environment need not be rectangular, any arrangement is acceptable as long as voxel faces are aligned.
2. Select boundary conditions for velocity and temperature similar to those in Table 1.
3. Consider viscosity, thermal expansion, and molecular diffusion, and set ν, β, and λ accordingly ($1/10 \Delta\tau$ or higher

for little visible turbulence, $1/100 \Delta\tau$ or lower for greater swirling).
4. Determine Δt from the minimum of $\frac{1}{30}^{th}$ of a second and the largest stable timestep given by (14) and (15).

After the parameters for the animation have been chosen, the automatic part of the process proceeds as follows:

5. Apply boundary conditions to the sides of objects chosen to simulate fans, heaters, sources, or sinks. Set the boundary velocity of other objects to zero, and set interior temperatures to the ambient temperature.
6. Use the finite difference approximations of (3) and (4) to update the temperature and velocity, $T_{i,j,k}$ and $\mathbf{u}_{i,j,k}$, for each cell (making use of ψ instead of pressure).
7. Use (10) to find the divergence field, $(\nabla \cdot \mathbf{u})$, for the gas to conserve mass.
8. While the iteration convergence condition, (12), is not satisfied,

   - Sweep the grid, calculating the relaxation adjustment, ψ, for each cell using (11).

9. Update the cell face velocities, $\mathbf{u}_{i,j,k}$, using (13).
10. Goto step 5.

This algorithm has been implemented on an SGI Indigo2 workstation using a simple interface to allow an animator to define obstacles, heat or steam sources and sinks, as well as moving fans, and to include them in an animation.

3.6. Rendering

There have been many approaches to rendering gaseous phenomena presented in recent years. A good discussion of them can be found in [17] and is not repeated here. To best illustrate the contributions of this paper, a rendering method involving suspended particles has been used. Massless particles are introduced into a scene and used to represent the local density of light-reflecting (or absorbing) matter. Once introduced, the particles are convected using the velocity field calculated from (4). The change in position of a particle k, at $\mathbf{x}_k$, over a single timestep is found from

$$\mathbf{x}_k^{n+1} = \mathbf{x}_k^n + \Delta t \, \mathbf{u}_\mathbf{x}^n,$$

where $\mathbf{u}_\mathbf{x}$ is found from the particle's position in the grid using linear interpolation. The particles themselves can be introduced as part of a boundary condition (proportional to T or $\mathbf{u}$ for example) or distributed however the animator wishes. The particles have no effect on the calculated motion, they are just used for rendering purposes to visualize how the density of smoke or steam changes as the gas medium moves.

Figure	Cell Resolution	Calc. Time (s/frame)	ψ cycles	Render Time (M/frame)
4	60x35x60	15.0	8	23
5	40x60x40	24.0	10	38
6	40x50x40	28.0	13	45
7	60x60x45	49.0	20	14

Table 2: *The calculation and rendering times for each of the examples. Cell resolution is approximate because the scenes are not rectangular. Cells that play only a small part in the motion of the gas are not used.*

For each frame of animation, the instantaneous distribution of particles is used as a density map for use with a volume renderer. There is no straightforward physics-based way to determine what density volume each particle represents or how many particles to use. This is dictated by the particular effect the animator wants (lots of very dense particles for smoke from burning tires, very few for smoke from a candle flame). The general formula for the examples shown here is to set each particle to represent $1/50^{th}$ of the volume of a single cell, and adjust its density according to the desired effect. The volume renderer used is similar to that described by Ebert and Parent [2]. For each pixel in an image, a viewing ray is cast through the density volume to find the effective opacity of the particle cloud as seen from the viewer. If desired, the ray can be subdivided, and for each subdivision, a ray is cast through the volume towards each light source. This significantly increases the cost of rendering, but it does allow for smoke and steam to self shadow and to fall under the shadow of other objects. This technique has been implemented as a volume shader for use with the BMRT implementation of the RenderMan Standard [7]. This shader was used for all the examples in this paper. It should be noted that the particle representation of suspended matter also makes the method ideal for rendering using Stam and Fiume's warped blobs [17].

4. Results

This paper has shown that the motion of a hot gas can be accurately calculated using an efficient low-resolution technique. In the following examples we illustrate the kind of rotational motion and gas/object interaction that is well suited to the method. All of the examples were calculated on an SGI Indigo2 with 64 Mb of memory. Table 2 gives the calculation times for each example, the approximate resolution of the environment, and the rendering time for a single image. Table 3 gives more specific information about each example including the width of each cell, the λ and ν coefficients, and the maximum gas velocity in the example.

Steam Valve

The images shown in Fig. 5 demonstrate the interaction of hot steam with solid objects. The voxel version of this environment is shown in Fig. 1. The steam is forced into the environment by setting both T and $\mathbf{u}$ boundary conditions on a set of voxels representing a pressure release valve. The input velocity is $0.3\,m/s$, and the steam temperature is $80^{\circ}C$. This is consistent with steam being vented from a boiler. The result is the billowing effect of the cloud of steam. In the animation, turbulence builds up just in front of the nozzle as the steam is vented at high velocity.

The same environmental conditions were also used to animate the interaction of steam from three separate valves. Three frames from this animation are shown in Fig. 6. The rotation caused by the cooling and mixing of the gas can be seen clearly in the full sequence. In both of the valve cases massless particles were introduced at an average rate of $2000/s$.

Figure	ν	$\Delta\tau$	λ	$|\mathbf{u}|$ max m/s
4	0.005	0.05	0.4	0.15
5	0.002	0.1	1.0	0.35
6	0.002	0.1	1.0	0.50
7	0.01	1.0	3.5	3.4

Table 3: *Parameters used to calculate each of the examples. In each case the thermal expansion coefficient, β, was 10^{-3}.*

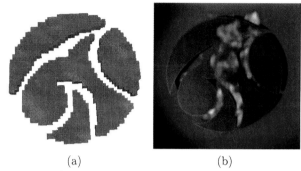

(a)   (b)

Figure 4: *a) A voxel approximation of the SIGGRAPH 97 logo. b) Smoke flowing smoothly around the approximation following the contours of the original shape.*

Smoke Stack

Figure 7 shows three frames from an animation of smoke rising from a chimney on a hot day. The boundary cells on the left of the grid are set to model a light wind of about $2\,m/s$ that occasionally gusts up to $3\,m/s$. We set the wind velocity to evolve according to the random-walk expression

$$\mathbf{u}_w^{n+1} = 0.98\,\mathbf{u}_w^n + 0.24\,\Delta t\;\phi(t),$$

where ϕ is a random number generator in the range [-1,1]. The value of $\mathbf{u}_w$ is clamped to lie in the range [2,3]. The constant coefficients have no physical significance, they are just parameters that have worked well for previous simulations. This wind is allowed to exit freely from the other end of the grid using the open window boundary condition from Table 2. The light wind sets up unstable conditions at the top of the tower causing the looping and swirling of the smoke as it moves. The smoke leaves the chimney at $0.8\,m/s$ with a boundary temperature of $46^{\circ}C$. From Table 2 it can be seen that nearly twice as many ψ iterations are required per frame. This is because the gusting windfield has a large component in every cell, so it takes longer for (11) to converge.

SIGGRAPH Logo

The final animation demonstrates that despite the low resolution voxel approximation, flow around complex objects can be accurately represented by our model. Figure 4a shows a voxel representation of the SIGGRAPH 97 logo, and Fig. 4b shows a frame from a sequence depicting smoke rising smoothly through it. The velocity along the boundary of the logo is set to zero to prevent smoke drifting into the artificial corners created by the approximation. When the smoke is released just beneath the symbol (with a temperature of $50^{\circ}C$) it flows over the object and conforms fairly closely to the original boundary.

5. Discussion of Limitations

The technique described in this paper derives efficiency by solving accurate equations at a low resolution. This is a compromise to try and preserve realism, and as such, it comes with some limitations. Primarily, the method can only resolve rotational motion at a resolution lower than or equal to the grid resolution. From the examples shown, good effects can be achieved, but this means that grid resolution has to be increased to get finer motion within an existing scene. If we double the resolution and halve $\Delta\tau$ to get the same sized environment, we also have to halve the timestep, Δt, so that the system remains stable (from (14) and (15)). This is an inherent problem with finite differences. It could be compensated for by using a multi-resolution grid which would impose less of an overhead than using a higher resolution everywhere, but that is left as a topic for future work.

A second limitation of a finite difference grid is that cell orientation can affect the results. A gas jet oriented so that it travels diagonally through the cubic cells will tend to exhibit more diffusion than if it were moving parallel to an axis. In general, differences due to such diffusion is not significant (see Fig. 6), but it is something that can often be avoided by selecting grid orientation based on desired gas motion rather than objects in the static environment.

It is also desirable to integrate the gas model with other computer graphics techniques so that dynamic objects can interact with a gas. There is some discussion about how an iterative relaxation step like that described in Sec. 3.3 can be used to incorporate moving objects into animations of liquids in Foster and Metaxas [6] and Metaxas [9]. The methods used there are also applicable to the algorithm described in this paper, although that has not been explored in any detail.

6. Concluding Remarks

Numerous techniques exist for animating hot gases for computer graphics. Nearly all of them concentrate on achieving a visual approximation to the characteristic motion of a gas while getting as high a frame rate as possible. This sacrifices rotational and turbulent motion and often requires the animator to micro-control the flow. In this paper we have presented a new, alternative approach that models different scales of gas motion directly. This method accurately animates gaseous phenomena involving hot and cold gases, turbulent flow around solid obstacles, and thermal buoyancy, while leaving enough freedom for the animator to produce many different effects. The model is physics-based and achieves efficient computational speeds by using a combination of scene approximation and low resolution volume calculation. We have shown that even at these low resolutions, the characteristics of complex motion in the model are retained, and that exciting results can be obtained.

7. Acknowledgements

Thanks to Larry Gritz for his advice on volume rendering with BMRT. This research is supported by ARPA DAMD17-94-J-4486, an NSF Career Award, National Library of Medicine N01LM-43551, and a 1997 ONR Young Investigator Award.

Appendix A: Finite Difference Form of the Motion Equations

The full expansion of (4) into first and second order derivatives is straightforward. Considering just the u velocity component for brevity, results in the following expression.

$$\frac{\partial u}{\partial t} = \nu\left(\frac{\partial^2 u}{\partial x^2} + \frac{\partial^2 u}{\partial y^2} + \frac{\partial^2 u}{\partial z^2}\right) - \frac{\partial u^2}{\partial x} - \frac{\partial uv}{\partial y} - \frac{\partial uw}{\partial z} - \frac{\partial p}{\partial x} \quad (16)$$

The finite difference scheme outlined in section 3.2 is then applied, (replacing p with ψ) giving the expression used to update the $u_{i+1/2,j,k}$ face velocity for cell i,j,k,

$$u^{n+1}_{i+1/2,j,k} = u^n_{i+1/2,j,k} + \Delta t\{(1/\Delta\tau)[(u^n_{i,j,k})^2 - (u^n_{i+1,j,k})^2$$

$$+(uv)^n_{i+1/2,j-1/2,k} - (uv)^n_{i+1/2,j+1/2,k} + (uw)^n_{i+1/2,j,k-1/2}$$

$$-(uw)^n_{i+1/2,j,k+1/2}] + (\lambda/\Delta\tau^2)(u^n_{i+3/2,j,k} - 2u^n_{i+1/2,j,k}$$

$$+u^n_{i-1/2,j,k} + u^n_{i+1/2,j+1,k} - 2u^n_{i+1/2,j,k} + u^n_{i+1/2,j-1,k}$$

$$+u^n_{i+1/2,j,k+1} - 2u^n_{i+1/2,j,k} + u^n_{i+1/2,j,k-1})$$

$$-\frac{1}{\Delta\tau}(\psi^n_{i,j,k} - \psi^n_{i+1,j,k})\}, \quad (17)$$

where values that aren't defined on the grid are found by averaging as before.

References

1. Chiba, N., Ohkawa, S., Muraoka, K., and Miura, M., "Two-dimensional Simulation of Flames, Smoke and the Spread of Fire", J. of Vis. and Comp. Animation, 5(1), 1994, pp. 37–54.

2. Ebert, D.S., and Parent, R.E., "Rendering and Animation of Gaseous Phenomena by Combining Fast Volume and Scanline A-buffer Techniques", SIGGRAPH '90, Computer Graphics, 24(4), 1990, pp. 357–366.

3. Ebert, D.S., Carlson, W.E., and Parent, R.E., "Solid Spaces and Inverse Particle Systems for Controlling the Animation of Gases and Fluids", The Visual Comp., 10, 1994, pp. 179–190.

4. Fletcher, C.A.J., "Computational Techniques for Fluid Dynamics," Springer Verlag, Sydney, 1990.

5. Foster, N., and Metaxas D., "Realistic Animation of Liquids," Graphical Models and Image Proc., 58(5), 1996, pp. 471–483.

6. Foster, N., and Metaxas D., "Controlling Fluid Animation," Proceedings of CGI '97, To appear, 1997.

7. Gritz, L., and Hahn, J.K., "BMRT: A Global Illumination Implementation of the RenderMan Standard", J. of Graphics Tools, to appear, 1997.

8. Harlow, F.H., and Welch, J.E., "Numerical Calculation of Time-Dependent Viscous Incompressible Flow," Phys. Fluids, 8, 1965, pp. 2182–2189.

9. Metaxas, D., "Physics-Based Deformable Models: Applications to Computer Vision, Graphics and Medical Imaging", Kluwer-Academic Publishers, 1996.

10. Yaeger, L., Upson, C., and Myers, R., "Combining Physical and Visual Simulation - Creation of the Planet Jupiter for the Film "2010" ", SIGGRAPH '86, Computer Graphics 20(4), 1986, pp. 85–93.

11. Reeves, W.T., and Blau, R., "Approximate and Probabilistic Algorithms for Shading and Rendering Structured Particle Systems", SIGGRAPH '85, Computer Graphics 19(3), 1985, pp. 313–322.

12. Sakas, G., "Modeling and Animating Turbulent Gaseous Phenomena Using Spectral Synthesis", The Visual Computer, 9, 1993, pp. 200–212.

13. Sims, K., "Particle Animation and Rendering Using Data Parallel Computation", SIGGRAPH '90, Computer Graphics 24(4), 1990, pp. 405–413.

14. Shaw, C.T., "Using Computational Fluid Dynamics", Prentice Hall, London, 1992.

15. Shinya, M., and Fournier, A., "Stochastic Motion - Motion Under the Influence of Wind", Proceeding of Eurographics '92, September 1992, pp. 119–128.

16. Stam, J., and Fiume, E., "Turbulent Wind Fields for Gaseous Phenomena", SIGGRAPH '93, 1993, pp. 369–376.

17. Stam, J., and Fiume, E., "Depicting Fire and Other Gaseous Phenomena Using Diffusion Processes", SIGGRAPH '95, 1995, pp. 129–136.

18. Wejchert, J., and Haumann, D., "Animation Aerodynamics", SIGGRAPH '91, Computer Graphics 25(3), 1991, pp. 19-22.

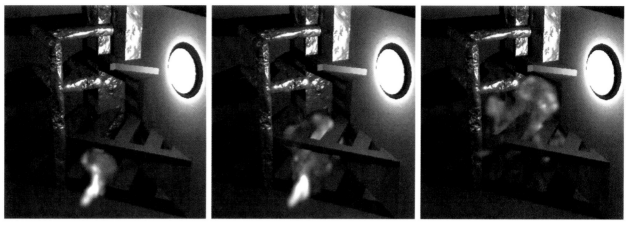

Figure 5: *An animation of steam discharge into a boiler room.*

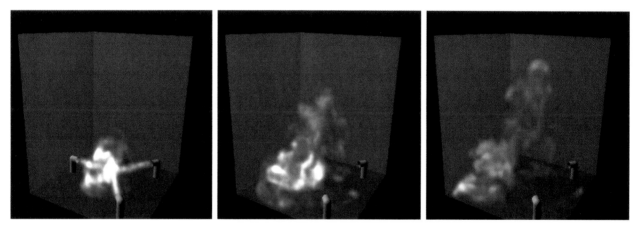

Figure 6: *Steam from three nozzles converges to cause vorticity and turbulence.*

Figure 7: *Turbulent smoke rolls out of a chimney into a light, gusting wind.*

View-Dependent Refinement of Progressive Meshes

Hugues Hoppe

Microsoft Research

ABSTRACT

Level-of-detail (LOD) representations are an important tool for real-time rendering of complex geometric environments. The previously introduced *progressive mesh* representation defines for an arbitrary triangle mesh a sequence of approximating meshes optimized for view-independent LOD. In this paper, we introduce a framework for selectively refining an arbitrary progressive mesh according to changing view parameters. We define efficient refinement criteria based on the view frustum, surface orientation, and screen-space geometric error, and develop a real-time algorithm for incrementally refining and coarsening the mesh according to these criteria. The algorithm exploits view coherence, supports frame rate regulation, and is found to require less than 15% of total frame time on a graphics workstation. Moreover, for continuous motions this work can be amortized over consecutive frames. In addition, smooth visual transitions (geomorphs) can be constructed between any two selectively refined meshes.

A number of previous schemes create view-dependent LOD meshes for height fields (e.g. terrains) and parametric surfaces (e.g. NURBS). Our framework also performs well for these special cases. Notably, the absence of a rigid subdivision structure allows more accurate approximations than with existing schemes. We include results for these cases as well as for general meshes.

CR Categories: I.3.3 [Computer Graphics]: Picture/Image Generation - Display algorithms; I.3.5 [Computer Graphics]: Computational Geometry and Object Modeling - surfaces and object representations.

Additional Keywords: mesh simplification, level-of-detail, multiresolution representations, dynamic tessellation, shape interpolation.

1 INTRODUCTION

Rendering complex geometric models at interactive rates is a challenging problem in computer graphics. While rendering performance is continually improving, significant gains are obtained by adapting the complexity of a model to its contribution to the rendered image. The ideal solution would be to efficiently determine the coarsest model that satisfies some perceptual image qualities. One common heuristic technique is to author several versions of a model at various *levels of detail* (LOD); a detailed triangle mesh is used when the object is close to the viewer, and coarser approximations are substituted as the object recedes [4, 8]. Such LOD meshes can be computed automatically using mesh simplification

Email: hhoppe@microsoft.com

Web: http://research.microsoft.com/~hoppe/

techniques (e.g. [5, 10, 19, 21]). The recently introduced *progressive mesh* (PM) representation [10] captures a continuous sequence of meshes optimized for view-independent LOD control, and allows fast traversal of the sequence at runtime.

Sets or sequences of view-independent LOD meshes are appropriate for many applications, but difficulties arise when rendering large-scale models, such as environments, that may surround the viewer:

- Many faces of the model may lie outside the view frustum and thus do not contribute to the image (Figure 12a). While these faces are typically culled early in the rendering pipeline, this processing incurs a cost.

- Similarly, it is often unnecessary to render faces oriented away from the viewer, and such faces are usually culled using a "back-facing" test, but again at a cost.

- Within the view frustum, some regions of the model may lie much closer to the viewer than others. View-independent LOD meshes fail to provide the appropriate level of detail over the entire model (e.g. as does the mesh in Figure 12b).

Some of these problems can be addressed by representing a graphics scene as a hierarchy of meshes. Parts of the scene outside the view frustum can then be removed efficiently using hierarchical culling, and LOD can be adjusted independently for each mesh in the hierarchy [4, 8]. However, establishing such hierarchies on continuous surfaces is a challenging problem. For instance, if a terrain mesh (Figure 11d) is partitioned into blocks, and these blocks are rendered at different levels of detail, one has to address the problem of cracks between the blocks [14]. In addition, the block boundaries are unlikely to correspond to natural features in the surface, resulting in suboptimal approximations. Similar problems also arise in the adaptive tessellation of smooth parametric surfaces [1, 13, 18].

Specialized schemes have been presented to adaptively refine meshes for the cases of height fields and parametric surfaces, as summarized in Section 2.1. In this paper, we offer a general runtime LOD framework for selectively refining arbitrary meshes according to changing view parameters. A similar approach was developed independently by Xia and Varshney [24]; their scheme is summarized and compared in Section 2.3.

The principal contributions of this paper are:

- It presents a framework for real-time selective refinement of arbitrary progressive meshes (Section 3).

- It defines fast view-dependent refinement criteria involving the view frustum, surface orientation, and screen-space projected error (Section 4).

- It presents an efficient algorithm for incrementally adapting the mesh refinement based on these criteria (Section 5). The algorithm exploits view coherence, supports frame rate regulation, and may be amortized over consecutive frames. To reduce popping, geomorphs can be constructed between any two selectively refined meshes.

- It shows that triangle strips can be generated for efficient rendering even though the mesh connectivity is irregular and dynamic (Section 6).

- Finally, it demonstrates the framework's effectiveness on the important special cases of height fields and tessellated parametric surfaces, as well as on general meshes (Section 8).

Notation We denote a triangle mesh M as a tuple (V, F), where V is a set of vertices v_j with positions $\mathbf{v}_j \in \mathbf{R}^3$, and F is a set of ordered vertex triples $\{v_j, v_k, v_l\}$ specifying vertices of triangle faces in counter-clockwise order. The *neighborhood* of a vertex v, denoted N_v, refers to the set of faces adjacent to v.

2 RELATED WORK

2.1 View-dependent LOD for domains in $\mathbf{R}^2$

Previous view-dependent refinement methods for domains in $\mathbf{R}^2$ fall into two categories: height fields and parametric surfaces.

Although there exist numerous methods for simplifying height fields, only a subset support efficient view-dependent LOD. These are based on hierarchical representations such as grid quadtrees [14, 23], quaternary triangular subdivisions [15], and more general triangulation hierarchies [3, 6, 20]. (The subdivision approach of [15] generalizes to 2-dimensional domains of arbitrary topological type.) Because quadtrees and quaternary subdivisions are based on a regular subdivision structure, the view-dependent meshes created by these schemes have constrained connectivities, and therefore require more polygons for a given accuracy than so-called *triangulated irregular networks* (TIN's). It was previously thought that dynamically adapting a TIN at interactive rates would be prohibitively expensive [14]. In this paper we demonstrate real-time modification of highly adaptable TIN's. Moreover, our framework extends to arbitrary meshes.

View-dependent tessellation of parametric surfaces such as NURBS requires fairly involved algorithms to deal with parameter step sizes, trimming curves, and stitching of adjacent patches [1, 13, 18]. Most real-time schemes sample a regular grid in the parametric domain of each patch to exploit fast forward differencing and to simplify the patch stitching process. Our framework allows real-time adaptive tessellations that adapt to surface curvature and view parameters.

2.2 Review of progressive meshes

In the PM representation [10], an arbitrary mesh $\hat{M}$ is simplified through a sequence of n *edge collapse* transformations (*ecol* in Figure 1) to yield a much simpler base mesh M^0 (see Figure 11):

$$(\hat{M}=M^n) \xrightarrow{ecol_{n-1}} \ldots \xrightarrow{ecol_1} M^1 \xrightarrow{ecol_0} M^0 \ .$$

Because each *ecol* has an inverse, called a *vertex split* transformation, the process can be reversed:

$$M^0 \xrightarrow{vsplit_0} M^1 \xrightarrow{vsplit_1} \ldots \xrightarrow{vsplit_{n-1}} (M^n=\hat{M}) \ .$$

The tuple $(M^0, \{vsplit_0, \ldots, vsplit_{n-1}\})$ forms a PM representation of $\hat{M}$. Each vertex split, parametrized as $vsplit(v_s, v_l, v_r, v_t, f_l, f_r)$, modifies the mesh by introducing one new vertex v_t and two new faces $f_l = \{v_s, v_t, v_l\}$ and $f_r = \{v_s, v_r, v_t\}$ as shown in Figure 1. The resulting sequence of meshes $M^0, \ldots, M^n=\hat{M}$ is effective for view-independent LOD control (Figure 11). In addition, smooth visual transitions (*geomorphs*) can be constructed between any two meshes in this sequence.

To create view-dependent approximations, our earlier work [10] describes a scheme for selectively refining the mesh based on a user-specified query function qrefine(v_s). The basic idea is to traverse the

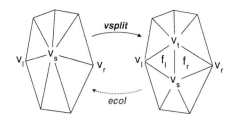

Figure 1: Original definitions of the refinement (*vsplit*) and coarsening (*ecol*) transformations.

$vsplit_i$ records in order, but to only perform $vsplit_i(v_{s_i}, v_{l_i}, v_{r_i}, \ldots)$ if

(1) $vsplit_i$ is a *legal* transformation, that is, if the vertices $\{v_{s_i}, v_{l_i}, v_{r_i}\}$ satisfy some conditions in the mesh refined so far, and

(2) qrefine(v_{s_i}) evaluates to *true*.

The scheme is demonstrated with a view-dependent qrefine function whose criteria include the view frustum, proximity to silhouettes, and screen-projected face areas.

However, some major issues are left unaddressed. The qrefine function is not designed for real-time performance, and fails to measure screen-space geometric error. More importantly, no facility is provided for efficiently adapting the selectively refined mesh as the view parameters change.

2.3 Vertex hierarchies

Xia and Varshney [24] use *ecol/vsplit* transformations to create a simplification hierarchy that allows real-time selective refinement. Their approach is to precompute for a given mesh $\hat{M}$ a *merge tree* bottom-up as follows. First, all vertices $\hat{V}$ are entered as leaves at level 0 of the tree. Then, for each level $l \geq 0$, a set of *ecol* transformations is selected to merge pairs of vertices, and the resulting proper subset of vertices is promoted to level $l + 1$. The *ecol* transformations in each level are chosen based on edge lengths, but with the constraint that their neighborhoods do not overlap. The topmost level of the tree (or more precisely, forest) corresponds to the vertices of a coarse mesh M^0. (In some respects, this structure is similar to the subdivision hierarchy of [11].)

At runtime, selective refinement is achieved by moving a vertex front up and down through the hierarchy. For consistency of the refinement, an *ecol* or *vsplit* transformation at level l is only permitted if its neighborhood in the selectively refined mesh is identical to that in the precomputed mesh at level l; these additional dependencies are stored in the merge tree. As a consequence, the representation shares characteristics of quadtree-type hierarchies, in that only gradual change is permitted from regions of high refinement to regions of low refinement [24].

Whereas Xia and Varshney construct the hierarchy based on edge lengths and constrain the hierarchy to a set of levels with non-overlapping transformations, our approach is to let the hierarchy be formed by an unconstrained, geometrically optimized sequence of *vsplit* transformations (from an arbitrary PM), and to introduce as few dependencies as possible between these transformations, in order to minimize the complexity of approximating meshes.

Several types of view-dependent criteria are outlined in [24], including local illumination and screen-space projected edge length. In this paper we detail three view-dependent criteria. One of these measures screen-space surface approximation error, and therefore yields mesh refinement that naturally adapts to both surface curvature and viewing direction.

Another related scheme is that of Luebke [16], which constructs a vertex hierarchy using a clustering octree, and locally adapts the complexity of the scene by selectively coalescing the cluster nodes.

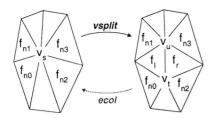

Figure 2: New definitions of *vsplit* and *ecol*.

3 SELECTIVE REFINEMENT FRAMEWORK

In this section, we show that a real-time selective refinement framework can be built upon an arbitrary PM.

Let a selectively refined mesh M^S be defined as the mesh obtained by applying to the base mesh M^0 a subsequence $S \subseteq \{0, \ldots, n-1\}$ of the PM *vsplit* sequence. As noted in Section 2.2, an arbitrary subsequence S may not correspond to a well-defined mesh, since a *vsplit* transformation is *legal* only if the current mesh satisfies some preconditions. These preconditions are analogous to the vertex or face dependencies found in most hierarchical representations [6, 14, 24]. Several definitions of *vsplit* legality have been presented (two in [10] and one in [24]); ours is yet another, which we will introduce shortly. Let $\mathcal{M}$ be the set of all meshes M^S produced from M^0 by a subsequence S of legal *vsplit* transformations.

To support incremental refinement, it is necessary to consider not just *vsplit*'s, but also *ecol*'s, and to perform these transformations in an order possibly different from that in the PM sequence. A major concern is that a selectively refined mesh should be unique, regardless of the sequence of (legal) transformations that leads to it, and in particular, it should still be a mesh in $\mathcal{M}$.

We first sought to extend the selective refinement scheme of [10] with a set of legality preconditions for *ecol* transformations, but were unable to form a consistent framework without overly restricting it. Instead, we began anew with modified definitions of *vsplit* and *ecol*, and found a set of legality preconditions sufficient for consistency, yet flexible enough to permit highly adaptable refinement. The remainder of this section presents these new definitions and preconditions.

New transformation definitions The new definitions of *vsplit* and *ecol* are illustrated in Figure 2. Note that their effects on the mesh are still the same; they are simply parametrized differently. The transformation $vsplit(v_s, v_t, v_u, f_l, f_r, f_{n0}, f_{n1}, f_{n2}, f_{n3})$, replaces the *parent* vertex v_s by two *children* v_t and v_u. Two new faces f_l and f_r are created between the two pairs of neighboring faces (f_{n0}, f_{n1}) and (f_{n2}, f_{n3}) adjacent to v_s. The edge collapse transformation $ecol(v_s, v_t, v_u, \ldots)$ has the same parameters as *vsplit* and performs the inverse operation. To support meshes with boundaries, face neighbors $f_{n0}, f_{n1}, f_{n2}, f_{n3}$ may have a special *nil* value, and vertex splits with $f_{n2} = f_{n3} = nil$ create only the single face f_l.

Let $\mathcal{V}$ denote the set of vertices in all meshes of the PM sequence. Note that $|\mathcal{V}|$ is approximately twice the number $|\hat{V}|$ of original vertices because of the vertex renaming in each *vsplit*. In contrast, the faces of a selectively refined mesh M^S are always a subset of the original faces $\hat{F}$. We number the vertices and faces in the order that they are created, so that $vsplit_i$ introduces the vertices $t_i = |V^0| + 2i + 1$ and $u_i = |V^0| + 2i + 2$. We say that a vertex or face is *active* if it exists in the selectively refined mesh M^S.

Vertex hierarchy As in [24], the parent-child relation on the vertices establishes a vertex hierarchy (Figure 3), and a selectively refined mesh corresponds to a "vertex front" through this hierarchy (e.g. M^0 and $\hat{M}$ in Figure 3). Our vertex hierarchy differs in two respects. First, vertices are renamed as they are split, and this

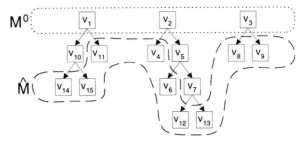

Figure 3: The vertex hierarchy on $\mathcal{V}$ forms a "forest", in which the root nodes are the vertices of the coarsest mesh (base mesh M^0) and the leaf nodes are the vertices of the most refined mesh (original mesh $\hat{M}$).

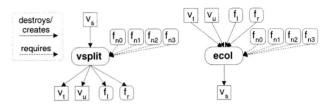

Figure 4: Preconditions and effects of *vsplit* and *ecol* transformations.

renaming contributes to the refinement dependencies. Second, the hierarchy is constructed top-down after loading a PM using a simple traversal of the *vsplit* records. Although our hierarchies may be unbalanced, they typically have fewer levels than in [24] (e.g. 24 instead of 65 for the bunny) because they are unconstrained.

Preconditions We define a set of preconditions for *vsplit* and *ecol* to be legal (refer to Figure 4).

A $vsplit(v_s, v_t, v_u, \ldots)$ transformation is legal if

(1) v_s is an active vertex, and

(2) the faces $\{f_{n0}, f_{n1}, f_{n2}, f_{n3}\}$ are all active faces.

An $ecol(v_s, v_t, v_u, \ldots)$ transformation is legal if

(1) v_t and v_u are both active vertices, and

(2) the faces adjacent to f_l and f_r are $\{f_{n0}, f_{n1}, f_{n2}, f_{n3}\}$, in the configuration of Figure 2.

Properties Let $\mathcal{M}^\star$ be the set of meshes obtained by transitive closure of legal *vsplit* and *ecol* transformations from M^0 (or equivalently from $\hat{M}$ since the PM sequence $M^0 \longleftrightarrow \hat{M}$ is legal). For any mesh $M = (V, F) \in \mathcal{M}^\star$, we observe the following properties:[1]

- If $vsplit(v_s, v_t, v_u, \ldots)$ is legal, then $\{f_{n0}, f_{n1}\}$ and $\{f_{n2}, f_{n3}\}$ must be pairwise adjacent and adjacent to v_s as in Figure 2.

- If the active vertex front lies below $ecol(v_s, v_t, v_u, \ldots)$ (i.e. $f_l, f_r \in F$), then $\{f_{n0}, f_{n1}, f_{n2}, f_{n3}\}$ must all be active.

- $M \in \mathcal{M}$, i.e. $M = M^S$ for some subsequence S, i.e. $\mathcal{M}^\star = \mathcal{M}$.

- $M = M^S$ is identical to the mesh obtained by applying to $\hat{M}$ the complement subsequence $\{n-1, \ldots, 0\} \setminus S$ of *ecol* transformations, which are legal.

Implementation To make these ideas more concrete, Figure 5 lists the C++ data structures used in our implementation. A selectively refinable mesh consists of an array of vertices and an array of faces. Of these vertices and faces, only a subset are active, as specified by two doubly-linked lists that thread through a subset of

---

[1]Although these properties have held for the numerous experiments we have performed, we unfortunately do not have formal proofs for them as yet.

```
struct ListNode {                 // Node possibly on a linked list
    ListNode* next;               // 0 if this node is not on the list
    ListNode* prev;
};
struct Vertex {
    ListNode active;              // list stringing active vertices V
    Point point;
    Vector normal;
    Vertex* parent;               // 0 if this vertex is in M^0
    Vertex* vt;                   // 0 if this vertex is in M̂; (vu=vt+1)
    // Remaining fields encode vsplit information, defined if vt ≠ 0.
    Face* fl;                     // (fr=fl+1)
    Face* fn[4];                  // required neighbors fn0,fn1,fn2,fn3
    RefineInfo refine_info;       // defined in Section 4
};
struct Face {
    ListNode active;              // list stringing active faces F
    int matid;                    // material identifier
    // Remaining fields are used if the face is active.
    Vertex* vertices[3];          // ordered counter-clockwise
    Face* neighbors[3];           // neighbors[i] across from vertices[i]
};
struct SRMesh {                   // Selectively refinable mesh
    Array<Vertex> vertices;       // set V of all vertices
    Array<Face> faces;            // set F̂ of all faces
    ListNode active_vertices;     // head of list V ⊆ V
    ListNode active_faces;        // head of list F ⊆ F̂
};
```

Figure 5: Principal C++ data structures.

the records. In the Vertex records, the fields *parent* and *vt* encode the vertex hierarchy of Figure 3. If a vertex can be split, its *fl* and *fn*[0..3] fields encode the remaining parameters of the *vsplit* (and hence the dependencies of Figure 4). Each Face record contains links to its current vertices, links to its current face neighbors, and a material identifier used for rendering.

4 REFINEMENT CRITERIA

In this section, we describe a query function qrefine(v_s) that determines whether a vertex v_s should be split based on the current view parameters. As outlined below, the function uses three criteria: the view frustum, surface orientation, and screen-space geometric error. Because qrefine is often evaluated thousands of times per frame, it has been designed to be fast, at the expense of a few simplifying approximations where noted.

function qrefine(v_s)
    // *Refine only if it affects the surface within the view frustum.*
    if outside_view_frustum(v_s) **return** *false*
    // *Refine only if part of the affected surface faces the viewer.*
    if oriented_away(v_s) **return** *false*
    // *Refine only if screen-projected error exceeds tolerance τ.*
    if screen_space_error(v_s) $\leq \tau$ **return** *false*
    return *true*

View frustum This first criterion seeks to coarsen the mesh outside the view frustum in order to reduce graphics load. Our approach is to compute for each vertex $v \in \mathcal{V}$ the radius r_v of a sphere centered at **v** that bounds the region of $\hat{M}$ supported by v and all its descendants. We let qrefine(v) return *false* if this bounding sphere lies completely outside the view frustum.

The radii r_v are computed after a PM representation is loaded into memory using a bounding sphere hierarchy as follows. First, we compute for each $v \in \hat{V}$ (the leaf nodes of the vertex hierarchy) a sphere S_v that bounds its adjacent vertices in $\hat{M}$. Next, we perform a postorder traversal of the vertex hierarchy (by scanning the *vsplit*

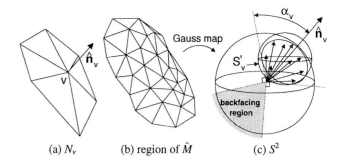

   (a) N_v (b) region of $\hat{M}$ (c) S^2

Figure 6: Illustration of (a) the neighborhood of v, (b) the region in $\hat{M}$ affected by v, and (c) the space of normals over that region and the cone of normals that bounds it.

sequence backwards) to assign each parent vertex v_s the smallest sphere S_{v_s} that bounds the spheres S_{v_t}, S_{v_u} of its two children. Finally, since the resulting spheres S_v are not centered on the vertices, we compute at each vertex v the radius r_v of a larger sphere centered at **v** that bounds S_v.

Since the view frustum is a 4-sided semi-infinite pyramid, a sphere of radius r_v centered at $\mathbf{v} = (v_x, v_y, v_z)$ lies outside the frustum if

$$a_i v_x + b_i v_y + c_i v_z + d_i < -r_v \quad \text{for any } i = 1 \ldots 4$$

where each linear functional $a_i x + b_i y + c_i z + d_i$ measures the signed Euclidean distance to a side of the frustum. Selective refinement based solely on the view frustum is demonstrated in Figure 12a.

Surface orientation The purpose of the second criterion is to coarsen regions of the mesh oriented away from the viewer, again to reduce graphics load. Our approach is analogous to the view frustum criterion, except that we now consider the space of normals over the surface (the Gauss map) instead of the surface itself. The space of normals is a subset of the unit sphere $S^2 = \{\mathbf{p} \in \mathbf{R}^3 : \|\mathbf{p}\| = 1\}$; for a triangle mesh $\hat{M}$, it consists of a discrete set of points, each corresponding to the normal of a triangle face of $\hat{M}$.

For each vertex v, we bound the space of normals associated with the region of $\hat{M}$ supported by v and its descendants, using a *cone of normals* [22] defined by a semiangle α_v about the vector $\hat{\mathbf{n}}_v = v.normal$ (Figure 6). The semiangles α_v are computed after a PM representation is loaded into memory using a *normal space hierarchy* [12]. As before, we first hierarchically compute at each vertex v a sphere S'_v that bounds the associated space of normals. Next, we compute at each vertex v the semiangle α_v of a cone about $\hat{\mathbf{n}}_v$ that bounds the intersection of S'_v and S^2. We let $\alpha_v = \frac{\pi}{2}$ if no bounding cone (with $\alpha_v < \frac{\pi}{2}$) exists.

Given a viewpoint **e**, it is unnecessary to split v if **e** lies in the *backfacing region* of v, that is, if

$$\frac{\mathbf{a}_v - \mathbf{e}}{\|\mathbf{a}_v - \mathbf{e}\|} \cdot \hat{\mathbf{n}}_v > \sin \alpha_v ,$$

where $\mathbf{a}_v$ is a cone *anchor point* that takes into account the geometric bounding volume S_v (see [22] for details). However, to improve both space and time efficiency, we approximate $\mathbf{a}_v$ by **v** (it amounts to a parallel projection approximation [13]), and instead use the test

$$(\mathbf{v} - \mathbf{e}) \cdot \hat{\mathbf{n}}_v > 0 \quad \textbf{and} \quad ((\mathbf{v} - \mathbf{e}) \cdot \hat{\mathbf{n}}_v)^2 > \|\mathbf{v} - \mathbf{e}\|^2 \sin^2 \alpha_v .$$

The effect of this test is seen in Figures 13c, 14, and 16c, where the backfacing regions of the meshes are kept coarse.

Screen-space geometric error The goal of the third criterion is to adapt the mesh refinement such that the distance between the approximate surface M and the original $\hat{M}$, when projected on the screen, is everywhere less than a screen-space tolerance τ.

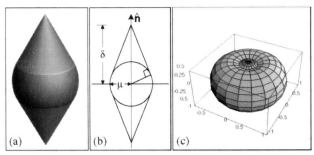

Figure 7: Illustration of (a) the deviation space $D_{\hat{n}}(\mu, \delta)$, (b) its cross-section, and (c) the extent of its screen-space projection as a function of viewing angle (with $\mu = 0.5$ and $\delta = 1$).

To determine whether a vertex $v \in V$ should be split, we seek a measure of the deviation between its current neighborhood N_v (the set of faces adjacent to v) and the corresponding region $\hat{N}_v$ in $\hat{M}$. One quantitative measure is the *Hausdorff distance* $\mathcal{H}(N_v, \hat{N}_v)$, defined as the smallest scalar r such that any point on N_v is within distance r of a point on $\hat{N}_v$, and vice versa. Mathematically, $\mathcal{H}(N_v, \hat{N}_v)$ is the smallest r for which $N_v \subset \hat{N}_v \oplus B(r)$ and $\hat{N}_v \subset N_v \oplus B(r)$ where $B(r)$ is the closed ball of radius r and $\oplus$ denotes the Minkowski sum[2]. If $\mathcal{H}(N_v, \hat{N}_v) = r$, the screen-space approximation error is bounded by the screen-space projection of the ball $B(r)$.

If N_v and $\hat{N}_v$ are similar and approximately planar, a tighter distance bound can be obtained by replacing the ball $B(r)$ in the above definition by a more general *deviation space D*. For instance, Lindstrom et al. [14] record deviation of height fields (graphs of functions over the **xy** plane) by associating to each vertex a scalar value δ representing a vertical deviation space $D_{\hat{z}}(\delta) = \{h\hat{z} : -\delta \le h \le \delta\}$. The main advantage of using $D_{\hat{z}}(\delta)$ is that its screen-space projection vanishes as its principal axis $\hat{z}$ becomes parallel to the viewing direction, unlike the corresponding $B(\delta)$.

To generalize these ideas to arbitrary surfaces, we define a deviation space $D_{\hat{n}}(\mu, \delta)$ shown in Figure 7a–b. The motivation is that most of the deviation is orthogonal to the surface and is captured by a directional component $\delta\hat{n}$, but a uniform component μ may be required when $\hat{N}_v$ is curved. The uniform component also allows accurate approximation of discontinuity curves (such as surface boundaries and material boundaries) whose deviations are often tangent to the surface. The particular definition of $D_{\hat{n}}(\mu, \delta)$ corresponds to the shape whose projected radius along a direction $\vec{v}$ has the simple formula $\max(\mu, \delta\|\hat{n} \times \vec{v}\|)$. As shown in Figure 7c, the graph of this radius as a function of view direction has the shape of a sphere of radius μ unioned with a "bialy" [14] of radius δ.

During the construction of a PM representation, we precompute μ_v, δ_v for deviation space $D_{\hat{n}_v}(\mu_v, \delta_v)$ at each vertex $v \in V$ as follows. After each $ecol(v_s, v_t, v_u, \ldots)$ transformation is applied, we estimate the deviation between N_{v_s} and $\hat{N}_{v_s}$ by examining the residual error vectors $E = \{e_i\}$ from a dense set of points X sampled on $\hat{M}$ that locally project onto N_{v_s}, as explained in more detail in [10]. We use $\max_{e_i \in E}(e_i \cdot \hat{n}_v) / \max_{e_i \in E} \|e_i \times \hat{n}_v\|$ to fix the ratio δ_v/μ_v, and find the smallest $D_{\hat{n}_v}(\mu_v, \delta_v)$ with that ratio that bounds E. Alternatively, other simplification schemes such as [2, 5, 9] could be adapted to obtain deviation spaces with guaranteed bounds.

Note that the computation of μ_v, δ_v does not measure parametric distortion. This is appropriate for texture-mapped surfaces if the texture is geometrically projected or "wrapped". If instead, vertices were to contain explicit texture coordinates, the residual computation could be altered to measure deviation parametrically.

Given viewpoint e, screen-space tolerance τ (as a fraction of viewport size), and field-of-view angle φ, qrefine(v) returns *true* if

---

[2]The Minkowski sum is simply $A \oplus B = \{a + b : a \in A, b \in B\}$.

the screen-space projection of $D_{\hat{n}_v}(\mu_v, \delta_v)$ exceeds τ, that is, if

$$\max\left(\mu_v, \delta_v \left\|\hat{n}_v \times \frac{v - e}{\|v - e\|}\right\|\right) / \|v - e\| \ge \left(2\cot\frac{\varphi}{2}\right)\tau .$$

For efficiency, we use the equivalent test

$$\mu_v^2 \ge \kappa^2 \|v - e\|^2 \quad \text{or}$$
$$\delta_v^2 \left(\|v - e\|^2 - ((v - e) \cdot \hat{n}_v)^2\right) \ge \kappa^2 \|v - e\|^4 ,$$

where $\kappa^2 = (2\cot\frac{\varphi}{2})^2\tau^2$ is computed once per frame. Note that the test reduces to that of [14] when $\mu_v = 0$ and $\hat{n}_v = \hat{z}$, and requires only a few more floating point operations in the general case. As seen in Figures 13b and 16b, our test naturally results in more refinement near the model silhouette where surface deviation is orthogonal to the view direction.

Our test provides only an approximate bound on the screen-space projected error, for a number of reasons. First, the test slightly underestimates error away from the viewport center, as pointed out in [14]. Second, a parallel projection assumption is made when projecting $D_{\hat{n}}$ on the screen, as in [14]. Third, the neighborhood about v when evaluating qrefine(v) may be different from that in the PM sequence since M is selectively refined; thus the deviation spaces $D_{\hat{n}}$ provide strict bounds only at the vertices themselves. Nonetheless, the criterion works well in practice, as demonstrated in Figures 12–16.

Implementation We store in each Vertex.RefineInfo record the four scalar values $\{-r_v, \sin^2\alpha_v, \mu_v^2, \delta_v^2\}$. Because the three refinement tests share several common subexpressions, evaluation of the complete qrefine function requires remarkably few CPU cycles on average (230 cycles per call as shown in Table 2).

5 INCREMENTAL SELECTIVE REFINEMENT ALGORITHM

We now present an algorithm for incrementally adapting a mesh within the selective refinement framework of Section 3, using the qrefine function of Section 4. The basic idea is to traverse the list of active vertices V before rendering each frame, and for each vertex $v \in V$, either leave it as is, split it, or collapse it. The core of the traversal algorithm is summarized below.

```
procedure adapt_refinement()
    for each v ∈ V
        if v.vt and qrefine(v)
            force_vsplit(v)
        else if v.parent and ecol_legal(v.parent) and
                not qrefine(v.parent)
            ecol(v.parent)     // (and reconsider some vertices)
procedure force_vsplit(v') {
    stack ← v'
    while v ← stack.top()
        if v.vt and v.fl ∈ F
            stack.pop()       // v was split earlier in the loop
        else if v ∉ V
            stack.push(v.parent)
        else if vsplit_legal(v)
            stack.pop()
            vsplit(v)         // (placing v.vt and v.vu next in list V)
        else for i ∈ {0...3}
            if v.fn[i] ∉ F
                // force vsplit that creates face v.fn[i]
                stack.push(v.fn[i].vertices[0].parent) ³
```

---

[3]Implementation detail: the vertex that should be split to create an inactive face f is found in $f.vertices[0].parent$ because we always set both $f_l.vertices[0] = v_t$ and $f_r.vertices[0] = v_t$ when creating faces, thereby obviating the need for a Face.*parent* field.

We iterate through the doubly linked list of active vertices V. For any active vertex $v \notin \hat{M}$, if qrefine(v) evaluates to *true*, the vertex should be split. If *vsplit*(v) is not legal (i.e. if any of the faces $v.fn[0..3]$ are not active), a chain of other vertex splits are performed in order for *vsplit*(v) to become legal (procedure force_vsplit), namely those that introduce the faces $v.fn[0..3]$, and recursively, any others required to make those vertex splits legal.

For any active vertex $v \notin M^0$, if qrefine($v.parent$) returns *false*, the vertex v should be collapsed. However, this edge collapse is only performed if it is legal (i.e. if the sibling of v is also active and the neighboring faces of $v.parent.fl$ and $v.parent.fr$ match those of $v.parent.fn[0..3]$).

In short, the strategy is to force refinement when desired, but to coarsen only when possible. After a *vsplit* or *ecol* is performed, some vertices in the resulting neighborhood should be considered for further transformations. Since these vertices may have been previously visited in the traversal of V, we relocate them in the list to lie immediately after the list iterator. Specifically, following *vsplit*(v), we add $v.vt, v.vu$ after the iterator; and, following *ecol*($v.parent$), we add $v.parent$ and relocate v_l, v_r after the iterator (where v_l and v_r are the current neighbors of v as in Figure 1).

Time complexity The time complexity for adapt_refinement, transforming M^A into M^B, is $O(|V^A| + |V^B|)$ in the worst case since $M^A \rightarrow M^0 \rightarrow M^B$ could possibly require $O(|V^A|)$ *ecol*'s and $O(|V^B|)$ *vsplit*'s, each taking constant time. For continuous view changes, V^B is usually similar to V^A, and the simple traversal of the active vertex list is the bottleneck of the incremental refinement algorithm, as shown in Table 2. Note that the number $|V|$ of active vertices is typically much smaller than the number $|\hat{V}|$ of original vertices. The rendering process, which has the same time complexity ($|F| \simeq 2|V|$), in fact has a larger time constant. Indeed, adapt_refinement requires only about 14% of total frame time, as discussed in Section 8.

Regulation For a given PM and a constant screen-space tolerance τ, the number $|F|$ of active faces can vary dramatically depending on the view. Since both refinement times and rendering times are closely correlated to $|F|$, this leads to high variability in frame rates (Figure 9). We have implemented a simple scheme for regulating τ so as to maintain $|F|$ at a nearly constant level. Let m be the desired number of faces. Prior to calling adapt_refinement at time frame t, we set $\tau_t = \tau_{t-1}(|F_{t-1}|/m)$ where $|F_{t-1}|$ is the number of active faces in the previously drawn frame. As shown in Figure 10, this simple feedback control system exhibits good stability for our terrain flythrough. More sophisticated control strategies may be necessary for heterogeneous, irregular models. Direct regulation of frame rate could be attempted, but since frame rate is more sensitive to operating system "hiccups", it may be best achieved indirectly using a secondary, slower controller adjusting m.

Amortization Since the main loop of adapt_refinement is a simple traversal of the list V, we can distribute its work over consecutive frames by traversing only a fraction of V each frame. For slowly changing view parameters, this reduces the already low overhead of selective refinement while introducing few visual artifacts.

With amortization, however, regulation of $|F|$ through adjustment of τ becomes more difficult, since the response in $|F|$ may lag several frames. Our current strategy is to wait several frames until the entire list V has been traversed before making changes to τ. To reduce overshooting, we disallow *vsplit* refinement if the number of active faces reaches an upper limit (e.g. $|F| \geq 1.2m$). but do count the number of faces that would be introduced towards the next adjustment to τ. In the flythrough example of Figure 10, where the average frame rate is 7.2 frames/sec, amortization increases frame rate to 8 frames/sec.

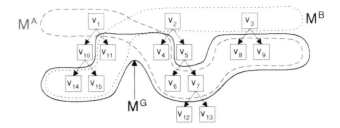

Figure 8: Illustration of two selectively refined meshes M^A and M^B, and of the mesh M^G used to geomorph between them.

Geomorphs The selective refinement framework also supports geomorphs between any two selectively refined meshes M^A and M^B. That is, one can construct a mesh $M^G(\alpha)$ whose vertices vary as a function of a parameter $0 \leq \alpha \leq 1$, such that $M^G(0)$ looks identical to M^A and $M^G(1)$ looks identical to M^B. The key is to first find a mesh M^G whose active vertex front is everywhere lower than or equal to that of M^A and M^B, as illustrated in Figure 8. Mesh $\hat{M}$ trivially satisfies this property, but a simpler mesh M^G is generally obtained by starting from either M^A or M^B and successively calling force_vsplit to advance the vertex front towards that of the other mesh. The mesh M^G has the property that its faces F^G are a superset of both F^A and F^B, and that any vertex $v_j \in V^G$ has a unique ancestor $v_{\rho^{G \rightarrow A}(j)} \in V^A$ and a unique ancestor $v_{\rho^{G \rightarrow B}(j)} \in V^B$. The geomorph $M^G(\alpha)$ is the mesh $(F^G, V^G(\alpha))$ with

$$\mathbf{v}_j^G(\alpha) = (1-\alpha)\mathbf{v}_{\rho^{G \rightarrow A}(j)} + (\alpha)\mathbf{v}_{\rho^{G \rightarrow B}(j)} \;.$$

In the case that M^B is the result of calling adapt_refinement on M^A, the mesh M^G can be obtained more directly. Instead of a single pass through V in adapt_refinement, we make two passes: a refinement pass $M^A \rightarrow M^G$ where only *vsplit* are considered, and a coarsening pass $M^G \rightarrow M^B$ where only *ecol* are considered. In each pass, we record the sequence of transformations performed, allowing us to backtrack through the inverse of the *ecol* sequence to recover the intermediate mesh M^G, and to construct the desired ancestry functions $\rho^{G \rightarrow A}$ and $\rho^{G \rightarrow B}$. Such a geomorph is demonstrated on the accompanying video. Because of view coherence, the number of vertices that require interpolation is generally smaller than the number of active vertices. More research is needed to determine the feasibility and usefulness of generating geomorphs at runtime.

6 RENDERING

Many graphics systems require triangle strip representations for optimal rendering performance [7]. Because the mesh connectivity in our incremental refinement scheme is dynamic, it is not possible to precompute triangle strips. We use a greedy algorithm to generate triangle strips at every frame, as shown in Figure 12e. Surprisingly, the algorithm produces strips of adequate length (on average, 10–15 faces per "generalized" triangle strip under IRIS GL, and about 4.2 faces per "sequential" triangle strip under OpenGL), and does so efficiently (Table 2).

The algorithm traverses the list of active faces F, and at any face not yet rendered, begins a new triangle strip. Then, iteratively, it renders the face, checks if any of its neighbor(s) has not yet been rendered, and if so continues the strip there. Only neighbors with the same material are considered, so as to reduce graphics state changes. To reduce fragmentation, we always favor continuing generalized triangle strips in a clockwise spiral (Figure 12e). When the strip reaches a dead end, traversal of the list F resumes. One bit of the Face.*matid* field is used as a boolean flag to record rendered faces; these bits are cleared using a quick second pass through F.

Recently, graphics libraries have begun to support interfaces for immediate-mode rendering of (V, F) mesh representations (e.g. Direct3D DrawIndexedPrimitive and OpenGL glArrayElementArrayEXT). Although not used in our current prototype, such interfaces may be ideal for rendering selectively refined meshes.

7 OPTIMIZING PM CONSTRUCTION FOR SELECTIVE REFINEMENT

The PM construction algorithm of [10] finds a sequence of *vsplit* refinement transformations optimized for accuracy, without regard to the shape of the resulting vertex hierarchy. We have experimented with introducing a small penalty function to the cost metric of [10] to favor balanced hierarchies in order to minimize unnecessary dependencies. The penalty for $ecol(v_t, v_u)$ is $c\,(n_{v_t} + n_{v_u})$ where n_v is the number of descendants of v (including itself) and c is a user-specified parameter. We find that a small value of c improves results slightly for some examples (i.e. reduces the number of faces for a given error tolerance τ), but that as c increases, the hierarchies become quadtree-like and the results worsen markedly (Figure 17). Our conclusion is that it is beneficial to introduce a small bias to favor balanced hierarchies in the absence of geometric preferences.

8 RESULTS

Timing results We constructed a PM representation of a Grand Canyon terrain mesh of 600^2 vertices (717,602 faces), and truncated this PM representation to 400,000 faces. This preprocessing requires several hours but is done off-line (Table 1). Loading this PM from disk and constructing the SRMesh requires less than a minute (most of it spent computing r_v and α_v). Figures 9 and 10 show measurements from a 3-minute real-time flythrough of the terrain without and with regulation, on an SGI Indigo2 Extreme (150MHz R4400 with 128MB of memory). The measurements show that the time spent in adapt_refinement is approximately 14% of total frame time. In the accompanying video, amortization is used to reduce this overhead to 8% of total frame time. For the flythrough of Figure 10, code profiling and system monitoring reveal the timing breakdown shown in Table 2. Note that triangle strip generation is efficient enough to keep CPU utilization below 100%; the graphics system is in fact the bottleneck. On another computer with the same CPU but with an Impact graphics system, the average frame rate increases from 7.2 to 14.0 frames/sec.

Space requirements Table 1 shows the disk space required to store the PM representations and associated deviation parameters; both are compressed using GNU gzip. Positions, normals, and deviation parameters are currently stored as floating point, and should be quantized to improve compression.

Since $|\mathcal{V}| \simeq 2|\hat{V}|$ and $|\hat{F}| \simeq 2|\hat{V}|$, memory requirement for SRMesh is $O(|\hat{V}|)$. The current implementation is not optimized for space, and requires about $224|\hat{V}|$ bytes. The memory footprint could be reduced as follows. Since only about half of all vertices $\mathcal{V}$ can be split, it would be best to store the split information $(fl, fn[0..3], refine\_info)$ in a separate array of "Vsplit" records indexed by vt. If space is always allocated for 2 faces per *vsplit*, the Vertex.*fl* field can be deleted and instead computed from vt. Scalar values in the RefineInfo record can be quantized to 8 bits with an exponential map as in [14]. Coordinates of points and normals can be quantized to 16 bits. Material identifiers are unnecessary if the mesh has only one material. Overall, these changes would reduce memory requirements down to about $140|\hat{V}|$ bytes.

For the case of height fields, the memory requirement per vertex far exceeds that of regular grid schemes [14]. However, the fully detailed mesh $\hat{M}$ may have arbitrary connectivity, and may therefore be obtained by pre-simplifying a given grid representation, possibly

Table 1: Statistics for the various data sets.

Model	Fully detailed $\hat{M}$		Disk (MB)		Mem.	V hier.	Constr.
	$|\hat{V}|$	$|\hat{F}|$	PM	$\{\mu, \delta\}$	(MB)	height	(mins)
canyon$_{200}$	40,000	79,202	1.3	0.3	8.9	29	47
canyon$_{400}$	160,000	318,402	5.0	1.1	35.8	32	244
canyon$_{600}$	360,000	717,602	11.0	2.6	80.6	36	627
" trunc.	200,600	400,000	6.6	1.5	44.9	35	627
sphere	9,902	19,800	0.3	0.1	2.2	19	11
teapot trunc.	5,090	10,000	0.2	0.0	1.1	20	12
gameguy	21,412	42,712	0.8	0.2	4.8	26	30
bunny	34,835	69,473	1.2	0.2	7.8	24	51

Table 2: CPU utilization (on a 150MHz MIPS R4400).

	procedure	% of frame time	cycles/call
User	adapt_refinement	14 %	-
	(vsplit)	(0 %)	2200
	(ecol)	(1 %)	4000
	(qrefine)	(4 %)	230
	render (tstrip/face)	26 %	600
	GL library	19 %	-
System	OS + graphics	21 %	-
	CPU idle	20 %	-

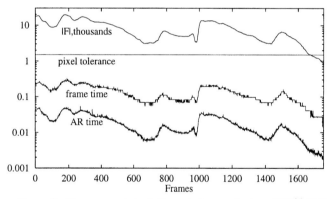

Figure 9: Measurements in flythrough for constant $\tau = 0.25\%$ (1.5 pixels in 600^2 window). From top: number of faces in thousands, τ in pixels, frame times and adapt_refinement times in seconds.

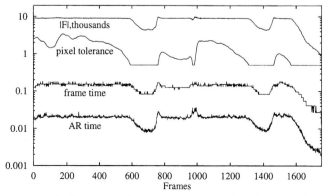

Figure 10: Same but with regulation to maintain $|F| \simeq 9000$. (τ is never allowed below 0.5 pixels.)

by an order of magnitude or more, without significant loss of accuracy. This pre-simplification may be achieved by simply truncating the PM representation, either at creation time or at load time.

Applications that use height fields often require efficient geometric queries, such as point search. Because the vertex hierarchies in our framework have $O(\log n)$ height in the average case (this can be enforced using the approach in Section 7), such queries can be performed in $O(\log n)$ time by iteratively calling force_vsplit on vertices in the neighborhood of the query point.

Parametric surfaces Our framework offers a novel approach to real-time adaptive tessellation of parametric surfaces. As a precomputation, we first obtain a dense tessellation of the surface, then construct from this dense mesh a PM representation, and finally truncate the PM sequence to a desired level of maximum accuracy. At runtime, we selectively refine this truncated PM representation according to the viewpoint (Figure 14). The main drawback of this approach is that the resolution of the most detailed tessellation is fixed a priori. However, the benefits include simplicity of runtime implementation (no trimming or stitching), efficiency (incremental, amortized work), and most importantly, high adaptability of the tessellations (accurate TIN's whose connectivities adapt both to surface curvature and to the viewpoint).

General meshes Figures 15 and 16 demonstrate selective refinement applied to general meshes. We expect this to be of practical use for rendering complex models and environments that do not conveniently admit scene hierarchies.

9 SUMMARY AND FUTURE WORK

We have introduced an efficient framework for selectively refining arbitrary progressive meshes, developed fast view-dependent refinement criteria, and presented an algorithm for incrementally adapting the approximating meshes according to these criteria. We have demonstrated real-time selective refinement on a number of meshes, including terrains, parametric surface tessellations, and general meshes. As the adaptive refinement algorithm exploits frame-to-frame coherence and is easily amortized, it consumes only a small fraction of total frame time. Because the selectively refined meshes stem from a geometrically optimized set of vertex split transformations with few dependencies, they quickly adapt to the underlying model, requiring fewer polygons for a given level of approximation than previous schemes.

There are a number of areas for future work, including:

- Memory management for large models, particularly terrains.
- Experimentation with runtime generation of geomorphs.
- Extension of refinement criteria to account for surface shading [24], or for surface velocity and proximity to gaze center [17].
- Adaptive refinement for animated models.
- Applications of selective refinement to collision detection.

ACKNOWLEDGMENTS

The Grand Canyon data is from the United States Geological Survey, with in-house processing by Chad McCabe of the Microsoft Geography Product Unit; the "gameguy" mesh is courtesy of Viewpoint DataLabs; the "bunny" is from the Stanford University Computer Graphics Laboratory. I also wish to thank Jed Lengyel, John Snyder, and Rick Szeliski for helpful comments, and Bobby Bodenheimer for useful discussions on control theory.

REFERENCES

[1] ABI-EZZI, S. S., AND SUBRAMANIAM, S. Fast dynamic tessellation of trimmed NURBS surfaces. *Computer Graphics Forum (Proceedings of Eurographics '94) 13*, 3 (1994), 107–126.

[2] BAJAJ, C., AND SCHIKORE, D. Error-bounded reduction of triangle meshes with multivariate data. *SPIE 2656* (1996), 34–45.

[3] CIGNONI, P., PUPPO, E., AND SCOPIGNO, R. Representation and visualization of terrain surfaces at variable resolution. In *Scientific Visualization '95* (1995), R. Scateni, Ed., World Scientific, pp. 50–68.

[4] CLARK, J. Hierarchical geometric models for visible surface algorithms. *Communications of the ACM 19*, 10 (October 1976), 547–554.

[5] COHEN, J., VARSHNEY, A., MANOCHA, D., TURK, G., WEBER, H., AGARWAL, P., BROOKS, F., AND WRIGHT, W. Simplification envelopes. *Computer Graphics (SIGGRAPH '96 Proceedings)* (1996), 119–128.

[6] DE FLORIANI, L., MARZANO, P., AND PUPPO, E. Multiresolution models for topographic surface description. *The Visual Computer 12*, 7 (1996), 317–345.

[7] EVANS, F., SKIENA, S., AND VARSHNEY, A. Optimizing triangle strips for fast rendering. In *Visualization '96 Proceedings* (1996), IEEE, pp. 319–326.

[8] FUNKHOUSER, T., AND SÉQUIN, C. Adaptive display algorithm for interactive frame rates during visualization of complex virtual environments. *Computer Graphics (SIGGRAPH '93 Proceedings)* (1993), 247–254.

[9] GUÉZIEC, A. Surface simplification with variable tolerance. In *Proceedings of the Second International Symposium on Medical Robotics and Computer Assisted Surgery* (November 1995), pp. 132–139.

[10] HOPPE, H. Progressive meshes. *Computer Graphics (SIGGRAPH '96 Proceedings)* (1996), 99–108.

[11] KIRKPATRICK, D. Optimal search in planar subdivisions. *SIAM Journal on Computing 12*, 1 (February 1983), 28–35.

[12] KUMAR, S., AND MANOCHA, D. Hierarchical visibility culling for spline models. In *Proceedings of Graphics Interface '96* (1996), pp. 142–150.

[13] KUMAR, S., MANOCHA, D., AND LASTRA, A. Interactive display of large-scale NURBS models. In *1995 Symposium on Interactive 3D Graphics* (1995), ACM SIGGRAPH, pp. 51–58.

[14] LINDSTROM, P., KOLLER, D., RIBARSKY, W., HODGES, L., FAUST, N., AND TURNER, G. Real-time, continuous level of detail rendering of height fields. *Computer Graphics (SIGGRAPH '96 Proceedings)* (1996), 109–118.

[15] LOUNSBERY, M., DEROSE, T., AND WARREN, J. Multiresolution surfaces of arbitrary topological type. *ACM Transactions on Graphics 16*, 1 (January 1997), 34–73.

[16] LUEBKE, D. Hierarchical structures for dynamic polygonal simplification. TR 96-006, Department of Computer Science, University of North Carolina at Chapel Hill, 1996.

[17] OHSHIMA, T., YAMAMOTO, H., AND TAMURA, H. Gaze-directed adaptive rendering for interacting with virtual space. In *Proc. of IEEE 1996 Virtual Reality Annual Intnl. Symp.* (1996), pp. 103–110.

[18] ROCKWOOD, A., HEATON, K., AND DAVIS, T. Real-time rendering of trimmed surfaces. In *Computer Graphics (SIGGRAPH '89 Proceedings)* (1989), vol. 23, pp. 107–116.

[19] ROSSIGNAC, J., AND BORREL, P. Multi-resolution 3D approximations for rendering complex scenes. In *Modeling in Computer Graphics*, B. Falcidieno and T. L. Kunii, Eds. Springer-Verlag, 1993, pp. 455–465.

[20] SCARLATOS, L. L. A refined triangulation hierarchy for multiple levels of terrain detail. In *Proceedings, IMAGE V Conference* (June 1990), pp. 115–122.

[21] SCHROEDER, W., ZARGE, J., AND LORENSEN, W. Decimation of triangle meshes. *Computer Graphics (SIGGRAPH '92 Proceedings) 26*, 2 (1992), 65–70.

[22] SHIRMAN, L., AND ABI-EZZI, S. The cone of normals technique for fast processing of curved patches. *Computer Graphics Forum (Proceedings of Eurographics '93) 12*, 3 (1993), 261–272.

[23] TAYLOR, D. C., AND BARRETT, W. A. An algorithm for continuous resolution polygonalizations of a discrete surface. In *Proceedings of Graphics Interface '94* (1994), pp. 33–42.

[24] XIA, J., AND VARSHNEY, A. Dynamic view-dependent simplification for polygonal models. In *Visualization '96 Proceedings* (1996), IEEE, pp. 327–334.

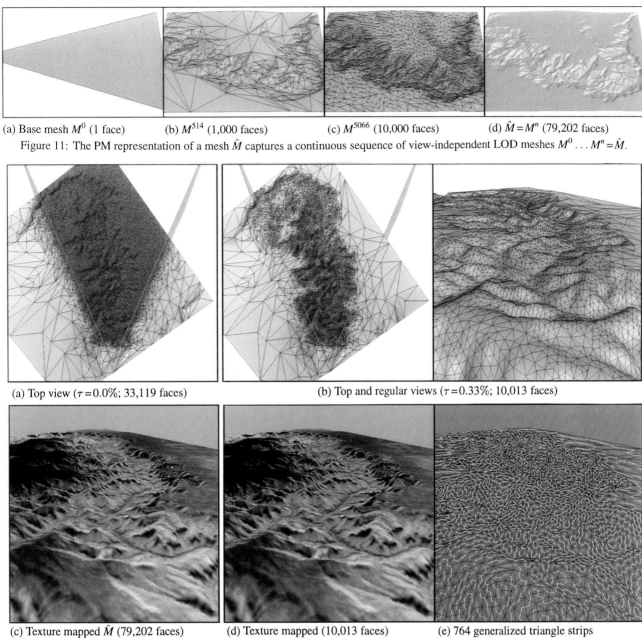

(a) Base mesh M^0 (1 face) (b) M^{514} (1,000 faces) (c) M^{5066} (10,000 faces) (d) $\hat{M} = M^n$ (79,202 faces)

Figure 11: The PM representation of a mesh $\hat{M}$ captures a continuous sequence of view-independent LOD meshes $M^0 \dots M^n = \hat{M}$.

(a) Top view ($\tau = 0.0\%$; 33,119 faces) (b) Top and regular views ($\tau = 0.33\%$; 10,013 faces)

(c) Texture mapped $\hat{M}$ (79,202 faces) (d) Texture mapped (10,013 faces) (e) 764 generalized triangle strips

Figure 12: View-dependent refinement of the same PM, using the view frustum (highlighted in orange) and a screen-space geometric error tolerance of (a) 0% and (b,d,e) 0.33% of window size (i.e. 2 pixels for a 600×600 image).

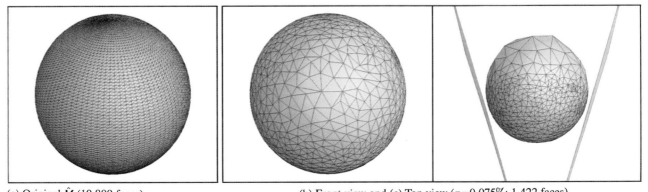

(a) Original $\hat{M}$ (19,800 faces) (b) Front view and (c) Top view ($\tau = 0.075\%$; 1,422 faces)

Figure 13: View-dependent refinement of a tessellated sphere, demonstrating (b) the directionality of the deviation space $D_{\hat{n}}$ (more refinement near silhouettes) and (c) the surface orientation criterion (coarsening of backfacing regions).

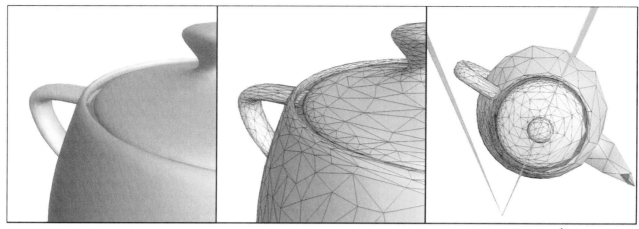

Figure 14: View-dependent refinement ($\tau = 0.15\%$; 1,782 faces) of a truncated PM representation (10,000 faces in $\hat{M}$) created from a tessellated parametric surface (25,440 faces). Interactive frame rate near this viewpoint is 14.7 frames/sec, versus 6.8 frames/sec using $\hat{M}$.

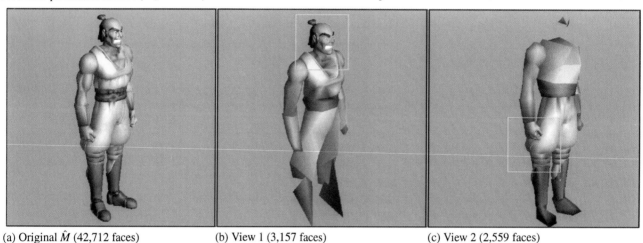

(a) Original $\hat{M}$ (42,712 faces)   (b) View 1 (3,157 faces)   (c) View 2 (2,559 faces)

Figure 15: Two view-dependent refinements of a general mesh $\hat{M}$ using view frustums highlighted in orange and with τ set to 0.6%.

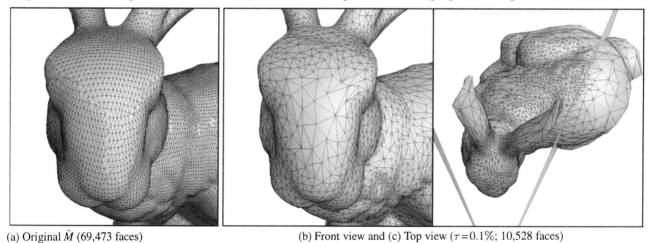

(a) Original $\hat{M}$ (69,473 faces)   (b) Front view and (c) Top view ($\tau = 0.1\%$; 10,528 faces)

Figure 16: View-dependent refinement. Interactive frame rate near this viewpoint is 6.7 frames/sec, versus 1.9 frames/sec using $\hat{M}$.

Figure 17: Height of vertex hierarchy, and number of faces in mesh of Figure 16b, as functions of the bias parameter c used in PM construction of bunny.

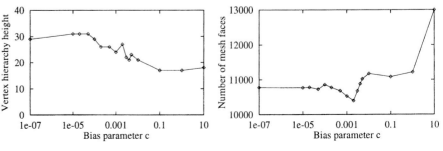

View-Dependent Simplification Of Arbitrary Polygonal Environments

David Luebke, Carl Erikson
Department of Computer Science
University of North Carolina at Chapel Hill

1. ABSTRACT

Hierarchical dynamic simplification (HDS) is a new approach to the problem of simplifying arbitrary polygonal environments. HDS operates dynamically, retessellating the scene continuously as the user's viewing position shifts, and adaptively, processing the entire database without first decomposing the environment into individual objects. The resulting system allows real-time display of very complex polygonal CAD models consisting of thousands of parts and hundreds of thousands of polygons. HDS supports various preprocessing algorithms and various run-time criteria, providing a general framework for dynamic view-dependent simplification.

Briefly, HDS works by clustering vertices together in a hierarchical fashion. The simplification process continuously queries this hierarchy to generate a scene containing only those polygons that are important from the current viewpoint. When the volume of space associated with a vertex cluster occupies less than a user-specified amount of the screen, all vertices within that cluster are collapsed together and degenerate polygons filtered out. HDS maintains an *active list* of visible polygons for rendering. Since frame-to-frame movements typically involve small changes in viewpoint, and therefore modify the active list by only a few polygons, the method takes advantage of temporal coherence for greater speed.

CR Categories: I.3.5 [Computer Graphics]: Computational Geometry and Object Modeling - surfaces and object representations.

Additional Keywords: polygonal simplification, level of detail, view dependent rendering.

2. INTRODUCTION

2.1 Polygons In Computer Graphics

Polygonal models currently dominate the field of interactive three-dimensional computer graphics. This is largely because their mathematical simplicity allows rapid rendering of polygonal datasets, which in turn has led to widely available polygon-rendering hardware. Moreover, polygons serve as a sort of lowest common denominator for computer models, since almost any model representation (spline, implicit-surface, volumetric) can be converted with arbitrary accuracy to a polygonal mesh.

In many cases the complexity of such models exceeds the capability of graphics hardware to render them interactively. Three approaches are used to alleviate this problem:

- Augmenting the raw polygonal data to convey more visual detail per polygon. Gouraud shading and texture mapping fall into this category.

- Using information about the model to cull away large portions which are occluded from the current viewpoint. The visibility processing approach of Teller and Sequin is an excellent example [Teller 91].

- *Polygonal simplification* methods simplify the polygonal geometry of small or distant objects to reduce the rendering cost without a significant loss in the visual content of the scene. HDS is one such method.

2.2 Polygonal Simplification

Polygonal simplification is at once a very current and a very old topic in computer graphics. As early as 1976, James Clark described the benefits of representing objects within a scene at several resolutions, and flight simulators have long used hand-crafted multi-resolution models of airplanes to guarantee a constant frame rate [Clark 76, Cosman 81]. Recent years have seen a flurry of research into generating such multi-resolution representations of objects automatically by simplifying the polygonal geometry of the object. This paper presents a new approach which simplifies the geometry of entire scenes dynamically, adjusting the simplification as the user moves around.

2.3 Motivation

The algorithm presented in this paper was conceived for very complex hand-crafted CAD databases, a class of models for which existing simplification methods are often inadequate. Real-world CAD models are often topologically unsound (i.e., non-manifold), and may entail a great deal of clean-up effort before many simplification algorithms can be applied. Sometimes such models even come in "polygon-soup" formats which do not differentiate individual objects, but instead describe the entire scene as an unorganized list of polygons. No existing algorithm deals elegantly with such models.

Even when the model format delineates objects, simplifying complex CAD datasets with current schemes can involve many man-hours. To begin with, physically large objects must be subdivided. Consider a model of a ship, for example: the hull of the ship should be divided into several sections, or the end furthest from the user will be tessellated as finely as the nearby hull. In addition, physically small objects may need to be combined, especially for drastic simplification. The diesel engine of that ship might consist of ten thousand small parts; a roughly engine-shaped block makes a better approximation than ten thousand tetrahedra. Finally, each simplification must be inspected for visual fidelity to the original object, and an appropriate switching threshold selected. This can be the most time-consuming step in the simplification of a complicated model with thousands of parts, but few existing techniques address automating the process.[1]

These considerations led to a new approach with three primary goals. First, the algorithm should be very general, making as few assumptions as possible about the input model. The algorithm must therefore deal robustly with degenerate and non-manifold models. Second, the algorithm should be completely automatic, able to simplify even a polygon-soup model without human

---

[1] Notable exceptions include work by Cohen et al, and by Shirley and Maciel [Cohen 96, Maciel 95].

intervention. This implies that the algorithm must simplify the entire scene adaptively rather than relying on simplifying objects within the scene. Third, the algorithm should be dynamically adjustable, supplying the system with a fine-grained interactive "dial" for trading off performance and fidelity. This final requirement implies that the algorithm must operate at least partially at run time.

2.4 Hierarchical Dynamic Simplification

Hierarchical dynamic simplification has some novel features. Rather than representing the scene as a collection of objects, each at several levels of detail, the entire model comprises a single large data structure. This is the *vertex tree*, a hierarchy of vertices which is queried dynamically to generate a simplified scene. The vertex tree contains information only about the vertices and triangles of the model; manifold topology is not required and need not be preserved. Each node in the vertex tree contains one or more vertices; HDS operates by collapsing all of the vertices within a node together to a single *representative vertex*. Triangles whose corners have been collapsed together become redundant and can be eliminated, decreasing the total polygon count. Likewise, a node may be expanded by splitting its representative vertex into the representative vertices of the node's children. Triangles filtered out when the node was collapsed become visible again when the node is expanded, increasing the polygon count.

The entire system is dynamic; nodes to be collapsed or expanded are continuously chosen based on their projected size. The screenspace extent of each node is monitored: as the viewpoint shifts, certain nodes in the vertex tree will fall below the size threshold. These nodes will be *folded* into their parent nodes and the now-redundant triangles removed from the display list. Other nodes will increase in apparent size to the user and will be *unfolded* into their constituent child nodes, introducing new vertices and new triangles into the display list. The user selects the screenspace size threshold and may adjust it during the course of a viewing session for interactive control over the degree of simplification. Nodes will be folded and unfolded each frame, so efficient methods for finding, adding, and removing the affected triangles are crucial.

3. STRUCTURES AND METHODS

3.1 Active Triangle List

The purpose of the active triangle list is to take advantage of temporal coherence. Frames in an interactive viewing session typically exhibit only incremental shifts in viewpoint, so the set of visible triangles remains largely constant. The active triangle list in its simplest form is just a sequence of those visible triangles. Expanding a node appends some triangles to the active triangle list; collapsing the node removes them. The active list is maintained in the current implementation as a doubly-linked list of triangle structures, each with the following basic structure:

```
struct Tri {
    Node *      corners[3];
    Node *      proxies[3];
    Tri         *prev, *next;
};
```

The **corners** field represents the triangle at its highest resolution, pointing to the three nodes whose representative vertices are the original corners of the triangle. The **proxies** field represents the triangle in the current simplification, pointing to the *first active ancestor* of each corner node [Figure 1].

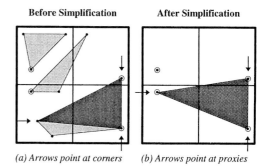

(a) Arrows point at corners   *(b) Arrows point at proxies*

*Figure 1: A triangle's **corners** reference the initial vertices; its **proxies** point to the current simplification of each corner. Clustering vertices to the representative vertex of their quadrant (circled) collapses all but the darkened triangle.*

3.2 Vertex Tree

Created during a preprocessing stage, the vertex tree controls the order in which vertices are collapsed and stores data necessary to collapse and uncollapse these vertices quickly. Unfolded nodes in the vertex tree are labeled *active*, and folded nodes are labeled *inactive*; the active nodes of the vertex tree comprise a contiguous region called the *active tree*. Active nodes with no active children are a special case; these nodes form the boundary of the active tree and are labeled *boundary* nodes[Figure 2].

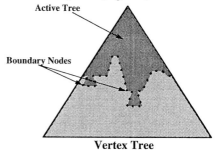

Figure 2: The vertex tree, active tree, and boundary nodes.

Each node in the vertex tree includes the basic structure described below (explanations of the individual fields follow):

```
struct Node {
    BitVec       id;
    Byte         depth;
    NodeStatus   label;
    Coord        repvert;
    Coord        center;
    float        radius;
    Tri *        tris;
    Tri *        subtris;
    Node *       parent;
    Byte         numchildren;
    Node **      children;
};
```

- **id**: a bit vector which labels the path from the root of the vertex tree to the node. In a binary vertex tree, each bit specifies the left or right branch at that level of the tree. For the vertex octree described in section 7.1, each 3-bit triple denotes the correct branch at that level.
- **depth**: the depth of the node in the vertex tree. The depth and id together uniquely identify the node.
- **label**: the node's status: *active*, *boundary*, or *inactive*.
- **repvert**: the coordinates of the node's representative vertex. All vertices in boundary and inactive nodes are collapsed to this vertex.

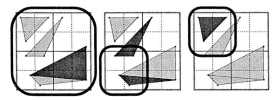

Figure 4: Showing the subtris of three nodes. These are the triangles which appear and vanish as the nodes fold and unfold. Here the subtris of each circled node are darkened.

- **center, radius**: the center and radius of a bounding sphere containing all vertices in this node.
- **tris**: a list of triangles with exactly one corner in the node. These are the triangles whose corners must be adjusted when the node is folded or unfolded.
- **subtris**: a list of triangles with two or three corners within the node, but no more than one corner within any child of the node [Figure 4]. These triangles will be filtered out if the node is folded, and re-introduced if the node is unfolded.
- **parent, numchildren, children**: the parent and children of this node in the vertex tree.

The fundamental operations associated with nodes in the vertex tree are *collapseNode()* and *expandNode()*. These functions add or remove the subtris of the specified node from the active triangle list and update the proxies of the node's tris:

```
collapseNode (Node *N)
    N->label = boundary;
    foreach child C of N
        // label all children inactive
        if (C->label == active)
            collapseNode(C);
        C->label = inactive;
    foreach triangle T in N->tris
        // update tri proxies
        foreach corner c of {1,2,3}
            T->proxies[c] =
                firstActiveAncestor(T->
                    corners[c]);
    foreach triangle T in N->subtris
        // remove subtris from active list
        removeTri(T);

expandNode (Node *N)
    foreach child C of N
        C->label = boundary;
    N->label = active;
    foreach triangle T in N->tris
        // update tri proxies
        foreach corner c of {1,2,3}
            T->proxies[c] =
                firstActiveAncestor(T->
                    corners[c]);
    foreach triangle T in N->subtris
        // add subtris to active list
        addTri(T);
```

4. VIEW-DEPENDENT SIMPLIFICATION

The data structures and methods described so far provide a framework for dynamic view-dependent simplification. Any criterion for run-time simplification may be plugged into this framework; each criterion takes the form of a function to choose which nodes are folded and unfolded each frame. The current implementation incorporates three criteria: a screenspace error threshold, a silhouette test, and a triangle budget.

4.1 Screenspace Error Threshold

The underlying philosophy of HDS is to remove triangles which are not important to the scene. Since importance usually diminishes with size on the screen, an obvious run-time strategy is

to collapse nodes which occupy a small amount of the screen. To formulate this strategy more precisely, consider a node which represents several vertices clustered together. The error introduced by collapsing the vertices can be thought of as the maximum distance a vertex can be shifted during the collapse operation, which equals the length of the vector between the two farthest vertices in the cluster. The extent of this vector on the screen is the *screenspace error* of the node. By unfolding exactly those nodes whose screenspace error exceeds a user-specified threshold t, HDS enforces a quality constraint on the simplification: no vertex shall move by more than t pixels on the screen.

Determining the exact screenspace extent of a vertex cluster can be a time-consuming task, but a conservative estimate can be efficiently obtained by associating a bounding volume with each node in the vertex tree. The current implementation uses bounding spheres, which allow an extremely fast screenspace extent test but often provide a poor fit to the vertex cluster. The function nodeSize(N) tests the bounding sphere of the node N and returns its extent projected onto the screen. The recursive procedure adjustTree() uses nodeSize() in a top-down fashion, evaluating which nodes to collapse and expand:

```
adjustTree(Node *N)
    size = nodeSize(N);
    if (size >= threshold)
        if (N->label == active)
            foreach child C of N
                adjustTree(C);
        else    // N->label == Boundary
            expandNode(N);
    else    // size < threshold
        if (N->label == active)
            collapseNode(N);
```

4.2 Silhouette Preservation

Silhouettes and contours are particularly important visual cues for object recognition. Detecting nodes along object silhouettes and allocating more detail to those regions can therefore disproportionately increase the perceived quality of a simplification [Xia 96]. A conservative but efficient silhouette test can be plugged into the HDS framework by adding two fields to the Node structure: **coneNormal** is a vector and **coneAngle** is a floating-point scalar. These fields together specify a *cone of normals* [Shirman 93] for the node which conservatively bounds all the normals of all the triangles in the subtree rooted at the node [Figure 5]. At run time a viewing cone is created that originates from the viewer position and tightly encloses the bounding sphere of the node [Figure 6]. Testing the viewing cone against the cone of normals determines whether the node is completely frontfacing, completely backfacing, or potentially lies on the silhouette. If any normal in the cone of normals is orthogonal to any direction contained within the viewing cone, the node is potentially on the silhouette [Figure 7]:

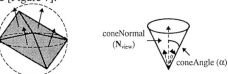

Figure 5: On the left, a node containing four triangles plus its bounding sphere. On the right, the node's cone of normals.

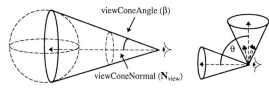

Figure 6: The viewing cone on the left originates from the viewer and tightly encloses the bounding sphere of the node. The angle between N_{cone} and N_{view} is denoted θ in the pseudocode below.

```
testSilhouette(Node *node, Coord eyePt)
    α = node->coneAngle;
    N_cone = node->coneNormal;
    β = calcViewConeAngle(eyePt, node);
    N_view = calcViewConeNormal(eyePt, node);
    θ = cos^-1(N_view • N_cone);
    if (θ - α - β > π/2)
        return FrontFacing;
    if (θ + α + β < π/2)
        return BackFacing;
    return OnSilhouette;
```

Silhouette preservation dovetails nicely with the screenspace error metric approach presented above: the testSilhouette() operation determines which nodes may be on the silhouette, and these nodes are then tested against a tighter screenspace error threshold than interior nodes [Plate 2]. The adjustTree() operation is easily modified to incorporate this test:

```
adjustTree(Node *N)
    size = nodeSize(N);
    if (testSilhouette(N) == OnSilhouette)
        testThreshold = T_s;
    else        // testSilhouette(N) == Interior
        testThreshold = T_i;
    if (size >= testThreshold)
        if (N->label == active)
            foreach child C of N
                adjustTree(C);
        else  // N->label == Boundary
            expandNode(N);
    else        // size < testThreshold
        if (N->label == active)
            collapseNode(N);
```

Note that *hierarchical backface culling* falls out of the silhouette preservation test if polygons of backfacing nodes are not rendered [Kumar 96].

4.3 Triangle-Budget Simplification

The screenspace error threshold and silhouette test allow the user to set a bound on the quality of the simplified scene, but often a bound on the complexity (and rendering time) is desired instead. *Triangle budget simplification* allows the user to specify how many triangles the scene should contain. HDS then minimizes the maximum screenspace error of all boundary nodes within this triangle budget constraint. The intuitive meaning of this process is easily put into words: "Vertices on the screen can move as far as *t* pixels from their original position. Minimize *t*."

The current system implements triangle budget simplification as a priority queue of boundary nodes, sorted by screenspace error. The node N with the greatest error is unfolded, removing N from the top of the queue and inserting the children of N back into the queue. This process iterates until unfolding the top node of the queue would exceed the triangle budget, at which point the maximum error has been minimized. The simplification could further refine the scene by searching the priority queue for the largest nodes which can still be unfolded without violating the triangle budget, but this is unnecessary in practice. The initial minimization step works extremely well on all models tested, and always terminates within twenty triangles of the specified budget. Pseudocode for this procedure is straightforward:

```
budgetSimplify(Node *rootnode)
    // Initialize Q to rootnode
    Heap *Q(rootnode);
    Node *topnode = rootnode;

    Q->initialize(root);
    while (topnode->nsubtris < tribudget)
        topnode = Q->removeTop();
        expandNode(topnode);
        Q->insert(topnode->children);
        tribudget -= topnode->nsubtris;
```

5. OPTIMIZING THE ALGORITHM

A straightforward implementation of the HDS algorithm runs with adequate speed on small models, no larger than 20,000 triangles or so. Three kinds of optimizations together increase the speed of the dynamic simplification by almost two orders of magnitude: exploiting temporal coherence, using visibility information, and parallelizing the algorithm.

5.1 Exploiting Temporal Coherence

HDS assumes a high degree of frame-to-frame coherence in the position of the viewer. The design of the active triangle list in particular is based on the assumption that relatively few triangles will be added or removed to the scene each frame. One especially frequent operation that can also take advantage of coherence is the firstActiveAncestor() function, used heavily by collapseNode() and expandNode(). FirstActiveAncestor(N) searches up the vertex tree for the nearest ancestor of node N which is tagged Active or Boundary. Storing the result of each search as a field of N and going up or down from that node speeds up the next search considerably. The **id** field of the Node structure provides the information necessary to traverse down the tree along the correct path.

5.2 Visibility: Culling the Active Triangle List

The active triangle list as described exploits temporal coherence but does not lend itself to efficient culling of invisible triangles. View-frustum culling techniques clump polygons together, often using a spatial hierarchy to quickly reject clumps which lie outside the view frustum, but clumping is hard to maintain in the ever-changing active list. A different approach for HDS would be to distribute the active triangles across the vertex tree, associating each triangle with the smallest node which contains all three of the triangle's corners. Rendering the scene would then consist of a top-down traversal of the vertex tree, evaluating each node's visibility and rendering the associated triangles of visible nodes. While enabling efficient visibility culling, this scheme loses the advantage of temporal coherence, since every visible active node must be visited every frame. On complex models the overhead of traversing a deep active tree undermines the benefit of rendering fewer triangles.

In practice a hybrid approach works well: the active triangle list is split into several lists, each associated with a high-level node of the vertex tree. Nodes with an active list are termed cullNodes; triangles added by expandNode() are appended to the active list of the smallest cullNode containing the corners of the triangle. Restricting cullNodes to the high levels of the vertex tree results in a coarse-grained culling without the overhead of a full active tree traversal, thus exploiting both visibility culling and temporal coherence.

5.3 Visibility: Avoiding Irrelevant Nodes

Distributing the active list across multiple nodes speeds up rendering, since invisible nodes are not visited. HDS may still need to examine such nodes, however, since the tris and subtris of an invisible node may still be visible [Figure 8]. Some nodes are not only invisible but *irrelevant*, that is, expanding or collapsing the node cannot possibly affect the scene. An invisible node is irrelevant if it does not contain a corner of any potentially visible triangle; the simplification traversal can save time by not visiting these nodes. In an interactive walkthrough session, the vast majority of invisible nodes are usually irrelevant, so testing for irrelevance provides a significant speedup. An exact test is difficult, but a conservative test for irrelevant nodes is easily constructed by adding a **container** field to each node in the vertex tree. The container node C of a node N is the smallest node which contains every tri and subtri of N and N's descendants. C thus contains every triangle which might be affected by operations on the subtree rooted at N. If C is invisible, N is irrelevant and can be safely ignored by the simplification traversal.

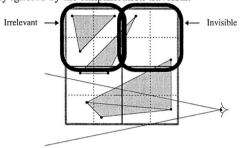

Figure 8: Invisible nodes are completely outside the view frustum. Irrelevant nodes are invisible and contain no vertices of visible triangles.

5.4 Asynchronous Simplification

An important strategy for speeding up any algorithm is to parallelize it, distributing the work over multiple processors. Computer graphics applications most commonly accomplish this by parallelizing the major stages of the rendering computation in a pipeline fashion. A traditional level-of-detail system might be divided into SELECT and RENDER stages: the SELECT stage decides which resolution of which objects to render and compiles them into a display list, which the RENDER process then renders. Meanwhile, the SELECT process prepares the display list for the next frame [Funkhouser 93, Rohlf 94]. If S is the time taken to select levels of detail and R is the time taken to render a frame, parallelizing the two processes as a pipeline reduces the total time per frame from R+S to max(R,S).

HDS also divides naturally into two basic tasks, SIMPLIFY and RENDER. The SIMPLIFY task traverses the vertex tree folding and unfolding nodes as needed. The RENDER task cycles over the active triangle list rendering each triangle. Let the time taken by SIMPLIFY to traverse the entire tree be S and the time taken by RENDER to draw the entire active list be R. The frame time of a uniprocessor implementation will then be R+S, and the frame time of a pipelined implementation will again be max(R,S). The rendering task usually dominates the simplification task, so the effective frame time often reduces to R. The exception is during large shifts of viewpoint, when the usual assumption of temporal coherence fails and many triangles must be added and deleted from the active triangle list. This can have the distracting effect of slowing down the frame rate when the user speeds up the rate of motion.

Asynchronous simplification provides a solution: let the SIMPLIFY and RENDER tasks run asynchronously, with the SIMPLIFY process writing to the active triangle list and the RENDER process reading it. This decouples the tasks for a total frame time of R, eliminating the slowdown artifact associated with large viewpoint changes. When the viewer's velocity outpaces the simplification rate in asynchronous mode, the SIMPLIFY process simply falls behind. As a result the scene rendered for the viewer

is somewhat coarse in quality until the SIMPLIFY process catches up, at which point the scene gradually sweetens back to the expected quality. This graceful degradation of fidelity is less distracting than sudden drops in frame rate.

A straightforward implementation of asynchronous simplification is relatively easy to code on a shared-memory multiprocessor system, but care must be taken to avoid "dropouts". Characterized by triangles that disappear for a frame, these transient artifacts occur when the RENDER process sweeps through a region of the active list being affected by the SIMPLIFY process. For example, the collapseNode() operation removes triangles and fills in the resulting holes by adjusting the corner positions of neighboring triangles. If those neighboring triangles have already been rendered during the frame when collapseNode() adjusts their corners, but the triangle to be removed has not yet been rendered, a hole will appear in the mesh for that frame.

Dropouts are fundamentally caused by failure to maintain a consistent shared database in an asynchronous system. They are difficult to eradicate with simple locking schemes. Locking the triangles to be affected before every collapseNode() and expandNode() operation will not suffice, since the triangles may not be near each other in the active triangle list. Since the active triangle list is divided among the high-level nodes for culling purposes, another possibility would be to lock all nodes affected by the collapse or expand operation.[2] This strategy prevents dropouts, but proves prohibitively expensive in practice.

The *update queue* provides one solution to the dropout problem. The update queue was motivated by the observation that the time spent performing collapseNode() and expandNode() operations is a small fraction of the time taken by the SIMPLIFY process to traverse the vertex tree and determine which nodes to fold and unfold. Rather than actually performing the updates, the SIMPLIFY process accumulates them into the update queue, marking the node Dirty and placing a Collapse or Expand entry in the queue. The update queue acts as a buffer: at the beginning of every frame the RENDER process performs the first n updates in the queue, collapsing or expanding each node before marking it Clean again.[3] All changes to the active triangle list take place as a batch before any triangles are rendered; the shared database is thus kept consistent and dropouts are eliminated.

6. PREVIOUS WORK

6.1 Constructing the Vertex Tree

Many excellent polygonal simplification algorithms have been described in the recent literature [Cohen 96, Hoppe 96, Eck 95]. HDS is not a competing algorithm, but a framework into which many existing algorithms can be incorporated. Any algorithm which can be expressed in terms of vertex collapse operations can be used to create the vertex tree. The construction of the vertex tree determines the order in which vertices are collapsed, which in turn determines the quality of the simplification HDS can create. In addition, the construction of the vertex tree affects the run-time performance of HDS, since a well-balanced tree will reduce the traversal time of the SIMPLIFY task. Possible algorithms form a spectrum, ranging from fast, simple approaches with moderate fidelity to slower, more sophisticated methods with superb fidelity. The choice of algorithm for constructing the vertex tree is heavily application-dependent. In a design-review setting, CAD

---

[2] This turns out to be the subtree rooted at the container node of the node being collapsed or expanded.

[3] As with any buffer, care must be taken to empty the update queue fast enough; n was set to 1000 for all models tested.

users may want to visualize their revisions in the context of the entire model several times a day. Preprocessing times of hours are unacceptable in this scenario. On the other hand, a walkthrough of the completed model might be desired for demonstration purposes. Here it makes sense to use a slower, more careful algorithm to optimize the quality of simplifications and prevent any distracting artifacts.

6.1.1 Simplest: Spatial Subdivision

One of the simplest techniques is to classify the vertices of the model with a space-partitioning structure such as an octree. An adaptive version of the spatial binning approach introduced by [Rossignac 92], the spatial subdivision method was first introduced for view-dependent simplification by [Luebke 96]. Vertices are ranked by importance using local criteria such as edge length and curvature. Beginning at the root of the octree, the most important vertex within each node is chosen as that node's representative vertex. The vertices are then partitioned among the node's eight children and the process is recursively repeated. In this way vertices are clustered roughly according to proximity. Neighboring vertices are likely to get collapsed almost immediately, whereas distant vertices tend to merge only at high levels of the tree.

Unless the vertices of the model are uniformly distributed, the straightforward approach just described will result in highly unbalanced octrees. CAD models are often locally dense but globally sparse, consisting of highly detailed components separated by areas of low detail or empty space. In this situation a more adaptive partitioning structure such as a K-D tree will produce a more balanced tree, yielding better run-time performance. An even simpler structure is the *tight octree*, in which each node of the octree is tightened to the smallest axis-aligned cube which encloses the relevant vertices before the node is subdivided. This approach seems to adapt very well to CAD models, and most results presented in this paper used tight-octree spatial subdivision to cluster vertices.

Top-down spatial subdivision clustering schemes possess many advantages. Their simplicity makes an efficient, robust implementation relatively easy to code. In addition, spatial partitioning of vertices is typically very fast, bringing the preprocess time of even large models down to manageable levels: preprocessing the 700,000 polygon torpedo room model, for example, takes only 158 seconds [Table 1]. Finally, spatial-subdivision vertex clustering is by its nature very general. No knowledge of the polygon mesh is used; manifold topology is neither assumed nor preserved. Meshes with degeneracies (such as cracks, T-junctions, and missing polygons) are unfortunately quite common. Spatial-subdivision vertex clustering schemes will operate despite the presence of degeneracies incompatible with more complex schemes.

6.1.2 Prettiest: Simplification Envelopes, Progressive Mesh Algorithm

On the other end of the spectrum, some very sophisticated recent simplification algorithms could be used to build the vertex cluster tree. Cohen et al present *Simplification Envelopes*, offset surfaces of a polygonal mesh modified to prevent self-intersection and bounded to a distance ε of the mesh. By generating a simpler triangulation of the surface without intersecting the simplification envelopes, the authors guarantee a simplification which preserves global topology and varies from the original surface by no more than ε [Cohen 96]. Simplification envelopes could be used to construct the vertex tree in HDS by applying successively larger values of ε, at each stage only clustering those vertices which do not cause the mesh to intersect the envelopes. The value of ε used to generate each cluster would then become the error metric

associated with that node in the vertex tree, resulting in an HDS simplification with excellent fidelity. Unfortunately, it is not clear how to extend simplification envelopes to allow merging between different objects, or to allow drastic topology-discarding collapse operations at high levels of the tree.

Hoppe describes an optimization approach which creates a series of edge collapses for the *Progressive Meshes* representation [Hoppe 96]. Each edge collapse corresponds to a node in HDS with two children and one or two subtris. The stream of edge collapse records in a progressive mesh contains an implicit hierarchy that maps directly to the HDS vertex tree. A progressive mesh may thus be viewed without modification in an HDS system, though this has disadvantages. A progressive mesh never collapses more than two vertices together at a time, which may result in an unnecessarily deep vertex tree. A modified optimization step which could collapse multiple vertices seems possible, and would address this problem. Also, progressive meshes collapse only vertices within a mesh, so separate objects never merge together. Finally, restricting edge collapses to those which preserve the manifold topology of the mesh limits the amount of simplification possible.[4] For these reasons, a direct embedding of a progressive mesh is not optimal for the drastic simplification necessary to visualize very complex models.

Along with progressive meshes, Hoppe introduces a very nice framework for handling surface attributes of a mesh during simplification. Such attributes are categorized as *discrete* attributes, associated with faces in the mesh, and *scalar* attributes, associated with corners of the faces in the mesh. Common discrete attributes include material and texture identifiers; common scalar attributes include color, normal, and texture coordinates. Hoppe's method of maintaining discrete and scalar attributes as vertices are collapsed extends directly to HDS, and is used without modification in the current implementation.

6.1.3 A Hybrid Approach

Both the simplification envelope and progressive mesh approaches can be combined with top-down spatial subdivision to allow drastic simplification and merging of objects. The result of either approach on a collection of objects in a scene is a collection of vertex trees. When the vertex tree for each object is adequate, the spatial subdivision algorithm unifies this "vertex forest" into a single tree. A tight octree or similar structure merges nearby vertices from the same or different object, without regard to topology. The final vertex tree exhibits both high fidelity (at low levels of the tree) and drastic simplification (at high levels).

The sphere and bunny simplifications in the color plates were generated with this type of hybrid approach. Since this model was intended to illustrate silhouette preservation as a run-time criterion, it was important to merge vertices so as to minimize the normal cones of the resulting vertex cluster. Also, the curvature of a non-manifold mesh is not well defined, so only adjacent vertices in the mesh could be collapsed. These considerations led to a two-stage clustering algorithm. First, a progressive mesh representation of the model was created, in which the edge collapse order was chosen to minimize normal cones and to maintain a balanced tree. Edge collapses which resulted in normal cone angles greater than $135°$ were disallowed. When the model could be simplified no further with these restrictions, a tight octree was applied to the remaining vertex clusters to produce a single HDS vertex tree.

---

[4] For example, our implementation could not reduce the 69,451-triangle bunny model beyond 520 triangles.

Model	Category	Vertices	Triangles	Preprocessing Time (Tight Octree)	(Hybrid)
Bone6	Medical	3,410,391	1,136,785	445 seconds	—
Sphere	Procedural	4,098	8,192	1.2 seconds	2.5 minutes
Bunny	Scanned	35,947	69,451	12 seconds	20 minutes
Sierra	Terrain	81,920	162,690	33 seconds	—
AMR	CAD	280,544	504,969	121 seconds	—
Torp	CAD	411,778	698,872	158 seconds	87 minutes

Table 1: Sizes and preprocessing times of models pictured in color plates. Note that the hybrid vertex clustering algorithm (described in Section 6.1.3) is not optimized for speed.

6.2 Other Related Work

Xia and Varshney use merge trees to perform view-dependent simplifications of triangular models in real-time [Xia 96]. A merge tree is similar to a progressive mesh, created off-line and consisting of a hierarchy of edge collapses. Selective refinement is applied based on viewing direction, lighting, and visibility. Xia and Varshney update an active list of vertices and triangles, using frame-to-frame coherence to achieve real-time performance. In addition, extra information is stored at each node of the merge tree to specify dependencies between edge collapse operations. These dependencies are used to eliminate folding artifacts during the visualization of the model, but also constrain the tessellation to change gradually between areas of high simplification and areas of low simplification. This restriction limits the degree of drastic simplification possible with a merge tree, as does the inability of merge trees to combine vertices from different objects. Xia and Varshney also assume manifold models, which together with the limited simplification available makes their approach less appropriate for large-scale CAD databases.

The error bounds described in Section 4 provide a useful indicator of the simplification fidelity, but screenspace error and silhouette preservation are only two of the many criteria that determine the view-dependent perceptual importance of a region of a scene. Ohshima et al. [Ohshima 96] investigate a gaze-directed system which allocates geometric detail to objects according to their calculated *visual acuity*. Objects in the center of vision have a higher visual acuity than objects in the periphery and are thus drawn at a higher level of detail. Similarly, stationary objects are assigned a higher visual acuity than rapidly moving objects, and objects at the depth of the user's binocular fusion are assigned a higher visual acuity than objects closer or farther than the distance at which the user's eyes currently converge. These techniques show promise for further reducing the polygon count of a scene in immersive rendering situations, and could be integrated into the HDS framework as additional run-time simplification criteria.

7. RESULTS

HDS has been implemented and tested on a Silicon Graphics Onyx system with InfiniteReality graphics.

The models tested span a range of categories. Bone6 is a medical model created from the Visible Man volumetric dataset. Sierra is a terrain database originally acquired from satellite topography. Torp and AMR are complex CAD models of the torpedo and auxiliary machine rooms on a nuclear submarine, each comprised of over three thousand individual objects. Bunny is a digitized model from a laser scanner. Finally, Sphere is a simple procedurally-generated sphere created to illustrate silhouette preservation and backface simplification. Table 1 details the size of each database along with the preprocessing time for the tight-octree algorithm of Section 6.1.1 and the hybrid algorithm of Section 6.1.3. Polygon counts and error thresholds

for specific views of each model are provided with the color plates.

8. REMARKS

Polygonal simplification is a process of approximation. As with any approximation, a simplification algorithm taken to the limit should recover the original object being approximated. This holds true for the HDS algorithm: as the screenspace area threshold approaches subpixel size, the visual effects of collapsing vertices become vanishingly small. Note that the polygon counts of large and complex enough scenes will be reduced even under these extreme conditions. This is important; with complex CAD models, finely tessellated laser-scanned objects, and polygon proliferating radiosity algorithms all coming into widespread use, databases in which many or most visible polygons are smaller than a pixel are becoming increasingly common.

View-dependent simplification is inherently an immediate-mode technique, a disadvantage since most current rendering hardware favors retained-mode display lists. Experiments on an SGI Onyx with InfiniteReality graphics, for example, indicate that Gouraud-shaded depth-buffered unlit triangles render two to three times faster in a display list than in a tightly optimized immediate mode display loop [Aliaga 97]. Relatively small models will prove more efficient to render using existing static multiresolution techniques, since the levels of detail for each object can be precompiled into a display list. As scenes approach the size and complexity of the AMR and Torp datasets, the speedups possible in an adaptive view-dependent framework begin to exceed the speedups provided by display lists. For very large, complex CAD databases, as well as for scenes containing degenerate or polygon-soup models, HDS retains the advantage even on highly display-list oriented hardware.

9. SUMMARY AND FUTURE WORK

HDS provides a framework for the dynamic view-dependent simplification of complex polygonal environments. This framework is robust, operating solely at the level of vertices and triangles and thus insensitive to topological degeneracies, and adaptive, able to merge objects within a scene or even operate on polygon-soup databases. Any simplification method reducible to a series of vertex clustering operations can be used by the preprocessing stage of HDS. The tight-octree spatial subdivision method described in section 7.1 and the two-stage hybrid approach described in section 7.3 have been implemented and demonstrate two such preprocessing strategies. Different run-time criteria for collapsing and expanding vertices may also be plugged into the HDS framework; the current system supports a screenspace error tolerance, a triangle budget, and silhouette preservation. Many optimizations of the HDS run-time algorithm have been incorporated, including an asynchronous simplification scheme which decouples the rendering and simplification tasks.

Many avenues for future work remain. HDS in its current form is limited to static scenes; even the fast spatial subdivision schemes for vertex tree construction cannot keep up with a model that changes significantly in real time. An incremental algorithm for creating and maintaining the vertex tree might allow simplification of truly dynamic scenes. More sophisticated run-time criteria are certainly possible. The bounding spheres in the current implementation can be a poor fit for the vertices of a cluster, resulting in unnecessarily conservative error estimates. More sophisticated bounding volumes such as ellipsoids or oriented bounding boxes would complicate the nodeSize() operation, but could provide a much better fit. Nodes might also be unfolded to devote more detail to regions containing specular highlights in the manner of [Cho 96] and [Xia 96], or to perceptually important regions using the gaze-directed heuristics described in [Oshima 96].

10. ACKNOWLEDGMENTS

Special thanks to Fred Brooks, Greg Turk, and Dinesh Manocha for their invaluable guidance and support throughout this project. Funding for this work was provided by DARPA Contract DABT63-93-C-0048, and Lockheed Missile and Space Co., Inc. Additional funding was provided by National Center for Research Resources Grant NIH/NCCR P4RR02170-13. David Luebke is supported by an IBM Cooperative Fellowship; Carl Erikson is supported by an NSF Graduate Fellowship.

11. REFERENCES

[Aliaga 97] Aliaga, Daniel. "SGI Performance Tips" (Talk). For more information see: *http://www.cs.unc.edu/~aliaga/IR-perf.html.*

[Cho 96] Cho, Y., U. Neumann, J. Woo. "Improved Specular Highlights with Adaptive Shading", *Computer Graphics International 96*, June, 1996.

[Clark 76] Clark, James H. "Hierarchical Geometric Models for Visible Surface Algorithms," *Communications of the ACM*, Vol 19, No 10, pp 547-554.

[Cohen 96] Cohen, J., A. Varshney, D. Manocha, G. Turk, H. Weber, P. Agarwal, F. Brooks, W. Wright. "Simplification Envelopes", *Computer Graphics*, Vol 30 (SIGGRAPH 96).

[Cosman 81] Cosman, M., and R. Schumacker. "System Strategies to Optimize CIG Image Content". *Proceedings Image II Conference* (Scotsdale, Arizona), 1981.

[Eck 95] Eck, M., T. DeRose, T. Duchamp, H. Hoppe, M. Lounsbery, W. Stuetzle. "Multiresolution Analysis of Arbitrary Meshes", *Computer Graphics*, Vol 29 (SIGGRAPH 95).

[Funkhouser 93] Funkhouser, Thomas, and Carlo Sequin. "Adaptive Display Algorithm for Interactive Frame Rates During Visualization of Complex Virtual Environments". *Computer Graphics*, Vol 27 (SIGGRAPH 93).

[Hoppe 96] Hoppe, Hugues. "Progressive Meshes", *Computer Graphics*, Vol 30 (SIGGRAPH 96).

[Kaufman 95] Taosong He, L. Hong, A. Kaufman, A. Varshney, and S. Wang. "Voxel-Based Object Simplification". *Proceedings Visualization 95*, IEEE Computer Society Press (Atlanta, GA), 1995, pp. 296-303.

[Kumar 96] Kumar, Subodh, D. Manocha, W. Garrett, M. Lin. "Hierarchical Backface Computation". *Proc. Of 7th Eurographics Workshop on Rendering*, 1996.

[Maciel 95] Maciel, Paulo, and Shirley, Peter. "Visual Navigation of Large Environments Using Textured Clusters", *Proceedings 1995 SIGGRAPH Symposium on Interactive 3D Graphics* (Monterey, CA), 1995, pp. 95-102.

[Luebke 96] Luebke, David. "Hierarchical Structures for Dynamic Polygonal Simplification". University of North Carolina Department of Computer Science Tech Report #TR96-006, January, 1996.

[Oshima 96] Ohshima, Toshikazu, H. Yamamoto, H. Tamura. "Gaze-Directed Adaptive Rendering for Interacting with Virtual Space." *Proc. of IEEE 1996 Virtual Reality Annual Intnl. Symposium.* (1996), pp 103-110.

[Rohlf 94] Rohlf, John and James Helman. "IRIS Performer: A High Performance Multiprocessing Toolkit for Real-Time 3D Graphics", *Computer Graphics*, Vol 28 (SIGGRAPH 94).

[Rossignac 92] Rossignac, Jarek, and Paul Borrel. "Multi-Resolution 3D Approximations for Rendering Complex Scenes", pp. 455-465 in *Geometric Modeling in Computer* Graphics, Springer-Verlag, Eds. B. Falcidieno and T.L. Kunii, Genova, Italy, 6/28/93-7/2/93. Also published as IBM Research Report RC17697 (77951) 2/19/92.

[Schroeder 92] Schroeder, William, Jonathan Zarge and William Lorenson, "Decimation of Triangle Meshes", *Computer Graphics*, Vol 26 (SIGGRAPH 92)

[Shirman 93] Shirman, L., and Abi-Ezzi, S. "The Cone of Normals Technique for Fast Processing of Curved Patches", Computer Graphics Forum (*Proc. Eurographics '93*) Vol 12, No 3, (1993), pp 261-272.

[Teller 91] Teller, Seth, and Carlo Sequin. "Visibility Preprocessing for Interactive Walkthroughs", *Computer Graphics*, Vol 25 (SIGGRAPH 91).

[Turk 92] Turk, Greg. "Re-tiling Polygonal Surfaces", *Computer Graphics,* Vol 26 (SIGGRAPH 92).

[Varshney 94] Varshney, Amitabh. "Hierarchical Geometry Approximations", Ph.D. Thesis, University of North Carolina Department of Computer Science Tech Report TR-050

[Xia 96] Xia, Julie and Amitabh Varshney. "Dynamic View-Dependent Simplification for Polygonal Models", *Visualization 96.*

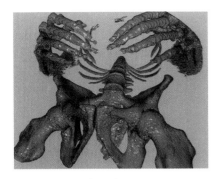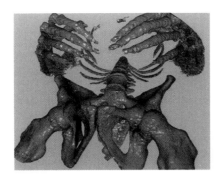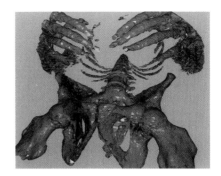

Plate 1: Bone6 model shown at original resolution (1,136,785 faces), 0.5% error tolerance (417,182 faces), and 1% error tolerance (172,499 faces).

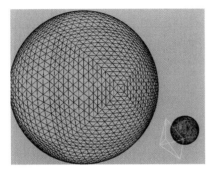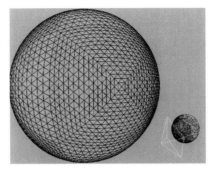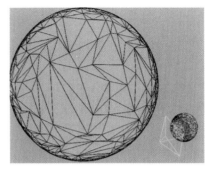

Plate 2: Sphere model shown at original resolution (8,192 faces), at 1% error threshold with backface simplification (3,388 faces), and at 1% silhouette error threshold with a 20% interior error tolerance (1,950 faces).

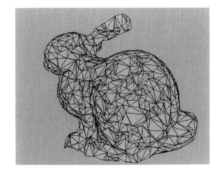

Plate 3: Bunny model shown at original resolution (69,451 faces), 1% error tolerance (19,598 faces), and 5% error tolerance (2,901 faces).

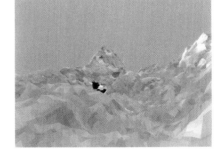

Plate 4: Bunny model shown with 1% silhouette, 6% interior (13,135 faces).

Plate 5: Sierra model shown at original resolution (154,153 faces) and 1.5% error tolerance (54,847 faces).

Plate 6: AMR model shown at original resolution (501,550 faces), 0.7% error tolerance (123,106 faces), and 2.5% error tolerance (34,128 faces).

Plate 7: AMR model shown at the same error tolerances as Plate 6, but drawn with wireframes on.

Plate 8: Torp model shown at original resolution (673,728 faces), 0.8% error tolerance (129,446 faces), and 1.5% error tolerance (76,404 faces).

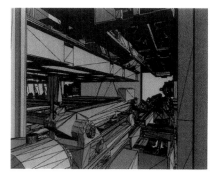 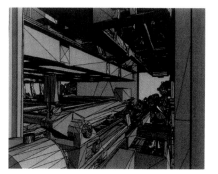 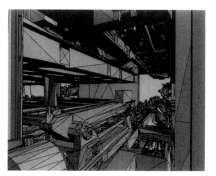

Plate 9: Torp model shown at the same error tolerances as Plate 8, but drawn with wireframes on.

Surface Simplification Using Quadric Error Metrics

Michael Garland*   Paul S. Heckbert[†]

Carnegie Mellon University

Abstract

Many applications in computer graphics require complex, highly detailed models. However, the level of detail actually necessary may vary considerably. To control processing time, it is often desirable to use approximations in place of excessively detailed models.

We have developed a surface simplification algorithm which can rapidly produce high quality approximations of polygonal models. The algorithm uses iterative contractions of vertex pairs to simplify models and maintains surface error approximations using quadric matrices. By contracting arbitrary vertex pairs (not just edges), our algorithm is able to join unconnected regions of models. This can facilitate much better approximations, both visually and with respect to geometric error. In order to allow topological joining, our system also supports non-manifold surface models.

CR Categories: I.3.5 [Computer Graphics]: Computational Geometry and Object Modeling—surface and object representations

Keywords: surface simplification, multiresolution modeling, pair contraction, level of detail, non-manifold

1 Introduction

Many computer graphics applications require complex, highly detailed models to maintain a convincing level of realism. Consequently, models are often created or acquired at a very high resolution to accommodate this need for detail. However, the full complexity of such models is not always required, and since the computational cost of using a model is directly related to its complexity, it is useful to have simpler versions of complex models. Naturally, we would like to automatically produce these simplified models. Recent work on surface simplification algorithms has focused on this goal.

As with most other work in this area, we will focus on the simplification of polygonal models. We will assume that the model consists of *triangles only*. This implies no loss of generality, since every polygon in the original model can be triangulated as part of a pre-processing phase. To achieve more reliable results, when corners of two faces intersect at a point, the faces should be defined as sharing a single vertex rather than using two separate vertices which happen to be coincident in space.

*garland@cs.cmu.edu; http://www.cs.cmu.edu/~garland/

[†]ph@cs.cmu.edu; http://www.cs.cmu.edu/~ph/

We have developed an algorithm which produces simplified versions of such polygonal models. Our algorithm is based on the iterative contraction of vertex pairs (a generalization of edge contraction). As the algorithm proceeds, a geometric error approximation is maintained at each vertex of the current model. This error approximation is represented using quadric matrices. The primary advantages of our algorithm are:

- *Efficiency:* The algorithm is able to simplify complex models quite rapidly. For example, our implementation can create a 100 face approximation of a 70,000 face model in 15 seconds. The error approximation is also very compact, requiring only 10 floating point numbers per vertex.

- *Quality:* The approximations produced by our algorithm maintain high fidelity to the original model. The primary features of the model are preserved even after significant simplification.

- *Generality:* Unlike most other surface simplification algorithms, ours is able to join unconnected regions of the model together, a process which we term *aggregation*. Provided that maintaining object topology is not an important concern, this can facilitate better approximations of models with many disconnected components. This also requires our algorithm to support non-manifold[1] models.

2 Background and Related Work

The goal of polygonal surface simplification is to take a polygonal model as input and generate a simplified model (i.e., an approximation of the original) as output. We assume that the input model (M_n) has been triangulated. The target approximation (M_g) will satisfy some given target criterion which is typically either a desired face count or a maximum tolerable error. We are interested in surface simplification algorithms that can be used in rendering systems for *multiresolution modeling* — the generation of models with appropriate levels of detail for the current context.

We do not assume that the topology of the model must be maintained. In certain application areas, medical imaging for example, maintaining the object topology can be essential. However, in application areas such as rendering, topology is less important than overall appearance. Our algorithm is capable of both closing topological holes as well as joining unconnected regions.

Many prior simplification algorithms have either implicitly or explicitly assumed that their input surfaces were, and ought to remain, manifold surfaces. Let us stress that we do not make this assumption. In fact, the process of aggregation will regularly create non-manifold regions.

2.1 Surface Simplification

In recent years, the problem of surface simplification, and the more general problem of multiresolution modeling, has received increas-

---

[1]A *manifold* is a surface for which the infinitesimal neighborhood of every point is topologically equivalent to a disk (or half-disk for a *manifold with boundary*).

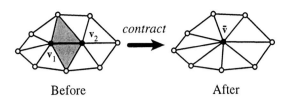

Before   After

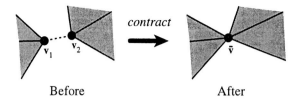

Before   After

Figure 1: Edge contraction. The highlighted edge is contracted into a single point. The shaded triangles become degenerate and are removed during the contraction.

Figure 2: Non-edge contraction. When non-edge pairs are contracted, unconnected sections of the model are joined. The dashed line indicates the two vertices being contracted together.

ing attention. Several different algorithms have been formulated for simplifying surfaces. Those algorithms which are most relevant to our work can be broadly categorized into 3 classes:

Vertex Decimation. Schroeder *et al.* [9] describe an algorithm which we would term *vertex decimation*. Their method iteratively selects a vertex for removal, removes all adjacent faces, and retriangulates the resulting hole. Soucy and Laurendeau [10] described a more sophisticated, but essentially similar algorithm. While they provide reasonable efficiency and quality, these methods are not really suited for our purpose. Both methods use vertex classification and retriangulation schemes which are inherently limited to manifold surfaces, and they carefully maintain the topology of the model. While these are important features in some domains, they are restrictions for multiresolution rendering systems.

Vertex Clustering. The algorithm described by Rossignac and Borrel [8] is one of the few capable of processing arbitrary polygonal input. A bounding box is placed around the original model and divided into a grid. Within each cell, the cell's vertices are clustered together into a single vertex, and the model faces are updated accordingly. This process can be very fast, and can make drastic topological alterations to the model. However, while the size of the grid cells does provide a geometric error bound, the quality of the output is often quite low. In addition, it is difficult to construct an approximation with a specific face count, since the number of faces is only indirectly determined by the specified grid dimensions. The exact approximation produced is also dependent on the exact position and orientation of the original model with respect to the surrounding grid. This uniform method can easily be generalized to use an adaptive grid structure, such as an octree [6]. This can improve the simplification results, but it still does not support the quality and control that we desire.

Iterative Edge Contraction. Several algorithms have been published that simplify models by iteratively contracting edges (see Figure 1). The essential difference between these algorithms lies in how they choose an edge to contract. Some notable examples of such algorithms are those of Hoppe [4, 3], Ronfard and Rossignac [7], and Guéziec [2]. These algorithms all seem to have been designed for use on manifold surfaces, although edge contractions can be utilized on non-manifold surfaces. By performing successive edge contractions, they can close holes in the object but they cannot join unconnected regions.

If it is critical that the approximate model lie within some distance of the original model and that its topology remain unchanged, the simplification envelopes technique of Cohen *et al.* [1] can be used in conjunction with one of the above simplification algorithms. As long as any modification made to the model is restricted to lie within the envelopes, a global error guarantee can be maintained. However, while this provides strong error limits, the method is inherently limited to orientable manifold surfaces and carefully pre-

serves model topology. Again, these are often limitations for the purposes of simplification for rendering.

None of these previously developed algorithms provide the combination of efficiency, quality, and generality that we desire. Vertex decimation algorithms are unsuitable for our needs; they are careful to maintain model topology and usually assume manifold geometry. Vertex clustering algorithms are very general and can be very fast. However, they provide poor control over their results and these results can be of rather low quality. Edge contraction algorithms can not support aggregation.

We have developed an algorithm which supports both aggregation and high quality approximations. It possesses much of the generality of vertex clustering as well as the quality and control of iterative contraction algorithms. It also allows faster simplification than some higher quality methods [3].

3 Decimation via Pair Contraction

Our simplification algorithm is based on the iterative contraction of vertex pairs; a generalization of the iterative edge contraction technique used in previous work. A *pair contraction*, which we will write $(v_1, v_2) \rightarrow \bar{v}$, moves the vertices v_1 and v_2 to the new position $\bar{v}$, connects all their incident edges to v_1, and deletes the vertex v_2. Subsequently, any edges or faces which have become degenerate are removed. The effect of a contraction is small and highly localized. If (v_1, v_2) is an edge, then 1 or more faces will be removed (see Figure 1). Otherwise, two previously separate sections of the model will be joined at $\bar{v}$ (see Figure 2).

This notion of contraction is in fact quite general; we can contract a set of vertices into a single vertex: $(v_1, v_2, \ldots, v_k) \rightarrow \bar{v}$. This form of generalized contraction can express both pair contractions as well as more general operations such as vertex clustering. However, we use pair contraction as the atomic operation of our algorithm because it is the most fine-grained contraction operation.

Starting with the initial model M_n, a sequence of pair contractions is applied until the simplification goals are satisfied and a final approximation M_g is produced. Because each contraction corresponds to a local incremental modification of the current model, the algorithm actually generates a sequence of models $M_n, M_{n-1}, \ldots, M_g$. Thus, a single run can produce a large number of approximate models or a multiresolution representation such as a progressive mesh [3].

3.1 Aggregation

The primary benefit which we gain by utilizing general vertex pair contractions is the ability of the algorithm to join previously unconnected regions of the model together. A potential side benefit is that it makes the algorithm less sensitive to the mesh connectivity of the original model. If in fact two faces meet at a vertex which is duplicated, the contraction of that pair of vertices will repair this shortcoming of the initial mesh.

Figure 3: On the left is a regular grid of 100 closely spaced cubes. In the middle, an approximation built using only edge contractions demonstrates unacceptable fragmentation. On the right, the result of using more general pair contractions to achieve aggregation is an approximation much closer to the original.

In some applications, such as rendering, topology may be less important than overall shape. Consider a shape such as that shown in Figure 3 which is made up of 100 closely spaced cubes in a regular grid. Suppose we wanted to construct an approximation of the model on the left for rendering at a distance. Algorithms based on edge contraction can close holes in objects, but they can never join disconnected components. In an algorithm using only edge contraction, the individual components are individually simplified into nothing, as in the model in the middle. Using pair contraction, the individual components can be merged into a single object, as in the model on the right. The result is a much more faithful approximation.

Allowing aggregation also requires us to support non-manifold surfaces. At the instant when two separate regions are joined, a non-manifold region is quite likely to be created. It would require a great deal of care and effort to ensure that a contraction never created a non-manifold region without severely limiting the kinds of contractions that we could perform.

3.2 Pair Selection

We have chosen to select the set of valid pairs at initialization time, and to consider only these pairs during the course of the algorithm. Our decision is based on the assumption that, in a good approximation, points do not move far from their original positions.

We will say that a pair $(\mathbf{v}_1, \mathbf{v}_2)$ is a *valid* pair for contraction if either:

1. $(\mathbf{v}_1, \mathbf{v}_2)$ is an edge, *or*

2. $\|\mathbf{v}_1 - \mathbf{v}_2\| < t$, where t is a threshold parameter

Using a threshold of $t = 0$ gives a simple edge contraction algorithm. Higher thresholds allow non-connected vertices to be paired. Naturally, this threshold must be chosen with some care; if it is too high, widely separated portions of the model could be connected, which is presumably undesirable, and it could create $O(n^2)$ pairs.

We must track the set of valid pairs during the course of iterative contraction. With each vertex, we associate the set of pairs of which it is a member. When we perform the contraction $(\mathbf{v}_1, \mathbf{v}_2) \to \bar{\mathbf{v}}$, not only does $\mathbf{v}_1$ acquire all the edges that were linked to $\mathbf{v}_2$, it also merges the set of pairs from $\mathbf{v}_2$ into its own set. Every occurrence of $\mathbf{v}_2$ in a valid pair is replaced by $\mathbf{v}_1$, and duplicate pairs are removed.

4 Approximating Error With Quadrics

In order to select a contraction to perform during a given iteration, we need some notion of the *cost* of a contraction. To define this cost, we attempt to characterize the error at each vertex. To do this, we associate a symmetric 4×4 matrix $\mathbf{Q}$ with each vertex, and we define the error at vertex $\mathbf{v} = [v_x\ v_y\ v_z\ 1]^\mathsf{T}$ to be the quadratic form $\Delta(\mathbf{v}) =$

$\mathbf{v}^\mathsf{T}\mathbf{Q}\mathbf{v}$. In Section 5, we will describe how the initial matrices are constructed. Note that the level surface $\Delta(\mathbf{v}) = \epsilon$, which is the set of all points whose error with respect to $\mathbf{Q}$ is ϵ, is a quadric surface.

For a given contraction $(\mathbf{v}_1, \mathbf{v}_2) \to \bar{\mathbf{v}}$, we must derive a new matrix $\bar{\mathbf{Q}}$ which approximates the error at $\bar{\mathbf{v}}$. We have chosen to use the simple additive rule $\bar{\mathbf{Q}} = \mathbf{Q}_1 + \mathbf{Q}_2$.

In order to perform the contraction $(\mathbf{v}_1, \mathbf{v}_2) \to \bar{\mathbf{v}}$, we must also choose a position for $\bar{\mathbf{v}}$. A simple scheme would be to select either $\mathbf{v}_1$, $\mathbf{v}_2$, or $(\mathbf{v}_1 + \mathbf{v}_2)/2$ depending on which one of these produces the lowest value of $\Delta(\bar{\mathbf{v}})$. However, it would be nice to find a position for $\bar{\mathbf{v}}$ which minimizes $\Delta(\bar{\mathbf{v}})$. Since the error function Δ is quadratic, finding its minimum is a linear problem. Thus, we find $\bar{\mathbf{v}}$ by solving $\partial\Delta/\partial x = \partial\Delta/\partial y = \partial\Delta/\partial z = 0$. This is equivalent[2] to solving:

$$\begin{bmatrix} q_{11} & q_{12} & q_{13} & q_{14} \\ q_{12} & q_{22} & q_{23} & q_{24} \\ q_{13} & q_{23} & q_{33} & q_{34} \\ 0 & 0 & 0 & 1 \end{bmatrix} \bar{\mathbf{v}} = \begin{bmatrix} 0 \\ 0 \\ 0 \\ 1 \end{bmatrix}$$

for $\bar{\mathbf{v}}$. The bottom row of the matrix is empty because $\bar{\mathbf{v}}$ is an homogeneous vector — its w component is always 1. Assuming that this matrix is invertible, we get that

$$\bar{\mathbf{v}} = \begin{bmatrix} q_{11} & q_{12} & q_{13} & q_{14} \\ q_{12} & q_{22} & q_{23} & q_{24} \\ q_{13} & q_{23} & q_{33} & q_{34} \\ 0 & 0 & 0 & 1 \end{bmatrix}^{-1} \begin{bmatrix} 0 \\ 0 \\ 0 \\ 1 \end{bmatrix} \qquad (1)$$

If this matrix is not invertible, we attempt to find the optimal vertex along the segment $\mathbf{v}_1\mathbf{v}_2$. If this also fails, we fall back on choosing $\bar{\mathbf{v}}$ from amongst the endpoints and the midpoint.

4.1 Algorithm Summary

Our simplification algorithm is built around pair contractions and error quadrics. The current implementation represents models using an adjacency graph structure: vertices, edges, and faces are all explicitly represented and linked together. To track the set of valid pairs, each vertex maintains a list of the pairs of which it is a member. The algorithm itself can be quickly summarized as follows:

1. Compute the $\mathbf{Q}$ matrices for all the initial vertices.

2. Select all valid pairs.

3. Compute the optimal contraction target $\bar{\mathbf{v}}$ for each valid pair $(\mathbf{v}_1, \mathbf{v}_2)$. The error $\bar{\mathbf{v}}^\mathsf{T}(\mathbf{Q}_1 + \mathbf{Q}_2)\bar{\mathbf{v}}$ of this target vertex becomes the *cost* of contracting that pair.

4. Place all the pairs in a heap keyed on cost with the minimum cost pair at the top.

5. Iteratively remove the pair $(\mathbf{v}_1, \mathbf{v}_2)$ of least cost from the heap, contract this pair, and update the costs of all valid pairs involving $\mathbf{v}_1$.

The only remaining issue is how to compute the initial $\mathbf{Q}$ matrices from which the error metric Δ is constructed.

---

[2]You can verify this for yourself by taking partial derivatives of

$$\begin{aligned} \mathbf{v}^\mathsf{T}\mathbf{Q}\mathbf{v} &= q_{11}x^2 + 2q_{12}xy + 2q_{13}xz + 2q_{14}x + q_{22}y^2 \\ &+ 2q_{23}yz + 2q_{24}y + q_{33}z^2 + 2q_{34}z + q_{44} \end{aligned}$$

Figure 4: A sequence of approximations generated using our algorithm. The original model on the left has 5,804 faces. The approximations to the right have 994, 532, 248, and 64 faces respectively. Note that features such as horns and hooves continue to exist through many simplifications. Only at extremely low levels of detail do they begin to disappear.

5   Deriving Error Quadrics

To construct our error quadrics, we must choose a heuristic to characterize the geometric error. We have selected a heuristic which is quite similar to the one given by Ronfard and Rossignac [7]. Following [7], we can observe that in the original model, each vertex is the solution of the intersection of a set of planes — namely, the planes of the triangles that meet at that vertex. We can associate a set of planes with each vertex, and we can define the error of the vertex with respect to this set as the sum of squared distances to its planes:

$$\Delta(\mathbf{v}) = \Delta([v_x\ v_y\ v_z\ 1]^{\mathsf{T}}) = \sum_{\mathbf{p}\in\text{planes}(\mathbf{v})} (\mathbf{p}^{\mathsf{T}}\mathbf{v})^2 \qquad (2)$$

where $\mathbf{p} = [a\ b\ c\ d]^{\mathsf{T}}$ represents the plane defined by the equation $ax + by + cz + d = 0$ where $a^2 + b^2 + c^2 = 1$. This approximate error metric is similar to [7], although we have used a summation rather than a maximum over the set of planes. The set of planes at a vertex is initialized to be the planes of the triangles that meet at that vertex. Note that if we were to track these plane sets explicitly, as [7] did, we would propagate planes after a contraction $(\mathbf{v}_1, \mathbf{v}_2) \rightarrow \bar{\mathbf{v}}$ using the rule: $\text{planes}(\bar{\mathbf{v}}) = \text{planes}(\mathbf{v}_1) \cup \text{planes}(\mathbf{v}_2)$. This can require a sizeable amount of storage that does not diminish as simplification progresses.

The error metric given in (2) can be rewritten as a quadratic form:

$$\begin{aligned}
\Delta(\mathbf{v}) &= \sum_{\mathbf{p}\in\text{planes}(\mathbf{v})} (\mathbf{v}^{\mathsf{T}}\mathbf{p})(\mathbf{p}^{\mathsf{T}}\mathbf{v}) \\
&= \sum_{\mathbf{p}\in\text{planes}(\mathbf{v})} \mathbf{v}^{\mathsf{T}}(\mathbf{p}\mathbf{p}^{\mathsf{T}})\mathbf{v} \\
&= \mathbf{v}^{\mathsf{T}}\left(\sum_{\mathbf{p}\in\text{planes}(\mathbf{v})} \mathbf{K_p}\right)\mathbf{v}
\end{aligned}$$

where $\mathbf{K_p}$ is the matrix:

$$\mathbf{K_p} = \mathbf{p}\mathbf{p}^{\mathsf{T}} = \begin{bmatrix} a^2 & ab & ac & ad \\ ab & b^2 & bc & bd \\ ac & bc & c^2 & cd \\ ad & bd & cd & d^2 \end{bmatrix}$$

This *fundamental error quadric* $\mathbf{K_p}$ can be used to find the squared distance of any point in space to the plane $\mathbf{p}$. We can sum these fundamental quadrics together and represent an entire set of planes by a single matrix $\mathbf{Q}$.

We implicitly track sets of planes using a single matrix; instead of computing a set union ($\text{planes}(\mathbf{v}_1) \cup \text{planes}(\mathbf{v}_2)$) we simply add two quadrics ($\mathbf{Q}_1 + \mathbf{Q}_2$). If the sets represented by $\mathbf{Q}_1$ and $\mathbf{Q}_2$ in the original metric are disjoint, the quadric addition is equivalent to the set union. If there is some overlap, then a single plane may be counted multiple times. However, any single plane can be counted at most 3 times since each plane is initially distributed only to the

vertices of its defining triangle. This may introduce some imprecision into the error measurement, but it has major benefits: the space required to track a plane set is only that required for a 4×4 symmetric matrix (10 floating point numbers), and the cost of updating the approximation is only that for adding two such matrices. If we are willing to sacrifice some additional storage, it would even be possible to eliminate this multiple counting using an inclusion-exclusion formula.

Thus, to compute the initial $\mathbf{Q}$ matrices required for our pair contraction algorithm, each vertex must accumulate the planes for the triangles which meet at that vertex. For each vertex, this set of planes defines several fundamental error quadrics $\mathbf{K_p}$. The error quadric $\mathbf{Q}$ for this vertex is the sum of the fundamental quadrics. Note that the initial error estimate for each vertex is 0, since each vertex lies in the planes of all its incident triangles.

5.1   Geometric Interpretation

As we will see, our plane-based error quadrics produce fairly high quality approximations. In addition, they also possess a useful geometric meaning[3].

The level surfaces of these quadrics are almost always ellipsoids. In some circumstances, the level surfaces may be degenerate. For instance, parallel planes (e.g., around a planar surface region) will produce level surfaces which are two parallel planes, and planes which are all parallel to a line (e.g., around a linear surface crease) will produce cylindrical level surfaces. The matrix used for finding optimal vertex positions (Eq. 1) will be invertible as long as the level surfaces are non-degenerate ellipsoids. In this case, $\bar{\mathbf{v}}$ will be at the center of the ellipsoid.

6   Additional Details

The general algorithm outlined so far performs well on most models. However, there are a few important enhancements which improve its performance on certain types of models, particularly planar models with open boundaries.

Preserving Boundaries.   The error quadrics derived earlier do not make any allowance for open boundaries. For models such as terrain height fields, it is necessary to preserve boundary curves while simplifying their shape. We might also wish to preserve discrete color discontinuities. In such cases, we initially label each edge as either normal or as a "discontinuity". For each face surrounding a particular discontinuity edge, we generate a perpendicular plane running through the edge. These constraint planes are then converted into quadrics, weighted by a large penalty factor, and

---

[3]Kalvin and Taylor [5] describe a somewhat similar use of quadrics to represent plane sets. They were tracking sets of planes which fit a set of points within some tolerance. They used ellipsoids in plane-space to represent the set of valid approximating planes.

Model	Faces	t	Init (s)	Simplify (s)
Bunny	69,451	0	3.3	12.0
Crater Lake	199,114	0	10.6	36.0
Cow	5,804	0	0.22	0.69
Cube Grid	1,200	0.12	0.25	0.17
Foot	4,204	0	0.16	0.41
Foot	4,204	0.318	0.43	0.76

Figure 5: Sample running times. All data reflects the time needed to make a 10 face approximation of the given model. Initialization time includes selecting valid pairs, computing initial error matrices, and choosing contraction targets. Simplification time includes the iterative contraction of pairs.

Faces (i)	Fixed (E_i)	Optimal (E_i)	Reduction
10	0.0062	0.0054	13.4%
100	0.00032	0.00025	21.7%
500	2.4e-05	1.3e-05	47.6%
1000	5.7e-06	3.4e-06	40.3%
2000	1.2e-06	7.9e-07	32.4%
3000	3.6e-07	2.6e-07	28.2%

Figure 6: Effect of optimal vertex placement. Choosing an optimal position, rather than a fixed choice amongst the endpoints and midpoint, can significantly reduce approximation error. Approximations are of cow model using $t = 0$.

added into the initial quadrics for the endpoints of the edge. We have found that this works quite well.

Preventing Mesh Inversion. Pair contractions do not necessarily preserve the orientation of the faces in the area of the contraction. For instance, it is possible to contract an edge and cause some neighboring faces to fold over on each other. It is usually best to try to avoid this type of mesh inversion. We use essentially the same scheme as others have before ([7] for example). When considering a possible contraction, we compare the normal of each neighboring face before and after the contraction. If the normal flips, that contraction can be either heavily penalized or disallowed.

6.1 Evaluating Approximations

In order to evaluate the quality of approximations produced by our algorithm, we need an error measurement which is a bit more rigorous than the heuristic error measurement employed by the algorithm itself. We have chosen a metric which measures the average squared distance between the approximation and the original model. This is very similar to the E_{dist} energy term used by Hoppe et al. [4]. We define the approximation error $E_i = E(M_n, M_i)$ of the simplified model M_i as:

$$E_i = \frac{1}{|X_n| + |X_i|} \left(\sum_{v \in X_n} d^2(v, M_i) + \sum_{v \in X_i} d^2(v, M_n) \right)$$

where X_n and X_i are sets of points sampled on the models M_n and M_i respectively. The distance $d(v, M) = \min_{p \in M} \|v - p\|$ is the minimum distance from v to the closest face of M ($\|\cdot\|$ is the usual Euclidean vector length operator). We use this metric for evaluation purposes only; it plays no part in the actual algorithm.

7 Results

Our algorithm can produce high fidelity approximations in fairly short amounts of time. Figure 5 summarizes the running time[4] of our current implementation using the models shown in this paper. Figure 4 shows a sample sequence of approximations generated by our algorithm. This entire sequence of cows was constructed in about a second. Notice that features such as horns and hooves remain recognizable through many simplifications. Only at extremely low levels of detail do they begin to disappear.

As described earlier, our algorithm attempts to optimize the placement of vertices after contractions. Figure 6 summarizes the effect of this policy on approximations for a representative model (the cow model of Fig. 4). At extremely low levels of detail, the

effect is modest. However, at more reasonable levels of detail the effect is substantial; optimal vertex placement can reduce the overall error by as much as 50%. In our experiments, we have also found that using optimal vertex placement tends to produce more well-shaped meshes.

Figures 8–13 demonstrate the performance of our algorithm on much larger models. Figure 9 represents a significant simplification (1.4%) of the original, but notice that all the major details of the original remain. In particular, notice that the contours on the interior of the ear and the large contours around the rear leg have been preserved. Figure 10 presents an even more drastic approximation: 100 faces or 0.14% of the original size. While most of the detail of the model has disappeared, the basic structure of the object is still intact; the major features such as the head, legs, tail, and ears are all apparent, albeit highly simplified. Figure 12 shows a very densely tessellated terrain model, and Figure 13 shows a highly simplified version. While the small scale texture of the terrain has largely disappeared, all the basic features of the terrain remain. Also note that the open boundary has been properly preserved. Without the boundary constraints described earlier, the boundary would have been significantly eroded.

Figure 11 illustrates the nature of the error quadrics accumulated during simplification. The level surface $\mathbf{v}^{\mathsf{T}} \mathbf{Q} \mathbf{v} = \epsilon$ is shown for each vertex. Each level surface is an ellipsoid centered around the corresponding vertex. The interpretation of these ellipsoids is that a vertex can be moved anywhere within its ellipsoid and have an error less than ϵ. The significant feature of the ellipsoids is that they conform to the shape of the model surface very nicely. They are large and flat on mostly planar areas such as the middle of the hind leg, and they are elongated along discontinuity lines such as the contours through the ear and along the bottom of the leg. In some sense, these ellipsoids can be thought of as accumulating information about the shape of the local surface around their vertex.

Figures 14–17 demonstrate the real benefits which aggregation via pair contractions can provide. The original model consists of the bones of a human's left foot. There are many separate bone segments, some of which even interpenetrate (obviously an error in model reconstruction). Three approximations are compared: one built by uniform vertex clustering, one built with edge contractions alone, and one built with pair contractions. When edge contractions alone are used, the small segments at the ends of the toes collapse into single points; this creates the impression that the toes are slowly receding back into the foot. On the other hand, using the more general pair contractions allows separate bone segments to be merged. As you can see in Figure 17, the toes are being merged into single long segments. Figure 19 shows some of the pairs initially selected as valid. Notice how they span the gaps between bone segments. Finally, Figure 18 shows another illustration of the level surfaces of the error quadrics accumulated during simplification (this is the model seen in Figure 16).

The benefits of aggregation are not solely visual. Aggregation can also produce objectively lower approximation error. Figure 7

---

[4]This data was collected on an SGI Indigo2 with a 195 MHz R10000 processor and 128 Mbytes of memory.

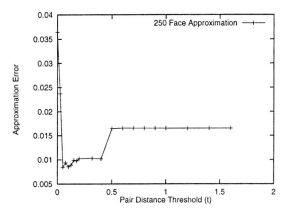

Figure 7: The effect of pair thresholds. Approximation error E_{250} is shown as a function of t for a 250 face approximation of the foot model (Fig. 14). Pair contractions resulting in aggregation can significantly reduce approximation error.

shows the error E_{250} for 250 face approximations of the foot model using various values of t. A fairly wide range of values all produce objectively better approximations than are achieved by the edge contraction only approximation ($t = 0$). Notice, however, that increasing t does not always improve the approximation. This is due to the nature of our quadric error metric. Locally, the distance to a set of planes is a reasonable approximation of the distance to a set of faces. However, because planes have infinite extent and faces do not, the error metric becomes less reliable as we move farther away.

8 Discussion

Our algorithm provides a mix of efficiency, quality, and generality not found in earlier algorithms. While certain other algorithms are faster or generate higher quality approximations than ours, they typically do not meet the capability of our algorithm in all three areas. The only algorithm capable of simplifying arbitrary polygonal models, vertex clustering [8], does not reliably produce high quality approximations. None of the higher quality methods available [2, 7, 3] support aggregation. Both [2] and [3] seem to be significantly more time consuming than our algorithm. The results of [7] are most similar to our own because we use a very similar error approximation. However, our system uses a more efficient means to track plane sets, and it incorporates some enhancements such as boundary preservation.

There remain various aspects of our algorithm that could be improved upon. We have used a fairly simple scheme for selecting valid pairs. It is quite possible that a more sophisticated adaptive scheme could produce better results. We have not addressed the issue of surface properties such as color. One possible solution is to treat each vertex as a vector (x, y, z, r, g, b), construct 7×7 quadrics, and simplify. We believe this could work well, but the added size and complexity make it less attractive than the basic algorithm.

Although it generally performs well, our algorithm has a couple of clear weaknesses. First, as mentioned earlier, measuring error as a distance to a set of planes only works well in a suitably local neighborhood. Second, the information accumulated in the quadrics is essentially implicit, which can at times be problematic. Suppose we join together two cubes and would like to remove the planes associated with the now defunct interior faces. Not only is it, in general, difficult to determine what faces are defunct, there is no clear way to reliably remove the appropriate planes from the quadrics. As a result, our algorithm does not do as good a job at simplification with

aggregation as we would like.

9 Conclusion

We have described a surface simplification algorithm which is capable of rapidly producing high fidelity approximations of polygonal models. Our algorithm uses iterative pair contractions to simplify models and quadric error metrics to track the approximate error of the model as it is being simplified. The quadrics stored with the final vertices can also be used to characterize the overall shape of the surface.

Our algorithm has the ability to join unconnected sections of models while still maintaining fairly high quality results. While most previous algorithms are also inherently limited to manifold surfaces, our system is quite capable of handling and simplifying non-manifold objects. Finally, our algorithm provides a useful middle ground between very fast, low-quality methods such as vertex clustering [8] and very slow, high-quality methods such as mesh optimization [3].

References

[1] Jonathan Cohen, Amitabh Varshney, Dinesh Manocha, Greg Turk, Hans Weber, Pankaj Agarwal, Frederick Brooks, and William Wright. Simplification envelopes. In *SIGGRAPH '96 Proc.*, pages 119–128, Aug. 1996. http://www.cs.unc.edu/~geom/envelope.html.

[2] André Guéziec. Surface simplification with variable tolerance. In *Second Annual Intl. Symp. on Medical Robotics and Computer Assisted Surgery (MRCAS '95)*, pages 132–139, November 1995.

[3] Hugues Hoppe. Progressive meshes. In *SIGGRAPH '96 Proc.*, pages 99–108, Aug. 1996. http://www.research.microsoft.com/research/graphics/hoppe/.

[4] Hugues Hoppe, Tony DeRose, Tom Duchamp, John McDonald, and Werner Stuetzle. Mesh optimization. In *SIGGRAPH '93 Proc.*, pages 19–26, Aug. 1993. http://www.research.microsoft.com/research/graphics/hoppe/.

[5] Alan D. Kalvin and Russell H. Taylor. Superfaces:polygonal mesh simplification with bounded error. *IEEE Computer Graphics and Appl.*, 16(3), May 1996. http://www.computer.org/pubs/cg&a/articles/g30064.pdf.

[6] David Luebke and Carl Erikson. View-dependent simplification of arbitrary polygonal environments. In *SIGGRAPH 97 Proc.*, August 1997.

[7] Rémi Ronfard and Jarek Rossignac. Full-range approximation of triangulated polyhedra. *Computer Graphics Forum*, 15(3), Aug. 1996. Proc. Eurographics '96.

[8] Jarek Rossignac and Paul Borrel. Multi-resolution 3D approximations for rendering complex scenes. In B. Falcidieno and T. Kunii, editors, *Modeling in Computer Graphics: Methods and Applications*, pages 455–465, 1993.

[9] William J. Schroeder, Jonathan A. Zarge, and William E. Lorensen. Decimation of triangle meshes. *Computer Graphics (SIGGRAPH '92 Proc.)*, 26(2):65–70, July 1992.

[10] Marc Soucy and Denis Laurendeau. Multiresolution surface modeling based on hierarchical triangulation. *Computer Vision and Image Understanding*, 63(1):1–14, 1996.

Figure 8: Original bunny model with 69,451 triangles. Rendered using flat shading just as in approximations below.

Figure 11: 1,000 face approximation. Error ellipsoids for each vertex are shown in green.

Figure 9: An approximation using only 1,000 triangles (generated in 15 seconds).

Figure 12: Terrain model of Crater Lake (199,114 faces).

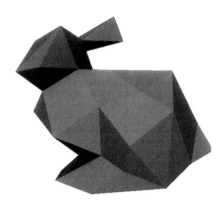

Figure 10: An approximation using only 100 triangles (generated in 15 seconds).

Figure 13: Simplified model with 999 faces (took 46 seconds).

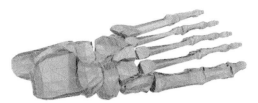

Figure 14: **Original.** Bones of a human's left foot (4,204 faces). Note the many separate bone segments.

Figure 15: **Uniform Vertex Clustering.** 262 face approximation ($11 \times 4 \times 4$ grid). Indiscriminate joining destroys approximation quality.

Figure 18: Level surfaces of the error quadrics at the vertices of the approximation shown in Figure 16.

Figure 16: **Edge Contractions.** 250 face approximation. Bone segments at the ends of the toes have disappeared; the toes appear to be receding back into the foot.

Figure 17: **Pair Contractions.** 250 face approximation ($t = 0.318$). Toes are being merged into larger solid components. No receding artifacts. This model now contains 61 non-manifold edges.

Figure 19: Pairs selected as valid during initialization (for Fig. 17). Red pairs are edges; green pairs are non-edges.

Progressive Simplicial Complexes

Jovan Popović*
Carnegie Mellon University

Hugues Hoppe
Microsoft Research

ABSTRACT

In this paper, we introduce the progressive simplicial complex (PSC) representation, a new format for storing and transmitting triangulated geometric models. Like the earlier progressive mesh (PM) representation, it captures a given model as a coarse base model together with a sequence of refinement transformations that progressively recover detail. The PSC representation makes use of a more general refinement transformation, allowing the given model to be an arbitrary triangulation (e.g. any dimension, non-orientable, non-manifold, non-regular), and the base model to always consist of a single vertex. Indeed, the sequence of refinement transformations encodes both the geometry and the topology of the model in a unified multiresolution framework. The PSC representation retains the advantages of PM's. It defines a continuous sequence of approximating models for runtime level-of-detail control, allows smooth transitions between any pair of models in the sequence, supports progressive transmission, and offers a space-efficient representation. Moreover, by allowing changes to topology, the PSC sequence of approximations achieves better fidelity than the corresponding PM sequence.

We develop an optimization algorithm for constructing PSC representations for graphics surface models, and demonstrate the framework on models that are both geometrically and topologically complex.

CR Categories: I.3.5 [Computer Graphics]: Computational Geometry and Object Modeling - surfaces and object representations.

Additional Keywords: model simplification, level-of-detail representations, multiresolution, progressive transmission, geometry compression.

1 INTRODUCTION

Modeling and 3D scanning systems commonly give rise to triangle meshes of high complexity. Such meshes are notoriously difficult to render, store, and transmit. One approach to speed up rendering is to replace a complex mesh by a set of level-of-detail (LOD) approximations; a detailed mesh is used when the object is close to the viewer, and coarser approximations are substituted as the object recedes [6, 8]. These LOD approximations can be precomputed automatically using mesh simplification methods (e.g. [2, 10, 14, 20, 21, 22, 24, 27]). For efficient storage and transmission, mesh compression schemes [7, 26] have also been developed.

The recently introduced *progressive mesh* (PM) representation [13] provides a unified solution to these problems. In PM form, an arbitrary mesh $\hat{M}$ is stored as a coarse base mesh M^0 together with a sequence of n detail records that indicate how to incrementally refine M^0 into $M^n = \hat{M}$ (see Figure 7). Each detail record encodes the information associated with a *vertex split*, an elementary transformation that adds one vertex to the mesh. In addition to defining a continuous sequence of approximations $M^0 \ldots M^n$, the PM representation supports smooth visual transitions (geomorphs), allows progressive transmission, and makes an effective mesh compression scheme.

The PM representation has two restrictions, however. First, it can only represent *meshes*: triangulations that correspond to orientable[1] 2-dimensional manifolds. Triangulated[2] models that cannot be represented include 1-d manifolds (open and closed curves), higher dimensional polyhedra (e.g. triangulated volumes), non-orientable surfaces (e.g. Möbius strips), non-manifolds (e.g. two cubes joined along an edge), and non-regular models (i.e. models of mixed dimensionality). Second, the expressiveness of the PM vertex split transformations constrains all meshes $M^0 \ldots M^n$ to have the same topological type. Therefore, when $\hat{M}$ is topologically complex, the simplified base mesh M^0 may still have numerous triangles (Figure 7).

In contrast, a number of existing simplification methods allow topological changes as the model is simplified (Section 6). Our work is inspired by vertex unification schemes [21, 22], which merge vertices of the model based on geometric proximity, thereby allowing genus modification and component merging.

In this paper, we introduce the *progressive simplicial complex* (PSC) representation, a generalization of the PM representation that permits topological changes. The key element of our approach is the introduction of a more general refinement transformation, the *generalized vertex split*, that encodes changes to both the geometry and topology of the model. The PSC representation expresses an arbitrary triangulated model M (e.g. any dimension, non-orientable, non-manifold, non-regular) as the result of successive refinements applied to a base model M^1 that always consists of a single vertex (Figure 8). Thus both geometric and topological complexity are recovered progressively. Moreover, the PSC representation retains the advantages of PM's, including continuous LOD, geomorphs, progressive transmission, and model compression.

In addition, we develop an optimization algorithm for constructing a PSC representation from a given model, as described in Section 4.

*Work performed while at Microsoft Research.
Email: jovan@cs.cmu.edu, hhoppe@microsoft.com
Web: http://www.cs.cmu.edu/~jovan/
Web: http://research.microsoft.com/~hoppe/

---

[1] The particular parametrization of vertex splits in [13] assumes that mesh triangles are consistently oriented.

[2] Throughout this paper, we use the words "triangulated" and "triangulation" in the general dimension-independent sense.

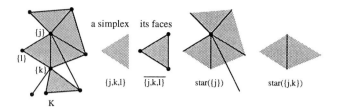

Figure 1: Illustration of a simplicial complex K and some of its subsets.

2 BACKGROUND

2.1 Concepts from algebraic topology

To precisely define both triangulated models and their PSC representations, we find it useful to introduce some elegant abstractions from algebraic topology (e.g. [15, 25]).

The geometry of a triangulated model is denoted as a tuple (K, V) where the *abstract simplicial complex* K is a combinatorial structure specifying the adjacency of vertices, edges, triangles, etc., and V is a set of vertex positions specifying the shape of the model in $\mathbf{R}^3$.

More precisely, an abstract simplicial complex K consists of a set of vertices $\{1, \ldots, m\}$ together with a set of non-empty subsets of the vertices, called the *simplices* of K, such that any set consisting of exactly one vertex is a simplex in K, and every non-empty subset of a simplex in K is also a simplex in K.

A simplex containing exactly $d+1$ vertices has *dimension d* and is called a *d-simplex*. As illustrated pictorially in Figure 1, the *faces* of a simplex s, denoted $\bar{s}$, is the set of non-empty subsets of s. The *star* of s, denoted $\text{star}(s)$, is the set of simplices of which s is a face. The *children* of a d-simplex s are the $(d-1)$-simplices of $\bar{s}$, and its *parents* are the $(d+1)$-simplices of $\text{star}(s)$. A simplex with exactly one parent is said to be a *boundary simplex*, and one with no parents a *principal simplex*. The dimension of K is the maximum dimension of its simplices; K is said to be *regular* if all its principal simplices have the same dimension.

To form a triangulation from K, identify its vertices $\{1, \ldots, m\}$ with the standard basis vectors $\{\mathbf{e}_1, \ldots, \mathbf{e}_m\}$ of $\mathbf{R}^m$. For each simplex s, let the *open simplex* $\langle s \rangle \subset \mathbf{R}^m$ denote the interior of the convex hull of its vertices:

$$\langle s \rangle = \{ \mathbf{b} \in \mathbf{R}^m \; : \; \mathbf{b}_j \geq 0 \, , \, \sum_{j=1}^{m} \mathbf{b}_j = 1 \, , \, \mathbf{b}_j > 0 \Leftrightarrow \{j\} \subseteq s \}.$$

The *topological realization* $|K|$ is defined as $|K| = \langle K \rangle = \cup_{s \in K} \langle s \rangle$. The *geometric realization* of K is the image $\phi_V(|K|)$ where $\phi_V : \mathbf{R}^m \rightarrow \mathbf{R}^3$ is the linear map that sends the j-th standard basis vector $\mathbf{e}_j \in \mathbf{R}^m$ to $\mathbf{v}_j \in \mathbf{R}^3$. Only a restricted set of vertex positions $V = \{\mathbf{v}_1, \ldots, \mathbf{v}_m\}$ lead to an embedding of $\phi_V(|K|) \subset \mathbf{R}^3$, that is, prevent self-intersections. The geometric realization $\phi_V(|K|)$ is often called a *simplicial complex* or *polyhedron*; it is formed by an arbitrary union of points, segments, triangles, tetrahedra, etc. Note that there generally exist many triangulations (K, V) for a given polyhedron. (Some of the vertices V may lie in the polyhedron's interior.)

Two sets are said to be *homeomorphic* (denoted $\cong$) if there exists a continuous one-to-one mapping between them. Equivalently, they are said to have the same *topological type*. The topological realization $|K|$ is a *d-dimensional manifold without boundary* if for each vertex $\{j\}$, $\langle \text{star}(\{j\}) \rangle \cong \mathbf{R}^d$. It is a *d-dimensional manifold* if each $\langle \text{star}(\{v\}) \rangle$ is homeomorphic to either $\mathbf{R}^d$ or $\mathbf{R}^d_+$, where $\mathbf{R}^d_+ = \{\mathbf{x} \in \mathbf{R}^d : \mathbf{x}_1 \geq 0\}$. Two simplices s_1 and s_2 are *d-adjacent* if they have a common d-dimensional face. Two d-adjacent $(d+1)$-simplices s_1 and s_2 are *manifold-adjacent* if $\langle \text{star}(s_1 \cap s_2) \rangle \cong \mathbf{R}^{d+1}$.

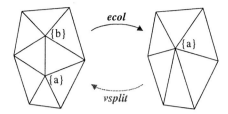

Figure 2: Illustration of the edge collapse transformation and its inverse, the vertex split.

Transitive closure of 0-adjacency partitions K into *connected components*. Similarly, transitive closure of manifold-adjacency partitions K into *manifold components*.

2.2 Review of progressive meshes

In the PM representation [13], a mesh with appearance attributes is represented as a tuple $M = (K, V, D, S)$, where the abstract simplicial complex K is restricted to define an orientable 2-dimensional manifold, the vertex positions $V = \{\mathbf{v}_1, \ldots, \mathbf{v}_m\}$ determine its geometric realization $\phi_V(|K|)$ in $\mathbf{R}^3$, D is the set of discrete material attributes d_f associated with 2-simplices $f \in K$, and S is the set of scalar attributes $s_{(v,f)}$ (e.g. normals, texture coordinates) associated with corners (vertex-face tuples) of K.

An initial mesh $\hat{M} = M^n$ is simplified into a coarser base mesh M^0 by applying a sequence of n successive edge collapse transformations:

$$(\hat{M} = M^n) \xrightarrow{ecol_{n-1}} \ldots \xrightarrow{ecol_1} M^1 \xrightarrow{ecol_0} M^0 .$$

As shown in Figure 2, each *ecol* unifies the two vertices of an edge $\{a, b\}$, thereby removing one or two triangles. The position of the resulting unified vertex can be arbitrary. Because the edge collapse transformation has an inverse, called the *vertex split* transformation (Figure 2), the process can be reversed, so that an arbitrary mesh $\hat{M}$ may be represented as a simple mesh M^0 together with a sequence of n *vsplit* records:

$$M^0 \xrightarrow{vsplit_0} M^1 \xrightarrow{vsplit_1} \ldots \xrightarrow{vsplit_{n-1}} (M^n = \hat{M})$$

The tuple $(M^0, \{vsplit_0, \ldots, vsplit_{n-1}\})$ forms a *progressive mesh* (PM) representation of $\hat{M}$.

The PM representation thus captures a continuous sequence of approximations $M^0 \ldots M^n$ that can be quickly traversed for interactive level-of-detail control. Moreover, there exists a correspondence between the vertices of any two meshes M^c and M^f ($0 \leq c < f \leq n$) within this sequence, allowing for the construction of smooth visual transitions (geomorphs) between them. A sequence of such geomorphs can be precomputed for smooth runtime LOD. In addition, PM's support progressive transmission, since the base mesh M^0 can be quickly transmitted first, followed the *vsplit* sequence. Finally, the *vsplit* records can be encoded concisely, making the PM representation an effective scheme for mesh compression.

Topological constraints Because the definitions of *ecol* and *vsplit* are such that they preserve the topological type of the mesh (i.e. all $|K^i|$ are homeomorphic), there is a constraint on the minimum complexity that K^0 may achieve. For instance, it is known that the minimal number of vertices for a closed genus g mesh (orientable 2-manifold) is $\lceil (7 + (48g+1)^{\frac{1}{2}})/2 \rceil$ if $g \neq 2$ (10 if $g = 2$) [16]. Also, the presence of boundary components may further constrain the complexity of K^0. Most importantly, $\hat{K}$ may consist of a number of components, and each is required to appear in the base mesh. For example, the meshes in Figure 7 each have 117 components. As evident from the figure, the geometry of PM meshes may deteriorate severely as they approach topological lower bound.

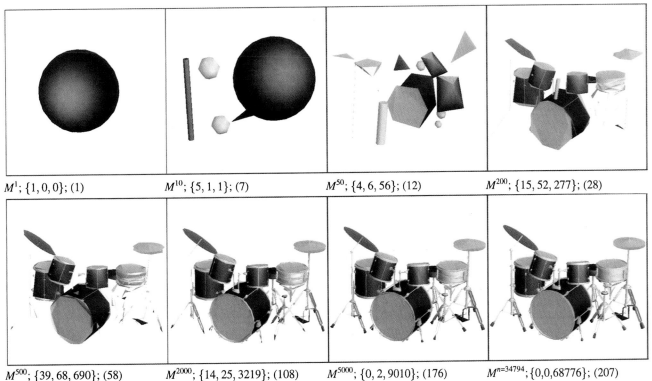

$M^1; \{1, 0, 0\}; (1)$ $M^{10}; \{5, 1, 1\}; (7)$ $M^{50}; \{4, 6, 56\}; (12)$ $M^{200}; \{15, 52, 277\}; (28)$

$M^{500}; \{39, 68, 690\}; (58)$ $M^{2000}; \{14, 25, 3219\}; (108)$ $M^{5000}; \{0, 2, 9010\}; (176)$ $M^{n=34794}; \{0,0,68776\}; (207)$

Figure 3: Example of a PSC representation. The image captions indicate the number of principal $\{0, 1, 2\}$-simplices respectively and the number of connected components (in parenthesis).

3 PSC REPRESENTATION

3.1 Triangulated models

The first step towards generalizing PM's is to let the PSC representation encode more general triangulated models, instead of just meshes.

We denote a triangulated model as a tuple $M = (K, V, D, A)$. The abstract simplicial complex K is not restricted to 2-manifolds, but may in fact be arbitrary. To represent K in memory, we encode the *incidence graph* of the simplices using the following linked structures (in C++ notation):

```
struct Simplex {
    int dim;          // 0=vertex, 1=edge, 2=triangle, ...
    int id;
    Simplex* children[MAXDIM+1];      // [0..dim]
    List<Simplex*> parents;
};
```

To render the model, we draw only the principal simplices of K, denoted $\mathcal{P}(K)$ (i.e. vertices not adjacent to edges, edges not adjacent to triangles, etc.). The discrete attributes D associate a material identifier d_s with each simplex $s \in \mathcal{P}(K)$. For the sake of simplicity, we avoid explicitly storing surface normals at "corners" (using a set S) as done in [13]. Instead we let the material identifier d_s contain a *smoothing group* field [28], and let a normal discontinuity (*crease*) form between any pair of adjacent triangles with different smoothing groups.

Previous vertex unification schemes [21, 22] render principal simplices of dimension 0 and 1 (denoted $\mathcal{P}_{01}(K)$) as points and lines respectively with fixed, device-dependent screen widths. To better approximate the model, we instead define a set A that associates an area $a_s \in A$ with each simplex $s \in \mathcal{P}_{01}(K)$. We think of a 0-simplex $s_0 \in \mathcal{P}_0(K)$ as approximating a sphere with area a_{s_0}, and a 1-simplex $s_1 = \{j, k\} \in \mathcal{P}_1(K)$ as approximating a cylinder (with axis $(\mathbf{v}_j, \mathbf{v}_k)$)

of area a_{s_1}. To render a simplex $s \in \mathcal{P}_{01}(K)$, we determine the radius r_{model} of the corresponding sphere or cylinder in modeling space, and project the length r_{model} to obtain the radius r_{screen} in screen pixels. Depending on r_{screen}, we render the simplex as a polygonal sphere or cylinder with radius r_{model}, a 2D point or line with thickness $2r_{screen}$, or do not render it at all. This choice based on r_{screen} can be adjusted to mitigate the overhead of introducing polygonal representations of spheres and cylinders.

As an example, Figure 3 shows an initial model $\hat{M}$ of 68,776 triangles. One of its approximations M^{500} is a triangulated model with $\{39, 68, 690\}$ principal $\{0, 1, 2\}$-simplices respectively.

3.2 Level-of-detail sequence

As in progressive meshes, from a given triangulated model $\hat{M} = M^n$, we define a sequence of approximations M^i:

$$M^1 \xleftrightarrow{op_1} M^2 \xleftrightarrow{op_2} \dots M^{n-1} \xleftrightarrow{op_{n-1}} M^n .$$

Here each model M^i has exactly i vertices. The simplification operator $M^i \xleftarrow{unify_i} M^{i+1}$ is the *vertex unification* transformation, which merges two vertices (Section 3.3), and its inverse $M^i \xrightarrow{gvspl_i} M^{i+1}$ is the *generalized vertex split* transformation (Section 3.4). The tuple $(M^1, \{gvspl_1, \dots, gvspl_{n-1}\})$ forms a *progressive simplicial complex* (PSC) representation of $\hat{M}$.

To construct a PSC representation, we first determine a sequence of *vunify* transformations simplifying $\hat{M}$ down to a single vertex, as described in Section 4. After reversing these transformations, we renumber the simplices in the order that they are created, so that each $gvspl_i(\{a_i\}, \dots)$ splits the vertex $\{a_i\} \in K^i$ into two vertices $\{a_i\}, \{i+1\} \in K^{i+1}$. As vertices may have different positions in the different models, we denote the position of $\{j\}$ in M^i as $\mathbf{v}_j^i$.

To better approximate a surface model $\hat{M}$ at lower complexity levels, we initially associate with each (principal) 2-simplex s an area a_s equal to its triangle area in $\hat{M}$. Then, as the model is simplified, we keep constant the sum of areas a_s associated with principal simplices within each manifold component. When 2-simplices are eventually reduced to principal 1-simplices and 0-simplices, their associated areas will provide good estimates of the original component areas.

3.3 Vertex unification transformation

The transformation $vunify(\{a_i\}, \{b_i\}, midp_i) : M^i \leftarrow M^{i+1}$ takes an arbitrary pair of vertices $\{a_i\}, \{b_i\} \in K^{i+1}$ (simplex $\{a_i, b_i\}$ need not be present in K^{i+1}) and merges them into a single vertex $\{a_i\} \in K^i$.

Model M^i is created from M^{i+1} by updating each member of the tuple (K, V, D, A) as follows:

K: References to $\{b_i\}$ in all simplices of K are replaced by references to $\{a_i\}$. More precisely, each simplex s in $\text{star}(\{b_i\}) \subset K^{i+1}$ is replaced by simplex $(s \setminus \{b_i\}) \cup \{a_i\}$, which we call the *ancestor simplex* of s. If this ancestor simplex already exists, s is deleted.

V: Vertex $\mathbf{v}_b$ is deleted. For simplicity, the position of the remaining (unified) vertex is set to either the midpoint or is left unchanged. That is, $\mathbf{v}_a^i = (\mathbf{v}_a^{i+1} + \mathbf{v}_b^{i+1})/2$ if the boolean parameter $midp_i$ is *true*, or $\mathbf{v}_a^i = \mathbf{v}_a^{i+1}$ otherwise.

D: Materials are carried through as expected. So, if after the vertex unification an ancestor simplex $(s \setminus \{b_i\}) \cup \{a_i\} \in K^i$ is a new principal simplex, it receives its material from $s \in K^{i+1}$ if s is a principal simplex, or else from the single parent $s \cup \{a_i\} \in K^{i+1}$ of s.

A: To maintain the initial areas of manifold components, the areas a_s of deleted principal simplices are redistributed to manifold-adjacent neighbors. More concretely, the area of each principal d-simplex s deleted during the K update is distributed to a manifold-adjacent d-simplex not in $\text{star}(\{a_i, b_i\})$. If no such neighbor exists and the ancestor of s is a principal simplex, the area a_s is distributed to that ancestor simplex. Otherwise, the manifold component $(\text{star}(\{a_i, b_i\}))$ of s is being squashed between two other manifold components, and a_s is discarded.

3.4 Generalized vertex split transformation

Constructing the PSC representation involves recording the information necessary to perform the inverse of each $vunify_i$. This inverse is the generalized vertex split $gvspl_i$, which splits a 0-simplex $\{a_i\}$ to introduce an additional 0-simplex $\{b_i\}$. (As mentioned previously, renumbering of simplices implies $b_i \equiv i+1$, so index b_i need not be stored explicitly.) Each $gvspl_i$ record has the form

$$gvspl_i(\{a_i\}, C_i^{\Delta K}, midp_i, (\Delta \mathbf{v})_i, C_i^{\Delta D}, C_i^{\Delta A}),$$

and constructs model M^{i+1} from M^i by updating the tuple (K, V, D, A) as follows:

K: As illustrated in Figure 4, any simplex adjacent to $\{a_i\}$ in K^i can be the *vunify* result of one of four configurations in K^{i+1}. To construct K^{i+1}, we therefore replace each ancestor simplex $s \in \text{star}(\{a_i\})$ in K^i by either **(1)** s, **(2)** $(s \setminus \{a_i\}) \cup \{i+1\}$, **(3)** s and $(s \setminus \{a_i\}) \cup \{i+1\}$, or **(4)** s, $(s \setminus \{a_i\}) \cup \{i+1\}$ and $s \cup \{i+1\}$. The choice is determined by a *split code* associated with s. These split codes are stored as a code string $C_i^{\Delta K}$, in which the simplices $\text{star}(\{a_i\})$ are sorted first in order of increasing dimension, and then in order of increasing simplex id, as shown in Figure 5.

V: The new vertex is assigned position $\mathbf{v}_{i+1}^{i+1} = \mathbf{v}_{a_i}^i + (\Delta \mathbf{v})_i$. The other vertex is given position $\mathbf{v}_{a_i}^{i+1} = \mathbf{v}_{a_i}^i - (\Delta \mathbf{v})_i$ if the boolean parameter $midp_i$ is *true*; otherwise its position remains unchanged.

D: The string $C_i^{\Delta D}$ is used to assign materials d_s for each new principal simplex. Simplices in $C_i^{\Delta D}$, as well as in $C_i^{\Delta A}$ below, are sorted by simplex dimension and simplex id as in $C_i^{\Delta K}$.

A: During reconstruction, we are only interested in the areas a_s for $s \in \mathcal{P}_{01}(K)$. The string $C_i^{\Delta A}$ tracks changes in these areas.

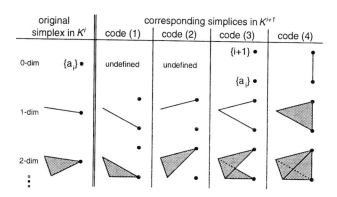

Figure 4: Effects of split codes on simplices of various dimensions.

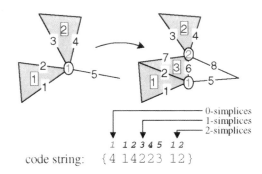

code string: $\{4\ 14223\ 12\}$

Figure 5: Example of split code encoding.

3.5 Properties

Levels of detail A graphics application can efficiently transition between models $M^1 \ldots M^n$ at runtime by performing a sequence of *vunify* or *gvspl* transformations. Our current research prototype was not designed for efficiency; it attains simplification rates of about 6000 *vunify*/sec and refinement rates of about 5000 *gvspl*/sec. We expect that a careful redesign using more efficient data structures would significantly improve these rates.

Geomorphs As in the PM representation, there exists a correspondence between the vertices of the models $M^1 \ldots M^n$. Given a coarser model M^c and a finer model M^f, $1 \le c < f \le n$, each vertex $\{j\} \in K^f$ corresponds to a unique ancestor vertex $\{\rho^{f \to c}(j)\} \in K^c$ found by recursively traversing the ancestor simplex relations:

$$\rho^{f \to c}(j) = \begin{cases} j & , j \le c \\ \rho^{f \to c}(a_{j-1}) & , j > c \end{cases}.$$

This correspondence allows the creation of a smooth visual transition (geomorph) $M^G(\alpha)$ such that $M^G(1)$ equals M^f and $M^G(0)$ looks identical to M^c. The geomorph is defined as the model

$$M^G(\alpha) = (K^f, V^G(\alpha), D^f, A^G(\alpha))$$

in which each vertex position is interpolated between its original position in V^f and the position of its ancestor in V^c:

$$\mathbf{v}_j^G(\alpha) = (\alpha)\mathbf{v}_j^f + (1-\alpha)\mathbf{v}_{\rho^{f \to c}(j)}^c.$$

However, we must account for the special rendering of principal simplices of dimension 0 and 1 (Section 3.1). For each simplex $s \in \mathcal{P}_{01}(K^f)$, we interpolate its area using

$$a_s^G(\alpha) = (\alpha)a_s^f + (1-\alpha)a_s^c,$$

where $a_s^c = 0$ if $s \notin \mathcal{P}_{01}(K^c)$. In addition, we render each simplex $s \in \mathcal{P}_{01}(K^c) \setminus \mathcal{P}_{01}(K^f)$ using area $a_s^G(\alpha) = (1-\alpha)a_s^c$. The resulting geomorph is visually smooth even as principal simplices are introduced, removed, or change dimension. The accompanying video demonstrates a sequence of such geomorphs.

Progressive transmission As with PM's, the PSC representation can be progressively transmitted by first sending M^1, followed by the *gvspl* records. Unlike the base mesh of the PM, M^1 always consists of a single vertex, and can therefore be sent in a fixed-size record. The rendering of lower-dimensional simplices as spheres and cylinders helps to quickly convey the overall shape of the model in the early stages of transmission.

Model compression Although PSC *gvspl* are more general than PM *vsplit* transformations, they offer a surprisingly concise representation of $\hat{M}$. Table 1 lists the average number of bits required to encode each field of the *gvspl* records.

Using arithmetic coding [30], the vertex id field $\{a_i\}$ requires $\log_2 i$ bits, and the boolean parameter $midp_i$ requires 0.6–0.9 bits for our models. The $(\Delta\mathbf{v})_i$ delta vector is quantized to 16 bits per coordinate (48 bits per $\Delta\mathbf{v}$), and stored as a variable-length field [7, 13], requiring about 31 bits on average.

At first glance, each split code in the code string $C_i^{\Delta K}$ seems to have 4 possible outcomes (except for the split code for 0-simplex $\{a_i\}$ which has only 2 possible outcomes). However, there exist constraints between these split codes. For example, in Figure 5, the code 1 for 1-simplex id 1 implies that 2-simplex id 1 also has code 1. This in turn implies that 1-simplex id 2 cannot have code 2. Similarly, code 2 for 1-simplex id 3 implies a code 2 for 2-simplex id 2, which in turn implies that 1-simplex id 4 cannot have code 1. These constraints, illustrated in the "scoreboard" of Figure 6, can be summarized using the following two rules:

(1) If a simplex has split code $c \in \{1, 2\}$, all of its parents have split code c.

(2) If a simplex has split code 3, none of its parents have split code 4.

As we encode split codes in $C_i^{\Delta K}$ left to right, we apply these two rules (and their contrapositives) transitively to constrain the possible outcomes for split codes yet to be encoded. Using arithmetic coding with uniform outcome probabilities, these constraints reduce the code string length in Figure 6 from 15 bits to 10.2 bits. In our models, the constraints reduce the code string from 30 bits to 14 bits on average.

The code string is further reduced using a non-uniform probability model. We create an array $T[0..dim][0..15]$ of encoding tables, indexed by simplex dimension (0..dim) and by the set of possible (constrained) split codes (a 4-bit mask). For each simplex s, we encode its split code c using the probability distribution found in $T[s.dim][s.codes\_mask]$. For 2-dimensional models, only 10 of the 48 tables are non-trivial, and each table contains at most 4 probabilities, so the total size of the probability model is small. These encoding tables reduce the code strings to approximately 8 bits as shown in Table 1. By comparison, the PM representation requires approximately 5 bits for the same information, but of course it disallows topological changes.

To provide more intuition for the efficiency of the PSC representation, we note that capturing the connectivity of an average 2-manifold simplicial complex (n vertices, $3n$ edges, and $2n$ triangles) requires $\sum_{i=1}^{n}(\log_2 i + 8) \simeq n(\log_2 n + 7)$ bits with PSC encoding, versus $n(12 \log_2 n + 9.5)$ bits with a traditional one-way incidence graph representation.

For improved compression, it would be best to use a hybrid PM + PSC representation, in which the more concise PM vertex split encoding is used when the local neighborhood is an orientable

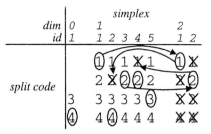

Figure 6: Constraints on the split codes for the simplices in the example of Figure 5.

Table 1: Compression results and construction times.

Object	#verts n	Space required (bits/n)							Trad. repr. bits/n	Con. time hrs.
		K		V		D	A	Σ		
		$\{a_i\}$	$C_i^{\Delta K}$	$midp_i$	$(\Delta\mathbf{v})_i$	$C_i^{\Delta D}$	$C_i^{\Delta A}$			
drumset	34,794	12.2	8.2	0.9	28.1	4.1	0.4	53.9	146.1	4.3
destroyer	83,799	13.3	8.3	0.7	23.1	2.1	0.3	47.8	154.1	14.1
chandelier	36,627	12.4	7.6	0.8	28.6	3.4	0.8	53.6	143.6	3.6
schooner	119,734	13.4	8.6	0.7	27.2	2.5	1.3	53.7	148.7	22.2
sandal	4,628	9.2	8.0	0.7	33.4	1.5	0.0	52.8	123.2	0.4
castle	15,082	11.0	1.2	0.6	30.7	0.0	-	43.5	-	0.5
cessna	6,795	9.6	7.6	0.6	32.2	2.5	0.1	52.6	132.1	0.5
harley	28,847	11.9	7.9	0.9	30.5	1.4	0.4	53.0	135.7	3.5

2-dimensional manifold (this occurs on average 93% of the time in our examples).

To compress $C_i^{\Delta D}$, we predict the material for each new principal simplex $s \in \text{star}(\{a_i\}) \cup \text{star}(\{b_i\}) \subset K^{i+1}$ by constructing an ordered set D_s of materials found in $\text{star}(\{a_i\}) \subset K^i$. To improve the coding model, the first materials in D_s are those of principal simplices in $\text{star}(s') \subset K^i$ where s' is the ancestor of s; the remaining materials in $\text{star}(\{a_i\}) \subset K^i$ are appended to D_s. The entry in $C_i^{\Delta D}$ associated with s is the index of its material in D_s, encoded arithmetically. If the material of s is not present in D_s, it is specified explicitly as a global index in D.

We encode $C_i^{\Delta A}$ by specifying the area a_s for each new principal simplex $s \in \mathcal{P}_{01}(\text{star}(\{a_i\}) \cup \text{star}(\{b_i\})) \subset K^{i+1}$. To account for this redistribution of area, we identify the principal simplex from which s receives its area by specifying its index in $\mathcal{P}_{01}(\text{star}(\{a_i\})) \subset K^i$.

The column labeled Σ in Table 1 sums the bits of each field of the *gvspl* records. Multiplying Σ by the number n of vertices in $\hat{M}$ gives the total number of bits for the PSC representation of the model (e.g. 500 KB for the destroyer). By way of comparison, the next column shows the number of bits per vertex required in a traditional "IndexedFaceSet" representation, with quantization of 16 bits per coordinate and arithmetic coding of face materials ($\simeq 3n \cdot 16 + 2n \cdot 3 \cdot \log_2 n$ + materials).

4 PSC CONSTRUCTION

In this section, we describe a scheme for iteratively choosing pairs of vertices to unify, in order to construct a PSC representation. Our algorithm, a generalization of [13], is time-intensive, seeking high quality approximations. It should be emphasized that many quality metrics are possible. For instance, the *quadric error* metric recently introduced by Garland and Heckbert [9] provides a different tradeoff of execution speed and visual quality.

As in [13, 20], we first compute a cost ΔE for each candidate *vunify* transformation, and enter the candidates into a priority queue ordered by ascending cost. Then, in each iteration $i = n-1 \ldots 1$, we perform the *vunify* at the front of the queue and update the costs of affected candidates.

4.1 Forming set $\mathcal{C}$ of candidate vertex pairs

In principle, we could enter all possible pairs of vertices from $\hat{M}$ into the priority queue, but this would be prohibitively expensive since simplification would then require at least $O(n^2 \log n)$ time. Instead, we would like to consider only a smaller set $\mathcal{C}$ of candidate vertex pairs. Naturally, $\mathcal{C}$ should include the 1-simplices of K. Additional pairs should also be included in $\mathcal{C}$ to allow distinct connected components of M to merge and to facilitate topological changes. We considered several schemes for forming these additional pairs, including binning, octrees, and k-closest neighbor graphs, but opted for the Delaunay triangulation because of its adaptability on models containing components at different scales.

We compute the Delaunay triangulation of the vertices of $\hat{M}$, represented as a 3-dimensional simplicial complex $\hat{K}_{DT}$. We define the initial set $\mathcal{C}$ to contain both the 1-simplices of $\hat{K}$ and the subset of 1-simplices of $\hat{K}_{DT}$ that connect vertices in different connected components of $\hat{K}$. During the simplification process, we apply each vertex unification performed on M to $\mathcal{C}$ as well in order to keep consistent the set of candidate pairs.

For models in $\mathbf{R}^3$, $\mathcal{C} \cap \text{star}(\{a_i\})$ has constant size in the average case, and the overall simplification algorithm requires $O(n \log n)$ time. (In the worst case, it could require $O(n^2 \log n)$ time.)

4.2 Selecting vertex unifications from $\mathcal{C}$

For each candidate vertex pair $(a, b) \in \mathcal{C}$, the associated $vunify(\{a\}, \{b\}) : M^i \leftarrow M^{i+1}$ is assigned the cost

$$\Delta E = \Delta E_{dist} + \Delta E_{disc} + E_{\Delta area} + E_{fold} .$$

As in [13], the first term is $\Delta E_{dist} = E_{dist}(M^i) - E_{dist}(M^{i+1})$, where $E_{dist}(M)$ measures the geometric accuracy of the approximate model M. Conceptually, $E_{dist}(M)$ approximates the continuous integral

$$\int_{\mathbf{p} \in \hat{M}} d^2(\mathbf{p}, M) ,$$

where $d(\mathbf{p}, M)$ is the Euclidean distance of the point $\mathbf{p}$ to the closest point on M. We discretize this integral by defining $E_{dist}(M)$ as the sum of squared distances to M from a dense set of points X sampled from the original model $\hat{M}$. We sample X from the set of principal simplices in K — a strategy that generalizes to arbitrary triangulated models.

In [13], $E_{disc}(M)$ measures the geometric accuracy of discontinuity curves formed by a set of sharp edges in the mesh. For the PSC representation, we generalize the concept of sharp edges to that of *sharp simplices* in K — a simplex is sharp either if it is a boundary simplex or if two of its parents are principal simplices with different material identifiers. The energy E_{disc} is defined as the sum of squared distances from a set X_{disc} of points sampled from sharp simplices to the discontinuity components from which they were sampled. Minimization of E_{disc} therefore preserves the geometry of material boundaries, normal discontinuities (creases), and triangulation boundaries (including boundary curves of a surface and endpoints of a curve).

We have found it useful to introduce a term $E_{\Delta area}$ that penalizes surface stretching (a more sophisticated version of the regularizing E_{spring} term of [13]). Let A_N^{i+1} be the sum of triangle areas in the neighborhood $\text{star}(\{a_i\}) \cup \text{star}(\{b_i\}) \subset K^{i+1}$, and A_N^i the sum of triangle areas in $\text{star}(\{a_i\}) \subset K^i$. The mean squared displacement over the neighborhood N due to the change in area can be approximated as $\overline{disp^2} = \frac{1}{2}(\sqrt{A_N^{i+1}} - \sqrt{A_N^i})^2$. We let $E_{\Delta area} = |X_N| \overline{disp^2}$, where $|X_N|$ is the number of points X projecting in the neighborhood.

To prevent model self-intersections, the last term E_{fold} penalizes surface folding. We compute the rotation of each oriented triangle in the neighborhood due to the vertex unification (as in [10, 20]). If

any rotation exceeds a threshold angle value, we set E_{fold} to a large constant.

Unlike [13], we do not optimize over the vertex position $\mathbf{v}_a^i$, but simply evaluate ΔE for $\mathbf{v}_a^i \in \{\mathbf{v}_a^{i+1}, \mathbf{v}_b^{i+1}, (\mathbf{v}_a^{i+1} + \mathbf{v}_b^{i+1})/2\}$ and choose the best one. This speeds up the optimization, improves model compression, and allows us to introduce non-quadratic energy terms like $E_{\Delta area}$.

5 RESULTS

Table 1 gives quantitative results for the examples in the figures and in the video. Simplification times for our prototype are measured on an SGI Indigo2 Extreme (150MHz R4400). Although these times may appear prohibitive, PSC construction is an off-line task that only needs to be performed once per model.

Figure 9 highlights some of the benefits of the PSC representation. The pearls in the chandelier model are initially disconnected tetrahedra; these tetrahedra merge and collapse into 1-d curves in lower-complexity approximations. Similarly, the numerous polygonal ropes in the schooner model are simplified into curves which can be rendered as line segments. The straps of the sandal model initially have some thickness; the top and bottom sides of these straps merge in the simplification. Also note the disappearance of the holes on the sandal straps. The castle example demonstrates that the original model need not be a mesh; here $\hat{M}$ is a 1-dimensional non-manifold obtained by extracting edges from an image.

6 RELATED WORK

There are numerous schemes for representing and simplifying triangulations in computer graphics. A common special case is that of subdivided 2-manifolds (meshes). Garland and Heckbert [12] provide a recent survey of mesh simplification techniques. Several methods simplify a given model through a sequence of edge collapse transformations [10, 13, 14, 20]. With the exception of [20], these methods constrain edge collapses to preserve the topological type of the model (e.g. disallow the collapse of a tetrahedron into a triangle).

Our work is closely related to several schemes that generalize the notion of edge collapse to that of vertex unification, whereby separate connected components of the model are allowed to merge and triangles may be collapsed into lower dimensional simplices. Rossignac and Borrel [21] overlay a uniform cubical lattice on the object, and merge together vertices that lie in the same cubes. Schaufler and Stürzlinger [22] develop a similar scheme in which vertices are merged using a hierarchical clustering algorithm. Luebke [18] introduces a scheme for locally adapting the complexity of a scene at runtime using a clustering octree. In these schemes, the approximating models correspond to simplicial complexes that would result from a set of *vunify* transformations (Section 3.3). Our approach differs in that we order the *vunify* in a carefully optimized sequence. More importantly, we define not only a simplification process, but also a new representation for the model using an encoding of $gvspl = vunify^{-1}$ transformations.

Recent, independent work by Schmalstieg and Schaufler [23] develops a similar strategy of encoding a model using a sequence of vertex split transformations. Their scheme differs in that it tracks only triangles, and therefore requires regular, 2-dimensional triangulations. Hence, it does not allow lower-dimensional simplices in the model approximations, and does not generalize to higher dimensions.

Some simplification schemes make use of an intermediate volumetric representation to allow topological changes to the model. He et al. [11] convert a mesh into a binary inside/outside function discretized on a three-dimensional grid, low-pass filter this function, and convert it back to a simpler surface using an adaptive "marching cubes" algorithm. They demonstrate that aliasing is reduced by rendering the filtered volume as a set of nested translucent surfaces. Similarly, Andújar et al. [1] make use of an inside/outside octree representation.

Triangulations of subdivided manifolds (and non-manifolds) of higher dimension are used extensively in solid modeling. Paoluzzi et al. [19] provide an overview of related work and analyze the benefits of representing such triangulations using (regular) simplicial complexes. Bertolotto et al. [3, 4] present hierarchical simplicial representations for subdivided manifolds, but these do not support changes of topological type.

Polyhedra can also be represented using more general representations. The simplicial set representation of Lang and Lienhardt [17] generalizes simplicial complexes to allow incomplete and degenerate simplices. Cell complexes, formed by subdividing manifolds into non-simplicial cells, can be represented using the radial edge structure of Weiler [29] or the cell tuple structure of Brisson [5].

7 SUMMARY AND FUTURE WORK

We have introduced the progressive simplicial complex representation, a new format for arbitrary triangulated models that captures both geometry and topology in a unified multiresolution framework. It defines a continuous-resolution sequence of approximating models, from the original model down to a single vertex. In addition, it allows geomorphs between any pair of models in this sequence, supports progressive transmission, and offers a concise storage format. We presented an optimization algorithm for constructing PSC representations for computer graphics surface models.

Although we restricted our examples in this paper to models of dimension at most 2, the PSC representation is defined for arbitrary dimensions, and we expect that it will find useful applications in the representation of higher dimensional models such as volumes, light fields, and bidirectional reflection distribution functions. In particular, it offers an avenue for level-of-detail control in volume rendering applications.

ACKNOWLEDGMENTS

We are extremely grateful to Viewpoint Datalabs for providing us with numerous meshes with which to experiment. We also wish to thank Tom Duchamp for helpful discussions on algebraic topology.

REFERENCES

[1] ANDÚJAR, C., AYALA, D., BRUNET, P., JOAN-ARINYO, R., AND SOLÉ, J. Automatic generation of multiresolution boundary representations. *Computer Graphics Forum (Proceedings of Eurographics '96) 15*, 3 (1996), 87–96.

[2] BAJAJ, C., AND SCHIKORE, D. Error-bounded reduction of triangle meshes with multivariate data. *SPIE 2656* (1996), 34–45.

[3] BERTOLOTTO, M., DE FLORIANI, L., BRUZZONE, E., AND PUPPO, E. Multiresolution representation of volume data through hierarchical simplicial complexes. In *Aspects of visual form processing* (1994), C. Arcelli, L. Cordella, and G. Sanniti di Baja, Eds., World Scientific, pp. 73–82.

[4] BERTOLOTTO, M., DE FLORIANI, L., AND MARZANO, P. Pyramidal simplicial complexes. In *Solid Modeling '95* (May 1995), pp. 153–162.

[5] BRISSON, E. *Representation of d-dimensional geometric objects*. PhD thesis, Dept. of Computer Science and Engineering, U. of Washington, 1990.

[6] CLARK, J. Hierarchical geometric models for visible surface algorithms. *Communications of the ACM 19*, 10 (October 1976), 547–554.

[7] DEERING, M. Geometry compression. *Computer Graphics (SIGGRAPH '95 Proceedings)* (1995), 13–20.

[8] FUNKHOUSER, T., AND SÉQUIN, C. Adaptive display algorithm for interactive frame rates during visualization of complex virtual environments. *Computer Graphics (SIGGRAPH '93 Proceedings)* (1993), 247–254.

[9] GARLAND, M., AND HECKBERT, P. Surface simplification using quadric error metrics. *Computer Graphics (SIGGRAPH '97 Proceedings)* (1997).

[10] GUÉZIEC, A. Surface simplification inside a tolerance volume. Research Report RC-20440, IBM, March 1996.

[11] HE, T., HONG, L., VARSHNEY, A., AND WANG, S. Controlled topology simplification. *IEEE Transactions on Visualization and Computer Graphics 2*, 2 (June 1996), 171–184.

[12] HECKBERT, P., AND GARLAND, M. Survey of polygonal surface simplification algorithms. Tech. Rep. CMU-CS-95-194, Carnegie Mellon University, 1995.

[13] HOPPE, H. Progressive meshes. *Computer Graphics (SIGGRAPH '96 Proceedings)* (1996), 99–108.

[14] HOPPE, H., DEROSE, T., DUCHAMP, T., MCDONALD, J., AND STUETZLE, W. Mesh optimization. *Computer Graphics (SIGGRAPH '93 Proceedings)* (1993), 19–26.

[15] HUDSON, J. *Piecewise Linear Topology*. W.A. Benjamin, Inc, 1969.

[16] JUNGERMAN, M., AND RINGEL, G. Minimal triangulations on orientable surfaces. *Acta Mathematica 145*, 1-2 (1980), 121–154.

[17] LANG, V., AND LIENHARDT, P. Geometric modeling with simplicial sets. In *Pacific Graphics '95* (August 1995), pp. 475–493.

[18] LUEBKE, D. Hierarchical structures for dynamic polygonal simplification. TR 96-006, Department of Computer Science, University of North Carolina at Chapel Hill, 1996.

[19] PAOLUZZI, A., BERNARDINI, F., CATTANI, C., AND FERRUCCI, V. Dimension-independent modeling with simplicial complexes. *ACM Transactions on Graphics 12*, 1 (January 1993), 56–102.

[20] RONFARD, R., AND ROSSIGNAC, J. Full-range approximation of triangulated polyhedra. *Computer Graphics Forum (Proceedings of Eurographics '96) 15*, 3 (1996), 67–76.

[21] ROSSIGNAC, J., AND BORREL, P. Multi-resolution 3D approximations for rendering complex scenes. In *Modeling in Computer Graphics*, B. Falcidieno and T. L. Kunii, Eds. Springer-Verlag, 1993, pp. 455–465.

[22] SCHAUFLER, G., AND STÜRZLINGER, W. Generating multiple levels of detail from polygonal geometry models. In *Virtual Environments '95 (Eurographics Workshop)* (January 1995), M. Göbel, Ed., Springer Verlag, pp. 33–41.

[23] SCHMALSTIEG, D., AND SCHAUFLER, G. Smooth levels of detail. In *Proc. of IEEE 1997 Virtual Reality Annual Intnl. Symp.* (1997), pp. 12–19.

[24] SCHROEDER, W., ZARGE, J., AND LORENSEN, W. Decimation of triangle meshes. *Computer Graphics (SIGGRAPH '92 Proceedings) 26*, 2 (1992), 65–70.

[25] SPANIER, E. H. *Algebraic Topology*. McGraw-Hill, New York, 1966.

[26] TAUBIN, G., AND ROSSIGNAC, J. Geometry compression through topological surgery. Research Report RC-20340, IBM, January 1996.

[27] TURK, G. Re-tiling polygonal surfaces. *Computer Graphics (SIGGRAPH '92 Proceedings) 26*, 2 (1992), 55–64.

[28] WAVEFRONT TECHNOLOGIES, INC. *Wavefront File Formats, Version 4.0 RG-10-004*, first ed. Santa Barbara, CA, 1993.

[29] WEILER, K. The radial edge structure: a topological representation for non-manifold geometric boundary modeling. In *Geometric modeling for CAD applications*. Elsevier Science Publish., 1988.

[30] WITTEN, I., NEAL, R., AND CLEARY, J. Arithmetic coding for data compression. *Communications of the ACM 30*, 6 (June 1987), 520–540.

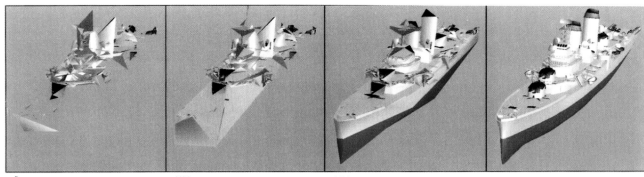

M^0; 1,154 verts; 2,522 tris M^{1739}; 2,893 verts; 6,000 tris M^{2739}; 3,893 verts; 8,000 tris $M^{n=82645}$; 83,799 verts; 167,744 tris

Figure 7: From a given mesh $\hat{M}$, the PM representation [13] captures a sequence of meshes $M^0 \ldots M^n = \hat{M}$. Because all approximations M^i must have the same topological type, the base mesh M^0 may still be complex.

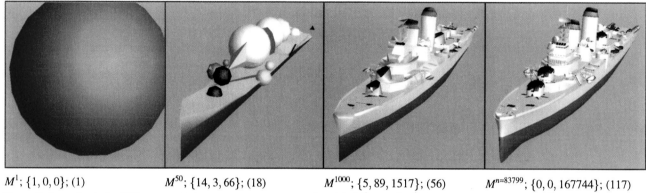

M^1; $\{1, 0, 0\}$; (1) M^{50}; $\{14, 3, 66\}$; (18) M^{1000}; $\{5, 89, 1517\}$; (56) $M^{n=83799}$; $\{0, 0, 167744\}$; (117)

Figure 8: In contrast, the PSC representation captures a sequence of models $M^1 \ldots M^n = \hat{M}$ in which the base model M^1 always consists of a single vertex. All geometric and topological information is encoded progressively by a sequence of generalized vertex split transformations. The image captions indicate the number of principal $\{0, 1, 2\}$-simplices respectively and the number of connected components (in parenthesis). Note that even M^{1000} looks markedly better than the 8000-triangle PM approximation.

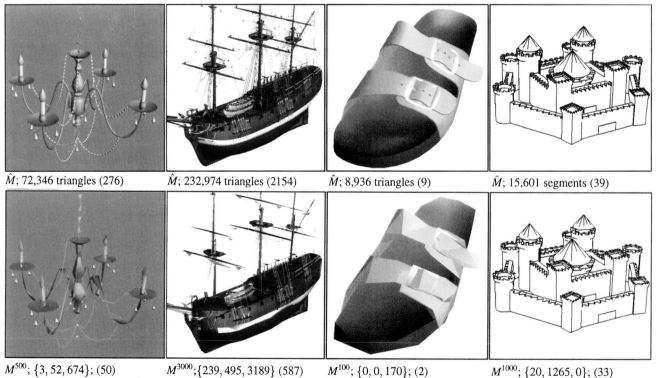

$\hat{M}$; 72,346 triangles (276) $\hat{M}$; 232,974 triangles (2154) $\hat{M}$; 8,936 triangles (9) $\hat{M}$; 15,601 segments (39)

M^{500}; $\{3, 52, 674\}$; (50) M^{3000}; $\{239, 495, 3189\}$ (587) M^{100}; $\{0, 0, 170\}$; (2) M^{1000}; $\{20, 1265, 0\}$; (33)

Figure 9: For each column, the top row shows the original model and the bottom row shows one approximation in the PSC sequence. The image captions indicate the number of principal $\{0, 1, 2\}$-simplices respectively and the number of connected components (in parenthesis).

Tour Into the Picture:

Using a Spidery Mesh Interface to Make Animation from a Single Image

Youichi Horry[*‡]   Ken-ichi Anjyo[†]   Kiyoshi Arai[*]

Hitachi, Ltd.

ABSTRACT

A new method called TIP (Tour Into the Picture) is presented for easily making animations from one 2D picture or photograph of a scene. In TIP, animation is created from the viewpoint of a camera which can be three-dimensionally "walked or flown-through" the 2D picture or photograph. To make such animation, conventional computer vision techniques cannot be applied in the 3D modeling process for the scene, using only a single 2D image. Instead a spidery mesh is employed in our method to obtain a simple scene model from the 2D image of the scene using a graphical user interface. Animation is thus easily generated without the need of multiple 2D images.

Unlike existing methods, our method is not intended to construct a precise 3D scene model. The scene model is rather simple, and not fully 3D-structured. The modeling process starts by specifying the vanishing point in the 2D image. The background in the scene model then consists of at most five rectangles, whereas hierarchical polygons are used as a model for each foreground object. Furthermore a virtual camera is moved around the 3D scene model, with the viewing angle being freely controlled. This process is easily and effectively performed using the spidery mesh interface. We have obtained a wide variety of animated scenes which demonstrate the efficiency of TIP.

CR Categories and Subject Descriptors: I.3.3 [Computer Graphics]: Picture/Image Generation - viewing algorithms; I.3.7 [Computer Graphics] Three-dimensional Graphics and Realism, Animation

Additional Keywords: graphical user interface, image-based modeling/rendering, vanishing point, field-of-view angle

1 INTRODUCTION

Making animation from one picture, painting, or photograph is not a new idea. Such animations have been mainly used for

[*]Central Research Laboratory, 1-280 Higashi-Koigakubo Kokubunji Tokyo 185
{horry, arai}@crl.hitachi.co.jp
[†]Visualware Planning Department, 4-6 Kanda-Surugadai Chiyoda Tokyo 101
anjyo@cm.head.hitachi.co.jp
[‡]Currently visiting INRIA Rocquencourt, Domaine de Volceau - Rocquencourt 78153 Le Chesnay Cedex France horry@bora.inria.fr

art and entertainment purposes, often with striking visual effects. For instance, 2D animations are commonly seen, where 2D figures of persons or animals in the original image move around, with the 2D background fixed. In relatively simple cases, these animations may be created using traditional cel animation techniques. If the animations are computer-generated, then 2D digital effects, such as warping and affine transformations, can also be employed.

However, it is still hard and tedious for a skilled animator to make computer animations from a single 2D image of a 3D scene without knowing its 3D structure, even if established digital techniques are fully available. When the input image is given in advance, first of all, the animator has to make the 3D scene model by trial and error until the projected image of the model fits well with the input image of the scene. At the very beginning of this process, the virtual camera position in 3D space must also be known as one of the conditions for the input image to be regenerated from the scene model. This poses the question, how is the camera position known by a single image ? Unfortunately existing approaches to create models directly from photographs, such as image-based techniques, require multiple input images of photographs, and the cases discussed in this paper are outside their scope. If animating a painting is desired, making the animation may become more difficult, because a painting does not give as precise information for creating the 3D scene model as a photograph does.

The best possible approach currently available to making animation from a single image therefore depends largely on the skill, sense, and eye of the animators, though this naivety may place an excessive and tedious task load on the animators. They can then develop the scene structure freely, using vague and incomplete information included in the input to animate the scene to their liking. The scene structure, however, may still be incomplete. A more straightforward method is thus desired for creating the scene animation, in which the 3D modeling process of the scene is rather simplified or skipped.

In this paper we propose a simple method, which we call TIP (Tour Into the Picture), for making animations from one 2D picture or photograph of a scene. This method provides a simple scene model, which is extracted from the animator's mind. Thus the scene model is not exactly 3D structured, but is geometrically just a collection of "billboards" and several 3D polygons. Therefore, the animations obtained with our method are not strictly three-dimensional. However, as we show, the proposed method allows easy creation of various animations, such as "walk-through" or "fly-through", while visually giving convincing 3D quality.

1.1 Related work

If a photograph is used as the 2D input image, then image-based methods, including [2, 4, 7] may be used effectively. In [2], the panoramic image is made from overlapping photographs taken by a regular camera to represent a virtual environment, so that real-time walk-through animations can be made with the viewpoint fixed. The method in [7] provides animations, with many closely spaced images being required as input, and its theoretical background largely relies on computer vision techniques. This work can also be considered to belong to the category of techniques for light field representation [6], which gives a new framework for rendering new views using large arrays of both rendered and digitized images. Similarly, in [4] a "sparse" set of photographs is used for existing architectural scenes to be animated. Though the input condition is improved due to architectural use, multiple input images are still required. Despite successful results with these image-based approaches, we need a new methodology, especially for dealing with the situations where the input is a single photograph.

For paintings or illustrations, there are relatively fewer research reports on their animation. A new rendering technique was presented in [8] for making painterly animations. Assuming that the 3D geometric models of the objects in a scene are known in advance, animations in a painterly style are then made by the method using 3D particles and 2D brush strokes.

Morphing techniques including [1] provide 3D effects visually, requiring at least two images as input, although actually only 2D image transformations are used. For example the view interpolation technique [3] is an efficient application of morphing, which generates intermediate images, from images prestored at nearby viewpoints. View morphing [9] also gives a strong sense of 3D metamorphosis in the transition between images of the objects. Then we note that most of these techniques require no knowledge of 3D shape in morphing.

Existing methods cited above work effectively, when multiple input images are available, or when the 3D geometric structure of a scene to be animated is known in advance. Our approach treats the cases when one input image of a scene is given without any knowledge of 3D shapes in the scene. Theoretically it is impossible to create an animation from a single view of the scene. Instead, our approach actually gives a new type of visual effect for making various animations, rather than constructing a rigid 3D model and animation of the scene.

1.2 Main Idea

If we consider traditional paintings or landscape photographs, their perspective views give a strong impression that the scenes depicted are 3D. It is hard for us to find an *exact* position for the vanishing point of the scene in the picture. In particular, for paintings or drawings, the vanishing point is not precisely prescribed, being largely dependent on the artist's imagination. Therefore, rigid approaches, such as computer vision techniques, are not valid for the purpose of exactly finding the vanishing point. However, it is relatively easy for us to *roughly* specify the vanishing point, by manually drawing guide lines for perspective viewing. Then we can expect that the "visually 3D" geometry of the scene's background is defined as a simple model (with polygons, for instance) centering around the *user-specified* vanishing point. Similarly, in many cases, we can easily tell the foreground objects from the background through our own eyes. A simple and intuitive model of the foreground object can then be like a "billboard" that stands on a polygon of the background model.

The main idea of the proposed method is simply to provide a user interface which allows the user to easily and interactively perform the following operations.

(1) Adding "virtual" vanishing points for the scene - The specification of the vanishing point should be done by the user, not automatically, as mentioned above.

(2) Distinguishing foreground objects from background - The decision as to whether an object in the scene is near the viewer should be made by the user, since no 3D geometry of the scene is known. In other words, this means that the user can freely position the foreground object, with the camera parameters being arranged.

(3) Constructing the background scene and the foreground objects by simple polygons - In order to approximate the geometry of the background scene, several polygons should be generated to represent the background. This model is then a polyhedron-like form with the vanishing point being on its base. The "billboard"-like representation and its variation are used for foreground objects.

These three operations are closely related to each other so that

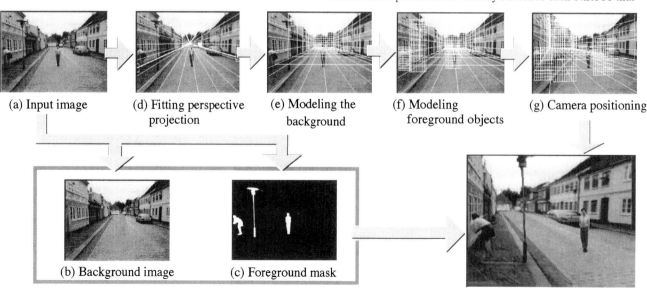

(a) Input image   (d) Fitting perspective projection   (e) Modeling the background   (f) Modeling foreground objects   (g) Camera positioning

(b) Background image   (c) Foreground mask

(h) Rendered image

Figure 1. Process flow diagram

the interactive user interface should be able to provide their easy and simultaneous performance. A *spidery mesh* is the key to fulfilling this requirement.

The proposed method is outlined as follows. Fig. 1 shows the process flow.

After an input image is digitized (Fig.1 (a)), the 2D image of the background and 2D mask image of the foreground objects are made (Figs. 1 (b), (c)). TIP uses a spidery mesh to prescribe a few perspective conditions, including the specification of a vanishing point (Fig. 1 (d)). In the current implementation of TIP, we can specify one vanishing point for a scene. This is not restrictive because many paintings, illustrations, or photographs can actually be considered one-point perspective, and because, as demonstrated later, the one-point perspective representation using spidery mesh works very well even for the cases where it is hard for us to tell if the input is one-point perspective or not.

Next, the background is modeled with less than five 3D rectangles (Fig. 1 (e)), and simple polygonal models for the foreground objects are also constructed (Fig. 1 (f)). Finally, by changing the virtual camera parameters (Fig. 1 (g)), images at different views are rendered (Fig. 1 (h)), so that the desired animation is obtained.

In section **2** the modeling process of the 3D scene (Figs. 1 (a) - (f)) in TIP is described. In section **3**, after the rendering technique (Figs. 1 (g), (h)) is briefly mentioned, several animation examples are shown, which demonstrate well the efficiency and usefulness of the proposed method. Conclusions and future research directions of the method are summarized in section **4**.

2   SCENE MODELING FROM A SINGLE IMAGE

In our method we use one picture or photograph of a 3D scene as input, from which we wish to make a computer animation. Then we specify one "virtual" (i.e. "user-specified") vanishing point for the scene. As described later, this does not always mean that the input image must be one-point perspective. For convenience, the line that goes through the vanishing point and view point is vertical to the view plane. As for camera positioning, default values of camera position, view-plane normal, and view angle (field-of-view angle) are assigned in advance (see [5] for technical terms). These parameters are changed later using our GUI (Graphical User Interface) in **3.1** for making animations. For simplicity, the input images used are taken by the virtual camera without tilting, (though actually this condition can easily be eliminated). This means that the view up vector, which is parallel to the view plane in this paper, is vertical to the ground of the 3D scene to be modeled.

2.1 Foreground Mask and Background Image

In the modeling process we first derive two types of image information from the input 2D image: *foreground mask* and *background image*. Let F_1, F_2 ,..., F_p be subimages of the input image I, each of which is supposed to correspond to a foreground object in the 3D scene and is relatively close to the virtual camera. In practice the subimages $\{F_i\}_{1 \leq i \leq p}$ are specified by a user and are modeled as polygonal objects in the corresponding 3D scene (see **2.3**). The *foreground mask* is then defined as the 2D image consisting of $\{\alpha_i\}_{1 \leq i \leq p}$, where α_i is a grey-scaled masking value (α-value) of F_i. The *background image* is the 2D image which is made from I by retouching the traces of $\{F_i\}$ after the subimages $\{F_i\}$ are removed from I. The retouching process consists of occluding the traces of these subimages using color information for the neighborhood of each point (pixel) in F_i.

There is commercially available software, such as 2D paint tools, that enable us to easily make 2D images for the foreground mask and the background, from an input image. Fig.1 presented an example. Fig.1(a) showed the input image (of a photograph). The background image in Fig. 1 (b), as well as the foreground mask in Fig. 1 (c), were obtained using a standard 2D paint tool. To get the foreground mask in Fig. 1 (c), a street lamp and two persons were selected by the user, as the subimages $\{F_i\}$ mentioned above.

2.2 Specifying the Vanishing Point and Inner Rectangle

In order to model the 3D scene from the input image, we use our software called TIP, starting with the specification of the vanishing point of this image. TIP employs a unique GUI with a spidery mesh, which plays an essential role not only in the specification process but also in the processes thereafter.

Fig. 2 (a) shows the initial state of the spidery mesh in applying it to the input image in Fig. 1 (a). In general, as illustrated in Fig. 2 (a), the spidery mesh is defined as the 2D figure consisting of: a vanishing point; and an inner rectangle, which intuitively means the window out of which we look at infinity; radial lines that radiate from the vanishing point; an outer rectangle which corresponds to the outer frame of the input image. Each side of the inner rectangle is made to be parallel to a side of the outer rectangle. In TIP, the specification of the inner rectangle is done as well as that of the vanishing point. It should then be noted that, as described later, the inner rectangle is also used to specify the *rear window* in the 3D space (see **2.3** and **2.4**). The rear window is a border that the virtual camera, which will be used in making an animation, cannot go through. The inner rectangle is consequently defined as the 2D projection of this window onto the 2D image space (i.e., the projection plane). In practice the 3D window is considered to be so distant from the current (initial) position of the virtual camera, that the camera does not zoom in beyond this window from the current position.

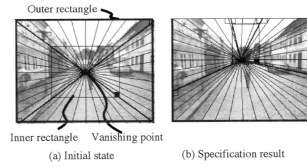

Outer rectangle

Inner rectangle   Vanishing point

(a) Initial state   (b) Specification result

Figure 2. Spidery mesh on the 2D image

We now describe how to use the spidery mesh in order to specify the vanishing point. As described above, we then position the inner rectangle, along with the vanishing point. First we consider typical cases where the vanishing point is located in the input image (i.e., within the outer rectangle of the spidery mesh). Fig. 3 (a) is such a case. Then, using a pointing device (a mouse in the current implementation), we can control the geometry of the spidery mesh using the following functions.

[a] Deformation of the inner rectangle - If the right-bottom edge of the inner rectangle is dragged with the pointing device, then the left-top edge of the rectangle is fixed, and the right-bottom edge is moved according

to the dragging (see Fig. 3 (a)).

[b] Translation of the inner rectangle - If we drag a point on one of the sides of the rectangle (except the point at the right-bottom corner), then the rectangle is moved by the dragging distance (Fig. 3 (b)).

[c] Translation of the vanishing point - If the vanishing point is dragged, then it is translated. The four radial lines, which are drawn boldly in Fig. 3, are also moved under the condition that these radial lines always go through the four edges of the inner rectangle, respectively (Fig. 3 (c)). If the cursor is dragged out of the inner rectangle, then the vanishing point is moved in the direction, and by the distance of, the dragging. Conversely, if one of these bold radial lines is translated by moving its edge on the outer rectangle, the vanishing point is moved based on a certain rule that we call *servility of the vanishing point* to the four (bold) radial lines. This means, for example, that, if we drag the edge of radial line L_1 in Fig. 3 (d) along the outer rectangle, then radial line L_2 is fixed and the vanishing point is moved along L_2. The dotted lines in Fig. 3 (d) show the new positions of the bold radial lines with the source point of the dotted lines obtained as a result for the vanishing point.

Using these functions in our GUI, we can specify the vanishing point and the inner rectangle. In practice the radial lines are very helpful in the specification process. For example a user can specify the vanishing point, while controlling the radial lines so that they go along the borderlines between buildings and roads (see Fig. 2 (b)). Then servility of the vanishing point in [c] is useful in controlling the radial lines. It should also be noted that the concept of the spidery mesh is totally 2D, which assures easy-to-use and real-time feedback in the specification process.

As for the cases when the vanishing point is out of the input image (outer rectangle), functions similar to those described above can be applied, so that the inner rectangle is specified in the outer rectangle.

2.3 Modeling the 3D Background

The next thing we do is to model the 3D background of the scene using very few polygons.

Let us suppose that the vanishing point and the inner rectangle are specified as shown in Fig. 4 (a). We can then

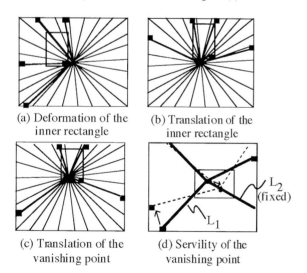

(a) Deformation of the inner rectangle

(b) Translation of the inner rectangle

(c) Translation of the vanishing point

(d) Servility of the vanishing point

Figure 3. Controlling the spidery mesh

make a 2D decomposition of the outer rectangle into five smaller regions each of which is a 2D polygon in the outer rectangle. As illustrated in Fig.4 (b), the five 2D rectangles may be deduced from these regions, and the rectangles are tentatively called the floor, right wall, left wall, rear wall, and ceiling, respectively (the rear wall is actually the inner rectangle). We define the textures of these 2D rectangles to be taken from the background image. Suppose that these rectangles are the projection of the 3D rectangles. We name each of these 3D rectangles the same as the 2D corresponding projection. We then define the 3D background model in 3D space as being these five 3D rectangles, assuming that the following conditions hold:

[A-1] Every adjacent 3D rectangle mentioned above is orthogonal to the others.

[A-2] The 3D rear wall is parallel to the view plane.

[A-3] The 3D floor is orthogonal to the view up vector.

[A-4] The textures of the 3D rectangles are inherited from those of the corresponding 2D rectangles.

The vertices of these 3D rectangles are therefore easily estimated. For simplicity, we set the coordinate system of the 3D space so that the view up vector = (0, 1, 0) and the 3D floor is on the plane y = 0. Then the vertices of the 3D rectangles, which are numbered as shown in Fig. 4 (c), are

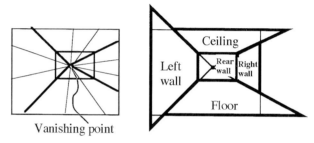

(a) Specified spidery mesh   (b) Deduced 2D polygons

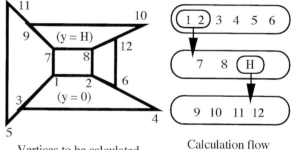

Vertices to be calculated   Calculation flow

(c) Estimating the vertices of the 3D rectangles

(d) 3D background model obtained

Figure 4. Modeling the 3D background

calculated as follows (also see calculation flow in Fig. 4 (c)). First we note that the 3D coordinate values of a point are easily obtained, if we know that it is on a certain (known) plane, and that its view plane coordinate values are known. Since we see the 2D positions of vertices 1 - 4 in Fig. 4 (c), we get the 3D positions of these four points, considering that these are on the plane y = 0. Similarly we get the values of vertices 5 and 6. Next we consider the plane which the 3D rear wall is on. The equation of this plane is then known, because it is vertical to the plane y = 0 containing the known vertices 1 and 2. Since vertices 7 and 8 are on this known plane, we can get the values of these two vertices. Then we estimate the "height" of the 3D ceiling. Since the 3D ceiling is on the plane parallel to the plane y = 0, we may assume that the 3D ceiling is on the plane y = H, for some H. If calculation of the y-values of vertices 7 and 8 contained no error, the y-values would be equal to H. However, in our implementation, we set H as the mean of the two y-values, in order to avoid errors. Thereafter, the y-values of vertices 7 and 8 are reset as being H. Consequently the remaining vertices 9 -12 are estimated.

The 3D background model described above employs five rectangles, as shown in Figs.4 (c), (d). There are, however, some other cases when the background model uses fewer 3D rectangles. Treatments including these special cases are briefly described later in **3.3**, along with the application examples.

2.4 Hierarchical Polygonal Models for the Foreground Objects

For the foreground objects in the scene, the foreground mask is prepared in advance. Based on the mask information, we construct the 3D polygonal model for a foreground object in the scene as described below. For simplicity, this model is hereafter referred to as a foreground object model.

First we consider the case in which the foreground object model is a quadrangle. The 2D quadrangle in the input image is then specified, so as to surround the 2D image of a foreground object (i.e., F_i in **2.1**). Next we specify the 3D position of the quadrangle in the 3D background model, under the condition that the quadrangle should be perpendicularly put on one of the five 3D regions: floor, right wall, left wall, rear wall, and ceiling. In the example of Fig. 5 (a), the person is a foreground object to be modeled, and is surrounded by the quadrangle (which is a rectangle in this case). The quadrangle in the 3D scene is perpendicularly attached to the 3D floor. By an argument similar to that in **2.3**, we know the 3D positions of P_0 and P_1 in Fig. 5 (b). Then we get the equation of the plane which the quadrangle is on, and consequently the 3D positions of P_2 and P_3 are known. Thus the 3D quadrangle, which is the polygonal model for the person in Fig. 5 (a), is explicitly specified. In Fig. 5 (c), each of the three foreground objects (see Fig. 1 (a)) is modeled with a single 3D polygon, which has a fine mesh for clarity.

If the foreground object models are all quadrangles, the models may be restrictive in dealing with more complicated objects. The foreground object models in our method are therefore endowed with a hierarchical structure in the sense that

1) Each model consists of one or more polygons. In particular a single polygon itself is a foreground object model.

2) For any polygon F_1 belonging to the model, another polygon F_2 can be added to the model, if F_2 is orthogonally attached to F_1 so that one side of F_2 is on F_1. Then F_2 is called a child of F_1 (or F_1 is a parent of F_2). This constitutes a hierarchy among the polygons belonging to a foreground object model.

3) If a polygon of the model is at the highest level in the hierarchy, it is orthogonally attached to one of the five 3D regions of the 3D background. Then only one side of the highest level is only on the region.

Fig. 6 illustrates how to construct the foreground object models. First, two quadrangles F_0 and F_1 are defined on the 3D floor (top sketch). Then F_2 is added to F_1 (middle sketch); and F_3 is added to F_2 (bottom sketch). In this way the

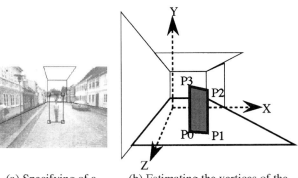

(a) Specifying of a foreground object   (b) Estimating the vertices of the foreground object model

(c) Three foreground object models

Figure 5. Modeling foreground objects

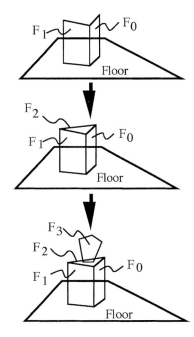

Figure 6. **Hierarchical positioning of the foreground objects**

foreground object models become more flexible (see **3.3** for a more concrete example).

3 ANIMATING AND RENDERING THE 3D SCENE

3.1 Camera Positioning

This section describes how to decide the virtual camera position for making an animation of the 3D scene. In using the virtual camera in our method, three parameters can be controlled: camera position, view-plane normal (vector), and view angle (i.e., field-of-view angle).

To visually control these parameters, the following commands are supported by our GUI in TIP, so that they are specified using pointing-device operations.

[a] Rotation: The view-plane normal is changed by rotations. This essentially means panning and tilting at a fixed camera position.

[b] Translation: With the view-plane normal fixed, the viewpoint (camera position) goes up and down; and right and left.

[c] Zoom: The viewpoint is moved in the direction of the fixed view-plane normal.

[d] View angle: The magnitude of the view angle is controlled with the viewpoint and the view-plane normal fixed.

[e] Look around: After selecting the center of attention at an object in the scene, the viewpoint is changed on a sphere whose center is the center of attention and whose radius is equal to the distance between the viewpoint and the center of attention.

3.2 Rendering via 2D-3D Transformations

The rendering method in TIP which is briefly described below is useful in making animation, particularly on a standard PC. The rendering procedure essentially involves an ordinary texture mapping technique. Of course much faster rendering techniques are available when using a powerful workstation.

Let (h_0, v_0) be an arbitrary point (pixel) in the 2D image to be rendered. Since we have the simple models for the 3D scene, as described in **2.3** and **2.4**, we can get the 3D point **P** which is projected to (h_0, v_0). We also know the 2D point (h_1, v_1) that is the 2D projection of **P** with the initial camera position. If **P** is a point on the 3D background model, then the color at (h_0, v_0) in the output image is the color C_A at (h_1, v_1) in the background image mentioned in **2.1**. (C_A is the mean value of the colors at the four pixels nearest to (h_1, v_1).) If **P** is a point on a foreground object model, we also know the color C_B at (h_1, v_1) in the input image and that there exists the subimage F_i including (h_1, v_1). The color at (h_0, v_0) in the output image is then defined as $(1 - \alpha_i) C_A + \alpha_i C_B$, where α_i is taken from the foreground mask.

3.3 Animation Examples

The camera positioning and the rendering processes described

(a) Input image   (b)-(d) Rendered images

Figure 7. Animation example preserving the view angle

above are performed by turns, in order to get a desired animation. The animation is then made by a key-framing method, based on the camera positioning information. The rendering process may still be rather time-consuming, compared to the camera positioning, and may be a bottleneck especially when performing a real-time walk-through by TIP on a standard PC. Previewing at lower resolutions would then be effective.

The following animations are TIP-implemented on a standard PC. The pixel resolutions of all the images in the animations have resolutions of 640×480 pixels. The wall clock time for rendering per frame is on average 0.1 sec, while real-time previewing is performed at 320×240 pixels.

The first animation example is made from the landscape painting in Fig. 7 (a)[§], which we can clearly take for a one-perspective projection. The frames in Figs. 7 (b) - (d), following the input image in Fig. 7 (a), are excerpts from the animation. Since the trees at the left-front of the input image are modeled as a foreground object (with a single quadrangle), the scene in Fig.7 (b) is generated by setting the virtual camera in front of the trees. In Fig. 7 (c) the camera goes up toward the top of the trees, using the translation of camera movement (see [b] in **3.1**). Then the camera zooms in toward the figures in the center, which are a foreground object model defined as a single quadrangle. The natural perspective views, with the view angle fixed, which cannot be achieved by traditional 2D image extension operations, are obtained in this animation. It should be noted that the vanishing point cannot be uniquely specified. This may be a drawback for knowing the exact position of the vanishing point. However, if we wish to have a variety of animations from one 2D picture, the non-uniqueness of the vanishing point is a big advantage. Actually, just by changing the geometry of the spidery mesh, different types of animations from the same input image are provided.

The next animation example is made from the input image in Fig. 8 (a), which is not clearly identified with a one-point perspective projection. However, we can model the scene from this image, by specifying the vanishing point. The dynamic changes in Figs. 8 (b)-(d) are then obtained by our method. Though we may apply the spidery mesh in Fig. 4 (a) to this case, specifying the five rectangles as the 3D background in Fig. 4 (c), a simplified spidery mesh in Fig. 8 (e) is more convenient for practical use. In addition, the 3D background model is rather simple, as shown in Fig. 8 (f). It actually consists of only two rectangles for the floor and the rear wall.

The third example in Fig. 9 illustrates the efficiency of the foreground object model. In Fig. 9 (a), the input image is shown, and the linework in Fig. 9 (b) presents the modeled scene. The box-like object and the plant in Fig. 9 (a) are then considered as one foreground object which has an hierarchical structure (see **2.4**). As shown with the linework, the box-like object is modeled with several polygons, while a single polygon is used for the plant. The polygonal models in Fig. 9 (c) are used for previewing, and then Fig. 9 (d) gives a different view in the obtained animation.

The final example in Fig. 10 shows view angle effects. It is very interesting that, in a one-point perspective view, the view angle can be specified independently of the other

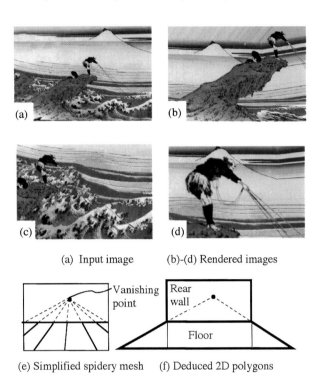

(a) Input image   (b)-(d) Rendered images

(e) Simplified spidery mesh   (f) Deduced 2D polygons

Figure 8. Animation example using the 3D background modeled with two rectangles

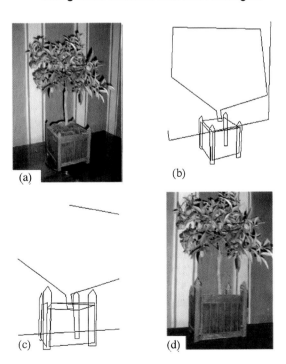

(a) Input image   (b) 3D scene model obtained
(c) Different view of the 3D scene model   (d) Rendered image

Figure 9. Animation example with the foreground object model hierarchically positioned

---

[§] Hitachi Viewseum image (http://www.viewsium.com); The Hudson River Portfolio Engraved by J.R. Smith (1775-1849) and John Hill (1770-1850) from watercolors by William GuyWall (1792-c.1862) View Near Fishkill, c. 1821-25
Engraving/acquatint with hand-painted watercolor, 13 15/16 x 21 1/8" (image only, no text) Published by Henry I. Megary & W.B. Gilley, New York, and John Mill, Charleston, S.C., 1823
Gift of Miss Susan D. Bliss Collection The Hudson River Museum of Westchester Photo: Quesada/Burke

parameters. Based on the photograph in Fig.10 (a), completely different animations can be generated just by changing the view angles. Figs.10 (b) and (c) show different views with different view angles, both of which are excerpts from the animations starting with the same frame in Fig. 10 (a).

4 CONCLUSION AND FUTURE WORK

Creating 3D animations from one 2D picture or photograph of a 3D scene is possible for a skilled animator but often very laborious, since precise information for making the 3D scene model cannot be extracted from the single 2D image. However, the incompleteness of 3D information derived from one image allows animators to create the 3D scene model in a more flexible way. In this paper we have proposed a new technique called TIP which provides a simple scene model that transforms the animator's imaginings into reality. The key to our method lies in the GUI using a spidery mesh, which allows animators to easily model the 3D scene. This lets animators utilize the incomplete 3D scene information to freely create scenery to their liking and obtain enjoyable and "visually 3D" animations.

In this paper we restricted ourselves to the cases where only one vanishing point is specified by the animator. The animation examples demonstrated that our method works very well, without insisting that an input image is strictly one-point perspective projection. Actually, we showed that relaxing use of the one-point perspective representation can allow new visual effects for animations. For example, we can get various background and foreground models just by changing the geometry of the spidery mesh, which therefore provides different types of animations from the same input image. Changing field-of-view angle also provides a new visual deformation effect.

Of course there are many things to do next. Hierarchical foreground mask information would be more powerful in describing the scenes with more complex foreground objects. Multiresolution images would support finer zooming. We are currently extending our method, in order to treat two-point perspective projections. Two-point perspective is commonly used in the various fields of engineering, industrial design and advertising drawings. Unlike one-point perspective, the field-of-view angle is uniquely fixed so that the animations obtained will be more rigid, but still have many applications. Such an extended version of TIP would thus be used mainly for engineering or industrial design, whereas the current version

provides new and easy-to-use visual effects for making animations in art and entertainment.

ACKNOWLEDGMENTS
We are very grateful to the anonymous reviewers for their invaluable suggestions which made this a significantly better paper. Many thanks go to Tsuneya Kurihara and Hiroyuki Nomura for discussions at the early stages of this work. Thanks to Carol Kikuchi and Peter Lee for proofreading and comments. Thanks also to KimuAyu for her help and encouragement.

REFERENCES

[1] Beier, T., and Neely, S. "Feature-Based Image Metamorphosis" Proc. SIGGRAPH '92 (Chicago, Illinois, July 26 - 31, 1992). In Computer Graphics, 26, 2 (July 1992), pp. 35-42.

[2] Chen, S. E. "Quicktime VR - An Image-based Approach to Virtual Environment Navigation" Proc. SIGGRAPH '95 (Los Angels, California, August 6 -11, 1995). In Computer Graphics Proceedings, Annual Conference Series, 1995. ACM SIGGRAPH, pp. 29-38.

[3] Chen, S. E. and Williams, L. "View Interpolation for Image Synthesis" Proc. SIGGRAPH '93 (Anaheim, California, August 1 - 6, 1993). In Computer Graphics Proceedings, Annual Conference Series, 1993. ACM SIGGRAPH, pp. 279-288.

[4] Devebec, P.E., Taylor C.A., and Malik J. "Modeling and Rendering Architecture from Photographs: A Hybrid Geometry- and Image- based Approach" Proc. SIGGRAPH '96 (New Orleans, Louisiana, August 4 - 9, 1996). In Computer Graphics Proceedings, Annual Conference Series, 1996. ACM SIGGRAPH, pp. 11-20.

[5] Foley, J.D., van Dam, A., Feiner, S.K., and Hughes, J.F. Computer Graphics: Principles and Practice, Addison-Wesley, Reading, Mass., 1990.

[6] Levoy, M. and Hanrahan, P. "Light Field Rendering" Proc. SIGGRAPH '96 (New Orleans, Louisiana, August 4 - 9, 1996). In Computer Graphics Proceedings, Annual Conference Series, 1996. ACM SIGGRAPH, pp. 31- 42.

[7] McMillan, L. and Bishop, G. "Plenoptic Modeling: An Image-based Rendering System" Proc. SIGGRAPH '95 (Los Angels, California, August 6 -11, 1995). In Computer Graphics Proceedings, Annual Conference Series, 1995. ACM SIGGRAPH, pp. 39-46.

[8] Meier, B.J. "Painterly Rendering for Animation" Proc. SIGGRAPH '96 (New Orleans, Louisiana, August 4 - 9, 1996). In Computer Graphics Proceedings, Annual Conference Series, 1996. ACM SIGGRAPH, pp. 477-484.

[9] Seitz, S. M., and Dyer, C.R. "View Morphing" Proc. SIGGRAPH '96 (New Orleans, Louisiana, August 4 - 9, 1996). In Computer Graphics Proceedings, Annual Conference Series, 1996. ACM SIGGRAPH, pp. 21-30.

(a) Input image

(b) View angle = 54 (deg.) (c) View angle = 150 (deg.)

Figure 10. View-angle effects

Rendering With Coherent Layers

Jed Lengyel and John Snyder
Microsoft Research

Abstract

For decades, animated cartoons and movie special effects have factored the rendering of a scene into layers that are updated independently and composed in the final display. We apply layer factorization to real-time computer graphics. The layers allow targeting of resources, whether the ink and paint artists of cartoons or the graphics pipeline as described here, to those parts of the scene that are most important.

To take advantage of frame-to-frame coherence, we generalize layer factorization to apply to both dynamic geometric objects and terms of the shading model, introduce new ways to trade off fidelity for resource use in individual layers, and show how to compute warps that reuse renderings for multiple frames. We describe quantities, called *fiducials*, that measure the fidelity of approximations to the original image. Layer update rates, spatial resolution, and other quality parameters are determined by geometric, photometric, visibility, and sampling fiducials weighted by the content author's preferences. We also compare the fidelity of various types of reuse warps and demonstrate the suitability of the affine warp.

Using Talisman, a hardware architecture with an efficient layer primitive, the work presented here dramatically improves the geometric complexity and shading quality of scenes rendered in real-time.

CR Categories and Subject Descriptors: I.3.3 [Computer Graphics]: Picture/Image Generation; I.3.7 [Computer Graphics]: Three-Dimensional Graphics and Realism.

Additional Keywords: sprite, affine transformation, image compositing, image-based rendering, Talisman

1 Introduction

The layered pipeline separates or *factor*s the scene into layers that represent the appearance of an object (e.g., a space ship separate from the star field background) or a special lighting effect (e.g., a shadow, reflection, highlight, explosion, or lens flare.) Each layer produces a 2D-image stream as well as a stream of 2D transformations that place the image on the display. We use *sprite* to refer to a layer's image (with alpha channel) and transformation together.

The layered pipeline decouples rendering of layers from their display. Specifically, the sprite transformation may be updated more frequently than the sprite image. Rendering (using 3D CG) updates the sprite image only when needed. Sprite transforming and compositing [Porter84] occur at display rates. The sprite transformation scales low-resolution sprites up to the display resolution, and transforms sprites rendered earlier to approximate their later appearance. In other words, the sprite transformation interpolates rendered image streams to display resolution in both space and time.

Layered rendering has several advantages for real-time CG. First, layered rendering better exploits coherence by separating fast-moving foreground objects from slowly changing background layers. Second, layered rendering more optimally targets rendering resources by allowing less important layers to be degraded to conserve resources for more important layers. Finally, layered rendering naturally integrates 2D elements such as overlaid video, offline rendered sprites, or hand-animated characters into 3D scenes.

As an architectural feature, decoupling rendering from compositing is advantageous. Compositing is 2D rather than 3D, requires no

Address: One Microsoft Way, Redmond, WA 98052-6399
Email: jedl@microsoft.com, johnsny@microsoft.com

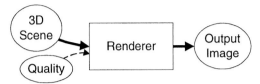

Figure 1: TRADITIONAL PIPELINE processes the entire scene database to produce each output image. The quality parameters for texture and geometry (such as level-of-detail) may be set independently for each object in the scene. However, the sampling resolutions in time (frame rate) and space (image resolution and compression) are the same for all objects in the scene.

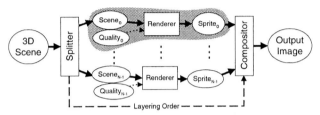

Figure 2: LAYERED PIPELINE partitions the scene into independent layers. A single layer's pipeline (highlighted at top) is similar to the traditional pipeline. By adjusting each layer's quality controls, the content author targets rendering resources to perceptually important parts of the scene. Slowly changing or unimportant layers are updated at lower frame rates, at lower resolution, and with higher compression.

z-buffer, no lighting computations, no polygon edge antialiasing, and must handle few sprites (which are analogous to texture-mapped polygons) relative to the number of polygons in the rendered geometry. This simplicity allows compositing hardware to be made with pixel fill rates much higher than 3D rendering hardware. Our investigation demonstrates that the saving in 3D rendering justifies the extra hardware expense of a compositor.

The layered pipeline augments the set of traditional rendering quality parameters such as geometric level-of-detail and shading model (e.g., flat-, Gouraud-, or Phong-shaded), with the temporal and spatial resolution parameters of each layer. The *regulator* adjusts the quality parameters in order to achieve optimal quality within fixed rendering resources. The regulator dynamically measures both the costs of changing the quality parameters – how much more or less of the rendering budget they will consume – and the benefits – how much improvement or loss in fidelity will occur.

The specific contributions of this paper include extending the generality of factoring. While some authors have considered factoring over static geometric objects [Regan94, Maciel95, Shade96, Schaufler96ab], we consider dynamic situations and factoring over shading expressions (Section 2). We describe how to render using the layered pipeline (Section 3). We investigate different types of sprite transformations and show why an affine transformation is a good choice (Section 4). We discuss low-computation measures of image fidelity, which we call *fiducials*, and identify several classes of fiducials (Section 5). We add the spatial and temporal resolution of layers as regulation parameters and propose a simple regulator that balances them to optimize image fidelity (Section 6). Finally, we demonstrate that the ideas presented here enhance performance of the Talisman architecture by factors of 3-10, by using interpolated triple-framing or by regulating the heterogeneous update of sprite images (Section 7).

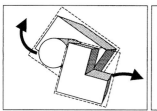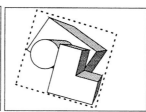

Figure 3: INDEPENDENT UPDATE depends on choice of factoring. The left and middle figures show how factoring the geometry into two separate layers allows each layer to be reused. The right figure shows a less effective partition.

1.1 The Layered Pipeline and Talisman

The Talisman reference hardware architecture was designed to support the layered pipeline (see [Torborg96] for details.) Rendering occurs within one 32×32 chunk at a time, so that z-buffer and fragment information for antialiasing can be stored on-chip. The resulting sprites with alpha channel are compressed and written to sprite memory. In parallel with 3D rendering, for every frame, the compositor applies an affine warp to each of an ordered set of sprites uncompressed from sprite memory and composites the sprites just ahead of the video refresh, eliminating the need for a frame buffer. Sprite composition is limited to the "over" operator [Porter84].

Although our experiments assume the Talisman reference architecture, the ideas can be usefully applied to traditional architectures. Layer composition can be emulated with rendering hardware that supports texture mapping with transparency by dedicating some of the pixel-fill rate of the renderer for sprite composition. This may be a good sacrifice if sprite rendering is polygon limited rather than pixel fill limited. Clearly though, Talisman is a superior layered pipeline in that sprite composition is "for free" (i.e., sacrifices few rendering resources) and very high speed (because of sprite compression and the simplicity of sprite composition in relation to rendering).[1]

1.2 Previous Work

To avoid visibility sorting of layers, alternative architectures use what are essentially sprites with z information per pixel [Molnar92, Regan94, Mark97]. Such systems are more costly in computation, bandwidth, and storage requirements since z must be stored and transmitted to a more complicated compositor. Z information is also difficult to interpolate and compress. We observe that z information per pixel is greatly redundant when used solely to determine a layering order. But such an ordering is necessary to ensure an antialiased result.[2] Our approach of factoring into layers allows warping per coherent object. It also avoids problems with uncovering of depth-shadowed information. Of course, sprites could store multiple z layers per pixel, a prohibitively costly approach for hardware, but one near to ours in spirit. Such a scheme stores all the layers within each pixel, rather than all the pixels for each layer.[3]

[Funkhouser93] adjusts rendering parameters to extract the best quality. We add sprite resolution and update rate to the set of regulated parameters and make photometric measurements rather than relying on *a priori* assignment of benefit to sampling rate. [Maciel95] takes a similar approach but use fiducials and impostor representations optimized for walkthroughs of static scenes.

Taking advantage of temporal coherence has been an ongoing theme in computer graphics [Hubschman81, Shelley82]. [Hofmann89] presents techniques for measuring how much camera movement is

allowed before changes in the projected geometry exceed a given tolerance. [Chen93, Chen95] show how to take advantage of coherence between viewpoints to produce nearly constant cost per frame walkthroughs of static environments. [McMillan95] re-projects images to produce an arbitrary view.

Our use of temporal coherence is most similar to [Regan94], who observed that not all objects need updating at the display rate. Rather than factoring globally across object sets requiring a common update rate, our scheme factors over geometric objects and shading model terms, and accounts for relative motion between dynamic objects.

[Shade96] and [Schaufler96ab] use image caches and texture-mapped quadrilaterals to warp the image. This is conceptually similar to our work, but does not include the factoring across shading or the idea of real-time regulation of quality parameters. We harness simpler image transformations (affine rather than perspective) to achieve greater fidelity (Section 4.2). Our work also treats dynamic geometry.

Shading expressions [Cook84, Hanrahan90] have been studied extensively. [Dorsey95] factors shading expressions by light source and linearly combines the resulting images in the final display. [Guenter95] caches intermediate results. [Meier96] uses image processing techniques to factor shadow and highlight regions into separate layers which are then re-rendered using painterly techniques and finally composited. The novel aspects of our technique are the independent quality parameters for each layer and warp of cached terms.

2 Factoring

The guiding principle of our approach is to factor into separate layers elements that require different spatial or temporal sampling rates. This section discusses guidelines for manually factoring across geometry and shading, visibility sorting of layers, and annotating models with layer information.

2.1 Factoring Geometry

Geometry factoring should consider the following properties of objects and their motions:

1. *Relative velocity* – A sprite that contains two objects moving away from each other must be updated more frequently than two sprites each containing a single object (Figure 3). Relative velocity also applies to shading.
2. *Perceptual distinctness* – Background elements require fewer samples in space and time than foreground elements, and so must be separated into layers to allow independent control of the quality parameters.
3. *Ratio of clear to "touched" pixels* – Aggregating many objects into a single layer typically wastes sprite area where no geometry projects. Finer decompositions are often tighter. Reducing wasted sprite space saves rendering resources especially in a chunked architecture where some chunks can be eliminated, and makes better use of the compositor, whose maximum speed limits the average depth complexity of sprites over the display.

2.2 Visibility Sorting

Visibility sorting of dynamic layer geometry can be automated. We have implemented a preliminary algorithm for which we provide a sketch here. A full discussion along with experimental results is in progress [Snyder97].

To determine visibility order for layers containing moving geometry, we construct an incrementally changing kd-tree based on a set of constant directions. A convex polyhedron bounds each layer's geometry, for which we can incrementally compute bounding extents

---

[1] In a prototype implementation of Talisman, the compositor is planned to run at 320M pixels/second compared to 40Mps for the renderer.
[2] Penetrating z-sprites will have a point-sampled and thus aliased boundary where visibility switches.
[3] Post-warping of unfactored z-images also fails to address the case of independently moving objects.

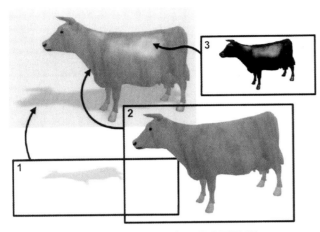

Figure 4: **FACTORED SHADING EXPRESSION** separates shadow, diffuse, and specular terms. In this example, the shadow and specular sprites are both computed at 25% (50% in x and y) of the display resolution. The shadow sprite modulates the color. The specular sprite adds to the output without changing alpha.

in each direction. The kd-tree quickly determines the set of objects that can possibly occlude a given object, based on these extents. Using this query, the visibility sort computes an incremental topological sort on the strongly connected components (which represent occlusion cycles) of the occlusion graph. Strongly connected components must be temporarily aggregated in the same layer, since a priority ordering does not exist.[4]

2.3 Factoring Shading

Shading may also be factored into separate layers. Figure 4 shows a typical multipass example, in which a shadow layer modulates the fully illuminated scene, and a reflection layer adds a reflection (in this case the reflection is the specular reflection from a light.) Figure 5 shows a schematic view of the steps needed to create the multipass image. The shadow layer is generated from a depth map rendered from the point of view of a light. The reflection layer is generated from a texture map produced by a separate rendering with a reflected camera. The layers shown in the figure represent post-modulation images using the same camera. With traditional architectures, the three layers are combined in the frame buffer using pixel blend operations supported by the 3D hardware, as described in [Segal92].

Shadows and reflections may instead be separated into layers as shown in Figure 6, so that the blend takes place in the compositor rather than the renderer. We call these *shade sprites* in reference to shade trees [Cook84]. To take advantage of temporal coherence, highlights from fast moving lights, reflections of fast moving reflected geometry, and animated texture maps should be in separate layers and rendered at higher frame rates than the receiving geometry. To take advantage of spatial coherence, blurry highlights, reflections, or shadows should be in separate layers and given fewer pixel samples.

For reflections, the correctness of using the compositor is evident because the reflection term is simply added to the rest of the shading. More generally, any terms of the shading expression that are combined with '+' or 'over' may be split into separate layers. 'A + B' can be computed using 'A over B' and setting A's alpha channel to zero.

The separation of shadows is slightly more difficult. The shadowing term multiplies each part of the shading expression that depends on a given light source. Many such terms can be added for

---

[4] At least, an ordering does not exist with respect to hulls formed by the set of bounding directions, which is a more conservative test than with the original bounding polyhedra. Note that visibility order for aggregated layers is computed simply by rendering into the same hardware z-buffer.

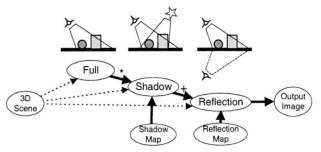

Figure 5: **MULTIPASS RENDERING** combines the results of several rendering passes to produce effects such as shadows and reflections. With a traditional architecture, the rendering passes are combined using blending operations in the 3D renderer (multiplication for shadow modulation and addition for adding reflections.)

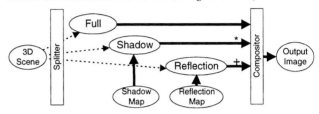

Figure 6: **SHADE SPRITES** are combined in the final composition phase to produce the multipass rendering. Each shading term may have different resolutions in space and time.

multiple shadowing light sources. We describe an approximation to multiplicative blending using the 'over' composition operator in an appendix.

Consider a simple example of a shading model with two textures and a shadow, $S(N \cdot L)(T_1 + T_2)$, where S is the shadowing term, N is the normal to the light, L is the light direction, and T_1 and T_2 are texture lookups. This shading model can be factored into three layers: S, $(N \cdot L)T_1$, and $(N \cdot L)T_2$, which are composited to produce the final image. The fact that this expression can be reordered and partial results cached is well known [Guenter95]. What we observe here is that each of these factors may be given different sampling resolutions in space and time, and interpolated to display resolutions.

As an aside, we believe shade sprites will be useful in authoring. When modifying the geometry and animation of a single primitive, the artist would like to see the current object in the context of the fully rendered and animated scene. By pre-rendering the layers that are not currently being manipulated, the bulk of the rendering resources may be applied to the current layer. The layers in front of the current layer may be made partially transparent (using a per-sprite alpha multiplier) to allow better manipulation in occluded environments. By using separate layers for each texture shading term, the artist can manipulate the texture-blending factors interactively at the full frame rate.

2.4 Model Annotation

The first step of model annotation is to break the scene into "parts" such as the base level joints in a hierarchical animated figure. The parts are containers for all of the standard CG elements such as polygon meshes, textures, materials, etc., required to render an image of the part. A part is the smallest renderable unit.

The second step is to group the parts into layers according to the guidelines described above. The distinction is made between parts and layers to allow for reuse of the parts, for example in both a shadow map layer and a shadow receiver layer.

The final step is to tag the layers with resource-use preferences relative to other layers in the scene. The preferences are relative so that total resource consumption can change when, for example, other applications are started (as discussed in Section 6).

3 Image Rendering

This section discusses how a layer's sprite image is created (i.e., rendered). Once created, the image can be warped in subsequent frames to approximate its underlying motion, until the approximation error grows too large. Although the discussion refers to the Talisman reference architecture with its 2D affine image warp, the ideas work for other warps as well.

3.1 Characteristic Bounding Polyhedron

The motion of the original geometry is tracked using a *characteristic bounding polyhedron*, usually containing a small number of vertices

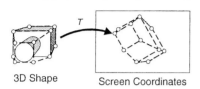

3D Shape   Screen Coordinates

Figure 7: CHARACTERISTIC BOUND-ING POLYHEDRON matches the shape of the geometry but has fewer vertices.

(Figure 7). For rigidly moving objects, the vertices of the characteristic polyhedron, called *characteristic points*, are transformed using the original geometry's time-varying transform. Nonrigidly deforming geometry can be tracked similarly by defining trajectories for each of the characteristic points. To group rigid bodies, we combine the characteristic bounding polyhedra, or calculate a single bounding polyhedron for the whole.

3.2 Sprite Extents

For a particular frame, there is no reason to render off-screen parts of the image. But in order to increase sprite reuse, it is often advantageous to expand the sprite image to include some off-screen area.

Figure 8a shows how clipping a sprite to the screen (solid box) prevents its later reuse because parts of the clipped image later become visible. In Figure 8b, the sprite extent (dashed box) has been enlarged to include regions that later become visible. The extra area to include depends on such factors as the screen velocity of the sprite

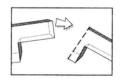

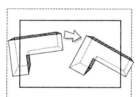

Figure 8: SPRITE EXTENTS enlarge the display extent to reuse sprites whose geometry lies partially off-screen.

(which suggests both where and how much the extents should be enlarged) and its expected duration of reuse.

3.3 Sprite Rendering Transformation

When creating a sprite image, we must consider a new transform in the pipeline in addition to the modeling, viewing, and projection transforms: a 2D affine transform that maps the sprite to the screen.

If T is the concatenation of the modeling, viewing, and projection matrices, a screen point p' is obtained from a modeling point p, by $p' = Tp$. For the sprite transformation, $p' = Aq$, where A is an affine transform and q is a point in sprite coordinates. To get the proper mapping of geometry to the display, the inverse 2D affine transform is appended to the projection matrix, so that $q = A^{-1}Tp$ results in the same screen point $p' = Aq = AA^{-1}Tp = Tp$ (Figure 9). The choice of matrix A determines how tightly the sprite fits the projected object. A tighter fit wastes fewer samples as discussed in Section 2.

To choose the affine transform that gives the tightest fit, we first project the vertices of the characteristic bounding polyhedron to the screen, clipping to the expanded sprite extent. Then, using discrete directions (from 2-30, depending on the desired tightness), we calculate 2D bounding slabs [Kay86]. Alternately, the slab directions may

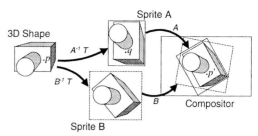

Figure 9: SPRITE RENDERING TRANSFORMATION maps the 3D shape into the sprite image. Affine transform B does not make the best use of image samples, while A fits the projected shape tightly.

be chosen by embedding preferred axes in the original model, and transforming the axes to screen space.

Using the bounding slabs, we find the bounding rectangle with the smallest area (Figure 10). The origin and edges of the rectangle determine the affine matrix. Initially, we searched for the smallest area parallelogram, but found the resulting affine transformation had too much anisotropy.

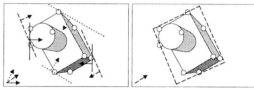

Figure 10: BOUNDING SLABS are obtained by taking the extremal values of the dot product of each slab direction with the characteristic points. A tight-fitting initial affine transform can be calculated by taking the minimum area rectangle or parallelogram that uses the slab directions.

3.4 Spatial Resolution

The choice of affine matrix A also determines how much the sprite is magnified on the display. Rendering using a sampling density less than the display's is useful for less important objects or for intentional blurring (Figure 11). The default is to use the same sampling density as the screen, by using the length in pixels of each side of the parallelogram from Section 3.3. See Figure 24 for an example of different sampling resolutions per sprite.

For a linear motion blur effect, the sprite sampling along one of the axes may be reduced to blur along that axis. The sprite rendering transformation should align one of the coordinate axes to the object's velocity vector by setting the bounding slab directions to the velocity vector and its perpendicular.

Figure 11: SPATIAL RESOLUTION is independent of the display resolution. The sampling density of the top sprite is the same as the screen. The middle sprite uses fewer samples than the screen, trading off pixel fill for blur. The bottom sprite aligns to the velocity vector and uses fewer samples along one dimension for a motion blur effect.

4 Image Warps

To reuse a rendered sprite image in subsequent frames, an image warp is used to approximate the actual motion of the object. We use the projected vertices of the bounding polyhedron (the characteristic points) to track the object's motion, as shown in Figure 12.

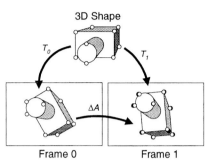

3D Shape

Frame 0   Frame 1

Figure 12: MATCHING CHARACTERISTIC POINTS on the 3D shape are projected to the screen to find a transform A that best matches the original points (white) to the points in the new frame (black).

To reuse images where objects are in transition from off-screen to on-screen, and to prevent large distortions (i.e., ill-conditioning of the resulting systems of equations), the characteristic bounding polyhedron is clipped to the viewing frustum, which may be enlarged from the display's as discussed in Section 3.2. The clipped points are added to the set of characteristic points (Figure 13) and used to determine an approximating sprite transformation as described below.

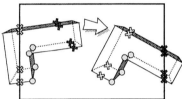

Figure 13: CLIPPED CHARACTERISTIC POLYHEDRON adds corresponding points introduced by clipping the characteristic polyhedron at the last-rendered and current frames.

4.1 Affine Warp

A 2D affine transform is represented by a 2x3 matrix, where the right column is translation and the left 2x2 is the rotation, scale, and skew.

$$A = \begin{bmatrix} a & b & t_X \\ c & d & t_Y \end{bmatrix}$$

Let P be the time-varying set of projected and clipped bounding polyhedron vertices, ignoring the z values and adding a row of 1's to account for the translation

$$P = \begin{bmatrix} x_0 & & x_{n-1} \\ y_0 & \cdots & y_{n-1} \\ 1 & & 1 \end{bmatrix}$$

where n is the number of points (at least 3 for the affine transform). Let $\hat{P}$ be the matrix of characteristic points at the initial time and P be the matrix at the desired time t. We solve for the best least-squares transform that matches the two sets of image-space points [Xie95].

In an affine transform, the x and y dimensions are decoupled and so may be solved independently. To solve $A\hat{P} = P$ at time t for the best A, in the least-squares sense, we use normal equations:

$$A\hat{P}\hat{P}^T = P\hat{P}^T$$
$$A = P\hat{P}^T\left(\hat{P}\hat{P}^T\right)^{-1}$$

The normal-equations technique works well in practice, as long as the projected points are reasonably distributed. Adding the clipped characteristic points ensures that $\hat{P}\hat{P}^T$ is not rank deficient. Much of the right hand side may be collected into a single vector K that may be reused for subsequent frames.

$$K = \hat{P}^T\left(\hat{P}\hat{P}^T\right)^{-1}$$
$$A = PK$$

To calculate K requires the accumulation and inverse of a symmetric 3×3 matrix.

4.2 Comparison of Warps

Clearly, other types of image warps can be used in place of the affine described above. In order to compare alternative image warps, we ran a series of experiments to

1. measure update rate as a function of maximum geometric error for various warps, and
2. measure perceptual quality as a function of update rate for various warps.

Each series involved the animation of a moving rigid body and/or moving camera to see how well image warping approximates 3D motion. We tried several types of rigid bodies, including nearly planar and non-planar examples. We also tried many animated trajectories for each body including translations with fixed camera, translations accompanied by rotation of the body along various axes with various rotation rates, and head turning animations with fixed objects.

The types of 2D image warps considered were

1. pure translation,
2. translation with isotropic scale,
3. translation with independent scale in x and y,
4. general affine, and
5. general perspective.

The fundamental simulation routine computes an animation given a geometric error threshold, attempting to minimize the number of renderings by approximating with an image warp of a particular type. A pseudo-code version is shown in Figure 14.

```
simulate(error-threshold, warp-type, animation)
{
    for each frame in animation
        compute screen position of characteristic points at current time
        compute transform (of warp-type) which best maps old
            cached positions to new positions
        compute maximum error for any characteristic point
        if error exceeds threshold
            re-render and cache current positions of characteristic points
        else
            display sprite with computed transformation
        endif
    endfor
    return total number of re-renderings
}
```

Figure 14: EXPERIMENT PSEUDOCODE shows steps used to compute update rates of various warps.

Ideally, we would like to compute approximations of each type that minimize the maximum error over all characteristic points, since this is the regulation metric. This is a difficult problem computationally, especially since the warping transformation happens at display rates for every layer in the animation. Minimizing the sum of squares of the error is much more tractable, yielding a simple linear system as we have already discussed. As a compromise, we simulated both kinds of error minimization: sum-of-squares and maximum error using an optimization method for L^∞ norms that iteratively applies the sum-of-square minimization, as described in [Gill81, pp. 96-98].

Further complicating matters, minimizing the error for perspective transformations is easier when done in homogeneous space rather than 2D space, again since the latter yields an 8×8 linear system rather than a difficult nonlinear optimization problem. We therefore included sum-of-square and maximum error methods for the first four (non-perspective) transformation types.

For perspective, we included sum-of-square minimization in homogeneous space (yielding a linear system as described above), maximum error in homogeneous space (using the technique of [Gill81]), and sum-of-square minimization in nonhomogeneous space (post-perspective divide), using gradient descent.[5] The starting point

---

[5] Minimization of the maximum nonhomogeneous error seemed wholly impractical for real-time implementation.

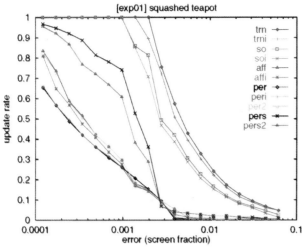

Figure 15 FLAT TEAPOT update-rate/error relations for the various warps show a surprisingly small difference between the affine and the perspective for a nearly flat object .

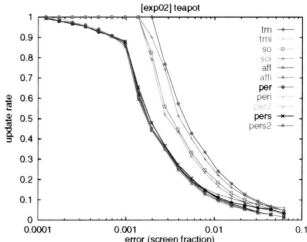

Figure 16 REGULAR TEAPOT update-rate/error relations show that affine and perspective are nearly indistinguishable.

for the gradient descent was the sum-of-squares-error-minimizing affine transformation.

We also included a perspective transformation derived using the method of [Shade96], in which objects are replaced by a quadrilateral placed perpendicular to the view direction and through the center of the object's bounding box. Our derivation projects the characteristic points onto this quadrilateral, bounds the projected points with a rectangle, and projects the corners of the rectangle to the screen. The perspective transformation that maps the old corners of the rectangle to their current locations is selected as the approximation. In yet another version, Shade's method is used as a starting point and then refined using gradient descent in nonhomogeneous space with the sum-of-square error metric.

Representative results of the first series of experiments are shown in Figure 15 and Figure 16. In both figures, the experiment involved a rotating and translating teapot which is scaled nearly flat[6] in Figure 15 and unscaled in Figure 16. Error thresholds ranging from 1/8 pixel to 64 pixels were used for each warp type/error minimization method, assuming an image size of 1024×1024, and the resulting rate of re-rendering measured via the simulation process described above. The meanings of the curve name keywords are as follows:

keyword	Warp type and minimization method
trn	translation, sum-of-square
trni	translation, max
so	translation with xy scale, sum-of-square
soi	translation with xy scale, max
aff	affine, sum-of-square
affi	affine, max
per	perspective, homogeneous, sum-of-square
peri	perspective, homogeneous, max
per2	perspective, nonhomogeneous, sum-of-square
pers	perspective, method of Shade
pers2	pers, followed by gradient descent

In the case of the flat teapot (Figure 15), note that the error/update curves cluster into groups – translation, translation with separate scale, Shade, affine, and perspective, in order of merit. Shade's method is significantly outperformed by affine. Note also that the

sum-of-square error minimization is not much different than maximum error minimization for any of the warp types. The difference between perspective and affine is much less than one might expect in this case, given that perspective exactly matches motions of a perfectly flat object. Figure 16 (regular teapot) is similar, except that the clusters are translation, translation with separate scale, and all other warp types. In this case, perspective yields virtually no advantage over affine, and in fact is slightly worse towards the high-error/low update rate end of the curves for the homogeneous space metrics (per and peri).[7] This is because the homogeneous metric weights the errors unevenly over the set of characteristic points. The method of Shade is slightly worse than affine in this case.

Since geometric error is a rather indirect measure of the perceptual quality of the warp types, the second series of experiments attempted to compare the perceptual quality of the set of warps given an update rate (i.e., an equal consumption of rendering resources). We used binary search to invert the relation between error threshold and update rate for each warp type, and then recorded the same animation, at the same update rate[8], for various image warp approximations. Although subjective, the results confirm the merit of the affine transformation over less general transformations and the lack of improvement with the more general perspective transformation in typical scenarios.

4.3 Color Warp

Images can be "warped" to match photometry changes as well as geometry changes. For example, Talisman provides a per-sprite color multiplier that can be used to match photometry changes. To solve for this multiplier, we augment each characteristic point with a normal so that shading results can be computed (see Section 5.2). The color multiplier is selected using a simple least-squares technique that best matches the original color values of the shaded characteristic points to the new color values.

---

[6] The teapot, a roughly spherical object, was scaled along its axis of bilateral symmetry to 5% of its previous size.

[7] In the second series of experiments, the animations that used the homogeneous-weighted metric to determine an approximating perspective transformation looked visibly worse than those that used the simple affine transformation.

[8] The update rate is the fraction of frames re-rendered; this balances the total consumption of rendering resources over the whole animation.

5 Fiducials

Fiducials measure the fidelity of the approximation techniques. Our fiducials are of four types. Geometric fiducials measure error in the screen-projected positions of the geometry. Photometric fiducials measure error in lighting and shading. Sampling fiducials measure the degree of distortion of the image samples. Visibility fiducials measure potential visibility artifacts.

We use conservative measurements where possible, but are willing to use heuristic measurements if efficient and effective. Any computation expended on warping or measuring approximation quality can always be redirected to improve 3D renderings, so the cost of computing warps and fiducials must be kept small relative to the cost of rendering.

5.1 Geometric Fiducials

Let $\hat{P}$ be a set of characteristic points from an initial rendering, let P be the set of points at the current time, and let W be the warp computed to best match $\hat{P}$ to P. The geometric fiducial is defined as

$$F_{geom} = \max_i \left\| P_i - W\hat{P}_i \right\|$$

Figure 17: GEOMETRIC FIDUCIAL measures maximum pointwise distance between the warped original and current characteristic points.

5.2 Photometric Fiducials

We use two approaches to approximately measure photometric errors. The first uses characteristic points augmented with normals as described in Section 4.3 to point sample the lighting. Let $\hat{C}$ be the colors that result from sampling the lighting at the characteristic points at the initial time, and C be the sampled colors at the current time. Let W_C be the color warp used to best match $\hat{C}$ to C[9]. Then the shading photometric fiducial is defined to be the maximum pointwise distance from the matched color to the current color.

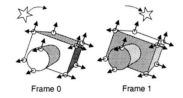

Figure 18: POINT-SAMPLED PHOTOMETRIC FIDUCIAL samples the shading at the initial and current characteristic points with normals.

$$F_{photo} = \max_i \left\| C_i - W_C\hat{C}_i \right\|$$

Another approach is to abandon color warping and simply measure the change in photometry from the initial time to the current. Many measures of photometric change can be devised. Ours measures the change in the apparent position of the light. Let $\hat{L}$ be the position of the light at the initial time and L its position at the current time (accounting for relative motion of the object and light). For light sources far away from the illuminated object, we can measure the angular change from $\hat{L}$ to L with respect to the object, and the change in distance to a representative object "center". For diffuse shading, the angular change essentially measures how much the object's terminator moves around the object, and the change in distance measures the increase or decrease in brightness. Light sources close to the object are best handled with a simple Euclidean norm. For specular shading, changes in the eye point can also be measured.

Figure 19: LIGHT SOURCE PHOTOMETRIC FIDUCIAL measures lighting change by the relative motion of light.

5.3 Sampling Fiducials

Sampling fiducials measure distortion of the samples in the image approximation. In Figure 20, both the geometric and photometric fiducials indicate high fidelity, but the image is blurry. The magnitudes of the singular values of the Jacobian of the image mapping function measure the greatest magnification and minification and the ratio measures the maximum anisotropy[10]. The affine warp has a spatially invariant Jacobian given by the left 2×2 part of the 2×3 matrix, for

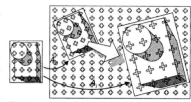

Figure 20: SAMPLING FIDUCIAL measures how the samples of a sprite are stretched or compressed.

which the two singular values are easily calculated [Blinn96]. For transforms with spatially varying Jacobians, such as the perspective warp, the singular values vary over the image. In this case, bounds on the singular values over the input domain can be computed.

5.4 Visibility Fiducials

Visibility fiducials measure potential visibility artifacts by tracking back-facing to front-facing transitions in the characteristic geometry (the simplified geometry makes these calculations tractable), and testing if the edges of clipped sprites become visible.

6 Regulation

A more complete treatment of regulation issues and directions may be found in [Horvitz96]. Our prototype regulator uses a simple cost-benefit scheduler and fiducial thresholds. The fiducial threshold provides a cutoff below which no attempt to re-render the layer is made (i.e., the image warp approximation is used). The regulator considers each frame separately, and performs the following steps:

1. Compute warp from previous rendering.
2. Use fiducials to estimate benefit of each warped layer.
3. Estimate rendering cost of each layer.
4. Sort layers according to benefit/cost.
5. Use fiducial thresholds to choose which layers to re-render.
6. Adjust parameters of chosen layers to fit within budget.
7. Render layers in order, stopping when all resources are used.

For a "budget-filling" regulator, the fiducial threshold is set to be small, on the order of a 1/1000 of the typical maximum error. All of the rendering resources are used in the attempt to make the scene as good as possible. For a "threshold" regulator, the threshold is raised to the maximum error that the user is willing to tolerate. This allows rendering resources to be used for other tasks.

Cost estimation [step 3] is based on a polygon budget, and measures the fraction of this budget consumed by the number of polygons in the layer's geometry. Parameter adjustments [step 6] are made to the sprite's spatial resolution using a budgeted total sprite size. This accounts for the rate at which the 3D rendering hardware can rasterize pixels.[11] Sprites that have been selected for re-rendering [step 5] are allocated part of this total budget in proportion to their desired area divided by the total desired area of the selected set. To dampen fluctuations in the regulation parameters which are perceptible when large, parameter changes are clamped to be no more than ±10% of their previous value at the time of last re-rendering. Note that factoring into many low-cost sprites allows smoother regulation.

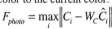

[9] Note that in architectures without color warping capability, W_C is the identity transform and we simply measure the maximum shading difference over all the characteristic points.

[10] The filtering capabilities of the hardware limit the amount of minification and anisotropy that can be handled before perceptible artifacts arise.

[11] A global average depth-complexity estimate is used to reduce the budget to account for rasterization of hidden geometry. Note that the depth complexity of factored geometry in a single layer is lower than would be the case for frame-buffer renderings of the entire scene.

7 Results

For the results presented here, we assume we have an engine that will composite all of the sprite layers with minimal impact on the rendering resources (as in the Talisman architecture.) We track the number of polygons and the amount of pixel fill used for rendering, but disregard compositing.

Both of the sequences described below are intended to represent typical content. For scenes with a moving camera, the typical speedup is 3-5 times what the standard graphics pipeline is capable of producing.

7.1 Canyon Flyby

This 250-frame sequence (Figure 25) used 10 sprite layers. We interpolated using affine warps and regulated the update rate with a geometric fiducial threshold of 4 pixels. Each sprite layer was re-rendered only when the geometric threshold was exceeded. The fiducial threshold of 4 pixels may seem large, but is acceptable for this sequence since the ships are well separated from the rest of the world.

The average update rate was 19%, and the cost-weighted average (based on polygon count) was 32%. About a third of the total polygons were rendered per frame.

In the canyon flyby scene, the entire background was placed in one sprite. Parallax effects from the rapidly moving camera make this a poor layering decision that yields a high update rate for the landscape sprite. In contrast, the sky is rendered just once

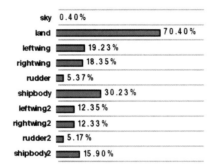

Figure 21: CANYON FLYBY AVERAGE UPDATE RATE for each sprite is the number of times each sprite was rendered divided by the number of frames in the sequence, 250

and then positioned with a new affine transformation each frame, and parts of the ships are updated relatively infrequently (5-30%).

7.2 Barnyard

The barnyard sequence (Figure 26) was chosen as an example in which a camera moves through a static scene[12]. This is a difficult case, because the eye is sensitive to relative motion between static objects. Approximation errors in sequences in which objects already have relative motion are far less perceptible (e.g., the ships in the canyon flyby above.) Even with this difficult case, our interpolation technique is dramatically better than triple framing.

The scene is factored into 119 standard layers, 2 shadow map layers, and 2 shadow modulation layers. The contiguous landscape geometry was split into separate sprites. As an authoring pre-process, the geometry along the split boundaries was expanded to allow for small separation of the warped sprites (the "seam" artifact.) This is similar to the expansion of the geometry along the split used by [Shade96]. More work is needed for automatic determination of the geometric expansion and better blending along the split boundaries.

The resource-use graph in Figure 22 shows three types of regulation. Simple triple framing, in which a frame is rendered and then

held for three frames, requires the most resources. Interpolated triple-framing requires the same amount of rendering resources, but interpolates through time using the warp described in Section 4.1 – the sprites are still rendered in lock-step but track the underlying characteristic geometry between renderings. The rest of the curves show threshold regulation with increasing geometric error threshold, from 0.1-0.8 pixels – the sprites are updated heterogeneously when the geometric error threshold is exceeded. The graph is normalized to the resource use of triple-framing.

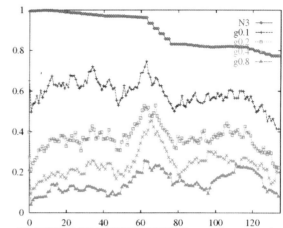

Figure 22: BARNYARD RESOURCE USE shows polygon counts as a 15-frame moving average. Pixel fill resource use is analogous. The top line is the triple-frame rendering. The lines below use threshold-regulation with increasing geometric threshold. As expected, as the pixel error tolerance goes up, the resource use goes down.

In the resulting animations, the most dramatic improvement in quality comes when the interpolation is turned on. The rest of the animations are nearly indistinguishable and use a fraction of the resources by rendering only those sprites whose geometric error exceeds the threshold.

Figure 23 shows the average pixel error for the same sequences shown in Figure 22. Each of the threshold-regulation sequences uses an error threshold smaller than the maximum error observed when triple-framing. Note that threshold-regulation is not the typical case and is shown here simply to demonstrate the performance advantage over the traditional graphics pipeline. Typically, all of the rendering resources are used to make the picture as good as possible.

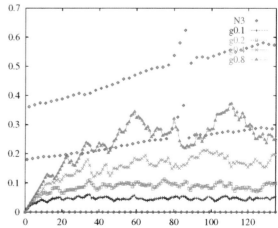

Figure 23: BARNYARD PIXEL ERROR shows average sprite pixel error per frame. Note that the triple-frame error is a saw-tooth that starts at 0, jumps to ½, and then jumps to full error value. The other curves oscillate below the given geometric threshold value.

---

[12] In the longer film from which the barnyard sequence is taken, many of the shots have fixed cameras. In these shots, only the main characters need to be updated, so the performance gain is extremely high. This is similar to the time-honored technique of saving the z-buffer for fixed camera shots.

8 Conclusions and Future Work

3D scenes should be factored into layers, with each layer having the proper sampling rates in both space and time to exploit the coherence of its underlying geometry and shading. By regulating rendering parameters using feedback from geometric, photometric, visibility, and sampling fiducials, rendering resources are applied where most beneficial. When not re-rendered, image warping suffices to approximate 3D motion of coherently factored layers. An affine warp provides a simple but effective interpolation primitive. These ideas yield 3-10 times improvement in rendering performance with the Talisman architecture with minor artifacts; greater performance can be controllably obtained with further sacrifices in fidelity.

Perceptual discontinuities may occur when a sprite's image is updated. Approximation with image warps captures the in-plane rotation, scale, and translation of an object, but not the out-of-plane rotation. The sprite image updates are sometimes perceived as a "clicking" or "popping" discontinuity. As the demand for higher quality 3D graphics increases display refresh rates, such artifacts will wane even at large factors of rendering amplification. More work is needed on the "seam" artifact (handling the boundaries of contiguous geometry placed in separate sprites.) Better modeling of the perceptual effects of regulation parameters is another area of future work [Horvitz97].

Factoring of shading terms is currently done using a fixed shading model that targets only the addition and over operations provided by hardware. Compilation of programmable shaders into layerable terms is an important extension. Many shading expressions, such as the shadow multiplication described in the appendix, can only be approximated with the over operator. We are interested in extending the system to target a fuller set of the image compositing operations.

Acknowledgements

The authors would like to thank the Microsoft Talisman Group and Microsoft Research, especially Jim Kajiya, Larry Ockene, Mark Kenworthy, Mike Toelle, Kent Griffin, Conal Elliott, Brian Guenter, Hugues Hoppe, Eric Horvitz, David Jenner, Andrew Glassner, Bobby Bodenheimer, Joe Chauvin, Howard Good, Mikey Wetzel, Susan O'Donnell, Mike Anderson, Jim Blinn, Steve Gabriel, Dan Ling, and Jay Torborg. Thanks to Nathan Myhrvold for the research direction and core ideas, and to Russell Schick for initial work on error-based sprite re-rendering. Thanks also to Allison Hart Lengyel and Julia Yang-Snyder.

Appendix: Shadow Sprites

For a fast-moving shadow on a slow-moving receiver, we update only the fast-moving shadow and use the compositor to compute the shadow modulation. Since the compositor supports only 'over', we use the following approximation.

Let $\mathbf{B}=[\beta B, \beta]$ be the receiver, where B is the color and β is the coverage. Let $\mathbf{A}=[\alpha A, \alpha]$ be the desired shadow sprite, where A is the color and α is the coverage. The compositor computes

$$\mathbf{A} \text{ over } \mathbf{B}=[\alpha A+(1-\alpha)\beta B, \; \alpha+(1-\alpha)\beta].$$

Let s be the shadow modulation obtained by scan-converting the geometry of the background while looking up values in the shadow map of the fast moving object, where 0 means fully in shadow and 1 means fully illuminated.

The desired result is $\mathbf{C'}=[s\beta B, \beta]$. By letting $\mathbf{A}=[0,(1-s)\beta]$, we get $\mathbf{C'}=\mathbf{A}$ over $\mathbf{B}$, or $\mathbf{C'}=[s\beta B+(1-s)(1-\beta)\beta B, \; \beta+(1-s)(1-\beta)\beta]$ which is close to the correct answer. Where there is no shadow, s is 1 and we get the correct answer of $[\beta B, \beta]$. Where coverage is complete, β is 1 and we get the correct answer of $[sB,1]$. The problem lies in regions of shadow and partial coverage.

Ideally, the shadow modulation needs a color multiply operator '$*$' defined by $s*[\beta B,\beta]=[s\beta B,\beta]$. This is a per-pixel version of the Porter-Duff 'darken' operator. Note that this operator is not associative, and so requires the saving of partial results when used in a nested expression.

References

[Blinn96]   Consider the Lowly 2x2 Matrix, Jim Blinn, *IEEE Computer Graphics and Applications*, March 1996, pp. 82-88.

[Chen93]   View Interpolation for Image Synthesis, Shenchang Eric Chen and Lance Williams, *SIGGRAPH* 93, pp. 279-288.

[Chen95]   QuickTime VR – An Image-Based Approach to Virtual Environment Navigation, Shenchang Eric Chen, *SIGGRAPH* 95, pp. 29-38.

[Cook84]   Shade Trees, Robert L. Cook, *SIGGRAPH* 94, pp. 223-232.

[Dorsey95]   Interactive Design of Complex Time Dependent Lighting, Julie Dorsey, Jim Arvo, Donald P. Greenberg, *IEEE Computer Graphics and Application*, March 1995, Volume 15, Number 2, pp. 26-36.

[Funkhouser93] Adaptive Display Algorithm for Interactive Frame Rates During Visualization of Complex Virtual Environments, Thomas A. Funkhouser and Carlo H. Séquin, *SIGGRAPH* 93, pp. 247-254.

[Gill81]   Practical Optimization, Philip E. Gill, Walter Murray, and Margaret H. Wright, Academic Press, London, 1981.

[Greene93]   Hierarchical Z-Buffer Visibility, Ned Greene, Michael Kass, Gavin Miller, *SIGGRAPH* 93, pp. 231-238.

[Greene94]   Error-Bounded Antialiased Rendering of Complex Environments, Ned Greene and Michael Kass, *SIGGRAPH* 94, pp. 59-66.

[Guenter95]   Specializing Shaders, Brian Guenter, Todd B. Knoblock, and Erik Ruf, *SIGGRAPH* 95, pp. 343-350.

[Hanrahan90]   A Language for Shading and Lighting Calculations, Pat Hanrahan and Jim Lawson, *SIGGRAPH* 90, pp. 289-298.

[Hofmann89]   The Calculus of the Non-Exact Perspective Projection, Scene-Shifting for Computer Animation. Georg Rainer Hofmann. *Tutorial Notes for Computer Animation, Eurographics '89*.

[Horvitz96]   Flexible Rendering of 3D Graphics Under Varying Resources: Issues and Directions, Eric Horvitz and Jed Lengyel, In *Symposium on Flexible Computation*, AAAI Notes FS-96-06, pp. 81-88. Also available as Microsoft Technical Report MSR-TR-96-18.

[Horvitz97]   Decision-Theoretic Regulation of Graphics Rendering, Eric Horvitz and Jed Lengyel, In *Thirteenth Conference on Uncertainty in Artificial Intelligence*, D. Geiger and P. Shenoy, eds., August 1997.

[Hubschman81] Frame to Frame Coherence and the Hidden Surface Computation: Constraints for a Convex World, Harold Hubschman, and Steven W. Zucker, *SIGGRAPH* 81, pp. 45-54.

[Kay86]   Ray Tracing Complex Scenes, Timothy L. Kay and James T. Kajiya, *SIGGRAPH* 86, pp. 269-278.

[Maciel95]   Visual Navigation of Large Environments Using Textured Clusters, Paolo W. C. Maciel and Peter Shirley, *Proceedings 1995 Symposium on Interactive 3D Graphics*, April 1995, pp. 95-102.

[Mark97]   Post-Rendering 3D Warping, William R. Mark, Leonard McMillan, and Gary Bishop, *Proceedings 1997 Symposium on Interactive 3D Graphics*, April 1997, pp. 7-16.

[Meier96]   Painterly Rendering for Animation, Barbara J. Meier, *SIGGRAPH* 96, pp. 477-484.

[Molnar92]   PixelFlow: High-Speed Rendering Using Image Composition, Steve Molnar, John Eyles, and John Poulton, *SIGGRAPH* 92, pp. 231-240.

[McMillan95]   Plenoptic Modeling: An Image-Based Rendering System, Leonard McMillan, Gary Bishop, *SIGGRAPH* 95, pp. 39-46.

[Porter84]   Compositing Digital Images, Thomas Porter and Tom Duff, *SIGGRAPH* 84, pp. 253-259.

[Regan94]   Priority Rendering with a Virtual Reality Address Recalculation Pipeline, Matthew Regan and Ronald Pose, *SIGGRAPH* 94, pp. 155-162.

[Segal92]   Fast Shadows and Lighting Effects Using Texture Mapping, Mark Segal, Carl Korobkin, Rolf van Widenfelt, Jim Foran, Paul Haeberli, *SIGGRAPH* 92, pp. 249-252.

[Schaufler96a] Exploiting Frame to Frame Coherence in a Virtual Reality System, Gernot Schaufler, *Proceedings of VRAIS '96*, April 1996, pp. 95-102.

[Schaufler96b] A Three Dimensional Image Cache for Virtual Reality, Gernot Schaufler and Wolfgang Stürzlinger, *Proceedings of Eurographics '96*, August 1996, pp. 227-235.

[Shade96]   Hierarchical Image Caching for Accelerated Walkthroughs of Complex Environments, Jonathan Shade, Dani Lischinski, David Salesin, Tony DeRose, John Snyder, *SIGGRAPH* 96, pp. 75-82.

[Shelley82]   Path Specification and Path Coherence, Kim L. Shelley and Donald P. Greenberg, *SIGGRAPH* 82, pp. 157-166.

[Snyder97]   Visibility Sorting for Dynamic, Aggregate Geometry, John Snyder, Microsoft Technical Report, MSR-TR-97-11.

[Torborg96]   Talisman: Commodity Real-time 3D Graphics for the PC, Jay Torborg, Jim Kajiya, *SIGGRAPH* 96, pp. 353-364.

[Xie95]   Feature Matching and Affine Transformation for 2D Cell Animation, Ming Xie, Visual Computer, Volume 11, 1995, pp. 419-428.

Figure 24: CHICKEN CROSSING sequence used 80 layers, some of which are shown separately (left and bottom) and displayed in the final frame with colored boundaries (middle). The sprite sizes reflect their actual rendered resolutions relative to the final frame. The rest of the sprites (not shown separately) were rendered at 40-50% of their display resolution. Since the chicken wing forms an occlusion cycle with the tailgate, the two were placed in a single sprite (bottom).

Figure 25: CANYON FLYBY used 10 layers with a geometric fiducial threshold of 4 pixels. The average sprite update rate was 19% with little loss of fidelity.

Figure 26: BARNYARD was factored into 119 geometry layers, 2 shadow map layers, and 2 shadow modulation layers. Threshold regulation for various geometric fiducial thresholds is compared in Figures 22 and 23.

Multiperspective Panoramas for Cel Animation

Daniel N. Wood[1]   Adam Finkelstein[1,2]   John F. Hughes[3]   Craig E. Thayer[4]   David H. Salesin[1]

[1]University of Washington   [2]Princeton University   [3]GVSTC   [4]Walt Disney Feature Animation

Figure 1 A multiperspective panorama from Disney's 1940 film *Pinocchio*. (Used with permission.)

Abstract

We describe a new approach for simulating apparent camera motion through a 3D environment. The approach is motivated by a traditional technique used in 2D cel animation, in which a single background image, which we call a *multiperspective panorama*, is used to incorporate multiple views of a 3D environment as seen from along a given camera path. When viewed through a small moving window, the panorama produces the illusion of 3D motion. In this paper, we explore how such panoramas can be designed by computer, and we examine their application to cel animation in particular. Multiperspective panoramas should also be useful for any application in which predefined camera moves are applied to 3D scenes, including virtual reality fly-throughs, computer games, and architectural walk-throughs.

CR Categories: I.3.3 [Computer Graphics]: Picture/Image Generation.

Additional Keywords: CGI production, compositing, illustration, image-based rendering, mosaics, multiplaning, non-photorealistic rendering.

1 Introduction

Walt Disney's 1940 feature animation, *Pinocchio* [14], opens with a long, continuous shot, in which the camera appears to fly over the rooftops of a small village and gradually descend into an alley facing Gepetto's cottage. This simulated 3D fly-through was actually accomplished via a stunning 2D effects shot. Instead of modeling a 3D scene, a single backdrop was painted that incorporated a kind of

"warped perspective" (Figure 1). The backdrop was then revealed just a little at a time though a small moving window. The resulting animation provides a surprisingly compelling 3D effect.

In this paper, we explore how such backdrops, which we call *multiperspective panoramas*, can be created from 3D models and camera paths. As a driving application, we examine in particular how such computer-generated panoramas can be used to aid in the creation of "Disney-style" 2D cel animation. To this end, we envision using the following four-step process (Figure 2):

1. A 3D modeling program is used to create a crude 3D scene and camera path. (Since only rough geometry is required, a modeler like SKETCH [24] might provide an ideal interface.)

2. Our program takes the 3D scene and camera path as input, and outputs one or more panoramas, each with a 2D *moving window* for viewing the panorama during each frame of the animation. When viewed as a whole, the panoramas may appear strangely warped. However, when taken together, the panoramas and moving windows should produce the illusion of 3D motion along the camera path. In the rest of this paper, we will use the term *layout* to refer to the panoramas taken together with their moving windows.

3. An illustrator then uses each computer-generated panorama as a guide to produce a high-quality artistic rendering of the distorted scene, called an *illustrated panorama*. The illustrated panorama may be created with any traditional media and scanned back into the computer. Alternatively, the illustrated panorama may be created with a digital paint system directly on the computer.

4. For each frame in the scene, images are extracted from the panoramas according to the moving windows. These images are composited (together with any additional foreground or computer-animated elements) to produce the final frames of the animation.

[3]NSF STC for Computer Graphics and Scientific Visualization, Brown University Site

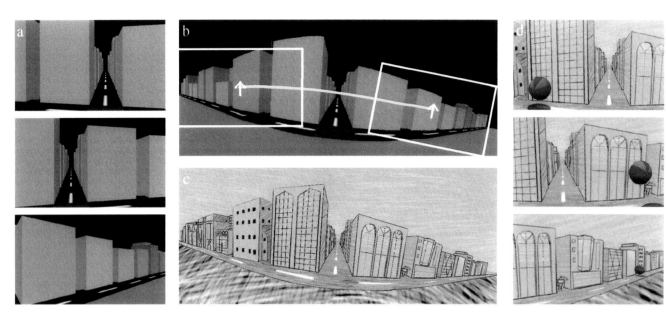

Figure 2 Pan. (a) Views from a 3D camera path. (b) Computer-generated layout. (c) Illustrated panorama. (d) Frames from the illustrated panorama with a computer-animated bouncing ball.

This process leverages the strengths of both the computer and the artist. The computer permits the use of much more complex camera paths than can be created by hand; in addition, it allows easier experimentation in designing them. The artist, on the other hand, is free to create the panorama in any artistic style, and is not limited by the availability of any particular computer rendering technique. Moreover, because the computer-generated layouts are created algorithmically from 3D models, they can be integrated with live-action or with conventional 3D computer-generated effects—something that it is extremely difficult to do with hand-drawn layouts, which often do not accurately correspond to any physical 3D scene or camera path. In addition, an automated process for creating such layouts should allow layout artists to work more efficiently and employ layouts more widely.

In addition to cel animation, the multiperspective panoramas described here should have applications to any situation in which "canned" camera moves are applied to 3D scenes, including virtual-reality fly-throughs, computer games like *Myst* [16], and architectural walk-throughs. In many internet-based applications, they may also be significantly faster to download and interact with than true 3D models, such as VRML.

1.1 Related work

The work described in this paper is related to several different threads of research in computer graphics.

First, our work is related to previous efforts on creating panoramas from multiple views [8, 20]. Our problem is in one sense simpler than that of these previous works, in that our source images are computer-generated. We therefore avoid solving the point-correspondence problem on images of real-world scenes. On the other hand, we allow for large changes in camera position and orientation across the panorama, and so we must accommodate a much greater sort of perspective distortion. Our problem is also related to Zorin and Barr's work on correcting distortion in perspective renderings [25, 26], although in our case we are concerned with the problem of making the distortions appear *locally* correct, rather than globally correct. (Much of Escher's art [6] also includes locally correct but globally distorted perspective.)

Our work also fits into the general framework of image-based rendering [3, 4, 5, 12, 15, 19], in which new views of a 3D scene are created from one or more source images. Our process differs from these previous image-based rendering approaches in that it generates a warped view (or set of views) that is optimized for the very simplest of extraction operations—that of selecting out a single rectangle for each frame. An advantage of using such multiperspective views is that the panorama created by the artist appears in the final frames in exactly the same way as it was painted—with no distortion in the shapes of the brush strokes, for example. In trade for this, however, our panoramas only allow this nice type of reconstruction along a single pre-specified path.

Another thread of research related to this paper is that of non-photorealistic rendering [10, 13, 17, 22, 23], in which 3D geometry is rendered in an artistically stylized form. The work in the paper is motivated by this same desire to create artistically rendered images of 3D geometry. However, the approach we take here is to output a flat design that can be rendered in any style, by hand, using traditional media. Alternatively, the panoramas that the program constructs can be given as input to an image-based non-photorealistic renderer, as described in Section 5.

This work is also related to previous results in automating the process of cel animation and digital compositing [7, 21], although we look at only a particular aspect of this process here—that of creating multiperspective panoramas—which has not been previously investigated.

1.2 Overview

In the next section, we approach the problem of generating arbitrary panoramas by first examining some simpler special cases. We then formulate a general solution in Section 3. We discuss our implementation in Section 4. Finally we conclude in Section 5 with some discussion and directions for future work.

2 An introduction to layouts

In this section, we describe panoramas produced in the simple cases of some basic camera moves: pan, tilt-pan, zoom, and truck [11].

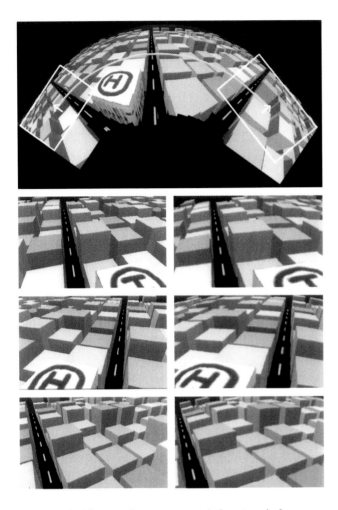

Figure 3 Tilt-pan. Computer-generated layout and frames (3D views on left, extracted frames on right).

Figure 4 Truck. Computer-generated layout (top two rows) and frames (3D views on left, extracted frames on right). The four panoramas at top are composited from front to back, starting with the upper left panorama, and proceeding in clockwise order.

Making layouts even for these relatively simple moves can be nontrivial.

2.1 Pan

Suppose that we wish to make a movie of a scene, taken by a camera rotating from left to right with its gaze always horizontal (a *pan*). We can ensure that the vertical centerline of each image is correct by unrolling a cylindrical projection for our panorama (as in QuicktimeVR [3]). Then the center vertical lines of extracted rectangles are perfect, but the vertical line segments on the left and right of the image appear too short. If the scene contains parallel horizontal lines, they become curved lines with vanishing points both to the left and to the right. Figure 2b demonstrates a pan panorama created by our application. With tight framing (Figure 2d) the bowed lines are not too objectionable.

2.2 Tilt-pan

As a more complex example, imagine that we are looking down and out across a city from the roof of a tall building, and wish to rotate our view from left to right. Our tripod is level, but the camera is tilted down as we pan. This *tilt-pan* requires a more complex layout.

If we simply use the cylindrical projection again, extracted rectangles from the lower portion of the cylinder will be deeply

unsatisfactory: not only will horizontal lines become bowed so that they all sag in the middle, but the extracted images will differ from the original ones by a "keystoning" transformation. A far better approximation is a conical projection [2].

Figure 3 shows a panorama created by our application for a tilt-pan. Notice that the vertical direction is not mapped to a single consistent direction in the panorama, and that the eventual sequence of extracted rectangles rotates about the cone-point of the flattened cone.

2.3 Zoom

Now suppose that instead of panning, we want to *zoom* (change the focal length of a stationary camera). Our panorama is simply a normal image from which we extract smaller and smaller windows. In a painting the brush strokes will be enlarged as we zoom in, and it may become necessary to cross-fade to a more detailed image. For example, the opening sequence of *Pinocchio* ends with a zoom toward the window of Gepetto's cottage followed by a crossfade to a detailed closeup of the cottage. (Of course, if the final panorama is generated digitally, tools like multiresolution paint [1] can help address this problem.)

2.4 Truck

If the camera's center of projection moves, occlusions may change. Cel animation has taken two approaches to changing occlusion. One approach is to ignore it—small errors in realism may well go unnoticed. This approach works for relatively small occlusion

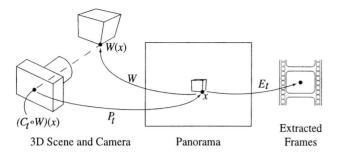

Figure 5 The coordinate systems and mapping between them.

changes (a hill in the far distance always occludes the same part of the mountain in the very far distance, for example). Alternatively, limited changes in occlusion can be suggested using *multiplaning*, in which objects in the scene are grouped roughly according to their depths, and each group appears on a separate panorama with its own moving window. The extracted frames are composited, back to front, to produce the final animation. This effect has also been widely used in computer games (*e.g.*, the backdrops of driving simulators).

In a scene with significant variation in depth, moving the camera perpendicular to the gaze direction (called *trucking*), creates the impression of objects at different depths moving at different relative speeds (called *parallax*). Figure 4 shows multiple panoramas created for a trucking scene, as well as some frames after compositing. If several objects are at the same depth, then an orthographic projection of the plane containing them can be used as the panorama with no distortion. To the extent that the scene has depth, objects in the same panorama will become distorted, as seen in the figure.

3 General formulation

In this section we describe a general solution for arbitrary camera paths, which specializes to the layouts we have already described for simpler camera moves like pan, tilt-pan, zoom, or truck. As previously stated, the goal for our layout is for the frames extracted from the panorama to match exactly the rendered images of the original camera path, which we will call *views* for contrast.

Historically, cel animators were limited to extracting rectangular sub-images from panoramas by their camera apparatus. We preserve this constraint for four reasons: it is simple; it meshes well mechanically with the existing animation process, and seamlessly with existing animations; it forces the resulting panorama to look (locally) like a traditional perspective view, making it easier for an artist to draw; and it preserves the artistic texture and composition of the panorama. Limiting extraction to rectangular windows with a fixed aspect ratio also tells us something about the relationships between neighboring frames in the resulting animation: any two will be related by a *similarity transform*—a transform involving a translation, rotation and uniform scale.

To create an image incorporating many perspectives, we begin with views of the scene taken from different perspectives and try to merge them. Regardless of how we merge them, each point $x \in \mathbb{R}^2$ of the resulting panorama corresponds to a world-space point $W(x) \in \mathbb{R}^3$ (Figure 5). For each time t, let C_t denote the map from world-space points to view points, and P_t denote the map from view points at time t onto the panorama. Let E_t be the map from a subset of the panorama to an image that is the extracted frame for time t. Finally, each point x of the panorama gets its color from a view at some particular time $S(x)$. From these definitions it follows that if $t = S(x)$, then $(P_t \circ C_t \circ W)(x) = x$.

If the extraction process produces the same picture as the original camera view, then $E_t(x) = (C_t \circ W)(x)$ for all points x in the domain of E_t. Hence $(P_t \circ E_t)(x) = (P_t \circ C_t \circ W)(x)$, which simplifies to $(P_t \circ E_t)(x) = x$ when $S(x) = t$. For points y in the domain of E_t for which $S(y) = s \neq t$, we have that $(E_t \circ P_s \circ C_s \circ W)(y) = E_t(y) = (C_t \circ W)(y)$.

If $(P_s \circ C_s \circ W)(y)$ differs much from $(P_t \circ C_t \circ W)(y)$, then the panorama will be distorted badly within the domain of E_t, and so the frame extracted at time t will look bad. In a perfect panorama (one in which the extracted frames look like the original views), $(P_t \circ C_t \circ W)(y) = (P_s \circ C_s \circ W)(y)$ for all points y in the domain of E_t such that $S(y) = s$. In this case $(E_t \circ P_t \circ C_t \circ W)(y) = (C_t \circ W)(y)$ for *all* y in the domain of E_t implying that in any perfect layout the (linear) extraction map E_t is the inverse of the linear placement map P_t. In our panorama, we therefore always choose E_t to be the inverse of P_t, since it is a necessary condition for a panorama to be perfect. For camera paths and scenes where no perfect panorama is possible, if the distortion is small the same sort of argument implies that E_t is *approximately* the inverse of P_t. Thus, if we can find a suitable rule for placing views into the panorama, then we will know how to extract frames from the panorama.

We now take our characterization of ideal panoramas and convert it from a descriptive one to a prescriptive one—one that tells us what the placement map P_t should be. We continue to be guided by the necessary condition for a perfect layout: for world points w visible at time t, $(P_t \circ C_t)(w) = (P_s \circ C_s)(w)$ for values of s near t. If we write $s = t + \epsilon$ and then expand both P and C in a first-order Taylor series about t, we get $(P_t \circ C_t)(w) \simeq ((P_t + \epsilon P_t') \circ (C_t + \epsilon C_t'))(w)$, which can be simplified to $(P_t \circ C_t')(w) + (P_t' \circ (C_t + \epsilon C_t'))(w) \simeq 0$, using the linearity of P_t and C_t. Taking the limit as $\epsilon \rightarrow 0$ gives $(P_t \circ C_t')(w) = (-P_t' \circ C_t)(w)$. In words, the rate at which w is moving across the film plane of the camera at the instant t is the negative of the rate at which the film-plane point $C_t(w)$ is being translated across the panorama. We want this true for every w, but because P_t must be a linear map, we compromise by requiring it only on average: we compute the similarity transform that is the least-squares approximation of the *optical flow*, the flow of world-space points across the image plane of the camera, and use its negative as the rate of change of the camera-placement map P_t. Choosing P_0 arbitrarily, we now find P_t by numerical integration. Since E_t is the inverse of P_t, all that is left for us to define is $S(x)$. In Section 4.2, we will describe a simple rule for $S(x)$ that works reasonably well in practice.

For sufficiently simple scenes, this formulation specializes to the layouts described in Section 2. In fact, the layouts for Figures 2 through 4 were created using the general formulation described in this section.

4 Implementation

In this section we describe our implementation of the general principles just described. We discretize the 3D camera path and render frames at finely spaced intervals. Then we find the placement transform for each of these views; finally, we select from among them in regions where they overlap.

4.1 Placement

The first view is arbitrarily placed at the origin of the panorama's coordinate system. We find a transform that places each subsequent view relative to its predecessor. The relative transform from any view $i + 1$ to i would ideally be the inverse of the optical flow between them. These transforms are composed to place each view on the panorama.

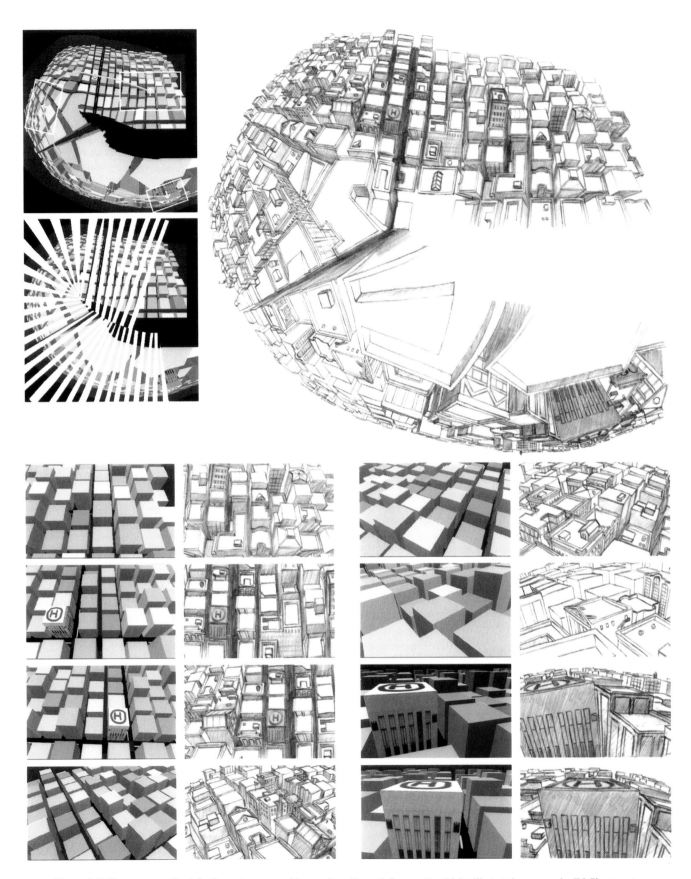

Figure 6 Helicopter scene. Top left: Computer-generated layout above Voronoi diagram. Top Right: Illustrated panorama by Ed Ghertner at Walt Disney Feature Animation. Bottom: Frames (3D views to the left of extracted frames.)

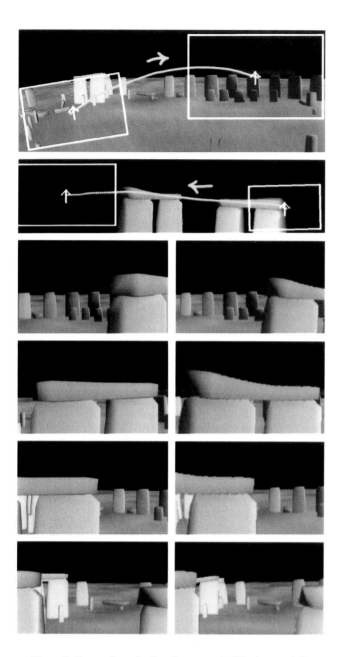

Figure 7 Frames from the Stonehenge movie (3D views on left, extracted frames on right).

Figure 8 Two frames extracted from the Helicopter layout, showing overlaid 3D axes and computer-animated rain.

coherence ensures that this assumption is reasonable.

Finally, we find the least-squares-best similarity transform that matches the source points to their corresponding target points. Horn [9] describes a closed-form solution to this least-squares problem. We sometimes clamp the scale-change of the resulting transform in order to restrict the amount by which portions of the panorama are magnified.

4.2 Selection

Having placed all the views in a single coordinate system, we must choose, for each point, which of the many overlapping views at that point should be included in the final panorama. We project the center of each view into the panorama (using the transformations of the previous section). This collection of points, shown in yellow in our panoramas, we call the *spine* of the camera path. Then, at every point, we simply select the view corresponding to the closest spine point. The selected portions of each view constitute the Voronoi diagram of the spine.

Figure 6 shows a layout in which a helicopter flies across town, descends while spinning around, and then approaches a helicopter pad to land. (Note that the building with the helicopter pad, in yellow, appears twice in the panorama from two different perspectives.) The spine for the camera path and Voronoi diagram appear are also shown. Observe that the first and last camera position contribute large areas of the panorama. Along the spine, the separations between the Voronoi regions are roughly perpendicular to the motion of the camera center. Each camera position contributes a narrow wedge to the overall panorama. (For illustrative purposes, the figure shows the Voronoi diagram for a spine sampled very coarsely; the actual spine was sampled much more finely.)

4.3 Multiplaning

As mentioned in Section 2.4, multiplaning uses several layers of panoramas in concert to create an impression of parallax. In our process, the 3D scene is partitioned into separate planes by hand, although a useful area for future work would be automatic partitioning of the scene. Our application generates panoramas for each plane using the same camera path. The panorama for each plane contains an alpha channel, and the final animation is produced by simply compositing the extracted frames from back to front.

The Stonehenge example shown in Figure 7 illustrates an important use of multiplaning. The two windows move in opposite directions giving the impression of a camera circling around the ring of stones, looking inward. This effect is difficult to achieve with a single panorama. (We ignored the ground when firing rays during the placement stage, on the assumption that its lack of features would make a poor fit unimportant.)

4.4 Integrating computer-animated elements

Figure 8 shows the Helicopter movie, overlaid with 3D axes and a computer-animated rain element whose motion is appropriate for

The optical flow function can be approximated by discrete sampling. We take an evenly spaced grid of nine points (*source points*) on view $i+1$ and find corresponding points (*target points*) on view i. We reject any source points that see no objects in the scene; if fewer than four points remain, we subdivide the source grid until we have at least four points. The rejection of some source points leads to variations in our approximation of optical flow, which is why Figure 2 and Figure 3 are not exact cylindrical and conical projections.

To find the target point x' corresponding to source point x, we simply fire a ray from camera $i+1$ through point x into the 3D scene. As mentioned above, if the ray hits nothing it is rejected. If the ray intersects an object at $W(x)$, then we let x' be the projection of $W(x)$ into the image plane of camera i. This correspondence assumes no change in occlusion; that is, we assume that if camera $i+1$ can see point $W(x)$ then camera i can see it as well. Frame-to-frame

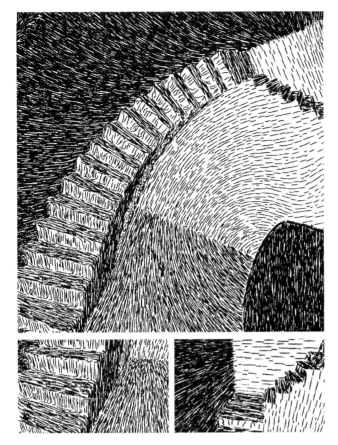

Figure 9 Pen-and-ink illustration of a panorama with two frames from from the resulting animation using warping.

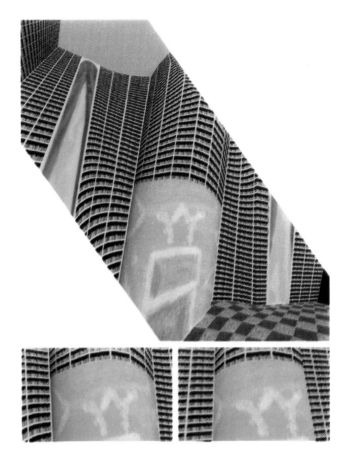

Figure 10 Library with curtains and fireplace. Excessive distortion in computer-generated panorama and unwarped frame (on left) is corrected in warped frame (on right).

the 3D model and camera. This alignment would have been difficult to achieve if the illustrated panorama had been designed by hand without a corresponding 3D model.

We have implemented two different techniques for integrating computer-animated foreground elements into our extracted frames. In both cases, the frames of the computer-animated elements are composited onto the layout movie. To generate the rain in the helicopter scene we simply make a standard 3D animation of rain using the 3D camera path. However, an element that interacts more closely with the background, like the bouncing ball (Figure 2d), requires a tighter match with the extracted frames. To generate the frame at time t, we take the world-space position w of the ball and find the corresponding location x on the panorama. To find x we look at the positions $P_s(w)$ on the panorama where w could have been placed at any time s. We solve $S(P_s(w)) = s$ for s, and let $x = P_s(w)$, which makes $w = W(x)$. We then render the ball using camera C_s. To create the final frame, we transform the rendered image of the ball with $E_t \circ P_s = E_t \circ E_s^{-1}$.

Incorporating a computer-animated element that interacts with the background and spans a significant number of views (*e.g.*, a flood of molasses) would require that the element share all of the multiple perspectives of the panorama.

5 Discussion and future work

Directly generating final panoramas. As our focus is on cel animation, the panoramas our program creates are drafts with rough transitions at the boundaries between views. Some applications, including integrating computer-animated elements for cel animation,

require high-quality computer generated panoramas. Our staircase panorama, Figure 9, generated using a computer pen-and-ink illustration system [18] demonstrates one way to automatically create a final panorama, but a program that renders ready-to-use panoramas would be useful.

Panorama-creation problems. There are situations where successful panorama-creation is impossible. When occlusions on a single object change drastically without the object leaving the camera frame (e.g., if a camera makes a 360-degree pass around a dinner table, always showing the centerpiece and the surrounding place-settings), each extracted frame will show not only the part of the object that ought to be visible, but "adjacent" parts that ought to be hidden in the current view. Even for objects with smooth boundaries, this problem can occur if the visible silhouette of the object changes radically with different views. This problem is also closely related to another difficult situation: radical perspective changes. An example is a bug's-eye view of the floor as the bug flies upwards from the floor to a table. In each case, the difficulty is that the aggregate optical flow is not well-approximated by a similarity transform. This can be addressed, in part, by warping, which is discussed below.

There are also situations where *our* algorithm does not produce successful layouts, even though such layouts can be hand-generated. Figure 10 shows an example: because of the strong linear elements of the scene, it is essential that certain large-scale geometric features—the horizontal shelves and the vertical dividers—be preserved. Our algorithm, whose selection scheme is purely local, cannot handle this type of constraint. Once again, warping can help address the problem, but an *ab initio* solution would be preferable.

Finally, there are two global issues not addressed by our method: first, the panorama can overlap itself as images from frames at widely separated times are placed (this almost happens in Figure 6); second, if the cumulative "scale" component of successive interframe transforms becomes too large or small, the artist may be compelled to render similar parts of the panorama at widely-differing scales, making a coherent artistic texture difficult. Allowing the extraction and placement maps to be adjusted by an arbitrary projective transformation might alleviate this; choosing the best correction would require global knowledge however.

Warping. If we store the world-space locations of points in the panorama, we can warp the panorama to produce a distortion-free animation. At time t, point x is warped to $(C_t \circ W)(x)$. This technique can be used with panoramas that would not produce a reasonable movie using the traditional technique, as demonstrated in the lower-right frame of Figure 10. (Warping is also used in the pen-and-ink example of Figure 9.) Unfortunately, using warping also has serious shortcomings. In particular, in some cases a warped view of the panorama may reveal world-space points that were not captured in the scene, leaving undesirable holes.

Fully exploring the potential of warping will surely expose a number of problems. Without the rectangular extraction constraint our general formulation will lead to a different algorithm for constructing the panorama. A good solution to the problems of occlusion and hole-filling for multiperspective panoramas should borrow from and extend related work in image-based rendering.

Acknowledgements

We would like to thank Scott Johnston for exposing us to the traditional use of panoramas in cel animation, and Ronen Barzel for suggesting the idea of generating such panoramas algorithmically. We also thank Tom Baker, Ed Ghertner, Dan Hansen, Kiran Joshi, Dan St. Pierre, Ann Tucker, and M.J. Turner from Disney for educating us further about cel animation and layouts. Particular thanks to Ed Ghertner for the illustrated panorama. Thanks to Brad deGraf and Protozoa for their VRML Stonehenge. Thanks to Michael Wong and Cassidy Curtis for helping to create the pen-and-ink staircase, and to Eric Stollnitz for creating the diagram and helping with the paper.

This work was supported by an Alfred P. Sloan Research Fellowship (BR-3495), an NSF Presidential Faculty Fellow award (CCR-9553199), an ONR Young Investigator award (N00014-95-1-0728) and Augmentation award (N00014-90-J-P00002), an NSF graduate fellowship, and an industrial gift from Microsoft.

References

[1] Deborah F. Berman, Jason T. Bartell, and David H. Salesin. Multiresolution painting and compositing. In *Proceedings of SIGGRAPH '94*, pages 85–90, New York, 1994. ACM.

[2] Nathaniel Bowditch. *Bowditch for Yachtsmen: Piloting; Selected from The American Practical Navigator*. David McKay Company, Inc., New York, 1976.

[3] Shenchang Eric Chen. Quicktime VR: An image-based approach to virtual environment navigation. In *Proceedings of SIGGRAPH '95*, pages 29–38, New York, 1995. ACM.

[4] Shenchang Eric Chen and Lance Williams. View interpolation for image synthesis. In *Proceedings of SIGGRAPH '93*, pages 279–288, New York, 1993. ACM.

[5] Paul E. Debevec, Camillo J. Taylor, and Jitendra Malik. Modeling and rendering architecture from photographs: A hybrid geometry- and image-based approach. In *SIGGRAPH 96 Conference Proceedings*, Annual Conference Series, pages 11–20. ACM SIGGRAPH, Addison Wesley, August 1996.

[6] Maurits C. Escher et. al. *M.C. Escher : His Life and Complete Graphic Work*. Harry N. Abrams, New York, 1992.

[7] Jean-Daniel Fekete, Érick Bizouarn, Éric Cournarie, Thierry Galas, and Frédéric Taillefer. TicTacToon: A paperless system for professional 2-D animation. In *SIGGRAPH 95 Conference Proceedings*, Annual Conference Series, pages 79–90. ACM SIGGRAPH, Addison Wesley, August 1995.

[8] Paul Haeberli. Grafica obscura web site. http://www.sgi.com/grafica/, 1997.

[9] Berthold K. P. Horn. Closed-form solution of absolute orientation using unit quaternions. *Journal of the Optical Society of America*, 4(4), April 1987.

[10] John Lansdown and Simon Schofield. Expressive rendering: A review of nonphotorealistic techniques. *IEEE Computer Graphics and Applications*, 15(3):29–37, May 1995.

[11] Lenny Lipton. *Independent Filmmaking*. Straight Arrow Books, San Francisco, 1972.

[12] Leonard McMillan and Gary Bishop. Plenoptic modeling: An image-based rendering system. In *Proceedings of SIGGRAPH '95*, pages 39–46, New York, 1995. ACM.

[13] Barbara J. Meier. Painterly rendering for animation. In *SIGGRAPH 96 Conference Proceedings*, Annual Conference Series, pages 477–484. ACM SIGGRAPH, Addison Wesley, August 1996.

[14] Walt Disney Productions. Pinocchio. Movie, 1940.

[15] Matthew Regan and Ronald Post. Priority rendering with a virtual reality address recalculation pipeline. In *Proceedings of SIGGRAPH '94*, Computer Graphics Proceedings, Annual Conference Series, pages 155–162. ACM SIGGRAPH, ACM Press, July 1994.

[16] Robyn and Rand Miller. Myst. Computer game, Cyan, Inc., 1993.

[17] Takafumi Saito and Tokiichiro Takahashi. Comprehensible rendering of 3-D shapes. In *Computer Graphics (SIGGRAPH '90 Proceedings)*, volume 24, pages 197–206, August 1990.

[18] Michael P. Salisbury, Michael T. Wong, John F. Hughes, and David H. Salesin. Orientable textures for image-based pen-and-ink illustration. In *SIGGRAPH 97 Conference Proceedings*. ACM SIGGRAPH, Addison Wesley, August 1997.

[19] Steven M. Seitz and Charles R. Dyer. View morphing: Synthesizing 3D metamorphoses using image transforms. In *SIGGRAPH 96 Conference Proceedings*, Annual Conference Series, pages 21–30. ACM SIGGRAPH, Addison Wesley, August 1996.

[20] Richard Szeliski. Video mosaics for virtual environments. In *IEEE Computer Graphics and Applications*, pages 22–30, March 1996.

[21] Bruce A. Wallace. Merging and transformation of raster images for cartoon animation. In *Computer Graphics (SIGGRAPH '81 Proceedings)*, volume 15, pages 253–262, August 1981.

[22] Georges Winkenbach and David H. Salesin. Computer-generated pen-and-ink illustration. In *Proceedings of SIGGRAPH '94*, pages 91–100, July 1994.

[23] Georges Winkenbach and David H. Salesin. Rendering free-form surfaces in pen and ink. In *SIGGRAPH 96 Conference Proceedings*, Annual Conference Series, pages 469–476. ACM SIGGRAPH, Addison Wesley, August 1996.

[24] Robert C. Zeleznik, Kenneth P. Herndon, and John F. Hughes. SKETCH: An interface for sketching 3D scenes. In *SIGGRAPH 96 Conference Proceedings*, Annual Conference Series, pages 163–170. ACM SIGGRAPH, Addison Wesley, August 1996.

[25] Denis Zorin. *Correction of Geometric Perceptual Distortions in Pictures*. California Institute of Technology, Pasadena, CA, 1995.

[26] Denis Zorin and Alan H. Barr. Correction of geometric perceptual distortion in pictures. In *SIGGRAPH 95 Conference Proceedings*, Annual Conference Series, pages 257–264. ACM SIGGRAPH, Addison Wesley, August 1995.

Creating Full View Panoramic Image Mosaics and Environment Maps

Richard Szeliski and Heung-Yeung Shum

Microsoft Research

Abstract

This paper presents a novel approach to creating full view panoramic mosaics from image sequences. Unlike current panoramic stitching methods, which usually require pure horizontal camera panning, our system does not require any controlled motions or constraints on how the images are taken (as long as there is no strong motion parallax). For example, images taken from a hand-held digital camera can be stitched seamlessly into panoramic mosaics. Because we represent our image mosaics using a set of transforms, there are no singularity problems such as those existing at the top and bottom of cylindrical or spherical maps. Our algorithm is fast and robust because it directly recovers 3D rotations instead of general 8 parameter planar perspective transforms. Methods to recover camera focal length are also presented. We also present an algorithm for efficiently extracting environment maps from our image mosaics. By mapping the mosaic onto an artibrary texture-mapped polyhedron surrounding the origin, we can explore the virtual environment using standard 3D graphics viewers and hardware without requiring special-purpose players.

CR Categories and Subject Descriptors: I.3.3 [Computer Graphics]: Picture/Image Generation - Viewing Algorithms; I.3.4 [Image Processing]: Enhancement - Registration.

Additional Keywords: full-view panoramic image mosaics, environment mapping, virtual environments, image-based rendering.

1 Introduction

Image-based rendering is a popular way to simulate a visually rich tele-presence or virtual reality experience. Instead of building and rendering a complete 3D model of the environment, a collection of images is used to render the scene while supporting virtual camera motion. For example, a single cylindrical image surrounding the viewer enables the user to pan and zoom inside an environment created from real images [4, 13]. More powerful image-based rendering systems can be built by adding a depth map to the image [3, 13], or using a larger collection of images [3, 6, 11].

In this paper, we focus on image-based rendering systems without any depth information, i.e., those which only support user panning, rotation, and zoom. Most of the commercial products based on this idea (such as QuickTime VR [22]

and Surround Video [23]) use cylindrical images with a limited vertical field of view, although newer systems support full spherical maps (e.g., PhotoBubble [24], Infinite Pictures [25], and RealVR [26]).

A number of techniques have been developed for capturing panoramic images of real-world scenes (for references on computer-generated environment maps, see [7]). One way is to record an image onto a long film strip using a panoramic camera to directly capture a cylindrical panoramic image [14]. Another way is to use a lens with a very large field of view such as a fisheye lens. Mirrored pyramids and parabolic mirrors can also be used to directly capture panoramic images [27, 28].

A less hardware-intensive method for constructing full view panoramas is to take many regular photographic or video images in order to cover the whole viewing space. These images must then be aligned and composited into complete panoramic images using an image mosaic or "stitching" algorithm [12, 17, 9, 4, 13, 18]. Most stitching systems require a carefully controlled camera motion (pure pan), and only produce cylindrical images [4, 13]. In this paper, we show how uncontrolled 3D camera rotation can be used.

The case of general camera rotation has been studied previously [12, 9, 18], using an 8-parameter planar perspective motion model. By contrast, our algorithm uses a 3-parameter rotational motion model, which is more robust since it has fewer unknowns. Since this algorithm requires knowing the camera's focal length, we develop a method for computing an initial focal length estimate from a set of 8-parameter perspective registrations. We also investigate how to close the "gap" (or "overlap") due to accumulated registration errors after a complete panoramic sequence has been assembled. To demonstrate the advantages of our algorithm, we apply it to a sequence of images taken with a handheld digital camera.

In our work, we represent our mosaic by a set of transformations. Each transformation corresponds to one image frame in the input image sequence and represents the mapping between image pixels and viewing directions in the world, i.e., it represents the *camera matrix* [5]. During the stitching process, our approach makes no commitment to the final output representation (e.g. spherical or cylindrical), which allows us to avoid the singularities associated with such representations.

Once a mosaic has been constructed, it can, of course, be mapped into cylindrical or spherical coordinates, and displayed using a special purpose viewer [4]. In this paper, we argue that such specialized representations are not necessary, and represent just a particular choice of geometry and texture coordinate embedding. Instead, we show how to convert our mosaic to an environment map [7], i.e., how to map our mosaic onto *any* texture-mapped polyhedron surrounding the origin. This allows us to use standard 3D graphics APIs and 3D model formats, and to use 3D graphics accelerators for texture mapping.

The remainder of our paper is structured as follows. Sections 2 and 3 review our algorithms for panoramic mosaic construction using cylindrical coordinates and general perspective transforms. Section 4 describes our novel direct rotation recovery algorithm. Section 5 presents our technique for estimating the focal length from perspective registrations. Section 6 discusses how to eliminate the "gap" in a panorama due to accumulated registration errors. Section 7 presents our algorithm for projecting our panoramas onto texture-mapped 3D models (environment maps). We close with a discussion and a description of ongoing and future work.

2 Cylindrical and spherical panoramas

Cylindrical panoramas are commonly used because of their ease of construction. To build a cylindrical panorama, a sequence of images is taken by a camera mounted on a leveled tripod. If the camera focal length or field of view is known, each perspective image can be warped into cylindrical coordinates. Figure 1a shows two overlapping cylindrical images—notice how horizontal lines become curved.

To build a cylindrical panorama, we map world coordinates $\mathbf{p} = (X, Y, Z)$ to 2D cylindrical screen coordinates (θ, v) using

$$\theta = \tan^{-1}(X/Z), \quad v = Y/\sqrt{X^2 + Z^2} \qquad (1)$$

where θ is the panning angle and v is the scanline [18]. Similarly, we can map world coordinates into 2D spherical coordinates (θ, ϕ) using

$$\theta = \tan^{-1}(X/Z), \quad \phi = \tan^{-1}(Y/\sqrt{X^2 + Z^2}). \qquad (2)$$

Once we have warped each input image, constructing the panoramic mosaics becomes a pure translation problem. Ideally, to build a cylindrical or spherical panorama from a horizontal panning sequence, only the unknown panning angles need to be recovered. In practice, small vertical translations are needed to compensate for vertical jitter and optical twist. Therefore, both a horizontal translation t_x and a vertical translation t_y are estimated for each input image.

To recover the translational motion, we estimate the incremental translation $\delta\mathbf{t} = (\delta t_x, \delta t_y)$ by minimizing the intensity error between two images,

$$E(\delta\mathbf{t}) = \sum_i [I_1(\mathbf{x}_i' + \delta\mathbf{t}) - I_0(\mathbf{x}_i)]^2, \qquad (3)$$

where $\mathbf{x}_i = (x_i, y_i)$ and $\mathbf{x}_i' = (x_i', y_i') = (x_i + t_x, y_i + t_y)$ are corresponding points in the two images, and $\mathbf{t} = (t_x, t_y)$ is the global translational motion field which is the same for all pixels [2].

After a first order Taylor series expansion, the above equation becomes

$$E(\delta\mathbf{t}) \approx \sum_i [\mathbf{g}_i^T \delta\mathbf{t} + e_i]^2 \qquad (4)$$

where $e_i = I_1(\mathbf{x}_i') - I_0(\mathbf{x}_i)$ is the current intensity or color error, and $\mathbf{g}_i^T = \nabla I_1(\mathbf{x}_i')$ is the image gradient of I_1 at $\mathbf{x}_i'$. This minimization problem has a simple least-squares solution,

$$\left(\sum_i \mathbf{g}_i \mathbf{g}_i^T\right) \delta\mathbf{t} = -\left(\sum_i e_i \mathbf{g}_i\right). \qquad (5)$$

Figure 1b shows a portion of a cylindrical panoramic mosaic built using this simple translational alignment technique. To handle larger initial displacements, we use a hierarchical coarse-to-fine optimization scheme [2]. To reduce

discontinuities in intensity and color between the images being composited, we apply a simple *feathering* algorithm, i.e., we weight the pixels in each image proportionally to their distance to the edge (or more precisely, their distance to the nearest invisible pixel) [18]. Once registration is finished, we can clip the ends (and optionally the top and bottom), and write out a single panoramic image.

Creating panoramas in cylindrical or spherical coordinates has several limitations. First, it can only handle the simple case of pure panning motion. Second, even though it is possible to convert an image to 2D spherical or cylindrical coordinates for a known tilting angle, ill-sampling at north pole and south pole causes big registration errors. Third, it requires knowing the focal length (or equivalently, field of view). While focal length can be carefully calibrated in the lab[19, 16], estimating the focal length of lens by registering two or more images is not very accurate, as we will discuss in section 5.

3 Perspective (8-parameter) panoramas

To overcome these limitations, several authors have suggested using full planar perspective motion models [12, 9, 18]. The planar perspective transform warps an image into another using 8 parameters,

$$\mathbf{x}' \sim \mathbf{M}\mathbf{x} = \begin{bmatrix} m_0 & m_1 & m_2 \\ m_3 & m_4 & m_5 \\ m_6 & m_7 & 1 \end{bmatrix} \begin{bmatrix} x \\ y \\ 1 \end{bmatrix}, \qquad (6)$$

where $\mathbf{x} = (x, y, 1)$ and $\mathbf{x}' = (x', y', 1)$ are homogeneous or projective coordinates, and $\sim$ indicates equality up to scale. This equation can be re-written as

$$x' = \frac{m_0 x + m_1 y + m_2}{m_6 x + m_7 y + 1} \qquad (7)$$

$$y' = \frac{m_3 x + m_4 y + m_5}{m_6 x + m_7 y + 1} \qquad (8)$$

(in translational motion, only the two parameters m_2 and m_5 are used).

To recover the 8 paramters, we iteratively update the transform matrix using

$$\mathbf{M} \leftarrow (\mathbf{I} + \mathbf{D})\mathbf{M} \qquad (9)$$

where

$$\mathbf{D} = \begin{bmatrix} d_0 & d_1 & d_2 \\ d_3 & d_4 & d_5 \\ d_6 & d_7 & 0 \end{bmatrix}. \qquad (10)$$

Resampling image I_1 with the new transformation $\mathbf{x}' \sim (\mathbf{I} + \mathbf{D})\mathbf{M}\mathbf{x}$ is the same as warping the resampled image $\tilde{I}_1(\mathbf{x}_i) = I_1(\mathbf{x}_i')$ by $\mathbf{x}'' \sim (\mathbf{I} + \mathbf{D})\mathbf{x}$, i.e.,

$$x'' = \frac{(1 + d_0)x + d_1 y + d_2}{d_6 x + d_7 y + 1} \qquad (11)$$

$$y'' = \frac{d_3 x + (1 + d_4)y + d_5}{d_6 x + d_7 y + 1}. \qquad (12)$$

Again, we wish to minimize

$$E(\mathbf{d}) = \sum_i [\tilde{I}_1(\mathbf{x}_i'') - I_0(\mathbf{x}_i)]^2 \qquad (13)$$

$$\approx \sum_i [\mathbf{g}_i^T \mathbf{J}_i^T \mathbf{d} + e_i]^2 \qquad (14)$$

where $\mathbf{d} = (d_0, \ldots, d_7)$ is the incremental update parameter, and $\mathbf{J}_i = \mathbf{J_d}(\mathbf{x}_i)$, where

$$\mathbf{J_d}(\mathbf{x}) = \frac{\partial \mathbf{x}''}{\partial \mathbf{d}} = \begin{bmatrix} x & y & 1 & 0 & 0 & 0 & -x^2 & -xy \\ 0 & 0 & 0 & x & y & 1 & -xy & -y^2 \end{bmatrix}^T \tag{15}$$

is the Jacobian of the resampled point coordinate $\mathbf{x}''_i$ with respect to $\mathbf{d}$. The entries in the Jacobian correspond to the optical flow induced by the instantaneous motion of a plane in 3D [2]. The least-squares minimization problem (14) is solved using *normal equations* analogous to (5)

$$\mathbf{Ad} = -\mathbf{b}, \tag{16}$$

where

$$\mathbf{A} = \sum_i \mathbf{J}_i \mathbf{g}_i \mathbf{g}_i^T \mathbf{J}_i^T \tag{17}$$

is the *Hessian*, and

$$\mathbf{b} = \sum_i e_i \mathbf{J}_i \mathbf{g}_i \tag{18}$$

is the *accumulated gradient* or *residual*.

The 8-parameter perspective transformation recovery algorithm works well provided that initial estimates of the correct transformation are close enough. However, since the motion model contains more free parameters than necessary, it suffers from slow convergence and sometimes gets stuck in local minima. For this reason, we prefer to use the 3-parameter rotational model described next.

4 Rotational (3-parameter) panoramas

For a camera centered at the origin, the relationship between a 3D point $\mathbf{p} = (X, Y, Z)$ and its image coordinates $\mathbf{x} = (x, y, 1)$ can be described by

$$\mathbf{x} \sim \mathbf{TVRp}, \tag{19}$$

where

$$\mathbf{T} = \begin{bmatrix} 1 & 0 & c_x \\ 0 & 1 & c_y \\ 0 & 0 & 1 \end{bmatrix}, \mathbf{V} = \begin{bmatrix} f & 0 & 0 \\ 0 & f & 0 \\ 0 & 0 & 1 \end{bmatrix}, \text{ and } \mathbf{R} = \begin{bmatrix} r_{ij} \end{bmatrix}$$

are the image plane translation, focal length scaling, and 3D rotation matrices. For simplicity of notation, we assume that pixels are numbered so that the origin is at the image center, i.e., $c_x = c_y = 0$, allowing us to dispense with $\mathbf{T}$ (in practice, mislocating the image center does not seem to affect mosaic registration algorithms very much). The 3D direction corresponding to a screen pixel $\mathbf{x}$ is given by $\mathbf{p} \sim \mathbf{R}^{-1}\mathbf{V}^{-1}\mathbf{x}$.

For a camera rotating around its center of projection, the mapping (perspective projection) between two images k and l is therefore given by

$$\mathbf{M} \sim \mathbf{V}_k \mathbf{R}_k \mathbf{R}_l^{-1} \mathbf{V}_l^{-1} \tag{20}$$

where each image is represented by $\mathbf{V}_k \mathbf{R}_k$, i.e., a focal length and a 3D rotation.

Assume for now that the focal length is known and is the same for all images, i.e, $\mathbf{V}_k = \mathbf{V}$. To recover the rotation, we perform an incremental update to $\mathbf{R}_k$ based on the angular velocity $\mathbf{\Omega} = (\omega_x, \omega_y, \omega_z)$,

$$\mathbf{M} \leftarrow \mathbf{V}\hat{\mathbf{R}}(\mathbf{\Omega})\mathbf{R}_k \mathbf{R}_l^{-1} \mathbf{V}^{-1} \tag{21}$$

where the incremental rotation matrix $\hat{\mathbf{R}}(\mathbf{\Omega})$ is given by Rodriguez's formula [1],

$$\hat{\mathbf{R}}(\hat{\mathbf{n}}, \theta) = \mathbf{I} + \sin\theta \mathbf{X}(\hat{\mathbf{n}}) + (1 - \cos\theta)\mathbf{X}(\hat{\mathbf{n}})^2 \tag{22}$$

with $\theta = \|\mathbf{\Omega}\|$, $\hat{\mathbf{n}} = \mathbf{\Omega}/\theta$, and

$$\mathbf{X}(\mathbf{\Omega}) = \begin{bmatrix} 0 & -\omega_z & \omega_y \\ \omega_z & 0 & -\omega_x \\ -\omega_y & \omega_x & 0 \end{bmatrix}$$

is the cross product operator. Keeping only terms linear in $\mathbf{\Omega}$, we get

$$\mathbf{M}' \approx \mathbf{V}[\mathbf{I} + \mathbf{X}(\mathbf{\Omega})]\mathbf{R}_k \mathbf{R}_l^{-1} \mathbf{V}^{-1} = (\mathbf{I} + \mathbf{D}_\Omega)\mathbf{M}, \tag{23}$$

where

$$\mathbf{D}_\Omega = \mathbf{V}\mathbf{X}(\mathbf{\Omega})\mathbf{V}^{-1} = \begin{bmatrix} 0 & -\omega_z & f\omega_y \\ \omega_z & 0 & -f\omega_x \\ -\omega_y/f & \omega_x/f & 0 \end{bmatrix}$$

is the deformation matrix which plays the same role as $\mathbf{D}$ in (9).

Computing the Jacobian of the entries in $\mathbf{D}_\Omega$ with respect to $\mathbf{\Omega}$ and applying the chain rule, we obtain the new Jacobian,

$$\mathbf{J}_\Omega = \frac{\partial \mathbf{x}''}{\partial \mathbf{\Omega}} = \frac{\partial \mathbf{x}''}{\partial \mathbf{d}} \frac{\partial \mathbf{d}}{\partial \mathbf{\Omega}} = \begin{bmatrix} -xy/f & f + x^2/f & -y \\ -f - y^2/f & xy/f & x \end{bmatrix}^T. \tag{24}$$

This Jacobian is then plugged into the previous minimization pipeline to estimate the incremental rotation vector $(\omega_x \ \omega_y \ \omega_z)$, after which $\mathbf{R}_k$ can be updated using (21).

Figure 2 shows how our method can be used to register four images with arbitrary (non-panning) rotation. Compared to the 8-parameter perspective model, it is much easier and more intuitive to interactively adjust images using the 3-parameter rotational model.

5 Estimating the focal length

In order to apply our 3D rotation technique, we must first obtain an estimate for the camera's focal length. A convenient way to obtain this estimate to deduce the value from one or more perspective transforms computed using the 8-parameter algorithm. Expanding the $\mathbf{V}_1 \mathbf{R} \mathbf{V}_0^{-1}$ formulation, we have

$$\mathbf{M} = \begin{bmatrix} m_0 & m_1 & m_2 \\ m_3 & m_4 & m_5 \\ m_6 & m_7 & 1 \end{bmatrix} \sim \begin{bmatrix} r_{00} & r_{01} & r_{02}f_0 \\ r_{10} & r_{11} & r_{12}f_0 \\ r_{20}/f_1 & r_{21}/f_1 & r_{22}f_0/f_1 \end{bmatrix} \tag{25}$$

where $\mathbf{R} = [r_{ij}]$.

In order to estimate focal lengths f_0 and f_1, we observe that the first two rows (columns) of $\mathbf{R}$ must have the same norm and be orthogonal (even if the matrix is scaled), i.e.,

$$m_0^2 + m_1^2 + m_2^2/f_0^2 = m_3^2 + m_4^2 + m_5^2/f_0^2. \tag{26}$$

$$m_0 m_3 + m_1 m_4 + m_2 m_5/f_0^2 = 0. \tag{27}$$

From this, we can compute the estimates

$$f_0^2 = \sqrt{\frac{m_0^2 + m_1^2 - m_3^2 - m_4^2}{m_5^2 - m_2^2}} \quad \text{if } m_5 \neq m_2$$

or

$$f_0^2 = -\frac{m_0 m_3 + m_1 m_4}{m_2 m_5} \quad \text{if } m_5 \neq 0 \text{ and } m_2 \neq 0.$$

Similar result can be obtained for f_1 as well. If the focal length is fixed for two images, we can take the geometric mean of f_0 and f_1 as the estimated focal length $f = \sqrt{f_1 f_0}$. When multiple estimates of f are available, the median value is used as the final estimate.

Alternative techniques for estimating the focal length are presented in [8, 16, 13, 10]. The first technique [8] uses more than two frames and assumes a more general camera model (e.g., unknown optical center and aspect ratio). The other techniques either assume known rotation angles or use a complete panorama (similar to the technique described in section 6).

Once an initial set of f estimates is available, we can improve these estimates as part of the image registration process, using the same kind of least squares approach as for the rotation [15].

6 Closing the gap in a panorama

Even with our best algorithms for recovering rotations and focal length, when a complete panoramic sequence is stitched together, there will invariably be either a gap or an overlap (due to accumulated errors in the rotation estimates). We solve this problem by registering the same image at both the beginning and the end of the sequence.

The difference in the rotation matrices (actually, their quotient) directly tells us the amount of misregistration. This error can be distributed evenly across the whole sequence by converting the error in rotation into a quaternion, and dividing the quaternion by the number of images in the sequence (for lack of a better guess).

We can also update the estimated focal length based on the amount of misregistration. To do this, we first convert the quaternion describing the misregistration into a *gap angle* θ_g. We can then update the focal length using the equation

$$f' = \frac{360° - \theta_g}{360°} * f. \tag{28}$$

Figure 3a shows the end of registered image sequence and the first image. There is a big gap between the last image and the first which are in fact the same image. The gap is $32°$ because the wrong estimate of focal length (510) was used. Figure 3b shows the registration after closing the gap with the correct focal length (468). Notice that both mosaics show very little visual misregistration (except at the gap), yet Figure 3a has been computed using a focal length which has 9% error.

Related approaches have been developed by [13, 16, 10] to solve the focal length estimation problem using pure panning motion and cylindrical images. In recent work, we have developed an alternative approach to removing gaps and overlaps which works for arbitrary image sequences (see Section 8).

7 Environment map construction

Once we have constructed a complete panoramic mosaic, we need to convert the set of input images and associated transforms into one or more images which can be quickly rendered or viewed.

A traditional way to do this is to choose either a cylindrical or spherical map (Section 2). When being used as an environment map, such a representation is sometimes called a latitude-longitude projection [7]. The color associated with each pixel is computed by first converting the pixel address to a 3D ray, and then mapping this ray into each input image through our known transformation. The colors picked up from each image are then blended using the weighting function (feathering) described earlier. For example, we can convert our rotational panorama to spherical panorama using the following algorithm:

1. for each pixel (θ, ϕ) in the spherical map, compute its corresponding 3D position on unit sphere $\mathbf{p} = (X, Y, Z)$ where $X = cos(\phi)sin(\theta), Y = sin(\phi)$, and $Z = cos(\phi)cos(\theta)$;

2. for each $\mathbf{p}$, determine its mapping into each image k using $\mathbf{x} \sim \mathbf{T}_k \mathbf{V}_k \mathbf{R}_k \mathbf{p}$;

3. form a composite (blended) image from the above warped images.

Unfortunately, such a map requires a specialized viewer, and thus cannot take advantage of any hardware texture-mapping acceleration (without approximating the cylinder's or sphere's shape with a polyhedron, which would introduce distortions into the rendering). For true full-view panoramas, spherical maps also introduce a distortion around each pole.

As an alternative, we propose the use of traditional texture-mapped models, i.e., environment maps [7]. The shape of the model and the embedding of each face into texture space are left up to the user. This choice can range from something as simple as a cube with six separate texture maps [7], to something as complicated as a subdivided dodecahedron, or even a latitude-longitude tesselated globe.[1] This choice will depend on the characteristics of the rendering hardware and the desired quality (e.g., minimizing distortions or local changes in pixel size), and on external considerations such as the ease of painting on the resulting texture maps (since some embeddings may leave gaps in the texture map).

In this section, we describe how to efficiently compute texture map color values for any geometry and choice of texture map coordinates. A generalization of this algorithm can be used to project a collection of images onto an arbitrary model, e.g., non-convex models which do not surround the viewer.

We assume that the object model is a triangulated surface, i.e., a collection of triangles and vertices, where each vertex is tagged with its 3D (X, Y, Z) coordinates and (u, v) texture coordinates (faces may be assigned to different texture maps). We restrict the model to triangular faces in order to obtain a simple, closed-form solution (projective map, potentially different for each triangle) between texture coordinates and image coordinates. The output of our algorithm is a set of colored texture maps, with undefined (invisible) pixels flagged (e.g., if an alpha channel is used, then $\alpha \leftarrow 0$).

Our algorithm consists of the following four steps:

1. paint each triangle in (u, v) space a unique color;

2. for each triangle, determine its $(u, v, 1) \rightarrow (X, Y, Z)$ mapping;

3. for each triangle, form a composite (blended) image;

4. paint the composite image into the final texture map using the color values computed in step 1 as a stencil.

---

[1]This latter representation is equivalent to a spherical map in the limit as the globe facets become infinitessimally small. The important difference is that even with large facets, an exact rendering can be obtained with regular texture-mapping algorithms and hardware.

These four steps are described in more detail below.

The pseudocoloring (triangle painting) step uses an auxilliary buffer the same size as the texture map. We use an RGB image, which means that 2^{24} colors are available. After the initial coloring, we grow the colors into invisible regions using a simple dilation operation, i.e., iteratively replacing invisible pixels with one of their visible neighbor pseudocolors. This operation is performed in order to eliminate small gaps in the texture map, and to support filtering operations such as bilinear texture mapping and MIP mapping [21]. For example, when using a six-sided cube, we set the (u, v) coordinates of each square vertex to be slightly inside the margins of the texture map. Thus, each texture map covers a little more region than it needs to, but operation such a texture filtering and MIP mapping can be performed without worrying about edge effects.

In the second step, we compute the $(u, v, 1) \rightarrow (X, Y, Z)$ mapping for each triangle T by finding the 3×3 matrix $\mathbf{M}_T$ which satisfies

$$\mathbf{u}_i = \mathbf{M}_T \mathbf{p}_i$$

for each of the three triangle vertices i. Thus, $\mathbf{M}_T = \mathbf{U}\mathbf{P}^{-1}$, where $\mathbf{U} = [\mathbf{u}_0|\mathbf{u}_1|\mathbf{u}_2]$ and $\mathbf{P} = [\mathbf{p}_0|\mathbf{p}_1|\mathbf{p}_2]$ are formed by concatenating the $\mathbf{u}_i$ and $\mathbf{p}_i$ 3-vectors. This mapping is essentially a mapping from 3D directions in space (since the cameras are all at the origin) to (u, v) coordinates.

In the third step, we compute a bounding box around each triangle in (u, v) space and enlarge it slightly (by the same amount as the dilation in step 1). We then form a composite image by blending all of the input images j according to the transformation $\mathbf{u} = \mathbf{M}_T \mathbf{R}_k^{-1} \mathbf{V}_k^{-1} \mathbf{x}$. This is a full, 8-parameter perspective transformation. It is *not* the same as the 6-parameter affine map which would be obtained by simply projecting a triangle's vertices into the image, and then mapping these 2D image coordinates into 2D texture space (in essence ignoring the foreshortening in the projection onto the 3D model). The error in applying this naive but erroneous method to large texture map facets (e.g., those of a simple unrefined cube) would be quite large.

In the fourth step, we find the pseudocolor associated with each pixel inside the composited patch, and paint the composited color into the texture map if the pseudocolor matches the face id.

Our algorithm can also be used to project a collection of images onto an arbitrary object, i.e., to do true inverse texture mapping, by extending our algorithm to handle occlusions. To do this, we simply paint the pseudocolored polyhedral model into each input image using a z-buffering algorithm (this is called an *item buffer* in ray tracing [20]). When compositing the image for each face, we then check to see which pixels match the desired pseudocolor, and set those which do not match to be invisible (i.e., not to contribute to the final composite).

Figure 4 shows the results of mapping a panoramic mosaic onto a longitude-latitude tesselated globe. The white triangles at the top are the parts of the texture map not covered in the 3D tesselated globe model (due to triangular elements at the poles). Figures 5–7 show the results of mapping three different panoramic mosaics onto cubical environment maps. We can see that the mosaics are of very high quality, and also get a good sense for the extent of viewing sphere covered by these full-view mosaics. Note that Figure 5 uses images taken with a hand-held digital camera.

Once the texture-mapped 3D models have been constructed, they can be rendered directly with a standard 3D graphics system. For our work, we are currently using a simple 3D viewer written on top of the Direct3D API running on a personal computer with no hardware graphics acceleration.

8   Discussion

In this paper, we have developed some new techniques for building full view panoramic image mosaics. Our system does not place constraints on how the input images are taken, and allows the images to be taken with hand held cameras. By taking many overlapping images, we can significantly increase the field of view of the constructed panorama and remove the need for expensive fisheye lenses. Our method is accurate and robust because we estimate only 3 unknowns in the rotation matrix instead of 8 parameters in the general perspective transforms. Our method greatly increases accuracy, flexibility, and ease of use of previous techniques. We have also developed techniques for estimating the focal length from an image sequence, and for recovering from accumulated registration errors when a full panoramic mosaic is completed.

When building an image mosaic from a long sequence of images, we have to deal with error accumulation problems. In this paper we have presented a "gap closing" technique which updates the focal length and rotation matrices after a complete panorama is constructed. More recently we have developed a new method based on *block adjustment* which simultaneously adjusts all rotation matrices and focal lengths so that the sum of registration errors between all matching pairs of images is minimized [15].

In theory, panoramas can only be constructed if all images are taken by a camera whose optical centers never moves. In practice, this depends on the amount of camera translation relative to the nearest objects in front of the camera. With our 3-D rotation mosaicing method, we have demonstrated that images taken by a hand held digital camera can be seamlessly stitched. To compensate for local misregistration caused by larger amounts of motion parallax (e.g., camera translation), we have recently developed a *deghosting* technique [15]. We divide each image into small patches and compute patch-based alignments. Each image is then locally warped so that the overall mosaic does not contain visible ghosting. This deghosting method has been used to build the image mosaic of the Space Shuttle flight deck (Figure 8) from a sequence of images (with significant motion parallax) taken by an astronant with a hand-held camera.

We have also presented an algorithm for extracting texture maps from the image mosaics. We can map image mosaics onto any 3-D model and exploit 3-D graphics hardware and APIs. Compared with using special purpose players (e.g., cylindrical and spherical viewers), our inverse texture mapping approach can be much more easily integrated as backdrops for virtual worlds and games. In the future, we would like to explore how to extract the three-dimensional world descriptions from full-view panoramic image mosaics.

References

[1] N. Ayache. *Vision Stéréoscopique et Perception Multisensorielle.* InterEditions., Paris, 1989.

[2] J. R. Bergen, P. Anandan, K. J. Hanna, and R. Hingorani. Hierarchical model-based motion estimation. In *Second European Conference on Computer Vision (ECCV'92)*, pages 237–252, Santa Margherita Liguere, Italy, May 1992. Springer-Verlag.

[3] S. Chen and L. Williams. View interpolation for image synthesis. *Computer Graphics (SIGGRAPH'93)*, pages 279–288, August 1993.

[4] S. E. Chen. QuickTime VR – an image-based approach to virtual environment navigation. *Computer Graphics (SIG-GRAPH'95)*, pages 29–38, August 1995.

[5] O. Faugeras. *Three-dimensional computer vision: A geometric viewpoint*. MIT Press, Cambridge, Massachusetts, 1993.

[6] S. J. Gortler, R. Grzeszczuk, R. Szeliski, and M. F. Cohen. The lumigraph. In *Computer Graphics Proceedings, Annual Conference Series*, pages 43–54, Proc. SIGGRAPH'96 (New Orleans), August 1996. ACM SIGGRAPH.

[7] N. Greene. Environment mapping and other applications of world projections. *IEEE Computer Graphics and Applications*, 6(11):21–29, November 1986.

[8] R. I. Hartley. Self-calibration from multiple views of a rotating camera. In *Third European Conference on Computer Vision (ECCV'94)*, volume 1, pages 471–478, Stockholm, Sweden, May 1994. Springer-Verlag.

[9] M. Irani, P. Anandan, and S. Hsu. Mosaic based representations of video sequences and their applications. In *Fifth International Conference on Computer Vision (ICCV'95)*, pages 605–611, Cambridge, Massachusetts, June 1995.

[10] S. B. Kang and R Weiss. Characterization of errors in compositing panoramic images. Technical Report 96/2, Digital Equipment Corporation, Cambridge Research Lab, June 1996.

[11] M. Levoy and P. Hanrahan. Light field rendering. In *Computer Graphics Proceedings, Annual Conference Series*, pages 31–42, Proc. SIGGRAPH'96 (New Orleans), August 1996. ACM SIGGRAPH.

[12] S. Mann and R. W. Picard. Virtual bellows: Constructing high-quality images from video. In *First IEEE International Conference on Image Processing (ICIP-94)*, volume I, pages 363–367, Austin, Texas, November 1994.

[13] L. McMillan and G. Bishop. Plenoptic modeling: An image-based rendering system. *Computer Graphics (SIGGRAPH'95)*, pages 39–46, August 1995.

[14] J. Meehan. *Panoramic Photography*. Watson-Guptill, 1990.

[15] H.-Y. Shum and R. Szeliski. Construction and refinement of panoramic mosaics with global and local alignment. Submitted for review, April 1997.

[16] G. Stein. Accurate internal camera calibration using rotation, with analysis of sources of error. In *Fifth International Conference on Computer Vision (ICCV'95)*, pages 230–236, Cambridge, Massachusetts, June 1995.

[17] R. Szeliski. Image mosaicing for tele-reality applications. In *IEEE Workshop on Applications of Computer Vision (WACV'94)*, pages 44–53, Sarasota, Florida, December 1994. IEEE Computer Society.

[18] R. Szeliski. Video mosaics for virtual environments. *IEEE Computer Graphics and Applications*, pages 22–30, March 1996.

[19] R. Y. Tsai. A versatile camera calibration technique for high-accuracy 3D machine vision metrology using off-the-shelf TV cameras and lenses. *IEEE Journal of Robotics and Automation*, RA-3(4):323–344, August 1987.

[20] H. Weghorst, G. Hooper, and D. P. Greenberg. Improved computational methods for ray tracing. *ACM Transactions on Graphics*, 3(1):52069, January 1984.

[21] L. Williams. Pyramidal parametrics. *Computer Graphics*, 17(3):1–11, July 1983.

[22] http://qtvr.quicktime.apple.com.

[23] http://www.bdiamon.com.

[24] http://www.omniview.com.

[25] http://www.smoothmove.com.

[26] http://www.rlspace.com.

[27] http://www.behere.com.

[28] http://www.cs.columbia.edu/cave/omnicam.

(a)

(b)

Figure 1: Construction of a cylindrical panorama: (a) two warped images; (b) part of cylindrical panorama composited from a sequence of images.

Figure 2: 3D rotation registration of four images taken with a hand-held camera.

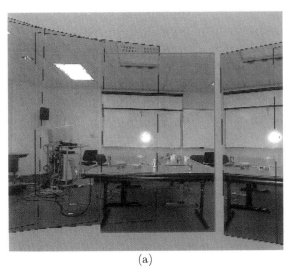 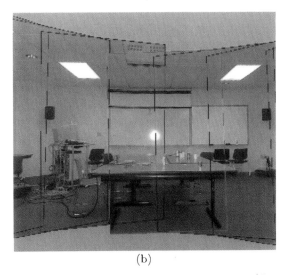

(a)   (b)

Figure 3: Gap closing after sequentially registering 24 images: (a) a gap is visible when the focal length is wrong ($f = 510$); (b) no gap is visible for the correct focal length ($f = 468$).

Figure 4: Tessellated spherical panorama covering the north pole (constructed from 54 images). The white triangles at the top are the parts of the texture map not covered in the 3D tesselated globe model (due to triangular elements at the poles).

Figure 5: Cubical texture-mapped model of conference room (from 75 images taken with a hand-held digital camera).

Figure 6: Cubical texture-mapped model of lobby (from 54 images).

Figure 7: Cubical texture-mapped model of hallway and sitting area (from 36 images).

Figure 8: Panorama of Space Shuttle flight deck from 14 images taken with a hand-held camera (using *deghosting* technique).

Interactive Multiresolution Mesh Editing

Denis Zorin*
Caltech

Peter Schröder†
Caltech

Wim Sweldens‡
Bell Laboratories

Abstract

We describe a multiresolution representation for meshes based on subdivision, which is a natural extension of the existing patch-based surface representations. Combining subdivision and the smoothing algorithms of Taubin [26] allows us to construct a set of algorithms for interactive multiresolution editing of complex hierarchical meshes of arbitrary topology. The simplicity of the underlying algorithms for refinement and coarsification enables us to make them local and adaptive, thereby considerably improving their efficiency. We have built a scalable interactive multiresolution editing system based on such algorithms.

1   Introduction

Applications such as special effects and animation require creation and manipulation of complex geometric models of arbitrary topology. Like real world geometry, these models often carry detail at many scales (cf. Fig. 1). The model might be constructed from scratch (ab initio design) in an interactive modeling environment or be scanned-in either by hand or with automatic digitizing methods. The latter is a common source of data particularly in the entertainment industry. When using laser range scanners, for example, individual models are often composed of high resolution meshes with hundreds of thousands to millions of triangles.

Manipulating such fine meshes can be difficult, especially when they are to be edited or animated. Interactivity, which is crucial in these cases, is challenging to achieve. Even without accounting for any computation on the mesh itself, available rendering resources alone, may not be able to cope with the sheer size of the data. Possible approaches include mesh optimization [15, 13] to reduce the size of the meshes.

Aside from considerations of economy, the choice of representation is also guided by the need for multiresolution editing semantics. The representation of the mesh needs to provide control at a large scale, so that one can change the mesh in a broad, smooth manner, for example. Additionally designers will typically also want control over the minute features of the model (cf. Fig. 1). Smoother approximations can be built through the use of patches [14], though at the cost of loosing the high frequency details. Such detail can be reintroduced by combining patches with displacement maps [17]. However, this is difficult to manage in the

*dzorin@gg.caltech.edu
†ps@cs.caltech.edu
‡wim@bell-labs.com

arbitrary topology setting and across a continuous range of scales and hardware resources.

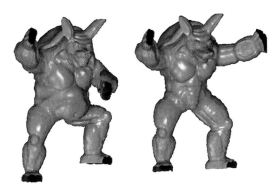

Figure 1: Before the Armadillo started working out he was flabby, complete with a double chin. Now he exercises regularly. The original is on the right (courtesy Venkat Krischnamurthy). The edited version on the left illustrates large scale edits, such as his belly, and smaller scale edits such as his double chin; all edits were performed at about 5 frames per second on an Indigo R10000 Solid Impact.

For reasons of efficiency the algorithms should be highly adaptive and dynamically adjust to available resources. Our goal is to have a single, simple, uniform representation with scalable algorithms. The system should be capable of delivering multiple frames per second update rates even on small workstations taking advantage of lower resolution representations.

In this paper we present a system which possesses these properties

- **Multiresolution control:** Both broad and general handles, as well as small knobs to tweak minute detail are available.

- **Speed/fidelity tradeoff:** All algorithms dynamically adapt to available resources to maintain interactivity.

- **Simplicity/uniformity:** A single primitive, triangular mesh, is used to represent the surface across all levels of resolution.

Our system is inspired by a number of earlier approaches. We mention multiresolution editing [11, 9, 12], arbitrary topology subdivision [6, 2, 19, 7, 28, 16], wavelet representations [21, 24, 8, 3], and mesh simplification [13, 17]. Independently an approach similar to ours was developed by Pulli and Lounsbery [23].

It should be noted that our methods rely on the finest level mesh having subdivision connectivity. This requires a remeshing step before external high resolution geometry can be imported into the editor. Eck et al. [8] have described a possible approach to remeshing arbitrary finest level input meshes fully automatically. A method that relies on a user's expertise was developed by Krishnamurthy and Levoy [17].

1.1   Earlier Editing Approaches

H-splines were presented in pioneering work on hierarchical editing by Forsey and Bartels [11]. Briefly, H-splines are obtained by adding finer resolution B-splines onto an existing coarser resolution B-spline patch relative to the coordinate frame induced by the coarser patch. Repeating this process, one can build very complicated shapes which are entirely parameterized over the unit square. Forsey and Bartels observed that the hierarchy induced coordinate frame for the offsets is essential to achieve correct editing semantics.

H-splines provide a uniform framework for representing both the coarse and fine level details. Note however, that as more detail is added to such a model the internal control mesh data structures more and more resemble a fine polyhedral mesh.

While their original implementation allowed only for regular topologies their approach could be extended to the general setting by using surface splines or one of the spline derived general topology subdivision schemes [18]. However, these schemes have not yet been made to work adaptively.

Forsey and Bartels' original work focused on the ab initio design setting. There the user's help is enlisted in defining what is meant by different levels of resolution. The user decides where to add detail and manipulates the corresponding controls. This way the levels of the hierarchy are hand built by a human user and the representation of the final object is a function of its editing history.

To edit an a priori given model it is crucial to have a general procedure to define coarser levels and compute details between levels. We refer to this as the *analysis* algorithm. An H-spline analysis algorithm based on weighted least squares was introduced [10], but is too expensive to run interactively. Note that even in an ab initio design setting online analysis is needed, since after a long sequence of editing steps the H-spline is likely to be overly refined and needs to be consolidated.

Wavelets provide a framework in which to rigorously define multiresolution approximations and fast analysis algorithms. Finkelstein and Salesin [9], for example, used B-spline wavelets to describe multiresolution editing of curves. As in H-splines, parameterization of details with respect to a coordinate frame induced by the coarser level approximation is required to get correct editing semantics. Gortler and Cohen [12], pointed out that wavelet representations of detail tend to behave in undesirable ways during editing and returned to a pure B-spline representation as used in H-splines.

Carrying these constructions over into the arbitrary topology surface framework is not straightforward. In the work by Lounsbery et al. [21] the connection between wavelets and subdivision was used to define the different levels of resolution. The original constructions were limited to piecewise linear subdivision, but smoother constructions are possible [24, 28].

An approach to surface modeling based on variational methods was proposed by Welch and Witkin [27]. An attractive characteristic of their method is flexibility in the choice of control points. However, they use a global optimization procedure to compute the surface which is not suitable for interactive manipulation of complex surfaces.

Before we proceed to a more detailed discussion of editing we first discuss different surface representations to motivate our choice of synthesis (refinement) algorithm.

1.2 Surface Representations

There are many possible choices for surface representations. Among the most popular are polynomial patches and polygons.

Patches are a powerful primitive for the construction of coarse grain, smooth models using a small number of control parameters. Combined with hardware support relatively fast implementations are possible. However, when building complex models with many patches the preservation of smoothness across patch boundaries can be quite cumbersome and expensive. These difficulties are compounded in the arbitrary topology setting when polynomial parameterizations cease to exist everywhere. Surface splines [4, 20, 22] provide one way to address the arbitrary topology challenge.

As more fine level detail is needed the proliferation of control points and patches can quickly overwhelm both the user and the most powerful hardware. With detail at finer levels, patches become less suited and polygonal meshes are more appropriate.

Polygonal Meshes can represent arbitrary topology and resolve fine detail as found in laser scanned models, for example. Given that most hardware rendering ultimately resolves to triangle scan-conversion even for patches, polygonal meshes are a very basic primitive. Because of sheer size, polygonal meshes are difficult to manipulate interactively. Mesh simplification algorithms [13] provide one possible answer. However, we need a mesh simplification approach, that is hierarchical and gives us shape handles for smooth changes over larger regions while maintaining high frequency details.

Patches and fine polygonal meshes represent two ends of a spectrum. Patches efficiently describe large smooth sections of a surface but cannot model fine detail very well. Polygonal meshes are good at describing very fine detail accurately using dense meshes, but do not provide coarser manipulation semantics.

Subdivision connects and unifies these two extremes.

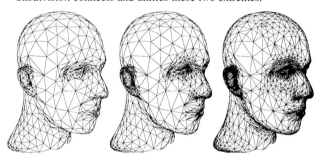

Figure 2: Subdivision describes a smooth surface as the limit of a sequence of refined polyhedra. The meshes show several levels of an adaptive Loop surface generated by our system (dataset courtesy Hugues Hoppe, University of Washington).

Subdivision defines a smooth surface as the limit of a sequence of successively refined polyhedral meshes (cf. Fig. 2). In the regular patch based setting, for example, this sequence can be defined through well known knot insertion algorithms [5]. Some subdivision methods generalize spline based knot insertion to irregular topology control meshes [2, 6, 19] while other subdivision schemes are independent of splines and include a number of interpolating schemes [7, 28, 16].

Since subdivision provides a path from patches to meshes, it can serve as a good foundation for the unified infrastructure that we seek. A single representation (hierarchical polyhedral meshes) supports the patch-type semantics of manipulation *and* finest level detail polyhedral edits equally well. The main challenge is to make the basic algorithms fast enough to escape the exponential time and space growth of naive subdivision. This is the core of our contribution.

We summarize the main features of subdivision important in our context

- **Topological Generality:** Vertices in a triangular (resp. quadrilateral) mesh need not have valence 6 (resp. 4). Generated surfaces are smooth everywhere, and efficient algorithms exist for computing normals and limit positions of points on the surface.

- **Multiresolution:** because they are the limit of successive refinement, subdivision surfaces support multiresolution algorithms, such as level-of-detail rendering, multiresolution editing, compression, wavelets, and numerical multigrid.

- **Simplicity:** subdivision algorithms are simple: the finer mesh is built through insertion of new vertices followed by *local* smoothing.

- **Uniformity of Representation:** subdivision provides a single representation of a surface at all resolution levels. Boundaries and features such as creases can be resolved through modified rules [14, 25], reducing the need for trim curves, for example.

1.3 Our Contribution

Aside from our perspective, which unifies the earlier approaches, our major contribution—and the main challenge in this program—is the design of highly adaptive and dynamic data structures and algorithms, which allow the system to function across a range of computational resources from PCs to workstations, delivering as much interactive fidelity as possible with a given polygon rendering performance. Our algorithms work for the class of 1-ring subdivision schemes (definition see below) and we demonstrate their performance for the concrete case of Loop's subdivision scheme.

The particulars of those algorithms will be given later, but Fig. 3 already gives a preview of how the different algorithms make up the editing system. In the next sections we first talk in more detail about subdivision, smoothing, and multiresolution transforms.

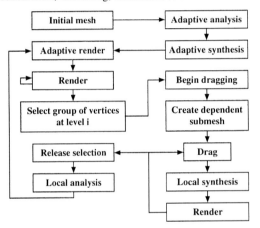

Figure 3: The relationship between various procedures as the user moves a set of vertices.

2 Subdivision

We begin by defining subdivision and fixing our notation. There are 2 points of view that we must distinguish. On the one hand we are dealing with an abstract *graph* and perform topological operations on it. On the other hand we have a *mesh* which is the geometric object in 3-space. The mesh is the image of a map defined on the graph: it associates a *point* in 3D with every *vertex* in the graph (cf. Fig. 4). A *triangle* denotes a face in the graph or the associated polygon in 3-space.

Initially we have a triangular graph T^0 with vertices V^0. By recursively *refining* each triangle into 4 subtriangles we can build a sequence of finer triangulations T^i with vertices V^i, $i > 0$ (cf. Fig. 4). The superscript i indicates the *level* of triangles and vertices respectively. A triangle $t \in T^i$ is a triple of indices $t = \{v_a, v_b, v_c\} \subset V^i$.

The vertex sets are nested as $V^j \subset V^i$ if $j < i$. We define *odd* vertices on level i as $M^i = V^{i+1} \setminus V^i$. V^{i+1} consists of two disjoint sets: *even* vertices (V^i) and *odd* vertices (M^i). We define the *level* of a vertex v as the smallest i for which $v \in V^i$. The level of v is $i + 1$ if and only if $v \in M^i$.

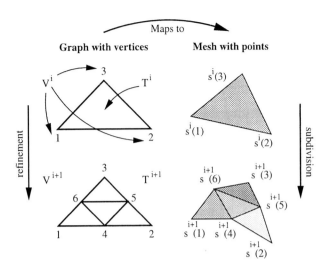

Figure 4: Left: the abstract graph. Vertices and triangles are members of sets V^i and T^i respectively. Their index indicates the level of refinement when they first appeared. Right: the mapping to the mesh and its subdivision in 3-space.

With each set V^i we associate a map, i.e., for each vertex v and each level i we have a 3D point $s^i(v) \in \mathbf{R}^3$. The set s^i contains all points on level i, $s^i = \{s^i(v) \mid v \in V^i\}$. Finally, a *subdivision scheme* is a linear operator S which takes the points from level i to points on the *finer* level $i + 1$: $s^{i+1} = S\, s^i$

Assuming that the subdivision converges, we can define a limit surface σ as

$$\sigma = \lim_{k \to \infty} S^k s^0.$$

$\sigma(v) \in \mathbf{R}^3$ denotes the point on the limit surface associated with vertex v.

In order to define our offsets with respect to a local frame we also need tangent vectors and a normal. For the subdivision schemes that we use, such vectors can be defined through the application of linear operators Q and R acting on s^i so that $q^i(v) = (Qs^i)(v)$ and $r^i(v) = (Rs^i)(v)$ are linearly independent tangent vectors at $\sigma(v)$. Together with an orientation they define a local orthonormal frame $F^i(v) = (n^i(v), q^i(v), r^i(v))$. It is important to note that in general it is not necessary to use precise normals and tangents during editing; as long as the frame vectors are affinely related to the positions of vertices of the mesh, we can expect intuitive editing behavior.

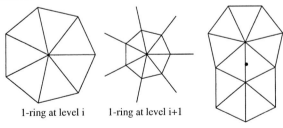

Figure 5: An even vertex has a 1-ring of neighbors at each level of refinement (left/middle). Odd vertices—in the middle of edges—have 1-rings around each of the vertices at either end of their edge (right).

Next we discuss two common subdivision schemes, both of which belong to the class of *1-ring schemes*. In these schemes points at level $i + 1$ depend only on 1-ring neighborhoods of points at level i. Let $v \in V^i$ (v even) then the point $s^{i+1}(v)$ is a function of only those $s^i(v_n)$, $v_n \in V^i$, which are immediate neighbors of v (cf. Fig. 5 left/middle). If $m \in M^i$ (m odd), it is the vertex inserted when splitting an edge of the graph; we call such vertices *middle vertices* of edges. In this case the point $s^{i+1}(m)$ is a function of the 1-rings around the vertices at the ends of the edge (cf. Fig. 5 right).

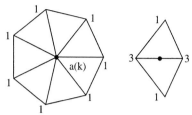

Figure 6: Stencils for Loop subdivision with unnormalized weights for even and odd vertices.

Loop is a non-interpolating subdivision scheme based on a generalization of quartic triangular box splines [19]. For a given even vertex $v \in V^i$, let $v_k \in V^i$ with $1 \le k \le K$ be its K 1-ring neighbors. The new point $s^{i+1}(v)$ is defined as $s^{i+1}(v) = (a(K) + K)^{-1}(a(K) s^i(v) + \sum_{k=1}^{K} s^i(v_k))$ (cf. Fig. 6), $a(K) = K(1-\alpha(K))/\alpha(K)$, and $\alpha(K) = 5/8 - (3 + 2\cos(2\pi/K))^2/64$. For odd v the weights shown in Fig. 6 are used. Two independent tangent vectors $t_1(v)$ and $t_2(v)$ are given by $t_p(v) = \sum_{k=1}^{K} \cos(2\pi(k+p)/K) s^i(v_k)$.

Features such as boundaries and cusps can be accommodated through simple modifications of the stencil weights [14, 25, 29].

Butterfly is an interpolating scheme, first proposed by Dyn et al. [7] in the topologically regular setting and recently generalized to arbitrary topologies [28]. Since it is interpolating we have $s^i(v) = \sigma(v)$ for $v \in V^i$ even. The exact expressions for odd vertices depend on the valence K and the reader is referred to the original paper for the exact values [28].

For our implementation we have chosen the Loop scheme, since more performance optimizations are possible in it. However, the algorithms we discuss later work for any 1-ring scheme.

3 Multiresolution Transforms

So far we only discussed subdivision, i.e., how to go from coarse to fine meshes. In this section we describe analysis which goes from fine to coarse.

We first need *smoothing*, i.e., a linear operation H to build a smooth coarse mesh at level $i - 1$ from a fine mesh at level i:

$$s^{i-1} = H s^i.$$

Several options are available here:

- **Least squares:** One could define analysis to be optimal in the least squares sense,

$$\min_{s^{i-1}} \| s^i - S s^{i-1} \|^2.$$

The solution may have unwanted undulations and is too expensive to compute interactively [10].

- **Fairing:** A coarse surface could be obtained as the solution to a global variational problem. This is too expensive as well. An alternative is presented by Taubin [26], who uses a *local* non-shrinking smoothing approach.

Because of its computational simplicity we decided to use a version of Taubin smoothing. As before let $v \in V^i$ have K neighbors $v_k \in V^i$. Use the average, $\bar{s}^i(v) = K^{-1} \sum_{k=1}^{K} s^i(v_k)$, to define the discrete Laplacian $\mathcal{L}(v) = \bar{s}^i(v) - s^i(v)$. On this basis Taubin gives a Gaussian-like smoother which does not exhibit shrinkage

$$H := (I + \mu \mathcal{L})(I + \lambda \mathcal{L}).$$

With subdivision and smoothing in place, we can describe the transform needed to support multiresolution editing. Recall that for multiresolution editing we want the difference between successive levels expressed with respect to a frame induced by the coarser level, i.e., the offsets are relative to the smoother level.

With each vertex v and each level $i > 0$ we associate a *detail vector*, $d^i(v) \in \mathbf{R}^3$. The set d^i contains all detail vectors on level i, $d^i = \{ d^i(v) \mid v \in V^i \}$. As indicated in Fig. 7 the detail vectors are defined as

$$d^i = (F^i)^t (s^i - S s^{i-1}) = (F^i)^t (I - S H) s^i,$$

i.e., the detail vectors at level i record how much the points at level i differ from the result of subdividing the points at level $i - 1$. This difference is then represented with respect to the local frame F^i to obtain coordinate independence.

Since detail vectors are sampled on the fine level mesh V^i, this transformation yields an overrepresentation in the spirit of the Burt-Adelson Laplacian pyramid [1]. The only difference is that the smoothing filters (Taubin) are not the dual of the subdivision filter (Loop). Theoretically it would be possible to subsample the detail vectors and only record a detail per odd vertex of M^{i-1}. This is what happens in the wavelet transform. However, subsampling the details severely restricts the family of smoothing operators that can be used.

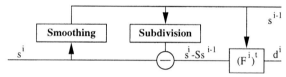

Figure 7: Wiring diagram of the multiresolution transform.

4 Algorithms and Implementation

Before we describe the algorithms in detail let us recall the overall structure of the mesh editor (cf. Fig 3). The analysis stage builds a succession of coarser approximations to the surface, each with fewer control parameters. Details or offsets between successive levels are also computed. In general, the coarser approximations are not visible; only their control points are rendered. These control points give rise to a *virtual surface* with respect to which the remaining details are given. Figure 8 shows wireframe representations of virtual surfaces corresponding to control points on levels 0, 1, and 2.

When an edit level is selected, the surface is represented internally as an approximation at this level, plus the set of all finer level details. The user can freely manipulate degrees of freedom at the edit level, while the finer level details remain unchanged relative to the coarser level. Meanwhile, the system will use the synthesis algorithm to render the modified edit level with all the finer details added in. In between edits, analysis enforces consistency on the internal representation of coarser levels and details (cf. Fig. 9).

The basic algorithms Analysis and Synthesis are very simple and we begin with their description.

Let $i = 0$ be the coarsest and $i = n$ the finest level with N vertices. For each vertex v and all levels i finer than the first level

Figure 8: Wireframe renderings of virtual surfaces representing the first three levels of control points.

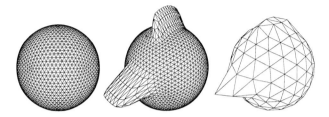

Figure 9: Analysis propagates the changes on finer levels to coarser levels, keeping the magnitude of details under control. Left: The initial mesh. Center: A simple edit on level 3. Right: The effect of the edit on level 2. A significant part of the change was absorbed by higher level details.

where the vertex v appears, there are storage locations $v.s[i]$ and $v.d[i]$, each with 3 floats. With this the total storage adds to $2 * 3 * (4N/3)$ floats. In general, $v.s[i]$ holds $s^i(v)$ and $v.d[i]$ holds $d^i(v)$; temporarily, these locations can be used to store other quantities. The local frame is computed by calling $v.F(i)$.

Global analysis and synthesis are performed level wise:

```
Analysis

   for i = n downto 1
      Analysis(i)
```

```
Synthesis

   for i = 1 to n
      Synthesis(i)
```

With the action at each level described by

```
Analysis(i)

   ∀v ∈ V^{i-1} : v.s[i-1] := smooth(v,i)
   ∀v ∈ V^i     : v.d[i] := v.F(i)^t * (v.s[i] - subd(v,i-1))
```

and

```
Synthesis(i)

   ∀v ∈ V^i : s.v[i] := v.F(i) * v.d[i] + subd(v,i-1)
```

Analysis computes points on the coarser level $i-1$ using smoothing (smooth), subdivides s^{i-1} (subd), and computes the detail vectors d^i (cf. Fig. 7). Synthesis reconstructs level i by subdividing level $i-1$ and adding the details.

So far we have assumed that all levels are uniformly refined, i.e., all neighbors at all levels exist. Since time and storage costs grow exponentially with the number of levels, this approach is unsuitable for an interactive implementation. In the next sections we explain how these basic algorithms can be made memory and time efficient.

Adaptive and *local* versions of these generic algorithms (cf. Fig. 3 for an overview of their use) are the key to these savings. The underlying idea is to use lazy evaluation and pruning based on

thresholds. Three thresholds control this pruning: ϵ_A for adaptive analysis, ϵ_S for adaptive synthesis, and ϵ_R for adaptive rendering. To make lazy evaluation fast enough several caches are maintained explicitly and the order of computations is carefully staged to avoid recomputation.

4.1 Adaptive Analysis

The generic version of analysis traverses entire levels of the hierarchy starting at some finest level. Recall that the purpose of analysis is to compute coarser approximations and detail offsets. In many regions of a mesh, for example, if it is flat, no significant details will be found. *Adaptive analysis* avoids the storage cost associated with detail vectors below some threshold ϵ_A by observing that small detail vectors imply that the finer level almost coincides with the subdivided coarser level. The storage savings are realized through *tree pruning*.

For this purpose we need an integer $v.finest := \max_i\{\|v.d[i]\| \geq \epsilon_A\}$. Initially $v.finest = n$ and the following precondition holds before calling Analysis(i):

- The surface is uniformly subdivided to level i,
- $\forall v \in V^i : v.s[i] = s^i(v)$,
- $\forall v \in V^i \mid i < j \leq v.finest : v.d[j] = d^j(v)$.

Now Analysis(i) becomes:

```
Analysis(i)

   ∀v ∈ V^{i-1} : v.s[i-1] := smooth(v,i)
   ∀v ∈ V^i :
      v.d[i] := v.s[i] - subd(v,i-1)
      if v.finest > i or ||v.d[i]|| ≥ ε_A then
         v.d[i] := v.F(i)^t * v.d[i]
      else
         v.finest := i-1
   Prune(i-1)
```

Triangles that do not contain details above the threshold are unrefined:

```
Prune(i)

   ∀t ∈ T^i : If all middle vertices m have m.finest = i-1
              and all children are leaves, delete children.
```

This results in an adaptive mesh structure for the surface with $v.d[i] = d^i(v)$ for all $v \in V^i$, $i \leq v.finest$. Note that the resulting mesh is not restricted, i.e., two triangles that share a vertex can differ in more than one level. Initial analysis has to be followed by a synthesis pass which enforces restriction.

4.2 Adaptive Synthesis

The main purpose of the general synthesis algorithm is to rebuild the finest level of a mesh from its hierarchical representation. Just as in the case of analysis we can get savings from noticing that in flat regions, for example, little is gained from synthesis and one might as well save the time and storage associated with synthesis. This is the basic idea behind *adaptive synthesis*, which has two main purposes. First, ensure the mesh is restricted on each level, (cf. Fig. 10). Second, refine triangles and recompute points until the mesh has reached a certain measure of local flatness compared against the threshold ϵ_S.

The algorithm recomputes the points $s^i(v)$ starting from the coarsest level. Not all neighbors needed in the subdivision stencil of a given point necessarily exist. Consequently adaptive synthesis

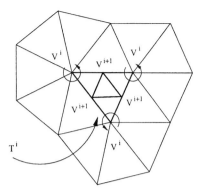

Figure 10: A restricted mesh: the center triangle is in T^i and its vertices in V^i. To subdivide it we need the 1-rings indicated by the circular arrows. If these are present the graph is restricted and we can compute s^{i+1} for all vertices and middle vertices of the center triangle.

```
Refine(t, i, dir)

  if t.leaf then  Create children for t
  ∀v ∈ t : if v.depth < i + 1 then
    GetRing(v, i)
    Update(v, i)
    ∀m ∈ N(v, i + 1, 1) :
      Update(m, i)
      if m.finest ≥ i + 1 then
        forced := true
    if dir and Flat(t) < ε_S and not forced then
    Delete children of t
  else
    ∀t ∈ current : t.restrict := true

Update(v, i)
  v.s[i + 1] := subd(v, i)
  v.depth := i + 1
  if v.finest ≥ i + 1 then
    v.s[i + 1] += v.F(i + 1) * v.d[i + 1]
```

lazily creates all triangles needed for subdivision by temporarily refining their parents, then computes subdivision, and finally deletes the newly created triangles unless they are needed to satisfy the restriction criterion. The following precondition holds before entering AdaptiveSynthesis:

- $\forall t \in T^j \mid 0 \le j \le i : t$ is restricted
- $\forall v \in V^j \mid 0 \le j \le v.depth : v.s[j] = s^j(v)$

where $v.depth := \max_i \{ s^i(v) \text{ has been recomputed} \}$.

```
AdaptiveSynthesis

  ∀v ∈ V⁰ : v.depth := 0
  for i = 0 to n − 1
    temptri := {}
    ∀t ∈ Tⁱ :
      current := {}
      Refine(t, i, true)
    ∀t ∈ temptri : if not t.restrict then
      Delete children of t
```

The list *temptri* serves as a cache holding triangles from levels $j < i$ which are temporarily refined. A triangle is appended to the list if it was refined to compute a value at a vertex. After processing level i these triangles are unrefined unless their *t.restrict* flag is set, indicating that a temporarily created triangle was later found to be needed permanently to ensure restriction. Since triangles are appended to *temptri*, parents precede children. Deallocating the list tail first guarantees that all unnecessary triangles are erased.

The function Refine(t, i, dir) (see below) creates children of $t \in T^i$ and computes the values $Ss^i(v)$ for the vertices and middle vertices of t. The results are stored in $v.s[i + 1]$. The boolean argument *dir* indicates whether the call was made directly or recursively.

The condition $v.depth = i + 1$ indicates whether an earlier call to Refine already recomputed $s^{i+1}(v)$. If not, call GetRing(v, i) and Update(v, i) to do so. In case a detail vector lives at v at level i ($v.finest \ge i + 1$) add it in. Next compute $s^{i+1}(m)$ for middle vertices on level $i + 1$ around v ($m \in N(v, i + 1, 1)$, where $N(v, i, l)$ is the l-ring neighborhood of vertex v at level i). If m has to be calculated, compute subd(m, i) and add in the detail if it exists and record this fact in the flag *forced* which will prevent unrefinement later. At this point, all s^{i+1} have been recomputed for the vertices and middle vertices of t. Unrefine t and delete its children if Refine was called directly, the triangle is sufficiently flat, and none of the middle vertices contain details (i.e., *forced* = false). The list *current* functions as a cache holding triangles from level $i - 1$ which are temporarily refined to build a 1-ring around the vertices of t. If after processing all vertices and middle vertices of t it is decided that t will remain refined, none of the coarser-level triangles from *current* can be unrefined without violating restriction. Thus *t.restrict* is set for all of them. The function Flat(t) measures how close to planar the corners and edge middle vertices of t are.

Finally, GetRing(v, i) ensures that a complete ring of triangles on level i adjacent to the vertex v exists. Because triangles on level i are restricted triangles all triangles on level $i - 1$ that contain v exist (precondition). At least one of them is refined, since otherwise there would be no reason to call GetRing(v, i). All other triangles could be leaves or temporarily refined. Any triangle that was already temporarily refined may become permanently refined to enforce restriction. Record such candidates in the *current* cache for fast access later.

```
GetRing(v, i)

  ∀t ∈ T^{i−1} with v ∈ t :
    if t.leaf then
      Refine(t, i − 1, false); temptri.append(t)
      t.restrict := false; t.temp := true
    if t.temp then
      current.append(t)
```

4.3 Local Synthesis

Even though the above algorithms are adaptive, they are still run everywhere. During an edit, however, not all of the surface changes. The most significant economy can be gained from performing analysis and synthesis only over submeshes which require it.

Assume the user edits level l and modifies the points $s^l(v)$ for $v \in V^{*l} \subset V^l$. This invalidates coarser level values s^i and d^i for certain subsets $V^{*i} \subset V^i, i \leq l$, and finer level points s^i for subsets $V^{*i} \subset V^i$ for $i > l$. Finer level detail vectors d^i for $i > l$ remain correct by definition. Recomputing the coarser levels is done by *local incremental analysis* described in Section 4.4, recomputing the finer level is done by *local synthesis* described in this section.

The set of vertices V^{*i} which are affected depends on the support of the subdivision scheme. If the support fits into an m-ring around the computed vertex, then all modified vertices on level $i + 1$ can be found recursively as

$$V^{*i+1} = \bigcup_{v \in V^{*i}} N(v, i+1, m).$$

We assume that $m = 2$ (Loop-like schemes) or $m = 3$ (Butterfly type schemes). We define the *subtriangulation* T^{*i} to be the subset of triangles of T^i with vertices in V^{*i}.

`LocalSynthesis` is only slightly modified from `AdaptiveSynthesis`: iteration starts at level l and iterates only over the submesh T^{*i}.

4.4 Local Incremental Analysis

After an edit on level l *local incremental analysis* will recompute $s^i(v)$ and $d^i(v)$ locally for coarser level vertices ($i \leq l$) which are affected by the edit. As in the previous section, we assume that the user edited a set of vertices v on level l and call V^{*i} the set of vertices affected on level i. For a given vertex $v \in V^{*i}$ we define

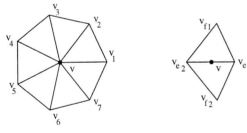

Figure 11: Sets of even vertices affected through smoothing by either an even v or odd m vertex.

$R^{i-1}(v) \subset V^{i-1}$ to be the set of vertices on level $i - 1$ affected by v through the smoothing operator H. The sets V^{*i} can now be defined recursively starting from level $i = l$ to $i = 0$:

$$V^{*i-1} = \bigcup_{v \in V^{*i}} R^{i-1}(v).$$

The set $R^{i-1}(v)$ depends on the size of the smoothing stencil and whether v is even or odd (cf. Fig. 11). If the smoothing filter is 1-ring, e.g., Gaussian, then $R^{i-1}(v) = \{v\}$ if v is even and $R^{i-1}(m) = \{v_{e1}, v_{e2}\}$ if m is odd. If the smoothing filter is 2-ring, e.g., Taubin, then $R^{i-1}(v) = \{v\} \cup \{v_k \mid 1 \leq k \leq K\}$ if v is even and $R^{i-1}(m) = \{v_{e1}, v_{e2}, v_{f1}, v_{f2}\}$ if v is odd. Because of restriction, these vertices always exist. For $v \in V^i$ and $v' \in R^{i-1}(v)$ we let $c(v, v')$ be the coefficient in the analysis stencil. Thus

$$(H s^i)(v') = \sum_{v \mid v' \in R^{i-1}(v)} c(v, v') s^i(v).$$

This could be implemented by running over the v' and each time computing the above sum. Instead we use the dual implementation, iterate over all v, accumulating (+=) the right amount to $s^i(v')$ for $v' \in R^{i-1}(v)$. In case of a 2-ring Taubin smoother the coefficients are given by

$$
\begin{aligned}
c(v, v) &= (1 - \mu)(1 - \lambda) + \mu \lambda / 6 \\
c(v, v_k) &= \mu \lambda / 6K \\
c(m, v_{e1}) &= ((1 - \mu)\lambda + (1 - \lambda)\mu + \mu \lambda / 3)/K \\
c(m, v_{f1}) &= \mu \lambda / 3K,
\end{aligned}
$$

where for each $c(v, v')$, K is the outdegree of v'.

The algorithm first copies the old points $s^i(v)$ for $v \in V^{*i}$ and $i \leq l$ into the storage location for the detail. If then propagates the incremental changes of the modified points from level l to the coarser levels and adds them to the old points (saved in the detail locations) to find the new points. Then it recomputes the detail vectors that depend on the modified points.

We assume that before the edit, the old points $s^l(v)$ for $v \in V^{*l}$ were saved in the detail locations. The algorithm starts out by building V^{*i-1} and saving the points $s^{i-1}(v)$ for $v \in V^{*i-1}$ in the detail locations. Then the changes resulting from the edit are propagated to level $i - 1$. Finally $S s^{i-1}$ is computed and used to update the detail vectors on level i.

```
LocalAnalysis(i)

  ∀v ∈ V*i : ∀v' ∈ R^{i-1}(v) :
    V*^{i-1} ∪= {v'}
    v'.d[i-1] := v'.s[i-1]
  ∀v ∈ V*i : ∀v' ∈ R^{i-1}(v) :
    v'.s[i-1] += c(v,v') * (v.s[i] - v.d[i])
  ∀v ∈ V*^{i-1} :
    v.d[i] = v.F(i)^t * (v.s[i] - subd(v,i-1))
    ∀m ∈ N(v,i,1) :
      m.d[i] = m.F(i)^t * (m.s[i] - subd(m,i-1))
```

Note that the odd points are actually computed twice. For the Loop scheme this is less expensive than trying to compute a predicate to avoid this. For Butterfly type schemes this is not true and one can avoid double computation by imposing an ordering on the triangles. The top level code is straightforward:

```
LocalAnalysis

  ∀v ∈ V*l : v.d[l] := v.s[l]
  for i := l downto 0
    LocalAnalysis(i)
```

It is difficult to make incremental local analysis adaptive, as it is formulated purely in terms of vertices. It is, however, possible to adaptively clean up the triangles affected by the edit and (un)refine them if needed.

4.5 Adaptive Rendering

The *adaptive rendering* algorithm decides which triangles will be drawn depending on the rendering performance available and level of detail needed.

The algorithm uses a flag $t.draw$ which is initialized to `false`, but set to `true` as soon as the area corresponding to t is drawn. This can happen either when t itself gets drawn, or when a set of its descendents, which cover t, is drawn. The top level algorithm loops through the triangles starting from the level $n - 1$. A triangle is always responsible for drawing its children, never itself, unless it is a coarsest-level triangle.

```
AdaptiveRender

for i = n − 1 downto 0
    ∀t ∈ T^i : if not t.leaf then
        Render(t)
    ∀t ∈ T^0 : if not t.draw then
        displaylist.append(t)
```

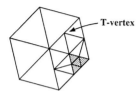

Figure 12: Adaptive rendering: On the left 6 triangles from level i, one has a covered child from level $i + 1$, and one has a T-vertex. On the right the result from applying Render to all six.

The Render(t) routine decides whether the children of t have to be drawn or not (cf. Fig.12). It uses a function edist(m) which measures the distance between the point corresponding to the edge's middle vertex m, and the edge itself. In the when case any of the children of t are already drawn or any of its middle vertices are far enough from the plane of the triangle, the routine will draw the rest of the children and set the draw flag for all their vertices and t. It also might be necessary to draw a triangle if some of its middle vertices are drawn because the triangle on the other side decided to draw its children. To avoid cracks, the routine cut(t) will cut t into 2, 3, or 4, triangles depending on how many middle vertices are drawn.

```
Render(t)

if (∃c ∈ t.child | c.draw = true
   or ∃m ∈ t.mid_vertex | edist(m) > ε_D) then
    ∀c ∈ t.child :
        if not c.draw then
            displaylist.append(c)
            ∀v ∈ c : v.draw := true
    t.draw := true
else if ∃m ∈ t.mid_vertex | m.draw = true
    ∀t' ∈ cut(t) : displaylist.append(t')
    t.draw := true
```

4.6 Data Structures and Code

The main data structure in our implementation is a forest of triangular quadtrees. Neighborhood relations within a single quadtree can be resolved in the standard way by ascending the tree to the least common parent when attempting to find the neighbor across a given edge. Neighbor relations between adjacent trees are resolved explicitly at the level of a collection of roots, i.e., triangles of a coarsest level graph. This structure also maintains an explicit representation of the boundary (if any). Submeshes rooted at any level can be created on the fly by assembling a new graph with some set of triangles as roots of their child quadtrees. It is here that the explicit representation of the boundary comes in, since the actual trees

are never copied, and a boundary is needed to delineate the actual submesh.

The algorithms we have described above make heavy use of container classes. Efficient support for sets is essential for a fast implementation and we have used the C++ Standard Template Library. The mesh editor was implemented using OpenInventor and OpenGL and currently runs on both SGI and Intel PentiumPro workstations.

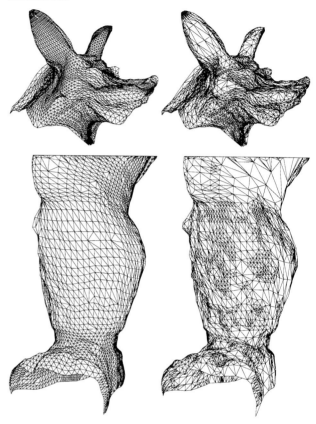

Figure 13: On the left are two meshes which are uniformly subdivided and consist of 11k (upper) and 9k (lower) triangles. On the right another pair of meshes mesh with approximately the same numbers of triangles. Upper and lower pairs of meshes are generated from the same original data but the right meshes were optimized through suitable choice of ϵ_S. See the color plates for a comparison between the two under shading.

5 Results

In this section we show some example images to demonstrate various features of our system and give performance measures.

Figure 13 shows two triangle mesh approximations of the Armadillo head and leg. Approximately the same number of triangles are used for both adaptive and uniform meshes. The meshes on the left were rendered uniformly, the meshes on the right were rendered adaptively. (See also color plate 15.)

Locally changing threshold parameters can be used to resolve an area of interest particularly well, while leaving the rest of the mesh at a coarse level. An example of this "lens" effect is demonstrated in Figure 14 around the right eye of the Mannequin head. (See also color plate 16.)

We have measured the performance of our code on two platforms: an Indigo R10000@175MHz with Solid Impact graphics, and a PentiumPro@200MHz with an Intergraph Intense 3D board.

We used the Armadillo head as a test case. It has approximately 172000 triangles on 6 levels of subdivision. Display list creation took 2 seconds on the SGI and 3 seconds on the PC for the full model. We adjusted ϵ_R so that both machines rendered models at 5 frames per second. In the case of the SGI approximately 113,000 triangles were rendered at that rate. On the PC we achieved 5 frames per second when the rendering threshold had been raised enough so that an approximation consisting of 35000 polygons was used.

The other important performance number is the time it takes to recompute and re-render the region of the mesh which is changing as the user moves a set of control points. This submesh is rendered in immediate mode, while the rest of the surface continues to be rendered as a display list. Grabbing a submesh of 20-30 faces (a typical case) at level 0 added 250 mS of time per redraw, at level 1 it added 110 mS and at level 2 it added 30 mS in case of the SGI. The corresponding timings for the PC were 500 mS, 200 mS and 60 mS respectively.

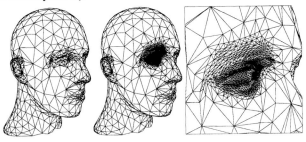

Figure 14: It is easy to change ϵ_S locally. Here a "lens" was applied to the right eye of the Mannequin head with decreasing ϵ_S to force very fine resolution of the mesh around the eye.

6 Conclusion and Future Research

We have built a scalable system for interactive multiresolution editing of arbitrary topology meshes. The user can either start from scratch or from a given fine detail mesh *with subdivision connectivity*. We use smooth subdivision combined with details at each level as a uniform surface representation across scales and argue that this forms a natural connection between fine polygonal meshes and patches. Interactivity is obtained by building both local and adaptive variants of the basic analysis, synthesis, and rendering algorithms, which rely on fast lazy evaluation and tree pruning. The system allows interactive manipulation of meshes according to the polygon performance of the workstation or PC used.

There are several avenues for future research:

- Multiresolution transforms readily connect with compression. We want to be able to store the models in a compressed format and use progressive transmission.

- Features such as creases, corners, and tension controls can easily be added into our system and expand the users' editing toolbox.

- Presently no real time fairing techniques, which lead to more intuitive coarse levels, exist.

- In our system coarse level edits can only be made by dragging coarse level vertices. Which vertices live on coarse levels is currently fixed because of subdivision connectivity. Ideally the user should be able to dynamically adjust this to make coarse level edits centered at arbitrary locations.

- The system allows topological edits on the coarsest level. Algorithms that allow topological edits on all levels are needed.

- An important area of research relevant for this work is generation of meshes with subdivision connectivity from scanned data or from existing models in other representations.

Acknowledgments

We would like to thank Venkat Krishnamurthy for providing the Armadillo dataset. Andrei Khodakovsky and Gary Wu helped beyond the call of duty to bring the system up. The research was supported in part through grants from the Intel Corporation, Microsoft, the Charles Lee Powell Foundation, the Sloan Foundation, an NSF CAREER award (ASC-9624957), and under a MURI (AFOSR F49620-96-1-0471). Other support was provided by the NSF STC for Computer Graphics and Scientific Visualization.

References

[1] BURT, P. J., AND ADELSON, E. H. Laplacian Pyramid as a Compact Image Code. *IEEE Trans. Commun. 31*, 4 (1983), 532–540.

[2] CATMULL, E., AND CLARK, J. Recursively Generated B-Spline Surfaces on Arbitrary Topological Meshes. *Computer Aided Design 10*, 6 (1978), 350–355.

[3] CERTAIN, A., POPOVIĆ, J., DEROSE, T., DUCHAMP, T., SALESIN, D., AND STUETZLE, W. Interactive Multiresolution Surface Viewing. In *SIGGRAPH 96 Conference Proceedings*, H. Rushmeier, Ed., Annual Conference Series, 91–98, Aug. 1996.

[4] DAHMEN, W., MICCHELLI, C. A., AND SEIDEL, H.-P. Blossoming Begets B-Splines Bases Built Better by B-Patches. *Mathematics of Computation 59*, 199 (July 1992), 97–115.

[5] DE BOOR, C. *A Practical Guide to Splines*. Springer, 1978.

[6] DOO, D., AND SABIN, M. Analysis of the Behaviour of Recursive Division Surfaces near Extraordinary Points. *Computer Aided Design 10*, 6 (1978), 356–360.

[7] DYN, N., LEVIN, D., AND GREGORY, J. A. A Butterfly Subdivision Scheme for Surface Interpolation with Tension Control. *ACM Trans. Gr. 9*, 2 (April 1990), 160–169.

[8] ECK, M., DEROSE, T., DUCHAMP, T., HOPPE, H., LOUNSBERY, M., AND STUETZLE, W. Multiresolution Analysis of Arbitrary Meshes. In *Computer Graphics Proceedings*, Annual Conference Series, 173–182, 1995.

[9] FINKELSTEIN, A., AND SALESIN, D. H. Multiresolution Curves. *Computer Graphics* Proceedings, Annual Conference Series, 261–268, July 1994.

[10] FORSEY, D., AND WONG, D. Multiresolution Surface Reconstruction for Hierarchical B-splines. Tech. rep., University of British Columbia, 1995.

[11] FORSEY, D. R., AND BARTELS, R. H. Hierarchical B-Spline Refinement. *Computer Graphics (SIGGRAPH '88 Proceedings)*, Vol. 22, No. 4, pp. 205–212, August 1988.

[12] GORTLER, S. J., AND COHEN, M. F. Hierarchical and Variational Geometric Modeling with Wavelets. In *Proceedings Symposium on Interactive 3D Graphics*, May 1995.

[13] HOPPE, H. Progressive Meshes. In *SIGGRAPH 96 Conference Proceedings*, H. Rushmeier, Ed., Annual Conference Series, 99–108, August 1996.

[14] HOPPE, H., DEROSE, T., DUCHAMP, T., HALSTEAD, M., JIN, H., MCDONALD, J., SCHWEITZER, J., AND STUETZLE, W. Piecewise Smooth Surface Reconstruction. In *Computer Graphics Proceedings*, Annual Conference Series, 295–302, 1994.

[15] HOPPE, H., DEROSE, T., DUCHAMP, T., MCDONALD, J., AND STUETZLE, W. Mesh Optimization. In *Computer Graphics (SIGGRAPH '93 Proceedings)*, J. T. Kajiya, Ed., vol. 27, 19–26, August 1993.

[16] KOBBELT, L. Interpolatory Subdivision on Open Quadrilateral Nets with Arbitrary Topology. In *Proceedings of Eurographics 96*, Computer Graphics Forum, 409–420, 1996.

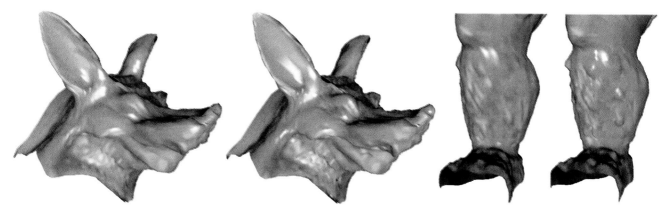

Figure 15: Shaded rendering (OpenGL) of the meshes in Figure 13.

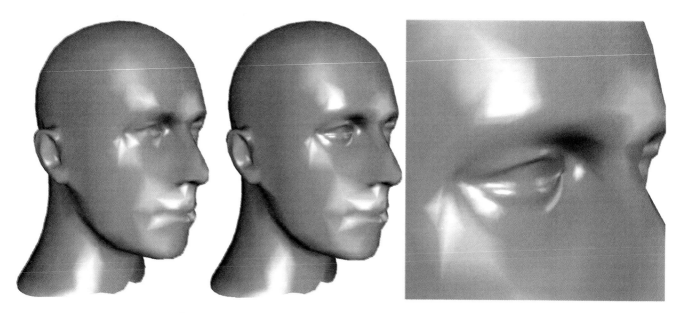

Figure 16: Shaded rendering (OpenGL) of the meshes in Figure 14.

[17] KRISHNAMURTHY, V., AND LEVOY, M. Fitting Smooth Surfaces to Dense Polygon Meshes. In *SIGGRAPH 96 Conference Proceedings*, H. Rushmeier, Ed., Annual Conference Series, 313–324, August 1996.

[18] KURIHARA, T. Interactive Surface Design Using Recursive Subdivision. In *Proceedings of Communicating with Virtual Worlds*. Springer Verlag, June 1993.

[19] LOOP, C. Smooth Subdivision Surfaces Based on Triangles. Master's thesis, University of Utah, Department of Mathematics, 1987.

[20] LOOP, C. Smooth Spline Surfaces over Irregular Meshes. In *Computer Graphics Proceedings*, Annual Conference Series, 303–310, 1994.

[21] LOUNSBERY, M., DEROSE, T., AND WARREN, J. Multiresolution Analysis for Surfaces of Arbitrary Topological Type. *Transactions on Graphics 16*, 1 (January 1997), 34–73.

[22] PETERS, J. C^1 Surface Splines. *SIAM J. Numer. Anal. 32*, 2 (1995), 645–666.

[23] PULLI, K., AND LOUNSBERY, M. Hierarchical Editing and Rendering of Subdivision Surfaces. Tech. Rep. UW-CSE-97-04-07, Dept. of CS&E, University of Washington, Seattle, WA, 1997.

[24] SCHRÖDER, P., AND SWELDENS, W. Spherical wavelets: Efficiently representing functions on the sphere. *Computer Graphics Proceedings, (SIGGRAPH 95)* (1995), 161–172.

[25] SCHWEITZER, J. E. *Analysis and Application of Subdivision Surfaces*. PhD thesis, University of Washington, 1996.

[26] TAUBIN, G. A Signal Processing Approach to Fair Surface Design. In *SIGGRAPH 95 Conference Proceedings*, R. Cook, Ed., Annual Conference Series, 351–358, August 1995.

[27] WELCH, W., AND WITKIN, A. Variational surface modeling. In *Computer Graphics (SIGGRAPH '92 Proceedings)*, E. E. Catmull, Ed., vol. 26, 157–166, July 1992.

[28] ZORIN, D., SCHRÖDER, P., AND SWELDENS, W. Interpolating Subdivision for Meshes with Arbitrary Topology. *Computer Graphics Proceedings (SIGGRAPH 96)* (1996), 189–192.

[29] ZORIN, D. N. *Subdivision and Multiresolution Surface Representations*. PhD thesis, Caltech, Pasadena, California, 1997.

Interactive Boolean Operations for Conceptual Design of 3-D Solids

Ari Rappoport   Steven Spitz[†]

Institute of Computer Science, The Hebrew University

Abstract

Interactive modeling of 3-D solids is an important and difficult problem in computer graphics. The Constructive Solid Geometry (CSG) modeling scheme is highly attractive for interactive design, due to its support for hierarchical modeling and Boolean operations. Unfortunately, current algorithms for interactive display of CSG models require expensive special-purpose hardware that is not easily available.

In this paper we present a method for interactive display of CSG models using standard, widely available graphics hardware. The method enables the user to interactively modify the affine transformations associated with CSG sub-objects. The application we focus upon is that of conceptual design, a stage in the design process in which rapid, interactive visualization of the model and high-level design operations are of crucial importance, while the objects are relatively simple.

The method converts the CSG graph to a novel *Convex Differences Aggregate(CDA)* representation. The CDA utilizes graph re-writing techniques, efficient geometric algorithms on convex objects and a built-in hierarchical acceleration scheme. The CDA rendering algorithm is very simple, takes advantage of standard graphics hardware, and makes efficient use of system resources by splitting the work between the graphics system and the CPU.

CR Categories and Subject Descriptors: I.3.3 [Computer Graphics]: Picture/Image Generation — Display algorithms; I.3.5 [Computer Graphics]: Computational Geometry and Object Modeling — CSG; J.6 [Computer Applications]: Computer-Aided Engineering — CAD.

Additional Key Words: geometric modeling, solid modeling, conceptual design, Boolean operations, convex differences, convex differences aggregate, convex polyhedra.

1 Introduction

Interactive design of 3-D geometric models is of major importance in computer graphics. The Constructive Solid Geometry (CSG)

Institute of Computer Science, The Hebrew University, Jerusalem 91904, Israel. http://www.cs.huji.ac.il/~arir, arir@cs.huji.ac.il

[†]Current address: Programmable Automation Laboratory, Computer Science Department, University of Southern California, Los Angeles, CA 90089-0781. http://www-pal.usc.edu/~spitz, spitz@usc.edu

solid representation scheme [Requicha80] is highly attractive for interactive design, because it lets the user compose objects hierarchically using Boolean operations. Unfortunately, current algorithms for interactive display of CSG models require expensive special-purpose hardware that is not widely available.

In this paper we address the problem of displaying CSG models at interactive rates using standard, off-the-shelf graphics hardware. The application we have in mind is that of conceptual design, a stage in the design process in which rapid, interactive visualization of the model and high-level design operations are of crucial importance, while the objects are relatively simple.

Background. A design process starts with conceptual design and progresses by iterative refinement stages until meeting the design goal [Smithers89]. In geometric design, the initial conceptual design phase is one of the most difficult to computerize. Other stages, such as detailed geometric design and physical analysis, are already supported in current modeling systems. Conceptual design is rarely supported.

The reason why conceptual design is so difficult to support is that it imposes the largest demands for interactivity. Initially, designers need to experiment with a large number of potential designs. This 'navigation in design space' must be done in a very intuitive and fast manner. The vocabulary by which designer intentions are expressed should be very high-level, and is translated into a large number of low-level operations that could be difficult to compute efficiently. Nonetheless, conceptual design is easier than detailed design in that (1) the number of geometric objects involved is usually much smaller, (2) it suffices to support model visualization (other operations are not strictly essential), and (3) interactive visualization is much more important than accuracy of the model.

Most conceptual design is currently done using pen and paper. When designing 3-D models, the great potential advantage of computer graphics is obvious, letting designers inspect their models from different viewpoints and at different scales and make fast modifications. We are interested in direct conceptual design of 3-D models.

Constructive Solid Geometry (CSG) [Requicha80, Hoffmann89] is a well-known representation scheme that represents 3-D solids by a graph whose leaves contain geometric primitives and whose nodes contain Boolean and affine operations. The arcs of the graph denote the fact that an operation uses an object as an argument. The native CSG modeling operations include: (1) instantiation of simple geometric primitives, (2) composition of objects from simpler objects in a hierarchical manner, using the union Boolean operation, (3) performing affine operations (translation, rotation and scaling) on objects, and (4) using one object to modify another by the Boolean difference and intersection operations. These relatively high-level modeling operations make CSG an attractive choice for conceptual design.

A CSG graph models a family of objects spanning a design space. Navigation through this design space is performed by modifying the numerical parameters defining the affine transformations. It is crucial that such navigation could be performed in an interactive manner, otherwise the design process is damaged to the point that pen and paper are more effective. Rapid display of CSG objects after modification of their affine parameters is the goal of this paper.

Previous work. Previous work on rendering CSG models can be classified into several categories according to the methods used. The most obvious method is to convert the CSG representation into a boundary representation, which is the native format accepted by virtually all interactive rendering systems. However, all boundary evaluation methods require considerable amounts of computation [Requicha85] and are too slow for interactive modification of the model.

Several well-known graphics algorithms have been customized for CSG display. This includes scanline methods [Atherton83, Bronsvoort87], ray tracing and ray casting [Roth82], image subdivision [Cameron94], octrees [Meagher84] and even point sampling and voxel reconstruction [Breen91]. Again, all of these methods do not provide interactive performance.

Binary Space Partitioning (BSP) trees, known in computer graphics for acceleration of many types of computations, were used for CSG [Thibault87, Naylor92, Naylor96]. Although the results are impressive, these method are basically an acceleration of complete boundary evaluation. They utilize standard graphics hardware only to a limited extent, and limit the range of modifications that can be done on the object.

Many methods were suggested for CSG display using special purpose hardware. These methods have progressed from a special kind of z-buffer [Okino84, VanHook86, Rossignac86] to usage of multiple z and frame buffers and multiple rendering passes [Goldfeather86, Jansen86, Jansen87, Goldfeather89, Rossignac90, Jansen91]. These methods do support real-time rendering of CSG models (naturally, depending upon the model size), but are not practical for every-day use because they require expensive special purpose hardware that is not easily available.

[Wiegand96] presents a method to emulate the algorithm of [Goldfeather89], designed for a parallel pixel-based architecture, on standard graphics hardware. In effect, double z and image buffers are emulated by using multiple passes and memory copying. This method, and a similar method detailed in [McReynolds96], are the most practical methods suggested so far. However, these multi-pass methods are brute-force ones, putting virtually all of the computational load on the graphics system. Demanding applications should try to use all the computational resources provided by the machine, especially considering that today's CPUs are rather powerful and that multi-processor machines are not uncommon. In addition, the brute-force methods do not support many kinds of geometric acceleration schemes.

In summary, none of the existing methods fulfills the goal of interactive display of CSG models while using standard graphics hardware. The methods that partially support that goal (e.g. [Wiegand96]) do not make efficient use of the overall architecture and are too low level and brute-force to provide satisfactory support for conceptual design.

Proposed approach. In this paper we present a method for displaying CSG models, which is particularly attractive for conceptual design. The method enables interactive modification of the numerical parameters of the affine transformations in the CSG graph. The major advantages of the method are:

1. Interactive performance,

2. Utilization of standard, widely available graphics hardware,

3. Splitting the work between the CPU and the graphics system.

In addition, our internal representation speeds up complete approximate boundary evaluation when desired, and possesses a built-in spatial hierarchy.

The method utilizes a combination of graph re-writing, efficient geometric algorithms and standard graphics hardware. The surfaces of solid CSG primitives are approximated by linear facets, and the primitives themselves are expressed as convex polyhedra or Boolean combinations of convex polyhedra. All traditional CSG primitives (box, tetrahedron, pyramid, sphere, cylinder, cone, torus) are easily supported. The torus is modeled as a union of several simple convex pieces. Note that constraints imposed by sub-object convexity are present in other interactive solutions as well [Wiegand96]. Support for free-form objects is more difficult, although there is no inherent reason why they could not be used.

The CSG graph is transformed into a novel *Convex Differences Aggregate (CDA)* representation. The CDA is a union of cells each of which is a containing convex polyhedron minus a set of contained convex polyhedra. Interactions between polyhedral faces that might affect visibility are efficiently detected and handled by a *face binding* mechanism. Display of an aggregate involves standard capabilities of the graphics system (polygon rasterization, z-buffer, a single stencil bit-plane). The process of building a CDA can be divided into two: structure and geometry. Structure is re-computed each time the structure of the corresponding CSG graph is modified. This computation is very fast. Geometry is updated each time visual feedback is needed, in particular when the user modifies the parameters defining the affine operations. This update is done by computing 3-D convex hulls of sets of points.

By itself, the CDA is a *lossy* modeling scheme [Rappoport95] because it approximates geometry using planar faces and because it loses the object hierarchy. However, the method as a whole is lossless, because the original CSG graph is retained.

The paper is structured as follows. The CDA representation is defined in Section 2. Rendering a CDA is detailed in Section 3. Conversion of a CSG object to a CDA is described in Section 4, and general system aspects and results are discussed in Section 5.

2 The Convex Differences Aggregate (CDA)

In this section we introduce the convex differences aggregate (CDA) representation. The CDA utilizes the difference between a containing convex polyhedron and other convex polyhedra. As such, it resembles the 2-D representations in [Sklansky72, Batchelor80, Tor84, Rappoport90, Rappoport92] and the 3-D and n-D representations in [Woo82, Kim90, Rappoport91]. However, the CDA is different from these representations in structure, geometric aspects, and the fact that it is optimized for computer graphics display.

A CDA A represents a pointset $Set(A)$ by a set of *cells* $A = \{C_1, \ldots, C_n\}$. Each cell C represents a pointset $Set(C)$. The pointset represented by the CDA is the union of the pointsets represented by the cells: $Set(A) = Set(C_1) \cup \ldots \cup Set(C_n)$. In principle, the CDA is a pure aggregate of cells and there are no relationships between the cells. Figure 1 shows a CDA consisting of two cells, C_1 and C_2.

A cell C is represented by a single *positive* cell $Pos(C)$, a set of *negative* cells $Neg(C) = \{N_1, \ldots, N_m\}$, and a set of *zero* cells $Zero(C) = \{Z_1, \ldots, Z_k\}$. We denote a cell by $C = \{P; N_1, \ldots, N_m; Z_1, \ldots, Z_k\}$. The pointset represented by a cell is the set difference between that

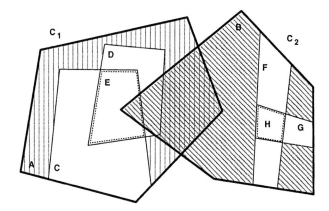

Figure 1 A 2-D CDA consisting of two cells, $C_1 = \{A; C, D; E\}$ and $C_2 = \{B; F, G; H\}$. Each cell has two negative cells intersecting in a single zero cell.

represented by its positive cell and the union of pointsets represented by its negative cells:

$$Set(C) = Set(P) \setminus (Set(N_1) \cup \ldots \cup Set(N_m)).$$

Negative cells represent holes in their positive cells. In Figure 1, C, D, F and G are negative cells. Zero cells do not affect the pointset represented by a cell; they exist solely to assist rendering. Unless stated otherwise, throughout this paper we assume regularized Boolean operations, ensuring the full dimensionality of CSG objects. The result of a regularized Boolean operation between two sets is the topological closure of the result of the Boolean operation when applied to the topological interior of the two sets [Requicha80].

The pointset represented by a positive, negative or zero cell H is given by a convex polyhedron associated with the cell. For simplicity, we will also denote the polyhedron by H. We will also call a face positive (negative, zero) when referring to a face of the polyhedron of a positive (negative, zero) cell. We assume that face normals of positive polyhedra consistently point out of the positive polyhedron, and that normals of negative faces consistently point into the negative polyhedron.

From a set-theoretic modeling point of view, the CDA is a special kind of CSG graph: it contains only the union and difference Boolean operations (no intersections, complements, and affine operations), it possesses a special structure (its depth is exactly three, the first and third levels contain union operations and the second level a difference operation), and all primitives are convex polyhedra.

The CDA imposes additional structural and geometric requirements from its ingredients, which are an integral part of its definition: (1) containment relationships between pointsets of positive and negative cells, (2) existence of zero cells and intersection relationships between their pointsets and that of negative cells, (3) binding between certain faces of negative and positive cells, and (4) binding between certain faces of zero and negative cells. The motivation for these requirements is optimizing the display operation while supporting fast affine modification of geometry.

Containment. Negative cells are required to be contained in their positive cell. Negative cells of dimensionality lower than 3 are redundant and should be discarded (recall that the Boolean operations are regularized).

Zero cells. A zero cell Z_{ij} exists for every intersecting pair of negative cells that belong to the same aggregate cell: $Set(Z_{ij}) =$

$Set(N_i) \cap Set(N_j)$. In Figure 1, each cell has two negative cells intersecting in a single zero cell. A zero cell may exist even when the intersection between the negative cells is of one dimension lower than the cell dimension (but see the definition of zero face bindings below). For example, if two negative 3-D convex polyhedra intersect only in a face, then the resulting zero cell is a degenerate polyhedron with two identical faces having opposite normals.

In Figure 2, negative cells M and N intersect in a zero cell Z which is of full dimensionality in (a) and (b) and of dimension one lower in (c).

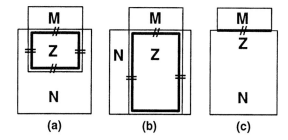

Figure 2 Two negative cells can yield a zero cell of full dimensionality (a, b) or of dimension one lower than themselves (c). Bound zero faces are crossed by two short line segments. Note that the lower face of the zero cell in (b) is not bound.

Positive-negative (P-N) face bindings. If a positive face and a negative face belonging to the same cell are co-planar, there is an explicit binding between these two faces. We say that the positive face is bound *downwards* and that the negative face is bound *upwards*. Note that since both polyhedra are convex, a negative face is bound to no more than a single positive face. However, it is certainly possible that two different negative cells will be co-planar with the same positive face. Thus, a positive face can be bound to several different negative faces.

Negative-zero (N-Z) face bindings. A face of a zero cell can be explicitly bound to a face of one of the two negative cells that yielded the zero cell. This binding exists in one of two situations:

1. The zero face is co-planar with exactly one negative face (e.g. the bound faces in Figure 2(a) and (b)), or

2. The zero face is co-planar with both negative faces, and the normals of the negative faces point in opposite directions (e.g. Figure 2(c)).

We say that the negative face is bound *downwards* and that the zero face is bound *upwards*. The lower zero face in Figure 2(b) is not bound because the normals of the originating negative faces point in the same direction. The bound faces of zero cells are exactly those that do not belong to the union of their two originating negative cells. Since negative polyhedra are convex, their intersection is also convex and a zero face is bound to no more than a single negative face. A negative face can be bound to several different zero faces.

3 Rendering a CDA

In this section we discuss CDA rendering, showing how the structural and geometric properties of a CDA make its rendering very simple. A CDA is rendered using a standard 3-D graphics API such as OpenGL. The graphics system should support polygon-based hidden surface removal (usually, using a z-buffer) and a stencil bitplane.

The rationale behind the convex differences aggregate representation is made clear when considering the rendering operation. We can render aggregate cells independently because their pointsets are unioned; from the point of view of the graphics system, these cells can be treated as separate objects. Positive faces can be rendered correctly because holes in them are modeled explicitly by face bindings. Negative faces can be rendered correctly because interactions between negative cells that might modify visibility relationships are represented by the existence of zero cells, and are handled by bindings between zero and negative faces.

The CDA rendering algorithm is shown in Figure 3. Rendering a CDA starts by clearing the frame buffer and the z-buffer, and then independently rendering all of its cells. Rendering a cell is done by rendering its positive cell and all its negative cells. Rendering a positive or negative cell is done by rendering its polyhedron. Rendering a polyhedron is done by rendering those of its faces that are front-facing (a simple optimization) and not bound upwards. This discards only negative faces bound to positive ones, because zero faces are not rendered directly. Rendering a face starts by clearing the stencil bit-plane. The faces bound to the rendered face (actually, only those that are bound downwards) are rendered onto the stencil; they leave no mark on the frame buffer and z buffers. Then the face itself is rendered on the parts of the frame and z buffers not masked by the stencil.

```
CDARender (CDA A):
      clear frame and z buffers.
      for all cells Ci of A
            CellRender (Ci).
◇

CellRender (Cell C):
      PolyhedronRender (Pos (C)).
      for all negative cells Ni of C
            PolyhedronRender (Ni)).
◇

PolyhedronRender (Polyhedron P):
      for all faces Fi of P
            if Fi is front-facing and not bound upwards
                  FaceRender (Fi).
◇

FaceRender (Face F):
      clear stencil bit-plane S.
      for all bound faces bj of F
            render bj on S.
      render F on the parts of the frame and z buffers
            not masked by S.
◇
```

Figure 3 Rendering a convex differences aggregate.

A formal proof of correctness of the rendering algorithm is given in [Spitz94]; here we only give an informal argument. First, note that since the pointset represented by the CDA is the union of the pointsets represented by the aggregate cells, the z-buffer automatically guarantees that if cells are rendered correctly then the results are combined correctly.

Next, consider positive faces. Because negative cells are contained in the positive cell, positive faces are never hidden by negative ones. At most, they coincide with them. Since negative cells are of full dimensionality, a negative face that coincides with a positive face represents a through-hole in the positive face. Such negative faces are bound (by definition of the CDA) to the positive face, and masked by the stencil. As a result, the visible pixels of positive faces are exactly those that are rendered.

Finally, consider negative faces. Negative faces that overlap positive faces represent holes in the positive face through which something may be visible. Such faces are bound upwards and are not directly rendered by the algorithm; they were rendered as holes in the stencil when rendering the positive face. Regarding other negative faces, if a negative face does not intersect any other negative face, it might be visible like any ordinary face of a non-convex polyhedron and is rendered similarly to positive faces (note that normals of negative faces by definition point in the correct direction, outside the object represented by the cell). If a face f of a negative cell N is intersected by a negative cell M, there are three cases:

1. The intersection between N and M is not along a co-planar face; the intersection is of full dimensionality. In this case the cell M cuts a through-hole in the face f. By definition, the face f is bound to a zero face having the exact geometry of the through-hole. When the face f is rendered, the stencil masks the through-hole.

2. The intersection between N and M is along a face g of M coplanar with f, and the normals of f and g point in opposite directions. This case is similar to the previous one, since g again comprises a hole in f. This is why we allow degenerate zero cells having lower dimensionality.

3. The intersection between N and M is along a face g of M coplanar with f, and the normals of f and g point in identical directions. In this case f and g can be rendered independently, since they do not hide or create through-holes in each other. This is why in this case there are no zero faces bound to either of them.

The requirement that cell polyhedra must be convex is not strictly necessary for rendering, and is needed only in order to efficiently recompute the geometry of the cells, as explained in Section 4.2. In addition, the fixed three-level depth of the CDA is not essential, but is more efficient for rendering. An arbitrary depth CDA-like representation for n-D polyhedra called the *extended convex differences tree* is described in [Rappoport91].

The deep reason why the rendering algorithm works is, of course, the fact that the CDA is a *solid* representation. Whenever a face has a through-hole, the hole is simply masked and the rest of the face is rendered ordinarily. Because the object is modeled as a solid, if the through-hole is not a real hole through the object, at some point some face will block it. For the same reason, our rendering algorithm will not work when the viewer is located inside the solid.

4 Conversion of CSG to CDA

In this section we show how to convert a CSG graph to a convex differences aggregate representation. Initially, the primitives are tessellated into linear polyhedra according to approximation parameters supplied by the user. The conversion proceeds in two parts: generation of the *structure* of the resulting CDA (Section 4.1), and computation of the *geometry* of the convex polyhedra present in the CDA (Section 4.2). The separation into different structure and geometry computations is only done in order to simplify the presentation. In practice, the two are intermixed to enable pruning optimizations [Spitz94].

4.1 CDA Structure Generation

Generation of the correct structure of a CDA corresponding to a CSG graph is done by a simple graph re-writing procedure. Many of the previous algorithms for rendering CSG objects [Rossignac90,

Goldfeather89, Wiegand96] utilize such procedures. Our graph rewriting is different from all of these, although it shares with them the fact that the top level of the resulting expression contains only union operations.

Initially, the CSG graph is converted into an equivalent binary tree by duplicating a node according to the number of its outcoming arcs and by splitting Boolean operations having more than two arguments to a series of binary operations. All affine operations in the resulting CSG tree are now propagated into its leaves and attached to the primitives. All these steps are standard CSG procedures. We now have a tree of Boolean operations in which every primitive is located in its final position.

The CDA is computed recursively (bottom-up computation is also possible). When visiting a node, we call the evaluation algorithm recursively for its children, and merge the returned CDAs to form the CDA returned by the node. Since CSG nodes contain only union, intersection and difference Boolean operations, it is enough to show how the union, intersection and difference of two CDAs can be transformed into a CDA. In the following, denote the two CDAs and their cells by $A = \bigcup_{i=1}^{n} C_i, B = \bigcup_{j=1}^{r} D_j$.

Aggregate union. The union of two aggregates is simply an aggregate containing all of their cells: $A \cup B = \bigcup_{i=1}^{n} C_i \bigcup_{j=1}^{r} D_j$. Obviously, the pointset represented by the new aggregate is indeed the union of the two pointsets represented by A and B. Since all cells are valid before executing the aggregate operation, they are also valid after its execution, and the result is a valid CDA.

Aggregate intersection. Since $\bigcup_{i=1}^{n} C_i \cap \bigcup_{j=1}^{r} D_j = \bigcup_{i=1..n, j=1..r} C_i \cap D_j$, the intersection of two CDAs is a CDA whose cells are the pairwise intersections between the cells of the two aggregates: $A \cap B = \{C_i \cap D_j, i = 1 \ldots n, j = 1 \ldots r\}$. Again, the pointset of the result is the intersection of the original pointsets. However, we also have to show how to implement the cell intersection operation so that the result possesses a valid structure.

Cell intersection. Denote the two cells to be intersected by $C = \{P; N_1, \ldots, N_m; Z_1, \ldots, Z_k\}$, and $D = \{Q; M_1, \ldots, M_s; X_1, \ldots, X_t\}$, and also denote $N = N_1 \cup \ldots \cup N_m, M = M_1 \cup \ldots \cup M_s$. Now, $Set(C) = P \setminus N, Set(D) = Q \setminus M$. We have $(P \setminus N) \cap (Q \setminus M) = (P \cap N^c) \cap (Q \cap M^c) = (P \cap Q \cap (N \cup M)^c) = (P \cap Q) \setminus (N \cup M) = (P \cap Q) \setminus (N_1 \cup \ldots \cup N_m \cup M_1 \ldots \cup M_s)$, which is of the structural form desired. The CDA also requires that negative cells are contained within their positive ones, so we intersect each negative cell with $P \cap Q$. P's original cells are already contained in P, so we only have to intersect them with Q; the same holds for Q's original cells. We obtain $C \cap D = \{(P \cap Q); (Q \cap N_1), \ldots, (Q \cap N_m), (P \cap M_1), \ldots, (P \cap M_s)\}$.

Now to the zero cells. Each original zero cell Z_{ij} of C has originated from an intersection between two negative cells N_i, N_j. Hence the new corresponding negative cells $(Q \cap N_i)$ and $(Q \cap N_j)$ may potentially intersect. We can thus intersect Z_{ij} with Q, and add the result (if it is not empty) to the zero cell list. This, however, is not sufficient, because there may be new zero cells arising from intersections of the form $(Q \cap N_i) \cap (P \cap M_j)$. Therefore, we add non-empty intersections of this form to the result as well. To summarize, the intersection between two cells is given by:

$$\{P; N_1..N_m; Z_1..Z_k\} \cap \{Q; M_1..M_s; X_1..X_t\} =$$

$$\{(P \cap Q); (Q \cap N_1)..(Q \cap N_m), (P \cap M_1)..(P \cap M_s);$$

$$(Q \cap Z_1)..(Q \cap Z_k), (P \cap X_1)..(P \cap X_t), (Q \cap N_i) \cap (P \cap M_j)\ldots\}.$$

Note that the only geometric operation in this expression is intersecting two convex polyhedra (all original positive, negative and zero cells are convex polyhedra). This operation will be detailed in Section 4.2.

Note that simple pruning optimizations are possible and should certainly be performed. If the two positive cells P, Q do not intersect, no other intersections calculations need be performed. If a positive cell P does not intersect a negative cell M_j of Q, it does not intersect the zero cells X_l of Q that originated from M_j.

Aggregate difference. $A \setminus B = (\bigcup_{i=1}^{n} C_i) \setminus B = \bigcup_{i=1}^{n} (C_i \setminus B)$. This expression is a union of differences between a cell and an aggregate. For a cell C, we have $C \setminus B = C \setminus \bigcup_{j=1}^{r} D_j = C \cap (\bigcup_{j=1}^{r} D_j)^c = C \cap (\bigcap_{j=1}^{r} D_j^c) = \bigcap_{j=1}^{r} (C \cap D_j^c) = \bigcap_{j=1}^{r} (C \setminus D_j)$. That is, a cell minus an aggregate can be expressed as the intersection of terms of the form $C \setminus D_j$, which is a cell difference operation.

Cell difference. For two cells $C, D, C \setminus D = C \setminus (Q \setminus \bigcup_{i=1}^{s} M_s)$. It is easy to see that, in general, $A \setminus (B \setminus C) = (A \setminus B) \cup (A \cap C)$. Hence, $C \setminus D = (C \setminus Q) \cup (C \cap \bigcup_{i=1}^{s} M_s) = (C \setminus Q) \cup (\bigcup_{i=1}^{s} (C \cap M_i))$. In other words, the difference between cells C and D is an aggregate whose cells are $\{C \setminus Q, C \cap M_1, \ldots, C \cap M_s\}$. The cell $C \setminus Q$ is computed by adding $P \cap Q$ to the negative cell list of C, updating the zero cells as well (Q cannot be added as is because it must be contained within C's positive cell, P). All others are easily handled by transforming the polyhedron M_j to a cell M_j' containing a single positive cell and intersecting the two cells C and M_j' using the cell intersection expression derived above.

In summary, we have seen that aggregate union, intersection and difference can all be reduced to a series of cell intersection operations, which in turn require a single geometric operation, intersection between two convex polyhedra.

In general, the size of the resulting aggregate (in terms of the number of cells that it contains) is usually larger than the combined sizes of the two input aggregates. Theoretically, an aggregate's size can be very large (see [Rossignac94]), but practically, during conceptual design, aggregates are of manageable sizes. The same statement holds for the number of the negative cells, and especially the zero cells, in a cell. Theoretically, all pairs of negative cells may intersect, resulting in a large number of zero cells. However, during the conceptual design stage features tend to be strong and geometric interactions between through-holes (resulting in zero cells) are kept to a minimum.

Example. Figure 4 shows a CSG graph describing a simple car. The car is built as follows. A circle primitive is scaled using an affine operation to provide a wheel frame. A rectangle primitive is instantiated twice, scaled and positioned to form vertical and horizontal wheel holes. The wheel frame minus the holes defines the final wheel. The wheel is instantiated twice to form a left wheel and a right wheel. Note that the geometries of the wheels are different, because a different affine transformation is used. Two rectangles are intersected to form a body frame. A window is subtracted from the body frame to generate the body, which is then positioned in place. The car is the union of the two wheels and the body. The object is of course very simple, but the situation is typical to a conceptual design session: parameterized primitives are instantiated and positioned at the desired locations in the desired scale. They are combined using Boolean operations to form sub-objects. Sub-objects are usually combined using the union operation.

The result after the initial graph re-write is shown in Figure 5(a). The graph was expanded into a tree. All primitives (marked by an internal P) are at their final positions and scale (in the actual data structure affine transformations are attached to the primitives; this is not shown in the figure because we do not consider them to be

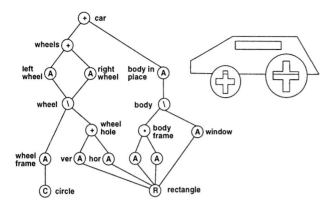

Figure 4 A CSG graph (left) describing a simple car object (right).

part of the tree anymore).

We now describe in a bottom-up fashion all intermediate CDAs computed during the conversion of the tree to a valid CDA. Capital letters denote CDAs, and capital letters with a hat denote CDA cells. The first two CDAs are simply $J = \{\hat{J}_1, \hat{J}_2\}, K = \{\hat{K}_1, \hat{K}_2\}$. $\hat{J}_1 = \{B; ; \}, \hat{J}_2 = \{C; ; \}, \hat{K}_1 = \{E; ; \}, \hat{K}_2 = \{F; ; \}$. The CDA L results from intersecting two cells: $L = \{\hat{L}_1\}, \hat{L}_1 = \{G \cap H; ; \}$. The CDA M results from the difference between two CDAs: $M = A \setminus J = \{\hat{M}_1\}, \hat{M}_1 = \{A; A \cap B, A \cap C; A \cap B \cap C\}$. M possesses a single cell, whose positive cell is A, two negative cells, and a single zero cell. Similarly, the CDA N is given by $N = D \setminus K = \{\hat{N}_1\}, \hat{N}_1 = \{D; D \cap E, D \cap F; D \cap E \cap F\}$. The CDA O also results from the difference between two CDAs: $O = L \setminus I = \{\hat{O}_1\}, \hat{O}_1 = \{G \cap H; G \cap H \cap I; \}$. The CDAs P and Q result from the union of two CDAs: $P = M \cup N = \{\hat{M}_1, \hat{N}_1\}, Q = P \cup O = \{\hat{M}_1, \hat{N}_1, \hat{O}_1\}$. Figure 5(b) shows the final CDA obtained. A single prime on a cell's name (e.g. M') denotes the fact that the cell corresponds to the intermediate CDA M. A double prime (e.g. B'') denotes the fact that the geometry of a negative CDA cell is *not* identical to the corresponding intermediate result having the same name, because it must be intersected by its positive cell.

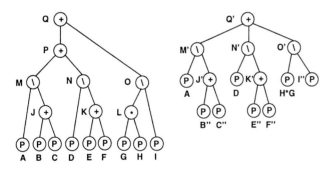

Figure 5 (a) The initial tree corresponding to the car CSG graph, without affine transformations. (b) The final CDA.

4.2 CDA Geometry Computation

The only operation needed in order to compute the geometry of a CDA whose structure was generated from a CSG graph is the intersection between two convex polyhedra. This problem has been extensively dealt with in the computational geometry literature [Muller78, Preparata85, Hertel84, Bieri88, Chazelle87, Chazelle92]. For the sake of completeness, we will briefly outline the algorithm in [Muller78, Preparata85], which is the one we have implemented. Generation of face bindings is a simple book-keeping matter during the execution of the algorithm.

Initially, a single point inside the intersection of the two polyhedra A, B is computed by linear programming. The two polyhedra are now translated so that the common intersection point lies at the origin. Each face is transformed to its dual point: if the plane equation of the face is $ax + by + cz + 1 = 0$, the dual point is (a, b, c). The 3-D convex hull of all dual points (belonging to both A and B) is computed. We have used an excellent available implementation of the QuickHull algorithm [Barber93]. The plane equations of the resulting convex hull are now dualized back to vertices. These are the vertices of the intersection $A \cap B$. The correctness of this algorithm is simple to prove [Preparata85].

The complexity of 3-D convex hull is $O(n \log n)$, so this step dominates the theoretical complexity of the algorithm. However, note that in our application the algorithm is repeatedly invoked on polyhedra whose relative geometries are almost unchanged. Therefore, there is reason to hope that incremental computation will reduce the complexity to linear time in practice.

We should note that there are efficient algorithms to *detect* a possible intersection between two convex polyhedra [Dobkin83]. In general, the fact that the CDA utilizes convex objects enables usage of the considerable amount of efficient algorithms for convex objects developed by the computational geometry community.

Note that a full boundary representation of the object represented by a single CDA cell can be computed by performing 2-D difference operations between bound faces. Thus, the CDA saves some computations when a complete boundary evaluation (with approximate primitives) needs to be performed. This is useful, for example, when converting the designed object to the VRML format.

5 Implementation and Results

In this section we give a brief description of our implementation. It is not our intention to describe a complete system; a complete discussion of system aspects would have to include important issues such as general user interface, direct 3-D manipulation of geometric primitives, visualization of the CSG graph structure, treatment at the object level, etc. All these are beyond the scope of the present paper. Our purpose in this section is only to let the reader understand the system context of our algorithms and data structures. A CSG system emphasizing user interface issues and direct 3-D manipulation is described in [Emmerik93].

The system was implemented on SGI workstations running Irix 5.3. Figure 6 shows the general system architecture. The user can perform four types of operations: (1) modification of the structure of the CSG graph, by adding or deleting nodes and arcs, (2) selection of sub-objects to manipulate, (3) modification of the affine operation associated with the selected sub-object, and (4) manipulation of the graphics view. All operations are done through a user interface module. Obviously, this general architecture suits many of the previous CSG display algorithms as well.

Operation 1 necessitates a re-computation of a CDA (both structure and geometry) from the modified CSG. This is the only operation requiring computation of CDA structure. The result of Operation 2, the current selected object, is stored in a separate data structure. In practice, this is a collection of pointers to CDA and CSG nodes. Operation 3 is the main one, triggering a re-computation of the geometry of the selected CDA nodes. Affine parameters are modified using a 'direct manipulation device' (DMD) [Emmerik93] for editing 3-D local coordinate systems (Figure 9, (a) and (e)). Operation 4 is done directly at the level of the graphics API and does not affect the CSG or CDA data structures.

Figures 7–9 show some objects designed using the system. We

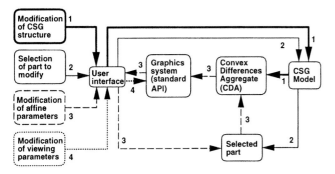

Figure 6 General system architecture.

found it useful to consistently use two different colors during editing to emphasize that the arguments of the difference operation do not have a symmetric role. In Figure 7 there are four cells, each containing a single difference operation. This is a common case, which is dealt with very efficiently by the CDA. In Figure 8, we see how the system can be used in order to investigate interesting geometric relationships between objects. In (c), there is a single CDA cell. Its positive cell is formed by the intersection of the two 'outer' cones, and it has two negative cells originating from the two subtracted cones. In (d), there are two cells, having one and two negative cells respectively. In Figure 9(a–g) we tried to convey the feeling of interactively moving a hole ((h) shows an intersection). The complexity of the CDA structure depends on whether the cube pattern is modeled using a union of nine small cubes or a single flat box minus four slabs. These examples show the advantage and pleasure derived from interactive 3-D Boolean operations using basic primitives.

Note that the relatively coarse tessellation of the cylinder in Figures 7 and 9 is not harmful for conceptual design, where dominant geometric features, their composition and interrelationships are the important issues.

The computational bottleneck in the system is the geometry update following modification of affine transformations of selected nodes. The current system implements only the raw conversion algorithm, without adding additional efficiency schemes. For example, all geometric computations on the geometric elements are repeated on every user event, even if the elements have not been modified, and no spatial acceleration scheme is used to prune possible intersections between negative cells (a quadratic number of such intersections is possible). To give some idea regarding the raw performance of the method, consider that the examples in Figures 7–9 run in about 5–30 frames per second on a 100 MHZ R4000 SGI Indigo with a GR2-XZ graphics board.

6 Discussion

Computer graphics and geometric modeling have not yet been able to provide adequate support for conceptual design. The CSG modeling operations, in particular the Boolean operations, are highly attractive for design. In this paper we presented a method that constitutes a step towards interactive conceptual design of 3-D solids, by allowing interactive modifications of affine transformations in CSG graphs.

Interactive editing and visualization of general CSG models is a truly difficult problem; in this paper we focused on the sub-problem of conceptual design of relatively simple 3-D solids, showing that interactive Boolean operations can be achieved for that purpose. Obviously, beyond a certain level of object complexity the method will no longer provide interactive performance. Because the present implementation incorporates virtually no efficiency schemes be-

yond that of the raw algorithm, it is difficult to assess at present the maximal object complexity supported. Two measures of object complexity are the number of products in the disjunctive form of the CSG tree and the number of negations in a product. The present system is useful mostly for cases when the maximal number of negations is very small (say, less than 10). Performance grows roughly linearly in the number of products.

In the future, we plan to extend our system in the following directions. First, we will try to improve efficiency by using incremental geometric algorithms, spatial acceleration schemes and integration with multi-pass methods. We believe that the combination of these techniques will provide better scaling to larger models and will take advantage of temporal coherence. Note that a spatial acceleration scheme can be naturally provided by the CDA itself, since each cell in the CDA possesses a two-level hierarchy: convex set minus contained convex sets. If two positive cells do not intersect, their negative children do not intersect as well. Thus, the CDA is suitable for efficient collision detection schemes such as the one described in [Ponamgi95].

Second, we will enhance the system with higher-level functionality, most notably by adding constraints to the set of modeling operations available to the designer. Constraints are also important for object positioning, since the visual feedback provided by tessellated models may not suffice for tangency, incidence and right angle relationships. Constraints may be defined between node coordinate systems or between entities of the object's boundary (such as vertices and edges). Supporting the latter while enabling the user to modify the degree of tessellation of non-planar surfaces may require efficient handling of the persistent naming problem [Rappoport96, Rappoport97], a challenging problem in geometric and solid modeling.

Finally, one of the main ideas in the CDA approach is that faces in a product are not represented explicitly, as done by most CAD systems, but are represented as the difference between an enclosing convex polygon and a set of possibly overlapping convex polygons. We intend to study other possible applications of this idea in geometric modeling.

Acknowledgements. I thank Eyal Ofek for his help with the images and the video, Michal Etzion and Ofir Amir for improving the implementation, Seth Teller for his polyhedra code, and Dani Lischinski, Ofri Sadowsky, Nadav Aharoni and the Siggraph reviewers for their comments on the paper.

References

[Atherton83] Atherton, P.R., A scan-line hidden surface removal procedure for constructive solid geometry. *Computer Graphics*, 17(3):73–82, 1983 (Siggraph '83).

[Barber93] Barber, C.B., Dobkin, D.P., Huhdanpaa, H.T., The Quickhull algorithm for convex hull, GCG53, The Geometry Center, Minneapolis, 1993 (ftp.geom.umn.edu/pub/software/qhull.tar.Z).

[Batchelor80] Batchelor, B.G., Hierarchical shape description based upon convex hulls of concavities. *J. of Cybernetics*, 10:205–210, 1980.

[Bieri88] Bieri, H., Nef, W., Elementary set operations with *d*-dimensional polyhedra. Computational Geometry and its Applications, LNCS 333, Springer-Verlag, 1988, pp. 97–112.

[Breen91] Breen, D.E., Constructive cubes: CSG evaluation for display using discrete 3-D scalar data sets. *Eurographics '91*, 127–142, 1991.

[Bronsvoort87] Bronsvoort, W.F., An algorithm for visible-line and visible-surface display of CSG models. *The Visual Computer*, 3:176–185, 1987.

[Cameron94] Cameron, S.A., Direct drawing from CSG models with hidden-line removal. *CSG 94, Set-Theoretic Solid Modeling: Techniques and Applications,* Information Geometers, 1994, pp. 179–192.

[Chazelle87] Chazelle, B., Dobkin, D., Intersection of convex objects in two and three dimensions, *Journal of the ACM,* 34(1):1–27, 1987.

[Chazelle92] Chazelle, B., An optimal algorithm for intersecting three-dimensional convex polyhedra. *SIAM J. Comput.,* 21(4):671–696, 1992.

[Dobkin83] Dobkin, D.P., Kirkpatrick, D.G., Fast detection of polyhedral intersection. *Theoret. Comput. Sci.,* 27:241–253, 1983.

[Emmerik93] Emmerik, M.J.G.M. van, Rappoport, A., Rossignac, J., Simplifying interactive design of solid models: a hypertext approach. *The Visual Computer,* 9:239–254, 1993.

[Goldfeather86] Goldfeather, J., Hultquist, J.P.M., Fuchs, H., Fast constructive solid geometry display in the pixel-power graphics system. *Computer Graphics,* 20(4):107–116, 1986 (Siggraph '86).

[Goldfeather89] Goldfeather, J., Molnar, S., Turk, G., Fuchs, H., Near real-time CSG rendering using tree normalization and geometric pruning. *IEEE CG&A,* 9:20–28, May 1989.

[Hertel84] Hertel, S., Mäntylä, M., Mehlhorn, K., Nievergelt, J., Space sweep solves intersection of convex polyhedra. *Acta Inform.,* 21:501–519, 1984.

[Hoffmann89] Hoffmann, C., Geometric and Solid Modeling: an Introduction. Morgan Kaufmann, 1989.

[Kim90] Kim, Y.S., Convex decomposition and solid geometric modeling. Ph.D. Thesis, Mech. Eng., Stanford University, 1990.

[Jansen86] Jansen, F.W., A pixel-parallel hidden surface algorithm for constructive solid geometry. *Eurographics '86,* Elsevier Science, NY, 29–40, 1986.

[Jansen87] Jansen, F.W., CSG hidden surface algorithms for VLSI hardware systems. In: *Advances in Computer Graphics Hardware I,* Springer-Verlag, 1987, pp. 75–82.

[Jansen91] Jansen, F.W., Depth-order point classification techniques for CSG display algorithms, *ACM Trans. on Graphics,* 10(1):40–70, 1991.

[Meagher84] Meagher, D.J., Interactive solids processing for medical analysis and planning. *Computer Graphics '84, NCGA Conference Proceedings,* vol. 2, NCGA, 1984, pp. 96–106.

[McReynolds96] McReynolds, T., Blythe, D., Programming with OpenGL: Advanced Rendering, course #23, Siggraph '96, pp. 36–40.

[Muller78] Muller, D.E., Preparata, F.P., Finding the intersection of two convex polyhedra. *Theoret. Comput. Sci.,* 7:217–236, 1978.

[Naylor92] Naylor, B., Interactive solid modeling using partitioning trees. *Graphics Interface '92,* pp. 11–18.

[Naylor96] Naylor, B., Destructive solid geometry for interactive entertainment and training, *CSG 96,* Cambridge, UK, 1996.

[Okino84] Okino, N., Kakazu, Y., Moritomo, M., Extended depth-buffer algorithms for hidden-surface visualization. *IEEE CG&A,* 4:79–88, 1984.

[Ponamgi95] Ponamgi, M., Manocha, D., Lin, M.C., Incremental algorithms for collision detection between solid models. Proceedings, *3rd ACM/Siggraph Symposium on Solid Modeling and Applications (Solid Modeling '95),* ACM Press, 1995, pp. 293–304.

[Preparata85] Preparata, F., Shamos, M. I., Computational Geometry: An Introduction, Springer-Verlag, New-York, 1985.

[Rappoport90] Rappoport, A., Using convex differences in hierarchical representations of polygonal maps. *Graphics Interface '90,* pp. 183–189.

[Rappoport91] Rappoport, A., The extended convex differences tree (ECDT) representation for n-dimensional polyhedra. *Intl. J. Comput. Geom. and App.,* 1(3):227–241, 1991. Also: proceedings, *ACM/Siggraph Symposium on Solid Modeling Foundations and CAD/CAM Applications (Solid Modeling '91),* ACM Press, 1991, pp. 139–148.

[Rappoport92] Rappoport, A., An efficient adaptive algorithm for constructing the convex differences tree of a simple polygon. *Computer Graphics Forum,* 11(4):235–240, 1992.

[Rappoport95] Rappoport, A., Geometric modeling: a new fundamental framework and its practical implications. Proceedings, *3rd ACM/Siggraph Symposium on Solid Modeling and Applications (Solid Modeling '95),* ACM Press, 1995, pp. 31–42.

[Rappoport96] Rappoport, A., Breps as displayable-selectable models in interactive design of families of geometric objects. *Theory and Practice of Geometric Modeling (Blaubeuren II),* Tübingen, Germany, October 1996. Proceedings to be published by Springer-Verlag.

[Rappoport97] Rappoport, A., The Generic Geometric Complex: a modeling scheme for families of decomposed pointsets. Proceedings, *4th ACM/Siggraph Symposium on Solid Modeling and Applications (Solid Modeling '97),* ACM Press, 1997, pp. 31–41.

[Requicha80] Requicha, A.G., Representations for rigid solids: Theory, methods and systems. *ACM Computing Surveys,* 12:437–464, 1980.

[Requicha85] Requicha, A.G., Voelcker, H.B., Boolean operations in solid modeling: boundary evaluation and merging algorithms, *Proc. of the IEEE* 73(1):30–44, 1985.

[Rossignac86] Rossignac, J.R., Requicha, A.A.G., Depth-buffering display techniques for constructive solid geometry. *IEEE CG&A,* 6:29–39, Sep. 1986.

[Rossignac90] Rossignac, J.R., Wu, J., Correct shading of regularized CSG solids using a depth-interval buffer. In: Grimsdale, R.L., Kaufman, A., (eds), *Advances in Computer Graphics Hardware V,* Springer-Verlag, Berlin, 1990, pp. 117–138.

[Rossignac94] Rossignac, J.R., Processing disjunctive forms directly from CSG graphs. *CSG 94, Set-Theoretic Solid Modeling: Techniques and Applications,* Information Geometers, 1994, pp. 55–70.

[Roth82] Roth, S.D., Ray casting for modeling solids. *CVGIP,* 18(2):109–144, 1982.

[Sklansky72] Sklansky, J., Measuring concavity on a rectangular mosaic. *IEEE Tran. Com.,* 21:1355–1364, 1972.

[Smithers89] Smithers, T., AI-based design versus geometry-based design, or why design cannot be supported by geometry alone. *Computer-Aided Design,* 21(3):141–150, 1989.

[Spitz94] Spitz, S., Interactive Boolean operations and collision detection on polyhedral solids. Amirim project report, Institute of Computer Science, The Hebrew University, July 1994.

[Thibault87] Thibault, W.C., Naylor, B.F., Set operations on polyhedra using binary space partitioning trees. *Computer Graphics,* 21(4):153–162, 1987 (Siggraph '87).

[Tor84] Tor, S.B., Middleditch A.E., Convex decomposition of simple polygons. *ACM Trans. on Graphics,* 3(4):244–265, 1984.

[VanHook86] Van Hook, T., Real-time shaded NC milling display. *Computer Graphics,* 20(4):15–20, 1986 (Siggraph '86).

[Wiegand96] Wiegand, T.F., Interactive rendering of CSG models. *Computer Graphics Forum,* 15(4):249–261, 1996.

[Woo82] Woo, T., Feature extraction by volume decomposition. Technical Report 82-4, Dept. of Indus. and Oper. Eng., The University of Michigan, 1982.

Figure 7 An abstract statue. The object is modeled as a union of the base and the three tubes. Each tube is the difference between two cylinders, and the base is the difference between two blocks. All the 'holes' can be moved, scaled and rotated in real time.

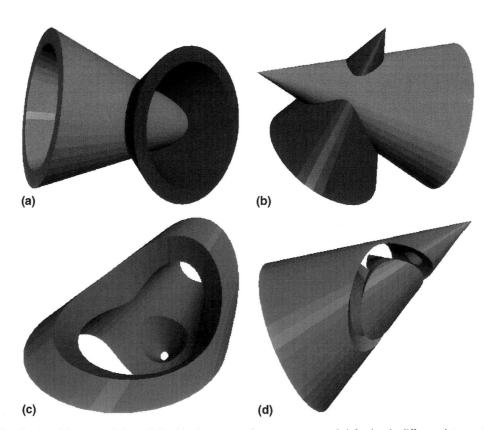

Figure 8 Visualization of the geometric interrelationships between two ice cream cones, each defined as the difference between two cones. (a) union, bottom view; (b) union, side view; (c) intersection; (d) difference. Affine operations can be executed on all constituents of this model in real time.

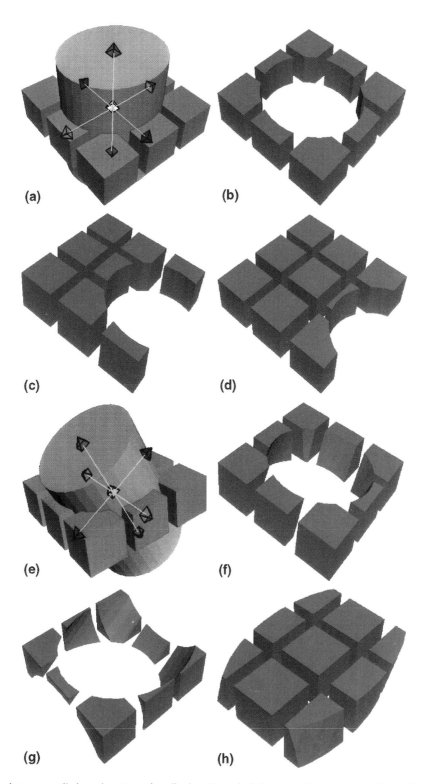

Figure 9 Interaction between a cylinder and a pattern of small cubes. (a) manipulation view; (b-d) moving a cylindrical hole; (e) manipulation view when scaling and rotating the cylinder; (f-g) rotating the hole; (h) intersection with a scaled-up cylinder.

Guaranteeing the Topology of an Implicit Surface Polygonization for Interactive Modeling

Barton T. Stander[1]   John C. Hart[2]

School of EECS

Washington State University

Abstract

Morse theory shows how the topology of an implicit surface is affected by its function's critical points, whereas catastrophe theory shows how these critical points behave as the function's parameters change. Interval analysis finds the critical points, and they can also be tracked efficiently during parameter changes. Changes in the function value at these critical points cause changes in the topology. Techniques for modifying the polygonization to accommodate such changes in topology are given. These techniques are robust enough to guarantee the topology of an implicit surface polygonization, and are efficient enough to maintain this guarantee during interactive modeling. The impact of this work is a topologically-guaranteed polygonization technique, and the ability to directly and accurately manipulate polygonized implicit surfaces in real time.

Descriptors: I.3.5 Computational Geometry and Object Modeling — Modeling packages. **General Terms:** Algorithms.
Keywords: catastrophe theory, critical points, implicit surfaces, Morse theory, polygonization, topology, interval analysis, interactive modeling, particle systems.

1 Introduction

Shapes are represented implicitly by a function that classifies points in space as inside the shape, outside the shape or on the shape's surface, called the implicit surface. This representation provides computer graphics with geometric models that can be easily and smoothly joined together, but the incorporation of the implicit representation into graphics systems can be problematic. Polygonization of implicit surfaces allows graphics systems to reap the powerful modeling benefits of the implicit representation while retaining the rendering speed and flexibility of polygonal meshes.

The *topology* (specifically the *homotopy type*) of an implicit surface refers to the connectedness of the shape, including the number of disjoint components and the number of holes in each component (*genus*). This should not be confused with other instances of topology in computer graphics, such as the connection patterns of a mesh of polygons or parametric patches. Thus, for a polygonization to accurately represent the topology of an implicit surface the number of components and the genus of each component of the polygonization need to agree with that of the implicit surface.

Implicit surfaces are commonly polygonized to a given degree of geometric accuracy. This accuracy is in some cases adaptively related to the local curvature of the implicit surface, reducing the number of polygons without affecting the appearance of the surface. This work instead focuses on a polygonization that accurately discerns the topology of an implicit surface. Topologically-accurate polygonization can reduce the number of polygons without affecting the structure of the surface.

Guaranteeing the topology of a polygonization does not necessarily yield an accurate polygonization. A coffee cup is topologically equivalent to a torus, but the torus provides a poor representation for the geometry of a coffee cup. The topological guarantee becomes useful when coupled with a geometrically accurate polygonization scheme.

Guaranteeing the topology of an implicit surface polygonization solves several open problems in computer graphics.

Polygonization topology is coordinate dependent. Polygonization schemes often discern topology from point samples. Different polygonizations of the same implicit surface may differ in topology, and the same polygonization algorithm may return different topological structures depending on the coordinate system of the implicit surface, as demonstrated in Figure 1. For example, the implicit surface might appear connected when polygonized in its modeling coordinate system but could then appear disconnected when polygonized in a scene's coordinate system.

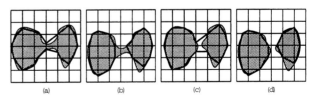

Figure 1: The topology of a connected implicit surface is correctly polygonized (a), but a translated instance is not (b). Two disjoint components are polygonized as a single component (c), but a translated instance is polygonized properly (d).

Interloping components. Some configurations of implicit surfaces can yield unexpected disjoint components. Such isolated components of the implicit surface occur because of an accumulation of neighboring potentials but do not themselves surround any "skele-

[1] Current address: Strata, 1562 El Vista Circle, Saint George, UT 84765, barts@strata3d.com
[2] Address: School of EECS, WSU, Pullman, WA 99164-2752, hart@eecs.wsu.edu

tal" geometry. For example, Figure 2 shows two blobby ellipsoids that produce a third component. Such components would not appear in a continuation-based polygonization[1], as might be used for modeling, but would appear as a surprise in a direct ray tracing of the implicit surface, as might be used for the final rendering.

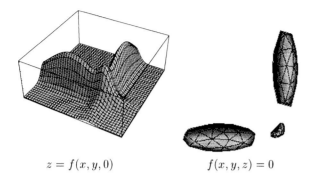

$$z = f(x, y, 0) \qquad\qquad f(x, y, z) = 0$$

Figure 2: An interloping component found at the intersection of the potential of two blobby ellipses (left) and two polygonized blobby ellipsoids (right). The algorithms described in this paper were used to correctly polygonize the interloping configuration on the right.

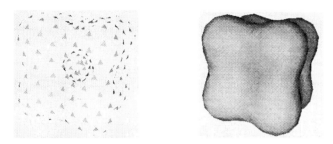

Figure 3: Implicit form displayed using a particle system (left) and polygonized (right).

Real-time implicit surface modeling. Implicit surfaces can be modeled and displayed in real-time using a particle system representation [35]. The viewer must then infer the shape of the implicit surface from the positions and orientations of the particles. Polygonization of the particles provides a better visual representation of the implicit surface, as demonstrated in Figure 3, but adding a polygonization step after every modeling change significantly degrades the otherwise real-time performance of the system. The ability to detect and correct topology changes allows the system to dynamically maintain the polygonization in real time by reconnecting the vertices of a polygonization only when a topology change has occurred, and only in the neighborhood of the topology change.

This work hence has two objectives. The first is to generate a polygonization of an implicit surface that is guaranteed to agree with its topology. The second objective is to maintain this topological guarantee during interactive manipulation of the surface. The topology of implicit surface polygonizations are guaranteed by tracking a few special points, called critical points, that dictate the topology of the implicit surface.

Section 2 examines previous polygonization techniques that consider topology. Section 3 describes critical points and adapts existing interval search methods and constraint techniques to the specific tasks of finding and tracking critical points. Section 4 analyzes the effect of critical points on topology and describes techniques for adjusting the topology of a polygonization to match the

topology of the implicit surface. Section 5 describes a new polygonization algorithm based on Morse theory that polygonizes an implicit surface with a guarantee that the topology of the polygonization matches the topology of the implicit surface. Section 6 describes several new algorithms for maintaining this topological guarantee fast enough to support direct manipulation at interactive speeds. Section 7 concludes with a summary, implementation details and directions for further investigation.

2 Previous Work

One method for interrogating an implicit surface subdivides space into cells and samples the implicit surface at the corners of these cells [22, 36, 16, 2, 20].

Some cellular polygonizations can guarantee that the implicit surface is contained in the union of a set of arbitrarily small cells, hence yielding a guarantee on surface topology accurate to a given geometric precision (e.g. the diameter of the smallest cells). Both the Lipschitz condition [14] and interval analysis [30, 17] can guarantee that an implicit surface does not pass through some cells. Cells for which this guarantee fails are "ambiguous" and can be subdivided until a given level of precision is reached and the implicit surface is assumed to lie within the union of the ambiguous cells. These ambiguous cells can then be further subdivided into "globally parameterizable" components [28]. The topology of the surface passing through such a component can be determined with a few point samples. Such cellular subdivision schemes yield a geometrically precise guaranteed representation of the implicit surface topology, though at the expense of a polygonization composed of an unnecessarily large number of small polygons.

An alternative method for interrogation constrains a particle system to the implicit surface [3, 33, 31, 9, 8]. When the implicit surface remains static, such as during a pause in user manipulation, it's particle system can be polygonized [6, 35].

A polygonization of the particle system can be maintained during user manipulation in a previous work [24]. Changes in topology were detected by comparing the interpolated polygonization normals to the implicit surface gradients at the vertices of the polygonization. Significant differences in these two vectors implied that the topology of the polygonization might not match the topology of the underlying implicit surface.

Critical points have also been used to determine implicit surface topology during a "shrinkwrap" polygonization [4]. A Lipschitz condition on the derivative of the function was used to guarantee the absence of critical points in a neighborhood, and upon failure, Newton's method was used to find the possible critical point. If Newton's method failed to converge, then the neighborhood was assumed to contain no critical points. The shrinkwrapping work also described a technique for repolygonizing the vertices surrounding a critical point based on the positions and orientations of the nearby polygons. Section 5 further explains and analyzes the shrinkwrap algorithm.

The analysis of topology using critical points is not entirely new to computer graphics. Critical points of vector and tensor fields are used to delineate topologically-distinct regions in the visualization of flow [13, 7]. Catastrophes have been used to understand caustics [18] and to interpret projections [15]. Morse theory has been used to reconstruct surfaces from cross sections [27] and to find surface-surface intersection curves [5].

3 Critical Points

The *implicit surface* defined by a function $f : \mathbb{R}^3 \to \mathbb{R}$ is the set of points $\mathbf{x} \in \mathbb{R}^3$ that satisfy $f(\mathbf{x}) = 0$. We assume the function

---

[1] The techniques developed in this paper could be used to assist a continuation-based polygonization schemes detect such isolated components.

returns positive values inside the object, so the *solid* modeled by the implicit surface is the set of points $\{\mathbf{x}|f(\mathbf{x}) \geq 0\}$.

This work requires the function f to be C^2 continuous, with continuous first and second derivatives, and its implicit surface must be a manifold with a well defined, continuously varying surface normal. These restrictions include exponential-based "blobby" models [1], but exclude some of the more efficient C^1 piecewise polynomial approximations [21, 36].

The implicit surface is extended into a family of surfaces defined by $f(\mathbf{x}; \mathbf{q})$ continuously parameterized by the vector $\mathbf{q}$ consisting of various model parameters (e.g. the locations of blobby elements). For some values of $\mathbf{q}$, the implicit surface defined by $f(\mathbf{x}; \mathbf{q}) = 0$ may contain a cusp, kink or crease, specifically when the implicit surface changes topology. We consider the implicit surfaces in this family before and after but not during such topology changes. An alternative technique exists for interactively manipulating implicit surfaces with cusps, kinks and creases [25].

The *critical points* of a function f occur where its gradient

$$\nabla f(\mathbf{x}) = (f_x(\mathbf{x}), f_y(\mathbf{x}), f_z(\mathbf{x})) \qquad (1)$$

vanishes. (The notation $f_x = \partial f/\partial x$.) A *critical value* is the value of the function f at a critical point.

The *Hessian* V (called the *stability matrix* in catastrophe theory) is defined as the Jacobian of the gradient

$$V(\mathbf{x}) = J(\nabla f(\mathbf{x})) = \begin{bmatrix} f_{xx}(\mathbf{x}) & f_{xy}(\mathbf{x}) & f_{xz}(\mathbf{x}) \\ f_{yx}(\mathbf{x}) & f_{yy}(\mathbf{x}) & f_{yz}(\mathbf{x}) \\ f_{zx}(\mathbf{x}) & f_{zy}(\mathbf{x}) & f_{zz}(\mathbf{x}) \end{bmatrix}. \qquad (2)$$

Since $f_{xy} = f_{yx}$, etc., the stability matrix is symmetric.

A critical point $\mathbf{x}$ is classified based on the signs of the three eigenvalues $l_1 \leq l_2 \leq l_3$ of $V(\mathbf{x})$ [32]. If all three eigenvalues are non-zero, then the critical point is called *non-degenerate* and is either a maximum, minimum or some kind of saddle point. In three dimensions, saddle points come in two varieties. Table 1 indicates this classification.

l_1	l_2	l_3	Critical Point
-	-	-	Maximum Point
-	-	+	2-Saddle
-	+	+	1-Saddle
+	+	+	Minimum Point

Table 1: Classification of critical points based on the sign of the eigenvalues of the stability matrix.

The critical points are continuously dependent on the parameter vector $\mathbf{q}$. As the parameter vector $\mathbf{q}$ changes, the critical points move in space. They can also appear spontaneously in pairs, or collide in pairs, annihilating each other. If any of the three eigenvalues of the stability matrix of a critical point equal zero then $\mathbf{x}$ is called a *degenerate critical point*. The creation and destruction of critical points occur at degenerate critical points Critical point creation/destruction is demonstrated in Figure 4.

Isolated degenerate critical points are unstable. In the rare event that an isolated degenerate critical point does appear, it can be removed by a small perturbation of the implicit surface parameters without affecting the implicit surface topology.

Some functions can yields non-isolated degenerate critical points (critical sets). For example, the cylinder defined by $f(x, y, z) = x^2 + y^2 - 1$ has a critical line along the z-axis. A small perturbation of the cylinder into an ellipsoid $f(x, y, z) = x^2 + y^2 + \epsilon z^2 - 1$ collapses the degenerate critical line into a single non-degenerate critical point at the origin. We assume the family of implicit surfaces is parameterized such that degenerate sets can be removed by such perturbation.

Figure 4: Creation of critical points in 1-D: $y = f(x, 0, 0)$. (a) Two summed Gaussian bumps, one large and one small, sufficiently close such that there is only a single maximum point in the domain shown. (b) Moving the smaller bump away from the larger creates a degenerate critical point. (c) Moving the smaller bump farther results in the creation of a pair of new critical points: a maximum point and a minimum point. Performing these steps in reverse demonstrates critical point annihilation.

3.1 Finding All Critical Points

Interval analysis searches can be guaranteed to find all points satisfying a given criterion in a given bounded domain to a desired degree of accuracy [19, 23]. Such a search can find all of the critical points of a given function to determine the topology of its implicit surface.

The interval search for critical points starts with an initial box bounding the space of interest. The simple interval search for critical points shown in Figure 5 eliminates large portions of space that cannot contain a critical point.

Given a box (a vector of intervals) $\mathbf{X} = [x_0, x_1] \times [y_0, y_1] \times [z_0, z_1]$ the algorithm checks whether the intervals returned by all of the partial derivatives contain zero. If not, then $\mathbf{X}$ contains no critical points. If so, then the algorithm subdivides $\mathbf{X}$ and tests each component individually. Note that $F_x(\mathbf{X})$ is an interval arithmetic implementation of $\partial f/\partial x$, and likewise for F_y, F_z.

Procedure SimpleSearch($\mathbf{X}$)
  If diam($\mathbf{X}$) $< \epsilon$ then indicate critical point in $\mathbf{X}$.
  If $0 \in F_x(\mathbf{X})$ and $0 \in F_y(\mathbf{X})$ and $0 \in F_z(\mathbf{X})$ then
    Subdivide $\mathbf{X}$ and continue the search recursively.

Figure 5: Simple interval divide and conquer search algorithm.

In these algorithms, subdivision means dividing into halves with respect to its widest axis, although any number of subdivision techniques could be used. The diameter of a box diam($\mathbf{X}$) is measured using the chessboard metric, and is simply the width of the widest interval-element in the vector $\mathbf{X}$.

Simple subdivision performs remarkably well, discarding large portions of space known not to contain critical points. This technique will eventually finds all critical points to any degree of accuracy within a given bounding box, but with only linear convergence.

When the box diameter reaches a given size, the quadratically-convergent interval Newton's method shown in Figure 6 refines and/or subdivides the box down to the desired numerical precision [28, 11].

Given two points $\mathbf{x}, \mathbf{y}$ there exist points $\mathbf{z}$ between[2] $\mathbf{x}$ and $\mathbf{y}$ such that

$$\nabla f(\mathbf{x}) + V(\mathbf{z})(\mathbf{y} - \mathbf{x}) = \nabla f(\mathbf{y}), \qquad (3)$$

where the stability matrix V is the Jacobian of ∇f. Let $\mathbf{m}(\mathbf{X})$ return the midpoint of box $\mathbf{X}$. The algorithm seeks $\mathbf{y} \in \mathbf{X}$ such that $\nabla f(\mathbf{y}) = 0$. Since both $\mathbf{x}, \mathbf{y} \in \mathbf{X}$, the $\mathbf{z}$ satisfying (3) must be in $\mathbf{X}$ as well. Thus, solving

$$\nabla f(\mathbf{m}(\mathbf{X})) + V(\mathbf{X})(\mathbf{Y} - \mathbf{m}(\mathbf{X})) = 0. \qquad (4)$$

yields $\mathbf{Y}$, a box containing all of the critical points in $\mathbf{X}$. Note that

```
Procedure NewtonSearch(X)
    Repeat.
        Solve V(X)(Y − m(X)) = −∇f(m(X)) for Y.
        If Y ⊃ X then subdivide X and search recursively.
        If Y ⊂ X then there is a unique c.p. in Y (and X).
        If Y ∩ X = ∅ then there is no c.p in X. Return.
        Otherwise let X = X ∩ Y.
    Until diam(X) < ε.
    Indicate critical point at m(X).
```

Figure 6: Interval Newton's method search for critical points.

$V(\mathbf{X})$ returns a matrix of intervals.

An interval version of Gauss-Seidel is recommended for solving (4), but this can lead to two problems. First, the diagonal elements of $V(\mathbf{X})$ might contain zero, requiring the interval arithmetic division operation to correctly perform a division by an interval containing zero. Division by intervals containing zero produce two intervals, leading to additional algorithm recursion [28, 10]. Solving the rows whose diagonal elements do not contain zero first reduces the occurrence of semi-infinite intervals [11].

Solving

$$V_c^{-1} V(\mathbf{X})(\mathbf{Y} - \mathbf{x}) = -V_c^{-1} \nabla f(\mathbf{m}(\mathbf{X})). \qquad (5)$$

where $V_c = m(V(\mathbf{X}))$ instead of (4) yields a much tighter bound and hastens the NewtonSearch performance [11]. Note that the expression $m(V(\mathbf{X}))$ returns a scalar matrix consisting of the midpoints of the intervals of $V(\mathbf{X})$.

When a critical point lies on an edge of the box, NewtonSearch's convergence is less quadratic. Extending $\mathbf{X}$ outward by a small percentage each iteration avoids this problem. Time may also be incorporated into the search by crossing $\mathbf{X}$ with the time interval $[t_0, t_1]$.

3.2 Tracking Critical Points

Altering an implicit surface's parameters changes the positions of some or all of the critical points.

The same techniques that constrain particles to adhere to the implicit surface [35], can also cause particles to adhere to any selected critical point.

Let $\mathbf{x} = \mathbf{x}(t)$ be a particle constrained to follow one of the critical points of the function f. Its partial derivatives $f_x(\mathbf{x})$, $f_y(\mathbf{x})$, and $f_x(\mathbf{x})$ are all constrained to zero. To ensure that they remain zero, their time derivatives $\dot{f}_x(\mathbf{x}) = \frac{d^2 f}{dx\,dt}(\mathbf{x})$, $\dot{f}_y(\mathbf{x})$ and $\dot{f}_z(\mathbf{x})$ must also be set to zero. Given the parameter vector $\mathbf{q}$ and its velocity $\dot{\mathbf{q}}$, one can solve these equations to determine the critical point velocity $\dot{\mathbf{x}}$. This velocity is then passed to a differential equation solver (such as fourth-order Runge-Kutta) to approximate the new location of the critical point. Newton's method refines the approximation.

4 Detecting and Correcting Topology Changes

The identification of critical points simplifies topologically-guaranteed direct manipulation of implicit surfaces through a polygonal representation. The key to solving the topology problem is that a change in the topology of a surface is always accompanied by a change in the sign of a critical value [12]. Monitoring the critical points greatly simplifies the burden of detecting topological changes, and divides the problem into classifying topological changes, identifying polygons to remove and reconnecting the verticed of the removed polygons.

---

[2]The notion of "between" for points in space means that $\mathbf{z}$ is in a box with corners at $\mathbf{x}$ and $\mathbf{y}$.

4.1 Classifying Topological Changes

Table 2 enumerates all of the possible critical-point/sign combinations and their corresponding implications on the implicit surface topology. When an implicit surface topology change is detected, the polygonization must be altered to properly represent the new topology.

Critical Point	Sign Changes To	Action
Maximum	−	Destroy
Maximum	+	Create
2-Saddle	−	Cut
2-Saddle	+	Attach
1-Saddle	−	Pierce
1-Saddle	+	Spackle
Minimum	−	Bubble
Minimum	+	Burst

Table 2: The affect of critical point sign on topology.

4.2 Identifying Polygons to Remove

Changes in maximum and minimum critical values cause entire simply-connected components of polygonization to be removed or created. Changes in saddle points require the determination of specific polygons to be removed such that their vertices may be properly reconnected. These polygons intersect a separatrix extending from the saddle point.

The separatrix may be efficiently approximated by a line for 2-saddles, or a plane for 1-saddles. These lines and planes described by the eigenvectors of the stability matrix of a critical point approximate the separatrix.

When separatrixes are linearly approximated by lines and planes, certain errors might occur. For example, a 2-saddle may connect two components, but the line approximating its separatrix might not intersect either component. One must then assume that the parameter vector $\mathbf{q}$ is sufficiently close to the parameter vector at the topology change $\mathbf{q}_*$ that the linear approximation correctly intersect the proper polygonized implicit surface components.

The separatrix extending from a 2-saddle can be treated as an initial value problem, using the positive eigenvector $\mathbf{v}_3(\mathbf{x})$ of the stability matrix to define the ordinary differential equation

$$\dot{\mathbf{x}} = \mathbf{v}_3(\mathbf{x}) \qquad (6)$$

and using numerical integration to trace out the path of the separatrix. The midpoint method provided sufficient numerical accuracy for this task in our experiments.

The case where a separatrix intersects a polygonization vertex can be removed with a topology-preserving perturbation.

4.3 Reconnection

The following procedures describe which polygons must be removed, and how their vertices are reconnected to update the topology of the polygonization.

Destroy. When the value at a maximum goes negative, an isolated component in the implicit surface disappears. A ray cast from the maximum point in any direction will first intersect a polygon in this simply-connected component. All polygons connected to this polygon are then removed. Figure 7 pseudocodes this algorithm.

Create. When the value at a maximum goes positive, a new, simply-connected component in the implicit surface appears. A sufficiently small tetrahedron may be placed around the maximum point, letting its vertices adhere to the implicit surface component and adding

```
Procedure Destroy/Burst
    Cast a ray from maximum point in any direction.
    Let p be the first polygon the ray intersects.
    Push p onto stack.
    While stack not empty.
        Let p be the result of popping the stack.
        For all polygons q sharing an edge with p.
            Push q onto stack.
        Remove p from polygonization.
```

Figure 7: The repolygonization algorithm for *Destroy* and *Burst*.

new polygons when necessary. Alternatively, a ray may be cast from the maximum point and intersected with the implicit surface. The first intersection denotes the location where any standard continuation polygonization technique may be applied. Figure 8 pseudocodes this algorithm.

```
Procedure Create/Bubble
    Cast a ray from maximum point in any direction.
    Let x ∈ f⁻¹(0) be the first ray intersection.
    Polygonize the component containing x.
```

Figure 8: The repolygonization algorithm for *Create* and *Bubble*.

Cut. When the value at a 2-saddle goes negative, part of the implicit surface disconnects. The separatrix surface extending from the 2-saddle is found by integrating the two negative eigenvalues of the stability matrix will intersect the polygons in a ring surrounding the 2-saddle. In practical cases, this separatrix is sufficiently approximated by a plane passing through the 2-saddle perpendicular to its positive eigenvector. The ring of polygons intersecting the separatrix surface are removed, yielding two disjoint rings of polygonization vertices. These rings are "sewn up" individually via triangulation. Figure 9 pseudocodes this algorithm, and Figure 10 illustrates the polygon configuration.

```
Procedure Cut/Spackle
    Let P be a plane containing the critical point x perpen-
        dicular to the uniquely-signed eigenvector of V(x).
    Cast a ray from x in any direction within P.
    Let p₀ be the first polygon intersected by the ray.
    Initialize i = 0 and repeat.
        Let pᵢ₊₁ be a polygon intersecting P, sharing an edge
            with pᵢ, and not equal to any pⱼ for j ≤ i.
        If no such pᵢ₊₁ exists, break.
        Increment i.
    Let v₀ be any vertex of p₀.
    Call Procedure Ring.
    Triangulate vᵢ.
    Let v₀ be any vertex of p₀ not currently triangulated.
    Call Procedure Ring.
    Triangulate vᵢ.

Procedure Ring
    Initialize i = 0 and repeat.
        Let e be an edge connecting vertex vᵢ to vᵢ₊₁
            separating a pₖ polygon from a non-pₖ polygon, and
            vertex vᵢ₊₁ not equal to any vⱼ for j ≤ i.
        If no such vᵢ₊₁ exists, break.
        Increment i.
```

Figure 9: The repolygonization algorithm for *Cut* and *Spackle*.

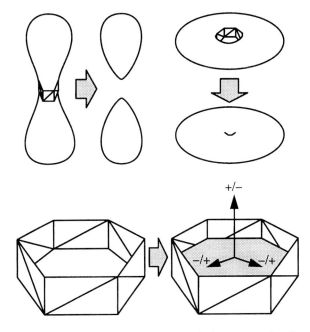

Figure 10: Polygons, eigenvalues and eigenvectors for *Cut* and *Spackle*.

Attach. When the value at a 2-saddle goes positive, two components of the implicit surface connect. The separatrix curve extends from the 2-saddle in the direction of its positive eigenvalue to a maximum point inside each component. The first polygon in each direction the separatrix intersects is removed. This leaves two disjoint rings of vertices that need to be connected. Proper correspondence algorithms between the two polygons can be found (e.g. [26]), but such techniques are not necessary if the polygonization is restricted to triangles. Figure 11 pseudocodes this algorithm.

```
Procedure Attach/Pierce
    Extend separatrix curves from the critical point.
    Let polygons p₀ and p₁ first intersect each separatrix.
    Connect the vertices of p₀ with the vertices of p₁.
    Remove p₀ and p₁.
```

Figure 11: The repolygonization algorithm for *Attach* and *Pierce*.

Pierce. When the value at a 1-saddle goes negative, a hole is pierced in the implicit surface. Similar to the *attach* case (a hole in the implicit surface of f is a connection in the implicit surface of $-f$), the two polygons that intersect the separatrix curve passing through the 1-saddle in the direction of the eigenvector corresponding to the one negative eigenvalue of the stability matrix are identified. These two polygons are removed and now form the ends of the hole. Corresponding and connecting the resulting two rings of vertices form the walls of the hole. The algorithm in Figure 11 also repolygonizes the *pierce* case.

Spackle. When the value at a 1-saddle goes positive, a hole in the implicit surface is filled. Similar to the *cut* case, the separatrix surface is constructed at the 1-saddle perpendicular to the eigenvector corresponding to the one negative eigenvalue of the stability matrix. The local polygons this surface pierces are removed, and the two resulting polygonal holes are "sewn up" by triangulation. The algorithm in Figure 9 also repolygonizes the *spackle* case and Figure 10 illustrates the polygon configuration.

Bubble. When the value at a minimum goes negative, a pocket of air forms inside the implicit solid. An air pocket in the implicit surface of f is a new component in the implicit surface of $-f$. This pocket of air may therefore be treated as a simply-connected implicit surface component, and polygonized using any of the existing techniques. The algorithm in Figure 8 also repolygonizes the *bubble* case.

Burst. When the value at a minimum goes positive, an air bubble within the implicit solid has burst. As in the Destroy case, a ray is cast from the minimum in any direction. The first polygon this ray intersects, as well as any other polygons with a connection to it, are then removed. The algorithm in Figure 7 also repolygonizes the *burst* case.

5 Polygonization

Morse theory provides the background for a topologically-guaranteed polygonization algorithm. Given a function f($\mathbf{x}$) implicitly defining the surface $f^{-1}(0)$, we consider the family of surfaces $f^{-1}(a)$ for non-negative a. Let a_0 be a value of sufficient magnitude such that the surface $f^{-1}(a_0) = \emptyset$. As a_0 decreases, it will pass critical values for maximum points, 2-saddles, 1-saddles and minimum points. As each critical value is encountered, the topology of the polygonization around its critical point is corrected. This "inflation" algorithm is pseudocoded in Figure 12.

Procedure Inflate
    X_c = Search $\mathbf{X}$ for $\{\mathbf{x} : \nabla f(\mathbf{x}) = \mathbf{0}\}$.
    Let $a_0 > \max_{\mathbf{x} \in X_c} f(\mathbf{x})$.
    Polygonize $f^{-1}(a_0)$.
    For $a = a_0 - \epsilon$ to 0 step $-\epsilon$.
        Adjust vertices to $f^{-1}(a)$.
        If $\exists \mathbf{x} \in X_c : a < f(\mathbf{x}) < a + \epsilon$ then
            Correct topology change in polygonization.
    Return polygonization of $f^{-1}(0)$.

Figure 12: The "Inflate" polygonization algorithm.

When a maximum point is passed, a new simply-connected component appears via the *create* routine. When a 2-saddle is passed, a connection formed via the *attach* routine. When a 1-saddle is passed, a hole is filled via the *spackle* routine. When a minimum point is passed, a hollow bubble is filled via the *burst* routine. The *Inflation* polygonization of a blobby cube is demonstrated in Figure 13.

Shrinkwrapping similarly polygonizes implicit surfaces but from the opposite direction, approaching the isovalue from the negative side [34]. Hence, the polygonization begins with a large simply-connected spheroid, which shrinks and appears to adhere to the final implicit surface. Morse theory can be incorporated to detect changes in topology during the shrinkwrapping process [4].

One problem with shrinkwrapping is that its outside-in processing fails to account for hollow bubbles within an implicit surface whereas *inflate's* inside-out processing correctly detects and polygonizes these regions. While such regions are typically hidden from the viewer, they become visible when the surface is rendered translucently or when the surface's polygonization is later intersected, trimmed, clipped or blended.

6 Interactive Repolygonization

The interaction algorithm consists of an initialization stage followed by an interactive loop of user input, model update, and model display. The system assumes it is initialized with a topologically correct polygonization, such as is described in Section 5.

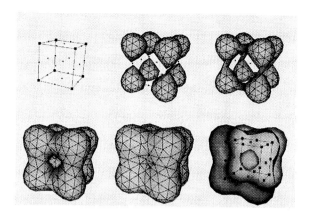

Figure 13: Polygonization via *Inflation* of the blobby cube. The last image illustrates the air bubble by only rendering back-facing polygons. Note that the definition of back facing may be the opposite of one's intuition for an air bubble.

Procedure Shrinkwrap
    X_c = Search $\mathbf{X}$ for $\{\mathbf{x} : \nabla f(\mathbf{x}) = \mathbf{0}\}$.
    Let $a_0 < \min_{\mathbf{x} \in X_c} f(\mathbf{x})$.
    Polygonize $f^{-1}(a_0)$.
    For $a = a_0 + \epsilon$ to 0 step ϵ.
        Adjust vertices to $f^{-1}(a)$.
        If $\exists \mathbf{x} \in X_c : a < f(\mathbf{x}) < a + \epsilon$ then
            Correct topology change in polygonization.
    Return polygonization of $f^{-1}(0)$.

Figure 14: The "Shrinkwrap" polygonization algorithm [4].

For each time step, the interaction algorithm performs the steps in Figure 15.

Procedure InteractionLoop
    Repeat.
        Alter model parameters based on user manipulation.
        Adjust vertex positions, fix mesh.
        Determine critical points.
        Correct polygonization topology.
        Render.

Figure 15: The interaction loop for interactive implicit surface modeling.

Figure 16 shows a critical point tracking algorithm. During user interaction, the critical points move and change sign. Furthermore, one or more of the eigenvalues of the stability matrix can change sign at some degenerate critical point $\mathbf{x}$, resulting in the creation or annihilation of a pair of critical points. Critical point annihilation is revealed by the collision of two critical-point tracking particles. Critical point creation occurs spontaneously and is not detected by the tracking particles.

Searching in four-dimensions, as shown in Figure 17, allows us to find the location in space and time of degenerate critical points. Since critical points can be tracked and annihilation can be detected, the interval search would serve to detect the spontaneous creation of critical points. Such occurrences rarely happen, but when they do occur they appear as double zeros (both $\nabla f(\mathbf{x})$ and $|V(\mathbf{x})| = 0$) which degrades convergence.

An alternative search shown in Figure 18 finds the location in space and time for singular points in the family of implicit surfaces. where the value of a critical point changes sign. Such occurrences

```
Procedure Track-n-Search
    Track critical points.
    Search X for {x : ∇f(x) = 0}.
```

Figure 16: The "Track-n-Search" critical point determination algorithm.

```
Procedure Track-n-SearchDegenerate
    Track critical points.
    Search X × [t₀, t₁] for {x : ∇f(x) = 0, |V(x)| = 0}.
```

Figure 17: The "Track-n-SearchDegenerate" critical point determination algorithm.

occur as rarely as degenerate critical points, so the interval search can quickly guarantee that such points do not exist. However, when they do exist, as with degenerate critical points, they appear as double zeros which degrades the rate of convergence.

7   Conclusion

Using techniques from catastrophe theory and Morse theory, the preceding sections developed (1) a new polygonization algorithm that can guarantee the topology of the polygonization matches that of the implicit surface, and (2) a new implicit surface modeling system capable of maintaining a topologically-accurate polygonized representation of the implicit surface during direct manipulation at interactive update rates.

Section 4 improves previous *ad hoc* geometry-only techniques [24, 4] by describing a mathematically sound method for using the separatrix to identify the polygons affected by a topology change, and robust algorithms for reconnecting the vertices of the polygonization.

Section 5 uses these techniques to polygonize an implicit surface. This method improves previous geometry-based interval methods [28] in that it is faster and does not return a large number of unnecessarily small polygons. The interval search is also guaranteed to find all critical points, which overcomes the uncertainty of previous methods [4], and also properly polygonizes hollow bubbles when they appear within an implicit surface.

Some initial experiments revealed that performance dropped below ten frames per second on scenes containing combinations of four or more interacting blobby ellipsoids. Modeling sessions that string a chain of blobby components operate in real time, but sessions with densely packed arrangements of blobby components appear sluggish in the current prototype implementation of the system. Even apparently simple configurations of blobby components can yield numerous nearly-degenerate critical points, and their detection is required for accurate topology management. This performance was measured using the SearchSingularity interaction loop, but is similar to the performance of the other interaction loop critical point search/tracking methods. This procedure becomes noticeably slow near topology changes. While any speed degradation and inconsistency is undesirable, the algorithm does focus its computation on the time and space where it is most needed.

```
Procedure SearchSingularity
    Search X × [t₀, t₁] for {x : f(x) = 0, ∇f(x) = 0}.
```

Figure 18: The "SearchSingularity" algorithm.

7.1   Some Implementation Tricks

One of the topological guarantee's restrictions was the lack of degenerate critical points. However, for speed, we were able to implement a C^2 cubic approximation to the exponential blobby model. The kernel of this approximation is uniform away from the center, and results in a three-dimensional degenerate critical set. We overcame this problem by assuming that the derivative intervals with zero for one endpoint did not contain a critical point, but instead contained a portion of this 3-D critical set. We avoided the possibility that a critical point fell on the boundary of the interval by expanding each interval by a small percentage.

Occasionally, the program errs in its attempt to process a topology change. In such cases, the system automatically initiates a full "inflation" repolygonization.

Further implementation details can be found in the dissertation [29].

7.2   Future Work

Tracking critical points is much faster than searching for them, but does not account for the pairs of critical points that can be created spontaneously. Tracking all of the derivatives of the function could detect degenerate critical points. This is not possible for exponentials because they are infinitely differentiable, and their derivatives become increasingly complex. Piecewise polynomials have finitely many derivatives that become increasingly simple, and might offer the opportunity to attempt such tracking.

Implicit surfaces still offer many challenges in modeling, texturing and animation due to the flexibility of their topology. This research solved the problem of interactive polygonization. Understanding the dynamics of critical points might lead to further solutions to other implicit surface problems, such as maintaining a consistent texturing during a topology change.

This research focused on 3-D implicit surfaces. Its application to the polygonization and modeling of 2-D implicit curves would be a useful, though perhaps now trivial, simplification.

7.3   Acknowledgments

This research was supported in part by the NSF Research Initiation Award #CCR-9309210. This research was performed in the Imaging Research Laboratory. The authors would like to thank the SIGGRAPH reviewers for their constructive criticism and positive comments. Further thanks are due to Dan Asimov, Jules Bloomethal and Jim Kajiya for their help in tracking down theorems in Morse theory. Special thanks to Andrew Glassner and Scott Lang for their assistance with the photoready copy of this paper.

REFERENCES

[1] BLINN, J. F. A generalization of algebraic surface drawing. *ACM Transactions on Graphics 1*, 3 (July 1982), 235–256.

[2] BLOOMENTHAL, J. Polygonization of implicit surfaces. *Computer Aided Geometric Design 5*, 4 (Nov. 1988), 341–355.

[3] BLOOMENTHAL, J., AND WYVILL, B. Interactive techniques for implicit modeling. *Computer Graphics 24*, 2 (Mar. 1990), 109–116.

[4] BOTTINO, A., NUIJ, W., AND VAN OVERVELD, K. How to shrinkwrap through a critical point: an algorithm for the adaptive triangulation of iso-surfaces with arbitrary topology. In *Proc. Implicit Surfaces '96* (Oct. 1996), pp. 53–72.

[5] CHENG, K.-P. Using plane vector fields to obtain all the intersection curves of two general surfaces. In *Theory and Practice of Geometric Modeling* (New York, 1989), Springer-Verlag.

[6] DE FIGUEIREDO, L. H., DE MIRANDA GOMES, J., TERZOPOULOS, D., AND VELHO, L. Physically-based methods for polygonization of implicit surfaces. In *Proceedings of Graphics Interface '92* (May 1992), pp. 250–257.

[7] DELMARCELLE, T., AND HESSELINK, L. The topology of symmetric, second-order tensor fields. *Proceedings IEEE Visualization '94* (October 1994), 140–147.

[8] DESBRUN, M., TSINGOS, N., AND GASCUEL, M.-P. Adaptive sampling of implicit surfaces for interactive modeling and animation. *Implicit Surfaces '95 Proceedings* (April 1995), 171–185.

[9] FLEISCHER, K. W., LAIDLAW, D. H., CURRIN, B. L., AND BARR, A. H. Cellular texture generation. In *Computer Graphics (Annual Conference Series)* (Aug. 1995), pp. 239–248.

[10] HANSEN, E. A globally convergent interval method for computing and bounding real roots. *BIT 18* (1978), 415–424.

[11] HANSEN, E. R., AND GREENBERG, R. I. An interval newton method. *Applied Mathematics and Computation 12* (1983), 89–98.

[12] HART, J. C. Morse theory for computer graphics. Tech. Rep. EECS-97-002, Washington State University, May 1997. Also in: SIGGRAPH '97 Course #14 Notes "New Frontiers in Modeling and Texturing".

[13] HELMAN, J. L., AND HESSELINK, L. Visualizing vector field topology in fluid flows. *IEEE Computer Graphics and Applications* (May 1991), 36–46.

[14] KALRA, D., AND BARR, A. H. Guaranteed ray intersections with implicit surfaces. *Computer Graphics 23*, 3 (July 1989), 297–306.

[15] KERGOSIEN, Y. L. Generic sign systems in medical imaging. *IEEE Computer Graphics and Applications 11*, 5 (Sep. 1991), 46–65.

[16] LORENSEN, W. E., AND CLINE, H. E. Marching cubes: A high resolution 3-d surface construction algorithm. *Computer Graphics 21*, 4 (July 1987), 163–170.

[17] MITCHELL, D. Three applications of interval analysis in computer graphics. In *Frontiers of Rendering.* SIGGRAPH '91 Course Notes, 1991.

[18] MITCHELL, D., AND HANRAHAN, P. Illumination from curved reflectors. *Computer Graphics 26*, 2 (July 1992), 283–291.

[19] MOORE, R. E. *Interval Analysis.* Prentice Hall, 1966.

[20] NING, P., AND BLOOMENTHAL, J. An evaluation of implicit surface tilers. *Computer Graphics and Applications 13*, 6 (Nov. 1993), 33–41.

[21] NISHIMURA, H., HIRAI, M., KAWAI, T., KAWATA, T., SHIRAKAWA, I., AND OMURA, K. Object modeling by distribution function and a method of image generation. In Proc. of *Electronics Communication Conference '85* (1985), pp. 718–725. (Japanese).

[22] NORTON, A. Generation and rendering of geometric fractals in 3-D. *Computer Graphics 16*, 3 (1982), 61–67.

[23] RATSCHEK, H., AND ROKNE, J. *Computer Methods for the Range of Functions.* John Wiley and Sons, 1984.

[24] RODRIAN, H.-C., AND MOOCK, H. Dynamic triangulation of animated skeleton-based implicit surfaces. In *Proc. Implicit Surfaces '96* (Oct. 1996), pp. 37–52.

[25] ROSCH, A., RUHL, M., AND SAUPE, D. Interactive visualization of implicit surfaces with singularities. In *Proc. Implicit Surfaces '96* (Oct. 1996), pp. 73–87.

[26] SEDERBERG, T. W., AND GREENWOOD, E. A physically based approach to 2-D shape blending. *Computer Graphics 26*, 2 (July 1992), 25–34.

[27] SHINAGAWA, Y., KUNII, T. L., AND KERGOSIEN, Y. L. Surface coding based on morse theory. *IEEE Computer Graphics and Applications 11*, 5 (Sep. 1991), 66–78.

[28] SNYDER, J. *Generative Modeling for Computer Graphics and CAD.* Academic Press, 1992.

[29] STANDER, B. T. *Polygonizing Implicit Surfaces with Guaranteed Topology.* PhD thesis, School of EECS, Washington State University, May 1997.

[30] SUFFERN, K., AND FACKERELL, E. Interval methods in computer graphics. In *Proc. AUSGRAPH 90* (1990), pp. 35–44.

[31] SZELISKI, R., AND TONNESEN, D. Surface modeling with oriented particle systems. In *Computer Graphics (SIGGRAPH '92 Proceedings)* (July 1992), E. E. Catmull, Ed., vol. 26, pp. 185–194.

[32] TAYLOR, A. E. *Advanced Calculus.* Ginn and Company, 1955.

[33] TURK, G. Generating textures for arbitrary surfaces using reaction-diffusion. In *Computer Graphics (SIGGRAPH '91 Proceedings)* (July 1991), T. W. Sederberg, Ed., vol. 25, pp. 289–298.

[34] VAN OVERVELD, C., AND WYVILL, B. Shrinkwrap: an adaptive algorithm for polygonizing and implicit surface. Tech. Rep. 93/514/19, University of Calgary, Dept. of Computer Science, March 1993.

[35] WITKIN, A. P., AND HECKBERT, P. S. Using particles to sample and control implicit surfaces. In *Computer Graphics (Annual Conference Series)* (July 1994), pp. 269–278.

[36] WYVILL, G., MCPHEETERS, C., AND WYVILL, B. Data structure for soft objects. *Visual Computer 2*, 4 (1986), 227–234.

Fast Construction of Accurate Quaternion Splines

Ravi Ramamoorthi
ravir@gg.caltech.edu

Alan H. Barr
barr@gg.caltech.edu

California Institute of Technology *

Abstract

In 1992, *Barr et al.* proposed a method for interpolating orientations with unit quaternion curves by minimizing covariant acceleration. This paper presents a simple improved method which uses cubic basis functions to achieve a speedup of up to three orders of magnitude. A new criterion for automatic refinement based on the Euler-Lagrange error functional is also introduced.

CR Categories: I.3.5 [*Computer Graphics*]: Computational Geometry and Object Modeling—Splines; G.1.6 [*Numerical Analysis*]: Optimization

Keywords: Euler-Lagrange error functional, Quaternions, Splines, Optimization

1 Introduction

In this paper, we discuss the interpolation of keyframe rotations with quaternion [6, 17] curves. Shoemake [16] introduced the idea of interpolating rotations with quaternions, but the constructed curves (slerps) did not satisfy an obvious variational principle [21] as splines [2] do in flat space. Gabriel and Kajiya [4] then proposed a method that solved the (intrinsic) Euler-Lagrange equations for minimization of covariant acceleration on a manifold with a metric and applied these ideas to interpolation of rotations. In Barr et al. [1], a simpler method to minimize covariant acceleration using an extrinsic formulation based on quaternions was given. However, their approach can take several minutes to hours to compute the optimal curve. Analytic construction schemes such as those of Kim et al [10] are significantly faster and often yield satisfactory curves.

This paper speeds up the method of Barr et al. [1] significantly, thus allowing minimization of covariant acceleration to be used as an interactive tool. We use simple cubic basis functions and unconstrained minimization instead of the finite difference constrained optimization approach in [1]. Near-optimal

* Address: MS 350-74, Caltech, Pasadena, Ca 91125.

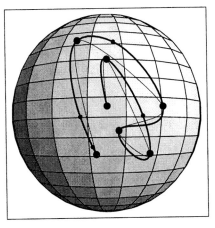

Figure 1: The interpolation problem in quaternion space. The large circles represent keyframes to be interpolated. The small circles show "variable frames" inserted by the system while computing the optimized path (shown with a solid line). A thin line shows the unoptimized path which is seen to have undue accelerations at the keyframes.

curves can be produced in a few seconds—two to three orders of magnitude faster than previous methods. Cubic basis functions can be replaced by other construction schemes so our technique can be used to refine analytic splining methods such as those in [7, 9, 10, 11, 19].

Our work is closely related to other areas of research that use optimization, such as spacetime constraints [3], dynamic nurbs [18] and variational surface modeling [20]. An important difference is the introduction of a new technique for automatic adaptive refinement based on the "error" as measured by the Euler-Lagrange error functional. Other differences include the use of "variable frames" (the system inserts these) and unconstrained minimization. In optimizing over a small number of variables for fast algorithms, our work is also similar to that of Liu and Cohen [12].

Although this paper describes the creation of quaternion splines primarily for animation, splining in curved spaces and constructing minimal energy motions is important to other communities such as computer aided geometric design, robotics and kinematics. A few related papers are found in [8, 15]. Our techniques can also be generalized easily to handle objective functions more complex than covariant acceleration for quaternions. Thus, our method can be used in conjunction with conventional animation techniques for rapid automatic improvement of "rough" animations or for sparser keyframing by interpolation[14].

The rest of this paper is organized as follows. In section 2, we formulate the quaternion interpolation problem. We present our solution in section 3 and discuss our results in section 4. Section 5 discusses future work and conclusions.

2 The Quaternion Interpolation Problem

As in [1], we want to minimize the net squared magnitude of the covariant (tangential) acceleration in quaternion space, while interpolating keyframe orientations and (if specified) angular velocities at the end frames. The normal component of the acceleration is not penalized since it is necessary for maintaining unit magnitude of the quaternions. This formulation is analogous to minimizing angular acceleration.

Let $q(t)$ denote the quaternion path as a function of time such that at keyframe times $t_1, t_2, ..., t_K$, $q(t_i) = Q^i$ where Q^i denotes the quaternion at keyframe i corresponding to time t_i. Further, if specified let ω_1 and ω_K denote the angular velocities at the end frames. Then, the problem we solve can be formulated thus:

$$minimize \int_{t_1}^{t_K} \| q'' \setminus q \|^2 \, dt \qquad (1)$$

subject to the constraints:

INTERPOLATION: $\quad \forall i : 1 \leq i \leq K : q(t_i) = Q^i$

UNITARINESS: $\quad \forall t : t_1 \leq t \leq t_K : q(t) \cdot q(t) = 1$

END-POINT ANGULAR VELOCITY:

$$2q'(t_1)q^{-1}(t_1) = \omega_1 \quad 2q'(t_K)q^{-1}(t_K) = \omega_K \qquad (2)$$

Here, $q'' \setminus q$ is the tangential or covariant acceleration[1] , and $\| q'' \setminus q \|$ is its norm or magnitude.

In this paper, we use cubic polynomials which do not in general lie on the unit sphere. We enforce the constraint of unit quaternions with a "soft constraint" and minimize the objective given below (with the integrand put explicitly in terms of quaternion components q_j)

$$OBJ = \int_{t_1}^{t_K} (\sum_{j=0}^{3} q_j'' q_j'' - \frac{(\sum_{k=0}^{3} q_k q_k'')^2}{\sum_{l=0}^{3} q_l q_l} + \alpha [1 - \sum_{n=0}^{3} q_n q_n]^2) \, dt$$
$$(3)$$

subject to the interpolation constraints. In the integrand in equation 3, the first two terms are the squared magnitude of the covariant acceleration (an expanded form of the integrand in equation 1). The third term maintains quaternion magnitude, and α is a positive constant that forces the quaternions to be nearly unitary. We also require the path $q(t)$ to be C^1 continuous.

Use of Soft Constraints   In this paper, we have used cubic basis functions for simplicity, and "soft constraints" to maintain the unitary constraint. While soft constraints are just a weighting term added to the objective, and do not ensure the constraint is exactly met, they are simple to use and often result in the constraint being met well enough for our purposes. Any simple unconstrained minimization package can be used, and the technique is faster than constrained optimization because the constraint does not need to be evaluated and differentiated at each iteration.

---

[1]As explained in [1], an explicit formula for the ith component of the covariant acceleration is:

$$(q'' \setminus q)_i = q_i'' - q_i \frac{\sum_{j=0}^{3} q_j'' q_j}{\sum_{k=0}^{3} q_k q_k}$$

The squared magnitude of the covariant acceleration, $\| q'' \setminus q \|^2$, is given by the first two terms of the objective in equation 3.

3 Our Algorithm

Figure 2 presents a summary of our method. A more detailed discussion of each step is given below.

Algorithm

1. *Input user-specified keyframes*, and number of ``variable frames'' (with optional angular velocities at the end frames).

2. *Guess quaternion velocities* at the interior keyframes and interpolate keyframes and velocities with C^1 continuous cubics.

3. *An optimizer adjusts velocities* at the interior keyframes to minimize the objective functional (equation 3).

4. *"Variable frames" are added* in a small number of ``segments'' having the largest average value for the Euler-Lagrange error functional (after the average Euler-Lagrange error functional in each ``segment'' has been computed).

5. *Readjust variable frame quaternions and velocities* in addition to keyframe velocities to minimize the objective functional again.

Figure 2: An overview of the algorithm.

Discussion of algorithm

Step 1: User provides keyframes   In part 1 of the algorithm, the user must provide the keyframes to be interpolated. In addition, angular velocities at the end frames may be provided if wanted. Angular velocities are converted internally to quaternion velocities: $q'(t) = (1/2)\omega q(t)$.

The value of the soft constraint weighting factor α need also be given. Since we want quaternions of nearly unit magnitude, α should be large. By making α approximately 1000 (with the time difference between key frames normalized to be of order 1), we tell the optimizer that maintaining unit magnitude is significantly more important than minimizing covariant acceleration. This works well in that maximum deviation from unitariness is frequently less than 1% (with the average deviation about one tenth of that), and the contribution to the objective from the soft constraint is about $1 - 2\%$ thus ensuring that the soft constraint does not dominate the objective.

Step 2: Assign initial guess for quaternion velocities   At all keyframes for which the user has not supplied angular velocities (interior keyframes and end-frames if the user has not specified angular velocities), the system guesses velocities with a very simple algorithm such as:

$$q_j'(t_i) = \frac{q_j(t_{i+1}) - q_j(t_{i-1})}{t_{i+1} - t_{i-1}}$$

With these velocities[2] , suitable basis functions are used to interpolate positions and velocities at the keyframes. In this paper we have used cubic polynomials, but there is no obstacle to using more advanced curves such as the hermite quaternion curves of [10]. Each component of the quaternion path is described by a piecewise cubic such that the position and velocity agree with those user-specified or system-inserted at the keyframes (or in the next stage, "variable frames"). Since both position and velocity are well-defined at the keyframes, the resulting paths must be C^1 continuous as required.

The integral in equation 3 is then evaluated by any simple numerical integration procedure.

Step 3: Minimization of the objective functional over keyframe velocities In part 3 of the algorithm, an unconstrained minimization package is used to alter our initial guess of the velocity at interior keyframes to minimize the objective OBJ given in equation 3. The variables over which the optimization is done are the velocities at the keyframe times; the user has not constrained the angular velocity at the interior keyframes. Note that since we have only C^1 continuity, the integrand in equation 3 may be discontinuous, but this will not affect the objective functional OBJ. We use the Sequential Quadratic Programming routine E04UCF in the NAG libraries [13]. We note that although the routine can do constrained optimization, it is significantly faster when using soft constraints as we have formulated the problem. To take advantage of sparseness in the problem, one may supply partial derivatives (for which one need evaluate only a small part of the region of integration since the cubic basis is local) instead of having the optimizer evaluate them. Since the method is fast enough even without this optimization, we have not used it in our tests.

Step 4: Checking of Euler-Lagrange error functional We divide the entire path into "segments" of time $\triangle t$ (segment n ranges from t_n to $t_n + \triangle t$). For each segment n, we compute the deviation (using the optimized path $Q(t)$ from step 3):

$$DEV(t_n) = \frac{1}{\triangle t} \int_{t_n}^{t_n + \triangle t} | EL(t) | \, dt \qquad (4)$$

where $| EL |$ stands for the length of the Euler-Lagrange vector in equation 7. We then pick the segments having the highest values for $DEV(t_n)$ (and such that t_n does not coincide with a keyframe), and add in a "variable frame" at time t_n. A "variable frame" is like a keyframe except that not only the velocities but also the positions q_i can be varied by the optimizer in step 5.

The number of regions in which we add variable frames is a tradeoff between accuracy (the more variable frames the better) and speed (the more variable frames the slower). For our applications, we have found that nearly optimal results can be produced with about 5 variable frames.

Some care must be taken in the way the path is divided into segments. If the segments are too short, there may be too many (and unnecessary) variable points inserted in one region at the expense of other regions. On the other hand, the segments should be near enough for multiple variable points to be concentrated in a region. For these reasons, we typically divide each time-interval between keyframes into 4 to 5 segments.

Note that we use an effectively continuous representation (with only fine-grain discretization for numerical integration). This is equivalent to saying numerical quadrature is done at several points within a segment. Further, since we generally want to add a small number of variable frames at the right places, it is appropriate to use a few segments in each interval between keyframes. Hence our recommendation above.

Since our method is relatively fast, the user may interactively modify the segment lengths if he wishes, but this should not be necessary in most cases.

Step 5: Optimizing again using variable frames We now repeat the optimization process of step 3 introducing some number M of additional optimization variables in the form of the positions and velocities at the variable frames. Thus, the minimizer now varies interior keyframe velocities as well as variable frame positions and velocities in order to minimize the objective functional. Figure 1 shows an example of an optimized quaternion spline along with keyframes, variable frames and the unoptimized "keyframish" path.

Euler-Lagrange Error functional

Let $F(q_i, q_i', q_i'')$ denote the integrand in equation 3 (the integral of which is the objective function OBJ). Then, the variational calculus [21] tells us that the optimal curve satisfies the corresponding Euler-Lagrange equations:

$$EL_i \equiv \frac{\partial F}{\partial q_i} - \frac{d}{dt}\frac{\partial F}{\partial q_i'} + \frac{d^2}{dt^2}\frac{\partial F}{\partial q_i''} = 0 \qquad (5)$$

There are four equations corresponding to each component q_i. By measuring the magnitude (Euler-Lagrange error) of the left-hand side of the equation above, we can get an idea of where to refine our coarse representation. The equations for the objective of equation 3 are given below.

Define:

$$a = \sum_{j=0}^{3} q_j q_j''$$

$$b = \sum_{j=0}^{3} q_j q_j$$

$$T = \frac{a}{b}$$

$$U(i) = q_i T^2 - q_i'' T$$

$$V(i) = q_i'' - q_i T$$

$$W(i) = 2\alpha(b - 1)q_i$$

$$\frac{d^2}{dt^2}V(i) \equiv q_i'''' - (q_i'' T + 2q_i' T' + q_i T'') \qquad (6)$$

In the notation of the canonical equation 5, $U(i)$ corresponds to the term $\partial F/\partial q_i$ for covariant acceleration. $W(i)$ is the corresponding term for maintenance of unitary quaternions. $V(i)$ corresponds to the term $\partial F/\partial q_i''$ in equation 5. The term $\partial F/\partial q_i' = 0$ since the objective function does not depend directly on q'.

The ith component of the Euler-Lagrange deviation or error is then:

$$EL_i = 2(U(i) + \frac{d^2}{dt^2}V(i) + W(i)) \qquad (7)$$

Since the first and second derivatives for T are complicated, and our calculations need only be accurate enough to order the

---

[2]At the end-points, we can only take one sided differences:

$$q_j'(t_1) = \frac{q_j(t_2) - q_j(t_1)}{t_2 - t_1} \qquad q_j'(t_K) = \frac{q_j(t_K) - q_j(t_{K-1})}{t_K - t_{K-1}}$$

segments by deviation, it may be simpler to differentiate T numerically rather than analytically. For reference, the analytic formulae (assuming cubic basis functions so the fourth derivative vanishes) are given below:

First, we must define:

$$
\begin{aligned}
d_{ij} &= d_{ji} = \sum_{k=0}^{3} q_k^{(i)} q_k^{(j)} \\
t1 &= \frac{2d_{13} + d_{22}}{d_{00}} - 4\frac{d_{01}(d_{12} + d_{03})}{(d_{00})^2} \\
t2 &= -2\frac{d_{02}(d_{02} + d_{11})}{(d_{00})^2} \\
t3 &= 8\frac{(d_{01})^2 d_{02}}{(d_{00})^3}
\end{aligned}
\tag{8}
$$

where the superscripts on the quaternions stand for the appropriate derivatives. Note that $d_{00} = b$, and $d_{02} = a$. We can now write:

$$
\begin{aligned}
T' &= \frac{d_{12} + d_{03}}{d_{00}} - 2\frac{d_{01}d_{02}}{(d_{00})^2} \\
T'' &= t1 + t2 + t3
\end{aligned}
\tag{9}
$$

As our "error" function for adaptive refinement (Step 4 in our algorithm), we use the length of the Euler-Lagrange vector $EL = \sqrt{\sum_{i=0}^{3} EL_i^2}$.

It should be noted that the Euler-Lagrange error functional vanishes as expected in case the path followed is a unit great circle (and thus has no covariant acceleration). For instance, consider the path:

$$
q_0(t) = \cos(t) \quad q_1(t) = \sin(t) \quad q_2(t) = q_3(t) = 0
$$

It is clear that for this path,

$$
q_i'' = -q_i \qquad b = 1 \qquad a = T = -1
$$

Using these relations, it can readily be verified that $U(i) = V(i) = W(i) = 0$, and the Euler-Lagrange error functional correctly recognizes that the path is optimal. Since all great circles can be constructed by rotating the example given, the Euler-Lagrange error functional vanishes for great circles as expected.

Euler-Lagrange Error Functional as a Metric for Adaptive Refinement We believe our use of Euler-Lagrange equations for adaptive refinement is an improvement over other approaches such as objective or constraint based subdivision [20] because the Euler-Lagrange equations should be 0 on complete minimization while the objective need not go to 0. Thus, a high objective does not necessarily indicate a large error while a "large" value for the Euler-Lagrange deviation is generally a sure indication of a "bad" region. This paper thus also shows how to combine Euler-Lagrange and gradient based methods effectively.

Here, we have used the Euler-Lagrange error functional only for adaptive refinement. An alternative approach that could be tried in the future is to solve the Euler-Lagrange equations directly or to minimize the Euler-Lagrange error functional instead of the objective function of equation 3. Note that while we have derived analytic formulae for the error functional, numerical approaches based on numerically approximating the left hand side of equation 5 can also be used, and may be necessary if more complicated objective functions than the one in this paper are used.

Advantages of Cubics There are a number of advantages that continuous (in our case cubic) basis functions possess over discrete methods [1, 4] of which some of the most important are given below.

- Accurate formulae for quaternion derivatives with respect to time are provided.

- An accurate representation of a curve can be made from a very small number of basis functions, leading to extremely fast algorithms.

Importance of Variable Frames Variable frames (where the optimizer can vary the position and velocity) have some advantages over approaches based on spline coefficients [3].

- Since variable frames correspond directly to frames on the actual animation path, they are easier to understand and deal with, especially for a user. Changes in variable frame positions or velocities usually correspond in a simple manner to changes in the actual animation. Large coefficient changes may balance each other, and may not correspond as directly and intuitively to the final animation.

- The use of variable frames ensures that keyframe interpolation is automatic. With coefficient based methods, constraints need to be added to ensure keyframe interpolation. This may require a more complex optimizer and/or a more time-consuming algorithm.

4 Results

We present a representative example with 7 keyframes. Figure 1 shows the path on the sphere (one quaternion component is zero always as are end-point velocities). Large dots represent keyframes; small dots are variable frames.

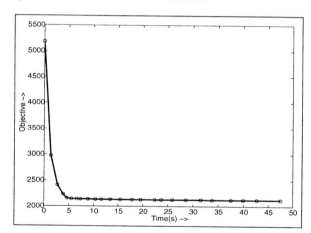

Figure 3: A very small number of variable frames can yield near-optimal results. As described in the text below, each circle represents an increasing number of variable frames or a higher level of optimization.

Performance

We show the decrease in objective (as a function of program execution time) as more variable frames are added in figure 3. Each circle on the graph shows a further level of optimization. The first circle shows no optimization, the second adjustment only of velocities at keyframes, the third addition of one variable frame, the fourth two variable frames and so on. We see that with 4 variable frames, we have a result that is only .1% away from optimal.

Unit Magnitude

In figure 4 we show the unit magnitude being maintained. The initial path (blue dotted) has many places where quaternions are far from unit magnitude. Our optimized path—4 variable frames and $\alpha = 1000$—(magenta dashdot) is within 1% of unit magnitude, while the solid red line shows the effect of making $\alpha = 10000$ and having 24 variable frames. We see that the quaternions are practically indistinguishable from having unit magnitude (The maximum deviation is .07% in the last example).

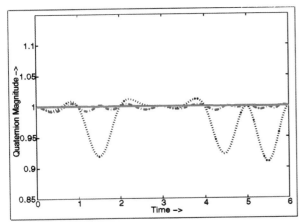

Figure 4: Maintaining unit magnitude. In the original path (blue dotted), there are significant deviations, while increasing levels of optimization (magenta dashdot and red solid line) bring the quaternions very close to unit magnitude.

Euler-Lagrange error functional

The Euler-Lagrange deviation before and after optimization are shown in figure 5. We see that our method has equidistributed the Euler-Lagrange error well.

Comparison to previous work

Our result with 4 variable frames took 4 seconds to compute. We did not make use of sparseness in the E04UCF routine. We also implemented a discrete method as in [1] where we used the formulae for derivatives given there [except that a factor of two must multiply their results for correctness]. Within this framework, we used the same optimization method and objectives as for the method described in this paper (but since we supplied derivatives, we did make use of sparseness in this case). The running time for the discrete method [1] was 8800 seconds, a factor of more than 2000 slower! (of course, the exact timings may vary depending on the specific machine and minimizer used). While we used 4 variable frames in our approach, we had to use the entire 600 frames over which the integral was evaluated in the discrete method. Our method is significantly faster because a much smaller number of variables are optimized.

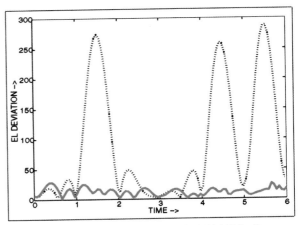

Figure 5: The blue dotted graph shows the initial Euler-Lagrange error. The solid red graph shows how this error is significantly decreased upon optimization.

Animations

The animations[3] accompanying this paper show some examples of rotational paths created using the methods in the paper. Our first example is the rotation of a rigid object similar to the example discussed above (except that there is more rotation which involves all four quaternion components). Figure 6 shows the (I-shaped) object rotating while moving in a parabola. The trunks are black for keyframes (which also have a dark circle behind them that makes their position clear), blue for variable frames and red for the few computed animation frames that are shown.

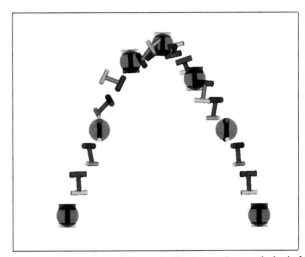

Figure 6: Showing the object path. Keyframes have a dark circle behind them. Variable frames have blue trunks and those for computed animation frames are red. The top and bottom of the object are shown in green and yellow consistently for all frames.

Our second example is derived from a molecular dynamics simulation (with exotic initial conditions). We resampled the rotations sparsely, interpolating to make animations. We show an example using 4 keyframes. A still is shown in figure 7.

---

[3] The animations are present on the CD-ROM accompanying the proceedings, and can be accessed via our website:
http://www.gg.caltech.edu/Animations/quaternions.html

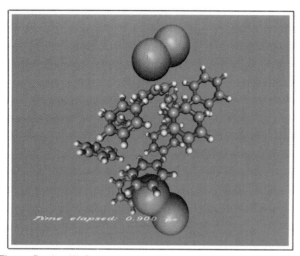

Figure 7: A still from an animation on the CD-ROM/website. The animation is derived from a molecular dynamics simulation of iodine and benzene molecules slowed down by a factor of approximately 10^{12}.

5   Conclusion and Future Work

We have shown how to construct quaternion splines orders of magnitude faster than previous methods and introduced a new technique for adaptive refinement based on the Euler-Lagrange error functional. While the results are encouraging, improvements can be made in the following areas:

- *Deriving theoretical bounds* on the error in the objective using the Euler-Lagrange error functional and comparing Euler-Lagrange based adaptive refinement to other methods. We [14] have derived a physical interpretation for the Euler-Lagrange error functional and some simple bounds, but these are currently too loose for meaningful error estimates.

- *Using more advanced basis functions.* Our current estimate for quaternion velocities (step 2 of the algorithm) can be improved. In addition, we use simple cubics. Using quaternion curves such as the B-spline quaternion curves of [10] for the initial guess of quaternion velocities and the corresponding hermite quaternion curves for interpolation instead of cubics might yield faster results. This would also allow the optimization procedure to be carried out on the quaternion sphere directly [5] instead of using soft constraints.

- *Higher degrees of continuity and better objective functions* This paper has discussed curves with C^1 continuity. A simple way of achieving C^2 continuity is with interpolating B-splines as in [14]. Perceptually (rather than mathematically) based objective functions also need to be investigated.

6   Acknowledgements

We would like to thank Julius Su (from Ahmed Zewail's femto-chemistry group at Caltech) for contributing the molecular dynamics simulation from which the video accompanying this paper was derived, Brian D'Urso for suggesting the particular initial conditions used, and the anonymous Siggraph reviewers for comments that were very helpful in preparing the final version of the paper. Thank also go to everyone at the Caltech graphics group for their help and encouragement.

This work was supported in part by grants from DEC, Hewlett Packard, and IBM. Additional support was provided by NSF (ASC-89-20219), as part of the NSF STC for Computer Graphics and Scientific Visualization. All opinions, findings, conclusions or recommendations expressed here are those of the authors only and do not necessarily reflect the views of the sponsoring agencies.

References

[1] A.H. BARR, B. CURRIN, S. GABRIEL, and J.F. HUGHES. Smooth interpolation of orientations with angular velocity constraints using quaternions. In *SIGGRAPH 92 proceedings*, pages 313–320, 1992.

[2] R. BARTELS, J. BEATTY, and B. BARSKY. *An Introduction to Splines for Use in Computer Graphics and Geometric Modeling.* Morgan Kaufman, Palo Alto, 1987.

[3] M.F. COHEN. Interactive spacetime control for animation. In *SIGGRAPH 92 proceedings*, pages 293–302, 1992.

[4] S. GABRIEL and J. KAJIYA. Spline interpolation in curved space. In *SIGGRAPH 85 course notes for State of the Art in Image Synthesis(#11)*, 1985.

[5] H.-J. HA. A new camera control method preserving view-up vectors. Master's thesis, KAIST, Taejon 305-701, Korea, 1996.

[6] W.R. HAMILTON. *Elements of Quaternions (Volume I, II).* Chelsea Publishing Company, 1969.

[7] B. JUTTLER. Visualization of moving objects using dual quaternion curves. *Computer & Graphics*, 18(3):315–326, 1994.

[8] B. JUTTLER and M.G. WAGNER. Computer-aided design with spatial rational B-spline motions. *Journal of Mechanical Design*, 118(2):193–201, June 1996.

[9] M.-J. KIM, M.-S. KIM, and S. SHIN. A C^2-continuous B-spline quaternion curve interpolating a given sequence of solid orientations. In *Computer Animation 95 Proceedings*, pages 72–81, 1995.

[10] M.-J. KIM, M.-S. KIM, and S. SHIN. A general construction scheme for unit quaternion curves with simple high order derivatives. In *SIGGRAPH 95 proceedings*, pages 369–376, 1995.

[11] M.-S. KIM and K.-W. NAM. Interpolating solid orientations with circular blending quaternion curves. *Computer Aided Design*, 27(5):385–398, 1995.

[12] Z. LIU and M.F. COHEN. Keyframe motion optimization by relaxing speed and timing. In 6th *Eurographics Workshop on Animation and Simulation (Maastricht 1995)*, pages 144–153, 1995.

[13] Numerical Algorithms Group, Ltd. *NAG Fortran Library Document*, 1988.

[14] R. RAMAMOORTHI, C. BALL, and A.H. BARR. Dynamic splines with constraints for animation. Technical Report CS-TR-97-03, California Institute of Technology, Included on CD-ROM, January 1997. ftp://ftp.cs.caltech.edu/tr/cs-tr-97-03.ps.Z.

[15] B. RAVANI and F. PARK. Bezier curves on riemannian manifolds and lie groups with kinematic applications. *Journal of Mechanical Design*, 117(1):36–40, March 1995.

[16] K. SHOEMAKE. Animating rotation with quaternion curves. In *SIGGRAPH 85 proceedings*, pages 245–254, 1985.

[17] K. SHOEMAKE. Quaternion calculus for animation. In *SIGGRAPH 91 course notes for Math for Siggraph (#2)*, 1991.

[18] D. TERZOPOULOS and H. QIN. Dynamic Nurbs with geometric constraints for interactive sculpting. *ACM Transactions on Graphics*, 13(2):103–136, April 1994.

[19] W. WANG and B. JOE. Orientation interpolation in quaternion space using spherical biarcs. In *Graphics Interface 93*, pages 24–32, 1993.

[20] W. WELCH and A. WITKIN. Variational surface modeling. In *SIGGRAPH 92 proceedings*, pages 157–166, 1992.

[21] D. ZWILLINGER. *Handbook of Differential Equations.* Academic Press, San Diego, 1989.

InfiniteReality: A Real-Time Graphics System

John S. Montrym, Daniel R. Baum, David L. Dignam, and Christopher J. Migdal

Silicon Graphics Computer Systems

ABSTRACT

The InfiniteReality™ graphics system is the first general-purpose workstation system specifically designed to deliver 60Hz steady frame rate high-quality rendering of complex scenes. This paper describes the InfiniteReality system architecture and presents novel features designed to handle extremely large texture databases, maintain control over frame rendering time, and allow user customization for diverse video output requirements. Rendering performance expressed using traditional workstation metrics exceeds seven million lighted, textured, antialiased triangles per second, and 710 million textured antialiased pixels filled per second.

CR Categories and Subject Descriptors: I.3.1 [Computer Graphics]: Hardware Architecture; I.3.3 [Computer Graphics]: Picture/Image Generation

1 INTRODUCTION

This paper describes the Silicon Graphics InfiniteReality architecture which is the highest performance graphics workstation ever commercially produced. The predecessor to the InfiniteReality system, the RealityEngine™, [Akel93] was the first example of what we term a third-generation graphics system. As a third-generation system, the target capability of the RealityEngine was to render lighted, smooth shaded, depth buffered, texture mapped, antialiased triangles. The level of realism achieved by RealityEngine graphics was well-matched to the application requirements of visual simulation (both flight and ground based simulation), location based entertainment [Paus96], defense imaging, and virtual reality. However, application success depends on two areas: the ability to provide convincing levels of realism and to deliver real-time performance of constant scene update rates of 60Hz or more. High frame rates reduce interaction latency and minimize symptoms of motion sickness in visual simulation and virtual reality applications. If frame rates are not constant, the visual integrity of the simulation is compromised.

InfiniteReality is also an example of a third-generation graphics system in that its target rendering quality is similar to that of RealityEngine. However, where RealityEngine delivered performance in the range of 15-30 Hz for most applications, the fundamental design goal of the InfiniteReality graphics system is to deliver real-time performance to a broad range of applications. Furthermore, the goal is to deliver this performance far more economically than competitive solutions.

Author contacts: {montrym | drb | dignam | migdal}@sgi.com

Most of the features and capabilities of the InfiniteReality architecture are designed to support this real-time performance goal. Minimizing the time required to change graphics modes and state is as important as increasing raw transformation and pixel fill rate. Many of the targeted applications require access to very large textures and/or a great number of distinct textures. Permanently storing such large amounts of texture data within the graphics system itself is not economically viable. Thus methods must be developed for applications to access a "virtual texture memory" without significantly impacting overall performance. Finally, the system must provide capabilities for the application to monitor actual geometry and fill rate performance on a frame by frame basis and make adjustments if necessary to maintain a constant 60Hz frame update rate.

Aside from the primary goal of real-time application performance, two other areas significantly shaped the system architecture. First, this was Silicon Graphics' first high-end graphics system to be designed from the beginning to provide native support for OpenGL™. To support the inherent flexibility of the OpenGL architecture, we could not take the traditional approach for the real-time market of providing a black-box solution such as a flight simulator [Scha83].

The InfiniteReality system is fundamentally a sort-middle architecture [Moln94]. Although interesting high-performance graphics architectures have been implemented using a sort-last approach [Moln92][Evan92], sort-last is not well-suited to supporting OpenGL framebuffer operations such as blending. Furthermore, sparse sort-last architectures make it difficult to rasterize primitives into the framebuffer in the order received from the application as required by OpenGL.

The second area that shaped the graphics architecture was the need for the InfiniteReality system to integrate well with two generations of host platforms. For the first year of production, the InfiniteReality system shipped with the Onyx host platform. Currently, the InfiniteReality system integrates into the Onyx2 platform. Not only was the host to graphics interface changed between the two systems, but the I/O performance was also significantly improved. Much effort went into designing a graphics system that would adequately support both host platforms.

The remainder of the paper is organized as follows. The next section gives an architectural overview of the system. Where appropriate, we contrast our approach to that of the RealityEngine system. Section 3 elaborates on novel functionality that enables real-time performance and enhanced video capabilities. Section 4 discusses the performance of the system. Finally, concluding remarks are made in Section 5.

2 ARCHITECTURE

It was a goal to be able to easily upgrade Onyx RealityEngine systems to InfiniteReality graphics. Accordingly, the physical partitioning of the InfiniteReality boardset is similar to that of

RealityEngine; there are three distinct board types: the Geometry, Raster Memory, and Display Generator boards (Figure 1).

The Geometry board comprises a host computer interface, command interpretation and geometry distribution logic, and four Geometry Engine processors in a MIMD arrangement. Each Raster Memory board comprises a single fragment generator with a single copy of texture memory, 80 image engines, and enough framebuffer memory to allocate 512 bits per pixel to a 1280x1024 framebuffer. The display generator board contains hardware to drive up to eight display output channels, each with its own video timing generator, video resize hardware, gamma correction, and digital-to-analog conversion hardware.

Systems can be configured with one, two or four raster memory boards, resulting in one, two, or four fragment generators and 80, 160, or 320 image engines.

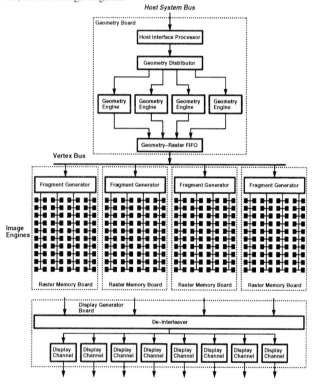

Figure 1: Board-level block diagram of the maximum configuration with 4 Geometry Engines, 4 Raster Memory boards, and a Display Generator board with 8 output channels.

2.1 Host Interface

There were significant system constraints that influenced the architectural design of InfiniteReality. Specifically, the graphics system had to be capable of working on two generations of host platforms. The Onyx2 differs significantly from the shared memory multiprocessor Onyx in that it is a distributed shared memory multiprocessor system with cache-coherent non-uniform memory access. The most significant difference in the graphics system design is that the Onyx2 provides twice the host-to-graphics bandwidth (400MB/sec vs. 200MB/sec) as does Onyx. Our challenge was to design a system that would be matched to the host-to-graphics data rate of the Onyx2, but still provide similar performance with the limited I/O capabilities of Onyx.

We addressed this problem with the design of the display list subsystem. In the RealityEngine system, display list processing had been handled by the host. Compiled display list objects were stored in host memory, and one of the host processors traversed the display list and transferred the data to the graphics pipeline using programmed I/O (PIO).

With the InfiniteReality system, display list processing is handled in two ways. First, compiled display list objects are stored in host memory in such a way that leaf display objects can be "pulled" into the graphics subsystem using DMA transfers set up by the Host Interface Processor (Figure 1). Because DMA transfers are faster and more efficient than PIO, this technique significantly reduces the computational load on the host processor so it can be better utilized for application computations. However, on the original Onyx system, DMA transfers alone were not fast enough to feed the graphics pipe at the rate at which it could consume data. The solution was to incorporate local display list processing into the design.

Attached to the Host Interface Processor is 16MB of synchronous dynamic RAM (SDRAM). Approximately 15MB of this memory is available to cache leaf display list objects. Locally stored display lists are traversed and processed by an embedded RISC core. Based on a priority specified using an OpenGL extension and the size of the display list object, the OpenGL display list manager determines whether or not a display list object should be cached locally on the Geometry board. Locally cached display lists are read at the maximum rate that can be consumed by the remainder of the InfiniteReality pipeline. As a result, the local display list provides a mechanism to mitigate the host to graphics I/O bottleneck of the original Onyx. Note that if the total size of leaf display list objects exceeds the resident 15MB limit, then some number of objects will be pulled from host memory at the reduced rate.

2.2 Geometry Distribution

The Geometry Distributor (Figure 1) passes incoming data and commands from the Host Interface Processor to individual Geometry Engines for further processing. The hardware supports both round-robin and least-busy distribution schemes. Since geometric processing requirements can vary from one vertex to another, a least-busy distribution scheme has a slight performance advantage over round-robin. With each command, an identifier is included which the Geometry-Raster FIFO (Figure 1) uses to recreate the original order of incoming primitives.

2.3 Geometry Engines

When we began the design of the InfiniteReality system, it became apparent that no commercial off-the-shelf floating point processors were being developed which would offer suitable price/performance. As a result, we chose to implement the Geometry Engine Processor as a semicustom application specific integrated circuit (ASIC).

The heart of the Geometry Engine is a single instruction multiple datapath (SIMD) arrangement of three floating point cores, each of which comprises an ALU and a multiplier plus a 32 word register file with two read and two write ports (Figure 2). A 2560 word on-chip memory holds elements of OpenGL state and provides scratch storage for intermediate calculations. A portion of the working memory is used as a queue for incoming vertex data. Early simulations of microcode fragments confirmed that high bandwidth to and from this memory would be required to get high utilization of the floating point hardware. Accordingly, each of the three cores can perform two reads and one write per instruction to working memory. Note that working memory allows data to be shared easily among cores. A dedicated float-to-fix converter follows each core, through which one floating point result may be written per instruction.

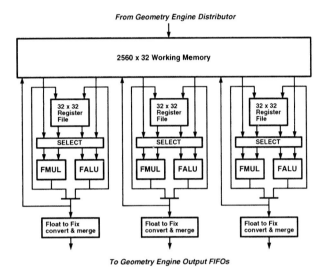

From Geometry Engine Distributor

To Geometry Engine Output FIFOs

Figure 2: Geometry Engine

We used a very simple scheduler to evaluate the performance effect of design trade-offs on critical microcode fragments. One of the trade-offs considered was the number of pipeline stages in the floating point arithmetic blocks. As we increased the depth of the pipeline from one to four stages, the machine's clock speed and throughput increased. For more than four stages, even though the clock speed improved, total performance did not because our code fragments did not have enough unrelated operations to fill the added computation slots.

Quite often machine performance is expressed in terms of vertex rates for triangles in long strips whereas application performance is much more likely to be determined by how well a system handles very short strips, with frequent mode changes. The problem of accelerating mode changes and other non-benchmark operations has enormous impact on the microcode architecture, which in turn influences aspects of the instruction set architecture.

To accelerate mode change processing, we divide the work associated with individual OpenGL modes into distinct code modules. For example, one module can be written to calculate lighting when one infinite light source is enabled, another may be tuned for one local point light source, and still another could handle a single spotlight. A general module exists to handle all cases which do not have a corresponding tuned module. Similarly, different microcode modules would be written to support other OpenGL modes such as texture coordinate generation or backface elimination. A table con-

sisting of pointers to the currently active modules is maintained in GE working memory. Each vertex is processed by executing the active modules in the table-specified sequence. When a mode change occurs, the appropriate table entry is changed. Vertex processing time degrades slowly and predictably as additional operations are turned on, unlike microcode architectures which implement hyper-optimized fast paths for selected bundles of mode settings, and a slow general path for all other combinations.

Since microcode modules tend to be relatively short, it is desirable to avoid the overhead of basic-block preamble and postamble code. All fields necessary to launch and retire a given operation, including memory and register file read and write controls, are specified in the launching microinstruction.

2.4 Geometry-Raster FIFO

The output streams from the four Geometry Engines are merged into a single stream by the Geometry-Raster FIFO. A FIFO large enough to hold 65536 vertexes is implemented in SDRAM. The merged geometry engine output is written, through the SDRAM FIFO, to the Vertex Bus. The Geometry-Raster FIFO contains a 256-word shadow RAM which keeps a copy of the latest values of the Fragment Generator and Image Engine control registers. By eliminating the need for the Geometry Engines to retain shadowed raster state in their local RAMs, the shadow RAM permits raster mode changes to be processed by only one of the Geometry Engines. This improves mode change performance and simplifies context switching.

2.5 Vertex Bus

One of our most important goals was to increase transform-limited triangle rates by an order of magnitude over RealityEngine. Given our desire to retain a sort-middle architecture, we were forced to increase the efficiency of the geometry-raster crossbar by a factor of ten. Whereas the RealityEngine system used a *Triangle Bus* to move triangle parameter slope information from its Geometry Engines to its Fragment Generators, the InfiniteReality system employs a *Vertex Bus* to transfer only screen space vertex information. Vertex Bus data is broadcast to all Fragment Generators. The Vertex Bus protocol supports the OpenGL triangle strip and triangle fan constructs, so the Vertex Bus load corresponds closely to the load on the host-to-graphics bus. The Geometry Engine triangle strip workload is reduced by around 60 percent by not calculating triangle setup information. However, hardware to assemble screen space primitives and compute parameter slopes is now incorporated into the Fragment Generators.

2.6 Fragment Generators

In order to provide increased user-accessible physical texture memory capacity at an acceptable cost, it was our goal to have only one copy of texture memory per Raster Memory board. A practical consequence of this is that there is also only one fragment generator per raster board. Figure 3 shows the fragment generator structure.

Connected vertex streams are received and assembled into triangle primitives. The Scan Converter (SC) and Texel Address Calculator (TA) ASICs perform scan conversion, color and depth interpolation, perspective correct texture coordinate interpolation and level-of-detail computation. Up to four fragments, corresponding to 2x2 pixel regions are produced every clock. Scan conversion is performed by directly evaluating the parameter plane equations at

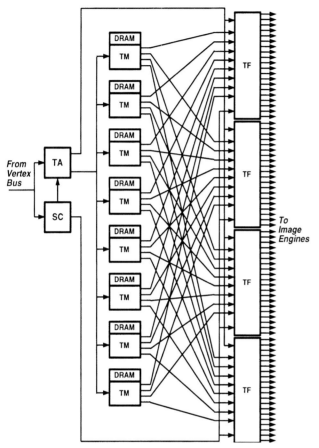

Figure 3: Fragment Generator

each pixel [Fuch85] rather than by using an interpolating DDA as was done in the RealityEngine system. Compared to a DDA, direct evaluation requires less setup time per triangle at the expense of more computation per pixel. Since application trends are towards smaller triangles, direct parameter evaluation is a more efficient solution.

Each texture memory controller (TM) ASIC performs the texel lookup in its four attached SDRAMs, given texel addresses from the TA. The TMs combine redundant texel requests from neighboring fragments to reduce SDRAM access. The TMs forward the resulting texel values to the appropriate TF ASIC for texture filtering, texture environment combination with interpolated color, and fog application. Since there is only one copy of the texture memory distributed across all the texture SDRAMs, there must exist a path from all 32 texture SDRAMs to all Image Engines. The TMs and TFs implement a two-rank omega network [Hwan84] to perform the required 32-to-80 sort.

2.7 Image Engines

Fragments output by a single Fragment Generator are distributed equally among the 80 Image Engines owned by that generator. Each Image Engine controls a single 256K x 32 SDRAM that comprises its portion of the framebuffer. Framebuffer memory per Image Engine is twice that of RealityEngine, so a single raster board system supports eight sample antialiasing at 1280 x 1024 or four sample antialiasing at 1920 x 1200 resolution.

2.8 Framebuffer Tiling

Three factors contributed to development of the framebuffer tiling scheme: the desire for load balancing of both drawing and video requests; the various restrictions on chip and board level packaging; and the requirement to keep on-chip FIFOs small.

In systems with more than one fragment generator, different fragment generators are each responsible for two-pixel wide vertical strips in framebuffer memory. If horizontal strips had been used instead, the resulting load imbalance due to display requests would have required excessively large FIFOs at the fragment generator inputs. The strip width is as narrow as possible to minimize the load imbalance due to drawing among fragment generators.

The Fragment Generator scan-conversion completes all pixels in a two pixel wide vertical strip before proceeding to the next strip for every primitive. To keep the Image Engines from limiting fill rate on large area primitives, all Image Engines must be responsible for part of every vertical strip owned by their Fragment Generator. Conversely, for best display request load balancing, all Image Engines must occur equally on every horizontal line. For a maximum system, the Image Engine framebuffer tiling repeat pattern is a rectangle 320 pixels wide by 80 pixels tall (320 is the number of Image Engines in the system and 80 is the number of Image Engines on one Raster Memory board).

2.9 Display Hardware

Each of the 80 Image Engines on the Raster Memory boards drives one or two bit serial signals to the Display Generator board. Two wires are driven if there is only one Raster Memory board, and one wire is driven if there are two or more. Unlike RealityEngine, both the number of pixels sent per block and the aggregate video band width of 1200 Mbytes/sec are independent of the number of Raster Memory boards. Four ASICs on the display board (Figure 4) de-serialize and de-interleave the 160 bit streams into RGBA10, RGB12, L16, Stereo Field Sequential (FS), or color indexes. The cursor is also injected at this point. A total of 32,768 color index map entries are available.

Color component width is maintained at 12 bits through the gamma table outputs. A connector site exists with a full 12 bit per component bus, which is used to connect video option boards. Option boards support the Digital Video Standard CCIR 601 and a digital pixel output for hardware-in-the-loop applications.

The base display system consists of two channels, expandable to eight. Each display channel is autonomous, with independent video timing and image resizing capabilities. The final channel output drives eight-bit digital-to-analog converters which can run up to a 220Mhz pixel clock rate. Either RGB or Left/Right Stereo Field Sequential is available from each channel.

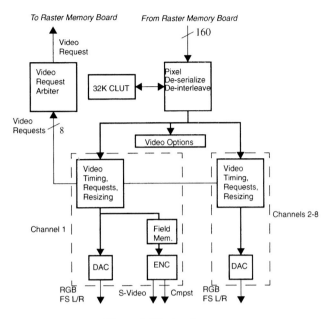

Figure 4: Display System

Video synchronization capabilities were expanded to support independent timing per channel (Figure 5). Swap events are constrained to happen during a common interval. Three different methods are used to synchronize video timing to external video sources. *Framelocking* is the ability to rate lock, using line rate dividers, two different video outputs whose line rates are related by small integer ratios. Line rate division is limited by the programmability of the phase-locked-loop gain and feedback parameters and the jitter spectrum of the input genlock source. The start of a video frame is detected by programmable sync pattern recognition hardware. Disparate source and displayed video formats which exceed the range of framelock are vertically locked by simply performing an asynchronous *frame reset* of the display video timing hardware. In this instance, the pixel clock is created by multiplying an oscillator clock. Identical formats may be *genlocked*. With frame lock or genlock, the frame reset from the pattern recognition hardware will be synchronous, and therefore cause no disturbance of the video signal being sent to the monitor.

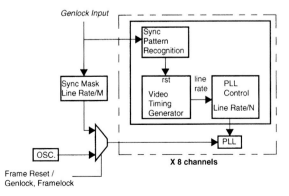

Figure 5: Video Synchronization

Certain situations require the synchronization of drawing between separate graphics systems. This is required in visual simulation installations where multiple displays are each driven by their own graphics system. If one graphics system takes longer than a frame time to draw a scene, the other graphics systems must be kept in lock step with the slowest one. InfiniteReality uses an external *swap ready* wire connecting all the graphics systems together in a wired AND configuration.

The video outputs of all the graphics systems are first locked together. Each pipe monitors the swap ready wire to determine if all the other pipes have finished drawing. A local buffer swap is only allowed to happen if all the graphics systems are ready to swap. In order to cope with slight pipe to pipe variations in video timing, a write exclusion window exists around the swap ready register to guarantee all pipes make the same decision.

Finally an NTSC or PAL output is available with any of the eight channels as the source. Resizing hardware allows for the scaling of any source resolution or windowed subset, to NTSC or PAL resolution.

3 FEATURES

3.1 Virtual Texture

The size of texture databases is rapidly increasing. Texture data that cover the entire world at one meter resolution will be commercially available in 1998. This corresponds to a texture size of 40,000,000 x 20,000,000 texels. Advanced simulation users need to be able to navigate around such large data in real-time. To meet this need, the InfiniteReality system provides hardware and software support for very large *virtual textures*, that is, textures which are too large to reside in physical texture memory.

Previous efforts to support texture databases larger than available texture memory required that the scene database modeler partition the original texture into a number of smaller tiles such that a subset of them fit into physical texture memory. The disadvantage of this approach is that the terrain polygons need to be subdivided so that no polygon maps to more than one texture tile. The InfiniteReality system, by contrast, allows the application to treat the original large texture as a single texture.

We introduce a representation called a *clip-map* which significantly reduces the storage requirements for very large textures. To illustrate the usefulness of the clip-map representation, we observe that the amount of texture data that can be viewed at one time is limited by the resolution of the display monitor. For example, using trilinear mip-map textures on a 1024x1024 monitor, the highest resolution necessary occurs just before a transition to the next coarser level of detail. In this case the maximum amount of resident texture required for any map level is no more than 2048 x 2048 for the finer map, and 1024x1024 for the coarser map, regardless of the size of the original map level. This is the worst case which occurs when the texture is viewed from directly above. In most applications the database is viewed obliquely and in perspective. This greatly reduces the maximum size of a particular level-of-detail that must be in texture memory in order to render a frame.

Recall that a mip-map represents a source image with a pyramidal set of two-dimensional images, each of which covers the full area of the source image at successively coarser resolution [Will83]. A clip-map can be thought of as a subset of the mip-map of the entire texture. It has two parts: a clip-map pyramid which is exactly the same as the coarser levels of the original mip-map, and a clip-map stack which holds a subset of the data in the original mip-map for the finest levels of detail. The clip-map stack levels all have the same size in texture memory, but each successively coarser level covers four times the source image area of the immediately finer level. Figure 6 illustrates the relationships between levels in a clip-map when viewed from above a textured database. The clip-map stack levels are centered on a common point. Each stack level represents larger and larger areas as the resolution of the data they contain becomes coarser and coarser. Figure 7 illustrates a clip-map for a 32K x 32K source image using a 2K x 2K clip-map tile size. Note that the clip-map representation requires about 1/64 the storage of the equivalent 32K x 32K mip-map.

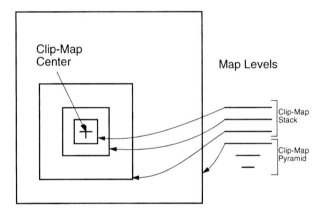

Figure 6: Clip-Map Levels

Because the clip-map stack does not contain the entire texture the position of the clip-map stack needs to be updated to track the viewer's position, or more optimally the center of the viewer's gaze. As the viewer's position or gaze moves, the contents of the clip-map stack should be updated to reflect this movement. New texture data is loaded into the texture memory to replace the texture data that is no longer required. The rate of update of texture data is highest for the finest clip-map stack level and becomes less for coarser stack levels of the clip-map. In the InfiniteReality system, it is not necessary to replace all data in a clip-map level when only a few texels actually need to be updated. The hardware loads new texture data over the old and automatically performs the correct addressing calculations using offset registers. Additionally, the Fragment Generators contain registers that define the clip-map center as it moves through the texture.

If the stack tile size is chosen correctly and the clip-map stack is updated properly as the viewpoint moves through the scene, the InfiniteReality system will produce images identical to those that would have been produced if the entire source mip-map had been resident in texture memory.

It cannot always be guaranteed that the texture data requested dur-

ing triangle rendering will be available at the requested level of detail. This may occur if the size of the clip-map tile has been chosen to be too small, or the update of the stack center failed to keep pace with the motion of the viewer. The InfiniteReality texture subsystem detects when texture is requested at a higher resolution than is available in texture memory. It substitutes the best available data which is data at the correct spatial position, but at a coarser level-of-detail than requested. As a result, the rendered scene will have regions where the texture will be coarser than if the entire mip-map were resident in texture memory. However, it will otherwise be rendered correctly. This substitution mechanism limits the required clip-map tile size and reduces the required texture update rate.

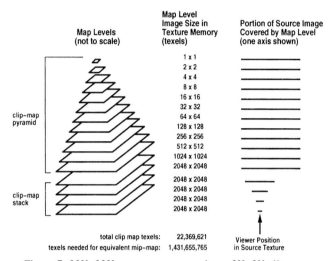

Figure 7: 32Kx32K texture represented as a 2Kx2K clip-map.

The Fragment Generator is limited to addressing a 32K x 32K clip-map. The addressability of clip-maps can be extended to arbitrary texture sizes through software. The software layer needs only to keep track of and implement a transformation from an arbitrarily large texture space into the texture space addressable by the hardware.

3.2 Texture Loading and Paging

We minimize the performance impact of large amounts of texture paging in the design of InfiniteReality system. The graphics subsystem interprets texture images directly as specified by the OpenGL programmer so no host processor translation is required. The front end of the Geometry Subsystem includes pixel unpacking and format conversion hardware; DMA hardware directly implements stride and padding address arithmetic as required by OpenGL. The Fragment Generators accept raster-order texture images at Vertex Bus-limited rates. To eliminate the need for the host computer to make and retain copies of loaded textures for context switching, the hardware supports texture image reads back to the host.

The Geometry-Raster FIFO maintains a separate path through which data bound for texture memory is routed. When the Fragment Generators are busy with fill-limited primitives, pending texture data is transferred over the Vertex Bus and routed to write queues in the TM ASICs. When a moderate amount of texture data is queued for a particular texture DRAM, the TM suspends draw access and writes the queue contents to that DRAM. Because total bandwidth to and from texture memory is an order of magnitude greater than that of the Vertex Bus, this action only slightly impacts fill rate. For fill-limited scenes, however, this approach utilizes Vertex Bus cycles which would otherwise go unused. Synchronization barrier primitives ensure that no texture is referenced until it has been fully loaded, and conversely, that no texture loading occurs until the data to be overwritten is no longer needed.

3.3 Scene Load Management

3.3.1 Pipeline Performance Statistics

Regardless of the performance levels of a graphics system, there may be times when there are insufficient hardware resources to maintain a real-time frame update rate. These cases occur when the pipeline becomes either geometry or fill rate limited. Rather than extending frame time, it is preferable for the application to detect such a situation and adjust the load on the pipeline appropriately.

The InfiniteReality system provides a mechanism for performing feedback-based load management with application-accessible monitoring instrumentation. Specifically, counters are maintained in the Geometry-Raster FIFO that monitor stall conditions on the Vertex Bus as well as wait conditions upstream in the geometry path. If the counters indicate that there is geometry pending in the Geometry-Raster FIFO, but writes to the Vertex Bus are stalled, then the system is fill rate limited. On the other hand, if the FIFO is empty, then the system is either host or geometry processing limited. By extracting these measurements, the application can take appropriate action whenever a geometry or fill rate bottleneck would have otherwise caused a drop in frame rate.

A common approach to a geometry limited pipeline is for the application to temporarily reduce the complexity of objects being drawn starting with those objects that are most distant from the viewer [Funk93][Rohl94]. This allows the application to reduce the polygon count being sent to the pipeline without severely impacting the visual fidelity of the scene. However, since distant objects do not tend to cover many pixels, this approach is not well-suited to the case where the pipeline is fill limited. To control fill limited situations, the InfiniteReality uses a novel technique termed *dynamic video resizing*.

3.3.2 Dynamic Video Resizing

Every frame, fill requirements are evaluated, and a scene is rendered to the framebuffer at a potentially reduced resolution such that drawing completes in less than one frame time. Prior to display on the monitor, the image is scaled up to the nominal resolution of the display format. Based on the current fill rate requirements of the scene, framebuffer resolution is continuously adjusted so that rendering can be completed within one frame time. A more detailed explanation follows.

Pipeline statistics are gathered each frame and used to determine if the current frame is close to being fill limited. These statistics are then used to estimate the amount by which the drawing time should be reduced or increased on the subsequent frame. Drawing

time is altered by changing the resolution at which the image is rendered in the framebuffer. Resolution is reduced if it is estimated that the new image cannot be drawn in less than a frame time. Resolution can be increased if it was reduced in prior scenes, and the current drawing time is less than one frame. The new frame may now be drawn at a different resolution from the previous one. Resolution can be changed in X or Y or both. Magnifying the image back up to the nominal display resolution is done digitally, just prior to display. The video resizing hardware is programmed for the matching magnification ratios, and the video request hardware is programmed to request the appropriate region of the framebuffer.

Finally, to ensure the magnification ratio is matched with the resolution of the frame currently being displayed, loading of the magnification and video request parameters is delayed until the next swap buffer event for that video channel. This ensures that even if scene rendering exceeds one frame time, the resizing parameters are not updated until drawing is finished.

Each channel is assigned a unique display ID, and the swap event is detected for each of these ID's. This swap forces the loading of the new resize parameters for the corresponding video channel, and allows channels with different swap rates to resize.

Note that the effectiveness of this technique is independent of scene content and does not require modifications to the scene data base.

3.4 Video Configurability

One of the goals for the InfiniteReality system was to enable our customers to both create their own video timing formats and to assign formats to each video channel.

This required that the underlying video timing hardware had to be more flexible than in the RealityEngine. Capabilities were expanded in the video timing and request hardware's ability to handle color field sequential, interlace, and large numbers of fields. The biggest change needed was an expanded capability to detect unique vertical sync signatures when genlocking to an external video signal. Since our customers could define vertical sync signatures whose structure could not be anticipated, the standard approach of simply hard-wiring the detection of known sync patterns would have been inadequate. Therefore, each video channel contains programmable pattern recognition hardware, which analyzes incoming external sync and generates resets to the video timing hardware as required.

In previous graphics systems, multi-channel support was designed as an afterthought to the basic single channel display system. This produced an implementation that was lacking in flexibility and was not as well integrated as it could have been. In the RealityEngine system, support for multiple channels was achieved by pushing video data to an external display board. The software that created multi-channel combinations was required to emulate the system hardware in order to precisely calculate how to order the video data. Ordering had to be maintained so each channel's local FIFO would not overflow or underflow. This approach was not very robust and made it impossible for our customers to define their own format combinations.

In the InfiniteReality system, every video channel was designed to be fully autonomous in that each has its own programmable pixel clock and video timing. Each video channel contains a FIFO, sized to account for latencies in requesting frame buffer memory. Video data is requested based on each channel's FIFO levels. A round robin arbiter is sufficient to guarantee adequate response time for multiple video requests.

Format combinations are limited to video formats with the same swap rate. Thus, the combination of 1280x1024@60Hz + 640x480@180Hz field sequential + 1024x768@120Hz stereo + NTSC is allowed but combining 1920x1080@72Hz and 50Hz PAL is not.

In order to achieve our design goal of moving more control of video into the hands of our customers, two software programs were developed. The first program is the Video Format Compiler or **vfc**. This program generates a file containing the microcode used to configure the video timing hardware. The source files for the compiler use a language whose syntax is consistent with standard video terminology. Source files can be generated automatically using templates. Generating simple block sync formats can be accomplished without any specific video knowledge other than knowing the width, height and frame rate of the desired video display format. More complex video formats can be written by modifying an existing source file or by starting from scratch. The Video Format Compiler generates an object file which can be loaded into the display subsystem at any time. Both the video timing hardware and the sync pattern recognition hardware are specified by the **vfc** for each unique video timing format.

The second program is the InfiniteReality combiner or **ircombine**. Its primary uses are to define combinations of existing video formats, verify that they operate within system limitations, and to specify various video parameters. Both a GUI and a command line version of this software are provided. Once a combination of video formats has been defined, it can be saved out to a file which can be loaded at a later time. The following is a partial list of **ircombine** capabilities:

o   Attach a video format to a specific video channel
o   Verify that the format combination can exist within system limits
o   Define the rectangular area in framebuffer memory to be displayed by each channel
o   Define how data is requested for interlace formats
o   Set video parameters (gain, sync on RGB, setup etc.)
o   Define genlock parameters (internal/external, genlock source format, horizontal phase, vertical phase)
o   Control the NTSC/PAL encoder (source channel, input window size, filter size)
o   Control pixel depth and size

4 PERFORMANCE

The InfiniteReality system incorporates 12 unique ASIC designs implemented using a combination of 0.5 and 0.35 micron, three-layer metal semiconductor fabrication technology.

Benchmark performance numbers for several key operations are summarized in Tables 1, 2, and 3. In general, geometry processing rates are seven to eight times that of the RealityEngine system and pixel fill rates are increased by over a factor of three. Note that the depth buffered fill rate assumes that every Z value passes the Z comparison and must be replaced which is the worst case. In practice, not every pixel will require replacement so the actual depth buffered fill rates will fall between the stated depth buffered and non depth buffered rate.

Although the benchmark numbers are impressive, our design goals focused on achieving real-time application performance rather than the highest possible benchmark numbers. Predicting application performance is a complex subject for which there are no standard accepted metrics. Some of the reasons that applications do not achieve peak benchmark rates include the frequent execution of mode changes (e.g. assigning a different texture, changing a surface material, etc.), the use of short triangle meshes, and host processing limitations. We include execution times for commonly performed mode changes (Table 4) as well as performance data for shorter triangle meshes (Table 5). Practical experience with a variety of applications has shown that the InfiniteReality system is successful in achieving our real-time performance goals.

We were pleasantly surprised by the utility of video resizing as a fill rate conservation tool. Preliminary simulations indicated that we could expect to dynamically reduce framebuffer resolution up to ten percent in each dimension without substantially degrading image quality. In practice, we find that we can frequently reduce framebuffer resolution up to 25% in each dimension which results in close to a 50% reduction in fill rate requirements.

unlit, untextured tstrips	11.3 Mtris/sec
unlit, textured tstrips	9.5 Mtris/sec
lit, textured tstrips	7.1 Mtris/sec

Table 1: Non Fill-Limited Geometry Rates

non-depth buffered, textured, antialiased	830 Mpix/sec
depth buffered, textured, antialiased	710 Mpix/sec

Table 2: Non Geometry-Limited Fill Rates (4 Raster Memory boards)

RGBA8	83.1 Mpix/sec (332 Mb/sec)

Table 3: Peak Pixel Download Rate

glMaterial	240,941/sec
glColorMaterial	337,814/sec
glBindTexture	244,537/sec
glMultMatrixf	1,110,779/sec
glPushMatrix/glPopMatrix	1,489,454/sec

Table 4: Mode Change Rates

Length 2 triangle strips	4.7 Mtris/sec
Length 4 triangle strips	7.7 Mtris/sec
Length 6 triangle strips	8.6 Mtris/sec
Length 8 triangle strips	9.0 Mtris/sec
Length 10 triangle strips	11.3 Mtris/sec

Table 5: Geometry Rates for Short Triangle Strips

The above numbers are for unlit, untextured triangle strips. Other types of triangle strips scale similarly.

The performance of the InfiniteReality system makes practical the use of multipass rendering techniques to enhance image realism. Multipass rendering can be used to implement effects such as reflections, Phong shading, shadows, and spotlights [Sega92]. Figure 8 shows a frame from a multipass rendering demonstration running at 60Hz on the InfiniteReality system. This application uses up to five passes per frame and renders approximately 40,000 triangles each frame.

5 CONCLUSION

The InfiniteReality system achieves real-time rendering through a combination of raw graphics performance and capabilities designed to enable applications to achieve guaranteed frame rates. The flexible video architecture of the InfiniteReality system is a general solution to the image generation needs of multichannel visual simulation applications. A true OpenGL implementation, the InfiniteReality brings unprecedented performance to traditional graphics-intensive applications. This underlying performance, together with new rendering functionality like virtual texturing, paves the way for entirely new classes of applications.

Acknowledgments

Many of the key insights in the area of visual simulation came from Michael Jones and our colleagues on the Performer team. Gregory Eitzmann helped architect the video subsystem and associated software tools. The multipass rendering demo in Figure 8 was produced by Luis Barcena Martin, Ignacio Sanz-Pastor Revorio, and Javier Castellar. Finally, the authors would like to thank the talented and dedicated InfiniteReality and Onyx2 teams for their tremendous efforts. Every individual made significant contributions to take the system from concept to product.

REFERENCES

[Akel93] K. Akeley, "RealityEngine Graphics", *SIGGRAPH 93 Proceedings*, pp. 109-116.

[Evan92] Evans and Sutherland Computer Corporation, "*Freedom Series Technical Report*", Salt Lake City, Utah, Oct. 92.

[Funk93] T. Funkhouser, C. Sequin, "Adaptive Display Algorithm for Interactive Frame Rates During Visualization of Complex Virtual Environments", *SIGGRAPH 93 Proceedings*, pp. 247-254.

[Fuch85] H. Fuchs, J. Goldfeather, J. Hultquist, S. Spach, J. Austin, F. Brooks, J. Eyles, and J. Poulton, "Fast Spheres, Shadows, Textures, Transparencies, and Image Enhancements in Pixel-Planes", *SIGGRAPH 85 Proceedings*, pp. 111-120.

[Hwan84] K. Hwang, F. Briggs, "*Computer Archetecture and Parallel Processing*", McGraw-Hill, New York, pp. 350-354, 1984.

[Moln92] S. Molnar, J. Eyles, J. Poulton, "Pixelflow: High-Speed Rendering Using Image Composition", *SIGGRAPH 92 Proceedings*, pp. 231-240.

[Moln94] S. Molnar, M. Cox, D. Ellsworth, H. Fuchs, "A Sorting Classification of Parallel Rendering", *IEEE Computer Graphics and Applications, July 94, pp. 23-32.*

[Paus96] R. Paush, J. Snoddy, R. Taylor, E. Haseltine, "Disney's Aladdin: First Steps Toward Storytelling in Virtual Reality", *SIGGRAPH 96 Proceedings*, pp. 193-203.

[Scha83] B. Schachter, "Computer Image Generation", John Wiley & Sons, New York, 1983.

[Sega92] M. Segal, C. Korobkin, R. van Widenfelt, J. Foran, P. Haeberli, "Fast Shadows and Lighting Effects Using Texture Mapping", *SIGGRAPH 92 Proceedings*, pp. 249-252.

[Rohl94] J. Rohlf, J. Helman, "IRIS Performer: A High Performance Multiprocessing Toolkit for Real-Time 3DGraphics, *SIGGRAPH 94 Proceedings*, pp. 381-394.

[Will83] L. Williams, "Pyramidal Parametrics", *SIGGRAPH 83 Proceedings*, pp. 1-11.

Figure 8: Example of a high-quality image rendered at 60 Hz using multipass techniques

Efficient Bump Mapping Hardware

Mark Peercy

John Airey

Brian Cabral

Silicon Graphics Computer Systems *

Abstract

We present a bump mapping method that requires minimal hardware beyond that necessary for Phong shading. We eliminate the costly per-pixel steps of reconstructing a tangent space and perturbing the interpolated normal vector by a) interpolating vectors that have been transformed into tangent space at polygon vertices and b) storing a precomputed, perturbed normal map as a texture. This represents a considerable savings in hardware or rendering speed compared to a straightforward implementation of bump mapping.

CR categories and subject descriptors: I.3.3 [Computer Graphics]: Picture/Image generation; I.3.7 [Image Processing]: Enhancement

Keywords: hardware, shading, bump mapping, texture mapping.

1 INTRODUCTION

Shading calculations in commercially available graphics systems have been limited to lighting at the vertices of a set of polygons, with the resultant colors interpolated and composited with a texture. The drawbacks of Gouraud interpolation [9] are well known and include diffused, crawling highlights and mach banding. The use of this method is motivated primarily by the relatively large cost of the lighting computation. When done at the vertices, this cost is amortized over the interiors of polygons.

The division of a computation into per-vertex and per-pixel components is a general strategy in hardware graphics acceleration [1]. Commonly, the vertex computations are performed in a general floating point processor or cpu, while the per-pixel computations are in special purpose, fixed point hardware. The division is a function of cost versus the general applicability, in terms of quality and speed, of a feature. Naturally, the advance of processor and application-specific integrated circuit technology has an impact on the choice.

Because the per-vertex computations are done in a general processor, the cost of a new feature tends to be dominated by additional per-pixel hardware. If this feature has a very specific application, the extra hardware is hard to justify because it lays idle in applications that do not leverage it. And in low-end or game systems, where every transistor counts, additional rasterization hardware is particularly expensive. An alternative to extra hardware is the reuse of existing hardware, but this option necessarily runs much slower.

* {peercy,airey,cabral}@sgi.com
2011 N. Shoreline Boulevard
Mountain View, California 94043-1389

Shading quality can be increased dramatically with Phong shading [13], which interpolates and normalizes vertex normal vectors at each pixel. Light and halfangle vectors are computed directly in eye space or interpolated, either of which requires their normalization for a local viewer and light. Figure 1 shows rasterization hard-

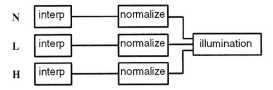

Figure 1. One implementation of Phong shading hardware.

ware for one implementation of Phong shading, upon which we base this discussion.[1] This adds significant cost to rasterization hardware. However higher quality lighting is almost universally desired in three-dimensional graphics applications, and advancing semiconductor technology is making Phong shading hardware more practical. We take Phong shading and texture mapping hardware as a prerequisite for bump mapping, assuming they will be standard in graphics hardware in the future.

Bump mapping [3] is a technique used in advanced shading applications for simulating the effect of light reflecting from small perturbations across a surface. A single component texture map, $f(u, v)$, is interpreted as a height field that perturbs the surface along its normal vector, $\mathbf{N} = (\mathbf{P}_u \times \mathbf{P}_v)/|(\mathbf{P}_u \times \mathbf{P}_v)|$, at each point. Rather than actually changing the surface geometry, however, only the normal vector is modified. From the partial derivatives of the surface position in the u and v parametric directions ($\mathbf{P}_u$ and $\mathbf{P}_v$), and the partial derivatives of the image height field in u and v (f_u and f_v), a perturbed normal vector $\mathbf{N}'$ is given by [3]:

$$\mathbf{N}' = ((\mathbf{P}_u \times \mathbf{P}_v) + \mathbf{D})/|(\mathbf{P}_u \times \mathbf{P}_v) + \mathbf{D}| \quad (1)$$

where

$$\mathbf{D} = -f_u(\mathbf{P}_v \times \mathbf{N}) - f_v(\mathbf{N} \times \mathbf{P}_u) \quad (2)$$

In these equations, $\mathbf{P}_u$ and $\mathbf{P}_v$ are not normalized. As Blinn points out [3], this causes the bump heights to be a function of the surface scale because $\mathbf{P}_u \times \mathbf{P}_v$ changes at a different rate than $\mathbf{D}$. If the surface scale is doubled, the bump heights are halved. This dependence on the surface often is an undesirable feature, and Blinn suggests one way to enforce a constant bump height.

A full implementation of these equations in a rasterizer is impractical, so the computation is divided among a preprocessing step, per-vertex, and per-pixel calculations. A natural method to support bump mapping in hardware, and one that is planned for a high-end graphics workstation [6], is to compute $\mathbf{P}_u \times \mathbf{P}_v$, $\mathbf{P}_v \times \mathbf{N}$, and $\mathbf{N} \times \mathbf{P}_u$ at polygon vertices and interpolate them to polygon interiors. The perturbed normal vector is computed and normalized as in Equation 1, with f_u and f_v read from a texture map. The resulting normal vector is used in an illumination model.

---

[1]Several different implementations of Phong shading have been suggested [11][10][4][5][7][2] with their own costs and benefits. Our bump mapping algorithm can leverage many variations, and we use this form as well as Blinn's introduction of the halfangle vector for clarity.

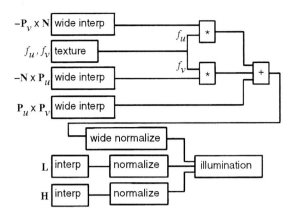

Figure 2. One possible implementation of bump mapping hardware.

Several implementations of this bump mapping method with minor variations are possible; the hardware for one approach based on Figure 1 is shown in Figure 2. Because $\mathbf{P}_u$ and $\mathbf{P}_v$ are unbounded, the three interpolators, the vector addition, vector scaling, and normalization must have much greater precision than those needed for bounded vectors. These requirements are noted in the figure. One approximation to this implementation has been proposed [8], where $\mathbf{P}_v \times \mathbf{N}$ and $\mathbf{N} \times \mathbf{P}_u$ are held constant across a polygon. While avoiding their interpolation, this approximation is known to have artifacts [8].

We present an implementation of bump mapping that leverages Phong shading hardware at full speed, eliminating either a large investment in special purpose hardware or a slowdown during bump mapping. The principal idea is to transform the bump mapping computation into a different reference frame. Because illumination models are a function of vector operations (such as the dot product) between the perturbed normal vector and other vectors (such as the light and halfangle), they can be computed relative to any frame. We are able to push portions of the bump mapping computation into a preprocess or the per-vertex processor and out of the rasterizer. As a result, minimal hardware is added to a Phong shading circuit.

2   OUR BUMP-MAPPING ALGORITHM

We proceed by recognizing that the original bump mapping approximation [3] assumes a surface is locally flat at each point. The perturbation is, therefore, a function only of the local tangent space. We define this space by the normal vector, $\mathbf{N}$, a tangent vector, $\mathbf{T} = \mathbf{P}_u / |\mathbf{P}_u|$, and a binormal vector, $\mathbf{B} = (\mathbf{N} \times \mathbf{T})$. $\mathbf{T}$, $\mathbf{B}$, and $\mathbf{N}$ form an orthonormal coordinate system in which we perform the bump mapping. In this space, the perturbed normal vector is (see appendix):

$$\mathbf{N}'_{TS} = (a, b, c) / \sqrt{a^2 + b^2 + c^2} \quad (3)$$

$$a = -f_u(\mathbf{B} \cdot \mathbf{P}_v) \quad (4)$$
$$b = -(f_v|\mathbf{P}_u| - f_u(\mathbf{T} \cdot \mathbf{P}_v)) \quad (5)$$
$$c = |\mathbf{P}_u \times \mathbf{P}_v| \quad (6)$$

The coefficients a, b, and c are a function of the surface itself (via $\mathbf{P}_u$ and $\mathbf{P}_v$) and the height field (via f_u and f_v). Provided that the bump map is fixed to a surface, the coefficients can be precomputed for that surface at each point of the height field and stored as a texture map (we discuss approximations that relax the surface dependence below). The texel components lie in the range -1 to 1.

The texture map containing the perturbed normal vector is filtered as a simple texture using, for instance, tri-linear mipmap filtering.

The texels in the coarser levels of detail can be computed by filtering finer levels of detail and renormalizing or by filtering the height field and computing the texels directly from Equations 3-6. It is well known that this filtering step tends to average out the bumps at large minifications, leading to artifacts at silhouette edges. Proper filtering of bump maps requires computing the reflected radiance over all bumps contributing to a single pixel, an option that is not practical for hardware systems. It should also be noted that, after mipmap interpolation, the texture will not be normalized, so we must normalize it prior to lighting.

For the illumination calculation to proceed properly, we transform the light and halfangle vectors into tangent space via a 3×3 matrix whose columns are $\mathbf{T}$, $\mathbf{B}$, and $\mathbf{N}$. For instance, the light vector, $\mathbf{L}$, is transformed by

$$\mathbf{L}_{TS} = \mathbf{L} \begin{pmatrix} \mathbf{T} & \mathbf{B} & \mathbf{N} \\ \downarrow & \downarrow & \downarrow \end{pmatrix} \quad (7)$$

Now the diffuse term in the illumination model can be computed from the perturbed normal vector from the texture map and the transformed light: $\mathbf{N}'_{TS} \cdot \mathbf{L}_{TS}$. The same consideration holds for the other terms in the illumination model.

The transformations of the light and halfangle vectors should be performed at every pixel; however, if the change of the local tangent space across a polygon is small, a good approximation can be obtained by transforming the vectors only at the polygon vertices. They are then interpolated and normalized in the polygon interiors. This is frequently a good assumption because tangent space changes rapidly in areas of high surface curvature, and an application will need to tessellate the surfaces more finely in those regions to reduce geometric faceting.

This transformation is, in spirit, the same as one proposed by Kuijk and Blake to reduce the hardware required for Phong shading [11]. Rather than specifying a tangent and binormal explicitly, they rotate the reference frames at polygon vertices to orient all normal vectors in the same direction (such as $(0, 0, 1)$). In this space, they no longer interpolate the normal vector (an approximation akin to ours that tangent space changes slowly). If the bump map is identically zero, we too can avoid an interpolation and normalization, and we will have a result similar to their approximation. It should be noted that the highlight in this case is slightly different than that obtained by the Phong circuit of Figure 1, yet it is still phenomenologically reasonable.

The rasterization hardware required for our bump mapping algorithm is shown in Figure 3; by adding a multiplexer to the Phong shading hardware of Figure 1, both the original Phong shading and bump mapping can be supported. Absent in the implementation of Figure 2, this algorithm requires transforming the light and halfangle vectors into tangent space at each vertex, storing a three-component texture map instead of a two-component map, and having a separate map for each surface. However, it requires only a multiplexer beyond Phong shading, avoids the interpolation of $(\mathbf{P}_v \times \mathbf{N})$ and $(\mathbf{N} \times \mathbf{P}_u)$, the perturbation of the normal vector at each pixel, and the extra precision needed for arithmetic on unbounded vectors. Effectively, we have traded per-pixel calculations cast in hardware for per-vertex calculations done in the general geometry processor. If the application is limited by the rasterization, it will run at the same speed with bump mapping as with Phong shading.

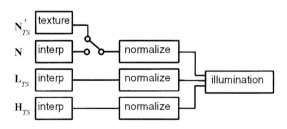

Figure 3. One implementation of our bump mapping algorithm.

Figure 4.The pinwheel height field is used as a bump map for the tesselated, bicubic surface.

2.1 Object-Space Normal Map

If the texture map is a function of the surface parameterization, another implementation is possible: the lighting model can be computed in object space rather than tangent space. Then, the texture stores the perturbed normal vectors in object space, and the light and halfangle vectors are transformed into object space at the polygon vertices and interpolated. Thus, the matrix transformation applied to the light and halfangle vectors is shared by all vertices, rather than one transformation for each vertex. This implementation keeps the rasterization hardware of Figure 3, significantly reduces the overhead in the geometry processor, and can coexist with the first formulation.

2.2 Removing the surface dependence

The primary drawback of our method is the surface dependence of the texture map. The dependence of the bumps on surface scale is shared with the traditional formulation of bump mapping. Yet in addition, our texture map is a function of the surface, so the height field can not be shared among surfaces with different parameterizations. This is particularly problematic when texture memory is restricted, as in a game system, or during design when a bump map is placed on a new surface interactively.

The surface dependencies can be eliminated under the assumption that, locally, the parameterization is the same as a square patch (similar to, yet more restrictive than, the assumption Blinn makes in removing the scale dependence [3]). Then, $\mathbf{P}_u$ and $\mathbf{P}_v$ are orthogonal ($\mathbf{P}_u \cdot \mathbf{P}_v = \mathbf{T} \cdot \mathbf{P}_v = 0$) and equal in magnitude ($|\mathbf{P}_u| = |\mathbf{P}_v|$). To remove the bump dependence on surface scale, we choose

Figure 6.Bump mapping with the hardware in Figure 3, and the texture map from Equations 3-6.

$|\mathbf{P}_u| = |\mathbf{P}_v| = k$, where k is a constant giving a relative height of the bumps. This, along with the orthogonality condition, reduce Equations 3-6 to

$$\mathbf{N}'_{TS} = (a, b, c)/\sqrt{a^2 + b^2 + c^2} \qquad (8)$$

$$a = -kf_u \qquad (9)$$
$$b = -kf_v \qquad (10)$$
$$c = k^2 \qquad (11)$$

The texture map becomes a function only of the height field and not of the surface geometry, so it can be precomputed and used on any surface.

The square patch assumption is good for several important surfaces, such as spheres, tori, surfaces of revolution, and flat rectangles. In addition, the property is highly desirable for general surfaces because the further $\mathbf{P}_u$ and $\mathbf{P}_v$ are from orthogonal and equal in magnitude, the greater the warp in the texture map when applied to a surface. This warping is typically undesirable, and its elimination has been the subject of research [12]. If the surface is already reasonably parameterized or can be reparameterized, the approximation in Equations 8-11 is good.

3 EXAMPLES

Figures 5-7 compare software simulations of the various bump mapping implementations. All of the images, including the height field, have a resolution of 512x512 pixels. The height field, Figure 4, was

Figure 5. Bump mapping using the hardware implementation shown in Figure 2.

Figure 7.Bump mapping with the hardware in Figure 3, and the texture map from Equations 8-11.

chosen as a pinwheel to highlight filtering and implementation artifacts, and the surface, Figure 4, was chosen as a highly stretched bicubic patch subdivided into 8x8x2 triangles to ensure that $\mathbf{P}_u$ and $\mathbf{P}_v$ deviate appreciably from orthogonal. The texture maps were filtered with trilinear mipmapping.

Figure 5 shows the image computed from the implementation of bump mapping from Figure 2. The partial derivatives, f_u and f_v, in this texture map and the others were computed with the derivative of a Gaussian covering seven by seven samples.

Figures 6 and 7 show our implementation based on the hardware of Figure 3; they differ only in the texture map that is employed. Figure 6 uses a texture map based on Equations 3-6. Each texel was computed from the analytic values of $\mathbf{P}_u$ and $\mathbf{P}_v$ for the bicubic patch. The difference between this image and Figure 5 is almost imperceptible, even under animation, as can be seen in the enlarged insets. The texture map used in Figure 7 is based on Equations 8-11, where the surface dependence has been removed. Minor differences can be seen in the rendered image compared to Figures 5 and 6; some are visible in the inset. All three implementations have similar filtering qualities and appearance during animation.

4 DISCUSSION

We have presented an implementation of bump mapping that, by transforming the lighting problem into tangent space, avoids any significant new rasterization hardware beyond Phong shading. To summarize our algorithm, we

- precompute a texture of the perturbed normal in tangent space
- transform all shading vectors into tangent space per vertex
- interpolate and renormalize the shading vectors
- fetch and normalize the perturbed normal from the texture
- compute the illumination model with these vectors

Efficiency is gained by moving a portion of the problem to the vertices and away from special purpose bump mapping hardware in the rasterizer; the incremental cost of the per-vertex transformations is amortized over the polygons.

It is important to note that the method of transforming into tangent space for bump mapping is independent of the illumination model, provided the model is a function only of vector operations on the normal. For instance, the original Phong lighting model, with the reflection vector and the view vector for the highlight, can be used instead of the halfangle vector. In this case, the view vector is transformed into tangent space and interpolated rather than the halfangle. As long as all necessary shading vectors for the illumination model are transformed into tangent space and interpolated, lighting is proper.

Our approach is relatively independent of the particular implementation of Phong shading, however it does require the per-pixel illumination model to accept vectors rather than partial illumination results. We have presented a Phong shading circuit where almost no new hardware is required, but other implementations may need extra hardware. For example, if the light and halfangle vectors are computed directly in eye space, interpolators must be added to support our algorithm. The additional cost still will be small compared to a straightforward implementation.

Phong shading likely will become a standard addition to hardware graphics systems because of its general applicability. Our algorithm extends Phong shading in such an effective manner that it is natural to support bump mapping even on the lowest cost Phong shading systems.

5 ACKNOWLEDGEMENTS

This work would not have been possible without help, ideas, conversations and encouragement from Pat Hanrahan, Bob Drebin, Kurt Akeley, Erik Lindholm and Vimal Parikh. Also thanks to the anonymous reviewers who provided good and insightful suggestions.

APPENDIX

Here we derive the perturbed normal vector in tangent space, a reference frame given by tangent, $\mathbf{T} = \mathbf{P}_u/|\mathbf{P}_u|$; binormal, $\mathbf{B} = (\mathbf{N} \times \mathbf{T})$; and normal, $\mathbf{N}$, vectors. $\mathbf{P}_v$ is in the plane of the tangent and binormal, and it can be written:

$$\mathbf{P}_v = (\mathbf{T} \cdot \mathbf{P}_v)\mathbf{T} + (\mathbf{B} \cdot \mathbf{P}_v)\mathbf{B} \qquad (12)$$

Therefore

$$\mathbf{P}_v \times \mathbf{N} = (\mathbf{B} \cdot \mathbf{P}_v)\mathbf{T} - (\mathbf{T} \cdot \mathbf{P}_v)\mathbf{B} \qquad (13)$$

The normal perturbation (Equation 2) is:

$$\mathbf{D} = -f_u(\mathbf{P}_v \times \mathbf{N}) - f_v(\mathbf{N} \times \mathbf{P}_u) \qquad (14)$$

$$= -f_u(\mathbf{P}_v \times \mathbf{N}) - f_v|\mathbf{P}_u|\mathbf{B} \qquad (15)$$

$$= -f_u(\mathbf{B} \cdot \mathbf{P}_v)\mathbf{T} - (f_v|\mathbf{P}_u| - f_u(\mathbf{T} \cdot \mathbf{P}_v))\mathbf{B} \qquad (16)$$

Substituting the expression for $\mathbf{D}$ and $\mathbf{P}_u \times \mathbf{P}_v = |\mathbf{P}_u \times \mathbf{P}_v|\mathbf{N}$ into Equation 1, normalizing, and taking $\mathbf{T}_{TS} = (1, 0, 0)$, $\mathbf{B}_{TS} = (0, 1, 0)$, and $\mathbf{N}_{TS} = (0, 0, 1)$ leads directly to Equations 3-6.

References

[1] AKELEY, K. RealityEngine graphics. In *Computer Graphics (SIGGRAPH '93 Proceedings)* (Aug. 1993), J. T. Kajiya, Ed., vol. 27, pp. 109–116.

[2] BISHOP, G., AND WEIMER, D. M. Fast Phong shading. In *Computer Graphics (SIGGRAPH '86 Proceedings)* (Aug. 1986), D. C. Evans and R. J. Athay, Eds., vol. 20, pp. 103–106.

[3] BLINN, J. F. Simulation of wrinkled surfaces. In *Computer Graphics (SIGGRAPH '78 Proceedings)* (Aug. 1978), vol. 12, pp. 286–292.

[4] CLAUSSEN, U. Real time phong shading. In *Fifth Eurographics Workshop on Graphics Hardware* (1989), D. Grimsdale and A. Kaufman, Eds.

[5] CLAUSSEN, U. On reducing the phong shading method. *Computers and Graphics 14*, 1 (1990), 73–81.

[6] COSMAN, M. A., AND GRANGE, R. L. CIG scene realism: The world tomorrow. In *Proceedings of I/ITSEC 1996 on CD-ROM* (1996), p. 628.

[7] DEERING, M. F., WINNER, S., SCHEDIWY, B., DUFFY, C., AND HUNT, N. The triangle processor and normal vector shader: A VLSI system for high performance graphics. In *Computer Graphics (SIGGRAPH '88 Proceedings)* (Aug. 1988), J. Dill, Ed., vol. 22, pp. 21–30.

[8] ERNST, I., JACKEL, D., RUSSELER, H., AND WITTIG, O. Hardware supported bump mapping: A step towards higher quality real-time rendering. In *10th Eurographics Workshop on Graphics Hardware* (1995), pp. 63–70.

[9] GOURAUD, H. Computer display of curved surfaces. *IEEE Trans. Computers C-20*, 6 (1971), 623–629.

[10] JACKEL, D., AND RUSSELER, H. A real time rendering system with normal vector shading. In *9th Eurographics Workshop on Graphics Hardware* (1994), pp. 48–57.

[11] KUIJK, A. A. M., AND BLAKE, E. H. Faster phong shading via angular interpolation. *Computer Graphics Forum 8*, 4 (Dec. 1989), 315–324.

[12] MAILLOT, J., YAHIA, H., AND VERROUST, A. Interactive texture mapping. In *Computer Graphics (SIGGRAPH '93 Proceedings)* (Aug. 1993), J. T. Kajiya, Ed., vol. 27, pp. 27–34.

[13] PHONG, B.-T. Illumination for computer generated pictures. *Communications of the ACM 18*, 6 (June 1975), 311–317.

Hardware Accelerated Rendering Of Antialiasing Using A Modified A-buffer Algorithm

Stephanie Winner[*], Mike Kelley[†], Brent Pease[**], Bill Rivard[*], and Alex Yen[†]

Apple Computer

ABSTRACT

This paper describes algorithms for accelerating antialiasing in 3D graphics through low-cost custom hardware. The rendering architecture employs a multiple-pass algorithm to perform front-to-back hidden surface removal and shading. Coverage mask evaluation is used to composite objects in 3D. The key advantage of this approach is that antialiasing requires no additional memory and decreases rendering performance by only 30-40% for typical images. The system is image partition based and is scalable to satisfy a wide range of performance and cost constraints.

CR Categories and Subject Descriptors: I.3.1 [Computer Graphics]: Hardware Architecture - raster display devices; **I.3.3** [Computer Graphics]: Picture/Image Generation - display algorithms; **I.3.7** [Computer Graphics]: Three-Dimensional Graphics and Realism - visible surface algorithms

Additional Key Words and Phrases: scanline, antialiasing, transparency, texture mapping, plane equation evaluation, image partitioning

1 INTRODUCTION

This paper describes a low-cost hardware accelerator for rendering 3D graphics with antialiasing. It is based on a previous architecture described by Kelley [10]. The hardware implements an innovative algorithm based on the A-buffer [3] that combines high performance front-to-back compositing of 3D objects with coverage mask evaluation. The hardware also performs triangle setup, depth sorting, texture mapping, transparency, shadows, and Constructive Solid Geometry (CSG) operations. Rasterization speed without antialiasing is 100M pixels/second, providing throughput of 2M texture-mapped triangles/second[1]. The degradation in speed when antialiasing is enabled for a complex scene is 30%, resulting in 70M pixels/second.

Several hardware algorithms have been developed which maintain either high quality or performance while reducing or eliminating the large memory requirement of supersampling [11,8]. An accumulation buffer requires only a fraction of the memory of supersampling, but requires several passes of the

---

[*] 3Dfx Interactive, San Jose, CA USA, winner@3dfx.com, rivard@edfx.com

[†] Silicon Graphics Computer Systems, Mountain View, CA USA, mwk@sgi.com, ayen@sgi.com

[**] Bungie West, San Jose, CA USA, brent@bungie.com

[1] 50 pixel triangles, with tri-linearly interpolated mip-mapped textures.

object data (one pass per subpixel sample) through the hardware rendering pipeline. The resulting image is very high quality, but the performance degrades in proportion to the number of subpixel samples used by the filter function.

An A-buffer implementation does not require several passes of the object data, but does require sorting objects by depth before compositing them. The amount of memory required to store the sorted layers is limited to the number of subpixel samples, but it is significant since the color, opacity and mask data are needed for each layer. The compositing operation uses a blending function which is based on three possible subpixel coverage components and is more computationally intensive than the accumulation buffer blending function. The difficulty of implementing the A-buffer algorithm in hardware is described by Molnar [12].

The A-buffer hardware implementation described in this paper maintains the high performance of the A-buffer using a limited amount of memory. Multiple passes of the object data are sometimes required to composite the data from front-to-back even when antialiasing is disabled. The number of passes required to rasterize a partition increases when antialiasing is used. However, only in the worst case is the number of passes equal to the number of subpixel samples (9, in our system). It is possible to enhance the algorithm as described in [2, 3] to correctly render intersecting objects. The current implementation does not include that enhancement. Furthermore, the algorithm correctly renders images of moderate complexity which have overlapping transparent objects without imposing any constraints on the order in which transparent objects are submitted.

2 SYSTEM OVERVIEW

The hardware accelerator is a single ASIC which performs the 3D rendering and triangle setup. It provides a low-cost solution for high performance 3D acceleration in a personal computer. A second ASIC is used to interface to the system bus or PCI/AGP. The rasterizer uses a screen partitioning algorithm with a partition size of 16x32 pixels. Screen partitioning reduces the memory required for depth sorting and image compositing to a size which can be accommodated inexpensively on-chip. No off-chip memory is needed for the z buffer and dedicated image buffer. The high bandwidth, low latency path between the rasterizer and the on-chip buffers improves performance.

The system's design was guided by three principles. We strove to:

1. Balance the computation between the processor and hardware 3D accelerator;

2. Minimize processor interrupts and system bus bandwidth; and

3. Provide good performance with as little as 2 MB of dedicated memory, but to have performance scale up in higher memory configurations.

The principles inspired the following features:

- The hardware accelerator implements triangle setup to reduce required system bandwidth and balance the computational load between the accelerator and the host processor(s). Multiple rendering ASICs can operate in parallel to match CPU performance.

- The hardware accelerator only interrupts the processor when it has finished processing a frame. This leaves the CPU free to perform geometry, clipping, and shading operations for the next frame while the ASIC is rasterizing the current frame.

- The partition size is 16x32 pixels so that a double-buffered z buffer and image buffer can be stored on-chip. This reduces cost and required memory bandwidth while improving performance. External memory is required for texture map storage, so texture map rendering performance scales with that memory's speed and bandwidth.

In addition to these three design principles, another goal was to provide hardware support for antialiased rendering. Two types of antialiasing quality were desired: a fast mode for interactive rendering, and a slower, high quality mode for producing final images.

For high quality antialiasing, the ASIC uses a traditional accumulation buffer method to antialias each partition by rendering the partition at every subpixel offset and accumulating the results in a off-chip buffer. Because this algorithm is well known [8], this high-quality antialiasing mode is not discussed in this paper.

The more challenging goal was to also provide high quality antialiasing for interactive rendering in less than double the time needed to render a non-antialiased image. We assumed that this type of antialiasing would only be used for playback or previewing, so it could only consume a small portion of the die area. Therefore the challenge in implementing antialiasing was how to properly antialias without maintaining the per pixel coverage and opacity data for each of the layers individually.

Our solution to this problem involves having the ASIC perform Z-ordered shading using a multiple pass algorithm (see the Appendix for psuedo-code of the rendering algorithm). This permits an unlimited number of layers to be rendered for each pixel as in the architecture presented by Mammen [11]. However, because Mammen's architecture performs antialiasing by integrating area samples in multiple passes to successively antialias the image, the number of passes is equal to the number of subpixel positions in the filter kernel. For example, rendering an antialiased image using a typical filter kernel of 8 samples would require 8 times as long as rendering it without antialiasing. Obviously this is too high a performance penalty for use in interactive rendering.

With our modified A-buffer algorithm, the number of passes required to antialias an image is a function of image complexity (opacity and subpixel coverage) in each partition, not the number of subpixel samples. The worst case arises when there are at least 8 layers which have 8 different coverage masks which each cover only one subpixel. This rarely, if ever, occurs in practice. In fact, we have found that an average of only 1.4 passes is required when rendering with a 16x32 partition and an 8 bit mask.

A discussion of the details of the system architecture follows the discussion of the antialiasing algorithm implementation.

2.1 Front-to-Back Antialiasing

The antialiasing algorithm is distributed among three of the major functional blocks of the ASIC (see Figure 1): the Plane Equation Setup, Hidden Surface Removal, and Composite Blocks.

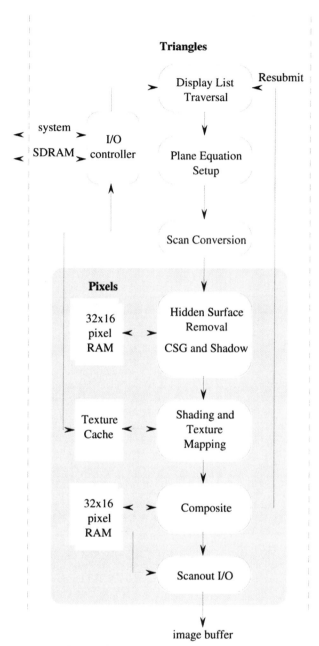

Figure 1. Rasterization ASIC pipeline

The Plane Equation Setup calculates plane equation parameters for each triangle and stores them for later evaluation in the relevant processing blocks. The Scan Conversion generates the subpixel coverage masks for each pixel fragment and outputs them to the rendering pipeline. During the Hidden Surface Removal, fragments of tessellated objects are flagged for specific blend operations during shading. The Composite Block shades pixels by merging the coverage masks and alpha values.

2.2 Coverage Mask Generation

We use a staggered subpixel mask, as shown in Figure 2. Each pixel is divided into 16 subpixels, but only half of the samples are used. The mask is stored as an 8 bit value using the bit assignments shown in Figure 2.

Figure 2. Staggered sub-pixel mask

This staggered mask is similar to the mask used in the triangle processor [5]. It uses only half the memory a grid-aligned 4x4 requires but offers nearly the same quality of antialiasing. Better antialiasing quality can be achieved by increasing the subpixel samples to 64 and using a 32 bit mask. To support that the on-chip image buffer would require nearly 60% more capacity.

The mask generation is performed by treating each scanline as 4 subscanlines and computing 4 coverage segments by using the scan conversion parameters. The triangle edge intersection with the scanline is calculated first. The edge intersection solves the following linear equations:

$$X_{begin} = Slope_{begin} * (CurrentY - Y_0) + X_0.$$

$$X_{end} = Slope_{end} * (CurrentY - Y_1) + X_1.$$

where Y_0, Y_1, X_0 and X_1 are the end points of the edges. Then the begin and end values for the 4 subscanlines are calculated and each pixel is clipped against those segments. The associated coverage mask bit is asserted if the subpixel is not clipped by the segment.

Figure 3 shows an example where each color represents the 16 subpixel samples. The column on the left represents the [begin, end] values of each segment. A subpixel's coverage mask bit is asserted when it is greater than or equal to the begin value and less than the end value. The coverage mask for each pixel is shown in the bottom of the figure.

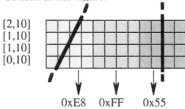

Figure 3. Coverage Mask Generation.

A single set of linear equation evaluators can achieve one pixel per clock output for even small size triangles such as 2X2. In hardware solving a linear equation is more efficient in terms of speed and area than using lookup tables as was done by Schilling [16]. As in Schilling's design [14] and the Reality Engine[2] we exploited the fact that the mask generation is closely related to scan conversion and reused much of the circuitry between those functions.

2.3 Fragment Merging

The Hidden Surface Removal block includes an on-chip buffer for two layers of pixel depth data (depth value and shadow and CSG state information). When objects are rendered in a single pass, only one layer is used. When multiple layers are needed, one layer contains the depth of the data composited during previous passes and the second layer contains the front-most depth of the data which has yet to be composited.

Pixels which are completely covered by opaque objects are resolved in a single pass. When a pixel contains portions of two or more triangles, it is desirable to merge the pixel fragments so that the pixel can be fully composited in one pass. We considered and explored several methods, but did not find a satisfactory solution which permits processing of pixel fragments in a single pass.

We considered using object tags that could be compared during sorting[3], but rejected that approach because of its limitations and the burden it places on software. Object tags require extra memory in the rasterizer as they must be stored along with the depth data for each pixel. The number of unique tags is thus limited by hardware memory. Software must assign a unique tag to each object and must determine how to best reuse tags when the number of objects exceeds the number of tags the hardware supports.

Another method which has been used for combining pixel fragments is to identify ones with similar depths and combine them if their colors are similar [17]. In our architecture the colors are not available during hidden surface removal, so the method of combining pixel fragments can only use the depth data. It is difficult to determine when two depths are similar and should be considered equal. Some software renderers use the minimum of the depth gradient to determine a tolerance within which objects are considered to have equal depth. Since the depth gradients in x and y are readily available, namely the a and b plane equation parameters (see Section 3.2), this seems to be a perfect option.

Unfortunately, in practice it is possible to create scenes in which small triangles, approaching a pixel in size, have large gradients which can not be properly sorted. The gradients output by the Plane Equation Setup are only accurate if the pixel is completely covered, so they are not representative of the actual gradient of a pixel fragment. It is more difficult to compute the true gradient of a pixel fragment, so we tried using a fixed tolerance. However, even when a fixed tolerance is used pixel data is incorrectly discarded during the multiple pass front-to-back depth sorting operation.

We decided that rather than implement a solution which causes serious artifacts we would prefer to have a robust solution and compromise on performance. The solution we used is to only consider two depths to be equal when they match precisely.

2.4 Shading For Antialiasing

Shading is implemented in the Composite Block, which, like the Hidden Surface Removal block, has a two-layer buffer for storing pixel colors and masks. Since the buffers occupy on-chip memory it is necessary to minimize the state information stored in them. Consequently, the pixel color, alpha, and mask for the previously composited data is stored as a single 40-bit value. In addition, a single bit controls the blending functions for color, alpha, and mask. The details of how the composite block functions as part of the pipeline are described later in this paper.

Consider the example of 3 layers of data as shown in Figure 4. Object A's data completely covers the pixel, having a mask of 0xff and an alpha of 0.5. At the end of the first pass the first layer contains A's color, alpha, and mask.

increasing depth

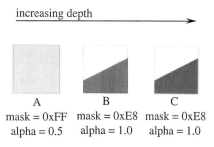

A
mask = 0xFF
alpha = 0.5

B
mask = 0xE8
alpha = 1.0

C
mask = 0xE8
alpha = 1.0

Figure 4. 3 layer composite example.

B's data is opaque, but does not completely cover the pixel, having a mask of 0xE8. First, B's color and alpha is scaled by its mask coverage, 0.5. The result is blended with the data from the previous pass using an AoverB operation [14] where:

$$I = I_{Front} + (1 - \alpha_{Front}) \cdot I_{Back}$$

I_{Back} is the color component intensity of the back object (B), I_{Front} is the color component intensity of the front object (A) pre-multiplied by α_{Front} (A's alpha), and $(1 - \alpha_{Front})$ is the transmission coefficient of the front object.

Blending the mask is a more complex operation. In the A-buffer algorithm the new mask is the bitwise OR of the two masks. In our algorithm, the coverage and transmission coefficients of the two objects are compared and the masks are either bitwise ORed or one mask is selected depending on the results of the comparison. When the front-most layer's mask completely covers the new mask and the new data is more opaque than the front-most layer's, the new mask replaces the previous mask. The opaqueMask flag is asserted for that pixel and is stored in the RAM.

Object C is composited during the third pass. It is opaque and has a mask of 0xE8. When the opaqueMask flag is asserted C's mask is clipped by the previously composited data's mask, resulting in a clipped mask of 0x0. Then C's color and alpha are scaled by the clipped mask coverage and blended behind the frontmost layer using the AoverB function.

Figure 5 shows an image generated with the opaqueMask flag. The scene contains a mostly-transparent layer covering an opaque black triangle which is closer than an identical opaque white triangle. The background is an opaque red layer. Figure 5 was generated with the opaqueMask feature disabled. Notice the fringing artifacts that result when the mask of the white triangle is not clipped by the black triangle.

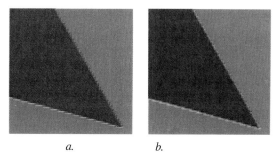

a.

b.

Figure 5. overlapping triangles (a) using the opaqueMask flag and (b) without using the opaqueMask flag.

Implementing the A-buffer algorithm in hardware requires saving the mask for each layer. Instead of combining the masks,

each layer's mask and alpha are saved to properly shade subsequent layers. Unfortunately, the number of layers is unbounded, as is the memory required to store them, so this is not an option. Using the opaqueMask flag to control the blending of the colors and masks allowed us to conserve memory and produce high quality images with some transparency.

Figure 6 shows a more common type of scene rendered with antialiasing enabled. The artifacts which appear where the blue cone overlaps the red cone are a result of the loss of per-layer mask and alpha data when the mask coverage is combined with the alpha as each layer is composited from front-to-back. As mentioned in [2], it is not possible to correctly antialias the intersection of the cones using an alpha antialiasing algorithm.

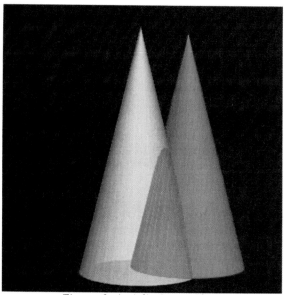

Figure 6. Antialiasing artifacts

Figure 7 shows a more complex scene rendered with and without antialiasing.

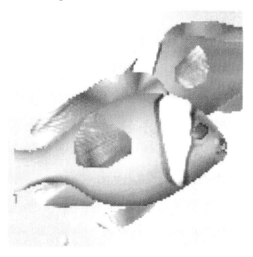

a.

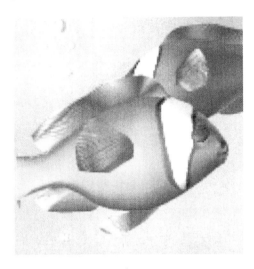

b.

Figure 7. Not antialiased (a) and antialiased (b).

2.5 Antialiased Intersections

It is possible to antialias the intersections by calculating or reconstructing subpixel depth values for each layer. Methods for doing this are described by [2] and [3]. The method described in the A-buffer algorithm works for the intersection of 2 objects, but breaks down when more than two objects intersect unless the Zmin and Zmax values are saved for each layer.

The method for antialiasing intersections used in the Reality Engine uses the x and y slope values and a single depth sample per layer to reconstruct subpixel depth values. This is more accurate than the A-buffer method, but is computationally intensive and requires storing subpixel depth values in the z-buffer.

Neither of these solutions was feasible to implement in an architecture with limited memory, particularly since antialiasing CSG and shadows requires maintaining subpixel CSG and shadow data in the depth buffer. A single CSG and shadow sample requires 12 bits of data, so 8 sub-samples would add 84 bits of data for each of the two layers for a total of 168 bits for each pixel. In order to accommodate that much data on-chip we would have to reduce the partition size which would decrease the performance of non-antialiased scenes.

If Perfection Is Required

There are two methods which can be used to render a high quality antialiased image. Supersampling can be achieved by rendering each partition at higher resolution and filtering it as a post-processing operation (using a separate image processing ASIC). An alternative is to use an accumulation buffer method to antialias the scene by rendering it several times using different subpixel offsets. The result of each rendering pass can be accumulated in a off-chip buffer for each partition.

2.6 Hidden surface removal

With this architecture, unlimited visible layers can be rasterized using multiple passes as in the algorithms described by [11] and [10]. Mammen's algorithm requires that all of the opaque objects be rasterized before transparent objects are rendered. As with the architecture described by Kelley, this does not require transparent objects to be rasterized separately from opaque objects. This is particularly important since a texture mapped

object's alpha values cannot be determined until they are retrieved from memory.

Unlike the architecture described by Kelley, objects in a partition are not depth sorted before shading. Kelley's architecture stored four layers of depth and required multiple passes to sort additional layers. Consequently, the number of layers that can occupy the same depth is limited to 3 or 4. This architecture can render an unlimited number of layers at any depth.

First Pass Sorting

Scenes that contain only opaque data and no shadows or CSG can be resolved in a single pass through the pipeline. Otherwise multiple passes are required to resolve the final color for each pixel in the scene. The operations that occur in the second and subsequent passes through the rendering pipeline differ from those that occur in the first.

During the first pass each input pixel depth is compared with the depth of the frontmost object received so far for the pass (see the Appendix for psuedo-code). The depth is a 25 bit floating point value with a 19 bit mantissa and a 6 bit exponent. Objects are not sorted before compositing begins. Instead, any object which passes the depth sort test is passed down the pipeline immediately.

When the compositing engine receives the coverage mask, opacity, and color data for a pixel, it stores the data in the image buffer. Any data already in the buffer it is overwritten (discarded) since it would fall behind the new data. Before being discarded, though, it is examined to determine if it would have contributed to the final pixel color. If so, a flag is set for that pixel which and is used at the end of the pass to initiate another rendering pass of the same partition.

After the last object enters the pipeline, the Display List Traversal sends a synchronization token before moving to the next partition. The Composite block interrupts the Display List Traversal when it receives that synchronization token (labeled Resubmit in Figure 1) and the Display List Traversal determines whether another pass is required before moving to the next partition. The latency incurred by waiting for the interrupt can be minimized with a predictive algorithm that begins re-fetching the data for another pass or pre-fetching data for the next partition.

Unlimited Equal Depth Layers

It is possible to composite an unlimited number of layers which have equal depth in a single pass. Equal layers are identified during the depth sort and are composited using additive blending after the new layer is clipped by the coverage mask of the existing layer.

In the current implementation, equality occurs when the depth values match precisely. Performance would be improved if a robust method for combining objects which have nearly equal depths could be used (refer to the previous section on fragment merging).

Subsequent Pass Sorting

The sort and composite operations are modified when multiple passes are required. The data in the depth and image buffers is retained at the end of each pass. Second depth and image buffers are used for storing the input pixel data.

During the depth sort, each object is compared with the final depth of the previous pass and the front-most depth of the current pass. If the object's depth falls between the two, or if it matches the front-most depth of the existing pass, it is passed to the composite block.

The composite block blends the colors of any objects which are equal in depth using an AoverB blend. The masks are combined and the results are stored in the second buffer. As in the case of the first pass, writing the second buffer sometimes causes data which was composited earlier during the same pass to be overwritten. It is necessary to determine if that discarded data would have contributed to the final pixel color. Again, a flag is set for that pixel which is used at the end of the pass to initiate another rendering pass of the same partition.

When the input object's depth is equal to that of the previously composited data, its coverage mask is clipped by the previous pass's coverage mask and blended (AoverB) with the data in the composite buffer.

This architecture requires all data for a partition to be submitted during each pass. In the case of equal depths it is also important that the data arrive in the same order since the first object at a particular depth is considered to be in front of any objects at the same depth which are received later (first-come-first-rendered).

2.7 Image Partitioning

Several screen partition based rasterizers have been proposed or built [13,6,15,18]. A motivating factor in using image partitioning is that the depth and image buffers can be stored on-chip. This improves performance and reduces the pin count of the ASIC (assuming the buffers would have dedicated ports for performance reasons). As in the case of other partition based renderers [10,17], performance is also improved since multiple passes are used to resolve the portions of the final image which contain the greatest depth complexity.

The primary disadvantage of partition based renderers is the inherent latency resulting for the need to construct a bucket sorted display list. Another disadvantage of partition based rasterizers is that data which appears in multiple partitions must be transferred from system memory multiple times or cached locally. Some partition based designs [5,10] used a one dimensional partition. In the best case an object had to be transferred once for every scanline it touched. It is important to exploit the inherent 2 dimensional image coherence to reduce the system memory bandwidth required to transfer the object data.

Two Dimensional Bucket Sorting

After the triangles are projected into screen space they are partitioned into each 16x32 partition that intersects with the triangle. Since determining which partition a triangle belongs in can be computationally expensive 2 different algorithms are used depending on the size of the triangle. Triangles that are approximately the size of a single partition or smaller are unlikely to span more than 1 or 2 partitions and are hence easier to sort. Small triangles are included in the bucket for each partition which is overlapped by the triangle's bounding box.

Triangles that are much larger than a partition are more difficult since their orientation will effect which partitions they intersect. It is important to avoid adding triangles to partitions that do not intersect the triangle, this can waste memory, bandwidth and performance. The edge slopes of large triangles are used to compute which partitions they cover.

In order to reduce the size of the display list, triangles can share vertices. Through the use of the QuickDraw ™ 3D and

QuickDraw™ 3D RAVE TriMesh data structures vertex sharing is easily achieved even after an object has been clipped and projected onto the screen. In the best case, vertex sharing permits each new vertex to define two new triangles. In that case the number of triangles is double the number of vertices.

3 SYSTEM ARCHITECTURE

The rendering tasks are divided between the host CPU and 3D accelerator to balance the overall system. The host CPU performs the transformation, clipping and shading functions. The algorithms which perform these functions are described in detail in [1,4,9]. It also generates the display list using a linked list structure to link the object lists for each partition. The hardware accelerator performs the rasterization by following the linked list. It DMAs the object data from system memory and only interrupts the CPU at the end of the list/frame.

The ASIC rasterizer is a pipelined design shown in figure 1. It reads triangle data and outputs texture mapped, shaded, pixels. The depth and image buffers are on-chip to minimize latency and maximize bandwidth. The ASIC is clocked at 100MHz.

3.1 Display List Traversal

This module reads the triangle vertex data by following a linked list which was constructed by software during the partition sort.

3.2 Plane Equation Setup

The scan conversion of the triangles is performed using plane equation evaluation as in the PixelPlanes design [7]. A plane equation is used to describe the relationship between a plane in screen space and any three points inside the plane. Algebraically, a plane can be described using this equation:

$$z = a * x + b * y + c.$$

The equation can be evaluated for any point (x,y,z) in screen space. The linear relationship between the three points (x_0, y_0, z_0), (x_1, y_1, z_1), (x_2, y_2, z_2) and the above plane equation is

$$\begin{pmatrix} z0 \\ z1 \\ z2 \end{pmatrix} = \begin{pmatrix} x0 & y0 & 1 \\ x1 & y1 & 1 \\ x2 & y2 & 1 \end{pmatrix} \begin{pmatrix} a \\ b \\ c \end{pmatrix}$$

The plane equation setup module takes the vertex data and generates the coefficients, a, b, and c, for each parameter's plane equation. The parameters include the color, alpha, depth, and texture map coordinates.

The plane equation setup eliminates the standard two passes of linear interpolation (lirp) in both x and y directions and is more accurate. The coefficient calculation is implemented in a systolic array, so the internal bandwidth is greater than a two pass lirp implementation [10].

Once the coefficients are calculated, they are passed down the pipeline and stored in the module where they will be used to evaluate the associated parameters; for example, the depth coefficients are stored in the Hidden Surface Removal module. The coefficients can be passed down a separate pipeline at a rate of one coefficient per clock cycle and double-buffered in the evaluation module, thus minimizing the overhead and bandwidth associated with plane equation parameter passing. The use of plane equation evaluation for a given shading parameter at a specific pipeline stage is more efficient than passing down the evaluated parameters for each pixel during every clock cycle.

3.3 Hidden Surface Removal

This module depth sorts a pixel per clock cycle. There is enough storage for two layers of depth, shadow, and CSG data. During the first pass of a partition only one layer is used.

3.4 Texture Map Lookup

The texture mapping module implements traditional mip-mapped bilinear and trilinear texturing [19]. A target square or non-square texture map can be up to 2048 texels on a side and either 16 or 32 bits per texel. Each texture mapped pixel produced by this system results from applying a filter function to either four (bilinear) or eight (trilinear) texels. The filter function is a linear interpolation between texel samples, weighted by the fractional portion of the horizontal (u) and vertical (v) lookup indices.

Our goal was to perform trilinear texture mapping at an average run rate of one pixel per clock cycle. The difficulty in achieving this performance goal arises from the fact that the interpolation operation needs an input feed rate of four or eight 32-bit texel colors per clock cycle. Building a texture memory subsystem that could sustain this bandwidth (1600 MBytes per second sustained random accesses for bilinear mapping, 3200 MBps for trilinear) is not feasible in a personal computer today. Instead, we chose to build an on-chip texel cache to provide most of the necessary bandwidth.

The texel cache harnesses two different types of pixel to pixel temporal locality from the bilinear texel access patterns. We refer to these types as "most recent four" and "line to line". Both patterns of temporal locality arise from our use of mip-mapping, which limits the pixel to pixel sampling stride through texture space. In our texel cache system, we use two different but coupled cache modules. One cache module captures most recent four reuse, and the other captures line to line reuse. Two such cache pairs provide the eight necessary texel samples for trilinear texture mapping.

The most recent four access pattern is illustrated in Figure 8. In this figure, a pixel associated with a particular draw object required the center 2x2 block of texels (shown in blue) for bilinear interpolation; the next pixel associated with that object will need a similar 2x2 block to be sampled (shown as a bolded square outline). But, because the sampling stride is constrained, we are sure to re-use at least one of the four texels from the previous pixel. On average we can expect to hit about two texels per pixel when caching the most recent four texels. The structure needed to implement this cache is a 4-entry, 4-port fully associative cache with an always-replace write policy for all four entries.

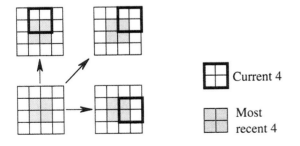

Figure 8. Most recent four texel reuse.

Line to line temporal locality is illustrated in Figure 9. The figure shows a triangle's bilinear sampling trace correspondence between screen and texture space. Each consecutive pixel on a scan line has an increasing X value (i.e., line A starts at X=1 and ends at X=8). There are six lines composing an example triangle in this figure (A through F). Bilinear sample points occur at the intersection of the A through F arrows and the X=1 through X=8 lines. The texels sampled for line A are shaded in the texture space portion of the figure. Those texels sampled by line A at x=4 and again by line B at x=4 are shaded in red.

Note that there is no simple spatial locality for a texture cache to utilize short of the cache itself embodying a texture lookup mechanism. However, given the fact that our rasterization is horizontally bounded (by our partition size), there is temporal locality which can be utilized by a relatively small associative-type cache.

A 4-port fully associative cache with LRU (least recently used) replacement policy could be used to capture both line to line and most recent four texel reuse, however such a structure would be unnecessarily large. The line to line texel reuse will always be correlated through X. As an example, in Figure 9 two of the texels sampled by line A (the upper two shown in red) were sampled at X=4; the remaining re-used texel was sampled at X=5. By limiting our associative search aperture to sampled texels adjacent to and including X (X+1, X, and X-1) we simplify the lookup and compare hardware. Only a three read port, one (or two) write port cache tag memory is needed, with twelve (maximum) comparators. A fully associative cache would require an N read port, four write port cache tag memory with N*4 comparators.

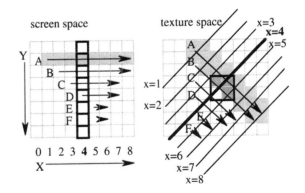

Figure 9.

By selectively saving one (or two) of the four texel samples for each pixel (indexed to X), it will be available for the next line of a particular draw object. The choice of which texel to save is easily determined by examining the sign bits of the object's u and v gradients. For example, if the next line in pixel space is going to sample down and to the right of the current line in texel space, then we save the bottom right of the four current texels (or bottom two texels with a two write port cache tag memory).

To determine if the line to line cache has a hit, the pixel space indices X+1, X, and X-1 are used to look up the previously stored addresses (stored as texel cache tags) for the one selected texel associated with that X value. A match indicates a hit. At the end of that cycle, a new cache tag (the selected texel address) is written to the cache tag store.

In our implementation, we chose to allow the line cache to report exactly one hit from the possible three texels examined at X+1, X and X-1. To minimize the overall cache performance degradation due to redundant hits between the most recent four and line caches, an inhibit signal is passed from the four cache module to the line cache module that suppresses reporting of redundant texel hits. In this way, the line cache will always report a unique hit if one is available.

With the four cache hitting an average of two texels per pixel, and the line cache frequently hitting a unique texel per pixel, an average of nearly three out of the needed four texels can be achieved in the high resolution mip-map. The low resolution map has a texel stride half that of the high resolution map and therefore achieves even better average hits. The remaining one to two average texels needed per trilinear pixel can be comfortably read from our pipelined SDRAM memory system.

Due to the 10 to 12 cycle read latency of the SDRAM memory system, it was necessary to split the cache tags and cache data in the pipeline. The cache tag control module shown in Figure 10 contains all of the cache tag state for data that will arrive and be cached some time later in the cache data controller. The synchronizer module aligns the arrival of texel color data from the SDRAM memory system with the arrival of cache tag data from the Texel Cache Tag Control module.

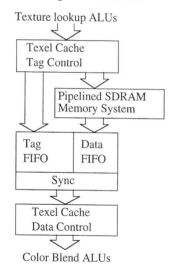

Figure 10. Split cache tag-data architecture.

The Texture Lookup CPUs in Figure 10 calculate texel sample addresses and pass these addresses to the Texel Cache Controller. Four addresses per cycle for each bilinear pixel are generated. Eight addresses per cycle are generated for each trilinear pixel. At the bottom of the texel cache pipeline a corresponding number of colors (four or eight) are presented to the Color Blend ALUs where color highlights and color modulation are applied to the raw bilinear or trilinear pixel color. The final rendered pixel color is passed further down the pipeline for compositing with other pixels.

3.5 Front-to-back Compositing

The final pixel processing is performed by compositing the incoming pixel layers in front-to-back order, after which the resulting ARGB values are output to the frame buffer. There is enough storage for 2 layers of image data. During the first pass only one layer is used. The second layer contains the final image data for the previous partition and can be scanned out of

the ASIC while the next partition is being composited (at least during the first pass). This is a standard double-buffering technique.

3.6 Scalable Performance

A low cost, single card implementation of the 3D accelerator is shown in figure 11. Texture map data is stored in the SDRAM connected to the 3D accelerator. The SDRAM connected to the I/O interface is optional; it can be used to store additional texture map data or vertex data. Storing the texture map data locally reducing the PCI bandwidth when texture mapping is used. Storing vertex data locally reduces the PCI bandwidth when triangles cross partition boundaries since they will only be loaded onto the card once. It also reduces PCI bandwidth if resubmission is required to resolve the final pixel values for a partition.

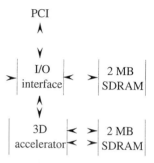

Figure 11. Low cost card implementation.

To improve performance it is possible to use multiple rasterizer ASICs in parallel as described by Fuchs in [6]. The I/O interface ASIC can drive up to 4 rasterizer ASICs as shown in Figure 12. The image buffer outputs of each rasterizer are merged by a Frame Buffer Interface (not designed as part of this project) which transfers each partition to the frame buffer (VRAM).

The frame buffer must be local to the rasterizer ASIC since PCI could not sustain the bandwidth required to support a 1280x1152 display at 30fps (177 MBytes/sec). A typical input bandwidth is 100 MBytes/sec which can be sustained by 32 bit 33MHz PCI.

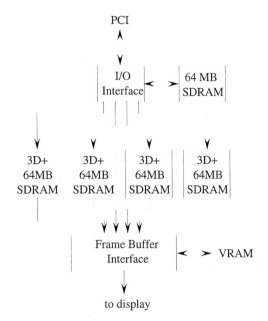

Figure 12. High performance card implementation

4 CONCLUSIONS

These are the main design goals met by the system:

High Performance Antialiasing

The performance when the modified A-buffer antialiasing is used is only 40% slower than when antialiasing is used. This is much better than performance degradation required for using an accumulation buffer or supersample method of antialiasing.

Low Memory Bandwidth and Capacity

The off-chip memory requirement for the depth buffer is eliminated. There is an on-chip image buffer so that the output is a write-only path to the frame buffer memory. Implementing these buffers on chip also reduces memory bandwidth. The on chip texture cache reduces the memory bandwidth needed for texture mapping. Dedicated memory can be used for texture and vertex data to further reduce the system memory bandwidth and improve rasterization performance.

Balance Between CPU and Rendering ASIC

The ASIC only interrupts the CPU at the end of each frame. This is required to process the 3D geometry as quickly as possible. Using dedicated memory with the 3D accelerator will also improve the system performance since it reduces the bandwidth load on the system memory.

5 FUTURE WORK

As mentioned it is necessary to develop a robust method for merging pixel fragments. This will reduce the number of passes required to perform antialiasing, improving image quality and performance. The quality of antialiasing can be further improved by increasing the number subpixel samples from 16 to 64. A method of antialiasing interpenetrating objects must also be incorporated. Finally, additional data should be included in the z and image buffers to properly antialias shadows and CSG.

ACKNOWLEDGMENTS

The authors wish to thank Paul Baker and Jack McHenry for supporting this project in Apple's Interactive 3D Graphics group. Thanks to Bill Garrett and Sun-Inn Shih for their reviews.

APPENDIX: PSEUDO-CODE

The following pseudo-code summarizes the rendering algorithm:

```
RenderFrame()
{
  /* object loop: transform, shade, sort */
  foreach (object)
  {
    Transform (object);
    Shade (object);
    PartitionSort (object);
  }

  /* partition loop: rasterize */
  foreach (partition)
  {
    InitPartition (partition);
    Rasterize (partition);
  }
}
```

The object loop is executed by the host CPU and the partition loop funtionality is embodied in the ASIC.

The following pseudo-code is a simplified version of the multipass rasterization loop:

```
/* rasterize loop: first layer */
foreach (object)
{
  foreach (pixel)
  {
    if (depth_pixel[x][y] <= depth_buf[x][y])
    {
      depth_buf[x][y] = depth_pixel[x][y];
      composite_buf[x][y] = Composite(pixel);
    }
  }
}
while ( Resubmit )
{
  firstDepth = depth_buf;
  firstComposite = composite_buf;
  clear(depth_buf);
  clear(composite_buf);

  foreach (object)
  {
    foreach (pixel)
    {
      if (depth_pixel[x][y] > firstDepth[x][y])
      {
        if (depth_pixel[x][y] !>
            depth_buf[x][y])
        {
          depth_buf[x][y] = depth_pixel[x][y];
```

```
        composite_buf[x][y] =
            CompositeFirst+pixel(pixel);
        }
      }
    }
  }
}
```

REFERENCES

[1] Kurt Akeley and T. Jermoluk. High-Performance Polygon Rendering. *Computer Graphics (SIGGRAPH 88 Conference Proceedings)*, volume 22, number 4, pages 239-246. August 1988.

[2] Kurt Akeley. RealityEngine Graphics. *SIGGRAPH 93 Conference Proceedings*, pages 109-116. August 1993. ISBN 0-89791-601-8.

[3] Loren Carpenter. The A-buffer, an Antialiased Hidden Surface Method. *Computer Graphics, (SIGGRAPH 84 Conference Proceedings)*, volume 18, number 3, pages 103-108. July 1984. ISBN 0-89791-138-5.

[4] Michael Deering and S. Nelson, Leo: A System for Cost Effective 3D Shaded Graphics. *SIGGRAPH 93 Conference Proceedings*, pages 101-108. August 1993.

[5] Michael Deering, S. Winner, B. Schediwy, C. Duffy and N. Hunt. The Triangle Processor and Normal Vector Shader: A VLSI System for High Performance Graphics. *Computer Graphics, (SIGGRAPH 88 Conference Proceedings)*, volume 22, number 4, pages 21-30. August 1988

[6] Henry Fuchs. Distributing a Visible Surface Algorithm over Multiple Processors. *Preceeding of the 6th ACM-IEEE Symposium on Computer Architecture*, pages 58-67. April, 1979.

[7] Henry Fuchs et al. Fast Spheres, Shadows, Textures, Transparencies, and Image Enhancements in Pixel-Planes. *Computer Graphics, (SIGGRAPH 85 Conference Proceedings)*, volume 19, number 3, pages 111-120. July 1985.

[8] Paul Haeberli and Kurt Akeley. The Accumulation Buffer: Hardware Support for High-Quality Rendering. *Computer Graphics, (SIGGRAPH 90 Conference Proceedings)*, volume 24, number 4, pages 309-318. August 1990. ISBN 0-89791-344-2.

[9] Chandlee Harrell and F. Fouladi. Graphics Rendering Architecture for a High Performance Desktop Workstation. *SIGGRAPH 93 Conference Proceedings*, pages 93-100. August 1993.

[10] Michael Kelley, K. Gould, B. Pease, S. Winner, and A. Yen. Hardware Accelerated Rendering of CSG and Transparency. *SIGGRAPH 94 Conference Proceedings*, pages 177-184. 1994.

[11] Abraham Mammen. Transparency and Antialiasing Algorithms Implemented with the Virtual Pixel Maps Technique. *IEEE Computer Graphics and Applications*, 9(4), pages 43-55. July 1989. ISBN 0272-17-16.

[12] Steven Molnar, John Eyles, and John Poulton. PixelFlow: High-Speed Rendering Using Image Composition. *Computer Graphics, (SIGGRAPH 92 Conference Proceedings)*, volume 26, number 2, pages 231-240. July 1992.

[13] F. Park. Simulation and Expected Performance Analysis of Multiple Processor Z-Buffer Systems. *Computer Graphics, (SIGGRAPH 80 Conference Proceedings)*, pages 48-56. 1980.

[14] Thomas Porter and Tom Duff. Compositing Digital Images. *Computer Graphics, (SIGGRAPH 84 Conference Proceedings)*, volume 18, number 3, pages 253-259. July 1984. ISBN 0-89791-138-5.

[15] PowerVR, NEC/VideoLogic 1996.

[16] Andreas Schilling. A New Simple and Efficient Antialiasing with Subpixel Masks. *Computer Graphics, (SIGGRAPH 91 Conference Proceedings)*, volume 25, number 4, pages 133-141. July 1991.

[17] Jay Torborg and James Kajiya. Talisman: Commodity Realtime 3D Graphics for the PC. *SIGGRAPH 96 Conference Proceedings*, pages 353-363. 1996.

[18] G. Watkins. A Real-Time Visible Surface Algorithm. Computer Science Department, University of Utah, UTECH-CSC-70-101. June 1970.

[19] Lance Williams. Pyramidal Parametrics. *SIGGRAPH 83 Conference Proceedings*, pages 1-11. July 1983.

Antialiasing of Curves by Discrete Pre-filtering

A.E. Fabris[†]   and   A.R. Forrest[*]
Universidade de São Paulo   University of East Anglia

ABSTRACT

Pre-filtering is generally considered the ideal approach to anti-aliasing but is difficult to perform exactly for complex geometries such as curves or for arbitrary choice of filters. We present a discrete pre-filtering technique for anti-aliasing Bézier curves using arbitrary filters which is numerically and geometrically robust and whose accuracy is controllable.

CR Categories and Subject Descriptors: I.3.3 [Computer Graphics]: Picture/Image Generation — antialiasing
Additional Keywords: Bézier curves, pre-filtering

1   INTRODUCTION

The causes of aliasing in computer generated imagery are well known and may be broken down into two components: aliasing due to inadequate sampling of the ideal image and aliasing due to incorrect or inadequate reconstruction of the displayed image from the samples. Many techniques have been proposed but there is no ideal or universal solution and compromises have to be made. As Mitchell and Netravali [29] point out, graphics has generally avoided the issues of reconstruction but with increasing use of non-c.r.t. displays it is now clear that anti-aliasing should take into account the reconstruction properties of the display device [22]. In this paper we describe an anti-aliasing technique for curves which not only avoids the geometric and numerical problems found in previous techniques but also permits the use of arbitrary filters thus enabling rendering to be tuned to specific output devices. This is achieved by combining the point containment approach of Corthout and Pol [6,7,8] with a pre-filtering technique akin to but more general than Gupta and Sproull [18]

2   PRE- AND POST-FILTERING

A naïve view of aliasing ascribes the problem to treating a pixel as a point rather than an area. Following this view, aliasing can be avoided by area sampling rather than point sampling: we compute the fractions of a pixel covered by components of the *ideal image* lying within the pixel and use these fractions to weight the fragment colours, accumulating the sum of fragment contributions

†   Instituto de Matématica e Estatistica, Caixa Postal 66281, CEP 05315-970, São Paulo - SP - Brazil, aef@ime.usp.br
*   School of Information Systems, Norwich NR4 7TJ, U.K. forrest@sys.uea.ac.uk

into the pixel value. Signal processing, on the other hand, shows that the problem lies in attempting to reconstruct an image which contains spatial frequencies higher than the maximum spatial frequency which the output device can display: we cannot correctly reconstruct an image which contains frequencies greater than or equal to half the sampling frequency. The solution is therefore to remove high frequency components before display by filtering. Area sampling can be shown to be a simple form of filtering—box filtering, but signal processing proves that better filters are possible.

There are two possible methods of filtering the ideal image: pre-filtering and post-filtering. In post-filtering the ideal image is point sampled at a higher rate than can be displayed, with multiple samples per pixel, and the samples are then numerically filtered by a discrete digital filter. Area sampling may be approximated numerically by averaging a regularly spaced super-sampling of a pixel. More sophisticated digital filters such as the Bartlett filter [10] give better results. However, regular super-sampling may still give rise to aliasing through missing important fragments. To overcome this, super-samples may be distributed in some stochastic manner [4] and reconstructed by a more complicated process, but the downside is the introduction of noise into the image. This may be considered more acceptable than jaggies although still highly visible.

The advantages of post-filtering lie largely in the simplicity of the process. In some applications, such as ray tracing, super-sampling followed by post-filtering is the only reasonable solution to aliasing. The disadvantages are the greatly increased costs of computation and the failure to eliminate aliasing completely.

If a precise geometric description of the ideal image is available, say analytic or piecewise analytic descriptions, then it is theoretically possible to filter the ideal image analytically to remove high frequency spatial components before sampling and then to point sample the bandwidth limited ideal image to produce alias-free images. For example, for simple geometries such as straight lines, we can pre-filter the geometry by a box filter by deriving expressions for pixel area coverage: sampling is then reduced to substitution of pixel coordinates in the expressions.

The advantages of pre-filtering are that once the ideal image has been analytically pre-filtered, a single sample per pixel suffices. The expectation is that if we can properly pre-filter the ideal image, then we will generate high quality displayed images. The main disadvantages heretofore have been the restricted range of geometries that could be pre-filtered and the restricted range of filters which could be employed. Pre-filtering will however remain a technique more appropriate to high quality two-dimensional images containing lines, regions and text rather than images of three-dimensional scenes.

3   PRIOR WORK ON PRE-FILTERING

Pitteway and Watkinson [33] describe the incorporation of area sampling in the Bresenham line algorithm, but do not handle line ends properly. Gupta and Sproull [18] developed an antialiased version of the Bresenham line algorithm in which, at least notionally, the ideal line is convolved with a circularly symmetric filter. In their implementation a lookup table is constructed which contains the fractions of the volume of the conical filter intercepted by the ideal line, indexed by the perpendicular distance of the pixel centre from the centre of the line. This table can be generated from a simply derived analytic expression. The circular symmetry enables a single one-dimensional table to cover lines at all possible angles. Analytic expressions for line ends, however, are difficult to derive and Gupta-Sproull resort to less precise two-dimensional tables. Whilst circular symmetry leads to a fast incremental algorithm, the conical filter does not give rise to a flat constant signal for constant sample values, thus exhibiting what Mitchell and Netravali call sample-frequency ripple. Forrest gives examples of this for various filter radii [16].

Feibush, Levoy and Cook [14] describe antialiasing of polygons in which polygons are first split into triangles; the volume of the filter intersected by each triangle is used as a weight. In effect this amounts to a discrete approximation to the convolution integral applied to polygon fragments. In one implementation a two-dimensional lookup table stores triangle-cone intersections. If the chosen filter is not circularly symmetric, the lookup table is considerably more complex, being four-dimensional. Abram, Westover and Whitted [1] develop a more complex approach in which polygon-filter convolution is classified in several different cases, each of which employs a discrete approximation to the convolution integral.

Duff's polygon scan conversion by exact convolution [11] numerically integrates the convolution integral to antialias simple polygons. Filters are more general than in other methods but are limited to bivariate polynomials which can be used to approximate sinc and other filters.

McCool [27] describes a method whereby an image consisting of Gouraud-shaded triangles can be represented by simplex splines; these can then be convolved with a box spline filter to form a set of prism splines representing the filtered image. This permits analytic filtering by filters which can be constructed from box spline basis functions, a special case being tensor product B-splines. Any further filtering for reconstruction is performed by digital post-processing.

4 PRIOR WORK ON ANTIALIASING CURVES

Aliased scan conversion of curves is still a topic for further research: whilst there exist efficient algorithms for circles and ellipses (although long thin ellipses still need special care), more general parametric, explicit or implicit curves generally require careful attention to both geometric and numerical detail in order to provide robust and efficient algorithms. In many cases the approach taken is to reduce the curve to a piecewise linear approximation which can then be antialiased; avoiding any visual evidence of polygonisation requires care.

Lien, Shantz and Pratt [26] develop an adaptive forward difference method for rendering curves and briefly mention a simple adaptation to their algorithm which enables an admittedly rough approximation to area sampling to be made. In effect the curve is approximated by short straight line segments. Klassen [23] emphasises the geometric problems found in rendering curves, particularly loops, cusps, and crossings, and goes on to develop a more robust approach than [26]. A curve is split into

monotonic sections (with respect to the x or y axes) then adaptive forward differencing is used to divide the curve into short straight line segments which may then be antialiased by the Gupta Sproull algorithm [18] or by any other filter which can be accessed from a lookup table in a similar manner. The transitions from x major to y-major line segments (and vice versa) need special attention to avoid "nicks" in the output. Klassen pays particular attention to numerical detail.

Field [15] describes a fast incremental method for antialiasing circles and ellipses based on a predictor-corrector method to compute filter values. The filter employed is an approximation to area sampling. Pitteway and Banissi [32] describe an integer algorithm for rendering antialiased ellipses which employs an approximation to area sampling sufficient for a two bit per pixel system, this giving a marked improvement in the rendering of fonts composed of conic segments.

Prior methods are seen to be restricted in terms of filters, employing either box or conical filters which are known to be poor. Curves, apart from circles and ellipses, are approximated by line segments rather than being antialiased directly as curves, and geometric special cases need careful treatment.

5 DISCRETE PRE-FILTERING

Consider the problem of pre-filtering an image as a three-dimensional problem in which the ideal image is a function $I(x,y)$ of the continuous spatial variables x and y, I representing the intensity (or colour) of the ideal image. The cross section of a line in a plane perpendicular to the line centre has a rectangular profile. Looking at the problem in this way, we can antialias by area sampling simply by convolving the intensity profile of the line with a box filter. Figure 1 shows several intensity profiles of three widths of lines (dark rectangles) with the corresponding box filtered profiles superimposed in gray. Area sampling is reduced to point sampling the convolved intensity profile. Figure 2 shows a three-dimensional view of a typical section of a 1.5 pixel-wide line after box filtering (the ruled surface end caps are not drawn).

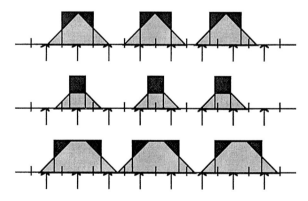

↑ pixel centre/sample point

ı pixel boundary

Figure 1

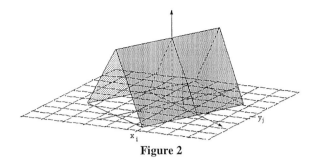

Figure 2

Lines and curves may be generated by continuous sweep of a brush along the mathematical centre of the line or curve [17]. Guibas et al. [19] refer to this process as convolving the curve with a brush, but in this paper we shall use the term *dilation* to denote the effect of brushing in order to avoid confusion with convolving a geometric object with a filter. Antialiased lines and curves of arbitrary width may similarly be generated by brushing with an ideal brush which has been convolved with some appropriate form of filter, resulting in intensity profiles of more complicated form than that shown in Figure 2 but of similar nature. Crow [9] describes line and character generation by an assembly of overlapping bump functions positioned to sub-pixel accuracy. The Quantel Paintbox painting system developed somewhat later uses a similar technique in which hand-drawn curves are painted as overlapping imprints of sub-pixel positioned cylindrical brushes convolved with an apparently ad hoc filter [34]. Whitted strokes curves with a brush of arbitrary footprint and intensity profile, using a Z-buffer technique to overwrite only those pixels where current position of the brush indexes a greater intensity than in previous writes [36]. In our approach however, we do not approximate the curve by a series of overlapping blobs or a series of straight line segments but sample the convolved ideal image by an approximate method whose accuracy is controllable both spatially and in terms of intensity [7,8,12,13].

6   POINT CONTAINMENT AND ANTIALIASING

The conventional approach to rendering would be to scan convert the convolved version of the curve but this as we have remarked earlier leads to numerical and geometric problems. Instead we chose to use the *point containment algorithm* developed by Corthout et al. to implement a pre-filtering algorithm along the lines of but more general than Gupta-Sproull [18]. Extension of their method to handle curves would involve computing the closest distance of a curve centre line to a pixel centre, a complex geometric calculation obviated by our approach. Brooks [3] quoting Poulton points out that if current hardware trends continue, the number of pixels per primitive rendered by hardware will approach unity, and in such circumstances we might as well compute pixels directly from the underlying geometry rather than first approximating the geometry by polygons or line segments. The point containment approach is an example of this strategy, generating pixels directly from Bézier curves and thus avoiding the difficulties in curve rendering tackled by Klassen [23] and Lien et al. [26]. In [5] Corthout and Jonkers describe an algorithm for determining the containment of a point within a region bounded by discrete Bézier curves. This is extended in [6] to encompass discrete rational Bézier curves and in [7,8] to support dilation and erosion of discrete Bézier curves and regions bounded by discrete Bézier curve by brushes which may be regions bounded by discrete Bézier curves. Extensions to the algorithm include the ability to transform the brush whilst stroking.

Corthout and Pol's thesis [8] contains full details of the mathematical theory of discrete Bézier curves, a version of the Jordan curve theorem for regions bounded by discrete curves, a formal development of the point containment algorithm and a description of its implementation in dedicated silicon, the Pharos chip. Recognising that at some stage we have to make the transition from the continuous world to the discrete, Corthout and Pol define discrete Bézier curves in a discrete model space which is of higher precision than device space. Discretisation is readily performed in a controlled fashion using a simple discrete integer space rather than floating point. [8] contains details of the overall integer precision required for rendering on a chosen device together with proofs of robustness and accuracy.

For each pixel in the image the point containment algorithm has to determine whether the pixel centre lies within the dilated curve. Rather than testing all pixels in the image, an obvious optimisation restricts testing to pixels lying within the bounding box of the curve dilated by the bounding box of the brush. Further optimisations of increasing complexity are described in [8]. Determining whether a pixel centre lies within the region defined by the dilated curve is non-trivial but fortunately the dual problem of determining whether the curve intersects the region defined by dilation of the pixel centre by the brush is rather simpler, Figure 3. Corthout and Pol describe an efficient recursive algorithm using integer arithmetic in [8].

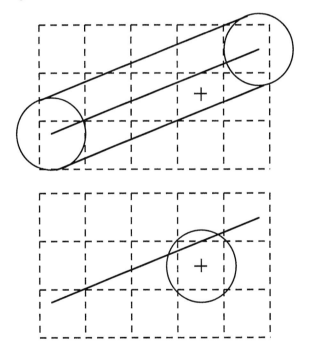

Figure 3

A discrete Bézier curve can be computed by subdivision on an integer grid of specified resolution. Figure 4 shows a typical 8-connected discrete curve computed on a grid with 4 times pixel resolution with a circular brush of radius 1.25 pixels centred on each point of the discrete curve to approximate the dilated curve. Pixels whose centre lie within the dilated curve are rendered by the point containment algorithm: inclusion of just one of the discrete curve points within a brush centred on a pixel will cause that pixel to be rendered, Figure 3. The accuracy of the discrete intersection test is a function of the sub-pixel resolution chosen for the discrete curve which reflects both the need to accommodate rounding errors [8] and the higher spatial resolution dictated by antialiasing [25].

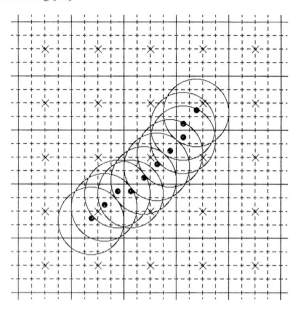

Figure 4

The algorithm relies on three predicates:

- `NotInDilatedBBox` — if the test pixel is outside the dilation of the bounding box of the discrete Bézier curve dilated by the bounding box of the brush, then NOT_COVERED is returned and the algorithm terminates.

- `At` — if the query point is covered by the brush placed at either end of the curve, COVERED is returned. For a circular or square brush this predicate is simply implemented, as in our initial system. More elaborate shapes are discussed in [8].

- `BaseCase` — if the curve is primitive, that is to say length of the curve is ≤1 measured in the discrete space selected, then TRUE is returned.

6.1 Standard Stroking

```
Discrete Curve C;
Brush B;
Pixel P;
{for(each pixel P in the image)
    if(Dilate(C,B,P)==COVERED) then Render(P);
}

Dilate(C,B,P)
/* returns COVERED if P is covered by C+B */
DiscreteCurve C
Brush B
Pixel P
{   if(Stroke(C-P,B)==COVERED) then
        return(COVERED)
    else return(NOT_COVERED);
}
```

```
Stroke(C,B)
/* detects whether the origin is covered */
/* by C+B */
DiscreteCurve C;
Brush B;
{  n=Length(C);
    if(NotInDilatedBBox(C,B))
return(NOT_COVERED);
/* test start point of curve */
    if(At(c[0],B)) return(COVERED);
/* test end point of curve */
    if(At(C[n],B)) return(COVERED);
    if(BaseCase(C)) return(NOT_COVERED);
    left=LeftHalf(C);
    right=RightHalf(C);
    if(Stroke(left,B)==COVERED)
        return(COVERED);
    if(Stroke(right,B)==COVERED)
        return(COVERED);
    return(NOT_COVERED);
}
```

`Dilate` translates the test pixel and the discrete curve so that the test pixel is centred at the origin. `Stroke` recursively splits the discrete curve into left and right halves when necessary using repeated halving of the polygon sides in a conventional manner, Figure 5. Control vertices are held at higher integer precision than the discrete space to allow for any accuracy loss in subdivision down to the `BaseCase`. Note that more than one point on the discrete curve may lie within a pixel but it suffices to find only one.

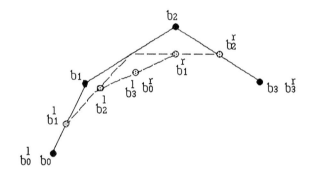

Figure 5

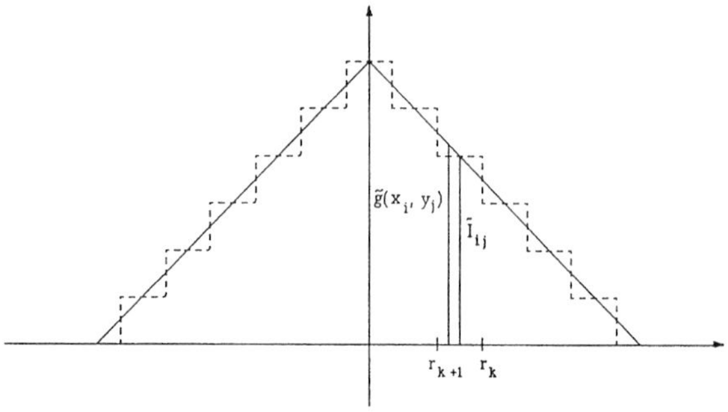

Figure 6

In our antialiasing version, we first convolve the brush with an antialiasing filter. The convolved brush is then approximated in a piecewise constant manner by a stack of nested brushes, as shown in Figure 6 for a box filter. The discrete Bézier curve is then dilated by the stack of brushes and the appropriate gray level (or antialiasing fraction) is determined by finding the smallest brush in the stack which is intersected by the discrete curve. A simple implementation of the algorithm uses the procedure Stroke as described above:

6.2 Antialiased Stroking

```
DiscreteCurve C;
StackOfBrushes SB;
Pixel P;
Index H;
/* H is an index to a brush in the brush */
/* stack */
/* Height(H) is the height of the brush */
/* in the stack and hence the fraction of */
/* the curve colour used for rendering */
for(each pixel P in the image)
{   if(AntialiasedDilate(C,SB,P,H))==COVERED
        then Render P with Height(H);
}


AntialiasedDilate(C,SB,P,H)
/* returns COVERED and H if P is covered*/
/* by C+SB(H) */
DiscreteCurve C;
StackOfBrushes SB;
Pixel P;
Index H;
{   n=number of brushes in stack SB
    H=0
    repeat with i=1 to n {
        if((Stroke(C-P,SB(H))==COVERED)
            then H=i;
        else exit repeat;
    }
    if(H==0) then return(NOT_COVERED);
    else return(COVERED);
}
```

In this version the brush stack is tested in order from bottom to top. Other strategies could be used: for example, test the largest brush for the NOT_COVERED case (early exit), then test the smallest brush. If this returns COVERED, we are done, otherwise we test the middle brush in the brush stack to determine whether the highest containing brush is larger or smaller than the middle brush, and so on, i.e. by interval halving. Details of the method employed for generation of the brush stack by optimal discrete stepwise approximation of the intensity profile of the filtered brush to a specified accuracy are given in [12,13]. On-demand generation of sections of the brush profile rather than using a pre-computed set of brush slices would enable a root finding procedure to determine the antialiasing fraction to arbitrary precision by interval halving—we have not yet implemented this approach.

7   RESULTS

Grayscale illustrations were computed at up to 6x6 sub-pixel resolution and viewed on an Apple Macintosh with a colour monitor using the "special gamma" setting. For reproduction, the images were saved as PostScript files and printed on a Hewlett-Packard LaserJet 4 Plus printer at 600 dpi using the "calibrated

colour/grayscale" option in the standard print dialogue. Images viewed on the screen are rather smoother as a consequence of the blurring effect of the gaussian-type reconstruction of the CRT. Differences between filters are less noticeable than in the printed versions. Laser printing allowed us more control over grayscale than would have been possible using photography. The illustrations are best viewed from approximately 0.5 metres using a strong incandescent bulb for lighting.

Plate 1 shows seven Bézier curves, parabolae and cubics, which are drawn aliased using the point containment algorithm (note the algorithm does not generate Bresenham lines). The curves are chosen to demonstrate particular geometric features such as near-vertical and near-horizontal portions, inflexion, low and high curvature, a cusp and its bordering configurations (a small loop and a curve with two inflexion points), and finally a large loop. In Plates 2-5 we use a circular brush convolved with a variety of filters to create stacks of circular brushes. Plate 2 shows the seven curves rendered as one pixel wide curves using a discrete version of the Mitchell-Netravali filter [29]. In Plate 3 we demonstrate the rendering of a low curvature parabola using a variety of filters. On balance the Mitchell-Netravali filter proved the best compromise between sharpness and smoothness or lack of braiding. The poor performance of box filtering is obvious. Plate 4 illustrates the ability of the algorithm to render curves with a variety of thicknesses and also the correct handling of a tight loop which is progressively filled in as the curve thickness increases. Plate 5 demonstrates the effect of gray level quantisation using a box filter and a truncated-sinc filter.

8   COMMENTS AND APPLICATIONS

Our technique follows the philosophy of the Corthout-Pol point containment technique [5,6,7,8] in which the problems of discretisation are acknowledged and tackled by casting the problem to be solved as a discrete integer problem from the outset rather than attempting to accommodate all the problems of numerical accuracy which follow from floating point discretisation, geometric approximation, or a less rigorous approach to discretisation later in the rendering process. Using their theory of discrete Bézier curves we are able to avoid the numerical problems which typically arise in computational geometry, especially with special cases. The Corthout-Pol point containment methods are provably accurate and robust. We gain the ability to use discrete approximations of any antialiasing filter. In [13] we describe how stacks of brushes can be generated to approximate the convolved brush to any required accuracy. We pay a price in terms of efficiency. At first sight, point containment is quadratic in terms of pixel resolution but Corthout and Pol [8] have shown that by exploiting area coherence and the convex hull properties of discrete Bézier curves, their method can be reduced to quasi-linear. Brooks' remarks cited earlier [3] are apposite. Furthermore, the method lends itself to hardware implementation: the Pharos chip fabricated by Philips implements the point containment algorithm in full and could be used serially or in a variety of parallel configurations for antialiasing. We make no claims for the efficiency of a software implementation.

Solution of the cases where the curve has more than one intersection with a pixel, for example where a curve crosses itself, need further discussion. There is a temptation to think of the problem in terms of area sampling but this is inappropriate as the convolved ideal image is point sampled: the issue is how convolved strokes should be merged prior to sampling. If we consider the case of aliased curve brushing, the ideal image is a union of the ideal strokes and hence it suffices to determine whether any one portion of the curve lies within the brush. By extension, if we consider one of the slices of a filtered brush, then we need to find containment in the union of the corresponding level set and hence the containment of at most one fragment of curve in the brush slice to determine whether that gray level has been reached within the pixel. Thus the approach we have taken is to detect the smallest (highest) brush intersected, computing a MAX value over all the curve's points within the pixel. There are no apparent problems with the looping curves in Plates 2 and 4. Where two fragments of curve run side by side without overlapping and together cover a complete pixel, the algorithm gives an incorrect rendering, requiring global knowledge of the curve configuration within the pixel rather than serial exploration, but this is expensive to implement. The problem is related to the bulge elimination problem discussed by Bloomenthal in the context of generating implicit branching surfaces by convolution of skeletons [2] and the solution may lie there or in investigation of level curves [28, 20].

Since our method is particularly suited to handling intricate details such as cusps and serifs in a robust fashion, an obvious application is in the generation of grayscale fonts from outline masters, at the requisite multiple sub-pixel positions if hardware is used, or pre-scanned and cached using an approach similar to that described by Naiman [30,31]. Hersch et al. [21] argue that for readability it is better to scan convert fonts using perceptually based tuning of the font outlines taking into account typographical features rather than to employ better filters, but their antialiasing is by post-filtering (simple averaging) of high resolution bitmaps (see also comments by Corthout and Pol [7]). Their approach ensures that similar typographical elements are, as far as possible, scan converted into identical groups of pixels rather than into varying sets of pixels which depend on sub-pixel positioning. Warnock, on the other hand, generated quite readable grayscale sub-pixel positioned fonts at small point sizes without perceptual tuning [35]. Our approach permits the use of sophisticated filters and does not require any geometric adjustment of font outlines before straightforward scan conversion. Whether text antialiased using our approach will prove to be as readable as Hersch's perceptually tuned fonts is a matter for future experiment. It is simple to modify our algorithm to allow the brush size to vary continuously whilst stroking curves [7] without the complication of computing offsets from the curve centreline [24]—a property which may be useful for generating Chinese and other brushed characters.

The implementation described in this paper covers only the antialiasing of curves as strokes and assumes black curves drawn over a white background permitting write-only image generation. The technique can of course be used in a simple manner for straight lines and polygons as well as parametric and rational spline curves. Future implementations will include antialiasing of region boundaries and the use of read-modify-write (lerping). More complex brushes such as orientable brushes and brushes defined by closed sequences of Bézier curves need investigation.

ACKNOWLEDGEMENTS

We wish to acknowledge the Advanced Technology Group, Apple Computer, Cupertino, for the provision of computing equipment and software through Apple Computer UK. The work of A.E. Fabris, on leave from the Instituto de Matématica e Estatistica, University of São Paulo (São Paulo, Brazil), was partially supported by a grant from the Conselho Nacional de Desenvolvimento Cientĺfico e Tecnológico (CNPq). The initial inspiration for this work is due to Marc Corthout and Evert-Jan Pol.

REFERENCES

[1] G.D. Abram, L. Westover, L. and J.T. Whitted. Efficient Alias-Free Rendering Using Bit-Masks and Look-up Tables. In Brian A. Barsky, editor, *Computer Graphics, (SIGGRAPH 85 Conference Proceedings),* volume 19, pages 53-60. ACM SIGGRAPH, July 1985. ISBN 0-89791-166-0.

[2] J.I. Bloomenthal. Bulge Elimination in Convolution Surfaces. *Computer Graphics Forum,* 16(1): 1-11, January 1997. ISSN 0167-7055.

[3] F.P. Brooks Jr. Springing into the Fifth Decade of Computer Graphics—Where We've Been and Where We're Going! In Holly Rushmeier, editor, *SIGGRAPH 96 Conference Proceedings*, Annual Conference Series, page 513. ACM SIGGRAPH, Addison Wesley, August 1996. ISBN 0-89791-746-4.

[4] R.L. Cook. Stochastic Sampling in Computer Graphics. *ACM Transactions on Graphics* 5(1): 51-72, January 1986. ISSN 0730-0301.

[5] M.E.A. Corthout and H.B.M. Jonkers. A New Point Containment Algorithm for B_Regions in the Discrete Plane. In R.A. Earnshaw, editor, *Theoretical Foundations of Computer Graphics and CAD,* NATO Advanced Study Institute Series F, F40, pages 297-306. Springer-Verlag, 1988. ISBN 0-387-19506-8.

[6] M.E.A. Corthout and E.-J.D. Pol. A Point Containment Algorithm for Regions in the Discrete Plane Outlined by Rational Bézier Curves. In J. André & R.D. Hersch, editors, *Raster Imaging and Digital Typography*, pages 169-179. Cambridge University Press, 1989. ISBN 0-521-37490-1.

[7] M.E.A. Corthout and E.-J.D. Pol. Supporting Outline Font Rendering in Dedicated Silicon: the PHAROS Chip. In R.A. Morris and J. André, editors, *Raster Imaging and Digital Typography II*, pages 177-189. Cambridge University Press, 1991. ISBN 0-521-41764-3.

[8] M.E.A. Corthout and E.-J.D. Pol. *Point Containment and the PHAROS Chip.* Joint Ph.D. Thesis, University of Leiden, The Netherlands, March 1992.

[9] F.C. Crow. The Use of Grayscale for Improved Raster Display of Vectors and Characters. In Richard L. Phillips, editor, *Computer Graphics, (SIGGRAPH 78 Conference Proceedings),* volume 12, pages 1-5. ACM SIGGRAPH, August 1978.

[10] F.C. Crow. A Comparison of Antialiasing Techniques. *IEEE Computer Graphics and Applications*, 1(1): 40-48, January 1981. ISSN 0272-1716.

[11] T.D.S. Duff. Polygon Scan Conversion by Exact Convolution. In J. André & R.D. Hersch, editors, *Raster Imaging and Digital Typography*, pages 154-168. Cambridge University Press, 1989. ISBN 0-521-37490-1.

[12] A.E. Fabris. *Robust Anti-aliasing of Curves.* Ph.D. Thesis, University of East Anglia, U.K., November 1995.

[13] A.E. Fabris and A.R. Forrest. *Robust Anti-aliasing of Curves.* December 1996, submitted for publication.

[14] E.A. Feibush, M. Levoy and R.L. Cook. Synthetic Texturing Using Digital Filters. In James J. Thomas, editor, *Computer Graphics, (SIGGRAPH 80 Conference Proceedings),* volume 14, pages 294-301. ACM SIGGRAPH, July 1980. ISBN 0-89791-1021-4.

[15] D.A. Field. Algorithms for Drawing Anti-aliased Circles and Ellipses. *Computer Vision Graphics and Image Processing*, 33(1): 1-15, January 1986. ISSN 0734-189X.

[16] A.R. Forrest. Antialiasing in Practice. In R.A. Earnshaw, editor, *Fundamental Algorithms for Computer Graphics,*

NATO Advanced Study Institute Series F, F17, pages 113-134. Springer-Verlag, 1985. ISBN 0-387-13920-6.

[17] P.K. Ghosh. A Mathematical Model for Shape Description using Minkowski Operators. Computer Vision, Graphics, and Image Processing, 44(3): 239-269, December 1988. ISSN 0734-189X.

[18] S. Gupta and R.F. Sproull. Filtering Edges for Gray-Scale Displays. In Henry Fuchs, editor, *Computer Graphics, (SIGGRAPH 81 Conference Proceedings)*, volume 15, pages 1-5. ACM SIGGRAPH, July 1981. ISBN 0-89791-045-1.

[19] L.J. Guibas, L.H. Ramshaw and J. Stolfi. A Kinetic Framework for Computational Geometry. In *Proceedings of the IEEE 1983 24th Annual Symposium on the Foundations of Computer Science*, pages 100-111. IEEE Computer Society Press, 1983.

[20] W. Heidrich, M.D. McCool and J. Stevens. Interactive Maximum Projection Volume Rendering. In G.M. Nielson and D. Silver, editors, *IEEE Visualization '95*, pages 11-18, CP-3. IEEE Computer Society Press, 1995. ISBN 0-8186-7187-4.

[21] R.D. Hersch, C. Bétrisey, J. Bur and A. Gürtler. Perceptually Tuned Generation of Grayscale Fonts. *IEEE Computer Graphics and Applications*, 15(6): 78-89, November 1995. ISSN 0272-1716.

[22] R.V. Klassen. *Device Dependent Image Construction for Computer Graphics*. Ph.D. Thesis, University of Waterloo, Waterloo, Ontario, July 1989.

[23] R.V. Klassen. Drawing Antialiased Cubic Spline Curves. *ACM Transactions on Graphics* 10(1): 92-108, January 1991. ISSN 0730-0301.

[24] R.V. Klassen. Variable Width Splines: a Possible Font Representation? *Electronic Publishing—Origination, Dissemination and Design (Special Issue, Proceedings of RIDT'94)*, 6(3): 183-194, September 1994. ISSN 0894-3982.

[25] W.J. Leler. Human Vision, Anti-Aliasing, and the Cheap 4000 Line Display. In James J. Thomas, editor, *Computer Graphics, (SIGGRAPH 80 Conference Proceedings)*, volume 14, pages 308-313. ACM SIGGRAPH, July 1980. ISBN 0-89791-021-4.

[26] S.-L. Lien, M. Shantz and V.R. Pratt. Adaptive Forward Differencing for Rendering Curves and Surfaces. In Maureen C. Stone, editor, *Computer Graphics, (SIGGRAPH 87 Conference Proceedings)*, volume 21, pages 111-118. ACM SIGGRAPH, July 1987. ISBN 0-89791-227-6.

[27] M.D. McCool. Analytic Antialiasing with Prism Splines. In Robert Cook, editor, *SIGGRAPH 95 Conference Proceedings*, Annual Conference Series, pages 429-436. ACM SIGGRAPH, Addison Wesley, August 1995. ISBN 0-89791-701-4.

[28] M.D. McCool. Private communication, September 1996.

[29] D.P. Mitchell and A.N. Netravali. Reconstruction Filters in Computer Graphics. In John Dill, editor, *Computer Graphics, (SIGGRAPH 88 Conference Proceedings)*, volume 22, pages 221-228. ACM SIGGRAPH, August 1988. ISBN 0-89791-275-6.

[30] A.C. Naiman. Grayscale Character Generator and Method. *United States Patent* 4,851,825, 25 July 1989.

[31] A.C. Naiman and A. Fournier. Rectangular Convolution for Fast Filtering of Characters. In Maureen C. Stone, editor, *Computer Graphics, (SIGGRAPH 87 Conference Proceedings)*, volume 21, pages 233-242. ACM SIGGRAPH, July 1987. ISBN 0-89791-227-6.

[32] M.L.V. Pitteway and E. Banissi. Soft Edging Fonts. In *Proceedings of Computer Graphics 87*, pages 133-154. Online Publications, 1987.

[33] M.L.V. Pitteway and D. Watkinson. Bresenham's Algorithm with Grey Scale. *Communications of the ACM*, 23(11): 625-626, November 1980. ISSN 0001-0782.

[34] I.C. Walker. Video Image Creation. *U.K. Patent* GB 2,089,625B, published 25 September 1985.

[35] J.E. Warnock. The Display of Characters Using Gray Level Sample Arrays. In James J. Thomas, editor, *Computer Graphics, (SIGGRAPH 80 Conference Proceedings)*, volume 14, pages 302-307. ACM SIGGRAPH, July 1980. ISBN 0-89791-021-4.

[36] J.T. Whitted. Anti-Aliased Line Drawing Using Brush Extrusion. In Peter Tanner, editor, *Computer Graphics, (SIGGRAPH 83 Conference Proceedings)*, volume 17, pages 151-156. ACM SIGGRAPH, July 1983. ISBN 0-89791-109-1.

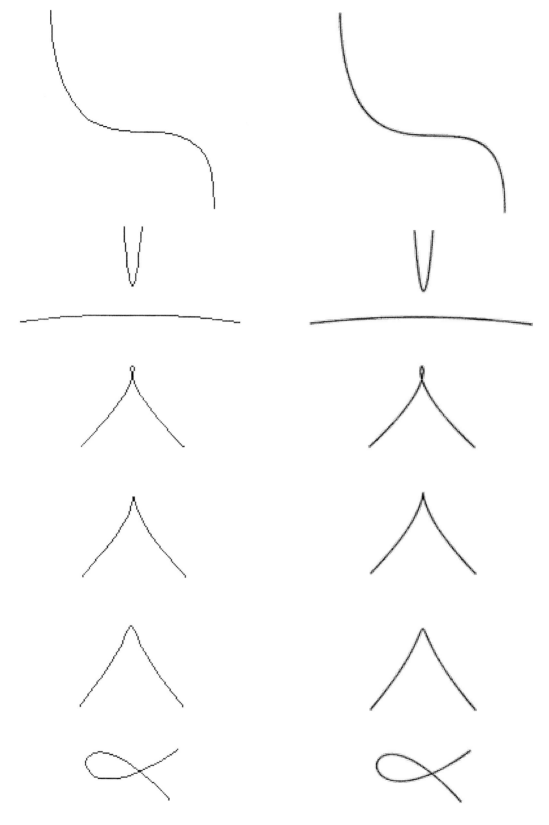

Plate 1: Aliased Test Curves   **Plate 2: Anti-aliased Test Curves**

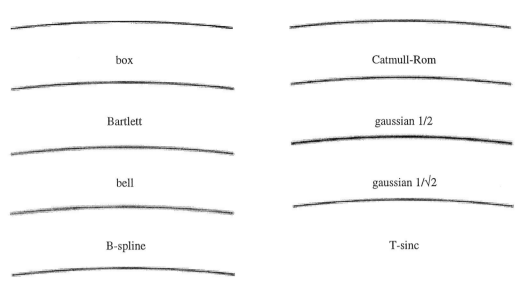

box

Catmull-Rom

Bartlett

gaussian 1/2

bell

gaussian 1/√2

B-spline

T-sinc

Mitchell-Netravali

Plate 3: Parabola rendered with a variety of filters.

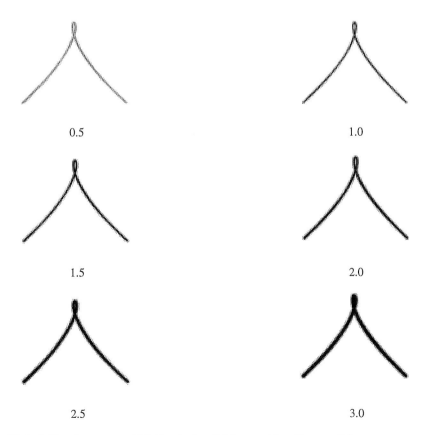

0.5

1.0

1.5

2.0

2.5

3.0

Plate 4: Varying curve width (in pixel units) for a cubic with a small loop near a cusp.

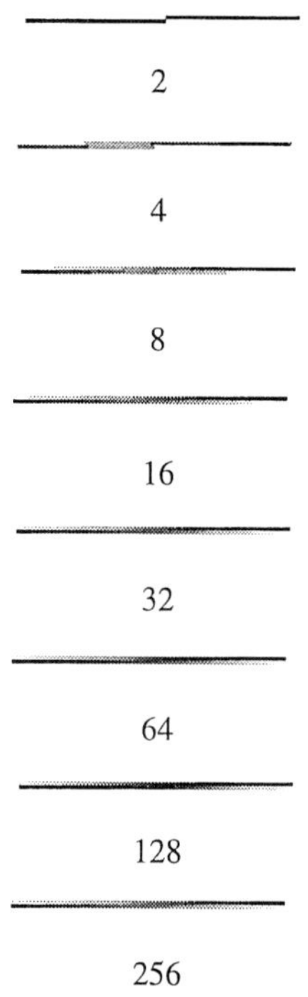

2	2
4	4
8	8
16	16
32	32
64	64
128	128
256	256
(a) box filter	**(b) T-sinc filter**

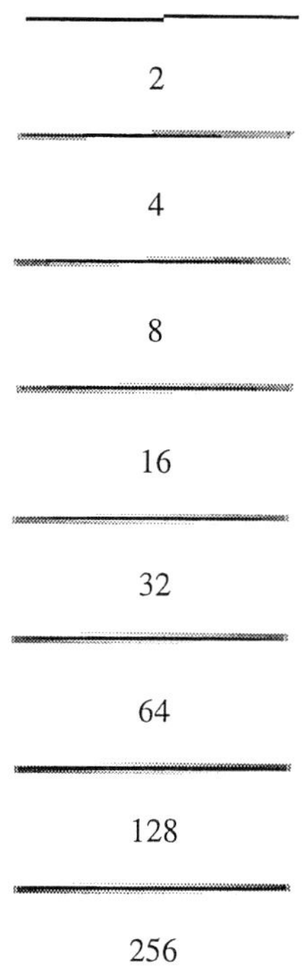

Plate 5: Varying number of grey levels.

The Two-User Responsive Workbench:
Support for Collaboration Through Individual Views of a Shared Space

Maneesh Agrawala*   Andrew C. Beers*   Bernd Fröhlich*   Pat Hanrahan*

Ian McDowall†   Mark Bolas†

*Stanford University
Stanford, CA

†Fakespace, Inc.
Mountain View, CA

Abstract

We present the two-user Responsive Workbench: a projection-based virtual reality system that allows two people to simultaneously view individual stereoscopic image pairs from their own viewpoints. The system tracks the head positions of both users and computes four images - one for each eye of each person. To display the four images as two stereo pairs, we must ensure each image is correctly presented to the appropriate eye. We describe a hardware solution to this display problem as well as registration and calibration procedures. These procedures ensure that when two users point to the same location on a virtual object, their fingers will physically touch. Since the stereo pairs are independent, we have the option of displaying specialized views of the shared virtual environment to each user. We present several scenarios in which specialized views might be useful.

CR Categories and Subject Descriptors: I.3.7 [Computer graphics]: Virtual Reality, I.3.1 [Computer graphics]: Three-Dimensional Displays.
Keywords: Virtual environments, Responsive Workbench.

1   Introduction

Many tasks require people to work together and there is great interest in using technology to improve the effectiveness of group activities. Groups, unlike individuals working alone, communicate and exchange information. For example, a whiteboard provides a single shared drawing surface that facilitates such collaborative interaction. Users can communicate by voice, gestures and by writing on the shared surface. A natural question is whether virtual environments can similarly provide a shared space in which collaborative interactions occur as easily and smoothly as they would in the real world.

Projection-based virtual reality systems such as the CAVE [4] and the Responsive Workbench [8] [7] are close analogues to whiteboards. In such systems, stereoscopic images are projected onto a large screen allowing groups of people to simultaneously view a virtual environment. As with whiteboards, the whole group is focused on the same display screen and can interact with one another in a natural manner. These systems track the head position of a single

Figure 1: Two users simultaneously view a shared virtual environment on the Responsive Workbench. Calibration ensures that when they point to the same feature on the virtual cube, their fingers touch. Note that the image on the Workbench is rendered for the point of view of the camera.

user and compute a stereoscopic image pair for that person's point of view. Unfortunately, when non-tracked users see these images, the virtual environment appears distorted. This distortion makes it difficult for non-tracked users to visually examine and refer to virtual objects.

In this paper, we describe an extension to the Responsive Workbench that allows *two* users to see individual stereoscopic images from their own viewpoint. Our two viewer display system is based on the common single viewer stereo display technique of *frame interleaving*. The system tracks the head positions of both users and computes four images - one for each eye of each person. The four images are displayed in sequence and we ensure each image is correctly presented only to the appropriate eye. Since both users see correct stereo images for their own point of view, they both see an undistorted, perspective correct view of the virtual environment. With proper calibration, when the users point to the same location on a virtual object their fingers will touch, as shown in figure 1.

At times users are interested in different aspects of a shared space. The ability to display two independent views offers the intriguing possibility of presenting different information in each view. As an example, consider a scenario in which an electrician and a plumber are discussing the plans for a new building. They must ensure that there is no interference between the wiring and plumbing. With a two-user Responsive Workbench, the electrician and plumber could see specialized views. Both would see the basic structure of the house, but only the electrician would see a detailed representation of the wiring and only the plumber would see a detailed representa-

(a)   (b)   (c)

Figure 2: (a) The view seen by a user standing on the left side of the table. (b) The view seen from the right side. (c) The view a user standing on the left side of the table would see if generated from the position of the view on the right. Even though the image on the Workbench is the same in (b) and (c), the cube appears sheared to the non-tracked user in (c).

tion of the water pipes. Regions in which the plumbing and wiring interfere would be shown in detail to both contractors. There are many interesting variations of this idea, and in this paper we discuss scenarios in which these specialized views might be useful.

The main contribution of our work is the development of a system that provides two users with perspective correct views of the same virtual environment on the Responsive Workbench. In sections 3 and 4, we describe the hardware and calibration required to create this shared space. In section 5, we present several scenarios that might benefit from specialized views of a virtual environment. We begin with a discussion of the problems with face-to-face collaboration in current projection-based virtual reality systems.

2 Support for Face-To-Face Collaboration

Face-to-face collaboration is difficult in current projection-based virtual reality systems because they do not provide a visually consistent shared space for all users. Before we analyze this problem in detail, let's consider what face-to-face collaboration entails.

Direct verbal communication is the most common type of interaction amongst a group of people. In a face-to-face situation, facial expressions and hand gestures provide important backchannels which create a sense of awareness and involvement within the group [2]. Other visual cues such as lip motions make it easier to understand what a speaker is saying. When a group performs a task in a shared physical space, gestures are often used to refer to objects. Such gestural interactions are important in establishing a shared context for the group [11]. When someone refers to an object by pointing to it, the object becomes the focus of the group. It is because of these visual cues that people often find it easier to communicate and collaborate when they are face-to-face than across a voice-only medium like a telephone [1]. Thus, face-to-face collaboration requires that participants can see some representation of one another and is best achieved when they share a single, visually consistent environment.

In projection-based virtual reality systems, users can see each other and therefore communicate face-to-face. However, current systems do not give the users a single visually consistent environment to discuss. Since the stereo images are perspective-correct only for the point of view of the tracked user, non-tracked users will notice two types of distortions (visual inconsistencies) in the stereo images:

- **Point of View Distortion:** For non-tracked users, virtual objects appear to shear or lean in some direction because they are not viewing the environment from the point of view for which it was rendered.

As shown in figure 2, a non-tracked user would see a distorted image when standing to the left of a tracked user. In the appendix, we analyze the point of view distortion in more detail.

- **Motion Distortion:** Since the stereoscopic image is computed for the tracked-user's head position, the image changes whenever the tracked user moves. To the non-tracked user who cannot predict the motions of the tracked user, these changes seem haphazard and cause disorientation.

Despite this distortion, it is possible for the users to talk about the general features of the virtual environment. The shear caused by the first distortion requires non-tracked users to stand close to tracked users to get an approximately correct view of the environment. If a tracked user points at a certain point on a virtual object, the non-tracked user will see the tracked user pointing at a different point in the virtual model, even though both see the tracked user pointing to the same point in physical space. For the users this is unintuitive and reduces the feeling of a shared space.

The second type of distortion can be jarring if the tracked user moves quickly. In normal use, tracked users will continuously move their heads by small amounts as they are examining the virtual objects. This motion causes the environment to continually swim for non-tracked users. We can solve both of these distortion problems by giving the users individual, viewpoint dependent, perspective-correct stereo image pairs.

3 Two-Viewer Display Method

The most common display technique for single viewer stereoscopic image displays uses two different frame buffers to store images computed for the left and right eyes. The display hardware alternates scanning out the two buffers at a typical rate of 120Hz, 60 images per eye per second. Shutter glasses are used to ensure that each eye sees only the appropriate image.

In order for two viewers to see individual stereoscopic image pairs, four different images must be rendered and displayed. We extended the single-viewer approach described above to two viewers by using four different frame buffers, one buffer for each eye of each user. As shown in figure 3, our current hardware consists of a Silicon Graphics Onyx2 workstation with four R10000 processors and two Infinite Reality graphics pipelines. Each pipeline generates two of the four images in parallel with the other pipeline. The generated frames are merged using custom hardware that interleaves two genlocked analog video streams. Our frame interleaving hardware supports a variety of resolutions and refresh rates, including a high refresh rate configuration with a screen size of 1280x492 at 144Hz, and a higher resolution configuration with a screen size of 1024x768 at 120Hz. The bandwidth of our current projector prevents us from using higher refresh rates or larger screen sizes than the ones described above.

We have also modified the design of the single viewer shutter glasses for use with this system. In addition to the two standard one eye open, one eye closed states, we added a third state in which both eyes are closed. This state is required whenever the images for the other viewer are displayed.

The main drawbacks of this two viewer approach are that we cut the display frame rate in half for each user compared to the single viewer approach, and that the images had a slight but noticeable flicker at the frame rates we were able to display. Also, half of the frames seen by each user are black while the views for the other user are shown. These black frames will reduce the perceived brightness of the images seen by the user, since the users see only half the amount of light as they would in a single user system.

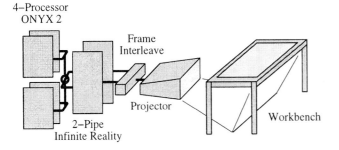

Figure 3: Two View Responsive Workbench System Overview.

The four images required for two users can be displayed in two fundamentally different sequences. Consider the four frame buffers and their corresponding images, which we name as follows: L1–left eye first viewer, R1–right eye first viewer, L2–left eye second viewer, R2–right eye second viewer. The two sequences are then:

- **Viewer Sequential:** ... L1 R1 L2 R2 ...The images for each viewer are displayed one after the other.

- **Viewer Interleaved:** ... L1 L2 R1 R2 ...The images of the two viewers are interleaved.

The viewer interleaved method exposes each viewer to an image at every other frame time, whereas with the viewer sequential method, each viewer receives two consecutive images, and then no image for two frame times. As expected, we found the flicker less perceptible for the viewer interleaved method.

We explored another display technique for a two user system that uses anaglyphic (i.e. red/blue) stereo, and is suitable for a prototyping system. One user wears a red filter over the left eye and a blue filter over the right, and the other does the opposite. Both users additionally wear shutter glasses. The shutter glasses ensure that only one of each user's eyes can see an image each frame, and the different colored filters ensure that the users see their own view. Note that one could combine this anaglyphic approach with the approach above to provide independent stereo views for four users.

4   Registration and Calibration

The methods of the previous section provide each user with an independent view onto a shared environment. In order for them to interact with this environment, we must calibrate the display and tracking systems so that a user can simply reach out and directly interact with virtual objects. This requires that the coordinate systems for the various devices are properly aligned. Our system uses three different coordinate systems: The user and the table top display exist within the real world, and therefore we can describe their positions within a *physical coordinate system*. Similarly, virtual objects are defined in

a *virtual coordinate system*. The user's head and hand motions are tracked with a tracking system, which reports coordinates in its own *tracker coordinate system*. Registration connects these three coordinate systems together to provide a common reference frame. We choose the physical coordinate system as our reference system, and affix it to the table top so that its origin is in the middle of the table, z is up and x and y are aligned with the edges of the table.

Accurately registering these three spaces to each other provides each user with a perspective correct image, and ensures that when both users point to the same virtual object, they also point to the same point in physical space above the tabletop. The three coordinate systems are registered in two steps: First, the virtual coordinate system is registered to the physical coordinate system, and then the tracker coordinate system to the physical coordinate system.

4.1   Registering the physical and virtual systems

We begin by aiming and aligning the projector so that the displayed image is centered on the table top and aligned parallel to the edges of the table. We then carefully linearize the display to ensure that virtual objects do not change size and shape when they are moved across the table. These two steps accurately register the virtual image plane with the physical xy-plane. Finally, we define our perspective projection so that the virtual and physical coordinate systems are aligned and use the same physical units. This projection depends on the physical size of the displayed image, which we measure with a ruler.

4.2   Registering the physical and tracking systems

The simplest way of registering the tracker and physical coordinate systems is to determine the transformation mapping the coordinate frame of the tracking system onto the coordinate frame of the physical table. This can be accomplished by measuring the location of three known points on the physical table using the tracking system. The corresponding points define a change-of-basis matrix between the two coordinate frames.

This method works well when there are no distortions in the tracker measurements. However, all tracking devices suffer distortions, and those present in magnetic systems like the Polhemus Fastrak can be quite large [10]. We have developed a look-up table approach for correcting these distortions, which is similar to methods developed by Bryson [3], Ghazisaedy et al. [6], and Livingston [9]. We begin by measuring points on a grid in physical space using a Polhemus 6DOF stylus. For each of these points, we save the corresponding location reported in tracker space. These measurements are samples of a function mapping physical space into tracker space. We compute the inverse of this function on a grid in tracker space, and then use trilinear interpolation to map positions reported by the tracker into our physical coordinate system.

We measured absolute position error in the space above the table surface and in front of the table where users normally stand. Using the above method, our position measurements have an average error of approximately 0.5cm and a maximum error of less than 3cm over the operating space of the Workbench, as compared to an average error of 3cm and a maximum error of 14cm or more without our distortion correction.

Combining the two registration steps yields accurate stereoscopic images for both users, and facilitates the interaction between the users and the virtual objects.

5   Specialized Views of a Shared Environment

In face-to-face collaborations, participants generally assume that the objects in the environment are visible to all the participants. If I see an object in the real world I can safely assume that you see it as well. Most of the examples we have designed for the two-user Responsive Workbench conform to this real world assumption and present exactly the same virtual environment to both users.

Sometimes, however, collaborators are interested in different aspects of a shared environment. One advantage of displaying individual stereo pairs with the two-user Responsive Workbench system is that each user can see a specialized view of the environment. We can independently display and highlight the information that is most important to each of them. This may keep the users from being overwhelmed by extraneous information and help to focus their attention on the most relevant details of the environment.

We have developed three scenarios that make use of such specialized views. The scenarios are described in figures 4–6 and are meant as simple demonstrations of situations in which specialized views might prove useful. The scenarios are based on more general strategies for partitioning information among multiple viewers of a shared environment. The strategies are not mutually exclusive and we expect applications to use different combinations of them.

Layer Partitioning. Many virtual models, simulations, or environments contain distinct layers of information that can be viewed independently or superimposed in combination to be viewed all at once. Typically each layer contains a very specific type of information and when all the layers are viewed at once, the spatial information density is so high that it is impossible to interpret or analyze the data. Moreover, in many cases each user will only be interested in a few layers of the model. Instead of displaying all the layers to every user, we can present individually specialized views of only the layers each user is most interested in. In figure 4, we develop a scenario that uses this layer partitioning strategy to facilitate a construction **Contractors' Meeting**. The layer partitioning technique does require some knowledge of the kinds of information users will be interested in during the modeling process. The approach is less useful for a user that needs information which is spread across many layers.

Given a model made up of information layers it is also possible to present different users with different representations of the same layer. In our contractors scenario (see figure 4), a bricklayer might see a detailed representation of each individual brick while the roof is represented as a single large slab. Simultaneously a roofer might see individual roof tiles while the walls are represented as slabs. Both users see both the walls and roof information layers, but the level of abstraction in the presentation of the layers is dependent on what each user is most interested in.

Spatial Partitioning. Some virtual environments can be spatially partitioned so that each user only sees a small region of the environment in exhaustive detail. We can deemphasize non-focus regions by presenting them at a lower level of geometric detail than the focus region. This type of partitioning works especially well for large display surfaces like the Responsive Workbench. If users stand close to the display surface, it provides a large field of view. Users tend to focus on subregions of the surface rather than viewing the entire surface. We develop an **Air Traffic** scenario in figure 5 that makes use of spatial partitioning.

Private Information. In some environments, some information is relatively independent of the shared space and of interest only to a single user. Such private information is not considered part of the general virtual environment, but may be very useful to a particular user. In figure 6, we describe a scenario in which a teacher uses private notes while giving an **Anatomy Lesson** to a student. Tang [11] describes meetings in which participants take notes or sketch ideas on a private notepad which they later make public and present to the rest of the group. Such private information spaces could be useful for developing one's own ideas in a group setting.

Carried to an extreme, specializing views can lead to a situation in which each user sees a completely different environment and there is no longer a shared space. With two-user technology, it is possible for each user to be engaged in a completely different application. In such cases, having two simultaneous users is probably not very useful. When displaying specialized information, the challenge is to ensure that the notion of a shared space is not lost.

6   Conclusions and Future Work

The two-user Responsive Workbench is a projection-based virtual reality system that supports tight, face-to-face collaborative interaction between two users. We have developed a hardware setup for enabling a two-user frame interleaved display, allowing us to present each user with a perspective-correct view of a shared virtual environment.

We are currently exploring methods for improving the display hardware and examining the feasibility of scaling this approach to support more than two users. We have encountered three limitations in our two-user display hardware: flicker, crosstalk and reduction of brightness. Flicker is caused by our current refresh rate of 144Hz, yielding only 36Hz per eye, per user. Crosstalk occurs because the CRT phosphors do not completely decay between the display of consecutive frames. Next generation video projectors promise higher refresh rates which should reduce flicker, but will necessitate faster phosphors or different technology. Higher refresh rates may also enable three or four user display systems. However, the ratio of time for which each user actually sees an image decreases as support for two or more users is added to the system. Users will experience this as a reduction in the brightness of the display.

As we discussed, specialized views is an interface paradigm that might be useful for reducing information overload or maintaining a boundary between public and private spaces. However, it is still unclear whether real-world applications supporting collaborative work would benefit from specialized views. Currently we are trying to identify such applications. We hope to assess the effectiveness of specialized views in aiding collaborative interactions within these applications.

Giving users the ability to view the same virtual environment while standing near one another allows them to communicate about the environment by voice and gesture. We are just beginning to explore the types of software tools and interfaces that might further assist such collaborative interaction. Cutler et al. [5] have shown that two-handed interaction tools can be useful in the Responsive Workbench environment. In a two user system, there are three or four hands possibly acting in a coordinated fashion. We are investigating how to extend their methods for this situation.

In this paper, we have demonstrated that a frame-interleaved stereo display on a projection-based system is possible for two simultaneous viewers. We expect that several simultaneous viewers will be possible in the near future. We believe that the advent of such technology will provide a great opportunity for developing tools, interfaces and paradigms that strengthen face-to-face collaborative interaction in a shared virtual environment.

7   Acknowledgments

We would like to thank Oliver Riedel of Fraunhofer for help with the initial hardware design. GMD, Germany's National Research Center for Information Technology, developed part of the basic workbench software that was used for this project. The air traffic data set is courtesy William F. Eddy and Shingo Oue. We would like to thank Larry Cutler and Yeva Fineberg for contributing ideas and for help with modeling objects. Jeff Feldgoise created the house model. The Stanford Instructional Television Network provided technical assistance with capturing video and images of the workbench. This work was supported by Interval Research Corporation.

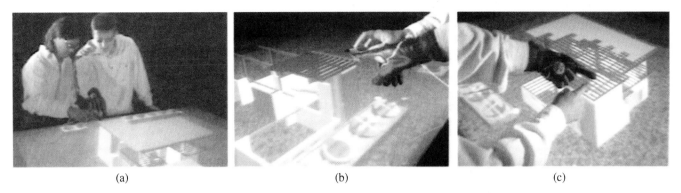

(a)   (b)   (c)

Figure 4: **The Contractors' Meeting.** Several contractors are responsible for designing and constructing various sections of a house. Each section is a different layer of information in our house model. One layer contains the wall support structure for the house, another contains the roof structure, still another contains the wiring and so on. (a) Two contractors are discussing modifications to a wall that supports part of the roof above. One contractor is responsible for the wall support structure, and the other for the roof. Both contractors see a basic model of the house, plus an additional information layer specific to their responsibilities. Areas where their work may come into conflict are shown to both contractors. (b) The wall contractor sees all walls that require modification in green and part of the roof that will be affected by the modifications. (c) The roofing contractor sees the entire roof and the wall that is being discussed for modification in green.

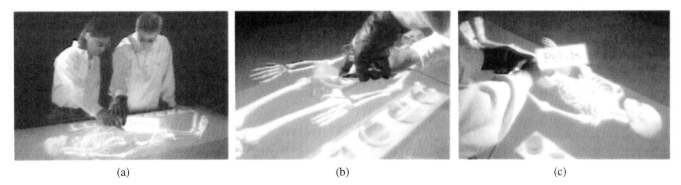

(a)   (b)   (c)

Figure 5: **The Anatomy Lesson.** (a) A teacher is using a virtual skeleton to teach anatomy. Both the student and teacher see the virtual skeleton, but only the teacher sees custom notes about the lesson. These notes include tags that appear when the teacher points to a bone. Here the teacher asks the student about a bone, indicating which one by pointing to it. (b) The student sees the indicated bone highlighted, but cannot see the notes about the bone. (c) In this case, the teacher privately see his notes about the pelvis.

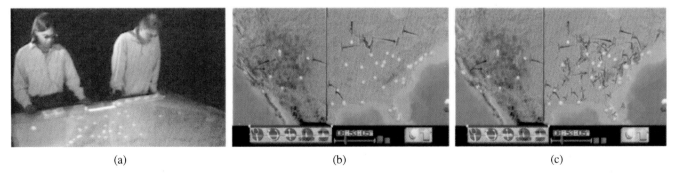

(a)   (b)   (c)

Figure 6: **Air Traffic.** (a) Two users monitor air traffic over the continental United States using an air traffic visualizer. They divide the responsibility by spatially partitioning the US into eastern and western regions. Under this spatial partitioning, both users see flights that cross over both regions. (b) Only the user responsible for the western half of the country sees flights that stay in the western region. (c) Only the user responsible for the eastern half sees those that stay in the eastern region. Flights that stay within a region leave purple trails while those that cross between regions leave blue trails. Note that (b) and (c) are overhead views.

Note: The images on the Workbench in the three establishing shots on the left were generated for the point of view of the camera.

References

[1] Sara A. Bly. A use of drawing surfaces in different collaborative settings. In *Proceedings of ACM CSCW'88 Conference on Computer-Supported Cooperative Work*, Synchronous Communication, pages 250–256, 1988.

[2] Susan E. Brennan. Conversation as direct manipulation: An iconoclastic view. In Brenda Laurel, editor, *The Art of Human Computer Interface Design*, pages 393–404. Addison-Wesley, 1990.

[3] Steve Bryson. Measurement and calibration of static distortion of position data from 3D trackers. In *Virtual Reality course notes, SIGGRAPH 93*, 1993.

[4] Carolina Cruz-Neira, Daniel J. Sandin, and Thomas A. DeFanti. Surround-screen projection-based virtual reality: The design and implementation of the cave. In James T. Kajiya, editor, *Computer Graphics (SIGGRAPH '93 Proceedings)*, volume 27, pages 135–142, August 1993.

[5] Lawrence D. Cutler, Bernd Fröhlich, and Pat Hanrahan. Two-handed direct manipulation on the responsive workbench. *1997 Symposium on Interactive 3D Graphics*, 1997.

[6] Morteza Ghadisaedy, David Adamczyk, Daniel J. Sandin, Robert V. Kenyon, and Thomas A. DeFanti. Ultrasonic calibration of a magnetic tracker in a virtual reality space. In *Proceedings of the IEEE Virtual Reality Annual International Symposium*, pages 179–188. IEEE, 1995.

[7] Wolfgang Krüger, Christina-A. Bohn, Bernd Fröhlich, Heinrich Schüth, Wolfgang Strauss, and Gerold Wesche. The responsive workbench: A virtual work environment. *IEEE Computer*, pages 42–48, July 1995.

[8] Wolfgang Krüger and Bernd Fröhlich. The responsive workbench. *IEEE Computer Graphics and Applications*, pages 12–15, May 1994.

[9] Mark A. Livingston and Andrei State. Magnetic tracker calibration for improved augmented reality registration. *To appear in Presence*, October 1998.

[10] Kennneth Meyer, Hugh. L. Applewhite, and Frank A. Biocca. A survey of position trackers. *Presence*, pages 173–198, 1992.

[11] J. C. Tang. *Listing, drawing and gesturing in design: A study of the use of shared workspaces by design teams*. Phd thesis, Mechanical Engineering, Stanford University, California, April 1989. Also available as research report SSL-89-3, Xerox Palo Alto Research Center, Palo Alto, California.

Appendix: The Point of View Distortion

The Responsive Workbench system displays images on the tabletop, which is therefore the image plane in our virtual world. Each image is a projection of the virtual environment onto this plane. Tracking the user's head position ensures that a virtual object always keeps the same shape and position independent of the user's viewpoint. However, to a non-tracked user viewing a stereoscopic image generated for a tracked user, the virtual world appears distorted. The perceived shape and position of virtual objects is dependent on the positions of the tracked and non-tracked users. The distortions can be large and if they are extreme it may not even be possible for the non-tracked user to fuse the stereoscopic images.

In Figure 7a, we analyze the distortion for a simple 2D situation and find that it is indeed a shear. The general 3D case as shown in Figure 7b is more complicated. Two images presented to the non-tracked viewer generally cannot be interpreted as the projection of a single 3D scene. For the Responsive Workbench, we have found that users almost always manage to fuse two such non-corresponding images and create a sensation of depth. If the tracked and the non-tracked users are standing next to each other and are about the same height, the 3D case reduces approximately to the simple 2D case and the untracked viewer experiences a sheared virtual world.

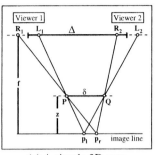 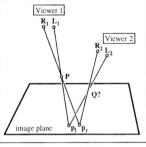

(a) A simple 2D case   (b) The general 3D case

Figure 7: The shearing distortion. Part (a) shows the distortion for a 2D case. Here a 2D world projects onto an image line instead of an image plane. We analyze the special case, in which the eye points of two viewers are on a line parallel to the image line, but the results for the general 2D case are similar. L_1, R_1, L_2 and R_2 denote the left and right eye positions for viewer 1 and 2 and we assume the interocular distance for both viewers is the same. Point P as seen by viewer 1 creates the projections p_l and p_r on the image line. Viewer 2 reconstructs point Q from looking at these projections. If z and f are the distance of P and the eyes from the image line, a distance of Δ in head positions results in a shift of δ in the perceived position of P. Using similar triangles we see that δ is related to Δ by the following simple formula: $\delta = \frac{\Delta}{f}z$, which is a shearing transformation. Part (b) shows the 3D case. In general the lines connecting the second viewer's eye points with the projection of point P do not intersect. Therefore no corresponding point Q exists.

SCAAT: Incremental Tracking with Incomplete Information

Greg Welch and Gary Bishop

University of North Carolina at Chapel Hill[†]

Abstract

We present a promising new mathematical method for tracking a user's pose (position and orientation) for interactive computer graphics. The method, which is applicable to a wide variety of both commercial and experimental systems, improves accuracy by properly assimilating sequential observations, filtering sensor measurements, and by concurrently autocalibrating source and sensor devices. It facilitates user motion prediction, multisensor data fusion, and higher report rates with lower latency than previous methods.

Tracking systems determine the user's pose by measuring signals from low-level hardware sensors. For reasons of physics and economics, most systems make multiple sequential measurements which are then combined to produce a single tracker report. For example, commercial magnetic trackers using the SPASYN (*Space Synchro*) system sequentially measure three magnetic vectors and then combine them mathematically to produce a report of the sensor pose.

Our new approach produces tracker reports as each new low-level sensor measurement is made rather than waiting to form a complete collection of observations. Because single observations under-constrain the mathematical solution, we refer to our approach as single-constraint-at-a-time or SCAAT tracking. The key is that the single observations provide some information about the user's state, and thus can be used to incrementally improve a previous estimate. We recursively apply this principle, incorporating new sensor data as soon as it is measured. With this approach we are able to generate estimates more frequently, with less latency, and with improved accuracy. We present results from both an actual implementation, and from extensive simulations.

CR Categories and Subject Descriptors: I.3.7 [Computer Graphics] Three-Dimensional Graphics and Realism—Virtual reality; I.4.4 [Image Processing] Restoration—Kalman filtering; I.4.8 [Image Processing] Scene Analysis—Sensor fusion; G.0 [Mathematics of Computing] General—Numerical Analysis, Probability and Statistics, Mathematical Software.

Additional Key Words and Phrases: virtual environments tracking, feature tracking, calibration, autocalibration, delay, latency, sensor fusion, Kalman filter.

---

† CB 3175, Sitterson Hall, Chapel Hill, NC, 27599-3175
welch@cs.unc.edu, http://www.cs.unc.edu/~welch
gb@cs.unc.edu, http://www.cs.unc.edu/~gb

1 INTRODUCTION

The method we present requires, we believe, a fundamental change in the way people think about estimating a set of unknowns in general, and tracking for virtual environments in particular. Most of us have the preconceived notion that to estimate a set of unknowns we need as many constraints as there are degrees of freedom at any particular instant in time. What we present instead is a method to constrain the unknowns *over time*, continually refining an estimate for the solution, a *single constraint at a time*.

For applications in which the constraints are provided by real-time observations of physical devices, e.g. through measurements of sensors or visual sightings of landmarks, the SCAAT method isolates the effects of error in individual measurements. This isolation can provide improved filtering as well as the ability to individually calibrate the respective devices or landmarks concurrently and continually while tracking. The method facilitates user motion prediction, multisensor or multiple modality data fusion, and in systems where the constraints can only be determined sequentially, it provides estimates at a higher rate and with lower latency than multiple-constraint (batch) approaches.

With respect to tracking for virtual environments, we are currently using the SCAAT method with a new version of the UNC wide-area optoelectronic tracking system (section 4). The method could also be used by developers of commercial tracking systems to improve their existing systems or it could be employed by end-users to improve custom multiple modality hybrid systems. With respect to the more general problem of estimating a set of unknowns that are related by some set of mathematical constraints, one could use the method to trade estimate quality for computation time. For example one could incorporate individual constraints, one at a time, stopping when the uncertainty in the solution reached an acceptable level.

1.1 Incomplete Information

The idea that one might build a tracking system that generates a new estimate with each individual sensor measurement or *observation* is a very interesting one. After all, individual observations usually provide only partial information about a user's complete state (pose), i.e. they are "incomplete" observations. For example, for a camera observing landmarks in a scene, only limited information is obtained from observations of any single landmark. In terms of control theory, a system designed to operate with only such incomplete measurements is characterized as *unobservable* because the user state cannot be observed (determined) from the measurements.

The notion of observability can also be described in terms of constraints on the unknown parameters of the system being estimated, e.g. constraints on the unknown elements of the system state. Given a particular system, and the corresponding set of unknowns that are to be estimated, let C be defined as the minimal number of independent simultaneous constraints necessary to uniquely determine a solution, let N be the number actually used to generate a new estimate, and let N_{ind} be the number of *independent* constraints that can be formed from the N constraints. For any $N \geq N_{ind}$ constraints, if $N_{ind} = C$ the problem is *well constrained*, if $N_{ind} > C$ it is *over constrained*, and if $N_{ind} < C$ it is *under-constrained*. (See Figure 1.)

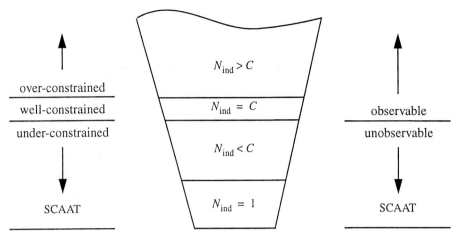

Figure 1: SCAAT and constraints on a system of simultaneous equations. C is the minimal number of independent simultaneous constraints necessary to uniquely determine a solution, N is the number of given constraints, and N_{ind} is the number of *independent* constraints that can be formed from the N. (For most systems of interest $C > 1$). The conventional approach is to ensure $N \geq N_{ind}$ and $N_{ind} \geq C$, i.e. to use enough measurements to well-constrain or even over-constrain the estimate. The SCAAT approach is to employ the smallest number of constraints available at any one time, generally $N = N_{ind} = 1$ constraint. From this viewpoint, each SCAAT estimate is severely under-constrained.

1.2 Landmark Tracking

Consider for example a system in which a single camera is used to observe known scene points to determine the camera position and orientation. In this case, the constraints provided by the observations are multi-dimensional: 2D image coordinates of 3D scene points. Given the internal camera parameters, a set of four known coplanar scene points, and the corresponding image coordinates, the camera position and orientation can be uniquely determined in closed-form [16]. In other words if $N = C = 4$ constraints (2D image points) are used to estimate the camera position and orientation, the system is completely observable. On the other hand, if $N < C$ then there are multiple solutions. For example with only $N = 3$ non-collinear points, there are up to 4 solutions. Even worse, with $N = 2$ or $N = 1$ points, there are infinite combinations of position and orientation that could result in the same camera images.

In general, for closed-form tracking approaches, a well or over-constrained system with $N \geq C$ is observable, an under-constrained system with $N < C$ is not. Therefore, if the individual observations provide only partial information, i.e. the measurements provide insufficient constraints, then multiple devices or landmarks must be excited and (or) sensed prior to estimating a solution. Sometimes the necessary observations can be obtained simultaneously, and sometimes they can not. Magnetic trackers such as those made by Polhemus and Ascension perform three *sequential* source excitations, each in conjunction with a complete sensor unit observation. And while a camera can indeed observe multiple landmarks simultaneously in a single image, the image processing to identify and locate the individual landmarks must be done sequentially for a single CPU system. If the landmarks can move independently over time, for example if they are artificial marks placed on the skin of an ultrasound patient for the purpose of landmark-based tracking [41], batch processing of the landmarks can reduce the effectiveness of the system. A SCAAT implementation might grab an image, extract a *single* landmark, update the estimates of both the camera *and* landmark positions, and then throw-away the image. In this way estimates are generated faster and with the most recent landmark configurations.

1.3 Putting the Pieces Together

Given a tracker that uses multiple constraints that are each individually incomplete, a *measurement model* for any one of incomplete constraints would be characterized as *locally unobservable*. Such a system must incorporate a sufficient set of these incomplete constraints so that the resulting overall system is observable. The corresponding aggregate measurement model can then be characterized as *globally observable*. Global observability can be obtained over *space* or over *time*. The SCAAT method adopts the latter scheme, even in some cases where the former is possible.

2 MOTIVATION

2.1 The Simultaneity Assumption

Several well-known virtual environment tracking systems collect position and orientation constraints (sensor measurements) sequentially. For example, tracking systems developed by Polhemus and Ascension depend on sensing a sequence of variously polarized electromagnetic waves or fields. A system that facilitated simultaneous polarized excitations would be very difficult if not impossible to implement. Similarly both the original UNC optoelectronic tracking system and the newer HiBall version are designed to observe only one ceiling-mounted LED at a time. Based on the available literature [25,27,37] these systems currently assume (mathematically) that their sequential observations were collected simultaneously. We refer to this as the *simultaneity assumption*. If the target remains motionless this assumption introduces no error. However if the target is moving, the violation of the assumption introduces error.

To put things into perspective, consider that typical arm and wrist motion can occur in as little as 1/2 second, with typical "fast" wrist tangential motion occurring at 3 meters/second [1]. For the current versions of the above systems such motion corresponds to approximately 2 to 6 centimeters of translation *throughout* the sequence of measurements required for a single estimate. For systems that attempt sub-millimeter accuracies, even slow motion occurring during a sequence of sequential measurements impacts the accuracy of the estimates.

The error introduced by violation of the simultaneity assumption is of greatest concern perhaps when attempting any form of system *autocalibration*. Gottschalk and Hughes note that motion during their autocalibration procedure must be severely restricted in order to avoid such errors [19]. Consider that for a multiple-measurement system with 30 milliseconds total measurement time, motion would have to be restricted to approximately 1.5 centimeters/second to confine the translation (throughout a measurement sequence) to 0.5 millimeters. For complete autocalibration of a large (wide-area) tracking system, this restriction results in lengthy specialized sessions.

2.2 Device Isolation & Autocalibration

Knowledge about source and sensor imperfections can be used to improve the accuracy of tracking systems. While intrinsic sensor parameters can often be determined off-line, e.g. by the manufacturer, this is generally not the case for extrinsic parameters. For example it can be difficult to determine the exact geometric relationship between the various sensors of a hybrid system. Consider that the coordinate system of a magnetic sensor is located at some unknown location inside the sensor unit. Similarly the precise geometric relationship between visible landmarks used in a vision-based system is often difficult to determine. Even worse, landmark positions can change over time as, for example, a patient's skin deforms with pressure from an ultrasound probe. In general, goals such as flexibility, ease of use, and lower cost, make the notion of self-calibration or *autocalibration* attractive.

The general idea for autocalibration is not new. See for example [19,45]. However, because the SCAAT method *isolates* the measurements provided by each sensor or modality, the method provides a new and elegant means to autocalibrate concurrently while tracking. Because the SCAAT method isolates the individual measurements, or measurement dimensions, individual source and sensor imperfections are more easily identified and dealt with. Furthermore, because the simultaneity assumption is avoided, the motion restrictions discussed in section 2.1 would be removed, and autocalibration could be performed *while concurrently tracking a target*.

The isolation enforced by the SCAAT approach can improve results even if the constraints are obtained simultaneously through multidimensional measurements. An intuitive explanation is that if the elements (dimensions) are corrupted by independent noise, then incorporating the elements independently can offer improved filtering over a batch or ensemble estimation scheme.

2.3 Temporal Improvements

Per Shannon's sampling theorem [24] the measurement or *sampling* frequency should be at least twice the true target motion bandwidth, or an estimator may track an alias of the true motion. Given that common arm and head motion bandwidth specifications range from 2 to 20 Hz [13,14,36], the *sampling* rate should ideally be greater than 40 Hz. Furthermore, the *estimate* rate should be as high as possible so that normally-distributed white estimate error can be discriminated from any non-white error that might be observed during times of significant target dynamics, and so estimates will always reflect the most recent user motion.

In addition to increasing the estimate rate, we want to reduce the latency associated with generating an improved estimate, thus reducing the overall latency between target motion and visual feedback in virtual environment systems [34]. If too high, such latency can impair adaptation and the illusion of presence [22], and can cause motion discomfort or sickness. Increased latency also contributes to problems with head-mounted display registration [23] and with motion prediction [4,15,29]. Finally, post-rendering

image deflection techniques are sometimes employed in an attempt to address latency variability in the rendering pipeline [32,39]. Such methods are most effective when they have access to (or generate) accurate motion predictions and low-latency tracker updates. With accurate prediction the best possible position and orientation information can be used to render a preliminary image. With fast tracker updates there is higher probability that when the preliminary image is ready for final deflection, recent user motion has been detected and incorporated into the deflection.

With these requirements in mind, let us examine the effect of the measurements on the estimate latency and rate. Let t_m be the time needed to determine one constraint, e.g. to measure a sensor or extract a scene landmark, let N be the number of (sequential) constraints used to compute a complete estimate, and let t_c be the time needed to actually compute that estimate. Then the estimate latency t_e and rate r_e are

$$t_e = Nt_m + t_c \ ,$$

$$r_e = \frac{1}{t_e} = \frac{1}{Nt_m + t_c} \ . \tag{1}$$

As the number of constraints N increases, equation (1) shows how the estimate latency and rate increase and decrease respectively. For example the Polhemus Fastrak, which uses the SPASYN (*Space Synchro*) method for determining relative position and orientation, employs $N = 3$ sequential electromagnetic excitations and measurements per estimate [25,27,37], the original University of North Carolina (UNC) optoelectronic tracking system sequentially observed $10 \leq N \leq 20$ beacons per estimate [3,44], and the current UNC hybrid landmark-magnetic tracking system extracts (from a camera image) and then incorporates $N = 4$ landmarks per update. The SCAAT method seeks to improve the latencies and data rates of such systems by updating the current estimate with each new (individual) constraint, i.e. by fixing N at 1. In other words, it increases the estimate rate to approximately the rate that individual constraints can be obtained and likewise decreases the estimate latency to approximately the time required to obtain a single constraint, e.g. to perform a single measurement of a single sensor, or to extract a single landmark.

Figure 2 illustrates the increased data rate with a timing diagram that compares the SPASYN (Polhemus Navigation Systems) magnetic position and orientation tracking system with a hypothetical SCAAT implementation. In contrast to the SPASYN system, a SCAAT implementation would generate a new estimate after sensing each *individual* excitation vector rather than waiting for a complete pattern.

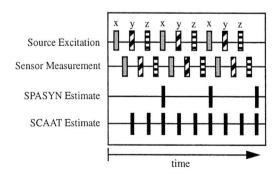

Figure 2: A timing diagram comparing the SPASYN (Polhemus Navigation Systems) magnetic position and orientation tracking system with a hypothetical SCAAT implementation.

2.4 Data Fusion & Hybrid Systems

The Kalman filter [26] has been widely used for data fusion. For example in navigation systems [17,30], virtual environment tracking systems [5,12,14], and in 3D scene modeling [20,42]. However the SCAAT method represents a new approach to Kalman filter based *multi-sensor data fusion*. Because constraints are intentionally incorporated one at a time, one can pick and choose which ones to add, and when to add them. This means that information from different sensors or modalities can be woven together in a common, flexible, and expeditious fashion. Furthermore, one can use the approach to ensure that each estimate is computed from the most recently obtained constraint.

Consider for a moment the UNC hybrid landmark-magnetic presented at SIGGRAPH 96 [41]. This system uses an off-the-shelf Ascension magnetic tracking system along with a vision-based landmark recognition system to achieve superior synthetic and real image registration for augmented reality assisted medical procedures. The vision-based component attempts to identify and locate multiple known landmarks in a single image before applying a correction to the magnetic readings. A SCAAT implementation would instead identify and locate only one landmark per update, using a new image (frame) each time. Not only would this approach increase the frequency of landmark-based correction (given the necessary image processing) but it would offer the added benefit that unlike the implementation presented in [41], no special processing would be needed for the cases where the number of visible landmarks falls below the number C necessary to determine a complete position and orientation solution. The SCAAT implementation would simply cycle through any available landmarks, one at a time. Even with only one visible landmark the method would continue to operate as usual, using the information provided by the landmark sighting to refine the estimate where possible, while increasing the uncertainty where not.

3 METHOD

The SCAAT method employs a *Kalman filter* (KF) in an unusual fashion. The Kalman filter is a mathematical procedure that provides an efficient computational (recursive) method for the least-squares estimation of a linear system. It does so in a *predictor-corrector* fashion, predicting short-term (since the last estimate) changes in the state using a *dynamic model*, and then correcting them with a measurement and a corresponding *measurement model*. The *extended* Kalman filter (EKF) is a variation of the Kalman filter that supports estimation of *nonlinear* systems, e.g. 3D position and orientation tracking systems. A basic introduction to the Kalman filter can be found in Chapter 1 of [31], while a more complete introductory discussion can be found in [40], which also contains some interesting historical narrative. More extensive references can be found in [7,18,24,28,31,46].

The Kalman filter has been employed previously for virtual environment tracking estimation and prediction. For example see [2,5,12,14,42], and most recently [32]. In each of these cases however the filter was applied directly and only to the 6D pose estimates delivered by the off-the-shelf tracker. The SCAAT approach could be applied to either a hybrid system using off-the-shelf and/or custom trackers, or it could be employed by tracker developers to improve the existing systems for the end-user graphics community.

In this section we describe the method in a manner that does not imply a specific tracking system. (In section 3.4 we present experimental results of a specific implementation, a SCAAT wide-area optoelectronic tracking system.) In section 3.1 we describe the method for tracking, and in section 3.2 we describe one possible method for concurrent autocalibration.

Throughout we use the following conventions.

$$
\begin{aligned}
x &= \text{scalar (lower case)} \\
\vec{x} &= \text{general vector (lower case, arrow) indexed as } \vec{x}[r] \\
\hat{x} &= \text{filter estimate vector (lower case, hat)} \\
A &= \text{matrix (capital letters) indexed as } A[r, c] \\
A^{-1} &= \text{matrix inverse} \\
I &= \text{the identity matrix} \\
\beta^- &= \text{matrix/vector } \textit{prediction} \text{ (super minus)} \\
\beta^T &= \text{matrix/vector transpose (super T)} \\
\alpha_i &= \text{matrix/vector/scalar identifier (subscript)} \\
E\{\bullet\} &= \text{mathematical expectation}
\end{aligned}
$$

3.1 Tracking

3.1.1 Main Tracker Filter

The use of a Kalman filter requires a mathematical (state-space) model for the dynamics of the process to be estimated, the target motion in this case. While several possible dynamic models and associated state configurations are possible, we have found a simple *position-velocity* model to suffice for the dynamics of our applications. In fact we use this same form of model, with different parameters, for all six of the position and orientation components $(x, y, z, \phi, \theta, \psi)$. Discussion of some other potential models and the associated trade-offs can be found in [7] pp. 415-420. Because our implementation is discrete with inter sample time δt we model the target's dynamic motion with the following linear difference equation:

$$\vec{x}(t + \delta t) = A(\delta t)\vec{x}(t) + \vec{w}(\delta t). \tag{2}$$

In the standard model corresponding to equation (2), the n dimensional Kalman filter *state vector* $\vec{x}(t)$ would completely describe the target position and orientation at any time t. In practice we use a method similar to [2,6] and maintain the complete target orientation externally to the Kalman filter in order to avoid the nonlinearities associated with orientation computations. In the internal state vector $\vec{x}(t)$ we maintain the target position as the Cartesian coordinates (x, y, z), and the *incremental* orientation as small rotations (ϕ, θ, ψ) about the (x, y, z) axis. Externally we maintain the target orientation as the *external quaternion* $\vec{\alpha} = (\alpha_w, (\alpha_x, \alpha_y, \alpha_z))$. (See [9] for discussion of quaternions.) At each filter update step, the incremental orientations (ϕ, θ, ψ) are factored into the external quaternion $\vec{\alpha}$, and then zeroed as shown below. Thus the incremental orientations are linearized for the EKF, centered about zero. We maintain the derivatives of the target position and orientation internally, in the state vector $\vec{x}(t)$. We maintain the angular velocities internally because the angular velocities behave like orthogonal vectors and do not exhibit the nonlinearities of the angles themselves. The target state is then represented by the $n = 12$ element internal state vector

$$\vec{x} = \begin{bmatrix} x & y & z & \dot{x} & \dot{y} & \dot{z} & \phi & \theta & \psi & \dot{\phi} & \dot{\theta} & \dot{\psi} \end{bmatrix}^T \tag{3}$$

and the four-element external orientation quaternion

$$\vec{\alpha} = (\alpha_w, (\alpha_x, \alpha_y, \alpha_z)), \tag{4}$$

where the time designations have been omitted for clarity.

The $n \times n$ *state transition matrix* $A(\delta t)$ in (2) projects the state forward from time t to time $t + \delta t$. For our linear model, the matrix implements the relationships

$$x(t + \delta t) = x(t) + \dot{x}(t)\delta t$$
$$\dot{x}(t + \delta t) = \dot{x}(t) \tag{5}$$

and likewise for the remaining elements of (3).

The $n \times 1$ *process noise vector* $\vec{w}(\delta t)$ in (2) is a normally-distributed zero-mean sequence that represents the uncertainty in the target state over any time interval δt. The corresponding $n \times n$ *process noise covariance matrix* is given by

$$E\{\vec{w}(\delta t)\vec{w}^T(\delta t + \varepsilon)\} = \begin{cases} Q(\delta t), & \varepsilon = 0 \\ 0, & \varepsilon \neq 0 \end{cases}. \tag{6}$$

Because our implementation is discrete with inter sample time δt, we can use the transfer function method illustrated by [7] pp. 221-222 to compute a *sampled* process noise covariance matrix. (Because the associated random processes are presumed to be time stationary, we present the process noise covariance matrix as a function of the inter-sample duration δt only.) The non-zero elements of $Q(\delta t)$ are given by

$$Q(\delta t)[i, i] = \vec{\eta}[i]\frac{(\delta t)^3}{3}$$
$$Q(\delta t)[i, j] = Q(\delta t)[j, i] = \vec{\eta}[i]\frac{(\delta t)^2}{2} \tag{7}$$
$$Q(\delta t)[j, j] = \vec{\eta}[i](\delta t)$$

for each pair

$$(i, j) \in \{(x, \dot{x}), (y, \dot{y}), (z, \dot{z}), (\phi, \dot{\phi}), (\theta, \dot{\theta}), (\psi, \dot{\psi})\}.$$

The $\vec{\eta}[i]$ in (7) are the *correlation kernels* of the (assumed constant) noise sources presumed to be driving the dynamic model. We determined a set of values using Powell's method, and then used these in both simulation and our real implementation. The values can be "tuned" for different dynamics, though we have found that the tracker works well over a broad range of values.

The use of a Kalman filter requires not only a dynamic model as described above, but also a *measurement model* for each available type of measurement. The measurement model is used to predict the ideal noise-free response of each sensor and source pair, given the filter's current estimate of the target state as in equations (3) and (4).

It is the nature of the measurement models and indeed the actual sensor measurements that distinguishes a SCAAT Kalman filter from a well-constrained one.

For each sensor *type* σ we define the $m_\sigma \times 1$ *measurement vector* $\vec{z}_\sigma(t)$ and corresponding *measurement function* $\vec{h}_\sigma(\cdot)$ such that

$$\vec{z}_{\sigma, t} = \vec{h}_\sigma(\vec{x}(t), \vec{b}_t, \vec{c}_t) + \vec{v}_\sigma(t). \tag{8}$$

Note that in the "purest" SCAAT implementation $m_\sigma = 1$ and the measurements are incorporated as single scalar values. However if it is not possible or necessary to isolate the measurements, e.g. to perform autocalibration, then multi-dimensional measurements can be incorporated also. Guidelines presented in [47] lead to the following heuristic for choosing the SCAAT Kalman filter measurement elements (constraints):

During each SCAAT Kalman filter measurement update one should observe a single sensor and source pair only.

For example, to incorporate magnetic tracker data as an end-user, $m_\sigma = 7$ for the three position and four orientation (quaternion)

elements, while if the manufacturer were to use the SCAAT implementation, $m_\sigma = 3$ for each 3-axis electromagnetic response to a single excitation. For an image-based landmark tracker such as [41] the measurement function would, given estimates of the camera pose and a single landmark location, transform the landmark into camera space and then project it onto the camera image plane. In this case $m_\sigma = 2$ for the 2D image coordinates of the landmark.

The $m_\sigma \times 1$ *measurement noise vector* $\vec{v}_\sigma(t)$ in (8) is a normally-distributed zero-mean sequence that represents any random error (e.g. electrical noise) in the measurement. This parameter can be determined from component design specifications, and (or) confirmed by off-line measurement. For our simulations we did both. The corresponding $m_\sigma \times m_\sigma$ *measurement noise covariance matrix* is given by

$$E\{\vec{v}_\sigma(t)\vec{v}_\sigma^T(t + \varepsilon)\} = \begin{cases} R_\sigma(t), & \varepsilon = 0 \\ 0, & \varepsilon \neq 0 \end{cases}. \tag{9}$$

For each measurement function $\vec{h}_\sigma(\cdot)$ we determine the corresponding Jacobian function

$$H_\sigma(\vec{x}(t), \vec{b}_t, \vec{c}_t)[i, j] \equiv \frac{\partial}{\partial \vec{x}[j]}\vec{h}_\sigma(\vec{x}(t), \vec{b}_t, \vec{c}_t)[i], \tag{10}$$

where $1 \leq i \leq m_\sigma$ and $1 \leq j \leq n$. Finally, we note the use of the standard (Kalman filter) $n \times n$ *error covariance matrix* $P(t)$ which maintains the covariance of the error in the estimated state.

3.1.2 Tracking Algorithm

Given an initial state estimate $\hat{x}(0)$ and error covariance estimate $P(0)$, the SCAAT algorithm proceeds similarly to a conventional EKF, cycling through the following steps whenever a discrete measurement $\vec{z}_{\sigma, t}$ from some sensor (type σ) and source becomes available at time t:

a. Compute the time δt since the previous estimate.

b. Predict the state and error covariance.

$$\hat{x}^- = A(\delta t)\hat{x}(t - \delta t)$$
$$P^- = A(\delta t)P(t - \delta t)A^T(\delta t) + Q(\delta t) \tag{11}$$

c. Predict the measurement and compute the corresponding Jacobian.

$$\hat{z} = \vec{h}_\sigma(\hat{x}^-, \vec{b}_t, \vec{c}_t)$$
$$H = H_\sigma(\hat{x}^-, \vec{b}_t, \vec{c}_t) \tag{12}$$

d. Compute the *Kalman gain*.

$$K = P^- H^T (H P^- H^T + R_\sigma(t))^{-1} \tag{13}$$

e. Compute the *residual* between the actual sensor measurement $\vec{z}_{\sigma, t}$ and the predicted measurement from (12).

$$\vec{\Delta z} = \vec{z}_{\sigma, t} - \hat{z} \tag{14}$$

f. Correct the predicted tracker state estimate and error covariance from (11).

$$\hat{x}(t) = \hat{x}^- + K\vec{\Delta z}$$
$$P(t) = (I - KH)P^- \tag{15}$$

g. Update the external orientation of equation (4) per the change indicated by the (ϕ, θ, ψ) elements of the state.[*]

$$\Delta\hat{\alpha} = \text{quaternion}(\hat{x}[\phi], \hat{x}[\theta], \hat{x}[\psi])$$
$$\hat{\alpha} = \hat{\alpha} \otimes \Delta\hat{\alpha} \qquad (16)$$

h. Zero the orientation elements of the state vector.

$$\hat{x}[\phi] = \hat{x}[\theta] = \hat{x}[\psi] = 0 \qquad (17)$$

The equations (11)-(17) may seem computationally complex, however they can be performed quite efficiently. The computations can be optimized to eliminate operations on matrix and vector elements that are known to be zero. For example, the elements of the Jacobian H in (12) that correspond to the velocities in the state $\hat{x}(t)$ will always be zero. In addition, the matrix inverted in the computation of K in (13) is of rank m_σ (2×2 for our example in section 3.4) which is smaller for a SCAAT filter than for a corresponding conventional EKF implementation. Finally, the increased data rate allows the use of the *small angle approximations* $\sin(\theta) = \theta$ and $\cos(\theta) = 1$ in $\hat{h}_\sigma(\bullet)$ and $H_\sigma(\bullet)$. The total *per estimate* computation time can therefore actually be less than that of a corresponding conventional implementation. (We are able to execute the SCAAT filter computations, with the autocalibration computations discussed in the next section, in approximately 100μs on a 200 MHz PC-compatible computer.)

3.1.3 Discussion

The key to the SCAAT method is the number of constraints provided by the measurement vector and measurement function in equation (8). For the 3D-tracking problem being solved, a unique solution requires $C = 6$ non-degenerate constraints to resolve six degrees of freedom. Because individual sensor measurements typically provide less than six constraints, conventional implementations usually construct a complete measurement vector

$$\vec{z}_t = \left[\vec{z}_{\sigma_1, t_1}^T \ \cdots \ \vec{z}_{\sigma_N, t_N}^T \right]^T$$

from some group of $N \geq C$ individual sensor measurements over time $t_1 \ldots t_N$, and *then* proceed to compute an estimate. Or a particular implementation may operate in a *moving-window* fashion, combining the most recent measurement with the $N - 1$ previous measurements, possibly implementing a form of a finite-impulse-response filter. In any case, for such well-constrained systems complete observability is obtained at each step of the filter. Systems that collect measurements sequentially in this way inherently violate the simultaneity assumption, as well as increase the time δt between estimates.

In contrast, the SCAAT method blends individual measurements that each provide incomplete constraints into a complete state estimate. The EKF inherently provides the means for this blending, no matter how complete the information content of each individual measurement $\vec{z}_{\sigma, t}$. The EKF accomplishes this through the Kalman gain K which is computed in (13). The Kalman gain, which is used to adjust the state and the error covariance in (15), is optimal in the sense that it minimizes the error covariance if certain conditions are met. Note that the inversion in (13) forms a ratio that reflects the relative uncertainties of the state and the measurement. Note too that the ratio is affected by the use of the measurement function Jacobian H. Because the Jacobian reflects the rate of change of each measurement with respect to the current state, it indicates a direction in state space along which a measurement could *possibly* affect the state. Because the gain is recomputed at each step with the appropriate

measurement function and associated Jacobian, it inherently reflects the amount and direction of information provided by the individual constraint.

3.2 Autocalibration

The method we use for autocalibration involves *augmenting* the *main tracker filter* presented in section 3.1 to effectively implement a distinct *device filter*, a Kalman filter, for each source or sensor to be calibrated. (We use the word "device" here to include for example scene landmarks which can be thought of as passive sources, and cameras which are indeed sensors.) In general, any constant device-related parameters used by a measurement function $\hat{h}_\sigma(\bullet)$ from (8) are candidates for this autocalibration method. We assume that the parameters to be estimated are contained in the device parameter vectors $\vec{b}_t$ and $\vec{c}_t$, and we also present the case where both the source and sensor are to be calibrated since omission of one or the other is trivial. We note the following new convention.

$$\widehat{\alpha} = \text{augmented matrix/vector (wide hat)}$$

3.2.1 Device Filters

For each device (source, sensor, landmark, etc.) we create a distinct device filter as follows. Let $\vec{\pi}$ represent the corresponding device parameter vector and $n_\pi = \text{length}(\vec{\pi})$.

a. Allocate an $n_\pi \times 1$ state vector $\hat{x}_\pi$ for the device, initialize with the best *a priori* device parameter estimates, e.g. from design.

b. Allocate an $n_\pi \times n_\pi$ noise covariance matrix $Q_\pi(\delta t)$, initialize with the expected parameter variances.

c. Allocate an $n_\pi \times n_\pi$ error covariance matrix $P_\pi(t)$, initialize to indicate the level of confidence in the *a priori* device parameter estimates from (a) above.

3.2.2 Revised Tracking Algorithm

The algorithm for tracking with concurrent autocalibration is the same as that presented in section 3.1, with the following exceptions. After step (a) in the original algorithm, we form augmented versions of the state vector

$$\widehat{x}(t - \delta t) = \left[\hat{x}^T(t - \delta t) \ \hat{x}_{b, t}^T(t - \delta t) \ \hat{x}_{c, t}^T(t - \delta t) \right]^T, \qquad (18)$$

the error covariance matrix

$$\widehat{P}(t - \delta t) = \begin{bmatrix} P(t - \delta t) & 0 & 0 \\ 0 & P_{b, t}(t - \delta t) & 0 \\ 0 & 0 & P_{c, t}(t - \delta t) \end{bmatrix}, \qquad (19)$$

the state transition matrix

$$\widehat{A}(\delta t) = \begin{bmatrix} A(\delta t) & 0 & 0 \\ 0 & I & 0 \\ 0 & 0 & I \end{bmatrix}, \qquad (20)$$

and the process noise matrix

$$\widehat{Q}(\delta t) = \begin{bmatrix} Q(\delta t) & 0 & 0 \\ 0 & Q_{b, t}(\delta t) & 0 \\ 0 & 0 & Q_{c, t}(\delta t) \end{bmatrix}. \qquad (21)$$

---

[*] The operation $\alpha \otimes \Delta\alpha$ is used to indicate a quaternion multiply [9].

We then follow steps (b)-(h) from the original algorithm, making the appropriate substitutions of (18)-(21), and noting that the measurement and Jacobian functions used in step (c) have become $\hat{h}_\sigma(\widehat{x}(t))$ and $H_\sigma(\widehat{x}(t))$ because the estimates of parameters $\hat{b}_t$ and $\hat{c}_t$ ($\hat{x}_{b,t}$ and $\hat{x}_{c,t}$) are now contained in the augmented state vector $\widehat{x}$ per (18). After step (h) we finish by extracting and saving the device filter portions of the augmented state vector and error covariance matrix

$$
\begin{aligned}
\hat{x}_{b,t}(t) &= \widehat{x}(t)[i...j] \\
P_{b,t}(t) &= \widehat{P}(t)[i...j, i...j] \\
\hat{x}_{c,t}(t) &= \widehat{x}(t)[k...l] \\
P_{c,t}(t) &= \widehat{P}(t)[k...l, k...l]
\end{aligned}
\tag{22}
$$

where

$$
\begin{aligned}
i &= n+1 \\
j &= n+n_b \\
k &= n+n_b+1 \\
l &= n+n_b+n_c
\end{aligned}
$$

and n, n_b, and n_c are the dimensions of the state vectors for the main tracker filter, the source filter, and the sensor filter (respectively). We leave the main tracker filter state vector and error covariance matrix in their augmented counterparts, while we swap the device filter components in and out with each estimate. The result is that individual device filters are updated less frequently than the main tracker filter. The more a device is used, the more it is calibrated. If a device is never used, it is never calibrated.

With respect to added time complexity, the computations can again be optimized to eliminate operations on matrix and vector elements that are known to be zero: those places mentioned in section 3.1, and see (19)-(21). Also note that the size of and thus time for the matrix inversion in (13) has not changed. With respect to added space complexity, the autocalibration method requires storing a separate state vector and covariance matrix for each device—a fixed amount of (generally small) space per device. For example, consider autocalibrating the beacon (LED) positions for an optical tracking system with 3,000 beacons. For each beacon one would need 3 words for the beacon state (its 3D position), $3 \times 3 = 9$ words for the noise covariance matrix, and $3 \times 3 = 9$ words for the error covariance matrix. Assuming 8 bytes per word, this is only $3,000 \times 8 \times (3 + 9 + 9) = 504,000$ bytes.

3.2.3 Discussion

The ability to simultaneously estimate two dependent sets of unknowns (the target and device states) is made possible by several factors. First, the dynamics of the two sets are very different as would be reflected in the process noise matrices. We assume the target is undergoing some random (constant) acceleration, reflected in the noise parameter η of $Q(\delta t)$ in (6). Conversely, we assume the device parameters are constant, and so the elements of $Q_\pi(\delta t)$ for a source or sensor simply reflect any allowed variances in the corresponding parameters: usually zero or extremely small. In addition, while the target is expected to be moving, the filter expects the motion between any two estimations to closely correspond to the velocity estimates in the state (3). If the tracker estimate rate is high enough, poorly estimated device parameters will result in what appears to be almost instantaneous target motion. The increased rate of the SCAAT method allows such motion to be recognized as unlikely, and attributed to poorly estimated device parameters.

3.3 Stability

Because the SCAAT method uses individual measurements with insufficient information, one might be concerned about the potential for instability or divergence. A linear system is said to be stable if its response to any input tends to a finite steady value after the input is removed [24]. For the Kalman filter in general this is certainly not a new concern, and there are standard requirements and corresponding tests that ensure or detect stability (see [18], p. 132):

a. The filter must be uniformly completely observable,

b. the dynamic and measurement noise matrices in equations (6) and (9) must be bounded from above and below, and

c. the dynamic behavior represented by $A(\delta t)$ in equation (2) must be bounded from above.

As it turns out, these conditions and their standard tests are equally applicable to a SCAAT implementation. For the SCAAT method the conditions mean that the user dynamics between estimates must be bounded, the measurement noise must be bounded, one must incorporate a sufficient set of non-degenerate constraints *over time*. In particular, the constraints must be incorporated in less than 1/2 the time of the user motion time-constant in order to avoid tracking an alias of the true motion. In general these conditions are easily met for systems and circumstances that would otherwise be stable with a multiple-constraint implementation. A complete stability analysis is beyond the scope of this paper, and is presented in [47].

3.4 Measurement Ordering

Beyond a simple round-robin approach, one might envision a measurement scheduling algorithm that makes better use of the available resources. In doing so one would like to be able to monitor and control uncertainty in the state vector. By periodically observing the eigenvalues and eigenvectors of the error covariance matrix $P(t)$, one can determine the directions in state-space along which more or less information is needed [21]. This approach can be used to monitor the stability of the tracker, and to guide the source/sensor ordering.

4 EXPERIMENTS

We are using the SCAAT approach in the current version of the UNC wide-area optoelectronic tracking system known as the *HiBall tracker*. The *HiBall*, shown below in Figure 3, incorporates six optical sensors and six lenses with infrared filters into one golf ball sized sensing unit that can be worn on a user's head or hand. The principal mechanical component of the HiBall, the senor housing unit, was fabricated by researchers at the University of Utah using their $\alpha 1$ modeling environment.

Because the HiBall sensors and lenses share a common transparent space in the center of the housing, a single sensor can actually sense light through more than one lens. By making use of all of these *views* we end up with effectively 26 "cameras". These cameras are then used to observe ceiling-mounted light-emitting diodes (LEDs) to track the position and orientation of the HiBall. This inside-looking-out approach was first used with the previous UNC optoelectronic tracking system [44] which spanned most of the user's head and weighed approximately ten pounds, not including a backpack containing some electronics. In contrast, the HiBall sensing unit is the size of a golf ball and weighs only five ounces, *including* the electronics. The combination of reduced weight, smaller packaging, and the new SCAAT algorithm results in a very ergonomic, fast, and accurate system.

In this section we present results from both simulations performed during the design and development of the HiBall, and

Figure 3: The HiBall is shown here with the internal circuitry exposed and the lenses removed. The sensors, which can be seen through the lens openings, are mounted on PC boards that fold-up into the HiBall upon assembly. The mechanical pencil at the bottom conveys an indication of the relative size of the unit.

preliminary results from the actual implementation. The simulations are useful because we have control over the "truth" and can perform controlled experiments. The results from the actual implementation serve to demonstrate actual operation and to provide some support for our accuracy and stability claims.

With respect to the SCAAT implementation, the tracker *sensors* are the HiBall cameras and the tracker *sources* are the ceiling-mounted 2D array of approximately 3000 electronic beacons (LEDs). The cameras provide a single 2D measurement vector, i.e. a 2D constraint, which is the (u, v) image coordinates of the beacon as seen by the camera. So for this example, $m_\sigma = 2$ and $\overset{\scriptscriptstyle\vee}{z}_\sigma = [u, v]^T$. The measurement function $\overset{\scriptscriptstyle\vee}{h}_\sigma(\bullet)$ transforms the beacon into camera coordinates and then projects it onto the camera's image plane in order to predict the camera response.

For the simulations we generated individual measurement events (a single beacon activation followed by a single camera reading) at a rate of 1000 Hz, and corrupted the measurements using the noise models detailed in [8]. We tested components of our real system in a laboratory and found the noise models in [8] to be reasonably accurate, if not pessimistic. We also perturbed the 3D beacon positions prior to simulations with a normally-distributed noise source with approximately 1.7 millimeters standard deviation. We controlled all random number generators to facilitate method comparisons with common random sequences.

To evaluate the filter performance we needed some reference data. Our solution was to collect motion data from *real-user* sessions with a conventional tracking system, and then to filter the data to remove high frequency noise. We then *defined* this data to be the "truth". We did this for seven such sessions.

The simulator operated by sampling the truth data, choosing one beacon and camera (round-robin from within the set of valid combinations), computing the corresponding camera measurement vector $\overset{\scriptscriptstyle\vee}{z}_{\sigma, t}$, and then adding some measurement noise. The (noisy) measurement vector, the camera parameter vector $\overset{\scriptscriptstyle\vee}{c}_t$ (position and orientation in user coordinates), and the beacon parameter vector $\overset{\scriptscriptstyle\vee}{b}_t$ (position in world coordinates) were then sent to the tracker.

For the tracking algorithm, we simulated both the SCAAT method (section 3.1, modified per section 3.2 for autocalibration) and several multiple-constraint methods, including the Collinearity method [3] and several variations of moving window (finite impulse response) methods. For each of the methods we varied the measurement noise, the measurement frequency, and the beacon position error. For the multiple constraint methods we also varied the number of constraints (beacon observations) per estimate N. In each case the respective estimates were compared with the truth data set for performance evaluation.

4.1 Tracker Filter

The 12 element state vector $\hat{x}(t)$ for the main tracker filter contained the elements shown in (3). Each of the 3000 beacon filters was allocated a 3 element state vector

$$\hat{x}_b = \begin{bmatrix} x_b & y_b & z_b \end{bmatrix}^T$$

where (x_b, y_b, z_b) represents the beacon's estimated position in cartesian (world) coordinates. The 12×12 state transition matrix for the main tracker filter was formed as discussed section 3.1, and for each beacon filter it was the 3×3 identity matrix. The 12×12 process noise matrix for the main tracker was computed using (7), using elements of $\overset{\scriptscriptstyle\rightarrow}{\eta}$ that were determined off-line using Powell's method and a variety of real motion data. For each beacon filter we used an identical noise covariance matrix

$$Q_b(\delta t)[i, j] = \begin{cases} \eta_b & \text{if } i = j \\ 0 & \text{otherwise} \end{cases}$$

for $1 \leq i, j \leq 3$, with beacon position variance η_b also determined off-line. (See [47] for the complete details.) At each estimate step, the *augmented* 15 element state vector, 15×15 process noise matrix, 15×15 state transition matrix, and 15×15 error covariance matrix all resembled (18)-(21) (without the camera parameter components). The measurement noise model was distance dependent (beacon light falls-off with distance) so $R_\sigma(t)$ from (9) was computed prior to step (d), by using a beacon distance estimate (obtained from the user and beacon positions in the predicted state $\widehat{x}^-$) to project a distance-dependent electrical variance onto the camera.

4.2 Initialization

The position and orientation elements of the main tracker state were initialized with the true user position and orientation, and the velocities were initialized to zero. The 3000 beacon filter state vectors were initialized with (potentially erroneous) beacon position estimates. The main tracker error covariance matrix was initialized to the null matrix. All beacon filter error covariance matrices were initialized to

$$P_b(0)[i, j] = \begin{cases} (0.001)^2 & \text{if } i = j \\ 0 & \text{otherwise} \end{cases}$$

for $1 \leq i, j \leq 3$, to reflect 1 millimeter of uncertainty in the initial beacon positions.

While for the presented simulations we initialized the filter state with the true user pose information, we also performed (but will not show here) simulations in which the state elements were initialized to arbitrary values, e.g. all zeros. It is a testament to the stability of the method that in most cases the filter completely converged in under a tenth of a second, i.e. with fewer than 100 measurements. (In a few cases the camera was facing away from the beacon, a condition not handled by our simulator.)

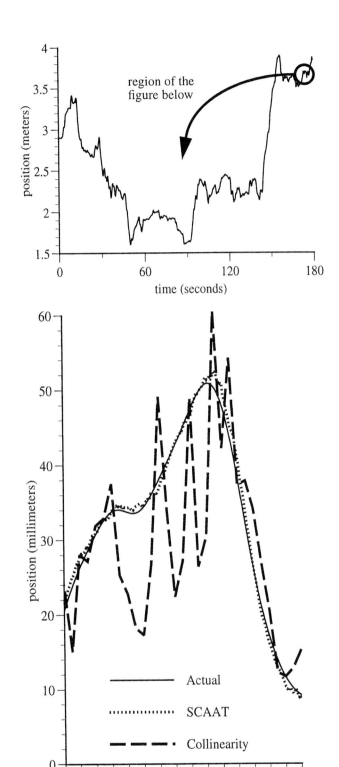

4.3 Simulation Results

We present here only comparisons of the SCAAT method with the Collinearity method, the "conventional approach" mentioned in the accompanying video. More extensive simulation results can be found in [47], including tests for stability under "cold starts" and periodic loss of data. All error measures reflect the RMS position error for a set of three imaginary points located approximately at arms length. This approach combines both position and orientation error into a metric that is related to the error a user would encounter in [HMD] screen space.

Figure 4 contains two related plots. The upper plot shows the entire three minutes (180 seconds) of the x-axis position for the first of seven data sets, data set 'a'. The lower plot shows a close-up of a particular segment of 300 milliseconds near the end. Notice that the Collinearity estimates appear very jerky. This is partially a result of the lower estimate rate, it is using $N = 10$ beacon observations to compute an estimate, and partially due to the method's inability to deal with the erroneous beacon position data. In contrast, the SCAAT method hugs the actual motion track, appearing both smooth and accurate. This is partly a result of the higher update rate (10 times Collinearity here), and partly the effects of Kalman filtering, but mostly the accuracy is a result of the SCAAT autocalibration scheme. With the autocalibration turned on, the initially erroneous beacon positions are being refined at the same high rate that user pose estimates are generated.

Figure 5 shows progressively improving estimates as the number of beacons N is reduced from 15 (Collinearity) down to 1 (SCAAT), and a clear improvement in the accuracy when autocalibration is on. Consider for a moment that the motion prediction work of Azuma and Bishop [4] was based on jerky Collinearity estimates similar to those in Figure 4. The smooth and accurate SCAAT estimation should provide a much better basis for motion prediction, which could in turn provide a more effective means for addressing other system latencies such as those in the rendering pipeline. The improved accuracy should also improve post-rendering warping or image deflection [32,39].

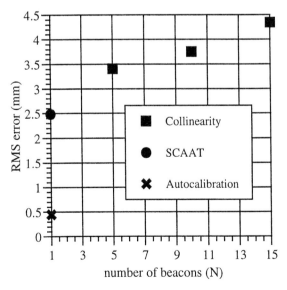

Figure 4: The upper plot depicts the entire 3 minutes of x-axis position data from user motion data set 'a' of sets 'a'-'f'. The lower plot shows a close-up of a short portion of the simulation. Collinearity here used $N = 10$ beacons per observation, hence its lower estimate rate. On the other hand, notice that the SCAAT estimates and the actual (truth) data are almost indistinguishable.

Figure 5: As the number of beacons N is reduced from 15 to 5, the Collinearity results improve slightly. (The Collinearity algorithm generally becomes unstable with $N \leq 4$.) The SCAAT results, with $N = 1$ beacons, are better, and especially good once autocalibration is turned on.

As further evidence of the smoothing offered by the SCAAT approach, Figure 6 presents an error spectra comparison between a Collinearity implementation with $N = 10$, and a SCAAT implementation with and without autocalibration. Even without autocalibration the SCAAT output has significantly less noise than collinearity, and with autocalibration it is better by more than a factor of 10. These reductions in noise are clearly visible to the HMD user as a reduction in the amount of jitter in virtual-world objects.

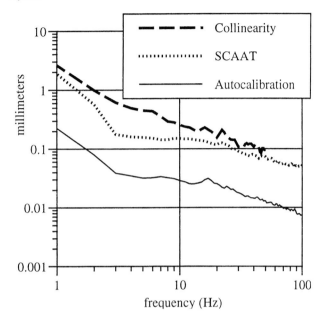

Figure 6: Here we show an error spectra comparison for the Collinearity method with $N = 10$ beacons, and the SCAAT method with and without autocalibration.

Figure 7 provides results for all seven of the real-user motion data sets. Again the Collinearity implementations observe $N = 10$ beacons per estimate, while the SCAAT implementations observe only $N = 1$. Because the beacon positions were being autocalibrated during the SCAAT run, we repeated each run, the second time using the beacon position estimation results from the first simulation. The more beacons are sighted during tracking, the better they are located. The second-pass simulation results are identified with the dagger (†) in Figure 7.

Figure 8 presents results that support the claim that the beacon location estimates are actually improving during tracking with autocalibration, as opposed to simply shifting to reduce spectral noise. Note that in the case of data set 'd', the beacon error was reduced nearly 60%.

Finally, we simulated using the SCAAT approach with tracking hardware that allowed truly simultaneous observations of beacons. For the Collinearity and other multiple-constraint methods we simply used the methods as usual, except that we passed them truly simultaneous measurements. For the SCAAT method we took the N simultaneous observations, and simply processed them one at a time with $\delta t = 0$. (See equation (2).) We were, at first, surprised to see that even under these ideal circumstances the SCAAT implementation could perform better, even significantly better than a multiple-constraint method with simultaneous constraints. The reason seems to be autocalibration. Even though the multiple-constraint methods were "helped" by the truly simultaneous observations, the SCAAT method still had the advantage in that it could still autocalibrate the beacons more

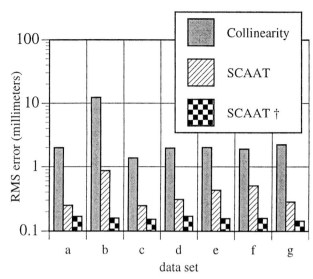

Figure 7: RMS error results for simulations of all seven real user motion data sets. The † symbol indicates a second pass through the motion data set, this time using the already autocalibrated beacons.

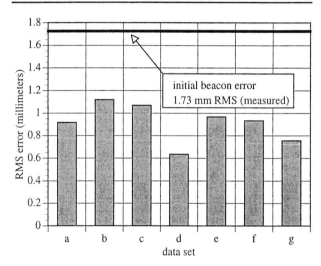

Figure 8: Autocalibration in action. Here we show the final beacon position error for runs through each of the seven user motion data sets.

effectively that any multiple-constraint method. This again arises from the method's inherent isolation of individual observations.

4.4 Real Results

We have demonstrated the SCAAT algorithm with the HiBall tracker, a head-mounted display, and a real application. However, at the time of the submission of this publication we have yet to perform extensive optimization and analysis. As such we present here only limited, albeit compelling results.

The SCAAT code runs on a 200 MHz PC-compatible computer with a custom interface board. With unoptimized code, the system generates new estimates at approximately 700 Hz. We expect the optimized version to operate at over 1000 Hz. Out of the approximately 1.4 millisecond period, the unoptimized SCAAT code takes approximately 100 microseconds and sampling of the sensors takes approximately 200 microseconds. The remaining time is spent on overhead including a significant amount of unoptimized code to choose an LED and to gather results.

In one experiment we set the HiBall on a flat surface under the ceiling beacons and collected several minutes worth of data. Given that the platform was relatively stable, we believe that the deviation of the estimates provides an indication of the noise in the system. Also, because the HiBall was not moving, we were able to observe the progressive effects of the autocalibration. The standard deviation of the position estimates for the first 15 seconds is shown in Figure 9. With autocalibration off, the estimates deviate approximately 6.0 millimeters in translation and 0.25 degrees in orientation (not shown). With autocalibration on, notice in Figure 9 how the deviation decreases with time, settling at approximately 0.3 millimeters in translation and 0.01 degrees in orientation (again not shown).

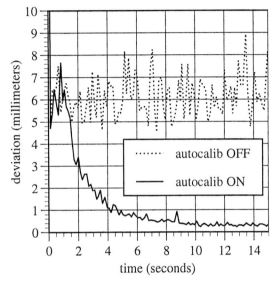

Figure 9: SCAAT position (only) estimate deviation for a Hiball sitting still on a flat surface, with and without autocalibration.

In another experiment we mounted the HiBall on a calibrated translation rail of length one meter, and slid (by hand) the HiBall from one end to the other and then back again. The disagreement between the HiBall and the calibrated position on the rail was less than 0.5 millimeters. The deviation of the measured track from co-linearity was 0.9 millimeters. Because the tolerances of our simple test fixture are of similar magnitude, we are unable to draw conclusions about how much of this disagreement should be attributed to error in the tracking system.

5 CONCLUSIONS

Stepping back from the details of the SCAAT method, we see an interesting relationship: Because the method generates estimates with individual measurements, it not only avoids the simultaneity assumption but it operates faster; by operating faster, it decreases the elapsed time since the previous state estimate; the more recent the previous estimate, the better the prediction in (12); the better the prediction, the more likely we can discriminate bad measurements; if we can discriminate bad measurements, we can autocalibrate the measurement devices; and if we can calibrate the measurement devices, we can improve the individual measurements, thus improving predictions, etc. In other words, the faster, the better.

Looking more closely, it is amazing that such a tracker can function at all. Consider for example the system presented in section 4. Any single beacon sighting offers so few constraints—

the user could be theoretically *anywhere*. Similarly, knowledge about where the user was a moment ago is only an indicator of where the user *might* be now. But used together, these two sources of information can offer more constraints than either alone. With a Kalman filter we can extract the information from the previous state and a new (individual) measurement, and blend them to form a better estimate than would be possible using either alone.

The SCAAT method is accurate, stable, fast, and flexible, and we believe it can be used to improve the performance of a wide variety of commercial and custom tracking systems.

Acknowledgements

We would like to thank the tracker team at UNC, in particular Vernon Chi, Steve Brumback, Kurtis Keller, Pawan Kumar, and Phillip Winston. This work was supported by DARPA/ETO contract no. DABT 63-93-C-0048, "Enabling Technologies and Application Demonstrations for Synthetic Environments", Principle Investigators Frederick P. Brooks Jr. and Henry Fuchs (University of North Carolina at Chapel Hill), and by the National Science Foundation Cooperative Agreement no. ASC-8920219: "Science and Technology Center for Computer Graphics and Scientific Visualization", Center Director Andy van Dam (Brown University). Principle Investigators Andy van Dam, Al Barr (California Institute of Technology), Don Greenberg (Cornell University), Henry Fuchs (University of North Carolina at Chapel Hill), Rich Riesenfeld (University of Utah).

References

[1] C.G. Atkeson and J.M. Hollerbach. 1985. "Kinematic features of unrestrained vertical arm movements," Journal of Neuroscience, 5:2318-2330.

[2] Ali Azarbayejani and Alex Pentland. June 1995. "Recursive Estimation of Motion, Structure, and Focal Length," *IEEE Trans. Pattern Analysis and Machine Intelligence*, June 1995, 17(6).

[3] Ronald Azuma and Mark Ward. 1991. "Space-Resection by Collinearity: Mathematics Behind the Optical Ceiling Head-Tracker," UNC Chapel Hill Department of Computer Science technical report TR 91-048 (November 1991).

[4] Ronald Azuma and Gary Bishop. 1994. "Improving Static and Dynamic Registration in an Optical See-Through HMD," SIGGRAPH 94 Conference Proceedings, Annual Conference Series, pp. 197-204, ACM SIGGRAPH, Addison Wesley, July 1994. ISBN 0-201-60795-6

[5] Ronald Azuma. 1995. "Predictive Tracking for Augmented Reality," Ph.D. dissertation, University of North Carolina at Chapel Hill, TR95-007.

[6] Ted J. Broida and Rama Chellappa. 1986. "Estimation of object motion parameters from noisy images," *IEEE Trans. Pattern Analysis and Machine Intelligence*, January 1986, 8(1), pp. 90-99.

[7] R. G. Brown and P. Y. C. Hwang. 1992. *Introduction to Random Signals and Applied Kalman Filtering, 2nd Edition*, John Wiley & Sons, Inc.

[8] Vernon L. Chi. 1995. "Noise Model and Performance Analysis of Outward-looking Optical Trackers Using Lateral Effect Photo Diodes," University of North Carolina, Department of Computer Science, TR 95-012 (April 3, 1995)

[9] Jack C.K. Chou. 1992. "Quaternion Kinematic and Dynamic Differential Equations," IEEE Transactions on Robotics and Automation, Vol. 8, No. 1, pp. 53-64.

[10] J. L. Crowley and Y. Demazeau. 1993. "Principles and Techniques for Sensor Data Fusion," *Signal Processing (EURASIP)* Vol. 32. pp. 5-27.

[11] J. J. Deyst and C. F. Price. 1968. "Conditions for Asymptotic Stability of the Discrete Minimum-Variance Linear Estimator," *IEEE Transactions on Automatic Control*, December, 1968.

[12] S. Emura and S. Tachi. 1994. "Sensor Fusion based Measurement of Human Head Motion," *Proceedings 3rd IEEE International Workshop on Robot and Human Communication, RO-MAN'94 NAGOYA* (Nagoya University, Nagoya, Japan).

[13] P. Fischer, R. Daniel and K. Siva. 1990. "Specification and Design of Input Devices for Teleoperation," *Proceedings of the IEEE Conference on Robotics and Automation* (Cincinnati, OH), pp. 540-545.

[14] Eric Foxlin. 1993. "Inertial Head Tracking," Master's Thesis, Electrical Engineering and Computer Science, Massachusetts Institute of Technology.

[15] M. Friedman, T. Starner, and A. Pentland. 1992. "Synchronization in Virtual Realities," *Presence: Teleoperators and Virtual Environments,* 1:139-144.

[16] S. Ganapathy. November 1984. "Camera Location Determination Problem," AT&T Bell Laboratories Technical Memorandum, 11358-841102-20-TM.

[17] G. J. Geier, P. V. W. Loomis and A. Cabak. 1987. "Guidance Simulation and Test Support for Differential GPS (Global Positioning System) Flight Experiment," National Aeronautics and Space Administration (Washington, DC) NAS 1.26:177471.

[18] A. Gelb. 1974. *Applied Optimal Estimation*, MIT Press, Cambridge, MA.

[19] Stefan Gottschalk and John F. Hughes. 1993. "Autocalibration for Virtual Environments Tracking Hardware," Proceedings of ACM SIGGRAPH 93 (Anaheim, CA, 1993), Computer Graphics, Annual Conference Series.

[20] A Robert De Saint Vincent Grandjean. 1989. "3-D Modeling of Indoor Scenes by Fusion of Noisy Range and Stereo Data," *IEEE International Conference on Robotics and Automation* (Scottsdale, AZ), 2:681-687.

[21] F. C. Ham and R. G. Brown. 1983. "Observability, Eigenvalues, and Kalman Filtering," *IEEE Transactions on Aerospace and Electronic Systems*, Vol. AES-19, No. 2, pp. 269-273.

[22] R. Held and N. Durlach. 1987. *Telepresence, Time Delay, and Adaptation.* NASA Conference Publication 10023.

[23] Richard L. Holloway. 1995. "Registration Errors in Augmented Reality Systems," Ph.D. dissertation, The University of North Carolina at Chapel Hill, TR95-016.

[24] O. L. R. Jacobs. 1993. *Introduction to Control Theory, 2nd Edition*. Oxford University Press.

[25] Roy S. Kalawsky. 1993. *The Science of Virtual Reality and Virtual Environments*, Addison-Wesley Publishers.

[26] R. E. Kalman. 1960. "A New Approach to Linear Filtering and Prediction Problems," Transaction of the ASME—Journal of Basic Engineering, pp. 35-45 (March 1960).

[27] J. B. Kuipers. 1980 "SPASYN—An Electromagnetic Relative Position and Orientation Tracking System," *IEEE Transactions on Instrumentation and Measurement*, Vol. IM-29, No. 4, pp. 462-466.

[28] Richard Lewis. 1986. *Optimal Estimation with an Introduction to Stochastic Control Theory*, John Wiley & Sons, Inc.

[29] J. Liang, C. Shaw and M. Green. 1991. "On Temporal-spatial Realism in the Virtual Reality Environment," *Fourth Annual Symposium on User Interface Software and Technology*, pp. 19-25.

[30] R. Mahmoud, O. Loffeld and K. Hartmann. 1994. "Multisensor Data Fusion for Automated Guided Vehicles," *Proceedings of SPIE - The International Society for Optical Engineering*, Vol. 2247, pp. 85-96.

[31] Peter S. Maybeck. 1979. *Stochastic Models, Estimation, and Control, Volume 1*, Academic Press, Inc.

[32] Thomas Mazuryk and Michael Gervautz. 1995. "Two-Step Prediction and Image Deflection for Exact Head Tracking in Virtual Environments," *EUROGRAPHICS '95*, Vol. 14, No. 3, pp. 30-41.

[33] K. Meyer, H. Applewhite and F. Biocca. 1992. A Survey of Position Trackers. *Presence,* a publication of the *Center for Research in Journalism and Mass Communication,* The University of North Carolina at Chapel Hill.

[34] Mark Mine. 1993. "Characterization of End-to-End Delays in Head-Mounted Display Systems," The University of North Carolina at Chapel Hill, TR93-001.

[35] National Research Council. 1994. "Virtual Reality, Scientific and Technological Challenges," National Academy Press (Washington, DC).

[36] P.D. Neilson. 1972. "Speed of Response or Bandwidth of Voluntary System Controlling Elbow Position in Intact Man," *Medical and Biological Engineering*, 10:450-459.

[37] F. H. Raab, E. B. Blood, T. O. Steiner, and H. R. Jones. 1979. "Magnetic Position and Orientation Tracking System," *IEEE Transactions on Aerospace and Electronic Systems*, Vol. AES-15, 709-718.

[38] Selspot Technical Specifications, Selcom Laser Measurements, obtained from Innovision Systems, Inc. (Warren, MI).

[39] Richard H. Y. So and Michael J. Griffin. July-August 1992. "Compensating Lags in Head-Coupled Displays Using Head Position Prediction and Image Deflection," *AIAA Journal of Aircraft*, Vol. 29, No. 6, pp. 1064-1068

[40] H. W. Sorenson. 1970. "Least-Squares estimation: from Gauss to Kalman," *IEEE Spectrum*, Vol. 7, pp. 63-68, July 1970.

[41] Andrei State, Gentaro Hirota, David T. Chen, Bill Garrett, Mark Livingston. 1996. "Superior Augmented Reality Registration by Integrating Landmark Tracking and Magnetic Tracking," SIGGRAPH 96 Conference Proceedings, Annual Conference Series, ACM SIGGRAPH, Addison Wesley, August 1996.

[42] J. V. L. Van Pabst and Paul F. C. Krekel. "Multi Sensor Data Fusion of Points, Line Segments and Surface Segments in 3D Space," TNO Physics and Electronics Laboratory, The Hague, The Netherlands. [cited 19 November 1995]. Available from http://www.bart.nl/~lawick/index.html.

[43] J. Wang, R. Azuma, G. Bishop, V. Chi, J. Eyles, and H. Fuchs. 1990. "Tracking a head-mounted display in a room-sized environment with head-mounted cameras," *Proceeding: SPIE'90 Technical Symposium on Optical Engineering & Photonics in Aerospace Sensing* (Orlando, FL).

[44] Mark Ward, Ronald Azuma, Robert Bennett, Stefan Gottschalk, and Henry Fuchs. 1992. "A Demonstrated Optical Tracker With Scalable Work Area for Head-Mounted Display Systems," *Proceedings of 1992 Symposium on Interactive 3D Graphics* (Cambridge, MA, 29 March - 1 April 1992), pp. 43-52.

[45] Wefald, K.M., and McClary, C.R. "Autocalibration of a laser gyro strapdown inertial reference/navigation system," *IEEE PLANS '84*. Position Location and Navigation Symposium Record.

[46] Greg Welch and Gary Bishop. 1995. "An Introduction to the Kalman Filter," University of North Carolina, Department of Computer Science, TR 95-041.

[47] Greg Welch, 1996. "SCAAT: Incremental Tracking with Incomplete Information," University of North Carolina at Chapel Hill, doctoral dissertation, TR 96-051.

[48] H. J. Woltring. 1974. *"New possibilities for human motion studies by real-time light spot position measurement,"* Biotelemetry, Vol. 1.

The Haptic Display of Complex Graphical Environments

Diego C. Ruspini[1], Krasimir Kolarov[2] and Oussama Khatib[1]

Stanford University[1]

Interval Research Corporation[2]

Abstract

Force feedback coupled with visual display allows people to interact intuitively with complex virtual environments. For this synergy of haptics and graphics to flourish, however, haptic systems must be capable of modeling environments with the same richness, complexity and interactivity that can be found in existing graphic systems. To help meet this challenge, we have developed a haptic rendering system that allows for the efficient tactile display of graphical information. The system uses a common high-level framework to model contact constraints, surface shading, friction and texture. The multi-level control system also helps ensure that the haptic device will remain stable even as the limits of the renderer's capabilities are reached.

CR Categories and Subject Descriptors: C.3 [Special Purpose and Application-Based Systems]: Real-time Systems; I.3.7 [Three-Dimensional Graphics and Realism]: Virtual Reality; I.3.4 [Graphics Utilities]: Device Drivers; I.6.8 [Simulation and Modeling]: Distributed.

Additional Keywords: haptic, force feedback, force shading, contact constraints, friction model, haptic texture, virtual environments.

1 INTRODUCTION

Haptic devices allow physical interaction with virtual environments, enhancing the ability of their users to perform a variety of complex computer interaction tasks [7,16,20]. Several technological advances are required, however, for haptic systems to achieve the ubiquity of graphic systems.

[1] Robotics Laboratory, Computer Science Department, Stanford University, Stanford, CA 94305
ruspini@cs.stanford.edu, khatib@cs.stanford.edu
[2] Interval Research Corporation 1801 Page Mill Road, Building C, Palo Alto, CA 94304
kolarov@interval.com

A successful haptic system must complement existing graphic devices. Current desktop graphic systems are capable of rendering over 20,000 shaded and textured polygonal surfaces at interactive (30Hz) rates. In comparison, most of the current haptic systems are only capable of representing a few dozen geometric primitives.

Because visual and tactile tasks are often closely intertwined, the haptic system should be capable of representing the surfaces and objects that are commonly found in graphic environments. These environments are usually composed of many zero-width polygons, lines and points. The haptic system should also make use of additional graphical information such as surface normals and texture maps which add to the complexity and richness of graphical environments.

Furthermore, graphic models often contain intersecting surfaces and gaps between primitives, and the topology of the model is seldom known. The haptic system should avoid, as much as possible, costly preprocessing steps that decrease the system's interactivity, such as those involved in the conversion or segmentation of a model.

In addition, the haptic controller should be robust and degrade gracefully as the limits of its performance are reached. Haptic devices require high controller servo rates—typically over 1000Hz—in order to achieve stability and high disturbance rejection. Failure to achieve these rates can lead to a system that is unstable, potentially causing device damage or user injury.

Finally, the haptic system should provide a high-level interface that hides many of the details of the haptic rendering process. Since graphic and haptic environments are often identical, it would be advantageous if the graphic and haptic specifications were similar.

This paper describes "HL," a new haptic interface library. The Application Programming Interface (API) of this library is almost identical to that of GL, the graphics hardware interface library of Silicon Graphics workstations. This allows haptic environments to be quickly and efficiently incorporated into graphics applications.

The HL library uses a multi-level control system to effectively simulate contacts with virtual environments. A key element of this control system is the notion of the virtual "proxy," similar to the "god-object" proposed by Zilles and Salisbury [27]. The virtual proxy is a representative object that substitutes for the physical finger or probe in the virtual environment. Figure 1 illustrates the motion of the virtual proxy, as the probe's position is altered. The motion of the proxy is akin to that of a robot greedily attempting to move toward a goal. When unobstructed, the robot moves directly towards the goal. When the robot encounters an obstacle, direct motion is not possible, but the robot may still be able to reduce the distance to the goal by moving along one or more of the constraint surfaces. The motion is chosen to locally minimize the distance to the goal. When the robot is unable to decrease its distance to the goal, it stops at the local minimum configuration.

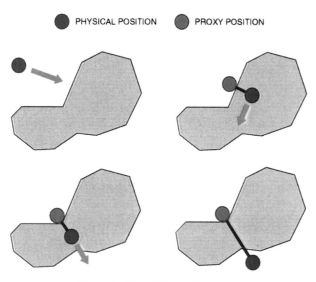

Figure 1: Virtual Proxy Example

Since a strong correspondence exists between the movement of the proxy and robot motion planning, many of the algorithms used in our implementation were developed originally for robotics applications. With this interaction model, the task of the haptic servo controller reduces to minimizing the error between the configuration of the proxy and the position of the haptic device. In effect, the haptic device is used to attempt to physically move the goal to the location of the proxy.

The remainder of this paper is organized as follows: In Section 2, we discuss previous work in haptic rendering. The basic algorithm employed to update the virtual proxy's position is presented in Section 3. In Section 4, we discuss the implementation of force shading—the haptic equivalent of Phong shading [21] in graphics—within the virtual proxy framework. Section 5 discusses methods to simulate static and dynamic friction, and other surface and atmospheric effects. An overview of the current implemented system is presented in Section 6, and the low-level haptic controller is presented in Section 7. Sections 8 and 9 are devoted to the presentation of results and the discussion of future work.

2 BACKGROUND AND RELATED WORK

In *penalty* methods, forces proportional to the amount of penetration into a virtual volume are applied to the haptic device. For simple geometries, like spheres and planes, the direction and amount of penetration are easy to determine. The simplicity of this approach has facilitated the study of many interesting situations such as those involving dynamic objects and surface effects. Massie and Salisbury extended this technique by subdividing the internal volume and associating each sub-volume with a surface toward which repulsion forces are exerted [17]. This approach has also been used successfully to allow haptic interactions with volumetric data [1,12].

These approaches, however, have a number of drawbacks. When multiple primitives touch or are allowed to intersect it is often difficult to determine which exterior surface should be associated with a given internal volume. In the worst case, a global search of all the primitives may be required to find the

nearest exterior surface, as seen in Figure 2(a). In addition, as a finger probe penetrates a surface it will eventually become closer to another surface of the object. The resultant force actively pushes the probe out through this second surface. This situation is illustrated in Figure 2(b). Finally, as shown in Figure 2(c), small or thin objects may have insufficient internal volume to generate the constraint forces required to prevent the probe from passing through the obstacle. This problem is particularly troublesome in graphics applications since most graphic models are constructed almost exclusively from infinitely thin polygons, lines and points.

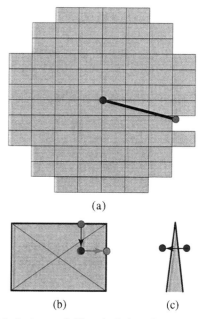

(a)

(b)   (c)

Figure 2: Limitations of "Penalty" based Haptic Rendering Methods. (a) Lack of locality: removal of primitive will create new nearest surface, (b) Force Discontinuities: application of force causes probe to be attracted toward other surfaces. (c) "Pop-Thru" of thin objects.

Constraint-based methods were first proposed for haptic applications by Zilles and Salisbury [27] to address the limitations of penalty-based approaches. These methods employ a god-object which, similar to the virtual proxy, is constrained by the objects in the environment. This approach has been used to model interactions between a point-size god-object and complex polygonal models. The virtual proxy is an extension of this idea. This paper presents how, in addition to surface constraints—force shading [19], friction, surface stiffness, and texture can be modeled by simply changing the position of the virtual proxy. Also, because the virtual proxy has a finite size, it does not slip through the tiny numerical gaps found in most polygonal meshes and can therefore operate without first having to reconstruct the topology of a surface as is required in the original god-object approach [27].

3 UPDATING PROXY POSITION

For simplicity, we will represent the virtual proxy as a massless sphere that moves among the objects in the environment. Because of small numerical errors, polygons that are intended to share a common edge often contain gaps. The radius of the proxy should therefore be large enough to avoid falling through the holes in the underlying model. In addition, the user will often wish to make the proxy large enough so that it is easily visible on a graphical display. We also assume that all the obstacles in the environment can be divided into a finite set of convex components.

During the update process, a goal configuration for the proxy is found at each time step and the proxy attempts to move to this configuration by direct linear motion. Initially, the goal configuration is the location of the end-point of the haptic device. This position, however, will change as the proxy encounters obstacles in the environment.

The volume swept by the virtual proxy, as it moves during a given time period, is checked to see if it penetrates any primitive in the environment. Because the path of the proxy is linear, this test involves determining whether a line-segment, specified by the proxy and goal configurations, falls within one radius of any object in the environment. Since many primitive objects may exist in the environment, an efficient means of determining which primitives intersect the proxy's path is required. Several fast, general purpose, algorithms have been developed for this purpose [15,10]. In our current implementation, we employ an algorithm originally developed for path-planning applications [22] that builds a bounding-sphere hierarchy for each object and is capable of quickly finding the shortest distance between non-convex bodies.

If the proxy's path does not collide with any obstacles, the proxy is allowed to move directly towards the goal. If one or more interfering primitives are found, the proxy's position is advanced until it makes contact with the first obstacle in its path. To model this interaction efficiently, we consider the configuration space of the proxy, where the *configuration-space obstacles* (C-obstacles) [14], consist of all points within one proxy radius of the original obstacles. Note that, in this space, the position of the proxy is identified by a point while all C-obstacles have continuously defined surfaces and non-zero thickness. A unique constraint plane can then be found where the line segment that represents the proxy's path intersects the C-obstacle. An example of configuration space, C-obstacles, and proxy constraint planes is shown in Figure 3.

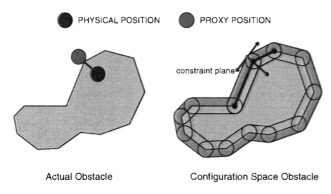

Figure 3: Configuration Space Obstacles & Constraint Planes

Introduction of the configuration space allows us to model the proxy as a point and the obstacles as uniquely defined local planar surfaces. The proxy is moved until it makes contact with the closest constraint plane. Planes that fall below this new position cannot affect the local motion of the proxy and may therefore be pruned. If the proxy reaches the user's position, no further movement is required. Otherwise, a new sub-goal is generated observing that each constraint plane limits the directions of motion to the half-space above the plane. The

intersection of all such half-spaces defines a convex, unbounded polyhedron. The desired solution is the point within this convex region (the local free-space) that minimizes the distance to the user's position. Since this problem is independent of coordinate translation, and since all the constraint planes go through the current proxy position, the problem can be written compactly as

$$\text{minimize } \|x - p\| \text{ subject to}$$

$$\hat{n}_1^T x \geq 0,$$
$$\hat{n}_2^T x \geq 0,$$
$$\vdots$$
$$\hat{n}_m^T x \geq 0.$$
(1)

where p is the vector from the current proxy position to the user's position, x is the new sub-goal, and $\hat{n}_i$, $0 \leq i \leq m$, are the unit normals of the constraint planes.

This problem may be solved using a standard quadratic programming package such as that introduced by Gill et. al [9]. In our case, however, there are many simplifications that make possible a simpler and faster solution. In our implementation, this problem is solved in two steps. The minimum set of active constraint planes is found first; this set is then used to find a new sub-goal position. If the desired solution lies on a face of the convex free space, then the solution lies on only one of the constraint planes. If the solution lies on an edge, then two constraint planes are required. If the solution lies on a vertex three planes are needed. Finally, if the user's position lies in the free space, then no constraint planes are required. This convex free space region has a dual space consisting of the points $-\hat{n}_i$, $0 \leq i \leq m$ (the outward normals of the planes forming the free-space region) and the origin (plane at infinity). The constraint planes that bound the solution can be found by determining the closest face, edge, or vertex on the convex hull of this region to a point $\hat{p}$, a unit vector with the same direction as p. This problem may be treated using the same algorithms employed in the collision detection process [8]. The vertices of the closest face, edge or vertex indicate that the corresponding constraint planes bound the solution. An example of this mapping is shown in Figure 4. As illustrated, the solution x is constrained by planes **a**, **b** and the plane at infinity **o**. In the dual, this corresponds to $\hat{p}$ being nearest the face $\{\mathbf{a}, \mathbf{b}, \mathbf{o}\}$.

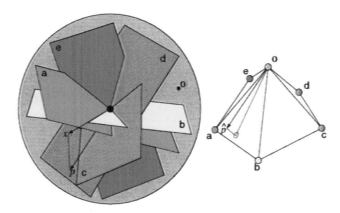

Figure 4: Constraint Planes and Equivalent Free Space Dual

Once the bounding planes have been determined, Equation 1 may be solved using only the active planes as constraints.

With the inequalities replaced by equalities, the problem can be solved easily using Lagrange multipliers as is described by Zilles in [27] to find the new sub-goal. Since at most three planes can be active at one time, the entire solution can be found in $O(m)$ time, where m is the original number of constraint planes. Once the new sub-goal is found, the iteration may continue.

Each iteration reduces the distance between the proxy and the user's position, thus ensuring that the movement of the proxy will be stable if the input from the user is stable.

4 FORCE SHADING

Most graphic interfaces permit the specification of surface normals on the vertices of polygonal surfaces. This information is used to alter the lighting model on the surface to give it the appearance of being smooth [11,21]. Morgenbesser and Srinivasan [19] were the first to demonstrate that a similar haptic effect may be created. Their solution changes the direction of the normal force while retaining the magnitude caused by the penetration of the original polygonal surface. While this technique produces compelling shading effects, it is unclear how to extend this approach to deal with multiple intersecting shaded surfaces or additional surface effects, such as friction or texture.

Our force shading approach handles situations involving multiple intersecting, shaded surfaces that are in contact with the proxy at the same time. These situations arise, for example, when two force-shaded cylinders are placed by side. In addition, the shading effect is created solely by moving the position of the proxy, thus helping to guarantee solution stability.

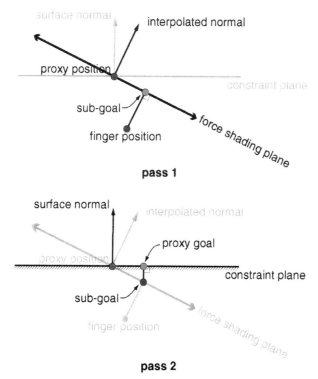

pass 1

pass 2

Figure 5: Two Pass Force Shading with Supplied Normals

When a polygonal surface with user specified normals is encountered a new local surface normal is calculated by interpolating the normals from the vertices of the polygon. Since the required interpolation weights have already been computed as part of the collision detection process, this determination requires little additional computation. This interpolation is very similar to that required for Phong shading in computer graphics applications [21]. The interpolated normal specifies a new constraint plane going through the contact point. The algorithm proceeds by first finding a new sub-goal using the interpolated planes instead of the original constraint planes. This sub-goal is then treated as the user's finger position and a second pass of the update procedure is performed to obtain the final sub-goal configuration for this iteration. This second pass is performed using the actual (non-interpolated) constraint planes. While this approach is slightly more computationally expensive than previous efforts [19,23], it properly considers the effect of all constraint surfaces in both passes and produces the correct result even if multiple force shaded surfaces exist. This process is illustrated in Figure 5.

If the sub-goal configuration is above all the true constraint planes after the first pass, the sub-goal is first projected back onto the nearest true constraint plane. This ensures that the new sub-goal point will always be on the object surface and that surface effects like friction and texture will be handled correctly.

Note that force shading may increase the distance between the user's finger position and the position of the proxy. This increase implies that the surface is active and can add energy to the haptic/user system. In graphic models the interpolated and the true surface normals typically differ by less then 30°. In this case, the added energy is very small, and is not noticed by the user. In all of our tests the motion was stable.

The difference between the force shaded surface and a flat surface is illustrated in Figure 6. In both figures the difference between the actual user position and the position of the virtual proxy are shown as the user's finger follows a circular path around a ten-sided polygonal approximation of a circular object.

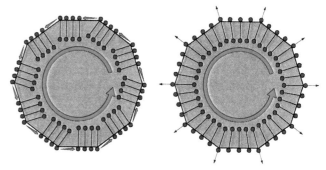

Figure 6: Effect of Flat (a) vs. Force Shaded (b) surface on proxy motion

As seen in Figure 6(a), a strong discontinuity occurs when the proxy finally reaches an obstacle edge. In Figure 6(b), surface normals have been specified on the vertices. The resulting movement of the proxy shows that the resultant force is always perpendicular to the interpolated circular object. This is what would be expected if the user were moving around a perfectly circular object. Although the proxy remains on the polygonal surface the motion of the proxy is continuous and therefore the resultant force feels smooth to the user.

5 SURFACE PROPERTIES

Several researchers [2,5,16,24,25] have proposed methods to simulate static, dynamic, viscous friction and texture. Unlike previous methods, our implementation creates all these effects solely by restricting the movement of the proxy. In this way the stability of the final solution can be better controlled.

5.1 Static Friction

Static friction (stiction) is particularly simple to model within the virtual proxy framework. The force exerted on the proxy by the user can be estimated by the equation $f = k_p(p-v)$, where p is the position of the proxy, v is the position of the finger and k_p is the proportional gain of the haptic controller. For a given constraint plane, let f_n and f_t be the components of the force on the proxy normal and tangential to the constraint plane, respectively. If the given constraint surface has a static friction parameter μ_s, then the proxy is in static contact if $\|f_t\| \le \mu_s \|f_n\|$, i.e., the user's position is in the friction cone of the surface. When any constraint surface is in static contact with the proxy, the proxy's position is prevented from changing by making the new sub-goal position equal to the current proxy position.

5.2 Viscous and Dynamic Friction

Our approach for modeling viscous damping and Coulomb friction is based on the observation of the motion of a one dimensional object. The equation of motion of an object with mass m moving in a viscous field, along a surface that exhibits dynamic friction is

$$f_t - \mu_d f_n = m\ddot{x} + b\dot{x}, \qquad (2)$$

where b is a viscous damping term, and μ_d is the coefficient of Coulomb friction. As the mass of the object approaches zero, the body quickly reaches its saturation velocity. In dynamic equilibrium, the velocity of the object is given by

$$\dot{x} = \frac{f_t - \mu_d f_n}{b}. \qquad (3)$$

This limit can be used to bound the amount that the proxy can travel in one clock cycle. When multiple constraint surfaces exist, the lowest velocity bound is taken as the limit of the proxy's movement. In the event that the maximum velocity is negative, then the dynamic friction term is sufficient to resist all movement and the proxy's position is not changed. If $b = 0$ no viscous term exists and the maximum velocity is not limited. Note that this method does not require computation of the finger velocity and is therefore not susceptible to errors caused from trying to estimate this value from a finite number of encoder values.

In the majority of current treatments, the stiffness of a surface is modeled by reducing the position gain of the haptic controller. This approach is undesirable in our system since the location of the proxy models many complex and intermixed phenomena. In addition, it is desirable to keep the haptic controller at settings that are chosen to optimize its performance based solely on the inertia, friction and stiffness of the mechanical system and not on the needs of the virtual environment.

Given a surface with stiffness s, $0 \le s \le 1$, it is possible to change the apparent stiffness of a surface without altering any of the controller's parameters by choosing a new point p' such that

$$p' = v + s(p - v), \qquad (4)$$

where p is the position of the proxy assuming an infinitely stiff surface and v is the position of the user's finger. The point p' is used as the proxy position for the haptic control loop. The old proxy position is still retained to allow the proxy to continue to follow the surface of the object. This approach is based on the intuitive physical observation that, as pressure is applied, the surface of a soft body will indent, resulting in the finger penetrating the volume of the un-deformed object, as seen in Figure 7. Caution should be taken when adjacent surfaces have different stiffnesses. As the proxy moves from a non-rigid surface to one with a higher stiffness, the distance between the proxy and the finger will increase, adding energy to the system. The result is that the user feels what appears to be an active unnatural surface. A more realistic effect can be created by altering the polygonal surface as it is affected by forces applied by the user. The surface can be deformed to reveal properties of the model's internal structure that are not possible to create solely by altering the stiffness of the boundary surface.

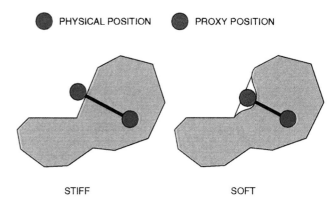

● PHYSICAL POSITION   ● PROXY POSITION

STIFF   SOFT

Figure 7: Physical Intuition Behind Stiffness Model

5.3 Texture

Haptic textures were first demonstrated by Minsky et al. [18] for the haptic display of height fields on a two degree of freedom planar haptic display. In our system, an image-based texture map can be used to modulate any of the surface parameters—friction, viscosity or stiffness—to create different haptic effects. At present, the texture values are only evaluated at the proxy position at the beginning of each clock cycle. This produces a convincing effect with slowly changing textures. Ideally, the texture values should be evaluated as the proxy moves along the surface of the object to ensure that a significant event is not missed as the proxy travels along that surface. This evaluation is required, for example, when layering a texture of thin high friction grid lines on a planar surface. Without evaluating the texture values along the path these grid-lines may be missed.

Another interesting approach to the modeling of textures is based on the modification of the force-shading constraint planes in a manner similar to that employed in bump mapping in computer graphics [4]. Our current texture bump-map technique can generate one additional constraint plane for each textured surface. This approach is adequate to model continuously differentiable textured surfaces. Grooved or cratered surfaces which contain sharp edges and corners may require additional constraint planes and the monitoring of the motion of the proxy to ensure that it is not constrained by other surface features as it moves along the surface.

6 SYSTEM IMPLEMENTATION

Our current system runs on two computers: the haptic server and the application client. The separation of the haptic and application/graphic processes was first proposed by Adachi et al. [2]. Decoupling the low-level force servo loop from the high-level control is important since the haptic servo loop must run at a very high rate, typically greater than 1000Hz, to achieve a high fidelity force display. Most application programs typically run at a much slower rate (~30Hz).

In our system the bulk of haptic rendering effort is placed on the haptic server, thus freeing the client machine to perform the tasks required by the user's application. The haptic server receives high level commands from the client, tracks the position of the haptic device, updates the position of the virtual proxy, and sends control commands to the haptic device. This arrangement places the performance bottle-neck on the haptic server CPU rather than on the I/O channel. This is desirable since CPU processor performance is increasing rapidly while the latency of I/O connections has been largely stagnant. In our current system, a SGI workstation is used as the haptic client, a Pentium Pro PC is used as the server, and communication between them is performed over a regular ethernet connection via TCP/IP packets.

6.1 The Client Application

Applications communicate to the haptic server through the HL network interface library. The current library supports a limited set of the functions provided by the GL graphics library. The HL Library allows users to define objects as a collection of primitive objects — points, line segments or polygons. Objects are retained until over-written. Transformations are provided to allow objects and primitives to be freely translated or rotated. Surface normals and texture coordinates can be associated with polygonal vertices to allow for the specification of smooth or textured surfaces. Object hierarchies and material properties such as friction and stiffness may also be defined.

6.2 Model Construction

Once the modeling commands are received from the client, they must be stored in a form suitable for haptic rendering. Vertices are transformed into local object frames and meshes and sequences of line segments are represented as a set of independent convex bodies.

Because each object is normally constructed from a large number of primitives, a naive test based on checking if each primitive is in the path of the proxy would be prohibitively expensive. In general, the proxy's path will be in contact with at most a small fraction of the underlying primitives. In our approach a hierarchical bounding representation for the object is constructed to take advantage of the spatial coherence inherent in the object. The bounding representation, based on spheres, is similar to that first proposed by Quinlan [22].

This hierarchy of bounding spheres is constructed by first covering each polygon with small spheres in a manner similar

to scan conversion in computer graphics. These spheres are the leaves of an approximately balanced binary tree. Each node of this tree represents a single sphere that completely contains all the leaves of its descendants. After covering the object, a divide and conquer strategy is used to build the interior nodes of the tree. This algorithm works in a manner similar to quick-sort. First an axis aligned bounding box that contains all the leaf spheres is found. The leaf spheres are then divided along the plane through the mid-point of the longest axes of the bounding box. Each of the resulting two subsets should be compact and contain approximately an equal number of leaf spheres. The bounding tree is constructed by recursively invoking the algorithm on each subset and then creating a new node with the two sub-trees as children. A cut-away view showing the leaf nodes (yellow) and bounding sphere hierarchy for a typical model is illustrated in Figure 8. Note that a node is not required to fully contain all the descendant internal nodes, only the descendant leaf nodes.

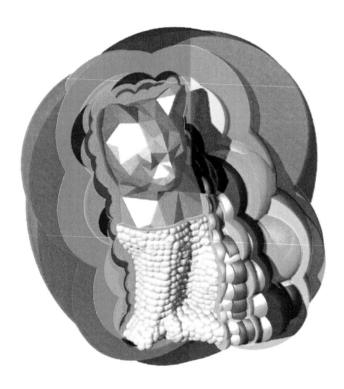

Figure 8: Cut-Away of the Bounding Hierarchy of a Cat Model

Two heuristics are used to compute the bounding sphere of a given node. The first heuristic finds the smallest bounding sphere that contains the spheres of its two children. The second method directly examines the leaf spheres. The center is taken as the mid-point of the bounding box already computed earlier. The radius is taken to be just large enough to contain all the descendant leaf nodes. The method that generates the sphere with the smallest radius is used for the given node. The first heuristic tends to work better near the leaves of the tree, while the second method produces better results closer to the root. This algorithm has an expected $O(n \lg n)$ execution time, where n is the number of leaf spheres.

7 HAPTIC CONTROLLER

Reliance on a virtual proxy reduces the task of the haptic servo controller to minimization of the error between the configuration of the proxy and position of the haptic device. Reducing position error of a mechanical system is a problem which has been discussed extensively in the robotics literature [6]. In our current implementation we rely on a simple operational space proportional derivative (PD) controller [13]. As all modeling effects are achieved by the movement of the proxy, controller gains and other parameters can be set by sole consideration of the properties of the mechanical system.

The low-level control loop may be separated from the contact/proxy update loop to guarantee stability of the system even in the presence of a large number of objects. By running the control loop at a high fixed clock rate, stability is easier to ensure and the fidelity of the haptic display degrades gracefully as the complexity of the environment is increased. If the proxy update procedure is unable to maintain the same rate as the controller, objects feel "sticky." While this effect may not be desirable, it is preferable to permitting unstable and dangerous behavior of the haptic device.

8 RESULTS

Our haptic library has been successfully tested on a large number of polygonal models, including some containing more than 24,000 polygonal primitives. In our tests the client computer was a SGI Indigo2 High Impact running IRIX 6.2 and the haptic server was a 200Mhz Pentium Pro running Linux 2.0.2. Communication between computers was made through a standard ethernet TCP/IP connection. The haptic device employed was a ground based PHANToM manipulator. This 3-degree-of-freedom force-feedback device has sufficiently high stiffness, low inertia and low friction for high fidelity force display. The server produced stable results with position gains over 1800 Newtons/meter with no artificial damping. The proxy update loop computation time is approximately $O(\lg n)$ where n is the number of polygons. This slow asymptotic growth is the consequence of the dependence of the proxy's movement on only its local environment. In contrast, the rendering time for a graphic display, where the entire world may be visible at one time, is inherently $O(n)$.

The current system is adept in modeling a large number of geometric models. Some examples are shown in Figures 9,10 and 11. Figure 9 shows a VRML model of an AT-AT from Star Wars containing over 11,000 polygons. The high level interface simplifies the implementation of applications like VRML browsers. Figure 10 shows a VRML model of the classic teapot, composed of 3416 triangular surfaces. Force shading is used to model the apparently curved surfaces of the underlying polygonal model. Figure 11 shows a sample test application where the user can click virtual buttons to select a variety of geometrical models with numerous different surface characteristics. These models can be moved to make them contact or overlap one another, creating possibly thousands of unexpected new intersections, edges, and corners.

In all cases, the location of the virtual proxy, rather than finger position, is displayed to the user, further adding to the sense of rigidity of the modeled environment [26].

Figure 9: Haptic AT-AT (11088 polygons)

Figure 10: Force Shaded Teapot (3416 polygons)

Figure 11: Interactive Haptic Environment

9 FUTURE WORK

While the current system is able to model a wide variety of objects and material properties, it only supports limited manipulation of the objects in the environment. As is the case with graphic systems, movement is simulated by re-rendering the moving objects at different locations. These discrete motion steps, which must be specified by the client processor, result in a discontinuous jerky motion. Furthermore, in some cases, it is possible for the proxy to lie outside of an object at one time step and within it the next. We are currently looking at several ways of allowing the application program to easily endow haptic objects with smooth, continuous and dynamic motions.

Finally, the virtual proxy framework can be expanded to handle implicit surfaces like splines, or even volumetric information directly without first transforming these representations into a polygonal surface model. This ability is beneficial because often the cost of this transformation can be prohibitively expensive, or can greatly reduce the interactivity of the application.

CONCLUSION

The system presented in this paper is capable of the haptic simulation of complex graphical environments. The common virtual proxy framework, used for modeling all haptic effects, reduces the low-level control of the haptic device to a simple positional controller. This controller may operate in real time if its operation is separated from the rest of the haptic rendering process, thus helping to ensure that the haptic controller's stability. The high level user interface allows graphic applications to quickly and easily incorporate haptic technology and increases the ability to manipulate and interact with virtual environments.

ACKNOWLEDGMENTS

We wish to thank Oliver Brock, Kyong-Sok Chang, Eugene Jhong, Karon MacLean, Robert Shaw and Bill Verplank for their helpful insights and discussion in preparing this paper. The AT-AT by H.H.C. is from Avalon Viewpoint archive. The reseach was supported by research grants from NASA/JSC, grant NGT-9-6, Boeing, Interval Research Corporation, and NSF, grant IRI-9320017.

REFERENCES

[1] Avila, R. S., Sobierajski, "A Haptic Interaction Method for Volume Visualization," *Visualization '96 Proceedings*, October 1996.

[2] Adachi, Y., Kumano, T., Ogino K., "Intermediate Representation for Stiff Virtual Objects." *Proc. IEEE Virtual Reality Annual Intl. Symposium '95*, (March 11-15), pp. 203-210.

[3] Baraff, D., "Analytical Methods for Dynamic Simulation of Non-penetrating Rigid Bodies," *SIGGRAPH 89 Proceedings*, (August 1989), pp. 223-232.

[4] Blinn, J., "Simulation of Wrinkled Surfaces," *SIGGRAPH 78 Proceedings*, (August 1978), pp. 286-292.

[5] Buttolo, P., Kung, D., Hannaford, B., "Manipulation in Real, Virtual and Remote Environments." *Proc. IEEE Conference on Systems, Man and Cybernetics* (August 1990), pp. 177-185.

[6] Craig, J., "Introduction to Robotics Mechanics and Control," *Addison-Wesley Pub. Co.,* 1989.

[7] Finch, M., Chi, V., Taylor, R. M. II, Falvo, M., Washburn, S., Superfine, R., "Surface Modification Tools in a Virtual Environment Interface to a Scanning Probe Microscope," *Proc. 1995 Symposium on Interactive 3D Graphics*, pp13-18, April 1995.

[8] Gilbert, E. G., Johnson, D.W., Keerthi, S. S., "A Fast Procedure for Computing the Distance Between Complex Objects in Three-Dimensional Space," *IEEE J. of Robotics and Automation*, Vol.4, No. 2, April 1988.

[9] Gill, P., Hammarling, S., Murray, W., Saunders, M., Wright, M., "User's Guide to LLSOL," *Stanford University Technical Report SOL 86-1*, (January 1986).

[10] Gottschalk, S., Lin, M. C., Manocha D., "OBBTree: A Hierarchical Structure for Rapid Interference Detection," *SIGGRAPH 96 Proceedings*, (August 1996), pp. 171-180.

[11] Gouraud, H. "Continuous Shading of Curved Surfaces." *IEEE Transactions on Computers*, C-20(6):pp 623-629, June 1971.

[12] Iwata H., Noma, H., "Volume Haptization," *IEEE 1993 Symposium on Research Frontiers in Virtual Reality*, pp. 16-23, October 1993.

[13] Khatib, O., "A Unified Approach to Motion and Force Control of Robot Manipulators: The Operational Space Formulation," *IEEE J. of Robotics and Automation*, Vol 3., No 1., 1987.

[14] Latombe, Jean-Claude, "Robot Motion Planning," Kluwer Academic Publishing, 1991, pp 58-152.

[15] Lin, M., Canny, J. F., "A Fast Algorithm for Incremental Distance Calculation," *International Conference on Robotics and Automation*, pp. 1008-1014, May 1991.

[16] Mark, W. R., Randolph,S. C., Finch M., Van Verth,J. M., Taylor II,R. M., "Adding Force Feedback to Graphics Systems: Issues and Solutions," *SIGGRAPH '96 Proceedings*, (August 1996), pp. 447-452.

[17] Massie, T.M., Salisbury, J.K., "The PHANToM Haptic Interface: A Device for Probing Virtual Objects." ASME Haptic Interfaces for Virtual Environment and Teleoperator Systems 1994, In *Dynamic Systems and Control 1994* (Chicago, Nov. 6-11), vol. 1, pp.295-301.

[18] Minsky, M. D. R., "Computational Haptics: The Sandpaper System for Synthesizing Texture for a Force-Feedback Display." PhD thesis, MIT, June 1995.

[19] Morgenbesser, H. B., "Force Shading for Haptic Shape Perception in Haptic Virtual Environments." M.Eng. thesis, MIT, September 1995.

[20] Ouh-Young, M., "Force Display in Molecular Docking," *Ph. D. Dissertation, University of North Carolina at Chapel Hill, UNC-CH CS TR90-004*, February, 1990.

[21] Phong, B. T., "Illumination for Computer Generated Pictures." *Communications of the ACM*, 18(6), pp311-317, June 1975.

[22] Quinlan, S., "Efficient Distance Computation between Non-Convex Objects," *Int. Conference on Robotics and Automation*, (April 1994).

[23] Ruspini, D., Kolarov, K., "Robust Haptic Display of Graphical Environments," Proc. of The First Phantom User's Group Workshop, September 1996

[24] Salcudean, S. E., Vlaar, T. D., "On the Emulation of Stiff Walls and Static Friction with a Magnetically Levitated Input/Output Device," ASME Haptic Interfaces for Virtual Environment and Teleoperator Systems, Dynamics Systems and Control, pp.123-130, April 1995.

[25] Salisbury, K., Brock, D., Massie, T., Swarup, N., Zilles, C., "Haptic Rendering: Programming Touch Interaction with Virtual Objects," Proc. 1995 Symposium on Interactive 3D Graphics, pp. 123-130, April 1995.

[26] Srinivasan, M. A., Beauregard, G. L., Brock, D. L., "The Impact of Visual Information of the Haptic Peception of Stiffness in Virtual Environments," ASME Winter Annual Meeting, November 1996.

[27] Zilles, C. B., Salisbury, J. K., "A Constraint-based God-object Method for Haptic Display." ASME Haptic Interfaces for Virtual Environment and Teleoperator Systems 1994, *Dynamic Systems and Control 1994* (Chicago, Illinois, Nov. 6-11), vol. 1, pp.146-150.

Video Rewrite: Driving Visual Speech with Audio

Christoph Bregler, Michele Covell, Malcolm Slaney

Interval Research Corporation

ABSTRACT

Video Rewrite uses existing footage to create automatically new video of a person mouthing words that she did not speak in the original footage. This technique is useful in movie dubbing, for example, where the movie sequence can be modified to sync the actors' lip motions to the new soundtrack.

Video Rewrite automatically labels the phonemes in the training data and in the new audio track. Video Rewrite reorders the mouth images in the training footage to match the phoneme sequence of the new audio track. When particular phonemes are unavailable in the training footage, Video Rewrite selects the closest approximations. The resulting sequence of mouth images is stitched into the background footage. This stitching process automatically corrects for differences in head position and orientation between the mouth images and the background footage.

Video Rewrite uses computer-vision techniques to track points on the speaker's mouth in the training footage, and morphing techniques to combine these mouth gestures into the final video sequence. The new video combines the dynamics of the original actor's articulations with the mannerisms and setting dictated by the background footage. Video Rewrite is the first facial-animation system to automate all the labeling and assembly tasks required to resync existing footage to a new soundtrack.

CR Categories: I.3.3 [Computer Graphics]: Picture/Image Generation—Morphing; I.4.6 [Image Processing]: Segmentation—Feature Detection; I.3.8 [Computer Graphics]: Applications—Facial Synthesis; I.4.10 [Image Processing]: Applications—Feature Transformations.

Additional Keywords: Facial Animation, Lip Sync.

1 WHY AND HOW WE REWRITE VIDEO

We are very sensitive to the synchronization between speech and lip motions. For example, the special effects in *Forest Gump* are compelling because the Kennedy and Nixon footage is lip synched to the movie's new soundtrack. In contrast, close-ups in dubbed movies are often disturbing due to the lack of lip sync. Video Rewrite is a system for automatically synthesizing faces with proper lip sync. It can be used for dubbing movies, teleconferencing, and special effects.

1801 Page Mill Road, Building C, Palo Alto, CA, 94304. E-mail: bregler@cs.berkeley.edu, covell@interval.com, malcolm@interval.com. See the SIGGRAPH Video Proceedings or http://www.interval.com/papers/1997-012/ for the latest animations.

Video Rewrite automatically pieces together from old footage a new video that shows an actor mouthing a new utterance. The results are similar to labor-intensive special effects in *Forest Gump*. These effects are successful because they start from actual film footage and modify it to match the new speech. Modifying and reassembling such footage in a smart way and synchronizing it to the new sound track leads to final footage of realistic quality. Video Rewrite uses a similar approach but does not require labor-intensive interaction.

Our approach allows Video Rewrite to learn from example footage how a person's face changes during speech. We learn what a person's mouth looks like from a video of that person speaking normally. We capture the dynamics and idiosyncrasies of her articulation by creating a database of video clips. For example, if a woman speaks out of one side of her mouth, this detail is recreated accurately. In contrast, most current facial-animation systems rely on generic head models that do not capture the idiosyncrasies of an individual speaker.

To model a new person, Video Rewrite requires a small number (26 in this work) of hand-labeled images. This is the only human intervention that is required in the whole process. Even this level of human interaction is not a fundamental requirement: We could use face-independent models instead [Kirby90, Covell96].

Video Rewrite shares its philosophy with concatenative speech synthesis [Moulines90]. Instead of modeling the vocal tract, concatenative speech synthesis analyzes a corpus of speech, selects examples of phonemes, and normalizes those examples. Phonemes are the distinct sounds within a language, such as the /IY/ and /P/ in "teapot." Concatenative speech synthesizes new sounds by concatenating the proper sequence of phonemes. After the appropriate warping of pitch and duration, the resulting speech is natural sounding. This approach to synthesis is data driven: The algorithms analyze and resynthesize sounds using little hand-coded knowledge of speech. Yet they are effective at implicitly capturing the nuances of human speech.

Video Rewrite uses a similar approach to create new sequences of visemes. Visemes are the visual counterpart to phonemes. Visemes are visually distinct mouth, teeth, and tongue articulations for a language. For example, the phonemes /B/ and /P/ are visually indistinguishable and are grouped into a single viseme class.

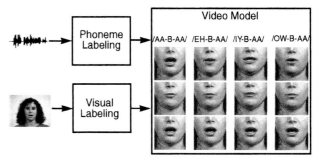

Figure 1: Overview of analysis stage. Video Rewrite uses the audio track to segment the video into triphones. Vision techniques find the orientation of the head, and the shape and position of the mouth and chin in each image. In the synthesis stage, Video Rewrite selects from this video model to synchronize new lip videos to any given audio.

353

Video Rewrite creates new videos using two steps: analysis of a training database and synthesis of new footage. In the *analysis* stage, Video Rewrite automatically segments into phonemes the audio track of the training database. We use these labels to segment the video track as well. We automatically track facial features in this segmented footage. The phoneme and facial labels together completely describe the visemes in the training database. In the *synthesis* stage, our system uses this video database, along with a new utterance. It automatically retrieves the appropriate viseme sequences, and blends them into a background scene using morphing techniques. The result is a new video with lip and jaw movements that synchronize to the new audio. The steps used in the analysis stage are shown in Figure 1; those of the synthesis stage are shown in Figure 2.

In the remainder of this paper, we first review other approaches to synthesizing talking faces (Section 2). We then describe the analysis and synthesis stages of Video Rewrite. In the analysis stage (Section 3), a collection of video is analyzed and stored in a database that matches sounds to video sequences. In the synthesis stage (Section 4), new speech is labeled, and the appropriate sequences are retrieved from the database. The final sections of this paper describe our results (Section 5), future work (Section 6), and contributions (Section 7).

2 SYNTHETIC VISUAL SPEECH

Facial-animation systems build a model of what a person's speech sounds and looks like. They use this model to generate a new output sequence, which matches the (new) target utterance. On the model-building side (analysis), there are typically three distinguishing choices: how the facial appearance is learned or described, how the facial appearance is controlled or labeled, and how the viseme labels are learned or described. For output-sequence generation (synthesis), the distinguishing choice is how the target utterance is characterized. This section reviews a representative sample of past research in these areas.

2.1 Source of Facial Appearance

Many facial-animation systems use a generic 3D mesh model of a face [Parke72, Lewis91, Guiard-Marigny94], sometimes adding texture mapping to improve realism [Morshima91, Cohen93, Waters95]. Another synthetic source of face data is hand-drawn images [Litwinowicz94]. Other systems use real faces for their source examples, including approaches that use 3D scans [Williams90] and still images [Scott94]. We use video footage to train Video Rewrite's models.

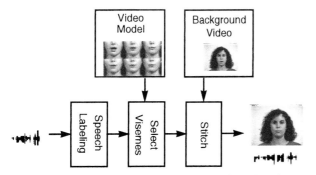

Figure 2: Overview of synthesis stage. Video Rewrite segments new audio and uses it to select triphones from the video model. Based on labels from the analysis stage, the new mouth images are morphed into a new background face.

2.2 Facial Appearance Control

Once a facial model is captured or created, the control parameters that exercise that model must be defined. In systems that rely on a 3D mesh model for appearance, the control parameters are the allowed 3D mesh deformations. Most of the image-based systems label the positions of specific facial locations as their control parameters. Of the systems that use facial-location labels, most rely on manual labeling of each example image [Scott94, Litwinowicz94]. Video Rewrite creates its video model by automatically labeling specific facial locations.

2.3 Viseme Labels

Many facial-animation systems label different visual configurations with an associated *phoneme*. These systems then match these phoneme labels with their corresponding labels in the target utterance. With synthetic images, the phoneme labels are artificial or are learned by analogy [Morshima91]. For natural images, taken from a video of someone speaking, the phonemic labels can be generated manually [Scott94] or automatically. Video Rewrite determines the phoneme labels automatically (Section 3.1).

2.4 Output-Sequence Generation

The goal of facial animation is to generate an image sequence that matches a target utterance. When phoneme labels are used, those for the target utterance can be entered manually [Scott94] or computed automatically [Lewis91, Morshima91]. Another option for phoneme labeling is to create the new utterance with synthetic speech [Parke72, Cohen93, Waters95]. Approaches, that do not use phoneme labels include motion capture of facial locations that are artificially highlighted [Williams90, Guiard-Marigny94] and manual control by an animator [Litwinowicz94]. Video Rewrite uses a combination of phoneme labels (from the target utterance) and facial-location labels (from the video-model segments). Video Rewrite derives all these labels automatically.

Video Rewrite is the first facial-animation system to automate all these steps and to generate realistic lip-synched video from natural speech and natural images.

3 ANALYSIS FOR VIDEO MODELING

As shown in Figure 1, the analysis stage creates an annotated database of example video clips, derived from unconstrained footage. We refer to this collection of annotated examples as a video model. This model captures how the subject's mouth and jaw move during speech. These training videos are labeled automatically with the phoneme sequence uttered during the video, and with the locations of fiduciary points that outline the lips, teeth, and jaw.

As we shall describe, the phonemic labels are from a time-aligned transcript of the speech, generated by a hidden Markov model (HMM). Video Rewrite uses the phonemic labels from the HMM to segment the input footage into short video clips, each showing three phonemes or a triphone. These triphone videos, with the fiduciary-point locations and the phoneme labels, are stored in the video model.

In Sections 3.1 and 3.2, we describe the visual and acoustic analyses of the video footage. In Section 4, we explain how to use this model to synthesize new video.

3.1 Annotation Using Image Analysis

Video Rewrite uses any footage of the subject speaking. As her face moves within the frame, we need to know the mouth position and the lip shapes at all times. In the synthesis stage, we use this information to warp overlapping videos such that they have the same lip shapes, and to align the lips with the background face.

Manual labeling of the fiduciary points around the mouth and jaw is error prone and tedious. Instead, we use computer-vision techniques to label the face and to identify the mouth and its shape. A major hurdle to automatic annotation is the low resolution of the images. In a typical scene, the lip region has a width of only 40 pixels. Conventional contour-tracking algorithms [Kass87, Yuille89] work well on high-contrast outer lip boundaries with some user interaction, but fail on inner lip boundaries at this resolution, due to the low signal-to-noise ratios. Grayscale-based algorithms, such as eigenimages [Kirby90, Turk91], work well at low resolutions, but estimate only the location of the lips or jaw, rather than estimating the desired fiduciary points. Eigenpoints [Covell96], and other extensions of eigenimages [Lanitis95], estimate control points reliably and automatically, even in such low-resolution images. As shown in Figure 3, eigenpoints learns how fiduciary points move as a function of the image appearance, and then uses this model to label new footage.

Video Rewrite labels each image in the training video using a total of 54 eigenpoints: 34 on the mouth (20 on the outer boundary, 12 on the inner boundary, 1 at the bottom of the upper teeth, and 1 at the top of the lower teeth) and 20 on the chin and jaw line. There are two separate eigenpoint analyses. The first eigenspace controls the placement of the 34 fiduciary points on the mouth, using 50×40 pixels around the nominal mouth location, a region that covers the mouth completely. The second eigenspace controls the placement of the 20 fiduciary points on the chin and jaw line, using 100×75 pixels around the nominal chin-location, a region that covers the upper neck and the lower part of the face.

We created the two eigenpoint models for locating the fiduciary points from a small number of images. We hand annotated only 26 images (of 14,218 images total; about 0.2%). We extended the hand-annotated dataset by morphing pairs of annotated images to form intermediate images, expanding the original 26 to 351 annotated images without any additional manual work. We then derived eigenpoints models using this extended data set.

We use eigenpoints to find the mouth and jaw and to label their contours. The derived eigenpoint models locate the facial features using six basis vectors for the mouth and six different vectors for the jaw. Eigenpoints then places the fiduciary points around the feature locations: 32 basis vectors place points around the lips and 64 basis vectors place points around the jaw.

Eigenpoints assumes that the features (the mouth or the jaw) are undergoing pure translational motion. It does a comparatively poor job at modeling rotations and scale changes. Yet, Video Rewrite is designed to use unconstrained footage. We expect rotations and scale changes. Subjects may lean toward the camera or turn away from it, tilt their heads to the side, or look up from under their eyelashes.

To allow for a variety of motions, we warp each face image into a standard reference plane, prior to eigenpoints labeling. We find the global transform that minimizes the mean-squared error between a large portion of the face image and a facial template. We currently use an affine transform [Black95]. The mask shown in Figure 4 defines the support of the minimization integral. Once the best global mapping is found, it is inverted and applied to the image, putting that face into the standard coordinate frame. We then perform eigenpoints analysis on this pre-warped image to find the fiduciary points. Finally, we back-project the fiduciary points through the global warp to place them on the original face image.

The labels provided by eigenpoints allow us automatically to (1) build the database of example lip configurations, and (2) track the features in a background scene that we intend to modify. Section 4.2 describes how we match the points we find in step 1 to each other and to the points found in step 2.

3.2 Annotation Using Audio Analysis

All the speech data in Video Rewrite (and their associated video) are segmented into sequences of phonemes. Although single phonemes are a convenient representation for linguistic analysis, they are not appropriate for Video Rewrite. We want to capture the visual dynamics of speech. To do so correctly, we must consider *coarticulation*, which causes the lip shapes for many phonemes to be modified based on the phoneme's context. For example, the /T/ in "beet" looks different from the /T/ in "boot."

Therefore, Video Rewrite segments speech and video into triphones: collections of three sequential phonemes. The word "teapot" is split into the sequence of triphones /SIL-T-IY/,[1] /T-IY-P/, /IY-P-AA/, /P-AA-T/, and /AA-T-SIL/. When we synthesize a video, we emphasize the middle of each triphone. We cross-fade the overlapping regions of neighboring triphones. We thus ensure that the precise transition points are not critical, and that we can capture effectively many of the dynamics of both forward and backward coarticulation.

Video Rewrite uses HMMs [Rabiner89] to label the training footage with phonemes. We trained the HMMs using the TIMIT speech database [Lamel86], a collection of 4200 utterances with phonemic transcriptions that gives the uttered phonemes and their timing. Each of the 61 phoneme categories in TIMIT is modeled with a separate three-state HMM. The emission probabilities of each state are modeled with mixtures of eight Gaussians with diagonal covariances. For robustness, we split the available data by gender and train two speaker-independent, gender-specific systems, one based on 1300 female utterances, and one based on 2900 male utterances.

We used these gender-specific HMMs to create a fine-grained phonemic transcription of our input footage, using forced Viterbi

---

1. /SIL/ indicates silence. Two /SIL/ in a row are used at the beginnings and ends of utterances to allow all segments—including the beginning and end—to be treated as triphones.

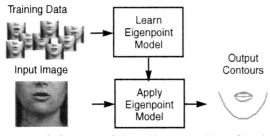

Figure 3: Overview of eigenpoints. A small set of hand-labeled facial images is used to train subspace models. Given a new image, the eigenpoint models tell us the positions of points on the lips and jaw.

Figure 4: Mask used to estimate the global warp. Each image is warped to account for changes in the head's position, size, and rotation. The transform minimizes the difference between the transformed images and the face template. The mask (left) forces the minimization to consider only the upper face (right).

search [Viterbi67]. Forced Viterbi uses unaligned sentence-level transcriptions and a phoneme-level pronunciation dictionary to create a time-aligned phoneme-level transcript of the speech. From this transcript, Video Rewrite segments the video automatically into triphone videos, labels them, and includes them in the video model.

4 SYNTHESIS USING A VIDEO MODEL

As shown in Figure 2, Video Rewrite synthesizes the final lip-synced video by labeling the new speech track, selecting a sequence of triphone videos that most accurately matches the new speech utterance, and stitching these images into a background video.

The background video sets the scene and provides the desired head position and movement. The background sequence in Video Rewrite includes most of the subject's face as well as the scene behind the subject. The frames of the background video are taken from the source footage in the same order as they were shot. The head tilts and the eyes blink, based on the background frames.

In contrast, the different triphone videos are used in whatever order is needed. They simply show the motions associated with articulation. For all the animations in this paper, the triphone images include the mouth, chin, and part of the cheeks, so that the chin and jaw move and the cheeks dimple appropriately as the mouth articulates. We use illumination-matching techniques [Burt83] to avoid visible seams between the triphone and background images.

The first step in synthesis (Figure 2) is labeling the new soundtrack. We label the new utterance with the same HMM that we used to create the video-model phoneme labels. In Sections 4.1 and 4.2, we describe the remaining steps: selecting triphone videos and stitching them into the background.

4.1 Selection of Triphone Videos

The new speech utterance determines the target sequence of speech sounds, marked with phoneme labels. We would like to find a sequence of triphone videos from our database that matches this new speech utterance. For each triphone in the new utterance, our goal is to find a video example with exactly the transition we need, and with lip shapes that match the lip shapes in neighboring triphone videos. Since this goal often is not reachable, we compromise by a choosing a sequence of clips that approximates the desired transitions and shape continuity.

Given a triphone in the new speech utterance, we compute a matching distance to each triphone in the video database. The matching metric has two terms: the *phoneme-context distance*, D_p, and the *distance between lip shapes* in overlapping visual triphones, D_s. The total error is

$$\text{error} = \alpha D_p + (1 - \alpha) D_s,$$

where the weight, α, is a constant that trades off the two factors.

The phoneme-context distance, D_p, is based on categorical distances between phoneme categories and between viseme classes. Since Video Rewrite does not need to create a new soundtrack (it needs only a new video track), we can cluster phonemes into viseme classes, based on their visual appearance.

We use 26 viseme classes. Ten are consonant classes: (1) /CH/, /JH/, /SH/, /ZH/; (2) /K/, /G/, /N/, /L/; (3) /T/, /D/, /S/, /Z/; (4) /P/, /B/, /M/; (5) /F/, /V/; (6) /TH/, /DH/; (7) /W/, /R/; (8) /HH/; (9) /Y/; and (10) /NG/. Fifteen are vowel classes: one each for /EH/, /EY/, /ER/, /UH/, /AA/ /AO/, /AW/, /AY/, /UW/, /OW/, /OY/, /IY/, /IH/, /AE/, /AH/. One class is for silence, /SIL/.

The phoneme-context distance, D_p, is the weighted sum of phoneme distances between the target phonemes and the video-model phonemes within the context of the triphone. If the phonemic categories are the same (for example, /P/ and /P/), then this distance is 0. If they are in different viseme classes (/P/ and /IY/), then the distance is 1. If they are in different phonemic categories but are in the same viseme class (/P/ and /B/), then the distance is a value between 0 and 1. The intraclass distances are derived from published confusion matrices [Owens85].

In D_p, the center phoneme of the triphone has the largest weight, and the weights drop smoothly from there. Although the video model stores only triphone images, we consider the triphone's original context when picking the best-fitting sequence. In current animations, this context covers the triphone itself, plus one phoneme on either side.

The second term, D_s, measures how closely the mouth contours match in overlapping segments of adjacent triphone videos. In synthesizing the mouth shapes for "teapot" we want the contours for the /IY/ and /P/ in the lip sequence used for /T-IY-P/ to match the contours for the /IY/ and /P/ in the sequence used for /IY-P-AA/. We measure this similarity by computing the Euclidean distance, frame by frame, between four-element feature vectors containing the overall lip width, overall lip height, inner lip height, and height of visible teeth.

The lip-shape distance (D_s) between two triphone videos is minimized with the correct time alignment. For example, consider the overlapping contours for the /P/ in /T-IY-P/ and /IY-P-AA/. The /P/ phoneme includes both a silence, when the lips are pressed together, and an audible release, when the lips move rapidly apart. The durations of the initial silence within the /P/ phoneme may be different. The phoneme labels do not provide us with this level of detailed timing. Yet, if the silence durations are different, the lip-shape distance for two otherwise-well-matched videos will be large. This problem is exacerbated by imprecision in the HMM phonemic labels.

We want to find the temporal overlap between neighboring triphones that maximizes the similarity between the two lip shapes. We shift the two triphones relative to each other to find the best temporal offset and duration. We then use this optimal overlap both in computing the lip-shape distance, D_s, and in cross-fading the triphone videos during the stitching step. The optimal overlap is the one that minimizes D_s while still maintaining a minimum-allowed overlap.

Since the fitness measure for each triphone segment depends on that segment's neighbors in both directions, we select the sequence of triphone segments using dynamic programming over the entire utterance. This procedure ensures the selection of the optimal segments.

4.2 Stitching It Together

Video Rewrite produces the final video by stitching together the appropriate entries from the video database. At this point, we have already selected a sequence of triphone videos that most closely matches the target audio. We need to align the overlapping lip images temporally. This internally time-aligned sequence of videos is then time aligned to the new speech utterance. Finally, the resulting sequences of lip images are spatially aligned and are stitched into the background face. We describe each step in turn.

4.2.1 Time Alignment of Triphone Videos

We have a sequence of triphone videos that we must combine to form a new mouth movie. In combining the videos, we want to maintain the dynamics of the phonemes and their transitions. We need to time align the triphone videos carefully before blending them. If we are not careful in this step, the mouth will appear to flutter open and closed inappropriately.

We align the triphone videos by choosing a portion of the overlapping triphones where the two lips shapes are as similar as possible. We make this choice when we evaluate D_s to choose the sequence of triphone videos (Section 4.1). We use the overlap duration and shift that provide the minimum value of D_s for the given videos.

4.2.2 Time Alignment of the Lips to the Utterance

We now have a self-consistent temporal alignment for the triphone videos. We have the correct articulatory motions, in the correct order to match the target utterance, but these articulations are not yet time aligned with the target utterance.

We align the lip motions with the target utterance by comparing the corresponding phoneme transcripts. The starting time of the center phone in the triphone sequence is aligned with the corresponding label in the target transcript. The triphone videos are then stretched or compressed such that they fit the time needed between the phoneme boundaries in the target utterance.

4.2.3 Combining of the Lips and the Background

The remaining task is to stitch the triphone videos into the background sequence. The correctness of the facial alignment is critical to the success of the recombination. The lips and head are constantly moving in the triphone and background footage. Yet, we need to align them all so that the new mouth is firmly planted on the face. Any error in spatial alignment causes the mouth to jitter relative to the face—an extremely disturbing effect.

We again use the mask from Figure 4 to help us find the optimal global transform to register the faces from the triphone videos with the background face. The combined tranforms from the mouth and background images to the template face (Section 3.1) give our starting estimate in this search. Re-estimating the global transform by directly matching the triphone images to the background improves the accuracy of the mapping.

We use a replacement mask to specify which portions of the final video come from the triphone images and which come from the background video. This replacement mask warps to fit the new mouth shape in the triphone image and to fit the jaw shape in the background image. Figure 5 shows an example replacement mask, applied to triphone and background images.

Local deformations are required to stitch the shape of the mouth and jaw line correctly. These two shapes are handled differently. The mouth's shape is completely determined by the triphone images. The only changes made to these mouth shapes are imposed to align the mouths within the overlapping triphone images: The lip shapes are linearly cross-faded between the shapes in the overlapping segments of the triphone videos.

 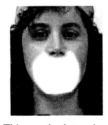

Figure 5: Facial fading mask. This mask determines which portions of the final movie frames come from the background frame, and which come from the triphone database. The mask should be large enough to include the mouth and chin. These images show the replacement mask applied to a triphone image, and its inverse applied to a background image. The mask warps according to the mouth and chin motions.

The jaw's shape, on the other hand, is a combination of the background jaw line and the two triphone jaw lines. Near the ears, we want to preserve the background video's jaw line. At the center of the jaw line (the chin), the shape and position are determined completely by what the mouth is doing. The final image of the jaw must join smoothly together the motion of the chin with the motion near the ears. To do this, we smoothly vary the weighting of the background and triphone shapes as we move along the jawline from the chin towards the ears.

The final stitching process is a three-way tradeoff in shape and texture among the fade-out lip image, the fade-in lip image, and the background image. As we move from phoneme to phoneme, the relative weights of the mouth shapes associated with the overlapping triphone-video images are changed. Within each frame, the relative weighting of the jaw shapes contributed by the background image and of the triphone-video images are varied spatially.

The derived fiduciary positions are used as control points in morphing. All morphs are done with the Beier-Neely algorithm [Beier92]. For each frame of the output image we need to warp four images: the two triphones, the replacement mask, and the background face. The warping is straightforward since we automatically generate high-quality control points using the eigenpoints algorithm.

5 RESULTS

We have applied Video Rewrite to several different training databases. We recorded one video dataset specifically for our evaluations. Section 5.1 describes our methods to collect this data and create lip-sync videos. Section 5.2 evaluates the resulting videos.

We also trained video models using truncated versions of our evaluation database. Finally, we used old footage of John F. Kennedy. We present the results from these experiments in Section 5.3.

5.1 Methods

We recorded about 8 minutes of video, containing 109 sentences, of a subject narrating a fairy tale. During the reading, the subject was asked to directly face the camera for some parts (still-head video) and to move and glance around naturally for others (moving-head video). We use these different segments to study the errors in local deformations separately from the errors in global spatial registration. The subject was also asked to wear a hat during the filming. We use this landmark to provide a quantitative evaluation of our global alignment. The hat is strictly outside all our alignment masks and our eigenpoints models. Thus, having the subject wear the hat does not effect the magnitude or type of errors that we expect to see in the animations—it simply provides us with a reference marker for the position and movement of her head.

To create a video model, we trained the system on all the still-head footage. Video Rewrite constructed and annotated the video model with just under 3500 triphone videos automatically, using HMM labeling of triphones and eigenpoint labeling of facial contours.

Video Rewrite was then given the target sentence, and was asked to construct the corresponding image sequence. To avoid unduly optimistic results, we removed from the database the triphone videos from training sentences similar to the target. A training sentence was considered similar to the target if the two shared a phrase two or more words long. Note that Video Rewrite would not normally pare the database in this manner: Instead, it would take advantage of these coincidences. We remove the similar sentences to avoid biasing our results.

We evaluated our output footage both qualitatively and quantitatively. Our qualitative evaluation was done informally, by a panel of observers. There are no accepted metrics for evaluating lip-synced footage. Instead, we were forced to rely on the qualitative judgements listed in Section 5.2.

Only the (global) spatial registration is evaluated quantitatively. Since our subject wore a hat that moved rigidly with her upper head, we were able to measure quantitatively our global-registration error on this footage. We did so by first warping the full frame (instead of just the mouth region) of the triphone image into the coordinate frame of the background image. If this global transformation is correct, it should overlay the two images of the hat exactly on top of one another. We measured the error by finding the offset of the correlation peak for the image regions corresponding to the front of the hat. The offset of the peak is the registration error (in pixels).

5.2 Evaluation

Examples of our output footage can be seen at http://www.interval.com/papers/1997-012/. The top row of Figure 6 shows example frames, extracted from these videos. This section describes our evaluation criteria and the results.

5.2.1 Lip and Utterance Synchronization

How well are the lip motions synchronized with the audio? We evaluate this measure on the still-head videos. There occasionally are visible timing errors in plosives and stops.

5.2.2 Triphone-Video Synchronization

Do the lips flutter open and closed inappropriately? This artifact usually is due to synchronization error in overlapping triphone videos. We evaluated this measure on the still-head videos. We do not see any artifacts of this type.

5.2.3 Natural Articulation

Assuming that neither of the artifacts from Sections 5.2.1 or 5.2.2 appear, do the lip and teeth articulations look natural? Unnatural-looking articulation can result if the desired sequence of phonemes is not available in the database, and thus another sequence is used in its place. In our experiments, this replacement occurred on 31 percent of the triphone videos. We evaluated this measure on the

still-head videos. We do not see this type of error when we use the full video model. Additional experiments in this area are described in Section 5.3.1.

5.2.4 Fading-Mask Visibility and Extent

Does the fading mask show? Does the animation have believable texture and motion around the lips and chin? Do the dimples move in sync with the mouth? We evaluated this measure on all the output videos. The still-head videos better show errors associated with the extent of the fading mask, whereas the moving-head videos better show errors due to interactions between the fading mask and the global transformation. Without illumination correction, we see artifacts in some of the moving-head videos, when the subject looked down so that the lighting on her face changed significantly. These artifacts disappear with adaptive illumination correction [Burt83].

5.2.5 Background Warping

Do the outer edges of the jaw line and neck, and the upper portions of the cheeks look realistic? Artifacts in these areas are due to incorrect warping of the background image or to a mismatch between the texture and the warped shape of the background image. We evaluated this measure on all the output videos. In some segments, we found minor artifacts near the outer edges of the jaw.

5.2.6 Spatial Registration

Does the mouth seem to float around on the face? Are the teeth rigidly attached to the skull? We evaluated this measure on the moving-head videos. No registration errors are visible.

We evaluated this error quantitatively as well, using the hat-registration metric described in Section 5.1. The mean, median, and maximum errors in the still-head videos were 0.6, 0.5, and 1.2 pixels (standard deviation 0.3); those in the moving-head videos were 1.0, 1.0, and 2.0 pixels (standard deviation 0.4). For comparison, the face covers approximately 85×120 pixels.

5.2.7 Overall Quality

Is the lip-sync believable? We evaluated this measure on all the output videos. We judged the overall quality as excellent.

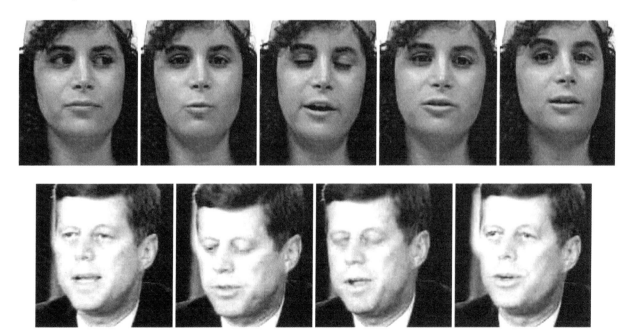

Figure 6: Examples of synthesized output frames. These frames show the quality of our output after triphone segments have been stitched into different background video frames.

5.3 Other Experiments

In this section, we examine our performance using steadily smaller training databases (Section 5.3.1) and using historic footage (Section 5.3.2).

5.3.1 Reduction of Video Model Size

We wanted to see how the quality fell off as the number of data available in the video model were reduced. With the 8 minutes of video, we have examples of approximately 1700 different triphones (of around 19,000 naturally occurring triphones); our animations used triphones other than the target triphones 31 percent of the time. What happens when we have only 1 or 2 minutes of data? We truncated our video database to one-half, one-quarter, and one-eighth of its original size, and then reanimated our target sentences. The percent of mismatched triphones increased by about 15 percent with each halving of the database (that is, 46, 58, and 74 percent of the triphones were replaced in the reduced datasets). The perceptual quality also degraded smoothly as the database size was reduced. The video from the reduced datasets are shown on our web site.

5.3.2 Reanimation of Historic Footage

We also applied Video Rewrite to public-domain footage of John F. Kennedy. For this application, we digitized 2 minutes (1157 triphones) of Kennedy speaking during the Cuban missile crisis. Forty-five seconds of this footage are from a close-up camera, about 30 degrees to Kennedy's left. The remaining images are medium shots from the same side. The size ratio is approximately 5:3 between the close-up and medium shots. During the footage, Kennedy moves his head about 30 degrees vertically, reading his speech from notes on the desk and making eye contact with a center camera (which we do not have).

We used this video model to synthesize new animations of Kennedy saying, for example, "Read my lips" and "I never met Forrest Gump." These animations combine the footage from both camera shots and from all head poses. The resulting videos are shown on our web site. The bottom row of Figure 6 shows example frames, extracted from these videos.

In our preliminary experiments, we were able to find the correct triphone sequences just 6% of the time. The lips are reliably synchronized to the utterance. The fading mask is not visible, nor is the background warping. However, the overall animation quality is not as good as our earlier results. The animations include some lip fluttering, because of the mismatched triphone sequences.

Our quality is limited for two reasons. The available viseme footage is distributed over a wide range of vertical head rotations. If we choose triphones that match the desired pose, then we cannot find good matches for the desired phoneme sequence. If we choose triphones that are well matched to the desired phoneme sequence, then we need to dramatically change the pose of the lip images. A large change in pose is difficult to model with our global (affine) transform. The lip shapes are distorted because we assumed, implicitly in the global transform, that the lips lie on a flat plane. Both the limited-triphone and pose problems can be avoided with additional data.

6 FUTURE WORK

There are many ways in which Video Rewrite could be extended and improved. The phonemic labeling of the triphone and background footage could consider the mouth- and jaw-shape information, as well as acoustic data [Bregler95]. Additional lip-image data and multiple eigenpoints models could be added, allowing larger out-of-plane head rotations. The acoustic data could be used in selecting the triphone videos, because facial expressions affect

voice qualities (you can hear a smile). The synthesis could be made real-time, with low-latency.

In Sections 6.1 through 6.3, we explore extensions that we think are most promising and interesting.

6.1 Alignment Between Lips and Target

We currently use the simplest approach to time aligning the lip sequences with the target utterance: We rely on the phoneme boundaries. This approach provides a rough alignment between the motions in the lip sequence and the sounds in the target utterance. As we mentioned in Section 4.1, however, the phoneme boundaries are both imprecise (the HMM alignment is not perfect) and coarse (significant visual and auditory landmarks occur within single phonemes).

A more accurate way to time align the lip motions with the target utterance uses dynamic time warping of the audio associated with each triphone video to the corresponding segment of the target utterance. This technique would allow us to time align the auditory landmarks from the triphone videos with those of the target utterance, even if the landmarks occur at subphoneme resolution. This time alignment, when applied to the triphone image sequence, would then align the visual landmarks of the lip sequence with the auditory landmarks of the target utterance.

The overlapping triphone videos would provide overlapping and conflicting time warpings. Yet we want to keep fixed the time alignment of the overlapping triphone videos, as dictated by the visual distances (Section 4.1 and 4.2). Research is needed in how best to trade off these potentially conflicting time-alignment maps.

6.2 Animation of Facial Features

Another promising extension is animation of other facial parts, based on simple acoustic features or other criteria. The simplest version of this extension would change the position of the eyebrows with pitch [Ohala94]. A second extension would index the video model by both triphone and expression labels. Using such labels, we would select smiling or frowning lips, as desired. Alternatively, we could impose the desired expression on a neutral mouth shape, for those times when the appropriate combinations of triphones and expression are not available. To do this imposition correctly, we must separate which deformations are associated with articulations, and which are associated with expressions, and how the two interact. This type of factorization must be learned from examples [Tenenbaum97].

6.3 Perception of Lip Shapes

In doing this work, we solved many problems—automatic labeling, matching, and stitching—yet we found many situations where we did not have sufficient knowledge of how people perceive speaking faces. We would like to know more about how important the correct lip shapes and motions are in lip synching. For example, one study [Owens85] describes the confusibility of consonants in vowel–consonant–vowel clusters. The clustering of consonants into viseme class depends on the surrounding vowel context. Clearly, we need more sophisticated distance metrics within and between viseme classes.

7 CONTRIBUTIONS

Video Rewrite is a facial animation system that is driven by audio input. The output sequence is created from real video footage. It combines background video footage, including natural facial movements (such as eye blinks and head motions) with natural footage of mouth and chin motions. Video Rewrite is the first facial-animation system to automate all the audio- and video-labeling tasks required for this type of reanimation.

Video Rewrite can use images from unconstrained footage both to create the video model of the mouth and chin motions and to provide a background sequence for the final output footage. It preserves the individual characteristics of the subject in the original footage, even while the subject appears to mouth a completely new utterance. For example, the temporal dynamics of John F. Kennedy's articulatory motions can be preserved, reorganized, and reimposed on Kennedy's face.

Since Video Rewrite retains most of the background frame, modifying only the mouth area, it is well suited to applications such as movie dubbing. The setting and action are provided by the background video. Video Rewrite maintains an actor's visual mannerisms, using the dynamics of the actor's lips and chin from the video model for articulatory mannerisms, and using the background video for all other mannerisms. It maintains the correct timing, using the action as paced by the background video and speech as paced by the new soundtrack. It undertakes the entire process without manual intervention. The actor convincingly mouths something completely new.

ACKNOWLEDGMENTS

Many colleagues helped us. Ellen Tauber and Marc Davis graciously submitted to our experimental manipulation. Trevor Darrell and Subutai Ahmad contributed many good ideas to the algorithm development. Trevor, Subutai, John Lewis, Bud Lassiter, Gaile Gordon, Kris Rahardja, Michael Bajura, Frank Crow, Bill Verplank, and John Woodfill helped us to evaluate our results and the description. Bud Lassiter and Chris Seguine helped us with the video production. We offer many thanks to all.

REFERENCES

[Beier92] T. Beier, S. Neely. Feature-based image metamorphosis. *Computer Graphics*, 26(2):35–42, 1992. ISSN 0097-8930.

[Black95] M.J. Black, Y. Yacoob. Tracking and recognizing rigid and non-rigid facial motions using local parametric models of image motion. *Proc. IEEE Int. Conf. Computer Vision*, Cambridge, MA, pp. 374–381, 1995. ISBN 0-8186-7042-8.

[Bregler95] C. Bregler, S. Omohundro. Nonlinear manifold learning for visual speech recognition. *Proc. IEEE Int. Conf. Computer Vision*, Cambridge, MA, pp. 494–499, 1995. ISBN 0-8186-7042-8.

[Burt83] P.J. Burt, E.H. Adelson. A multiresolution spline with application to image mosaics. *ACM Trans. Graphics*, 2(4): 217–236, 1983. ISSN 0730-0301.

[Cohen93] M.M. Cohen, D.W. Massaro. Modeling coarticulation in synthetic visual speech. In *Models and Techniques in Computer Animation*, ed. N.M Thalman, D. Thalman, pp. 139–156, Tokyo: Springer-Verlag, 1993. ISBN 0-3877-0124-9.

[Covell96] M. Covell, C. Bregler. Eigenpoints. *Proc. Int. Conf. Image Processing*, Lausanne, Switzerland, Vol. 3, pp. 471–474, 1996. ISBN 0-7803-3258-x.

[Guiard-Marigny94] T. Guiard-Marigny, A. Adjoudani, C. Benoit. A 3-D model of the lips for visual speech synthesis. *Proc. ESCA/IEEE Workshop on Speech Synthesis*, New Paltz, NY, pp. 49–52, 1994.

[Kass87] M. Kass, A. Witkin, D. Terzopoulos. Snakes: Active contour models. *Int. J. Computer Vision*, 1(4):321–331, 1987. ISSN 0920-5691.

[Kirby90] M. Kirby, L. Sirovich. Application of the Karhunen-Loeve procedure for the characterization of human faces. *IEEE PAMI*, 12(1):103–108, Jan. 1990. ISSN 0162-8828.

[Lamel86] L. F. Lamel, R. H. Kessel, S. Seneff. Speech database development: Design and analysis of the acoustic-phonetic corpus. *Proc. Speech Recognition Workshop (DARPA)*, Report #SAIC-86/1546, pp. 100–109, McLean VA: Science Applications International Corp., 1986.

[Lanitis95] A. Lanitis, C.J. Taylor, T.F. Cootes. A unified approach for coding and interpreting face images. *Proc. Int. Conf. Computer Vision*, Cambridge, MA, pp. 368–373, 1995. ISBN 0-8186-7042-8.

[Lewis91] J.Lewis. Automated lip-sync: Background and techniques. *J.Visualization and Computer Animation*, 2(4):118–122, 1991. ISSN 1049-8907.

[Litwinowicz94] P. Litwinowicz, L. Williams. Animating images with drawings. *SIGGRAPH 94*, Orlando, FL, pp. 409–412, 1994. ISBN 0-89791-667-0.

[Morishima91] S. Morishima, H. Harashima. A media conversion from speech to facial image for intelligent man-machine interface. *IEEE J Selected Areas Communications*, 9 (4):594–600, 1991. ISSN 0733-8716.

[Moulines90] E. Moulines, P. Emerard, D. Larreur, J. L. Le Saint Milon, L. Le Faucheur, F. Marty, F. Charpentier, C. Sorin. A real-time French text-to-speech system generating high-quality synthetic speech. *Proc. Int. Conf. Acoustics, Speech, and Signal Processing*, Albuquerque, NM, pp. 309–312, 1990.

[Ohala94] J.J. Ohala. The frequency code underlies the sound symbolic use of voice pitch. In *Sound Symbolism*, ed. L. Hinton, J. Nichols, J. J. Ohala, pp. 325–347, Cambridge UK: Cambridge Univ. Press, 1994. ISBN 0-5214-5219-8.

[Owens85] E. Owens, B. Blazek. Visemes observed by hearing-impaired and normal-hearing adult viewers. *J. Speech and Hearing Research*, 28:381–393, 1985. ISSN 0022-4685.

[Parke72] F. Parke. Computer generated animation of faces. *Proc. ACM National Conf.*, pp. 451–457, 1972.

[Rabiner89] L. R. Rabiner. A tutorial on hidden markov models and selected applications in speech recognition. In *Readings in Speech Recognition*, ed. A. Waibel, K. F. Lee, pp. 267–296, San Mateo, CA: Morgan Kaufmann Publishers, 1989. ISBN 1-5586-0124-4.

[Scott94] K.C. Scott, D.S. Kagels, S.H. Watson, H. Rom, J.R. Wright, M. Lee, K.J. Hussey. Synthesis of speaker facial movement to match selected speech sequences. *Proc. Australian Conf. Speech Science and Technology*, Perth Australia, pp. 620–625, 1994. ISBN 0-8642-2372-2.

[Tenenbaum97] J. Tenenbaum, W. Freeman. Separable mixture models: Separating style and content. In *Advances in Neural Information Processing 9*, ed. M. Jordan, M. Mozer, T. Petsche, Cambridge, MA: MIT Press, (in press).

[Turk91] M. Turk, A. Pentland. Eigenfaces for recognition. *J. Cognitive Neuroscience*, 3(1):71–86, 1991. ISSN 0898-929X

[Viterbi67] A. J. Viterbi. Error bounds for convolutional codes and an asymptotically optimal decoding algorithm. *IEEE Trans. Informat. Theory*, IT-13:260–269, 1967. ISSN 0018-9448.

[Waters95] K. Waters, T. Levergood. DECface: A System for Synthetic Face Applications. *J. Multimedia Tools and Applications*, 1 (4):349–366, 1995. ISSN 1380-7501.

[Williams90] L. Williams. Performance-Driven Facial Animation. *Computer Graphics* (Proceedings of SIGGRAPH 90), 24(4):235–242, 1990. ISSN 0097-8930.

[Yuille89] A.L. Yuille, D.S. Cohen, P.W. Hallinan. Feature extraction from faces using deformable templates. *Proc. IEEE Computer Vision and Pattern Recognition*, San Diego, CA, pp. 104–109, 1989. ISBN 0-8186-1952-x.

Multiresolution Sampling Procedure
for Analysis and Synthesis
of Texture Images

Jeremy S. De Bonet *

Learning & Vision Group
Artificial Intelligence Laboratory
Massachusetts Institute of Technology

EMAIL: jsd@ai.mit.edu
HOMEPAGE: http://www.ai.mit.edu/~jsd

Abstract

This paper outlines a technique for treating input texture images as probability density estimators from which new textures, with similar appearance and structural properties, can be sampled. In a two-phase process, the input texture is first analyzed by measuring the joint occurrence of texture discrimination features at multiple resolutions. In the second phase, a new texture is synthesized by sampling successive spatial frequency bands from the input texture, conditioned on the similar joint occurrence of features at lower spatial frequencies. Textures synthesized with this method more successfully capture the characteristics of input textures than do previous techniques.

1 Introduction

Synthetic texture generation has been an increasingly active research area in computer graphics. The primary approach has been to develop specialized procedural models which emulate the generative process of the texture they are trying to mimic. For example, models based on reaction-diffusion interactions have been developed to simulate seashells [15] or animal skins [14]. More recently work has been done which considers textures as samples from probabilistic distributions. By determining the form of these distributions and sampling from them, new textures that are similar to the originals can, in principle, be generated. The success of these methods is dependent upon the structure of the probability density estimator used in the sampling procedure. Recently several attempts at developing such estimators have been successful in limited domains. Most notably Heeger and Bergen [10] iteratively resample random noise to coerce it into having particular multiresolution oriented energy histograms. Using a similar distribution, and a more rigorous resampling method Zhu and Mumford [16] have also achieved some success. In work by Luettgen, et al [12] multiresolution Markov random fields are used to model relationships between spatial frequencies within texture images.

In human visual psychophysics research, the focus of texture perception studies has been on developing physiologically plausible models of texture discrimination. These models involve determining to which measurements of textural variations humans are most sensitive. Typically based on the responses of oriented filter banks, such models are capable of detecting variations across some patches perceived by humans to be different textures ([1, 2, 3, 4, 6, 9, 11],

for example.) The approach presented here uses these resulting psychophysical models to provide constraints on a statistical sampling procedure.

In a two-phase process, the input texture is first analyzed by computing the joint occurrence, across multiple resolutions, of several of the features used in psychophysical models. In the second phase, a new texture is synthesized by sampling successive spatial frequency bands from the input texture, conditioned on the similar joint occurrence of features at all lower spatial frequencies.

The sampling methodology is based on the hypothesis that texture images differ from typical images in that that there are regions within the image which, to some set of feature detectors, are less discriminable at certain resolutions than at others. By rearranging textural components at locations and resolutions where the discriminability is below threshold, new texture samples are generated which have similar visual characteristics.

2 Motivation

The goal of probabilistic texture synthesis can be stated as follows: to generate a new image, from an example texture, such that the new image is sufficiently different from the original yet still appears as though it was generated by the same underlying stochastic process as was the original texture.

If successful, the new image will differ from the original, yet have perceptually identical texture characteristics. This can be measured psychophysically in texture discrimination tests. To satisfy both criteria, a synthesized image should differ from the original in the same way as the original differs from itself.

From an input texture patch, such as that shown in Figure 1, there are infinitely many possible distributions which could be inferred as the generative process. Sampling from such distributions results in different synthesized textures, depending on the priors assumed. Depending on the accuracy of these assumptions, the resulting textures may, or may not, satisfy the above criteria for "good" synthesis.

One possible prior over the distribution of pixels is that the original texture is the only sample in the distribution, and that no other images are texturally similar. From this assumption, simple tiling results, as shown in Figure 2. Clearly this fails the "sufficiently different" criteria stated above.

Another feasible – though also clearly inadequate – prior is to assume that the pixels in the input texture are independently sampled from some distribution. Textures generated with this model do not capture the non-random structure within the original. The result of such an operation is shown in Figure 3. As expected it fails

---
*Research supported in part by DARPA under ONR contract No. N00014-95-1-0600 and by the Office of Naval Research under contract No. N00014-96-1-0311.

Figure 1: An example texture image for input to a texture synthesis process.

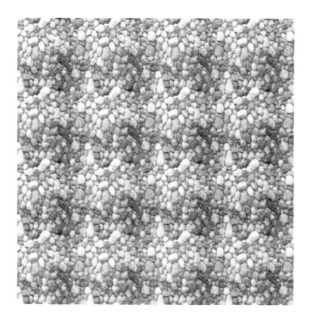

Figure 2: Simple repetition of the image does not result in a texture which appears to have come from the same stochastic distribution as the original.

Figure 3: Textures that contain randomness not present in the original are perceptually different textures. This texture was generated by uniformly sampling the pixel values of the original. The original texture superimposed on the synthetic one is easily identified.

Figure 4: Sampling each spatial frequency band from the corresponding band in the original does not capture the detail which is characteristic of the input texture, indicating that relationships between frequencies is critical. The synthesized texture is different from the superimposed original texture, which is clearly discriminable.

Figure 5: The objective is to generate a patch such as the one above which is different from the original yet appears as though it could have been generated by the same underlying stochastic process. This texture, which was synthesized using the technique described in this paper, is perceptually very similar to the original, and the superimposed original is not readily located.

to capture the character of the original and is perceptually different. This is evidenced by the ease with which the original can be located when superimposed on the synthesized texture. This effect, commonly known as "popout" ([3, 9, 11], e.g.), occurs because the textures are perceptually different and do not appear to have been generated by the same process.

The goal of texture synthesis is to generate a texture, such as that shown in Figure 5, which is both random, and indiscriminable from the original texture. Figure 5 satisfies these criteria in that it differs significantly from the original yet appears to have been generated by the same physical process. Because of the perceptual similarity between this texture, which was synthesized by the procedure in this paper, and the input texture (generated by some other process) it is difficult to locate the region which contains the superimposed original.

3 Functional synthesis framework

Mathematically, the goal of texture synthesis is to develop a function, F, which takes a texture image, I_{input}, to a new texture sample, I_{synth}, such that the difference between I_{input} and I_{synth} is above some measure of visual difference from the original, yet is texturally similar. Formally,

$$F(I_{\text{input}}) = I_{\text{synth}} \tag{1}$$

subject to the constraints that

$$D^* \left(I_{\text{input}}, I_{\text{synth}} \right) < T_{\text{max disc}} \tag{2}$$

and

$$V^* \left(I_{\text{input}}, I_{\text{synth}} \right) > T_{\text{min diff}} \tag{3}$$

where D^* is a perceptual measure of the perceived difference of textural characteristics, and V^* a measure of the perceived visual difference between the input and synthesized images. To be acceptable, the perceived difference in textural characteristics must fall below a maximum texture discriminability threshold $T_{\text{max disc}}$, and the perceived visual difference must be above a minimum visual difference threshold, $T_{\text{min diff}}$.

The success of a synthesis technique is measured by its ability to minimize $T_{\text{max disc}}$ while maximizing $T_{\text{min diff}}$.

Human perception of texture differences, indicated by the hypothetical function D^*, depends on our prior beliefs about how textures should vary. These beliefs incorporate much of human visual experience; therefore, determining a computable metric, D, to approximate D^*, is a complex and often ill-defined task. Devising a good approximation for V^* is an even more difficult task. For texture synthesis purposes however, a poor approximation such as direct correlation, is sufficient.

The difficulty of determining a function D, to approximate D^*, depends on the structure and textual complexity of the two images. Many psychophysically based approximations have been proposed (e.g. [4, 6].)

Clearly, more complex textures can be represented in larger images; therefore, determining a discrimination function, say D_{small}, between images which have few pixels is less difficult than determining a similar function D_{large} over larger images.

Using a multiresolution approach, this work approximates D^* with a process which begins from low resolution – small – images. By decomposing the function F into a set of functions F_i which each generate a single spatial frequency band of the new texture, I_{synth}.

The domain of the each function F_i is a subset of the domain of F, as F_i's need only be a function of the information contained in the low spatial frequency bands of I_{input}. An intuitive proof

of this is given by the following induction. Consider a new image, I'_{input}, which is generated from an image I_{input} by removing its high frequencies by low pass filtering with a Gaussian kernel. With just I'_{input}, and without knowledge of the additional information in I_{input}, one could still consider generating a new image I'_{synth} which is similar in textural appearance to I'_{input}. Thus, the process of generating I'_{synth} from I'_{input} is independent of highest frequency band of I_{input}. This argument can be repeated to show that I''_{synth} can be generated from I''_{input} without knowledge of I'_{input}, and so on. F_i is then given by:

$$\begin{aligned} F_i \left(I'^{\cdots'}_{\text{input}} \right) &= \\ &= F_i \left[L_i \left(I_{\text{input}} \right), L_{i+1} \left(I_{\text{input}} \right), \cdots, L_n \left(I_{\text{input}} \right) \right] \quad (4) \\ &= L_i \left(I_{\text{synth}} \right) \end{aligned}$$

where $L_i \left(I_{\text{synth}} \right)$ is the ith spatial frequency octave (or equivalently the ith level of the Laplacian pyramid decomposition.) The original function, F, in equation (1) is then constructed by combining the spatial frequency bands generated by F_0 through F_N. The method presented here simplifies the difficulty of minimizing (approximate) D^* difference by initially synthesizing textures which are similar at low spatial frequencies, and then maintaining that similarity as it progresses to higher frequencies. A new texture is synthesized by generating each of its spatial frequency bands so that as higher frequency information is added textural similarity is preserved.

4 Texture generation procedure

4.1 Hypothesis of texture structure

The sampling procedure used by this method is dependent upon the accuracy of the following hypothesis. Images perceived as textures differ from other images in that below some resolution they contain regions which differ by less than some discrimination threshold. Further, if the threshold is strict enough, randomization of these regions does not change the perceived characteristics of the texture. In other words, at some low resolution texture images contain regions whose difference measured by D^* is small, and reorganizing these low frequency regions, while retaining their high frequency detail will not change its textural (D^*) characteristics yet will increase its visual (V^*) difference.

In Figure 6, at each resolution examples of potentially interchangeable regions are highlighted. Rearranging the image at these resolutions and locations, while retaining their high resolution structure, corresponds to moving whole textural units (which in Figure 6 are individual pebbles.)

4.2 Analysis and Synthesis Pyramids

A new texture is synthesized by generating each of its spatial frequency bands so that as higher frequency information is added textural similarity is preserved. Each synthesized band is generated by sampling from the corresponding band in the input texture, constrained by the presence of local features. The general flow of this process is outlined in Figure 7.

In a first phase the input image is decomposed into multiple resolutions. This is done using the standard Laplacian pyramid formulation where band pass information at the point (x, y) at level i, in the image I, is given by:

$$L_i (I, x, y) = (G_i (I) - 2\uparrow[G_{i+1} (I)]) (x, y) \tag{5}$$

Figure 6: The synthesis procedure is based upon the hypothesis that at lower resolutions there are regions which are below some threshold of discriminability and that the randomness within a texture is in the locations of these regions.

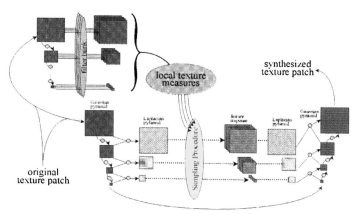

Analysis Pyramid   Synthesis Pyramid

Figure 7: Multiple regions in the analysis pyramid can be candidate values for a location in the synthesis pyramid (as shown in Figure 8).

where $G_i(I)$ is a low-pass down-sampling operation:

$$G_i(I) = 2{\downarrow}[G_{i-1}(I) \otimes g] \qquad (6)$$

where $2{\uparrow}[\cdot]$ and $2{\downarrow}[\cdot]$ are the $2\times$ up- and down-sampling operations respectively; g is a two dimensional Gaussian kernel; and $G_0(I) = I$.

Each level of the Laplacian pyramid contains the information from a one octave spatial frequency band of the input For a complete discussion of Laplacian and Gaussian pyramids, the reader is referred to [5].

From each level of this Laplacian pyramid a corresponding level of a new pyramid is sampled. If this sampling is done independently at each resolution, as shown in Figure 4, the synthesized image fails to capture the visual organization characteristic of the original, indicating that the values chosen for a particular spatial frequency should depend on the values chosen at other spatial frequencies. From the iterative proof, above, we can also infer that these values only depend values at that and at lower spatial frequencies.

However, using only the Laplacian information in the lower frequency bands to constrain selection is also insufficient. Such a procedure which samples from a distribution conditioned exclusively on lower resolutions only loosely constrains the relationship between the 'child' nodes of different 'parents.' Sampling from such a distribution can result in high frequency artifacts which are not present in the intended distribution. To prevent this, constraints must be propagated across children of different parents; however, constraint propagation on a two dimensional network results in dependency cycles, from which sampling requires iterative procedures, and which is not, in general, guaranteed to converge in finite time. This technique constrains the selection process within a spatial frequency band without creating cycles by using image features to constrain sampling.

Because the objective is to synthesize textures that contain the

same textural characteristics as the original, yet vary from it in global form, it is assumed that global structure within the input texture is coincidental and should not constrain synthesis. Given this assumption it is sufficient to use the responses of a set of *local* texture measures as features which provide the basis for an approximation to the human perceptual texture-discriminability function D^*. A filter bank of oriented first and second Gaussian derivatives – simple edge and line filters – were used in addition to Laplacian response. At each location (x, y) in the analysis pyramid level i, the response of each feature j, is computed for use in constraining the sampling procedure. When, at the lowest resolutions, the pyramid layers are too small, the features cannot be computed, and a constant value is used.

$$F_i^j(I, x, y) = \begin{cases} (G_i(I) \otimes f_j)(x, y) & \text{if size of } G_i(I) \geq f_j \\ 0 & \text{otherwise} \end{cases}$$

$$(7)$$

The constraints provided by these features are stronger than just the "parent" value, because they capture some of the relationships between pixels within a local neighborhood. This "analysis pyramid" which contains the multiresolution band-pass and feature response information, is directly computed from the input image.

4.3 Sampling procedure

A "synthesis pyramid" is generated by sampling from the analysis pyramid conditioned on the joint occurrence of similar feature response values at multiple resolutions. When the synthesized pyramid has been completely generated, the band-pass information is combined to form the final synthesized texture.

Initially the top level – lowest resolution – of the analysis pyramid, which is a single pixel, is copied directly into the synthesis pyramid. When synthesizing a texture larger than the original, the top level of the synthesis pyramid is larger that in the analysis pyramid; in this case the analysis level is simply repeated to fill the synthesis level.

Subsequent levels of the synthesis pyramid are sampled from the corresponding level of the analysis pyramid. At each location in the synthesis pyramid, the local "parent structure" is used to constrain sampling. The parent structure, $\vec{S}_i$, of a location, (x, y), in image I, at resolution i, is a vector which contains the local response for features 1 through M, at every lower resolution from $i + 1$ to N:

$$\begin{aligned}
\vec{S}_i(I, x, y) = \\
\left[\; F_{i+1}^0\left(\tfrac{x}{2}, \tfrac{y}{2}\right), F_{i+1}^1\left(\tfrac{x}{2}, \tfrac{y}{2}\right), \cdots, F_{i+1}^M\left(\tfrac{x}{2}, \tfrac{y}{2}\right), \right. \\
F_{i+2}^0\left(\tfrac{x}{4}, \tfrac{y}{4}\right), F_{i+2}^1\left(\tfrac{x}{4}, \tfrac{y}{4}\right), \cdots, F_{i+2}^M\left(\tfrac{x}{4}, \tfrac{y}{4}\right), \\
\cdots, \\
F_N^0\left(\tfrac{x}{2^N}, \tfrac{y}{2^N}\right), F_N^1\left(\tfrac{x}{2^N}, \tfrac{y}{2^N}\right), \cdots, \\
\left. F_N^M\left(\tfrac{x}{2^N}, \tfrac{y}{2^N}\right) \right]^T
\end{aligned} \qquad (8)$$

The parent structure of a location in a synthesis pyramid is depicted in Figure 8; in this schematic, each cell represents the set of local feature responses.

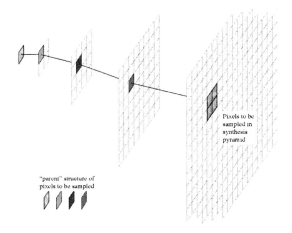

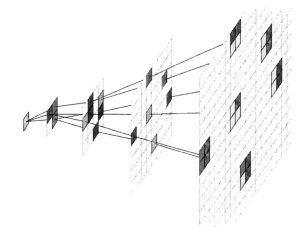

Figure 8: The distribution from which pixels in the synthesis pyramid are sampled is conditioned on the "parent" structure of those pixels. Each element of the parent structure contains a vector of the feature measurements at that location and scale.

Figure 9: An input texture is decomposed to form an analysis pyramid, from which a new synthesis pyramid is sampled, conditioned on local features within the pyramids. A filter bank of local texture measures, based on psychophysical models, are used as features.

Two locations are considered indistinguishable if the square difference between every component of their parent structures is below some threshold. For a given location (x', y') in the synthesis image, I_{synth}, the set of all such locations in the input image can be computed:

$$C_i\left(x', y'\right) = \left\{ (x, y) \left| D\left(\begin{array}{c} \vec{S}_i\left(I_{\text{synth}}, x', y'\right), \\ \vec{S}_i\left(I_{\text{input}}, x, y\right) \end{array} \right) \leq \vec{T}_i \right. \right\} \quad (9)$$

Where the distance function D, between two parent structures u and v, is given by:

$$D\left[u, v\right] = \frac{(u - v)^T (u - v)}{Z} \quad (10)$$

where Z is a normalization constant which eliminates the effect of contrast, equal to $\sum_{x,y} \vec{S}_i\left(I_{\text{input}}, x, y\right)$.

To be a member of set $C_i\left(x', y'\right)$ the distance between each component of the parent structures must be less than the corresponding component in a vector of thresholds for each resolution and feature:

$$\vec{T}_i = \begin{bmatrix} T_{i+1}^0 & T_{i+1}^1 & \cdots & T_{i+1}^M \\ T_{i+2}^0 & T_{i+2}^1 & \cdots & T_{i+2}^M \\ \cdots & & & \\ T_N^0 & T_N^1 & \cdots & T_N^M \end{bmatrix}^T \quad (11)$$

Where each element T_i^j is a threshold for the jth filter response at the ith resolution.

The values for new locations in the synthesis pyramid are sampled uniformly from among all regions in the analysis pyramid that have a parent structure which satisfies equation (??). This yields a probability distribution over spatial frequency band values conditioned on the joint occurrence of features at lower spatial frequencies:

$$P\left(L_i\left(I_{\text{synth}}, x', y'\right) \Rightarrow L_i\left(I_{\text{input}}, x, y\right) \left| (x, y) \in C_i\left(x', y'\right) \right.\right)$$

$$= \quad 1 / \|C_i\left(x', y'\right)\| \quad (12)$$

Variations between the analysis and synthesis pyramids occur when multiple regions in the analysis pyramid satisfy the above criterion. The parent structure of such a group of candidate locations is depicted in Figure 9. As the thresholds increase, the number of candidates from which the values in the synthesis pyramid will be sampled, increases. The levels of the thresholds, T_i^j, mediate the rearrangement of spatial frequency information within the synthesized texture, and encapsulate a prior belief about the degree of randomness in the true distribution from which the input texture was generated.

Algorithmically, this sampling procedure can be described with the pseudo-code:

SynthesizePyramid
```
Loop i from top_level-1 downto 0
  Loop (x',y') over Pyr_synth[level i]
    C = ∅
    Loop (x,y) over Pyr_analysis[level i]
      C = C ∪ {(x,y)}
      Loop v from top_level downto i + 1
        Loop j for each feature
          if D ( Pyr_analysis[v][j](x/2^(v-i), y/2^(v-i)),
                 Pyr_synth[v][j](x'/2^(v-i), y'/2^(v-i)) )
            < threshold[level v][feature j]
          then
            C = C - {(x,y)}
            break to next (x,y)

  selection = UniformRandom[0, ||C||]
  (x,y) = C[selection]
  Pyr_synth[v](x',y') = Pyr_analysis[v](x,y)
```

With more complex code, additional efficiency can be obtained by skipping whole regions which share a parent structure element that is above threshold difference.

Upon the completion of this sampling process for each level of the synthesis pyramid the synthesized band-pass information is combined to form the new texture using a standard **CollapsePyramid** procedure.

Though each band is sampled directly from the input image, the image which results from the recombination of each of these synthesized layers contains pixel values (i.e. RGB colors) not present

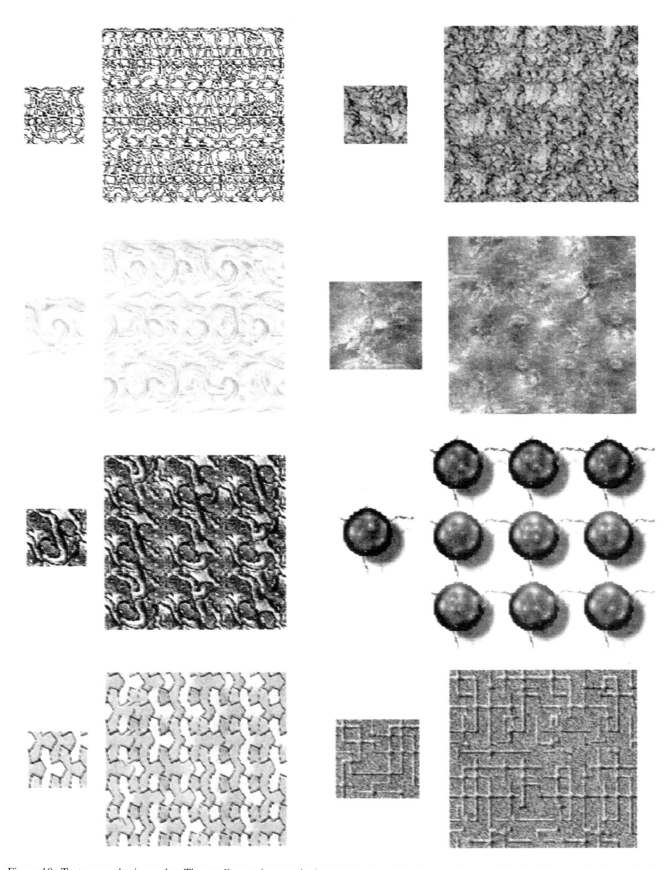

Figure 10: Texture synthesis results. The smaller patches are the input textures, and to their right are synthesized images which are 4 or 9 times larger.

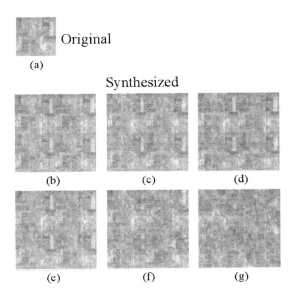

Figure 11: This series of 6 images (b-g) was generated from the original (a). For each a single threshold is used for all features and resolutions. Thresholds increase from 0.05 to 0.3 from (b) to (g).

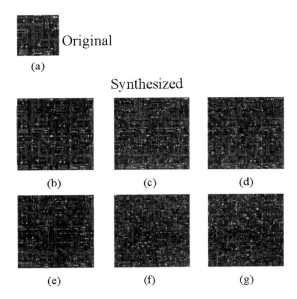

Figure 12: A series of synthesized textures for which the thresholds are inversely proportional to the spatial frequency and proportional to 0.05 in (b) to 0.3 in (g).

in the original, because non-zero thresholds allow synthesized spatial frequency hierarchies which differ from those in the original.

Because the Laplacian pyramid representation is over-complete, i.e. the space spanned by Laplacian pyramids is 4/3 larger than that spanned by images, it is possible to synthesize pyramids that are off of the manifold of real-images. When this occurs, the pyramid is projected onto the closest point on this manifold before reconstruction. This is done by collapsing the pyramid using full precision images, then replacing values above or below the range of legal pixel values with the closest legal value.

5   Examples of texture synthesis

For 800 full color input textures, we synthesized new textures, each four times larger than the original. Some typical results are shown in Figure 10. The results from these examples are indicative of the synthesis performance on the entire set and were chosen only because they reproduce well on paper. The results of all 800 textures are available on the world wide web via the URL:

http://www.ai.mit.edu/~jsd/Research/TextureSynthesis

In the synthesis examples through out this paper thresholds of the form:

$$T_i^j = \alpha/i^\beta \qquad (13)$$

were used with $\alpha \in [0, 0.4]$ and $\beta \in \{0, 1\}$. The parameter α establishes the prior belief about the sensitivity of D^*, the threshold $T_{\max \text{disc}}$ in equation (2); larger β incorporates the belief that the 'true' distribution which generated the input texture is spatially homogeneous, and that the low frequency structure within the input image should not be an influential factor in region discrimination.

Shown in Figure 11 are a series of synthesized textures for $\beta = 0$ and $\alpha = \{0.05, 0.10, 0.15, 0.20, 0.25, 0.30\}$. As the threshold increases, progressively more locations in the original become indistinguishable, and the amount of variation from the original increases. For this texture, the synthesized image which balances sufficient difference from the original with perceptual similarity, lies somewhere between $\alpha = .15$ and $\alpha = .20$ (images d-e.) For different images, the ideal threshold is different, reflecting our prior

belief about the randomness implied by the original. Another synthesis series for a different input image is shown in Figure 12. In this case $\beta = 1$, α varies over the same range, and the ideal threshold is somewhere around $\alpha = 0.25$ (image f.)

6   Discussion

Because it uses only local constraints, the estimator presented here cannot model, texture images with complex visual structures. Such structures include: reflective and rotational symmetry; progressive variations in size, color, orientation, etc.; and visual elements with internal semantic meaning (such as symbols) or which have meaning in their relative positions (such as letters.)

Simply adding additional complex features to attempt to capture these sorts of visual structures over conditions the sampling procedure, and simple tiling results. If appropriate thresholds could be determined through additional analysis of the input image, the effects of complex features could be mediated, and they might provide useful constraints.

Because it samples exclusively from the input image, this model assumes that the 'true' distributions from which each spatial frequency band in the input was generated, can be accurately approximated by only those values present in that image. If there were a model for the probability of values not present in the original, synthesized textures could possibly be generated which contain additional variation from the original which does not increase texture (D^*) difference yet increases the visual (V^*) difference.

7   Conclusion

We have presented a method for synthesis of a novel image from an input texture by generating and sampling from a distribution. This multiresolution technique is capable of capturing much of the important visual structure in the perceptual characteristics of many texture images; including artificial (man-made) textures and more natural ones, as shown in Figure 13. The input texture is treated as probability density estimator by using the joint occurrence of fea-

Original   Synthesized

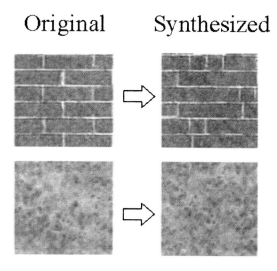

Figure 13: The characteristics of both artificial / man-made and natural textures can be captured and replicated with this process.

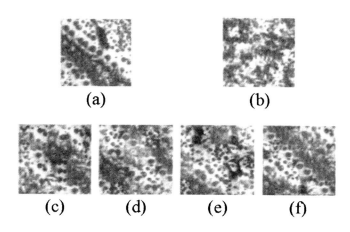

Figure 14: An input texture (a) which is beyond the limitations of Heeger and Bergen (1995) model (b), can be used successfully by this techniques to synthesize many new images. Four such synthesized images, using the same set of thresholds, are shown in (c) - (f).

tures across multiple resolutions to constrain sampling. Prior beliefs about the 'true' randomness in the input are incorporated into the model through the settings of thresholds which control the level of constraint provided by each feature. Many of the textures generated by sampling from this estimator can simultaneously satisfy two the two criteria of successful texture synthesis: the synthesized textures are sufficiently different from the original, and appear to have been created by the same underlying generative process. These textures can be synthesized from more intricate input examples, and produce textures which appear more akin to the originals, than those produced by earlier techniques (Figure 14.)

References

[1] J. R. Bergen. Theories of visual texture perception. In D. Regan, editor, *Vision and Visual Dysfunction*, volume 10B, pages 114–134. Macmillian, New York, 1991.

[2] J. R. Bergen and E. H. Adelson. Early vision and texture perception. *Nature*, 333(6171):363–364, 1988.

[3] J. R. Bergen and B. Julesz. Rapid discrimination of visual patterns. *IEEE Transactions on Systems Man and Cybernetics*, 13:857–863, 1993.

[4] J. R. Bergen and M. S. Landy. Computational modeling of visual texture segregation. In M. S. Landy and J. A. Movshon, editors, *Computational Models of Visual Perception*, pages 253–271. MIT Press, Cambridge MA, 1991.

[5] P. J. Burt and E. H. Adelson. The laplacian pyramid as a compact image code. *IEEE Transactions on Communications*, 31:532–540, 1983.

[6] C. Chubb and M. S. Landy. Orthogonal distribution analysis: A new approach to the study of texture perception. In M. S. Landy and J. A. Movshon, editors, *Computational Models of Visual Perception*, pages 291–301. MIT Press, Cambridge MA, 1991.

[7] A. Gagalowicz. Texture modelling applications. *The Visual Computer*, 3:186–200, 1987.

[8] A. Gagalowicz and S. D. Ma. Model driven synthesis of natural textures for 3-D scenes. *Computers and Graphics*, 10:161–170, 1986.

[9] N. Graham, A. Sutter, and C. Venkatesan. Spatial-frequency and orientation-selectivity of simple and complex channels in region segregation. *Vision Research*, 33:1893–1911, 1993.

[10] D. J. Heeger and J. R. Bergen. Pyramid based texture analysis/synthesis. In *Computer Graphics*, pages 229–238. ACM SIGGRAPH, 1995.

[11] B. Julesz. Visual pattern discrimination. *IRE Transactions on Information Theory*, IT–8:84–92, 1962.

[12] M. R. Luettgen, W. C. Karl, A. S. Willsky, and R. R. Tenney. Multiscale representations of markov random fields. *IEEE Trans. on Signal Processing*, 41(12):3377–3396, 1995.

[13] S. D. Ma and A. Gagalowicz. Determination of local coordinate systems for texture synthesis on 3-D surfaces. *Computers and Graphics*, 10:171–176, 1986.

[14] G. Turk. Genereating textures on arbitrary surfaces using reaction-diffusion. In *Computer Graphics*, volume 25, pages 289–298. ACM SIGGRAPH, 1991.

[15] A. Witkin and M. Kass. Reaction–diffusion textures. In *Computer Graphics*, volume 25, pages 299–308. ACM SIGGRAPH, 1991.

[16] S. C. Zhu, Y. Wu, and D. Mumford. Filters random fields and maximum entropy(frame): To a unified theory for texture modeling. *To appear in Int'l Journal of Computer Vision*, 1996.

Recovering High Dynamic Range Radiance Maps from Photographs

Paul E. Debevec   Jitendra Malik

University of California at Berkeley[1]

ABSTRACT

We present a method of recovering high dynamic range radiance maps from photographs taken with conventional imaging equipment. In our method, multiple photographs of the scene are taken with different amounts of exposure. Our algorithm uses these differently exposed photographs to recover the response function of the imaging process, up to factor of scale, using the assumption of reciprocity. With the known response function, the algorithm can fuse the multiple photographs into a single, high dynamic range radiance map whose pixel values are proportional to the true radiance values in the scene. We demonstrate our method on images acquired with both photochemical and digital imaging processes. We discuss how this work is applicable in many areas of computer graphics involving digitized photographs, including image-based modeling, image compositing, and image processing. Lastly, we demonstrate a few applications of having high dynamic range radiance maps, such as synthesizing realistic motion blur and simulating the response of the human visual system.

CR Descriptors: I.2.10 [**Artificial Intelligence**]: Vision and Scene Understanding - *Intensity, color, photometry and thresholding*; I.3.7 [**Computer Graphics**]: Three-Dimensional Graphics and Realism - *Color, shading, shadowing, and texture*; I.4.1 [**Image Processing**]: Digitization - *Scanning*; I.4.8 [**Image Processing**]: Scene Analysis - *Photometry, Sensor Fusion*.

1 Introduction

Digitized photographs are becoming increasingly important in computer graphics. More than ever, scanned images are used as texture maps for geometric models, and recent work in image-based modeling and rendering uses images as the fundamental modeling primitive. Furthermore, many of today's graphics applications require computer-generated images to mesh seamlessly with real photographic imagery. Properly using photographically acquired imagery in these applications can greatly benefit from an accurate model of the photographic process.

When we photograph a scene, either with film or an electronic imaging array, and digitize the photograph to obtain a two-dimensional array of "brightness" values, these values are rarely

---

[1] Computer Science Division, University of California at Berkeley, Berkeley, CA 94720-1776. Email: debevec@cs.berkeley.edu, malik@cs.berkeley.edu. More information and additional results may be found at: http://www.cs.berkeley.edu/~debevec/Research

true measurements of relative radiance in the scene. For example, if one pixel has twice the value of another, it is unlikely that it observed twice the radiance. Instead, there is usually an unknown, nonlinear mapping that determines how radiance in the scene becomes pixel values in the image.

This nonlinear mapping is hard to know beforehand because it is actually the composition of several nonlinear mappings that occur in the photographic process. In a conventional camera (see Fig. 1), the film is first exposed to light to form a latent image. The film is then developed to change this latent image into variations in transparency, or *density*, on the film. The film can then be digitized using a film scanner, which projects light through the film onto an electronic light-sensitive array, converting the image to electrical voltages. These voltages are digitized, and then manipulated before finally being written to the storage medium. If prints of the film are scanned rather than the film itself, then the printing process can also introduce nonlinear mappings.

In the first stage of the process, the film response to variations in exposure X (which is $E\Delta t$, the product of the irradiance E the film receives and the exposure time Δt) is a non-linear function, called the "characteristic curve" of the film. Noteworthy in the typical characteristic curve is the presence of a small response with no exposure and saturation at high exposures. The development, scanning and digitization processes usually introduce their own nonlinearities which compose to give the aggregate nonlinear relationship between the image pixel exposures X and their values Z.

Digital cameras, which use charge coupled device (CCD) arrays to image the scene, are prone to the same difficulties. Although the charge collected by a CCD element is proportional to its irradiance, most digital cameras apply a nonlinear mapping to the CCD outputs before they are written to the storage medium. This nonlinear mapping is used in various ways to mimic the response characteristics of film, anticipate nonlinear responses in the display device, and often to convert 12-bit output from the CCD's analog-to-digital converters to 8-bit values commonly used to store images. As with film, the most significant nonlinearity in the response curve is at its saturation point, where any pixel with a radiance above a certain level is mapped to the same maximum image value.

Why is this any problem at all? The most obvious difficulty, as any amateur or professional photographer knows, is that of limited dynamic range—one has to choose the range of radiance values that are of interest and determine the exposure time suitably. Sunlit scenes, and scenes with shiny materials and artificial light sources, often have extreme differences in radiance values that are impossible to capture without either under-exposing or saturating the film. To cover the full dynamic range in such a scene, one can take a series of photographs with different exposures. This then poses a problem: how can we combine these separate images into a composite radiance map? Here the fact that the mapping from scene radiance to pixel values is unknown and nonlinear begins to haunt us. The purpose of this paper is to present a simple technique for recovering this response function, up to a scale factor, using nothing more than a set of photographs taken with varying, known exposure durations. With this mapping, we then use the pixel values from all available photographs to construct an accurate map of the radiance in the scene, up to a factor of scale. This radiance map will cover

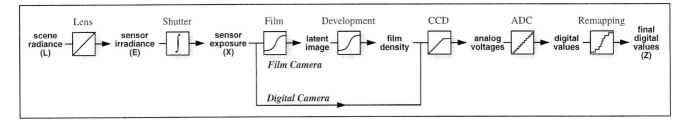

Figure 1: **Image Acquisition Pipeline** *shows how scene radiance becomes pixel values for both film and digital cameras. Unknown nonlinear mappings can occur during exposure, development, scanning, digitization, and remapping. The algorithm in this paper determines the aggregate mapping from scene radiance L to pixel values Z from a set of differently exposed images.*

the entire dynamic range captured by the original photographs.

1.1 Applications

Our technique of deriving imaging response functions and recovering high dynamic range radiance maps has many possible applications in computer graphics:

Image-based modeling and rendering

Image-based modeling and rendering systems to date (e.g. [11, 15, 2, 3, 12, 6, 17]) make the assumption that all the images are taken with the same exposure settings and film response functions. However, almost any large-scale environment will have some areas that are much brighter than others, making it impossible to adequately photograph the scene using a single exposure setting. In indoor scenes with windows, this situation often arises within the field of view of a single photograph, since the areas visible through the windows can be far brighter than the areas inside the building.

By determining the response functions of the imaging device, the method presented here allows one to correctly fuse pixel data from photographs taken at different exposure settings. As a result, one can properly photograph outdoor areas with short exposures, and indoor areas with longer exposures, without creating inconsistencies in the data set. Furthermore, knowing the response functions can be helpful in merging photographs taken with different imaging systems, such as video cameras, digital cameras, and film cameras with various film stocks and digitization processes.

The area of image-based modeling and rendering is working toward recovering more advanced reflection models (up to complete BRDF's) of the surfaces in the scene (e.g. [21]). These methods, which involve observing surface radiance in various directions under various lighting conditions, require absolute radiance values rather than the nonlinearly mapped pixel values found in conventional images. Just as important, the recovery of high dynamic range images will allow these methods to obtain accurate radiance values from surface specularities and from incident light sources. Such higher radiance values usually become clamped in conventional images.

Image processing

Most image processing operations, such as blurring, edge detection, color correction, and image correspondence, expect pixel values to be proportional to the scene radiance. Because of nonlinear image response, especially at the point of saturation, these operations can produce incorrect results for conventional images.

In computer graphics, one common image processing operation is the application of synthetic motion blur to images. In our results (Section 3), we will show that using true radiance maps produces significantly more realistic motion blur effects for high dynamic range scenes.

Image compositing

Many applications in computer graphics involve compositing image data from images obtained by different processes. For example, a background matte might be shot with a still camera, live action might be shot with a different film stock or scanning process, and CG elements would be produced by rendering algorithms. When there are significant differences in the response curves of these imaging processes, the composite image can be visually unconvincing. The technique presented in this paper provides a convenient and robust method of determining the overall response curve of any imaging process, allowing images from different processes to be used consistently as radiance maps. Furthermore, the recovered response curves can be inverted to render the composite radiance map as if it had been photographed with any of the original imaging processes, or a different imaging process entirely.

A research tool

One goal of computer graphics is to simulate the image formation process in a way that produces results that are consistent with what happens in the real world. Recovering radiance maps of real-world scenes should allow more quantitative evaluations of rendering algorithms to be made in addition to the qualitative scrutiny they traditionally receive. In particular, the method should be useful for developing reflectance and illumination models, and comparing global illumination solutions against ground truth data.

Rendering high dynamic range scenes on conventional display devices is the subject of considerable previous work, including [20, 16, 5, 23]. The work presented in this paper will allow such methods to be tested on real radiance maps in addition to synthetically computed radiance solutions.

1.2 Background

The photochemical processes involved in silver halide photography have been the subject of continued innovation and research ever since the invention of the daguerretype in 1839. [18] and [8] provide a comprehensive treatment of the theory and mechanisms involved. For the newer technology of solid-state imaging with charge coupled devices, [19] is an excellent reference. The technical and artistic problem of representing the dynamic range of a natural scene on the limited range of film has concerned photographers from the early days – [1] presents one of the best known systems to choose shutter speeds, lens apertures, and developing conditions to best coerce the dynamic range of a scene to fit into what is possible on a print. In scientific applications of photography, such as in astronomy, the nonlinear film response has been addressed by suitable calibration procedures. It is our objective instead to develop a simple self-calibrating procedure not requiring calibration charts or photometric measuring devices.

In previous work, [13] used multiple flux integration times of a CCD array to acquire extended dynamic range images. Since direct CCD outputs were available, the work did not need to deal with the problem of nonlinear pixel value response. [14] addressed the problem of nonlinear response but provide a rather limited method of recovering the response curve. Specifically, a parametric form of the response curve is arbitrarily assumed, there is no satisfactory treatment of image noise, and the recovery process makes only partial use of the available data.

2 The Algorithm

This section presents our algorithm for recovering the film response function, and then presents our method of reconstructing the high dynamic range radiance image from the multiple photographs. We describe the algorithm assuming a grayscale imaging device. We discuss how to deal with color in Section 2.6.

2.1 Film Response Recovery

Our algorithm is based on exploiting a physical property of imaging systems, both photochemical and electronic, known as *reciprocity*.

Let us consider photographic film first. The response of a film to variations in exposure is summarized by the characteristic curve (or Hurter-Driffield curve). This is a graph of the optical density D of the processed film against the logarithm of the exposure X to which it has been subjected. The exposure X is defined as the product of the irradiance E at the film and exposure time, Δt, so that its units are Jm^{-2}. Key to the very concept of the characteristic curve is the assumption that only the product $E\Delta t$ is important, that halving E and doubling Δt will not change the resulting optical density D. Under extreme conditions (very large or very low Δt), the reciprocity assumption can break down, a situation described as reciprocity failure. In typical print films, reciprocity holds to within $\frac{1}{3}$ stop[1] for exposure times of 10 seconds to 1/10,000 of a second.[2] In the case of charge coupled arrays, reciprocity holds under the assumption that each site measures the total number of photons it absorbs during the integration time.

After the development, scanning and digitization processes, we obtain a digital number Z, which is a nonlinear function of the original exposure X at the pixel. Let us call this function f, which is the composition of the characteristic curve of the film as well as all the nonlinearities introduced by the later processing steps. Our first goal will be to recover this function f. Once we have that, we can compute the exposure X at each pixel, as $X = f^{-1}(Z)$. We make the reasonable assumption that the function f is monotonically increasing, so its inverse f^{-1} is well defined. Knowing the exposure X and the exposure time Δt, the irradiance E is recovered as $E = X/\Delta t$, which we will take to be proportional to the radiance L in the scene.[3]

Before proceeding further, we should discuss the consequences of the spectral response of the sensor. The exposure X should be thought of as a function of wavelength $X(\lambda)$, and the abscissa on the characteristic curve should be the integral $\int X(\lambda)R(\lambda)d\lambda$ where $R(\lambda)$ is the spectral response of the sensing element at the pixel location. Strictly speaking, our use of irradiance, a radiometric quantity, is not justified. However, the spectral response of the sensor site may not be the photopic luminosity function V_λ, so the photometric term *illuminance* is not justified either. In what follows, we will use the term irradiance, while urging the reader to remember that the

quantities we will be dealing with are weighted by the spectral response at the sensor site. For color photography, the color channels may be treated separately.

The input to our algorithm is a number of digitized photographs taken from the same vantage point with different known exposure durations Δt_j.[4] We will assume that the scene is static and that this process is completed quickly enough that lighting changes can be safely ignored. It can then be assumed that the film irradiance values E_i for each pixel i are constant. We will denote pixel values by Z_{ij} where i is a spatial index over pixels and j indexes over exposure times Δt_j. We may now write down the film reciprocity equation as:

$$Z_{ij} = f(E_i \Delta t_j) \tag{1}$$

Since we assume f is monotonic, it is invertible, and we can rewrite (1) as:

$$f^{-1}(Z_{ij}) = E_i \Delta t_j$$

Taking the natural logarithm of both sides, we have:

$$\ln f^{-1}(Z_{ij}) = \ln E_i + \ln \Delta t_j$$

To simplify notation, let us define function $g = \ln f^{-1}$. We then have the set of equations:

$$g(Z_{ij}) = \ln E_i + \ln \Delta t_j \tag{2}$$

where i ranges over pixels and j ranges over exposure durations. In this set of equations, the Z_{ij} are known, as are the Δt_j. The unknowns are the irradiances E_i, as well as the function g, although we assume that g is smooth and monotonic.

We wish to recover the function g and the irradiances E_i that best satisfy the set of equations arising from Equation 2 in a least-squared error sense. We note that recovering g only requires recovering the *finite* number of values that $g(z)$ can take since the domain of Z, pixel brightness values, is finite. Letting Z_{min} and Z_{max} be the least and greatest pixel values (integers), N be the number of pixel locations and P be the number of photographs, we formulate the problem as one of finding the $(Z_{max} - Z_{min} + 1)$ values of $g(Z)$ and the N values of $\ln E_i$ that minimize the following quadratic objective function:

$$\mathcal{O} = \sum_{i=1}^{N}\sum_{j=1}^{P}[g(Z_{ij}) - \ln E_i - \ln \Delta t_j]^2 + \lambda \sum_{z=Z_{min}+1}^{Z_{max}-1} g''(z)^2 \tag{3}$$

The first term ensures that the solution satisfies the set of equations arising from Equation 2 in a least squares sense. The second term is a smoothness term on the sum of squared values of the second derivative of g to ensure that the function g is smooth; in this discrete setting we use $g''(z) = g(z-1) - 2g(z) + g(z+1)$. This smoothness term is essential to the formulation in that it provides coupling between the values $g(z)$ in the minimization. The scalar λ weights the smoothness term relative to the data fitting term, and should be chosen appropriately for the amount of noise expected in the Z_{ij} measurements.

Because it is quadratic in the E_i's and $g(z)$'s, minimizing $\mathcal{O}$ is a straightforward linear least squares problem. The overdetermined

---

[1] 1 stop is a photographic term for a factor of two; $\frac{1}{3}$ stop is thus $2^{\frac{1}{3}}$

[2] An even larger dynamic range can be covered by using neutral density filters to lessen to amount of light reaching the film for a given exposure time. A discussion of the modes of reciprocity failure may be found in [18], ch. 4.

[3] L is proportional E for any particular pixel, but it is possible for the proportionality factor to be different at different places on the sensor. One formula for this variance, given in [7], is $E = L\frac{\pi}{4}\left(\frac{d}{f}\right)^2 cos^4\alpha$, where α measures the pixel's angle from the lens' optical axis. However, most modern camera lenses are designed to compensate for this effect, and provide a nearly constant mapping between radiance and irradiance at f/8 and smaller apertures. See also [10].

[4] Most modern SLR cameras have electronically controlled shutters which give extremely accurate and reproducible exposure times. We tested our Canon EOS Elan camera by using a Macintosh to make digital audio recordings of the shutter. By analyzing these recordings we were able to verify the accuracy of the exposure times to within a thousandth of a second. Conveniently, we determined that the actual exposure times varied by powers of two between stops ($\frac{1}{64}$, $\frac{1}{32}$, $\frac{1}{16}$, $\frac{1}{8}$, $\frac{1}{4}$, $\frac{1}{2}$, 1, 2, 4, 8, 16, 32), rather than the rounded numbers displayed on the camera readout ($\frac{1}{60}$, $\frac{1}{30}$, $\frac{1}{15}$, $\frac{1}{8}$, $\frac{1}{4}$, $\frac{1}{2}$, 1, 2, 4, 8, 15, 30). Because of problems associated with vignetting, varying the aperture is not recommended.

system of linear equations is robustly solved using the singular value decomposition (SVD) method. An intuitive explanation of the procedure may be found in Fig. 2.

We need to make three additional points to complete our description of the algorithm:

First, the solution for the $g(z)$ and E_i values can only be up to a single scale factor α. If each log irradiance value $\ln E_i$ were replaced by $\ln E_i + \alpha$, and the function g replaced by $g + \alpha$, the system of equations 2 and also the objective function $\mathcal{O}$ would remain unchanged. To establish a scale factor, we introduce the additional constraint $g(Z_{mid}) = 0$, where $Z_{mid} = \frac{1}{2}(Z_{min} + Z_{max})$, simply by adding this as an equation in the linear system. The meaning of this constraint is that a pixel with value midway between Z_{min} and Z_{max} will be assumed to have unit exposure.

Second, the solution can be made to have a much better fit by anticipating the basic shape of the response function. Since $g(z)$ will typically have a steep slope near Z_{min} and Z_{max}, we should expect that $g(z)$ will be less smooth and will fit the data more poorly near these extremes. To recognize this, we can introduce a weighting function $w(z)$ to emphasize the smoothness and fitting terms toward the middle of the curve. A sensible choice of w is a simple hat function:

$$w(z) = \begin{cases} z - Z_{min} & \text{for } z \leq \frac{1}{2}(Z_{min} + Z_{max}) \\ Z_{max} - z & \text{for } z > \frac{1}{2}(Z_{min} + Z_{max}) \end{cases} \quad (4)$$

Equation 3 now becomes:

$$\mathcal{O} = \sum_{i=1}^{N} \sum_{j=1}^{P} \{w(Z_{ij})[g(Z_{ij}) - \ln E_i - \ln \Delta t_j]\}^2 + \lambda \sum_{z=Z_{min}+1}^{Z_{max}-1} [w(z)g''(z)]^2$$

Finally, we need not use every available pixel site in this solution procedure. Given measurements of N pixels in P photographs, we have to solve for N values of $\ln E_i$ and $(Z_{max} - Z_{min})$ samples of g. To ensure a sufficiently overdetermined system, we want $N(P-1) > (Z_{max} - Z_{min})$. For the pixel value range $(Z_{max} - Z_{min}) = 255$, $P = 11$ photographs, a choice of N on the order of 50 pixels is more than adequate. Since the size of the system of linear equations arising from Equation 3 is on the order of $N \times P + Z_{max} - Z_{min}$, computational complexity considerations make it impractical to use every pixel location in this algorithm. Clearly, the pixel locations should be chosen so that they have a reasonably even distribution of pixel values from Z_{min} to Z_{max}, and so that they are spatially well distributed in the image. Furthermore, the pixels are best sampled from regions of the image with low intensity variance so that radiance can be assumed to be constant across the area of the pixel, and the effect of optical blur of the imaging system is minimized. So far we have performed this task by hand, though it could easily be automated.

Note that we have not explicitly enforced the constraint that g must be a monotonic function. If desired, this can be done by transforming the problem to a non-negative least squares problem. We have not found it necessary because, in our experience, the smoothness penalty term is enough to make the estimated g monotonic in addition to being smooth.

To show its simplicity, the MATLAB routine we used to minimize Equation 5 is included in the Appendix. Running times are on the order of a few seconds.

2.2 Constructing the High Dynamic Range Radiance Map

Once the response curve g is recovered, it can be used to quickly convert pixel values to relative radiance values, assuming the exposure Δt_j is known. Note that the curve can be used to determine radiance values in any image(s) acquired by the imaging process associated with g, not just the images used to recover the response function.

From Equation 2, we obtain:

$$\ln E_i = g(Z_{ij}) - \ln \Delta t_j \quad (5)$$

For robustness, and to recover high dynamic range radiance values, we should use all the available exposures for a particular pixel to compute its radiance. For this, we reuse the weighting function in Equation 4 to give higher weight to exposures in which the pixel's value is closer to the middle of the response function:

$$\ln E_i = \frac{\sum_{j=1}^{P} w(Z_{ij})(g(Z_{ij}) - \ln \Delta t_j)}{\sum_{j=1}^{P} w(Z_{ij})} \quad (6)$$

Combining the multiple exposures has the effect of reducing noise in the recovered radiance values. It also reduces the effects of imaging artifacts such as film grain. Since the weighting function ignores saturated pixel values, "blooming" artifacts[5] have little impact on the reconstructed radiance values.

2.2.1 Storage

In our implementation the recovered radiance map is computed as an array of single-precision floating point values. For efficiency, the map can be converted to the image format used in the RADIANCE [22] simulation and rendering system, which uses just eight bits for each of the mantissa and exponent. This format is particularly compact for color radiance maps, since it stores just one exponent value for all three color values at each pixel. Thus, in this format, a high dynamic range radiance map requires just one third more storage than a conventional RGB image.

2.3 How many images are necessary?

To decide on the number of images needed for the technique, it is convenient to consider the two aspects of the process:

1. *Recovering the film response curve:* This requires a minimum of two photographs. Whether two photographs are enough can be understood in terms of the heuristic explanation of the process of film response curve recovery shown in Fig. 2. If the scene has sufficiently many different radiance values, the entire curve can, in principle, be assembled by sliding together the sampled curve segments, each with only two samples. Note that the photos must be similar enough in their exposure amounts that some pixels fall into the working range[6] of the film in both images; otherwise, there is no information to relate the exposures to each other. Obviously, using more than two images with differing exposure times improves performance with respect to noise sensitivity.

2. *Recovering a radiance map given the film response curve:* The number of photographs needed here is a function of the dynamic range of radiance values in the scene. Suppose the range of maximum to minimum radiance values that we are

---

[5]Blooming occurs when charge or light at highly saturated sites on the imaging surface spills over and affects values at neighboring sites.

[6]The *working range* of the film corresponds to the middle section of the response curve. The ends of the curve, in which large changes in exposure cause only small changes in density (or pixel value), are called the *toe* and the *shoulder*.

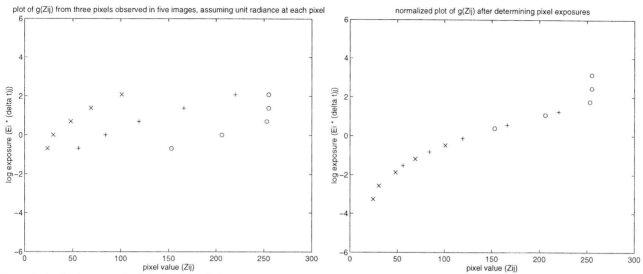

Figure 2: *In the figure on the left, the $\times$ symbols represent samples of the g curve derived from the digital values at one pixel for 5 different known exposures using Equation 2. The unknown log irradiance $\ln E_i$ has been arbitrarily assumed to be 0. Note that the shape of the g curve is correct, though its position on the vertical scale is arbitrary corresponding to the unknown $\ln E_i$. The $+$ and $\circ$ symbols show samples of g curve segments derived by consideration of two other pixels; again the vertical position of each segment is arbitrary. Essentially, what we want to achieve in the optimization process is to slide the 3 sampled curve segments up and down (by adjusting their $\ln E_i$'s) until they "line up" into a single smooth, monotonic curve, as shown in the right figure. The vertical position of the composite curve will remain arbitrary.*

interested in recovering accurately is R, and the film is capable of representing in its working range a dynamic range of F. Then the minimum number of photographs needed is $\lceil \frac{R}{F} \rceil$ to ensure that every part of the scene is imaged in at least one photograph at an exposure duration that puts it in the working range of the film response curve. As in recovering the response curve, using more photographs than strictly necessary will result in better noise sensitivity.

If one wanted to use as few photographs as possible, one might first recover the response curve of the imaging process by photographing a scene containing a diverse range of radiance values at three or four different exposures, differing by perhaps one or two stops. This response curve could be used to determine the working range of the imaging process, which for the processes we have seen would be as many as five or six stops. For the remainder of the shoot, the photographer could decide for any particular scene the number of shots necessary to cover its entire dynamic range. For diffuse indoor scenes, only one exposure might be necessary; for scenes with high dynamic range, several would be necessary. By recording the exposure amount for each shot, the images could then be converted to radiance maps using the pre-computed response curve.

2.4 Recovering extended dynamic range from single exposures

Most commericially available film scanners can detect reasonably close to the full range of useful densities present in film. However, many of these scanners (as well as the Kodak PhotoCD process) produce 8-bit-per-channel images designed to be viewed on a screen or printed on paper. Print film, however, records a significantly greater dynamic range than can be displayed with either of these media. As a result, such scanners deliver only a portion of the detected dynamic range of print film in a single scan, discarding information in either high or low density regions. The portion of the detected dynamic range that is delivered can usually be influenced by "brightness" or "density adjustment" controls.

The method presented in this paper enables two methods for recovering the full dynamic range of print film which we will briefly

outline[7]. In the first method, the print negative is scanned with the scanner set to scan slide film. Most scanners will then record the entire detectable dynamic range of the film in the resulting image. As before, a series of differently exposed images of the same scene can be used to recover the response function of the imaging system with each of these scanner settings. This response function can then be used to convert individual exposures to radiance maps. Unfortunately, since the resulting image is still 8-bits-per-channel, this results in increased quantization.

In the second method, the film can be scanned twice with the scanner set to different density adjustment settings. A series of differently exposed images of the same scene can then be used to recover the response function of the imaging system at each of these density adjustment settings. These two response functions can then be used to combine two scans of any single negative using a similar technique as in Section 2.2.

2.5 Obtaining Absolute Radiance

For many applications, such as image processing and image compositing, the relative radiance values computed by our method are all that are necessary. If needed, an approximation to the scaling term necessary to convert to absolute radiance can be derived using the ASA of the film[8] and the shutter speeds and exposure amounts in the photographs. With these numbers, formulas that give an approximate prediction of film response can be found in [9]. Such an approximation can be adequate for simulating visual artifacts such as glare, and predicting areas of scotopic retinal response. If desired, one could recover the scaling factor precisely by photographing a calibration luminaire of known radiance, and scaling the radiance values to agree with the known radiance of the luminaire.

2.6 Color

Color images, consisting of red, green, and blue channels, can be processed by reconstructing the imaging system response curve for

---

[7]This work was done in collaboration with Gregory Ward Larson

[8]Conveniently, most digital cameras also specify their sensitivity in terms of ASA.

each channel independently. Unfortunately, there will be three unknown scaling factors relating relative radiance to absolute radiance, one for each channel. As a result, different choices of these scaling factors will change the color balance of the radiance map.

By default, the algorithm chooses the scaling factor such that a pixel with value Z_{mid} will have unit exposure. Thus, any pixel with the RGB value $(Z_{mid}, Z_{mid}, Z_{mid})$ will have equal radiance values for R, G, and B, meaning that the pixel is achromatic. If the three channels of the imaging system actually do respond equally to achromatic light in the neighborhood of Z_{mid}, then our procedure correctly reconstructs the relative radiances.

However, films are usually calibrated to respond achromatically to a particular color of light C, such as sunlight or fluorescent light. In this case, the radiance values of the three channels should be scaled so that the pixel value $(Z_{mid}, Z_{mid}, Z_{mid})$ maps to a radiance with the same color ratios as C. To properly model the color response of the entire imaging process rather than just the film response, the scaling terms can be adjusted by photographing a calibration luminaire of known color.

2.7 Taking virtual photographs

The recovered response functions can also be used to map radiance values back to pixel values for a given exposure Δt using Equation 1. This process can be thought of as taking a virtual photograph of the radiance map, in that the resulting image will exhibit the response qualities of the modeled imaging system. Note that the response functions used need not be the same response functions used to construct the original radiance map, which allows photographs acquired with one imaging process to be rendered as if they were acquired with another.[9]

3 Results

Figures 3-5 show the results of using our algorithm to determine the response curve of a DCS460 digital camera. Eleven grayscale photographs filtered down to 765×509 resolution (Fig. 3) were taken at f/8 with exposure times ranging from $\frac{1}{30}$ of a second to 30 seconds, with each image receiving twice the exposure of the previous one. The film curve recovered by our algorithm from 45 pixel locations observed across the image sequence is shown in Fig. 4. Note that although CCD image arrays naturally produce linear output, from the curve it is evident that the camera nonlinearly remaps the data, presumably to mimic the response curves found in film. The underlying registered $(E_i \Delta t_j, Z_{ij})$ data are shown as light circles underneath the curve; some outliers are due to sensor artifacts (light horizontal bands across some of the darker images.)

Fig. 5 shows the reconstructed high dynamic range radiance map. To display this map, we have taken the logarithm of the radiance values and mapped the range of these values into the range of the display. In this representation, the pixels at the light regions do not saturate, and detail in the shadow regions can be made out, indicating that all of the information from the original image sequence is present in the radiance map. The large range of values present in the radiance map (over four orders of magnitude of useful dynamic range) is shown by the values at the marked pixel locations.

Figure 6 shows sixteen photographs taken inside a church with a Canon 35mm SLR camera on Fuji 100 ASA color print film. A fisheye 15mm lens set at f/8 was used, with exposure times ranging from 30 seconds to $\frac{1}{1000}$ of a second in 1-stop increments. The film was developed professionally and scanned in using a Kodak PhotoCD film scanner. The scanner was set so that it would not individually

---

[9]Note that here we are assuming that the spectral response functions for each channel of the two imaging processes is the same. Also, this technique does not model many significant qualities of an imaging system such as film grain, chromatic aberration, blooming, and the modulation transfer function.

Figure 3: **(a)** *Eleven grayscale photographs of an indoor scene acquired with a Kodak DCS460 digital camera, with shutter speeds progressing in 1-stop increments from $\frac{1}{30}$ of a second to 30 seconds.*

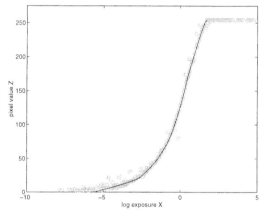

Figure 4: *The response function of the DCS460 recovered by our algorithm, with the underlying $(E_i \Delta t_j, Z_{ij})$ data shown as light circles. The logarithm is base e.*

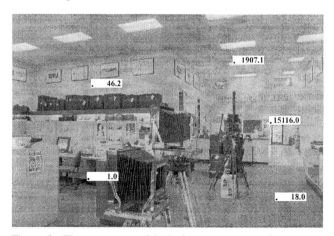

Figure 5: *The reconstructed high dynamic range radiance map, mapped into a grayscale image by taking the logarithm of the radiance values. The relative radiance values of the marked pixel locations, clockwise from lower left: 1.0, 46.2, 1907.1, 15116.0, and 18.0.*

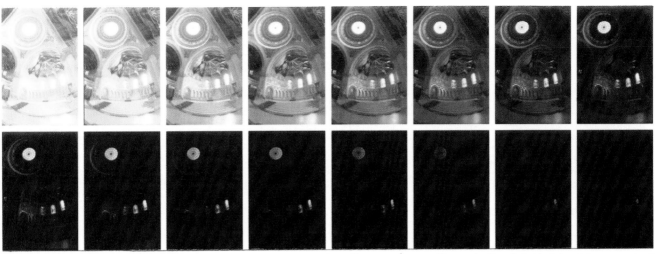

Figure 6: *Sixteen photographs of a church taken at 1-stop increments from 30 sec to $\frac{1}{1000}$ sec. The sun is directly behind the rightmost stained glass window, making it especially bright. The blue borders seen in some of the image margins are induced by the image registration process.*

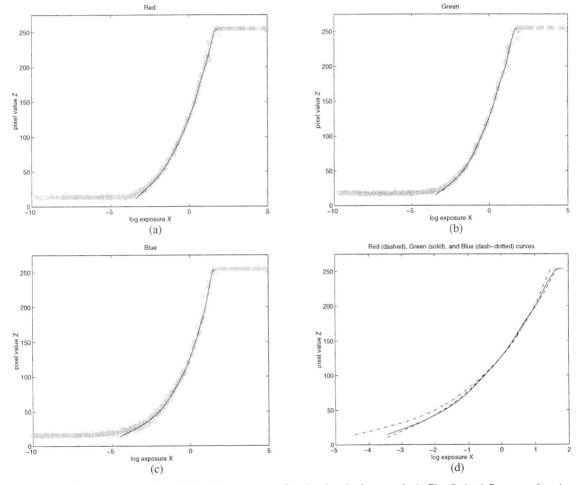

Figure 7: *Recovered response curves for the imaging system used in the church photographs in Fig. 8.* (**a-c**) *Response functions for the red, green, and blue channels, plotted with the underlying* $(E_i \Delta t_j, Z_{ij})$ *data shown as light circles.* (**d**) *The response functions for red, green, and blue plotted on the same axes. Note that while the red and green curves are very consistent, the blue curve rises significantly above the others for low exposure values. This indicates that dark regions in the images exhibit a slight blue cast. Since this artifact is recovered by the response curves, it does not affect the relative radiance values.*

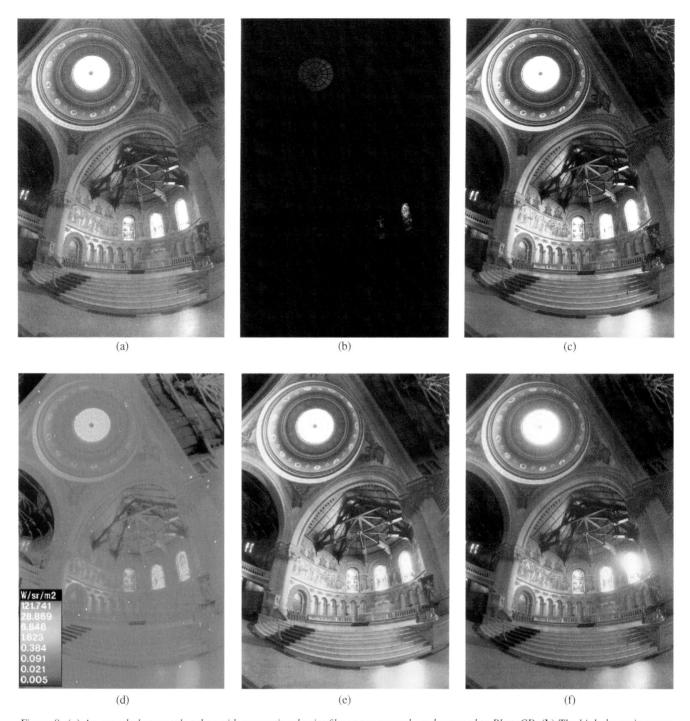

(a)

(b)

(c)

(d)

(e)

(f)

Figure 8: **(a)** *An actual photograph, taken with conventional print film at two seconds and scanned to PhotoCD.* **(b)** *The high dynamic range radiance map, displayed by linearly mapping its entire dynamic range into the dynamic range of the display device.* **(c)** *The radiance map, displayed by linearly mapping the lower 0.1% of its dynamic range to the display device.* **(d)** *A false-color image showing relative radiance values for a grayscale version of the radiance map, indicating that the map contains over five orders of magnitude of useful dynamic range.* **(e)** *A rendering of the radiance map using adaptive histogram compression.* **(f)** *A rendering of the radiance map using histogram compression and also simulating various properties of the human visual system, such as glare, contrast sensitivity, and scotopic retinal response. Images (e) and (f) were generated by a method described in [23]. Images (d-f) courtesy of Gregory Ward Larson.*

adjust the brightness and contrast of the images[10] to guarantee that each image would be digitized using the same response function.

An unfortunate aspect of the PhotoCD process is that it does not scan precisely the same area of each negative relative to the extents of the image.[11] To counteract this effect, we geometrically registered the images to each other using a using normalized correlation (see [4]) to determine, with sub-pixel accuracy, corresponding pixels between pairs of images.

Fig. 7(a-c) shows the response functions for the red, green, and blue channels of the church sequence recovered from 28 pixel locations. Fig. 7(d) shows the recovered red, green, and blue response curves plotted on the same set of axes. From this plot, we can see that while the red and green curves are very consistent, the blue curve rises significantly above the others for low exposure values. This indicates that dark regions in the images exhibit a slight blue cast. Since this artifact is modeled by the response curves, it will not affect the relative radiance values.

Fig. 8 interprets the recovered high dynamic range radiance map in a variety of ways. Fig. 8(a) is one of the actual photographs, which lacks detail in its darker regions at the same time that many values within the two rightmost stained glass windows are saturated. Figs. 8(b,c) show the radiance map, linearly scaled to the display device using two different scaling factors. Although one scaling factor is one thousand times the other, there is useful detail in both images. Fig. 8(d) is a false-color image showing radiance values for a grayscale version of the radiance map; the highest listed radiance value is nearly 250,000 times that of the lowest. Figs. 8(e,f) show two renderings of the radiance map using a new tone reproduction algorithm [23]. Although the rightmost stained glass window has radiance values over a thousand times higher than the darker areas in the rafters, these renderings exhibit detail in both areas.

Figure 9 demonstrates two applications of the techniques presented in this paper: accurate signal processing and virtual photography. The task is to simulate the effects of motion blur caused by moving the camera during the exposure. Fig. 9(a) shows the results of convolving an actual, low-dynamic range photograph with a 37×1 pixel box filter to simulate horizontal motion blur. Fig. 9(b) shows the results of applying this same filter to the high dynamic range radiance map, and then sending this filtered radiance map back through the recovered film response functions using the same exposure time Δt as in the actual photograph. Because we are seeing this image through the actual image response curves, the two left images are tonally consistent with each other. However, there is a large difference between these two images near the bright spots. In the photograph, the bright radiance values have been clamped to the maximum pixel values by the response function. As a result, these clamped values blur with lower neighboring values and fail to saturate the image in the final result, giving a muddy appearance.

In Fig. 9(b), the extremely high pixel values were represented properly in the radiance map and thus remained at values above the level of the response function's saturation point within most of the blurred region. As a result, the resulting virtual photograph exhibits several crisply-defined saturated regions.

Fig. 9(c) is an actual photograph with real motion blur induced by spinning the camera on the tripod during the exposure, which is equal in duration to Fig. 9(a) and the exposure simulated in Fig. 9(b). Clearly, in the bright regions, the blurring effect is qualitatively similar to the synthetic blur in 9(b) but not 9(a). The precise shape of the real motion blur is curved and was not modeled for this demonstration.

---

[10]This feature of the PhotoCD process is called "Scene Balance Adjustment", or SBA.

[11]This is far less of a problem for cinematic applications, in which the film sprocket holes are used to expose and scan precisely the same area of each frame.

(a) Synthetically blurred digital image

(b) Synthetically blurred radiance map

(c) Actual blurred photograph

Figure 9: **(a)** *Synthetic motion blur applied to one of the original digitized photographs. The bright values in the windows are clamped before the processing, producing mostly unsaturated values in the blurred regions.* **(b)** *Synthetic motion blur applied to a recovered high-dynamic range radiance map, then virtually rephotographed through the recovered film response curves. The radiance values are clamped to the display device after the processing, allowing pixels to remain saturated in the window regions.* **(c)** *Real motion blur created by rotating the camera on the tripod during the exposure, which is much more consistent with (b) than (a).*

4 Conclusion

We have presented a simple, practical, robust and accurate method of recovering high dynamic range radiance maps from ordinary photographs. Our method uses the constraint of sensor reciprocity to derive the response function and relative radiance values directly from a set of images taken with different exposures. This work has a wide variety of applications in the areas of image-based modeling and rendering, image processing, and image compositing, a few of which we have demonstrated. It is our hope that this work will be able to help both researchers and practitioners of computer graphics make much more effective use of digitized photographs.

Acknowledgments

The authors wish to thank Tim Hawkins, Carlo Séquin, David Forsyth, Steve Chenney, Chris Healey, and our reviewers for their valuable help in revising this paper. This research was supported by a Multidisciplinary University Research Initiative on three dimensional direct visualization from ONR and BMDO, grant FDN00014-96-1-1200.

References

[1] ADAMS, A. *Basic Photo*, 1st ed. Morgan & Morgan, Hastings-on-Hudson, New York, 1970.

[2] CHEN, E. QuickTime VR - an image-based approach to virtual environment navigation. In *SIGGRAPH '95* (1995).

[3] DEBEVEC, P. E., TAYLOR, C. J., AND MALIK, J. Modeling and rendering architecture from photographs: A hybrid geometry- and image-based approach. In *SIGGRAPH '96* (August 1996), pp. 11–20.

[4] FAUGERAS, O. *Three-Dimensional Computer Vision*. MIT Press, 1993.

[5] FERWERDA, J. A., PATTANAIK, S. N., SHIRLEY, P., AND GREENBERG, D. P. A model of visual adaptation for realistic image synthesis. In *SIGGRAPH '96* (1996), pp. 249–258.

[6] GORTLER, S. J., GRZESZCZUK, R., SZELISKI, R., AND CO-HEN, M. F. The Lumigraph. In *SIGGRAPH '96* (1996), pp. 43–54.

[7] HORN, B. K. P. *Robot Vision*. MIT Press, Cambridge, Mass., 1986, ch. 10, pp. 206–208.

[8] JAMES, T., Ed. *The Theory of the Photographic Process*. Macmillan, New York, 1977.

[9] KAUFMAN, J. E., Ed. *IES Lighting Handbook; the standard lighting guide*, 7th ed. Illuminating Engineering Society, New York, 1987, p. 24.

[10] KOLB, C., MITCHELL, D., AND HANRAHAN, P. A realistic camera model for computer graphics. In *SIGGRAPH '95* (1995).

[11] LAVEAU, S., AND FAUGERAS, O. 3-D scene representation as a collection of images. In *Proceedings of 12th International Conference on Pattern Recognition* (1994), vol. 1, pp. 689–691.

[12] LEVOY, M., AND HANRAHAN, P. Light field rendering. In *SIGGRAPH '96* (1996), pp. 31–42.

[13] MADDEN, B. C. Extended intensity range imaging. Tech. rep., GRASP Laboratory, University of Pennsylvania, 1993.

[14] MANN, S., AND PICARD, R. W. Being 'undigital' with digital cameras: Extending dynamic range by combining differently exposed pictures. In *Proceedings of IS&T 46th annual conference* (May 1995), pp. 422–428.

[15] MCMILLAN, L., AND BISHOP, G. Plenoptic Modeling: An image-based rendering system. In *SIGGRAPH '95* (1995).

[16] SCHLICK, C. Quantization techniques for visualization of high dynamic range pictures. In *Fifth Eurographics Workshop on Rendering (Darmstadt, Germany)* (June 1994), pp. 7–18.

[17] SZELISKI, R. Image mosaicing for tele-reality applications. In *IEEE Computer Graphics and Applications* (1996).

[18] TANI, T. *Photographic sensitivity : theory and mechanisms*. Oxford University Press, New York, 1995.

[19] THEUWISSEN, A. J. P. *Solid-state imaging with charge-coupled devices*. Kluwer Academic Publishers, Dordrecht; Boston, 1995.

[20] TUMBLIN, J., AND RUSHMEIER, H. Tone reproduction for realistic images. *IEEE Computer Graphics and Applications* 13, 6 (1993), 42–48.

[21] WARD, G. J. Measuring and modeling anisotropic reflection. In *SIGGRAPH '92* (July 1992), pp. 265–272.

[22] WARD, G. J. The radiance lighting simulation and rendering system. In *SIGGRAPH '94* (July 1994), pp. 459–472.

[23] WARD, G. J., RUSHMEIER, H., AND PIATKO, C. A visibility matching tone reproduction operator for high dynamic range scenes. Tech. Rep. LBNL-39882, Lawrence Berkeley National Laboratory, March 1997.

A Matlab Code

Here is the MATLAB code used to solve the linear system that minimizes the objective function $\mathcal{O}$ in Equation 3. Given a set of observed pixel values in a set of images with known exposures, this routine reconstructs the imaging response curve and the radiance values for the given pixels. The weighting function $w(z)$ is found in Equation 4.

```
%
% gsolve.m - Solve for imaging system response function
%
% Given a set of pixel values observed for several pixels in several
% images with different exposure times, this function returns the
% imaging system's response function g as well as the log film irradiance
% values for the observed pixels.
%
% Assumes:
%
%   Zmin = 0
%   Zmax = 255
%
% Arguments:
%
%   Z(i,j) is the pixel values of pixel location number i in image j
%   B(j)   is the log delta t, or log shutter speed, for image j
%   l      is lambda, the constant that determines the amount of smoothness
%   w(z)   is the weighting function value for pixel value z
%
% Returns:
%
%   g(z)   is the log exposure corresponding to pixel value z
%   lE(i)  is the log film irradiance at pixel location i
%

function [g,lE]=gsolve(Z,B,l,w)

n = 256;

A = zeros(size(Z,1)*size(Z,2)+n+1,n+size(Z,1));
b = zeros(size(A,1),1);

%% Include the data-fitting equations

k = 1;
for i=1:size(Z,1)
  for j=1:size(Z,2)
    wij = w(Z(i,j)+1);
    A(k,Z(i,j)+1) = wij;  A(k,n+i) = -wij;    b(k,1) = wij * B(i,j);
    k=k+1;
  end
end

%% Fix the curve by setting its middle value to 0

A(k,129) = 1;
k=k+1;

%% Include the smoothness equations

for i=1:n-2
  A(k,i)=l*w(i+1);         A(k,i+1)=-2*l*w(i+1);   A(k,i+2)=l*w(i+1);
  k=k+1;
end

%% Solve the system using SVD

x = A\b;

g = x(1:n);
lE = x(n+1:size(x,1));
```

Object Shape and Reflectance Modeling from Observation

Yoichi Sato[1], Mark D. Wheeler[2], and Katsushi Ikeuchi[1]

[1]Institute of Industrial Science
University of Tokyo

[2]Apple Computer Inc.

ABSTRACT

An object model for computer graphics applications should contain two aspects of information: shape and reflectance properties of the object. A number of techniques have been developed for modeling object shapes by observing real objects. In contrast, attempts to model reflectance properties of real objects have been rather limited. In most cases, modeled reflectance properties are too simple or too complicated to be used for synthesizing realistic images of the object.

In this paper, we propose a new method for modeling object reflectance properties, as well as object shapes, by observing real objects. First, an object surface shape is reconstructed by merging multiple range images of the object. By using the reconstructed object shape and a sequence of color images of the object, parameters of a reflection model are estimated in a robust manner. The key point of the proposed method is that, first, the diffuse and specular reflection components are separated from the color image sequence, and then, reflectance parameters of each reflection component are estimated separately. This approach enables estimation of reflectance properties of real objects whose surfaces show specularity as well as diffusely reflected lights. The recovered object shape and reflectance properties are then used for synthesizing object images with realistic shading effects under arbitrary illumination conditions.

CR Descriptors: I.2.10 [**Artificial Intelligence**]: Vision and Scene Understanding - *Modeling and recovery of physical attributes*; I.3.7 [**Computer Graphics**]: Three-Dimensional Graphics and Realism - *Color, shading, shadowing, and texture*; I.3.3 [**Computer Graphics**]: Picture/Image Generation - *Digitizing and scanning*

1 INTRODUCTION

As a result of significant advancement of graphics hardware and image rendering algorithms, the 3D computer graphics capability has become available even on low-end computers. In addition, the rapid spread of the internet technology has caused a significant increase in the demand for 3D computer graphics. For instance, a new format for 3D computer graphics on the internet, called VRML, is becoming an industrial standard format, and the number of applications using the format is increasing quickly.

However, it is often the case that 3D object models are created manually by users. That input process is normally time-consuming and can be a bottleneck for realistic image synthesis. Therefore, techniques to obtain object model data automatically by observing real objects could have great significance in practical applications.

An object model for computer graphics applications should contain two aspects of information: shape and reflectance properties of the object. A number of techniques have been developed for modeling object shapes by observing real objects. Those techniques use a wide variety of approaches which includes range image merging, shape from motion, shape from shading, and photometric stereo. In contrast, attempts to model reflectance properties of real objects have been rather limited. In most cases, modeled reflectance properties are too simple or too complicated to be used for synthesizing realistic images of the object. For example, if only observed color texture or diffuse texture of a real object surface is used (e.g., texture mapping), correct shading effects such as highlights cannot be reproduced correctly in synthesized images. If highlights on the object surface are observed in original color images, the highlights are treated as diffuse texture on the object surface and, therefore, remain on the object surface permanently regardless of illuminating and viewing conditions. On the other hand, object reflectance properties can be represented accurately by a bidirectional reflectance distribution function (BRDF). If a BRDF is available for the object surface, shading effects can be, in principle, reproduced correctly in synthesized images. However, the use of BRDF is not practical because measurement of BRDF is usually very expensive and time-consuming. In practice, we cannot obtain a BRDF for real objects with various reflectance properties.

Recently, several techniques to obtain object surface shapes and reflectance properties only from intensity images have been developed. Sato and Ikeuchi [15] introduced a method to analyze a sequence of color images taken under a moving light source. They successfully estimated reflectance function parameters, as well as object shape, by explicitly separating the diffuse and specular reflection components. Lu and Little [11] developed a method to estimate a reflectance function from a sequence of black and white images of a rotating smooth object, and the object shape was successfully recovered using the estimated reflectance function. Since the reflectance function is measured directly from the input image sequence, the method does not assume a particular reflection model such as the Lambertian model which is commonly used in computer vision. However, their algorithm can be applied to object surfaces with uniform reflectance properties, and it cannot be easily extended to overcome this limitation.

Another interesting attempt for measuring a reflectance function from intensity images has been reported by Ward [20]. Ward designed a special device with a half-silvered hemisphere and a CCD video camera, which can measure a BRDF of anisotropic reflection.

[1] Department of Electrical Engineering and Electronics, Institute of Industrial Science, University of Tokyo, 7-22-1 Roppongi, Minato-ku, Tokyo 106, Japan. {ysato, ki}@iis.u-tokyo.ac.jp. See also http://www.cvl.iis.u-tokyo.ac.jp/~ysato.

[2] Apple Computer Inc., 1 Infinite Loop, MS:301-3M, Cupertino, CA 95014. mdwheel@apple.com.

The main advantage of the device is that it takes significantly less time to measure a BRDF than a conventional gonioreflectometer. A BRDF of a real object surface has been measured by the device and highly realistic images have been synthesized. However, this approach cannot be easily extended for modeling real objects with various reflectance properties. This approach still requires a small piece of test material for measuring the material's BRDF.

Techniques to measure object surface shape and reflectance properties simultaneously by using both range images and black and white intensity images have been studied by other researchers. Ikeuchi and Sato [7] originally developed a method to measure object shapes and reflection function parameters from a range image and intensity image pair. In their attempt, the surface shape is recovered from the range image at first, and then surface normals of the recovered object surface are used for reflectance parameter estimation. The main drawback of the method is that it assumes uniform reflectance properties over the object surface. Additionally, only partial object shape was recovered because only one range image was used.

Baribeau, Rioux, and Godin [1] measured three reflectance parameters that they call the diffuse reflectance of the body material, the Fresnel reflectance of the air-media interface, and the slope surface roughness of the interface, by using their polychromatic laser range sensor which can produce a pair of range and color images. Their method could estimate more detailed reflectance properties than the one developed by Ikeuchi and Sato [7]. However, their method still required uniform reflectance properties over each object surface, and only partial object shape was recovered.

Kay and Caelli [9] introduced another method to use a range image and 4 or 8 intensity images taken under different illumination conditions. By increasing the number of intensity images, they estimated reflection function parameters locally for each image pixel. Unlike the algorithm proposed by Sato and Ikeuchi, the method can handle object surfaces with varying reflectance properties. However, it is reported that parameter estimation can be unstable, especially when the specular reflection component is not observed strongly.

More recently, Sato and Ikeuchi developed a method to measure object surface shape and reflectance properties from a sequence of range and color images [16]. The method has an advantage over other methods in that it can handle objects with non-uniform reflectance properties. However, the method relies on region segmentation on object surfaces, and each of the segmented regions must have uniform reflectance properties. Therefore, the method cannot be applied to highly textured objects.

In this paper, we propose a new method for modeling object reflectance properties, as well as object shapes, from multiple range and color images of real objects. Unlike previously proposed methods, our method can create complete object models, i.e., not partial object shape, with non-uniform reflectance properties. First, the object surface shape is reconstructed by merging multiple range images of the object. By using the reconstructed object shape and a sequence of color images of the object, parameters of a reflection model are estimated in a robust manner. The key point of the proposed method is that, first, the diffuse reflection components and the specular reflection component are separated from the color image sequence, and then, reflectance parameters of each reflection component are estimated separately. Unlike previously reported methods, this approach enables reliable estimation of surface reflectance properties which are not uniform over the object surface, and which include specularity as well as diffusely reflected

lights. We demonstrate the capability of our object modeling technique by synthesizing object images with realistic shading effects under arbitrary illumination conditions.

This paper is organized as follows: Section 2 describes our image acquisition system for obtaining a sequence of range and color images of the object. Section 3 explains reconstruction of the object surface shape from the range image sequence. Section 4 describes our method for estimating reflectance properties of the object using the reconstructed object shape and the color image sequence. Object images synthesized using the recovered object shape and reflectance properties are shown in Section 5. Concluding remarks are presented in Section 6.

2 IMAGE ACQUISITION SYSTEM

The experimental setup for the image acquisition system used in our experiments is illustrated in Figure 1. The object whose shape and reflectance information is to be recovered is mounted on the end of a robotic arm. The object used in our experiment is a ceramic mug whose height is about $100mm$. Using the system, a sequence of range and color images of the object is obtained as the object is rotated at a fixed angle step. Twelve range images and 120 color images were used in our experiment shown in this paper.

A range image is obtained using a light-stripe range finder with a liquid crystal shutter and a color CCD video camera [14]. 3D locations of points in the scene are computed at each image pixel using optical triangulation. Each range-image pixel represents an (X, Y, Z) location of a corresponding point on an object surface. The same color camera is used for acquiring range images and color images. Therefore, pixels of the range images and the color images directly correspond.

The range finder is calibrated to produce a 3×4 projection matrix Π which represents the projection transformation between the world coordinate system and the image coordinate system. The location of the PUMA 560 manipulator with respect to the world coordinate system is also found via calibration. Therefore, the object location is given as a 4×4 transformation matrix T for each digitized image.

A single incandescent lamp is used as a point light source. In our experiments, the light source direction and the light source color are measured by calibration. The gain and offset of outputs from the video camera are adjusted so that the light source color becomes $(R, G, B) = (1, 1, 1)$.

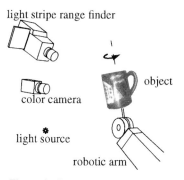

light stripe range finder

object

color camera

light source

robotic arm

Figure 1 *Image acquisition system*

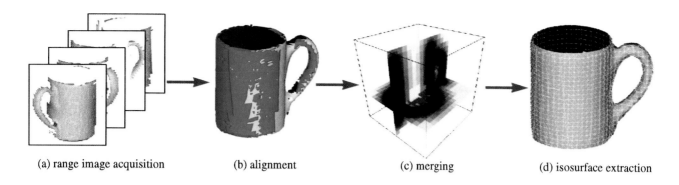

(a) range image acquisition   (b) alignment   (c) merging   (d) isosurface extraction

Figure 2 Shape reconstruction by merging range images: (a) Input surface patches (4 out of 12 patches are shown), (b) Result of alignment, (c) Obtained volumetric data (two cross sections are shown), (d) Generated triangular mesh of the object shape (3782 triangles)

3 SURFACE SHAPE MODELING

A sequence of range images of the object is used to construct the object shape as a triangular mesh. Then, the number of triangles used for the object shape model is reduced by simplifying the object shape without losing its details for efficient storage and rendering of the object.

One disadvantage of using the simplified object model is that a polygonal normal computed from the simplified triangular mesh model does not accurately approximate the real surface normal even though the object shape is preserved reasonably well. Thus, rather than using polygonal normals, we compute surface normals at dense grid points within each triangle of the object surface mesh by using the lowest level input, i.e., 3D points measured in range images.

In Section 3.1, we describe reconstruction of a triangular mesh model of the object from a sequence of range images. Estimation of dense surface normals is explained in Section 3.2.

3.1 Shape modeling from range image merging

For reconstructing object shapes as a triangular mesh model from multiple range images, we used the volumetric method developed by Wheeler, Sato, and Ikeuchi [21]. The method consists of the following four steps, each of which is briefly described in this section.

1. Surface acquisition from each range image

The range finder in our image acquisition system cannot measure the object surface itself. In other words, the range finder can produce only images of 3D points on the object surface. Because of this limitation, we need to somehow convert the measured 3D points into a triangular mesh which represents the object surface shape. This is done by connecting two neighboring range image pixels based on the assumption that those points are connected by a locally smooth surface. If those two points are closer in a 3D distance than some threshold, then we consider them to be connected on the object surface.

In Figure 2 (a), 4 out of 12 input range images of the mug are shown as triangular meshes.

2. Alignment of all range images

All of the range images are measured in the coordinate system fixed with respect to the range finder system, and they are not aligned to each other initially. Therefore, after we obtain the triangular surface meshes from the range images, we need to transform all of the meshes into a unique object coordinate system.

To align the range images, we use a transformation matrix T which represents the object location for each range image (Section 2). Suppose we select one of the range images as a key range image to which all other range images are aligned. We refer to the transformation matrix for the key range image as T_{merge}. Then, all other range images can be transformed into the key range image's coordinate system by transforming all 3D points $P = (X, Y, Z, 1)$ as $P' = T_{merge}T_f^{-1}P$ where $f = 1 \ldots n$ is a range image frame number.

3. Merging based on a volumetric representation

After all of the range images are converted into triangular patches and aligned to a unique coordinate system, we merge them using a volumetric representation. First, we consider imaginary 3D volume grids around the aligned triangular patches. Then, in each voxel,[3] we store the value, $f(x)$, of the signed distance from the center point of the voxel, x, to the closest point on the object surface. The sign indicates whether the point is outside, $f(x) > 0$, or inside, $f(x) < 0$, the object surface, while $f(x) = 0$ indicates that x lies on the surface of the object.

This technique has been applied to surface extraction by several researchers [5], [3], [4]. The novel part of our technique is the robust computation of the signed distance. Our technique computes the signed distance by using a new algorithm called *the consensus surface algorithm* [21]. In the consensus surface algorithm, a quorum of consensus of locally coherent observation of the object surface is used to compute the signed distance correctly, which eliminates many of the troublesome effects of noise and extraneous surface observations in the input range images, for which previously developed methods are susceptible.

One drawback of using a volume grid for merging range images is the amount of memory required for the volume grid, which is $O(n^3)$ and therefore quickly becomes prohibitively large as the resolution n increases. Curless and Levoy's method [3] used

---

3. **voxel:** volume element

a run-length encoding to overcome this problem. In our technique, an oct-tree structure [8] is used, and the required memory was reduced to $4 - 23$ % for several examples reported in [21]. Further study is needed to determine whether the use of oct-trees as in our technique is more or less efficient than the run-length encoding in Curless and Levoy's method.

Figure 2 (c) shows two cross sections of the volumetric data constructed from the input range images of the mug. A darker color represents a shorter distance to the object surface, and a brighter color represents a longer distance.

4.   Isosurface extraction from volumetric grid

The volumetric data is then used to construct the object surface as a triangular mesh. The marching cubes algorithm [10] constructs a triangular mesh by traversing zero crossings of the implicit surface, $f(x) = 0$, in the volume grid. Here, the marching cube algorithm was modified so that it handles holes and missing data correctly [21].

Figure 2 (d) shows the result of triangular mesh reconstruction. In this example, 3782 triangles were generated from the volumetric data.

The marching cube algorithm generally produces a large number of triangles whose sizes vary significantly. Thus, it is desirable to simplify the reconstructed object surface shape by reducing the number of triangles. We used the mesh simplification method developed by Hoppe et al. [6] for this purpose. In our experiment, the total number of triangles was reduced from 3782 to 488 (Figure 3).

Figure 3   Simplified shape model: The object shape model was simplified from 3782 to 488 triangles.

3.2 Surface normal estimation

Polygonal normals computed from a triangular surface mesh model can approximate real surface normals fairly well when the object surface is relatively smooth and does not have high curvature points. However, accuracy of polygonal normals becomes poor when the object surface has high curvature points and the resolution of the triangular surface mesh model is low, i.e., a smaller number of triangles to represent the object shape.

This becomes a problem especially for the task of reflectance parameter estimation. For estimating reflectance parameters at a surface point, we need to know three directions at the surface point: the viewing direction, the light source direction, and the surface normal. As a result, with incorrectly estimated surface normals, small highlights observed within each triangle cannot be analyzed accurately, and therefore they cannot be reproduced in synthesized images. For this reason, we compute surface normals at regular grid points (20×20 points in our experiment) within each triangle

using the 3D points from the range images. The resolution of regular grid points should be changed depending on the size of each triangle, so that the density of grid points becomes more or less uniform over the object surface. The adaptive resolution of grid points is yet to be implemented in our object modeling system.

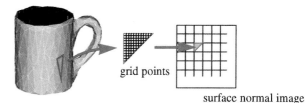

Figure 4   Dense surface normal estimation

The surface normal at a grid point P_g is determined from a least squares best fitting plane to all neighboring 3D points whose distances to the point P_g are shorter than some threshold. This surface normal estimation method has been used by other researchers for other applications. Cromwell [2] used a similar method for choosing the best direction for viewing a cloud of small particles, e.g., molecules, in computer graphics. Hoppe et al. [5] used the surface normal estimation method for surface reconstruction from a cloud of 3D points.

The surface normal is computed as an eigen vector of the covariance matrix of the neighboring 3D points; specifically, the eigen vector associated with the eigenvalue of smallest magnitude (Figure 5). The covariance matrix of n 3D points $[X_i, Y_i, Z_i]^T$, with centroid $[\bar{X}, \bar{Y}, \bar{Z}]^T$, is defined as

$$C = \sum_{i=1}^{n} \begin{bmatrix} (X_i - \bar{X}) \\ (Y_i - \bar{Y}) \\ (Z_i - \bar{Z}) \end{bmatrix} \begin{bmatrix} (X_i - \bar{X}) & (Y_i - \bar{Y}) & (Z_i - \bar{Z}) \end{bmatrix} . \quad (1)$$

The surface normals computed at regular grid points within each triangle are then stored as a three-band surface normal image which is later used for mapping dense surface normals to the triangular mesh of the object shape. The mapped surface normals are used both for reflectance parameter estimation and for rendering color images of the object.

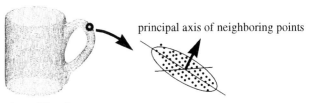

Figure 5   *Surface normal estimation from input 3D points*

4   SURFACE REFLECTANCE MODELING

After the object shape is reconstructed, we measure reflectance properties of the object surface using the reconstructed shape and the input color images. First, the two fundamental reflection components (i.e., the diffuse and specular reflection components) are separated from the input color images. Then, the parameters for the two reflection components are estimated separately. Separation of the two reflection components enables us to obtain a reliable estimation of the specular reflection parameters. Also, the specular reflection component (i.e., highlight) in the color images does not affect estimated diffuse reflection parameters of the object surface.

In Section 4.1 we introduce the reflection model used in this analysis. Then, in Section 4.2 we describe how to determine an observed color sequence for a 3D point on the object surface from the input color images. Using the observed color sequence, the algorithm for separating the diffuse and specular reflection components is explained in Section 4.3. We explain the measurement of the diffuse reflection parameters in Section 4.4. Finally, we describe the estimation of the specular reflection parameters in Section 4.5.

4.1 Reflection model

A general reflection model is described in terms of three reflection components, namely the diffuse lobe, the specular lobe, and the specular spike [12]. In many computer vision and computer graphics applications, reflection models are represented by linear combinations of two of those reflection components: the diffuse lobe component and the specular lobe component. The specular spike component can be observed only from mirror-like smooth surfaces where reflected light rays of the specular spike component are concentrated in a specular direction. It is thus difficult to observe the specular spike component from a coarsely sampled set of viewing directions.

The diffuse lobe component and the specular lobe component are normally called the diffuse reflection component and the specular reflection component, respectively. This reflection model was formally introduced by Shafer as the dichromatic reflection model [17].

In our analysis, the Torrance-Sparrow model [19] is used for representing the diffuse and specular reflection components. As Figure 1 illustrates, the illumination and viewing directions are fixed with respect to the world coordinate system. The reflection model used in our analysis is given as

$$I_m = K_{D,m} cos\theta_i + K_{S,m} \frac{1}{cos\theta_r} e^{-\alpha^2/2\sigma^2} \quad m = R, G, B \tag{2}$$

where θ_i is the angle between the surface normal and the light source direction, θ_r is the angle between the surface normal and the viewing direction, α is the angle between the surface normal and the bisector of the light source direction and the viewing direction, $K_{D,m}$ and $K_{S,m}$ are constants for the diffuse and specular reflection components, and σ is the standard deviation of a facet slope of the Torrance-Sparrow model.

This reflection model represents reflections which bounce only once from the light source. Therefore, the reflection model is valid only for convex objects, and it cannot represent interreflections on concave object surfaces. However, we empirically determined that interreflection did not affect our analysis significantly.

In this paper, we refer to $K_{D,R}$, $K_{D,G}$, and $K_{D,B}$ as the diffuse reflection parameters, and $K_{S,R}$, $K_{S,G}$, $K_{S,B}$, and σ as the specular reflection parameters.

4.2 Mapping color images onto object surface shape

For separating the diffuse and specular reflection components and for estimating parameters of each reflection component, we need to know a sequence of observed colors at each point on the object surface as the object is rotated. In this section, we describe how to obtain an observed color sequence of a surface point (X,Y,Z) from the input color image sequence.

We represent world coordinates and image coordinates using homogeneous coordinates. A point on the object surface with Euclidean coordinates (X, Y, Z) is expressed by a column vector $P = [X, Y, Z, 1]^T$. An image pixel location (x, y) is represented by $p = [x, y, 1]^T$. As described in Section 2, the camera projection transformation is represented by a 3×4 matrix Π, and the object location is given by a 4×4 object transformation matrix T. We denote the object transformation matrix for the input color image frame f by T_f ($f = 1...n$). Thus, using the projection matrix Π and the transformation matrix T_{merge} for the key range image (Section 3.1), the projection of a 3D point on the object surface in the color image frame f is given as

$$p_f = \Pi T_f T_{merge}^{-1} P \qquad (f = 1...n) \tag{3}$$

where the last component of p_f has to be normalized to give the projected image location (x, y).

The observed color of the 3D point in the color image frame f is given as the (R, G, B) color intensity at the pixel location (x, y). If the 3D point is not visible in the color image (i.e., the point is facing away from the camera, or it is occluded), the observed color for the 3D point is set to $(R, G, B) = (0, 0, 0)$. By repeating this procedure for all frames of the input color image sequence, we get an observed color sequence for the 3D point on the object surface.

Figure 6 shows the result of mapping the input color images onto the reconstructed object surface shape.

4.3 Reflection component separation from color image sequence

We now describe the algorithm for separating the two reflection components. This separation algorithm was originally introduced for the case of a moving light source by Sato and Ikeuchi [15]. In this paper, a similar algorithm is applied for the case of a moving object.

Using three color bands, red, green, and blue, the coefficients $K_{D,m}$ and $K_{S,m}$, in Equation (2), generalize to two linearly independent vectors,

$$K_D = \begin{bmatrix} K_{D,R} & K_{D,G} & K_{D,B} \end{bmatrix}^T \quad K_S = \begin{bmatrix} K_{S,R} & K_{S,G} & K_{S,B} \end{bmatrix}^T \tag{4}$$

unless the colors of the two reflection components are accidentally the same.

input color image sequence

Figure 6 *Color image mapping result: 6 out of 120 color images are shown here.*

First, the color intensities in the R, G, and B channels from input images of the object are measured for each point on the object surface as described in Section 4.2. The three sequences of intensity values are stored in the columns of an $n \times 3$ matrix M. Considering the reflectance model (Equation (2)) and two color vectors in Equation (4), the intensity values in the R, G, and B channels can be represented as

$$
\begin{aligned}
M &= \begin{bmatrix} M_R & M_G & M_B \end{bmatrix} \\
&= \begin{bmatrix} \cos\theta_{i1} & E(\theta_{r1}, \alpha_1) \\ \cos\theta_{i2} & E(\theta_{r2}, \alpha_2) \\ . & . \\ . & . \\ \cos\theta_{in} & E(\theta_{rn}, \alpha_n) \end{bmatrix} \begin{bmatrix} K_{D,R} & K_{D,G} & K_{D,B} \\ K_{S,R} & K_{S,G} & K_{S,B} \end{bmatrix} \\
&= \begin{bmatrix} G_D & G_S \end{bmatrix} \begin{bmatrix} K_D^T \\ K_S^T \end{bmatrix} \\
&\equiv GK
\end{aligned}
\tag{5}
$$

where $E(\theta_r, \alpha) = \exp(-\alpha^2/2\sigma^2)/\cos\theta_r$, and the two vectors G_D and G_S represent the intensity values of the diffuse and specular reflection components with respect to the illuminating/viewing directions θ_i, θ_r, and α. The vectors K_D and K_S represent the diffuse and the specular reflection color vectors, respectively.

Suppose we have an estimate of the matrix K. Then, the two reflection components represented by the matrix G are obtained by projecting the observed reflection stored in M onto the two color vectors K_D and K_S as

$$
G = MK^+
\tag{6}
$$

where K^+ is the 3×2 pseudoinverse matrix of the color matrix K.

The derivation shown above is based on the assumption that the matrix K is known. In our experiments, the specular reflection color vector K_S is directly measured as the light source color by a calibration procedure. Therefore, only the diffuse color vector K_D is unknown and needs to be determined.

From Equation (2), it can be seen that the distribution of the specular reflection component is limited to a fixed angle, depending

on σ. Thus, if the angle α is sufficiently large at a point on the object surface, an observed color at the point should represent the color of the diffuse reflection component. The angles α, θ_i, and θ_r are computed using the object transformation matrix T_f ($f = 1 \ldots n$) and the camera projection matrix Π as follows. The light source location is acquired via calibration, and the camera projection center can be computed from the projection matrix Π. Also, the surface normal at the surface point of the object model for the color image frame f can be computed by rotating the surface normal at the surface point by the object transformation matrix T_f. Using the light source direction, the viewing direction and the surface normal, α, θ_i, and θ_r are computed.

Once we get the matrix K, the matrix G can be calculated from Equation (6). Each of the diffuse and specular reflection components is given as

$$
M_D = G_D K_D^T \qquad M_S = G_S K_S^T .
\tag{7}
$$

Figure 7 (a) illustrates a typical observed color sequence with specularity. The separation algorithm was applied to the observed color sequence, and the separation result is shown in Figure 7 (b).

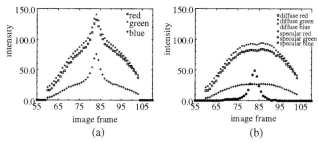

(a)　　　　　　　　　(b)

Figure 7 *(a) observed color sequence and (b) separation result*

Another technique for separating the diffuse and specular reflection components is the use of polarization filters [13] [22]. The technique could be used for separating reflection components instead of the one described in this section. However, the use of polarization generally requires more samplings of images by using a more complex image acquisition system. Thus, we have not explored this direction in our study.

4.4 Diffuse reflection parameter estimation

Using the diffuse reflection component separated from the observed color sequence, we now can estimate the diffuse reflection parameters ($K_{D,R}$, $K_{D,G}$, and $K_{D,B}$) without undesirable effects from the specular reflection component (i.e., highlights). Using the angle θ_i computed as stated in the previous section, the diffuse reflection parameters are estimated by fitting the reflection model (the first term of Equation (2)) to the separated diffuse reflection component. Hence, the estimated diffuse reflection parameters are not affected by the particular shadings in the observed images, e.g., the effect of the light source can be factored out. In other words, the diffuse reflection parameters can be estimated correctly even if the object appears dark or bright in the color images.

The diffuse reflection parameters are estimated at regular grid points within each triangle just as the surface normals in Section 3.2 are estimated. The resolution of the grid of points is 80×80 in our experiment, while it is 20×20 for the surface normal estimation. The higher resolution is necessary to capture details of the diffuse reflection texture on the object surface. The resolution for the diffuse reflection parameter estimation should be determined by the average number of pixels which fall onto one triangle of the object shape model in the observed color images. Resolution higher than the average number does not capture any more information than that in the observed color images, but it increases the required storage for the diffuse reflection parameters unnecessarily. Figure 8 shows the result of the diffuse reflection parameter estimation where the estimated parameters are visualized as surface texture on the mug.

Figure 8   Estimated diffuse reflection parameters

4.5 Specular reflection parameter estimation

As in the diffuse reflection parameter estimation, the specular reflection parameters ($K_{S,R}$, $K_{S,G}$, $K_{S,B}$, and σ) are also computed using the angle θ_r and the angle α. However, there is a significant difference between estimation of the diffuse and specular reflection parameters. The diffuse reflection parameters can be estimated as long as the object surface is illuminated and viewed from the camera. On the other hand, the specular reflection component is usually observed only from a limited range of viewing directions. For a finite set of views, the specular reflection component will only be observed over a small portion of the object surface in the input color image sequence. For much of the object surface, we cannot estimate the specular reflection parameters. Even if the specular reflection component is observed, the parameter estimation can become unreliable if the specular reflection component is not observed strongly, or if the separation of the two reflection components is not performed well.

For the above reasons, we decided to use a slightly different strategy for estimating the specular reflection parameters. Since the specular reflection parameters may only be estimated sparsely over the object surface, we use interpolation to infer the specular reflection parameters over the entire surface.

In Section 4.5.1, we describe how to select object surface points which are suitable for estimating the specular reflection parameters. Interpolation of the estimated specular reflection parameters on the object surface is explained in Section 4.5.2.

4.5.1 Selection of Surface Points for Parameter Estimation

For the specular reflection parameters to be estimated reliably, the following three conditions are necessary at a point on the object surface. All of the three conditions contribute to reliable separation of the diffuse and specular reflection components.

1.   The two reflection components must be reliably separated. Because the diffuse and specular reflection components are separated using the difference of the colors of the two components (Section 4.3), these color vectors should differ as much as possible. This can be examined by saturation of the diffuse color (Figure 9). Since the light source color is generally close to white (saturation = 0), if the diffuse color has a high saturation value, the diffuse and specular reflection colors will be different.

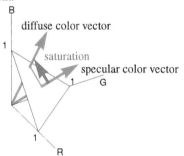

Figure 9   Diffuse saturation shown in the RGB color space

2.   The magnitude of the specular reflection component is as large as possible.

3.   The magnitude of the diffuse reflection component is as large as possible. Although this condition might seem to be unnecessary, we empirically found that the specular reflection parameters can be obtained more reliably if this condition is satisfied.

Figure 10   Selected vertices for specular parameter estimation: 100 out of 266 vertices were selected.

An evaluation measure: v = *diffuse saturation * max specular intensity * max diffuse intensity* is used to represent how well these three conditions are satisfied. In our experiments, we used the vertices of the triangular surface mesh as candidates for parameter estimation. Then, *100* vertices with the largest values were chosen according to our evaluation measurement v. Figure 10 illustrates 100 selected vertices for specular parameter estimation out of 266 vertices. Note that the use of the triangular vertices as initial candidates for specular parameter estimation is not essential in our method. In practice, we found that this choice was sufficient to find suitable points for specular parameter estimation.

4.5.2 Interpolation of Estimated Specular Parameters

In our experiment, the camera output is calibrated so that the specular reflection color (i.e., the light source color) has the same value from the three color channels (Section 2). For instance, the separated specular reflection component shown in Figure 7 (b) has more or less the same output from the three color channels. Therefore, only one color band was used to estimate the specular reflection parameters (K_S and σ) in our experiment.

After the specular reflection parameters K_S and σ were estimated at the 100 selected vertices, the estimated values were linearly interpolated based on a distance on the object surface, so that the specular reflection parameters were obtained at regular grid points within each triangle of the object surface mesh. The resolution of the grid points was 20×20 in our experiment, while the resolution was 80×80 for the diffuse reflection parameter estimation. In general, specular reflectance does not change so rapidly as diffuse reflectance, i.e., diffuse texture on the object surface. Therefore, the resolution of 20×20 was enough to capture the specular reflectance of the mug.

Interpolated values of the two specular reflection parameters are shown in Figure 11. The obtained specular reflection parameters were then stored in two specular reflection parameter images (a K_S image and a σ image) just as estimated surface normals were stored in the surface normal image.

Figure 11   Interpolated K_S and σ

5   IMAGE SYNTHESIS

Using the reconstructed object shape (Section 3.1), the surface normal image (Section 3.2), the diffuse reflection parameter image (Section 4.4), the specular reflection parameter image (Section 4.5), and the reflection model (Equation (2)), we can synthesize color object images under arbitrary illumination/viewing conditions.

Figure 12 shows synthesized images of the object with two point light sources. Note that the images represent highlights on the object surface naturally. For comparing synthesized images with the input color images of the object, the object model was rendered using the same illumination and viewing directions as some of the input color images. Figure 13 shows two frames of the input color image sequence as well as two synthesized images that were generated using the same illuminating/viewing condition as the input color images. It can be seen that the synthesized images closely resemble the corresponding real images. In particular, highlights,

which generally are a very important cue of surface material, appear on the side and the handle of the mug naturally in the synthesized images.

However, we can see that the synthesized images are slightly more blurred than the original color images, e.g., the eye of the painted fish in frame 50. That comes from slight error in the measured object transformation matrix T (Section 2) due to imperfect calibration of the robotic arm. Because of the error in the measured transformation matrix T, the projected input color images (Section 4.2) were not perfectly aligned on the reconstructed object surface. As a result, the estimated diffuse reflection parameters were slightly blurred. This blurring effect can be avoided if, after a color image is projected onto the object surface, the color image is aligned with previously projected images by a local search on the surface. However, we have not yet tested this idea in our implementation.

6   CONCLUSION

We have explored automatic generation of photorealistic object models from observation. Achieving photorealism in synthesized object images requires accurate modeling of shape and reflectance properties of the object. In this paper, we have presented a new paradigm for acquiring object shape and reflectance parameters from range and color images.

The object surface shape is reconstructed by merging multiple range images of the object. By using the reconstructed object shape and multiple color images of the object, parameters of the Torrance-Sparrow reflection model are estimated. For estimating reflectance parameters of the object robustly, our method is based on separation of the diffuse and specular reflection components from a color image sequence. Using separated reflection components, reflection model parameters for each of the two components were estimated separately. In particular, the specular reflection parameters were successfully obtained by identifying suitable surface points for estimation and by interpolating estimated parameters over the object surface.

Our experiments have shown that our object modeling method can be effectively used for synthesizing realistic object images under arbitrary illumination and viewing conditions.

Acknowledgment: The authors thank Marie Elm for her valuable comments of the draft of the paper.

REFERENCES

[1]   R. Baribeau, M. Rioux, and G. Godin, "Color reflectance modeling using a polychromatic laser sensor," *IEEE Trans. on Pattern Analysis and Machine Intelligence*, vol. 14, no. 2, pp. 263-269, 1992.

[2]   R. L. Cromwell, "Efficient eigenvalues for visualization," in P. S. Heckbert, editor, *Graphics Gems IV*, Academic Press, San Diego, 1994.

[3]   B. Curless and M. Levoy, "A volumetric method for building complex models from range images," *Computer Graphics (SIGGRAPH '96 Proceedings)*, pp. 303-312, 1996.

[4]   A. Hilton, J. Stoddart, J. Illingworth, and T. Windeatt, "Reliable surface reconstruction from multiple range images," *Proceedings of European Conference on Computer Vision '96*, pp. 117-126, 1996.

[5]   H. Hoppe, T. DeRose, T. Duchamp, J. McDonald, and W. Stuetzle,

"Surface reconstruction from unorganized points," *Computer Graphics (SIGGRAPH '92 Proceedings)*, pp. 71-78, 1992.

[6] H. Hoppe, T. DeRose, T. Duchamp, J. McDonald, and W. Stuetzle, "Mesh Optimization," *Computer Graphics (SIGGRAPH '93 Proceedings)*, pp. 19-26, 1993.

[7] K. Ikeuchi and K. Sato, "Determining reflectance properties of an object using range and brightness images," *IEEE Trans. on Pattern Analysis and Machine Intelligence*, vol. 13, no. 11, pp. 1139-1153, 1991.

[8] C. L. Jackins and S. L. Tanimoto, "Oct-trees and their use in representing three-dimensional objects," *Computer Graphics Image Processing*, vol. 14, no. 3, pp. 249-270, 1980.

[9] G. Kay and T. Caelli, "Inverting an illumination model from range and intensity maps," *CVGIP: Image Understanding*, vol. 59, pp. 183-201, 1994.

[10] W. E. Lorensen and H. E. Cline, "Marching cubes: a high resolution 3D surface construction algorithm," *Computer Graphics (SIGGRAPH '87 Proceedings)*, vol. 21, no. 4, pp. 163-169, 1987.

[11] J. Lu and J. Little, "Reflectance function estimation and shape recovery from image sequence of a rotating object," *Proceedings of International Conference on Computer Vision*, pp. 80-86, June 1995.

[12] S. K. Nayar, K. Ikeuchi, and T. Kanade, "Surface reflection: physical and geometrical perspectives," *IEEE Trans. on Pattern Analysis and Machine Intelligence*, vol. 13, no. 7, pp. 611-634, 1991.

[13] S. K. Nayar, X. Fang, and T. E. Boult, "Removal of specularities using color and polarization," *Proceedings of Computer Vision and Pattern Recognition '93*, pp. 583-590, New York City, NY, June 1993.

[14] K. Sato, H. Yamamoto, and S. Inokuchi, "Range imaging system utilizing nematic liquid crystal mask," *Proceedings of International Conference on Computer Vision*, pp. 657-661, 1987.

[15] Y. Sato and K. Ikeuchi, "Temporal-color space analysis of reflection," *Journal of Optical Society of America A*, vol. 11, no. 11, pp. 2990-3002, November 1994.

[16] Y. Sato and K. Ikeuchi, "Reflectance analysis for 3D computer graphics model generation," *Graphical Models and Image Processing*, vol. 58, no. 5, pp. 437-451, September 1996.

[17] S. Shafer, "Using color to separate reflection components," *COLOR Research and Application*, vol. 10, no. 4, pp. 210-218, 1985.

[18] R. Szelski at Micro Soft Co., *personal communication*.

[19] K. E. Torrance and E. M. Sparrow, "Theory for off-specular reflection from roughened surface," *Journal of Optical Society of America*, vol. 57, pp. 1105-1114, 1967.

[20] G. J. Ward, "Measuring and modeling anisotropic reflection," *Computer Graphics (SIGGRAPH 92 Proceedings)*, vol. 26, no. 2, pp. 265-272, 1992.

[21] M. D. Wheeler, Y. Sato, and K. Ikeuchi, "Consensus surfaces for modeling 3D objects from multiple range images," *DARPA Image Understanding Workshop*, 1997.

[22] L. B. Wolff, T. E. Boult, "Constraining object features using a polarization reflectance model," *IEEE Trans. on Pattern Analysis and Machine Intelligence*, vol. 13, no. 6, pp. 635-657, 1991.

 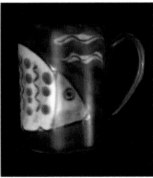  

Figure 12   *Synthesized object images*

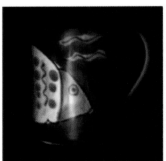 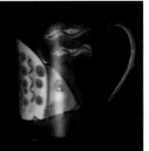    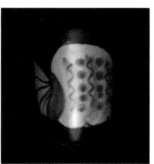

input   frame 50   **synthesized**   **input**   frame 80   **synthesized**

Figure 13   *Comparison of input color images and synthesized images*

Design Galleries: A General Approach to Setting Parameters for Computer Graphics and Animation

J. Marks*	B. Andalman	P.A. Beardsley	W. Freeman	S. Gibson	J. Hodgins	T. Kang
MERL	Harvard Univ.	MERL	MERL	MERL	Georgia Tech.	CMU

B. Mirtich	H. Pfister	W. Ruml	K. Ryall	J. Seims	S. Shieber
MERL	MERL	Harvard Univ.	Harvard Univ.	Univ. of Washington	Harvard Univ.

Abstract

Image rendering maps scene parameters to output pixel values; animation maps motion-control parameters to trajectory values. Because these mapping functions are usually multidimensional, nonlinear, and discontinuous, finding input parameters that yield desirable output values is often a painful process of manual tweaking. Interactive evolution and inverse design are two general methodologies for computer-assisted parameter setting in which the computer plays a prominent role. In this paper we present another such methodology. *Design Gallery*^{TM} (DG) interfaces present the user with the broadest selection, automatically generated and organized, of perceptually different graphics or animations that can be produced by varying a given input-parameter vector. The principal technical challenges posed by the DG approach are *dispersion*, finding a set of input-parameter vectors that optimally disperses the resulting output-value vectors, and *arrangement*, organizing the resulting graphics for easy and intuitive browsing by the user. We describe the use of DG interfaces for several parameter-setting problems: light selection and placement for image rendering, both standard and image-based; opacity and color transfer-function specification for volume rendering; and motion control for particle-system and articulated-figure animation.

CR Categories: I.2.6 [Artificial Intelligence]: Problem Solving, Control Methods and Search—heuristic methods; I.3.6 [Computer Graphics]: Methodology and Techniques—interaction techniques; I.3.7 [Computer Graphics]: Three-Dimensional Graphics and Realism.

Keywords: Animation, computer-aided design, image rendering, lighting, motion synthesis, particle systems, physical modeling, visualization, volume rendering.

---

*Address: MERL – A Mitsubishi Electric Research Laboratory, 201 Broadway, Cambridge, MA 02139, U.S.A. E-mail: marks@merl.com.

1 Introduction

Parameter tweaking is one of the vexations of computer graphics. Finding input parameters that yield a desirable output is difficult and tedious for many rendering, modeling, and motion-control processes. The notion of having the computer assist actively in setting parameters is therefore appealing. One such computer-assisted methodology is interactive evolution [11, 21, 23]: the computer explores the space of possible parameter settings, and the user acts as an objective-function oracle, interactively selecting computer-suggested alternatives for further exploration. A more automatic methodology is inverse design, e.g., [10, 12, 14, 19, 22, 25, 27]: the computer searches for parameter settings that optimize a user-supplied, mathematically stated objective function.

Unfortunately, there are many interesting and important graphics processes for which interactive evolution and inverse design are not very useful. These processes share two common characteristics:

- High computational cost: if the process cannot be computed in near real time, interactive evolution becomes unusable.

- Unquantifiable output qualities: even though desirable graphics may be readily identified by inspection, it may not be possible to quantify a priori the qualities that make them desirable. This lack of a suitable objective function rules out the use of inverse design.

In this paper we present a third methodology for computer-assisted parameter setting that is especially applicable to graphics processes that exhibit one or both of these characteristics. *Design Gallery* (DG) interfaces present the user with the broadest selection, automatically generated and organized, of perceptually different graphics or animations that can be produced by varying a given input-parameter vector. Because the selection is generated automatically, it can be done as a preprocess so that any high computational costs are hidden from the user. Furthermore, the DG approach requires only a measure of similarity between graphics, which can often be quantified even when optimality cannot.

A DG system includes several key elements. The *input vector* is a list of parameters that control the generation of the output graphic via a *mapping* process. The *output vector* is a list of values that summarizes the subjectively relevant qualities of the output graphic. The *distance metric* on the space of output vectors approximates the perceptual similarity of the corresponding output graphics. The *dispersion* method is used to find a set of input vectors that map to a well-distributed set of output vectors, and hence output graphics. The dispersed graphics are presented to the user through a perceptually reasonable *arrangement* method that makes use of the distance metric. These six elements — input vector, mapping, output vector, distance metric, dispersion, and arrangement — characterize a DG system. The creator of a DG system chooses the input vector, output vector, and the distance metric for a specific mapping process. For particular instances of the process, the computer performs the dispersion, the mapping of input vectors to output vectors, and the arrangement of final graphics in a gallery. The end user need only recognize and select appealing graphics from the gallery.

We explain and illustrate the use of DGs for several common parameter-setting problems: light selection and placement for image rendering, both standard and image-based; opacity and color transfer-function specification for volume rendering; and motion control for particle-system and articulated-figure animation. During the discussion, we describe the input and output vectors for each mapping process, and present various methods for dispersion and arrangement that we have used in building DG systems.

2 Light Selection and Placement

Setting lighting parameters is an essential precursor to image rendering. Previous attempts at computer-assisted lighting specification have used inverse design. For example, the user can specify the location of highlights and shadows in the image [15], pixel intensities [19], or subjective impressions of illumination [10]; the computer then attempts to determine lighting parameters that best meet the given objectives, using geometric [15] or optimization [10, 19] techniques. Unfortunately, the formulation of lighting specification as an inverse problem has some significant drawbacks. High-quality image rendering (e.g., raytracing or radiosity) is costly; to make the computer's search task tractable, the user may have to fix the light positions [10, 19], thereby grossly limiting the illuminations that can be considered. A more intrinsic difficulty is that of requiring the user to quantify a priori the desired illuminative characteristics of the resulting image. This requirement may be satisfiable in an architectural context [10], but seems very challenging in a more general cinematographic context [8]. The most difficult lighting parameters to set are those relating to light type and placement, so they have been the focus of our efforts.

2.1 Input and Output Vectors

For the light selection and placement problem, we begin with a scene model comprising surfaces and viewing parameters. The goal is to explore different ways of lighting the scene, so the input vector includes a light position, a light type, and a light direction if needed. The light position is located somewhere on one of the surfaces distinguished as a *light hook* surface by the user. The light type comes from a user-defined group, and describes attributes of the light: its basic class (e.g., point, area, or spotlight); whether or not it casts shadows; its falloff behavior (e.g., none, linear, or quadratic); and class-specific parameters (e.g., the beam angle of a spotlight). Directional lights are aimed at randomly chosen points on designated *light target* surfaces.

The output vector should be a concise, efficiently computed set of values that summarizes the perceptual qualities of the final image. Thus, output vectors are based on pixel luminances from several low-resolution thumbnail images (32×25 pixels and smaller). The luminances at resolution ρ are weighted by a factor $f(\rho)$. The distance metric on

the output vector is the standard L^1 (Manhattan) distance. As a result, the distance between output vectors corresponding to images q and r is

$$\sum_{\rho \in \{1, \frac{1}{16}, \frac{1}{16^2}, \ldots\}} \sum_{x,y} f(\rho) |Y_q^\rho(x,y) - Y_r^\rho(x,y)| \qquad (1)$$

where $Y_q^\rho(x,y)$ is the luminance of the pixel at location (x,y) in image q at resolution ρ.[1]

2.2 Dispersion

The dispersion phase selects an appropriate subset of input vectors from a random sample over the input space. Specifically, T lights are generated at each of H positions distributed uniformly over the light hook surfaces. This procedure yields a set L of $H \times T$ input vectors. Typical values are $H = 500$ and $T = 8$, in which case $|L| = 4000$.[2] For each input vector in L, thumbnail images are generated, and the corresponding output vector is determined as described above. The dispersion algorithm outlined in Figure 1 then finds a set $I \subset L$ with good spread among output vectors. The first step is the elimination of lights that dimly illuminate the visible part of the scene, because they are obscured or point away from the scene geometry; these lights are unlikely to be of interest to the user and can confound the rest of the dispersion process. Thumbnail images whose average luminance is less than a cutoff factor c are eliminated from the set L. (Typical useful values of c are in the range 1%–5% of the maximum luminance value.) The subset I is assembled by repeatedly adding to I the light in L whose output vector is most different from its closest match in the nascent I. The size of I is determined by the interface, as described below; $|I| = 584$ for the examples we discuss in the paper.

2.3 Arrangement

We would like the set of lights I to be large, so that the user will have many complementary lights from which to choose. However, the greater the size of I, the more difficult it will be for the user to browse the lights effectively. We accommodate these contradictory requirements by arranging the set I in a fully balanced hierarchy in which lights that produce similar illumination effects are grouped together. We accomplish this goal of the arrangement phase by graph partitioning. A complete graph is formed in which the vertices correspond to the lights in I, and edge costs are given by the inverse of the distance metric used in the dispersion phase. An optimal w-way partition of this graph would comprise w disjoint vertex subsets of equal cardinality such that the cost of the cut set, the total cost of all edges that connect vertices in different subsets, is minimized. Optimal graph partitioning is NP-hard [4], but many good heuristics have

---

[1] Since we start with a low-resolution thumbnail, the filtered images of even lower resolution called for in the expression will be truly tiny. Nevertheless, they do contain useful information: two barely nonoverlapping narrow-beam spotlights will generate a high (and somewhat misleading) difference score at the highest resolution, but smaller, more appropriate difference scores at lower resolutions because the beams will overlap in the lower-resolution images. The effect of the weighting function $f(\rho)$ is subtle, but we have found it preferable to weight higher-resolution images slightly more than lower-resolution ones.

[2] We picked these numbers to allow overnight batch processing of the entire DG process for one scene on a single MIPS R10000 processor.

```
Input:
    L, a set of lights and corresponding thumbnail images.
    n < |L|, the size of the selected subset.
    c, an average-luminance cutoff factor.

Output:
    I ⊂ L, a set of n dispersed lights and their images.

Procedure:
    SELECTION_DISPERSE(L, n, c) {
        L ← L \ find_dims(c, L);
        I ← ∅;
        for i ← 1 to n do {
            p_score ← −∞;
            foreach q ∈ L do {
                q_score ← ∞;
                foreach r ∈ I do
                    if image_diff(q, r) < q_score then
                        q_score ← image_diff(q, r);
                if q_score > p_score then {
                    p_score ← q_score;
                    p ← q;
                }
            }
            I ← I ∪ {p};
            L ← L \ {p};
        }
    }

Notes:
    \ denotes set difference.
    find_dims(c, L) returns those lights in L with average
    luminance less than c.
    image_diff(q, r) returns the value computed by Equa-
    tion 1.
```

Figure 1: A selection-based dispersion heuristic.

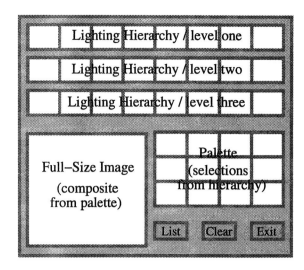

Figure 2: User-interface map.

2.4 Results

The DG in Figure 9 contains a scene inspired by an example from [8]. The floor, ceiling, and all four walls (only the rear one is visible) were designated light-hook surfaces. The surfaces comprising the figures were designated light-target surfaces, as was the back wall. The 584 lights in the gallery were selected from 5,000 randomly generated lights in the dispersion phase. The cost of computing this and the other light-selection-and-placement DGs shown here was dominated by the cost of raytracing the 584 full-size images used in the display, which took approximately five hours on a MIPS R10000 processor.

Figure 10 contains a scene with richer geometry. The ceiling, and the area around the base of the statue were designated light-hook surfaces. The surfaces of the two heads, the doors, the tree, and the statue were designated light-target surfaces. The gallery lights were selected from 3,000 randomly generated lights in the dispersion phase.

Finally, Figure 11 shows a DG for synthetic lighting of a photograph (inset at lower right). A point- and line-based 3D model is extracted from a triplet of scene images, each taken from a different viewpoint. This reconstruction process is completely automatic, as described in [2]. Points and lines are then aggregated semi-automatically into planes. An illumination of the final recovered model is used to modulate intensity in one of the original photographs.

been developed for this problem [1]. Our partitioning code is based on an algorithm and software developed by Karypis and Kumar [9]. Once the initial w-way partition is formed, representative lights for each partition are selected, and installed in the hierarchy. The partitioned subsets, minus their representative vertices, are then processed recursively until a hierarchy with branching factor w and height h is completed.

The values for w and h are dictated by the user interface, whose structure is depicted in Figure 2, and actual examples of which are shown in Figures 9–11. For each light in the final set I, medium-size (128×100 pixels) and full-size (512×400 pixels) images are generated for use in the interface. The user is presented with a row of eight images that serve as the first level of the light hierarchy. Clicking on one of these images causes its eight children in the hierarchy to be presented in the next row of images. The third and final level in the hierarchy is accessed by clicking on an image from the second row. Thus $w = 8$ and $h = 3$. In turn, these parameters determine the cardinality of I: $|I| = \sum_{j=1}^{h} w^j = 584$. This particular interface provides additional application-specific functionality that exploits the additive nature of light [6]. Images can be dragged to the palette, where light intensity and temperature can be varied interactively. Multiple images are composited to form a full-size image in the lower left.

3 Opacity and Color Transfer Functions for Volume Rendering

Choosing the opacity and color transfer functions for volume rendering is another tedious and difficult manual task amenable to a DG approach.[3] We developed DG interfaces for two data sets: the simulated electron density of a protein, and a CT scan of a human pelvis.

---

[3]The application of both interactive evolution and inverse design to this problem is the subject of [7].

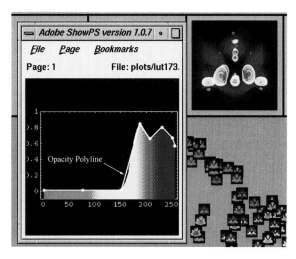

Figure 3: Pop-up display depicting transfer functions.

3.1 Input and Output Vectors

The protein data set contains values in the interval $[0, 255]$. The opacity transfer function over this domain is parameterized by a polyline with eight control points, for a total of 16 values. The polyline is low-pass filtered before it is used. The color transfer function is parameterized by five values that segment the data into six subranges, which are arbitrarily assigned the colors red, yellow, green, cyan, blue, and magenta. Thus color is being used only to identify subranges of the data, and not to convey any quantitative relations among the data. Figure 3 illustrates a sample opacity and color transfer function. The complete input vector comprises 23 parameters.

For the scene-lighting DG, the output vector contains approximately 850 weighted pixel luminances. This kind of resolution is necessary because lights can cause completely local illumination effects in a synthetically rendered image, effects that should be representable in the output vector. In comparison, changes to transfer functions will generally affect many pixels throughout a volume-rendered image. We can take advantage of this homogeneity by including only a handful of pixels in the output vector. Currently we use eight pixels, selected manually for each data set. Representing all of their YUV values requires 24 values in the output vector, and standard Euclidean distance is used as the output-space metric. Dispersion on the basis of eight pixels from different parts of the image produces excellent dispersion of complete images at a much reduced computational cost.

3.2 Dispersion

The dispersion heuristic in Figure 1 works by distilling a set of randomly generated input vectors down to a well-dispersed subset. Although simple, this method has the drawback of not utilizing what is learned via random sampling about the mapping from input to output vectors. In contrast, the dispersion heuristic in Figure 4 uses an evolutionary strategy that adapts its sampling over time in response to what it implicitly learns, and consequently performs much better. It starts with an initial set of random input vectors. These vectors are then perturbed randomly. Perturbed vectors are substituted for existing vectors in the set if the substitution improves dispersion. The key notion

of dispersion used is nearest-neighbor distance in the space of output vectors.

Input:
A random set of input vectors, I, and their corresponding output vectors, O. $|I| = |O| = n$.

A trial count, t.

Output:
Modified sets of input and output vectors, I and O.

Procedure:
$EVOLUTION\_DISPERSE(I, O, t)$ {
    for $i \leftarrow 1$ **to** t **do** {
        $j \leftarrow rand\_int(1, n)$;
        $u \leftarrow perturb(I[j], i)$;
        $map(u, v)$;
        $k \leftarrow worst\_index(O)$;
        if $is\_better(v, O[k], O)$ **then** {
            $I[k] \leftarrow u$;
            $O[k] \leftarrow v$;
        }
        else if $is\_better(v, O[j], O)$ **then** {
            $I[j] \leftarrow u$;
            $O[j] \leftarrow v$;
        }
    }
}

Notes:
$rand\_int(1, n)$ returns a random integer in the range $[1, n]$.

$perturb(I[j], i)$ returns a copy of $I[j]$ in which all the elements have been perturbed. The magnitude of the perturbations is inversely proportional to i.

$map(u, v)$ maps input vector u to output vector v using an application-specific mapping process.

$worst\_index(O)$ returns the index of the output vector in O with minimum nearest-neighbor distance. Ties are broken using the average distance to all other vectors in O.

$is\_better(v, O[k], O)$ returns true if the nearest neighbor to v in $O \setminus \{O[k]\}$ is further away than the nearest neighbor to $O[k]$ in O. Ties are broken using average distance to all other vectors in the relevant set.

Figure 4: An evolutionary dispersion heuristic.

3.3 Arrangement

The arrangement method based on graph partitioning that is presented in §2.3 results in a simple and easy-to-use interface. Unfortunately, sometimes the partition contains anomalies, e.g., dissimilar lights placed in the same subset of the partition. This problem is due to limitations of the partitioning method (no heuristic partitioning strategy guarantees an optimal partition), and to the structure of the set of output vectors, which may not map well to any regular hierarchical partition.

For the volume-rendering application, we used an alternative arrangement method that eschews a partition-based or hierarchical framework and instead illustrates the structure of the set of output vectors graphically in a 2D layout. An interface for this arrangement method is shown in

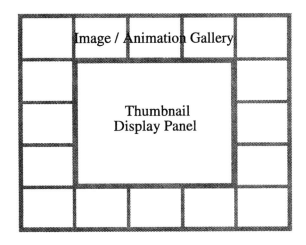

Figure 5: A more flexible user interface.

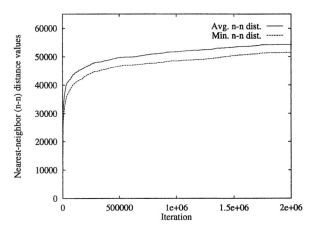

Figure 6: Nearest-neighbor distances over time.

Figure 5. A thumbnail, which in this case is a small, low-resolution volume-rendered image, is generated for each final output vector. The thumbnails are arranged in the center display panel, in a manner that correlates the distance between thumbnails with the distance between the associated output vectors. The thumbnail display panel can be panned and zoomed. Selecting a thumbnail brings up a full-size image, which can then be moved to the surrounding image gallery. Mousing on an image in the gallery highlights its associated thumbnail, and vice versa.

Thumbnail layout is accomplished using a multidimensional scaling (MDS) [3] method due to Torgerson [24].[4] Given a matrix of distances between points, MDS procedures compute an embedding of the points in a low-dimensional Euclidean space (2D in our case) such that the interpoint distances in the embedding closely match those in the given matrix. Torgerson's "classical scaling" method, although simpler and less general than iterative methods, is fast and robust. When the interpoint distances come from an embedding of the points in a high-dimensional Euclidean space (which is true for the applications we discuss here, although it need not be true in general), classical scaling is equivalent to an efficient technique for computing a principal-component analysis of the points [5, 13].

The layouts computed by classical scaling are not without anomalies — as we are using it, this MDS method is a projection from a high-dimensional space onto a 2D space, which cannot be done without loss of information — but they do reflect the underlying structure of the output vectors well enough to allow effective browsing. One important practical detail: since full-size versions of all the images returned by the dispersion procedure must be rendered anyway, it is convenient and better to compute distances from these full-size images in the arrangement phase, instead of from the eight pixels used in the dispersion phase.

3.4 Results

Figure 12 illustrates the DG for the volume rendering of the protein data set. The dispersion procedure returned 256 dispersed input and output vectors. A selection of images is shown in the surrounding image galleries. The lines that connect images with their thumbnails give some indication of how images congregate in the thumbnail display. (During interactive use the association between thumbnails and images is done preferably by dynamic highlighting, as described above.) Figure 3 shows the result of clicking on one of the images in the image gallery: the corresponding opacity and color transfer functions are depicted in a pop-up window, allowing the user to see how image and data relate.

The performance of the dispersion heuristic from this experiment is documented in Figure 6; this data is representative of all the DG experiments that use the evolutionary dispersion heuristic. The curves show how two values, the minimum and average nearest-neighbor distances in the set of output vectors, increase over time. Improvement is rapid at first: the minimum and average nearest-neighborhood distances in the initial random set are 184 and 7,789, respectively. However, the rate of improvement drops quickly. Although we used a trial count of $t = 2,000,000$ (see Figure 4), it is clear that relatively little improvement occurred after $t = 500,000$. To reach this point requires $8 \times 500,000 = 4,000,000$ raycast operations and takes less than 40 minutes on a single MIPS R10000 processor. This duration is roughly one-sixth of that needed to render the 256 full-size images (300×300 pixels) for the DG.

A second volume-rendering experiment was performed using a computed tomography (CT) data set for a human pelvis. These data values are presegmented into four disjoint subranges, one each for air, fat, muscle, and bone. The input vector specifies the y-coordinates of 12 opacity control points; the x-coordinates are held fixed. The input vector does not specify a color transfer function, since standard colors are used for the different tissue types. The output vector, distance metric, dispersion, and arrangement were identical to the protein-rendering experiment. Figure 13 illustrates the DG for the volume rendering of the pelvis data set.

4 Animation Applications

Motion control in animation involves extensive parameter tuning because the mapping from input parameters to graphical output is nonintuitive, unpredictable, and costly to compute.[5] For these reasons, motion control is very

---

[4]The use of more sophisticated MDS techniques for arranging a database of images is being investigated by Rubner et al. [18].

[5]Both interactive evolution [26] and inverse design [12, 14, 22, 25, 27] have been applied previously to motion control.

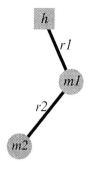

Figure 7: Articulated linkages.

amenable to a DG approach. Building a DG interface for animation is similar to building one for still images (we reuse the dispersion and arrangement code from §3 virtually without change); the major differences are in computing the output-vector components. We now discuss three DG systems for animation tasks, focusing on this latter issue.

4.1   2D Double Pendulum

The 2D double pendulum is a simple dynamic system with rich behavior that makes it an ideal test case for parameter-setting methodologies.[6] A double pendulum consists of an attachment point h, two bobs of masses m_1 and m_2, and two massless rods of lengths r_1 and r_2, connected as shown in Figure 7. Our pendulum also includes motors at the joints at h and m_1 that can apply sinusoidal time-varying torques. The input vector comprises the rod lengths, the bob masses, the initial angular positions and velocities of the rods, and the amplitude, frequency, and phase of both sinusoidal torques, for a total of 14 parameters.

Choosing a suitable output vector proved to be the most difficult part of the DG process for the double pendulum, as well as for the other motion-control applications; several rounds of experimentation were needed (see §5 for more details). The output vector must capture the behavior of the system over time. For the double pendulum, the output vector has 12 parameters: the differences in rod lengths and bob masses, the average Cartesian coordinates of each bob, and logarithms of the average angular velocity, the number of velocity reversals, and the number of revolutions for each rod. Euclidean distance is used as the distance metric on this output space.

The mapping from input vector to output vector is accomplished by dynamically simulating 20 seconds of the pendulum's motion, and using the algorithm in Figure 4 for dispersion. Arrangement is accomplished using the MDS layout method of §3.3. The displayed thumbnails are static images of the final state of the pendulum, along with a trail of the lower bob over the final few seconds. We found that these images give enough clues about the full animation to enable effective browsing. Thumbnails can be dragged into gallery slots, all of which can be animated simultaneously by clicking on any occupied slot.

Figure 14 shows the DG for the double pendulum. As before, the overlaid lines show where animations in the gallery are located in the thumbnail display. The plateau in nearest-neighbor distance is reached after 170,000 dispersion itera-

---

[6] Even without the application of external torques at its joints, the 2D double pendulum exhibits chaotic behavior [20].

tions, which take 6.5 hours on a single MIPS R10000 processor.

4.2   3D Hopper Dog

The previous DG is useful in finding and understanding the full range of motions possible for the pendulum under a given control regime. However, complete generality is not always a useful goal: the animator may have some preconceived idea of a motion that needs subtle refinement to add nuance and detail. The 3D hopper dog, shown in Figure 7, is an articulated linkage with rigid links connected by rotary joints. It has a head, ears, and tail, and moves by hopping on its single leg. It has 24 degrees of freedom (DOF). The hopper dog is actuated by a control system that tries to maintain a desired forward velocity and hopping height, as well as desired positions for joints in some of the appendages. The equations of motion for the system are generated using a commercially available package[17]; dynamic simulation is used to produce the animations.

We started with a basic hopping motion, and then used a DG approach to explore seven input quantities in order to achieve stylistic, physically attainable gaits. The seven quantities are: the forward velocity, the hopping height, and the positions of 2-DOF ear joints, a 2-DOF tail joint, and a 1-DOF neck joint. For each of these seven, a time-varying sinusoid specifies the desired trajectory, with the minimum value, maximum value, and frequency specified in the input vector, which therefore contains 21 values.

In this particular case, the elements of the output vector correspond closely to those of the input vector. The 14-element output vector contains the averages and variances of the same seven quantities, and is obtained by dynamically simulating 30 seconds of the hopper dog's motion. (Output vectors from simulations in which the hopper dog falls are discarded automatically.) As for the previous two applications, the output-space distance metric is Euclidean, and the arrangement method and interface from §3.3 are used. The hopper-dog DG is illustrated in the video proceedings.

4.3   Particle Systems

Particle systems are useful for modeling a variety of phenomena such as fire, clouds, water, and explosions [16]. A useful particle-system editor might have 40 or more parameters that the animator can set, so achieving desired effects can be tedious. As in the previous subsection, we use a DG interface to refine an animator's rough approximation to a desired animation.

The subject for our experiment is a hypothetical beam weapon for NASA space shuttles. A first draft was produced by hand using a regular particle-system editor; a still from midway through the animation is shown in Figure 8. The input vector contains the subset of particle-system controls that the animator wishes to have tweaked. In this example the controls govern: the mean and variance of particle velocities, particle acceleration, rate of particle production, particle lifetime, resilience and friction coefficient of collision surfaces, and perturbation vectors for surface normals. Among the parameters that are held fixed are the origin, average direction, and color of the beam.

For efficiency reasons, DG output vectors are based on subsampled versions of the final graphic where possible, thereby reducing computational costs and allowing more of the space to be explored. For example, static images can be rendered at low resolution (§2 and §3). The subsampling

Figure 8: A still from a particle-system animation.

strategy for the particle animation is to simulate only every 500th particle generated during the dispersion phase, and to examine the state of the particle system at just two distinct points in time: once midway through the simulation, and once at the end. The output vector comprises measures of the number of particles, their average distance from the origin and the individual variation in this distance, their spread from the average beam, the average velocity of the entire system, and the individual variation from this average (we take logs of all of these quantities except for the beam spread). These six measures are included for each of the two distinguished times, resulting in 12 output parameters. Euclidean distance is the metric on the output space.

Figure 15 shows the DG of variations on the animator's original sketch from Figure 8. The dispersion and arrangement methods from §3 are used to generate the DG. Each thumbnail is the midway still from the corresponding animation. (The user can optionally select thumbnails from different stages in the animation.) As with the double-pendulum DG, thumbnails can be dragged to gallery slots and animated therein. Also as before, lines connect animation stills with their associated thumbnails. The dispersion heuristic ran for $t = 100,000$ iterations, at which point it appeared to reach a plateau. This number of trials took approximately six hours on a MIPS R10000 processor. Generating the 256 animations in the DG with their full complement of particles took a little under five hours on the same processor.

5   Discussion

Table 1 summarizes the DGs described in this paper, in terms of the six basic elements of a DG system. Some of the variation in this table is application specific, while the remainder stems from our investigation of alternative dispersion and arrangement methods. All of the galleries described in the paper produce a useful variety of output graphics.

Using a DG for a particular instance of a design problem is fairly straightforward for the end user. Aside from browsing the final DG, the user's only other task may be to loosely focus the dispersion process by, for example, selecting suitable light-hook and light-target surfaces (§2), or by specifying a relevant subset of particle-control parameters (§4.3). However, creating a DG system for an entire

class of design problems is more difficult. The DG-system creator is responsible for choosing the structure of the input and output vectors, and the distance metric on the output space. Thus, the creator needs a better understanding of the design problem than the end user. Of the creator's tasks, the simplest is choosing the distance metric: very standard metrics sufficed for all applications we tried. Choosing the input vector is also straightforward. Even when there are many possible ways to parameterize the input, our experience is that choosing an acceptable parameterization is not hard.

The most difficult task of the DG-system creator is devising an output vector. The first two DGs in Table 1 work on static images. In these examples, the perceptual similarity between images correlates well with subsampled image or pixel differences, hence the output vectors comprise subsampled image and pixel values. An added advantage is that the ranges of all components of the output vector are bounded and known. Finding measures that capture the perceptual qualities of a complete animation is harder. The DG systems for animation tasks required several experiments to get a suitable output vector, although the process became easier for each successive system. Among the lessons learned in developing output vectors for motion-control problems, the two most important precepts are, with hindsight, fairly obvious:

- Take the log of quantities that have a large dynamic range. For many such quantities, e.g., velocity, human ability to resolve changes in magnitude diminishes as the magnitude increases. To uniformly sample the perceptual space, one must therefore sample the lower end of the dynamic range more thoroughly.

- The relative weights of the output-vector parameters matter. In general, the output-vector parameters should be scaled so that they each have approximately the same dynamic range, otherwise only the parameters with the largest ranges will be dispersed effectively.

What inevitably happened with a poorly chosen output vector was that the dispersion algorithm found a malicious way to get unfortunate and unexpected spread in one of the vector coordinates, usually through a degenerate set of input parameters, e.g., pendulums with extremely short links and very high rpm's, and particle systems with only a few particles, but very high variance in velocity.

In our experiments, we investigated two dispersion methods and two arrangement methods. The dispersion method of Figure 4 is more complex, but performs better. However, an advantage of the simpler method in Figure 1 is that it may be easier to parallelize. Two arrangement methods were also tried, one based on graph partitioning and the other on MDS. Both allowed the user to navigate through the output graphics effectively, and both had their fans among our group of informal testers. Layout and organizational anomalies were occasionally evident in both interfaces, but they did not hinder the user's ability to peruse the output graphics.

6   Conclusion

Design Gallery interfaces are a useful tool for many applications in computer graphics that require tuning parameters to achieve desired effects. The basic DG strategy is to extract from the set of all possible graphics a subset with optimal coverage. A variety of dispersion and arrangement methods can be used to construct galleries. The construction phase

Application	Light selection & placement	Volume rendering	Double pendulum	Particle system	Hopper dog
Input Vector	Light type, location, and direction	Control points for opacity/color transfer functions	Pendulum dimensions, initial conditions, motor torques	Animator-specified subset of particle control parameters	Desired trajectory sinusoids
Output Vector	Luminances of thumbnail pixels	YUV values for eight pixels	Trajectory statistics (mainly logs of time averages and variances)		
Distance Metric	Manhattan	Euclidean			
Mapping	Raytracing	Volume rendering	2D dynamic simulation	3D particle simulation	3D dynamic simulation
Dispersion	Selection from random sample over neighborhood	Evolution from full random sample		Evolution from random sample over neighborhood	
Arrangement	Graph partitioning	Multidimensional scaling			

Table 1: Summary of Design Gallery experiments.

is typically computationally intensive and occurs off-line, for example, during an overnight run. After the gallery is built, the user is able to quickly and easily browse through the space of output graphics.

Inverse design is one technique for setting parameters, but it is only feasible when the user can articulate or quantify what is desired. DGs replace this requirement with the much weaker one of quantifying similarity between graphics. Unlike interactive evolution, DGs are feasible even when the graphics-generating process has high computational cost. Finally, DGs are useful even when the user has absolutely no idea what is desired, but wants to know what the possibilities are. This is often the first step in the creative design process.

7 Acknowledgments

The protein data set used in §3 was made available by the Scripps Clinic, La Jolla, California. Volume rendering was performed using the VolVis system from SUNY Stony Brook, as modified by T. He. D. Allison, R. Kaplan, a. shelat, Y. Siegal, and R. Surdulescu provided helpful comments and code. The university participants were supported in part by grants from MERL and from the NSF (Grants No. IRI-9350192 and No. IRI-9457621), and by a Packard Fellowship.

References

[1] C. J. Alpert and A. B. Kahng. Recent directions in netlist partitioning: a survey. *Integration: The VLSI Journal*, 19:1–81, 1995.

[2] P. A. Beardsley, A. P. Zisserman, and D. W. Murray. Sequential updating of projective and affine structure from motion. *International Journal of Computer Vision*, 1997. In press.

[3] I. Borg and P. Groenen. *Modern Multidimensional Scaling: Theory and Applications*. Springer, 1997.

[4] M. R. Garey, D. S. Johnson, and L. Stockmeyer. Some simplified NP-complete graph problems. *Theoretical Computer Science*, 1(3):237–267, 1976.

[5] J. C. Gower. Some distance properties of latent root and vector methods used in multivariate analysis. *Biometrika*, 53:325–338, 1966.

[6] P. Haeberli. Synthetic lighting for photography. URL http://www.sgi.com/grafica/synth/index.-html, Jan. 1992.

[7] T. He, L. Hong, A. Kaufman, and H. Pfister. Generation of transfer functions with stochastic search techniques. In *Proc. of Visualization 96*, pages 227–234, San Francisco, California, Oct. 1996.

[8] J. Kahrs, S. Calahan, D. Carson, and S. Poster. Pixel cinematography: a lighting approach for computer graphics. Notes for Course #30, SIGGRAPH 96, New Orleans, Louisiana, Aug. 1996.

[9] G. Karypis and V. Kumar. Multilevel k-way partitioning scheme for irregular graphs. Technical report, Dept. of Computer Science, Univ. of Minnesota, 1995. See also URL http://www.cs.umn.edu/~karypis/-metis/metis.html.

[10] J. K. Kawai, J. S. Painter, and M. F. Cohen. Radioptimization – goal-based rendering. In *SIGGRAPH 93 Conf. Proc.*, pages 147–154, Anaheim, California, Aug. 1993.

[11] S. Kochhar. A prototype system for design automation via the browsing paradigm. In *Proc. of Graphics Interface 90*, pages 156–166, Halifax, Nova Scotia, May 1990.

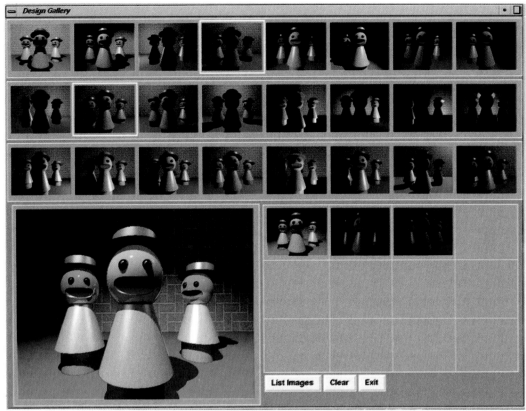

Figure 9: A DG for light selection and placement.

[12] Z. Liu, S. J. Gortler, and M. F. Cohen. Hierarchical spacetime control. In *SIGGRAPH 94 Conf. Proc.*, pages 35–42, Orlando, Florida, July 1994.

[13] H. Murakami and B. V. K. V. Kumar. Efficient calculation of primary images from a set of images. *IEEE Trans. on Pattern Analysis and Machine Intelligence*, PAMI-4(5):511–515, Sept. 1982.

[14] J. T. Ngo and J. Marks. Spacetime constraints revisited. In *SIGGRAPH 93 Conf. Proc.*, pages 343–350, Anaheim, California, Aug. 1993.

[15] P. Poulin and A. Fournier. Lights from highlights and shadows. In *Proc. of the 1992 Symposium on Interactive Graphics*, pages 31–38, Boston, Massachusetts, Mar. 1992. In *Computer Graphics* 25(2), 1992.

[16] W. T. Reeves. Particle systems – a technique for modeling a class of fuzzy objects. *ACM Trans. on Graphics*, 2:91–108, Apr. 1983.

[17] D. E. Rosenthal and M. A. Sherman. High performance multibody simulations via symbolic equation manipulation and Kane's method. *Journal of Astronautical Sciences*, 34(3):223–239, 1986.

[18] Y. Rubner, L. J. Guibas, and C. Tomasi. The earth mover's distance, multi-dimensional scaling, and color-based image retrieval. In *Proc. of the DARPA Image Understanding Workshop*, New Orleans, May 1997.

[19] C. Schoeneman, J. Dorsey, B. Smits, J. Arvo, and D. Greenberg. Painting with light. In *SIGGRAPH 93 Conf. Proc.*, pages 143–146, Anaheim, California, Aug. 1993.

[20] T. Shinbrot, C. Grebogi, J. Wisdom, and J. A. Yorke. Chaos in a double pendulum. *American Journal of Physics*, 60(6):491–499, 1992.

[21] K. Sims. Artificial evolution for computer graphics. In *Computer Graphics (SIGGRAPH 91 Conf. Proc.)*, volume 25, pages 319–328, Las Vegas, Nevada, July 1991.

[22] K. Sims. Evolving virtual creatures. In *SIGGRAPH 94 Conf. Proc.*, pages 15–22, Orlando, Florida, July 1994.

[23] S. Todd and W. Latham. *Evolutionary Art and Computers*. Academic Press, London, 1992.

[24] W. S. Torgerson. *Theory and Methods of Scaling*. Wiley, New York, 1958. See especially pages 254–259.

[25] M. van de Panne and E. Fiume. Sensor-actuator networks. In *SIGGRAPH 93 Conf. Proc.*, pages 335–342, Anaheim, California, Aug. 1993.

[26] J. Ventrella. Disney meets Darwin – the evolution of funny animated figures. In *Proc. of Computer Animation 95*, pages 35–43, Apr. 1995.

[27] A. Witkin and M. Kass. Spacetime constraints. In *Computer Graphics (SIGGRAPH 88 Conf. Proc.)*, volume 22, pages 159–168, Atlanta, Georgia, Aug. 1988.

Figure 10: Another DG for light selection and placement.

Figure 11: Light selection and placement for synthetic lighting of a photograph.

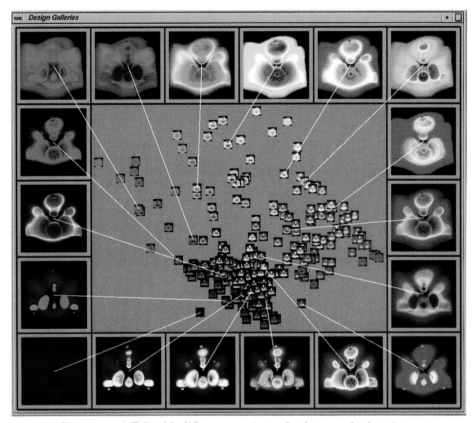

Figure 12: A DG with different opacity and color transfer functions.

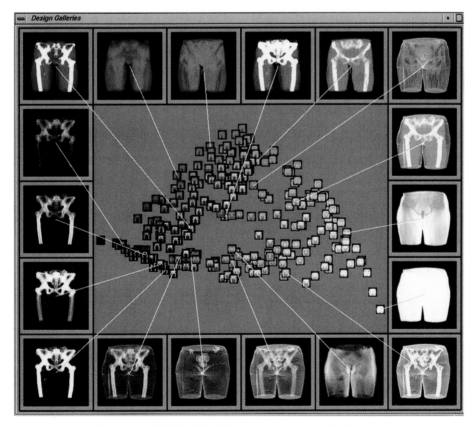

Figure 13: A DG with different opacity transfer functions.

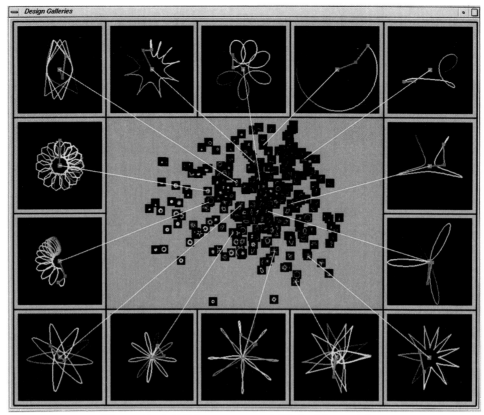

Figure 14: A DG for an actuated 2D double pendulum.

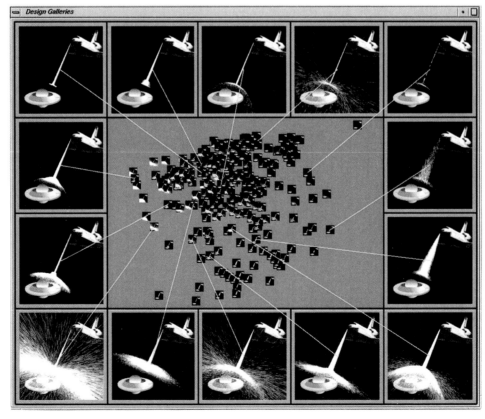

Figure 15: A DG for a particle system.

Orientable Textures for Image-Based Pen-and-Ink Illustration

Michael P. Salisbury   *Michael T. Wong*   *John F. Hughes**   *David H. Salesin*

University of Washington   *GVSTC

Abstract

We present an interactive system for creating pen-and-ink-style line drawings from greyscale images in which the strokes of the rendered illustration follow the features of the original image. The user, via new interaction techniques for editing a direction field, specifies an orientation for each region of the image; the computer draws oriented strokes, based on a user-specified set of example strokes, that achieve the same tone as the image via a new algorithm that compares an adaptively-blurred version of the current illustration to the target tone image. By aligning the direction field with surface orientations of the objects in the image, the user can create textures that appear attached to those objects instead of merely conveying their darkness. The result is a more compelling pen-and-ink illustration than was previously possible from 2D reference imagery.

CR Categories and Subject Descriptors: I.3.3 [Computer Graphics]: Picture/Image Generation — Display algorithms. I.4.3 [Image Processing] Enhancement — Filtering

Additional Key Words: Controlled-density hatching, direction field, image-based rendering, non-photorealistic rendering, scale-dependent rendering, stroke textures.

1   Introduction

Illustrations offer many advantages over photorealism, including their ability to abstract away detail, clarify shapes, and focus attention. In recent years, a number of systems have been built to produce illustrations in a pen-and-ink style. These systems can be classified into two broad categories, depending on their input: *geometry-based systems* [1, 2, 7, 12, 16, 17, 18], which take 3D scene descriptions as input; and *image-based systems* [10, 13], which produce their illustrations directly from greyscale images. The main advantage of geometry-based systems is that—because they have full access to the 3D geometry and viewing information—they can produce illustrations whose strokes not only convey the tone and texture of the surfaces in the scene, but—by placing strokes along the natural contours of surfaces—they can also convey the 3D forms of the surfaces. Existing image-based systems, on the other hand, have no knowledge of the underlying geometry or viewing transformations behind the images they are rendering, and until now have been able to convey 3D information only by having a user draw individual strokes or specify directions for orienting particular collections of strokes across the image.

University of Washington, Box 352350, Seattle, WA 98195-2350
{ salisbur | mtwong | salesin }@cs.washington.edu
*NSF STC for Computer Graphics and Scientific Visualization, Brown University Site, PO Box 1910, Providence, RI 02912
jfh@cs.brown.edu

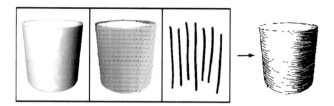

Figure 1 The three components of a layer are from left to right tone, direction, and a stroke example set. An illustration (far right) is rendered based upon one or more such layers.

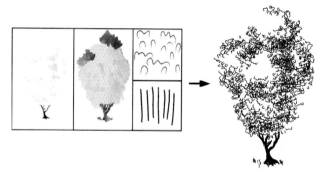

Figure 2 A tree with curved strokes for leaves and straight strokes for branches and trunk.

In this paper, we introduce the notion of "orientable textures" and show how they can be used to readily convey 3D information in an image-based system for pen-and-ink illustration. In our interactive system, a user creates an illustration from a reference image by specifying three components: a greyscale *target image* that defines the desired tone at every point in the illustration, a *direction field* that defines the desired orientation of texture at every point, and a *stroke example set*, or set of strokes, to fill in the tone areas (see figures 1 and 2). Given these three components and a scale for the final illustration, the system creates an *orientable texture*—generated procedurally—that conveys the tone, texture, and forms of the surfaces in the scene. An illustration is composed of one or more such layers of orientable textures, allowing an illustration to be rendered with several, potentially overlapping, types of strokes.

The ability to generate comparable illustrations with an image-based system rather than a geometry-based system offers several advantages. First, using an image-based system greatly reduces the tasks of geometric modeling and of specifying surface reflectance properties, allowing much more complicated models (such as furry creatures and human faces) to be illustrated. Second, an image-based system provides the flexibility of using *any* type of physical photograph, computer-generated image, or arbitrary scalar, vector, or tensor field as input, allowing visualization of data that is not necessarily even physical in nature. Finally, image-based systems offer more direct user control: the ability to much more easily modify tone, texture, or stroke orientation with an interactive digital-paint-style interface.

Although this paper is, to our knowledge, the first to use orientable textures for image-based pen-and-ink illustration (in which the strokes must convey not only orientation, but texture and tone), the idea of orienting strokes for illustration dates back at least as far as the seminal papers by Saito and Takahashi [11] and Haeberli [6] in SIGGRAPH 90. Winkenbach and Salesin [17] and Meier [9] also make use of oriented strokes for geometry-based illustration.

Supporting orientable textures for image-based pen-and-ink illustration requires solutions to several new subproblems, which we discuss in this paper. These problems include: creating interactive techniques that facilitate the specification of the kind of piecewise-continuous vector fields required for illustration; rendering strokes and stroke textures according to a vector field in such a way that they also produce the proper texture and tone; and efficiently estimating tone as new oriented strokes are progressively applied.

The next section describes the user interface for specifying the components of an illustration. Section 3 discusses the rendering of illustrations with oriented textures. Section 4 presents our results.

2 The interactive system

We provide an editor, similar to a conventional paint program, that allows the user to interactively alter the tone and direction components of a layer.[1] The user can view and edit arbitrary portions of a component at varying levels of zoom, superimpose multiple components, and paint directions directly on top of the target image. For an example of the high-level control afforded by our system, refer to figure 3.

Editing tone. Our tone editor is similar to existing paint programs. It supports lightening, darkening, and other image-processing operations, as well as painting. The user can load a reference image and designate it as a "cloning source." Selected portions of this reference may then be painted into a given layer's tone component. Tone may also be transferred between layers by painting. A negative cloning brush allows the user to freely and creatively reverse tonal relationships in a reference image.

Editing direction. Since we represent a direction field as a grid of direction values, much like an image of pixels, the direction-field editor is similar to the tone editor.[2]

The user "paints" directions on the image with a collection of tools, a few of which we describe here. The basic tool is the *comb*, which changes the directions of pixels beneath the cursor to match the direction of motion of the cursor. If a user wishes to smooth out discontinuities in the direction field, there is a *blending tool* that smooths a region of directions by convolving each point under the brush with a 3×3 filter.[3] There are also various region-filling tools. One tool lets the user fill a region with a constant direction. Another provides *interpolated fill*: the user draws two curves, after which the region between them is filled with directions that are tangents of linear interpolants of the curves. A third provides *source fill*, which orients directions away from a selected point.

The current state of the direction field is shown in two ways: first, a grid of line segment indicators covers the image and everywhere points in the direction of the field; second, a color-coded direction image is superimposed on the tone image

Applying the stroke example set. A *stroke* is a mark to be placed on the page. Each stroke is *oriented*, in the sense that it can be rotated to any angle to follow the direction field where it is placed. The *stroke example set* is a collection of strokes, all drawn with respect to the vertical orientation, that serve as prototypes for the strokes in the final image. Each such stroke is represented as a cubic

---

[1]The stroke example set is created in a separate program and can be loaded by name.

[2]We represent directions as values from 0 to 255, with 0 down, 128 up, and values increasing counter-clockwise. The resolution of the direction grid is the same as that of the tone image.

[3]We filter directions by first converting them into unit vectors, then performing a weighted sum of those vectors with the weights $(1, 2, 1; 2, 4, 2; 1, 2, 1)$, and then converting the resulting vector back into a direction.

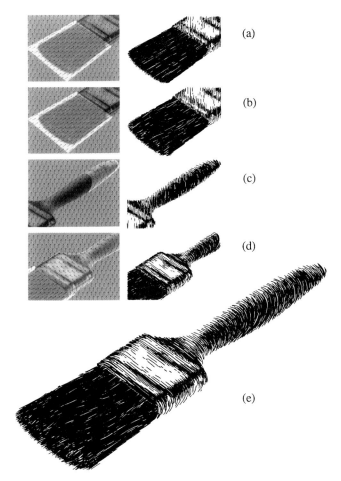

(a)

(b)

(c)

(d)

(e)

Figure 3 The steps in specifying the direction field for a paintbrush illustration. Shown in inset at various stages during the development of the illustration are, on the left, the user interface, and on the right, the corresponding rendered illustration. By default, the direction field is oriented downward. In (a) we see the effect of an interpolated fill between two lines on either side of the brush bristles. Panel (b) shows the state of the direction field and illustration after some irregularities were introduced to the bristles by nine coarse strokes of the direction comb along the length of the bristles, and thirty fine strokes at the bristle tips. Panel (c) shows the state of the brush handle after interpolating fills between four curves drawn to reflect its surface orientation. In (d), the last section of the direction field covering the metal ferrule has been defined with six mouse strokes. Panel (e) shows the completed brush illustration.

B-spline with knot sequence $(0, 0, 0, 1, 2, \ldots, n - 1, n, n, n)$, making it endpoint-interpolating. Thus a stroke example set for "parallel hatching" would contain many nearly vertical line segments, as shown in the third panel of figure 1, while for the leaves in figure 2, the strokes are wavy to suggest the edges of masses of foliage. When a stroke is drawn at a point in the illustration, it is rotated so that the vertical vector in the stroke texture aligns with the direction vector at that point; it is further warped so that this relation is true all along the stroke (see Section 3.1).

The repeated use of strokes from the example set to achieve tone with a specified orientation is a kind of procedural stroke texture. Non-procedural stroke textures were used by Salisbury *et al.* [13, 14]. In this previous work, the textures tiled the plane, and the stroke selected for drawing at a point was the one that happened to pass through that point. By contrast, in this new system the placement of strokes on the final illustration is independent of their relative position in the texture. Spacing between strokes is instead maintained indirectly by the rendering system (see Section 3). Dynamic placement of strokes is an important feature, for if we have

Figure 4 Magnifying a low-resolution direction field using (left) a standard symmetric resampling kernel, and (right) the modified kernel used by Salisbury *et al.* [14]. The same sharp tone component was used for both illustrations.

a direction field that diverges (say, for drawing the water spraying outwards from a fountain) and a stroke texture of parallel straight-line strokes that we wish to have follow the diverging field, a simple plane-tiling will not follow the field, and an embedding of the stroke texture that *does* follow the field will be stretched at the divergent end, necessarily causing the strokes to become more sparse. By contrast, our new method will insert additional strokes as the field widens, thus maintaining the density. In trade for this, we lose the texture-wide coherence that was available in our previous work.

3 Rendering

Once the user has specified the three components of a layer (tone, direction, and texture) our pen-and-ink renderer combines all of the components of each layer to generate the pen strokes of the final illustration. The user need only be concerned with the overall high-level aspects of the illustration such as tone and stroke direction; the system does the tedious work of placing all the strokes. Besides providing easy control over essential elements of an illustration, this separation of components until rendering allows us to produce illustrations at any size by first rescaling the components and then rendering, as described by Salisbury *et al.* [14]. Figure 4 demonstrates magnification of the direction field that respects edge discontinuities.

The rendering process is driven by a notion of "importance." We define the *importance* of a point as the fraction of its intended darkness that has not yet been accumulated at that point. By drawing in order of importance, we make all areas approach their target darkness at the same rate. Rendering therefore consists, roughly, of looking for the location with greatest importance, placing a stroke there, updating an image that records the importance, and repeating, until the importance everywhere is below a termination threshold. Each step of the process has subtleties, which are discussed below.

Matching the illustration to the target. We aim to place strokes in the illustration so that the tone of the illustration "matches" that of the tone image. Matching is necessarily approximate, because the illustration is purely black and white, whereas the tone image is greyscale. To facilitate this approximate matching, we think of each stroke as adding darkness to a *region* of the illustration. Moreover, since strokes in dark areas will be closely spaced and those in light areas will be sparse, the size of each region must be inversely proportional to the darkness. One way of spreading the darkness of a stroke over a region is to blur the image of the stroke when considering the effect of its darkness. To measure the progress of our illustration towards the target image, we therefore compare a blurred version of the illustration with the tone image, where the blurring consists of applying averaging filters of variable size across the illustration, with the size increasing with the target lightness in a region. The diameter of the blurring filter is the same as the average inter-stroke distance required to achieve the target lightness.

We record our success at matching the illustration to the tone image by maintaining a *difference image*, updated after each stroke is drawn, whose value at each pixel is the difference between the tone image and a blurred version of the illustration. The *importance image* is derived from the difference image; its value at each point is

Figure 5 Stacked books (after illustration by Frank Lohan [8].)

the current difference divided by the initial value of the difference.[4]

Drawing strokes in the right place. One of the basic rules of pen-and-ink illustration is that strokes should be placed evenly: close together in dark areas, widely spaced in light areas [8]. In the computation of the difference image, the importance-image values at points within some distance of a stroke are lowered when the stroke is drawn, with points near the stroke being lowered most; the size of the region affected is determined by the target tone (see Section 3.2). This algorithm tends to maintain stroke separation.

To help determine where to draw the next stroke, i.e., the location with greatest importance, we maintain a quadtree on the importance image, updated locally whenever a stroke is drawn.

Deciding when to stop. We do not actually try to drive the importance image to zero: even our filtered version of the strokes cannot hope to match the values in the tone image exactly. Instead, we try to drive the importance image to within a narrow tolerance around zero.[5] When the maximum value in the importance image is below a termination threshold, the renderer declares the illustration complete and stops drawing strokes.

3.1 Drawing a Stroke

The lowest-level activity is the actual drawing of a stroke, in itself a complex task. Once the algorithm knows where to place it, the stroke must be oriented, bent, and drawn. It must also be clipped if extending it further would make the illustration too dark. We discuss these processes in turn.

Orienting and bending. To start, the algorithm randomly selects a prototype stroke from the stroke example set. We would like to map this stroke into the direction field so that, at every point along its length, the stroke's new angle relative to the direction field is the same as the prototype stroke's angle with respect to the vertical direction. Since this mapped stroke is not easy to find, we approximate it by mapping the control hull of the prototype stroke into the direction field in an angle-preserving way, as described below. This process produces a mapped stroke that is close to our ideal stroke and is easy to compute, although it is the *control hull* of the stroke that passes through the target point rather than the stroke itself. The errors thus introduced are small as long as the control hull fits the stroke closely and the direction field does not change too fast.

To map the control hull into the direction field, we first pin a random control point P_i of the stroke onto the target location X in the

---

[4]If the initial difference is zero (i.e., if the target tone is white), the importance is set to zero.

[5]The storage values 0 to 255 correspond to importance values of -0.14 to 1.0. This range is a compromise between providing enough resolution in the positive values to distinguish differences in importance, and allowing negative values so that slightly overdarkened areas can be accommodated.

Figure 6 A visualization of four quantities from a symmetric tensor field. The integral curves of the principle-direction field are shown by strokes; the density of the strokes in each direction is related to the magnitude of the principle value associated with that direction.

Figure 7 Hair and face (after untitled photograph by Ralph Gibson [3].)

illustration. To find the location of P_{i+1}, we need to map the points along the segment P_iP_{i+1} to locations $\gamma_i(s)$ in the illustration, for $0 \leq s \leq 1$. To define γ_i, let θ_i denote the angle between the vector $v_i = P_{i+1} - P_i$ and the vertical; for each s, we want the angle between the tangent $\gamma_i'(s)$ and the direction field at $\gamma_i(s)$, called $d(\gamma_i(s))$, to be θ_i as well. In addition, we want the arclength of $\gamma_i(s)$ between $s = 0$ and $s = 1$ to be the length of v_i. In summary, we want

$$\gamma_i(0) = X$$
$$\text{angle}(\gamma_i'(s), d(\gamma_i(s))) = \theta_i$$
$$\| \gamma_i'(s) \| = \| v_i \|$$

We solve this set of differential equations numerically, using Euler integration, and record $\gamma_i(1)$ as the place to map P_{i+1}. We repeat this process to place the remaining points of the hull. Because our strokes have many control points, this approach effectively warps the stroke so that at every point its angle to the direction field in the illustration is very similar to its angle to the vertical in the stroke example set.

Clipping. Pen-and-ink artists have various rules for clipping strokes. One widely-accepted convention is that strokes do not cross object boundaries or boundaries between semantically different portions of objects, such as the edges of hard shadows [15]. We adhere to this convention by clipping strokes when they reach places where the direction field turns rapidly.[6] Strokes are also clipped when continuing to draw them would over-darken some region of the image. If a stroke is sufficiently short and has been clipped for this latter reason, it is removed altogether—pen-and-ink artists do not generally use short strokes to fill in every little bit of a dark area—and the importance value there is set to "below threshold" so that no further strokes will be draw into that area.

After the stroke is followed as far as possible in each direction from the pinned location, it is added to the illustration, and the difference and importance images are updated.

3.2 Updating the difference image

To quickly update the difference image with each added stroke, we sacrifice accuracy for efficiency through two approximations that seem to work well in practice.

The first approximation is that instead of blurring the current illustration after adding each stroke and subtracting the result from the tone image, we subtract a blurred version of the stroke from

the difference image. This assumption amounts to presuming that the blurred version of multiple strokes will be the same as the sum of blurred versions of the individual strokes, which is fine when strokes do not overlap; when they do, we lighten the blurred version of the stroke as described below.

The second approximation is in our computation of the filtered image of a stroke. Instead of rendering the stroke itself, we render its control hull as a wide blurry line. The width w is computed as $2h/t$ mm, where h is the stroke thickness (in mm) and t is the desired tone value between 0.0 (white) and 1.0 (black), and then clamped to the range 1–10 mm. We use Gupta-Sproull antialiased line drawing [4], but we supply the algorithm with a modified "darkness look-up table," whose width is as specified above, and whose height is twice the reciprocal of the width.[7] If the strokes are drawn with even spacing w, a nearly-constant blurred tone of average value t results. In our Gupta-Sproull computation, we treat neither the endpoints nor major-axis-direction changes as exceptional cases. In practice, these simplifications seem to have had no discernible effect.

Overlapping strokes and darkness adjustment. For light areas in the final illustration, strokes rarely overlap, whereas in dark areas they will often overlap. If each stroke in a dark region is counted as contributing as much darkness as a comparable stroke in a light area, the dark-area strokes will be overcounted: points where strokes cross will count as having been darkened twice or more. We therefore compute a *lightening factor*, which is a function of tone and the stroke example set. These lightening factors are computed in a preprocessing step: we draw many strokes into a buffer and record the buffer's darkness after each stroke. When we finish, we will know that, for instance, in an area of 50% grey, only 90% of the pixels drawn end up being visible; the rest overlap with other black pixels. In that case, when filling a region with a target tone of 50% grey, we would reduce the darkness of the filtered strokes to 90% before adding them to the blurred image, assuming that on average only 90% of their area does not overlap with other strokes in that region and will therefore actually contribute darkness to the illustration.

This approximation is not only faster than drawing-then-blurring, it also allows us to render a new stroke directly into the difference image without using a separate buffer. The lightening factor described above is incorporated into the "darkness look-up table" so that each stroke is drawn by looking at the underlying target tones. These tones determine which portion of the darkness look-up table

---

[6]Some automated assistance in detecting object boundaries would be valuable. We also intend to let the user draw into an "outline image," which would be used for both drawing outlines and truncating hatching strokes.

[7]For width w, height h and distance from stroke center x, the look-up value is $(0.884/h)e^{-2.3(x/w)^2}$, which is simply a bump function that tapers to nearly zero.

(a)   (b)   (c)

Figure 8 A teapot at three different scales (after illustration by Arthur Guptill [5].)

to use, and the values found there are directly incorporated into the difference image.

3.3 Output enhancements

The strokes to be drawn are deposited in a PostScript file, along with an interpreter that converts B-splines into drawable PostScript Bézier segments. We can also add two "stroke character" enhancements to the B-splines before printing (see the stroke detail inset of Figure 9).

The first enhancement is to render strokes with variable width.[8] Each stroke has three widths associated with it—one at each end and one in the middle. These widths are adjustable on a per-layer basis from the editing interface, and impart subtle expressive effects. Tapering the ends of strokes is ideal for rendering hair, but inappropriate for rendering hard shadows, for example.

The second enhancement is the addition of small "wiggles" to strokes more than 5mm long, to simulate a hand-drawn appearance. This effect is achieved by first resampling the control hull (except for the endpoints, which we copy), placing points with random spacing of about 4mm ±1mm. We then randomly perturb each interior control point slightly along the angle bisector of its two adjacent sides, and perturb the two end control points both along and orthogonal to the control hull segments that they terminate. In the current system, the perturbations are uniformly distributed between −0.15mm and 0.15mm.

4 Results

The pen-and-ink illustration system was written in two linked parts: the user interface was written in C++, and the rendering engine was written in Modula-3. The interface runs at interactive speed, and the pen-and-ink renderer takes a few minutes to render the illustrations presented here (see Table 1).

We have produced several illustrations to test the capabilities of our system. Figures 5 and 8 are attempts to closely follow examples of real pen-and-ink drawings from illustration texts. Figure 8 also shows that our system can rescale illustrations while maintaining the character of their texture.

---

[8]The adjustments that are made are ignored in the computation of darkness—they are to be thought of as merely embellishments.

Fig	Content	% Reduction	# Strokes	Time (sec)
5	Books	58	16722	258
6	Vectors	35	665	25
7	Hair/Face	79	37618	788
8a	Teapot small	65	2924	50
8b	Teapot	65	8361	77
8c	Teapot closeup	65	13617	200
9	Raccoon	62	55893	960

Table 1 Illustration statistics and rendering timings measured on a Silicon Graphics workstation with a 180MHz R5000 processor.

Figure 6 shows a way of visualizing measured or computed vector fields using our system. It was created by bypassing the interactive stage of the system and feeding directions and tones directly into the renderer. Figures 7 and 9 show our ability to render non-smooth, difficult-to-model surfaces such as hair and fur. Our stroke lengths are approximately 1–10cm in the original PostScript rendering. This scale is similar to that at which pen-and-ink artists typically work. These artists often reduce their work for final presentation to achieve a finer, more delicate feel. We have done the same with our illustrations; the reductions are reported in Table 1.

5 Future work

Our current system suggests two principle areas for future research.

Interactive illustrations. Currently the user interacts with the components of the underlying representation of the illustration. It would be nice for the user to have the option of interacting instead with the pen-and-ink illustration itself. Modifications to the illustration would be immediately reflected by corresponding changes in the tone or direction. While previous interactive systems [13] have allowed the user to directly manipulate the illustration, they do not—as does our system—allow the user to specify abstract high-level attributes of the illustration, and thus are not required to make a large number of changes as the result of a simple user action. With our system, changing the directions underneath the cursor can easily require removing and reapplying hundreds of strokes. Much of the incremental update mechanism needed for such behavior is already supported by our system, but we currently would require a considerable increase in rendering speed to make such an interface responsive enough to be usable.

Figure 9 Raccoon with detail inset showing stroke character.

Coherent textures. Many pen-and-ink drawings make use of textures such as bricks or shingles or fabrics that require strokes to appear in locally coherent patterns. Many artists also draw small groups of parallel hatches together in coherent clusters when filling in large areas of tone. We would like to support these kinds of coherent textures in our illustrations. The biggest difficulty is in dealing with diverging direction fields, since it is not obvious how to maintain local coherence and scale while following such a field without tearing the texture at some point.

Acknowledgments

This work was supported by an Alfred P. Sloan Research Fellowship (BR-3495), an NSF Presidential Faculty Fellow award (CCR-9553199), an ONR Young Investigator award (N00014-95-1-0728) and Augmentation award (N00014-90-J-P00002), and an industrial gift from Microsoft.

References

[1] Debra Dooley and Michael Cohen. Automatic illustration of 3D geometric models: Lines. In *Computer Graphics (1990 Symposium on Interactive 3D Graphics)*, pp. 77–82, March 1990.

[2] Gershon Elber. Line art rendering via a coverage of isoparametric curves. *IEEE Transactions on Visualization and Computer Graphics*, 1(3):231–239, September 1995.

[3] Ralph Gibson. *Tropism: photographs*. Aperture, New York, 1987.

[4] S. Gupta and R. F. Sproull. Filtering edges for gray-scale displays. *Computer Graphics (SIGGRAPH '81 Proceedings)*, 15(3):1–5, August 1981.

[5] Arthur L. Guptill. *Rendering in Pen and Ink*. Watson-Guptill Publications, New York, 1976.

[6] Paul Haeberli. Paint by numbers: Abstract image representations. *Computer Graphics*, 24(4):207–214, August 1990.

[7] John Lansdown and Simon Schofield. Expressive rendering: A review of nonphotorealistic techniques. *IEEE Computer Graphics and Applications*, 15(3):29–37, May 1995.

[8] Frank Lohan. *Pen and Ink Techniques*. Contemporary Books, Inc., Chicago, 1978.

[9] Barbara J. Meier. Painterly rendering for animation. In Holly Rushmeier, editor, *SIGGRAPH 96 Conference Proceedings*, pp. 477–484. Addison Wesley, August 1996.

[10] Yachin Pnueli and Alfred M. Bruckstein. **Dig**^i_D*ürer* — a digital engraving system. *The Visual Computer*, 10(5):277–292, 1994.

[11] Takafumi Saito and Tokiichiro Takahashi. Comprehensible rendering of 3-D shapes. *Computer Graphics*, 24(4):197–206, August 1990.

[12] Takafumi Saito and Tokiichiro Takahashi. NC machining with G-buffer method. *Computer Graphics*, 25(4):207–216, July 1991.

[13] Michael P. Salisbury, Sean E. Anderson, Ronen Barzel, and David H. Salesin. Interactive pen-and-ink illustration. In Andrew Glassner, editor, *Proceedings of SIGGRAPH '94*, pp. 101–108. ACM Press, July 1994.

[14] Mike Salisbury, Corin Anderson, Dani Lischinski, and David H. Salesin. Scale-dependent reproduction of pen-and-ink illustrations. In Holly Rushmeier, editor, *SIGGRAPH 96 Conference Proceedings*, pp. 461–468. Addison Wesley, August 1996.

[15] Gary Simmons. *The Technical Pen*. Watson-Guptill Publications, New York, 1992.

[16] Thomas Strothotte, Bernhard Preim, Andreas Raab, Jutta Schumann, and David R. Forsey. How to render frames and influence people. *Computer Graphics Forum*, 13(3):455–466, 1994. Eurographics '94 Conference issue.

[17] Georges Winkenbach and David H. Salesin. Computer-generated pen-and-ink illustration. In Andrew Glassner, editor, *Proceedings of SIGGRAPH '94*, pp. 91–100. ACM Press, July 1994.

[18] Georges Winkenbach and David H. Salesin. Rendering free-form surfaces in pen and ink. In Holly Rushmeier, editor, *SIGGRAPH 96 Conference Proceedings*, pp. 469–476. Addison Wesley, August 1996.

Processing Images and Video for An Impressionist Effect

Peter Litwinowicz

Apple Computer, Inc.

ABSTRACT

This paper describes a technique that transforms ordinary video segments into animations that have a hand-painted look. Our method is the first to exploit temporal coherence in video clips to design an automatic filter with a hand-drawn animation quality, in this case, one that produces an Impressionist effect. Off-the-shelf image processing and rendering techniques are employed, modified and combined in a novel way. This paper proceeds through the process step by step, providing helpful hints for tuning the off-the-shelf parts as well as describing the new techniques and bookkeeping used to glue the parts together.

1. INTRODUCTION

In the 1800's, Claude Monet created paintings that attempted to "catch the fleeting impression of sunlight on objects. And it was this out-of-doors world he wanted to capture in paint -- as it actually was at the moment of seeing it, not worked up in the studio from sketches." [Kingston80].

Impressionist paintings provide the inspiration for the work presented here. We have produced images that are *impressions* of an input image sequence, that give a sense of an original image without reproducing it. These images have a "painterly" feel; that is, they appear as if they have been hand-painted. Furthermore, we have produced entire animations with these same qualities.

Producing painterly animations from video clips *automatically* was the goal of this work. Our technique requires that the user specify a few parameters at the start of the process. After the first frame is produced to the user's liking, our technique processes a whole video segment without further user intervention. Previous painterly techniques require much user interaction and have only been presented in the context of modifying a single frame (with the exception of a technique applied to 3D animated scenes).

While this technique is not the first to produce images with an Impressionist look, our method has several advantages. Most significantly, this paper presents a process that uses optical flow fields to push brush strokes from frame to frame in the direction of pixel movements. This is the first time pixel motion has been tracked to produce a temporally coherent painterly style animation from an input video sequence. Brush strokes are distributed over an input image and then drawn with antialiased lines or with supplied textures to produce an image in the Impressionist style. Randomness is used to perturb the brush stroke's length, color and orientation to enhance the hand-touched look. Strokes are clipped to edges detected in the original image, thus preserving object silhouettes and fine detail. A new technique is described to orient strokes using gradient-based techniques. In the course of being moved from frame to frame, brush strokes may become too sparse to cover the image. Conversely, brush strokes may become overly dense. The necessary algorithms for adding and deleting brush strokes as they are pushed too close or too far apart by the optical flow field are described within this paper.

The following section describes previously presented painterly techniques. Then we present the details of our technique:

    1) the stroke rendering and clipping technique,
    2) the algorithm for producing brush stroke orientations,
    3) the algorithm for moving, adding and deleting brush strokes from frame to frame.

In conclusion, we discuss limitations of the algorithm and possible future directions.

2. BACKGROUND

Techniques for computer-assisted transformations of pictures are presented in [Haeberli90]. Many of those techniques involve extensive human interaction to produce the final images. More specifically, the user determines the number of strokes as well as their positions. The user controls the orientation, size and color of the strokes using combinations of interactive and non-interactive input. Examples of interactive input include cursor location, pressure and velocity; and non-interactive input include the gradient of the original image or other secondary images. Brush strokes can be selected from a palette and include both 2D and 3D brushes.

Painting each image in a sequence is labor intensive, and even more work is necessary to produce a sequence that is temporally coherent. "Obvious" modifications can be made to Haeberli's technique, but each has their drawbacks. For example, imagine keeping the same strokes from frame to frame and modifying the color and direction of the strokes as the underlying image sequence dictates. Doing so produces a final animation that looks as if it has been shot through a pane of glass because brush strokes don't follow the movement of the objects in the scene. Conversely, generating the random strokes from scratch for each frame often produces animation with too much jitter. Modifying Haeberli's approach to produce temporally coherent animations is a primary focus for the work presented here.

An interactive paint-like system for producing pen-and-ink illustrations is described in [Salisbury94]. The user specifies

Peter Litwinowicz
1 Infinite Loop, MS 301-3J
Cupertino, CA 95014
email: litwinow@apple.com

regions that are filled with chosen pen-and-ink patterns. Regions can be determined by hand, or specified as portions of a supplied secondary image. Similarly, tone can be supplied by hand or from some portion of an underlying reference image. Random variations are added to help produce a hand-drawn look. Building upon this work, [Salisbury96] presents a computer-assisted technique for producing scale-dependent pen-and-ink reproductions of images. In this work, tone from an image is used in conjunction with edges (detected from the same image) to produce a pen-and-ink format that is resolution-independent. The final rendered pen-and-ink images seek to preserve discontinuous shading across the edges that appeared in the original image, and to produce continuous shading in other areas. As with the techniques presented in [Haeberli90], applying the pen-and-ink techniques to sequences of images to produce a temporally coherent result is not straightforward. Motivated by this work, our technique also preserves perceived edges when transforming an input image.

The aforementioned techniques were only applied to single images. A system for producing 2-1/2D animations using "skeletal strokes" was presented in [Hsu94]. "Skeletal strokes" is a term used by the authors to describe a brush and stroke metaphor that uses arbitrary pictures as ink. However, all animation is key-framed by the user; that is, there is no automatic processing of an underlying image sequence.

In [Meier96], a system for transforming 3D geometry into animations with a painterly look is presented. 3D objects are animated and "particles" on the 3D surfaces are tracked. After the objects are projected into 2D (via a camera transformation), the particles are sorted by depth from the eye and then serve as positions for 2D brush strokes (painted back to front). Orientations are determined by using the surface normals as projected into the image plane. Brush size and texture is specified by the user. If desired, brush size may vary across a particular 3D object. This work demonstrates that temporal coherence of brush strokes is both interesting and important, but did not use video sequences as its input.

3. THE PROCESS

In this section we present our algorithm for overcoming some of the shortcomings of the previously described techniques. First, we describe the rendering technique, then the orientation algorithm, and finally the technique used to move brush strokes from frame to frame to produce temporally coherent animations. Color Plate 1 shows an example image that is used in demonstrating the process. (All color plates are located near the end of the paper so the reader may compare successive stages of the algorithm).

In order to create a final image there are many facets to our technique that work in concert with each other. However, explaining all the details at once would be confusing. We will first describe a very simple method to generate an image. As the paper progresses we will continue to describe modifications until the entire process has been explained.

A. Rendering strokes
Stroke Generation

To create the image shown in Color Plate 2, brush strokes are generated which, when rendered, cover the output image. Assume that each brush stroke is rendered with an antialiased line centered at (**cx,cy**), with a given length **length**, a given brush thickness **radius**, and a given orientation, **theta**. Assume that the brush strokes are generated with centers (**cx,cy**) positioned every two pixels in both the X and Y directions for the image. This spacing will assure coverage of the entire image with rendered brush strokes (brush radii and lengths shown in Table 1). In practice, the user sets the initial spacing distance. Then **cx** and **cy** are stored as floating point numbers for subpixel positioning. An orientation, **theta**, for each stroke is also needed. Discussion of the orientation calculation is deferred, so assume a constant direction of 45° (an arbitrary orientation chosen for demonstration purposes). The color for a particular stroke is assigned the bilinearly interpolated color of the original image at (**cx,cy**). Color components (r,g,b) are in the range [0,255]. Last, the order that the strokes are drawn is randomized to help create a hand-touched look (it helps break up the spatial coherence that would otherwise occur).

	Color Plates 2-5	Color Plates 6-8
Brush stroke radius (or offset for textured brushes)	1.5-2.0	4.0-4.5
Length	4-10	8-20

Table 1. Ranges for brush stroke radius and length.

Random Perturbations

Adding random variations and perturbations to a stroke helps to create a hand-crafted look. Much of the previous work on painterly renderings contain some form of random variation. We assign random amounts to **length** and **radius** in ranges supplied by the user (see Table 1). We perturb the color by a random amount for Δ**r**, Δ**g** and Δ**b**, each in the range [-15,15] (a range empirically found to be useful). We scale the perturbed color by a random amount, Δ**intensity**, in the range [.85,1.15]. After the originally sampled color is modified, the resulting color is clamped to the valid range [0,255]. We also

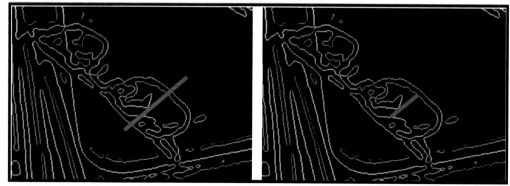

Figure 1. As shown at the left, previous methods have drawn brush strokes without regard to edges.
The same brush stroke clipped to edges in the image is shown on the right.

perturb **theta**, the orientation for the stroke, and do so by adding Δ**theta**, a random amount in the range [-15°,15°] (a range used for all images shown in the paper). **length**, **radius**, Δ**r**, Δ**g**, Δ**b**, Δ**intensity** and Δ**theta** are stored in the brush stroke's data structure and are used from frame to frame. We do not generate new values for each frame as this results in animations with too much jitter.

Clipping and Rendering

To render a brush stroke, an antialiased line is drawn through its center in the appropriate orientation. In order to preserve detail and silhouettes, strokes are clipped to edges that they encounter in the original image (see Figure 1). In this way, edges in the original image are more or less preserved. This is accomplished by starting at the center of the stroke and growing the stroke (in its orientation) until edges in the original image are detected. Color Plate 2 shows the results of drawing strokes while *not* trying to preserve edges, in contrast to Color Plate 3, which demonstrates the results of clipping the strokes against edges in the original image.

The stoke clipping technique is motivated in part by the work presented in [Salisbury94], in which stroke textures are clipped to edges provided by the user. Edges may be drawn or derived from an underlying image. [Salisbury94] presents an interactive system; the regions for stroke textures are specified by the user (using the original and secondary images, such as an edge enhanced version of the image). In our system there is no user interaction to specify edges; we rely solely on standard image processing techniques to locate edges.

The line clipping and drawing process proceeds as follows:

1. An intensity image is derived from the original color image. If the color value at a pixel is stored as red, green and blue components (r,g,b) in the range [0,255], then the intensity at each pixel is calculated as (30*r + 59*g + 11*b)/100 (standard conversion of r,g,b values to intensity value [Foley84]).

2. The intensity image is blurred with a Gaussian kernel [Jain95]. This blur helps reduce noise in the original video images. A larger kernel reduces noise, but at the expense of losing fine detail. A smaller kernel helps preserve fine detail, but may retain unwanted noise in the image. In this implementation, a B-spline approximation to the Gaussian is used. The width of the kernel should really depend on the content of the original sequence, so we let the user choose the kernel width. (A blurred image is shown in Figure 2, and uses a kernel that goes to zero at a radius of 11 pixels).

3. The resulting blurred image is Sobel filtered [Jain95]. The gradient (**Gx,Gy**) is calculated at each pixel and the value of the Sobel filter at any given pixel is:

Sobel(x,y) = Magnitude (**Gx, Gy**)

See Figure 2 for the Sobel filtered image of the example image.

4. Given the center (**cx,cy**), the orientation of the stroke, theta and the Sobel filtered image, endpoints of the stroke (**x1,y1**) and (**x2,y2**) need to be determined. The process starts at (**cx,cy**) and "grows" the line in its orientation until the maximum length is reached or an edge is detected in the smoothed image. An edge is considered found if the magnitude of the gradient (the Sobel value) decreases in the direction the stroke is being grown. See Appendix A for the pseudo-code for stroke clipping. This is similar to the edge detection process used in the Canny operator. For details of the Canny operator the reader is referred to [Jain95].

Determination of the stroke orientation, **theta**, is described in the following section. For Color Plate 3 we used a constant 45° orientation, with perturbations added.

5. The stroke is rendered with endpoints (**x1,y1**) and (**x2,y2**). The color of the stroke is assigned the color of the original image at the center of the stroke. The stored perturbations are used to modify this color, and then the color is clamped. The strokes in Color Plates 2 through 5 are rendered as antialiased lines using a stroke radius in the range [1.5,2.0] (again, a number used for example purposes). A linear falloff is used in a 1.0 pixel radius region (alpha, for compositing, transitions from a value of 1.0 to 0.0 linearly). Figure 3 shows how the values are used to render the stroke.

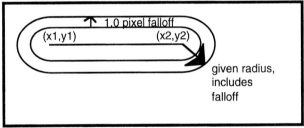

Figure 3. Antialiased stroke rendering.

Note that the drawing process touches pixels past the clipped endpoints of the line. Drawing slightly past the endpoints, along with the random ordering of strokes, creates a non-perfect line along edges. This helps to produce the hand-touched slightly wandering edges in the final image (shown in Color Plate 3) rather than an absolute hard edge.

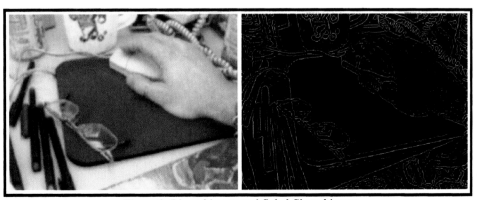

Figure 2. Blurred image and Sobel filtered image.

It is important to note that, at the very least, a circle is drawn of the given brush radius, even if there are edges in the image that clip a particular stroke to zero length. This means that something will be drawn for each stroke even if the stroke's center is surrounded by edges in the original image.

Using Brush Textures

Brush strokes may also be rendered with textured brush images that have r,g,b and alpha components. A given offset is provided (akin to the radius given for the antialiased lines) and a rectangle surrounding the clipped line is constructed (see Figure 4). The brush stroke texture is then rendered into this rectangle. Each component of the color of the brush stroke texture is multiplied by the color assigned to the stroke. In the current implementation, the given offset is used regardless of the length of the clipped line. Another approach would be to scale the offset based on the length of the stroke. Color Plates 7 and 8 demonstrate the use of brush stroke textures.

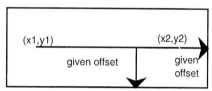

Figure 4. Rectangle for rendering textured brushes

B. Brush Stroke Orientation

In the previous section, a 45° constant orientation was used for all strokes (before the random variations were added). An artist, however, may not want to have all the strokes drawn in the same direction. We provide the user the option of drawing brush strokes in the direction of constant color, or near constant color, of the original image. This has the real world metaphor of strokes painted in a medium where a stroke does not change color as it is painted. This orientation can be approximated automatically by drawing strokes normal to the gradient direction (of the intensity image). Differentially, the gradient is the direction of most change, and normal to the gradient is the direction of zero change. Using this information, we assume that the image can be approximated locally with a relatively short stoke of constant color in the gradient-normal direction.

In our first implementation, the same Gaussian kernel used in the edge finding process was used for smoothing the image for the gradient calculation. However, using the same kernel did not produce a gradient that was smooth enough. A greater kernel width is used for the orientation calculation; in fact, the Gaussian filter used has a radius that is 4 pixels greater than the filter used for the edge finding process. Of course the user could

supply this parameter, but for the video sequences we processed, the slightly larger kernel provided an adequately smoothed orientation field (and eliminated one more choice for the user).

The gradient direction is used to guide brush strokes in the work presented in [Haeberli90]. However, the user must interactively supply the position and length of the strokes. Using equally spaced brush strokes and the normal to the gradient of a smoothed version of the original image, Color Plate 4 was produced. However, when the magnitude of gradient is near zero we cannot rely on the gradient direction to be useful. We introduce a novel technique which modifies the gradient field so that brush strokes in a region of constant color (or near constant color) smoothly interpolate the directions defined at the region's boundaries (the difference is shown between Color Plates 4 and 5).

To accomplish this, gradient values are "thrown out" at pixel locations where the Magnitude($(\mathbf{Gx},\mathbf{Gy})$) is near zero. In this implementation, this is approximated by the test: $|\mathbf{Gx}|<3.0$ and $|\mathbf{Gy}|<3.0$, which was empirically found to be useful. The gradient at pixels with near zero gradient magnitude are then replaced by interpolating surrounding "good" gradients. The "good" values do not necessarily lie on a uniform grid, so generating points with cubic interpolation (or other closed-form solution) does not work here. An interpolant that does not assume uniformly spaced data in both directions is needed. In our implementation, $\mathbf{Gx}$ and $\mathbf{Gy}$ are interpolated using a thin-plate spline [Franke79], which is chosen for its smoothness characteristics.

Finally, at each brush stroke center ($\mathbf{cx},\mathbf{cy}$), the modified gradient field components ($\mathbf{Gx},\mathbf{Gy}$) are bilinearly interpolated. A direction angle is computed from this vector as arctan($\mathbf{Gy}/\mathbf{Gx}$), 90° is added to it (to draw it normal to the gradient direction), and the Δtheta stored with the stroke is added to produce **theta**, the orientation of the drawn stroke (see Color Plate 5).

Using the normal to the gradient causes strokes to look glued to objects in a scene (it helps define their shape), especially when the objects are moving, rotating or changing shape. Keeping stroke orientation the same from frame to frame does not provide the same amount of perceived spatial and temporal coherence that is provided by using the normal to the gradient direction. Of course, keeping the strokes oriented along a particular constant direction remains an option.

C. Frame-to-Frame Coherence

In [Meier96], a temporally coherent technique is presented which employed "particles" on 3D objects as centers for brush

Figure 5. Two frames and the optical flow field that maps pixels from one frame to another.

strokes. By transforming these points into 2D, using the normal direction of 3D surfaces as guides for brush stroke orientations, and rendering strokes back to front as seen from the camera, temporally coherent animations were produced. However, input to our process is a video clip with no a priori information about pixel movement in the scene. Our technique uses standard vision techniques to produce an automatic technique to guide brush strokes in the direction of pixel movement.

To render the first frame, we use the process described in the previous two sections. In order to move the brush strokes from one frame to the next, we first calculate the optical flow between the two images. Optical flow methods are a subclass of motion estimation techniques and are based on the assumptions that illumination is constant and that occlusion can be ignored, that is, that the observed intensity changes are only due to the motion of the underlying objects. It should be noted that this assumption is quite invalid for many of our test sequences. However, the artifacts of these assumptions produce interesting results even when the assumptions aren't true. When objects appear or disappear, optical flow methods tend to mush together or stretch apart the image portions corresponding to these objects. This provides a pleasing temporal coherence when portions of objects appear or disappear.

We chose the algorithm presented in [Bergen90] for its speed. This algorithm uses a gradient-based multi-resolution technique, employing a pyramid of successively low-passed versions of the gradient to help compute the optical flow. Presenting details concerning this optical flow method is beyond the scope of this paper.

The optical flow vector field is used as a displacement field to move the brush strokes (specifically, their centers) to new locations in a subsequent frame. The optical flow technique we implemented provides subpixel positioning, and this feature is exploited by moving brush strokes to subpixel locations. See Figure 5 for two images and the flow field that maps pixels in the first one to pixels in the second. After application of the displacements, some of the strokes may have been pushed from the edge of the image. The best match for a pixel will not be outside the image, but the algorithm may map edge pixels in one frame to an interior point in the next. We must make sure to generate new strokes near the image boundaries when this happens.

After application of the flow field to move the strokes, there also may be regions away from image boundaries that become unnecessarily dense with brush strokes or not dense enough. We want full coverage of the image with rendered brush strokes, so brush strokes are "too sparse" in our algorithm when there are pixels left untouched in the final rendered image.

To generate new brush strokes in regions that are too sparse, a Delaunay triangulation [Preparata85] using the previous frame's brush stroke centers (after application of the optical flow field) is generated using the methods described in [Shewchuk96] using source code available at [TriangleCode] (see Figures 6a,b,c). The particulars of the Delaunay triangulation is beyond the scope of this paper; however, it is important to know that the Delaunay triangulation covers the convex hull of the submitted points with triangles. By including the corners of the image in the point set, it is assured that the entire image will be covered with triangles (remember, as stated above, the optical flow may push strokes far away from the image boundaries).

The Delaunay triangulation by itself does not generate new points for brush strokes. However, after the Delaunay triangulation is performed, the mesh is subdivided so that there are no triangles with an area larger than maximum supplied area (as presented in [Shewchuk96]). By supplying an appropriate maximal area, new vertices are created which fill in the sparse areas and are subsequently used as new brush stroke centers. To produce Color Plate 5, the specific maximal area we supplied was 2.0 in pixels units squared (the antialiased lines for this plate were rendered with brush radii with a range of 1.5 to 2.0), a number found empirically to provide dense enough vertices. The maximum area may be tuned by the user if desired; for example, if the user wishes to have areas of the final image untouched by strokes. New brush strokes are created for the new vertices and a new random length and new variations for angle, color, intensity are determined and stored. See Figure 6d for the subsequent subdivision of the initial triangulation shown in Figure 6c.

Eliminating brush strokes in regions that are overly dense is desirable. After pushing strokes around frame after frame, brush strokes collect in image regions that "shrink." Over time this results in overly dense brush stroke regions, which then causes the rendering process to slow down tremendously. The amount of brush buildup depends of course on the specific video

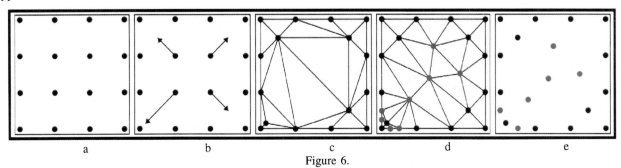

Figure 6.

a) Initial brush stroke positioning.
b) The four middle strokes are to be moved as shown.
c) Delaunay triangulation of the moved strokes
d) Red points show new vertices introduced as a result of satisfying the maximal area constraint.
e) The updated list of brush strokes. The original lower left corner brush stoke has been deleted because the distance between it and another original stroke satisfies the closeness test. Two of the potentially added new brush strokes have also been removed from the list.

sequence. To dispose of brush strokes, the edge list of the triangulation is traversed (remember, each point in the triangulation is the center for an associated brush stroke). If the distance between the two points of an edge is less than a user-specified length, the corresponding brush stroke that is drawn closer to the back is discarded (a display list of strokes is kept, so there is an implicit front to back ordering). For Figure 6e and Color Plate 5, strokes were discarded when their centers were closer than 0.25 pixel units. As the edge list of the triangulation is traversed, if a point has been discarded we must be sure to perform the distance calculation with the point (and associated stroke) that replaced it. The triangulation provides the closest neighboring points to a given point, enabling a great reduction in the number of distance and comparison calculations.

At this point there are two lists of brush strokes: a list of "old" strokes (strokes moved and subsequently kept) from the previous frame, and the "new" strokes generated in sparse regions. Old stroke ordering (after throwing out unwanted strokes) is kept to provide temporal coherence. To place the new strokes on the list with the old strokes, the new strokes' order is randomized with respect to themselves. Then the new strokes are uniformly distributed among the old strokes. If the new strokes are simply painted behind the old strokes, undesirable effects can occur.

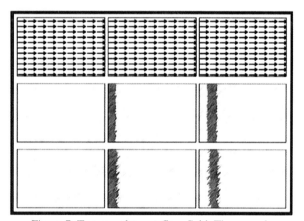

Figure 7. Top row shows a flow field. The second row shows the effects of placing new strokes behind old strokes, where new strokes are alternately coded dark and light. The third row demonstrates the effects of uniformly distributing the new strokes among the old ones.

For instance, in Figure 7 shows a flow field representing a pan of a video camera. The same figure demonstrates the results of putting new strokes behind old ones as well as uniformly distributing them. New strokes from frame to frame are alternately coded light and dark. Very clear edges appear if the new strokes are drawn behind the old ones. This is a problem, producing edges in the rendered image that may not be present in the original image. Uniformly distributing the new strokes produces much better results, effectively eliminating the problems encountered by painting new strokes behind the old ones. Distributing new strokes uniformly produces some temporal scintillation (strokes popping on top) but this was found to be preferable to the spatial anomalies that may otherwise occur.

After strokes are created, deleted and placed in their new positions, the base color of the stroke is retrieved from the image at the stroke center. The gradient field is determined for the new image in the sequence and used to calculate each brush's orientation. The stored delta values are then used to perturb these sampled values as described above and the next image in the rendered sequence is produced.

4. DISCUSSION

An algorithm for producing painterly animations from video clips has been presented. Brush strokes are clipped to edges detected in the original image sequence in an attempt to maintain silhouettes and other details present in the original images. Brush strokes are oriented normal to the gradient direction of the original image; a scattered data interpolation technique is used to interpolate the gradient field in areas where the magnitude of the gradient is near zero. Finally, a brush stroke list is maintained and manipulated through the use of optical flow fields to enhance temporal coherence.

The numbers presented in the paper represent a particular implementation. For the image sequence represented by the technique to produce Color Plate 5 (brush radii in the range [1.5-2.0], brush lengths in the range [4,10] and a maximal area constraint of 2.0), 76800 strokes were used to start the process (= 640/2 * 480/2). As the process continued, the stroke count averaged 120,000. Time to produce each frame averaged 81 seconds on a Macintosh 8500 running at 180 MHz.

Of course the specific parameters to the brush and the specific image processing and rendering techniques may be manipulated to produce different results. A fatter brush stroke radius of 8 produced the image in Color Plate 6, and textured brush strokes produced Color Plates 7 and 8. In the future different color assignment techniques are planned (such as averaging the colors under a particular brush stroke to generate its color).

We see this algorithm as an important step in automatically producing temporally coherent "painterly" animations. However, because we paint some of the new strokes in front of old strokes, the animations can scintillate. Whether we can avoid this and not introduce spatial anomalies remains to be determined. Also, because we clip lines to edges in the original video sequence, the presence of noise in the original video will cause the derived edges to scintillate, which in turn causes the brush stokes to scintillate. The brush stroke placement from frame to frame is not perfect either, and is only as good as the underlying motion estimation technique used. The technique we used does fairly well but can only do so much without any advanced knowledge of the objects in the scene. In particular, brush strokes can sometimes seem to swim in areas of near constant intensity.

Further directions may include implementing other rendering, image processing and vision techniques to produce other artistic styles. Applying the techniques to 3D objects to produce painterly renderings would be interesting (as in [Meier96]), and would enable animations with much greater temporal coherence since object movement is known a priori.

For the first time, temporal coherence in video segments is used to drive brush stoke placement for a painterly style effect. After a few initial decisions, such as what the brush stroke length, radius and texture should be; whether or not to use the gradient for brush stroke orientation; what filter kernels should be used; providing distances and areas for the closeness and sparseness tests, our system process the video *automatically*. Hopefully this technique proves easy enough for those who do

Color Plate 1. An original image. Plates 1-8 are 640x480 pixels.

Color Plate 2. Processed image using no brush stroke clipping and a constant base stroke orientation of 45°.

Color Plate 3. Technique of Color Plate 2 is modified so that brush strokes are cliped to edges detected in the original image.

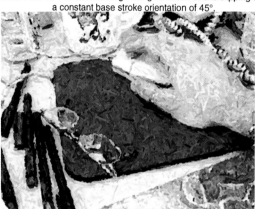

Color Plate 4. Technique of Color Plate 3 is modified to orient strokes using a gradient-based technique.

Color Plate 5. Technique of Color Plate 4 is modified such that regions with vanishing gradient magnitude are interpolated from surrounding regions.

Color Plate 6. Image produced using larger brush stroke radii and lengths.

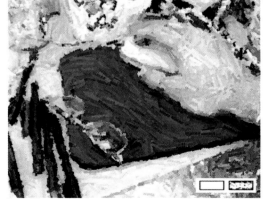

Color Plate 7. Brush stroke textures are used. Lower right corner shows basic brush intensity and alpha.

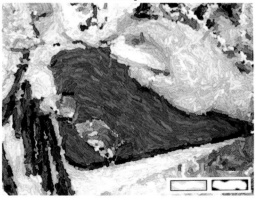

Color Plate 8. Another brush stroke texture is demonstrated.

not have the time, desire, or talent to hand-animate a sequence, but is also powerful enough to be part of the battery of tools a trained artist might use.

5. ACKNOWLEDGEMENTS

Thanks to Apple Research Labs for sponsoring this work, Gavin Miller for many ideas, and the reviewers who provided a careful reading of this paper.

6. REFERENCES

[Bergen90] Bergen, J. R. and R. Hingorani. "Hierarchical motion-based frame rate conversion," David Sarnoff Research Center, Princeton, N. J.

[Foley84] Foley, James and Adries Van Dam. Fundamentals of Interactive Computer Graphics. Addison-Wesley, Reading, Massachusetts, 1984.

[Franke79] Franke, F. "A Critical Comparison of Some Methods for Interpolation of Scattered Data," Report NPS-53-79-03 of the Naval Postgraduate School, Monterey, CA. Obtained from the U.S Department of Commerce, National Technical Information Service.

[Haeberli90] Haeberli, Paul. "Paint By Numbers: Abstract Image Representations," Computer Graphics, SIGGRAPH Annual Conference Proceedings 1990, pp. 207-214.

[Hsu94] Hsu, Siu Chi and Irene Lee. "Drawing and Animation Using Skeletal Strokes," Computer Graphics, SIGGRAPH Annual Conference Proceedings 1994, pp. 109-118.

[Jain95] Jain, Ramesh, Rangachar Kasturi, and Brian Schunck. Machine Vision. McGraw-Hill, Inc. New York, 1995.

[Kingston80] Kingston, Jeremy. Arts and Artists. Book Club Associates, London, 1980. pp. 98-99.

[Meier96] Meier, Barbara. "Painterly Rendering for Animation," Computer Graphics, SIGGRAPH Annual Conference Proceedings 1996, pp. 477-484.

[Preparata85] Preparata, Franco, Michal Ian Shamos, Computational Geometry, An Introduction, Springer-Veralg, 1985.

[Salisbury94] Salisbury, Michael, Sean Anderson, Ronen Barzel, and David Salesin. "Interactive Pen-and-Ink Illustration", Computer Graphics, SIGGRAPH Annual Conference Proceedings 1994, pp. 101-108.

[Salisbury96] Salisbury, Mike, Corin Anderson, Dani Lischinski, and David Salesin. "Scale-Dependent Reproduction of Pen-and-Ink Illustrations", Computer Graphics, SIGGRAPH Annual Conference Proceedings 1996, pp. 461-468.

[Shewchuk96] ShewChuk, Jonathan. "Triangle: Engineering a 2D Quality Mesh Generator and Delaunay Triangulator," First Workshop on Applied Computational Geometry, Association for Computing Machinery, May, 1996, pp. 124-133.

[TriangleCode] Code for reference [Shewchuk96] available at http://www.cs.cmu.edu/~quake/triangle.html.

Appendix A. STROKE CLIPPING

The center of the stroke is given by (**cx**,**cy**) and the direction of the stroke is given by (**dirx**,**diry**). This process determines (**x1**,**y1**) and (**x2**,**y2**), the endpoints of the stroke clipped to edges in the image.

The Sobel filtered intensity image is sampled in steps of unit length in order to detect edges. To determine (**x1**,**y1**):

    a. set (**x1**,**y1**) to (**cx**,**cy**)

    b. bilinearly sample the Sobel filtered intensity image at (**x1**,**y1**), and set **lastSample** to this value

    c. set (**tempx**,**tempy**) to (**x1**+**dirx**, **y1**+**diry**), taking a unit step in the orientation direction.

    d. if (dist((**x1**,**y1**),(**tempx**,**tempy**))) > (**length** of stroke)/2, then stop

    e. bilinearly sample the Sobel image at (**tempx**,**tempy**), and set **newSample** to this value

    f. if (**newSample** < **lastSample**) then stop

    g. set (**x1**,**y1**) to (**tempx**,**tempy**)

    h. set **lastSample** to **newSample**

    i. go to step c

At the end of this process, the endpoint (**x1**,**y1**) of the line in one direction has been determined. To find (**x2**,**y2**), the endpoint in the other direction, set (**dirx**,**diry**) to (-**dirx**, -**diry**) and repeat the above process.

Color Plate 9. Another image produced with the technique.

Real-Time Nonphotorealistic Rendering

Lee Markosian   Michael A. Kowalski   Samuel J. Trychin   Lubomir D. Bourdev

Daniel Goldstein   John F. Hughes

Brown University site of the
NSF Science and Technology Center for
Computer Graphics and Scientific Visualization
Providence, RI 02912

Abstract

Nonphotorealistic rendering (NPR) can help make *comprehensible* but simple pictures of complicated objects by employing an economy of line. But current nonphotorealistic rendering is primarily a batch process. This paper presents a real-time nonphotorealistic renderer that deliberately trades accuracy and detail for speed. Our renderer uses a method for determining visible lines and surfaces which is a modification of Appel's hidden-line algorithm, with improvements which are based on the topology of singular maps of a surface into the plane. The method we describe for determining visibility has the potential to be used in any NPR system that requires a description of visible lines or surfaces in the scene. The major contribution of this paper is thus to describe a tool which can significantly improve the performance of these systems. We demonstrate the system with several nonphotorealistic rendering styles, all of which operate on complex models at interactive frame rates.

CR Categories and Subject Descriptors: I.3.3 [Computer Graphics]: Picture/Image Generation — Display algorithms;

Additional Key Words: non-photorealistic rendering

1   Introduction

Computer graphics is concerned with the production of images in order to convey visual information. Historically, research in computer graphics has focused primarily on the problem of producing images which are indistinguishable from photographs. But graphic designers have long understood that photographs are not always the best choice for presenting visual information. A simplified diagram is often preferred when an image is required to delineate and explain. Lansdown and Schofield [10] make this point in the context of a repair manual, asking, "How much use is a photograph to mechanics when they already have the real thing in front of them?" Strothotte et al. [17] note that architects often trace over computer renderings of their initial designs to create a sketchier look, because they want to avoid giving their clients a false impression of completeness. In general, the question of whether to use photorealistic imagery depends on the *visual effect intended by the designer.*

A growing body of research in computer graphics has recognized the power and usefulness of nonphotorealistic imagery [21, 20, 13, 22, 10, 17, 11, 7, 16, 3]. Until now, though, nonphotorealistic rendering (NPR) methods have primarily been batch-oriented rather than interactive. (An exception is Zeleznik's SKETCH system [22], which makes crude nonphotorealistic renderings using tricks in the standard polygon-rendering pipeline). One obstacle to achieving real-time nonphotorealistic rendering is the problem of determining visibility, since a straightforward use of z-buffering may give incorrect results. This can occur when what is drawn on the screen does not correspond literally to the geometry of the scene. For example, a line segment between two vertices of a triangle mesh may be rendered in a wobbly, hand-drawn style. Any part of the wobbly line which does not directly correspond to the original line segment may be clipped out during z-buffering.

This paper presents a new real-time NPR technique based on an *economy of line* – the idea that a great deal of information can be effectively conveyed by very few strokes. Certain key features of images can convey a great deal of information; our algorithm preferentially renders silhouettes, certain user-chosen key features (e.g., creases), and some minimal shading of surface regions. To accomplish this at interactive rates, we rely on approximate data: not every silhouette is rendered in every frame, although large silhouettes are rendered with high probability. The key ideas that support this scheme are

- rapid (probabilistic) identification of silhouette edges,

- using interframe coherence of silhouette edges, and

- fast visibility determination using improvements and simplifications in Appel's hidden-line algorithm [1].

We demonstrate the use of these techniques to support a variety of rendering styles, all of which are produced at interactive rates. These include a spare line-rendering style suitable for illustrations (including optional rendering of hidden lines), a variety of sketchy hand-drawn styles suitable for approximate models, and a technique for adding shading strokes to basic visible-line renderings in order to better convey 3D information while preserving an artistic effect. This last technique uses a method for determining hidden surfaces which is a simple extension of the hidden-line algorithm. Using the methods we describe, our renderer is able to produce basic visible line drawings of free-form (tesselated) surfaces at an effective rate of over 1 million model polygons per second on a modern workstation.

The overall structure of our algorithm is: (i) determine the silhouette curves in the model, (ii) determine the visibility of silhouette and other feature edges by a modified Appel's algorithm, (iii) render the silhouette and feature edges. The basic algorithm can be extended to perform some shading over surface regions, in which case step (ii) is extended to determine visibility of surfaces. We explain the first two parts in detail, and then describe the final part in Section 5.

2 Assumptions and Definitions

First, we assume the model to be rendered is represented by a non-self-intersecting polygon mesh, no edge of which has more than two adjacent faces – i.e., the mesh is a topological manifold. To make our second assumption precise, we need some definitions:

Definition 1 *A polygon is* **front-facing** *if the dot product of its outward normal and a vector from a point on the polygon to the camera position is positive. Otherwise the polygon is* **back-facing**. *A* **silhouette edge** *is an edge adjacent to one front-facing and one back-facing polygon. A* **border edge** *is an edge adjacent to just one face. A silhouette edge is* **front-facing** *if its adjacent face nearest the camera is front-facing. Other silhouette edges are* **back-facing**.

Our second assumption is that in every image that we render, the view is *generic* in the following sense:

Definition 2 *A view is* **generic** *if (i) the multiplicity of the image of the silhouette curves is everywhere one, except at a finite number of points where it is two; (ii) these multiplicity-two points do not coincide with the projection of any vertices of the mesh; and (iii) their number is invariant under small changes in viewing direction.* [1]

Our method may fail for non-generic views, but we have not observed this in practice when computations are performed with double-precison (64 bit) floating point numbers.

3 Appel's Algorithm

Appel's hidden-line algorithm, as well as those of Galimberti [6] and Loutrel [12], is based on a notion of *quantitative invisibility* (QI), which counts the number of front-facing polygons between a point of an object and the camera. The algorithm is applied to the entire mesh of edges in a polyhedral model to determine QI at all points; those with QI = 0 are visible and are drawn. Good descriptions of the basic algorithm can be found in [5, 2, 18]. We summarize a few key ideas here.

The algorithm first identifies all silhouette edges, because as we traverse the interior of an edge, QI changes only when the edge crosses behind a silhouette. In a generic view, QI can also change at a vertex, but only when the vertex lies on a silhouette edge. This fact is characterized by several authors [18, 5] as a "complication" of the algorithm; we'll discuss this further below.

The algorithm proceeds by determining (via raytracing, for example), the QI of some point in each connected set of edges, and then propagating QI out from this point, taking care to note changes as the edge along which it is propagated passes behind silhouettes, or when a vertex through which it is propagated lies on a silhouette. In this way the number of ray tests is minimized by exploiting "edge coherence."

4 Improving Appel's algorithm

4.1 A fast randomized algorithm for finding silhouettes

Since we focus primarily on rendering silhouettes, and because of their prominence in Appel's algorithm, it's important to find them quickly. But the straightforward approach to finding silhouettes requires an exhaustive search, which conflicts with our goal of achieving interactive frame rates while rendering complex models.

We therefore compromise, and have developed a randomized algorithm for rapidly detecting silhouette edges. We examine a small fraction of the edges in the model, and if we find a silhouette edge, it is easy (by stepping along adjacent silhouette edges) to trace out the entire silhouette curve. If a typical silhouette has 100 edges, we are likely to detect it if we examine only 1% of the edges in the object. Thus the likelihood that a silhouette will be detected is proportional to its length, so that long ones, which are more significant, are more likely to be detected. [2]

If we order the edges by dihedral angle θ, and assign probabilities that decrease as θ increases, we can increase our chances of finding silhouette edges, because given a randomly chosen view, the probability that an edge is a silhouette is proportional to $\pi - \theta$ (in radians).

Given sufficiently small changes in camera position and orientation, it's often the case that a silhouette curve in one frame contains edges that were also silhoutte edges in the previous frame. We exploit this frame-to-frame coherence of silhouettes by always checking every silhouette edge of the previous frame. To further increase the chance of finding silhouettes in the current frame, we select a small fraction of silhouette edges from the previous frame as the starting point for a limited search, traversing edges toward or away from the camera depending on whether the start point lies within a back-facing or front-facing region of surface, respectively. The search stops when a silhoutte edge is found or when the number of edges traversed exceeds a pre-set bound.

When we remove the "seed-and-seek" approach to silhouette-finding and instead check every edge of the model, we observe up to a five-fold increase in total running time for finely-tessellated models (see Section 6).

4.2 Silhouettes and cusps

The "complication" in Appel's algorithm arises because the mapping from the surface to the plane is singular along silhouette edges. Understanding this complicated case better allows us to avoid some unneeded computation. To this end, we first (following [4]) redefine QI to be the number of layers of surface (front- and back-facing) obscuring a point. We then observe that, for generic views, QI along a silhouette curve can change at a vertex only if that vertex is of a special type, which we call a *cusp*:

Definition 3 *A vertex is called a* **cusp vertex** *(or* **cusp***) if one of the following holds (see figure 1):*

1. *it is adjacent to exactly 2 silhouette edges, one front-facing and the other back-facing,*

2. *it is adjacent to more than 2 silhouette edges, or*

3. *it is adjacent to a border edge* [3].

The QI along a non-silhouette curve which intersects a silhouette curve at a vertex can change as it passes through the vertex. Appel's algorithm thus requires a local test at every vertex belonging to a silhouette. But we are interested primarily in propagating QI *along*

---

[1] This definition is adopted from [19].

[2] Suppose an object's tessellation is refined using a scheme with the following properties: with each subsequent refinement, the total number of edges quadruples, the number of distinct silhouette curves (connected sets of silhouette edges) remains constant, and the number of edges in each silhouette curve doubles. Then it is not hard to show that a constant probability of detecting a silhouette is maintained while checking $O(\sqrt{n})$ edges, where n is the number of edges in a given refinement of the object.

[3] This case is necessary, as shown by figure 1(c), which contradicts corollary 5.1.5 of [4].

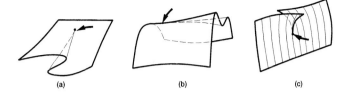

Figure 1 Arrows indicate cusps. (a) A typical cusp. (b) A more exotic cusp. (c) A border cusp (the two edges meeting at the center of the sheet are border edges).

silhouette curves, so testing for changes in QI just at cusp vertices provides a significant savings in computation time. [4]

4.3 Avoiding ray tests

Next, we show how to avoid some of the ray tests required by Appel's algorithm. First, if we assume that all objects in the scene are completely in view of the camera, then any edge which touches the 2D bounding box (in image space) of all silhouettes does not require a ray test – it is automatically visible. Hence, no ray test is required for any connected set (or **cluster**) of silhouette edges containing such an edge.

Appel's algorithm would now proceed with (1) a ray test to establish QI at some distinguished point on each cluster, followed by (2) the propagation step in which QI is assigned to the remaining points of each cluster. By reversing this order, we can sometimes eliminate the need for a ray test altogether, since the second step is often sufficient to determine that an entire silhouette curve is occluded. (See figure 2).

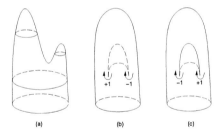

Figure 2 (a) A surface: side view. (b) Smaller branch is in rear. (c) Smaller branch is in front. The change in QI at cusps is indicated. Traversing the inner silhouette in (b) is sufficient to determine that the silhouette is totally occluded.

For each connected cluster of silhouette edges, we first choose an edge and a point on it infinitesimally close to one of its vertices. We call this point the **base point** of the cluster. Let b denote QI at the base point. QI at all other points of the cluster will be defined via offsets from b. We assign a preliminary lower-bound value of 0 to b. We then calculate the offsets with a graph search, taking into account image space intersections of edges of the current cluster with any silhouette edges, as well as cusp vertices encountered in the traversal. (A curve's QI increases by two when it passes behind a silhouette, and may change by an arbitrary, locally measurable amount at a cusp vertex). We record the minimum QI, m, encountered during the search. If $m < 0$, we may safely increment b by $-m$. It's easy to show that on a closed surface, front-facing silhouette edges must have even QI and back-facing silhouette edges must

---

[4] Note that front-facing and back-facing silhouette edges (used in identifying cusps) can be detected according to whether the surface along the edge is convex or concave; the convexity of each edge can be determined in a pre-process step once-and-for-all.

have odd QI. For such surfaces, we add 1 to b if needed to correct its parity. (In that case the cluster is totally occluded – figure 2 shows an example of this).

Finally, we examine each intersection involving edges from different clusters. In this situation, if n is the QI of the occluding edge, and m is the QI of the occluded edge along its unobscured portion, then we must have $m \geq n$. If we find that for our estimated QI values $m < n$, we can increment the base QI of the cluster containing the occluded edge by $n - m$, and propagate this information to other clusters as well.

In practice, these observations often account for all clusters, and consequently no ray tests are required in the current frame. In the remaining cases we perform the needed ray tests efficiently through a technique we call **walking**.

4.4 Walking

Once relative QI values at all points of a silhouette cluster have been determined with respect to the QI b at the base point, we must determine the correct value of b. The following technique does this, assuming all objects in the scene are in front of the camera. (We briefly discuss how to render immersive scenes below).

When one silhouette cluster is totally enclosed by another (in image space), the enclosing silhouette may be the boundary of a region which may totally obscure the enclosed silhouette. (See figure 2 (b) and (c). In (b), the enclosed silhouette is totally occluded, in (c) it is not). We detect such enclosures and their consequent occlusions as follows. First, we disregard silhouette curves which are already known to be totally occluded. We also disregard any silhouette curve which touches the image space box, B, that bounds all silhouette edges (as it can't be totally enclosed). On each remaining silhouette curve, we choose a point U with currently assigned QI of 0. Let U_p denote the projection of U. We identify enclosing silhouettes by tracing a path in image space from U_p toward the boundary of B. From each enclosing silhouette curve S encountered at an image space point V_p, we find the corresponding point V on S. We choose a branch of surface adjacent to S at V along which we can begin tracing a path whose projection heads back toward U_p, if such a branch of surface exists. (Either both branches of surface satisfy this condition or both do not – in which case we proceed to the next enclosing silhouette). We then traverse the surface from V along the path whose projection retraces (in reverse direction) the original path from U_p. If this surface walk succeeds in arriving at a point which projects to U_p, a depth test determines whether U is occluded by that portion of surface.

Our walking method does not work in general for immersive scenes in which geometry may surround the camera. An alternative approach is to perform ray tests efficiently with the use of an octree data structure which can be used to find intersections of a line segment with any triangles in the scene. One problem with this approach is that if there are any silhouette curves in the scene which have gone undetected by the randomized algorithm for finding silhouettes, it's possible for a small region of occlusion in a detected silhouette to be propagated (incorrectly) throughout the entire silhouette. This can occur since intersections with the undetected silhouettes are not taken into account, but the ray test may count occlusions due to surfaces bounded by the undetected silhouettes. (The walking method does not count such surfaces). Taking steps to decrease the probability of missing silhouette curves that lie within the viewing frustum is one approach for minimizing this problem.

The discussion to this point has tacitly assumed that edges of interest are all silhouette edges. These methods easily accomodate border edges and other non-silhouette edges (such as creases or decorative edges) as well. Border edges cause a change of ± 1 in

QI of edges passing behind them. Other edges cause no change in QI of edges passing behind them.

4.5 Implementation details

We follow Loutrel's [12] approach of projecting the silhouette edges into image space and finding their intersections there. This can be done with a sweep-line algorithm in $O(k \log k)$ time, where k is the number of silhouette edges (see e.g. [15]). We found it more convenient to use a spatial subdivision data structure which divides the image space bounding box of the silhouette edges into a grid of cells. Each silhouette edge is "scan converted" into the grid; only edges which share a cell need be tested for intersection. This method has worst-case complexity of $O(k^2)$ but performs well on average. We re-use the spatial subdivision grid in the walking step, in order to find enclosing silhouettes whose projection intersects the image-space path from U_p.

5 Rendering visible lines and surfaces

We demonstrate the use of our visibility algorithm to produce several styles of nonphotorealistic renderings at interactive rates. The accompanying video shows our system in action, and still images produced by the renderer are included at the end of this paper.

World-space polylines to be rendered are first projected into the film plane. Artistic or expressive strokes are then generated by modifying the resulting 2D polylines. We use three techniques for generating expressive strokes: drawing the polylines directly, with slight enhancements such as variations in line width or color (see figure 3(a)); high-resolution "artistically" perturbed strokes defined by adding offsets to the polyline (figure 3(b)); and texture-mapped strokes which follow the shape of the polyline (figure 3(c)). A variation on the first method is to render occluded lines in a style which depends on the number of layers of surface occluding them (figure 3(e)).

In the second method we first parameterize the polyline by arc length. We then define a new parametric curve $\mathbf{q}(t)$ based on the original parametric curve $\mathbf{p}(t)$ by adding a vector offset $\mathbf{v}(t)$ defined in the tangent-normal basis, i.e.:

$$\mathbf{q}(t) = \mathbf{p}(t) + v_x(t)\mathbf{p}'(t) + v_y(t)\mathbf{n}(t).$$

The use of vector offsets allows $\mathbf{q}(t)$ to double back on itself or form loops. Using the tangent-normal basis allows perturbation patterns to follow silhouette curvature. These offset vectors can either be precomputed and stored in lookup tables or computed on the fly. (We have implemented both techniques).

For precomputed offsets, we use a file format which specifies vector offsets. This format also incorporates "break" tags which signal the renderer to leave selected adjacent vertices unconnected in $\mathbf{q}(t)$, allowing strokes to incorporate disconnected shapes, such as circles, dashes, or letters. Variations on a small number of fundamental stroke classes (sawtooth, parabolic undulations, noise) produce a wide variety of stroke styles: high frequency sawtooth curves produce a charcoal style; low-frequency parabolic curves produce a wandering, lazy style; high-frequency, low-magnitude noise applied along the stroke normal and tangent directions produces a jittery hand-drawn style; low-frequency, high-magnitude offsets along the stroke tangent produces a jerky, rough-sketched look.

An alternative method for computing offsets is to use a spatially-coherent noise function indexed by screen-space location. We use a Perlin noise function [14] to define displacements along visible lines. [5]

The third method builds a texture-mapped mesh using the polyline as a reference spine. Each texture map represents a single brushstroke. We repeat the texture along the reference spine, approximately preserving its original aspect ratio. In order to generate the mesh, we walk along the spine adding a perpendicular crossbar at each vertex in the polyline and at each seam between repeating brushstrokes. Additionally, the width of the stroke can be made to vary with lighting computed at the polyline vertices, becoming thicker in darker areas and thinner in lighter areas. Our simple implementation does not handle self-intersections of the texture map mesh due to areas of high curvature.

Lastly we demonstrate a technique for generating curved shading strokes in order to produce a richer artistic effect and to better convey 3D information. (See figure 3(d)). Here, the principle of "economy of line" supports both the esthetic goals and that of maintaining interactive frame rates. We use an extension of the hidden line algorithm which allows us to derive visibility information across surface regions. This method was described by Hornung [9].

We place shading strokes (or *particles*) in world space (on the surface) rather than define them in screen space. This is the approach used by Meier [13] in her "painterly rendering" system. One advantage of this approach is that it maintains frame-to-frame coherence. We make the simplifying assumption that lighting comes from a point source located at the camera position. This greatly simplifies the task of computing stroke placement and density to achieve a target tone. An even distribution of strokes on the surface produces higher apparent densities in regions slanting away from the light – which is exactly where we want a darker tone. Our initial implementation assigns one stroke particle to the center of each triangle, which assumes a sufficiently even triangulation. Strokes are not drawn when occluded or when the computed gray value (using a lambertian shading model) falls below a threshhold.

Stroke directions are defined by the cross product of local surface normal and the ray from the camera to the stroke location, so that strokes line up with silhouette lines. Strokes have a preset world-space length; those with sufficiently large screen-space length are drawn as polylines. The direction of each segment of the polyline is computed as above, with local surface normal taken as a blend of normals at the vertices of the triangle at which the stroke is centered. Finally, we render the strokes using any of the artistic rendering methods described above.

6 Performance

We treat our models as subdivision surfaces, which allows us to refine a given mesh so that it approximates a smooth surface with an arbitrary degree of accuracy. (See [8] for a description of the type of subdivision surfaces we use). The following tables list performance statistics for our renderer operating on models which have been subdivided to the indicated number of polygons. Our test machine is a 200 MHz Sun Ultra ™ 2 Model 2200 with Creator 3D graphics. [6] Our method performs particularly well on smooth meshes, since these have fewer cusps and intersecting silhouette edges than irregular or bumpy surfaces.

In contrast, Winkenbach's [21] pen-and-ink rendering system produces decidedly finer images, but takes several minutes per frame to do so. (Over half that time is spent on visibility determination).

---

[5] We thank Paul Haeberli for this rendering method and the source code for implementing it.

[6] We use the graphics capabilities for rendering lines only.

Model	Triangles	Frames/sec	Triangles/sec
Two torii	65,536	30.58	2,004,091
Mechanical part	64,512	14.69	947,681
Venus	90,752	17.83	1,618,108

Table 1 Performance of basic visible-line renderer. Times were measured on a 200 MHz Ultrasparc.

Model	Triangles	Frames/sec	Slowdown
Two torii	65,536	5.27	5.8
Mechanical part	64,512	4.30	3.4
Venus	90,752	3.47	5.1

Table 2 Performance of basic line renderer when checking all edges each frame – the slowdown is in comparison with the same models listed in table 1.

Model	Triangles	Frames/sec	Triangles/sec
Blobby teddy bear	7,776	6.37	49,588
Venus	5,672	9.2	52,195

Table 3 Performance of shaded line renderer. Models are those shown in the accompanying video.

7 Future Work

We envision several avenues for future work. Our handling of shading strokes is restrictive and could be generalized to support arbitrary lighting conditions and to better control the density of strokes in screen space to match a target gray value. The shaded stroke renderings would be further enhanced by the addition of cast shadows, which our visibility algorithm can easily be extended to find. (The technique for computing shadow regions is straightforward, and was used in [21]).

More generally, we feel that our exploration of rendering styles can be developed much further. The rendering styles we have demonstrated in this paper take a simple, automated approach in which renderings are produced without regard to the content of the 3D scene, or to the intent of its designer. A rich, unexplored area for future research in NPR is the use of additional information in model definitions which can be used to produce nonphotorealistic renderings which reflect information about a model beyond basic geometric attributes, or which target particular esthetic effects.

8 Acknowledgments

We thank Mark Oribello and Seung Hong for help with images and video, Christine Waggoner for help with modelling, Loring Holden for lending Dan a shell, and Paul Haeberli for the idea and source code for displacing lines with Perlin noise. Also thanks to our sponsors: NSF Graphics and Visualization Center, Alias/Wavefront, Autodesk, Microsoft, Mitsubishi, NASA, Sun Microsystems, and TACO.

References

[1] A. Appel. The notion of quantitative invisibility and the machine rendering of solids. In *Proceedings of ACM National Conference*, pp. 387–393, 1967.

[2] J. Blinn. *Jim Blinn's Corner*, chapter 10, pp. 91–102. Morgan Kaufmann, 1996.

[3] D. Dooley and M. Cohen. Automatic illustration of 3d geometric models: Lines. In *Proceedings of the 1990 Symposium on Interactive 3D Graphics*, pp. 77–82, March 1990.

[4] G. Elber and E. Cohen. Hidden curve removal for free form surfaces. In *Proceedings of SIGGRAPH '90*, pp. 95–104, August 1990.

[5] J. Foley, A. van Dam, S. Feiner, and J. F. Hughes. *Computer Graphics: Principles and Practice*, chapter 15, pp. 666–667. Addison-Wesley, 1992.

[6] R. Galimberti and U. Montanari. An algorithm for hidden line elimination. *Communications of the ACM*, 12(4):206–211, April 1969.

[7] P. Haeberli. Paint by numbers: Abstract image representations. In *Proceedings of SIGGRAPH '90*, pp. 207–214, August 1990.

[8] H. Hoppe, T. DeRose, T. Duchamp, M. Halstead, H. Jin, J. McDonald, J. Schweitzer, and W. Stuetzle. Piecewise smooth surface reconstruction. *Proceedings of SIGGRAPH '94*, pp. 295–302, July 1994.

[9] C. Hornung. A method for solving the visibility problem. *IEEE Computer Graphics and Applications*, pp. 26–33, 1984.

[10] J. Lansdown and S. Schofield. Expressive rendering: A review of nonphotorealistic techniques. *IEEE Computer Graphics and Applications*, 15(3):29–37, May 1995.

[11] W. Leister. Computer generated copper plates. *Computer Graphics Forum*, 13(1):69–77, 1994.

[12] P. Loutrel. A solution to the hidden-line problem for computer-drawn polyhedra. *IEEE Transactions on Computers*, C-19(3):205–213, March 1970.

[13] B. Meier. Painterly rendering for animation. In *Proceedings of SIGGRAPH '96*, pp. 477–484, August 1996.

[14] K. Perlin. An image synthesizer. In *Proceedings of SIGGRAPH '85*, pp. 287–296, July 1985.

[15] F. P. Preparata and M. I. Shamos. *Computational Geometry: An Introduction*, chapter 7. Springer-Verlag, 1985.

[16] T. Saito and T. Takahashi. Comprehensible rendering of 3d shapes. In *Proceedings of SIGGRAPH '90*, pp. 197–206, aug 1990.

[17] T. Strothotte, B. Preim, A. Raab, J. Schuman, and D. Forsey. How to render frames and influence people. *Computer Graphics Forum*, 13(3):455–466, September 1994.

[18] I. Sutherland, R. Sproull, and R. Schumacker. A characterization of ten hidden-surface algorithms. *Computing Surveys*, 6(1):1–55, March 1974.

[19] L. R. Williams. Topological reconstruction of a smooth manifold-solid from its occluding contour. Technical Report 94-04, University of Massachusetts, Amherst, MA, 1994.

[20] G. Winkenbach and D. Salesin. Computer-generated pen-and-ink illustration. In *Proceedings of SIGGRAPH '94*, pp. 91–100, July 1994.

[21] G. Winkenbach and D. Salesin. Rendering parametric surfaces in pen and ink. In *Proceedings of SIGGRAPH '96*, pp. 469–476, August 1996.

[22] R. Zeleznik, K. Herndon, and J. F. Hughes. Sketch: An interface for sketching 3d scenes. In *Proceedings of SIGGRAPH '96*, pp. 163–170, August 1996.

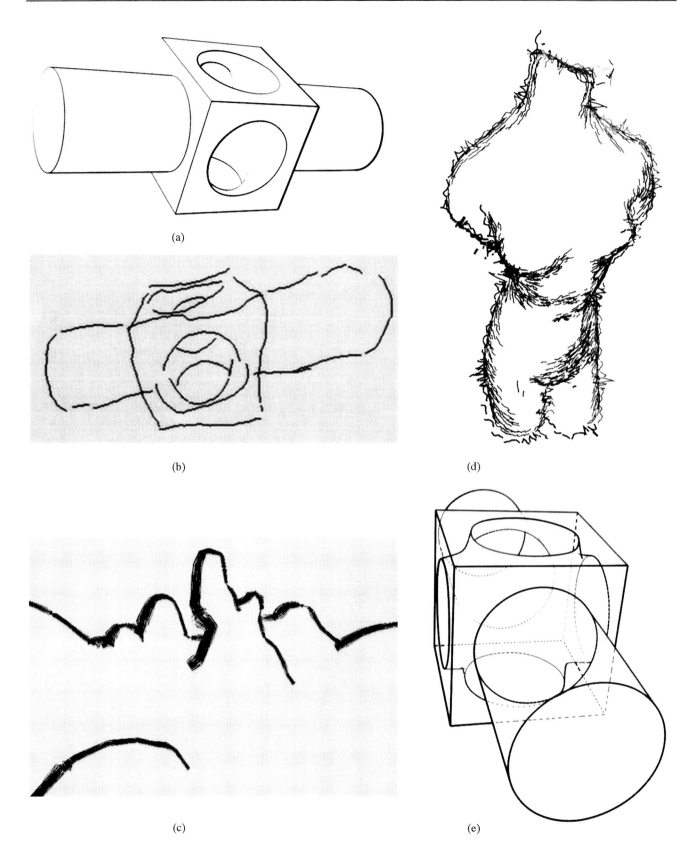

Figure 3 (a) A mechanical part (model courtesy of the University of Washington). (b) Mechanical part rendered with *sketchy lines*. (c) A charcoal-like rendering of terrain with texture-mapped strokes. (d) Human figure with expressive outline and shading strokes. (e) Mechanical part with hidden lines in varied styles.

Computer-Generated Watercolor

Cassidy J. Curtis   Sean E. Anderson*   Joshua E. Seims   Kurt W. Fleischer†   David H. Salesin

University of Washington   *Stanford University   †Pixar Animation Studios

Abstract

This paper describes the various artistic effects of watercolor and shows how they can be simulated automatically. Our watercolor model is based on an ordered set of translucent glazes, which are created independently using a shallow-water fluid simulation. We use a Kubelka-Munk compositing model for simulating the optical effect of the superimposed glazes. We demonstrate how computer-generated watercolor can be used in three different applications: as part of an interactive watercolor paint system, as a method for automatic image "watercolorization," and as a mechanism for non-photorealistic rendering of three-dimensional scenes.

CR Categories: I.3.3 [Computer Graphics]: Picture/Image Generation; I.6.3 [Simulation and Modeling]: Applications.

Additional Keywords: Fluid simulation, glazing, illustration, Kubelka-Munk, non-photorealistic rendering, optical compositing, painting, pigments, watercolor.

1 Introduction

Watercolor is like no other medium. It exhibits beautiful textures and patterns that reveal the motion of water across paper, much as the shape of a valley suggests the flow of streams. Its vibrant colors and spontaneous shapes give it a distinctive charm. And it can be applied in delicate layers to achieve subtle variations in color, giving even the most mundane subject a transparent, luminous quality.

In this paper, we characterize the most important effects of watercolor and show how they can be simulated automatically. We then demonstrate how computer-generated watercolor can be used in three different applications: as part of an interactive watercolor paint system (Figure 7), as a method for automatic image "watercolorization" (Figure 10), and as a mechanism for non-photorealistic rendering of three-dimensional scenes (Figures 14 and 13).

The watercolor simulator we describe is empirically-based: while it does incorporate some physically-based models, it is by no means a strict physical simulation. Rather, our emphasis in this work has been to re-create, synthetically, the most salient artistic features of watercolor in a way that is both predictable and controllable.

1.1 Related work

This paper follows in a long line of important work on simulating artists' traditional media and tools. Most directly related is Small's groundbreaking work on simulating watercolor on a Connection Machine [34]. Like Small, we use a cellular automaton to simulate fluid flow and pigment dispersion. However, in order to achieve

even more realistic watercolor effects, we employ a more sophisticated paper model, a more complex shallow water simulation, and a more faithful rendering and optical compositing of pigmented layers based on the Kubelka-Munk model. The combination of these improvements enables our system to create many additional watercolor effects such as edge-darkening, granulation, backruns, separation of pigments, and glazing, as described in Section 2. These effects produce a look that is closer to that of real watercolors, and captures better the feeling of transparency and luminosity that is characteristic of the medium.

In the commercial realm, certain watercolor effects are provided by products such as Fractal Design Painter, although this product does not appear to give as realistic watercolor results as the simulation we describe. In other related work, Guo and Kunii have explored the effects of "Sumie" painting [13], and Guo has continued to apply that work to calligraphy [12]. Their model of ink diffusion through paper resembles, to some extent, both Small's and our own water simulation techniques.

Other research work on modeling thick, shiny paint [2] and the effects of bristle brushes on painting and calligraphy [30, 36] also bears relation to the work described here, in providing a plausible simulation of traditional artists' tools.[1] The work described here also continues in a growing line of non-photorealistic rendering research [5, 6, 9, 16, 22, 23, 26, 33, 39, 40], and it builds on previous work on animating the fluid dynamics of water [1, 10, 19] and the effects of water flow on the appearance of surfaces [7, 8, 28].

1.2 Overview

The next section describes the physical nature of the watercolor medium, and then goes on to survey some of its most important characteristics from an artist's standpoint. Section 3 discusses how these key characteristics can be created synthetically. Section 4 describes our physical simulation of the dispersion of water and pigment in detail. Section 5 discusses how the resulting distributions of pigment are rendered. Section 6 presents three different applications in which we have used our watercolor simulation and provides examples of the results produced. Finally, Section 7 discusses some ideas for future research.

2 Properties of watercolor

For centuries, ground pigments have been combined with water-soluble binding materials and used in painting. The earliest uses of watercolor were as thin colored washes painstakingly applied to detailed pen-and-ink or pencil illustrations. The modern tradition of watercolor, however, dates back to the latter half of the eighteenth century, when artists such as J. M. W. Turner (1775–1851), John Constable (1776–1837), and David Cox (1783–1859) began to experiment with new techniques such as wiping and scratching out, and with the immediacy and spontaneity of the medium [35].

To simulate watercolor effectively, it is important to study not only the physical properties of the medium, but also the characteristic phenomena that make watercolor so popular to artists. A simulation is successful only if it can achieve many of the same effects. In the

---

[1]This approach is essentially the same as the "minimal simulation" approach taken by Cockshott et al. [2], whose "wet & sticky" paint model is designed to behave like the real medium as far as the artist can tell, without necessarily having a real physical basis.

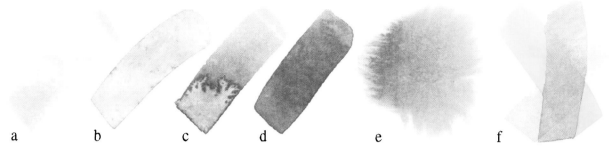

Figure 1 Real watercolor effects: drybrush (a), edge darkening (b), backruns (c), granulation (d), flow effects (e), and glazing (f).

rest of this section, we therefore discuss the physical nature of watercolor, and then survey some of the most important characteristics of watercolor from an artist's standpoint.

2.1 Watercolor materials

Watercolor images are created by the application of watercolor paint to paper. *Watercolor paint* (also called, simply, *watercolor*) is a suspension of pigment particles in a solution of water, binder, and surfactant [17, 25, 35]. The ingredients of watercolor are described in more detail below.

Watercolor paper is typically not made from wood pulp, but instead from linen or cotton rags pounded into small fibers. The paper itself is mostly air, laced with a microscopic web of these tangled fibers. Such a substance is obviously extremely absorbent to liquids, and so the paper is impregnated with *sizing* so that liquid paints may be used on it without immediately soaking in and diffusing. Sizing is usually made of cellulose. It forms a barrier that slows the rate of water absorption and diffusion. For most watercolor papers, sizing is applied sparingly and just coats the fibers and fills some of the pores, leaving the paper surface still rough.

A *pigment* is a solid material in the form of small, separate particles. Watercolor pigments are typically ground in a milling process into a powder made of grains ranging from about 0.05 to 0.5 microns. Pigments can penetrate into the paper, but once in the paper they tend not to migrate far. Pigments vary in *density*, with lighter pigments tending to stay suspended in water longer than heavier ones, and thus spreading further across paper. *Staining power*, an estimate of the pigment's tendency to adhere to or coat paper fibers, also varies between pigments. Certain pigments exhibit *granulation*, in which particles settle into the hollows of rough paper. Others exhibit *flocculation*, in which particles are drawn together into clumps usually by electrical effects. (Since flocculation is similar in appearance to granulation, we discuss the modeling of granulation only in this paper.)

The two remaining ingredients, *binder* and *surfactant*, both play important roles. The binder enables the pigment to adhere to the paper (known as "adsorption of the pigment by the paper"). The surfactant allows water to soak into sized paper. A proper proportion of pigment, binder, and surfactant is necessary in order for the paint to exhibit the qualities desired by artists. (However, as these proportions are controlled by the paint manufacturer and not the artist, we have not made them part of our model.)

The final appearance of watercolor derives from the interaction between the movements of various pigments in a flowing medium, the adsorption of these pigments by the paper, the absorption of water into the paper, and the eventual evaporation of the water medium. While these interactions are quite complex in nature, they can be used by a skilled artist to achieve a wide variety of effects, as described in the next section.

2.2 Watercolor effects

Watercolor can be used in many different ways. To begin with, there are two basic brushing techniques. In *wet-in-wet* painting, a brush loaded with watercolor paint is applied to paper that is already saturated with water, allowing the paint to spread freely. When the brush is applied to dry paper, it is known as *wet-on-dry* painting. These techniques give rise to a number of standard effects that can be reliably employed by the watercolor expert, including:

- *Dry-brush* effects (Figure 1a): A brush that is almost dry, applied at the proper grazing angle, will apply paint only to the raised areas of the rough paper, leaving a stroke with irregular gaps and ragged edges.

- *Edge darkening* (Figure 1b): In a wet-on-dry brushtroke, the sizing in the paper, coupled with the surface tension of water, does not allow the brushstroke to spread. Instead, in a gradual process, the pigment migrates from the interior of the painted region towards its edges as the paint begins to dry, leaving a dark deposit at the edge. This key effect is one that watercolor artists rely upon and that paint manufacturers take pains to ensure in their watercolor paint formulations [17].

- Intentional *backruns* (Figure 1c): When a puddle of water spreads back into a damp region of paint, as often happens when a wash dries unevenly, the water tends to push pigment along as it spreads, resulting in complex, branching shapes with severely darkened edges.

- *Granulation* and *separation* of pigments (Figure 1d): Granulation of pigments yields a kind of grainy texture that emphasizes the peaks and valleys in the paper. Granulation varies from pigment to pigment, and is strongest when the paper is very wet. Separation refers to a splitting of colors that occurs when denser pigments settle earlier than lighter ones.

- *Flow patterns* (Figure 1e): In wet-in-wet painting, the wet surface allows the brushstrokes to spread freely, resulting in soft, feathery shapes with delicate striations that follow the direction of water flow.

One other very important technique in watercolor is the process of *color glazing* (Figure 1f). Glazing is the process of adding very thin, pale layers, or *washes*, of watercolor, one over another, to achieve a very clear and even effect. Each layer of watercolor is added after the previous layer has dried. More expensive watercolor paints are specially formulated to have a low *resolubility*, which not only allows thin uniform washes to be overlaid, but in fact allows any type of brushing technique to be employed over a dried wash (including dry-brush and wet-on-wet) without disturbing the underlying layers.

Glazing is different from ordinary painting in that the different pigments are not mixed physically, but optically—in their superposition on the paper. Glazes yield a pleasing effect that is often described as "luminous," or as "glowing from within" [4, 32]. We suspect that this subjective impression arises from the edge-darkening effect. The impression is intensified with multiple super-

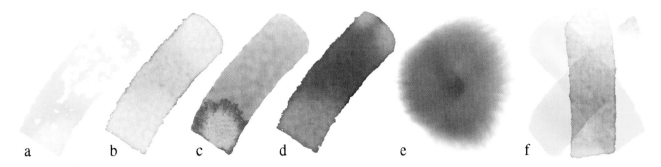

Figure 2 Simulated watercolor effects created using our system.

imposed wet-on-dry washes.

Figure 1 shows scanned-in images of real watercolors. Figure 2 illustrates similar effects obtained from our watercolor simulations.

3   Computer-generated watercolor

Implementing all of these artistic effects automatically presents an interesting challenge, particularly given the paucity of available information on the physical processes involved.[2] In this section, we propose a basic model for the physical and optical behavior of watercolors. The details of this model are then elaborated in the next two sections.

We represent a complete painting as an ordered set of washes over a sheet of rough paper. Each wash may contain various pigments in varying quantities over different parts of the image. We store these quantities in a data structure called a "glaze."

Each glaze is created independently by running a fluid simulation that computes the flow of paint across the paper. The simulation takes, as input, parameters that control the physical properties of the individual pigments, the paper, and the watercolor medium. In addition, the simulation makes use of *wet-area masks*, which represent the areas of paper that have been touched by water. These masks control where water is allowed to flow by limiting the fluid flow computation. The next section describes this fluid simulation in detail.

Once the glazes are computed, they are optically composited using the Kubelka-Munk color model to provide the final visual effect, as described in Section 5.

4   The fluid simulation

In our system, each individual wash is simulated using a three-layer model (Figure 3). From top to bottom, these three layers include:

- The *shallow-water layer* — where water and pigment flow above the surface of the paper.

- The *pigment-deposition layer* — where pigment is deposited onto ("adsorbed by") and lifted ("desorbed") from the paper.

- The *capillary layer* — where water that is absorbed into the paper is diffused by capillary action. (This layer is only used when simulating the backrun effect.)

---

[2]Indeed, As Mayer points out in his 1991 handbook [25, p. 13]: "The study of artists' materials and techniques is hampered by the lack of systematic data of an authentic nature based on modern scientific laboratory investigations with which to supplement our present knowledge—the accumulation of the practical experience of past centuries, necessarily quite full of principles which rest on the shaky foundations of conjecture and consensus. . . . We await the day when a sustained activity, directed from the viewpoint of the artists, will supply us with more of the benefits of modern science and technology."

In the shallow-water layer (Figure 3a), water flows across the surface in a way that is bounded by the wet-area mask. As the water flows, it lifts pigment from the paper, carries it along, and redeposits it on the paper. The quantities involved in this simulation are:

- The wet-area mask M, which is 1 if the paper is wet, and 0 otherwise.

- The velocity u, v of the water in the x and y directions.

- The pressure p of the water.

- The concentration g^k of each pigment k in the water.

- The slope ∇h of the rough paper surface, defined as the gradient of the paper's height h.

- The physical properties of the watercolor medium, including its *viscosity* μ and *viscous drag* κ. (In all of our examples, we set $\mu = 0.1$ and $\kappa = 0.01$.)

Each pigment k is transferred between the shallow-water layer and the pigment-deposition layer by adsorption and desorption. While pigment in the shallow-water layer is denoted by g^k, we will use d^k for any deposited pigment. The physical properties of the individual pigments, including their density ρ, staining power ω, and granularity γ—all affect the rates of adsorption and desorption by the paper. (The values of these parameters for our examples are shown in the caption for Figure 5.)

The function of the capillary layer is to allow for expansion of the wet-area mask due to capillary flow of water through the pores of the paper. The relevant quantities in this layer are:

- The *water saturation s* of the paper, defined as the fraction of a given volume of space occupied by water.

- The *fluid-holding capacity c* of the paper, which is the fraction of volume not occupied by paper fibers.

All of the above quantities are discretized over a two-dimensional grid representing the plane of the paper.

We will refer to the value of each quantity, say p, at a particular cell using subscripts, such as $p_{i,j}$. We will use bold-italics (such as p) to

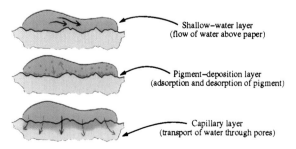

Figure 3 The three-layer fluid model for a watercolor wash.

Figure 4 Example paper textures.

denote the entire array of discretized values.

4.1 Paper generation

In real watercolor, the structure of the paper affects fluid flow, backruns, and granulation. The mechanics underlying these effects may be quite complex, and may depend on the precise connections among the individual fibers, as well as the exact slopes of the fine-scale peaks and valleys of the paper. We use a much simpler model in our system. Paper texture is modeled as a height field and a fluid capacity field. The height field h is generated using one of a selection of pseudo-random processes [29, 41], and scaled so that $0 < h < 1$. Some examples of our synthetic paper textures can be seen in Figure 4. The slope of the height field is used to modify the fluid velocity u, v in the dynamics simulation. In addition, the fluid capacity c is computed from the height field h, as $c = h * (c_{max} - c_{min}) + c_{min}$.

4.2 Main loop

The main loop of our simulation takes as input the initial wet-area mask M; the initial velocity of the water u, v; the initial water pressure p; the initial pigment concentrations g^k; and the initial water saturation of the paper s. The main loop iterates over a specified number of time steps, moving water and pigment in the shallow-water layer, transferring pigment between the shallow-water and pigment-deposition layers, and simulating capillary flow:

```
proc MainLoop(M, u, v, p, g¹, ..., gⁿ, d¹, ..., dⁿ, s):
    for each time step do:
        MoveWater(M, u, v, p)
        MovePigment(M, u, v, g¹, ..., gⁿ)
        TransferPigment(g¹, ..., gⁿ, d¹, ..., dⁿ)
        SimulateCapillaryFlow(M, s)
    end for
end proc
```

4.3 Moving water in the shallow water layer

For realism, the behavior of the water should satisfy the following conditions:

1. The flow must be constrained so that water remains within the wet-area mask.

2. A surplus of water in one area should cause flow outward from that area into nearby regions.

3. The flow must be damped to minimize oscillating waves.

4. The flow must be perturbed by the texture of the paper to cause streaks parallel to flow direction.

5. Local changes should have global effects. For example, adding water in a local area should affect the entire simulation.

6. There should be outward flow of the fluid toward the edges to produce the edge-darkening effect.

The first two conditions are satisfied directly by the basic shallow-water equations using appropriate boundary conditions [24, 38]:

$$\frac{\partial u}{\partial t} = -\left(\frac{\partial u^2}{\partial x^2} + \frac{\partial uv}{\partial y^2}\right) + \mu \nabla^2 u - \frac{\partial p}{\partial x} \quad (1)$$

$$\frac{\partial v}{\partial t} = -\left(\frac{\partial v^2}{\partial y^2} + \frac{\partial uv}{\partial x^2}\right) + \mu \nabla^2 v - \frac{\partial p}{\partial y} \quad (2)$$

These equations are implemented in the *UpdateVelocities*() subroutine. Conditions 3 and 4 are met by adding terms to the fluid flow simulation involving the viscous drag κ and the paper slope ∇h, as shown in the *UpdateVelocities*() pseudocode. Conditions 5 and 6 are accomplished by two additional subroutines, *RelaxDivergence*() and *FlowOutward*(). All three of these routines are used to implement the movement of water in the shallow-water layer:

```
proc MoveWater(M, u, v, p):
    UpdateVelocities(M, u, v, p)
    RelaxDivergence(M, u, v, p)
    FlowOutward(M, p)
end proc
```

4.3.1 Updating the water velocities

To update the water velocities, we discretize the equations (1) and (2) spatially on a staggered grid (as in Foster [10]). An effect of this discretization is that our solution is resolution-dependent. Generalizing to a resolution-independent model is an important goal for future work.

The staggered grid representation stores velocity values at grid cell boundaries and all other values (pressure, pigment concentrations, etc.) at grid cell centers. We use the standard notation for staggered grids, referring to quantities on cell boundaries as having "fractional" indices. For example, the velocity u at the boundary between the grid cells centered at (i, j) and $(i + 1, j)$ is called $u_{i+.5, j}$. Furthermore, we will use the shorthand notation $(uv)_{i,j}$ to denote $u_{i,j} v_{i,j}$. We will also use indices to denote quantities that are not represented directly, but computed implicitly from their two immediate neighbors instead. For instance,

$$p_{i+.5, j} \equiv (p_{i,j} + p_{i+1,j}) / 2$$
$$u_{i,j} \equiv (u_{i-.5,j} + u_{i+.5,j}) / 2$$

In the pseudocode below, we discretize equations (1) and (2) in time and solve forward using Euler's Method with an adaptive step size. The step size Δt is set to ensure that velocities do not exceed one pixel per time step:

```
proc UpdateVelocities(M, u, v, p):
    (u, v) ← (u, v) − ∇h
    Δt ← 1/⌈maxᵢ,ⱼ {|u|, |v|}⌉
    for t ← 0 to 1 by Δt do
        for all cells (i, j) do
            A ← u²ᵢ,ⱼ − u²ᵢ₊₁,ⱼ + (uv)ᵢ₊.₅,ⱼ₋.₅ − (uv)ᵢ₊.₅,ⱼ₊.₅
            B ← (uᵢ₊₁.₅,ⱼ + uᵢ₋.₅,ⱼ + uᵢ₊.₅,ⱼ₊₁ + uᵢ₊.₅,ⱼ₋₁ − 4uᵢ₊.₅,ⱼ)
            u'ᵢ₊.₅,ⱼ ← uᵢ₊.₅,ⱼ + Δt (A − μB + pᵢ,ⱼ − pᵢ₊₁,ⱼ − κuᵢ₊.₅,ⱼ)
            A ← v²ᵢ,ⱼ − v²ᵢ,ⱼ₊₁ + (uv)ᵢ₋.₅,ⱼ₊.₅ − (uv)ᵢ₊.₅,ⱼ₊.₅
            B ← (vᵢ₊₁,ⱼ₊.₅ + vᵢ₋₁,ⱼ₊.₅ + vᵢ,ⱼ₊₁.₅ + vᵢ,ⱼ₋.₅ − 4vᵢ,ⱼ₊.₅)
            v'ᵢ,ⱼ₊.₅ ← vᵢ,ⱼ₊.₅ + Δt (A − μB + pᵢ,ⱼ − pᵢ,ⱼ₊₁ − κvᵢ,ⱼ₊.₅)
        end for
        (u, v) ← (u', v')
        EnforceBoundaryConditions(M, u, v)
    end for
end proc
```

The *EnforceBoundaryConditions*() procedure simply sets the velocity at the boundary of any pixel not in the wet-area mask to zero.

4.3.2 Relaxation

Following Foster et al. [10], we also relax the divergence of the velocity field $\partial u / \partial x + \partial v / \partial y$ after each time step until it is less than some tolerance τ by redistributing the fluid into neighboring grid cells. In our implementation of the following pseudocode, we have used $N = 50$, $\tau = 0.01$ and $\xi = 0.1$:

proc $RelaxDivergence(\boldsymbol{u}, \boldsymbol{v}, \boldsymbol{p})$:

  $t \leftarrow 0$
  repeat
    $(\boldsymbol{u}', \boldsymbol{v}') \leftarrow (\boldsymbol{u}, \boldsymbol{v})$
    $\delta_{max} \leftarrow 0$
    for all cells (i, j) **do**
      $\delta \leftarrow \xi(u_{i+1/2, j} - u_{i-1/2, j} + v_{i, j+1/2} - v_{i, j-1/2})$
      $p_{i,j} \leftarrow p_{i,j} + \delta$
      $u'_{i+.5, j} \leftarrow u'_{i+.5, j} + \delta$
      $u'_{i-.5, j} \leftarrow u'_{i-.5, j} - \delta$
      $v'_{i, j+.5} \leftarrow v'_{i, j+.5} + \delta$
      $v'_{i, j-.5} \leftarrow v'_{i, j-.5} - \delta$
      $\delta_{max} \leftarrow \max(|\delta|, \delta_{max})$
    end for
    $(\boldsymbol{u}, \boldsymbol{v}) \leftarrow (\boldsymbol{u}', \boldsymbol{v}')$
    $t \leftarrow t + 1$
  until $\delta_{max} \leq \tau$ **or** $t \geq N$
end proc

4.3.3 Edge darkening

In a wet-on-dry brushstroke, pigment tends to migrate from the interior towards the edges over time. This phenomenon occurs in any evaporating suspension in which the contact line of a drop is pinned in place by surface tension [3]. Because of this geometric constraint, liquid evaporating near the boundary must be replenished by liquid from the interior, resulting in outward flow. This flow carries pigment with it, leading to edge darkening as the water evaporates. In our model, we simulate this flow by decreasing the water pressure near the edges of the wet-area mask.

The $FlowOutward()$ routine removes at each time step an amount of water from each cell according to the cell's distance from the boundary of the wet-area mask, with more water removed from cells closer to the boundary. The distance to the boundary is approximated by first performing a Gaussian blur with a $K \times K$ kernel on the wet-area mask $\boldsymbol{M}$. Then an amount of water is removed from each cell according to the value of the resulting Gaussian-blurred image $\boldsymbol{M}'$:

$$\boldsymbol{p} \leftarrow \boldsymbol{p} - \eta(1 - \boldsymbol{M}')\boldsymbol{M} \tag{3}$$

In our examples, $K = 10$ and $0.01 \leq \eta \leq 0.05$.

An example of the edge-darkening effect is shown in Figure 2b.

4.4 Moving pigments

Pigments move within the shallow-water layer as specified by the velocity field $\boldsymbol{u}, \boldsymbol{v}$ computed for the water above. In this part of the simulation, we distribute pigment from each cell to its neighbors according to the rate of fluid movement out of the cell:

proc $MovePigment(\boldsymbol{M}, \boldsymbol{u}, \boldsymbol{v}, \boldsymbol{g}^1, \ldots, \boldsymbol{g}^n)$:

  $\Delta t \leftarrow 1/\lceil \max_{i,j}\{|\boldsymbol{u}|, |\boldsymbol{v}|\}\rceil$
  for each pigment k **do**
    for $t \leftarrow 0$ **to** 1 **by** Δt **do**
      $\boldsymbol{g}' \leftarrow \boldsymbol{g} \leftarrow \boldsymbol{g}^k$
      forall cells (i, j) **do**
        $g'_{i+1, j} \leftarrow g'_{i+1, j} + \max(0, u_{i+.5, j}\, g_{i,j})$
        $g'_{i-1, j} \leftarrow g'_{i-1, j} + \max(0, -u_{i-.5, j}\, g_{i,j})$
        $g'_{i, j+1} \leftarrow g'_{i, j+1} + \max(0, v_{i, j+.5}\, g_{i,j})$
        $g'_{i, j-1} \leftarrow g'_{i, j-1} + \max(0, -v_{i, j-.5}\, g_{i,j})$
        $g'_{i,j} \leftarrow g'_{i,j} - \max(0, u_{i+.5, j}\, g_{i,j}) + \max(0, -u_{i-.5, j}\, g_{i,j})$
          $+ \max(0, v_{i, j+.5}\, g_{i,j}) + \max(0, -v_{i, j-.5}\, g_{i,j})$
      end for
      $\boldsymbol{g}^k \leftarrow \boldsymbol{g}'$
    end for
  end for
end proc

4.5 Pigment adsorption and desorption

At each step of the simulation, pigment is also adsorbed by the pigment-deposition layer at a certain rate, and desorbed back into the fluid at another rate (in a process similar to the one described by Dorsey *et al.* [8] for weathering patterns due to fluid flow.) The *density* ρ^k and *staining power* ω^k are scalars that affect the rate at which each pigment k is adsorbed and desorbed by the paper. The *granulation* γ^k determines how much the paper height h affects adsorption and desorption.

proc $TransferPigment(\boldsymbol{g}^1, \ldots, \boldsymbol{g}^n, \boldsymbol{d}^1, \ldots, \boldsymbol{d}^n)$:

  for each pigment k **do**
    for all cells (i, j) **do**
      if $M_{i,j} = 1$ **then**
        $\delta_{down} \leftarrow g^k_{i,j}(1 - h_{i,j}\gamma^k)\rho^k$
        $\delta_{up} \leftarrow d^k_{i,j}(1 + (h_{i,j} - 1)\gamma^k)\rho^k/\omega^k$
        if $(d^k_{i,j} + \delta_{down}) > 1$
          then $\delta_{down} \leftarrow \max(0, 1 - d^k_{i,j})$
        if $(g^k_{i,j} + \delta_{up}) > 1$
          then $\delta_{up} \leftarrow \max(0, 1 - g^k_{i,j})$
        $d^k_{i,j} \leftarrow d^k_{i,j} + \delta_{down} - \delta_{up}$
        $g^k_{i,j} \leftarrow g^k_{i,j} + \delta_{up} - \delta_{down}$
      end if
    end for
  end for
end proc

4.6 Backruns: diffusing water through the capillary layer

Backruns occur only when a puddle of water spreads slowly into a region that is drying but still damp [37]. In a *damp* region, the only water present is within the pores of the paper. In this situation, flow is dominated by capillary effects, not by momentum as in the shallow water equations.

In the backrun simulation, water is absorbed from the shallow-water layer above at the absorption rate α, and diffuses through the capillary layer. Each cell transfers water to its four neighbors until they are saturated to capacity c. If any cell's saturation exceeds a threshold σ, then the wet-area mask is expanded to include that cell. In this way, capillary action within the paper can enable a puddle to spread. The variation in cell capacity from pixel to pixel results in an irregular branching pattern. Other parameters affecting this process are ϵ, the minimum saturation a pixel must have before it can diffuse to its neighbors, and δ, a saturation value below which a pixel will not receive diffusion.

proc $SimulateCapillaryFlow(s, M)$:

  forall cells (i, j) **do**
    if $(M_{i,j} > 0)$ **then**
      $s_{i,j} \leftarrow s_{i,j} + \max(0, \min(\alpha, c_{i,j} - s_{i,j}))$
  end for
  $s' \leftarrow s$
  for all cells (i, j) **do**
    for each cell $(k, \ell) \in neighbors(i, j)$ **do**
      if $s_{i,j} > \epsilon$ **and** $s_{i,j} > s_{k,\ell}$ **and** $s_{k,\ell} > \delta$ **then**
        $\Delta s \leftarrow \max(0, \min(s_{i,j} - s_{k,\ell}, c_{k,\ell} - s_{k,\ell})/4)$
        $s'_{i,j} \leftarrow s'_{i,j} - \Delta s$
        $s'_{k,\ell} \leftarrow s'_{k,\ell} + \Delta s$
      end if
    end for
  end for
  $s \leftarrow s'$
  for all cells (i, j) **do**
    if $s_{i,j} > \sigma$ **then**
      $M_{i,j} \leftarrow 1$
  end for
end proc

4.7 Drybrush effects

The drybrush effect occurs when the brush is applied at the proper angle and is dry enough to wet only the highest points on the paper surface. We model this effect by excluding from the wet-area mask any pixel whose height is less than a user-defined threshold. An example of simulated drybrush is shown in Figure 1a.

5 Rendering the pigmented layers

We use the Kubelka-Munk (KM) model [14, 20] to perform the optical compositing of glazing layers. (The same model was also used by Dorsey and Hanrahan to model the transmission of light through layers of copper patina [7].)

In our use of the KM model, each pigment is assigned a set of *absorption coefficients* K and *scattering coefficients* S. These coefficients are a function of wavelength, and control the fraction of energy absorbed and scattered back, respectively, per unit distance in the layer of pigment. In our implementation, we use three coefficients each for K and S, representing *RGB* components of each quantity.

5.1 Specifying the optical properties of pigments

In typical applications of KM theory, the K and S coefficients for a given colorant layer are determined experimentally, using spectral measurements from layers of known thicknesses. However, in our application we have found it to be much more convenient to allow a user to specify the K and S coefficients interactively, by choosing the desired appearance of a "unit thickness" of the pigment over both a white and a black background. Given these two user-selected *RGB* colors R_w and R_b, respectively, the K and S values can be computed by a simple inversion of the KM equations:

$$S = \frac{1}{b} \cdot \coth^{-1} \left(\frac{b^2 - (a - R_w)(a - 1)}{b(1 - R_w)} \right)$$
$$K = S(a - 1)$$

where

$$a = \frac{1}{2} \left(R_w + \frac{R_b - R_w + 1}{R_b} \right), \qquad b = \sqrt{a^2 - 1}$$

The above computations are applied to each color channel of S, K, R_w, and R_b independently. In order to avoid any divisions by zero, we require that $0 < R_b < R_w < 1$ for each color channel. This restriction is reasonable even for opaque pigments, since the user is specifying reflected colors through just a thin layer, which should still be at least partially transparent. While for most valid combinations of specified colors the computed K and S values fall in the legal range of 0 to 1, for certain very saturated input colors the absorption or scattering coefficients computed by this method may actually exceed the value of 1 in some color channels. Though such a large value of K or S is clearly not possible for any physical pigment, we have not noticed any ill effects in our simulation from allowing such "out-of-range" values. The situation is somewhat analogous to allowing an "alpha" opacity to lie outside the range 0 to 1, another non-physical effect that is sometimes useful [15].

We have found this method of specifying pigments to be quite adequate for creating a wide range of realistic paints (see Figure 5). In addition, the method is much easier than taking the kind of extremely careful measurements that would otherwise be required. By specifying the colors over black and white, the user can easily create different types of pigments. As examples:

- *Opaque paints*, such as Indian Red, exhibit a similar color on both white and black. Such paints have high scattering in the same wavelengths as their color, and high absorption in complementary wavelengths.

- *Transparent paints*, such as Quinacridone Rose, appear colored on white, and nearly black on black. Such paints have low scattering in all wavelengths, and high absorption in wavelengths complementary to their color.

- *Interference paints*, such as Interference Lilac, appear white (or transparent) on white, and colored on black. Such paints have high scattering in the same wavelengths as their color, and low absorption in all wavelengths. Such pigments actually get their color from interference effects involving the phase of light waves, which have been modeled accurately by Gondek *et al.* [11]. While our simple model does not simulate phase effects, it nevertheless manages to produce colors similar in appearance to the interference paints used in watercolor painting.

Our method also makes it easy to simulate real paints that exhibit slightly different hues over black than white, such as Hansa yellow. Figure 5(i) shows a simulated swatch of this pigment over both black and white backgrounds.

5.2 Optical compositing of layers

Given scattering and absorption coefficients S and K for a pigmented layer of given thickness x, the KM model allows us to compute reflectance R and transmittance T through the layer [20]:

$$\begin{aligned} R &= \sinh bSx/c \\ T &= b/c \end{aligned} \qquad \text{where} \qquad c = a \sinh bSx + b \cosh bSx$$

We can then use Kubelka's optical compositing equations [20, 21] to determine the overall reflectance R and transmittance T of two abutting layers with reflectances R_1, R_2 and T_1, T_2, respectively:

$$R = R_1 + \frac{T_1^2 R_2}{1 - R_1 R_2} \qquad\qquad T = \frac{T_1 T_2}{1 - R_1 R_2}$$

This computation is repeated for each additional glaze. The overall reflectance R is then used to render the pixel.

For individual layers containing more than one pigment of thicknesses $x^1, \ldots, x^n$, the S and K coefficients of each pigment k are weighted in proportion to that pigment's relative thickness x^k. The overall thickness of the layer x is taken to be the sum of the thicknesses of the individual pigments.

In our fluid simulation (see Section 4), we use g^k to denote the concentration of pigment in the shallow-water layer, and d^k for the concentration of pigment deposited on the paper. These values are summed to compute the thickness parameter x^k used by the Kubelka-Munk equations.

5.3 Pigment examples

Figure 5 shows the palette of colors used in the examples, with each pigment shown as a swatch painted over a black stripe. The colors we chose for these pigments were based on fairly casual observations of the colors of the actual paints over black and white backgrounds. The K and S coefficients were then derived from these colors by the procedure outlined in Section 5.1. As the thickness of a layer of pigment increases, its color traces a complex curve through color space. For example, Figure 6 shows the range of colors obtainable by glazing "Hansa Yellow" over both white and black backgrounds. Note the difference in hue between the two curves, and the change in both hue and saturation along each curve. This complexity is one of the qualities that gives these pigments their rich appearance.

5.4 Discussion of Kubelka-Munk model

The KM model appears to give very plausible and intuitive results in all the cases we have tried. On the one hand, these results are not very surprising, considering that the KM model was specifically designed for situations akin to watercolor in which there are multiple pigmented layers that scatter and absorb light. It is, however,

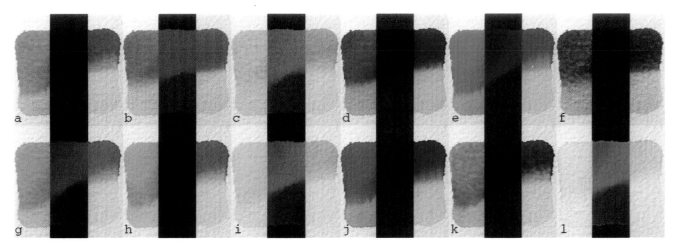

Figure 5 Various synthetic pigments. The swatches were all created using identical initial conditions, with thicker pigment in the top half, and extra water in the upper left and lower right corners. The only changes from swatch to swatch are the pigments' optical and physical parameters, shown at right. The swatches are painted over a black stripe to distinguish the more opaque pigments such as "Indian Red" (b) from the more transparent ones such as "Brilliant Orange" (h).

	PIGMENT	K_r	K_g	K_b	S_r	S_g	S_b	ρ	ω	γ
a	"Quinacridone Rose"	0.22	1.47	0.57	0.05	0.003	0.03	0.02	5.5	0.81
b	"Indian Red"	0.46	1.07	1.50	1.28	0.38	0.21	0.05	7.0	0.40
c	"Cadmium Yellow"	0.10	0.36	3.45	0.97	0.65	0.007	0.05	3.4	0.81
d	"Hookers Green"	1.62	0.61	1.64	0.01	0.012	0.003	0.09	1.0	0.41
e	"Cerulean Blue"	1.52	0.32	0.25	0.06	0.26	0.40	0.01	1.0	0.31
f	"Burnt Umber"	0.74	1.54	2.10	0.09	0.09	0.004	0.09	9.3	0.90
g	"Cadmium Red"	0.14	1.08	1.68	0.77	0.015	0.018	0.02	1.0	0.63
h	"Brilliant Orange"	0.13	0.81	3.45	0.005	0.009	0.007	0.01	1.0	0.14
i	"Hansa Yellow"	0.06	0.21	1.78	0.50	0.88	0.009	0.06	1.0	0.08
j	"Phthalo Green"	1.55	0.47	0.63	0.01	0.05	0.035	0.02	1.0	0.12
k	"French Ultramarine"	0.86	0.86	0.06	0.005	0.005	0.09	0.01	3.1	0.91
l	"Interference Lilac"	0.08	0.11	0.07	1.25	0.42	1.43	0.06	1.0	0.08

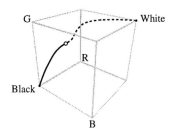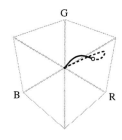

Figure 6 The range of colors obtainable by compositing varying thicknesses of "Hansa Yellow" over black (solid curve) and over white (dashed curve). The point where the two curves meet is R_∞, the color of an infinitely thick layer. At left, the RGB cube is viewed in perspective; at right, we look directly down the luminance axis, showing the difference in hue between the two curves.

worth noting that there are a number of fine points in the basic KM assumptions that are satisfied, at best, only partially in our situation:

1. *All colorant layers are immersed in mediums of the same refractive index.* This assumption is in fact violated at both the "air to pigment-layer" and "pigment-layer to paper" boundaries (although a fairly simple correction term has been proposed [18], that could be used to increase accuracy).

2. *The pigment particles are oriented randomly.* This assumption is satisfied for most watercolor paints, although not all. For example, metallic paint pigments have mostly horizontal flakes.

3. *The illumination is diffuse.* Our simulated watercolors will obviously not look entirely correct under all lighting and viewing conditions. Duntley [20] has a more general theory with four parameters instead of two that can account for more general lighting conditions.

4. *The KM equations apply only to one wavelength at a time.* Fluorescent paints violate this assumption.

5. *There is no chemical or electrical interaction between different pigments, or between the pigment and medium, which would* *cause clumping of pigment grains and a non-uniform particle size.* These assumptions are violated for most watercolor pigments.

In summary, the fact that the KM model appears to work so well could actually be considered quite surprising, given the number of basic assumptions of the model violated by watercolor. We suspect that while the results of the model are probably not very physically accurate, they at least provide very plausible physical approximations, which appear quite adequate for many applications.

6 Applications

In this section, we briefly discuss three different applications of computer-generated watercolor: interactive painting, automatic image "watercolorization," and 3D non-photorealistic rendering.

6.1 Interactive painting with watercolors

We have written an interactive application that allows a user to paint the initial conditions for the watercolor simulator. The user sets up one or more glazes for the simulator, where each glaze has sub-layers for pigments, water, and a wet-area mask. Common to all glazes are a reference image and a shaded paper texture. There are slider controls to adjust the physical parameters for each glaze (including viscous drag κ, edge darkening η and kernel size K) as well as the number of times to iterate the simulation.

The glaze's pigment channels are represented by colored images in the glaze. Each pigment is painted independently using a circular brush with a Gaussian intensity drop-off. The brush size, penumbra, and overall intensity parameters are adjustable. A palette of pigments associated with a glaze may be defined by specifying the color of each pigment over black and over white, as described in Section 5.1, using an HSV color picker—or by loading predefined pigments from files. For each pigment, the density ρ, staining power ω, and granulation γ may also be controlled using sliders.

The wet-area mask can be painted directly using a similar brush, or by selecting regions from the reference image using "intelligent scissors" [27]. The user can achieve drybrush effects by setting the

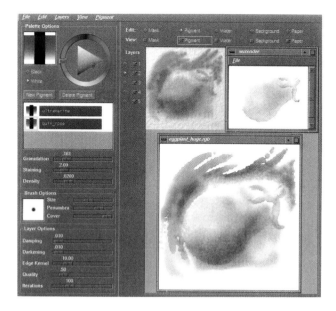

Figure 7 An interactive painting application. At top center are the initial conditions painted by the user; at top right, a watercolor simulation in progress, showing two of the painting's five glazes. The large image is the finished painting.

depth to which the brush is allowed to touch the paper.

Although our watercolor simulator runs too slowly for interactive painting, compositing many glazes of pigments using the KM model is feasible in real-time, and provides the user with valuable feedback about the colors resulting from the simulation. The reference image, paper texture, and set of glazes and their sublayers can be independently toggled on and off, and displayed in any combination. Another helpful feature is a rendering window that displays the progress of running the simulator on a (possibly scaled-down) set of glazes. Lower-resolution simulations are enlarged for display in the viewing window, and each frame of the simulator's animation is typically displayed in a fraction of a second to a few minutes. A screenshot from the application appears in Figure 7, showing several simulations at different stages of completion.

6.2 Automatic image "watercolorization"

Another application we have built allows a color image to be automatically converted into a watercolor illustration, once mattes for the key elements have been extracted and an ordered set of pigments has been chosen, with one pigment per glaze. In our tests, we generated these regions quickly using a commercial paint program. We have also chosen the pigments by hand in our examples, although for further automation, the choice of pigments could instead be computed through an optimization process [31].

The conversion is executed in two stages: *color separation* (Figure 8), in which the ideal distribution of pigment in each glaze is calculated to produce the desired image; and *brushstroke planning* (Figure 9), in which each glaze is painted in an attempt to re-create the desired pigment distribution by adding brushstrokes of water and pigment, taking into account the behavior of the medium. The result is an image that approximates the original but has the flow patterns and texture of a watercolor painting.

Color separation. Color separations are calculated using a brute-force search over a discrete set of thicknesses for each pigment. Given an ordered list of n pigments, the thickness range for each pigment is first divided into m steps, using a binary subdivision by Manhattan distance in the six-dimensional space of the R_i and T_i Kubelka-Munk parameters. Using the KM optical compositing model, a composite color is then computed for each of the m^n combinations, and the color is stored in a $3d$-tree according to its RGB color values. (The tree is pruned so that the difference between

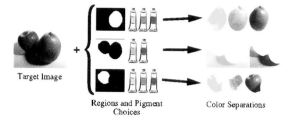

Figure 8 Overview of the color separation process.

Figure 9 Brushstroke planning. At given intervals, the planner identifies regions containing too much pigment (a) and thins them out by adding plain water (b). The planner can also compensate for a lack of pigment (c) by adding a pigmented wash (d).

colors is less than 1/255.) For the separations used for Figures 10 and 14, $m = 20$, and $n = 3$. Color separations are computed by searching the tree for each pixel to find the pigment combination yielding the closest color to the desired color. These colors are stored in an image called the *target glaze*.

Brushstroke planning. A painter can somewhat control the concentration and flow of pigment in a wash by carefully monitoring the relative wetness of brush and paper, knowing that spreading water carries pigment with it and tends to thin it out. Similarly, we control a glaze by adding incremental brushstrokes of pigment, and we control the direction of flow by increasing or decreasing water pressure wherever pigment is added.

The overall process works by repeatedly querying and manipulating the state of the glaze at a user-specified interval (30 to 100 steps in our examples) during the simulation, using user-controlled parameters δ_g, ϕ_g, and ϕ_p. In our examples, the steps below were repeated between 2 and 5 times, and we used the following values: $0.01 \leq \delta_g \leq 0.2$, $\phi_g = -\delta_g$, and $\phi_p = 1.0$. At each step, the current pigment distribution is compared to the target glaze, ignoring high frequency details, by performing a low-pass filter on the difference between the two. Then one of two actions is performed:

1. In areas where the current glaze does not have enough pigment (by more than δ_g), increment g by δ_g, and increment p by ϕ_g.

2. In areas where the current glaze has too much pigment (by more than δ_g), increment p by ϕ_p.

As a final step, highlights are created by removing paint from areas defined by the user in the form of mattes. This step is analogous to the "lifting out" technique used by artists for similar effects. Figure 10 shows the final results, and Figure 11 shows the appearance of the painting in progress as glazes are added.

Figure 10 An automatic watercolorization (left) of a low resolution image captured using a poor-quality video camera (above). The finished painting consists of 11 glazes, using a total of 2750 iterations of the simulator, rendered at a resolution of 640 by 480 pixels in 7 hours on a 133 MHz SGI R4600 processor.

6.3 Non-photorealistic rendering of 3D models

A straightforward extension of the automatic watercolorization of the previous section is to perform non-photorealistic watercolor rendering directly from 3D models.

Given a 3D geometric scene, we automatically generate mattes isolating each object. These mattes are used as input to the watercolorization process, along with a more traditional "photorealistic" rendering of the scene as the target image. The pigment choices and brushstroke planning parameters are supplied by the user. As shown in Figure 12, even a very primitive "photorealistic" image can thus be converted into a richly textured painting (seen in Figure 14). Figure 13 shows several frames from a painterly animation of clouds generated using only a few dozen spheres.

7 Future Work

Other effects. There are several techniques we do not model, such as spattering and some aspects of the drybrush technique. One way to simulate the appearance of bristle patterns in drybrush would be to integrate hairy brushes [36] with the watercolor simulator. The integration of watercolor with other media such as pen-and-ink would also be interesting.

Automatic rendering. We would like to explore further the idea of automatic watercolorization of images in a more general sense. An algorithm to automatically specify wet areas so that hard edges are placed properly would be especially useful, as well as a color-separation algorithm to calculate the optimal palette of pigments to use for various regions of the image [31]. Other possibilities include automatic recognition and generation of textures using drybrush, spattering, scraping, and other techniques.

Generalization. Our model treats backruns and wet-in-wet flow patterns as two separate processes. In real watercolor, however, they are just two extremes of a continuum of effects, the difference between them being simply the degree of wetness of the paper. A model that could integrate these two effects, parametrized by wetness, would be a significant improvement.

Animation issues. When an animated sequence is converted to watercolor one frame at a time, the resulting animation exhibits certain temporal artifacts, such as the "shower door" effect [26]. In the future we would like to develop a system that takes into account the issue of coherency over time and allows the user to control these artifacts.

Acknowledgements

The 3D target animation for Figures 12–14 was created by Siang Lin Loo. We would also like to thank Ron Harmon of Daniel Smith Artists' Materials for connecting us to reality; John Hughes, Alan Barr, Randy Leveque, Michael Wong, and Adam Finkelstein for many helpful discussions; and Daniel Wexler and Adam Schaeffer for assistance with the images.

This work was supported by an Alfred P. Sloan Research Fellowship (BR-3495), an NSF Presidential Faculty Fellow award (CCR-9553199), an ONR Young Investigator award (N00014-95-1-0728) and Augmentation award (N00014-90-J-P00002), and an industrial gift from Microsoft.

References

[1] Jim X. Chen and Niels da Vitoria Lobo. Toward interactive-rate simulation of fluids with moving obstacles using navier-stokes equations. *Graphical Models and Image Processing*, 57(2):107–116, March 1995.

[2] Tunde Cockshott, John Patterson, and David England. Modelling the texture of paint. *Computer Graphics Forum (Eurographics '92)*, 11(3):217–226, September 1992.

[3] Robert D. Deegan, Olgica Bakajin, Todd F. Dupont, Greg Huber, Sidney R. Nagel, and Thomas A. Witten. Contact line deposits in an evaporating drop. *James Franck Institute (University of Chicago) preprint*, October 1996.

[4] Jeanne Dobie. *Making Color Sing*. Watson-Guptill, 1986.

[5] Debra Dooley and Michael F. Cohen. Automatic illustration of 3D geometric models: Lines. *Computer Graphics*, 24(2):77–82, March 1990.

[6] Debra Dooley and Michael F. Cohen. Automatic illustration of 3D geometric models: Surfaces. In *Proceedings of Visualization '90*, pages 307–314. October 1990.

[7] Julie Dorsey and Pat Hanrahan. Modeling and rendering of metallic patinas. In *SIGGRAPH '96 Proceedings*, pages 387–396. 1996.

[8] Julie Dorsey, Hans Køhling Pedersen, and Pat Hanrahan. Flow and changes in appearance. In *SIGGRAPH '96 Proceedings*, pages 411–420. 1996.

[9] Gershon Elber. Line art rendering via a coverage of isoparametric curves. *IEEE Transaction on Visualization and Computer Graphics*, 1(3):231–239, September 1995.

Figure 12 The target image for Figure 14.

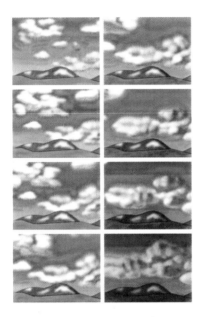

Figure 11 Steps in the rendering of Figure 10.

Figure 13 Several frames from a non-photorealistic animation of moving clouds.

Figure 14 Detail of one frame from Figure 13.

[10] Nick Foster and Dimitri Metaxas. Realistic animation of liquids. In *Graphics Interface '96*, pages 204–212. 1996.

[11] Jay S. Gondek, Gary W. Meyer, and Jonathan G. Newman. Wavelength dependent reflectance functions. In *SIGGRAPH '94 Proceedings*, pages 213–220. 1994.

[12] Qinglian Guo. Generating realistic calligraphy words. *IEICE Transactions on Fundamentals of Electronics Communications and Computer Sciences*, E78A(11):1556–1558, November 1996.

[13] Qinglian Guo and T. L. Kunii. Modeling the diffuse painting of sumie. In T. L. Kunii, editor, *IFIP Modeling in Comnputer Graphics*. 1991.

[14] Chet S. Haase and Gary W. Meyer. Modeling pigmented materials for realistic image synthesis. *ACM Trans. on Graphics*, 11(4):305, October 1992.

[15] Paul Haeberli and Douglas Voorhies. Image processing by linear interpolation and extrapolation. *IRIS Universe Magazine*, (28), Aug 1994.

[16] Paul E. Haeberli. Paint by numbers: Abstract image representations. In *SIGGRAPH '90 Proceedings*, pages 207–214. 1990.

[17] Ron Harmon. *personal communication*. Techical Manager, Daniel Smith Artists' Materials, 1996.

[18] D. B. Judd and G. Wyszecki. *Color in Business, Science, and Industry*. John Wiley and Sons, New York, 1975.

[19] Michael Kass and Gavin Miller. Rapid, stable fluid dynamics for computer graphics. In *SIGGRAPH '90 Proceedings*, pages 49–57. 1990.

[20] G. Kortum. *Reflectance Spectroscopy*. Springer-Verlag, 1969.

[21] P. Kubelka. New contributions to the optics of intensely light-scattering material, part ii: Non-homogeneous layers. *J. Optical Society*, 44:330, 1954.

[22] John Lansdown and Simon Schofield. Expressive rendering: A review of nonphotorealistic techniques. *IEEE Computer Graphics and Applications*, 15(3):29–37, May 1995.

[23] Wolfgang Leister. Computer generated copper plates. *Computer Graphics Forum*, 13(1):69–77, 1994.

[24] James A. Liggett. Basic equations of unsteady flow. *Unsteady Flow in Open Channels, Vol. 1*, eds: K. Mahmood and V. Yevjevich, Water Resources Publications, Fort Collins, Colorado, 1975.

[25] Ralph Mayer. *The Artist's Handbook of Materials and Techniques*. Penguin Books, 5 edition, 1991.

[26] Barbara J. Meier. Painterly rendering for animation. In *SIGGRAPH '96 Proceedings*, pages 477–484. 1996.

[27] Eric N. Mortensen and William A. Barrett. Intelligent scissors for image composition. In *SIGGRAPH '95 Proceedings*, pages 191–198. 1995.

[28] F. Kenton Musgrave, Craig E. Kolb, and Robert S. Mace. The synthesis and rendering of eroded fractal terrains. In *SIGGRAPH '89 Proceedings*, pages 41–50. 1989.

[29] Ken Perlin. An image synthesizer. In *SIGGRAPH '85 Proceedings*, pages 287–296. July 1985.

[30] Binh Pham. Expressive brush strokes. *CVGIP: Graphical Models and Image Processing*, 53(1), 1991.

[31] Joanna L. Power, Brad S. West, Eric J. Stollnitz, and David H. Salesin. Reproducing color images as duotones. In *SIGGRAPH '96 Proceedings*, pages 237–248. 1996.

[32] Don Rankin. *Mastering Glazing Techniques in Watercolor*. Watson-Guptill, 1986.

[33] Takafumi Saito and Tokiichiro Takahashi. Comprehensible rendering of 3D shapes. *Computer Graphics*, 24(4):197–206, August 1990.

[34] David Small. Simulating watercolor by modeling diffusion, pigment, and paper fibers. In *Proceedings of SPIE '91*. February 1991.

[35] Ray Smith. *The Artist's Handbook*. Alfred A. Knopf, 1987.

[36] Steve Strassmann. Hairy brushes. In *SIGGRAPH '86 Proceedings*, pages 225–232. August 1986.

[37] Zoltan Szabo. *Creative Watercolor Techniques*. Watson-Guptill, 1974.

[38] C. B. Vreugdenhil. *Numerical Methods for Shallow-Water Flow*. Kluwer Academic Publishers, 1994.

[39] Georges Winkenbach and David H. Salesin. Computer–generated pen–and–ink illustration. In *SIGGRAPH '94 Proceedings*, pages 91–100. 1994.

[40] Georges Winkenbach and David H. Salesin. Rendering free-form surfaces in pen and ink. In *SIGGRAPH '96 Proceedings*, pages 469–476. 1996.

[41] Steven P. Worley. A cellular texturing basis function. In *SIGGRAPH '96 Proceedings*, pages 291–294. 1996.

The Implications of a Theory of Play for the Design of Computer Toys

Organizer
Bill Kolomyjec

Panelists
Justine Cassell (MIT Media Lab)
Yasmine B. Kafai (University of California, Los Angeles)
Mary Williamson (University of California, Berkeley)

"Action in the imaginative sphere, in an imaginary situation, the creation of voluntary intentions, and the formation of real-life plans and volitional motives — all appear in play and make it the highest level of preschool development. The child moves forward essentially through play activity... Play [can] be considered a leading activity that determines the child's development." Lev Vygotsky, *Mind in Society* (pg. 102-103)

1. The nature of play

It is easy to underestimate the importance of play for the child. Play is ubiquitous in a child's life as well as culturally universal. It is also difficult to overemphasize the differences between what play is for the *child* and what the adult *supposes* that play is for the child. Many adults regard a child as an "adult-in-training" (Sutton-Smith, 1989) and suppose that the child at play either is "merely playing" (i.e. doing something trivial and unimportant) or is "practicing" (i.e. modeling future adult roles). While play doesn't entail the same import and consequences as many adult activities, and while imitating an adult is an aspect of some genres of play, these observations about play miss the importance of play *for the child.*

In this position paper, we draw on social theory to create a model of the child's world of play and use it to understand the importance of play activities on a child's individual and cultural development. As an adult, we can all look back on play during our childhood. What we want high-tech content providers to do is to remember what it was like to play as a child. From this perspective, the designer can recognize the importance of play.

We also stress that we don't believe that all children experience play the same way nor that all cultures have the same play activities. One of the most salient differences in the way that children experience play differently has to do with differences in gender. There are well-documented and persistent differences in types of play and manner of play between boys and girls (Turkle and Papert, 1991; Schofield, 1995; Kafai, 1996; Sutton-Smith, 1986). Additionally, play activities vary across cultures (Sutton-Smith, 1986). The existence of gender and cultural differences strengthens our central thesis: in play, the child becomes emancipated from immediate circumstances, those in a particular gendered and cultural context, and becomes able to envision alternative circumstances, those in an alternatively gendered and cultural context. It is the *options* for gender and cultural norms and values that a child can experience in play.

2. Play is more than make-believe

The child is immersed in play. For the child, play is the medium through which everyday life is experienced. Like air or water, play is the environment through which and with which the child experiences her world. For the content provider, this means that the imagination of the child is readily available (the "willing sus-

pension of disbelief"). It is important to stress, however, that it also means that it is the *child's* imagination which is available, not what the adult may believe the child to be imagining. During play, the *child's* experience of the world is transformed from an immediate experience to an imaginative experience. The nature of the child's imagination and its immersive character leads to two considerations for designers and content providers of play events.

First, it is practically impossible to determine which play activities will capture and hold the child's imagination. We have all been surprised by the child who ignores the expensive new toy because she is enthralled with its box. Apparently it is the box that sparks the the chld's imagination. Second, it is impossible to determine when play events start and stop (Sutton-Smith, 1989). The context of a play event is much broader than may appear to the adult observer.

A social theory of play can provide insight into the phenomenon of immersion and imagination in play. From within the play event, beginning around three years old, when the child starts to experience unrealizable desires, play mediates these desires by allowing the child to create an imaginary world where those desires *can* be met (Vygotsky, 1978). Since childhood is a time of learning to defer gratification and desire, the child spends *most* of her time in her imaginary world. However, it is also important that the child is always immersed in a *local* world. In other words, the child's imagination is constrained by the boundaries of the cultural world in which the child is playing; a child can't invent an imaginary world characterized by cultural experiences untraceable to the child's own world (although the child's ability to use imagination in this way may become more developed in later childhood).

The social theorist studying play and the content provider enabling play can learn a lot about play by looking at real play activities. For example, in our Western culture, "tea party" is a common game among girls in early elementary school. The child with limited control over the adult world can become a "mother" playing tea party. By taking up the "mother" role, the child realizes the desire to have increased control over real world events. By looking at how girls play act as "mothers," it is possible to learn quite a bit about how girls think and feel about themselves and others in their world. It is important to notice, however, that "real" mothers in most Western cultures, including the American culture, don't themselves participate in "real" tea parties. Why do their daughters? What is the relationship between an imaginary and socially non-existent practice like the tea party and the playing child's social transformation?

It is less the content of the specific play activity which matters than the "rules" (implicit or explicit) of the activity which mediate or link the child and her imagination to the outcomes of the play activity. It is this mediating function which allows the child to develop, while playing, important cognitive, social and affective skills that the child will use later as an adult living in a particular, for example Western, culture. Of course, the child in another culture — Bali, for example, or Iran — might not play tea party. Instead, that child might chose a different play activity with different roles and different rules.

Vygotsky introduces the notion of the "zone of proximal development of play" (we shorten this to the ZPD of play below) to describe the model in which the developmental progression of the relationships among the child and the play event is represented. The child "enters" the ZPD of play by participating in a play activity. During play, the child interacts with others in the ZPD, some of whom will be more competent and some less, and uses play objects (see section 3 below). The relationships among the children, the individual child's imagination and the objects are *always* governed by rules within a ZPD of play, and these rules will mirror the social values of the culture in which the ZPD is embedded. It is the *rules* of the tea party activity which make it a transformative event. The child will become able to learn the rules of a particular activity as the child becomes developmentally able to do so and as the rules are taught to her by another person (child or adult). As the child becomes competent in the activity, the child is transformed *by* the activity. In this way, the child learns the rules of her society. As long as the rules of the tea party mirror social values such as women's conversational styles and attitudes about women's social roles, tea parties will continue to take place (and girls will continue to play Barbies).

3. The progression of play and the development of thinking

There are always objects in the ZPD of play. Vygotsky calls these objects "pivot objects." A "pivot object" is the object with which the child actually plays (the "play tool," such as the cup, saucer and tea pot in the tea party activity). The nature of a particular pivot object turns out to be quite different, depending on the age of the child, the "location" of the play activity in the ZPD of play (determined by the relationships among the child, other people and the rules of the activity) and the nature of the larger culture in which the play activity takes place. It is primarily the *differences* among pivot objects which can be observed, analyzed and extrapolated into principles of software design (and it is the potentially different uses of available pivot objects which a child makes use of in imagining alternative circumstances).

For our purpose of elaborating on how an understanding of play is important for design, we will stress two intertwined characteristics of pivot objects: their "representational" nature (i.e. how they take on meaning for children) and their "pragmatic" nature (i.e. how they are used by real children in real play). *Play facilitates the development of the child's ability to mediate between thinking (representation) and creating (pragmatics or use).* It does so in three ways.

First, all objects take on a meaning independent of their meaning as objects. In the tea party activity, a cup is not just a cup, it is part of a tea set; in checkers, the round, red plastic tokens are "men" on a battlefield.

Second, the older child comes to be guided by the meaning in the (imaginary) situation and not by the objects in it at all. For the youngest children in play, the pivot objects themselves set up the boundaries of the play activity. A tea set will be used for a tea party. For the older child, the situation will determine the perception of the pivot objects. For example, the round, red piece of plastic can be a "man" on a battlefield but it can also be a poker chip.

Third, the rules anchor play behavior and determine the shape of the imagination possible during that activity. As the child matures, the rules become more abstract but also more explicit. Also, as the child matures, the rules place more (not fewer) constraints on behavior. The characteristics of favorite play events change over time as the child matures. In Vygotskian terms, play transforms from being an "overt imaginary situation with covert rules" (like a tea party activity) to a "covert imaginary situation with overt rules" (like a checkers game).

4. Play is always learning

What a child does in play is *under the control of the child*, not under the control of the adults in the child's life and not under the control of the activity designer. But that doesn't mean we shouldn't care about the activities we give to children. What it does mean is that it's important to understand what play is and is not. Play is neither trivial nor an activity supplied by adults to "train" children into the adults they should become (but which the adults around them are not). Play is a complex social phenomenon which serves the crucial social function of nurturing a child's imagination and ability to envision and create alternative social and material circumstances.

All play is learning. *All play has educational value as a means of developing complex thinking and acting.* Let us emphasize our claim: all play, irrespective of genre, including Dungeons and Dragons, Toy Story Animated Storybook, tea parties, and board games like checkers, have educational value.

Play can be systematically deconstructed into elements which can serve as building blocks for educational software activities and game design; looking at play activities from a Vygotskian point of view can highlight cognitive and social relationships that a designer can drawn on. The tea party activity and the game of checkers promote social values and attitudes, albeit somewhat sexist and imperialist ones. The child playing tea party is using the tea party objects to practice a socially defined role, practice imposing a meaning on an object (a meaning which is still largely determined by the object itself), and practice sustaining a type of social interaction, a type often associated with women (cf. Tannen, 1990). The child playing checkers is also practicing a socially defined role (to design and carry out a battle plan), practicing imposing a meaning on an object (in this case, the meaning is almost completely arbitrarily imposed on the object), and practicing winning or losing (the battle). In checkers, the child is sustaining a type of moral reasoning, a type often associated with men (cf. Gilligan on Piaget, 1982).

5. Play as a cultural event

Play is a mirror of a wider sphere of cultural value. This is true of both tea party and checkers. In the tea party activity, the child creates an imaginary world in which she participates in "polite" conversation and in an activity of the "leisured" class. There are conventionalized conversational topics to refer to such as the day's events, and conventionalized conversational rules such as to avoid serious and disturbing topics, compliment the hostess, apologize for spills, and tell an amusing story, but the content is flexible and mistakes are tolerated and accommodation and compromise are stressed. (Other examples of this kind of open-ended play activity include image creating software, simulations and activity centers.)

Checkers, on the other hand, is an example of a play activity called a "game." In checkers, the child also creates an imaginary world. In this world, she can act out a battle scene in which the object is to conquer the opponent's territory by subduing all his or her men, again rewarding competition and maneuvering for tactical advantage. The rules are fixed and inflexible and violations are sanctioned, supporting a highly rationalized understanding of moral reasoning. (Other examples of the game kind of activity include most card and board games, adventure games and Dungeon and Dragon games.)

Our work on play, and our understanding of play as an immersive and culturally-embedded event, has led us to an understanding that designing play activities requires more than merely "tacking on" desirable elements to the design process. Play tools created and used by children in play *always already* serve the prevailing culture's cognitive, affective and social values. Play tools will continue to serve these values because that is their nature. Socially responsible design requires an awareness of these existing values and a willingness to change them.

6. Play is a kid thing

Play is not what adults think it is because adults have developed beyond remembering how immersed in play they were as children. In this position paper we remind adults about the role play played in our lives. Play was serious, consuming and ubiquitous but paradoxically fun. Through play we developed as individuals and learned how to fit into our particular societies and cultures. As we, as adult high-tech content providers and designers, persist in designing computer toys for our children then we must be aware of the consequences and implications of putting them into the context of children at play. The toys we give children may affect them differently than we intend. So, the next time you observe kids at play see their play as it really is — a kid thing.

References

Gilligan, C. (1982) In a different voice: Psychological theory and women's development. Cambridge, MA: Harvard University Press.

Kafai, Y. B. (1996) Electronic play worlds: Gender differences in children's construction of video games. In Kafai, Y and ., M. (Eds.) Constructionism in practice: Designing, thinking and learning in a digital world. New Jersey: Lawrence Erlbaum Associates. p. 97-123.

Schofield, J. W. (1995) Computers and classroom culture. New York: Cambridge University Press.

Sutton-Smith, B. and Magee, M. A. (1989) Reversible Childhood. Play and Culture, 1989, 2, 52-63.

Sutton-Smith, B. (1986) Toys as culture. New York: Gardner Press.

Tannen, Deborah (1990) You just don't understand : women and men in conversation. New York : Morrow, c1990.

Turkle, S. and, Papert, S. (1991) Epistemological pluralism and the revaluation of the concrete. In Harel, I. and Papert, S. (Ed.) Constructionism. Norwood, NJ: Ablex Publishing Co. p. 161-191.

Vygotsky, L. S. (1978) Mind in Society: The development of higher psychological processes. Cambridge, Mass: Harvard University Press.

Facial Animation: Past, Present and Future

Organizers
Demetri Terzopoulos (University of Toronto)
Barbara Mones-Hattal (George Mason University)

Panelists
Beth Hofer (Pacific Data Images)
Frederic Parke (Texas A&M University)
Doug Sweetland (Pixar)
Keith Waters (Digital Equipment Corporation)

Panel Overview

Facial animation is now attracting more attention than ever before in its 25 years as an identifiable area of computer graphics. Imaginative applications of animated graphical faces are found in sophisticated human-computer interfaces, interactive games, multimedia titles, VR telepresence experiences, and, as always, in a broad variety of production animations. Graphics technologies underlying facial animation now run the gamut from keyframing to image morphing, video tracking, geometric and physical modeling, and behavioral animation. Supporting technologies include speech synthesis and artificial intelligence. Whether the goal is to synthesize realistic faces or fantastic ones, representing the dynamic facial likeness of humans and other creatures is giving impetus to a diverse and rapidly growing body of cross-disciplinary research. The panel will present a historical perspective, assess the state of the art, and speculate on the exciting future of facial animation.

Frederic Parke
A Historical Perspective

Human facial expression has been the subject of scientific investigation for more than one hundred years. Computer based facial expression modeling and animation is not a new endeavor [1]. Initial efforts in this area go backwell over 25 years. Increasingly complex computer animated characters demand expressive, articulate faces. It is interesting that most of the currently employed techniques involve principles developed in the research community some years ago – in some cases, several decades ago.

The earliest work with computer based facial representation was done in the early 1970's. In 1971 Chernoff proposed the use of two-dimensional faces as a way to represent k-dimensional data. The first three-dimensional facial animation was created by Parke in 1972. In 1973 Gillenson developed an interactive system to assemble and edit line drawn facial images. And in 1974, Parke developed a parameterized three-dimensional facial model.

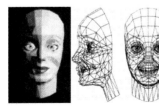

The early 1980's saw the development of the first physically based muscle-controlled face model by Platt and the development of techniques for facial caricatures by Brennan. In 1985, the short animated film ``Tony dePeltrie'' was a landmark for facial animation. In it for the first time computer facial expression and speech animation were a fundamental part of telling the story.

The late 1980's saw the development of a new muscle based model by Waters, the development of an abstract muscle action model by Magnenat-Thalmann and colleagues, and approaches to automatic speech synchronization by Lewis and by Hill.

The 1990's have seen increasing activity in the development of facial animation techniques and the use of computer facial animation as a key storytelling component as illustrated in the recent film ``Toy Story.''

If past trends are a valid indicator of future developments, the next decade should be a very exciting time to be involved in computer facial animation. Driven by increases in computational power, the development of more effective modeling and animation techniques, and the insatiable need of animation production companies for ever more capable computer animated characters, the quantity and quality of facial animation will increase manyfold.

Doug Sweetland
A Pixar Animator's Approach to Facial Animation

At Pixar, facial animation is achieved by moving individual muscles on the face. This gives the animator incredibly acute control over the aesthetics and choreography of the face. With all of these controls to oversee, an animator has to have a complete sense of the result desired on screen. The Pixar studio produces broad-based acting in feature animation; hence, the most important considerations are facial appearance and the meaning that the face conveys. Hopefully, before an animator begins working on the face, the character's body has been well animated and/or possess the proper attitude. A good strategy is to draw ``thumbnails,'' small sketches of the desired appearance of the face. Here an animator should think about the graphic design both in the small and in the large; from the relationship of one eyebrow to the other, to the interrelationship of all the facial features, to how the face relates to head position relative to the camera and perhaps even in the context of adjacent shots. The goal is to compose a graphic design with all its elements in place. None of the components are arbitrary and they all contribute towards the final effect.

A keen awareness of the character and its position at that point in the story – for example, the ability to answer questions such as "What has the character been through up to this point?," "What is this character thinking right now?," "What does this character want?" – enables the facial animator to make sensible choices about the desired effect and how to compose the character to achieve the effect. The idea here is to make an intellectual decision about a character's behavior instead of trying to feel your way through it or drawing solely from a reading of the dialogue. Without the proper planning, the result can often seem hackneyed or inconsistent and the performance frequently goes lifeless once the line has been read. Mastering a character's thoughts, even if they are really quite simple or few, is a key to achieving a compelling performance that makes sense in the context of the entire film.

The overall goal in animating the face is to give the illusion that the poses and expressions are motivated by the character instead of being topically manipulated by the animator, despite the fact that the performance is premeditated and requires microscopic attention to detail. Making informed decisions on what the face needs to express and understanding natural facial composition are fundamental to the making of a believable facial performance.

Demetri Terzopoulos
Realistic Facial Modeling for Animation

It was hard enough to model and animate the faces of the toy characters in "Toy Story." An even more formidable task was to animate the face of Andy, the nice boy who owned the toys, along with the faces of the other members of Andy's family and Sid, the evil boy next door. This ranks prominently among the reasons for the brevity of the "people scenes" in the landmark film.

Indeed, a grand challenge in facial animation is the synthesis of artificial faces that look and act like your mother, or like some celebrity, or like any other real and perhaps familiar person. The solution to this challenge will involve not just computer graphics, but also other scientific disciplines such as psychology and artificial intelligence. In recent years, however, good progress has been made in realistic facial modeling for animation.

Creating artificial faces begins with a high fidelity geometric model suitable for animation that accurately captures the facial shape and appearance of a person. Traditionally, this job has been extremely laborious. Fortunately, animators are now able to digitize facial geometries and textures through the use of scanning range sensors, such as the one manufactured by Cyberware, Inc. Facial meshes can be adapted in a highly automated fashion by exploiting image analysis algorithms from computer vision.

A promising approach to realistic facial animation is to create facial models that take into account facial anatomy and biomechanics [2]. Progress has been made on developing facial models

that are animated through the dynamic simulation of deformable facial tissues with embedded contractile muscles of facial expression rooted in a skull substructure with a hinged jaw. Facial control algorithms hide the numerous parameters and coordinate the muscle actions to produce meaningful dynamic expressions. When confronting the synthesis of realistic faces, it is also of paramount importance to adequately model auxiliary structures, such as the mouth, eyes, eyelids, teeth, lips, hair, ears, and the articulate neck, each a nontrivial task.

Sophisticated biomechanical models of this sort are obviously much more computationally expensive than traditional, purely geometric models. They can tax the abilities of even the most powerful graphics computers currently available. The big challenge is to make realistic facial models flawless, a joy for animators to use. An intriguing avenue for future work is to develop brain and perception models that can imbue artificial faces with some level of intelligent behavior. Then perhaps computer animators can begin to employ realistic artificial faces the way film directors employ human faces.

Keith Waters
Real-Time Facial Animation for Human-Computer Interaction

Facial animation has progressed significantly over the past few years and a variety of algorithms and techniques now make it possible to create highly realistic looking characters: 3D scanners and photometric techniques are capable of creating highly detailed geometry of the face, algorithms are capable of emulating muscle and skin that approximates real facial expressions, and synthetic and real speech can be accurately synchronized to graphical faces.

Despite the technological advances, facial animation is humbled by some simple issues. As the realism of the face increases (making the synthetic face look more like a real person), we become much less forgiving of imperfections in the modeling and animation: If it looks like a person we expect it to behave like a person. This is due to the fact that we are extremely sensitive to reading small and very subtle facial characteristics in everyday life. Evidence suggests that our brains are even ``hard-wired''to interpret facial images.

An alternative is to create characters that have non-human characteristics, such as dogs and cats. In this case we are desensitized to imperfections in the modeling and animation because we have no experience of talking dogs and cats. Taking this further, two dots and an upward curving line can convey as much information about the emotion of happiness as a complex 3D facial model-whose facial muscles extend simulated skin at the corners of the mouth.

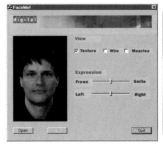

Understanding where some of these boundaries in facial animation exist helps us build new and exciting artifacts. We have constructed two scenarios to explore such novel forms of human computer interaction with real-time faces. The first is a talking face on the desktop [3]. The second is a Smart Kiosk, where the human-computer interaction is governed by the visual sensing of users in the environment [4].

Beth Hofer
Character Facial Animation at PDI

Creating character animation in a production environment presents many challenges to the animator. The wide variety of projects presents diverse needs and requirements. PDI has concentrated on character animation for years, working on many different types of characters. With each new character, the character's design, its animation style, and the length of the project are all factors in developing the facial animation system. A facial animation system for a cartoon character who has exaggerated, extreme facial expressions, may not be appropriate for a character who must display very subtle, human-like expressions. Two recent projects at PDI demonstrate two very different facial animation solutions.

The ``Simpsons'' project involved animating a character with distinct, recognizable, exaggerated facial expressions. In addition, with limited lead time, we had to develop a solution in a relatively short time frame. We created a shape interpolation-based system with layered high-level deformation controls. This

allowed animators to specify exaggerated expressions with relative ease. They could then use lower-level controls to refine the animation of individual facial features.

Our upcoming ``ANTZ'' film project, on the other hand, requires a wide variety of detailed, human-based expressions. The lead time for the film project is much greater, allowing the development of a more elaborate, robust facial animation system. We created an anatomically-based facial muscle system for ANTZ. Higher-level expression libraries are used to block in the main expressions. Lower-level muscle controls are then animated as the motion is refined.

Each system achieved the desired results for their particular project. The common element was to provide a layered approach for the animators. High-level controls block out overall expressions and timing, allowing the animator to easily refine overall timing without having to adjust many controls. Mid-range controls are used to start offsetting timing of individual features and to begin to include unique movements to the expressions. Finally, low-level controls allow the animator to introduce a final level of detail to the animation. Layered controls allow facial animators to work efficiently, no matter what type of underlying animation system is being used.

References

[1] F.I. Parke and K. Waters, ``Computer Facial Animation,'' A K Peters, 1996.

[2] Y. Lee, D. Terzopoulos, and K. Waters, ``Realistic modeling for facial animation,'' Proc. ACM SIG-GRAPH 95 Conf., pp. 55-62, 1995.

[3] K. Waters and T. Levergood, ``DECface: A System for Synthetic Face Applications,'' Multimedia Tools and Applications, 1, pp. 349-366, 1995.

[4] K. Waters, J. Rehg, M. Loughlin, S. B. Kang, and D. Terzopoulos, ``Visual Sensing of Humans for Active Public Interfaces,'' Digital Cambridge Research Lab TR 95/6, March 1996.

Can We Get There From Here?: Current Challenges in Cloth Design, Modeling and Animation

Organizer
Dr. David E. Breen (California Institute of Technology)

Panelists
Jeffrey W. Eischen (North Carolina State University)
Michael Kass (Pixar)
Nadia Magnenat Thalmann (University of Geneva)
Maurizio Vecchione (ModaCAD Inc.)

Summary

This panel will address the technical, economic and marketing hurdles that inhibit the widespread use of cloth/clothing modeling, design and animation technology. Many of the fundamental technologies needed to support cloth modeling have already been developed. Still, we do not see computer-animated characters wearing realistic clothing, and clothing designers are not creating new fashions with computer-based 3-D design systems. The CAD industry is capable of providing the systems for designing the Boeing 777, but almost none of the clothing we wear is designed with 3-D CAD tools. The panel will explore the reasons that the design of cloth and clothing, a material that has been a part of the human experience for thousands of years, has not yet been fully computerized.

A variety of issues related to cloth/clothing modeling will be explored. Are there fundamental technological barriers preventing us from fully deploying computer technology when modeling, designing, or animating cloth/clothing? Have the technical problems been solved and our computers are just not fast enough? Do we simply need good user interfaces to solve this difficult modeling problem? Is realism always important when modeling cloth? Does computer-based manufacturing place special demands on cloth modeling? Are designers, artists and clothing makers resisting the computerization of their "black art"? Can the average user even afford to do cloth modeling? Is the technology too expensive? These are some of the questions that the panelists will address.

Before describing the challenges involved in modeling and animating clothing, the panelists will provide a snapshot of the state-of-the-art in the field. Topics will include the detailed modeling of cloth, the research involved in clothing virtual actors, bringing clothing animation to the entertainment industry, textile mechanics and engineering applications, and the latest in apparel CAD software and technology. Each speaker will briefly describe their work in the field, augmenting their talks with images, animations and live demonstrations.

The panel will strive to achieve several goals. It will highlight cloth/clothing modeling as a separate field of study. Very often cloth modeling is seen as simply another application of deformable models. Cloth is a unique material with unusual properties that requires new and different modeling methods. In the CAD field, software systems for designing clothing are certainly different from conventional CAD systems that model collections of rigid parts. Given the unique nature of the field, it is important to seed the SIGGRAPH community with new ideas and challenges. The panel will educate the audience in a way that stimulates future research in cloth/clothing modeling. Another goal of the panel is to expose the SIGGRAPH community to those people working in the field of cloth/clothing modeling who are interested in more than just visual effects. The panel includes speakers who have a broader view of cloth modeling, including

those working within the textile engineering and CAD communities. They are more concerned with accurately modeling cloth as an engineering material and bringing powerful CAD tools to the marketplace than the making of pretty pictures. The panel also consists of an international participant, in recognition that some of the best clothing modeling research is being conducted overseas.

David E. Breen

My main interest in cloth modeling has focused on accurately capturing and modeling the unique mechanical properties and behavior of woven cloth. When modeling cloth, it is customary to assume that cloth is simply a special kind of continuous deformable sheet. In fact, cloth is a complex mechanical structure. I believe that conventional computer graphics continuum models are inadequate for accurately simulating the mechanical behavior of woven cloth. My research has addressed this inadequacy in two ways. First, I have developed a microstructural model of cloth which directly represents the important low-level features of cloth, namely the thread crossing. Second, I have developed methods for incorporating non-linear mechanical empirical data into my model. This removes the need to make the assumption of linearity when defining the model, and produces a model that more accurately represents woven cloth. My talk will briefly describe my novel approach to modeling cloth. Images and animations will be used to present my research results. When modeling cloth, I will discuss what I think it takes to "get it right". All of the details of my microstructural approach have not been worked out, though. Many components of the approach are still not fully developed. I will described these unfinished components that, when completed, will make my model fast and dynamic, as well as, accurate.

Jeffrey W. Eischen

My talk will focus on the physical aspects of cloth modeling. A brief review of the work which properly accounts for the mechanical properties of cloth will be presented. The difficulties encountered when attempting to realistically model cloth will also be presented. The various applications of such computer modeling will be discussed: modeling of cloth on the human body (static and dynamic), modeling of cloth on inanimate objects such as furniture and automobiles, modeling of cloth during manufacturing operations such as: cutting, picking, placing, folding, sewing, etc.

Michael Kass

The rigors of computer-graphics production place severe demands on physically-based computer graphics techniques. They must be fast, stable, and predictable. But above all, the techniques must be controllable if they are to be useful in storytelling. In this talk, I will discuss some of the issues in bringing such techniques for cloth modeling and animation into the environment of an animation studio. In studio animation, absolute realism is not necessarily the goal, even in a seemingly realistic piece; there may be a great deal of exaggeration for a desired effect. Nonetheless, physical simulation, perhaps with exaggerated parameters, offers the opportunity to achieve a level of complexity in clothing animation that is difficult or impossible to achieve with traditional techniques. The clothing animation in Toy Story was done without simulation, and became so tedious that the animators were unable to achieve the level of quality they hoped for. Since then, we have developed tools for the physically-based simulation of cloth. I will describe our experience with these tools, and with the process of melding clothing simulation into our production environment.

Nadia Magnenat Thalmann

It is a far cry from simulating a flag, or draping a rectangular cloth on a table, to the animation of clothed virtual humans. First, garment cloth tends to be of rather complex form, so that modeling it as a deformable surface requires consideration of many component elements, greatly augmenting computation time. Second, collisions with the environment (the body, other clothing) must be analyzed when determining the shape of the garment as it is worn and changes during animation.

We present a selection of work on simulated clothing, one of our major research areas as early as 1988. First we show our remake of a scene from "The Seven Year Itch", in which a virtual Marilyn holds down her skirt against the air current from a subway vent. Then we discuss technical issues involved in decreasing the calculation time, illustrated by our film of Marilyn receiving the Golden Camera Award in Berlin (1996), in the simulation of armored costumes for the terra cotta soldiers from Xian, and using VLNET (Virtual Life System) for the collaborative interactive design of a virtual dress.

Maurizio Vecchione

In my talk I will present a brief review of the current state of graphical design technology applied to the textile/apparel industry with special focus on the technologies deployed for apparel

design. "Did you realize that 70% of today's apparel is partially designed on computers? What are the limits of today's Computer Based Apparel Design? Why is 2-D king and the industry does not want to accept 3-D design technology?" A discussion of the industry's trends and needs, and a review of the elements making up realistic cloth simulation with special discussion of the emerging rendering and modeling techniques specifically focused to amorphous materials behaviors will also be included. Cloth-like surface detail may also be added by deploying special rendering techniques without complicating the model itself. I will show how. Additional topics will include new rendering approaches to the problems of textile simulations with a special discussion of the unique problems associated with texture mapping textiles and the importance of proper control over UV parameters. The talk will close with the presentation of major directions of future expansion and major challenges driven by the industry, including the emergence of knowledge-based technologies for cloth simulation. I plan to show live demos and examples, and will take an industry approach, combining the technical approaches with the business forces motivating the realization of certain technical options.

Fabrics designed, modeled and rendered onto a lifelike model photorealistically in ModaCAD.

Relevant URLs

A summary of Breen's Ph.D. work on cloth models.

`www.gg.caltech.edu/~david/david_pbm.html`

The abstracts for IEEE CG&A's special issue on Computer Graphics in Textiles and Apparel, an issue guest-edited by Breen.

`www.computer.org/pubs/cg%26a/`
`    backissu.htm#september1996`

National Textile Center Home Page Eischen is part of NTC, a university consortium exploring textile-related technologies.

`ntc.tx.ncsu.edu/ntc.html`

Computer-Aided Engineering and Mechantronics in the Design of Apparel Systems A report on an NTC project.

`ntc.tx.ncsu.edu/html/REPORTS/`
`    SUMMER-FOLDER/1.html`

A summary of past and present cloth animation research supervised by Magnenat Thalmann.

`miralabwww.unige.ch/Research/Research_areas/`
`    Rcloth.html`

ModaCAD Home Page An overview of the apparel and textile CAD products offered by Vecchione's company.

`ns.sip.net/modacad/home.html`

Bibliography

M. Aono, P. Denti, D.E. Breen and M. Wozny, "Fitting a Woven Cloth Model to a Curved Surface: Dart Insertion," IEEE Computer Graphics and Applications, Vol. 16, No. 5, pp. 60-70, September 1996.

D.H. House, R.W. DeVaul and D.E. Breen, "Towards Simulating Cloth Dynamics Using Interacting Particles," International Journal of Clothing Science and Technology, Vol. 8, No. 3, pp. 75-94, 1996.

D.E. Breen, D.H. House and M.J. Wozny, "Predicting the Drape of Woven Cloth Using Interacting Particles," SIGGRAPH '94 Conference Proceedings, (Orlando, FL, July 1994) pp. 365-372.

J. Eischen, S. Deng and T.G. Clapp, "Finite Element Modeling and Control of Flexible Fabric Parts," IEEE Computer Graphics and Applications, Vol. 16, No. 5, pp. 71-80, September 1996.

J. Eischen, S.D. McWaters and T.G. Clapp, "Computer Simulation of Fabric Deformation for the Design of Equipment," International Journal of Clothing Science and Technology, Vol. 6, No. 5, 1994.

J. Eischen and T. McDevitt, "Simulation of Fabric Draping and Manipulation with Arbitrary Contact Surfaces and Adaptive Meshing," Proceedings of the 4th Annual Academic Apparel Research Conference, Raleigh, NC, February 1993.

P. Volino, N. Magnenat Thalmann, S. Jianhua and D. Thalmann, "An Evolving System for Simulating Clothes on Virtual Actors," IEEE Computer Graphics and Applications, Vol. 16, No. 5, pp. 42-51, September 1996.

P. Volino, M. Courchesne, N. Magnenat-Thalmann, "Versatile and Efficient Techniques for Simulating Cloth and Other Deformable Objects," SIGGRAPH '95 Conference Proceedings, (Los Angeles, August 1995) pp. 137-144.

M. Carignan, Y. Yang, N. Magnenat Thalmann, D. Thalmann, "Dressing Animated Synthetic Actors with Complex Clothes," Computer Graphics (Proc. SIGGRAPH '92), Vol. 26, No. 2, pp. 99-104, July 1992.

J.W.S. Hearle, "Virtual Reality and Fabric Mechanics (Part I)," Textile Horizons, Vol. 15, No. 2, pp. 12-17, April 1995.

J.W.S. Hearle, "Virtual Reality and Fabric Mechanics (Part II)," Textile Horizons, Vol. 15, No. 3, pp. 10-14, June 1995.

H.N. Ng and R.L. Grimsdale, "Computer Graphics Techniques for Modeling Cloth," IEEE Computer Graphics and Applications, Vol. 16, No. 5, pp. 28-41, September 1996.

NARRATIVE ENVIRONMENTS: VIRTUAL REALITY AS A STORYTELLING MEDIUM

Organizer
Celia Pearce (Momentum Media Group)

Panelists
Jim Ludtke (CD-ROM Artist)
C. Scott Young (Dimensional Graphics)
Brad deGraf (Protozoa, Inc.)
Athomas Goldberg (New York University)

OMNI-DIRECTIONAL STORYTELLING: THE INTER-ACTIVE CONUNDRUM
Celia Pearce, Creative Director/Principal (Panel Chair)
Momentum Media Group

What is a narrative environment? Simply put, it is a space that facilitates a story. Although this art has been perfected in the real world by theme park designers, in the virtual world, space as a narrative medium is just beginning to be explored. Current applications focus on three dimensions, but ignore the fourth—time. Thus much of cyerspace is, at present, a ghost town in which aimless avatars wander about in search of meaning. The potential for dynamic, interactive storytelling in cyberspace is enormous when you consider the multi-user realms now available, and the level of user responsiveness that can be created within a virtual world. Furthermore, the unique immersive, first person perspective afforded by Virtual Reality creates the opportunity for emotional impact through empathy, discovery and personal choice. Traditionally, interactive narrative has been synonymous with "nonlinear storytelling," or branching, video-based genres. Virtual reality offers a more interactive alternative: "omnidirectional storytelling."   But therein lies the challenge. For indeed the more interactivity, the more challenging it becomes to facilitate the story. What does it mean to give up this control? Must we form an entirely new paradigm for story structure? How can we harmonize the seeming contradition between "interactive" and "narrative"? For the dramatic conclusion, tune in to the next episode of "Narrative Environments: Virtual Reality as a Storytelling Medium..."

FROM HOMER TO FREAK SHOW: CREATING A NEW GENRE OF STORYTELLING
Jim Ludke, Digital Artist

In 1991, I began a collaboration with the San-Francisco alternative rock/performance art group The Residents that became one of the most creatively satisfying periods in my career and resulted in two highly acclaimed "alternative" CD-ROM products, "Freak Show" & "Bad Day on the Midway." The Residents had already spent 20 years creating bizarre, iconoclastic musical works that wed the sacred and profane. They had been innovators in live performance, and in the formative years of music video, helped defined the genre. We began to discuss ways to bring their "story-worlds" into a form of immersible and challenging digital entertainment.

Interactive media was starting to boom. Low-cost, easy to use authoring tools had arrived, and it seemed that a new era was upon us. The Residents saw this as a way to reach a wider audience; I saw it as a way to appropriate and subvert a medium in danger of becoming strictly the domain of computer games and corporate presentations.

Our first collaboration, "Freak Show", attempted to fill what we saw as a gaping void in the existing CD-ROM lineup. The

Residents objective was to bring an emotional context to the work, a quality strictly avoided in the emerging "computer game" culture. My goal was to create an alternative to games entirely—to ingore the rules, and annoy those coming to the party with preconceived expectations. This had been what the Residents had been doing musically for years, and I gladly joined in to help foster this anarchy. We created a CD-ROM that was not a game, that you couldn't garner points from, and had no goal other than to take you into a place of The Residents creation, full of very human and often upsetting tales deliberately designed to confound the participant. Combine this with human grotesquery and geeking (in it's classic sense), and we assured ourselves a place among the "most hated" by complacent marketing executives.

We were strictly niche market, but it was worth it. When I saw a storytelling timeline in Details magazine that began with Homer's "Oddysey" and ended with "Freak Show", I knew we had succeeded in creating a new genre.

Today it has become virtually impossible to have independent experimental works published in the hit-driven world of disk-based publishing. The market that I envisioned thriving parallel to the game industry never came into its own. The good news is, interactive media is in a healthy state of flux. Self expression in the interactive realm has found a new home on the Web. The means have arrived. Authoring environments for graphics, animation and virtual reality on the web, are making it possible for small garage productions to compete directly with heavily funded on-line networks for the same audience. The infrastructure is in place for a new age to begin. This time, I think it will work.

QUALITIES OF THE INTER ACTIVE ENVIRONMENT
C.Scott Young, VRML Knight

There are more factors involved in creating the interactive environment than what our technology or a program can define, through reactive nodes, sound or animation.

The creation of 'real' worlds does not lie totally in the technology but in what we draw from ourselves to take into this new realm of the multidimensionalomniverse.

Now in this time of the human the universe seeks to divide itself into another dimension of expression using Us as the template. In the creation of this place known as Cyberspace we will need to take certain aspects of this reality with us so that there is familiarity. Quality content will have to come from within the deep of what we take from ourselves, if We are to create meaning.

We are all a part of a great rhyme being told. The universe takes on our shape as an Avatar from out of the storm of manifestation and creation. We are the universe seeking understanding of itself. Our lives are the stories that define ourselves as individuals and as one tribe and one nation. We define our portion of the universe in the living of life. This is the rhyme of our time. VRML allows us to take our thoughts and experience and put them in a place that anyone from anywhere can come and share. This sharing of common experience and individual experiences brings about an event which creates the 'commun- effect' the act of communication, the formation of community, a creation of common understanding and compassion. (even though compassion is comp- more so than commun- it belongs here if We are to make effective interactive environments.)

All of these factors and more play an important part in quality content communicated in the interactive environment. You may have all the effects imaginable but if nothing is being said, who will stay to listen?

CHARACTERS AS WORLDS
Brad deGraf, Chief Executive, Organism Protozoa, Inc.

"World" is a somewhat overused term for a container of geometric descriptions of objects and their relationships to each other ("nodes") and to time ("behavior"). "3D scene" or "scene graph" say effectively the same thing, but somewhat less evocatively. In Protozoa's use of the term, a world is simply a 3D media type. A world might be "architectural", such as a model of a building, but it need not be. A character is a world, as is the character's shoe. Worlds can be nested, containing other worlds. In fact, a fundamental feature of the 3D media type is that it is recursive, i.e. the child of a world can be another world.

A world is "live" if it has "behavior". Behavior is a fairly broad term, but it essentially encompasses a range of qualities that allow the world to be more than a static collection of objects. Such qualities include: animation of all kinds; editability, where the structure of the world can change; shape change; user interaction; multi-user interaction; events; audio; etc. There is no single quality that makes a static world become live.

By these definitions, a character is a world. It is a collection of objects that relate to each other, to which animation functions are attached. It can be contained in a larger world that includes other characters and objects as well. There really is no difference between a rich character that talks, wags its tail, and looks at the camera, and a door that opens when the knob is touched.

Live 3D worlds can be applied to a variety of forms, including linear animation; live cartoon characters; incarnations of users in virtual world and chat environments; incarnations of autonomous entities such as agents and game characters; shared virtual environments; interface elements such as navigators; virtual toys; interactive advertising; and high-performance theme-park installations.

As chat environments and multi-user domains become more three-dimensional, the quality expectations for each user's incarnation will rise, which will create a demand for richer characters with more expressiveness. Additionally, agents or bots (software that autonomously performs functions) will become more commonplace within the 3D environment.

As part of this presentation, we will show some new Protozoa projects, including our new game engine, procedurally animated and motion-capture animated VRML characters, and some of the work we are doing in the are of character-driven story environments.

DESIGNING NARRATIVE SPACES Athomas Goldberg, Research Scientist, Media Research Lab, New York University

Narrative. As a noun it refers to a narrated account or story; or the act, technique or process of telling a story. As an adjective, it refers to the something consisting of, or characterized by, the telling of a story.

Interactive Narrative. For some time now this term has been treated as an oxymoron in need of reconciliation. How can you tell a story if the audience can alter what happens? How do you give people the power to do whatever they want and still follow the narrative? How, as an author, can you possibly anticipate everything the audience might try to do, while ensuring the events necessary to the plot still occur at the right moment?

Many of these questions arise from an attempt to adapt traditional narrative structures to interactive media. The central issue revolves around maintaining narrative integrity while giving the audience something meaningful to do. The inherent obstacle to this is the fact that traditional narrative structures offer a specific model for interaction that is, in many ways, diametrically opposed to the model proposed by many who are interested in developing interactive media, that of active audience participation in the unfolding of events within the story. One of the most powerful tools available to the narrative author is the ability to construct and control the sequence of events through which the story is conveyed. As soon as user interaction is introduced, this ability to define the narrative is compromised. As one can see, these forms, which include the novel, theater and dramatic film, make poor models for interactive media, as they all rely on the creation of an explicit narrative, in which the characters and events have all been defined ahead of time.

In this presentation, we'll be discussing structures which may more easily lend themselves to the creation of interactive narrative spaces. We'll show how setting, character, relationships, goals, obstacles and resolution, the elements of most traditional narratives, can be used to convey a story without the author defining the specific sequence of events ahead of time. More importantly, we'll show how audience interaction, rather than an obstacle to narrative storytelling, can be an essential element in conveying an author's intentions.

Motion Capture and CG Character Animation

Organizer
Gordon Cameron (SOFTIMAGE Inc.)

Panelists
Andre Bustanoby (Digital Domain)
Ken Cope (Ones and Zeros Surreal Estate)
Steph Greenberg (Independent Animator)
Craig Hayes (Tippett Studios)
Olivier Ozoux (SOFTIMAGE Special Projects)

Abstract

Are classical animation techniques better suited to imparting life to computer animated characters than capturing a performance from an actor or puppeteer via motion capture or a digital input device?

Panel Overview

This panel will focus it's discussion on the application and worth of motion capture (mocap) technology, in its many forms, within the CG character animation field. These forms include full body motion capture systems, digital and stop-motion armatures, and other real-time physical input media.

There is much debate as to whether "Satan's Rotoscope" (footnote - the "affectionate" term for motion capture coined by Steph and Ken, amongst others!) is indeed a force for good, or evil (as the nickname may suggest) within the evolving field of CG character animation.

Detractors point to the difficulty of getting mocap to 'perform well' and produce good results in the animation process, it's cheapening of an art form, it's distancing of the animator from the creative process, and the threat it poses to their artistic livelihood as factors against the technology. Proponents state that there is nothing inherently bad in motion capture technology, and that, used appropriately, it serves as just another tool in the animator's bag of tricks, expanding the range of possibilities for artistic creativity and freedom.

We hope to cover several aspects in the panel, including asking questions such as : does motion capture have anything to do with animation at all?; is mocap more akin to digital puppetry?; does mocap save money in production ?; can mocap achieve as rich an aesthetic result as hand-crafted character animation ?; does mocap pose a threat to the animator's job ?; does using mocap mean a surrendering of artistic ideals by the animator in favour of the director and performer, or does it instead open up possibilities for a new range of artistic expression?; what will the future roles of puppeteer, motion capture specialist, digital performance artist, character animator and director be ?; what are the ethics of capturing and reusing an actor's performance, and many more.

This topic is one that should be of great interest and relevance to SIGGRAPH attendees - up until recently, motion capture technology has been thought of being too expensive and esoteric a solution to be of interest to the majority of animators. However - things are beginning to change with the pervasion of cheap, quality animation software packages, many of these having the ability to interface with a wider range of cheaper motion capture technology than previously available. The question remains, however : is this technology an interesting, valid, or positive contribution to the world of animation?

Position Statements

Andre Bustanoby

Actors and traditional performers are beginning to author digital characters.

This is not to say, however, that all digital characters should be done with capture technology. In fact, some characters should be traditionally key-framed. But, as I recognize the limitations of Performance Capture for some characters, so animators should recognize the limitations of traditional key-frame techniques. Characters are being written into stories that require extremely realistic and subtle performances. Furthermore, cost and schedule realities are continuing to pressure traditional means of animation. Performance Capture, when properly deployed, promises to open avenues of motion and emotion never before explored by actors, directors or animators.

Traditionally, actors haven't really played in the animator's technological and artistic backyard...until now. Performance Capture is enabling this change in the traditional animation paradigm. The future promises to expand the creative palette of animator and actor alike and honest education in the appropriate uses of the new capture technology will benefit everyone.

Gordon Cameron

I feel that there is a future for the use of motion capture in the creation of believable characters, and that tools developed can help talented CG character animators bring their vision to the screen. However, there is a worrying trend - and I believe it is just that, a trend that will pass - towards seeing and using motion capture as the be-all-and-end-all of character animation - the 'digital holy grail'. This assertion is clearly not the case, but if such an attitude becomes pervasive, the animator's livelihood and art will suffer.

The argument is oft-made that motion capture is more akin to puppeteering than animation, but, for me this is just terminology. There is significant overlap in the intended end-result that the two disciplines must somehow work together, and I believe that this can best happen with the development of tools that take into account the artistic, as well as technical aspects involved. Such tools will need to allow the animator to work with the results of motion capture without disrupting their artistic workflow or limiting their creative vision, integrating capture data seamlesssly into the animation process.

It is also worthwhile noting that motion capture can encompass many forms of real-time physical input media - not just the "people jumping around in suits" class of device. I strongly believe that, by integrating support for such devices within animation software - not as an afterthought, but at the core - the workflow for animators can truly be enhanced. As a developer who works on, among other things, 'motion capture' tools in a package geared towards animation, I have a strong interest in ensuring that the next-generation tools that see the light are tools that enable and encourage the creative process rather than stifling it.

Ken Cope

"I'm Not Buying Satan's Rotoscope, But The Suits Are."

Motion capture is more closely related to the cinematographer's medium than to that of the animator. Its allure lies in the capacity to isolate a subject's gross skeletal movement from accidents of lighting, camera angle, costuming, flesh, even final casting. Now a director can postpone decisions about those details until the last conceivable moment. Typically lacking even the slightest benefit of the animator's unique expertise, a director must coax a performance (the one he'll know he wants when he sees it) from a capture-rigged movement specialist. The motion is recorded, not created, by a technical director. At this point, that TD is acting more like a film magazine loader than an animator.

Motion Capture is a product too frequently used to promote freedom from animators, not freedom for them. Opportunities for animators to prepare themselves to explore what is unique about an exciting new medium are rare. Too many aspiring animators find their job options limited to the role of captured data processors.

Animators, for decades, have understood the use of silhouette, volume, timing, mass, isolation and exaggeration, elements that motion capture alone does not begin to address. An animator knows when to break a bone to make a character strike a more compelling pose that no human could ever hold. An animator knows how to fly impossible hair and drapery; misdirecting and focusing your attention like any other magician. Exploiting the notion of movement rather than its literal recitation, an animator shifts n-dimensional shadows through, around and outside time. We celebrate a living language of graphic cheats spoken by neither meat puppets nor engineers.

Steph Greenberg

Animation is a deliberately interpreted "illusion of life." It has been practiced for the last 70 years in both drawn and stop motion animation, and as such, is not an attempt to mimic human and animal life exactly.

This is not a pathology, as many in the computer animation industry maintain. The means to copy human life in drawn form have existed since the invention by the Fleischer brothers of the "Rotoscope" in the 1920s. Designed as an aid to match animation to live action film, and employed as a means to study human and animal movement, the Fleischers knew that the results of copying human motion directly yielded motion that was smooth but lacked life. Hence their most memorable characters, like Betty Boop and Popeye, were drawn from artists' imagination, their movement not copied from live human actors. 1939s "Gulliver's Travels" had a whole town full of hand animated characters, with the hero, Gulliver, "rotoscoped". Most critics of animation consider Gulliver's rotoscoped sequences to be lifeless and uninspired. The same view is held for more recent uses of the Rotoscope and direct tracing of "live action reference" by Ralph Bakshi in "Fire and Ice" and "Lord of the Rings."

What motion capture has allowed is not just the tracing of live action reference to characters, but the direct application of live action actors' movement to computer generated models. The result is the same as that previously created using the Fleischers' "Rotoscope." Motion capture is not animation. It is a form of live action film making using computer generated costumes. The result can be likened to comparing the lively and animated Disney character Goofy to the person wearing a Goofy costume at the Disney theme parks.

An animated character has capabilities that no human can replicate without possible injury. Hand keyframed characters can "snap" into position, their movements deliberate and uncompromising - their athletic abilities simply can't be matched. Digitally puppeteered characters are not animated - their expression and movement are determined by the real time abilities of the puppeteers. No matter what the CG character's costume, the character will still look like it is a puppet.

Does all this invalidate motion capture and digital puppeteering as exciting new art forms? Certainly not. I can envision a time when all future film making is done using a more refined form of motion capture. For real time performances and digital puppeteering, motion capture offers some intriguing possibilities, particularly in the area of costuming. This also applies to digital puppeteering. However, lumping these newly developed techniques into the category of animation, regardless of the dictionary definition of the word, is an insult to people who have studied and practiced in the deliberate and painstaking art of animation. I believe the use of the word "animation" in describing these techniques is only designed to bestow a type of instant credibility not yet earned, rather than "confuse" the marketplace with a new and unfamiliar term that better describes them.

Craig Hayes

My own position is somewhat ambiguous. I do feel motion capture tends to be used as a crutch, or even worse, to create performances/images that could have been created with filmed, live actors. One of our forms of motion input at Tippett, the digital-input device, usually operates at far less than real-time, enabling the stop-motion animators to work at a pace more to their style. At the same time, we have had good luck in applying the motion of theatrical performers to slightly different anatomies.

We have also had great success in using motion capture as a training base for less experienced animators. These people have gone on to be excellent CG animators in short order, and this is undeniably due, in part, to their exposure to the curves of motion capture performances.

Probably my biggest influence in the whole mess has been the reaction to these technologies by many of the talented animators I have had the great pleasure of working with. Some of these people have 20-30 years experience in the field of stop-motion animation, an art definitely not for the faint of heart! These people are thrilled at the opportunity to have another way of expressing their creative ideas.

Olivier Ozoux

Motion Capture is here to stay. As any emerging technology, it currently shows more promise than results, and will most probably be misused more often than not.

However, just as Photography did not replace Painting, but rather made it stronger by liberating it from the constraints of realism and reproduction, Motion Capture will free keyframe animators from having to create realistic animation, allowing them to focus on more creative endeavors.

Motion Capture should not (and *cannot*) be used as a replacement for keyframe animation. It can find its own place in the animators palette, between keyframing, simulation, and behavioral animation. Although each of these techniques can be used to tell the same story, the "feel" of each is different - just as photography is different from painting.

Biographies

Andre Bustanoby is currently Performance Capture Manager at Digital Domain in Venice, CA. He is responsible for implementing and deploying new capture methodology and technologies for the feature film, commercial and new media divisions at DD. He worked previously at Boss Film Studios as Head of Integration and Chief Engineer where he was responsible for the design and manufacture of equipment for digital imaging, motion control and motion capture.

With nearly 7 years of experience in feature film, commercial and special venue visual effects, Bustanoby sees the promise of properly deployed technology working in concert with digital artists. This will serve to bring the ever expanding digital world to the tool box of the traditional filmmaker.

Gordon Cameron is a software engineer with SOFTIMAGE, Inc., and editor of SIGGRAPHs 'Computer Graphics' quarterly magazine. He has been working on Softimage|3D since early 1995, mainly on tools for motion capture/control (Channels and SI-Live), and real-time viewing.

Previous to this, he worked for several years at the Edinburgh Parallel Computing Centre (EPCC), developing scientific visualisation tools and methodologies, and parallel applications. Prior to EPCC, he worked at the Department of Artificial Intelligence at the University of Edinburgh, in the field of robot vision.

Pencil and computer animator *Ken Cope* has feature credits on The Secret of NIMH, Robocop II, and Beauty and the Beast. He worked on He-Man and Shera, and for Filmation's last series, Bravestarr, was rotoscoped as the bad guy, Tex Hex. After generating environments and a pixel puppet for two motion-based theme park attractions, he was the first animator hired to model and animate Disney characters for Imagineering's Virtual Reality project.

He moved to the San Francisco Bay Area in 1995 to work in computer game development. While working for GameTek on Nintendo 64 titles, private projects, using Softimage, include a 3D collaboration with psychedelic printmaker and Zap Comix co-founder Victor Moscoso.

Steph Greenberg started working with computer animation in 1987 when he bought his first Amiga computer to do cel animation while confined to a bed as the result of a back injury. In 1991 he was hired by Mr. Film to work on the ill fated after school special, "The Magic Seven" which was slated to feature 53 minutes of character animation employing motion capture technology. Homer and Associates hired him in 1993 where he worked on various projects including Vince Neil's music video, "Sister of Pain", which also employed motion capture, as well as some hand animation.

Joining Walt Disney Imagineering's Virtual Reality Lab (later renamed Virtual Reality Studio) in 1994 , Greenberg worked on the "preview" release of "Aladdin's Virtual Reality Adventure", where an attempt was made to employ motion capture - it quickly proved to be more trouble than it was worth to get the characters to move like animated characters instead of humans with CG costumes. For the "release" version, veteran animation director Robert Taylor and Greenberg worked out a system that ultimately enabled 3-4 animators plus Taylor to create over 25 minutes of animation in about 9 months. Greenberg was promoted to Supervising Animator in 1995.

Craig Hayes has been working with Tippett Studio for the past 11 years. The collaboration started with the movie Robocop, with the design & construction of ED 209, Robocop's robotic nemesis. Following this, Tippett Studio created characters & visual effects for the following following feature films: Honey, I Shrank the Kids, Robocop 2, Robocop 3, Jurassic Park (animatics & motion-input animation), Three Wishes, (the studio's first entirely computer-graphic production), Dragonheart (character design & animatics), and currently, Starship Troopers, an epic space picture directed by Paul Verhoven.

While working at Tippett Studio, Craig's responsibilities have included character design & construction, visual effects art direction, mechanical design, and, most applicably, the development of motion input technologies. One aspect of this developement, the digital-input device, developed for work on Jurassic Park, recently recieved a scientific/technical award from the Academy of Motion Picture Sciences. Another aspect of motion input used by Tippett Studio is the body suit, an exo skeleton for real time recording of an actors performance. Currently, input animation acounts for approximately 30% of animation being generated, the remaining being done by animators on computers.

Olivier Ozoux is currently working as an Animation Consultant and Project Leader in SOFTIMAGE's Special Projects office in Los Angeles. He has been involved with Motion Capture since 1991 when SOFTIMAGE introduced it's 'Channels' architecture.

He has also worked with virtual sets and virtual characters on the ELSET project (virtual set software which was later sold to Accom), and helped SOFTIMAGE implement it's own version of a real-time performance system, the Virtual Theater. For more information, see
http://www.beachnet.com/~/o_ozoux/resume.html

References

Books

* "The Illusion of Life - Disney Animation", Frank Thomas and Ollie Johnston
* "Industrial Light & Magic - The Art of Special Effects", Thomas G. Smith
* "ILM Book II"
* "[digital] character animation" - George Maestri
* "Animation From Script to Screen" by Shamus Culhane
* "The Animation Workbook" by Tony White
* "The History of Animation: Enchanted Drawings" by Charles Solomon
* "Chuck Amuck" by Chuck Jones
* "Tex Avery, King of Cartoons" by Joe Adamson

* "Timing for Animation" by Harold Whitaker and John Halas
* "How to Animate Film Cartoons" by Preston Blair
* "The Animation Book" by Kit Laybourne
* "Serious Business, the Art and Commerce of Animation in America from Betty Boop to Toy Story" by Stefan Kanfer
* "The Illusion of Life, Essays on Animation" edited by Alan Cholodenko.

Most of these cover traditional drawn animation techniques, but the principles apply to CG animation as well.

Web
* http://www.3dsite.com (Great starting place for 3d)
* http://www.cinenet.net/users/rickmay/CGCHAR/ main.htm (CG Character Animation List)

Movies/Videos : The supplementary material appended to Laserdiscs from Disney contains much valuable material, specifically the CAV LD releases of Snow White and the Seven Dwarves, Cinderella, and Alice in Wonderland, all of which contain rare live action footage of voice and motion reference actors, used much differently than did the Fleischer Studios. Films which contained notable rotoscoped footage include the 1931 Betty Boop short subject Snow White (where Cab Calloway moonwalked as a cartoon long before Michael Jackson turned into one), the Fleischer feature film Gulliver's Travels, and of course, Ralph Bakshi's Lord of the Rings.

The difference between here and there: what graphic design brings to e-space.

Organizer
Lisa Koonts

Panelists
Andrew Blauvelt (North Carolina State University)
Edwin Utermohlen (North Carolina State University)
Laura Kusumoto (LVL Interactive)
Anne Burdick (The Offices of Anne Burdick)
Louise Sandhaus (California Institute of the Arts)
Natalie Buda (Flagler College)

SUMMARY

What does the practice of graphic design have to offer a medium originally created within the technical-scientific community? In the fluid medium of e-space, a primary difference between hypermedia, broadcast media, and print is the visual structure of information and the levels of interactivity. The designers in this panel discuss the interdisciplinary processes involved in designing interfaces, graphical precedents for visualizing information, and the structuring of electronic spaces.

OVERVIEW

Everything changes. Everything stays the same. Electronic spaces offer designers almost unprecedented opportunities for design. A closer look at this new medium reveals that we are still grappling with the same problems and processes of how we structure, arrange, and perceive information. Designing for e-space is similar to solving an equation with an increasingly large and diverse set of variables. Each solution contains different visual, structural and technical considerations. In e-space there is no intrinsic difference between here and there. Difference is realized through the visual form given to information regardless of its location or source. In the absence of specific environmental cues, the user's relationship to information is determined by its visual structure.

What does the practice of graphic design offer to the electronic medium? How can visual and information designers and engineers best collaborate to create workable interfaces within an increasingly more complex environment? What is the future of writing and the book in e-space? How do we communicate the concepts and processes of e-space in design curriculm?

Lisa Koonts, panel organizer

Lisa Koonts is a print and digital graphic designer. She has a BS in computer science, master's degree in graphic design, and a background in technical theatre. She has been working both as a web designer and with a virtual reality stage company.

Andrew Blauvelt & Edwin Utermohlen

Andrew Blauvelt is Chair of the Department of Graphic Design at NC State University. He has written and lectured about information design and digital technology in numerous venues.

Edwin Utermohlen is a Visiting Professor in Graphic Design at NC State University. He designs interactive media and web sites and creates digital prints through his company; RED.

Graphic design evolved out of the division of labor associated with bringing messages to the public. The activity of designing such messages traditionally fell to those who controlled the means of producing them: namely typesetters and printers. Not until the twentieth century did the means of producing messages become segmented so that the creation of designs became distinct from their reproduction and distribution. As such, graphic designers acted as "gatekeepers" to mass communications, mediating between clients and those capable of reproducing and distributing messages. Graphic designers exist as mediating agents between specific content "here" and specific audiences "there." With the personal computer the distinct activities of design, production, and distribution are re-integrated. Therefore, it might seem as if graphic designers are no longer a necessary component in the communications equation. But this notion would be problematic because it confuses technology with design; the means of doing things with a way of thinking and making things.

Part of what graphic designers can bring to e-space is their practical experience in print. Part of this legacy includes information design, namely the graphical representation of information through typography and imagery.

Until recently, information design has been largely limited to translating three-dimensional and four-dimensional content into the two-dimensional space of print. For example, maps give us a two-dimensional representation of space, while a calendar gives us a graphical representation of time. The advent of digital multimedia—sound, time, motion, interaction—allows us to "decompress" static, two-dimensional displays with the hope of enriching the users' experience by enhancing comprehension without sacrificing the complexity of the content.

Giving information visual form, ordering content, and orchestrating interaction suggests a narrative, or ways of reading. Sometimes readings are simple like the "rise and fall" of a typical graph and sometimes complex "stories" with multiple content and varied interpretations. As interaction with information expands, the opportunities for developing multiple narrative approaches to the same information grow. Importantly, by expanding the ways users can interact with information, we more accurately reveal that information is constructed to be interpreted and is not merely self-evident.

Laura Kusumoto

Laura Kusumoto is Director of Production at LVL Interactive, a Web site design and development company. Her background spans 18 years of software engineering and multimedia production in such diverse areas as artificial intelligence and virtual reality.

New media are the catalyst for merging applied arts and applied sciences. As an electronic space, the Web pushes designers and engineers to the forefront of this convergence. Like a car or a toaster, a Web site must look good, work correctly, and sell. Building a commercial site mixes the disciplines of graphic design, engineering, and business—and this sometimes feels like a convergence of water, oil, and milk. Taking cues from industrial design, Web teams can work synergistically to deliver value and enjoyment to the consumer.

How many of us like waiting 60 seconds to download an animated graphical doodad that struts its moment on the stage, full of sound and fury but meaning nothing? Today, we use the Web mainly to retrieve information in the form of text. As the Web matures, we will more often consume multimedia content. Web surfers prefer convenient access to all types of content, through an interface that immerses us in the flow of interactions. Any break in that flow is irritating.

Some Web designers obstruct usability at the very moment they are in a position to facilitate it. They are in this enviable position for a reason: the Web is visual. After all, it was the graphical browser that popularized the Internet. Without graphics, it was a cold and inconvenient place. Corporations today are enlisting professionals to help shift the focus of Web design from self-expression to usability and market value.

There is no user manual for the Web. With few conventions to follow, Web designers are groping to create interfaces with the right balance of form and functionality—to make a Web site as easy to use as a toaster that delivers tasty contents.

The field of industrial design offers insights for Web designers. It devotes equal reverence to form and functionality. Separate, yet interdependent, design processes yield a sleek-looking car with superb performance. In commercial Web development, visual design (graphic and information design) combines with engineering to create a product. This presentation will review examples of industrial and Web design with an eye towards how these disciplines interplay in the development process.

At past SIGGRAPH conferences we've heard the plea: "We are the visual communicators! Empower us to do the design!" Now, Web teams are concerned not with whether, but how, we make this happen. We need to communicate with each other to bring out the best in both visual and engineering design. This presentation concludes by looking at the different disciplinary cultures of graphic designers and engineers, focusing on how to deal with each.

Anne Burdick & Louise Sandhaus

Anne Burdick is a graphic designer, critic and educator. Her firm, The Offices of Anne Burdick, is located in Los Angeles, where she teaches in the graduate programs at Art Center College of Design and the California Institute of the Arts. Anne is Visual Editor of the ELECTRONIC BOOK REVIEW (ebr), an on-line literary journal <www.altx.com/ebr> and co-editor of ebr6, an upcoming issue on image and narrative in new media.

Louise Sandhaus is a consultant in user-interface design and the Associate Director of the Graphic Design Program at the California Institute of the Arts. Recently, she was co-organizer of "Bit x Bit: Rebuilding Design Education in the Digital Context," part of a 3-day event on design education sponsored by the School of Visual Arts, NY. She was also co-organizer of the Los Angeles-based panel discussion, "Authoring Options: Who is the (Author)ity in New Media?"

What is the future of writing and the book in e-space? And what does this have to do with graphic design?

Anne Burdick and Louise Sandhaus will present work from new media projects that explore these questions. Looking at the history of the book and its role in shaping Western culture—as an object, a technology, and a metaphor for intelligence—Anne and Louise ponder how the forms of the future will shape what we know and how we know it. As form-makers, organizers, and visualizers, graphic designers have the ability to imagine new possibilities for form which enable new constructs for thought.

Louise will present the work of two recent interdisciplinary courses, "Mutant Design: The Future of the Book" and "The Apple Design Project '97: The Future of Libraries," sponsored by the Apple Research Laboratories and conducted at the California Institute of the Arts.

Anne will be presenting her collaboration with the writers and editors of the ELECTRONIC BOOK REVIEW, an on-line forum committed to reviewing all aspects of book culture in the context of emerging media, promoting translations and transformations from print to screen, and covering literary work that is designed to be read in electronic formats. As Visual Editor, Anne is responsible for establishing structural parameters that will both limit and enable the kinds of writing that can take place at the site.

Natalie Buda

Natalie Buda is an Assistant Professor of Graphic Design at Flagler College in St. Augustine, Florida, where she developed the Flagler Graphics Lab for student experimentation in electronic spaces. She has an undergraduate degree in film and video, a master's degree in graphic design, and professional experience in corporate video. Recently, she presented "The Electronic Muse: Rethinking Originality and Ownership in the Digital Age" at a national symposium at the Cummer Museum of Art.

Mastery of visual language, composition, and space are some of the devices graphic designers use to create and steer the messages audiences receive from a variety of media. Electronic media (e-space) embody the elements of variable time and space, which are not a part of traditional print media. These two variables make a difference in conceptualizing and designing for e-space because they allow for greater control over how the audience receives and navigates through communication.

The visual mapping of an electronic space portrays a sense of time and place within the electronic production, and differentiates it from its surrounding environment. Processes used in designing information to establish a place and time include creating visual hierarchy, navigation through trail marking, and pacing. Some of these methods used in authoring visual messages spring from older conventions in cinema and print media and are reinterpreted and expanded in e-space.

Using the procedures of visual language and the skills developed in a graphic design curriculum, students in the Flagler Graphics Lab (FGL) address the concepts and processes for designing in new media. For example, can one use graphic design to influence what happens cognitively and visually on the screen as well as between the screens. Experiments from the FGL will be presented to demonstrate how visual direction makes a difference between "here" and "there" in electronic space.

Interfacing Reality:
Exploring Emerging Trends between Humans and Machines

Organizer
Eric Paulos (University of California, Berkeley)

Panelists
John Canny (University of California, Berkeley)
Eduardo Kac (School of the Art Institute of Chicago)
Ken Goldberg (University of California, Berkeley)
Mark Pauline (Survival Research Laboratories)
Stelarc (Performance Artist)

"[My project] is something we're all intimately interested in: the reshaping of the human body by modern technology."
— Vaughan in *Crash* by J.G. Ballard (1973)

Summary

The spontaneous growth of the World Wide Web (WWW) over the past several years has resulted in a plethora of remote controlled mechanical devices, all of them accessible from any networked computer in the world. This panel brings together a diverse collection of pioneers who are actively engaged in exploring future directions and implications of internet based robots and machinery, in essence the newly emerging human-machine interface. The panel will discuss current and future applications of such technology and several extremely relevant social issues including: cultural impact, human acceptance, interaction, authenticity, responsibility, privacy, and security.

Introduction

There is little doubt that the world of computer graphics will be enriched with renderings and interactions beyond the virtual and into the real by employing robots and other mechanical systems. This panel hopes to begin the discussion of this evolution of technology at SIGGRAPH. We chose SIGGRAPH because it is the premiere international forum devoted to exploring cutting edge interactive techniques. This goal is reflected directly in the title, SIGGRAPH: Special Interest Group on Computer Graphics and Interactive Techniques. Most of SIGGRAPH is aimed at the discovery and development of breathtakingly realistic visual sensations of modern computer graphics and the playful interactions of humans in the resulting virtual worlds. The participants of this panel have employed techniques from computer graphics and extended the tools used to interact with virtual worlds, to allow humans to interact with real remote worlds. Researchers on this panel are extremely adept and inventive at incorporating the latest elements of technology from a variety of fields: computer graphics, robotics, networking, and human interaction, into entirely new interactive systems. All of the panelist have developed several such systems, pushing the limits of technology at the crossroads of computer graphics, networking, and telerobotics. Each panelist will detail the technological elements, development, economic impact, and human interaction of the various systems they have created as well as addressing related issues in the field.

Cultural/Economic Impact and Human Interaction

Over the past several years, users have become increasingly more comfortable interacting within three dimensional virtual words. However, the graphic rich tele-presence and robotic systems created by these panelists allow users to begin exploring real spaces distant from themselves. In addition many of these systems allow users to observe and in many cases physically alter the real world and/or its inhabitants. It is still unclear when and how users will adopt such systems, to what extent they will blur the line with virtual worlds, and the scope of their economic and social impact, particularly as new forms of communication and useful household/industrial tools. The panelists will comment on possible future directions for this technology and the development of the newly emerging human-machine interface.

Authenticity

With virtual and real worlds equally accessible, new issues of authenticity arise. While developers of tele-robotic sites on the internet strive to create the most realistic impression of "presence" in the remote space, users are still left wondering if what is on the other end is real. All of the information delivered to the end user is digital due to the underlying transport mechanism. As a result, images and even video can be faked by clever methods of fetching pre-stored images. In fact there have been a number of creators of purportedly tele-robotic sites in the last few years that have been exposed as charlatans. This panel will discuss fundamental obstacles related to this issue and attempts (failed and successful) to overcome this ambiguity.

Responsibility, Privacy, and Security

So far most of the WWW based tele-robotic systems have been intentionally designed to be safe. Although many of these systems have been developed on standard industrial robots where safety is an issue, they are typically kept behind locked doors, preventing an unsuspecting person from accidentally placing some part of their body in harm's way of the robot. However, fundamentally, there is nothing preventing people from intentionally or accidentally creating systems where physical structural damage or human injury is possible. In fact such systems have already been developed by several of the panelists. What are the issues of responsibility in terms of property damage and human injury with such systems? Does the responsibility rest in the hands of the creator of such a system or in the remote individual controlling the system? In the case of the latter it is entirely possible, due to the easy of anonymity on the internet, that the identity of the remote user may never be know. We are all aware of the interest in hacking into computers and manipulating, stealing, or destroying digital data. One can easily image the fascination of taking control of a potentially dangerous device, to use to one's only ends. There are more questions than answers in this area, only that extreme precautions should be taken when developing such systems. This panel will directly address the inevitable future collision of this research with these issues in the years ahead as universal control of various mechanical systems evolve.

John Canny

John Canny is a Professor in the Computer Science Department at the University of California, Berkeley. A large portion of his research is in RISC robotics - on minimalist designs for hardware and software in robotic devices. Recently, he has been adopting this design methodology to WWW based tele-robotics in the hopes of creating new tools for home consumers and industry. He is also the recipient of several major awards including the Presidential Young Investigator Award, the David and Lucille Packard Foundation Fellowship, and the ACM Doctorial Dissertation Award.

Eduardo Kac

Rara Avis, a networked telepresence installation by Eduardo Kac (1996)

Eduardo Kac is an artist and writer who works with electronic and photonic media. His work has been exhibited widely in the United States, Europe, and South America. Kac's works belong to the permanent collections of the Museum of Modern Art in New York, the Museum of Holography in Chicago, and the Museum of Modern Art in Rio de Janeiro, Brazil, among others. He is a member of the editorial board of the journal Leonardo. His anthology "New Media Poetry: Poetic Innovation and New Technologies" was published in 1996 as a special issue of the journal Visible Language, of which he was a guest editor. Eduardo Kac was the Chair of SIGGRAPH's Artist Sketches in 1995. His writings have appeared in several books and journals in many languages, including French, German, English, Portuguese, Spanish, Hungarian, Finnish and Russian. He is an Assistant Professor of Art and Technology at the School of the Art Institute of Chicago and has received numerous grants and awards for his work.

Ken Goldberg

The Telegarden: An Interactive Installation on the WWW. (Ken Goldberg 1995) (Photo by Robert Wedermeyer)

"We must rediscover a commerce with the world and a presence to the world that is older than intelligence." Merleau-Ponty (1945)

I'm interested in the distance between the viewer and what is being viewed. How does technology alter our perceptions of distance, scale, and structure? Technologies for viewing continue to evolve, from the camera obscura to the telescope to the atomic force microscope; each new technology raises questions about what is real versus what is an artifact of the viewing process. I've become increasingly interested in the epistemological question: "How do I know this is real?" The visitor acts and perceives this "reality" throught an instrument with no objective scale. How does the framed vision of the microscope differ from the framing induced by the World Wide Web? Discontinuities induced by these media can undermine what Husserl calls the "inner" and "outer" horizons of experience. These horizons are vital to architecture and to what we might call "telepistemology": how distance influences belief, truth, and perception.

Ken Goldberg is an artist and engineer on the faculty at UC Berkeley. He has exhibited technology based artwork internationally including exhibitions at New Langton Arts '97, Ars Electronica '96, Dutch Electronic Art Festival '96, and LAX '92. His installations have won juried awards at the Interactive Media Festival, the Festival for Interactive Arts, New Voices/New Visions, and the National Information Infrastructure Awards. He was named an NSF Presidential Faculty Fellow in 1995.

Mark Pauline

The Unexpected Destruction of Elaborately Engineered Artifacts: A Misguided Adventure in Risk Eradication, Happening Without Known Cause, in Connection with Events that are Not Necessarily Related (SRL / Austin, Texas / March 1997) (Photo by Alan Anzalone)

Survival Research Laboratories (SRL) was conceived of and founded by Mark Pauline in November 1978. Since its inception, SRL has operated as an organization of creative technicians dedicated to re-directing the techniques, tools, and tenets of industry, science, and the military away from their typical manifestations in practicality, product or warfare. Since 1979, SRL has staged over 50 mechanized presentations in the United States and Europe. Each performance consists of a unique set of ritualized interactions between machines, robots, and special effects devices, employed in developing themes of socio-political satire. Humans are present only as audience or operators.

Eric Paulos

Tele-Embodiment: Space Browser and Surface Cruiser (Paulos 1997)

Eric Paulos is a Graduate Student in the Computer Science Department at the University of California, Berkeley. His researchinterests revolve around robotics and WWW based telepresence, particulary human centered robotics. He has developed several WWW based tele-operated robots including, Mechanical Gaze (1995), Space Browsers (1996), and Surface Cruisers (1997). With Mark Pauline, Judith Donath, and John Canny, he designed and implemented Legal Tender (1996), a WWW tele-robotic system that allows users to examine a pair of $100 bills and experiment on them to determine their authenticity. His work has has been exhibited internationally, including SIGGRAPH, the Dutch Electronic Art Festival (DEAF) in Rotterdam, the Blasthaus Gallery, and a performance for the opening of the Whitney Museum of American Art's 1997 Biennial Exhibition.

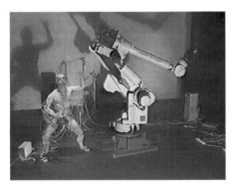

Stelarc

Host Body / Coupled Gestures (Stelarc)

Stelarc is a performance artist who is interested in alternate aesthetic strategies. He has used medical, robot and virtual reality systems to explore, extend and enhance the body's performance parameters. In the past he has acoustically and visually probed the body - amplifying his brainwaves, heartbeat, bloodflow and muscle signals and filming the inside of his lungs, stomach and colon.

Having experimented with the limitations of the body, he has developed strategies to augment its capabilities, interfacing the body with prosthetics and computer technologies. For the fifth Australian Sculpture Triennale in 1993 he inserted an electronic object into his stomach cavity and tracked its operation with video endoscopy. Recently he has developed a touch-screen interfaced muscle stimulation system that enabled the remote actuation of the body. The Ping Body software stimualtes the body o move to the ebb and flow of internet activity. He has performed extensively overseas with his Third Hand, Virtual Arm, Virtual Body and industrial robot arms in art events, including new music, dance festivals and experimental theatre. Stelarc's artwork is solely represented by the Sherman Galleries in Sydney. Between 1995-1997 he received an Australia Council Arts/Craft Board Fellowship.

Contact Information

John Canny
Professor
University of California, Berkeley
jfc@cs.berkeley.edu
http://www.cs.berkeley.edu/~jfc

Ken Goldberg
Assistant Professor
Industrial Engineering and Operations Research Department
University of California at Berkeley
goldberg@ieor.berkeley.edu
http://www.ieor.berkeley.edu/~goldberg

Eduardo Kac
Assistant Professor of Art and Technology
The School of the Art Institute of Chicago
ekac@artic.edu
http://www.uky.edu/FineArts/Art/kac/kachome.html

Mark Pauline
Founder/Director
Survival Research Laboratories
markp@srl.org
http://www.srl.org

Eric Paulos
Computer Science Graduate Student
University of California at Berkeley
paulos@cs.berkeley.edu
http://www.cs.berkeley.edu/~paulos/

Stelarc
Performance Artist
Research into muscle stimulation and
remote actuation of the body
stelarc@peg.apc.org
http://www.merlin.com.au/stelarc/

References

Ballard, J. G. Crash, Noonday Press, 1973.

Benjamin, W. Art in the Age of Mechanical Reproduction, 1939.

Legal Tender http://www.counterfeit.org

Goertz, R. and Thompson, R. "Electronically controlled manipulator," Nucleonics, 1954.

Goldberg, K., Mascha, M., Gentner, S., Rothenberg, N., Sutter, C., and Wiegley, J. "Robot Teleoperation Via the WWW," International Conference on Robotics and Automation, 1995.

Kac, Edwardo. "Interactive Art on the Internet", Wired World, Proceedings of the Ars Electronica Symposium, Peter Weibel, 1995.

Paulos, E. and Canny, J. "Ubiquitous Tele-embodiment: Applications and Implications", Special Issue on Innovative Applications of the World Wide Web, International Journal of Human-Computer Studies, 1997.

Ping Body http://www.merlin.com.au/stelarc/pingbody/

PRoP: Personal Roving Presence http://vive.cs.berkeley.edu/prop

Rara Avis http://www.uky.edu/FineArts/Art/kac/raraavis.html

Survival Research Laboratories http://www.srl.org

The Telegarden http://telegarden.aec.at

What 3D API for Java should I use and why?

Organizer
Dave Nadeau (San Diego Supercomputer Center)

Panelists
Brad Grantham (Silicon Graphics, Inc.)
Colin McCartney (Microsoft Corporation)
Mitra (Mitra Internet Consulting)
Henry Sowizral (Sun Microsystems Inc.)

The Java[tm] slogan "Write once, run anywhere" has attracted a great deal of attention. Today, 3D graphics professionals are wondering if the slogan can apply to 3D graphics application development as well. This panel brings together representatives from groups developing 3D APIs for Java and challenges them to compare and contrast their products, discussing product features, differences, performance, portability, and limitations.

Brad Grantham, Silicon Graphics Inc.

Silicon Graphics provides a number of solutions to application developers and users desiring the Java language and high-performance interactive 3D graphics.

Application programmers may use Java bindings to OpenGL++, a scene graph toolkit for OpenGL[tm], to render and to provide interaction with 3D objects and scenes. OpenGL++ provides interaction features similar to the Inventor interactive toolkit and features derived from Silicon Graphics' experience with the high-performance Performer visual simulation toolkit. Developers have control over their 3D application from as high a level as "load and render this VRML 2.0 database" to as low a level as "draw these polygons with these colors, viewed from this location".

The Cosmo Worlds[tm] VRML 2.0 authoring application in conjunction with the multi-platform Cosmo Player[tm] VRML 2.0 navigator provides VRML 2.0 content authors with powerful modeling features. Embedded Java script nodes can directly control and manipulate the VRML 2.0 scene graph and access standard Java packages and language features. Java applets may control VRML 2.0 content through the External Authoring Interface (EAI).

Java bindings to OpenGL on both Silicon Graphics workstations and Windows 95/NT PCs can be used in a variety of domains where the overhead of frequent Java method calls is acceptable, including education, experimentation, and the prototype conversion of OpenGL code from other languages.

A developer's choice of 3D API for Java must be based on the developer's requirements and the available features.

Java bindings for OpenGL and OpenGL++ provide access to advanced features on workstations which may be important to a developer requiring, for example, high polygon counts, advanced texture capabilities, or machine-specific extensions. On the other hand, the use of these advanced features may preclude using a Windows NT/95 PC. Java3D, as a required part of Java, can be relied upon to be ubiquitous. Any operating system that provides the JavaMedia APIs will provide Java3D, and that may be important to users from games developers to teachers to intranet application developers.

The VRML 2.0 EAI and scripting nodes provide an efficient interface to controlling active VRML 2.0 content that exists on any VRML 2.0 browser. The EAI provides simple application control of databases. This may be important, for example, to customers providing kiosk applications which must direct user interaction with the database. Scripting nodes, on the other hand, provide intelligent content that can be readily referenced and included as URLs in larger databases, which may be important for vendors building multi-user VRML worlds.

Silicon Graphics brings a substantial amount of expertise in interactive high-performance 3D graphics to the table. SGI provides a range of solutions for Java developers from detailed OpenGL pipeline control to high-level VRML 2.0 navigation.

To state that any particular solution is the best, however, is as inappropriate as claiming a Lotus is always a better choice of vehicle than a Geo Metro. OpenGL++ and alternative 3D APIs all have advantages and disadvantages. A developer's choice of 3D Java API can only be made after consideration of the merits of each solution and the developer's requirements.

Colin McCartney, Microsoft Corp.

 Microsoft's commitment to 3D graphics is founded on the principals of flexibility and choice for developers, giving them the ability to select the appropriate tools for the task in hand. Microsoft offers a full range of integrated 3D graphics options from the high to low end, enabling developers to create the full spectrum of 3D applications.

The company's Java[tm] strategy embraces these same principals of choice and flexibility, enabling developers to create applications in the languages of their choice through features such as ActiveX/Beans integration and cross-language debugging, allowing them to leverage their existing experience and code bases while taking advantage of Java. To enhance the developer's Java experience, Microsoft is focused on providing the fastest, most secure, most robust Java VM, the richest, most fully featured suite of Java class libraries and the best tools for Java development.

Microsoft's DirectX J[tm] suite of multimedia Java class libraries gives developers access to the power of DirectX's highly optimised native code and enables them to take advantage of hardware acceleration in their Java applications. DirectX J is Microsoft's multimedia solution for Java, and includes the following technologies for comprehensive, cross-platform 3D graphics in Java:

  * Direct3D[tm] J: Direct3D J gives Java developers both low-overhead to-the-metal access via its Immediate Mode API, and interoperable access to a higher-level suite of functionality, including a full world management system,

via its Retained Mode API.

* DirectAnimation™: DirectAnimation is a higher level media integration API that allows developers to integrate media compoments such as 3D graphics, video, 2D graphics and audio with ease.

* VRML 97: Following Microsoft's acquisition of DimensionX, developers can not only build tools and applications using Microsoft's Liquid Reality™-based Java VRML viewer; they can now take advantage of Java and VRML-specific 3D capabilities that will be integrated into the Direct3D J class libraries.

Mitra, Mitra Internet Consulting

When choosing an API to use for programming 3D and Java, the most important thing is to know what you are trying to achieve. Each of the API's presented in this panel has their strengths and weaknesses.

As I see it, the biggest distinction between the API's is what I call "Who's on top".

* If you see yourself as writing a 3D application (for example a game), then one of the lower level API's (Direct3D, Java3D, or OpenGL++) might make sense. At the time of this writing, Direct3D has only just added Java bindings, and the specifications for Java3D and OpenGL++ are not available, so comparisom is not really useful.

* If, on the other hand, you see yourself as modelling a world of active, independent, or inter-dependant, objects, then you should probably be building the world in VRML, and adding behavior to the VRML objects via VRML2.0's Java scripting API (not to be confused with JavaScript scripting).

* Alternatively, if you are building a Web page, that needs a 3D image, for example to graph some results, then using VRML's Java or Javascript External Application Interface (EAI) probably makes sense.

The biggest advantage that the VRML/Java scripting API gives you is its simplicity. Essentially your Java program is mostly manipulating the fields and nodes of a standard VRML 2.0 scene graph. In Java3D or OpenGL++ I understand that you will have intimate control of the lighting, and other rendering characteristics. In VRML's API's you don't worry about these things, leaving them to the browser. This allows the behavior author to concentrate on what they do best, writing programs, leaving a modeler to do what they do best, using an authoring tool to set up a visual effect.

Of course, in the VRML API, as in anything else the author has full access to everything you expect in Java, for example to AWT classes, or to Threads, or the network.

Henry Sowizral, Sun Microsystems Inc.

The Java 3D Graphics API is a scene graph-based and Java-based API designed with graphics performance in mind. Its inheritance model removes as much graphic state information from the interior of a scene graph as possible and moves that information to the scene-graph's leaves. By placing the state information at the leaves, Java 3D can use scene graphs as carriers of graphics information. It need not treat them as a computational structure. Efficient processing of a Java 3D scene graph will require that a Java 3D renderer build and use ancillary data structures.

The Java 3D API provides programmers with three rendering modes: immediate, retained, and compiled retained. Programmers can use any one, two, or even all three modes at the same time to render a scene. The immediate mode defines a higher level abstraction of low-level functionality by providing programmers with a means to change graphic attributes and to render sets of points, lines, or triangles directly to a canvas. The retained mode allows programmers to specify a scene-graph and to inform the Java 3D renderer that it should render that scene graph. The compiled retained mode allows programmers to identify a scene graph fragment as a candidate for compilation. That fragment may have mutable components identified as such by the programmer. Such information allows a Java 3D compiler to analyze a scene-graph fragment and replace it with a opaque representation subject to the programmer specified mutability constraints.

The API includes a number of unique features including a more complete view model (one that supports more exotic viewing environments such a immersive and fish-tank VR applications), an extended input model that permits access to real-time inputs such as six-degree-of-freedom trackers and joysticks, and a behavior execution and execution-culling model that uses Java as its base language and the registration of "wakeup criteria" to permit culling. As a runtime API, Java 3D programs must construct their scene-graphs programatically. The API does not specify an external file format for scene graphs. It does however, make it quite straightforward to build object loaders and scene-graph loaders. As an example, we rapidly built a wavefront ".obj" format loader and a VRML 1.0 loader. In future, we anticipate the availability of many other loaders including a VRML 2.0 loader. In the case of VRML 2.0, the Java 3D API specifies a uniform technique for processing VRML 2.0 routes and fields. That specification relies on a Java 3D behavior that triggers at each frame and propagates any changes associated with a route. Applications that do not use VRML 2.0 routes pay no cost for runtime support of routes and fields.

The Java 3D Graphics API was initially designed by a small group of partner companies. Sun distributed the design resulting from that effort to its Java licensees as a 0.9 specification of the Java 3D API. Interested Java licensees provided feedback that resulted in changes to the 0.9 specification. Sun incorporated those updates into the specification and then distributed the updated 0.95 specification of the Java 3D API to the general public for feedback. Comments from the public will change the 0.95 specification and culminate in the 1.0 specification of the Java 3D API.

community/content/interface: creative online journalism

Organizer
Mark Tribe (Rhizome Internet)

Panelists
Armin Medosch (Telepolis Journal)
Kathy Rae Huffman (Telepolis Journal)
Lev Manovich (University of California, San Diego)
Gary Wolf (HotWired)

Introduction

The age of information has opened wide the ideological doors of the Internet for Online Journalism. New topics, new forms and revised (and often simply updated) formats of traditional print media have sprung up around the world like digital weeds. The Web is determined by the cultural fabric of our moment, it is a product of the zeitgeist of the age of information. The question, "How does the technology of the Web determine the quality of online journalism?" will be only one of the questions addressed by each panelist, who will not only relate his or her experience in online journalism but will bring key issues at hand to illustrate, demonstrate and investigate the topics that challenge creative online journalism.

Repurposing Print

Until recently, many online journals were simply Web versions of pre-existing print publications. But in the past year, most of these publications have started to provide online content and information services that are not available in print. How is this changing the nature of journalism, and what questions does this repurposing raise from the perspective of access?

Community Killers

What appears as a new "e-zine" topic is sometimes just a reframed old-timer, an issue that has been around on the Net for years, and discussed online but not in hypertext markup graphics form (HTML), but as net culture discussions in the form of mailing lists and newsgroups. The radical content of what were formerly these "insider news forums" have been treated with off-the-shelf formatting for a wider audience, and often with the hope to lure a lucrative consumer audience. Does the design, plug-ins, bells and whistles attract or detract those who seek challenging content. Is there any profit to be made from these conversions, and if not, how will these online communities survive in the future.

Hyperconsciousness

Hypertext is a key to the easy online information retrieval, and an interface that informs and reacts is what brings 'em back. But, how does interface design affect content? Is information simply hyped-up with new online jargon, and designed into a new format, constitute online journalism? .... seek a new level of consciousness?

New Media Vanguard or Digital Cess Pool?

New hot topics in online journalism, like net culture, cyber feminism digital rights and privacy effect society as a whole, but tend to emerge as topics in online first, finding a place later in print and broadcast forms that reach a wider public. Does online journalism represent an informational vanguard, or a breeding ground for trencly issues that only affect a privileged few? The demographics of the Web are changing rapidly, with women gaining significant numbers, in some surveys they even amount to 42%. But the online population is still 87% white, 64% have college degrees, and the average income is $60,000 per year. Still, one in ten person is under the age of 18 years old, and is growing up interacting with media, rather than receiving it passively. The need for content and creativity in online journalism is imperative in order to influence this new audience of game conscious, peer pressured youth.

Connected readers

Under what circumstances do consumer politics take the voice away from the publishers, influence attitudes towards online publishing, and at what point do readers cease to become no more interactive than they do with traditional print media? We discuss the Net, the Global Brain, and International Connectivity as if everyone was online, yet how can we be a global online community considering that industrialized Germany still has only 2 percent of its population wired, and using internet accounts? How do online journals find their audience, and do they need to actually develop loyal communities. What are the various target audiences for the new online journalism, and how does stratigically does development market topics to new online readers. What constitutes an online community? And who are the connected readers of net culture, artists, art critics and culture studies online journals?

Panelists

Mark Tribe, Founder, Rhizome Internet, New York
http://www.rhizome.com

Mark studied Visual Art at the University of California, San Diego (MFA 1994) and received a BA, Phi Beta Kappa, in Visual Art from Brown University in 1990. He was a designer at Pixelpark GmbH in Gerlin, where he helped implement the Wildpart web site. As founder and CEO of Rhizome Internet in 1996, he created a fourm for the exchange of ideas crucial for new media art to emerge as a significant contribution to the boom of the broader concerns of contemporary art.

Rhizome is geographically dispersed, bringing people together in three forums, a web site, and two mailing lists, Rhizome Raw and Rhizome Digest. As a forum for the exchange of ideas, Rhizome is a comprehensive resource for information and critical writing about what's going on at the intersection of emerging technology and contemporary art. As a business venture, Rhizome seeks innovative solutions to market artists' images online as a contribution to the expanding need for content and creativity, and to develop an image bank for Net design.

Armin Medosch, Editor, Telepolis Journal, London
http://www.ix.de/tp/

A creative writer, curator and producer, Armin is Editor and founder the online venture of Heise Verlag (Hannover, Germany): Telepolis - Das Magazin der Netzkultur. Heise Verlag, a significant publisher of German language technical journals (notably ix and Ct) seeded Telepolis as a creative project to develop online publishing, and since itís premiere in Spring 1996, it has become the largest online net culture fourm. Considering that Germany is far behind America in the population being wired (in 1996 only 2% had a private email account), the readership of Telepolis has climbing steadily during the past year. In response to general reader interest, Telepolis also publishes a quarterly review of selected online texts - a tactical reverse strategy.

Important issues for Armin are not how much money big publishers can earn, but rather how writers are paid adequately, how copyright issues are handled properly, and the overall conditions for critical discourses and investigative journalism. With the position that online publishing will not replace newspapers anytime soon, Telepolis seeks to understand how society as a whole influences online publishing. Specifically, in 96 widespread panic over pornography and terrorism swept journalists away. Although in the early fantasy era of Web deleria it was felt that everybody on the net was not just a consumer, but also a producer (a pro-sumer), the tendency has retreated back to consumer mentality.

Kathy Rae Huffman, Correspondent pop~TARTS, Telepolis, Vienna
http://www.ix.de/tp/po/4005/fhome.htm

A curator, net communicator, and media art critic based in Austria since 1991, Kathy created the pop~TARTS column for Telepolis with Margarete Jahrmann, a multi-media artist and Theoretician. Based in Vienna, pop~TARTS brings to Telepolis a multimedia forum for special topics and Net-women. Using a palaver style, the column encourages an exchange of dialogue between Net personalites, and the subjects it features. In 1997, a group of pop~AGENTS was selected to react to pop~TOPICS and pop~EVENTS. The community of women between 18 - 25 is the fastest growing Internet user in Europe. Pop~TARTS engages grrls and boyx in topical Net issues like *micronations* and *data_set: the uploaded body*.

A graduate of the School of Design, California State Universtiy Long Beach (MFA 1979), Kathy has been active in media art since her student days. As former curator at the Long Beach Museum of Art, and the ICA Boston, she brings to Net culture her history of video art, art television, and interactive art, topics on which she now lectures widely in Europe. In Vienna she also collaborates on the female Net artwork FACE SETTINGS with Eva Wohlgemuth (http://thing.at/face/) which brings cooking, connectivity and community together in real and virtual events. She has curated dar~LINKS for the Ars Electronica Center, Linz, and cooperates with media organizations like Van Gogh TV, Hamburg, Internationale Stadt, Berlin and V2_Organization, Rotterdam.

Gary Wolf, Executive Producer, HotWired, San Francisco
http://www.hotwired.com

One of the team that launched HotWired in 1994, Gary is currently developing Wired channels for the new generation of browser technology. In the fall of 1995, he led the launce of theWired News channel on Pointcast. He is also the author of Aether Madness: An Offbeat Guide to the Online World, and a frequent contributor to Wired Magazine.

HotWired is a network of smart Web sites recognized as the premier source for original, interactive, multimedia content on the World Wide Web. Soon after its launch, it already started receiving 10 hits per minute, and it has only leaped on from there. Recognized as the first to move style into the extremely limited constraints of HTML, HotWired combines text, sound, image and interactivity to vitalize the medium. It is a model of cross-cultural discourse, technical innovation and design. In addition to coverage of health, arts, politics and digital culture, HotWired offers HotBot, a comprhensive search tool for the web, including a complete fully searchable archive of back issues of WIRED magazine.

Lev Manovich, Theorist and critic of new media, University of California, San Diego
http://jupiter.ucsd.edu/~manovich

Lev was born in Moscow, where he began his studies in fine arts and computer science. He received an M.A. in experimental psychology from NYU, and a Ph.D. in Visual and Cultural Studies from the University of Rochester. His writings have been published in seven countries, as well as in cyberspace. He has contributed to Rhizome Internet, Telepolis, and C Theory, to name only a few. In 1995, Lev was awarded a Mellon Fellowship in Art Criticism by the California Institute of the Arts. He is currently working on two books: a collection of essays on digital realism and a history of the social and cultural origins of computer graphics technologies tentatively entitled "The Engineering of Vision from Constructivism to Computer" (forthcoming from University of Texas Press).

One of the few theorists who seeks feedback consistently, Lev analyses the phenomena of interactive art, and media, as a shift between representation to manipulation. He is able to bring a unique perspective to the topic of Internet communication. Although he grew up in a Communist society ruled by Breznev, he brings a great sense of humor to his analysis, he calls it the "..giant garbage site for the information society...with everybody dumping their used products of intellectual labor and nobody is cleaning it up." He points out "the complete transparency of the medium (which was already realized in communist societies) that everybody can track everybody else."

Educating the Digital Artist for the Entertainment Industry:
The Collision of Academia and Business

Organizer
Charles S. Swartz (UCLA Extension)

Panelists
Edwin E. Catmull (Pixar)
Robin King (Sheridan College)
Richard Weinberg (University of Southern California)
Jane Veeder (San Francisco State University)

DESCRIPTION

The entertainment industry has historically neglected education and training, perhaps believing that the supply of eager creative talent would always exceed the demand. But the explosive growth of digital technology applied to special visual effects and animation has created a desperate need for digital artists to work in film, television, video, computer games, and interactive media.

Much has been said recently about the urgency of creating a talent pipeline to fill this shortage. At first glance, it might seem educators on the one hand, and production and post-production companies on the other, would share a commonality of interests and goals. But deeper issues may reflect the different goals of academia and business. This panel proposes to air and address these issues, so that each side can better understand the other, and resulting work will be of higher quality and will produce more personal satisfaction.

Panel Chair

Charles S. Swartz is Program Manager of the Department of Entertainment Studies and Performing Arts at UCLA Extension, the continuing education division of UCLA, where he is responsible for professional training programs in Multimedia and Digital Technologies and the Business and Management of Entertainment, and shares responsibility for programs in film, television, video, and music. He led the efforts of UCLA Extension with IBM that resulted in establishing the UCLA Extension/IBM Media Lab, a multimedia teaching lab at the UCLA Extension Metropolitan Center on Universal CityWalk. He attended the University of Southern California, Department of Cinema-Television, as a graduate student and received his B.A., Magna Cum Laude, from Yale University.
Panel Members:

Dr. Edwin E. Catmull is a graduate of the University of Utah with a B.S. in Computer Science and in Physics, and holds a Ph.D in Computer Science. Dr. Catmull was awarded two Scientific and Technical Engineering Awards from The Academy of Motion Picture Arts and Sciences for his part in pioneering digital compositing and helping to develop RenderMan Software. Dr. Catmull received the Steven Anson Coons Award in recognition of his important research contributions and inspiring leadership in the computer graphics field. Dr. Catmull is a member of the Academy of Motion Picture Arts and Sciences and the Sciences and Technical Awards Committee.

Robin King is Currently Director of the School of Animation and Design at Sheridan College where he has been a member of the Faculty since 1971. He was responsible for the development of the graduate programs in Computer Animation and Computer Graphics which were launched in 1980. Professor King has lectured at SIGGRAPH and many other international conferences

and is working on several educational projects in the Far East. Currently, he is working on the design and development of a new, $24 million centre for Animation and Communications at Sheridan in partnership with the Government of Ontario.

Carl Rosendahl is President of PDI, which he founded in 1980 to combine his interest in film making and computer graphics; the company's core mission to generate fully computer animated imagery for entertainment products. Over the past 17 years, the company has successfully expanded from being a specialty production facility to one of the most respected computer animation and visual effects studios in the industry. A Los Angeles native, Rosendahl holds a BSEE from Stanford University (1979). He is an expert source for industry and the trade press, appearing as guest speaker at numerous industry conferences and symposiums, and is a frequent guest editor for Animation Magazine. Rosendahl also taught a graduate level course entitled, Computer Animation and Visual Effects for Film and Television at USC Film School in 1993 and 1994. He is a member of the governing board of directors of the Visual Effects Society and a long-standing member of ACM SIGGRAPH. Rosendahl is executive producer of the first Dreamworks/PDI computer-animated feature film, Ants.

Jane Veeder began in 1976 her long career in electronic media arts and was a member of the pioneering Chicago computer art scene in the early 1980's. She was one of the leaders of the artist group that developed high A/V standards for SIGGRAPH conferences and has served on the SIGGRAPH executive committee and as an organizer or contributor on many conferences. She currently teaches computer animation and interactive multimedia at San Francisco State University, where she is Associate Professor in the College of Creative Arts. She recently served a year as director of animation at Time Warner Interactive, Games Division.

Richard Weinberg is the Director of the USC Computer Animation Laboratory, which he established in 1985, and is a Research Associate Professor in the USC School of Cinema-Television. He co-designed the original curriculum for USC's MFA in Animation and Digital Arts program, and established the CG Hatchery at USC's Annenberg Center Multimedia Incubator.

He obtained a Ph.D. and M.S. from the University of Minnesota, and a B.A. from Cornell University, all in the area of computer science / computer graphics. His interests include computer animation, multimedia, scientific visualization and entertainment technology.

The Panel will discuss, among others, the following issues. Preliminary responses to questions raised by some of these issues follow.

* Educators tend to emphasize the process of learning, while companies look at the end product. A more polished portfolio/demo reel may actually reflect a less adventurous and imaginative student, who took fewer chances in order to protect the commercial appeal of the end result.

* What is the optimum balance between theory and practice in computer graphics education? Too little practice may lower the "hiring desirability quotient." Too little theory may produce a student adequately fluent in today's software but less able to adapt to the future.

* Production and post-production companies are engaged in collaborative activity, where strong teamwork skills and effective management and organizational abilities must complement artistic and technical strengths. Do educators give these skill sets sufficient attention?

"In general, computer animation and related programs are faced with major tasks in educating students in the theoretical and practical aspects of production and post production. The individual skill set required for a specialist in this arena to become productive demands more training than can usually be achieved in college and university programs. Educators must create environments in which shared skills are essential to the development of each student's capabilities. However, the shift from individual production to collaborative group work requires more complex methodologies which are often idiosyncratic to a company's creative environment, specialization and client base. Institutions should certainly give more attention to group work, but companies themselves need to ensure that the transition to the work environment includes further enhancement of the student's collaborative skill. Work placement and a "farm team" arrangements are approaches which should be seriously considered.

Students need to be highly competent with hardware and software but, more than anything else, they need to be creative, imaginative, adaptable, and thoroughly skilled in the fundamental aspects of storyboarding, character development, animation dynamics as well as familiar with technical and creative demands of the industry. Personal development is continuous throughout the individual's career. Companies must also be more committed to providing an environment which encourages the growth and development of their employees skills." — *Robin King*

* "I need 25 digital artists and I need them yesterday!" Can educators increase the number of highly talented graduates in a rapid fashion? Are there limits imposed by the quality of the applicant pool, maximum effective class size, availability of qualified faculty, and funding?

"The rapidly expanding computer animation and special effects

industry is asking: "Where are the animators?" For those of us sitting on years of rejected equipment donation requests, it's about time and I'm grateful. But they should also be asking a more long range question: "Where are the animation teachers?"

Skilled industry professionals who may teach software skills part-time have much to contribute but won't supply the complete solution. The best academics have a real commitment to helping

students develop creative individuality, a repertoire of creative strategies and inventive design methodologies. Additionally, animation academics today must teach a wide range of topics and media, run animation studios and computer labs, pursue ongoing research and development to translate their discipline across evolving technologies, and commit themselves to lifelong learning to keep up with new creative and production opportunities. The resulting role is a tall order for anyone!

Working in animation production is so lucrative and exciting today that rarely are graduating students attracted to teaching. The decline in fine arts funding and declining public support for education make this role even less attractive. Industry can help by partnering with academic programs in concrete ways such as team-teaching courses using cutting-edge technology and new production paradigms, student and faculty internship programs, donations of slightly less-than-cutting edge technology, and production advising and support for faculty personal work." — *Jane Veeder*

* When evaluating artistic talent, imagination, and creativity, how do educators measure the unmeasurable? Do assessment instruments exist that are meaningful to employers?

"Real methods for assessment do exist, but they are rarely in the students' grades and transcripts. Critical tools an employer has for evaluating the important aspects of students are the faculty and staff of the school as well as curriculum. We consider various programs of study to satisfy the different needs of production. What an employer wants to know typically is not measured in today's grading system. Qualities such as the individual's passion for the work, their innate talent and their "eye," their strengths and weaknesses, their ability to work with a team, these are the kinds of things we want to know about the students.

Our most successful recruiting of students comes from schools where we have built a relationship with the faculty and staff. These relationships are built over time which involves ongoing communication and support between employer and school. — *Carl Rosendahl*

* For film and television especially, computer graphics work product rarely stands alone; images must be integrated with live-action footage and advance the underlying narrative. Do educational institutions teaching computer graphics and digital imaging place sufficient emphasis in their curricula on filmic narrative, storyboarding, cinematography, and editing?

"The USC School of Cinema-Television represents a highly unusual case, having an extremely close relationship with the Hollywood community, and academy award winning faculty members in cinematography and editing teaching students. Our students have strong interests in the integration of live action and digital images, and are producing several such projects each semester in 35mm film and video formats, making heavy use of digital compositing, film scanning, animation and nonlinear editing. Students in our MFA in Animation and Digital Arts program take screenwriting, life drawing, and study the entire filmmaking process in a production-oriented curriculum so that they will understand the relationship of their work to the larger whole. Being successful in this educational arena requires extensive infrastructure, a critical mass of faculty and staff, substantial corporate support, and recognition on the part of the educational institution of the escalating importance of this field. When these resources come together with the right students in a creative environment, a new breed of digital artist can emerge, that we hope will push the envelope of the industry." — *Richard Weinberg*

Medical Visualization - Why We Use CG
and Does It REALLY Make a Difference in Creating Meaningful Images

Co-Organizers:
Virginia E. McArthur (Engineering Animation, Inc.)
Carrie L. DiLorenzo (Engineering Animation, Inc.)

Panelists
Marsha Jessup (UMDNJ-Robert Wood Johnson Medical School)
Patrick Lynch (Yale University School of Medicine),
Casey Herbert (Flying Foto Factory)
Jane Hurd (Hurd Studios)

Summary

Creating effective illustration depends on having a clear grasp of the information to be conveyed as well as a visual strategy for adapting the message for the audience. As image-makers versed in the "visual language of science", medical illustrators may spend as much time gathering information as finding ways to make the message accessible to particular audiences. With 3D animation technology, and tools for creating interactive and simulation products, a greater variety of visual solutions are possible in biomedical communication than with traditional art media. This round table discussion is intended to promote critique and evaluation of the ways in which using computer graphics has made a difference in how we present visual information.

Introduction

Somewhere between the structured discipline of scientific inquiry and the more ephemeral business of entertainment lies the profession of medical illustration, an endeavor that demands both rigor and creativity. Unlike the scientist or entertainment animator, the medical illustrator is faced with communication problems almost completely constrained by the content, the audience, the schedule, the budget, and the presentation format. This presents the illustrator with the creative challenge of meeting all these needs without sacrificing aesthetic standards. Constantly faced with the questions of "What information needs to be included?" and "How should it be presented?", we have the responsibility for insuring that the communication objectives of a particular illustration, animation, or interactive product are met.

Trained as artists and instructional designers for the medical profession, the domain of the medical illustrator encompasses research, conceptualization, design, and application. While content such as anatomy hardly changes in a lifetime, alternatives for application have exploded with the accessibility of computer graphic tools. More than likely, questions that arise regarding how best to use new technology are common to all image-makers trying to convey information accurately while maintaining a coherent story line or conveying a logical train of thought. This generation of tools has almost usurped our notion of artistic craftsmanship with an abundance of technical alternatives and shortcuts, while not liberating us from the task of developing visual strategies. We are still responsible for identifying the communication objective and designing the visual manifestation of the concepts. The question is whether developments in computer graphics have had an impact on the types of concepts we choose to portray, or the strategies we invoke to portray them. Verisimilitude, focus, coherence, and mood are all qualities of visual presentations intended to facilitate a particular type of understanding. While medical illustrators as a group aim to incorporate some or all of these along with other characteristics of images in their work, these particular topics shall be used as a vehicle for discussion among the members of the panel.

In aiming for verisimilitude we seek to effect recognition of a likeness, perhaps to simulate a view or an experience. The depiction of light and shadow, volume relationships in space, depth cues, color, textures, transparency, or surface perturbations all are components of an image or scene that the traditional artist can manipulate with ease by using computer graphic tools. As we focus, we seek to emphasize what is unique by highlighting specific information at the exclusion of other details, or distinguishing one thing from another. Differential three-dimensional rendering, multilayered images in a two dimensional format, and the orchestrated choices for camera lenses, motion, and timing can all provide the visual communicator with numerous options for setting up contrasts or placing emphasis. With coherence, we intend to make comprehensible the relationships between separate elements to show logical cause and effect or explain the evolution of a story. The modeling of anatomically related structures, the composition of shapes and color in a two dimensional format, the layout of events and transitions within a storyboard, and the organization of interfaces within an interactive document all can benefit from the convenience of the computer as a production tool. Finally, with mood, we mean to suggest the most compelling emotive quality of a subject. By intensifying or diminishing visual cues, areas of focus, the coherence of relationships, the connection between cause and effect, or the apparent rate of the passage of time with the flexibility and control of digital tools, a visual presentation can be made to captivate or persuade. Still, while computer graphics can be demonstrated to have an effect on our ability to to achieve certain qualities, it is impossible to judge the significance of the tools without an understanding of the cognitive skills an illustrator must develop and exercise. Discerning when to use computer graphics over traditional media can be a simple matter of weighing cost and efficiency against the tradeoffs in visual quality. But judging which tool is most suitable, what qualities the image needs, and how best to achieve them to meet the communication objective are all at the core of developing a visual presentation. These decisions most likely derive, in part, from pregraduate training in fundamental artistic principles of color, light and shadow, form, composition, and design. Our expertise, however, evolves with an understanding of the content, an ability to develop a rationale for the artistic decisions that are made, and through experience in doing the work.

The training of a medical illustrator includes graduate level human gross anatomy, cellular biology, embryology, neuroscience, pathology as well as observation and practice in surgical technique. This background gives the medical illustrator the means to consider content in terms of its visual qualities. Experience in drawing anatomic relationships, rendering tissue quality, and developing image sequences to communicate the steps of a surgical procedure are all exercises that give the illustration student the opportunity to identify concepts, develop strategies, and execute them in a variety of media. Regular faculty critiques engage the student in a dialog about the reasons why certain colors are chosen, highlights added, edges enhanced, or diagonals offset in terms of the message that is intended. Being able to articulate the reasons for every artistic decision becomes another essential part of the illustrator's tool kit. Finally, practice in the field becomes the ultimate test of effectiveness. However realistic, focused, detailed, or dramatic an illustration may be, its success lies in whether the intended audience can demonstrate an understanding of the message that was intended.

The fact that digital tools speed up rote processes, provide infinite revisability and considerably expand the range of output options can free the medical illustrator to concentrate more on information delivery. While the technology incurs its own expense for the individual enterpreneur, it has heightened the demand for digital media in institutional and commercial settings. This makes a stronger case for medical illustrators to identify more readily what to communicate and to be more efficient in expressing it. For many illustrators, the biggest advantage of access to computer graphic tools may be the opportunity to specialize in one particular market of visual presentation. The development of surgical simulators, volume rendered images, and segmentation of anatomic datasets are all activities that strive for verisimilitude or authenticity by generating images from real data. Medical-legal graphics and educational media are usually developed to provide visual focus on certain details at the specific exclusion of information which is not relevant. Animation and interactive multimedia may depend on the coherence of information presented in a temporal format, or in a logical, step-by-step sequence. And images, whether static or in motion, developed for advertisement, entertainment, or patient education often rely on the communicability of a mood or feeling related to a subject to lure or usher the audience in and hold their attention.

With representation from several branches of biomedical communication, this panel has been modeled as a round table discussion among a small group selected for their expertise. By using these general aspects of visual presentation as a framework, a series of questions about the impact of computer graphic technology will be used as a springboard for discussion. Comments or questions arising from the audience or from electronic dialogue via the Internet prior to the meeting will be incorporated into the discussion. The round table format has been selected to allow free discussion among the panelists and attendees.

Marsha Jessup: The use of three-dimensional computer graphics in health care training and practice has taken medical visualization out of a flat, static world of two-dimensional snapshots of reality into a multi-dimensional, dynamic experiential environment. What has traditionally been visualized and manipulated in multiple iterations in the mind is now seen in front of the eyes and interacted with physically. This new direction in medical visualization has vast implications for health care training and health industry manufacturing. Visualizing the interaction of three-dimensional human anatomy and medical devices with specific physical properties in an animated electronic workspace is becoming common to both endeavors. The design, virtual prototyping, and manufacture of medical devices closely parallels surgical planning, simulation, and practice. The common denominator and critical point of intersection is knowledge-based, medical visualization which has an inherent capacity to make health care and health industry manufacturing more efficient, responsive, and cost effective.

Patrick Lynch: The evolution of 2D digital medical illustration will be characterized by the increasing density of information. Today's layered Photoshop files are progenitors of tomorrow's informated illustrations, deeply layered 2D visuals that may contain multiple illustrations, diagnostic images, and multimedia content. Informated illustrations might be thought of as smart objects within larger digital documents, or small, stratified visual databases capable of producing an almost infinite variety of 2D "illustrations," depending on how the relationships between components are manipulated. Layers might have programmed logical relationships to one another. Possible components of the various layers might include preliminary artwork and references, extensive anatomic labels with descriptive text, 3D models, multiple diagnostic imaging references, or digital audiovisual references.

Casey Herbert: As a designer, I've had the opportunity to adapt my skills and interests in visual communication to the peculiarities of the computer as a method of ideation and production. This process has presented many challenges which with them has brought an array of possibilities that have enriched the work I produce. The iterative nature of our tools opens up unlimited possibilities, benefiting all involved in the process.

As a communicator, and the interpreter of clients' concepts and wishes, the designing and developing of 3-dimensional static and motion images has many stages. The foremost of these is the understanding of the subject matter adequately to apply my skills to develop an accurate, appealing, and instructive product. This requires that I coax from my clients, be they engineers, surgeons, or program producers that which is crucial to the presentation— our product. This requires I be student to client at some points in the process, as well as trusted teacher, vendor and practitioner of a somewhat mysterious craft. This in and of itself is always an interesting dynamic.

The 3D toolsets we use at Flying Foto Factory offer our designers the creative freedom far beyond what traditional media has allowed. These same tools offer an economy in practice to our clients, allowing for experimentation in alternatives which otherwise would be prohibitive with traditional tools in terms of time and budgets. As hired guns, we're always pressed for meeting deadlines and budget.

Jane Hurd: Most medical illustration is visual storytelling with an educational objective. To do this effectively, first we must be skilled in using the visual language. Second, we must have clarity of vision. This includes 1) knowledge of the content to be communicated, 2) a point of view about the content, 3) knowledge of the audience's intellectual and emotional capacities and biases, 4) a coherent, meaningful illustration "style" designed for that audience and befitting the client's identity and 5) a desired outcome of the communication - an objective. Finally, execution must not lose sight of the vision. Execution decisions with CG should be no different than with "traditional" media. Only the mechanics are different. Computer graphics are simply different and rapidly changing tools with many more options but also pitfalls.

Prior to CG, illustrators had to create the illusion of motion in still images. The option of motion provided by computer animation has greatly enhanced storytelling. Also, we had to spend inordinate time deriving data from gross or microscopic photos, reading text descriptions of relationships, processes and concepts and then using our imaginations to portray structures that we had never really seen in the way that we wanted to portray them for a particular communication objective. Then we had to use our imaginations to create specific views, perspective, lighting and color to create the illusion of form and space. The 3D environment has made this process much easier. But herein lies one pitfall. The 3D environment still has limitations. Frequently, functionality does not take advantage of many of the insights gained by artists over thousands of years in creating the illusion of space on a 2D surface. This is evident in the default settings of light positions, camera lenses and shadow colors. Much of this knowledge of how visual cues effect our perception of space and form must still be applied in the 3D environment, because ultimately the final images still end up on a 2D plane. The fact that creation takes place in a 3D computer environment is no guarantee that the final 2D image will successfully convey the illusion of space. Many artists trained in 3D CG, never having had to use their imaginations to create the illusion of space on a 2D plane could benefit from the knowledge of their "traditional" predecessors.

Many medical illustrators have always had to fight the temptation of "overdoing" illustrations with too much decorative clutter not relevant to the objective. This tendency becomes an even greater pitfall with CG, because it is easy to be seduced by the glitter and glitz of the many special effects available and lose sight of the original clarity of vision.

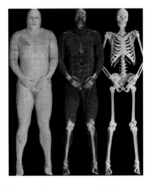

Figure 1. Volume-Renderings of Visible Human Male, Engineering Animation, Inc.

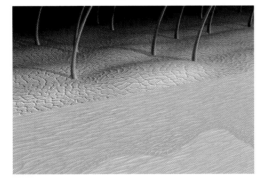

Figure 2. Epidermis, Casey Herbert, Flying Foto Factory.

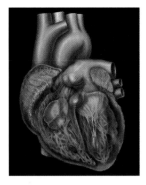

Figure 3. Anterior Heart, Patrick Lynch, Yale University School of Medicine.

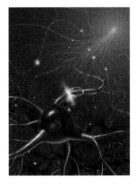

Figure 4. Blood Brain Barrier, Engineering Animation, Inc.

Figure 5. Cataract Surgery (IOL)

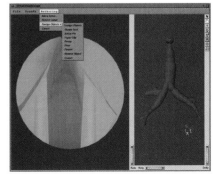

Jane Hurd/Art Dir., Time Life Medical.
Figure 6. Virtual Bronchoscopy, Engineering Animation, Inc.

Putting a Human Face on Cyberspace: Designing Avatars and the Virtual Worlds They Live In

Organizer
Bruce Damer (Contact Consortium)

Panelists
Steve DiPaola (OnLive! Technologies)
Joannis Paniaras (University of Art and Design)
Kirk Parsons (Black Sun Interactive)
Bernie Roel (University of Waterloo)
Moses Ma (Internet Game Inc.)

Figure 1:User avatars in conversation in the voice supported Onlive Traveler virtual world, August 1996

The Emergence of a New Design Medium

Who do you want to be today? As thousands of Internet users begin new lives as 'avatars' in virtual worlds, a new design industry is being born. SIGGRAPH 1996 had several panels, BOFs, exhibits, and discussions on VRML, character animation and multi user virtual communities. These forums introduced the medium we term "avatar cyberspace" to the SIGGRAPH community. Since SIGGRAPH, conferences such as Virtual Humans, Earth to Avatars 96, World Movers, and VRML 97 began to flesh out some of the major issues in designing for avatar worlds. In addition, avatar standards efforts such as Living Worlds, Universal Avatars and Open Community have been initiated.

Avatars and the worlds they live in comprise a vast new design medium attracting a wide range of professionals including: anthropologists, 3D and multimedia designers, character animators, musicians, voice and facial expression specialists, performance artists, architects, business workgroup and work-flow experts, and educators involved in distance learning.

The Discussants

We have assembled a group of experts to discuss the technologies underlying avatars, design tools and approaches to build avatars and the worlds they live in, and the psychological relationship of users to their avatars.

Bruce Damer: Bruce Damer is co-director of the Contact Consortium, the world's leading forum on avatar virtual worlds. Bruce speaks and writes extensively on new Internet frontiers and is completing a book on avatar worlds.

Steve DiPaola: Steve DiPaola leads a team of artists, architects, UI designers and musicians in designing and developing 3D Avatars and virtual spaces at Onlive! Technologies the creators of the Traveler voice-supported virtual world.

Moses Ma: Moses Ma is an Internet and computer gaming visionary and was the originator of the Universal Avatars specification with IBM. He recently became co-author of the Open Community VRML multi-user specification proposal with Mitsubishi Electronics.

Ioannis Paniaras: Ioannis Paniaras is completing graduate research at the Media Lab of the University of Art and Design Helsinki UIAH. Ioannis is studying virtual communities and avatar fashion trends and their influence on social life in Cyberspace.

Kirk Parsons: Kirk Parsons is a developer of avatar authoring software and has served as a chief avatar technologist for a number of companies including Black Sun Interactive.

Bernie Roehl: Bernie Roehl is a software developer based at the University of Waterloo in Ontario, Canada. Bernie has written several books and dozens of articles on virtual worlds and currently chairs the Virtual Humans Architecture Group.

Issue Areas

Figure 2: Avatar wedding in AlphaWorld, May 8, 1996

The design of multi-user graphical virtual environments is one of the most challenging new areas in computer science and consumer on-line services. Supporting tens of thousands of users in simultaneous communication in a shared virtual environment, within which they can build their own spaces and shape their own faces might seem like an impossible task. Yet, a dozen such environments are running today, hosting over 350,000 users dialing in from home PCs.

The number one question asked by users entering these virtual environments is: how can I design my own "avatar" (their virtual embodiment)? The success or failure of these environments in research or commercial settings can hinge on avatar design issues. Basic design decisions often involve trade-offs: in the basic technology choices (2D versus 3D, polygonal versus photorealistic), in the methods of communication (text versus voice, gesture versus facial animation) and in the use of standards (VRML versus proprietary 3D, IRC versus custom communication backbones). The most difficult design criteria to pin down are aesthetic: what makes one person 'like' or 'identify' with their avatar can be often very personal and subjective.

The panelists will focus on design approaches for avatars within the emergent 'avatar cyberspace'. Some panelists will give an overview of the underlying technologies of avatars, some will describe their experiences designing and using avatar virtual worlds and others will address aesthetic and psychological issues surrounding avatars.

We encourage you to download and try some of these virtual worlds. There is a comprehensive gateway to the medium of Avatar Cyberspace at http://www.digitalspace.com/avatars. Additional information on projects and debates within Avatar Cyberspace can be found at the Contact Consortium home page at: http://www.ccon.org.

Summaries of the Individual Presenters

Bruce Damer, Panel Moderator

What the moderator will contribute to the panel

In my task as moderator, I will guide the panelists through the major themes and provide a continuity to the work done over the past year, making sense of the trends and technologies for the audience. I also plan to act to discipline panelists to stay focused on the issues of avatar design (as this topic area is so broadly connected to other interesting subjects).

The moderator's viewpoint on the panel topic

I feel that the panel topic will emerge into a whole discipline of design, emerging from the synthesis of many different fields. To take a cue from Nicholas Negroponte, the question we face is no longer: "are you being digital?" but is now "what is your digital being?"

Figure 3: Avatars meeting in street scenes in OZ Virtual, March 1997

The Panelists

Steve DiPaola

What Steve will contribute to the panel

I will speak about design approaches which rely heavily on techniques to make users feel that they are really interacting in the virtual space: 3D attenuated voice and sound, 3D navigation,

an immersive first person U.I., individualized 3D head avatars with emotions and lip sync, 3D space design. I will then cover how well Onlive has transposed this experience to consumer based PC platforms connected to the Internet at dial-up speeds. During the panel, I will connect live to a virtual world allowing panelists to query users and ask for themselves how effective the design approaches are.

The panelist's viewpoint on the panel topic

The design approach to avatar cyberspace that I bring is born of experience trying to emulate natural social paradigms and provide immersion in a 3D visual and sound landscapes. Three more-detailed examples of design choices we have made might spark interest and debate within the panel and the audience:

* *Does community come from communication?* I hold that the structural process of a community and socialization, real or virtual is communication and that the most natural human form of communication is verbal. Therefore, 3D spatial multi-participant voice with distance attenuation, and stereo positioning is the best tool for the development of virtual cocktail parties and virtual communities alike. Other panelists or the audience may choose to challenge this view based on their experience in text-based virtual community.
* *You are your avatar, but can we use just heads?* A fundamental goal of avatar cyberspace is to bind the Real Person at their computer ~with~ the Virtual Avatar in cyberspace. Given the finite CPU/polygon/bandwidth resources, we need to invest in the most natural form of socialization first: face to face. I posit that the body (hand gestures, body language) is secondary for human communication and can be added later. Would anyone care to challenge this?
* *Major Design Issue: physically based spiral of infinite betterment* Given the natural emulation goal, one might assume that the design choice is to strive to make things more and more realistic, this is not so. A major truth in computer graphics and simulation (and well known for facial modeling) is the more realistic you make something, the more open to criticism it is for not being realistic enough. So we emulate natural paradigms just enough to achieve recognition of familiarness. Is 'just good enough for all practical purposes' just good enough?

Moses Ma

What Moses will contribute to the panel

I will contribute my background and experience in attempting to develop and promote a standard set of formats, protocols and design methodologies for avatars. Until now, avatars have been system and browser dependent, which meant that an avatar created for one virtual world wasn't necessarily compatible with other worlds. A number of people in the VRML business have put together a proposal, called Universal Avatars, which details a way to standardize what avatars are and do.

By using this proposed standard, avatars will be able to move from one world to another, keeping the same appearance and behavior. This means that users will be able to recognize other users' avatars that they met in other worlds. And their avatars will have individualized automatic actions, moods, and even pets.

And they'll be able to tell how their friends, from around the world, are feeling today, just by the look on their avatar's faces.

The latest draft of our proposal now deals with a variety of issues, which begin with 3D models and behaviors, but now ventures forth to discuss other important issues, such as persistent identity, interworld communications, database concerns, and support for additional emerging standards such T-120, H-323 and Versit. We believe that this is an early basis for an emerging "operating system" for socialization.

The panelist's viewpoint on the panel topic

Clearly, it would be useful to have a standardized avatar representation for the purpose of visiting all virtual worlds with a user's preferred avatar representation and openly tendered identity profile. This has many benefits, including the reduction of the workload on the user, the standardization of global search for other people through their public avatar presentation, and the ability to create new business opportunities for VR vendors. The Universal Avatar system, if adopted, could have a fundamental impact on the design of avatars in the medium of virtual

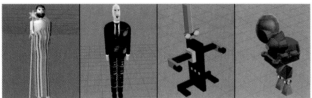

worlds on the Internet.

Figure 4: Various avatars designed by Ioannis Paniaras

Ioannis Paniaras

What Ioannis will contribute to the panel

As an artist, designer, and researcher in CMC (computer mediated communication) I will focus on issues related with the aesthetics, the design, the visual management of the avatar, its identity and the community of avatars and their cultural manifestations through a design perspective. I will pose the following provocative questions to the panel:

* What is a virtual persona and how does one design for and manage a virtual persona?
* How do the aesthetics and the visual appearance of an avatar can contribute to a didactic state of virtual life and communication in the virtual community?
* How does the design of the avatar influences the identity and the perception of the self in real life?
* What is an ideal interface for human contact?

I will also demonstrate some design examples of avatars with articulation and expressions.

The panelist's viewpoint on the panel topic

This medium is not understood well but has demonstrated the power to defragment the solid identity [the modern notion of the identity] and sustain the emergence of a plethora of virtual identities. Avatars are part of the visual and behavioral grammar of the emerging cultures in virtual communities, and by analyz-

ing the design structure of the avatar we help understand the direction we might heading in human contact. I would like to ask the audience think about new visions for avatar mediated communication which originate in knowledge of human behavior.

Kirk Parsons

What Kirk will contribute to the panel

I will focus on avatar representation issues, including avatar animation. My presentation will be done from a technical perspective, with the goal being to relate the key technical trade-offs to avatar authoring possibilities. This presentation will be complementary with Ioannis' in that he will be focusing on top level artistic issues, while I'll focus on how the underlying technology affects an artist's choices in the design process.

* Expressiveness in avatars - how is it achieved
* Suspension of Disbelief
* Morph based animations
* Keyframe animations
* Real-time motion technologies
* Artificial Intelligence and Avatars

The panelist's viewpoint on the panel topic

I believe that any designer of avatars must have a solid understanding of underlying technologies, not only to enable them to function within narrow bandwidth constraints, but also to create effective and aesthetically pleasing designs. The use of photorealism to reduce polygon count, texture mapping and morphing to create facial expression and other 'tricks' must be in the designer's grab bag of techniques.

Bernie Roehl

What Bernie will contribute to the panel

What I will contribute to the panel is a strong background in the technology of virtual reality, as well as insight into the activities of various groups (Living Worlds and the Virtual Humans Architecture Group) which are relevant to our efforts at avatar standards definition and avatar design. I feel it's important that we acknowledge the need to create expressive and communicative avatars within the constraints imposed by bandwidth, latency and rendering performance.

The panelist's viewpoint on the panel topic

My viewpoint on the panel is that it should attempt to identify and prioritize the most important issues related to avatars, as a first step towards dealing with those issues. My own personal feeling is that the key issues are:

* defining standards that enable the creation of interoperable avatars
* creating tools that allow users to create their own avatars
* provide avatars with as much expressive power as possible, using voice and gesture and facial expressions
* find effective methods for integrating speech, expression and movement
* issues surrounding identity and the ownership of one's virtual self

Sounding Off on Audio: The Future of Internet Sound

Organizer
Paul Godwin (New Dog Music)

Panelists
Eythor Arnolds (Oz Interactive Inc.)
William L. Martens (University of Aizu)
Tim Cole (SSEYO Ltd.)
James Grunke (Onlive Technologies)

The following is a compilation of ideas and writings from three of the four panelists and from myself as host. I have been involved with music and audio on a professional level for some 17 years. As a professional sound designer for theater I created hundreds of complex sound effects which were reproduced and mixed live in a sophisticated surround sound environment— before the term "surround sound' was ever in use. Theatre sound is certainly one of the most significant pre-cursors to the concepts of 3D or immersive audio we find being discussed and occasionally implemented in today's computer oriented media. As a composer, I created soundtracks in an "after-the-fact" production routine for documentary films and television commercials. The power and influence of effective soundtracks in those media are uncontested, though as Bill Martens will point out, also under appreciated, under funded and under scheduled. While Bill is also quite opinionated about what he calls "the neglected sibling" syndrome, that is, sound as the under appreciated kid sibling to graphics, I have had other experience with this subject. In my transition from traditional broadcast media to interactive media, I found a community that was actually much more receptive and appreciative of excellent sound design and intelligent music, than I had encountered in the broadcast field. Many projects actually have included the sound designers and composers in design phase meetings, not only for their opinions on their subject, but for their overall design suggestions.

Upon landing in San Francisco in 1994, I was invited to become a featured artist at the launch of HotWired, Wired magazine's online magazine. The simplest move was to provide digitized audio files of some far out sound design I had done for commercials and other media and due to their short deadlines and low budget, that is just what I provided. As the year went on, I was contacted several other times by HotWired, who began to engage my services to create a RealAudio tour for surfing their site. In this case the music was actually the on-screen model which allowed the user to move forward and backward on a net tour. Finally, we were involved in developing an OnNet audio logo which was structured out of modem sounds turned into music. I was actually quite disappointed with the approach I saw developing there, a broadcast model, a publishing model, being enforced on the web, which seemed to have infinitely greater possibilities as a tool for communication.

The next significant milestone in this progression was my exposure to a talk which Mark Pesce, the co-creator of VRML, gave at a San Francisco VERGE (virtual reality group) meeting. Pesce spoke of "WorldSong", a concept not clearly defined, but clearly implying the entire world using sound for some kind of spiritual communion over the Internet. I befriended Pesce and began to try and hammer out just how this WorldSong would be realized. Pesce introduced me to Dr. William Martens, one of our four panelists, who did pioneering research at Northwestern University in an anechoic chamber on the subject of Psychoacoustics. Dr. Martens went on to work at E-Mu Systems where he developed 3D code which wound up incorporated in E-

Mu's parent company's PC-based sound card, the Creative Labs AWE-32. Dr. Martens then wrote the specification for audio which was included (in a minimized form) in VRML 2.0.

But how could we get the entire world to hear each other at once, or better yet, how could we hear the sounds that already existed in the web, and use them to navigate. Pesce and I came up with an elaborate distributed system concept for hearing the sounds of the web and using them to navigate. We demonstrated a prototype of this system at the Doors of Perception conference in Amsterdam in November of 1995.

Enter the Avatar community. Upon seeing the Onlive Traveler interface at work, a 3D rendered environment with real-time avatars speaking to each other over the net, albeit at a resolution of 8bit/8KHz. The leap had been made - sound communities on the Web! This was the most exciting interactive experience so far. And the key was sound. It became quite clear that Onlive could serve as the environment to beta test Pesce's WorldSong. And again, it was at SIGGRAPH that we pulled it off. Just one year ago in the Digital Bayou, we created a Sound Community consisting of 15 people in New Orleans doing a vocal toning exercise with 5 people in San Francisco. This structured improvisation was not only possible across great distances and low bandwidth, but a great deal of fun. With Onlive, we went on to create to subsequent "proof of concepts". One of them linked 7 cities including 2 European and 2 Canadian all making sounds together on the Web. The group assembled at the base site was comprised of 60-70 computer professionals, and I felt my work was well made. Implanting the meme into these designers heads had been my goal from the start.

It was at this time that I encountered James Grunke. As Director of Audio at Onlive Technologies, James was developing a very elegant GUI for the creation of interactive audio. All I could think of was "where can I get a hold of this tool?" Fortunately, in the true 'net spirit' evidenced by much of the web community, James was suggesting his R.A.S. or Random Audio Sequencer as a specification for the creation of interactive audio. As chairman of the MIDI Manufacturer's Association and as former Director of Audio at Atari Corporation, I was certain James was the man for the job of putting across this spec.

Also that week in New Orleans, I encountered Eythor Arnalds, the sound visionary for the Icelandic startup OZ Interactive. Eythor spoke to me of his concept of using Levels of Detail in audio on the web. Why shouldn't sound be played in increasingly complex iterations, just as graphics could download in increasingly detailed streams?

Tim Cole is not known to me personally but his company SSEYO has launched a device called KOAN which allows end users, musicians or not, to create some of the most beautiful music I have heard, on or off the web. This recombinant music can last for hours without repeating itself. Tim's vision is of

MIDI as the grand connector, a system so low in bandwidth as to turn all other musical solutions into great and sluggish lumbering giants. MIDI will surely be a key component in the future of web audio and if you haven't yet tried KOAN, download it at once!

Moving audio and the web in general beyond a broadcast or publishing model is my greatest desire as a designer and as one who envisions the future. It is in that spirit that I have gathered together these four individuals whose work has most impressed me in this field. Following will be some statements by the panelists, in their own words which outline their interests and concerns for the future of internet audio.

"Spatial Sound Design for Interaction and Immersion"

William L. Martens, Ph.D.
Human Interface Lab University of Aizu

High quality 3D graphics has typically been regarded as the most important component in the design of interactive and immersive new media. The second most important ingredient would have to be real-time rendering of 3D sound (the neglected sibling of the industry's gifted child, 3D graphics). Yet spatial sound design is virtually never given the attention it requires and deserves. Of course, the problem is actually more fundamental than this. Audio production, in general, has always played a role subsidiary to visual production. Just as in film production, the sound design for multimedia production has often been left until near the end of the time allotted for development. And the budget, both in terms of financial resources and computational resources, has often been in far too small a proportion. Yet in comparison to the visuals, good sound design has more power to produce emotional responses in the user.

One of the primary differences between the contribution of improved graphics and improved sound in creating a powerful experience from multimedia software is that the contribution of the sound is less obvious to the user. They just don't seem to be able to "see" how the sound has enriched their experience. On the other hand, it is much more "apparent" how improved graphics have contributed. However, it is by the very unobtrusiveness of good sound design that it gains it's power. In a market where consumers have become jaded by exquisite imagery, it takes a lot for interactive graphics to give rise to any emotional response. However, good sound design can, and often does, produce emotional responses such as awe, suspense, and serenity, and the consumer doesn't seem to notice that it was the music that shaped these responses.

Tim Cole, SSEYO Ltd.

The music of the future is uncertain

A continuous experience?

Do you imagine an Internet future where all music content is predefined or precomposed and streamed and therefore also likely to have many joins and gaps? Or, like the endless journey you rejoin each time you use the Internet, do you imagine an Internet future where all music content is created fresh for you, part of a rich and seamless interactive personal experience? The near term reality probably lies somewhere in between, but is certainly moving towards the latter as 'the experience' becomes ever more important.

Creating the content - consumers as producers?

With an ever increasing audience online, people will be looking to provide their own low-bandwidth musical experiences to accompany their websites. Creating great sounding music has always been the domain of talented musicians, but getting copyright clearances for the use of recordings of this music on the internet will be a big obstacle for the greater public (and has many bandwidth implications). In the same way that graphics packages/clip art and desktop publishing software gave people the freedom to easily design and publish their own materials, generative music software will allow them to create their own musical environments (high bandwidth recorded or low-bandwidth continuous). With the launch of the easy to use Koan X drag 'n' mix generative music powertool, low-bandwidth (2-20k) personal musical creativity for the wider audience is now a reality.

One way - both ways

Is Internet music going to be one way push (like current TV) or will it be two way as people expect to have more interaction with it? To some extent this will depend on the resources available to the site. If two way interaction is the way ahead, then what is Internet interactive music? * Is it multiple streamed audio files where you choose and mix the source? * Or is it like the looping music found in many games where (often long) fixed phrases and added sound effects are juxtaposed at play time, and that you will be able to trigger with a mouse click? * Or does it go even further than this, allowing users to genuinely experience a personal dynamic music environment where they would have the power to affect it and customize it to their liking and where they feel a sense of involvement? In this case, where the music contains a degree of uncertainty/freshness, it will be composed locally and so requires an intelligent music engine to do the composition.

* For VRML worlds, will it be a collaboration between the two (interactive/streaming), where the a server hosts an interactive music composition engine, the output of which visitors can 'affect', and which is then streamed to create a *shared* musical experience.

MIDI standards

MIDI is a natural choice for interactive music but is hampered by widely varying soundsets on host machines. For Internet MIDI music to be in widespread use a consistent listener experience is required. Is this to be achieved through DLS or SoundFonts, more powerful soft-synths or will installed hardware base hardware accelerators (soundcards/proprietary DSP chips) still be the overriding driver?

  * Can DLS/SoundFonts by itself be considered a low-bandwidth solution (a multi-download scenario if you go to many sites, as each would have its own samples) or will it require traditional distribution media to carry the audio samples and the player software?

  * Or, is a larger, once off high quality Softsynth download a better bet in the long run?

  * Or, will the onboard MIDI synthesis hardware (and software) on motherboards hold the key.

In any case, the installed base of any player technology will have a marked bearing on the outcome - and listeners have ever less time or inclination for software/hardware installations. Who will win the battle of the player standards? It may all come down to player distribution and installed base at the end of the day....

James Grunke
Director of Audio, Onlive Technologies
Chairman, MIDI Manufacturer's Assn.

I have seen the enemy and it is twisted copper pairs.

Living in the local loop of the phone system, twisted copper pair wire is what links the broad consumer base via analog connection to the Internet. Certain new technologies are pressing closer to the curb but many industry experts still claim that mass market broadband connections to the home are years if not decades away. This is the reality, this is the gating factor to bringing hi-fi music and audio effects to VRML worlds.

New narrow band delivery techniques are needed, standards and recommended practices must be developed, and embraced. The Downloadable Sounds recommended practice was recently released by the IASIG of the MIDI Manufacturers Association. This new protocol deals with many of the shortcomings in General MIDI by allowing authors to create their own custom sound files and articulation parameters insuring consistent cross platform performance. What is the integration path to use this new technology in VRML?

Combining industry standards with VRML specific audio playback mechanisms is the convergence needed to bring sophisticated soundscapes to the 3D Internet.

Image-Based Rendering: Really New or Déjà Vu?

Organizer
Michael Cohen (Microsoft Research)

Panelists
Marc Levoy (Stanford University)
Jitendra Malik (University of California, Berkeley)
Leonard McMillan (Massachusetts Institute of Technology)
Eric Chen (Live Picture)

Michael F. Cohen

Image Based Rendering (IBR), techniques which generate new images from other images rather than geometric primitives, appeared to burst onto the computer graphics scene in the last few years. IBR seems to hold the promise of leaping right over the difficulties of traditional modeling and rendering or at a minimum hiding the latency between rendered frames. This panel will first define what is meant by image based rendering and place this emerging technology in the context of a continuum of developments. The panel of IBR researchers will then speculate on the long-term impact of IBR on computer graphics by addressing issues such as:

* what is IBR good for?
* will IBR replace polygons?
* what could IBR mean for graphics on the net?
* what is the relationship between IBR and traditional computer vision research?

Perhaps the first task is to redefine our own understanding of the terms "image", "model", and "rendering". Traditional image synthesis rendering has meant simulating the flow of light from a source, reflecting it from a geometric and material description of a model, into a simulated camera and onto a film plane to produce an image. (Of course all this is done backwards if you are a ray tracer.)

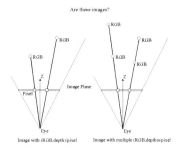

In particular, the result of this process, an "image", has generally been considered a 2D array of RGB valued pixels (or if you prefer, a continuous RGB valued function in 2D). What if a depth value is added at each pixel (or point in 2D)? Is this still an image? Or is this now a model consisting of colored points floating in 3D? What if instead of a single RGB and Z (depth value) per pixel, there is a list of these? Is this still an image, or a sparse volume? What is a 4D light field (or lumigraph) relative to an image?

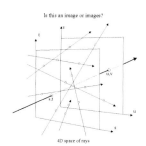

The computer graphics community is already familiar with concepts such as texture mapping, and environment mapping. These are certainly a form of image based rendering. What is the new excitement all about?

To begin to answer these questions, it is important to look at what has been achieved in the computer vision community as well. Vision researchers have struggled with the problems of producing accurate models from images, while the graphics community has tried to both create models through sophisticated user interfaces and to render these models. Vision technology continues to have a difficult time producing the rich detail in complex geometric models (but does have the visual effects of the detail in the original images). Meanwhile, graphics technology has difficulty in producing the same geometric detail and also in rendering its effects. However, by placing the partial results of computer vision methods end to end with those from graphics, we seem to be able to (in some cases) simply skip both difficulties. To a great extent, this has been the cause of the excitement. However, this paradigm is not yet well understood and its limitations are even less well understood. Hopefully, this panel will help clarify the questions if not the answers in this emerging research endeavor.

Marc Levoy

The study of image-based modeling and rendering techniques is essentially the study of sampled representations of 3D objects. This idea has been around for a long time in the form of textures, sprites, shadow and environment maps, range images, movie maps, and so on. In computer vision, classic examples include reflectance maps, disparity maps, optic flow fields, and epipolar volumes. The new vigor in this area seems to arise from two factors: a marked increase in the dimensionality and size of the representations - 3D volumes, 4D light fields, 5D plenoptic functions, and hierarchical image caches to name a few - and a shift toward fast, robust algorithms that combine techniques from graphics and vision.

Numerous engineering challenges must be overcome to make image-based techniques practical, including acquisition, compression, fast display, and software interface. The research community will undoubtedly respond to these challenges, leading to many SIGGRAPH papers in this area.

In this panel, I would like to address a different question: what are the outer boundaries of image-based modeling and rendering? In other words, how far can we push this paradigm? This question can be approached from several viewpoints (no pun intended):

* What other sampled *representations* of 3D objects are possible?

  Light fields were recently introduced into computer graphics as a 4D scalar field, but Adelson's plenoptic function, which inspired them, is a 5D scalar field, and Gershun's original light field was a 3D vector field. What other definitions are possible? As another example, light fields store radiance. Is there a place for irradiance fields? How about importance fields?

* What *operations* are possible on image-based representations?

  For example, to what extent can objects be edited via images of them? Can one write a paint program or a 3D modeler that operates entirely on light fields? Is knowledge of surface orientation essential in order to compute reflection, or depth in order to compute occlusion? Are there weaker forms of knowledge that suffice for these tasks?

* Recent work in image-based rendering has focused on walkthroughs; what are other *applications* exist for these techniques?

  The vision problem - determining shape from images - is known to be hard. If we are willing to represent shape as images, perhaps as a set of inconsistent range maps rather than as a geometric model, does this simplify the vision problem? Another hard problem is computing global illumination in complex environments. The inverse global illumination problem - determining surface reflectance from measured radiance in the presence of interreflections - is even harder; it has never been solved except on very simple scenes. Can image-based representations help solve these problems?

* Finally, any change in paradigm engenders a crisis in *scholarly methodology*; how shall we judge and compare the results of the new paradigm?

  For geometry-based representations, the graphics and computational geometry communities have developed analytical tools (e.g. visibility aspect graphs), measures of rendering cost (e.g. numbers of polygons, depth complexity, pixel count), and measures of image quality (e.g. aliasing, variance, discrepancy). Image-based representations will require new analytical tools and new metrics.

Leonard McMillan

At this early stage in the development of image-based rendering (IBR) it is worthwhile to ask several pertinent questions:

> What good is it?
> How will it be delivered?
> Where is it going?

IBR can be utilized in many of the same applications where conventional geometry-based computer graphics is employed today. The advantages of IBR methods include the easy acquisition of models from images, computational requirements that are independent of scene complexity, and the delivery of photorealism while avoiding the costs of physical simulation. IBR also holds promise in many new applications such as latency reduction in the network transmission of three-dimensional environments, and in virtual and augmented reality applications (with an emphasis on reality).

In order for IBR methods to be widely adopted in the computer-graphics industry their advantages over geometry-based systems must be realized. This will undoubtedly require the development of special-purpose hardware. It is interesting to speculate on the form that such hardware systems might take. Luckily, we can draw upon our more than 25 years of experience building geometry-based computer-graphics systems. There are striking similarities between IBR methods and the traditional rendering pipeline and the texture mapping approaches used today. In the short term, I expect to see evolutionary modifications to existing geometry-based systems that will render them "IBR capable." However, in the longer term we can expect to see far more revolutionary systems that capitalize on the strengths of the IBR method in representing scenes with apparently high geometric complexity.

Finally, it is interesting to speculate on future directions in IBR research. For instance; how do the image-warping and viewing interpolation approaches compare to the light field and lumigraph methods? Can they be viewed as limiting cases within a common framework? Instead, might image warping be considered as a compression method for the database of rays represented in light-fields and lumigraphs? What are the computational implications of these various approaches? Another class of issues revolves around the dependence of IBR methods on difficult computer vision problems such as image-correspondence and camera calibration. We must first ask if this dependence necessary, and how might we successfully avoid these problems? This will lead to the fundamental issue of whether the problem of visualization is fundamentally a metric (and thus geometric) problem.

Jitendra Malik

Image based modeling and rendering has been presented in its purest form in the Light Field and Lumigraph work. In some ways this has very much the flavor of 'What you see is what you get'. The flip side is, of course, 'What you see is all you get'. In order to go further, one needs to recover geometric and reflectance structure from the collection of images. Barrow and Tennenbaum had proposed producing such a factorization—they called the result 'intrinsic images'—as an agenda for computer vision research way back in 1978. To the extent one is able to perform such a factorization, the ability to produce renderings from novel viewpoints and in novel lighting conditions follows directly. Unfortunately, twenty years of computer vision research in this framework has shown the problem to be much harder than originally suspected and fully automated, general purpose solutions are not yet available. I shall argue that the way forward is with hybrid approaches based on partial factorization into geometric and reflectance structure and representation of the remaining information in the form of unfactored image maps. Practical solutions are likely to be domain dependent. Requirements for geometric fidelity and/or photorealism, as well as what is possible given current computer vision technology, will vary according to the application.

Eric Chen

As the Web gradually moves from pure text-based pages toward multimedia enriched sites, the demand for using virtual reality to enhance the Web browsing experience is increasing. This is evident from the popularity VRML has received so far. However, real-time 3D rendering running on a PC typically does not offer very high image quality. The difficulty in creating good 3D content also presents a hurdle for the wide adoption of traditional 3D environment descriptions.

Image based rendering offers an attractive alternative. The use of images and photographs to "model" virtual environment is easier than 3D modeling in most cases. The rendering speed of IBR has weak correlation with scene complexity and is usually fast enough even on low-end PCs. IBR also allows a virtual environment to be transmitted with fairly constant bandwidth and can use standard image compression methods to reduce the data size. IBR is thus more likely to be accepted as the virtual reality method for the Web and the consumer markets.

IBR already has wide applications on the Web. Travel and real estate sites are using panoramic image rendering to create photorealistic location-based browsing. Image based objects (objects represented with images shot from different directions) are used to create interactive product catalogs. The merging of IBR and 3D rendering allows the creation of a virtual environment that is both photorealistic and dynamic.

The Rhetoric of the Synthetic:
Images of the Body in Technology, Business and Culture

Organizer
Lorne Falk (Archeon)

Panelists
Bill Kroyer (Warner Digital Studios)
Heidi Gilpin (University of Hong Kong)
Val Marmillion (Pacific Visions Communications)
Mark Resch (Xerox)

Introduction

We organized this panel for SIGGRAPH for several reasons. Even as new technologies are absorbed deeper and deeper into culture, we note that content is a concern in the emerging digital world that refuses to go away. We are excited to see that community is also a hot topic right now, but we don't like the trend to create "people free communities" on the Web. We believe that subjects which provoke technologists, influence voters, motivate consumers, help teachers, inspire artists - what we call "tide pool subjects" because they gather disciplines and professional fields together rather than isolate them from one another - are especially important right now.

The representation of the human body is a tide pool subject. It is a practice that is as old as civilization and that has a lot to do with the future of content, community, and every field of endeavor that involves people.

The Rhetorical Landscape

What is it that makes Barbie, Terminator and the Cyborg icons of popular culture? How and why are we using these symbols to represent the human body - our body - as beautiful, invincible and immortal? How does Cyberpunk, which existed only as literature, become an actual subculture with its own fashion, language and values?

To explore questions like these more deeply, this panel will look at the rhetoric of synthetic images as they currently appear in technology, business and culture. Specifically, the panelists will discuss the strategies and motives for representing the body in their respective professions - animation, business documents, communications, and comparative literature - as one way of figuring out what is happening to us in the emerging world of digital culture.

Understanding the rhetoric of synthetic images is increasingly central to the development and analysis of content and community in digital culture. Unlike philosophy, which is preoccupied with real truth and meaning, rhetoric is interested in what moves and persuades people to believe something is true and meaningful. In other words, the rhetorical landscape is a social and political landscape. From a philosophical perspective, we ask questions like "What is technology?" From the rhetorical perspective, we ask questions like: What are the givens of digital technology? What are the facts it commands, the procedures it trusts, and the socially and politically constructed values it expresses and extends? Are we self-consciousness and critical enough to discern in digital images of the body the partisan aims they hide from view? Do the attributes we find in the synthesized body make it an eternal object? Or is it an artifact whose fundamental design we regularly alter according to our personal, public and commercial needs? Understanding the rhetoric of the synthetic does not distort the facts about content and community, but helps us to discover them.

But whatever we discover about digital culture, the rhetoric of the synthetic is still a tricky landscape. Because (in postmodern thought anyway) all technology and all possibilities for its application have been written on the body in some fashion and at some time, digital technologies will be written into and on the body in some way. As philosopher and webmaster Byron Henderson writes, "The body becomes like a hard disk. We still believe that a message instantiated in a body is a more truthful message, more real and more permanent. Even if we stored it there ourselves. Even if it is only a cryptogram of pixels and voltages. The body is still the privileged locus for reading and writing the messages of the eternal. So we come full circle. By synthesizing our messages on the body, we "prove" that the messages were not made by man. Synthetic becomes genetic. Rhetoric becomes truth. Encrypted becomes intelligible. Virtual is real. (And because more truths is a better truth, virtual becomes the preferred reality.)"

Henderson points out how tricky rhetoric can be. In a sense, he is asking a fundamental question that takes us back to Barbie, Terminator and the Cyborg: What is the object of digital representation? By exploring the rhetoric of synthetic images of the body in technology, business and culture, we hope to articulate this question in a way that is useful to other professionals in the field.

Points of View

Lorne Falk (Archeon)

The surface which forms the common boundary between physical and digital matter is increasingly permeable to the human body and its senses. This "affective interface" is already used by real people living in telepresent neighborhoods, live buildings, and hot rooms to input and output information carrying expression, intelligence, and personality. Moreover, these people regard the possibilities of interrelations between themselves and artificial life-forms as symbiotic, as something mutually beneficial and natural to do. They are eager to model and ultimately bring to life their own computer presences, which currently exist as dull, unintelligent data scrolls (credit histories, medical histories, email and chat room personalities, etc.). What will happen when people are able to form, reform, and transform their computer presence? Will these synthesized bodies be sensing, affecting, and generous with feedback? What are the strategies used in recent computer-integrated media to enable people to transfer their disposition into a digital environment, to create dynamic digital identities, to manifest agency? What are the rhetorical strategies that bring these digital identities to life?

Bill Kroyer (Warner Digital Studios)

The rhetoric of synthetic images of the body triggers a strong connection to an old principle of design: Visual Grammar. Human beings sort and process the grammar of visual imagery as precisely as they sort the meaning of words and phrases. People communicate by symbols. Through the ages, artists (and others) have learned that specific symbols elicit specific responses. The art of communication might be measured by the facility of a person to convey precise ideas through pictures alone. Are there universal rules of Visual Grammar that apply to all people, through all ages? Do cave paintings and avatars share an identical code of conveying ideas? How many of these "rules" are logical? How many are constant, and how many change and evolve with culture and technology? In the age of digital precision, if a picture is worth a thousand words, can a picture be worth one word... or forty-two words? Is it possible, in other words, to limit the focus or meaning of a visual image?

If the medium is the message, how does digital imagery affect the rules of Visual Grammar? In a quantum universe, where each observer perceives a different reality, can there be such a thing as a constant rule of Visual Grammar? To put it another way: given the chance to recreate yourself visually, will your self-created image bear any resemblance whatsoever to the image perceived by your audience?

And don't forget the Animator's greatest tool: the FOURTH DIMENSION OF DESIGN, i.e., motion. The movement of any object tends to take precedence over any other aspect of its appearance in sending messages of Visual Grammar to the viewer. To a lesser degree, the visual image is affected by two other non-visual elements: Sound and Context. Sound might be a character's voice that supports or contrasts the personality of the image; background music or sound effects that create a mood, or even a vocal narration that explains the image. Context implies the positioning of the image within a sequence of other images, or its placement in the physical world - that is, a public viewing versus a private viewing.

Heidi Gilpin (University of Hong Kong)

Bodies speak rhetoric in a variety of ways that demand our attention in the development of digital culture. In this presentation, I will focus on a few of the constructions and functions of bodily rhetoric. How do the body and its senses operate in the act of witnessing? How has the digital codification - rhetoric - of the senses affected witnessing? I will address the relation between the consciousness of corporeality in motion and the memory of that motion as witnessed in digital space. Issues to be explored include kinesthesia as cultural artifact, forms of bodily rhetoric (physical and mental) in various interface systems, and performative digitalia. Material will be drawn from the medical and theoretical work of Oliver Sacks, Cathy Caruth, Gilles Deleuze, Jean-Francois Lyotard, and Shoshana Felman, and the performance work of Bob Flanagan, William Forsythe, and Pina Bausch, among others. If the performative transmits motion and its simultaneous vanishing, how can new media projects convey such performativity in the interactivity they impose, and the witness-consciousness they desire? The digital reincorporates the desiring body in ways that expose the inherently kinesthetic nature of perception. In its ability to synchronize material and immaterial realms, being digital reveals a fear of the very agency it proposes: the ability to be virtually everywhere is mediated by the condition of actually not being anywhere. Does being digital risk eliminating the possibility of bearing witness? Or is the body's

rhetoric transposed enough to allow the digital witness to perform?

Val Marmillion (Pacific Visions Communications)

What are the political devices embedded in a body-image? How do representations of the body - and of particular bodies - affect the perception of figures in political contexts. What makes a body political? How are politics represented through rhetorical configurations of the body? This presentation will expose the workings of the political images of bodies, as well as the body images of politics. Specific attention will be paid to the rhetorical strategies used by various media to elect, name, or characterize well-known political figures.

Mark Resch (Xerox)

What are the business opportunities arising from the absorption of technology into culture? How does this change the relationship of business and the body? Are there unique implications because of the renewed interrelations of technology, business and culture? What are some of the business opportunities arising from the synthetic that are compelling now and that dramatize the absorption of technology into culture? This presentation will address these general questions as well as more specific issues about business and the body such as: How does our disembodied business culture comprehend doing business with multiple avatars? How can we take advantage of new opportunities, such as developing educational software that takes advantage of hitherto unknown opportunities like dynamic "shared knowledge spaces"? As we experience the voracious appetite of culture for technology, how will we cope with a software with more than 1 billion users?

Experiences with Virtual Reality Applications

Organizer
William R. Sherman (The National Center for Supercomputing Applications)

Panelists
Nina Adams (Adams Consulting Group)
Rita Addison, M. A.
R. Bowen Loftin (University of Houston and NASA/Johnson Space Center)
Ben Britton (University of Cincinnati)
Donna Cox (The National Center for Supercomputing Applications)
Robert Patterson (The National Center for Supercomputing Applications)

Introduction

Research in virtual reality is turning the corner from being focused primarily on technology to focusing more and more on what we experience in VR — the content.

The content of virtual reality comes from many different areas of application, including: education, business and manufacturing, art, visualization, training, etc. The people creating these applications are helping VR move from a primarily technology based research effort, to one that is exploring the possibilities of what can be done in this emerging medium.

As more content creators join the VR community, they discover application constraints, and make design choices that influence how the users of their application interface with a virtual world. A common lexicon (or user-interface) arises (generally from other existing media) and evolves from the accumulation of the constraints and choices of the content creators.

We can push the evolution of the language of VR by discussing our ideas and methodologies in a public forum, and inviting the SIGGRAPH community to participate in the discussion. Perhaps this will help members of the VR community (content providers and technology researchers alike) to learn, discover and push forward new ways to work in this emerging medium.

Nina Adams
Motorola Assembly Line Training

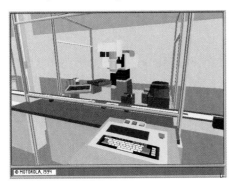

The manufacturing line of the '90's is dramatically different from the manufacturing line of the '70's. Today's manufacturing work-cell probably works because a computer, or series of computers, sends a series of pre-programmed instructions to a control unit within the work-cell. Human intervention may be needed only to replenish parts and to diagnose problems. Although the operator from previous generations also had to diagnose problems, they did not have to understand advanced robotics, nor computer technology.

Many of the workers in today's factories don't have the skills needed to operate state-of-the-art equipment. Leading many organizations to face the question:

> * How can we efficiently upgrade the skills of our workers so they are able to operate technologically advanced manufacturing equipment?

One answer being implemented by Motorola University comes from a research study we conducted in conjunction with the staff of Motorola University.

Our hypothesis was:

> A Virtual Reality simulation can be used to orient new employees to plant operations as effectively as the current method of new employee orientation.

When this study began, orientation to robotics plant operations was frequently gained by associates attending a three day class - MFG451: An Introduction to Advanced Manufacturing Concepts. When the course was conducted in Schaumburg, IL, the class consisted of lecture, classroom activities, and hands-on activities on a 5 station manufacturing line set up for training at Motorola University.

When the course was conducted at Motorola University locations outside of Schaumburg, no manufacturing line was present. Instead of hands-on activities, participant's watch a video of equipment operations.

Numerous studies have shown that learning retention is greatest when participants are involved with hands-on activities. Our study was set up to answer the natural questions which followed:

> * Is there any way to provide an activity which simulates hands-on equipment operation without setting up equipment at all Motorola University sites?
> * Would participants who learn in the simulated environment be able to perform as well as those who learn in a real environment?

Since we wanted to limit the number of variables we were analyzing, we designed the simulation to replace the current hands on activity; It was not designed as a stand-alone training program.

Based on the favorable results of the study, Motorola implemented 4 other class-room based Virtual Reality programs as well as 3 programs which may be used as self-paced instruction.

Rita Addison
"Empathy as evoked by Virtual Reality technology"

Virtual Reality is truly a way to make dreams come true. It is multi-sensory, interactive, realtime 3D graphics, spatialized sound, kinesthetic and soon, we hope, olfactory input and output facilitate an experiential event.

I use "experiential" to mean that a person perceives the VR event as a subjective reality. There in a strong correlation between this and our sense of presence, i.e., a strong sense of being in a place.

At the Electronic Visualization Laboratory at the University of Illinois at Chicago, directed by Tom DeFanti and Dan Sandin, students and I created "DETOUR: Brain Deconstruction Ahead," a program for SIGGRAPH 1994.

Displayed in EVL's CAVE[tm] (an immersive, room size VR environment) this application was built to simulate perceptual anomalies I'd sustained due to an automobile accident and subsequent brain injury. A walk through gallery of my pre-accident photography, followed by an abstract rendering of the car crash culminated in a return to the gallery post-brain damage only to encounter the images which were this time, distorted and deformed.

The 3D stereo glasses and head-tracking immerse the participant to the degree that many experienced a sense of being "out of control;" making comments such as "I wanted to rub my eyes and get refocused, but I couldn't. I was seeing and hearing just the way you were."

Often people would comment, "Finally, I understand what my loved one is trying to communicate. They had a stroke (migraine, psychosis, Alzheimer's) and I've felt so isolated because I know they view the world differently, but I just couldn't imagine it - until I could feel like it was my own world, as I felt in 'DETOUR.'"

"DETOUR" documents that VR technology can evoke empathy. Empathy is the quality associated with such sayings as, "If I could walk a mile in your shoes; if only I could see through your eyes." Empathy is a means by which we robustly identify with another who has differing perceptual and physical states.

Empathy is a powerful tool of communication in rehabilitation, story telling, educating - in sharing the condition of being human. I've chosen to use the earth's natural forces, images and seasons as metaphors in my VR work so that they can transcend boundaries of language, gender, regionalism, etc.

I am now working with health organizations, private businesses,

education centers to further this evocation of empathy through virtual reality.

R. Bowen Loftin
Virtual Environment Applications in Training and Education

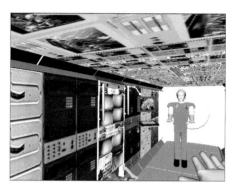

Since 1991 we have been exploring the use of virtual environments to address training needs with NASA. In the past two years this work has focused on the International Space Station. The figure above shows a portion of the interior of one of the Station's science modules through the eyes of an astronaut. The avatar of a second astronaut is also shown in this figure. The two astronauts, actually located at different sites, are training to perform a maintenance task on the Biotechnology Facility Rack shown in the left portion of the view. Thus, members of a team can train to perform cooperative tasks without the wear and tear of travel and separation from home. Within the next two years this technology will become available in the on-board setting for "just-in-time" training.

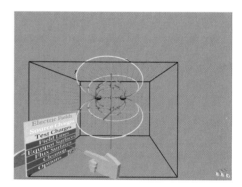

In addition to developing training applications with virtual environments, we have been creating educational virtual worlds. Project ScienceSpace, funded by the National Science Foundation and carried out in collaboration with colleagues at George Mason University, is providing interactive, immersive, multisensory environments for students of physics and chemistry. This figure shows a view of MaxwellWorld—a virtual world for the study of electrostatics. Students can build charge configurations and interactively explore the electric fields and potentials that they create. Surfaces of equipotential and trajectories of free charges can also be examined at will. Research with both high school and college students has shown that students using MaxwellWorld have superior mastery of critical concepts when compared with those using two-dimensional simulations with similar context.

These applications of virtual environments in training and education have demonstrated extraordinary potential to deliver training and experiences in more effective and more efficient ways than the traditional routes of simulations and lectures. The continuing improvement in graphics and communications technologies insures that this approach will become commonplace in the not too distant future.

For additional information visit our website at www.vetl.uh.edu.

Ben Britton
LASCAUX: A Practical Review of its Project Development

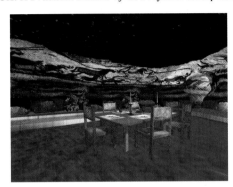

LASCAUX is a virtual reality art installation about the ancient painted French Cave of Lascaux. The purpose of the LASCAUX project is to explore the relationship of our culture's role and relationship to human culture of the past and the future, and to provide a link for viewers to connect personally to the cultural traditions of humankind by echoing the past to suggest the future.

The first and most important aspect of its design, from the day of its original conception, is the nature of the interactivity for the viewer. Interactivity enables the viewer to become invested in their experience. The composition of interactivity determines the relationship of the viewer to the material of the work. Artificial intelligence and interactivity are, to my thinking, equivalent or coexistent. The maker of an interactive artwork must build an attitude or personality into the work, engaging viewers in a way that may be considered entertainment. Entertainment, the dirty 13-letter word, has noble roots, stemming from the middle-French; it comes from the words "entre" (between) and "tenir" (to hold"), and it originally meant a performance of the sacred rites of the Church.

Building a relationship with a viewer, the maker of an interactive composition must intrigue, engage and involve the viewer to bring them to make a personal commitment, a leap of logic to the point of immersion. This has become important because of the capacity of a computer to respond to viewers. This capacity existed before in music and performance, but never before in objects of art. Using this fact requires new skills and a particular sensitivity, a willingness and ability to anticipate viewer response. All art is interactive (Marcel Duchamp; "The viewer makes the picture"), but computer art can be more interactive than many traditional art media, and this gives a capacity, a challenge and an opportunity to artists to use this interactivity for expressive effect. The key to this engagement is to build mystery to activate the viewer's fascination with the unknown.

I learned many things from LASCAUX about the importance of cultural icons and the responsibility of an artist when treating elements of the community's cultural legacy. This is not theoreti-

cal, but practical; the treatment "sticks" to the artist, and the artist wears it like a tattoo forever. The treatment sticks also in the mind of the viewer, and the artist contributes to the definition of meaning that the material holds for the community. I have learned to treat material with respect; even seemingly imaginary elements have associative value, and we build meaning in the physical world as we treat these seemingly mere virtual ideas in our work. Art thus builds meaning, definition and value.

Virtual reality can simulate the physics of the real world. New computers will hopefully increase in capacity to provide photorealistic image quality by providing more texture memory. I believe 256 MB of texture memory is needed to achieve relative photorealism. Some have said naturalistic verisimillitude is unnecessary, but it is surely not; building on a base of naturalism, the viewer becomes engaged in a work (and we remember that even abstract images have associative value and therefore trigger expectations of real-world, naturalistic physics). Once immersed, the viewer can encounter mystery and achieve a recognition of the supernatural as the artist selectively breaks the laws of physics in this virtual model. The supernatural is achieved by building on a base of naturalism and by composing situations in which naturalism is subverted.

To make LASCAUX, it was necessary to build a custom virtual reality authoring program. Limited though it is, it is better and faster to use than any tool currently on the commercial market. We built this in C++ with Sense8 WorldToolKit and OpenGL graphics libraries. Tools today for the creation of virtual reality projects are primitive, undeveloped and overly engineer-driven. I feel that toolmakers should listen and work with artists and producers rather than dictating what they insist we use; we cannot use tools that do not enable us to achieve our goals. Better tools need to be developed, and I am exploring Java-based approaches now, to enable authoring of Net-based projects.

I found that the economic (and therefore the logistic) realities of computing affected my project in some ways. At a certain point it became clear that LASCAUX had to be made as a state-of-the-art project; garage VR would not do. Expecting to use SGI's reality engine, models were built and mapped, but image quality of the model exceeded the capacity of their computers to display, because of the low amounts of texture memory (16mb at that time). I am very appreciative of Intergraph's technical foresight in computer architecture, their price/performance, as well as their responsibility in helping to bring LASCAUX to the public without sacrificing its essentially non-commercial nature. Corporations do well who prove their capacity to contribute to the community in the real world. Artists can contribute in return by their objective-oriented research and by broad public exposure.

In my new work, I am exploring VRML, DVD, the Internet and proprietary or custom solutions vs. open or public standards for creating a new virtual reality project. Will VRML become useful as a state-of-the-art tool, or will it be a diversion, as CD-ROMs diverted the attention of the public from interactive laserdisc? And will DVD bring us back to the good old days of the 80's when we could compose interactive full-motion, broadcast quality video? How can we link it to the Internet and mutual reality worlds? How can we use peer-to-peer or client-server architectures for multi-user VR? What is the relationship between home and museum viewing environments. How shall we make art on the Net? And most importantly, to understand the context for virtual reality in society, what is the relationship between a physical and a virtual world?

Donna Cox / Bob Patterson
The Virtual Director: a 3D Interface for a 3D Problem

Standing in the CAVE virtual environment, Robert Patterson and Donna
Cox use the Virtual Director to previsualize a galaxy collision choreography for the Cosmic Voyage IMAX film. They use a wireless microphone
to enter over 50 voice commands and a magnetically tracked wand to
navigate around the simulation and position the camera.

The standard 2D mouse and keyboard interface to computer
graphics production is limiting and creates many problems for
the user. The Virtual Director is a virtual camera choreographer
where the users employ voice and gesture to navigate around a
scene and control a virtual camera. The focus of the creators,
Donna Cox, Robert Patterson, and Marcus Thiebaux, has been to
solve the camera choreographer interface problem using virtual
reality.

The presenters will discuss what they learned taking the early
version of Virtual Director from a prototype using Fakespace
BOOM^{tm} technology to the current production tool that was used
to choreograph visualizations for the "Cosmic Voyage" IMAX
film. Today the Virtual Director employs the CAVE, an immersive virtual environment with multi-screen, rear-projected stereo
imagery, head-tracked liquid crystal shutter glasses, and a magnetically tracked hand-held wand. The user is free to move about
the CAVE and interact with the synthetic environment in a spatially direct manner.

Specifically, there are interface design issues such as the advantages of voice-driven interaction with hand-gesture to input, capture, edit and playback computer graphics camera spline paths.
For example, voice commands and wand gestures can be customized for intuitive control over a wide variety of functionality.
The focus here is to highlight techniques employed, present what
we have learned and touch on future plans.

A Framework for Realistic Image Synthesis

Donald P. Greenberg*   Kenneth E. Torrance*   Peter Shirley†

James Arvo‡   James A.Ferwerda*   Sumanta Pattanaik*

Eric Lafortune*   Bruce Walter*   Sing-Choong Foo**

                         Ben Trumbore*

Program of Computer Graphics*
Cornell University

Abstract

Our goal is to develop physically based lighting models and perceptually based rendering procedures for computer graphics that will
produce synthetic images that are visually and measurably indistinguishable from real-world images. Fidelity of the physical simulation is of primary concern. Our research framework is subdivided
into three sub-sections: the local light reflection model, the energy
transport simulation, and the visual display algorithms. The first two
subsections are physically based, and the last is perceptually based.

We emphasize the comparisons between simulations and actual
measurements, the difficulties encountered, and the need to utilize
the vast amount of psychophysical research already conducted. Future research directions are enumerated. We hope that results of this
research will help establish a more fundamental, scientific approach
for future rendering algorithms. This presentation describes a chro-
nology of past research in global illumination and how parts of our
new system are currently being developed.

CR Categories and Subject Descriptors: I.3.0 [Computer Graph-
ics]: General; I.3.6 [Computer Graphics]: Methodology and Techniques.

Additional Key Words and Phrases: Realistic Image Synthesis, Light
Reflection, Perception.

1   INTRODUCTION

From its infancy in the late 1960's, the quality of computer graphics
images have improved at fantastic rates. The initial renderings of
simple environments with only direct lighting have been transformed
into pictures of complex scenes with shadows, shading, and global
interreflections. For several decades now, high quality simulations

*580 Frank H.T. Rhodes Hall, Ithaca, NY 14853

† Department of Computer Science, University of Utah

‡ Department of Computer Science, California Institute of Technology

** Currently with Blue Sky Studios, Harrison, NY

have been used for a large number of tasks such as pilot training, automotive design, and architectural walkthroughs [GREE91]. The entertainment industry has developed techniques for creating startling special effects and realistic simulations with dramatic results. Even virtual reality games use convincing imagery with great success.

But are these images correct? Would they accurately represent the scene
if the environment actually existed? In general, the answer is no; yet
the results are appealing because the resulting images are believable.

If we could generate simulations that were guaranteed to be correct,
where the algorithms and resulting pictures were accurate representations, then the simulations could be used in a predictive manner.
This would be a major paradigm shift for the computer graphics
industry, but would have much broader applicability than just picture making.

A look at how accurate simulations are used in other areas might
clarify this point. The entire electronics industry is now based on
simulations for chip design; these simulations are standardly used
for testing and modifications prior to fabrication. In color science,
we utilize the response matching functions for color transformations without recreating the matching experiments. Why can't we
use computer graphics algorithms for the testing and development
of printing technologies, photographic image capture or display devices? Why can't these accurate but artificial scenes be used for algorithmic development in image processing, robotics and machine
vision? If we knew that the simulated images were correct, we could
easily control and isolate the variables, obtain any precision or resolution desired, and avoid the difficulties and constraints of experimental measurements.

However, in order to be *predictive*, we must prove that the simulations are correct. *Fidelity* is the key. This difficult task requires a
major multi-disciplinary effort between physicists, computer scientists, and perception psychologists and also requires experimental
measurements and comparisons. Unfortunately to date there has been
relatively little work done in correlating the results of computer
graphics simulations with real scenes. However, with more accurate
image acquisition and measurement devices, these compaisons will
be achievable if we can generate adequate computer simulations.

From early computer generated images such as the Phong goblet
(1975) to the synthesized pictures of today, there has been an exponential growth in the complexity of environments (Figure 1). This
increased complexity has also led to an exponential growth in computational costs for realistic rendering (Figure 2). But the available
processing power has also increased exponentially.

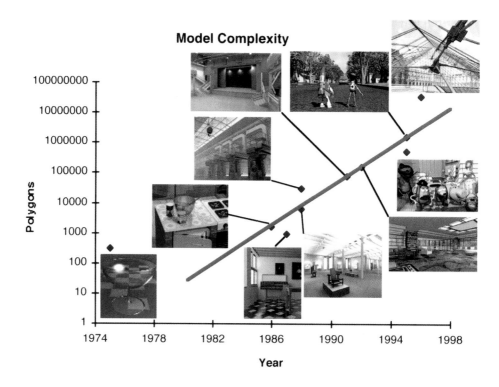

Figure 1: *The polygonal complexity of several familiar models is plotted against the year in which the images were generated. Each scene may be considered "complex" for the time when it was rendered. The number of polygons in complex scenes is increasing exponentially as the years go by. Some polygon counts are estimated from available information [DISN97], and are for illustrative purposes only.*

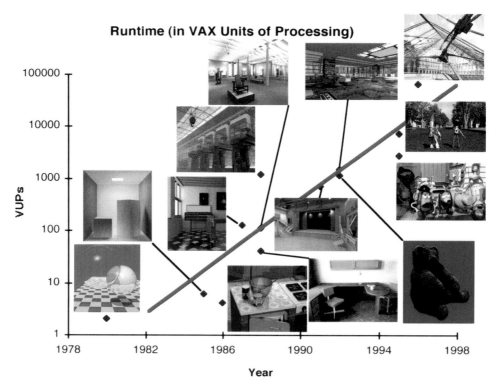

Figure 2: *The computation time for images of "complex" scenes is plotted against the year in which the images were generated. Computation time is presented in VAX Units of Processing (VUPs) [HENN97], which approximate the number of hours a DEC VAX 11/780 would require to perform the same computation. The processing power used to generate complex images is increasing exponentially with passing years. Some computation times are estimated from available information [DISN97], and are for illustrative purposes only.*

According to Moore's Law, with a doubling of chip density every 18 months, we now have approximately 4000 times the processing power that was available when the first graphics algorithms were developed (Figure 3). There has also been a concomitant increase in memory capacity, which offsets the constraint on environment complexity, as well as a vast reduction in cost per compute cycle. As we look toward the future a combination of increasing computation power and algorithmic improvements will certainly allow us to compute images that are physically and perceptually correct.

The purpose of this monograph is to describe in general terms our long-term development efforts attempting to achieve these tasks, to describe the difficulties encountered, and to encourage the computer graphics community to develop physically based algorithms of great realism and fidelity. Although there are many frontiers for future research in computer graphics, for physically based realistic image synthesis, three areas are especially critical: local light reflection models, light transport simulation, and perceptually based issues.

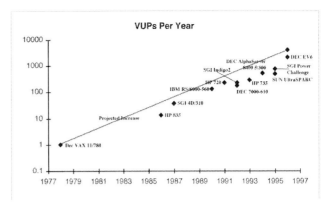

Figure 3: *The computational power of common computers is plotted against the year they were introduced. Computational power is presented in VAX Units of Processing (VUPs) [HENN97], which approximate how many times more powerful a machine is relative to a DEC VAX 11/780. The line represents a doubling of processing power every 18 months. VUPs were calculated using the LINPACK benchmark [DONG97]. Some machine introduction dates are approximate.*

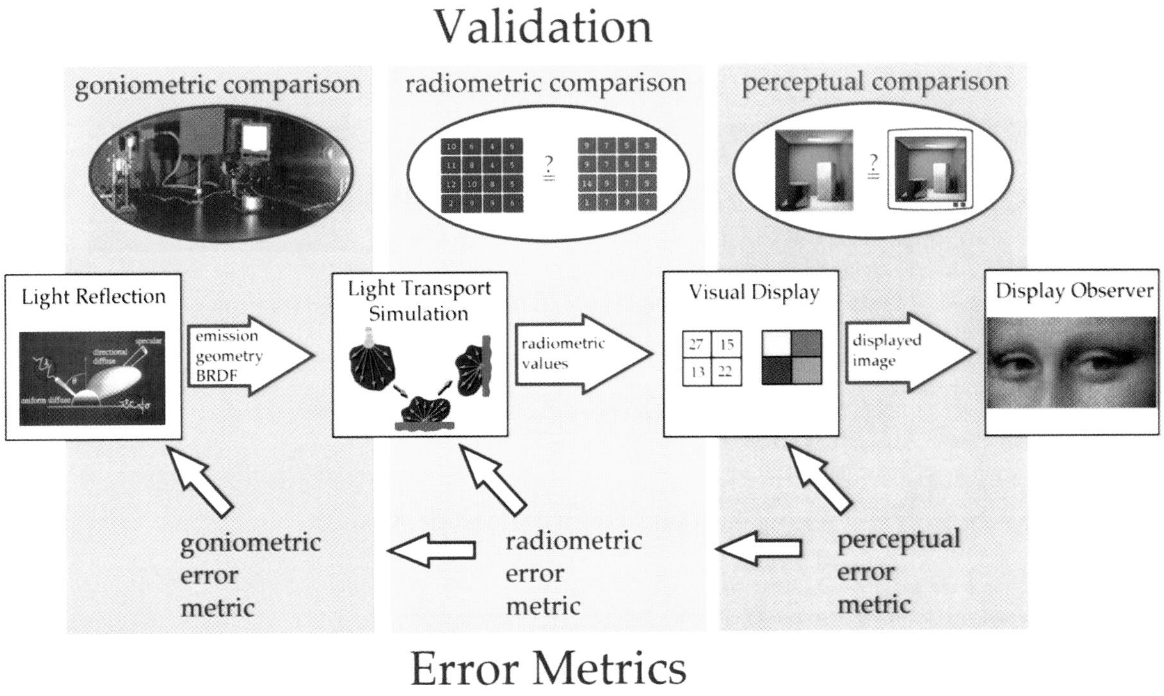

Validation

goniometric comparison   radiometric comparison   perceptual comparison

Light Reflection — emission geometry BRDF → **Light Transport Simulation** — radiometric values → **Visual Display** — displayed image → **Display Observer**

goniometric error metric ← radiometric error metric ← perceptual error metric

Error Metrics

Figure 4: *The entire system is subdivided into three separate stages, the local light reflection model, the global light transport simulations, and the image display procedures. The first two stages simulate and compare physical processes, whereas the last stage occurs in the perceptual domain. Note that the squares represent processes and simulations, the ovals represent comparison measurements, and the bold arrows contain only data. As shown in the smaller arrows (bottom) each stage is related to itself and its predecessor stage by providing a "feedback loop" to reduce computations, resolution, or representations when below a given error threshold.*

Our specific long term goals are:

Light Reflection Models

- The development of a general purpose wavelength-dependent model or models for arbitrary reflectance functions including the effects of subsurface scattering and re-emission, texturing and surface anisotropy
- Validation of the local light reflection model through comparisons with measured physical experiments
- A means for representing this model in a compact, data-efficient form useful for progressive rendering algorithms
- Establishment and distribution of the reflectance characteristics of materials whose accuracy has been verified by measurements

Light Transport Simulation

- Creation of global illumination procedures capable of accurately simulating the light energy transport within complex geometric environments composed of surfaces with arbitrary reflection functions

- Validation of the global energy transport algorithms through comparisons to measured physical environments
- Creation of automatic and adaptive techniques for progressive energy transport algorithms
- Development of physical error estimates for radiometric computations

Perceptual Issues

- Creation of photorealistic synthetic images which are perceptually indistinguishable from real scenes
- Use of perceptual metrics to establish realistic visual display methods for a wide variety of display devices and viewing conditions
- Improving the efficiency of global illumination algorithms through the utilization of perceptual error bounds

For the past decade or more we have been developing a system to test, validate, and improve the fidelity and efficiency of computer graphics algorithms. An overview of this system is shown in Figure 4. This system is structured into three separate sub-sections dealing with the local light reflection model, the global light transport simulation, and the image display. Each of these stages is discussed in greater detail in following sections. What is of paramount importance is that at each stage, simulations are compared with measured experiments.

For the first stage, our ultimate goal is to derive an accurate, physically based local light reflection model for arbitrary reflectance functions. A measurement laboratory has been assembled to goniometrically measure and compare the local reflection model with a large number of samples. If the simulation model is correct, it becomes possible to send accurate data in terms of geometry, emission, and reflectance functions to the next stage.

With this information, it is then necessary to accurately simulate the physical propagation of light energy throughout the environment. For arbitrary reflectance functions and complex geometries, current simulation procedures are computationally excessive to say the least. As will be described later, most global illumination algorithms use simplifying assumptions, and although images of spectacular quality have been achieved, none have really guaranteed physical accuracy. If, however, it were feasible to simulate these reflection and transport processes, then once again we could measure and compare the resulting radiometric scene values.

Two factors are worth emphasizing. One is that the first two stages deal with physically based simulations only. The second is that we have not yet created a "picture", but are only comparing measured and simulated radiant energy on an image plane with full dynamic range and infinite resolution.

If the results of the first two physical stages are accurate, we then can proceed to the third phase of creating and perceptually comparing images. Since any comparison must utilize the human vision system, this stage occurs entirely in the perceptual domain. The computational processes must account for the limited dynamic range, limited spatial resolution, and limited color gamut of the display or printing devices. But the "mappings" should also account for the viewer's position and focus, state of adaptation, and the vast, complex, and mostly unknown relationships between the spatial, temporal and chromatic attributes of the scene.

One major benefit of this research will be to reduce the computational expense of the global illumination algorithms. An inherent cause of the slowness of these algorithms is that an excessive amount of time is spent computing scene features that are measurably unimportant and perceptually below the visible thresholds of the average human observer. Algorithms could be substantially accelerated if we can develop error metrics that correctly predict the perceptual thresholds of scene features. The establishment of these techniques will not only allow realistic visual display, but will also provide a feedback loop for reducing the magnitude of the physical computations. This will improve the *efficiency* of the global illumination algorithms.

In the following three sections, each of these stages, and the inherent difficulties in the measurement, testing and simulations are described. The light reflection stage is presented in the most detail since the research is relatively mature, though not yet "mainstream" in the computer graphics community. The light transport stage is described in less detail since the field is now mature, and the algorithms are generally well-known to the SIGGRAPH audience. The third stage dealing with perceptual investigations is an area of research just beginning, and results have not yet been achieved, as they depend on the accuracy of the prior two stages.

2 LIGHT REFLECTION

2.1 Light Reflectance Models

Light reflectance models have always been of great interest to the computer graphics community. The most commonly used model was derived approximately twenty-five years ago at the University of Utah [PHON75]. The Phong direct lighting model is a clever scheme using a simple representation, but it is neither accurate in the sense that it represents the true reflection behavior of surfaces, nor is it energy consistent. The arbitrary nature in which we assign the specular and diffuse coefficients and the associated energy of these components is not physically correct. Yet the entire industry is based on these early investigations, and all major manufacturers today use the same computationally efficient but overly simplified shading model.

Blinn [BLIN77] introduced a more accurate model, based on earlier work by Torrance and Sparrow [TORR67]. The model was based on geometric optics, thus accounting for self-shadowing effects from surface facets, and for the off-specular peaks that occur at grazing angles. By 1981, Cook [COOK81] further improved the reflection model by relating the solid angle of the illuminating light source and incorporating the Fresnel color shift effects of the specular at grazing angles. The work was particularly successful in depicting metallic objects.

None of these models, however, was sufficiently general. A comprehensive model of how light reflects or transmits when it hits a surface, including its subsurface interactions, needs to be developed. The resulting bidirectional reflectance distribution function (BRDF) is a function of the wavelength, surface roughness properties, and the incoming and outgoing directions. The BRDF should correctly predict the diffuse, directional diffuse, and specular components of the reflected light.

In 1991, He [HE91] presented a sophisticated model based on physical optics and incorporating the specular, directional diffuse, and uniform diffuse reflections by a surface. The reflected light pattern depends on wavelength, incidence angle, two surface roughness parameters, and a surface refractive index. The formulation is self-consistent in terms of polarization, surface roughness, masking/shadowing, and energy. However, the model is extremely cumbersome to compute, since it contains an infinite summation that converges very slowly. This infinite summation term can be closely approximated by a spline surface and stored as a small look-up table of control points, vastly accelerating the computation of the full BRDF [HE92].

Poulin and Fournier [POUL90] constructed a similar model assuming a surface of cylindrical facets. Oren and Nayar [OREN94] also derived a model for more non-Lambertian diffuse reflection, based on diffuse micro-facets.

These models are applicable to a wide range of materials and surface finishes. For more complex surfaces, such as layered surfaces or thin films, analytical derivations are often too complicated. In those cases, Monte Carlo methods have been applied for simulating the local reflectance properties on a micro-scale [KAJI85] [CABR87] [HANR93] [GOND94]. For these models, and for reflectance models and measurements in general, a good means of representation is important.

2.2 Light Reflectance Measurement

In attempting to simulate the reflection and transport processes of light propagation, it is first necessary to measure and compare the material light reflection models (BRDF's) as well as measure the goniometric diagrams and spectral distribution of the illumination sources. For this reason it was necessary to set up a sophisticated light measurement laboratory (Figure 5).

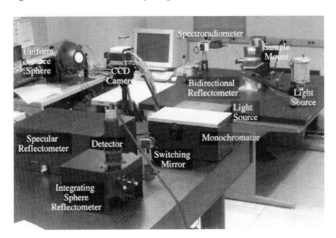

Figure 5: *Light Measurement Laboratory (1995)*

Difficulties for the measurement experiments are numerous and basically fall into three categories:

- Information on the calibration and precision of measurement equipment is scarce
- Physical constraints sometimes make the measurement a complex task, particularly for systems involving dense data sets
- Certain phenomena play a large role in reflection models, and yet are extremely difficult to measure

We would like to address each of these issues, at least by example, to show the problems.

To show the difficulties with the calibration and precision of the measurement equipment, let us just examine the tasks that had to be completed to use our high-resolution liquid-cooled camera, with a 1280 x 1024 CCD array. If you have either a guaranteed flat field illumination source, or a guaranteed flat field reflection from a surface, every pixel in the liquid cooled camera should yield an identical numerical intensity value. Using an integrating sphere uniform light source, we could produce a flat field, but there was considerable variation in the camera on a pixel by pixel basis. This could be caused by a variation in the sensors across the image plane or possibly by unequal thermal distribution.

Discrepancies could also be caused by lens effects, such as aberration or defects in the lens geometry, focusing and depth of field effects, selective absorption at different wavelengths, scattering within the lens and, most evident, the electronic and mechanical shutter effects. In either case, it was necessary to determine the behavior and response of the entire camera system over its full dynamic range before using the measurements. We did this with painstaking care so that we ultimately obtained different calibration factors for each pixel for each wavelength band.

Furthermore, if we wanted to deal with recording the intensities across the full spectral range of visible light we had to use a significant number of filters. We found that using eight band pass filters presented us with satisfactory data (Figure 6). Although this is not sufficient to reconstruct a continuous spectral distribution, we are sure of the accuracy of the individual basis functions. However, since we can compare the simulation of radiant energy at each one of these individual wavelength bands, we can make experimental comparisons without having to reconstruct the full spectrum image.

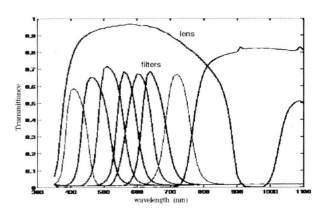

Figure 6: *Spectral transmittance of filters used in spectral image reconstruction*

Let us now look at some of the physical constraints which make reflectance measurement a complex task. A gonioreflectometer is used to measure the full bidirectional reflectance distribution function (BRDF) for every wavelength and for every incidence or reflectance direction on the material surface. To do this the gonioreflectometer must have three degrees of freedom for an isotropic sample. Two of these are obtained by allowing the plane of the sample to be rotated and tilted. The third pivots the direction of the light source. For each position the sample must be illuminated by a constant light source with a uniform illuminating field (Figure 7).

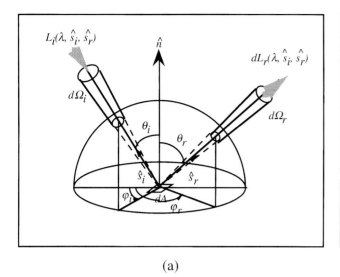

(a)

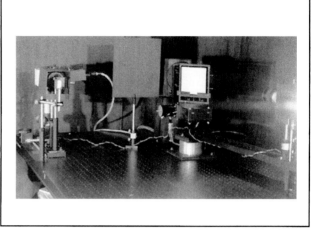

(b)

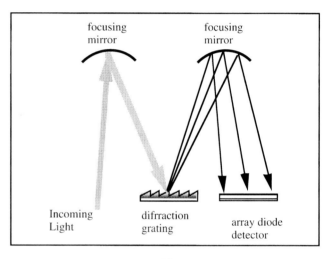

(c)

(d)

Figure 7:
a) Diagram of incidence and reflection geometry
b) Photograph of gonioreflectometer
c) Schematic of gonioreflectometer
d) Schematic of array diode spectrometer, the detector for the gonioreflectometer

Difficulties arise because of mechanical and optical constraints; for example, holding the sample in place can physically obscure the light source under particular conditions. We had to modify our equipment several times to obtain almost all of the hemispherical values. High grazing angles are also difficult since a small detector solid angle is required to measure the reflected energy. Unfortunately, this grazing region is where some of the most interesting characteristics occur, such as the off-specular peak (Figure 8).

To complicate the situation, the variation of the BRDF is relatively gradual in the diffuse and directional diffuse regions, but we need to take very closely spaced samples in the specular direction. Thus, the patterns used to measure the samples should not be uniform, but concentrate in the areas of greatest change (Figure 9).

Of even greater concern, perhaps, is the large role that phenomena which are difficult to model play in the BRDF's. Polarization has a very large effect and we have had to measure our isotropic samples

with two measurements after depolarizing the source and correcting for the bias of the detector. Measuring the anisotropy of the surface is difficult and we do not have the equipment within our laboratory to actually measure the microscopic deviations in the surface roughness, although we can make some statistical straight-line stylus probe measurements.

Since the reflection models are statistically based, we need to at least have the parameters describing the surface geometry. Fluorescence and phosphorescence also have substantial effects and these phenomena are material dependent. Even worse with fluorescence, light which may enter at a given wavelength may be re-emitted at many other wavelengths as there is crosstalk between color channels. Subsurface scattering depends on how far the light penetrates underneath the surface, and is a material property usually defined by the coefficient of extinction, but we have no mechanism for measuring this. Thus many problems still exist.

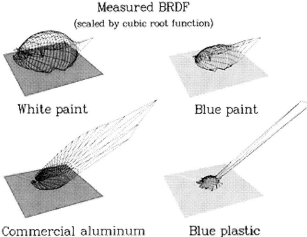

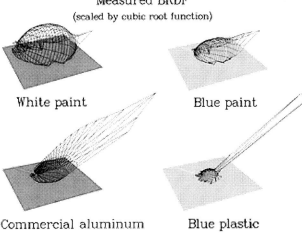

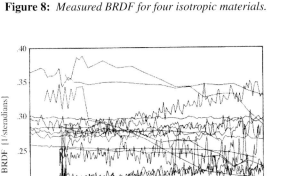

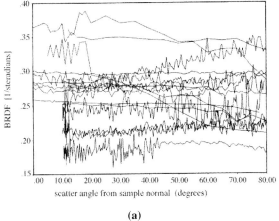

Figure 8: *Measured BRDF for four isotropic materials.*

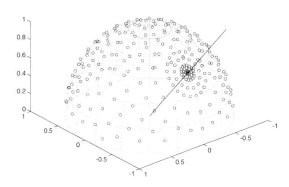

Figure 9: *Sampling positions of BRDF measurements on the hemisphere above the sample surface. The solid line indicates the specular reflection direction.*

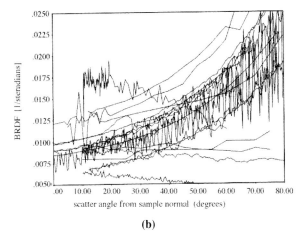

(a)   **(b)**

Figure 10: *(from Leonard, 1988)*
(a) Measured BRDF curves for the diffuse white sample by various facilities participating in the BRDF round robin. The specular beam would be located at 10°.
(b) Measured BRDF curves of the diffuse black sample

Once we have set up a BRDF experiment, the reflected light is measured in many directions on the reflection hemisphere. At each sample point the light is reflected through a diffraction grating so that we can measure the response at a thousand different wavelengths simultaneously. This creates a data explosion and thus both data storage and time for measurement become large[1]. However, despite all of these difficulties, we are now attempting to correlate our simulated light reflection model with our measured experimental results. Initial tests look very promising, at least for a small number of samples.

As stated previously, we are not the only ones to have difficulties with these measurements [LEON88] [LEON89]. In 1988, eighteen "scatter" measurement facilities participated in a round robin measuring four two-inch diameter samples of a white diffuse surface, a black diffuse surface, an industrial grade molybdenum mirror and an aluminum mirror, both very smooth. The results showed an enormous range of deviation, confirming the difficulty of the task (Figure 10).

2.3   Light Reflectance Representation

Ultimately, what is necessary is a compact representational scheme which can accurately describe the dominant behavior of a BRDF. The functions must capture the diffuse, directional diffuse and specular characteristics, including the off-specular peaks, but must also be energy consistent and obey the laws of reciprocity. Furthermore, the representation method should be suitable for progressive algorithms, monotonically converging to a correct solution. Several researchers have used spherical harmonics with some success, but this representation has problems with ringing and negative values in the approximation [CABR87] [SILL91] [WEST92]. Work based on wavelets has been presented by Schröder [SCHR95]. This representation seems ideally suited for progressive algorithms and shows

---

[1]A typical set of data for a single isotropic material at 10 degree intervals for the incoming directions, with 800 outgoing directions for each incoming direction, at 8 wavelengths yields approximately 230 Kbytes. The potential size of accumulated material data indicates the utility of an accurate reflectance model with a compact means of representation.

great promise. Fournier [FOUR95] proposed the use of separable bicubic polynomials, and recently Koenderink etal. [KOEN96] presented a compact scheme based on Zernike polynomials. Ward [WARD92] and Lafortune [LAFO97] presented models with an emphasis on computational efficiency, taking into account that reflectance functions are generally only known to a limited accuracy that is sufficient for global illumination computations.

3 LIGHT TRANSPORT

3.1 Light Transport Theory and History

Once the emission, geometry, and reflection functions (BRDF's) are known, we can then simulate the light transport. The general equations have been well known [KAJI86], but until recently neither the processing power nor the physically based reflection models were available to perform accurate simulations.

The following equation is a modified form of Kajiya's rendering equation [IMME86] which expresses the outgoing radiance at a surface point x in terms of the emission from x and incoming radiance at x.

$$L\_o(\omega) = E(\omega) + \int \rho(\omega, \omega') L\_i(\omega') d\omega' \quad (1)$$

In the equation, ω', ω are respectively the hemispherical incoming and outgoing directions, $L\_o(\omega)$, $E(\omega)$ are respectively the total radiance and emitted radiance along w, $L\_i(\omega')$ is the incoming radiance along ω', and $\rho(\omega, \omega')$ is the bidirectional reflectance distribution function (BRDF). Incoming radiance at any surface point x along ω' in a scene is due to the outgoing radiance at another surface point x' visible to x along the direction opposite to ω' in the same scene. In a complex scene the computation of the BRDF function and the visibility along the hemispherical directions itself is computationally expensive. To compute the solution of Equation (1), with complex BRDF and accurate visibility along all incoming and outgoing directions, for the outgoing radiances at all points in the scene is a formidable problem. Most algorithms make simplifying assumptions, for the BRDF function, for the visibility computation, and for the solution of the integral equation, yet still produce images of startling quality and realism. The two most common methods used are ray-tracing, introduced to the graphics community in 1979 [WHIT80], and radiosity, first presented five years later [GORA84]. Although during the past fifteen years many improvements have been made, neither of these commonly used algorithms are exact, each neglecting various and significant mechanisms of light transport.

3.1.1 Ray Tracing

View-dependent ray tracing methods originally computed only some of the transport paths, but accounted for specular transport in a visually compelling manner [WHIT80]. In essence, ray tracing reduces the BRDF expression to only include the path in specular direction [KAJI86], thus simplifying the computations but ignoring diffuse-diffuse and specular-diffuse interactions [WALL87]. Cook added a probabilistic framework to ray tracing to account for more physical effects [COOK84]. Kajiya extended Cook's framework to include all transport paths for a probabilistic view-dependent solution [KAJI86]. The main limitation of Kajiya's method in practice is that it takes a great deal of computation time. Many researchers have attempted to improve the methods of gathering statistics in Kajiya's methods, and this is still an active and fruitful area of work [LAFO96] [VEAC95]. The main theoretical limitation of Kajiya's method is that although it is an unbiased method, meaning it will converge to the correct answer, its variance is unknown. The variance can itself be statistically estimated, but important statistical outliers can cause these error estimates to be misleading [LEE85].

Another important extension to Cook's framework was brought out by Ward [WARD88][WARD94a] from the observation that illumination due to diffuse-diffuse interactions changes gradually over surfaces and it is possible to reuse the computation at any surface point for points in close proximity. Though Ward's method ignores other indirect interactions such as specular-diffuse interactions, it provides a practical method for near accurate view-dependent solution of Equation (1) for many complex scenes.

3.1.2 Boundary Element Methods

Traditionally, view-independent radiosity-type solutions have been computed by boundary element methods. These methods work by interleaving the computation of the global light transport and the local lighting representation. In essence, these approaches model the transport processes by determining the "form-factor", the percentage of illumination leaving one surface element and reaching another. With the typical assumption of diffuse (Lambertian) reflection only, computations are based on geometric relationships only (shape, size, orientation, distance, and occlusion).

Although computationally expensive due to the complex visibility problem in real scenes, and matrices which are large due to the number of elements, equations can be solved (by Gaussian elimination) due to diagonal dominance [COHE85]. For complex environments, it is not practical to explicitly solve the full set of energy equations. Thus most solutions iteratively compute a portion of the global transport and update local representations until some convergence criteria are reached. To create high quality images, the requirement of very fine local representations, particularly in areas of high illumination gradients, e.g. shadow boundaries, gives rise to an exponential increase in elements. This combination of operations involving high global and high local complexity causes an explosion in resource consumption in terms of both memory and time.

Much research has gone into improving the basic finite element or boundary element method. Several techniques such as hierarchical radiosity [HANR91] and clustering [SMIT94] greatly reduce the time required at the expense of additional data structures and greater memory usage. Consequently, it is usually memory that limits the maximum input size and solution quality. To overcome this problem, researchers have tried various ways to reduce global or local complexity. Discontinuity meshing [CAMP90] [LISC93] attempts to precompute the potential locations of shadows to allow for a more compact local representation. This can produce dramatically better shadows, but it does not handle other lighting features, such as caustics and shadows from secondary sources, and does not scale well to large environments. Teller et al. [TELL94] try to partition the environment into small, weakly interacting subsets to lower the effective global complexity. If such a partitioning can be found then the computation can be ordered to use virtual memory efficiently; however such a partitioning may not exist (e.g., a hotel atrium). Smits et al. [SMIT94] reduce the local complexity by abandoning the idea of displaying the solution directly. Instead, the solution is computed at a low resolution and a computationally expensive local-gather pass is required to display the solution.

However, despite these impressive advances in reducing computational tasks, most of these schemes to date have been restricted to diffuse environments and static scenes. For more exact solutions, what is necessary is a physically based approach that can handle complex geometric environments with arbitrary reflectance functions, resulting in accurate solutions with known error characteristics.

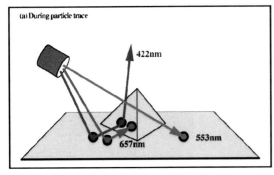

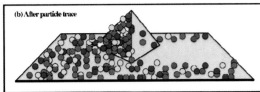

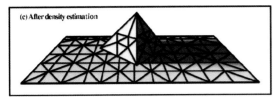

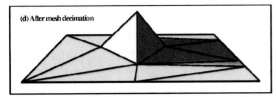

Figure 11: *(a) and (b) Particle Tracing: Power-carrying particles, each with a specific wavelength, are emitted from each luminaire using an appropriate spectral radiant intensity distribution and tracked as they travel through the environment until they are absorbed. Each time a particle hits a surface it is probabilistically absorbed or scattered in a new direction according to the BRDF of the surface. A list of all particle "hit points" is generated and saved. (c) Density Estimation: The stored hit points are used to construct approximate lighting functions on each surface. The illumination on a surface is proportional to the density of the hit points. To reconstruct luminous and chromatic exitance, the hits are weighted by the surface reflectance and the CIE XYZ response functions and local linear density estimation is applied. The result is a Gouraud-shaded mesh of triangles with three color channels suitable for direct display.*
(d) Mesh Decimation: The initial mesh is generated conservatively and can be decimated by progressively removing vertices as long as the resulting change is below a perceptually-based threshold. Although not part of the simulation/measurement paradigm, it is useful to have the capability to rapidly display the rendered scene.

3.2 Density Estimation Framework

For our predictive simulations, we have chosen a density estimation framework which avoids the combination of high local and global complexity by splitting light transport and lighting representation into separate computational stages [WALT97a]. In the transport stage we compute the flow of light between surfaces without ever explicitly reconstructing the lighting on surfaces. Particle tracing is a natural and robust way to simulate this light flow. The representation stage then uses information from the transport stage to explicitly reconstruct the lighting on each surface. Since the intensity of the lighting is proportional to the density of light particles, the reconstruction is a density estimation problem [SILV86]. It should be emphasized that this is not a practical way to generate synthetic images, but does allow us to achieve the accuracy desired for complex environments with arbitrary reflectance functions.

Particle tracing has been used by many other researchers [APPE68] [ARVO86] [PATT93] to compute illumination, and Heckbert [HECK90] first noted that reconstructing lighting from particles is a density estimation problem. Since then a variety of different density estimation techniques have been applied, including histograms [HECK90], kernel methods [CHEN91] [COLL94], and splines [REDN95]. However, the fundamental difference between our framework and previous work is the separation of the transport and reconstruction stages.

The particle tracing stage computes a statistical simulation of global light transport. Since light particles do not interact there is no need to explicitly reconstruct the lighting function, and instead we simply record some information about the particle histories. Thus the particle tracing can work directly with the raw input geometry and has high global complexity but minimal local complexity.

The lighting reconstruction stage uses the recorded particle histories to estimate the lighting function on each surface. Because all of the global transport was handled in the previous phase, we can reconstruct the lighting on each surface independently. Reconstruction on a surface has high local complexity but no global complexity. Because each stage has only high global or high local complex

(e) An example scene rendered using Particle Tracing and Density estimation framework

ity but not both, the individual stages require fewer resources than finite element methods, especially in terms of memory. But we have not completely escaped the complexity problem. The combined high global and high local complexity is contained in the voluminous particle history data.

Our specific implementation is composed of three phases as shown in Figure 11. The system has been implemented because it is the only physically-based method we know which can handle complex geometries, general reflection functions, and whose error can be characterized. Although computational requirements are enormous, a major benefit of this approach is that particle tracing can easily exploit coarse-grain parallelism, thus reducing computation time.

The current implementation reconstructs irradiance function over the surfaces, which amounts to the reconstruction of radiance function for Lambertian surfaces only. However, the density estimation framework could be extended to reconstruct the radiance function for non-diffuse surfaces as well. The particle tracing phase already handles non-diffuse light transport. Depending on the degree of non-

diffuseness, more particles would be required to get an acceptable solution. The major unresolved issue is to find an efficient mechanism for storing the directional information. Solutions to this problem are currently being investigated. [WALT97b].

3.3 Light Transport Measurement and Image Validation

In keeping with our goal of comparing photorealistic image simulations against real world scenes, several steps are required. These include accurately measuring the input physical data, as well as acquiring a CCD camera image of the scene. The input data include scene geometry, light sources, and material reflectance properties, measured with appropriate equipment. The CCD measurement is acquired with our calibrated camera previously described. Some of the equipment for these measurements has been shown in Figure 5. The objective is to directly compare a simulation with a calibrated physical measurement.

Accurate simulations require accurate input data. We use the gonioreflectometer (Figure 7) to obtain the reflectance of surfaces with complex, strongly directional behavior. For surfaces that are specular or nearly ideal diffuse, we can use either a specular reflectometer or an integrating sphere reflectometer. Schematics are shown in Figure 12. These provide fast, accurate spectral measurements of the reflectance. The two reflectometers can also be used for transmission measurements, and the monochromator and detectors can be arranged for light source measurements. For measurements of scene geometry, we have relied on direct mensuration, or for small objects, a Cyberware scanner.

The CCD camera is used to acquire a 2D image of a scene. After calibration, twelve-bit images at any wavelength band can be obtained. An example image obtained through a 550nm filter is shown in Figure 13.

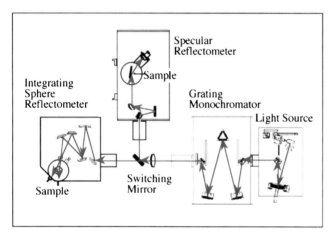

Figure 12: *Schematics of equipment for measuring the diffuse and specular reflectances.*

(a)

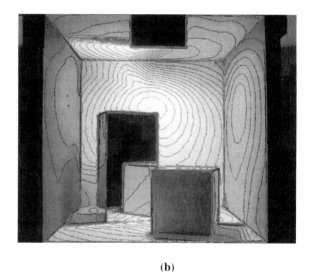

(b)

Figure 13:
(a) Calibrated CCD camera image via 550nm (Δλ = 80nm) filter
(b) The same camera image showing radiance contours

3.4   Future Directions

Before describing the perceptual issues, it is worthwhile examining our future directions in modeling the physical behavior of light reflection and light transport. Though significant progress has been made in modeling the surface BRDF, the model is far from complete. Properties such as polarization and anisotropy need to be well accounted for. Subsurface scattering which contributes towards the diffuse component of the BRDF is not well understood and is being handled empirically. Surface properties other than the BRDF which affect light interaction such as transmission, fluorescence, phosphorescence are either completely ignored or are being modeled empirically. These need to be correctly accounted for.

In the context of the simulation of light transport, we have introduced particle tracing and the density estimation framework. This framework can in principle handle all types of surface properties accurately. However, as mentioned earlier, further research is necessary to efficiently store and estimate the radiance function resulting from such accurate simulations.

4   PERCEPTION

A major goal of realistic image synthesis is to create an image that is perceptually indistinguishable from an actual scene. This is illustrated in Figure 14. This is not a trick photograph. The person in the figure is holding a real physical image generated by the rules of photographic tone reproduction.

Generating a visual image is the last stage of realistic image synthesis. At the end of the light transport process outlined in Figure 4 we have a global illumination solution that represents the radiometric values at every point in a three-dimensional scene. The final stage in image synthesis involves mapping these simulated scene radiances to display radiances to produce a visual image. This is an underappreciated and very important part of the image synthesis process that must take into account the physical characteristics of the display device, the perceptual characteristics of the observer, and the conditions under which the image will be viewed.

While the physically-based rendering methods described in the previous sections make it possible to accurately simulate the radiometric properties of scenes, this physical accuracy does not guarantee that the images displayed at the end of the process will have a realistic visual appearance. There are two reasons for this. First, current display devices are limited in a number of ways including spatial resolution, temporal resolution, absolute and dynamic luminance range, and color gamuts. Second, the scene observer and the display observer may be in very different visual states and this can affect how they perceive the visual information before them.

Current display technologies place fundamental limits on the fidelity of the display process. In the spatial domain, displays have fixed addressability and resolution, and are bounded in extent. In the temporal domain, they have fixed refresh rates and discrete update intervals. In luminance, both the absolute and dynamic ranges producible on displays are small relative to the ranges that can be measured in real scenes. Finally, in color the displays are trichromatic and have limited gamuts. The fact that display devices work as well as they do in creating acceptable visual representations of scenes is due to the fact that the human visual system is limited as well.

4.1   Psychophysical Models Of Vision

For the last 150 years psychophysicists have measured the characteristics of human visual function. The contrast sensitivity function (CSF) shown in Figure 15 plots the spatial transfer properties of vision. The high frequency cutoff of the CSF indicates the spatial resolution of the visual system which is on the order of 60 cycles/degree or 1 minute of visual angle. The temporal contrast sensitivity function shown in Figure 16 plots the temporal response properties of the visual system.

In this case the high frequency cutoff indicates the limit of flicker sensitivity which at high levels of illumination is approximately 75-80 Hz. In the luminance domain, the threshold-versus-intensity functions show the relationship between just noticeable differences in intensity (JND) and the background illumination level. Over a wide range of illumination levels the visual system obeys Weber's law which states that the size of the JND is a constant proportion of the background

Figure 14: *The goal of realistic image synthesis: an example from photography [STRO86].*

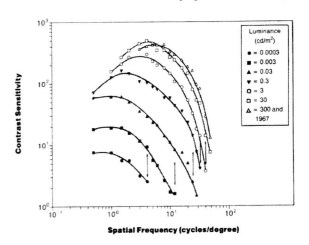

Figure 15: *The spatial contrast sensitivity function. The curves plot the relationship between contrast sensitivity and spatial frequency for detection of sine-wave gratings. The different curves reflect contrast sensitivity at the different levels of illumination shown in the inset, after [EVANN67], [BOFF86].*

level (Figure 17). In color vision the shapes and sizes of the MacAdam ellipses on the CIE chromaticity diagram indicate that color discrimination is not uniform within the spectral gamut, but varies with chromaticity and with the direction of the chromatic difference (Figure 18). Lastly, our visual acuity decreases dramatically with the distance from the central fovea. Although acuity can be as good as 20/10 in the central field, at only 10 degrees in the periphery (roughly a palm's width at arm's length) acuity is reduced to 20/80 (Figure 19). This is an important phenomenon, especially when considering the necessary resolution for immersive displays.

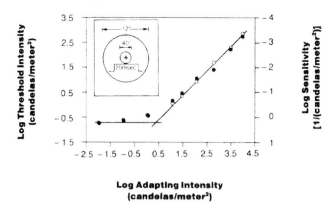

Log Adapting Intensity (candelas/meter²)

Figure 17: *Contrast threshold-versus-intensity function for the disk target and adapting annulus background shown in the inset. The abscissa shows the luminance of the background. The ordinate shows the threshold luminance necessary to detect the target. At low adapting luminances the background has no effect on the target. At higher luminances the threshold increases in constant proportion to the background luminance following Weber's law: $^l threshold = {}^{kl} background$. After [MUEL50], from [BOFF86].*

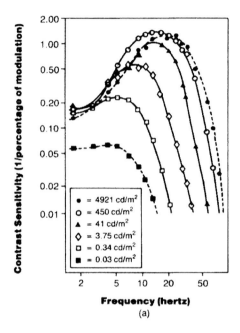

Figure 16: *The temporal contrast sensitivity function. The curves plot the relationship between contrast sensitivity and temporal frequency for a large white disk modulated sinusoidally . The curves reflect contrast sensitivity at the different levels of illumination shown in the inset. After [KELL61], from[BOFF86].*

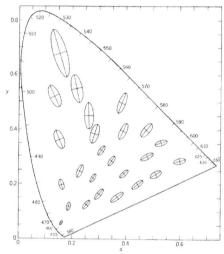

Figure 18: *The MacAdam's ellipses for color discrimination plotted on the CIE chromaticity diagram. Ellipses show measured color difference thresholds at different chromaticities. The axes of the plotted ellipses are ten times their actual length [WYSZ82].*

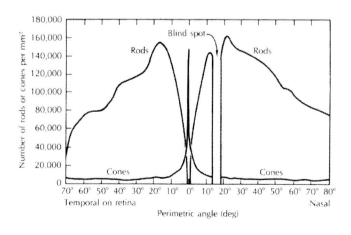

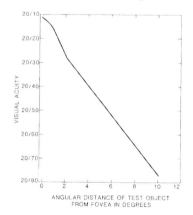

Figure 19: *Densities of rods and cones across the retina. Cone density is highest in the central fovea and falls off rapidly with eccentricity. Rod density is minimal in the fovea, increasing rapidly out to approximately 20 degrees peripherally and declining thereafter. The blind spot is a region devoid of photoreceptors located at about 17 degrees on the nasal retina. From Pirenne (1967). The graph on the right shows how acuity varies with retinal eccentricity. Acuity is approximately 20/10 in the fovea, this has dropped to about 20/80 ten degrees peripherally[Boff86].*

4.2 Use of Psychophysical Models In Imaging Systems

Reliance on psychophysical measurements is not new. Imaging system designers have used visual models for decades to improve the quality and reduce the bandwidth and computational load of imaging systems. In photography, subjective tone reproduction and preferred gamma curves incorporate Weber's law and simultaneous contrast effects. In color printing, knowledge of the trichromatic nature of vision allows full color reproduction from a small number of inks, while an awareness of spatial integration in vision has led to halftoning and color dithering techniques. Designers of simulation systems have taken advantage of differences in resolution across the visual field to reduce the level of detail for objects outside of the focal region. Finally, designers of image coding and compression systems such as NTSC, JPEG, and MPEG have used the spatial, temporal, and chromatic limits of vision to determine bandwidths and quantization levels for visual features of different scales, choose refresh rates and motion prediction methods for image sequences, and guide the choice of color coding schemes.

4.3 Using Psychophysical Models In Realistic Image Synthesis

In computer graphics we are only beginning to take similar advantage of visual perception in realistic image synthesis. Meyer [MEYE80] [MEYE86] has used results from color vision to develop color reproduction and spectral sampling strategies. Mitchell [MITC87] used a visual model to generate antialiased images at low sampling densities. Tumblin [TUMB93], Ward [WARD94b] and Ferwerda [FERW96] have developed tone reproduction schemes based on models of brightness and contrast perception and on a model of visual adaptation to realistically map the results of global illumination solutions to display devices. Spencer [SPEN95] developed a model of visual glare to both simulate the disabling effects of glare on visibility and to increase the apparent dynamic range of displayed images. Bolin [BOLI95] developed a frequency-based ray tracer that decides where to send rays based on the a model of the visibility of sampling artifacts. Recently Ferwerda [FERW97] has introduced a model of visual masking to predict when textures will hide visible artifacts in rendered scenes.

To improve the visual realism of synthetic images, it will be necessary to continue to "mine" the psychophysics literature for visual models that can be applied in computer graphics. A better understanding of the spatial, temporal, chromatic, and three-dimensional properties of vision can lead to more realistic and more efficient graphics algorithms.

4.4 Research Directions In Perceptually-Based Realistic Image Synthesis

To produce realistic images we need to model not only the physical behavior of light, but also the parameters of perceptual response. By modeling the transformations that occur during visual processing we can develop mappings from simulated scene radiances to display radiances to produce images that are as realistic as possible. Our goal is to show that these images can be predictive of what a observer standing in the physical scene would see. Validation of the

predictive aspect of the images is a key component of the framework. Models of visual processing will also allow us to create perceptually-based error metrics for our rendering algorithms that reduce the computational demands of rendering while preserving the visual fidelity of the rendered images.

For our research framework, the approach used is based on the idea of a tone *reproduction operator* introduced by Tumblin [TUMB93] (Figure 20). The oval on the left represents the scene radiances simulated by our light transport algorithms. A hypothetical scene observer receiving these radiances will have a particular visual experience. On the right is a display observer looking at a display device driven by a graphics frame buffer. Our goal in realistic image synthesis is to have the display observer have the same visual experience as the scene observer. The tone reproduction operator maps the simulated scene radiances to the display radiances with the goal of producing a perceptual match between the display and the scene. There are two major components; the first is a model of the physical transfer properties of the display device including information about the absolute and dynamic range limits of the display, gamma correction factors, monitor white point, and color gamut. The second component of the tone reproduction operator is a visual model of the scene and display observers.

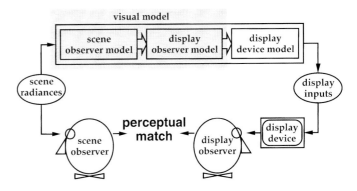

Figure 20: *The tone reproduction operator. A scene observer shown on the left receives the scene radiances and has a particular visual experience. We wish to have the display observer shown on the right have the same visual experience so the displayed image is a perceptual match to the scene. The tone reproduction operator maps the (simulated) scene radiances to display radiances taking into account the limits of the display device and the visual states of the scene and display observers. After [TUMB93].*

An accurate visual model is the essential component of a tone reproduction operator. The model allows us to characterize the visual states of the scene and display observers and allows us to relate them to determine the mapping from simulated scene radiances to display radiances.

Because the tone reproduction operator produces a perceptual match between the image and the scene this allows the images to be used predictively. Images produced by this method can be used quantitatively in areas such as illumination engineering, transportation and safety design, and visual ergonomics.

To claim that images generated by our visually-based tone reproduction operators are predictive, we have to validate this in comparison experiments. The results of such experiments will allow us to tune the visual models so the images we create are truly predictive. Furthermore, an experimentally validated visual model will also allow us to use the model in lieu of actual comparison experiments for the development of perceptually-based error metrics. These perceptually-based error metrics along with the previously determined physically-based error metrics will allow us to create more realistic and efficient image synthesis algorithms. If the end product of a simulation is a visual image then an efficient "steepest ascent" path can be derived to obtain a high fidelity visual solution with fewer computational demands.

We are just beginning this work but we believe that predictive visual models of phenomena like these are at the heart of future advances in computer graphics. To develop these models we will need to work together with experimental psychologists. But part of the difficulty in using the results of psychophysical experiments in graphics is that the experiments are typically carried out under extremely reductionistic conditions that only probe one dimension of visual function at a time. This makes it very difficult to generalize from these results to determine their effects in complex computer generated images, where there are significant interactions between the different dimensions of visual experience, and "crosstalk" between visual mechanisms is the rule rather than the exception. Two examples will make this clear.

The first example is Benham's top [HURV81]. Here a toy top is painted with the black and white pattern shown on the left in Figure 21. When the top is spun an observer sees red, yellow, and green rings even though there is no color in the pattern. The effect is due to interactions between the spatial, temporal, and chromatic mechanisms in vision. Current psychophysical models are only beginning to be able to explain these kinds of interactions. The second example shows that these interactions occur at even higher levels in the visual system. In Figure 22, adapted from the work of Adelson [ADEL93], the elements of the checkerboard block on the left and the flat pattern on the right have the same reflectances but the three-dimensional organization of the block makes us perceive them very differently.

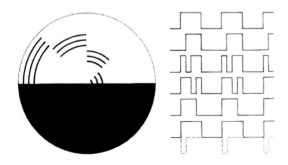

Figure 21: *Benham's top. When the black and white patterned top shown on the left is rotated at 5-10 rev./sec. colored rings are seen. The light intensity distribution of the rotating pattern as a function of time is shown on the right. Spatiotemporal interactions between antagonistic, spectrally-opponent color mechanisms account for the phenomenon. Thus while it is a convenient fiction for vision scientists to measure and characterize the visual system in terms of its simple responses to pattern, motion, and color, in fact the system is unified and the same visual mechanisms are at work in all cases [HURV81].*

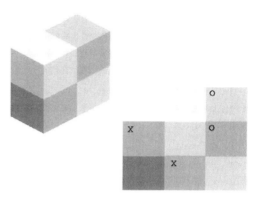

Figure 22: *Interactions between apparent reflectance, apparent illumination, and 3d spatial organization. The two patterns have the same reflectances. The 3d spatial organization of the block produces differing interpretations of the shaded regions in terms of lightness and brightness The two regions marked with X's have the same reflectance, but in the block they are perceived as different colors under different levels of illumination. The regions marked O's show another effect. Here the two regions have different reflectances but appear to be the same color, again under different illumination levels. After [ADEL93].*

Thus there are complex interactions between apparent reflectance, apparent illumination, and three-dimensional spatial organization that dramatically affect our perceptions of the identical visual stimulus. These interactions have implications for object recognition, color constancy, and other higher order visual phenomena. The quantitative aspects of these relationships are still not well understood.

In order to better understand normal vision outside the laboratory, vision researchers need to work with natural, complex, dynamic, three-dimensional visual displays. In the past, the problem has been that in these environments there has been little control to change the features of the environment, which has made careful experimentation difficult. By using the physically-based global illumination image synthesis methods, we should be able to provide rich visual environments for perceptual experiments that also allow precise control over the environmental features. Through this collaboration we hope to develop a better understanding of the complex interacting processes that underlie visual perception, which will allow us to develop more comprehensive visual models for computer graphics that will improve the realism and efficiency of our algorithms.

5   CONCLUSION

Our quest has been to develop physically based lighting models and perceptually based rendering procedures to produce synthetic images visually indistinguishable from real world scenes. To obtain *fidelity* we have subdivided our research into three parts: the local light reflection model, the energy transport phase, and the display procedures. The first two portions occur entirely in the physical domain, whereas the last is based entirely in the perceptual domain. All sections involve the testing and measurement necessary to guarantee *fidelity* and thus *predictive* algorithms. Since each stage is related to the next, feedback loops enable errors to be evaluated, a subsequent reduction in computational expense, and ultimately, we hope, more *efficient* algorithms.

The approaches and algorithms utilized are not currently practical, and require excessive computational resources. They do, however, yield important scientific insights into the physical processes of light reflection and light transport and clarify the computational bottlenecks. And because the algorithms are physically correct, they have already been used for simulating radiant heat exchange in turbine design, canopy detection in aerial reconnaissance, theater lighting and architectural and automotive design. With computing power increasing exponentially, global illumination algorithms will eventually become the norm. We hope that this research will ultimately help provide a better scientific foundation for future rendering algorithms.

Although the work presented has primarily been derived from research at one university, the effort is expanding to other universities, and there have been significant contributions by private and national laboratories. The research efforts should now be enlarged to a greater portion of the SIGGRAPH community. Only with a greater concentrated focus on these issues can we hope to improve the fidelity of our rendering algorithms.

Acknowledgments

This work was supported by National Science Foundation grants ASC-9523483 (Greenberg) and CCR-9401961 (Shirley), as well as by the support of all authors through the NSF Science and Technology Center for Computer Graphics and Scientific Visualization (ASC-8920219). Much of the research was performed on workstations generously provided by the Hewlett Packard Corporation.

The authors thank Linda Stephenson for her patience and skill assembling the final manuscript.

References

[ADEL93] E.H. Adelson. Perceptual Organization and the Judgment of Brightness. In *Science*, vol. 262, pp. 2042-2044, 1993.

[APPE68] A. Appel. Some Techniques for Shading Machine Renderings of Solids. In *AFIPS 1968 Spring Joint Computing Conference*, pp. 37-49, 1968.

[ARVO86] James Arvo. Backward Ray Tracing. Developments in Ray Tracing. In *Computer Graphics* Course Notes, Annual Conference Series, 1986, ACM SIGGRAPH, pp. 259-263, 1986.

[BLIN77] James F. Blinn. Models of Light Reflection for Computer Synthesized Pictures. In *Computer Graphics*, Proceedings, Annual Conference Series, 1977, ACM SIGGRAPH, pp. 192-198.

[BOFF86] Kenneth R. Boff, Lloyd Kaufman, James P. Thomas. *Handbook of Perception and Human Performance*. John Wiley and Sons, 1986.

[BOLI95] Mark R. Bolin and Gary W. Meyer. A Frequency Based Ray Tracer. In *Computer Graphics*, Proceedings, Annual Conference Series, 1995, ACM SIGGRAPH, pp. 409-418.

[CABR87] Brian Cabral, Nelson Max and Rebecca Springmeyer. Bidirectional Reflectance Functions from Surface Bump Maps. In *Computer Graphics*, 21(4), Proceedings, Annual Conference Series, 1987, ACM SIGGRAPH, pp. 273-282.

[CAMP90] A. T. Campbell III, and Donald Fussel. Adaptive Mesh Generation for Global Diffuse Illumination. In *Computer Graphics*, 24(4), Proceedings, Annual Conference Series, 1990, ACM SIGGRAPH, pp. 155-164.

[CHEN91] Shenchang Eric Chen, Holly Rushmeier, Gavin Miller, and Douglass Turner. A Progressive Multi-Pass Method for Global Illumination. In *Computer Graphics*, 25(4), Proceedings, Annual Conference Series, 1991, ACM SIGGRAPH, pp. 165-174.

[COHE85] Michael Cohen and Donald Greenberg. The HEMI-CUBE, A Radiosity Solution for Complex Environments. In *Computer Graphics*, 19(3), Proceedings, Annual Conference Series, 1985, ACM SIGGRAPH, pp. 31-40.

[COLL94] Steven Collins. Adaptive Splatting for Specular to Diffuse Light Transport. In *Proceedings of the Fifth Eurographics Workshop on Rendering*, pp. 119-135, June 1994.

[COOK81] Robert L. Cook and Kennneth E. Torrance. A Reflectance Model for Computer Graphics. In *Computer Graphics*, 15(3), Proceedings, Annual Conference Series, 1981, ACM SIGGRAPH, pp. 307-316.

[COOK84] Robert L. Cook, Thomas Porter, and Loren Carpenter. Distributed Ray Tracing. In *Computer Graphics*, Proceedings, Annual Conference Series, 1984, ACM SIGGRAPH, pp. 137-145.

[DISN97] Anonymous, "About The Film," Walt Disney Home Video, 1996. http://www.disney.com/DisneyVideos/ToyStory/about/abfilm.htm.

[DONG97] Dongarra, Jack, "Linpack Benchmark," The Performance Database Server, May 5, 1997. http://performance.netlib.org/performance/html/linpack.data.col0.html.

[FERW96] J.A. Ferwerda, S. Pattanaik, P. Shirley, and D.P. Greenberg. A Model of Visual Adaptation for Realistic Image Synthesis. In *Computer Graphics*, Proceedings, Annual Conference Series, 1996, ACM SIGGRAPH, pp. 249-258.

[FERW97] J.A. Ferwerda, S. Pattanaik, P. Shirley, and D.P. Greenberg. A Model of Visual Masking for Computer Graphics. In *Computer Graphics*, Proceedings, Annual Conference Series, 1997, ACM SIGGRAPH, in press.

[FOUR95] A. Fournier. Separating reflection functions for linear radiosity. In Proceedings of the *Sixth Eurographics Workshop on Rendering*, pp. 383-392, Dublin, Ireland, June 1995.

[GOND94] J.S. Gondek, G.W. Meyer, and J.G. Newman. Wavelength dependent reflectance functions. In *Computer Graphics,* Proceedings, Annual Conference, 1994, ACM SIGGRAPH, pp. 213-220, Orlando, Florida.

[GORA84] Cindy M. Goral, Kenneth E. Torrance, and Donald P. Greenberg. Modeling the Interaction of Light between Diffuse Surfaces. In *Computer Graphics,* 18(4), Proceedings, Annual Conference Series, 1984, ACM SIGGRAPH, pp. 213-222.

[GREE91] Donald P. Greenberg. Computers in Architecture. In *Scientific American,* pp. 104-109, February 1991.

[HANR91] Pat Hanrahan, David Salzman, and Larry Aupperle. A Rapid Hierarchical Radiosity Algorithm. In *Computer Graphics,* 25(4), Proceedings, Annual Conference Series, 1991, ACM SIGGRAPH, pp. 197-206.

[HANR93] P. Hanrahan and W. Krueger. Reflection from layered surfaces due to subsurface scattering. In *Computer Graphics,* Proceedings, Annual Conference Series, 1993, ACM SIGGRAPH, pp. 165-174, Anaheim, California.

[HE91] Xiao D. He, Kenneth E. Torrance, Francois X. Sillion, and Donald P. Greenberg. A Comprehensive Physical Model for Light Reflection. In *Computer Graphics,* 25(4), Proceedings, Annual Conference Series, 1991, ACM SIGGRAPH, pp. 175-186.

[HE92] Xiao D. He, Patrick O. Heynen, Richard L. Phillips, Kenneth E. Torrance, David H. Salesin, and Donald P. Greenberg. A Fast and Accurate Light Reflection Model. In *Computer Graphics,* 26(2), Proceedings, Annual Conference Series, 1992, ACM SIGGRAPH, pp. 253-254.

[HECK90] Paul S. Heckbert. Adaptive Radiosity Textures for Bidirectional Ray Tracing. In *Computer Graphics,* 24(3), Proceedings, Annual Conference Series, 1990, ACM SIGGRAPH, pp. 145-154.

[HENN97] Henning, John L., "How Many VUPS Is That Alpha In The Window?" Digital Equipment Corporation, Feb. 1997. http://www.europe.digital.com/info/alphaserver/performance/vups_297.html.

[HURV81] L.M. Hurvich. In *Color Vision.* Sunderland MA: Sinauer Assoc. Inc., 1981.

[IMME86] David S. Immel, Michael F. Cohen, and Donald P. Greenberg. A Radiosity Method for Non-diffuse Environment. In *Computer Graphics,* 20(4), Proceedings, Annual Conference Series, 1986, ACM SIGGRAPH, pp. 133-142.

[KAJI85] J. Kajiya. Anisotropic reflectance models. In *Computer Graphics,* 19(4), Proceedings, Annual Conference, 1985, ACM SIGGRAPH , pp. 15-21.

[KAJI86] James T. Kajiya. The Rendering Equation. In *Computer Graphics,* 20(4), Proceedings, Annual Conference Series, 1986, ACM SIGGRAPH, pp. 143-150.

[KELL61] D.H. Kelly. Visual Response to Time-Dependent Stimuli. I. Amplitude Sensitivity Measurements. In *J. Opt. Soc. Am.* 51, pp. 422-429, 1961.

[KOEN96] J.J. Koenderink, A.J. van Doorn, and M. Stavridi. Bidirectional reflection distribution function expressed in terms of surface scattering modes. In *European Conference on Computer Vision,* pp. 28-39, 1996.

[LAFO96] Eric Lafortune. Mathematical Methods and Monte Carlo Algorithms for Physically Based Rendering. In Ph.D. Thesis, Katholieke Universiteit Leuven, Belgium, February 1996.

[LAFO97] E. Lafortune, S.C. Foo, K.E. Torrance, D.P. Greenberg. Non-Linear Approximation of Reflectance Functions. In *Computer Graphics,* Proceedings, Annual Conference Series, 1997, ACM SIGGRAPH, Los Angeles, California.

[LEE85] M.E. Lee, R. A. Redner, and S.P. Uselton. Statistically Optimized Sampling for Distributed Ray Tracing. In *Computer Graphics,* 19(3), Proceedings, Annual Conference Series, 1985, ACM SIGGRAPH, pp. 61-67.

[LEON88] Thomas A. Leonard and Michael Pantoliano. BRDF Round Robin, Stray Light and Contamination in Optical Systems. In S.P.I.E. Vol. 967, Society of Photo-Optical Instrumentation Engineers, 1988.

[LEON89] Thomas A. Leonard, Michael Pantoliano, and James Reilly. Results of a CO2 BRDF Round Robin, Scatter from Optical Components. In S.P.I.E. Vol 1165, Society of Photo-Optical Instrumentation Engineers, 1989.

[LISC93] Dani Lischinski, Filippo Tampieri, and Donald P. Greenberg. Combining Hierarchical Radiosity and Discontinuity Meshing. In *Computer Graphics,* Proceedings, Annual Conference Series, 1993, ACM SIGGRAPH, pp. 199-208.

[MEYE80] G.W. Meyer and D.P. Greenberg. Perceptual Color Spaces for Computer Graphics. In *Computer Graphics* Proceedings, Annual Conference Series, 1980, ACM SIGGRAPH, pp. 254-261.

[MEYE86] G.W. Meyer. Color Calculation for and Perceptual Assessment of Computer Graphic Images. In Unpublished Ph.D. thesis, Cornell University, 1986.

[MITC87] D.P. Mitchell. Generating Antialiased Images at Low Sampling Densities. In *Computer Graphics,* 21(4), Proceedings, Annual Conference Series, 1987, ACM SIGGRAPH, pp. 463-474.

[MUEL50] C.G. Mueller. Frequency of Seeing Functions for Intensity Discriminations at Various Levels of Adapting Intensity. In *J. Gen. Psych.,* 1950.

[OREN94] M. Oren and S.K. Nayar. Generalization of Lambert's reflectance model. In *Computer Graphics, Proceedings, Annual Conference Series, 1994*, ACM SIGGRAPH, pp. 239-246, Orlando, Florida, July 1994.

[PATT93] S. N. Pattanaik. Computational Methods for Global Illumination and Visualization of Complex 3D Environments. In Ph.D. thesis, Birla Institute of Technology & Science, Computer Science Department, Pilani, India, February 1993.

[PHON75] Bui-Tuong Phong. Illumination for Computer Generated Images. In *Communications of the ACM*, 18(6):311-317, June 1975.

[PIRE67] M.H. Pirenne. In *Vision and the Eye*, 2nd edition. London: Associated Book Publishers, 1967.

[POUL90] P. Poulin and A. Fournier. A Model for Anisotropic Reflection. In *Computer Graphics, Proceedings, 24(4), Annual Conference Series, 1990*, ACM SIGGRAPH, pp. 273-282, August 1990.

[REDN95] R.A. Redner, M.E. Lee, and S.P. Uselton. Smooth B-Spline Illumination Maps for Bidirectional Ray Tracing. In *ACM Transactions on Graphics*, 14(4), October 1995.

[SCHR95] Peter Schröder, Win Sweldens. Spherical Wavelets: Efficiently Representing Functions on the Sphere. In *Computer Graphics*, Proceedings, Annual Conference Series, 1995, ACM SIGGRAPH, pp. 161-171.

[SILL91] Francois X. Sillion, James Arvo, Stephen Westin, and Donald Greenberg. A Global Illumination Algorithm for General Reflection Distributions. In *Computer Graphics*, 25(4), Proceedings, Annual Conference Series, 1991, ACM SIGGRAPH, pp. 187-196.

[SILV86] B. W. Silverman. In *Density Estimation for Statistics and Data Analysis*. Chapman and Hall, London, 1986.

[SMIT94] Brian E. Smits, James R. Arvo, and Donald P. Greenberg. A Clustering Algorithm for Radiosity in Complex Environments. In *Computer Graphics*, 28(3), Proceedings, Annual Conference Series, 1994, ACM SIGGRAPH, pp. 435-442.

[SPEN95] G. Spencer, P. Shirley, K. Zimmerman, and D.P. Greenberg. Physically-Based Glare Effects for Computer Generated Images. In *Computer Graphics*, Proceedings, Annual Conference Series, 1995, ACM SIGGRAPH, pp. 325-334.

[BREA88] Robert P. Breault. Stray Light and Contamination in Optical Systems. In S.P.I.E., 1988, p.234.

[STRO86] L. Stroebel, J. Compton, I. Current, and R. Zakia. In *Photographic Materials and Processes*. Boston: Focal Press, 1986.

[TELL94] Seth Teller, Celeste Fowler, Thomas Funkhouser, and Pat Hanrahan. Partitioning and Ordering Large Radiosity Calculations. In *Computer Graphics*, 28(3), Proceedings, Annual Conference Series, 1994, ACM SIGGRAPH, pp. 443-450.

[TORR67] K.E. Torrance and E.M. Sparrow. Theory for Off-Specular Reflection from Roughened Surfaces. In *Journal of the Optical Society of America* 57(9), September 1967.

[TUMB93] J. Tumblin and H. Rushmeier. Tone Reproduction for Realistic Images. In *IEEE Computer Graphics and Applications*, 13(6), pp. 42-48, 1993.

[VANN67] F.L. Van Nes and M.A. Bouman. Spatial Modulation Transfer in the Human Eye. In *J. Opt. Soc. Am.* 57, pp. 401-406, 1967.

[VEAC95] Eric Veach and Leonidus J. Guibas. Optimally Combining Sampling Techniques for Monte Carlo Rendering. In *Computer Graphics*, Proceedings, Annual Conference Series, 1995, ACM SIGGRAPH, pp. 419-428.

[WALL87] John Wallace, Michael Cohen, and Donald Greenberg. A Two-Pass Solution to the Rendering Problem. In *Computer Graphics*, 21(4), Proceedings, Annual Conference Series, 1987, ACM SIGGRAPH, pp 311-320.

[WALT97a] Bruce Walter, Philip M. Hubbard, Peter Shirley, and Donald P. Greenberg. Global Illumination Using Local Linear Density Estimation. In *ACM Transactions on Graphics*, 1997.

[WALT97b] Bruce Walter, Gun Alppay, Eric Lafortune, Sebastian Fernandez, and Donald P. Greenberg. Fitting Virtual Light for Non-Diffuse Walkthroughs. In *Computer Graphics*, Proceedings, Annual Conference Series, 1997, ACM SIGGRAPH.

[WARD88] Gregory Ward, Francis Rubinstein and Robert Clear, A Ray Tracing Solution for Diffuse Interreflection. In *Computer Graphics*, Proceedings, Annual Conference Series, 1988, 22(4), ACM SIGGRAPH.

[WARD92] G.J. Ward. Measuring and Modeling Mnisotropic Reflection. In *Computer Graphics*, 26(2), Proceedings, Annual Conference Series, 1992, ACM SIGGRAPH, pp. 265-272.

[WARD94a] Gregory Ward. The RADIANCE Lighting Simulation and Rendering System. In *Computer Graphics*, Proceedings, Annual Conference Series, 1994, 28(4), ACM SIGGRAPH, pp 459-472.

[WARD94b] G. Ward. A Contrast-Based Scalefactor for Luminance Display. In P.S. Heckbert (Ed.). In *Graphics Gems IV*, Boston: Academic Press Professional, 1994.

[WEST92]   S.H. Westin, J.R. Arvo, and K.E. Torrance. Predicting
           Reflectance Functions from Complex Surfaces. In *Com-
           puter Graphics,* 26(2), Proceedings, Annual Conference
           Series, 1992, ACM SIGGRAPH, pp. 255-264, July
           1992.

[WHIT80]   Turner Whitted. An Improved Illumination Model for
           Shaded Display. In *Communications of the ACM,* 23(6),
           pp. 343-349, June 1980.

[WYSZ82]   G. Wyszecki and W.S. Stiles. In *Color Science: Con-
           cepts and Methods, Quantitative Data and Formulae
           (2nd edition).* New York: Wiley, 1982.

SIGGRAPH 97 Committee

Conference Chair
G. Scott Owen
Georgia State University

Conference Chief Staff Executive
Dino Schweitzer
Capstone Management Group, Inc.

Accounting
Smith, Bucklin, & Associates, Inc.

Audio/Visual Support
AVW Audio Visual, Inc.

Community Outreach
Jackie White
California State University, Los Angeles

Computer Animation Festival
Judith Crow
Digital Domain

Conference Administration
Capstone Management Group, Inc.

Conference Management
Smith, Bucklin, & Associates, Inc.

Copy Coordination
Smith, Bucklin, & Associates, Inc.

Courses
Barb Helfer
The Ohio State University

Creative Applications Laboratory
Steve Anderson
Silicon Graphics, Inc.

Educators Program
Rosalee Wolfe
DePaul University

Electric Garden
Rick Hopkins
Side Effects Software

Exhibition Management
Hall-Erickson, Inc.

Graphic Design/Editing
Q LTD

International Chair
Alain Chesnais
Alias|Wavefront Paris

Marketing and Media
Smith, Bucklin, & Associates, Inc.

Networking
Steven M. Van Frank
Van Frank Consulting

Ongoings: The Fine Arts Gallery
Lynn Pocock
Pratt Institute

Online Technologies
Janet McAndless
Sony Pictures Imageworks

Panels
Barbara Mones-Hattal
George Mason University

Papers
Turner Whitted
Numerical Design Limited

Director for Publications
Stephen N. Spencer
The Ohio State University

Registration
Smith, Bucklin, & Associates, Inc.

Service Contractor
Freeman Decorating Company

SIGGRAPH TV
David Tubbs
Evans & Sutherland Computer
Corporation

Sketches
David S. Ebert
University of Maryland Baltimore County

Student Volunteers
Mk Haley
Walt Disney Imagineering

Travel Agent
Flying Colors

SIGGRAPH 96 Conference Chair
John Fujii
Hewlett-Packard Company

SIGGRAPH 98 Conference Chair
Walt Bransford
Thrillistic LLC

SIGGRAPH 99 Conference Chair
Warren Waggenspack
Louisiana State University

SIGGRAPH Chair
Steve Cunningham
California State University, Stanislaus

Conference Advisory Group

SIGGRAPH 96 Conference Chair
John Fujii
Hewlett-Packard Company

SIGGRAPH 97 Conference Chair
G. Scott Owen
Georgia State University

SIGGRAPH 98 Conference Chair
Walt Bransford
Thrillistic, LLC

SIGGRAPH 99 Conference Chair
Warren Waggenspack
Louisiana State University

SIGGRAPH Conference
Chief Staff Executive (Ex officio)
Dino Schweitzer
Capstone Management Group, Inc.

SIGGRAPH Organization Chair
Steve Cunningham
California State University, Stanislaus

SIGGRAPH Executive Committee

Chair
Steve Cunningham
California State University, Stanislaus

Vice Chair
Alain Chesnais
Alias|Wavefront Paris

Director for Communications
John C. Hart
Washington State University

Director for Education
Marc J. Barr
Middle Tennessee State University

Director for Professional Chapters
Scott Lang
Academy for the Advancement of
Science & Technology

Director for Publications
Stephen N. Spencer
The Ohio State University

Directors-at-Large
Chuck Hansen
University of Utah

Theresa-Marie Rhyne
Lockheed Martin Technical Services/
US EPA Scientific Visualization Center

Treasurer
Nan Schaller
Rochester Institute of Technology

Past Chair
Mary C. Whitton
University of North Carolina at Chapel Hill

SIGGRAPH 97 Conference Chair
G. Scott Owen
Georgia State University

SIGGRAPH Conference
Chief Staff Executive (ex officio)
Dino Schweitzer
Capstone Management Group, Inc.

Papers Committee

Chair
Turner Whitted
Numerical Design Limited

Administrative Assistant
Nereida Segura-Rico
University of North Carolina at Chapel Hill

Committee

Frederick P. Brooks, Jr.
University of North Carolina at Chapel Hill

Edwin Catmull
Pixar Animation Studios

Michael Cohen
Microsoft Research

Frank Crow
Interval Research Corporation

Julie Dorsey
Massachusetts Institute of Technology

Eugene Fiume
University of Toronto and Alias|Wavefront

Alain Fournier
University of British Columbia

Thomas Allen Funkhouser
Bell Laboratories

Jessica Hodgins
Georgia Institute of Technology

John F. Hughes
Brown University

R. Victor Klassen
Xerox Corporation

Bill Lorensen
GE Corporate R&D

Gavin S. P. Miller
Interval Research Corporation

J. Michael Moshell
University of Central Florida

Alyn P. Rockwood
Arizona State University

Holly Rushmeier
IBM TJ Watson Research Center

Hans-Peter Seidel
Universität Erlangen

John M. Snyder
Microsoft Research

Maureen Stone
Xerox Palo Alto Research Center

Richard Szeliski
Microsoft Research

Demetri Terzopoulos
University of Toronto

Greg Turk
Georgia Institute of Technology

Douglas Voorhies
Silicon Graphics Computer Systems

Andy Witkin
Carnegie Mellon University

Panels Committee

Chair
Barbara Mones-Hattal
George Mason University

Administrative Assistant
Dawn Truelsen
TrueMedia

Committee

Leo Hourvitz
Pixar Studios

Alyce Kaprow
New Studio

Mike Mcgrath
Colorado School of Mines

Celia Pearce
Momentum Media Group

Theresa-Marie Rhyne
Lockheed Martin Technical Services/
US EPA Scientific Visualization Center

Carl Rosendahl
Pacific Data Images

Alan Turransky
USA Today

Mary Whitton
University of North Carolina at Chapel Hill

Courses Committee

Chair
Barbara Helfer
The Ohio State University

Administrative Assistant
Viki Dennis
The Ohio State University

Committee

Andrew Daniel
Alliance Semiconductor

Jeffrey J. McConnell
Canisius College

Nan Schaller
Rochester Institute of Technology

Andrew Scott
Central State University

Scott Senften
SGI - Houston

Harry Smith
University of North Carolina at Wilmington

Courses Reviewers

Dr. Thomas Alexander
Steve Anderson
Peter Anderson
Daniel Bergeron
Daniel J. Bicket
Jack Bresenham
Wayne Carlson
Pete Carswell
Alan Commike
Larry Coon
Andy Daniel
Viki Dennis
David Ebert
Steven Feiner
Ken Flurchick
Robert Geitz
Peter Grestman
Barb Helfer
Larry Hodges
Donald House
Kathy Kershaw Barshatzky
Midori Kitagawa-DeLeon
Kris Laszlo
Tom Ledoux
Mark Lee
Matt Lewis
Steve May
Jeffrey J. McConnell
Bonnie Mitchell
Steven Mullins
Dave Reed
Phil Ritzenthaler
Evelyn Rozanski
Nan Schaller
Marla Schweppe
Andrew Scott
Thomas Sederberg
Scott Senften
Dennis Sessanna
Alvy Ray Smith
Harry Smith
Leslie Southern
Don Stredney
Al Stutz
Sara Susskind
Traci Temple
Sam Uselton
Patricia Wenner
Mary Whitton
Barbara Woodall

Paper Reviewers

Salim Abi-Ezzi
Kurt Akeley
John Amanatides
P. Anandan
Jacques Andre
Greg Angelini
Masaki Aono
Tony Apodaca
James Arvo
Ian Ashdown
Lisa Avial
Ricardo Avila
Ali Azarbayajani
Norm Badler
Larry Baird
Chandrajit Bajaj
Harlyn Baker
Sanjay Bakshi
Kavita Bala
David Banks
David Baraff
Richard Bartels
Lyn Bartram
Ronen Barzel
Dan Baum
Ben Bederson
Thaddeus Beier
James Bergen
Krishna A. Bharat
Charles Bigelow
Gary Bishop.
Frederic Blaise
Brian S. Blau
Avi Bleiweiss
Jim Blinn
Jules Bloomenthal
Bruce Blumberg
Silviu Borac
Christoph C. Borel
Jean-Yves Bouguet
Ronan Boulic
Terrance Boult
David Brainard
Scott Brave
Eric Brechner
David E. Breen
Normand Briere
David Brogan
Alfred Bruckstein
Armin Bruderlin
Steve Bryson
John Buchanan
Bob Buckley
Robert Buckley
Christina Burbeck
Ed Burton
Bill Buxton
Brian Cabral
Swen Campagna
Stu Card
Wayne E. Carlson
Eric Chen
Jim Chen
Per Christensen
Tom Clarke
Jonathan Cohen
Michael M. Cohen
Perry R. Cook
Rob Cook
Satyan Coorg
William Cowan
Michael Cox
James Cremer
Brian Curless
Niels da Vitoria Lobo
Larry Davis
Mark de Berg
Paul Debevec

Michael Deering
Tony DeRose
Oliver Deussen
Paul Diefenbach
Paul Dizio
Yoshinori Dobashi
Steven Dollins
Shane Dorosh
George Drettakis
Tom Duff
Charles Dyer
David S. Ebert
Matthias Eck
Zair Chems Eddine
Jenny Ehrlich
Gershon Elber
Matthew Eldridge
Jihad Ell-Sana
Paul Emerson
Nick England
Carl Erikson
Irfan A. Essa
Joyce Farrell
Olivier Faugeras
Steven K. Feiner
Bob Ferguson
Helaman Ferguson
Adam Finkelstein
Ken Fishkin
Kurt Fleischer
Jim Foran
A.R. Forrest
Dave Forsey
Scott Foster
Deborah Fowler
Henry Fuchs
Don Fussell
Tinsley Galyean
Geoffrey Gardner
Jeff Gardner
Michael Garland
Marie-Paule Gascuel
W. Gates
Dariu M. Gavrila
Reid Gershbein
Sherif Ghali
Simon Gibson
Andrew Glassner
Mike Gleicher
Steven Gortler
Craig Gotsman
Hans Peter Graf
Mark Green
Ned Greene
Guenther Greiner
Cindy Grimm
Larry Gritz
Andy Gruber
Radek Grzeszczuk
Brian Guenter
André Guéziec
Baining Guo
Paul Haeberli
Michael Halle
Bernd Hamann
Jim Hannan
Pat Hanrahan
Andrew J. Hanson
Ken Hardis
John Hart
David Haumann
Paul Heckert
Wolfgang Heidrich
Jeremy Heiner
Jim Helman
Sheila Hemani
Daryl Hepting
Roger D. Hersch

Larry Hodges
Jessica Hodgins
Kenneth Hoff
Dave Holliday
Michael J. Holst
Hugues Hoppe
Geoffrey Howell
Helen Hu
Philip M. Hubbard
Charles E. Hughes
Homan Igehy
Victoria Interrante
Hiroshi Ishii
Ramesh Jain
Kalpana Janamanchi
Fran Janucik
Allan Jepson
Chris Johnson
Keith Johnson
Michael Jones
Peter Jones
Bert Juettler
Zafer Kadi
Jim Kajiya
Prem Kalra
Takeo Kanade
Lina Karam
Michael Kass
Arie Kaufman
Tim Kay
Myung-Soo Kim
Dave Kirk
Reinhard Klein
Brian Knep
Bruce Knerr
Leif Kobbelt
Jeff Koechling
Hans-Juergen Koglin
Evangelos Kokkevis
Craig Kolb
David Koller
Cary Kornfeld
Thiemo Krink
Venkat Krishnamurthy
Subodah Kumar
Tosiyasu L. Kunii
Tsuneya Kurihara
Winfried Kurth
Jim Lackner
Phil Lacroute
Eric Lafortune
David Laidlaw
Paul Lalonde
Don Lampton
Olin Lathrop
Mark Leather
Yvan Leclerc
Jed Lengyel
Apostolos Lerios
David Levin
Marc Levoy
Bob Lewis
John Lewis
J. Bryan Lewis
Peter Liepa
Ming Lin
James S. Lipscomb
Dani Lischinski
Jim Little
Pete Litwinowicz
Mark Livingston
Charles Loop
Michael Lounsbery
William Luken
Jock Mackinlay
Nadia Magnenat-Thalmann
Jerome Maillot
Jitendra Malik

Tom Malzbender
Stephen Mann
Steve Mann
Dinesh Manocha
Dan Mapes
Bill Mark
Lee Markosian
Joe Marks
Paul Martin
Kenji Mase
Thomas Massie
Nelson Max
David McAllister
Michael McCarthy
Michael McCool
Michael McKenna
Dave McKeown
Leonard McMillan
Barbara Meier
Jai Menon
Dimitri Metaxas
Ron Metoyer
Gary Meyer
Mark Mine
Brian Mirtich
Don Mitchell
Gary Monheit
Michael Monks
Mark Montague
Claudio Montani
John Montrym
Henry Moreton
Shigeo Morishima
F. Musgrave
Michael Nagy
Vishvjit S. Nalwa
Sandy Napel
Shree Nayar
Bruce Naylor
Shawn Neely
Ferd Neves
Gregory B. Newby
Fabrice Neyret
Krates Ng
Victor Ng-Thow-Hing
Tom Ngo
Gregory Nielson
Jeffry Nimeroff
Tomoyuki Nishita
Alan Norton
D. Nuesch
James O'Brien
Paul Oiefenbach
John Oliensis
John Owens
Dinesh K. Pai
Yakup Paker
Alex Pang
Richard Parent
Frederic I. Parke
Jim Parsons
Kimberly Parsons
Alexander Pasko
Nick Patrikalakis
Sumant Pattanaik
Randy Pausch
Darwyn Peachey
Andrew Pearce
Hans Pedersen
Catherine Pelachaud
Sandy Pentland
Ken Perlin
Pietro Perona
Joerg Peters
Preston Pfarner
Matt Pharr
Christine Piatko
Steve Pieper

Jean Ponce
Zoran Popović
Mike Potmesil
Helmut Pottmann
Pierre Poulin
Charles Poynton
Guru Prasad
Hartmut Prautzsch
Dennis Profitt
Przemek Prusinkiewicz
Steve Putz
Ari Rappoport
Matthew Regan
Wes Regian
Jim Rehg
Ulrich Reif
Craig Reynolds
Bill Ribarsky
Richard Robb
George Robertson
Warren Robinett
John Rohlf
Jannick P. Rolland
Chuck Rose
Dan Rosenthal
Jarek Rossignac
Gerhard Roth
Malcolm Sabin
Mark Sagar
David Salesin
Kenneth Salisbury
Hanan Samet
Daniel Sandin
Radim Sara
Yoichi Sato
Stefan Schaal
Robert Schaback
Rob Scharein
Gernot Schauffler
Christopher Schlick
Chris Schoeneman
Peter Schröder
Will Schröder
Roberto Scopigno
Tom Sederberg
Mark Segal
Steve Seitz
Carlo H. Séquin
Jonathan Shade
Michael Shantz
Albert Sheffer
Michael Sherman
Peter Shirley
Harry Shum
François Sillion
Karl Sims
Gurminder Singh
Karan Singh
Mel Slater
Ken Sloan
Philipp Slusallek
David Small
Brian Smits
Christa Sommerer
Greg Spencer
Mandayam Srinivasan
Jos Stam
Kay Stanney
Andrei State
James Stewart
Jorge Stolfi
Eric Stollnitz
Tim Strotman
Oded Sudarsky
Martin Suter
Guno Sutiono
Wim Sweldens
Filippo Tampieri

Takala Tapio
Gabriel Taubin
C J Taylor
Bob Taylor
Russell Taylor
Brice Tebbs
Seth Teller
Patrick Teo
Daniel Thalmann
Carlo Tomasi
David Tonnesen
Ken Torrance
Xiaoyuan Tu
Matthew Turk
Ken Turkowskim
Brygg Ullmer
Sam Uselton
Andy van Dam
Michael van de Panne
Mark VandeWettering
Tamas Varady
Amitabh Varshney
Luiz Velho
Dennis Venable
Vincent John Vincent
Dave Vining
Jensen Wann
Greg Ward
Joe Warren
Keith Waters
Kevin Weiler
Will Welch
Stephen Westin
Dan Wexler
Scott Whitman
Mary Whitton
Greg Wiatrowski
Jane Wilhelms
Kent E. Williams
Lance Williams
Kayle Wilson
Georges Winkenbach
Matthias Wloka
George Wolberg
Larry Wolff
Hans Wolters
Andrew Woo
Wayne Wooten
Steven P. Worley
Brian Wyvill
Roni Yagel
Naokazu Yokoya
David Zeltzer
Hansong Zhang
Ben Zhu
Denis Zorin
Mike Zyda

Exhibitors

(As of 14 May 1997)

(Art)^n Laboratory
3D Construction Company
3Dlabs, Inc.
3Name3D
4DVISION
5D Ltd.

A K Peters, Ltd.
Academic Press, Inc.
AccelGraphics, Inc.
Accom, Inc.
Acuris Inc.
Adaptive Media
Addison-Wesley Publishing Company
Adobe Systems Inc.
Advanced Media Production Center
Advanced Rendering Technology
Advanced Visual Systems Inc.
Alias|Wavefront
Alien Skin Software, LLC
American Cinematographer Magazine
Animation Science
Anthro Corporation
AP PROFESSIONAL
Artbeats Software, Inc.
Ascension Technology Corporation
ASK LCD
ATLIGHTSPEED, Inc.
auto.des.sys, Inc.
AutoMedia Ltd.
Autometric Inc.
Avid Technology Inc.
Aztek, Inc.

B-H Photo Video
Balboa Capital
BARCO, Inc.
BioVision
Bit 3 Computer Corporation
Blue Sky Studios
Bushey Virtual Construction

CADCrafts
Caligari Corporation
Cambridge Animation Systems
Carrera Computers
Cartesia Software
CBS News Archives
CELCO
CGI
CGSD Corporation
Chroma Graphics, Inc.
Chromatek Inc.
Chyron Corporation
Cinebase Software
Ciprico Inc.
CIRAD - Unite de modelisation des plantes
Cirrus Logic, Inc.
Cogswell Polytechnical College
Communications Specialties Incorporated

Compaq Computer Corporation
Computrend
The Coriolis Group
Coryphaeus Software, Inc.
CRC Press, Inc.
Crystal River Engineering
Cyberware

Denim Software
Depthography/Upgrade Technology
Desktop Engineering Magazine
Desktop Images
Diamond Multimedia Systems
Diaquest Inc.
Digimation, Inc.
Digital Domain
Digital Equipment Corporation
Digital Processing Systems Inc.
Digital Semiconductor
Digital Wisdom Inc.
Digits 'n Art Software, Inc.
Discreet Logic
DreamWorks Animation
Dynamic Pictures, Inc.

Eastman Kodak Company
ElectricImage, Inc.
Electronic Arts
ELSA Inc.
ENCAD, Inc.
Engineering Animation, Inc.
Ensemble Designs Inc.
Equilibrium
Evans & Sutherland Computer Corporation
Eye on Software

Falcon Systems, Inc.
Fast Electronic U.S., Inc.
Floating Images
Folsom Research Inc.
Fractal Design Corporation
Fujitsu Microelectronics, Inc.

Graham-Patten Systems, Inc.

GW Hannaway & Associates
Hash Inc.
Hewlett-Packard Company
Hitachi America, Ltd.
House of Moves
HPCwire

IBM Corporation
IdN
IMAGICA Corporation of America
Immersion Corporation
Industrial Light + Magic, Lucas Digital
InnovMetric Software, Inc.
Intel Corporation
Interactive Effects
Intergraph Corporation
InterSense

IRIS Graphics, Inc.
ITU Research, Inc.

Jazz Media Network

Ketiv Technologies
Kinetix
Kingston Technology Corporation

LambSoft, Inc.
Leadtek Research, Inc.
LEGASYS International, Inc.
Leitch Incorporated
Lightscape Technologies, Inc.
Lightwave Communications, Inc.
LightWork Design Ltd.
Linker Systems, Inc.
Logitech
Lucent Technologies

Macmillan Computer Publishing, USA
Macromedia
Mainframe Entertainment, Inc.
Management Graphics, Inc.
Matrox Electronic Systems Ltd.
Matrox Graphics
Maxon Computer GmbH
MAXSTRAT
Robert McMeel & Associates
Medea Corporation
Media 100/Data Translation
Media PEGS
MegaDrive Systems, Inc.
MetaTools, Inc.
Microboards Technology
Micropolis Corp.
Microsoft
Miller Freeman Inc.
Minicomputer Exchange
Minolta Corporation
Miranda Technologies Inc.
Mitsubishi Electronics America, Inc.
MMS Multi Media Systems GmbH
Montpellier Technopole
Morgan Kaufmann Publishers
Motion Analysis Corporation
MountainGate
Moving Pixels
MultiGen Inc.
MuSE Technologies, Inc.

n-Vision, Inc.
National Animation and Design Centre
(NAD Centre)
NEC Electronics Inc.
NeTPower
Newfire, Inc.
NewTek, Inc.
NHK (Japan Broadcasting System)
Nichimen Graphics, Inc.
Northern Digital Inc.
nStor Corporation

Exhibitors

NTT Optical Network Systems Laboratory
Numerical Algorithms Group, Inc.
NVision, Inc.

Odyssey Productions
Omnicomp Graphics
Omniview, Inc.
Onyx Computing, Inc.
Optia
Oxberry LLC

P.E. Photron
Pacific Bell
Panasonic Broadcast & Television
 Systems Company
PC Graphics and Video
PC Video Conversion
Phobus Corporation
Pixar Animation Studios
Play Incorporated
Polhemus
Positron
Produccion & Distribucion
ProMax Technology
Proxima Corporation
Pthalo Systems, Inc.
Pyramid Systems, Inc.

Quantel, Inc.
Quantum 3D, Inc.
Quantum Corporation
Questar Productions
QuVIS Inc.

Radiance Software International
Radius Inc.
Real-Time Geometry
Real 3D
Realax Corporation
REM INFOGRAFICA, S.A.
Resolution Technologies, Inc.
RGB Spectrum
Rhythm & Hues Studios

S-MOS Systems, Inc.
Savannah College of Art and Design
Screen Actors Guild
SensAble Technologies, Inc.
Sense8 Corporation
Side Effects Software
Sierra Design Labs
Sigma Electronics, Inc.
Silicon Graphics, Inc.
Society of Motion Pictures and
 Television Engineers (SMPTE)
Softimage
Solid Systems CAD Services
Solomon Volumetric Imaging, Inc.
Sony Electronics Inc.
Sony Pictures Imageworks
Sony/Tektronix Corporation
Sound Ideas

Spacetec IMC
Springer-Verlag
Sprint
Square L.A. Inc.
StereoGraphics Corporation
Storage Concepts
Strata, Inc.
StreamLogic Corporation
Sun Microsystems Inc.
Sun Microsystems Inc.
Superscape
Sven Technologies
Symmetric

Techexport, Inc.
Tektronix, Inc.
Template Graphics Software, Inc.
Texas Memory Systems, Inc.
The Republic Group, Inc.
Toon Boom Technologies Inc.
Transoft Technology Corporation
Transom Technologies
Tri-Star Computer
Trinity Animation
TV One Multimedia Solutions

Unlimited Potential

Vangard Technology, Inc.
Ventana
Vicon Motion Systems
Videomedia, Inc.
Viewpoint DataLabs International, Inc.
Viewsonic
VIFX
Virtual Technologies, Inc.
Visible Productions

Wacom Technology Corporation
Walt Disney Company
Western Scientific, Inc.
Wiley Computer Publishing
Winsted Corporation
Worlds, Inc.

SIGGRAPH Professional Chapters

California

Los Angeles ACM SIGGRAPH
Aliza Corson
PO Box 9399
Marina del Rey, CA 90295
los_angeles_chapter@siggraph.org
http://siggraph.allen.com/

San Diego ACM SIGGRAPH
Nancy Collier
4822 Santa Monica Ave, Suite 179
San Diego, CA 92107
san_diego_chapter@siggraph.org
http://www.SDSC.edu/sdsiggraph

San Francisco ACM SIGGRAPH
Richard Cox
P.O. Box 1495
El Cerrito, CA 94530-4495
san_francisco_chapter@siggraph.org
http://www.best.com/~siggraph/

Silicon Valley ACM SIGGRAPH
Alesh Jancarik
PO Box 1205
Mountain View, CA 94042-1205
silicon_valley_chapter@siggraph.org
http://www.best.com/~siggraph

Colorado

Denver/Boulder ACM SIGGRAPH
Mike McCarthy
PO Box 61402
Cherry Creek Station
Denver, CO 80206-8402
denver-boulder_chapter@siggraph.org

Florida

Ft. Lauderdale ACM SIGGRAPH
Garry M. Paxinos
Metro Link Inc
4711 N. Powerline Road
Fort Lauderdale, FL 33309
fort_lauderdale_chapter@siggraph.org
http://www.flsig.org/ftl/

Orlando ACM SIGGRAPH
Colleen Cleary
PO Box 2208
Winter Park, FL 32790-2208
orlando_chapter@siggraph.org
http://www.flsig.org/os/

Tampa Bay ACM SIGGRAPH
Steve Pidgeon
Pulse Productions
12551 Indian Rocks Road S Suite 13
Largo, FL 34644
tampa_bay_chapter@siggraph.org
http://www.flsig.org/tampa/

Georgia

Atlanta ACM SIGGRAPH
Mark Feldman
PO Box 769182
Roswell, GA 30076-9182
atlanta_chapter@siggraph.org
http://www.acm.org/chapters/atlanta

Massachusetts

Boston ACM SIGGRAPH
Olin Lathrop
PO Box 194
Bedford, MA 01730
boston_chapter@siggraph.org
http://www.v-site.net/siggraph-ne

Minnesota

Minneapolis/St. Paul ACM SIGGRAPH
Stan Bissinger
School of Communication Arts
2526 27th Ave South
Minneapolis, MN 55406
minneapolis-stpaul_chapter@siggraph.org
http://www.pixel8.com/siggraph/

New Jersey

Princeton ACM SIGGRAPH
Douglas Dixon
P.O. Box 1324
Princeton, NJ 08542
princeton _chapter@siggraph.org

New Mexico

Rio Grande ACM SIGGRAPH
David Callahan
P.O. Box 8352
Albuquerque, NM 87108-8352
rio_grande_chapter@siggraph.org

New York

New York City ACM SIGGRAPH
Debra Herschmann c/o Valerie Castleman
60 Gramercy Park, #9A
New York, NY 10010
new_york_city_chapter@siggraph.org

North Carolina

NC Research Triangle ACM SIGGRAPH
Randy Brown
SAS
Campus Drive RA 459
Cary, NC 27513
research_triangle_chapter@siggraph.org

Texas

Dallas Area ACM SIGGRAPH
Aaron Hightower
Paradigm Simulation Inc.
14900 Landmark Suite 400
Dallas, TX 75240
dallas_area_chapter@siggraph.org
http://acm.org/~aaronh/das.html

Houston ACM SIGGRAPH
Tom Ledoux
2501 Tanglewilde #203
Houston, TX 77063
houston_chapter@siggraph.org
http://www.cogniseis.com/HAS/

Washington

Seattle ACM SIGGRAPH
Steve Hollasch
Microsoft
One Microsoft Way
Redmond, WA 98052-6399
seattle_chapter@siggraph.org
http://www.research.microsoft.com/siggraph/

Tri-Cities Washington ACM SIGGRAPH
Donald R. Jones
Pacific Northwest Lab
MS K1-96
PO Box 999
Richland, WA 99352
tri-cities_chapter@siggraph.org

Brazil

Sao Paulo ACM SIGGRAPH
Sergio Martinelli
Digital Group
Rua Bairi 294
SP-05059
Sao Paulo, Brazil
sao_paulo_chapter@siggraph.org

SIGGRAPH Professional Chapters

Bulgaria

Sofia ACM SIGGRAPH
Gospodin Jelev
Dept of Prog & Computer Appl
Technical Univ. of Sofia
1756 Sofia, Bulgaria
sofia_chapter@siggraph.org

Canada

Vancouver B.C. ACM SIGGRAPH
Tom Berryhill
PO Box 29147
1996 W. Broadway
Vancouver BC
V6J-3SI Canada
vancouver_bc_chapter@siggraph.org
http://fas.sfu.ca/cs/research/groups/GMRL/
ACM-SIGGRAPH

France

Paris ACM SIGGRAPH
Thierry Frey c/o SUPINFOCOM - Terita 3000
2, rue Henri Matisse
59300
Aulnoye-lez- Valenciennes, France
paris_chapter@siggraph.org

Israel

Central Israel ACM SIGGRAPH
Daniel Cohen-Or
Dept of Computer Science
Tel Aviv University
Ramat Aviv, Israel
central_israel_chapter@siggraph.org
http://www.cs.technion.ac.il/~sudar/icgf.html

Japan

Tokyo ACM SIGGRAPH
Masa Inakage c/o Yukiko Ozaki
Image Systems Engineering Division
IMAGICA Corporation
2-14-1,Higashi-Gotanda,Shinagawa-ku
Tokyo,141 Japan
tokyo_chapter@siggraph.org

Mexico

Mexico City ACM SIGGRAPH
Eduardo Llaguno Velasco
Calzada de las Aguilas #1124-E-202
Col. San Clemente
Mexico City
01740 D.F. Mexico
mexico_city_chapter@siggraph.org
http://www.spin.com.mx/sigmex/sighome.htm

In-Formation Chapters

Brussels ACM SIGGRAPH - In Formation
Jean-Yves Roger
Project Officer
European Commission Directorate
General III - Industry Rue de la
loi/Wetstraat 200
B-1049
Bruxelles/Brussel
Belgium
brussels_chapter@siggraph.org

London ACM SIGGRAPH - In Formation
Len Breen c/o Department of Design
Brunel University
Runnymede Campus
Englefied Green
Surrey TW20 0JZ
United Kingdom
london_chapter@siggraph.org

New Orleans ACM SIGGRAPH - In
Formation
Irving Blatt
4700 Wichers Drive
Marrero, LA 70072
new_orleans_chapter@siggraph.org

Rotterdam ACM SIGGRAPH - In
Formation
Richard E. Ouwerkerk
Department of Arts and Architecture
Hogeschool Rotterdam & Omstreken
Scheepmakersstraat 7
PO Box 1272
3000 BG
Rotterdam
The Netherlands
rotterdam_chapter@siggraph.org

Singapore ACM SIGGRAPH - In
Formation
Yong Tsui Lee
Nanyang Technological University
Nanyang Avenue
Singapore
639798
Republic of Singapore
singapore_chapter@siggraph.org

Toronto ACM SIGGRAPH - In Formation
Greg Blair
8 Corley Avenue
Toronto, Ontario
M4E IT9
Canada
toronto_chapter@siggraph.org

Index

Pages marked with * denote panel summaries.
Pages marked with † denote special session.

Index

Cover Image Credits

Front Cover

"Stacked Books"
Copyright © 1997 Michael Salisbury, Michael Wong, John Hughes and David Salesin.

This computer rendered pen-and-ink style illustration began life as a low resolution Apple QuickTake 100 image. A tear in the book binding was added using Adobe Photoshop before the image was imported for further manipulation within our system. Once imported, greyscale tone from this reference image was selectively transferred to six illustration layers: two each for the book covers, book pages, and table surface. With our high-level direction field editing tools, direction fields to orient hatching strokes were then specified for each of these layers. As a final touch, stroke example sets and stroke characters were specified for each layer to help differentiate materials and add visual interest to the rendering.

Reference: "Orientable Textures for Image-Based Pen-and-Ink Illustration," *Michael P. Salisbury, Michael T. Wong, John F. Hughes, David H. Salesin, pp. 401–406.*

Frontispiece

"Metropolitan Wavelets"

Caustics in a pool of water, viewed indirectly through the ripples on the surface. It is difficult for unbiased Monte Carlo algorithms to sample the important light transport paths, since they must be generated starting from the eye – and in this scene the light source occupies only about one percent of the hemisphere, as seen from the pool bottom (which is curved). This image was computed using the Metropolis light transport algorithm, which can efficiently sample these paths by means of an appropriate set of "light-seeking" path mutations.

Reference: "Metropolis Light Transport," *Eric Veach, Leonidas J. Guibas, pp. 65–76.*

Back Cover, Top Left

"Painted Spheres and Q-Panel"
Copyright © 1997, Eric Lafortune, Cornell University.

This picture illustrates the use of a new, compact representation of surface reflectance. The reflectance distribution functions of the blue latex paint and the steel panel were measured and then represented using the model. The scene was rendered using Monte Carlo path tracing, for which the representation is particularly well suited. The sphere on the left was rendered with a Lambertian approximation, while the sphere on the right was rendered using the more accurate approximation. It successfully captures the forward scattering at grazing angles, which is visible in the colored highlights on the sphere. The steel Q-panel exhibits a metallic gloss, which is also captured by the representation.

Reference: "Non-Linear Approximation of Reflectance Functions," *Eric P.F. Lafortune, Sing-Choong Foo, Kenneth E. Torrance, Donald P. Greenberg, pp. 117–126.*

Back Cover, Top Right

A Dalmatian puppy rendered at low resolution using a probabilistic 'fake fur' shader. Model: Geoff Campbell, Kyle Odermatt, Wayne Kennedy. Textures: Carol Hayden.

Reference: "Fake Fur Rendering," *Dan B. Goldman, pp. 127–134.*

Back Cover, Middle Left

"Still Life"
Cassidy Curtis

This still life was created by applying a semi-automatic watercolor painting process to a poor-quality video image. The artist created a matte, chose pigments, and chose a glazing "style" for each piece of fruit and the shadow areas. The painting was then rendered automatically using a watercolor simulation.

Reference: "Computer-Generated Watercolor," *Cassidy J. Curtis, Sean E. Anderson, Joshua E. Seims, Kurt W. Fleischer, David H. Salesin, pp. 421–430.*

Back Cover, Middle Right

"Brown Nose Smoke"
Copyright © 1997 Nick Foster and Dimitris Metaxas, University of Pennsylvania

This image shows smoke pouring through everyone's favorite SIGGRAPH logo. It is a frame from an animation demonstrating that despite the approximations in our model for animating hot gases, interaction between a turbulent gas and a curved surface is handled in a visually realistic way. The image was created using the Blue Moon Rendering Tools' implementation of the RenderMan standard.

Reference: "Modeling the Motion of a Hot, Turbulent Gas," *Nick Foster, Dimitris Metaxas, pp. 181–188.*

Back Cover, Bottom Left

"Sushi Time"
Matt Pharr

This image is from the paper, "Rendering Complex Scenes with Memory-Coherent Ray Tracing." The scene is highly complex, comprised of over 43 million primitives, and the complex illumination is modelled accurately with Monte Carlo ray tracing algorithms. In spite of the complexity of the scene, it can be rendered efficiently on a standard desktop workstation using the algorithms presented in the paper. Craig Kolb and Reid Gershbein helped develop the scene and offered aesthetic advice, and Eric Veach shared artwork for the walls.

Reference: "Rendering Complex Scenes with Memory-Coherent Ray Tracing," *Matt Pharr, Craig Kolb, Reid Gershbein, Pat Hanrahan, pp. 101–108.*

Back Cover, Bottom Right

This texture was synthesized from an input texture which is 1/9 the size, and contains a single pink swirl. The input texture was modeled as a probabilistic multiresolution distribution. This image was synthesized by sampling from this distribution using a procedure which incorporates joint feature constraints across multiple resolutions.

Reference: "Multiresolution Sampling Procedure for Analysis and Synthesis of Texture Images," *Jeremy S. De Bonet, pp. 361–368.*